THE EDUCATION
OF POOR
AND MINORITY
CHILDREN

THE EDUCATION OF POOR AND MINORITY CHILDREN

A World Bibliography

Volume 2

Compiled by Meyer Weinberg

GREENWOOD PRESS
WESTPORT, CONNECTICUT • LONDON, ENGLAND

Library of Congress Cataloging in Publication Data

Weinberg, Meyer, 1920-
    The education of poor and minority children.

    Includes index.
    1. Educational equalization—United States—Bib-
liography.   2. Minorities—Education—United States—
Bibliography.   3. Educational equalization—Bibliography.
4. Socially handicapped—Education—Bibliography.
I. Title.
Z5814.E68W44   [LC214.2]   370.19'34'0973   80-29441
ISBN 0-313-21996-6 (lib. bdg.) (set)
ISBN 0-313-23023-4 (lib. bdg.) (vol. 1)
ISBN 0-313-23024-2 (lib. bdg.) (vol. 2)

Library of Congress Catalog Card Number: 80-29441
ISBN: 0-313-21996-6 (set)
ISBN: 0-313-23023-4 (vol. 1)
ISBN: 0-313-23024-2 (vol. 2)

First published in 1981

Greenwood Press
A division of Congressional Information Service, Inc.
88 Post Road West, Westport, Connecticut 06881

Printed in the United States of America

10 9 8 7 6 5 4 3 2 1

To
Monroe Nathan Work,
Pioneer bibliographer

CONTENTS

THE EDUCATION
OF POOR
AND MINORITY
CHILDREN

17.
LAW AND GOVERNMENT

Legislation

A. Philip Randolph Institute. The Reluctant Guardians: A Survey of the Enforcement of Federal Civil Rights Laws. Springfield, VA: Clearinghouse for Federal Scientific and Technical Information, D, 1969.

Administrative Repeal of Civil Rights Laws: A Case Study. HEW's Record of Non-Enforcement of School Desegregation in the South, 1972. The Potomac Institute, Inc., 1501 Eighteenth Street, N.W., Washington, DC 20036.

American Friends Service Committee and NAACP Legal Defense and Education Fund. Report on the Implementation of Title VI of the Civil Rights Act of 1964 in Regard to School Desegregation. N 15, 1965.

American Friends Service Committee and Others. The Emergency School Assistance Program. An Evaluation. Washington, DC: The Washington Research Project, 1970.

Aubry, Ernest L. "Remedies for Malfeasance in Title I Administration." Clearinghouse Review 7(Mr, 1974):658-660. [National Clearinghouse for Legal Services]

Avins, A. "De Facto and De Jure School Segregation: Some Reflected Light on the Fourteenth Amendment from the Civil Rights Act of 1875." Mississippi Law Journal 38(Mr, 1967):179.

_____. "Federal Aid to Education Policies, 1865-1888. Some Reflected Light on School Segregation and the Fourteenth Amendment." Alabama Law Review 21(Fall, 1968):61.

Bailey, Stephen K., and Mosher, Edith. ESEA: The Office of Education Administers a Law. New York: Syracuse U. Press, 1968.

_____ and _____. "Implementation of Title VI of the Civil Rights Act." Phi Delta Kappan, F, 1968.

Baker, O. W., Jr. "Trend of Civil Rights Statutes and Cases." National Bar Association Journal 1(Jl, 1941):75-86.

Barkin, David, and Hettich, Walter. The Elementary and Secondary Education Act: A Distributional Analysis. St Louis, MO: Institute for Urban and Regional Studies, Washington U., Ap, 1968.

Bickel, Alexander. "The Civil Rights Act of 1964." Commentary, Ag, 1964.

_____. "Forcing Desegregation Through Title VI." New Republic, Ap 9, 1966.

_____. "Sleepers in the Civil Rights Bill." New Republic, F 29, 1964.

"A Bill on Negro History." Document. Integrated Education, Mr-Ap, 1969.

Bolner, James. "Legislative Problems Surrounding Racially Balanced Public Schools: A Critical Examination of the Responses and the Prospects." Vanderbilt Law Review 22(1968-69): 1253-1274.

Bork, Robert H. Constitutionality of the President's Busing Proposals, My, 1972. American Enterprise Institute, 1150 17th Street, N.W., Washington, DC 20036.

Bonpua, Jose L., Jr. "The Law of 1866 and Ethnic Educators' Right to Fair Treatment." Intellect 103(F, 1975):330-332.

Braddock, Clayton. "Title III: The Tempo of Change." Southern Education Report, N, 1966. [Title III of the Elementary and Secondary Education Act]

Bureau of National Affairs. The Civil Rights Act of 1964...Legislative History...BNA Operations Manual. Washington, DC, 1964.

Carter, Robert L. "The Law and Racial Equality in Education." Journal of Negro Education, Summer, 1968.

"Civil Rights/Civil Liberties, 1977." ADA Legislative Newsletter 6(Ag 1-15, 1977). [Congressional role in civil rights]

"Civil Rights: Recession Layoffs and Title VII: Rightful Place or Status Quo?" _University of Florida Law Review_ 28(Winter, 1976): 604-610.

"Civil Rights Responsibilities of Federal Government." _Civil Rights Digest_, S, 1967.

"Civil Rights--The Supreme Court's Terrible Swift Sword: The Civil Rights Act of 1866 and the Reconstruction of Private Schools." _Washington Law Review_ 52(O, 1977):955-974.

Cole, Elizabeth R. "Public Education and the Civil Rights Act of 1964." _Journal of Family Law_, Fall, 1964.

"Comment: Title VI of the Civil Rights Act of 1964--Implementation and Impact." _George Washington Law Review_, My, 1968.

Comptroller General of the United States. _Need to Improve Policies and Procedures for Approving Grants Under the Emergency School Assistance Program_. Reprinted in U.S. Congress, 92nd, 1st Session, House of Representatives, Committee on Education and Labor, General Subcommittee on Education, _Emergency School Aid Act. Hearings..._, pp. 89-162. Washington, DC: GPO, 1971.

"Congress and Federal School Racial Policy." _Congressional Digest_ 49(Ap, 1970):99-107, 128.

"Constitutionality of a Statute Compelling the Color Line in Private Schools." _Harvard Law Review_ 22(1909):217-218.

Cooper, George, and Sobol, Richard B. "Seniority and Testing Under Fair Employment Laws: A General Approach to Objective Criteria of Hiring and Promotion." _Harvard Law Review_ 82(1969):1598-1679.

Cousens, Frances Reissman. _Public Civil Rights Agencies and Fair Employment_. New York: Praeger, 1968.

Crocker, Stephen and others. _Title IV of the Civil Rights Act of 1964: A Review of Program Operations_. Santa Monica, CA: Rand, Ag, 1976.

Cunningham, Luvern L. "A Critique--Federal Intervention in Education," parts 1 and 2. _American School Board Journal_, Ap and My, 1966.

Determan, Dean W., and Ware, Gilbert. "New Dimensions in Education: Title VI of the Civil Rights Act of 1964." _Journal of Negro Education_, Winter, 1966.

Drew, Elizabeth Brenner. "Education's Billion-Dollar Baby." _Atlantic Monthly_, Jl, 1966. [Problems of Title I of the Elementary and Secondary Education Act of 1965, with some emphasis upon Chicago]

DuBois, W. E. B. "Civil Rights Legislation Before and After the Passage of the 14th Amendment." _Lawyers Guild Review_ 6(N-D, 1946): 640-642.

Dunn, James R. "Title VI, the Guidelines and School Desegregation in the South." _Virginia Law Review_ 53(1967).

Elden, G. "'Forty Acres and a Mule' With Interest: The Constitutionality of Black Capitalism, Benign School Quotes and Other Statutory Racial Classification." _Journal of Urban Law_ 47(1969-1970).

Egerton, John. _Title IV of the 1964 Civil Rights Act: A Program in Search of a Policy_, Mr, 1970. Race Relations Information Center, Nashville, TN 37212.

"The Equal Educational Opportunity Act of 1967." _Saturday Review_, D 17, 1966. [Excerpts from a U.S. Office of Education staff paper relating to possible legislation on the subject]

Finch, Robert H. "Establishing a Nation-Wide School Desegregation Program Under Title VI of the Civil Rights Act of 1964." _Integrated Education_, My-Je, 1969.

Flaxman, Erwin, and Mosley, Doris. "Title VI in the 60's." _IRCD Bulletin_ 8(My-S, 1972).

Foster, G. W. "Title VI: Southern Education Faces the Facts." _Saturday Review_, Mr 20, 1965.

_____. "Who Pulled the Teeth from Title VI." _Saturday Review_, Ap 16, 1966.

Glickstein, Howard A. "Federal Educational Programs and Minority Groups." _Journal of Negro Education_, Summer, 1969.

Gordon, I. A. "Nature and Uses of Congressional Power Under Section Five of the Fourteenth Amendment to Overcome Decisions of the Supreme Court." _Northwestern University Law Review_ 72(N-D, 1977):656-705. [Busing]

Gousha, Richard P., and Row, Howard E. "Federal Guidelines on Desegregation of Schools: A Constructive Criticism of the Guidelines." _NEA Journal_, Mr, 1967. [See Seeley, below]

Hagman, Donald G. _Standards for Incorporation and Municipal Boundary Change: Recommendations Based on a Study of Statutory and Case Law in the United States, 1970_. League of Minnesota Municipalities, 3300 University Avenue, S.E., Minneapolis, MN 55414.

"HEW is Required to Make a Progam-by-Program Finding of Discrimination in Order to Terminate Federal Funds." _Vanderbilt Law Review_ 23(D, 1969).

"H.E.W. School Desegregation Guidelines." Harvard Civil Rights-Civil Liberties Law Review, 1966.

"Interpreting the Anti-Busing Provisions of the Education Amendment of 1972." Harvard Journal of Legislation 10(1973).

Kennedy, Edward M. "The Case for New Desegregation Legislation." Integrated Education, Je-Jl, 1966.

"The Kennedy Bill, S. 2829." Integrated Education, Ap-My, 1966.

King, Micelima J. "Social Intervention in Title IV Technical Assistance." Doctoral dissertation, U. of California, Los Angeles, 1976. Univ. Microfilms Order No. 77-9346.

Knoll, Erwin. "There's Room for Negotiation." Southern Education Report, My-Je, 1966. [Regarding the new "Guidelines" to Title VI of the Civil Rights Act, released in March, 1967]

Kovarsky, Irving. "Some Social and Legal Aspects of Testing under the Civil Rights Act." Labor Law Journal 20(1969):346-356.

Lane, Russell Adrian. "The Legal Trend Toward Equalization of Racial Opportunity for Education in the United States." Master's thesis, U. of Indiana, 1930.

_____. "Legal Trend Toward Increased Provisions for Negro Education in the United States Between 1920 and 1930." Journal of Negro Education 1(O, 1932):396-399.

Leeson, Jim. "The Deliberate Speed of Title VI." Saturday Review, D 17, 1966. [Desegregation in the South]

_____. "Title IV. The 'Help' Program is Expanded." Southern Education Report, My, 1968. [Title IV of the Civil Rights Act of 1964]

"Legal Backing for the Guidelines." Southern Education Report, Jl-Ag, 1966. [Account of a legal memorandum on the 1966 Office of Education guidelines to the Civil Rights Act]

Levin, Roger E. National Institute of Education: Preliminary Plan for the Proposed Institute. Santa Monica, CA: Rand, F, 1971. [Reprinted in U.S. Congress, 92nd, 1st Session, House of Representatives, Committee on Education and Labor, Select Subcommittee on Education, To Establish a National Institute of Education. Hearings..., pp. 518-615. Washington, DC: GPO, 1971]

Lytle, Clifford. "Resurrecting the 1866 Civil Rights Act." Civil Rights Digest 9(Summer, 1977):28-31. [Discrimination in the private sector]

Martin, Ruby S. "Chronology of the Nixon Administration's School Desegregation Actions and Inactions." In U.S. Congress, 92nd, 2nd Session, House of Representatives, Committee on Education and Labor, Equal Educational Opportunities Act. Hearings..., pp. 458-465. Washington, DC: GPO, 1972. [Ja 29, 1969-Mr 16, 1972]

_____. "The Civil Rights Act of 1964 and the Urban Crisis." Urban West, Jl, 1968.

_____. "Title VI of the Civil Rights Act of 1964 and Education." Educational Horizons, Fall, 1968.

"Materials on U.S. Department of Agriculture Civil Rights Enforcement." In U.S. Congress, 91st, 1st Session, Senate, Select Committee on Nutrition and Human Needs, Nutrition and Human Needs...Hearings, Part 8, pp. 2684-2718. Washington, DC: GPO, 1969.

Menacker, Julius. "The Organizational Behavior of Congress in the Formation of Educational Support Policy." Phi Delta Kappan, O, 1966.

Meranto, Philip J. Metropolitanism and Federal Aid to Education--The Passage and Impact of the 1965 Aid to Education Act, 1967. ERIC ED 010 799.

Morsell, John A. "Legislation [for Educational Equality] and Its Implementation." Journal of Negro Education, Summer, 1965.

Murray, Pauli. "The Historical Development of Race Laws in the United States." Journal of Negro Education 22(Winter, 1953):4-15.

_____. "Roots of the Racial Crisis: Prologue to Policy." J.S.D. thesis, Yale U., 1965.

National Advisory Committee on Education. Federal Relations to Education. Part I. Committee Findings and Recommendations; Part II, Basic Facts. Washington, DC: The Committee, 1931.

Neidt, Charles O., and French, Joseph L. Guide To Evaluation of Title I Projects. Washington, DC: GPO, O, 1966. [Title I of the Elementary and Secondary Education Act of 1965]

"New Crackdown on Local Schools." U.S. News and World Report, My 2, 1966. [U.S. government enforcement of Title VI of the Civil Rights Act of 1964]

"Now Under Fire: Guidelines for Integration." U.S. News and World Report, O 17, 1966.

Orfield, Gary. "Nixon's First Test." Nation, Ja 20, 1969. [Enforcement of school desegregation regulations]

_____. The Reconstruction of Southern Education. The Schools and the 1964 Civil Rights Act. New York: Wiley-Interscience, 1969.

Pettigrew, Thomas F. "Racial Implication of Title III, ESEA." Integrated Education, O-N, 1967.

_____. "Urban and Metropolitan Considerations: With Special Focus on Civil Rights." In U.S. Congress, 90th, 1st Session, Senate, Committee on Labor and Public Welfare, Sub-committee on Education. Notes and Working Papers Concerning the Administration of Pro-grams Authorized under Title III of Public Law 89-11. The Elementary and Secondary Education Act of 1965 as Amended by Public Law 89-750, pp. 153-163. Washington, DC: GPO, 1967. [The relative lack of concern for integration in projects approved under Title I and III of the ESEA]

"The Powell Bill, H.R. 13079." Integrated Ed-ucation, Ap-My, 1966.

Quattlebaum, Charles (ed.). Federal Educational Policies, Programs and Proposals, 3 volumes. Washington, DC: GPO, 1968.

"Racial Imbalance in the Public Schools--Leg-islative Motive and the Constitution." Virginia Law Review 50(1964):464-534.

Reams, Bernard D., Jr., and Wilson, Paul E. (eds.). Segregation and the Fourteenth Amendment in the States: A Survey of State Segregation Laws 1865-1953: Prepared for United States Supreme Court in re: Brown v. Board of Education of Topeka. Buffalo, NY: Hein, 1975.

Reed, Glen A. "Section 1981 and Private Groups: The Right to Discriminate versus Freedom from Discrimination." Yale Law Journal 84(Je, 1975):1441-1476.

Roller, G. "Congress and the President Against the Courts: Busing as a Viable Tool for Desegregation." Wayne Law Review 19(S, 1973).

Rosenberg, Max. "Proposed: An Equal Oppor-tunity Amendment to the U.S. Constitution." Phi Delta Kappan 55(Mr, 1974):442-443, 467.

"Rules and Regulations: Civil Rights Act." Integrated Education, D, 1965-Ja, 1966.

Sargentich, Lewis D., and Seymour, Richard T. "The Congress Has No Power Under the Consti-tution to Enact the Administration Propo-sals." In U.S. Congress, 92nd, 2nd Session, House of Representatives, Committee on Ed-ucation and Labor, Equal Education Opportun-ities Act. Hearings..., pp. 553-561. Wash-ington, DC: GPO, 1972.

"School Desegregation and the Office of Educa-tion Guidelines." Duquesne University Law Review, Summer, 1968.

"School Desegregation and the Office of Educa-tion Guidelines." George Washington Law Re-view 55(1966):325-351.

Scott, D. "Busing to Desegregate Schools: The Perspective from Congress." University of Richmond Law Review 8(Winter, 1974).

Seeley, David S. "Desegregation Guidelines. Do They Go Far Enough?" American Education, F, 1967.

_____. "Federal Guidelines on Desegregation of Schools: Total or Trojan Horse?" NEA Journal, Mr, 1967. [See Gousha and Row, above]

"Segregated Academies, Section 1981, and an Exemption for Truly Private Groups." Connecticut Law Review 8(1976).

Sherrill, Robert G. "Guidelines to Frustration." Nation, Ja 16, 1967. [A critique of federal administration of the school provisions of the Civil Rights Act of 1964]

"Should Congress Define Racial Imbalance?" Hastings Law Journal, 1966.

Sky, Theodore. "Concentration Under Title I of the Elementary and Secondary Act: The New Part C." Journal of Law and Education 1(Ap, 1972):171-211.

Southern Regional Council. School Desegregation. Old Problems Under a New Law [Civil Rights Act of 1964]. Atlanta: Southern Regional Council, 1965.

Slippen, Richard I. "Administrative Enforcement of Civil Rights in Public Education: Title VI, HEW, and the Civil Rights Reviewing Au-thority." Wayne Law Review 21(1975).

Stephenson, G. T. "Race Distinctions in Amer-ican Law--Civil Rights of Negroes and Legis-lation Thereon; in Schools, in Public Con-veyances." American Law Review 43(1909): 547, 695.

"Title VI of the Civil Rights Act of 1964--Implementation and Import." George Washing-ton Law Review, My, 1968.

U.S. Commission on Civil Rights. Civil Rights Act of 1964. Civil Rights Under Federal Pro-grams. An Analysis of Title VI. Washington, DC: GPO, Ja, 1966.

_____. Federal Civil Rights Enforcement Effort: A Report of the United States Commission on Civil Rights, 1970. Washington, DC: GPO, 1970.

_____. The Federal Civil Rights Enforcement Effort: One Year Later. Washington, DC: GPO, N, 1971.

_____. The Federal Civil Rights Enforcement Effort--Seven Months Later. Washington, DC: The Commission, My 10, 1971.

_____. Federal Enforcement of School Desegre-gation. Washington, DC: GPO, 1969.

_____. Federal Rights under School Desegre-
gation Law. Washington, DC: GPO, Je, 1966.
[Informative questions and answers, includes
text of Mr, 1966, Office of Education Guide-
lines]

_____. HEW and Title VI. A Report on the
Development of the Organization, Policies,
and Compliance Procedures of the Department
of Health, Education and Welfare Under Title
VI of the Civil Rights Act of 1964. Washington, DC: GPO, 1970.

_____. Title IV and School Desegregation. A
Study of a Neglected Federal Program. Washington, DC: GPO, Ja, 1973.

_____. Title VI...One Year After. A Survey
of Desegregation of Health and Welfare Services in the South. Washington, DC: U.S.
Commission on Civil Rights, 1966. [Includes
section on segregation within the Head
Start Program]

U.S. Congress, 88th, 1st Session, House of Representatives, Committee on Judiciary, Subcommittee No. 5. Hearings...on Miscellaneous Proposals Regarding the Civil Rights
of Persons Within the Jurisdiction of the
United States, May 8, 1963-October 16, 1963.
Washington, DC: GPO, 1963-1964.

U.S. Congress, 88th, 1st Session, Senate, Committee on the Judiciary. Civil Rights, the
President's Program, 1963. Hearings, July
16-September 11, 1963. Washington, DC:
GPO, 1964.

U.S. Congress, 89th, 2nd Session, House of Rep-
resentatives, Committee on the Judiciary,
Subcommittee No. 5. Civil Rights, 1966.
Hearings...on Miscellaneous Rights of Per-
sons within the Jurisdiction of the United
States. Washington, DC: GPO, 1966.

U.S. Congress, 89th, 2nd Session, House of Representatives, Committee on the Judiciary,
Special Subcommittee on Civil Rights.
Guidelines for School Desegregation...Hear-
ings...December 14, 15 and 16, 1966. Washington, DC: GPO, 1966.

U.S. Congress, 90th, 1st Session, House of Representatives, Committee on Education and
Labor. Elementary and Secondary Education
Amendments of 1967, Hearings...Parts 1 and
2. Washington, DC: GPO, 1967.

U.S. Congress, 90th, 1st Session, Senate, Committee on Labor and Public Welfare. Enact-
ments by the 89th Congress Concerning Education and Training, 2 parts. Washington, DC:
GPO, 1967.

U.S. Congress, 90th, 1st Session, Senate, Committee on the Judiciary, Subcommittee on
Constitutional Rights. Civil Rights Act of
1967. Hearings. Washington, DC: GPO,
1967.

U.S. Congress, 90th, 2nd Session, House of Representatives, Committee on Appropriations,
Subcommittee... Departments of State, Justice, and Commerce, the Judiciary, and Related Agencies Appropriations for 1969.
Hearings. Washington, DC: GPO, 1968.
[Hearings on civil rights educational activities of Office of Education and U.S.
Commission on Civil Rights]

U.S. Congress, 91st, 1st Session, House of Representatives, Committee on Education and
Labor. House Report No. 91-114. Elementary
and Secondary Education Amendments of 1969.
Washington, DC: GPO, 1969.

U.S. Congress, 91st, 2nd Session, House of Representatives, Report No. 91-937. Elementary
and Secondary Education Amendments of 1969...
Conference Report, Mr 24, 1970.

U.S. Congress, 91st, 2nd Session, Senate, Select
Committee on Equal Educational Opportunity.
Equal Educational Opportunity. Hearings...
Part 1A--Equality of Educational Opportunity.
An Introduction. Part 1B--Equality of Educa-
tional Opportunity. Appendix. Part 2--Equal-
ity of Educational Opportunity. An Introduc-
tion--Continued. Parts 3A, 3B, 3C, and 3D--
Desegregation Under Law. Washington, DC:
GPO, 1970.

U.S. Congress, 92nd, 1st Session, House of Representatives, Committee on Education and Labor, Select Subcommittee on Education. To
Establish a National Institute of Education.
Hearings... Washington, DC: GPO, 1971.

U.S. Congress, 92nd, 1st Session, Senate, Select
Committee on Equal Educational Opportunity.
Equal Educational Opportunity. Hearings...
Part 11. Status of School Desegregation Law.
Washington, DC: GPO, 1971.

U.S. Congress, 92nd, 1st Session, Senate, Select
Committee on Nutrition and Human Needs.
Nutrition and Human Needs--1971. Part 5--
Implementation of Public Law 91-248, National
School Lunch Act of 1970, in Michigan. Wash-
ington, DC: GPO, 1971.

U.S. Congress, 92nd, 2nd Session, House of Representatives. Report No. 92-1335. Equal
Educational Opportunities Act of 1972, Ag
14, 1972.

U.S. Congress, 92nd, 2nd Session, House of Representatives, Committee on Education and
Labor. Equal Educational Opportunities Act.
Hearings..., 2 parts. Washington, DC: GPO,
1972.

U.S. Congress, 92nd, 2nd Session, House of Representatives, Committee on Education and Labor. Equal Educational Opportunities Act.
Hearings..., Part 3. Washington, DC: GPO,
1972.

U.S. Congress, 92nd, 2nd Session, House of Representatives, Committee on Education and Labor, General Subcommittee on Education. Equal Educational Opportunities Act. Hearing... Washington, DC: GPO, 1972.

U.S. Congress, 92nd, 2nd Session, House of Representatives, Committee on Education and Labor, General Subcommittee on Education. Indian Education Act of 1971. Hearings... Washington, DC: GPO, 1972.

U.S. Congress, 92nd, 2nd Session, House of Representatives, Committee on Education and Labor, General Subcommittee on Education. Public and Private Education Assistance Act of 1972. Hearings... Washington, DC: GPO, 1972. [MI and IL]

U.S. Congress, 92nd, 2nd Session, Senate, Report No. 92-798. Education Amendments of 1972. Conference Report, My 22, 1972. [Pp. 212-220 contain discussion of Emergency School Aid Act, concerning desegregation]

U.S. Congress, 93rd, 1st Session, Senate, Committee on the Judiciary. Nomination of J. Stanley Pottinger To Be Assistant Attorney General In Charge of The Civil Rights Division. Hearings... Washington, DC: GPO, 1973.

U.S. Congress, 93rd, 2nd Session, House of Representatives, Report No. 93-805. Elementary and Secondary Education Amendments of 1974, F 21, 1974.

U.S. Congress, 93rd, 2nd Session, Senate, Committee on Labor and Public Welfare, Subcommittee on Education. Neighborhood Schools Act, 1974. Hearings... Washington, DC: GPO, 1975.

U.S. Congress, 94th, 1st Session, House of Representatives, Committee on the Judiciary, Subcommittee on Civil and Constitutional Rights. Civil Rights Aspects of General Revenue Sharing. Hearings... Washington, DC: GPO, 1975.

U.S. Department of Health, Education and Welfare, Office of the General Counsel. Memorandum on Points Raised by Senator Stennis Concerning School Desegregation Policies Under Title VI of the Civil Rights Act of 1964. Washington, DC: U.S. Office of Education, F 24, 1967.

_____. Policies on Elementary and Secondary School Compliance with Title VI of the Civil Rights Act of 1964. Washington, DC: GPO, Mr, 1968.

U.S. Equal Employment Opportunity Commission. Legislative History of Titles VII and XI of Civil Rights Act of 1964. Washington, DC: GPO, 1968.

U.S. Office of Education. History of Title I ESEA. Washington, DC: Department of Health Education and Welfare, Je, 1969.

Williams, George W. "Negro School Laws, 1619-1860." In History of the Negro Race in America from 1619 to 1880, II. New York: G.P. Putnam's Sons, 1883.

Wirt, Frederick M. "What State Laws Say About Local Control." Phi Delta Kappan (Ap, 1978): 517-520.

Wise, Michael B. "Congress, Busing, and Federal Law. The Roots of Antibusing Laws and How They Grew." Civil Rights Digest 5(Summer, 1973):28-35.

Litigation

Abel, David. "Can a Student Sue the Schools for Educational Malpractice?" Harvard Educational Review 44(N, 1974):416-436.

"Achieving Integration by Bussing Only Black Children is Not Proper." Harvard Civil Rights-Civil Liberties Law Journal 5(1971).

"The Affirmative Duty to Integrate in Higher Education." Yale Law Journal 79(1970):666-697.

"Albertson v. School Board of Fenway: Is Racial Imbalance in Public Schools Unconstitutional? --No." Missouri Law Review 31(1966):411-432.

Allen, James E. "The Supreme Court and Public Education." New York State Bar Journal 38 (1966):364-369; 435-441; and 516-522; 39(1967): 61-66.

Allen, Richard C. Legal Rights of the Disabled and Disadvantaged. Washington, DC: GPO, 1969.

Allen, Robert L. "The Bakke Case and Affirmative Action." Black Scholar 9(S, 1977):9-16.

"Alternatives to Case-by-Case Attacks on School Segregation." Harvard Law Journal 16(Spring, 1971).

Amaker, Norman C. "Milliken v. Bradley: The Meaning of the Constitution in School Desegregation Cases." Hastings' Constitutional Law Quarterly 2(1975).

_____. "Public School Desegregation: Legal Perspectives." Negro History Bulletin 33(N, 1970):174-177.

"Ameliorative Racial Classification Under the Equal Protection Clause. DeFunis v. Odegaard." Duke Law Journal (1973):1126-1153.

Anderson, Donald Louis. "The Problem of Implementing the 1954 Decision in Public Schools." Quarterly Review of Higher Education Among Negroes 28(O, 1960):265-291.

Armstrong, Robert G. "A Reply to Herbert Wechsler's Holmes Lecture 'Toward Neutral Principles of Constitutional Law.'" Phylon, Fall, 1960. [See Wechsler, below]

Ashmore, Harry and others. "Segregation in the Public Schools—A Symposium." Journal of Public Law 3(Spring, 1954):5-170.

Auer, A. "Public School Desegregation and the Color-Blind Constitution." Southwestern University Law Journal 27(Ag, 1973):454-489.

Auster, Paul. "De Facto Segregation." William and Mary Law Review, Ja, 1965.

Avins, A. "Black Studies, White Separation, and Reflected Light on College Segregation and the Fourteenth Amendment from Early Land Grant College Policies." Washburn Law Journal 10(Winter, 1971).

Badger, William V. "A Systematic Analysis of the U.S. Supreme Court Cases Dealing with Education: 1790-1951." Doctoral dissertation, Florida State U., 1953. Univ. Microfilms Order No. 5391.

Balbus, Isacc D. The Dialectics of Legal Repression. Black Rebels Before the American Criminal Courts. New York: Basic Books, 1973.

Ball, C. L. "Constitutionality of the Proposed Plan for Professional Education of the Southern Negro." Vanderbilt Law Review 1(Ap, 1948):403-424.

Bannon, John. "Legitimizing Segregation: The Supreme Court's Recent School Decisions." Civil Rights Digest 9(Summer, 1977):12-17.

Bardolph, Richard (ed.). The Civil Rights Record: Black Americans and the Law, 1849-1970. New York: Crowell, 1970.

Bell, Derrick A., Jr. "The Burden of Brown on Blacks: History-Based Observations on a Landmark Decision." North Carolina Central Law Journal 7(1975):27-39.

_____. "The Curse of Brown on Blacks." First World 2(Spring, 1978):14-18.

_____. "Is Brown Obsolete? Yes!" Integrateducation 14(My-Je, 1976):28.

_____. "Legacy of W.E.B. DuBois: A Rational Model for Achieving Public School Equity for America's Black Children." Creighton Law Review 11(D, 1977):409-431.

_____. "Racial Remediation: An Historical Perspective on Current Conditions." Notre Dame Lawyer 52(O, 1976):5-29.

_____. "School Litigation Strategies for the 1970's: New Phases in the Continuing Quest for Equality Schools." Wisconsin Law Review, 1970.

_____. "Serving Two Masters: Integration Ideals and Client Interest in School Desegregation Litigation." Yale Law Journal 85 (1976):470-516. [Reprinted in Limits of Justice. The Courts' Role in School Desegregation. Edited by Howard I. Kalodner and James J. Fishman. Cambridge, MA: Ballinger, 1978. See also letter from Nathaniel R. Jones, pp. 614-618]

_____. "Waiting on the Promise of Brown." Law and Contemporary Problems 39(Spring, 1975):341-383.

Benson, Charles S. "How to Beat Serrano: Rules for the Rich." Saturday Review, D 9, 1972.

Berman, Daniel M. It Is So Ordered. New York: Norton, 1967. [A history of the Brown school desegregation case]

"Beyond the Law—to Equal Educational Opportunities for Chicanos and Indians." New Mexico Law Review 1(1971).

Bickel, Alexander. "The Decade of School Desegregation—1954-1964: Progress and Prospects." Columbia Law Review 60(1964):193-229.

_____ and others. "Education in a Democracy: The Legal and Practical Problems of School Busing: A Symposium." Human Rights 3(Summer, 1973):53-92.

Bickel, Robert D., and Vandercreek, William. "Class Action Aspects of Federal Employment Discrimination Litigation." Journal of College and University Law 2(Winter, 1974-75): 143-156.

Binion, G. "Racial Discrimination by Alteration on Refusal to Alter School District Boundaries." Journal of Urban Law 54(Spring, Summer, 1977):811-848.

Bishop, David W. "Plessy v. Ferguson: A Reinterpretation." Journal of Negro History 62 (Ap, 1977):125-133.

Black, Charles L., Jr. "The Lawfulness of the Segregation Decisions." Yale Law Journal, Ja, 1960.

"Black, White, Brown and Green: Color Consciousness in Public School Desegregation." Georgia Law Review 3(Summer, 1969).

Blackwell, Randolph T. "Perspective on the Brown Decision." New South 28(Winter, 1973):9-17.

Blauner, Robert. "Sociology in the Courtroom: The Search for White Racism in the Voir Dire." In The Voir Dire Conducted by Charles R. Garry in People of California v. Huey P. Newton, pp. 43-73. Edited by Ann F. Ginger, 1969. National Lawyers Guild, P.O. Box 673, Berkeley, CA 94701.

Bloch, Charles J. "Does the Fourteenth Amendment Forbid De Facto Segregation?" Western Reserve Law Review, Ap, 1965.

Bloomfield, N. J. "Equality of Educational Opportunity: Judicial Supervision of Public Education." Southern California Law Review 43(1970).

Blumrosen, Alfred W. "Quotas, Common Sense, and Law in Labor Relations: Three Dimensions of Equal Opportunity." Rutgers Law Review 27 (Spring, 1974):675-703.

Bolmeier, Edward C. Landmark Supreme Court Decisions on Public School Issues. Charlottesville, VA: Michie Co., 1973.

Bolner, James. "The Supreme Court and Racially Imbalanced Public Schools in 1967." Journal of Negro Education, Spring, 1969.

Bolner, James, and Shanley, Robert. Busing: The Political and Judicial Process. New York: Praeger, 1974.

Bosma, Roland Boyd. "Civil and Constitutional Rights of Public School Teachers As Citizens." Doctoral dissertation, Wayne State U., 1971.

Boykin, L., Jr. "'Separate But Equal' Concept in Education--A Legal Fallacy." Notre Dame Law 23(Ja, 1948):220-226.

Brinkman, Dale T. "'Intention' as a Requirement for De Jure School Segregation." Ohio State Law Journal 37(1976).

Broderick, A. "Preferential Admissions and the Brown Heritage." North Carolina Central Law Journal 8(Spring, 1977):123-187.

"Brown and Busing." Journal of Urban Law, Summer, 1967.

Brown, Richard W. "Freedom of Choice in the South: A Constitutional Perspective." Louisiana Law Review 28(Ap, 1968):455-468.

Brown, Ronald W. "Busing and the Search for Equal Educational Opportunity." Journal of Law and Education 1(Ap, 1972):257-288.

_____. "Busing as a Permissible Tool in Desegregation." Black Law Journal 1(Winter, 1971):222-233.

Browning, R. Stephen (ed.). From Brown to Bradley: School Desegregation, 1954-1974. Cincinnati, OH: Jefferson, 1975.

Buitrago y Goodall, Ann Mari. "The Political Role of Lower Federal Courts: Race Relations Cases in the Fifth Circuit, 1954-1967." Doctoral dissertation, City U. of New York, 1978. Univ. Microfilms Order No. 7902541.

Bullock, Charles S. III. "Federal Law and School Discrimination in the North." Journal of Negro Education 47(Spring, 1978):113-131.

_____. "The Justice Department and School Desegregation: The Importance of Developing Trust." Journal of Politics 39(N, 1977): 1036-1043.

Bunche, Ralph J. "Social Attitudes and the Constitution." Quarterly Review of Higher Education Among Negroes 7(Jl, 1939):191-194.

Burns, Haywood. "Black People and the Tyranny of American Law." Annals 407(My, 1973): 156-166.

Bushnell, George E., Jr., Jones, Richard A., and Olmstead, David J. "Litigation and the Quest for Equal Educational Opportunity." Inequality in Education 1, Nos. 3-4(1970): 15-16, 27-29.

"Busing and the Search for Equal Educational Opportunity." Journal of Law and Education 1(Ap, 1972):251-288.

"Busing--A Permissible Tool of School Desegregation." Journal of Urban Law 49(N, 1971).

"Busing, Swann v. Charlotte-Mecklenburg and the Future of Desegregation in the Fifth Circuit." Texas Law Review 49(My, 1971).

"By Any Other Name: Meiklejohn, the First Amendment and School Desegregation." Connecticut Law Review 3(Winter, 1970-1971).

Calkins, Hugh, and Gordon, Jeffrey. "Right to Choose an Integrated Education: Voluntary Regional Integrated Schools--A Partial Remedy for De Facto Segregation." Harvard Civil Rights Law Review 9(Mr, 1974):171-225.

Campbell, Robert F. "Busing Decisions Provide Leeway." Race Relations Reporter 2(S 7, 1971):4-6.

Carol, Lila N. "Court-Mandated Citizen Participation in School Desegregation." Phi Delta Kappan 59(N, 1977):171-173.

Carter, Robert L. "De Facto School Segregation: An Examination of the Legal and Constitutional Questions Presented." Western Reserve Law Review, Ap, 1965.

_____. "Equal Educational Opportunity for Negroes--Abstraction or Reality?" University of Illinois Law Forum 160, Summer, 1968.

_____. "School Integration Is Still on the Agenda." Saturday Review, O 21, 1967. [Implications of Hobson v. Hansen, the Washington, DC school case]

_____. "The Warren Court and Desegregation." Michigan Law Review 67(1968).

Carter, Robert L., and Marshall, Thurgood. "The Meaning and Significance of the Supreme Court Decree." Journal of Negro Education 24(Summer, 1955):397-404. [Brown v. Board of Education of Topeka]

Chachkin, Norman J. "Metropolitan School Desegregation: Evolving Law." Integrated Education, Mr-Ap, 1972, pp. 13-26.

Chambers, Julius L. "Implementing 'Brown.'" Educational Forum 41(My, 1977):415-429.

_____. "Implementing the Promise of Brown: Social Science and the Courts in Future School Litigation." In Education, Social Science and the Judicial Process, pp. 27-37. Washington, DC: National Institute of Education, Je, 1976.

Champagne, Anthony M. "The Segregation Academy and the Law." Journal of Negro Education 42 (Winter, 1973):58-66.

Chanin, Robert H. Protecting Teacher Rights. A Summary of Constitutional Developments. Washington, DC: National Education Association, 1970.

Clark, L. D., and Burns, W. H. "Realpolitik of Racial Segregation in Northern Public Schools: Some Pragmatic Approaches." Howard Law Review, Summer, 1968.

Clotfelter, Charles T. "Detroit Decision and 'White Flight.'" Journal of Legal Studies 5 (1976).

_____. "Implications of 'Resegregation' for Judicially Imposed School Segregation Remedies." Vanderbilt Law Review 31(My, 1978):829-854.

_____. "Twenty Years After the Brown Decision: Does Integration Have a Future." Harvard Crimson, My 21, 1974.

Cobb, J. A. "Race Distinctions in American Law." National Bar Association, 1930, pp. 34-37.

Cohen, David K. "Defining Racial Equality in Education." U.C.L.A. Law Review 16(F, 1969): 255.

_____. "Jurists and Educators on Urban Schools: The Wright Decision and the Passow Report." Record, D, 1968. [D.C.]

_____. "Segregation, Desegregation, and Brown." Society, N-D, 1974.

Collins, Charles W. "The Fourteenth Amendment and the Negro Race Question." American Law Review 45(N-D, 1911):830-856.

Committee on Civil Rights. Racial Imbalance in the Public Schools: The Current Status of Federal and New York Law. New York State Bar Association, 99 Washington Avenue, Albany, NY, O 20, 1964.

"Congress and the President Against the Courts: Busing as a Viable Tool for Desegregation." Wayne Law Review 19(S, 1973):1483-1549.

"Consolidation for Desegregation: The Unresolved Issue of the Inevitable Sequel." Yale Law Journal 82(J1, 1973).

"Constitutional Law—De Facto Segregation— the Courts and Urban Education." North Carolina Law Review, D, 1967.

"Constitutional Law—Defenses—Segregation Is a Defense to Parents' Prosecution Under Compulsory School Attendance Law— (People v. Serna, Cal. 1977)." Western State University Law Review 4(Spring, 1977).

"Constitutional Law—Desegregation—Brown v. Board of Education Applies to Mexican-American Students and Any Other Readily Identifiable Ethnic-Minority Group or Class." Texas Law Review 49(Ja, 1971).

"Constitutional Law/Equal Protection of the Laws—State's Affirmative Duty to Desegregate Higher Educational Facilities Not Discharged by Good Faith but Unsuccessful 'Open Door' Policy." Harvard Law Review 82(Je, 1969).

"Constitutional Law—Equal Protection of the Laws—Statute Requiring Redrawing of School Attendance Zones to Achieve Racial Imbalance Violates Equal Protection Clause of Fourteenth Amendment." Harvard Law Review, Ja, 1968.

"Constitutional Law—Equal Protection—Zoning to Avoid Perpetuating De Facto Segregation." Tennessee Law Review 43(Fall, 1975):133-147.

"Constitutional Law—Freedom of Speech—Withdrawal of Funds from College Newspaper Advocating Segregationalist Policy Deemed Violative of First and Fourteenth Amendments— Joyner v. Whiting, 477 F. 2nd 456 (4th Cir. 1973)." University of Richmond Law Review 8(Winter, 1974);297-302.

"Constitutional Law—Race Relations—Achieving Integration by Busing Only Black and Puerto Rican Children is Proper." Harvard Civil Law Review 5(Ap, 1970).

"Constitutional Law—Racial Imbalance in Public Schools: The Affirmative Duty to Integrate Administrators." North Carolina Law Review 49(Je, 1971).

"Constitutional Law—School Desegregation— Constitutional Duty to Desegregate—De Facto Segregation." Emory Law Journal 23 (Winter, 1974).

"Constitutional Law—School Desegregation—the Conundrum of De Facto and De Jure Segregation." De Paul Law Review 18(Autumn, 1968).

"Constitutional Law—School Desegregation— Failure to Revamp Segregated School District Attenuates the Milliken v. Bradley Barrier to Federal Inter-district Remedies." Texas Law Review 54(1976).

"Constitutional Right of Bilingual Chilldren to an Equal Educational Opportunity." Southern California Law Review 47(1974).

"Constitutionality of Adventitious Segregation in the Public Schools." University of Illinois Law Forum, Fall, 1967.

"Constitutionality of De Facto Segregation." North Dakota Law Review, Mr, 1965.

"The Constitutionality of Sex Separation in School Desegregation Plans." University of Chicago Law Review 37(Winter, 1970).

Cook, G. "School Desegregation: To Brown and Back Again—the Great Circle." Baylor Law Review 23(Summer, 1971).

Coons, John E. and others. "Affirmative Integration: Studies of Efforts to Overcome De Facto Segregation in the Public Schools. A Symposium." Law and Society Review, N, 1967. [Eight cities]

Countryman, Vern (ed.). Discrimination and the Law. Chicago, IL: U. of Chicago Press, 1965.

"The Courts, HEW, and Southern School Desegregation." Yale Law Journal 77(D, 1967):321-365.

Cox, Archibald. "After Twenty Years. Reflections Upon the Constitutional Significance of Brown v. Board of Education." Civil Rights Digest 6(Summer, 1974):38-45.

_____. "Constitutional Adjudication and the Promotion of Human Rights." Harvard Law Review 80(1966):91.

Cox, Archibald, Howe, Mark De Wolfe, and Wiggins, J. R. Civil Rights, the Constitution and the Courts. Cambridge, MA: Harvard U. Press, 1967.

Craven, J. Braxton. "Integrating the Desegregation Vocabulary—Brown Rides North, Maybe." West Virginia Law Review 1(1971).

Dauterive, Verna B. "Historical Legal Development of Integration in Public Schools." Doctoral dissertation, U. of Southern California, 1966. Univ. Microfilms Order No. 66-10538.

Davies, Alfred T. "Law and Morality in Race Relations." Christian Century, O 13, 1965.

Davis, Abraham L. "Pro and Con Arguments Concerning the Judicial Use of Sociological Data in the Historic Desegregation Decision of May 17, 1954: An Evaluation." Journal of Social and Behavioral Sciences 18(Fall, 1972):45-55.

"De Facto Segregation—A Study in State Action." Northwestern University Law Review 57(1963):722-737.

"De Facto Segregation and Brown—A Constitutional Duty or Continual Despair?" Howard Law Journal 15(Winter, 1969).

"De Facto Segregation and the Neighborhood School." Wayne Law Review 9(1963):514-523.

"De Facto Segregation: Racial Concentration as a Consideration in School Districting." Rutgers Law Review 19(1965).

"De Facto Segregation—The Elusive Spectre of Brown." Villanova Law Review 9(1964):283-294.

"De Facto Segregation: Two Views." Res Ipsa Loquitur 18, pp. 10-13.

Delano, W. "Grade School Segregation: The Latest Attack on Racial Discrimination." Yale Law Journal 61(1952):730-744.

"Demise of the Neighborhood School Plan." Cornell Law Review 55(Ap, 1970).

"Desegregating Private Schools Under Section 1981." Albany Law Review 41(1977):759-787.

Deutsch, E. P. "Views from Many Bridges on School Segregation and Integration." American Bar Association Journal, Mr, 1965.

Dickens, Milton, and Schwartz, Ruth E. "Oral Argument Before the Supreme Court: Marshall v. Davis in the School Segregation Cases." Quarterly Journal of Speech 57(F, 1971):32-42.

Dimond, Paul R. "The Constitutional Right to Education: The Quiet Revolution." Hastings Law Journal 24(1973).

_____. "Reform of the Government of Education: A Resolution of the Conflict between 'Integration' and 'Community Control.'" Wayne Law Review 16(Summer, 1970).

_____. "School Segregation in the North: There Is But One Constitution." Harvard Civil Rights-Civil Liberties Law Review 7(Ja, 1972):1-55.

_____. "Segregation, Northern Style." Clearinghouse Review 5(1972).

"Discrimination in the Hiring and Assignment of Teachers in Public School Systems." Michigan Law Review, F, 1966.

Dobbin, John E. Guidelines for Service as an Expert Witness in Civil Suits Pertaining to School Desegregation, S, 1970. ERIC ED 043 692.

Dorsen, Norman (ed.). "Arthur Garfield Hays Conference. Northern School Segregation." Howard Law Journal, Fall, 1964. [Participants included Will Maslow, Robert Carter, John Kaplan and Stanley H. Lowell.]

Douglass, Frederick. "Important [Ohio] Decision for Colored Persons of Anglo-American Descent." Douglass' Monthly, Ag, 1859. [How much "white blood" defines a "white man"?]

Doyle, William E. "Social Science Evidence in Court Cases." In Education, Social Science and the Judicial Process, pp. 11-17. Washington, DC: National Institute of Education, Je, 1976.

Drinan, Robert, S.J. "Direct-Non-Violent Action and the Law." Integrated Education, Ag-S, 1964.

_____. "Racially Balanced Schools: Psychological and Legal Aspects." Catholic Lawyer, Winter, 1965.

Ducharme, Gerald D., and Eickholt, Eugene H. "Brown and Busing." Journal of Urban Law 44 (Summer, 1967):635-652.

Dunn, John C. "American Educational Jurisprudence: A Study of the Influence of State Statutes and Federal Courts on Public Schools and the Desegregation Process in the United States." Doctoral dissertation, Ohio State U., 1978. Univ. Microfilms Order No. 7902112.

Dworkin, Ronald. "The De Funis Case: The Right to Go to Law School." New York Review of Books, F 5, 1976.

_____. "Social Sciences and Constitutional Rights--The Consequences of Uncertainty." In Education, Social Science and the Judicial Process, pp. 19-26. Washington, DC: National Institute of Education, Je, 1976.

Edelman, Marian Wright. "Twenty Years After Brown: Where Are We Now?" New York University Education Quarterly 5(Summer, 1974):2-10.

_____. Twenty Years After "Brown": Where Are We Now?, Ap 4, 1974. ERIC ED 094 015.

Edmonds, Ronald R. "Advocating Inequity: A Critique of the Civil Rights Attorney in Class Action Desegregation Suits." Black Law Journal 3(1974).

Education, Social Science and the Judicial Process. Washington, DC: National Institute of Education, Je, 1976.

"Educational Malpractice." University of Pennsylvania Law Review 124(Ja, 1976):755-805.

Edwards, George. "Desegregation: A View From the Federal Bench." Crisis 83(N, 1976): 321-325.

Elden, Gary. "'Forty Acres and a Mule,' With Interest: The Constitutionality of Black Capitalism, Benign School Quotas, and Other Statutory Racial Classifications." Journal of Urban Law 47(1969-1970):591-652.

Elliff, John T. "Aspects of Federal Civil Rights Enforcement; The Justice Department and the FBI, 1939-1964." In Law in American History. Edited by Donald Fleming and Bernard Bailyn. Boston: Little, Brown, 1972.

Emerson, T. I. et al. "Segregation and the Equal Protection Clause. Brief for Committee of Law Teachers Against Segregation in Legal Education." Minnesota Law Review 34(Mr, 1950):289-329.

"Equal Educational Facilities under Equal Protection Clause of Fourteenth Amendment." Washington University Law Quarterly, D, 1950, pp. 594-616.

"Equal but Segregated Facilities for Negroes in Education--A Study in Discrimination." Intramural Law Review (N.Y.U.) 6(My, 1951): 273-284.

"Equivalence of Educational Facilities Extended by Public School System to Members of White and Members of Colored Race." A.L.R. 103 (1936):713.

Ethridge, Samuel B. "Court Decisions: Impact on Staff Racial Balance." Educational Leadership, D, 1968.

"Exclusion of Negroes from State Supported Schools." Yale Law Journal 45(1936):1296.

Falk, Gail. "12 Judges Hear School Arguments." Southern Courier, Mr 18, 1967. [Hearings by 12-judge U.S. Circuit Court of Appeals]

Fallows, James M. "Klan on Trial in U.S. Court." Southern Courier, Ag 10, 1968. [Crenshaw County, AL]

Fierst, Edith U. "Constitutionality of Educational Segregation." George Washington Law Review 17(F, 1949):208-225.

"Finding Intent in School Segregation Constitutional Violations." Case Western Reserve Law Review 28(Fall, 1977):119-165.

Finn, Chester E., and Lenkowsky, Leslie. "'Serrano' vs. the People." Commentary 54 (S, 1972):68-72.

Fiss, Owen M. "Charlotte-Mecklenburg Case-- And Its Significance for Northern School Desegregation." University of Chicago Law Review 38(Summer, 1971).

_____. "The Jurisprudence of Busing." Law and Contemporary Problems 39(Winter, 1975): 194-216.

_____. "Racial Imbalance in the Public Schools: The Constitutional Concepts." Harvard Law Review, Ja, 1965.

_____. "School Desegregation: The Uncertain Path of the Law." Philosophy and Public Affairs 4(Fall, 1974):3-39.

_____. "School Desegregation: The Uncertain Path of the Law." In Equality and Preferential Treatment. Edited by Marshall Cohen and Others. Princeton: Princeton U. Press, 1977. .

Fitt, Alfred B. "In Search of a Just Outcome." Change 9(O, 1977):22-25, 59. [Bakke case]

Flannery, J. Harold. "De Jure Desegregation: The Quest for Adequacy." Journal of Law and Education 4(Ja, 1975):141-157.

_____. School Desegregation Law: Development, Status, and Propsects: Ohio Department of Education, Office of Equal Educational Opportunity, Ap, 1972. ERIC ED 062 489.

_____. "School Desegregation Law: Recent Developments." Integrated Education, My-Je, 1972, pp. 11-19.

Fleischer, H. W. "Study of Circumvention: The Enforceability of 'Brown.'" Denver Law Center Journal, My-Je, 1964.

Forkosch, M. D. "Desegregation Opinion Revisited: Legal or Sociological?" Vanderbilt Law Review, D, 1967.

"Foreseeable Racial Segregation--A Presumption of Unconstitutionality." Nebraska Law Review 55(1975).

Freund, Paul A. "Civil Rights and the Limits of the Law." Buffalo Law Review, Winter, 1964.

Friedman, Leon (ed.). Argument. New York: Chelsea House, 1969. [Essays by Kenneth B. Clark and Yale Kamisar; copy of complete oral argument before Supreme Court in 1954 desegregation decision]

Garber, Lee O. "Courts Rule Both Ways on De Facto Segregation." U. of Pennsylvania Press, 1966.

Gegan, B. E. "De Jure Integration in Education." Catholic Lawyer, Winter, 1965.

Gellhorn, Walter. "A Decade of Desegregation...Retrospect and Prospect." Utah Law Review, Summer, 1964.

Gibson, Eddie. "Thurgood Marshall, the NAACP and the Gradual Erosion of the 'Separate But Equal Theory' in Education." Texas Southern University Law Review 4(1977).

Giles, Michael W., and Walker, Thomas G. "Judicial Policy-Making and Southern School Segregation." Journal of Politics 37(1975):917-936.

Gill, Robert L. "The Afro-American Before the Warren Court: 1953-1969." Journal of Social and Behavioral Sciences 19(Summer-Fall, 1972):21-34.

Gittell, Marilyn. [School Desegregation and the Courts] Social Policy 6(Ja-F, 1976): 36-41.

Glickstein, Howard A. "Equal Educational Opportunity: The State of the Law." Howard Law Journal 20(1977):100-127.

Goldman, Roger L. "Benign Racial Classifications: A Constitutional Dilemma." University of Cincinnati Law Review 35(1966):349-375.

Goldstein, R. D. "Swann Song for Remedies: Equitable Relief in the Burger Court." Harvard Civil Rights Law Review 13(Winter, 1978):1-80.

Goodman, Frank. "De Facto School Segregation: A Constitutional and Empirical Analysis." California Law Review 60(1972).

Gordon, I. A. "Nature and Uses of Congressional Power Under Section Five of the Fourteenth Amendment to Overcome Decisions of the Supreme Court." Northwestern University Law Review 72(N-D, 1977):656-705.

"Government Agency's Color Consciousness in Selection of Supervisory Personnel Not Unlawful [Porcelli v. Titus, D. N.J. (1969)]." Seton Hall Law Review 1(Spring, 1970).

Graglia, Lino A. Disaster by Decree. The Supreme Court Decisions on Race and the Schools. Ithaca, NY: Cornell U. Press, 1976.

"Grade School Segregation--Latest Attack on Racial Discrimination." Yale Law Journal 61 (My, 1952):730-744.

Graham, Howard Jay. "The Fourteenth Amendment and School Segregation." Buffalo Law Review 3(Winter, 1953):1-24.

Graham, Robert L., and Kravitt, Jason H. "The Evolution of Equal Protection--Education, Municipal Services and Wealth." Harvard Civil Rights-Civil Liberties Law Review 7 (Ja, 1972):103-199.

Greenawalt, Kent. "Judicial Scrutiny of 'Benign' Racial Preference in Law School Admissions." Columbia Law Review 75(Ap, 1975):559-602.

Greenberg, Jack. "Integration or Segregation?" University of Pennsylvania Law Review 118 (My, 1970).

_____. "The Meaning of Bakke's 'Window.'" Nation, Jl 22-29, 1978.

_____. Race Relations and American Law. New York: Columbia U. Press, 1959.

Gregor, A. James. "The Law, Social Science and School Segregation: An Assessment." Western Reserve Law Review, S, 1963.

Gross, M. P. "Cast Aside by the Burger Court: Blacks in Quest of Justice and Education." Notre Dame Lawyer 49(O, 1973).

Guillory, L. Marie. "The Impact of the Constitution on Segregation in Church Schools." In Catholic Schools and Racial Integration: Perspectives, Directions, Models, pp. 11-16. Washington, DC: National Catholic Conference for Interracial Justice, 1977.

Guthrie, James W. "The Educational Implications of Serrano." Education and Urban Society 5(F, 1973):197-209.

Hagman, Donald G., and Disco, Sally Grant. "One-Man One-Vote as a Constitutional Imperative for Needed Reform of Incorporation and Boundary Change Laws." The Urban Lawyer 2 (Fall, 1970):459-479.

Handler, Joel F. Social Reform Groups and the Legal System: Enforcement Problems. Madison: Institute for Research on Poverty, U. of Wisconsin, Je, 1974.

Harris, Norene, and Jackson, Nathaniel. "The Court and Desegregation: An Interview with United States District Judge Robert R. Merhige, Jr." In Norene Harris, Nathaniel Jackson, and Carl Rydingsword and Contributors, The Integration of American Schools: Problems, Experiences, Solutions, pp. 120-128. Boston: Allyn & Bacon, 1975.

_____ and _____. "Why Integration. An Interview with Judge Alfred Gitelson." In Norene Harris, Nathaniel Jackson, and Carl Rydingsword and Contributors, The Integration of American Schools: Problems, Experiences, Solutions, pp. 268-273. Boston: Allyn & Bacon, 1975.

Harrison, H. W., Jr. "Metropolitan School Desegregation: Discrimination Intent." Temple Law Quarterly 51(1978):41-68.

Hastie, William H. "Toward an Equalitarian Legal Order: 1930-1950." Annals 407(My, 1973):18-31.

"Hayes v. United States: Private Interference with School Desegregation." Harvard Civil Rights Law Review 8(My, 1973).

Henderson, Hoke F. "Separation of Races in Schools." Law Notes 32(1928):147.

Herbst, Robert L. "The Legal Struggle to Integrate Schools in the North." Annals 407(My, 1973):43-62.

Higgenbotham, A. Leon, Jr. In the Matter of Color. Race and the American Legal Process: The Colonial Period. New York: Oxford U. Press, 1978.

_____. "'To the Scale and Standing of Men.'" Journal of Negro History 60(Jl, 1975):347-396.

Hilton, Paul. "Race, Religion, and Constitutional Restraints on Private Schools." Rutgers Law Review 30(Winter, 1977).

Hirsch, Herbert, and Donohew, Lewis. "A Note on Negro White Differences in Attitutdes Toward the Supreme Court." Social Science Quarterly 49(D, 1968):557-562.

Hirschoff, M.-M. U. "Runyon v. McCrary and Regulation of Private Schools." Indiana Law Journal 52(Summer, 1977):747-760.

"Hobson v. Hansen: Judicial Supervision of the Color-Blind School Board." Harvard Law Review, My, 1968.

"Hobson v. Hansen." Reporter, Jl 13, 1967.

"Hobson v. Hansen: The De Facto Limits on Judicial Power." Stanford Law Review, Je, 1968.

Hogan, John C. "School Desegregation--North, South, East, West: Trends in Court Decision, 1849-1973." Phi Delta Kappan 55(S, 1973): 58-63.

_____. The Schools, the Courts, and the Public Interest. Lexington, MA: Heath, 1973.

Hogue, C. D., Jr. "Constitutional Law--Racial Discrimination--Discriminatory Salary Schedules of Negro School-Teachers Prohibited by Fourteenth Amendment." North Carolina Law Review 21(F, 1943):217-223.

Holley, W. H., and Feild, H. S. "Law and Performance Evaluation in Education: A Review of Court Cases and Implications for Use." Journal of Law and Education 6(O, 1977):427-448.

Holmes, E. D. "Effective Desegregation Without Busing: The Constitutionality of Anti-Injunction Legislation." Urban Law Annual 7 141-179.

Hooker, Clifford P. "The Richmond Decision--an Expansion of the White Majority Thesis." NOLPE School Law Journal 2(F, 1972):42-56.

_____ (ed.). The Courts and Education. Chicago: U. of Chicago Press, 1978.

Horowitz, H. W. "Discriminatory Fraternities at State Universities--A Violation of the Fourteenth Amendment?" Southern California Law Review 25(Ap, 1952):289-296.

_____. "Unseparate But Unequal--The Emerging Fourteenth Amendment Issue in Public Education." UCLA Law Review 13(1966):114.

"Housing Remedies in School Desegregation Cases: The View from Indianapolis." Harvard Civil Rights Law Review 12(Summer, 1977):649-691.

Houston, Charles H. "Educational Inequalities Must Go." Crisis 42(O, 1935).

_____. "How to Fight for Better Schools." Crisis 43(F, 1936).

Howard, M. E. "The Social Scientists, the Courts, and 'the School Segregation Cases': A Historical Review." Doctoral dissertation, Stanford U., 1972.

Hubbard, Maceo W., and Alexander, Raymond P. "Types of Potentially Favorable Court Cases Relative to the Separate School." Journal of Negro Education 4(Jl, 1935):375-405.

Hudgins, H. C., Jr. "Desegregation: Where Schools Stand With the Courts as the New Year Begins." American School Board Journal, Ja, 1969.

_____. "The Many Voices of the Burger Court and School Desegregation." Phi Delta Kappan (N, 1978):165-168.

Hudgins, H. C., Jr., with Gorodetzer, Marshall B. Public School Desegregation: Legal Issues and Judicial Decisions. Topeka, KS: National Organization on Legal Problems of Education, 1973.

Hughes, Michael. The Struggle for Equality in Education: From Brown to 1975, 1975. ERIC ED 139 872.

Hunsaker, David M. "The Rhetoric of Brown v. Board of Education: Paradigm for Contemporary Social Protest." Southern Speech Communication Journal 43(Winter, 1978):91-109.

Hunter, E. F. and others. "Public School Desegregation: Legal Perspectives." Georgia State Bar Journal 87(Ag, 1970).

Hyman, Jacob D., and Newhouse, Wade J., Jr. "Desegregation of the Schools: The Present Legal Situation." Urban Education, Summer, 1964.

"Implications of Recent Cases on Education of Minority Racial Groups." University of Florida Law Review 3(Fall, 1950):358-367.

"'Integrate Now': A Study of Alexander v. Holmes County Bd. of Ed'n." Notre Dame Lawyer 45(Spring, 1970).

"Interdistrict Desegregation: The Remaining Options." Stanford Law Review 28(1976).

"Interdistrict School Desegregation Remedies After Milliken v. Bradley." Boston University Law Review 56(1976).

"Is Racial Segregation Consistent with Equal Protection of the Laws? Plessy v. Ferguson Re-examined." Columbia Law Review (My, 1949):629-639.

Jacobs, Clyde E. The Eleventh Amendment and Sovereign Immunity. Westport, CT: Greenwood Press, 1972.

Jefferson, W. "School Desegregation and the Black Teacher: A Search for Effective Remedies." Tulane Law Review 48(D, 1973): 55-84.

Jencks, Christopher. "Busing--The Supreme Court Goes North." New York Times Magazine, N 19, 1972.

Jones, Butler Alfonso. "Law and Social Change: A Study of the Impact of New Legal Requirements Affecting Equality of Educational Opportunities for Negroes Upon Certain Customary Official Behaviors in the South, 1938-1952." Doctoral dissertation, New York U., 1955.

Jones, Donald J. "An Analysis of Selected Court Cases which Have Applied the Principle of Metropolitan School Desegregation as a Means of Achieving Equality of Educational Opportunity." Doctoral dissertation, U. of Michigan, 1976.

Jones, Nathaniel R. "An Anti-Black Strategy and the Supreme Court." Journal of Law and Education 4(1975).

_____. "Implications of the Weinstein Decision." Integrateducation 13(My-Je, 1975):143-146. [N.Y.C.]

_____. "Is Brown Obsolete? No!" Integrateducation 14(My-Je, 1976.

Kahng, Anthony. "University of California v. Bakke. Who Won?" Bridge 6(Fall, 1978):4-14. [An Asian-American perspective]

Kalodner, Howard I., and Fishman, James J. (eds.). Limits of Justice. The Courts' Role in School Desegregation. Cambridge, MA: Ballinger, 1978.

Kanner, S. B. "From Denver to Dayton: The Development of a Theory of Equal Protection Remedies." Northwestern University Law Review 72(Jl-Ag, 1977):382-406.

Kaplan, John. "Equal Justice in an Unequal World: Equality for the Negro--The Problem of Special Treatment." Northwestern University Law Review, Jl-Ag, 1966.

_____. "Segregation Litigation and the Schools--Part I: The New Rochelle Experience," and Part II: "The General Northern Problem." Northwestern University Law Review, Mr-Ap and My-Je, 1963.

Karst, Kenneth L., and Horowitz, Harold W. "Emerging Nationwide Standards--Charlotte and Mobile, 1971." Black Law Journal 1 (Winter, 1971):197-205.

Katzenbach, Nicholas De B. "Guidelines for Enforcement of Title IV." Integrated Education, F-Mr, 1966.

_____. "School Integration: The Bitter Realities." Integrated Education, Ag-N, 1965.

Kelly, Alfred H. "The Fourteenth Amendment Reconsidered: The Segregation Question." Michigan Law Review 54(Je, 1956):1049-1086.

"Keyes v. School District No. 1: Unlocking the Northern Schoolhouse Doors." Harvard Civil Rights Law Review 9(Ja, 1974):124-155.

Kievits, E. "Equal Protection, Negro Educational Facilities." Southern California Law Review 13(N, 1939):68-75.

Kilpatrick, William H. "Resort to Courts by Negroes to Improve Their Schools: A Conditional Alternative." Journal of Negro Education 4(Jl, 1935):412-418.

King, Donald B., and Quick, Charles W. (eds.). Legal Aspects of the Civil Rights Movement. Detroit, MI: Wayne State U. Press, 1965.

Kinney, Bradford L. "Catalyst for a Revolution--A Rhetorical Analysis of the Oral Debates on School Segregation Leading to the Supreme Court Decision of 1954." Doctoral dissertation, U. of Pittsburgh, n.d.

Kinoy, Arthur. "The Constitutional Right of Negro Freedom." Rutgers Law Review, Spring, 1967.

Kirp, David L. "Equal Education?" Yale Law Journal 78, n.d.

_____. "Law, Politics, and Equal Educational Opportunity: The Limits of Judicial Involvement." Harvard Educational Review 47 (My, 1977):117-137.

Kirp, David L., Buss, W., and Kuriloff, P. "Legal Reform in Special Education: Empirical Studies and Procedural Proposals." California Law Review 62(1974):40-155.

Kluger, Richard. Simple Justice: The History of Brown v. Board of Education and Black America's Struggle for Equality. New York: Knopf, 1976.

Konvitz, Milton R. "Law Restricting Teaching of Foreign Languages Held Unconstitutional." Common Ground 9(Winter, 1949):99-101. [Law aimed at "after-school" instruction in Chinese and Japanese]

Kovarsky, I. "Testing and the Civil Rights Act." Howard Law Review 15(Winter, 1969).

Kraft, Ivor. [Du Funis v. Odegaard] Race, Merit, and the Fourteenth Amendment, 1976. Uncommon Lawyers Workshop, P.O. Box 160636, Sacramento, CA 95816.

Kurland, P. B. "Equal Educational Opportunity: the Limits of Constitutional Jurisprudence Undefined." University of Chicago Law Review 38(Summer, 1968):583.

Kishner, James A., and Werner, Frances E. "Metropolitan Desegregation After Milliken v. Bradley: The Case for Land Use Litigation Strategies." Catholic University Law Review 24(1975).

Lawrence, C. R. III. "Segregation 'Misunderstood': The Milliken Decision Revisited." University of San Francisco Law Review 12 (Fall, 1977):15-56.

Leeson, Jim. "The Crumbling Legal Barriers to School Desegregation." Southern Education Report, O, 1966. [Southern anti-desegregation statutes]

_____. "Desegregation." Southern Education Report, Jy-Je, 1966. [New trend in southern desegregation court cases to remedy effects of past "unequal and inferior educational opportunities"]

_____. "Desegregation Guidelines and a New Court." Southern Education Report, Ja-F, 1967.

_____. "How Powerful a Weapon Did Wright Provide?" Southern Education Report, S, 1967. [The Hobson v. Hansen (Washington, DC) ruling by Judge J. Skelly Wright]

Leflar, Robert A., and Davis, Wylie H. "Segregation in the Public Schools." Harvard Law Review 67(Ja, 1954):377-435.

"Legality of Race Segregation in Educational Institutions." University of Pennsylvania Law Review 82(1933):157.

Leibowitz, Arnold H. "English Literacy: Legal Sanctions for Discrimination." Notre Dame Lawyer 45(1969).

Leubsdorf, John. "Completing the Desegregation Remedy." Boston University Law Review 57 (Ja, 1977).

Levin, Betsy, and Moise, Philip. "School Desegregation Litigation in the Seventies and the Use of Social Science Evidence: An Annotated Guide." Law and Contemporary Problems 39(Winter, 1975):50-133.

Levin, Betsy, and Hawley, Willis D. (eds.). The Courts, Social Science, and School Desegregation. New Brunswick, NJ: Transaction Books, 1976.

Lewis, John. "Black Voter Registration in the South." In Issues of Electoral Reform. Edited by Richard J. Carlson. New York: National Municipal League, 1973.

Lewis, Ovid C. "Parry and Ripose to Gregor's, 'The Law, Social Science, and School Segregation: An Assessment.'" Western Reserve Law Review, S, 1963, followed by commentary by James Gregor. [See Gregor, above]

Lichtman, Elliott C. "Title VI of the Civil Rights Act. Prospects for Enforcement Through Litigation." Civil Rights Digest 4 (Spring, 1971):25-29. [Adams v. Richardson]

Lichtman, Richard. "The Ethics of Compensatory Justice" (45-minute tape). Center for the Study of Democratic Institutions, Box 4068, Santa Barbara, CA. [Philosopher and Center staff member]

_____. "The Ethics of Compensatory Justice." Law in Transition Quarterly, 1965, pp. 73-103.

Lindquist, Robert. "Bradley v. Milliken: Was Busing Really the Question?" Educational Researcher 4(Mr, 1975):16-20.

Lindsay, Beverly, and Harris, John III. "Desegregation, the Judicial System and Social Science Research: Educational Stratagems for Black Child Development." Negro Educational Review 29(Ap, 1978):68-79.

Lubenow, Gerald C. "The Action Lawyers." Saturday Review 55(Ag 26, 1972):36-42. [Serrano v. Priest]

Lucas, Jo Desha. "Serrano and Rodriguez--an Overextension of Equal Protection." NOLPE School Law Journal 2(F, 1972):18-41.

Lucas, Louis R. "The Law and Desegregation: What Board Members and Administrators Must Understand." In School Desegregation: Making It Work, pp. 31-38. East Lansing, MI: College of Urban Development, Michigan State U., 1976.

Lundsgaarde, Henry P. "Racial and Ethnic Classifications: An Appraisal of the Role of Anthropology in the Lawmaking Process." Houston Law Review 10(Mr, 1973.

McAuliffe, D. J. "School Desegregation: The Problem of Compensatory Discrimination." Virginia Law Review 57(F, 1971).

McCarrick, E. M. "Desegregation and the Judiciary: The Role of the Federal District Court in Educational Desegregation in Louisiana." Journal of Public Law 16,

McCord, John H. (ed.). With All Deliberate Speed. Urbana, IL: U. of Illinois Press, My, 1970.

McGovney, D. O. "Race Discrimination in Naturalization." Iowa Law Bulletin 8(1923):129-211.

McMahon, William Otis. "The Litigation of the National Association for the Advancement of Colored People, 1910-1942." Master's thesis, Howard U., 1942.

Manley, R. E. "Litigation and Metropolitan Integration." Urban Law 10(Winter, 1978):73-114.

_____. "School Desegregation in the North: A Post-Milliken Strategy for Obtaining Metropolitan Relief." St. Louis University Law Journal 20(1976):585-609.

Marshall, Margaret H. "The Standard of Intent: Two Recent Michigan Cases." Journal of Law and Education 4(1975). [Kalamazoo and Grand Rapids]

Marshall, Thurgood. "Address by Solicitor General Marshall at the White House Conference on Civil Rights." Washington, DC: U.S. Department of Justice, Je 1, 1966 (mimeographed).

_____. "An Evaluation of Recent Efforts to Achieve Racial Integration in Education through Resport to the Courts." Journal of Negro Education 21(Summer, 1952):316-327.

_____. "Equal Justice Under the Law." Crisis 46(Jl, 1939):199-201.

_____. "Law and the Quest for Equality." Washington, DC: U.S. Department of Justice, Mr 8, 1967 (mimeographed).

_____. "The Legal Attack to Secure Civil Rights." In Negro Protest Though Twentieth Century. Edited by Francis L. Broderick and August Meier. Indianapolis, IN: Bobbs-Merrill, 1965. [Address given in 1944]

Martin, A. T. "Segregation of Negroes." Michigan Law Review 32(Ap, 1934):721-742.

Martinez, Susanne. "Poor People and Public Education in America: An Overview of the Impact of OEO Legal Services Agencies on Public Education." Journal of Law and Education 4(Ap, 1975):337-354.

Mathews, Donald R., and Prothro, James W. "Stateways versus Folkways: Critical Factors in Southern Reactions to Brown v. Board of Education." In Essays on the American Constitution. Edited by Gottfried Dietze. Englewood Cliffs, NJ: Prentice-Hall, 1964.

May, Henry Stratford, Jr. "Busing, Swann v. Charlotte-Mecklenburg, and the Future of Desegregation in the Fifth Circuit." Texas Law Review 49(My, 1971):884-910.

"Mexican-Americans and the Desegregation of Schools in the Southwest." Houston Law Review 8(My, 1971).

Meyer, Howard N. The Amendment that Refused to Die. Radner, PA: Chilton, 1973. [14th Amendment]

Milchen, Joseph A. "Unconstitutional Racial Classification and De Facto Segregation." Michigan Law Review, Mr, 1965.

Miller, Arthur S. Racial Discrimination and Private Education: A Legal Analysis. Chapel Hill, NC: U. of North Carolina Press, 1957.

Miller, Barry A. "Proof of Racially Discriminating Purpose Under the Equal Protection Clause: Washington v. Davis, Arlington, Mt. Healthy, and Williamsburg." Harvard Civil Rights-Civil Liberties Law Review 12 (Summer, 1977):725-770.

Miller, Loren. The Petitioners: The Story of the Supreme Court of the United States and the Negro. New York: Pantheon, 1966.

"Milliken v. Bradley in Historical Perspective: The Supreme Court Comes Full Circle." Northwestern University Law Review 69(1974).

Mills, Roger. "Justice Delayed and Denied. HEW and Northern School Desegregation." Civil Rights Digest 7(Fall, 1974):11-21.

Monaghan, P. "Law and the Negro Revolution: Ten Years Later." Boston University Law Review, Fall, 1964.

Moody, Charles D., Vergon, Charles B., and Taylor, John A. (eds.). Proceedings of Conference on Developments in School Desegregation and the Law. Ann Arbor, MI: Program for Educational Opportunity, School of Education, U. of Michigan, n.d.

Moore, Howard, Jr. "Brown v. Board of Education. The Court's Relationship to Black Liberation." In Law Against the People. Edited by Robert Lefcourt. New York: Random House, 1971.

Morgan, Douglas F. "American Blacks and the North Atlantic State Supreme Courts, 1790-1860." Doctoral dissertation, U. of Chicago, 1972.

Morris, Arval A. "Equal Educational Opportunity, Constitutional Uniformity and the 'Defunis' Reward." Washington Law Review 50(Je, 1975):565-595.

Myers, Phyllis. "Second Thoughts on the Serrano Case." City, Winter, 1971.

Nash, A. E. Keir. "Negro Rights and Judicial Behavior in the Old South." Doctoral dissertation, Harvard U., 1968.

N.A.A.C.P. "Can White Students Be Excluded?" Integrated Education, D, 1963-Ja, 1964. [Balaban case, New York City]

"The Negro Citizen in the Supreme Court." Harvard Law Review 52(Mr, 1939):823-832.

"Neighborhood School System That Causes Segregation, Whether Called De Facto or De Jure, Is Unconstitutional." Alabama Law Review 25 (Spring, 1973).

"New Perspectives on Court Ordered Busing." Columbia Journal of Law and Social Problems 8(Spring, 1972):321-355.

Norton, Eleanor Holmes. "Comment on the Bakke Decision." Personnel Administrator 23 (Ag, 1978):26-28.

O'Brien, Kenneth B., Jr. "The Supreme Court and Education." Doctoral dissertation, Stanford U., 1956. Univ. Microfilms Order No. 17732.

"On Insulating Busing from Congressional Review: The Swann Right to a Racial Mixture." American University Law Review 22(Summer, 1973).

O'Neil, Robert M. Discriminating Against Discrimination: Preferential Admissions and the De Funis Case. Bloomington, IN: Indiana U. Press, 1975.

Ortega, Joe C., and Roos, Peter D. "Chicanos in the Schools: An Overview of the Problems and the Legal Remedies." Notre Dame Lawyer 51(1975).

Papale, A. E. "Judicial Enforcement of Desegregation: Its Problems and Limitations." Northwestern University Law Review 52 (Jl-Ag, 1957):301-319.

Peterson, Gladys T. "The Present Status of the Negro Separate School as Defined by Court Decisions." Journal of Negro Education 4 (Jl, 1935):351-374.

Pfeffer, Leo. "The Courts and De Facto Segregation." Parts I and II, CLSA Reports, F 1, 1964 and Mr 15, 1964. Commission on Law and Social Action of the American Jewish Congress, 15 East 84th Street, New York, NY 10028.

Phillips, James E. "The Legal Requirement of Intent to Segregate: Some Observations." NOLPE School Law Journal 7(1977):111-125.

Pindur, Wolfgang. "Professional Comment: Legislative and Judicial Roles in the Detroit School Decentralization Controversy." Journal of Urban Law 50(1972).

Poindexter, Robert C. "An Analysis of Recent Federal Court Decisions Concerning Public School Desegregation in the United States." Doctoral dissertation, Indiana U., 1968.

Polier, Justine Wise. "Dispositional Delays Due to Segregated and Unequal Services for Non White Children." In A View from the Bench: The Juvenile Court. New York: National Council on Crime and Delinquency, 1964.

Poling, James. "Thurgood Marshall and the Fourteenth Amendment." Collier's, F 23, 1952.

Pottinger, J. Stanley. "HEW Enforcement of Swann." Inequality in Education 9(Ag 3, 1971).

Powe, R. "Constitutionality of Segregation in Elementary Public Schools." Law Guild Review 11(Summer, 1951):151–155.

Pratt, John H. "HEW Ordered to Defer Funds." Integrated Education 11(Ja–F, 1973):65–71. [Adams v. Richardson]

"Problems and Responsibilities of Desegregation: A Symposium." Notre Dame Lawyer 34 (1959):607–770.

"Problems in the Cure of De Jure Segregation in in Education: Equal Protection of the Laws or Fundamental Human Right?" New England Law Review 6(Fall, 1970).

"Public Housing and Integration: A Neglected Opportunity." Columbia Journal of Law and Social Problems 6(My, 1970).

Puryear, P. L. "Equity Power and the School Desegregation Cases." Harvard Educational Review, Fall, 1963.

"Racial Discrimination in Church Schools." Louisiana Law Review 38(Spring, 1978):874–890.

R., E. J. "Legality of Race Segregation in Educational Institutions." University of Pennsylvania Law Review 82(D, 1933):157–164.

"Racial Discrimination—Discriminatory Salary Schedules of Negro Schoolteachers Prohibited by Fourteenth Amendment." North Carolina Law Review 21(F, 1943):217–223. [Thomas v. Hibbitts 46 Supp. 368]

"Racial Imbalance and Municipal Boundaries—Educational Crisis in Morristown. Rutgers Law Review 24(Winter, 1970).

"Racial Imbalance in the Public Schools." Portia Law Journal, Fall, 1966.

"Racial Imbalance in the Public Schools: Constitutional Dimensions and Judicial Response." Vanderbilt Law Review, Je, 1965.

"Racially Disproportionate Impact of Facially Neutral Practices—What Approach Under 42 U.S.C. Sections 1981 and 1982?" Duke Law Journal 1977(Ja, 1977):1267–1288.

Ratner, Gershon M. "Inter-Neighborhood Denials of Equal Protection in the Provision of Municipal Services." Harvard Civil Rights-Civil Liberties Law Review, Fall, 1968.

Read, Frank T. "Judicial Evolution of the Law of School Integration Since Brown v. Board of Education." Law and Contemporary Problems 39(Winter, 1975):7–49.

Read, Frank T., and McGough, Lucy S. Let Them Be Judged: The Judicial Integration of the Deep South. Metuchen, NJ: Scarecrow Press, 1978.

"Reading the Mind of the School Board: Segregative Intent and the De Facto/De Jure Distinction." Yale Law Journal 86 (D, 1976):317–355.

Reid, I. S. "Cast Aside by the Burger Court: Blacks in Quest of Justice and Education." Notre Dame Lawyer 49 (O, 1973).

Reutter, E. Edmund, Jr. "The Constitutional Duty of School Boards to Eliminate Segregated Schools." IAR Research Bulletin 14(Je, 1974):1, 12–14.

Rice, Pamela H. "Racial Discrimination in Education under the United States Constitution." Doctoral dissertation, U. of Wisconsin, 1953.

Rices, C. E. "Legality of De Facto Segregation." Catholic Lawyer, Autumn, 1964.

Richardson, Elliot L. "Judicial Intervention in the Civil Rights Movement." Boston University Law Review, Winter, 1966.

Richardson, S. "Changing Concepts of the Supreme Court as They Affect the Legal Status of the Negro." National Bar Association Journal 1(O, 1941):113–129.

Roach, Stephen F. "The Federal Courts and Racial Imbalance in Public Schools." Phi Delta Kappan, Ja, 1966.

Rodgers, Harrell R., Jr. "The Supreme Court and School Desegregation: Twenty Years Later." Political Science Quarterly 89(Winter, 1974–1975):751–776.

Romanoli, Peter J. "School Attendance Areas and the Courts Relative to De Facto Segregation." Doctoral dissertation, U. of Pittsburgh, 1964. Univ. Microfilms Order No. 65-8314.

Rousselot, Peter F. "Achieving Equal Educational Opportunity for Negroes in the Public Schools of the North and West: The Emerging Role of Private Constitutional Litigation." George Washington Law Review 35(1967):698.

Sanborn, R. T. "Constitutionality of Segregation of Negroes in Public Schools." Law and Society Journal 13(N, 1948):93–101.

Sandalow, T. "Judicial Protection of Minorities." Michigan Law Review 75(Ap–My, 1977): 1162–1195.

"School Desegregation: 1954-1974." Journal of Law and Education 4(Ja, 1975):1-241.

"School Desegregation after Swann: A Theory of Government Responsibility." University of Chicago Law Review 39(1972).

"Schools and School Districts: School District Lines No Barrier to Commissioner When Seeking to Eliminate Racial Imbalance." Seton Hall Law Review 3(1971).

Schroeder, Oliver, Jr., and Smith, David T. (eds.). De Facto Segregation and Civil Rights--Struggle for Legal and Social Equality. New York: Hein, 1965.

"Section 1981 After Runyon v. McCrary (96 Sup. Ct. 2586): The Free Exercise of Private Sectarian Schools to Deny Admission to Blacks on Account of Race." Duke Law Journal 1977(Ja, 1977):1219-1266.

Sedler, Robert Allen. "Metropolitan in the Wake of Milliken--On Losing Big Battles and Winning Small Wars: The View Largely From Within." Washington University Law Quarterly, 1975.

Seegert, N. "Fourteenth Amendment--Equal Protection of the Laws--Racial Segregation in Public Educational Institutions." Michigan Law Review 46(Mr, 1948):639-645.

"Segregation in Law and Graduate School." University of Pittsburgh Law Review 12 (Winter, 1951):261-269.

"Segregation Litigation in the 1960's: Is There an Affirmative Duty to Integrate the Schools?" Indiana Law Journal, Spring, 1964.

"Segregation of Poor and Minority Children into Classes for the Mentally Retarded by Use of IQ Tests." Michigan Law Review 71(My, 1973).

"Separate-but-Equal: A Study of the Career of a Constitutional Concept." Race Relations Law Reporter 1(1956):283.

Shannon, Thomas A. "The Denver Decision: Death Knell for De Facto Segregation?" Phi Delta Kappan 55(S, 1973):6-9.

_____. "Has the Fourteenth Done It Again?" Phi Delta Kappan 53(Ap, 1972):466-471. [Serrano v. Priest]

Sherrer, C. W., and Rosten, R. A. "Some Legal and Psychological Concerns About Personality Testing in the Public Schools." Federal Bar Journal 30(Spring, 1971).

Silard, John. "Toward Nationwide School Desegregation: A 'Compelling State Interest' Test of Racial Concentration in Public Education." North Carolina Law Review 51 (Mr, 1973).

Silard, J., and White, S. "Intrastate Inequalities in Public Education: The Case for Judicial Relief Under the Equal Protection Clause." Wisconsin Law Review 7 (1970).

Simon, L. G. "Racially Prejudiced Governmental Actions: A Motivation Theory of the Constitutional Ban Against Racial Discrimination." San Diego Law Review 15(Ag, 1978).

Sindler, Allan P. Bakke, De Funis, and Minority Admissions: The Quest for Equal Opportunity. New York: Longman, 1979.

Singleton, Robert. "Impact of Serrano on Minority Pupils." Education Finance Reform Project, 1972, unpublished.

Smedley, Theodore A. "Developments in the Law of School Desegregation." Vanderbilt Law Review 26(Ap, 1973).

_____. "Legal Aspects of Desegregation." In School Desegregation: Retrospect and Prospect, pp. 15-27. Edited by Eugene C. Lee. Southern Newspaper Publishers Association Foundation, P.O. Box 11606, Atlanta, GA 30305, 1971.

_____. Race Relations Law Index 1973-74. A Listing of Federal Court Decisions Involving Race. Atlanta: Southern Regional Council, Mr, 1975.

Smith, J. E. "Post-Brown Private White Schools--An Imperfect Dualism." Vanderbilt Law Review 26(Ap, 1973):587-624.

Smith, Charles W. "Public School Desegregation and the Law." Social Forces 54(D, 1975):317-327.

Smith, H. Stuart, Jr. "An Analysis of Court-Ordered Desegregation." NASSP Bulletin 57 (Ap, 1973):34-42.

Speer, Hugh W. A Historical and Social Perspective on Brown v. Board of Education of Topeka with Present and Future Implications. Final Report, My, 1968. ERIC ED 024 747.

Spivak, Jonathan. "Desegregation Drive--Schools in North, South Face U.S. Aid Cutoffs if Integration Lags." Wall Street Journal, D 11, 1967.

Spurlock, Clark. Education and the Supreme Court. Urbana, IL: U. of Illinois Press, 1955.

Steel, Lewis M. "Nine Men in Black Who Think White." New York Times Magazine, O 13, 1968.

Stevens, Leonard B. "Neighborhood School Faces N.A.A.C.P. Test." Education News, Ag 5, 1968.

Stockard, Robert M. "The United States Supreme Court and the Legal Aspects of Busing for Public School Desegregation." Doctoral dissertation, U. of North Carolina at Greensboro, 1978. Univ. Microfilms Order No. 7824903.

Stone, I. F. "Moving the Constitution to the Back of the Bus." New York Review of Books 18(Ap 20, 1972):4-11.

Strother, David B. "Evidence, Argument and Decision in Brown vs. Board of Education." Doctoral dissertation, U. of Illinois, 1958. Univ. Microfilms Order No. 59-587.

Styles, Fitzhugh L. Negroes and the Law in the Race's Battle for Liberty, Equality and Justice Under the Constitution of the United States; With Cause Celebres. Boston: Christopher, 1937.

Sugarman, Stephen D. "Accountability through the Courts." School Review 82(F, 1974):233-259.

_____. "Equal Protection for Non-English-Speaking School Children: Lau v. Nichols." California Law Review 62(Ja, 1974):157-182.

Sullivan, Harold J. "De Facto" School Segregation: Private Choice or Public Policy?" Doctoral dissertation, City U. of New York, 1978. Univ. Microfilms Order No. 7900812.

"Swann v. Charlotte-Mecklenburg Board of Education: Roadblocks to the Implementation of Brown." William and Mary Law Review 12 (Summer, 1971).

Taylor, William L. "The Supreme Court and School Litigation." Integrateducation 15 (N-D, 1977):67-69.

_____. "The Supreme Court and Urban Reality: A Tactical Analysis of Milliken v. Bradley." Wayne Law Review 21(Mr, 1975):751-778.

Taylor, William L., Benjes, John E., and Wright, Eric E. "School Desegregation and the Courts." Social Policy 6(Ja-F, 1976):32-35.

"Text of Justice Department's Brief in Baake Case." Chronicle of Higher Education, S 26, 1977.

Thompson, Charles H. "Court Action the Only Reasonable Alternative to Remedy Immediate Abuses of the Negro Separate School." Journal of Negro Education 4(Jl, 1935):419-434.

Thompson, Frank, Jr., and Pollitt, Daniel H. "Congressional Control of Judicial Remedies: President Nixon's Proposed Moratorium on 'Busing' Orders." North Carolina Law Review 50(1972):809-841.

Tobier, Arthur, Inger, Morton, Carter, Robert, Rein, David, and Cline, Marvin. "Hobson v. Hansen--What Is Law For?" The Center Forum, Jl 5, 1967.

Tollett, Kenneth S. "The Viability and Reliability of the U.S. Supreme Court as an Institution for Social Change and Progress Beneficial to Blacks" (2 parts). Black Law Journal 2(1972) and 3(1973).

U.S. Commission on Civil Rights. The Federal Civil Rights Enforcement Effort--1974. Vol. I: To Regulate in the Public Interest. Washington, DC: The Commission, N, 1974.

_____. The Federal Civil Rights Enforcement Effort--1974. Vol. III: To Ensure Equal Educational Opportunity. Washington, DC: The Commission, Ja, 1975.

_____. The Federal Civil Rights Enforcement Effort--1974. Vol. IV: To Provide Fiscal Assistance. Washington, DC: The Commission, F, 1975.

_____. Milliken v. Bradley: The Implications for Metropolitan Desegregation. Washington, DC: GPO, 1975.

_____. Twenty Years After Brown: Equality of Educational Opoortunity. Washington, DC: The Commission, Mr, 1975.

"Unconstitutional Racial Classification and De Facto Segregation." Michigan Law Review, Mr, 1965.

U.S. Congress, 87th, 2nd session, Senate, Committee on the Judiciary. Hearings... on Nominating Thurgood Marshall, of New York, to be United States Circuit Judge for the Second Circuit. Washington, DC: GPO, 1962.

U.S. Congress, 89th, 1st session, Senate, Committee on the Judiciary. Hearings... on Nomination of Thurgood Marshall to be Solicitor General of the United States. Washington, DC: GPO, 1965.

U.S. Congress, 90th, 1st session, Senate, Committee on the Judiciary. Hearings... on Nomination of Thurgood Marshall, of New York, to be an Associate Justice of the Supreme Court of the United States. Washington, DC: GPO, 1967.

U.S. Department of Justice, Community Relations Service. Activities Relating to the Desegregation of Public Schools. August 15, 1970 to February 15, 1971. Washington, DC: GPO, 1972.

Vacca, Richard S. "The Federal Courts and Faculty Desegregation." Clearing House 46 (Ja, 1972):312-316.

Van den Haag, Ernest. "Social Science Testimony in the Desegregation Cases--A Reply to Professor Kenneth Clark." Villanova Law Review, Fall, 1960.

van Geel, Tyll. The Policy-Making Process in the Supreme Court: Problems and Solutions. Rochester, NY: College of Education, U. of Rochester, 1974.

Venable, Thelma C. "Decisions of the State Courts Involving the Rights of Negroes, 1877-1900." Master's thesis, Howard U., 1948.

Vieira, Norman. "Racial Imbalance, Black Separation, and Permissible Classification by Race." Michigan Law Review 67(Je, 1969): 1553-1626.

Vines, Kenneth N. "Southern State Supreme Courts and Race Relations." Western Political Quarterly, Mr, 1965.

von Euler, Mary, and Parham, David L. A Citizen's Guide to School Desegregation Law. Washington, DC: National Institute of Education, Jl, 1978.

Vose, Clement E. "The NAACP's Legal Strategy to Overturn Restrictive Covenants in Housing." In Law, Politics, and the Federal Courts, pp. 5-16. Edited by Herbert Jacob. Boston: Little, Brown, 1967.

Waite, Edward F. "The Negro in the Supreme Court." Minnesota Law Review 30(Mr, 1946): 219-304.

Walker, John W. "An Attorney's Viewpoint." In School Desegregation: Retrospect and Prospect, pp. 28-41. Edited by Eugene C. Lee. Southern Newspaper Publishers Association Foundation, P.O. Box 11606, Atlanta, GA 30305, 1971.

Walker, Paul. "Court Decisions Dealing with Legal Relationships between American Colleges and Universities and Their Students." Doctoral dissertation, U. of Southern California, 1961. Univ. Microfilms Order No. 61-406.

Warren, Earl. "Inside the Supreme Court. The Momentous School Desegregation Decision." Atlantic 239(Ap, 1977):35-40. [Brown]

Wasby, Stephen L, D'Amato, Anthony A., and Metrailer, Rosemary. Desegregation from Brown to Alexander: An Exploration of Supreme Court Strategies. Carbondale, IL: Southern Illinois U., 1977. [1954-1969]

Washington Research Project. What the Supreme Court Has Said About School Desegregation Ag, 1972. Leadership Conference on Civil Rights, Project One Nation, 2027 Massachusetts Avenue, N.W., Washington, DC 20036.

Weaver, Harold D. "The Law and Education for Minority Groups in Seventeen Southern States." Doctoral dissertation, Pennsylvania State College, 1946.

Wechsler, Herbert. "Toward Neutral Principles of Constitutional Law." Harvard Law Review, N, 1959. [See Armstrong, above]

Wechstein, Paul. "Legal Challenges to Educational Testing Practices." Inequality in Education 15(N, 1973):92-101.

Wiley, Walter E. "The Influence of the State and the United States Supreme Court Decisions on the Education of the Negro." Doctoral dissertation, Ohio State U., 1951.

Wilkinson, J. H. III. "Supreme Court and Southern School Desegregation, 1955-1970: A History and Analysis." Virginia Law Review 64(My, 1978):485-559.

Williams, Jamye C. "A Rhetorical Analysis of Thurgood Marshall's Arguments before the Supreme Court in the Public School Segregation Controversy." Doctoral dissertation, Ohio State U., 1959. Univ. Microfilms Order No. 59-5949.

Williams, W. T. B. "Court Action by Negroes to Improve Their Schools a Doubtful Remedy." Journal of Negro Education 4(Jl, 1935):435-441.

Wilson, Paul E. "Brown v. Board of Education Revisited." Kansas Law Review 12(1964):509-524.

Wisdom, John Minor. "Random Remarks on the Role of Social Sciences in the Judicial Decision-Making Process in School Desegregation Cases." Law and Contemporary Problems 39 (Winter, 1975):134-149.

Wise, Michael B. (ed.). Desegregation in Education: A Directory of Reported Federal Decisions. Notre Dame, IN: Center for Civil Rights, U. of Notre Dame Law School, Ap, 1977. [1954-1976]

Wright, J. Skelly. "The Courts Have Failed the Poor." New York Times Magazine, Mr 9, 1969.

_____. "De Facto School Segregation: Constitutional Issues and Scope of Remedial Action." Western Reserve Law Review, Ap, 1965.

_____. "Public School Desegregation: Legal Remedies for De Facto Segregation." New York University Law Review, Ap, 1965.

Yudof, Mark. "Equal Educational Opportunity and the Courts." Texas Law Review 51(Mr, 1973).

_____. "Title I and Empowerment: A Litigation Strategy." Inequality in Education 5(Je 30, 1970). [Title I, Elementary and Secondary Education Act of 1965]

Public Finance

Adams, John Kay. "California School Tax Ruling. What Does It Mean?" Opportunity 2(Ja-F, 1972):2-7.

Advisory Commission on Intergovernmental Relations. "Financing Local Schools--A State Responsibility." In State Aid to Local Government, pp. 31-60. Washington, DC: GPO, Ap, 1969.

_____. Public Opinion and Taxes. Washington, DC: The Commission, My, 1972.

_____. State-Local Finances: Significant Features and Suggested Legislation. 1972 ed. Washington, DC: GPO, 1972.

_____. Who Should Pay for Public Schools? Washington, DC: GPO, 1971.

Aiken, John S., and Clune, William H. III. "Economic and Legal Justifications of Fiscal Neutrality." Education and Urban Society 5 (F, 1973):177-195.

Aptheker, Herbert. "Education, Money, and Democracy." Political Affairs, Je, 1973.

Barlow, Robin. "Efficiency Aspects of Local School Finance." Journal of Political Economy 78(S-O, 1970):1028-1040.

Bendixsen, Marion F. "School Finance: A Matter of Equal Protection?" Special Report, National Committee for Support of the Public Schools, F, 1970.

Benson, Charles S. "Developing a Workable Response in Education Finance to Serrano v. Priest." Education and Urban Society 5 (F, 1973):211-222.

_____. "Education Finance and Its Relation to School Opportunities of Underprivileged Groups." Unpublished study for U.S. Commission on Civil Rights, 1966.

Benson, Charles S. and others. Final Report to the Senate Select Committee on School District Finance, Vol. I. Sacramento, CA: State Senate, Je 12, 1972.

Berke, Joel S. Answers to Inequity: An Analysis of the New School Finance. Berkeley, CA: McCutchan, 1974.

_____. "Recent Adventures of State School Finance: A Saga of Rocket Ships and Glider Planes." School Review 82(F, 1974): 184-206.

_____. "The Role of Federal Aid in the Post-Rodriguez Period." Education and Urban Society 5(F, 1973):239-254.

Berke, Joel S., Bailey, Stephen K., Campbell, Alan K., and Sachs, Seymour. Federal Aid to Public Education: Who Benefits? Syracuse, NY: Policy Institute of the Syracuse U. Research Corporation, Ja 31, 1971.

Berke, Joel S., Campbell, Alan K., and Goettel, Robert J. Financing Equal Educational Opportunity: Alternatives for State Finance. Berkeley, CA: McCutchan, 1972.

Berke, Joel S., and Kirst, Michael. "The Federal Role in American School Finance: A Fiscal and Administrative Analysis." Georgetown Law Journal 61(Mr, 1973).

Berke, Joel S. and others. "The Texas School Finance Case: A Wrong in Search of a Remedy." Journal of Law and Education 1(N, 1972).

Blair, Patricia W. General Revenue Sharing in American Cities: First Impressions, D, 1974. National Clearinghouse on Revenue Sharing, 1785 Massachusetts Avenue, N.W., Washington, DC 20036.

Bond, Horace M. "Shall Federal Funds Be Spent for Adult Negro Relief or the Education of Negro Children?" School and Society 36(Ag 13, 1932):223-224.

Boulding, Kenneth, and Pfaff, Martin (eds.). Redistribution to the Rich and the Poor. The Grants Economics of Income Distribution. Belmont, CA: Wadsworth, 1972.

Bowles, Samuel. "The Efficient Allocation of Resources in Education." Quarterly Journal of Economics, My, 1967.

Burkhead, Jesse. Public School Finance. Economics and Politics. Syracuse, NY: Syracuse U. Press, 1964.

Cable, George Washington. "Does the Negro Pay for His Education?" Forum 13(J1, 1892):640-649.

Callahan, John. Metropolitan Disparities--A Second Reading. Washington, DC: Advisory Commission on Intergovernmental Relations, Ja, 1970.

Callahan, John J., Wilken, William H., and Sillerman, M. Tracy. Urban Schools and School Finance Reform: Promise and Reality. Washington, DC: National Urban Coalition, N, 1973.

Campbell, Alan K. "Educational Policy-Making Studied in Large Cities." American School Board Journal, Mr, 1967. [Fiscal aspects]

_____. "Inequities of School Finance." Saturday Review, Ja 11, 1969.

Campbell, Alan K., and Sacks, Seymour. Metropolitan America. Fiscal Patterns and Governmental Systems. New York: The Free Press, 1967.

Campbell, Alan K., and Meranto, Philip. "The Metropolitan Education Dilemma: Matching Resources to Needs." Urban Affairs Quarterly, Fall, 1966.

Chu, M. "Political Efficacy: The Problem of Money, Race, and Control in the Schools." Wisconsin Law Review (1977):989-1033.

Clark, Wayne A. Discrimination in General Revenue Sharing in the South. Atlanta: Southern Regional Council, D, 1975.

Cleghorn, Reese. "Segregation by Tax Exemption." Nation, Je 29, 1970.

Cohen, David K., McCann, Walter J., Murphy, Jerome T., and van Geel, Tyll R. The Effects of Revenue Sharing and Black Grants on Education. Cambridge, Ma: Harvard Graduate School of Education, O 31, 1970.

Conant, James B. "Financing the Public Schools." School & Society 100(Ap, 1972): 219-222.

Coon, Charles L. Public Taxation and Negro Schools. Cheyney, PA: n.p., 1909.

Coons, John E., Clune, William H. III, and Sugarman, Stephen D. "Dollars, Scholars and Constitution." Nation, O 16, 1972, pp. 338-340.

_____, _____ and _____. Private Wealth and Public Education. Cambridge, MA: Harvard U. Press, 1970.

_____, _____ and _____. "A Workable Constitutional Test for State Financial Structures." California Law Review, Winter, 1969.

"Constitutional Implications of Withdrawal of Federal Tax Benefits from Private Segregated Schools." Maryland Law Review 33(1973).

Davis, O. A., and Kortanek, K. O. "Centralization and Decentralization: The Political Economy of Public School Systems." American Economic Review 61(My, 1971):456-462.

"Distribution of Costs and Benefits in an Urban Public School System." National Tax Journal 24(Mr, 1971).

Dye, Thomas R. "Income Inequality and American State Politics." American Political Science Review, Mr, 1969.

Eggerz, Solveig. "Federal Funding No Help to Education." Human Events, Ap 27, 1974.

"The Emergency School Aid Act." American Education 9(J1, 1973):9-11.

Fay, J. Michael. Comparability v. Community Resources: A New Wrinkle in the Intra-District Resource Allocation Controversy. Los Angeles: Education of Finance Project, 1975. [Los Angeles]

"Federal Income Tax: Exemptions and Deductions --The Validity of Tax Benefits to Private Segregated Schools." Michigan Law Review 68(Je, 1970).

"Federal Money in Public Schools." U.S. News and World Report, D 5, 1966. [Interview with Harold Howe II]

"Federal Tax Benefits to Segregated Private Schools." Columbia Law Review, My, 1968.

Financing Public Schools, 1972. Public Information Center, Federal Reserve Bank of Boston, Boston, MA 02106.

Fleming, Patsy. "New Directions for Aid to Poverty Schools." Focus 2(Je, 1964):4-5.

Fox, Lynn H., and Hurd, Gordon E. Finances of Large-City School Systems. A Comparative Analysis. Washington, DC: GPO, 1971.

Freeman, Roger A. "Should States Finance the Schools?" Wall Street Journal, Mr 31, 1972.

Friedman, Nathalie. The Federal Educational Opportunity Grant Program. New York: Bureau of Applied Social Research, Columbia U., My, 1971.

Froomkin, J. "Cost-Effectiveness and Cost-Benefit Analysis of Educational Programs." Socio-Economic Planning Services 2(1969): 381-388.

Galambos, Eva. State and Local Taxes in the South, 1973. Atlanta: Southern Regional Council, D, 1973.

_____. The Tax Structure of the Southern States: An Analysis. Atlanta: Southern Regional Council, N, 1969.

Garms, Walter I., and Smith, Mark C. "Educational Need and Its Application to State School Finance." Journal of Human Resources 5 (Summer, 1970):304-317.

Gilmore, Richard G. "The Financing of Elementary and Secondary Public School Education." Congressional Record, Ap 18, 1972, E 3886-3890.

Gittell, Marilyn, Hollander, T. Edward, and Vincent, William S. Investigation of Fiscally Independent and Dependent City School Districts. New York: City U. Research Foundation, 1967.

Goldberg, F. T. "Equalization of Municipal Services: The Economics of Serrano & Shaw." Yale Law Journal 82(N, 1972).

Goldsheid, Rudolf. "A Sociological Approach to Problems of Public Finance." In Classics in the Theory of Public Finance. Edited by Richard A. Musgrave and Alan T. Peacock. New York: St. Martin's Press, 1964.

Goldstein, S. "Interdistrict Inequalities in School Financing: A Critical Analysis of Serrano v. Priest and Its Progeny." University of Pennsylvania Law Review 120 (1972).

Government Consulting Service. Special Education and Fiscal Requirements of Urban School Districts in Pennsylvania. A Research Inquiry: The Impact of Social and Economic Conditions on Urban Education and State Fiscal Policy. Philadelphia: Fels Institute of Local and State Government, U. of Pennsylvania, 1964.

Green, Edith. "Backer of Federal Aid Asks, 'What Went Wrong?'" New York Times, Ja 16, 1974.

Grier, Boyce M. "Legal Bases for Salary Differentials of White and Negro Teachers." Doctoral dissertation, George Peabody College for Teachers, 1948.

Gordon, Edmund W. "The Political Economics of Effective Schooling." In Equality of Educational Opportunity, pp. 445-460. Edited by La Mar P. Miller and Edmund W. Gordon. New York: AMS Press, 1974.

Grubb, W. Norton. "The Purposes of Education and the Patterns of School Finance: Historical Implications." Forensic Quarterly 46(Ag, 1972):261-275.

Grubb, W. Norton, and Michelson, Stephan. "Public School Finance in a Post-Serrano World." Harvard Civil Rights-Civil Liberties Law Review 8(My, 1973).

_____ and _____. States and Schools: The Political Economy of Public School Finance. Lexington, MA: Heath, 1974.

Guthrie, James W. "School Finance Reform: Acceptable Remedies for Serrano." School Review 82(F, 1974):207-232.

Guthrie, James W., and Lawton, S. B. "The Distribution of Federal School Aid Funds: Who Wins? Who Loses?" Educational Administrative Quarterly, Winter, 1970.

Guthrie, James W., Kleindorfer, George B., Levin, Henry M., and Stout, Robert T. Schools and Inequality. Cambridge, MA: MIT Press, 1971. [Michigan]

Guthrie, James W. and others. Educational Inequality, School Finance, and a Plan for the 70's, Ap, 1970. ERIC ED 042 257.

Hansen, W. Lee (ed.). Education, Income, and Human Capital. New York: Columbia U. Press, 1970.

Hansen, W. Lee, and Weisbrod, Burton A. Benefits, Costs, and Finance of Public Higher Education. Chicago, IL: Markham, 1969.

Hickrod, G. Alan and others. Definition, Measurement, and Application of the Concept of Equalization in School Finance. An Integration and Critique of School Finance Research Conducted on the Subject of Equal Educational Opportunity. An Occasional Paper, F, 1972. ERIC ED 060 544.

_____. Further Explorations in Human Resource Migration Among School Districts in Metropolitan Areas and the Effect of This Migration Upon School Finance. Final Report, S, 1969. ERIC ED 037 963.

Hirsch, Werner Z. and others. Fiscal Pressures on the Central City... New York: Praeger, 1971.

Iannaccone, Laurence. Problems of Financing Inner City Schools. Columbus, OH: The Ohio State Research Foundation, 1972.

James, H. Thomas, Kelly, James A., and Garms, Walter I. Determination of Educational Expenditures in Large Cities of the United States. Stanford, CA: School of Education, Stanford U., 1966.

James, H. Thomas, and Levin, Henry M. "Financing Community Schools." In Community Control of Schools. Edited by Henry M. Levin. Washington, DC: Brookings, 1970.

Katzman, Martin T. The Political Economy of Urban Schools. Cambridge, MA: Harvard U. Press, 1971.

Kengla, N. D. "Federal Grants-in-Aid and Unconstitutional Conditions." George Washington Law Review 10(N, 1941):64-92.

"Keppel Tips His Hand, Shows What Federal Aid Really Means." Human Events, O 23, 1965.

Kershaw, Joseph A., and Mood, Alex M. "Resource Allocation in Higher Education." American Economic Review, My, 1970.

Kester, Donald L. Social Demand Analysis, Cost-Benefit Analysis, and Manpower Analysis Converge to Present a Clear Mandate--The Open Door Must Remain Open, 1970. ERIC ED 045 070.

Kim, Sung, Clark, Elsie, Donaldson, John, Jordan, Joseph, King, Margery, and McDowell, Eugene. The Process of Funds Allocation Under Title I of the Elementary and Secondary Education Act of 1965. Second Interim Report, Mr, 1973. Technical Analysis Division, National Bureau of Standards, Washington, DC 20234.

Kirst, M. W. "Delivery Systems for Federal Aid to Disadvantaged Children: Problems and Prospects." In U.S. Congress, 92nd, 1st session, Senate, Select Committee on Equal Educational Opportunity, Equal Educational Opportunity--1971. Part 17--Delivery Systems for Federal Aid to Disadvantaged Children, pp. 8645-8673. Washington, DC: GPO, 1971.

Le Roy, S. F., and Brockschmidt, P. "Who Pays the School Property Tax?" Federal Reserve Bank of Kansas City Monthly Review (N, 1972).

Levin, Betsy, Muller, Thomas, Scanlon, William, and Cohen, Michael. Public School Finance: Present Disparities and Fiscal Alternatives, 1972. Urban Institute, 2100 M Street, N.W., Washington, DC 20037.

Levin, Henry M. "Alternatives to the Present System of School Finance: Their Problems and Prospects." Georgetown Law Journal 61 (Mr, 1973).

_____. "The Effect of Different Levels of Expenditure of Educational Output." In U.S. Congress, 91st, 2nd session, Senate, Select Committee on Equal Educational Opportunity, Equal Educational Opportunity, Part 7--Inequality of Economic Resources, pp. 3626-3644. Washington, DC: GPO, 1970.

_____. "Equal Educational Opportunity and the Distribution of Educational Expenditures." Education and Urban Society 5(F, 1973): 149-176.

_____. "Financing Education for the Urban Disadvantaged." In U.S. Congress, 91st, 2nd session, Senate, Select Committee on Equal Educational Opportunity, Equal Educational Opportunity, Part 7--Inequality of Economic Resources, pp. 3612-3621. Washington, DC: GPO, 1970.

_____. Social Utility, Equal Educational Opportunity, and Educational Investment Policy. Albany, NY: New York State Commission on the Quality, Cost and Financing of Elementary and Secondary Education, Jl, 1971.

Levy, Frank S., Meltsner, Arnold J., and Wildovsky, Aaron. Urban Outcomes. Schools, Streets, and Libraries. Berkeley, CA: U. of California Press, 1974. [Oakland, CA]

Little, Arthur D., Inc. A Study of Property Taxes and Urban Blight. Washington, DC: GPO, Ap 23, 1973. [U.S. Congress, 93rd, 1st session, Senate, Committee on Government Operations, Subcommittee on Intergovernmental Relations, Committee Print]

McLure, William P. "The 'Conant Plan' for State Financing of All Public Schools." Integrated Education 7(S-O, 1969):52-59.

_____. "The Urgent Need for Education Finance Reform in the Seventies." Phi Delta Kappan, N, 1969.

McMurrin, Sterling M. (ed.). Resources for Urban Schools. Lexington, MA: D. C. Heath, 1971.

Meltsner, Arnold J. Political Feasibility of Reform in School Financing. New York: Prager, 1973.

Meyers, Alfred V. "The Financial Crisis in Urban Schools: Patterns of Support and Non-Support Among Organized Groups in an Urban Community." Doctoral dissertation, Wayne State U., 1964. Univ. Microfilms Order No. 65-1840.

Michelson, Stephan. "For the Plaintiffs--Equal School Resource Allocation." Journal of Human Resources 7(Summer, 1972):283-306.

_____. "The Political Economy of Public School Finance." In Schooling in a Corporate Society. The Political Economy of Education in America, pp. 140-174. Edited by Martin Carnoy. New York: McKay, 1972.

Milner, Murray. Effects of Federal Aid to Higher Education on Social and Educational Inequality, Je, 1970. ERIC ED 046 363.

Murphy, Jerome T. "Title V of ESEA: The Impact of Discretionary Funds on State Education Bureaucracies." Harvard Educational Review 43(Ag, 1973):362-385.

Need to Improve Policies and Procedures for Approving Grants Under the Emergency School Assistance Program. Report to the Select Committee on Equal Educational Opportunity, United States Senate, Mr 5, 1971. ERIC ED 049 322.

Netzer, Dick. Impact of the Property Tax. Washington, DC: GPO, MY, 1968. (U.S. Congress, 90th, 2nd session, Joint Economic Committee.)

"Note. A Statistical Analysis of the School Finance Decisions: On Winning Battles and Losing Wars." Yale Law Journal, 1972.

O'Connor, James. The Fiscal Crisis of the State. New York: St. Martin's Press, 1973.

O'Neill, Dave M. and others. "For the Defendants --Educational Equality and Expenditure Equalization." Journal of Human Resources 7(Summer, 1972):307-325.

Osborne, John. "Paying for Integration." New Republic, Je 6, 1970.

Owen, J. D. "The Distribution of Educational Resources in Large American Cities." Journal of Human Resources 7(Winter, 1972).

Parker, Frank R. "Federal Boost for Segregation." Civil Rights Digest, Fall, 1968. [On tax-exemption status of privately funded segregated schools]

Pechman, Joseph A., and Okner, Benjamin A. "Individual Income Tax Erosion by Income Classes." In U.S. Congress, 92nd, 2nd session, Joint Economics Committee, The Economics of Federal Subsidy Programs. Part Part 1--General Study Papers, pp. 13-40. Washington, DC: GPO, 1972.

Preece, P. F. W. "The Economics of Education."
Science and Society 34(Fall, 1970):303-318.

President's Commission on School Finance.
Progress Report. Washington, DC: GPO,
Mr 22, 1971.

Public Opinion and Taxes. Washington, DC:
Advisory Commission on Intergovernmental
Relations, My, 1972.

Quindry, Kenneth E. State and Local Revenue
Potential, 1970. Atlanta, GA: Southern
Regional Education Board, 1971.

Quindry, Kenneth E., and Engels, Richard A.
State and Local Revenue Potential
Atlanta, GA: Southern Regional Education
Board, 1974.

Ribich, Thomas. "Education and Poverty Revisited." Bulletin of the National
Association of Secondary School Principals
55(Ap, 1971):17-28.

Richards, D. "Equal Opportunity and School
Financing: Towards a Moral Theory of
Constitutional Adjudication." University
of Chicago Law Review 41(Fall, 1973).

Sacks, Seymour, with Ranney, David, and Andrew,
Ralph. City Schools/Suburban Schools. A
History of Fiscal Conflict. Syracuse, NY:
Syracuse U. Press, 1972.

Sacks, Seymour, and Ranney, David C. "Suburban Education: A Fiscal Analysis."
Urban Affairs Quarterly, Fall, 1966.

St. Louis, Larry, and McNamara, James F.
"Economics of Scale in a State System of
Public School Districts." Socio-Economic
Planning Sciences 7(Je, 1973):295-303.
[Model applied to Oregon]

School Finance Project. Title I Comparability:
A Preliminary Evaluation, S, 1972.
School Finance Project, Lawyers' Committee
for Civil Rights Under Law, 520 Woodward
Bldg., Washington, DC 20005.

Sclar, Elliott, Behr, Ted, Torto, Raymond, and
Edid, Maralyn. "Taxes, Taxpayers, and
Social Change: The Political Economy of the
State Sector." Review of Radical Political
Economics 6(Spring, 1974):134-153.

Shannon, Thomas A., and Benson, Charles. Schools
Without Property Taxes: Hope or Illusion?
Fastback Series, No. 1, 1972. ERIC ED
062 724.

Sklar, Morton H. "The Impact of Revenue
Sharing on Minorities and the Poor."
Harvard Civil Rights-Civil Liberties Law
Review (Winter, 1975):104-112.

Smith, Annie Tolman. "The Support of Colored
Public Schools." Independent 43(Ap 2,
1891):7.

Solmon, Lewis C. "A Note on Equality of
Educational Opportunity." American Economic
Review 60(S, 1970):768-771.

Spengler, J. J. "Economic Malfunctioning in the
Educational Industry." American Journal of
Economics and Sociology 31(Jl, 1972).

Spratlen, Thaddeus H. "Financing Inner City
Schools: Policy Aspects of Economics,
Political and Racial Disparities." Journal
of Negro Education 42(Summer, 1973):283-307.

Spratt, J. M., Jr. "Federal Tax Exemption for
Private Segregated Schools: The Crumbling
Foundation." William and Mary Law Review 1
(Fall, 1970).

Steinhilber, August W. "The Judicial Assault
on State School Aid Laws: Problems and
Prognosis." Phi Delta Kappan, N, 1969.

Stern, David. "Some Speculations on School
Finance and a More Egalitarian Society."
Education and Urban Society 5(F, 1973):
223-238.

Turner, Willie L. "Federal Aid to Negro
Education." Master's thesis, Howard U.,
1930.

U.S. Advisory Commission on Intergovernmental
Relations. Fiscal Balance in the American
Federal System. 2 vols. Washington, DC:
GPO, O, 1967 [1968] [Vol. II is entitled:
"Metropolitan Fiscal Disparities."]

U.S. Commission on Civil Rights. Inequality
in School Financing: The Role of the Law.
Washington, DC: GPO, Ag, 1972.

_____. Making Civil Rights Sense Out of
Revenue Sharing Dollars. Washington, DC:
The Commission, F, 1975.

U.S. Congress, 90th, 2nd session, Senate,
Committee on Government Operations, Sub-
committee on National Security and Inter-
national Operations. Planning-Programming-
Budgeting. Uses and Abuses of Analysis.
By James R. Schlesinger. Washington, DC:
GPO, 1968.

U.S. Congress, 91st, 1st session, Joint Economic
Committee, Subcommittee on Economy in Government. Guidelines for Estimating the Benefits
of Public Expenditures. Hearings. Washington, DC: GPO, 1969.

U.S. Congress, 91st, 2nd session, House of
Representatives, Committee on Education and
Labor, General Subcommittee on Education.
Emergency School Aid Act of 1970. Hearings...
Washington, DC: GPO, 1970.

U.S. Congress, 91st, 2nd session, House of
Representatives, Report No. 91-1634.
Emergency School Aid Act of 1969. Washington,
DC: GPO, n.d.

U.S. Congress, ilst, 2nd session, Senate, Committee on Labor and Public Welfare, Subcommittee on Education. Emergency School Aid Act of 1970. Hearings... Washington, DC: GPO, 1970.

U.S. Congress, 91st, 2nd session, Senate, Select Committee on Equal Educational Opportunity, Equal Educational Opportunity. Hearings... Part 3E. Washington, DC: GPO, 1970.

U.S. Congress, 91st, 2nd session, Senate, Select Committee on Equal Educational Opportunity. Equal Educational Opportunity. Part 6--Racial Imbalance in Urban Schools. Washington, DC: GPO, 1970.

U.S. Congress, 91st, 2nd session, Senate, Select Committee on Equal Educational Opportunity. Equal Educational Opportunity. Part 7--Inequality of Economic Resources. Washington, DC: GPO, 1970.

U.S. Congress, 92nd, 1st session, House of Representatives, Committee on Education and Labor, General Subcommittee on Education. Emergency School Aid Act. Hearings... Washington, DC: GPO, 1971.

U.S. Congress, 92nd, 1st session, House of Representatives, Committee on Education and Labor. Emergency School Aid Act of 1971. Report No. 92-576.

U.S. Congress, 92nd, 1st session, Senate, Report No. 92-17. Authorizing Additional Expenditures by the Select Committee on Equal Educational Opportunity for Inquiries and Investigations, F 19, 1971.

U.S. Congress, 92nd, 1st session, Senate, Committee on Labor and Public Welfare, Subcommittee on Education. Emergency School Aid, 1971. Hearings... Washington, DC: GPO, 1971.

U.S. Congress, 92nd, 1st session, Senate, Report No. 92-61, Committee on Labor and Public Welfare. Emergency School Aid and Quality Integrated Education Act of 1971. Report..., Ap 16, 1971. Washington, DC: GPO, 1971.

U.S. Congress, 92nd, 1st session, Senate, Select Committee on Equal Educational Opportunity. Equal Educational Opportunity --1971. Part 16A: Inequality in School Finance. Washington, DC: GPO, 1971.

U.S. Congress, 92nd, 1st session, Senate, Select Committee on Equal Educational Opportunity. Equal Educational Opportunity --1971. Hearings... Part 16B: Inequality in School Finance. Washington, DC: GPO, 1971.

U.S. Congress, 92nd, 1st session, Senate, Select Committee on Equal Educational Opportunity. Equal Educational Opportunity-- 1971. Part 16C: Inequality in School Finance. Appendix I. Schools and Inequality. [Reprint of Guthrie, Kleindorfer, Levin, and Stout, Schools and Inequality, 1969]

U.S. Congress, 92nd, 1st session, Senate, Select Committee on Equal Educational Opportunity. Equal Educational Opportunity-- 1971. Part 16D-1: Inequality in School Finance: General Appendixes. Part 16D-2: Inequality in School Finance: General Appendixes. Part 16D-3: Inequality in School Finance: General Appendixes. Washington, DC: GPO, 1971.

U.S. Congress, 92nd, 1st session, Senate, Select Committee on Equal Educational Opportunity. Equal Educational Opportunity-- 1971. Hearings... Part 18: Pupil Transportation Costs. Washington, DC: GPO, 1971.

U.S. Congress, 92nd, 2nd session, Joint Economic Committee. The Economics of Federal Subsidy Programs. Part 1: General Study Papers. Washington, DC: GPO, 1972.

U.S. Congress, 92nd, 2nd session, Joint Economic Committee, Subcommittee on Fiscal Policy. Studies in Public Welfare. Paper No. 4. Income Transfer Programs: How They Tax the Poor. Washington, DC: GPO, D 22, 1972.

U.S. Congress, 92nd, 2nd session, Joint Economic Committee. The Value-Added Tax. Hearings... Washington, DC: GPO, 1972.

U.S. Congress, 92nd, 2nd session, Senate, Select Committee on Equal Educational Opportunity. The Financial Aspects of Equality of Educational Opportunity and Inequities in School Finance. Washington, DC: GPO, 1972.

U.S. Congress, 92nd, 2nd session, Senate, Select Committee on Equal Educational Opportunity. Issues in School Finance. Washington, DC: GPO, 1972.

U.S. Congress, 92nd, 2nd session, Senate, Committee on Government Operations, Subcommittee on Intergovernmental Relations. Property Taxes. Hearings... on the Impact and Administration of the Property Tax. Washington, DC: GPO, 1973.

U.S. Congress, 93rd, 1st session, House of Representatives, Committee on the Judiciary, Civil Rights Oversight Subcommittee (Subcommittee No. 4). Budgetary Cutbacks in Community Relations Service. Hearings... Washington, DC: GPO, 1973.

U.S. Department of Health, Education, and Welfare, Office of Education, Bureau of Elementary and Secondary Education, Division of Equal Educational Opportunities. Policies and Procedures Manual for Grants to School Boards Washington, DC: The Division, O, 1969.

U.S. Department of Health, Education, and Welfare. Toward a Long-Range Plan for Federal Financial Support for Higher Education. Washington, DC: GPO, Ja, 1969.

Ware, Gilbert, and Determan, Dean W. "The Federal Dollar, the Negro College, and the Negro Student." Journal of Negro Education, Fall, 1966.

Weil, R. A. "Tax Exemptions for Racial Discrimination in Education." Tax Law Review, Mr, 1968.

Weiss, Steven J. Existing Disparities in Public School Finance and Proposals for Reform. Research Report to the Federal Reserve Bank of Boston No. 46, F, 1970. [Reprinted as pp. 7789-7933 in U.S. Congress, 92nd, 1st session, Senate, Select Committee on Equal Educational Opportunity, Equal Educational Opportunity--1971, Part 16D-2. Inequality in School Finance. General Appendixes. Washington, DC: GPO, 1971.]

_____. "The Need for Change in State Public School Finance Systems." New England Economic Review, Ja-F, 1970, pp. 3-22.

Weitz, A. S. "Race and Equal Educational Opportunity in the Allocation of Public School Teachers." George Washington Law Review 39(D, 1970).

White, Sharon. Law and Equal Rights for Educational Opportunity, 1970. ERIC ED 042 243.

Wildavsky, Aaron. "The Political Economy of Efficiency: Cost-Benefit Analysis, Systems Analysis, and Program Budgeting." Public Administration, D, 1966.

Williamson, Dorothy, Colburn, Kenneth S., and Kacser, Pamela. The Black Community and Revenue Sharing, Ja, 1973. Joint Center for Political Studies, 1426 H Street, N.W., Suite 926, Washington, DC 20005.

Willis, Benjamin C. "The Cost of Compliance with the Spirit and Letter of Federal Programs." Integrated Education, Je-Jl, 1966. [Reprint of following article]

_____. [Interview on federal aid] U.S. News and World Report, N 8, 1965.

Wise, Arthur E. "The Constitutional Challenge to Inequities in School Finance." Phi Delta Kappan, N, 1969.

_____. Rich Schools, Poor Schools. The Promise of Equal Educational Opportunity. Chicago: U. of Chicago Press, 1968.

Woodhall, Maureen. Cost-Benefit Analysis in Educational Planning. Paris: UNESCO, 1970.

Wren, Christopher S. "What Better Schools Will Cost." Look, My 17, 1966. [An interview with H.E.W. Secretary John W. Gardner; touches on problems of school desegregation]

Yudof, Mark G. "What Happened to Comparability?" Inequality in Education 5, Je 30, 1970. [Comparability of expenditures per student in poverty and non-poverty schools]

Zukosky, Jerome. "Taxes and Schools." New Republic 166(Je 17, 1972):20-23.

General

Abrams, Elliott. "The Quota Commission." Commentary 54(O, 1972):54-57. [Equal Employment Opportunity Commission]

Advisory Commission on Intergovernmental Relations. Metropolitan America: Challenge to Federalism. Washington, DC: GPO, 1966.

_____. Metropolitan Social and Economic Disparities: Implications for Intergovernmental Relations in Central Cities and Suburbs. Washington, DC: GPO, 1965.

Allen, James E. "Crisis in City Schools" (interview). U.S. News and World Report, Je 30, 1969.

_____. An Interview. Phi Delta Kappan, Ap, 1969.

_____. "An Interview with James Allen." Harvard Educational Review 40(N, 1970): 533-546.

Arnold, Mark R. "How a County Grapples with School Guidelines." National Observer, Ap 15. 1967.

Asbell, Bernard. "Does Robert Finch Have Soul?" New York Times Magazine, Ap 6, 1969.

_____. "Pat Moynihan: 'Too Much!' and 'Too Little!'" New York Times Magazine, N 2, 1969.

Ashley, G. E., and Randall, M. L. "Constitutionality of the Proposed Regional School." Missouri Law Review 13(Je, 1948):286-311.

Ball, Markham. "Dealing with Racial Imbalance in the Public Schools: A Study of the Governing Legal Principles." Appendix A in Nelson Associates, Inc., Achieving and Maintaining Ethnic Balance in the High Schools of Queens. New York: Board of Education, Ag, 1967.

Banfield, Edward. "Why Government Cannot Solve the Urban Problem." Daedalus, Fall, 1968.

Barker, Horace. The Federal Retreat in School Desegregation. Atlanta: Southern Regional Council, D, 1969.

Barry, Marion S., Jr., and Garman, Betty. A Special Report on Southern School Desegregation, O, 1965. Student Nonviolent Coordinating Committee, 107 Rhode Island Avenue N.W., Washington, DC.

Bartley, Glenda, Anderson, Robert E., Jr., Gignilliat, William R. III, and Horwitz, Kenneth M. Lawlessness and Disorder. Fourteen Years of Failure in Southern School Desegregation. Atlanta: Southern Regional Council, 1968.

Batten, James K. "Desegregation: A View from Washington." Integrated Education 8(S-O, 1970):36-41.

_____. "The Nixonians and School Desegregation." Southern Education Report, Je, 1969.

Beck, Rochelle, and Butler, John. "An Interview with Marian Wright Edelman." Harvard Educational Review 44(F, 1974):33-73.

Bell, D. "Congressional Response to Busing." Georgetown Law Journal 61(Mr, 1973).

Bell, Derrick A., Jr. Race, Racism, and American Law. Boston: Little, Brown, n.d.

Benson, Charles S. "Why the Schools Flunk Out." Nation, Ap 10, 1967.

Benson, Charles S., and Lund, Peter B. Neighborhood Distribution of Local Public Services. Berkeley, CA: Institute of Governmental Studies, U. of California, 1969.

Berger, Raoul. "The Imperial Court." New York Times Magazine, O 9, 1977.

Berry, Mary Frances. Black Resistance/White Law: A History of Constitutional Racism in America. New York: Appleton-Century-Crofts, 1971.

Bevan, C. E. "Racial Discrimination in Education." JBA Kansas 10(F, 1942):285-287.

Bickel, Alexander. "Beyond Tokenism." New Republic, Ja 4, 1964.

_____. "Busing: What's To Be Done?" New Republic, S 30, 1972.

_____. "The Debate Over School Desegregation." New Republic, Mr 21, 1970.

_____. "Desegregation: Where Do We Go from Here?" New Republic, F 7, 1970.

_____. Politics and the Warren Court. New York: Harper & Row, 1966.

_____. "Speeding Up School Integration." New Republic, My 15, 1965.

_____. "Untangling the Busing Snarl" (2 parts). New Republic, S 23, 30, 1972.

Biddle, Francis. "Democracy and Racial Minorities." Common Ground 4(Winter, 1944): 3-12.

Black, Guy. The Decentralization of Urban Government. Washington, DC: Programs of Policy Studies in Science and Technology, George Washington U., Ag, 1968.

Black, Hugo. "Just Schools for all Children..." Integrated Education 7(N-D, 1969):17-19.

Black, Virginia. "The Erosion of Legal Principles in the Creation of Legal Policies." Ethics 84(Ja, 1974):93-115. [On "reverse discrimination"]

Bland, Randall W. Private Pressure on Public Law. The Legal Career of Justice Thurgood Marshall. Port Washington, NY: Kennikat Press, 1973.

Bolner, James. "Defining Racial Imbalance in Public Educational Institutions." Journal of Negro Education, Spring, 1968.

Bond, Horace M. "The Extent and Character of Separate Schools in the United States." Journal of Negro Education 4(Jl, 1935):321-327.

_____. "Redefining the Relationship of the Federal Government to the Education of Racial and Other Minority Groups." Journal of Negro Education 7(Jl, 1938):454-460.

_____. "Shall Federal Funds Be Spent for Adult Negro Relief or the Education of Negro Children?" School and Society 36(Ag 13, 1932):223-224.

Brown, Cynthia. "Busing: Leaving the Driving to U.S...." Inequality in Education 10(D, 1971):3-6.

_____. "Nixon Administration Desegregation." Inequality in Education 9, Ag 3, 1971.

Buchanan, Patrick J. "Memorandum to the President." Harper's 244(Je, 1972):66-67. [Dated F, 1970]

Burkhead, Jesse, assisted by Fox, Thomas G., and Holland, John W. Input-Output Relations in Large City High Schools. Large City Education Systems Study, Metropolitan Studies Program, Maxwell Graduate School, Syracuse U., Syracuse, NY, 1967.

Burt, Lorin A. "The Legal Status of the Neighborhood School." I and II. American School Board Journal, Je, Jl, 1965.

"Busing, the Courts, and the Politics of Integration." Commentary 54(Jl, 1972):6-31. [Replies to Nathan Galzer, "Is Busing Necessary?" Mr, 1972 issue, and rejoinder]

Buss, William G., Jr. "The Law and the Education of the Urban Negro." In Educating an Urban Population. Edited by Marilyn Gittell. Beverly Hills, CA: Sage Publications, 1967.

Byer, Harold L. "The Legal Status of Pupil Placement in the Public Schools in the United States." Doctoral dissertation, Duke U., 1965. Univ. Microfilms Order No. 66-92.

Cahill, Robert S., and Hencley, Stephen P. (eds.). The Politics of Education in the Local Community. Danville, IL; Interstate Printers and Publishers, 1964.

Calhoun, Lillian S. "Senator Mondale, a Fighter for Integration." Integrated Education 8(N-D, 1970):51-52.

Caliver, Ambrose. "The Office of Education and Negro Schools." Southern Workman 62 (My, 1933):218-231.

_____. Supervision of the Education of Negroes as a Function of State Departments of Education. Washington, DC: GPO, 1941.

Calkins, Carl F. and others. "Children's Rights: An Introductory Sociological Overview." Peabody Journal of Education 50 (Ja, 1973):89-109.

Campbell, E. "Defining and Attaining Equal Educational Opportunity in a Pluralistic Society." Vanderbilt Law Review 26(Ap, 1973).

Campbell, Roald F. "The Folklore of Local School Control." School Review, Spring, 1959.

Canby, W. "'Northern' School Segregation: Minority Rights to Integrate and Separate." Law and Social Order, 1971.

Carol, Lila N. Viewpoints and Guidelines on Court Appointed Citizens Monitoring Commissions in School Desegregation, 1978. ERIC ED 153 364.

Carol, Lila N., and Day, Robert. Court Mandated Citizen Participation in School Desegregation: Monitoring Commissions, 1977. ERIC ED 151 470.

Carter, Robert L. "Equal Educational Opportunity." Black Law Journal 1(Winter, 1971):197-205.

_____. "Equal Educational Opportunity for Negroes--Abstraction or Reality." University of Illinois Law Forum, Summer, 1968.

Carter, Robert L. and others. Equality. New York: Pantheon, 1965. [On quotas and preferential treatment]

Carter, Robert L. The Legal Responsibilities of Public Schools for Dealing with Minority Group Members, Ag, 1967. Paper presented at Conference on the Disadvantaged (U. of Wisconsin-Milwaukee, Je 8-9, 1967), 21 pp. ERIC ED 022 805.

_____. "The Right to Equal Educational Opportunity." In The Rights of Americans. Edited by Norman Dorsen. New York: Pantheon, 1971.

_____. "Toward Apartheid." Integrated Education 8(N-D, 1970):27-32.

_____. "The University and the Racial Crisis." In The Campus Crisis. Edited by William M. Birenbaum. New York: Practicing Law Institute, 1969.

Center for Law and Education. Classification Materials. Rev. ed. Cambridge, MA: Center for Law and Education, Harvard U., S, 1973.

Chesteen, Richard D. "Bibliographical Essay: The Legal Validity of Jim Crow." Journal of Negro History 56(O, 1971):284-293.

Cheung, S. N. "Property Rights in Children." Economic Journal 82(Je, 1972).

Clair, Joseph. "Urban Education and the Exceptional Child: A Legal Analysis." Journal of Negro Education 42(Summer, 1973): 351-359.

Clark, Kenneth B. "Fifteen Years of Deliberate Speed." Saturday Review, D 20, 1969.

_____. "Social Science, Constitutional Rights and the Courts." In Education, Social Science and the Judicial Process, pp. 3-9. Washington, DC: National Institute of Education, Je, 1976.

Clark, R. "Education: Integration or Catastrophe?" Seton Hall Law Review 1(Fall, 1970.

Clayton, Claude F., Jr. "Equal Protection and Standardized Testing." Mississippi Law Journal 44(N, 1973):900-927.

Clymer, Adam. "John W. Gardner, An Interview." Integrated Education, D, 1965-Ja, 1966.

Cohen, David K. "Defining Equal Educational Opportunity." Georgetown Law Journal 61 (Mr, 1973).

_____. "The Economics of Inequality." Saturday Review, Ap 19, 1969.

Cohen, David K., and van Geel, Tyll R. "Public Education." In The State and the Poor. Edited by Samuel H. Beer and Richard E. Barringer. Cambridge, MA: Winthrop Publishers, 1970.

Cohen, Wilbur J. "Education and Learning." Annals, S, 1967. [The need for indicators to measure progress toward goals]

Combating Discrimination in the Schools. Legal Remedies and Guidelines. Washington, DC: National Educational Association, 1973.

"Community Control of the Public School--Practical Approach for Achieving Equal Educational Opportunity: A Socio-Legal Perspective." Suffolk University Law Review 3(Spring, 1969).

"Community Resistance to School Desegregation: Enjoining the Undefinable Class." University of Chicago Law Review 44(Fall, 1976):111-167.

"Completing the Job of School Desegregation: A Symposium." Howard Law Journal 19(1975).

Coons, John E. "Recreating the Family's Role in Education." Inequality in Education 1, Nos. 3-4(1970):1-5.

Coons, John E. and Others. "Reslicing the School Pie." Teachers College Record 72(My, 1971): 485-493.

Council of Chief State School Officers. State and Local Responsibilities for Education. Washington, DC: The Council, 1968.

Cover, Robert M. Justice Accused: Antislavery and the Judicial Process. New Haven, CT: Yale U. Press, 1975.

Craven, J. Braxton, Jr. "The Impact of Social Science Evidence on the Judge: A Personal Comment." Law and Contemporary Problems 39 (Winter, 1975):150-156.

_____. "Through a Looking Glass: The Constitutional Imperative." In School Desegregation: Retrospect and Prospect, pp. 7-14. Edited by Eugene C. Lee. Southern Newspaper Publishers Association Foundation, P.O. Box 11606, Atlanta, GA 30305, 1971.

Crockett, George W., Jr. "Justice, the Courts, and Change." Journal of Applied Behavioral Science 10(1974):361-366.

_____. "The United Nations--The American Negro and His Government." Freedomways, Spring, 1965.

"Cultural Pluralism." Harvard Civil Rights Law Review 13(Winter, 1978):133-173.

Cunningham, Luvern L. "Educational Governance and Policy Making in Large Cities." Public Adminstration Review 30(Jl-Ag, 1970):333-339.

Cunningham, Luvern L., and Carol, Lila N. "Court Ordered Monitoring of School Desegregation." Theory Into Practice 17(F, 1978): 81-85.

Daly, Charles U. (ed.). The Quality of Inequality: Urban and Suburban Public Schools. Chicago: U. of Chicago Center for Policy Study, 1968.

Davis, Gordon J., and Hawes, Amanda. "Toward an Understanding of Decision Making in the Office of Economic Opportunity: the CDMG Affair." Harvard Civil Rights-Civil Liberties Law Review, Spring, 1967. [Child Development Group of Mississippi Head Start Program]

De Lone, Richard H. "Cool Man in a Hot Seat." Saturday Review, S 20, 1969. [U.S. Commissioner of Education James E. Allen, Jr.]

Delgado, Richard. "Minority Students and the Legal Curriculum: An Experiment at Berkeley." California Law Review 63(1975).

"Demise of Race Distinctions in Graduate Education." Duke B Journal 1(Je, 1951):135-169.

Denison, Edward F. "An Aspect of Inequality of Opportunity." Journal of Political Economy 78(S-O, 1970):1195-1202.

Desegregation Studies Staff (ed.). School Desegregation: A Report of State and Federal Judicial and Administrative Activity As of September 1977. Washington, DC: National Institute of Education, O, 1977.

Dimond, Paul R. "The Law of School Classification." Inequality in Education 12(Jl, 1972): 30-38.

_____. "Segregation, Northern Style." Inequality in Education 9, Ag 3, 1971.

Directory of Federal Programs for Schools and Communities. New York: Basic Systems, Inc., 1966.

"Discrimination Against Negroes in Public Education." International Juridical Association Bulletin 10(O, 1941).

"Discrimination in Employment, Housing, and Education: Constitutional Concepts and Social Theories." The Catholic Lawyer 16(Spring, 1970).

Document. "Senate Quizzes Richardson." Integrated Education 8(N-D, 1970):52-55.

Dorsen, Norman. "Racial Discrimination in 'Private' Schools." William and Mary Law Review, Fall, 1967.

_____. "The Role of the Lawyer in America's Ghetto Society." In Vern Countryman and others, Law in Contemporary Society. Austin, TX: U. of Texas Press, 1973.

Douglass, Frederick. "Citizenship of Colored Americans." Douglass' Monthly, F, 1863.

Drew, Elizabeth Brenner. "The [U.S.] Civil Rights Commission." Atlantic, Ag, 1967. [The Commission's problems in studying urban problems]

Dreyfuss, Joel. "The Verdict Was 'Too Negative.'" Washington Post, S 30, 1973. [How a book on minority lawyers and judges was dis-sponsored by the Practicing Law Institute]

Du Bois, W. E. B. "Does 'All Deliberate Speed' Mean 338 Years?" National Guardian 10(N 4, 1957).

_____. "The Negro Citizen." In Charles S. Johnson, The Negro in American Civiliza-tion, pp. 461-470. New York: Holt, 1930.

Dulles, Foster Rhea. The Civil Rights Commission, 1957-1965. East Lansing, MI: Michigan State U. Press, 1968.

Dunbaugh, Frank. "The Justice Department and Northern Integration." Integrateducation 13 (My-Je, 1975):11-13.

Dunnaway, Edin E. and others. "Affirmative Discrimination: I. Schools and Housing" (50-minute tape). Center for the Study of Democratic Institutions, Box 4068, Santa Barbara, CA. [Former Supreme Court Justice of Arkansas]

DuValle, A. "The Legal Status of Negro Education." Master's thesis, U. of Indiana, 1920.

Dworkin, Ronald. "The Jurisprudence of Richard Nixon." New York Review of Books, My 4, 1972.

Dye, Thomas R. "Governmental Structure, Urban Environment, and Educational Policy." Midwest Journal of Political Science, Ag, 1967.

Edelman, Marian Wright. "The Debate Over School Desegregation." New Republic, Mr 21, 1970.

Edelstein, Frederick S. "Federal and State Roles in School Desegregation." Education and Urban Society 9(My, 1977):303-326.

Eisner, Mary. "Courts, Schools, Race." New Republic 169(Jl 21, 1973):13-14.

Ellickson, Bryan. "Jurisdictional Fragmenta-tiob and Residential Choice." American Economic Review 61(My, 1971):334-339.

Emerson, Thomas I., Haber, David, and Dorsen, Norman. Political and Civil Rights in the Untied States, II, pp. 1607-1792. Boston: Little, Brown, 1967.

Equal Educational Opportunities; Annual Re-port, Fiscal Year 1969. Washington, DC: Office of Education (DHEW), 1970. ERIC ED 042 855.

Equal Educational Opportunity Policy Research Project. Federal Policies for Equal Educa-tional Opportunity: Conflict and Confusion. Austin, TX: Lyndon B. Johnson School of Public Affairs, U. of Texas, 1977.

"Equal Protection and Intelligence Classifica-tion." Stanford Law Review 26(1974).

"Equality of Educational Opportunity: Are Compensatory Programs Constitutionally Re-quired?" Southern California Law Review 42 (Fall, 1968).

Equivalence of Educational Facilities Extended by Public School System to Members of White and Members of Colored Race." American Law Reports 103(1936):713-719.

ERIC (comp.). Educational Finance. An ERIC Bibliography, 1972. Macmillan Library Services, 866 Third Avenue, New York, NY 10022.

Fain, Robert P. "Attitudes of School Board Members Toward Inter-School District Coopera-tion." Doctoral dissertation, U. of Missouri, Kansas City, 1970.

Fairley, Richard L. "Comparability." American Education 6(O, 1970):20.

"A Federal Hand on Local Schools?" U.S. News and World Report, N 8, 1965.

Fields, Cheryl M. "57 Rights Groups Hit HEW on Anti-Bias Enforcement." Chronicle of Higher Education, D 22, 1975.

Finch, Robert H. "New Approach to Integration?" (Interview). U.S. News and World Report, Mr 10, 1969.

"Finch's Guidelines." New Republic, My 3, 1969.

Foster, G. W., Jr. "Color Conscious, Color Blind." Progressive, Mr, 1966.

_____. "Statement...in Support of the Nomination of Judge Clement F. Haynsworth, Jr Jr." In U.S. Congress, 91st, 1st session, Senate, Committee on the Judiciary, Clement F. Haynsworth, Jr. Hearings, pp. 602-611. Washington, DC: GPO, 1969.

Foster, William P. "Bilingual Education: An Educational and Legal Survey." Journal of Law and Education 5(1976).

Frieden, Bernard J. "Can Federal Programs Help Negroes Leave the Ghetto?" In U.S. Commission on Civil Rights. Papers Prepared for National Conference on Equal Educational Opportunity in America's Cities. Washington, DC: GPO, 1968.

"From All Deliberate Speed to Deliberate Slow-down." I. F. Stone's Bi-Weekly, Ap 6, 1970.

Fuller, Edgar, and Pearson, Jim Berry (eds.). Education in the States: Historical Development and Outlook. Washington, DC: National Education Association, 1969.

_____ and _____ (eds.). Education in the States: Nationwide Development Since 1900. Washington, DC: National Education Association, 1969.

Gall, Peter. "Mores of Protest." In Blowing the Whistle: Dissent in the Public Interest, pp. 168-181. Edited by Charles Peters and Taylor Branch. New York: Praeger, 1972.

Garber, Lee O. Current Legal Concepts in Education. Philadelphia: U. of Pennsylvania Press, 1966.

_____. "How Courts Look at Pupil and Faculty Desegregation." Nation's Schools, N, 1969.

_____. Yearbook of School Law. Danville, IL: Interstate Printers and Publishers, 1966.

Garfinkle, Herbert. "Social Science Evidence and the School Segregation Cases." Journal of Politics, F, 1959.

Garnett, Bernard. "Blacks in HEW Form Caucus." Race Relations Reporter 2(O 18, 1971):8-9.

Ginger, Ann Fagan (ed.). Civil Liberties Docket XIII: 1967-1968, 1968. The National Lawyers Guild, Box 673, Berkeley, CA 94701. [Comprehensive listing of cases on civil liberties, due process, civil rights, and law of the poor]

Giles, Micheal W. "H.E.W. versus the Federal Courts: A Comparison of School Segregation Enforcement." American Politics Quarterly 3 (Ja, 1975):81-90.

Gittell, Marilyn. "The Illusion of Affirmative Action." Change 7(O, 1975):39-43.

Glazer, Nathan. "Affirmative Action vs. Quotas." Harvard Crimson, Mr 20, 1973.

_____. "Is Busing Necessary?" Commentary 53 (Mr, 1972):39-52.

Glickstein, Howard. "Political and Legal Progress Since 1964." Integrateducation 13 (My-Je, 1975):16-17.

Goettel, Robert J., and Andrew, Ralph. "School-by-School Expenditures and Educational Need in Three Urban Districts." Planning and Changing 3(F, 1972):11-23.

Goodman, Paul. "What Rights Should Children Have?" New York Review 17(S 23, 1971):20-22.

Goodman, Walter. "The Return of the Quota System." New York Times Magazine, S 10, 1972.

"Government's Plan to Desegregate the Suburbs." U.S. News and World Report, O 10, 1966.

Graham, Howard Jay. Everyman's Constitution. New York: Norton, 1968.

Grant, William. "Judge on the Firing Line." Nation, D 24, 1973. [U.S. Distri Judge Damon J. Keith]

Grayzel, J. A. "Using Social Science Concepts in the Legal Fight Against Discrimination: Servant or Sorcerer's Apprentice?" American Bar Association Journal 64(Ag, 1978):1238-1244.

Green, Edith S. "The Federal Government and School Desegregation." Social Action, S, 1965.

Green, Philip. "Science, Government, and the Case of RAND, A Singular Pluralism." World Politics, Ja, 1968. [On the politics in social scientific studies performed for the federal government]

Greenberg, Gary, Jr. "Revolt at Justice." University of Chicago Magazine, Mr-Ap, 1970. [Movement within U.S. Dept. of Justice on behalf of desegregation policy]

Greenberg, Jack. "Legal Problems--North and South." Intergrateducation 13(My-Je, 1975):6-7.

_____. "The Tortoise Can Beat the Hare." Saturday Review, F 17, 1968. [Recent developments in the law of desegregation]

Greene, Maxine. "The Visibility of Harold Howe." School and Society, Ja 21, 1967.

Greenfield, Meg. "What is Racial Balance in the Schools?" Reporter, Mr 23, 1967.

Greenhaus, Jeffrey H., and Gavin, James F. "The Relationship between Expectancies and Job Behavior for White and Black Employees." Personnel Psychology 25(Autumn, 1972):449-455.

Grieder, Calvin. "Why Bully Schoolmen for Not Giving Instant Desegregation?" Nation's Schools, S, 1966.

Griffith, Katherine S. "U.S.D.A. It Remains Government's Worst Rights Offender." South Today, N, 1969.

Gross, M. "Reckoning for Legal Services: A Case Study of Legal Assistance in Indian Education." Notre Dame Lawyer 49(O, 1973).

Groves, H. E. "Revolt of Black Students." Utah Law Review, Ja, 1969.

Grubb, W. Norton. "Breaking the Language Barrier: The Right to Bilingual Education." Harvard Civil Rights Law Review 9(Ja, 1974).

Guidelines for the Collection, Maintenance, and
Dissemination of Pupil Records. Report of
a Conference on the Ethical and Legal Aspects
of School Record Keeping. New York: Russell
Sage Foundation, 1970.

Hahn, Jeanne. "The NAACP Legal Defense and Ed-
ucational Fund: Its Judicial Strategy and
Tactics." In Stephen L. Wasby, American
Government and Politics. New York:
Scribner's, 1973.

Hall, Em. "On the Road to Educational Failure:
A Lawyer's Guide to Tracking." Inequality
in Education 5, Je 30, 1970.

_____. "The Politics of Special Education."
Inequality in Education 1, Nos. 3-4(1970):
17-25.

Hamilton, Charles V. The Black Experience in
American Politics. New York: Putnam, 1973.

Hansen, C. E. "Central City and Suburb: A
Study of Educational Opportunity." Doctoral
dissertation, U. of California, Berkeley,
1969.

Hansen, W. Lee. "Income Distribution Effects
of Higher Education." American Economic
Review, My, 1970.

Harbaugh, William H. Lawyer's Lawyer. The
Life of John W. Davis. New York: Oxford
U. Press, 1973.

Hahn, Harlan, and Holland, R. William.
American Government: Minority Rights
Versus Majority Rule. New York: Wiley,
1975.

Hare, Nathan. "The Attitudes and Behavior of
the Government Towards Minorities."
Social Education 36(O, 1972):586-589.

Harris, Richard. "Annals of Politics (The
Department of Justice--III)." New York,
N 22, 1969.

_____. Decision. New York: Dutton, 1971.
[The rejected nomination of G. Harrold
Carswell to the U.S. Supreme Court]

Hartman, Robert W. "A Comment on the Pechmann-
Weisbrod Controversy." Journal of Human
Resources 5(F, 1970):519-523.

Havemann, Joel. "Torn By Parents and Courts on
Busing, Candidates Go With the Parents."
National Journal 4(Ap 15, 1972):630-641.

HEW Urban Education Task Force. Urban School
Crisis. The Problem and Solutions.
Washington, DC: National School Public
Relations Association, 1970.

Healy, Timothy S. "The Debate Over School
Desegregation." New Republic, Ap 4, 1970.

Hedgepeth, William. "America's Concentration
Camps: The Rumors and the Realities."
Look, My 28, 1968.

Hicks, Donald Albert. "An Analysis of Patterns
of Change in the Evaluation of the Federal
Role in School Desegregation: 1956-1972."
Doctoral dissertation, U. of North Carolina,
1976. Univ. Microfilms Order No. 77-2048.

Hirsch, Werner Z. "Planning Education Today
for Tomorrow." Urban Affairs Quarterly,
S, 1966.

Hickrod, G. Alan, and Hubbard, Ben C. "Social
Stratification, Educational Opportunity, and
the Role of State Departments of Education."
Educational Administration Quarterly, Winter,
1969.

Hobson, Julius W. "Uncle Sam, the Biased
Employer." Integrated Education 8(S-O,
1970):27-30.

Horowitz, H. W. "Equal Protection Aspects of
Inequalities in Public Education and Public
Assistance Programs from Place to Place
Within a State." University of California,
Los Angeles Law Review, Ap, 1968.

Houston, Charles H. "Educational Inequalities
Must Go!" Crisis 42(O, 1935):300-301, 316.

_____. "How to Fight for Better Schools."
Crisis 43(F, 1936):52, 59

Howe, Harold II. "Education's Most Crucial
Issue." Integrated Education, Je-Jl, 1966.

_____. "How New Desegregation Rules Will
Work." Nation's Schools, Ap, 1968.

_____. The Human Frontier: Remarks on
Equality in Education. Washington, DC:
GPO, 1966. [Four articles]

_____. "Test for Schoolmen: Action on
Segregation." American Federationist, Ag,
1966.

Howie, Donald L. W. "The Image of Black People
in Brown v. Board of Education." Journal of
Black Studies 3(Mr, 1973):371-384.

Huebner, Lee W. "Nixon and the Blacks. An
Exclusive Statement from the White House."
The Black Politician, Fall, 1969.

Hughes, Graham. "The Right to Special
Treatment." In The Rights of Americans.
What They Are—What They Should Be, pp. 94-
109. Edited by Norman Dorsen. New York:
Pantheon, 1971.

"Inequality in Desegregation: Black School
Closings." University of Chicago Law
Review, 1972.

"Integration: A Tool for the Achievement of
the Goal of Quality Education." Howard Law
Journal, Summer, 1968.

"Integration of Higher Education in the South." _Columbia Law Review_ 69(Ja, 1969): 112.

Jacobson, Robert L. "U.S. Campaign on College Bias Seen Faltering." _Chronicle of Higher Education_, Mr 9, 1970.

James, H. Thomas. "Politics and Community Decision Making in Education." _Review of Educational Research_, O, 1967.

Jenkins, Timothy L. "Study of Federal Effort to End Job Bias: A History, a Status Report, and a Prognosis." _Howard Law Journal_ 14 (Summer, 1968):259-329.

Johnson, Tobe. _Metropolitan Government: A Black Analytical Perspective_. Washington, DC: Joint Center for Political Studies, 1972.

Joint Legislative Committee on Metropolitan and Regional Areas Study. _Governing Urban Areas: Realism and Reform_. Legislative Document (1967), No. 42. Albany, NY: The Committee, Mr 31, 1967.

Jones, Butler A. "Law and Social Change: A Study of the Impact of New Legal Requirements Affecting Equality of Educational Opportunities for Negroes upon Certain Customary Official Behavior in the South, 1938-1952." Doctoral dissertation, New York U., 1955. Univ. Microfilms Order No. 24441.

Kahn, Alfred J., Kamerman, Sheila B., and McGowan, Brenda G. _Child Advocacy. Report of a National Baseline Study_. Washington, DC: GPO, 1973.

Kalish, James A. "Flim-Flam, Double-Talk, and Hustle: The Urban Problems Industry." _The Washington Monthly_, N, 1969.

Kaplan, John. "A Legal Look at Prosocial Behavior: What Can Happen for Failing to Help or Trying to Help Someone." _Journal of Social Issues_ 28(1972):219-226.

Karmin, Monroe W. "Integrating Classes: Federal Officials Now Favor End to Tradition of Neighborhood Schools." _Wall Street Journal_, Ag 12, 1966.

Kelley, Florence. "The Sterling Discrimination Bill." _Crisis_ 26(O, 1923).

Keppel, Francis. "Thank God for the Civil Rights Movement." _Integrated Education_, Ap-My, 1964.

Kiesling, Herbert. "The Value to Society of Integrated Education and Compensatory Education." _Georgetown Law Journal_ 61(Mr, 1973).

King, David L. "A Critique of Wise's Thesis." _Phi Delta Kappan_, N, 1969. [Ref. to Arthur E. Wise]

Kinsley, Susan F. "Can Feminine Muscle Lift Faculty Job Barriers?" _Harvard Crimson_, Ap 18, 1972.

Kirp, David L. "Community Control, Public Policy, and the Limits of the Law." _Michigan Law Review_ 68(Je, 1970).

_____. "Desegregation and the Limits of Legalism." _Public Interest_ 47(Spring, 1977): 101-128.

_____. "The Great Sorting Machine." _Phi Delta Kappan_ 55(Ap, 1974):521-525.

_____. "The Poor, the Schools, and Equal Protection." _Harvard Educational Review_, Fall, 1968.

_____. "Race, Class, and the Limits of Schooling." _Urban Review_ 4(1970):10-13.

_____. "The Role of Law in Educational Policy." _Social Policy_ 2(S-O, 1971):42-47.

_____. "Schools as Sorters: The Constitutional and Policy Implications of Student Classification." _University of Pennsylvania Law Review_ 121(Ap, 1973).

Klein, Steven N. "Desegregation of Private Schools: Pursuit and Challenge." _Intramural Law Review_ (N.Y.U. School of Law), Mr, 1966.

Knoll, Erwin. "Still Separate, Still Unequal." _Progressive_, S, 1969.

Kohler, Mary. "The Rights of Children--An Unexplored Constituency." _Social Policy_ 1 (Mr-Ap, 1971):36-43.

Kotin, L. "Equal Educational Opportunity: The Emerging Role of the State Board of Education." _Buffalo University Law Review_ 211 (Spring, 1970).

Krislov, Samuel. "Constituency vs. Constitutionalism: The Desegregation Issue and Tensions and Aspirations of Southern Attorneys General." _Midwest Journal of Political Science_ 3(1959):75-92.

Kunstler, William M. _Deep in My Heart_. New York: Morrow, 1966.

Large, Arlene J. "The Senate Debates School Segregation." _Wall Street Journal_, F 13, 1970.

"The Law-and-Order Man." _Newsweek_, S 8, 1969. [U.S. Attorney General John N. Mitchell]

Lawyers' Committee on Civil Rights Under Law. _State Legal Standards for the Provision of Public Education_. Washington, DC: National Institute of Education, N, 1978. [Part 1 of Compendium of State Legal Standards for the Provision of Public Education]

Leadership Conference on Civil Rights. "The Carter Administration and Civil Rights: An Assessment of the First 18 Months." Integrateducation 16(N-D, 1978):9-19.

Leeson, Jim. "The Attention Now Turns to 'Balance.'" Southern Education Report, Je, 1967. [The U.S. Commission on Civil Rights' report, Racial Isolation in the Public Schools]

_____. "Desegregation: A New Approach, A New Deadline." Southern Education Report, Ja-F, 1968.

_____. "Desegregation. Checking on College Compliance." Southern Education Report, Ap, 1968.

_____. " Desegregation Guidelines--A Repeat Performance." Southern Education Report, O, 1966.

_____. "Desegregation. Violence, Intimidation, and Protest." Southern Education Report, D, 1966.

_____. "Equality of Educational Opportunity: Some Basic Beliefs Challenged." Southern Education Report, My, 1967. [Discussion of the "Coleman Report"]

_____. "Herbert Wey: Consultant to Southern Schoolmen." Southern Education Report, Jl-Ag, 1966.

_____. "Questions, Controversies and Opportunities." Southern Education Report, N-D, 1965. [The Educational Opportunities Survey]

Lefkowitz, Benjamin, and D'Esopo, Donato A. Analysis of Alternative Methods of Improving Racial Balance in a School District. Menlo Park, CA: Stanford Research Institute, 1967.

Leflar, R. A. "Legal Education: Desegregation in Law Schools." American Bar Association Journal 43(F, 1957):145.

Leonard, Jerris. "Some Considerations of Policy in the Enforcement of Civil Rights Laws." Your Schools, O, 1969. [Letter to all attorneys, Civil Rights Division, U.S. Department of Justice, S 18, 1969]

Levin, Henry M. "Education, Life Chances, and the Courts: The Role of Social Science Evidence." Law and Contemporary Problems 39 (Spring, 1975):217-240.

Lieberman, Myron. "The Civil Rights Fiasco in Public Education." Phi Delta Kappan, My, 1966.

Lindegren, Alina M. "The Federal Government in American Education." Doctoral dissertation, U. of Wisconsin, 1928.

Littlewood, Tom. "David S. Seeley: An Interview." Integrated Education, D, 1965-Ja, 1966.

Lobenthal, Joseph, Jr. "The Benched Community." Center Forum, My 15, 1969. [The courts and community control]

Lockard, Duane. The Perverted Priorities of American Politics. New York: Macmillan, 1971.

Lowe, William T. and others. Strategies for Metropolitan Cooperation in Education. Final Report, n.d. ERIC ED 052 545.

Lyke, Robert F. "Representation and Urban School Boards." In Community Control of Schools. Edited by Henry M. Levin. Washington, DC: Brookings, 1970.

Lynn, Conrad J. There is a Fountain: The Autobiography of a Civil Rights Lawyer. Westport, CT: L. Hill, 1978.

McCain, R. Ray. "Reactions to the United States Supreme Court Segregation Decision of 1954." Georgia Historical Quarterly, D, 1968.

McCaskill, James L. "How the Kelley Bill Was Lost and Why." NEA Journal 65(S, 1956): 363-366. [In re: the Powell Amendment against use of federal aid for discriminatory purposes]

McClung, Merle. "School Classification: Some Legal Approaches to Labels." Inequality in Education 14(Jl, 1973):17-37.

McClure, Phyllis. "New Legal Strategies for School Equality." Civil Rights Digest, Fall, 1968.

McGivney, Joseph H., and Bowles, B. Dean. "The Political Aspects of PPBS." Planning and Changing 3(Ap, 1972):3-12.

McKay, Robert B. "Racial Discrimination in the Electoral Process." Annals 407(My, 1973): 102-118.

_____. "Social Science, Segregation, and the Law." School and Society, Ap 8, 1961.

Mackler, Bernard. "The Right, or Is It a Privilege, to Attend Public School." Journal of Special Education 4(Spring, Summer, 1970):129-137.

McMillan, James B. "Social Science and the District Court. The Observations of a Journeyman Trial Judge." Law and Contemporary Problems 39(Winter, 1975):157-163.

McPherson, R. Bruce. "Will Classrooms and Schools Built with Federal Funds Be Integrated?" Phi Delta Kappan, S, 1966.

Maddocks, Lewis I. "Justice John Marshall Harlan: Defender of Individual Rights." Doctoral dissertation, Ohio State U., 1959. Univ. Microfilms Order No. 59-5918.

Malikail, J. S. "Challenge to Local Control of Education in U.S.A." Journal of Educational Administration and History 3(Je, 1971):53-56.

Mangum, Charles S., Jr. "Education." In The Legal Status of the Negro, pp. 78-137. Chapel Hill, NC: U. of North Carolina Press, 1940.

Mann, Dale. "Political Representation and Urban School Advisory Councils." Teachers College Record 75(F, 1974):279-307.

Mardian, Robert C. "School Desegregation." Integrated Education 8(My-Je, 1970):15-22.

Martin, Ruby G. "Getting Desegregation Done." Integrated Education 8(S-O, 1970):41-47.

Martinez, S. "Poor People and Public Education in America: An Overview of the Impact of OEO Legal Services Agencies on Public Education." Journal of Law and Education 4 (Ap, 1975).337-354.

Meranto, Philip J. The Policies of Federal Aid to Education in 1965: A Study in Political Innovation. Syracuse, NY: Syracuse U. Press, 1967.

Mikva, Abner J. and others. A Report by the Lawyers' Review Committee to Study the Department of Justice, J1, 1972. The Committee, Suite 704, 1424 Sixteenth Street, N.W., Washington, DC 20036.

Mills, Nicolaus. "Busing: Who's Being Taken for a Ride?" Commonweal, Mr 24, 1972.

Mills, Roger. Justice Delayed Denied. HEW and Northern School Desegregation. Washington, DC: Center for National Policy Review, Catholic U. of America, S, 1974.

Mitchell, John N. Meet the Press (transcript). Washington, DC: Merkle Press, N 2, 1969.

Mogin, Bert. The State Role in School Desegregation. Menlo Park, CA: Stanford Research Institute, J1, 1977.

Mondale, Walter F. "Busing in Perspective." New Republic, Mr 4, 1972.

Morgan, Charles, Jr. "Schools: Bickel's 'New Paternalism' Masks a National Retreat." South Today 1(1970):9. [Critique of Bickel article, New Republic, F 7, 1970]

Morse, H. T. "White House Meeting on Schools." Integrated Education, O-N, 1963.

Motley, Constance Baker. "The Continuing American Revolution." Journal of Negro History 41(Ja, 1976):7-15.

"Mr. Finch Gets Letters" (letters to and from Hon. Robert H. Finch, Secretary of the Department of Health, Education, and Wefare). Integrated Education 40(J1-Ag, 1969):42-45. [From Neil V. Sullivan and others]

Mulholland, Paige. "An Interview with Father Hesburgh." Civil Rights Digest 5(Summer, 1973):42-48.

Murphy, Jerome T. "Bureaucratic Politics and Poverty Politics." Inequality in Education 6(1970). [Title I, Elementary and Secondary Education Act]

_____. "Title I of ESEA: The Politics of Implementary Federal Education Reform." Harvard Educational Review 41(F, 1971):35-63.

Murray, Pauli (ed.). States' Laws on Race and Color, and Appendices Containing International Documents, Federal Laws and Regulations, Local Ordinances and Charts. Cincinnati, OH: Women's Division of Christian Service, Board of Missions and Church Extension, Methodist Church, 1950. 1955 Supplement, by Verge Lake and Pauli Murray.

Mykkeltvedt, Roald, and Mathis, Doyle. Courts as Political Instruments: The Politics of School Consolidation. Athens, GA: Institute of Government, U. of Georgia, 1970.

National Conference of State Legislators. Leadership for Education. Proceedings of the Conference. Washington, DC, D 4-6, 1966. Washington, DC: National Committee for Support of the Public Schools, 1967.

National Education Association and U.S. Office of Education. Report of Task Force Appointed to Study the Problem of Displaced School Personnel Related to School Desegregation and the Employment Status of Recently Prepared Negro College Graduates Certified to Teach in Seventeen States. Washington, DC: National Education Association, D 13, 1965.

National Science Board, Special Commission on the Social Sciences. Knowledge Into Action: Improving the Nation's Use of the Social Sciences. Washington, DC: GPO, 1969.

National Urban League. A Call to Action. Recommendations on the Urban and Racial Crisis Submitted to President Richard M. Nixon. New York: National Urban League, Ja 20, 1969.

Navasky, Victor S. "The Greening of Griffin Bell." New York Times Magazine, F 27, 1977.

"The Negro Teacher in Desegregated Schools." New York University Law Review, N, 1967.

Nelson, Jack. The U.S. Commission on Civil Rights. Nashville, TN: Race Relations Information Center, Je, 1971.

Newbold, N. C. "Common Schools for Negroes in the South." Annals of the American Academy of Political and Social Science 140(N, 1928): 209-224.

Newby, I. A. Challenge to the Court. Social Scientists and the Defence of Segregation, 1954-1966. Baton Rouge, LA: Louisiana State U. Press, 1967. 2nd edition, 1969.

Newman, Frank C. and others. "New International Tribunal on Racial Discrimination." California Law Review 56(N, 1968).

Nixon, Richard. "A Presidential Letter." Integrated Education 8(N-D, 1970):21.

_____. Statement on Desegregation. New York Times, Mr 25, 1970.

Norton, Eleanor Holmes, Hoffman, Philip E., and S., W. "More on 'Quotas.'" Jewish Currents, F, 1973.

Nussbaum, Michael. "Student Rights Are Civil Rights." Civil Rights Digest, Spring, 1969.

O'Brien, Conor Cruise. "What Rights Should Minorities Have?" New Community 2(Spring, 1973):109-116.

O'Brien, Kenneth B., Jr. "The Supreme Court and Education." Doctoral dissertation, Stanford U., 1956.

Office for Civil Rights. Department of Health, Education, and Welfare Progress Report on Civil Rights. Washington, DC: The Department, S 14, 1969.

Office of Children's Services. Juvenile Injustice, O, 1973. Judicial Conference of the State of New York, 270 Broadway, New York, NY 10007.

Office of General Counsel, U.S. Commission on Civil Rights. "Legal Aspects of Metropolitan Solutions for Problems of Racial Isolation." In U.S. Commission on Civil Rights. Papers Prepared for National Conference on Equal Educational Opportunity in America's Cities. Washington, DC: GPO, 1968.

Officer, James E. "The Role of the United States Government in Acculturation and Assimilation." Annuario Indigenista (Mexico) 25(1965).

Olander, Joseph D. "Black Americans and the Politics of Justice in their Years of Travail." Doctoral dissertation, Indiana U., 1971.

"On the Refusal of White Authority to Enforce the Law." New South, Spring, 1969.

Orfield, Gary. "Congress, the President, and Anti-Busing Legislation, 1966-1974." Journal of Law and Education 4(Ja, 1975):81-139.

_____. "The Court, the Schools, and the Southern Strategy." Saturday Review, D 20, 1969.

_____. "Federal Policy, Local Power, and Metropolitan Segregation." Political Science Quarterly 89(Winter, 1974-75):777-802.

_____. "The Politics of Resegregation [in the South]." Saturday Review, S 20, 1969.

_____. [Testimony in opposition to the Nomination of Clement F. Haynsworth, Jr. to the U.S. Supreme Court] In U.S. Congress, 91st, 1st session, Senate, Committee on the Judiciary, Clement F. Haynsworth, Jr. Hearings, pp. 554-579. Washington, DC: GPO, 1969.

_____. [Testimony in opposition to Nomination of George Harrold Carswell to be Associate Justice of the U.S. Supreme Court] U.S. Congress, 91st, 2nd session, Senate, Committee on the Judiciary, George Harrold Carswell. Hearings... Washington, DC: GPO, 1970.

Osborne, John. "Busing and Politics." New Republic 164(My 29, 1971):19-20.

_____. "Chicken, Southern Fried." New Republic, F 21, 1970. [Cabinet committee on school integration]

_____. "Integrating Friends." New Republic, Ap 18, 1970.

_____. "More Desegregation." New Republic 164(Je 12, 1971):15-16.

_____. "The Rise of Harry Dent." New Republic, Je 14, 1969. [Former aide to Senator Strom Thurmond; later Special Assistant to President Nixon]

_____. The Second Year of the Nixon Watch. New York: Liveright, 1971.

_____. "Truth and Busing." New Republic 165 (S 11, 1971):11-12.

Osborne, John, and Bickel, Alexander M. [Two Articles on President Nixon's Desegregation Speech of March 24, 1970] New Republic, Ap 4, 1970.

Overlan, S. Francis. "An Equal Chance to Learn." New Republic 166(My 13, 1972):19-21.

Panetta, Leon E. " Alexander Bickel Is Wrong." New Republic, F 28, 1970. [In re: Bickel, New Republic, F 7, 1970]

_____. "A Nation of Men...and Laws." Antioch Review, Summer, 1970.

_____. "Why Civil Rights Progress Is at a Snail's Pace." Los Angeles Times, D 13, 1974.

Panetta, Leon E., and Gall, Peter. *Bring Us Together. The Nixon Team and the Civil Rights Retreat*. Philadelphia: Lippincott, 1971.

Participation in USDA Programs by Ethnic Groups. Washington, DC: Department of Agriculture, Jl, 1971, 96 pp. ERIC ED 052 881.

Passell, Peter, and Ross, Leonard. *State Policies and Federal Programs: Priorities and Constraints*. New York: Praeger, 1978.

Pfeffer, Leo. "The Case for and Against Quotas, Compensations, and Demonstrations." *Law Commentary*, Spring, 1964.

Platt, Patricia F. "HEW Race Data Hits Urban North." *Education News*, Ag 5, 1968.

Poinsett, Alex. "Class Patterns in Black Politics." *Ebony* 28(Ag, 1973):35-42.

_____. "Crusader for Justice." *Ebony* 29 (Mr, 1974):72-82. [U.S. District Judge Damon J. Keith]

_____. "'The Joint.'" *Ebony* 28(Ap, 1973). [Joint Center for Political Studies]

_____. "Whatever Happened to School Desegregation?" *Ebony* 29(My, 1974):104-114.

Polier, Justine Wise. *The Rule of Law and the Role of Psychiatry*. Baltimore, MD: The Johns Hopkins Press, 1968.

Pottinger, J. Stanley. "Discrimination and Denial Due to National Origin." *Integrated Education* 8(Jl-Ag, 1970).

_____. "HEW and the Schools: An In-Depth Look" (interview). *The State* (Columbia, SC), Jl 18, 1971.

_____. "The Nixon Administration: A View from Inside." In *School Desegregation: Retrospect and Prospect*, pp. 62-67. Edited by Eugene C. Lee. Southern Newspaper Publishers Association Foundation, P.O. Box 11606, Atlanta, GA 30305, 1971.

_____. "Non Discrimination in Elementary and Secondary School Staffing Practices." *Integrated Education* 9(My-Je, 1971):52-54.

"Prevention of Discrimination in Private Educational Institutions." *Columbia Law Review* 47(Jl, 1947):821-827.

Punke, H. H. "Teacher Assignment in School Desegregation." *Alabama Lawyer*, Jl, 1968.

"Racial Discrimination in Fraternities and Sororities State Action?" *University of Illinois Law Forum*, Fall, 1964.

"Racial Imbalance." *School Management*, Je, 1965.

Radin, Beryl. *Implementation, Change, and the Federal Bureaucracy. School Desegregation Policy in HEW, 1964-1968*. New York: Teachers College Press, 1977.

Reagan, Michael D. *The New Federalism*. New York: Oxford U. Press, 1972.

Real, Manuel L. "Pilgrims to a New Experience." *Integrated Education* 8(N-D, 1970):55-59.

Report of President Nixon's Task Force on Education. *Congressional Record*, Mr 12, 1969. H 1658-H 1667.

The Report of the White House Conference. "To Fulfill These Rights." June 1-2, 1966. Washington, DC: GPO, 1966.

"Response to President Nixon's Busing Statement by the Black Law Students of Harvard University." *Congressional Record*, Ap 11, 1972, E 3523.

Reutter, E. Edmund, Jr. *The Law, Race, and School Districting*, Jl 10, 1968. ERIC ED 030 692.

Ribicoff, Abraham A. "Do Most Americans Secretly Want Segregation?" *Look*, S 8, 1970.

_____. "The Future of School Integration in the United States." *Journal of Law and Education* 1(Ja, 1972):1-21.

Richardson, Elliot L. "Desegregation Progress, Fall, 1970." *Integrated Education* 9(Ja-F, 1971):50-51.

Risen, Maurice L. "Legal Aspects of Separation of Races in the Public Schools." Doctoral dissertation, Teachers College, Temple U., 1935.

Rivlin, Alice M. "Measuring Performance in Education." In *The Measurement of Economic and Social Performance*, pp. 411-428. Edited by Milton Moss. New York: Columbia U. Press, 1973.

Roche, J. P. "Education, Segregation, and the Supreme Court--A Political Analysis." *University of Pennsylvania Law Review* 99 (My, 1951):949-959.

Rosen, P. *The Supreme Court and Social Science*. N.p.: n.p., 1972.

Ruch, Floyd L., and Ash, Philip. "Comments on Psychological Testing." *Columbia Law Review* 69(Ap, 1969):608-618.

Salisbury, Robert H. "Education and Urban Politics." In *Planning for a Nation of Cities*. Edited by Sam B. Warner, Jr. Cambridge, MA: M.I.T. Press, 1966.

_____. "Schools and Politics in the Big City." *Harvard Educational Review*, Summer, 1967.

Sandow, Stuart A. Emerging Education Policy Issues in Law: Fraud. Syracuse, NY: Educational Policy Research Center, N, 1970.

Sansing, John. "A Student Describes Guidelines to Southern School Districts." Virginia Law Weekly, O, 1966.

Saunders, Socrates W. "Legal Aspects of the Education of Negroes with Special Emphasis on the Equalization Principle." Doctoral dissertation, U. of Pittsburgh, 1943.

Schardt, Arlie. "[Anti-Busing] Amendment Drive Threatens Schools." Civil Liberties (A.C.L.U.), Ja, 1972.

_____. "Bad Week in the Senate." Nation, Mr 20, 1972. [Debate on school busing]

_____. "The Busing Battle." Civil Liberties 289(S, 1972):1-2.

"School Decentralization: Legal Paths to Local Control." Georgetown Law Journal, My, 1969.

Shea, Thomas E. "An Educational Perspective of the Legality of Intelligence Testing and Ability Grouping." Journal of Law and Education 6(Ap, 1977):137-158.

Schueler, H. "Education in the Modern Urban Setting." Law and Contemporary Problems, Winter, 1965.

Schwarzschild, Henry. "Fighting 'Resegregation': Another Southern Strategy." Civil Liberties, Mr, 1971.

Schwelb, Egon. "The International Convention on the Elimination of All Forms of Racial Discrimination." International and Comparative Law Quarterly 15(1966).

Seeley, David S. "The Schools and Civil Rights." Integrated Education, Ap-My, 1966.

_____. "Southern Desegregation: A Look at the Bright Side." Nation's Schools, Je, 1967.

_____. "Where the Office of Education Stands on Enforcing Desegregation." Nation's Schools, N, 1966.

Seligman, Daniel. "How 'Equal Opportunity' Turned Into Employment Quotas." Fortune, Mr, 1973.

Sellers, Barney. "Civil Rights, the Nixon Fiddle." Nation, O 6, 1969.

_____. "Ebb Tide of Integration." Nation, D 9, 1968. [Enforcement of desegregation efforts]

Semple, Robert B., Jr. "Busing and the President: The Evolution of a Policy." New York Times, Mr 19, 1972.

Shalala, Donna E., and Kelley, James A. "Politics, the Courts, and Educational Policy." Teachers College Record, D, 1973.

Shanks, Herschel. "Equal Education and the Law." American Scholar 39(Spring, 1970):255-269.

Shellow, Robert. "Social Scientists and Social Action from Within the Establishment." Journal of Social Issues 26(Winter, 1970):207-220.

Sherrill, Robert. "The Real Robert Finch Stands Up." New York Times Magazine, Jl 5, 1970.

Siggers, Kathleen (ed.). With Justice for All. Riverside, CA: Western Regional School Desegregation Projects, U. of California, Je, 1972.

Silverman, William (ed.). "Legal Developments in Urban Education." Education and Urban Society 3(Ag, 1971):478-485.

Slippen, Richard I. "Administrative Enforcement of Civil Rights in Public Education: Title VI, HEW, and the Civil Rights Reviewing Authority. Wayne Law Review 21(Mr, 1975):931-954.

Smith, Charles H. "The U.S.O.E. and Urban Education." Phi Delta Kappan, S, 1968. [Interview]

Smith, James McCune. "Citizenship." Douglass' Monthly, Je, 1859.

Southern Regional Council. School Desegregation, 1966: The Slow Undoing. Atlanta: Southern Regional Council, D, 1966.

Special Review Staff, Manpower Administration. Review of the Rural Manpower Service. Washington, DC: U.S. Department of Labor, 1972. [Report of investigation of charges that the R.M.S. engaged in discriminatory practices]

"Specific Steps Toward Quality Integrated Schools: White House Conference Recommendations." Integrated Education, O-N, 1966.

Spivak, Jonathan. "'Good Faith' Slows School Integration." Wall Street Journal, My 21, 1970.

Steif, William. "The Anti-Busing Crusade Reaches Congress." Race Relations Reporter 3(Ja 3, 1972):15-17.

_____. "The New Look in Civil Rights Enforcement." Southern Education Report, S, 1967.

_____. "Why is Desegregation of Schools Slowing Down?" (Interview with Leon Panetta). National Catholic Reporter, Je 25, 1969.

Stephenson, George. Race Distinctions in American Law. New York: Russell and Russell, 1969 (orign. 1910).

Strauss, G., and Ingerman, S. "Public Policy and Discrimination in Apprenticeship." Hastings Law Journal, F, 1965.

Strum, Philippa. "'Forward Together. The Nixon Administration on Integration." Afro-American Studies 1(0, 1970):161-171.

Sugarman, S. D., and Kirp, David L. "Rethinking Collective Responsibility for Education." Law and Contemporary Problems 39(Summer, 1975).

Sullivan, Neil V. Desegregation Strategies-- The Classroom and the Courtroom. Riverside, CA: Western Regional School Desegregation Projects, U. of California, Je, 1971.

Swanson, Austin D., and Lamatie, Robert E. "Project 1990: Educational Planning at the Metropolitan Level." Socio-Economic Planning Sciences 5(D, 1971):535-545.

Taylor, William L. Hanging Together. Equality in An Urban Nation. New York: Simon and Shuster, 1971.

_____. "The Justice Department and Race Relations." Integrated Education 12(My-Je, 1974):5-8.

_____. "Metropolitan Approaches to Desegregation." Integrateducation 13(My-Je, 1975): 131-134.

Thomas, Cynthia A. "Civil Rights Participation and Attitudes of Militancy in the Negro Ghetto Community." Doctoral dissertation, U. of Rochester, 1971.

"Tough New Man at Justice." Time, F 1, 1971. [Robert C. Mardian]

Trachtenberg, Stephen J. "The Federal Government and School Desegregation." Changing Education, Fall, 1966.

Tribe, Laurence H. American Constitutional Law. Mineola, NY: Foundation Press, 1978.

Trister, Michael B., and Spriggs, P. Kent. "The Debate Over School Segregation." New Republic 162(1970):25-28. [Contra Alexander M. Bikel]

Tyack, David, Orfield, Gary, Hamilton, Charles, and Brest, Paul. "The Debate Over School Segregation." New Republic, Mr 7, 1970. [Replies to Alexander M. Bickel, New Republic, F 7, 1970]

U.S. Commission on Civil Rights. Civil Rights, '63. 1963 Report of the United States Commission on Civil Rights. Washington, DC: CPO, 1963.

_____. Education, Vol. II of the 1961 U.S. Commission on Civil Rights Report. Washington, DC: GPO, 1961.

_____. Federal Enforcement of School Desegregation. Washington, DC: The Commission, S 11, 1969.

_____. First Annual Conference [on problems of desegregation in public schools], Nashville, Tennessee, March 5-6, 1959. Washington, DC: GPO, 1959.

_____. Second Annual Conference [on desegregation in public schools]. Washington, DC: GPO, 1960.

_____. Third Annual Conference on Problems of Schools in Transition from the Educator's Viewpoint. Washington, DC: GPO, 1961.

_____. Fourth Annual Education Conference on Problems of Segregation and Desegregation of Public Schools, May 3-4, 1962. Washington, DC: GPO, 1962.

_____. The National Conference and the Reports of the State Advisory Committee to the U.S. Commission on Civil Rights, 1959. Washington, DC: GPO, 1959.

_____. 1963 Staff Report, Public Education. Washington, DC: GPO, 1963.

_____. 1964 Staff Report, Public Education. Washignton, DC: GPO, 1964.

_____. Problems of Segregation and Desegregation of Public Schools. Synopsis of a Conference...May 3-4, 1962. Washington, DC: GPO, 1962.

_____. Statement on Affirmative Action for Equal Employment Opportunities. Washington, DC: GPO, 1973.

_____. Survey of School Desegregation in the Southern and Border States, 1965-6. Washington, DC: GPO, 1966.

_____. To Know or Not to Know. Collection and Use of Racial and Ethnic Data in Federal Assistance Programs. Washington, DC: GPO, F, 1973.

_____. With Liberty and Justice for All. An Abridgment of the Report of the U.S. Commission on Civil Rights, 1959. Washington, DC: GPO, 1959.

U.S. Congress, 90th, 1st session, House of Representatives, Committee on Education and Labor, Special Subcommittee on Education. Study of the United States Office of Education. Washington, DC: GPO, 1967.

U.S. Congress, 91st, 1st session, House of Representatives, Committee on kducation and Labor. Extension of Elementary and Secondary Education Programs. Hearings. Parts 2-4. Washington, DC: GPO, 1969.

U.S. Congress, 91st, 1st session, Senate, Committee on Labor and Public Welfare. Nominations. James E. Allen, Jr., of New York, to be Commissioner of Education and an Assistant Secretary for Health, Education, and Welfare, Ap 15, 1969. Washington, DC: GPO, 1969.

U.S. Congress, 91st, 2nd session, House of Representatives, Committee on Interstate and Foreign Commerce, Subcommittee on Communications and Power. Films and Broadcasts Demeaning Ethnic, Racial, or Religious Groups. Hearing... Serial No. 91-73. Washington, DC: GPO, 1970.

U.S. Congress, 91st, 2nd session, House of Representatives, Committee on Education and Labor, General Subcommittee on Education. To Authorize a White House Conference on Education. Hearings... Washington, DC: GPO, 1970.

U.S. Congress, 91st, 2nd session, Senate, Select Committee on Equal Educational Opportunity. Equal Educational Opportunity. Hearings... Part 5: De Facto Segregation and Housing Discrimination. Washington, DC: GPO, 1971.

U.S. Congress, 92nd, 1st session, Senate, Committee on the Judiciary. Nominations of William H. Rehnquist and Lewis F. Powell, Jr. Hearings... Washington, DC: GPO, 1971.

U.S. Congress, 92nd, 1st session, Senate, Select Committee on Equal Educational Opportunity. Equal Educational Opportunity--1971. Hearings... Part 22: Education Information. Washington, DC: GPO, 1972.

U.S. Congress, 92nd, 2nd session, Senate, Committee on the Judiciary. Richard G. Kleindienst... Hearings... 2 parts. Washington, DC: GPO, 1972.

U.S. Congress, 92nd, 2nd session, Senate, Committee on the Judiciary. Richard G. Kleindienst--Resumed. Hearings... Part 3. Washington, DC: GPO, 1972.

U.S. Congress, 93rd, 1st session, House of Representatives, Committee on the Judiciary, Subcommittee on Civil Rights and Constitutional Rights. Budgetary Cuts in the Community Relations Service. Hearings... Serial No. 21. Washington, DC: GPO, 1973.

U.S. Congress, 95th, 1st session, Senate, Committee on the Judiciary. Griffin B. Bell. Hearings... Washington, DC: GPO, 1977.

U.S. Department of Health, Education, and Welfare. HEW and Civil Rights. Washington, DC: GPO, 1971.

U.S. Dept. of HEW, Office for Civil Rights. HEW and Civil Rights. Washington, DC: GPO, 1968.

U.S. Department of Justice. Community Relations Service. Annual Report 1971. Washington, DC: GPO, 1972.

"United States Government and Negro Education." School and Society 32(S 27, 1930):421. [Appointment of Ambrose Caliver]

"U.S. Integration Rule Seen Harmful to Negro Colleges." Chronicle of Higher Education, Mr 16, 1970.

U.S. Office of Education. "New Guidelines for School Desegregation." Integrated Education, Ap-My, 1966.

_____. Status of Compliance. Public School Districts. Seventeen Southern and Border States. Report No. 6. Washington, DC: GPO, My, 1967.

Usdan, Michael D., Minar, David W., and Hurwitz, Emanuel, Jr. Education and State Politics. The Developing Relationship Between Elementary-Secondary and Higher Education. New York: Teachers College Press, 1969.

_____, _____ and _____. The Politics of Elementary-Secondary and Higher Education, 1968. Education Commission of the States, 822 Lincoln Tower, 1860 Lincoln Street, Denver, CO 80203.

Van den Berghe, Pierre. "The Benign Quota: Panacea or Pandora's Box?" American Sociologist 6(Je, 1971).

Van Geel, Tyll. "Does the Constitution Establish a Right to an Education?" School Review 82(F, 1974):293-326.

Von Pfeifil, H. (comp.). Juvenile Rights Since 1967. South Hackensack, NJ: Rothman, 1974.

Wall, Robert. "Special Agent for the FBI." New York Review, Ja 27, 1972.

Wallace, P. A. "Economic Position and Prospects for Urban Blacks." American Journal of Agricultural Economics 53(My, 1971).

"Walls of Racial Separation: The Role of Private and Parochial Schools in Racial Integration." New York University Law Review, My, 1968.

Waltz, Jon R. "The Burger/Blackmun Court." New York Times Magazine, D 6, 1970.

Ware, Gilbert (ed.). From the Black Bar: Voice for Equal Justice. New York: Putnam, 1976.

Watters, Pat. "To Fulfill These Rights." New South, Summer, 1966. [Account of the White House Conference, "To Fulfill These Rights," Je, 1966]

Weaver, Robert C. "The Public Works Administration School Building Program and Separate Negro Schools." Journal of Negro Education 7 (Jl, 1938):366-374.

Weinberg, Meyer. "The Courts are Doing their Duty." Intergroup 2(Je, 1972).

_____. "De Facto Segregation: Fact or Artifact?" Integrated Education, Ap, 1963.

_____. Race and Place: A Legal History of the Neighborhood School. Washington, DC: GPO, 1968.

_____. "Schooling and the New Parenthood." Journal of Negro Education 40(Summer, 1971): 207-215.

What Is Affirmative Action? Combating Discrimination in Employment. Washington, DC: National Education Association, 1973.

"White Curtain: Racially Disadvantaging Local Government Boundary Practices: A Symposium." Journal of Urban Law 54(Spring and Summer, 1977):681-1073.

"The White House Conference on Education." American Education, Jl-Ag, 1965.

"White House Panel on Education." Integrated Education, F-Mr, 1966.

Williams, John Bell. "School Desegregation Problems: Are Federal Courts Educators?" Vital Speakers of the Day 36(Mr 1, 1970): 306-309.

Wilson, Charles H. "The Myth of Local Control." School Management 15(My, 1971):34-35, 48.

Wise, Arthur E. "Is Denial of Equal Opportunity Constitutional?" Administrator's Notebook (Midwest Administration Center, U. of Chicago), F, 1965.

Wise, Arthur E., and Manley-Casimir, Michael. "Law, Freedom and Equality: Implications for Schooling." Association for Supervision and Curriculum Development 1971 Yearbook.

Wise, Michael B. "School Desegregation: The Court, the Congress, and the President." School Review 82(F, 1974):159-182.

Witherspoon, Joseph P. Administrative Implementation of Civil Rights. Austin, TX: U. of Texas Press, 1968.

Wolf, Eleanor P. "Courtrooms and Classrooms." Educational Forum 41(My, 1977):431-453.

_____. "Northern School Desegregation and Residential Choice." Supreme Court Review 1977 (1977):63-85.

Wolk, Allan. The Presidency and Black Civil Rights. Cranbury, NJ : Fairleigh Dickinson U. Press, 1971.

Wolman, Harold L., and Thomas, Norman C. "Black Interest, Black Groups, and Black Influence in the Federal Policy Process: The Cases of Housing and Education." Journal of Politics, N, 1970.

Wright, J. Skelly. "Promises to Keep." Integrateducation 12(S-O, 1974):1-8.

Wright, Marian A. "Sociology, Psychology and Civil Rights." North Carolina Law Review, 1963.

Yudof, Mark G. "Suspension and Expulsion of Black Students from the Public Schools: Academic Capital Punishment and the Constitution." Law and Contemporary Problems 39 (Spring, 1975):374-411.

Yudof, Mark G., Coons, John E., and Carey, Sarah C. "Serrano and Segregation." Integrated Education (Mr-Ap, 1972):71-71.

Zeitlin, Harry. "Federal Relations in American Education, 1933-1943. A Study of New Deal Efforts and Innovations." Doctoral dissertation, Columbia U., 1958.

Zeitz, L. "Survey of Negro Attitudes toward Law." Rutgers Law Review, Winter, 1965.

Zimmerman, Joseph H. "Metropolitan Reform in the U.S.: An Overview." Public Administration Review (S-O, 1970):531-543.

Bibliographies

Ohio Civil Rights Commission. De Facto Segregation, Suggested Readings. Columbus, OH, 1964.

Phillips, M. R., and Miller, C. L. (comps.). "Selected Annotated Bibliography on Relationship of the Federal Government to Negro Education." Journal of Negro Education 7(Jl, 1938): 468-472.

Reference Department, Oxon Hill Branch. Selective List of Government Publications About the American Negro, 1970. Administrative Offices, Prince George's County Memorial Library, 6532 Adelphi Road, Hyattsville, MD 20782.

Ross, Larry L. Taxation in Public Education. Analysis and Bibliography Series, No. 12. Eugene, OR: U. of Oregon, Clearinghouse on Educational Administration, Mr, 1971, 17 pp. ERIC ED 049 516.

Smedley, T. A. (ed.). Race Relations Law Index, 1972-1973. Nashville, TN: Race Relations Information Center, D, 1973.

Tompkins, Dorothy C. (comp.). Local Public Schools: How to Pay for Them? Berkeley, CA: Institute of Governmental Studies, U. of California, 1972.

Troop, Warren F., and MacDonald, A. F., Jr. "Internal-External Locus of Control: A Bibliography." Psychological Reports 28 (F, 1971):175-190.

U.S. Congress, 90th, 1st session, House of
Representatives, Committee on Education and
Labor. A Compendium of Federal Education
Laws. Washington, DC: GPO, My, 1967.

U.S. Congress, 91st, 2nd session, Senate,
Committee on Government Operations, Sub-
committee on Intergovernmental Relations.
Bibliography of Federal Grants-In-Aid to
State and Local Governments 1964-1969.
Washington, DC: GPO, O 2, 1970.

U.S. Congress, 92nd, 1st session, House of
Representatives, Committee on the Judiciary.
Leading Court Decisions Pertinent to Public
School Desegregation. Washington, DC:
GPO, 1972.

U.S. Congress, 92nd, 2nd session, Senate,
Select Committee on Equal Educational
Opportunity. Selected Court Decisions Re-
lating to Equal Educational Opportunity.
Washington, DC: GPO, Mr, 1972.

U.S. Office of Education. Bibliography of Publications of the United States Office of
Education, 1867-1959. Reprint edition,
1971. Rowman and Littlefield, 81 Adams
Drive, Totowa, NJ 07512.

_____. Fact Book, Office of Education
Programs. Washington, DC: GPO, 1967.

Wise, Michael B. and others. "Desegregation
Education: A Legal Bibliography." Notre
Dame Lawyer 52(Ap, 1977):733-790. [Law
review articles]

18.
CHURCH

General

'Abd-al-'Aziz' Abd-al-Qadir Kamil. Islam and the Race Question. Paris: UNESCO, 1970.

Abrahamson, Harold J. Ethnic Diversity in Catholic America. New York: Wiley, 1973.

Agatha, Mother M. "Catholic Education and the Negro." In Essays on Catholic Education in the United States, pp. 500-522. Edited by Roy Joseph Defenari. Washington, DC: Catholic U. of America Press, 1942.

Ahmann, Mathew. "The Church and the Urban Negro." America, F, 1968.

Ahmann, Mathew, and Roach, Margaret (eds.). The Church and the Urban Racial Crisis. Divine Word Publications, 1968.

"An Awakening of Black Nun Power." Ebony, O, 1968.

Baily, Flavius J. "The Policies of the American Missionary Association in Relation to Negro Education." Master's thesis, Howard U., 1933.

"Being Black on a Catholic Campus." National Catholic Reporter, Je 4, 1969.

Bernal, Helen H., and Bernal, Ernest M., Jr. "Teaching Religion to Minority Groups: Content, Method, and Cultural Compatibility." Notre Dame Journal of Education 5(Fall, 1974): 232-236.

Billings, Sr. Cora Marie, R.S.M. "Facet of a Mosaic." Dimension 3(Winter, 1971):156-164. [A black nun]

Billington, Ray Allen. The Protestant Crusade, 1800-1860. New York: Macmillan, 1938.

Boardman, Richard. "Public and Parochial." Urban Review, N, 1966.

Boney, F. N. "Dilemma for Parochial Schools." America, S 13, 1969. [Catholic schools in the South]

Bowen, Trevor. Divine White Right: A Study of Race Segregation and Interracial Cooperation in Religious Organizations and Institutions in the United States. New York: Harper and Row, 1934.

Braddock, Clayton. "Catholics and Ghettos." Southern Education Report, Jl-Ag, 1968.

Brawley, James P. Two Centuries of Methodist Concern: Bondage, Freedom, and Education of Black People. New York: Vantage Press, 1974.

Brecht, David L. "Black Catholic High School: How Realistic the Possibility?" Today's Catholic Teacher, F, 1976.

Bringhurst, Newell G. "Forgotten Mormon Perspectives: Slavery, Race, and the Black Man as Issues Among Non-Utah Latter-Day Saints, 1844-1873." Michigan History 61(Winter, 1977):353-370.

Brownson, Orestes A. "Public and Parochial Schools." Brownson's Quarterly Review (N.Y. Series) 4(1859):324-342.

Brunner, Clarence V. "The Religious Instruction of the Slave in the Antebellum South." Doctoral thesis, George Peabody College for Teachers, 1933.

Buchanan, Henry A., and Brown, Bob W. "Integration: Great Dilemma of the Church." Ebony, Je, 1966.

Buetow, Harold A. Of Singular Benefit: The Story of Catholic Education in the United States. New York: Macmillan, 1970.

_____. "The Underprivileged and Roman Catholic Education." Journal of Negro Education 40 (Fall, 1971):373-389.

Bullock, Paul. "On Organizing the Poor. Problems of Morality and Tactics." Dissent, Ja-F, 1968.

Burns, Charles D. "A Critical Analysis of the Treatment of School Integration in the American Catholic Press." Master's thesis, Catholic U. of America, 1962.

Burns, James A. The Catholic School System in the United States, Its Principles, Origin, and Establishment. New York: Benziger Bros., 1908.

_____. The Growth and Development of the Catholic School System in the United States. New York: Benziger Bros., 1912.

Calam, John. "Parsons and Pedagogues: The S.P.G. Adventure in American Education." Doctoral dissertation, Columbia U., 1969.

Caldwell, Gilbert H. "Black Folk in White Churches." Christian Century, F 12, 1969.

Campbell, James D. "Parochial Schools: A Delay in Desegregation." Civil Rights Digest 4 (Winter, 1971):21-25.

Cantwell, Daniel M. "Letter to My Friends." New City, Ag 1, 1965.

Cantwell, Daniel M., Heaney, Thomas W., Mallette, Daniel, and Prater, Boniface. "Why I Did or Did Not Participate in Chicago's Anti-Willis Demonstrations." Community, N, 1965.

Caravaglios, Maria Genoina. The American Catholic Church and the Negro Problem in the XVIII-XIX Centuries. Edited by Ernest L. Unterkoefler. Charleston, SC: Caravaglios, 1974.

Catholic Schools and Racial Integration: Perspectives, Directions, Models. Washington, DC: National Catholic Conference for Interracial Justice, 1977.

Chmielewska, Annette. "A History of the Educational Activities of the Sisters of the Resurrection in the United States from 1900 to the Present." Master's thesis, Fordham U., 1958.

Claret, Sr. M. Anthony, O.S.F. "A Sister's Survey." Community, Mr, 1967.

Clark, Dennis. A Catholic Answer to the Race Problem. National Catholic Conference, 21 West Superior Street, Chicago, IL, n.d.

_____. "Color and Catholic Classrooms." Integrated Education, Je, 1963.

Clark, Henry. The Church and Residential Desegregation. New Haven, CT: College and University Press, 1965.

Cleage, Albert B., Jr. The Black Messiah. New York: Sheed & Ward, 1968.

Clement, Rufus E. "The Educational Work of the African Methodist Episcopal Zion Church, 1820-1920." Master's thesis, Northwestern U., 1922.

The Committee of Religious Leaders of the City of New York. Proceedings of the Metropolitan New York Conference on Religion and Race, F 25, 1964.

Cone, James H. "Failure of the Black Church." Liberator, My, 1969.

Congress of Colored Catholics of the United States. Three Catholic Afro-American Congresses. New York: Arno Press, 1978. [1889, 1890, and 1892]

Cotton, June Rosella. "The Historical Development of United Presbyterian Schools for Southern Negroes." Master's thesis, U. of Cincinnati, 1938.

Cronin, Joseph M. "Negroes in Catholic Schools." Commonweal, O 7, 1966.

Cross, Robert. "Origins of Catholic Parochial Schools in America." American Benedictine Review 16(1965):194-209.

Czuba, Natalie A. History of the Ukranian Catholic Parochial Schools in the United States. Chicago, IL: DePaul U., 1956.

Davis, Joseph M. "The Black Revolution and Black Catholics." Homilectic and Pastoral Review 71(O, 1970).

Davis, Joseph. "NCEA Ignores Minorities." National Catholic Reporter, Ap 28, 1972. [National Catholic Educational Association]

"De Facto Segregation in Public Schools--A Position Paper for the Guidance of Jewish Communities and Agencies." In Joint Program Plan for Jewish Community Relations, 1965-1966, n.d. National Community Relations Advisory Council, 55 West 42nd Street, New York, NY 10036.

Diffley, Jerome Edward. "Catholic Reaction to American Public Education, 1792-1852." Doctoral dissertation, U. of Notre Dame, 1959.

Diggs, Margaret A. Catholic Negro Education in the United States. Washington, DC: Author, 1936.

"Divine Word Province to Join Black Struggle." National Catholic Reporter, Ja 8, 1969.

Donohue, James C. "Nonpublic Schools and Equal Educational Opportunity." In U.S. Commission on Civil Rights, Papers Prepared for National Conference on Equal Educational Opportunity in America's Cities. Washington, DC: GPO, 1968.

_____. "New Priorities in Catholic Education." America, Ap 13, 1968.

Dorey, Frank D. "The Church and Segregation in Washington, D.C. and Chicago, Illinois." Doctoral dissertation, U. of Chicago, 1951.

Drinan, Robert F., S.F. "Catholics and Racially Balanced Schools." In The Committee of Religious Leaders of the City of New York, F 25, 1964.

Du Bois, W. E. B. "Negro Education and Evangelization." In The New Schaff-Herzog Religious Encyclopedia, vol. 8, pp. 100-108. Edited by S. M. Jackson. New York: Funk & Wagnalls, 1910.

Egan, John J. "The Human Side of Neighborhoods." Integrated Education, Je, 1963.

Eighmy, John Lee. "The Baptists and Slavery. An Examination of the Origins and Benefits of Segregation." Social Science Quarterly, D, 1968.

Fackre, Gabriel. Second Fronts in Metropolitan Mission. Grand Rapids, MI: Eerdmans Publishing Co., 1968.

Fell, Sr. Marie Léonore. The Foundations of Nativism in American Textbooks, 1783-1860. Washington, DC: Catholic U. of America Press, 1941.

Fichter, Joseph H. "American Religion and the Negro." Daedalus, Fall, 1965.

_____. "Chicago's Archdiocesan Office of Urban Affairs." America, O 23, 1965.

Flinn, Sr. Patricia. "I Teach in a Racist School." America, S 26, 1970. [Catholic high school in Midwest]

Fukiyama, Yoshito. "The Parishioners--A Sociological Interpretation." Research Department, United Church Board for Homeland Ministries, 287 Park Avenue South, New York, NY, O, 1966.

Fumet, Stanilas. Life of St. Martin de Porres: Patron Saint of Interracial Justice. Garden City, NY: Doubleday, 1964.

Gabert, Glen, Jr. In Hoc Signo? A Brief History of Catholic Parochial Education in America. Kennikat Press, 1973.

Ganley, William (ed.). Catholic Schools in America. Elementary and Secondary, 1972 edition. The Franklin Press, P.O. Box 10397, Denver, CO 80210.

Gannon, Arthur Seymour [pseud.] "The Desegregation of Catholic Schools, A Case Study--Diocese of Fairview." In Catholic Schools and Racial Integration: Perspectives, Directions, Models, pp. 48-62. Washington, DC: National Catholic Conference for Interracial Justice, 1977.

Gannon, Thomas M., S.F. "Parochial Education and the Inner City." Urban Review, Je, 1967.

Garinger, Louis. "Christianity and 'Black Power.'" Christian Science Monitor, N 26, 1968.

Garnett, Bernard E. Black Protest: Will It Split the United Methodists?, N, 1969. Race Relations Information Center, Nashville, TN 37212.

_____. Invaders from the Black Nation. The "Black Muslims" in 1970. Nashville, TN: Race Relations Information Center, Jl, 1970.

Garvin, Richard, and Garvin, Carol. "What Has God Done for Black People?" Liberator, O, 1968.

Geaney, Dennis J. "What Do We Owe Our Children?" Community, My, 1964.

Gist, Grace Perry. "The Educational Work of the African Methodist Episcopal Church Prior to 1900." Master's thesis, Howard U., 1949.

Gitlin, Todd. "The Racial Potential of the Poor." International Socialist Journal, D, 1967.

Gorsuch, Richard L., and Aleshire, Daniel. "Christian Faith and Ethnic Prejudice: A Review and Interpretation of Research." Journal for the Scientific Study of Religion 13(S, 1974):281-307.

Greeley, Andrew M. "Catholic Schools Are Committing Suicide." New York Times Magazine, O 21, 1973.

Griffin, John Howard. The Church and the Black Man. Pflaum Press,

Hadden, Jeffrey K., and Rymph, Raymond C. "Social Structure and Civil Rights Involvement: A Case Study of Protestant Ministers." Social Forces, S, 1966.

Hallman, George H. and Others. Louisville and Jefferson County Community Action Commission Evaluation. Louisville, KY: Je 9, 1967.

Harlow, Harold C., Jr. "Racial Integration of the Y.M.C.A." Doctoral dissertation, Hartford Seminary Foundation, 1961. Univ. Microfilms Order No. 61-4570.

Harper, L. Alexander. "School Integration--Search for a Christian Context." Social Action, S, 1965.

_____. "Where's the Action in School Reform? Some Guidelines for Churchmen." Social Action, S, 1968.

Harrison, Violet Gertrude. "A Study of Negro Colleges and other Educational Institutions Founded by the Methodist Episcopal Church." Master's thesis, U. of Cincinnati, 1937.

Haughey, John C. "Black Catholicism." America, Mr 22, 1969.

Haynes, Leonard L., Jr. The Negro Community Within American Protestantism, 1619-1844. Boston: Christophers, 1953.

Henkel, Milford F. "History of the Christian Day Schools Affiliated with the National Union of Christian Schools [Since 1850]." Doctoral dissertation, U. of Pittsburgh, 1959.

Hilton, Bruce. The Delta Ministry. New York: Macmillan, 1969.

Holland, Timothy J. "The Catholic Church and the Negro in the United States Prior to the Civil War." Doctoral dissertation, Fordham U., 1950.

Hough, Joseph C., Jr. Black Power and White Protestants. New York: Oxford, 1968.

Howes, Robert B. and others. Baltimore Urban Parish Study, N, 1967. Archdiocesan Office of Planning and Development, 320 Cathedral Street, Baltimore, MD 21201.

Hronek, Mary Linda (ed.). "A Catholic High School Integrates." I and II, Interracial Review, D, 1963 and F, 1964.

Hunt, L. L., and Hunt, J. G. "Black Catholicism and Occupational Status in Northern Cities." Social Science Quarterly 58(Mr, 1978).

Ingram, T. Robert. "Why Integration is Un-Christian!" Citizen, Je, 1962.

"I've Learned You Shouldn't Judge White People By Their Color." Education Age, My–Je, 1968.

Johns, Elizabeth (ed.). "In the North Also. School Segregation." Social Action, S, 1965.

Johnson, Henry M. "The Methodist Episcopal Church and the Education of Southern Negroes (1862–1900)." Doctoral dissertation, Yale U., 1939.

Jones, John. "Priests, Sisters, and Martin Luther King." Community, S, 1965.

Jones, James M. and others. New Roads to Faith: Black Perspectives in Church Education. Educating Black People for Liberation and Collective Growth, 1972. ERIC ED 091 473.

Jones, Miles J. "Why a Black Seminary?" Christian Century, F 2, 1972.

Kaiser, Sr. M. L. The Development of the Concept and Function of the Catholic Elementary School in the American Parish. Washington, DC: Catholic U. of America Press, 1955.

Kealey, Robert J. "Why Do Catholic Black and Hispanic Women Support Catholic Schools?" Notre Dame Journal of Education 6(Spring, 1975):32–35.

Kelly, George A. The Catholic Church and the American Poor. New York: Alba House, 1976.

Kiely, Pat. "A Cry for Black Nun Power." Commonweal, S 27, 1968.

Kleffner, John. "An Experiment in Integration." National Catholic Education Association Bulletin, F, 1968.

Kohlbrenner, Bernard. A History of Catholic Education in the United States. New York: n.p., 1937.

Labbé, Dolores Egger. Jim Crow Comes to Church: The Establishment of Segregated Catholic Parishes in South Louisiana. 2nd ed. Lafayette, LA: U. of Southwestern Louisiana, 1971.

Lecky, Robert S., and Wright, H. Elliott (eds.). Black Manifesto, Religion, Racism, and Reparations. New York: Sheed & Ward, 1969.

Lee, Robert, and Galloway, Russell. The Schizophrenic Church. Westminster, 1969. [Saul Alinsky in San Francisco Bay area]

Leonard, J. T. Theology and Race Relations. Milwaukee: Bruce, 1964.

Lewis, Elmer C. "A History of Secondary and Higher Education in Negro Schools Related to the Disciples of Christ." Doctoral dissertation, U. of Pittsburgh, 1957. Univ. Microfilms Order No. 22853.

Long, John C. "The Disciples of Christ and Negro Education." Doctoral dissertation, U. of Southern California, 1960. Univ. Microfilms Order No. 60-2779.

Lucas, Lawrence E. "Response to 'Harlem Catholic Schools Cool to Transfers.'" Interracial Review, Mr, 1964.

McAvoy, Thomas T. "The Formation of the Catholic Minority in the United States, 1820–1860." Review of Politics 10(Ja, 1948):13–34.

_____. A History of the Catholic Church in the United States. Notre Dame, IN: U. of Notre Dame Press, 1969.

McClory, Robert. "Now For the Good News." National Catholic Reporter, F 11, 1977. [Black Catholic parishes and parish schools]

McCluskey, Neil G. Catholic Viewpoint on Education. Garden City, NY: Doubleday, 1962.

McDermott, John A. "A Chicago Catholic Asks: Where Does My Church Stand on Racial Justice?" Look, N 1, 1966.

_____. "Let's Desegregate Catholic Schools." National Catholic Reporter, Mr 29, 1978.

MacEoin, Gary. "Blacks in Rome: To Tell Things the Way They Are." National Catholic Reporter, O 22, 1971. [Interview with Father Lawrence E. Lucas]

McLinden, James E., and Doyle, Joseph M. "Negro Students and Faculty on Catholic College Campuses." National Catholic Education Association Bulletin, F, 1966.

McPheeters, A. A. "Interest of the Methodist Church in the Education of Negroes." Phylon 10(1949):343-350. [1856-1949]

Mallette, Daniel J. "Black Priests Denounce the Church." Liberator, My, 1968.

Maroney, T. B. "Catholic Education Effort for the Negroes." Educational Review 18, pp. 511-523.

Marx, Gary T. "Religion: Opiate or Inspiration of Civil Rights Militancy Among Negroes?" American Sociological Review, F, 1967.

Mary, Sr. of the Holy Child, S.B.S. "The School in the Urban Apostolate." Catholic School Journal, Mr, 1965.

Mayo, A. D. "The Work of Certain Northern Churches in the Education of the Freedmen, 1861-1900." In U.S. Bureau of Education Report of 1902. Washington, DC: GPO, 1903.

Mays, Benjamin E. "The Education of Negro Ministers." Journal of Negro Education 2(J1, 1933):342-351.

Megan, John. "Milwaukee, An Interim Report." Community, Ap, 1966.

Meyer, Albert Cardinal. "Integration in Church Schools." Integrated Education, Je-J1, 1964.

Miller, Leroy. "Negro Churches and Public Schools." Center Forum, My 15, 1968. [Black Ministers and Teachers Conference, Detroit, Ap, 1968]

Miller, Steven I., and Kavanagh, Jack. "Catholic School Integration and Social Policy: A Case Study." Journal of Negro Education 44(Fall, 1975):482-492.

Miller, Thomas V. Ghetto Fever. Milwaukee, WI: Bruce, 1968.

Minnesota Council on Religion and Race, and the Minneapolis Urban Coalition. "Text of Report on Face Attitudes in Hennepin [County] Churches." Minneapolis Tribune, N 18, 1968.

Misch, Edward J. "The Catholic Church and the Negro, 1865-1884." Integrateducation 12(N-D, 1974):36-40.

Mitchell, Henry H. "Key Term in Negro: 'Compensatory.'" Christian Century, Ap 26, 1967.

More, Thomas (pseud.). "The Challenge of Desegregation, A Diocesan Case Study Diocese of Utopia." In Catholic Schools and Racial Integration: Perspectives, Directions, Models, pp. 63-75. Washington, DC: National Catholic Conference for Interracial Justice, 1977.

Moss, James A. "The Negro Church and Black Power." Journal of Human Relations, First Quarter, 1969.

Muir, Sr. Mary Alice, S.N.D. De N. "Catholic-Jewish Team Reviews Textbook [for Evidences of Anti-Semitism]." Christian Century, Ja 15, 1969.

Mufassir, Sulayman S. "Return of the Prodigal: The Rise of Orthodox Islam in Black America." Black World 22(N, 1972):59-61.

Murdick, Olin J. "Catholic Schools vs. Inner-City Apostolate." Catholic School Journal, Ja, 1969.

National Catholic Educational Association. "Characteristics of Catholic School Students—Race and Religion." In A Report on U.S. Catholic Schools, 1970-71, pp. 36-50. Washington, DC: The Association, 1971.

National Office for Black Catholics. "The Crisis of Catholic Education in the Black Community." Integrateducation 14(N-D, 1976).

Neuwien, Reginald A. (ed.). Catholic Schools in Action. Notre Dame, IN: The Notre Dame Press, 1966.

"New Commitments of Religions in Civil Rights." America, F 26, 1966.

New HOPE, Church and Private School Task Force. Is Your Church Planning a Private School to Avoid Integration?, 1970. New HOPE, 1401 Peachtree Street, N.E., Room 300, Atlanta, GA 30309. [HOPE = Help Our Public Schools]

Nobilis, M. "The School Sisters of Notre Dame in Polish-American Education." Polish American Studies 12(1955).

Nuesse, Celestine J. The Social Thought of American Catholics, 1634-1829. Washington, DC: Catholic U. of America Press, 1945.

Obenhaus, Victor, with Blount, Ross. And See the People. A Study of the United Church of Christ. Chicago: Chicago Theological Seminary, 1968.

O'Neill, Frank. "How Catholic? A Universal Church's Response to Southern 'Isms' of Race." South Today 2(O, 1970):4-5.

Oriez, Katherine. "Integration in Reverse." Our Sunday Visitor, My 29, 1966.

Osborne, William A. "The Race Problem in the Catholic Church in the United States between the Time of the Second Plenary Council (1866) and the Founding of the Catholic Interracial Council of New York (1934)." Doctoral dissertation, Columbia U., 1954. Univ. Microfilms Order No. 10273.

_____. The Segregated Covenant. N.p.: Herder and Herder, 1967.

Park, J. Philip. "Black Nuns Relate to Black Power." Christian Century, O 16, 1968.

Parker, James H. "The Interaction of Negroes and Whites in an Integrated Church Setting." Social Forces, Mr, 1968.

Pasquariello, Ronald D. "Catholic Schools and the Challenge of Intercultural Education-- An Interview with Geno Baroni." Momentum 6 (O, 1975):5-11.

Patterson, Joseph N. "A Study of the History of the Contribution of the American Missionary Association to the Higher Education of the Negro--With Special Reference to Five Selected Colleges Founded by the Association, 1865-1900." Doctoral dissertation, Cornell U., n.d. Univ. Microfilms Order No. 20423.

Pawlikowski, John T. Cathetics and Prejudice. How Catholic Teaching Materials View Jews, Protestants, and Racial Minorities. Paramus, NJ: Paulist Press, 1973.

Pleasant, Charles, Sr. "The Educative Functions of the Black Church." Notre Dame Journal of Education I(Summer, 1970):153-163.

Poinsett, Alex. "The Black Revolt in White Churches." Ebony, S, 1968.

Pool, Frank K. "The Southern Negro in the Methodist Episcopal Church." Doctoral dissertation, Cornell U., 1939.

Reimers, David M. White Protestantism and the Negro. New York: Oxford U. Press, 1965.

Ricau, Jackson G. "The Revealing Story of My Excommunication--An Act of Desperation by the Race Mixers!" Citizen, Ap, 1962.

Roche, Richard J. "Catholic Colleges and the Negro Students." Doctoral dissertation, Catholic U. of America, 1948.

Rogers, Cornish. "Black Theological Education: Successes and Failures." Christian Century, Ja 27, 1971.

Rooks, C. Shelby. "Theological Education and the Black Church." Christian Century, F 12, 1969.

Rouse, Michael Francis. A Study of the Development of Negro Education under Catholic Auspices in Maryland and the District of Columbia. Johns Hopkins U., 1933.

Salten, David G. "Education in Race Relations." Religious Education, Ja-F, 1964.

Schachern, Harold. "Negro Seminarians Cheer for All Black Theology Schools." National Catholic Reporter, N 20, 1968.

Schockley, Grant S. "Ultimatum and Hope." Christian Century, F 12, 1969.

Schwalm, Vernon F. "The Historical Development of the Denominational Colleges of the Old Northwest to 1870." Doctoral dissertation, U. of Chicago, 1928.

Scudden, Henry Martyn. The Catholics and the Public Schools. New York: n.p., 1873.

Sernett, Milton C. "Black Religion and American Evangelicalism: White Protestants, Plantation Missions, and the Independent Negro Church, 1787-1865." Doctoral dissertation, U. of Delaware, 1972.

Shalaby, Ibrahim M. "The Role of the School in Cultural Renewal and Identity Development in the Nation of Islam in America." Doctoral dissertation, U. of Arizona, 1967.

Shea, John Gilmary. The History of the Catholic Church in the United States. 4 vols. New York: n.p., 1886-1892.

Sheedy, Morgan M. "The Catholic Parochial Schools of the United States." In Report of the Commissioner of Education for 1903, pp. 1079-1101. N.p., n.d.

Sherrill, Lewis Joseph. Presbyterian Parochial Schools, 1846-1870. New Haven, CT: Yale U. Press, 1932.

Sims, David H. "Religious Education in Negro Colleges and Universities." Journal of Negro History 5(Ap, 1920):166-207.

Sklba, Richard J. "The Bible and Integration." Integrateducation 15(Mr-Ap, 1977.

Smith, Sandra N. "Parochial Schools in the Black Cities." Journal of Negro Education 42(Summer, 1973):379-391.

Sorohan, David K. "What About Desegregation in Catholic Schools?" Momentum 8(D, 1977).

Spalding, David. "The Negro Catholic Congresses, 1889-1894." Catholic Historical Review 55(O, 1969):337-357.

Steif, William. "Catholic Schools Cited for Segregation." Integrated Education, Ap-My, 1967.

Stephenson, George M. The Religious Aspects of Swedish Immigration--A Study of Immigrant Churches. Minneapolis, MN: U. of Minnesota Press, 1932.

Stowell, Jay Samuel. Methodist Adventures in Negro Education. New York: Cincinnati Methodist Book Concern, 1922.

Taylor, Olive A. "The Protestant Episcopal Church and the Negro in Washington, D.C.: A History of the Protestant Episcopal Church and its Nexus to the Black Population from the Seventeenth through the Nineteenth Centuries." Doctoral dissertation, Howard U., 1973. Univ. Microfilms Order No. 74-16,342.

Teresita, Sister. "A Black Nun Thinks Black." America, S 21, 1968.

Thibodeaux, Sister Mary Roger, S.B.S. A Black Nun Looks at Black Power. New York: Sheed and Ward, 1972.

Thompkins, Robert E. "A History of Religious Education Among Negroes in the Presbyterian Church in the United States of America." Doctoral dissertation, U. of Pittsburgh, 1951.

Thompson, Ernest Trice. "Black Presbyterians, Education and Evangelism after the Civil War." Journal of Presbyterian History, Summer, 1973.

Traxler, Sr. Margaret Ellen. "American Catholics and Negroes." Phylon, Winter, 1969.

_____. "The Sin of Segregation." Integrated Education, Je-Jl, 1966.

_____. Split-Level Lives. American Nuns Speak on Race. Techny, IL: Divine Word Publications, 1967.

Turner, Thomas W. "Actual Conditions of Catholic Education among the Colored Lay-men." Catholic Educational Association Bulletin 16(N, 1919):431.

Tyack, David. "Catholic Power, Black Power, and the Schools." Educational Forum, N, 1967.

Tyms, James D. The Rise of Religious Education Among Negro Baptists. New York: n.p., 1965.

Walsh, J. D. "Educational Work of the M.E. Church in the South." Methodist Quarterly Review 46(1886):329.

Ward, Hiley H. Prophet of the Black Nation. Philadelphia, PA: Pilgrim Press, 1970. [Rev. Albert B. Cleage]

Weatherford, Willis D. American Churches and the Negro. An Historical Study from Early Slave Days to the Present. Boston: Chrisopher Publishing House, 1957.

Weber, Chris, and Weber, Mary. "Racial Dis-crimination on Catholic College Campuses." Ave Maria, Ja 15, 1966.

Weinberg, Meyer. "Religion and Race: A Conference." Integrated Education, Ap, 1963.

Westhues, Kenneth. "An Alternative Model for Research on Catholic Education." American Journal of Sociology 77(S, 1971):279-292.

White, Edward A. "The Educational Crisis for the Urban Church." Religious Education, Ja-F, 1967.

White, John Taylor. "Survey of Organized Catholic Activities Among the Negroes in the St. Louis District, 1719-1937." Master's thesis, St. Louis U., 1937.

Williams, Daniel Jenkins. One Hundred Years of Welsh Calvinistic Methodism in America. Philadelphia, PA: Westminister Press, 1937. [Sunday school movement]

Wilson, Robert L. The Effect of Racially Changing Communities on the Methodist Churches in Thirty-Two Cities in the Southeast. New York: Department of Research and Survey, National Division, Board of Missions, Methodist Church, 1968.

Wilson, Robert L., and Davis, James H. The Church in the Racially Changing Community. Abingdon Press, 1966.

Winter, Gibson. "A Theology of Demonstration." Christian Century, O 13, 1965.

Witt, Raymond H. It Ain't Been Easy, Charlie. New York: Pageant, 1965.

Wood, James R., and Zald, Mayer N. "Aspects of Racial Integration in the Methodist Church: Sources of Resistance to Organizational Policy." Social Forces, D, 1966.

Woodson, Carter G. The History of the Negro Church. Washington, DC: Associated Publishers, 1921.

Ziegenhals, Walter E. Urban Churches in Transition. New York: Pilgrim Press, 1978. [Chicago]

Zollmann, Carl. "The Historical Background of Religious Day Schools." Marquette Law Review, 1925.

Bibliographies

Billington, Ray Allen. "Tentative Biblio-
graphy of Anti-Catholic Propaganda in the
United States (1800-1860)." Catholic
Historical Review 18(1933):492-513.

Burr, Nelson. Critical Bibliography of
Religion in America. N.p: n.p.,
n.d.

Ellis, John Tracy. A Guide to American
Catholic History. Milwaukee, WI:
Bruce, 1959.

Leffall, Dolores C. (comp.). The Black
Church. An Annotated Bibliography.
Washington, DC: Minority Research
Center, 1973.

Vollmar, Edward R. The Catholic Church in
America: An Historical Bibliography.
2nd edition. New York: Scarecrow Press,
1963.

19.
COMMUNITY

Housing

Abrams, Charles. "The Housing Problem and the Negro." Daedalus, Winter, 1966.

Ackerman, Bruce L. "Integration for Subsidized Housing and the Question of Racial Occupancy Controls." Stanford Law Review 26(Ja, 1974):245-309. [Quotas]

Aleinikoff, T. A. "Racial Steering: The Real Estate Broker and Title VIII." Yale Law Journal 85(My, 1976).

American Bar Association Advisory Commission on Housing and Urban Growth. Housing for All Under Law: New Directions in Housing, Land Use, and Planning Law. Cambridge, MA: Ballinger, 1978.

Atkinson, Reilly. "Housing Deprivation." Integrateducation 13(My-Je, 1975):85-86.

Barker, Horace, and Anderson, Robert E., Jr. Equal Housing Opportunities in the South. A Challenge. Report on Government and Citizen Action. Atlanta, GA: Southern Regional Council, Jl, 1971.

Barresi, Charles M. Neighborhood Patterns of Invasion and Succession, S, 1971. ERIC ED 055 124.

_____. "Racial Transition in an Urban Neighborhood." Growth and Change 3(Jl, 1972).

Beauchamp, Murray A. "Processual Indices of Segregation: Some Preliminary Comments." Behavioral Science, My, 1966. [A mathematical theory of residential segregation]

Berger, Stephen D. The Social Consequences of Residential Segregation of the Urban American Negro. New York: Metropolitan Applied Research Center, 1970.

Bish, Musa, Bullock, Jean, and Milgram, Jean. Racial Steering: The Dual Housing Market and Multiracial Neighborhoods, Je, 1973. National Neighbors, 5 Longford Street, Philadelphia, PA 19136.

Blumberg, Leonard. "Segregated Housing, Marginal Location, and the Crisis of Confidence." Phylon, Winter, 1964.

Blume, Norman. "Open Housing Referenda." Public Opinion Quarterly 35(Winter, 1971-1972):563-570. [Black views on residential integration]

Bogen, David S., and Falcon, Richard V. "The Use of Racial Statistics in Fair Housing Cases." Maryland Law Review 34(1974).

Boston, John, Rigsby, Leo C., and Zald, Mayer N. "The Impact of Race on Housing Markets: A Critical Review." Social Problems 19(Winter, 1972):382-393.

Boyer, Brian D. Cities Destroyed for Cash. Chicago: Follett, 1973.

Bradburn, Norman M., Sudman, Seymour, and Gockel, Galen, L., with Noel, Joseph R. Racial Integration in American Neighborhoods. Chicago: National Opinion Research Center, U. of Chicago, 1970.

Bradburn, Norman M., Sudman, Seymour, and Gockel, Galen L. Side by Side: Integrated Neighborhoods in America. Chicago: Quadrangle, 1971.

Bradford, Calvin. "Real Estate Underwriting, Discrimination and Neighborhood Change: Their Impact on Education." Integrateducation 15(N-D, 1977):70-74.

Bradford, Calvin, and others. Redlining and Disinvestment as a Discriminatory Practice in Residential Mortgage Loans. Washington, DC: GPO, 1977.

_____ and others. *Maintaining Viable Communities: The Investment-Disinvestment Process and Some Strategies for Housing Maintenance and Rehabilitation in the Pilsen Community of Chicago.* Evanston, IL: Center for Urban Studies and Metropolitan Resources, Northwestern U., 1976.

Brown, William H., Jr. "Access to Housing: The Role of the Real Estate Industry." *Economic Geography* 48(Ja, 1972):66-78.

Buehl, Stephen T., Peel, Norman D., and Pickett, Garth E. "Racial Discrimination in Public Housing Site Selection." *Stanford Law Review* 23(N, 1970).

Bullough, Bonnie. *Social-Psychological Barriers to Housing Desegregation.* Los Angeles, CA: Housing, Real Estate, and Urban Land Studies Program and Center for Real Estate and Urban Economics, 1969.

Cagle, Lawrence T. "Interracial Housing: A Reassessment of the Equal-Status Contact Hypothesis." *Sociology and Social Research* 57(Ap, 1972):342-355.

Cagle, Lawrence T., and Deutscher, Irwin. "Housing Aspirations and Housing Achievement: The Relocation of Poor Families." *Social Problems* 18(Fall, 1970):243-256.

Center for Urban and Regional Studies. *Black Residents in Five New Communities and Two Suburban Control Communities.* Chapel Hill, NC: U. of North Carolina, 1974.

Clemence, Theodore G. "Residential Segregation in the Mid-Sixties." *Demography* 4(1967): 562-568.

Clotfelter, Charles T. "An Economic Analysis of the Effect of School Desegregation on Residential Location and Private School Enrollment." Doctoral dissertation, Harvard U., 1974.

_____. "The Effect of School Desegregation on Housing Prices." *Review of Economics and Statistics* 57(N, 1975).

Cohen, Oscar. "The Case for Benign Quotas in Housing." *Phylon* 21(Spring, 1960):20-29.

Comarov, Avery. "It Pays to Stay When Blacks Move In." *Money*, N, 1973.

Combs, John Paul. "The Economics of Information Discrimination in the Real Estate Market and the Open Housing Law of 1968." Doctoral dissertation, North Carolina State U. at Raleigh, 1974. Univ. Microfilms Order No. 75-15,916.

Cooper, Gary Douglas. "The Economics of Ghetto Expansion: A Study of Residential Segregation." Doctoral dissertation, U. of Michigan, 1974. Univ. Microfilms Order No. 74-25,198.

Coral Anniversary History. Dover, DE: National Congress of Colored Parents and Teachers, 1961.

Cortese, Charles F. and others. "Further Consideration on the Methodological Analysis of Segregation Indices." *American Sociological Review* 41(Ag, 1976):630-637.

Courant, Paul N. *Urban Residential Structure and Racial Prejudice.* Ann Arbor, MI: Institute of Public Policy Studies, U. of Michigan, 1974.

Crowson, Robert L. "Hills v. Gautreaux: Implications for Education." *Phi Delta Kappan*, Mr, 1977, pp. 550-552.

Crull, Sue Ramsay. "Cultural Aspects of Housing Consumption." *Illinois Teacher of Home Economics* 20(N-D, 1976):73-76.

Danielson, Michael N. *The Politics of Exclusion.* New York: Columbia U. Press, 1976. [Suburban exclusion policies]

Davidoff, Paul. "Opening the Suburbs to Minorities." *Integrateducation* 13(My-Je, 1975):87-90.

Davis, O. A., Eastman, C. M., and Hua, C. I. "The Shrinkage in the Stock of Low-Quality Housing in the Central City: An Empirical Study of the U.S. Experience over the Last Ten Years." *Urban Studies* 11(F, 1974).

De Friese, Gordon H., and Ford, W. Scott, Jr. "Open Occupancy--What Whites Say, What They Do." *Trans-action*, Ap, 1968.

Devine, Richard. "Institutional Mortgage in an Area of Racial Transition: Bronx County, 1969-1970." Doctoral dissertation, New York U., 1973.

Downs, Anthony. "Residential Segregation: Its Effects on Education." *Civil Rights Digest* 3 (Fall, 1970):2-8.

Du Bois, W. E. B. "The Negro in the Large Cities." *New York Evening Post*, S 30, 1907.

_____. "The Problem of Housing the Negro." (six articles). *Southern Workman* 30(Je, S, O, N, D, 1901) and 31(F, 1902).

Erbe, Brigitte Mach. "Race and Socioeconomic Segregation." *American Sociological Review* 40(D, 1975):801-812.

Erber, Ernest. *Jobs and Housing. A Two-Year Study of Employment and Housing Opportunities for Racial Minorities in Suburban Areas of the New York Metropolitan Region.* New York: National Committee Against Discrimination in Housing, Mr, 1972.

Erskine, Hazel. "The Polls: Negro Housing." *Public Opinion Quarterly* 31(1967):482-498.

Farley, Reynolds. "Components of Suburban Population Growth." In The Changing Face of the Suburbs, pp. 3-38. Edited by Barry Schwartz. Chicago: U. of Chicago, 1976. [Racial segregation in the suburbs]

_____. "Residential Segregation and Its Implications for School Integration." Law and Contemporary Problems 39(Winter, 1975): 164-193.

_____. "Residential Segregation in Urbanized Areas of the United States in 1970: An Analysis of Social Class and Racial Differences." Demography 14(N, 1977):497-518.

Ford, W. Scott. Interracial Public Housing in Border City: A Situational Analysis of the Contact Hypothesis. Lexington, MA: Lexington Books, 1972.

Freeman, Linton, and Sunshine, Morris. Patterns of Residential Segregation. Cambridge, MA: Schenkman, 1970.

Fried, Marc, and Gleicher, Peggy. "Some Sources of Residential Satisfaction in an Urban Slum." In Urban Renewal: People, Politics and Planning. Edited by Jewel Bellush and Murray Hansknecht. Garden City, NY: Doubleday, 1967.

Fuerst, J. S., and Petty, Roy. "The Quota Approach to Housing." Nation, Ap 9, 1977. [Providence, RI]

Gardner, M. "Race Segregation in Cities." Kentucky Law Journal 29(Ja, 1941):213-219.

Gillingham, Robert F. Place to Place Rent Comparisons Using Hedonic Quality Adjustment Techniques Research. Washington, DC: Office of Prices and Living Conditions, Bureau of Labor Statistics, U.S. Department of Labor, Mr, 1973.

Goering, John M. "Neighborhood Tipping and Racial Transition: A Review of Social Science Evidence." Journal of the American Institute of Planners 44(1978):68-78.

Goodman, Walter. "The Battle of Forest Hills-- Who's Ahead?" New York Times Magazine, F 20, 1972. [NYC]

Gottlieb, Harry N. "The Ultimate Solution: Desegregated Housing." School Review 84 (My, 1976):463-478.

Greene, Kenneth Roger. "Black Demands for Open Housing: The Responses of Three City Governments." Doctoral dissertation, Michigan State U., 1971. Univ. Microfilms Order No. 72-08657.

Grier, G. C. "The Negro Ghettos and Federal Housing Policy." Law and Contemporary Problems, Summer, 1967.

Guest, Avery M., and Zuiches, James J. "Another Look at Residential Turnover in Urban Neighborhoods: A Note on 'Racial Change in a Stable Community' by Harvey Molotch." American Journal of Sociology 77 (N, 1971):457-467. [See reply by Molotch, pp. 468-471.]

Hamilton, David L., and Bishop, George D. "Attitudinal and Behavioral Effects of Initial Integration of White Suburban Neighborhoods." Journal of Social Issues 32 (1976):47-67.

Hammer, Charles. "Racially Changing Neighborhoods." New Republic 169(S 15, 1973): 19-21.

Harrison, Bennett. "Suburbanization and Ghetto Dispersal: A Critique of the Conventional Wisdom." In Controversies of State and Local Political Systems, pp. 401-408. Edited by Mavis M. Reeves and Parris N. Glendening. Boston: Allyn and Bacon, 1972.

Hartman, Chester W. Housing and Social Policy. Englewood Cliffs, NJ: Prentice-Hall, 1975.

Harvey, David. "Revolutionary and Counter-Revolutionary Theory in Geography and the Problems of Ghetto Formation." Antipode 4 (1972).

Harvey, James. "Equal Opportunity Housing." Integrateducation 13(My-Je, 1975):95-97.

Hawkins, Homer C. "Urban Housing and the Black Family." Phylon 37(Mr, 1976):73-84.

Hawley, Amos H., and Rock, Vincent P. (eds.). Segregation in Residential Areas. Papers on Racial and Socioeconomic Factors in Choice of Housing. Washington, DC: National Academy of Sciences, 1973.

Hecht, James L. Because It Is Right. Boston: Little, Brown, 1970. [The fair housing movement]

_____. "Mixed Housing in the Suburbs." Nation, Mr 6, 1972.

Helper, Rose. Racial Policies and Practices of Real Estate Brokers. Minneapolis: U. of Minnesota Press, 1969.

Hermalin, Albert I., and Farley, Reynolds. "The Potential for Residential Integration in Cities and Suburbs: Implications for the Busing Controversy." American Sociological Review 38(O, 1973):595-610.

Hoeber, Elizabeth. "Open Housing Through Legal Action." Integrateducation 13(My-Je, 1975): 105-106.

"Housing." Black Enterprise 3(Ag, 1972):19-48, 55.

The Housing Advertisers. Violators of U.S.
Fair Housing Law and Advertising Guidelines--
A Study of Selected Advertisers in the
National Capital Area, Ap, 1973. Housing
Opportunities Council of Metropolitan
Washington, 1522 K Street, N.W., Suite 406,
Washington, DC 20005.

Housing Analysis in Oakley, Bond Hill, and
Evanston: Financial Investment Patterns,
1974. Coalition of Neighborhoods, 3930
Reading Road, Cincinnati, OH 45229.

How the Federal Government Builds Ghettos.
New York: National Committee Against Discrimination in Housing, F, 1967.

Hoyt, Homer. Where the Rich and the Poor
People Live: The Location of Residential
Areas Occupied by the Highest and Lowest
Income Families In American Cities.
Washington, DC: Urban Land Institute, 1966.

Jacobs, Paul, and Landau, Saul (eds.). The
Permanent Ghettos. New York: Random House,
1968.

Kahn, Terry D. "Optimal Distribution of Residence Locations by Race: A Linear Programming Approach." Doctoral dissertation, U.
of California, Berkeley, 1970.

Kain, John. "Housing Segregation, Negro Employment, and Metropolitan Decentralization."
Quarterly Journal of Economics, My, 1968.

_____. "The Impact of Housing Segregation on
Blacks." Integrateducation 13(My-Je, 1975):
81-84.

_____. Racial Discrimination in Urban Housing
Markets and Goals for Public Policy, 0, 1974.
ERIC ED 126 221.

Kain, John F., and Quigley, John M. Housing
Markets and Racial Discrimination: A
Microeconimic Analysis. New York: Columbia
U. Press, 1975.

Keller, Suzanne. The Urban Neighborhood.
New York: Random House, 1968.

Kenyon, James B. "Patterns of Residential
Integration in the Bicultural Western City."
Professional Geographer 28(F, 1976):40-44.

_____. "Spatial Associations in the Integra-
tion of the American City." Economic
Geography 52(0, 1976):287-303. [Atlanta,
San Antonio, and Honolulu]

Lawson, Simpson F. Above Property Rights.
Prepared for the U.S. Commission on Civil
Rights. Washington, DC: GPO, D, 1972.

League of Women Voters Education Fund. What
Ever Happened to Open Housing: A Handbook
for Fair Housing Monitors. Washington, DC:
League of Women Voters, 1974.

Leasure, J. William, and Stern, David H.
"A Note on Housing Segregation Indexes."
Social Forces, Mr, 1968.

Lee, Douglass B., Jr. Analysis and Description
of Residential Segregation. An Application
of Centrographic Techniques to the Study of
the Spatial Distribution of Ethnic Groups in
Cities. Ithaca, NY: Division of Urban
Studies, Center for Housing and Environmental
Studies, Cornell U., N, 1967.

Lester, David. "Residential Segregation and
Completed Suicide." Crisis Intervention 3
(1971):7-9.

Levine, S. N. "A Model of Racially Changing
Neighborhoods." Socio-Economic Planning
Sciences 1(1968):477-480.

Listokin, David C. "The Urban Financing Prob-
lem: An Evaluation of the Economic and
Eco-Race Models of Lender Behavior."
Doctoral dissertation, Rutgers U., 1978.
Univ. Microfilms Order No. 7901286.
[Chicago]

Little, James T. and others. The Contemporary
Neighborhood Succession Process. St. Louis,
MO: Institute for Urban and Regional
Studies, Washington U., 1975.

Long, Laila. "Barriers to Equalizing Housing
Opportunities." Integrateducation 13(My-
Je, 1975):101-104.

McAllister, Ronald J. "Neighborhood Integration
and Prospective Residential Mobility. A
Study of the Impact of Social Relationships
on Moving and Staying Plans Among a National
Sample of Metropolitan Area Residents."
Doctoral dissertation, U. of North Carolina,
1970.

McAllister, Ronald J., Kaiser, Edward J., and
Butler, Edgar W. "Residential Mobility of
Blacks and Whites: A National Longitudinal
Survey." American Journal of Sociology 77
(N, 1971):445-456.

McGee, H. W., Jr. "Illusion and Contradiction
in the Quest for a Desegregated Metropolis."
University of Illinois Law Forum (1976):948-
1015.

McKay, David H. Housing and Race in Industrial
Society: Civil Rights and Urban Policy in
Britain and the United States. Totowa, NJ:
Rowman and Littlefield, 1977.

McPherson, James Alan. "The Story of the
Contract Buyers League." Atlantic Monthly,
Ap, 1972. [Chicago, IL]

Marando, Vincent L. "A Metropolitan Lower
Income Housing Allocation Policy." American
Behavioral Scientist 19(S-O, 1975):75-103.

Marcus, M. "Racial Composition and Home Price Changes: A Case Study," Journal of the American Institute of Planners 34(S, 1968): 334-338. [Plainfield, NJ]

Margolis, Richard J. "Last Chance for Desegregation?" Dissent 19(Winter, 1972):249-256.

Marshall, Harvey, and Jiobu, Robert. "Residential Segregation in United States Cities: A Causal Analysis." Social Forces 53(Mr, 1975):449-459.

Meyer, David R. "Interurban Differences in Black Housing Quality." Annals of the Association of American Geographers 63 (S, 1973):347-352.

_____. Spatial Variation of Black Urban Households. Chicago: Department of Geography, U. of Chicago, 1970.

Milgram, Jean Gregg. "Integrated Neighborhood and Integrated Education." Integrated Education 12(My-Je, 1974):29-30.

Milgram, Morris. Good Neighborhood, The Challenge of Open Housing. New York: Norton, 1977.

Milgram, Morris, and Beilenson, Roger N. Racial Integration in Housing, 1968. Contract H-926 with Department of Housing and Urban Development on behalf of the National Commission on Urban Problems.

Minnis, Mhyra S., and McWilliams. Tornado: The Voice of the People in Disaster and After. A Study in Residential Integration. Lubbock, TX: Texas Tech U., 1971.

Mitchell, Robert E. "Sociological Research on the Economic Myths of Housing." Social Problems 22(D, 1974):259-279.

Mooney, Joseph D. "Housing Segregation, Negro Employment and Metroplitan Decentralization: An Alternative Perspective." Quarterly Journal of Economics, My, 1969.

Moore, Eric G. Residential Mobility in the City. Washington, DC: Association of American Geographers, 1972.

Morris, David C. "Racial Attitudes of White Residents in Integrated and Segregated Neighborhoods." Sociological Focus 6(Spring, 1973):74-91.

Morris, Steven. "Home Was Where the Bulldozer Is." Chicago Tribune Magazine, Ap 18, 1971. [Urban renewal in Chicago]

Morrison, K. C. "Federal Aid to Housing and Discrimination." Journal of Social and Behavioral Sciences 14(Spring, 1969):42-50.

Mortl, Patty. "A Plan to End 'Racial Steering'--From One Who Knows How It Works." Los Angeles Times, My 17, 1974. [Los Angeles]

Murray, Clyde E. Human Needs in Public Housing. A Survey of Social Welfare and Health Services and Needs of Residents in Public Housing Developments Serving Families in Chicago. Chicago: Welfare Council of Metropolitan Chicago, My, 1970.

National Conference on Legal Rights of Tenants. Tenants' Rights, Legal Tools for Better Housing. Washington, DC: GPO, 1967.

Neimark, Paul. "Integration Moves to the Suburbs." Sepia 26(Mr, 1977).

Nelson, Susan Cordine. "Housing Discrimination and Black Employment Opportunities." Doctoral dissertation, Princeton U., 1976. Univ. Microfilms Order No. 76-23868.

Nicholas, J. C. "Racial and Ethnic Discrimination in Rental Housing." Review of Social Economy 36(Ap, 1970).

Northwood, Lawrence K., and Barth, Ernest A. T. Urban Desegregation, Negro Pioneers and Their White Neighbors. Seattle, WA: U. of Washington Press, 1965.

O'Connell, George Edward. "Residential Segregation by Racial-Ethnic Background and Socio-Economic Status in Four Standard Metropolitan Statistical Areas, 1970." Doctoral dissertation, U. of Minnesota, 1974. Univ. Microfilms Order No. 75-2134.

Onderdonk, Dudley, De Marco, Donald, and Cardona, Kathy. Integration in Housing: A Plan for Racial Diversity, 1977. Planning Division, Village of Park Forest, 200 Forest Blvd., Park Forest, IL 60466. [South suburb in Chicago area]

Orbell, John M., and Uno, Toru. "A Theory of Neighborhood Problem Solving: Political Action vs. Residential Mobility." American Political Science Review 66(Je, 1972):471-489.

Parker, Kallis E. "Black Ghetto Housing: Serving the Unserved." Current History 67 (N, 1974).

Pascal, Anthony H. The Analysis of Residential Segregation. Santa Monica, CA: Rand, 1969.

_____. The Economics of Housing Segregation. Santa Monica, CA: Rand, 1967.

Peabody, Malcolm E., Jr. "Custom Changing: Fundamental Change Required, HUD Tells Realtors." Journal of Intergroup Relations 2(Summer, 1973):46-58.

Peach, Ceri (ed.). Urban Social Segregation. London: Longman, 1975.

Pearce, Diana May. "Black, White, and Many Shades of Gray: Real Estate Brokers and their Racial Practices." Doctoral dissertation, U. of Michigan, 1976. Univ. Microfilms Order No. 77-08009.

Pettigrew, Thomas. "Attitudes on Race and Housing." In Segregation in Residential Areas: Papers on Racial and Socioeconomic Factors in Choice of Housing. Edited by Amos Hawley and Vincent Rock. Washington, DC: National Academy of Sciences, 1973.

Phares, Donald. "Racial Change and Housing Values: Transition in an Inner Suburb." Social Science Quarterly 52(D, 1971):560-573. [University City, MO]

Polikoff, Alexander. Housing the Poor. The Case for Heroism. Cambridge, MA: Ballinger, 1978.

Potomac Institute. Metropolitan Housing Desegregation, 1966. The Potomac Institute, Inc., 1501 Eighteenth Street, N.W., Washington, DC 20036.

Pottinger, J. Stanley. "Open Housing: Making the Promise a Reality." Integrated Education 12(Ja-Ap, 1974):26-28.

Pryor, Franklin. "An Empirical Note on the Tipping Point." Land Economics 47(1971): 413-417.

Rabushka, Alvin, and Weissert, William G. Caseworkers or Police? How Tenants See Public Housing. Stanford, CA: Hoover Institution Press, 1978.

"Racial Steering: The Real Estate Broker and Title VIII." Yale Law Journal 85(My, 1976):808-825.

Rainwater, Lee. "Poverty, Race and Urban Housing." In The Social Impact of Urban Design, pp. 7-30. Chicago: Center for Policy Study, U. of Chicago, 1971.

Real Estate Research Corporation. The Dynamics of Neighborhood Change. Washington, DC: U.S. Department of Housing and Urban Development, 1975.

Rent, George S., and Lord, J. Dennis. "Neighborhood Racial Transition and Property Value Trends in a Southern Community." Social Science Quarterly 59(Je, 1978):51-59.

Rice, Roger L. "Residential Segregation by Law, 1910-1917." Journal of Southern History 34(My, 1968):180-199.

Ricciardi, D. Robert, Rosenberg, Milton, and Smith, Julienne. Black Population and Housing in New York State, 1970. New York: State Division of Human Rights, 1972.

Robertson, Douglas L. "Cognitive Images of Neighborhood in a Transitional Residential Area." Master's thesis, Syracuse U., 1975.

Roof, W. Clark. "Residential Segregation of Blacks and Racial Inequality in Southern Cities: Toward a Causal Model." Social Problems 19(Winter, 1972):393-407.

_____ and others. "Residential Segregation in Southern Cities: 1970." Social Forces 55 (1976):59-71.

Rose, Harold M. "The All-Black Town: Suburban Prototype or Rural Slum?" In People and Politics in Urban Society, pp. 397-431. Edited by Harlan Hahn. Beverly Hills, CA: Sage, 1972.

_____. "The All-Negro Town: Its Evolution and Function." Geographical Review 55(Jl, 1965): 262-381.

_____. The Black Ghetto: A Spatial Behavioral Perspective. New York: McGraw-Hill, 1971.

_____. Black Suburbanization: Access to Improved Quality of Life or Maintenance of the Status Quo? Cambridge, MA: Ballinger, 1976.

_____. Social Processes in the City: Race and Urban Residential Choice. Washington, DC: Association of American Geographers, 1969.

_____. "The Spatial Development of Black Residential Subsystems." Economic Geography 48(Ja, 1972):43-65. [Denver, Boston, Indianapolis, Milwaukee, San Francisco, Seattle, and Minneapolis]

Rose-Ackerman, S. "The Political Economy of a Racist Housing Market." Journal of Urban Economics 4(Ap, 1977).

Roseman, Curtis C., and Knight, Prentice L. III. "Residential Environment and Migration Behavior of Urban Blacks." Professional Geographer 27(My, 1975):160-165.

Ross, Myron H. "Prices, Segregation, and Racial Harmony." Journal of Black Studies 2(D, 1971):225-243.

Rothman, Jack. Housing Urban America. Chicago: Aldine, 1974.

Rubinowitz, Leonard S. Low Income Housing: Suburban Strategies. Cambridge, MA: Ballinger, 1974.

Rubinowitz, Leonard S., and Dennis, Roger J. "School Desegregation versus Public Housing Desegregation: The Local School District and the Metropolitan Housing District." Urban Law Annual 10(1975):145-175.

Saltman, Juliet Z. "Implementing Open Housing Laws through Social Action." Journal of Applied Behavioral Science 11(1975):39-61.

_____. Open Housing as a Social Movement: Challenges, Conflict and Change. Lexington, MA: D. C. Heath, 1972.

Sanoff, Henry, Sawhney, Man, Burgwyn, King, and Ellinwood, George. Residential Patterns of Racial Change: A Study of a Southern City, Je, 1970. National Technical Information Service, Springfield, VA 22151.

Schelling, Thomas C. "A Process of Residential Segregation: Neighborhood Tipping." In Racial Discrimination in Economic Life. Edited by Anthony H. Pascal. Lexington, MA: Lexington Books, 1972.

Schnore, Ann B. Residential Segregation by Race in U.S. Metropolitan Areas: An Analysis Across and Over Time. Washington, DC: Office of Policy Development and Research, Department of Housing and Urban Development, F, 1977.

Schnore, L. F., and Everson, P. C. "Segregation in Southern Cities." American Journal of Sociology 72(Jl, 1966):58-67.

Schnore, Leo F. "Social Class Segregation Among Nonwhites in Metropolitan Centers." Demography, II, 1965.

Schorr, Alvin L. "National Community and Housing Policy." Social Service Review, D, 1965.

Scott, Herbert Amos. "Politics, Economics, and Race: A Comparative Analysis of Urban Public Housing Service Delivery and Distributional Patterns." Doctoral dissertation, Ohio State U., 1978. Univ. Microfilms Order No. 7819661.

Seeley, John. "The Slum: Its Nature, Use, and Users." In Urban Renewal: People, Politics and Planning. Edited by Jewel Bellush and Murray Hausknecht. Garden City, NY: Doubleday, 1967.

Setlow, Marcie Louise. "Metropolitan Open Housing Ordinances in Ellinois: Their Effectiveness as a Deterrent to Segregated Housing." Master's thesis, U. of Chicago, 1968.

Shaffer, Richard. "Interracial Neighborhood Mix and Aspirations: The Influence of Contact." Doctoral dissertation, U. of Notre Dame, 1976. Univ. Microfilms Order No. 76-10,521.

Sheppard, Nathaniel, Jr. "Race Discrimination Found Pervasive in Rental of Manhattan Apartments." New York Times, Je 28, 1976.

Social Science Panel of the Advisory Committee to the Department of Housing and Urban Development. Freedom of Choice in Housing--Opportunities and Constraints. Washington, DC: National Academy of Sciences, 1972.

Sorensen, Annemette, Taeuber, Karl E., and Hollingsworth, Leslie J., Jr. Indexes of Racial Residential Segregation for 109 Cities in the United States, 1940 to 1970. Madison, WI: Institute for Research on Poverty, U. of Wisconsin, 1974.

_____, _____, and _____. "Indexes of Racial Residential Segregation for 109 Cities in the United States, 1940 to 1970." Sociological Focus 8(Ap, 1975):125-142.

Stengel, Mitchell. "Racial Price Discrimination in the Urban Rental Housing Market." Doctoral dissertation, Harvard U., 1970.

_____. Racial Rent Differentials: Market Separation and the Ghetto Housing Market. East Lansing, MI: Graduate School of Business, Michigan State U., 1976.

Stephens, John D., and Wittick, Robert I. "An Instructional Unit for Simulating Urban Residential Segregation." Professional Geographer 27(Ag, 1975):340-346.

Stephenson, Gilbert T. "The Segregation of the White and Negro Races in Cities by Legislation." National Municipal Review 3(Jl, 1914):496-504.

Stone, Michael E. "The Housing Crisis, Mortgage Lending, and Class Struggle." Antipode 7 (1975):22-37.

Straszheim, Mahlon R. "Housing Market Discrimination and Black Housing Consumption." Quarterly Journal of Economics, F, 1974, pp. 19-43.

Sudman, Seymour, and Bradburn, Norman. Social Psychological Factors in Intergroup Housing. Report No. 111-A National Opinion Research Center, U. of Chicago, My, 1966. [Pilot study of integrated neighborhoods in Washington, DC, Atlanta and San Jose]

Sudman, Seymour, Bradburn, Norman, and Gockel, Galen. "The Extent and Characteristics of Racially Integrated Housing in the United States." Journal of Business, U. of Chicago, Ja, 1969.

Sutker, Sara Smith. Relationships Between Changing Residence Location and Labor Force Performance for Black New Resident Households in an Inner Suburb. PB-209-569. Springfield, VA: National Technical Information Service, F, 1972.

Taeuber, Karl E. "Demographic Perspectives on Housing and School Segregation." Wayne Law Review 21(Mr, 1975):833-849.

_____. "The Effect of Income Redistribution on Racial Residential Segregation." Urban Affairs Quarterly 4(S, 1968):5-14. [Cleveland]

_____. "Negro Residential Segregation: Trends and Measurement." Social Problems, Summer, 1964.

_____. Patterns of Negro-White Residential Segregation. Santa Monica, CA: Rand Corporation, 1970.

_____. "Population Trends and Residential Segregation Since 1960." Science, Mr 1, 1968.

_____. "The Problems of Residential Segregation." Proceedings, Academy of Political Science, 1968.

_____. "Racial Segregation: The Persisting Dilemma." Annals 422(N, 1975):87-96.

_____. "Residential Segregation." Scientific American, Ag, 1965.

_____. "Social and Demographic Trends: Focus on Race." In The Future of the Metropolis: People, Jobs, Income. Edited by E. Ginzberg. N.p., n.p., 1975.

Thumin, Fred J. "Demographic and Attitudinal Differences Between Negro and White Neighbors." Perceptual and Motor Skills 33 (O, 1971):423-427.

U.S. Commission on Civil Rights. Equal Opportunity in Suburbia. Washington, DC: The Commission, Jl, 1974.

_____. Hearing Held in Washington, D.C., June 14-17, 1971. Washington, DC: GPO, 1972. [On the bearing of federal programs upon racial polarization in the nation's metropolitan areas]

_____. Home Ownership for Lower Income Families. A Report on the Racial and Ethnic Impact of the Section 235 Program. Washington, DC: GPO, Je, 1971.

_____. Mortgage Money: Who Gets It? A Case Study in Mortgage Lending Discrimination in Hartford, Connecticut. Washington, DC: GPO, Je, 1974.

_____. Twenty Years After Brown: Equal Opportunity in Housing. Washington, DC: The Commission, D, 1975.

_____. Understanding Fair Housing. Washington, DC: GPO, F, 1973.

U.S. Congress, 90th, 1st session, Senate Committee on Banking and Currency, Subcommittee on Housing and Urban Affairs. Progress Report on Federal Housing Programs. Washington, DC: GPO, My 9, 1967.

U.S. Congress, 93rd, 2nd session, House of Representatives, Committee on the Judiciary, Subcommittee on Civil Rights and Constitutional Rights. Equal Opportunity in Housing. Hearing... Serial No. 57. Washington, DC: GPO, 1975.

U.S. Congress, 94th, 1st session, Senate, Committee on Banking, Housing and Urban Affairs. The Home Mortgage Disclosure Act of 1975--To Improve Public Understanding of Depository Institutions in Home Financing. 2 vols. Washington, DC: GPO, 1975. [On redlining]

U.S. Congress, 94th, 2nd session, House of Representatives, Committee on the Judiciary, Subcommittee on Civil and Constitutional Rights. Equal Opportunity in Housing. Hearings... Washington, DC: GPO, 1976.

U.S. Department of Housing and Urban Development. Fair Housing, An American Idea. Washington, DC: HUD, 1977.

_____. Insurance Crisis in Urban America. Washington, DC: U.S. Department of Housing and Urban Development, Je, 1978. [Redlining]

Urban Systems Research and Engineering. The Barriers to Equal Opportunity in Rural Housing Markets. Washington, DC: GPO, 1977.

_____. The Barriers to Equal Opportunity in Rural Housing Markets. Vol. 3. Washington, DC: Department of Housing and Urban Development, Office of Policy Development and Research, 1977.

Von Valey, Thomas L., Roof, Wade Clark, and Wilcox, Jerome E. "Trends in Residential Segregation: 1960-1970." American Journal of Sociology 82(Ja, 1977):826-844.

Vandell, Kerry D. and others. Financial Institutions and Neighborhood Decline: A Review of the Literature. Washington, DC: Federal Home Loan Board, N, 1974.

Varady, David P. "The Migration Decision in Racially Changing Neighborhoods." Doctoral dissertation, U. of Pennsylvania, 1971.

Vaughn, G. A. "The Role of Residential Racial Segregation in Causing and Perpetuating Inferior Housing for Lower-Income Nonwhites." Journal of Economics and Business 25(Fall, 1972).

Walden, W. Charles. Differences in the Quality of Housing Occupied by Black and White Households in Rural Areas of South Central Tennessee, 1968. Washington, DC: U.S. Department of Agriculture, Ap, 1972.

Warren, Michael. "Integration and Housing Prices." Master's thesis, Wharton School of Finance, 1968.

Weaver, Robert. "Housing Problems of Minorities." Integrateducation 13(My-Je, 1975):74-80.

_____. "The Impact of Housing on Jobs and Education." Integrateducation 14(Ja/F, 1976).

Winer, M. L. "White Resistance and Negro Insistence: An Ecological Analysis of Urban Desegregation." Cambridge, MA: Unpublished honors thesis, Harvard U., 1964.

Wurster, Catherine Bauer. "Housing Policy and the Educational System." Annals, N, 1955.

Yinger, John. The Black-White Price Differential in Housing: Some Further Evidence, D, 1975. ERIC ED 123 313.

_____. "The Black-White Price Differential in Housing: Some Further Evidence." Land Economics 54(My, 1978):187-206.

Zelder, Raymond E. "Racial Segregation in Urban Housing Markets." Journal of Regional Science 10(Ap, 1970):93-105.

Zeul, Carolyn, and Humphrey, Craig R. "The Integration of Black Residents in Suburban Neighborhoods. A Reexamination of the Contact Hypothesis." Social Problems 18 (Spring, 1971):462-474.

Zonn, Leo Edward. "Residential Search Patterns of Black Urban Households: A Spatial Behavioral View." Doctoral dissertation, U. of Wisconsin-Milwaukee, 1975. Univ. Microfilms Order No. 76-13,773.

Parent Participation

Aberbach, Joel D., and Walker, Jack L. "Citizen Desires, Policy Outcomes, and Community Control." Urban Affairs Quarterly 8(S, 1972):55-75.

Burgess, Tyrrell. Home and School. London: Penguin Press, 1973. [England]

Altshuler, Alan A. Community Control: The Black Demand for Participation in Large American Cities. New York: Pegasus, 1970.

Antonetty, Evalina, and Lurie, Ellen. Parent and Community Leadership Training Program. Bronx, NY: United Bronx Parents, 608 Union Avenue, Ap 1, 1967.

Armstrong, Marjorie. "Community Participation by Blacks: Its Relationship to School Achievement." Master's thesis, Northeastern Illinois U., 1971.

Aronowitz, Stanley. "The Dialectics of Community Control." Social Policy, My-Je, 1970.

Bauer, Raymond and others. Urban Education: Eight Experiments in Community Control, O 31, 1969. ERIC ED 135 876. [D.C., Illinois, Massachusetts and New York]

Beck, Bertram M. "Community Control: A Distraction, Not An Answer." Social Work 14(1969):14-20.

Beezer, B. G. "Title I Parent Advisory Councils: To What Extent Must They Be Involved?" Journal of Law and Education 7(Ap, 1978): 151-163.

Berube, Maurice R. "Community Control: Key to Educational Achievement." Social Policy, Jl-Ag, 1970.

Billings, Charles E. "Community Control of the School and the Quest for Power." Phi Delta Kappan 53(Ja, 1972):277-278.

Bostford, Michael L. "A Study to Determine the Need for Community Control of Education in Low-Income Urban Areas." Master's thesis, California State U., Long Beach, 1971.

Bourgeois, A. Donald. "Community Control and Urban Conflict." Theory Into Practice 8 (O, 1969):243-249.

Brown, Frank. "Three Slants on Parents and Curriculum." Integrateducation 13(S-O, 1975):30-32.

Burnes, Donald W. "Community Controlled Schools: Politics and Education." Civil Rights Digest, Fall, 1969.

Carol, Lila N. "Court-Mandated Citizen Participation in School Desegregation." Phi Delta Kappan 59(N, 1977):171-173.

Carpenter, Frank H. "Analysis of Negro Parents' Goals for the Educational System." Master's thesis, Wichita State U., 1967.

Center for Governmental Studies. Community Participation in Public Elementary Schools. S, 1970. The Center, 1701 K Street, N.W., Suite 906, Washington, DC 20006.

Cheng, Charles W. "Minority Parents and Teachers' Collective Bargaining." Integrateducation 15(N-D, 1977):112-115.

Chu, Morgan. Neighborhood and Political Influence: A Study of ESEA, Title I, Ap, 1974. ERIC ED 091 496.

Cohen, David K. "The Price of Community Control." Theory Into Practice 8(O, 1969): 231-241.

Cook, Paul W., Jr. Modernizing School Governance for Educational Equality and Diversity. Boston: Massachusetts Advisory Council on Education, 1972.

Crain, Robert L., and Rosenthal, Donald B. "Community Status as a Dimension of Local Decision-Making." American Sociological Review, D, 1967.

Cuban, Larry. "Community Participation and Urban School Reform." Changing Education 6 (Summer, 1974):24-26, 38.

Datta, Lois-ellin. Parent Involvement in Early Childhood Education: A Perspective from the United States, O, 1973. ERIC ED 088 587.

David, Miriam. "The Citizen's Voice in Education." New Society, Ag 30, 1973. [Community control in U.S.]

Davies, Don. "The Emerging Third Force in Education." Inequality in Education 15(N, 1973):5-12.

_____ (ed.). Schools Where Parents Make a Difference. Boston: Institute for Responsive Education, 1976.

Dawson, Roy J., Jr. "A Study of Title I Parent Council Member Participation in Selected Title I Programs." Doctoral dissertation, Rutgers U., 1977. Univ. Microfilms Order No. 7804590. [Camden County, NJ]

De'ath, Colin E. "Patterns of Participation and Exclusion: A Poor Italian and Black Urban Community and Its Response to a Federal Poverty Program." Doctoral dissertation, U. of Pittsburgh, 1970. Univ. Microfilms Order No. 71-7991.

Deschin, Celia S. "Community Control: Myth or Reality?" American Journal of Orthopsychiatry 40(O, 1970):740-743.

Dodson, Dan W. Power Conflict and Community Organizations. New York: Council for American Unity, 1967.

Edwards, Babette, and Wilcox, Preston. "Community Control for Whites Only." Amsterdam News, D 11, 1971.

Elazar, Daniel J. "Community Self-Government and the Crisis of American Politics." Ethics 81(Ja, 1971):91-106.

_____. "School Decentralization in the Context of Community Control: Some Neglected Considerations." Phylon 36(D, 1975): 385-394.

Eugster, Carla. "Field Education in West Heights: Equipping a Deprived Community to Help Itself." Human Organization, Fall, 1964.

Estes, Sidney H. "The Plight of Black Parents." Educational Leadership 29(F, 1972):451-453.

Fainstein, Norman I., and Fainstein, Susan S. Urban Political Movements: The Search for Power by Minority Groups in American Cities. Englewood Cliffs, NJ: Prentice-Hall, 1974.

Falkson, Joseph, and Grainer, Marc A. "Neighborhood School Politics and Contributing Organizations." School Review 81(N, 1972): 35-61.

Fantini, Mario. "Afterword. The Relationship Between Participation, Decentralization, and Quality Education." In Naomi Levine with Richard Cohen, Ocean Hill-Brownsville--A Case History of Schools in Crisis. New York: Popular Library, 1969.

_____. "Community Control and Quality Education in Urban School Systems." In Community Control of Schools. Edited by Henry M. Levin. Washington, DC: Brookings, 1970.

_____. "Community Participation: Many Faces, Many Directions." Educational Leadership 29 (My, 1972):674-680.

_____. "Participation, Decentralization, and Community Control." National Elementary Principal, Ap, 1969.

_____. The People and Their Schools: Community Participation. Bloomington, IN: Phi Delta Kappa Educational Foundation, 1975.

Fantini, Mario, Gittell, Marilyn, and Magat, Richard. Community Control and the Urban School. New York: Praeger, 1970.

Farley, Ena L. "The Equal Education Game: Reflections on a Timeless Conflict." Integrateducation 14(N/D, 1976).

Fein, Leonard J. "Community Schools and Social Theory: The Limits of Universalism." In Community Control of Schools. Edited by Henry M. Levin. Washington, DC: Brookings, 1970.

_____. The Ecology of the Public Schools. An Inquiry into Community Control. New York: Pegasus, 1971.

Firestone, William. "Community Organizations and School Reform: A Case Study." School Review 81(N, 1972):108-120.

Francy, Robert C. "Processes and Practices of Parent Advisory Councils: A Study in Twenty-Five Elementary Schools." Doctoral dissertation, U. of Utah, 1978. Univ. Microfilms Order No. 7821672. [California]

Friesina, H. Paul. "Black Control of Central Cities: The Hollow Prize." Journal of the American Institute of Planners 35(Mr, 1969): 75-77.

Gittell, Marilyn. "The Balance of Power and the Community School." In Community Control of Schools. Edited by Henry M. Levin. Washington, DC: Brookings, 1970.

_____. "The Potential for Change: Community Roles." Journal of Negro Education 40(Summer, 1971):216-224.

Glasgow, Douglas. "Black Power through Community Control." Social Work 17(My, 1972):59-64.

Glass, Thomas E., and Sanders, William. Community Control in Education: A Study in Power Transition. Midland, MI: Pendell Publishing Co., 1978.

Glazer, Nathan. "For White and Black, Community Control Is the Issue." New York Times Magazine, Ap 27, 1969.

Goldberg, Herman R. Community Control at the Crossroads, F 22, 1971, 12 pp. Paper, American Association of School Administrators. ERIC ED 049 557.

Goodman, Paul. "The Limits of Local Liberty." New Generation, Summer, 1969.

Goolsby, Thomas M., Jr. and others. School Integration Questionnaire for Parents. Athens, GA: U. of Georgia, Center for Educational Improvement, S, 1971, 6 pp. ERIC ED 057 099.

Gordon, I. J. Parent Involvement in Compensatory Education. Urban, IL: U. of Illinois Press, 1972.

Green, Vera M. "The Confrontation of Diversity Within the Black Community." Human Organization 29(1970):267-272.

Greenstone, J. David, and Peterson, Paul E. Race and Authority in Urban Politics. Community Participation and the War on Poverty. New York: Basic Books, 1973.

Grether, J. "Voluntary Participation of Parents in School Activities and Academic Achievement of Their Children." Master's thesis, Cornell U., 1968.

Grigsby, Eugene III. "Stratification in American Society: A Case for Reappraisal." Journal of Black Studies 2(D, 1971): 157-169.

Gross, Norman Nathan. "Participation of the Poor in Educational Decision Making: A Comparative Case Study." Doctoral dissertation, Univ. Microfilms Order No. 75-22,795.

Guthrie, James W. "Public Control of Public Schools: Can We Get It Back?" Public Affairs Report 15(Je, 1974):1-5. [Institute of Governmental Studies, U. of California, Berkeley]

Guttentag, Marcia. "Group Cohesiveness, Ethnic Organization, and Poverty." Journal of Social Issues 26(Spring, 1970): 105-132.

Hammer, Charles. "A Fresh Approach to Integrated Housing: Racially Changing Neighborhoods." New Republic 169(S 15, 1973):19-21.

Hammonds, Robinson Roy. "A Case Study of the Views of Key Participants in Local School Affairs Relative to Community Participation Under Decentralization." Doctoral dissertation, U. of Michigan, 1974. Univ. Microfilms Order No. 75-707.

Hanes, Robert W., and Bryuarm, Samuel W. "The Effect of a Voluntary Community Improvement Program on Local Race Relations." Phylon, Spring, 1965.

Haskins, Kenneth W. "A Black Perspective on Community Control." Inequality in Education 15(N, 1973):23-34.

_____. "The Case for Local Control." Saturday Review, Ja 11, 1969.

Hatton, Barbara R. "Schools and Black Communities: A Problem Formulation." Doctoral dissertation, Stanford U., 1976.

_____. "Schools and Black Community Development. A Reassessment of Community Control." Education and Urban Society 9(F, 1977):215-233.

Hawley, Willis D. Blacks and Metropolitan Governance: The Stakes of Reform. Berkeley, CA: Institute of Governmental Studies, U. of California, 1972.

Hentoff, Nat. "Who's to Blame? The Politics of Educational Malpractice." Learning 6(O, 1977):40-49.

Herman, Barry E. "Community Involvement—A Positive Approach in Education." Integrated Education 9(Mr-Ap, 1971):28-30.

_____. "Community School: New Thrust in Education." Educational Leadership 28 (Ja, 1971):419-423.

Holden, Dorothy H. "Academic Achievement of Black Students: A Black Parent's View." Integrateducation 14(Jl-Ag, 1976):39-43.

How Good Is Your Child's School?, Mr, 1972. United Bronx Parents, 791 Prospect Avenue, Bronx, NY 10455.

Howe, Elizabeth. "Community Control." In A Symposium of the Urban Crisis, pp. 300-383. Edited by Leonard J. Duhl. Berkeley, CA: Center for Planning and Development, U. of California, 1969.

Hunt, Martin H. "Parents-Teachers Alliance: An Alternative to Community Control." Integrateducation 14(Mr-Ap, 1976):35-37.

Jenkins, Jeanne Kohl. "Advisory Councils and Principals in Los Angeles." Integrateducation 14(Ja-F, 1976.

Kaplan, Bernard A., and Forgione, Pascal D., Jr. Parent Involvement in Compensatory Education Programs: Problems and Potential Strategies Across 32 School Districts, Mr, 1978. ERIC ED 155 242.

Kohl, Herbert. "Community Control--Failed or Undermined?" Phi Delta Kappan 57(F, 1976): 370, 429. [NYC]

Koslin, Sandra and others. Guidelines for the Evaluation of Desegregation Programs in School Districts, S, 1972. ERIC ED 094 042.

Kroth, Roger L. Getting Schools Involved With Parents. Reston, VA: Council for Exceptional Children, 1978.

Kunreuther, Sylvia C. A Ghetto Exchange: Parents Speak, A Teacher Listens, and Children Learn. Chicago: Institute for Juvenile Research, 1969.

Larson, Calvin J., and Hill, Richard J. "Segregation, Community Consciousness, and Black Power." Journal of Black Studies 2 (Mr, 1972):263-276.

Lessons from the Damned. Class Struggle in the Black Community, by the Damned. Washington, NJ: Times Change Press, 1973 (Distributed by Monthly Review Press).

Levin, Henry M. "The Case for Community Control." In New Models for American Education. Edited by James W. Guthrie and Edward Wynne. Englewood Cliffs, NJ: Prentice-Hall, 1971.

_____ (ed.). Community Control of Schools. Washington, DC: Brookings Institution, 1970.

Levine, Daniel M. and others. "Are the Black Poor Satisfied with Conditions in their Neighborhoods?" Journal of the American Instiute of Planners 38(My, 1972):168-171.

Lipset, Seymour M. "The Ideology of Local Control." In Education and Social Policy: Local Control of Education, pp. 21-42. Edited by A. Bowers, I. Housego and D. Dyke. New York: Random House, 1970.

Litak, Eugene, and Meyer, Henry J. School, Family, and Neighborhood. New York: Columbia U. Press, 1973.

Lopate, Carol, Flaxman, Erwin, Bynum, Effie M., and Gordon, Edmund W. "Decentralization and Community Participation in Public Education." Review of Educational Research 40(F, 1970): 135-150.

Lurie, Ellen. How to Change the Schools: Parent's Action Handbook on How to Fight the System. New York: Random House, 1971.

McMillan, Charles B. "The Changing Schools: A Look At Community Control." Freedomways 13 (1973):63-68.

Mann, Dale. A Principal's Handbook for Shared Control in Urban Community Schools. Washington, DC: National Center for Educational Communications, National Institute of Education, 1973.

Masotti, Louis H. "Patterns of White and Nonwhite School Referenda." In Educating an Urban Population. Edited by Marilyn Gittell. Beverly Hills, CA: Sage, 1967.

Merelman, Richard M. "On the Neo-Elitist Critique of Community Power." American Political Science Review, Je, 1968.

Merrimack Education Center. Parents and Title I: A Resource Package, F, 1978. ERIC ED 159 294.

Mogulof, Melvin B. Citizen Participation: A Review and Commentary on Federal Policies and Practices. Washington, DC: The Urban Institute, Ja, 1970.

_____. Citizen Participation: The Local Perspective. Washington, DC: The Urban Institute, Mr, 1970.

National Committee for Citizens in Education. Public Testimony on Public Schools. Berkeley, CA: McCutchan, 1975.

Office of Education and Management Assessment. An Evaluation: School-Community Advisory Councils. Los Angeles: Los Angeles Unified School District, 1972.

O'Shea, David W. "Social Science and School Decentralization." In Indeterminacy in Education, pp. 309-336. Edited by John E. McDermott. Berkeley, CA: McCutchan, 1976.

Ozmon, Howard. "Local Control of Schools-- A Case Against." GW (George Washington University) 6(Fall, 1970):15-16.

Pfautz, Harold W. "The Black Community, the Community School, and the Socialization Process: Some Caveats." In Community Control of Schools. Edited by Henry M. Levin. Washington, DC: Brookings, 1970.

Pollard, William L. A Study of Black Self Help. Palo Alto, CA: R & E Research Associates, 1978.

Pomfret, Alan. "Parental Involvement in Inner City Schools." Master's thesis, U. of Toronto, 1972.

Ravitch, Diane. "The Rhetoric of Decentralization." New York Affairs 1(Spring, 1974): 102-110.

Rein, Martin, and Miller, S. M. "Citizen Participation and Poverty." Connecticut Law Review I, No. 2, 1969.

Rempson, Joe L. "Community Control of Local School Boards." Teachers College Record, Ap, 1967.

Repo, Marjaleena. "The Fallacy of 'Community Control.'" In Participatory Democracy for Canada, pp. 59-77. Edited by Gerry Hunnius. Montreal, Canada: Black Rose Books, 1971.

Reyes, Ramiro. "The Role of School District Advisory Committee in the Educational Decision-Making Process of ESEA, Title I Programs for Disadvantaged Children in California." Doctoral dissertation, Michigan State U., 1972.

Riessman, Frank, and Gartner, Alan. "Community Control and Radical Social Change." Social Policy, My-Je, 1970.

Rustin, Bayard. "Community Control: Separation Repackaged." New Leader, Je 12, 1972. [Reprinted, New York Times, Je 11, 1972]

Salisbury, Robert H. Citizen Participation in the Public Schools, My, 1977. ERIC ED 153 161. [Six St. Louis area school districts]

Scott, Hugh J. "Community Control and Education Accountability: The Thrust of Blacks for Representation in the Management of Public Education for Blacks." In Restructuring the Educational Process: A Black Perspective. Edited by Lawrence E. Gary and Aaron Favors. Washington, DC: Insitute for Urban Affairs and Research, Howard U., 1975.

Sedlack, John William, Jr. "An Analysis and Evaluation of Local School Council Guidelines Established by the Chicago Board of Education." Doctoral dissertation, U. of Northern Colorado, 1973.

Shalala, Donna E. Neighborhood Governance: Proposals and Issues. New York: American Jewish Committee, My, 1971, 56 pp. ERIC ED 053 234.

Sharing the Power? A Report on the Status of School Councils in the 1970's. Boston: Institute for Responsive Education, D, 1977.

Smith, Calvert H. "Organizational Model for Parental Participation in Inner City Schools." Journal of Afro-American Issues 1(F, 1972):247-256.

Smith, David Horton, and McGrail, Richard Francis. "Community Control of Schools: A Review of Issues and Options." Urban and Social Change Review 3(1969):2-9.

Sobin, Dennis P. "Why Increase Citizen Participation Among Ghetto Residents?" Journal of Black Studies 2(Mr, 1972):359-370.

Spivak, Harriet. School Decentralization and Community Control: Policy in Search of a Research Agenda, 1973. ERIC ED 157 953.

Stanwick, Mary Ellen. Patterns of Participation. Report of a National Survey of Citizen Participation in Educational Decision-Making. Boston: Institute for Responsive Education, Ap, 1976.

Stoneman, Dorothy. "Parent Control As It Works at the East Harlem Block Schools." Master's thesis, Bank Street College of Education, 1973.

Strandt, Patricia. "Decentralization, Community Control--Where Do We Go From Here?" American Teacher, My, 1969.

Stanford Research Institute. Parent Involvement in Compensatory Education Programs, Ag, 1973. ERIC ED 088 588.

Strickman, Leonard P. "Community Control: Some Constitutional and Political Reservations." Inequality in Education 15(N, 1973):35-38.

Stuart, Reginald. "Parents Granted Voice in Schools." Race Relations Reporter 2(Je 7, 1971):11-12.

_____. "School Control Movement Dying." Race Relations Reporter 2(Je 21, 1971):10-11.

Summerfield, Harry L. The Neighborhood-Based Politics of Education. Columbus, OH: Merrill, 1971.

Task Force on Parent Participation. Parents As Partners in Department Programs for Children and Youth. Washington, DC: GPO, Ag, 1968.

Tax, Sol (ed.). The People vs. the System: A Dialogue in Urban Conflict. Chicago: Acme Press, 1968.

Thomas, Arthur E., and Burgin, Ruth W. Community School Council, Philosophy and Framework for Urban Educational Change, My, 1970. [Write: Dr. Ames W. Chapman, Central State U., Wilberforce, OH 45384.]

U.S. Commission on Civil Rights. A Time to Listen...A Time to Act. Voices from the Ghettos of the Nation's Cities. Washington, DC: GPO, N, 1967.

Usdan, Michael D., and Nystrand, Raphael O. "Towards Participative Decision-Making: The Impact of Community Action Programs [on Local Schools]." Teachers College Record, N, 1966.

Vallado, Andres Nicolas. "Parent Involvement in Compensatory Education through Title I ESEA Parent Advisory Committees in Selected School Districts in Texas." Doctoral dissertation, 1975. Univ. Microfilms Order No. 75-23950.

Van Geel, Tyll. "Parental Preferences and the Politics of Spending Public Educational Funds." Teachers College Record 79(F, 1978):339-363.

Walker, Joe. "Community Control Advocate, 'Saddened' at Black Miseducation." Muhammad Speaks, S 6, 1974. [Rev. C. Herbert Oliver, former chairman of Ocean Hill-Brownsville Governing Board]

Warren, Donald I. Black Neighborhoods. An Assessment of Community Power. Ann Arbor, MI: U. of Michigan Press, 1974. [Detroit]

Watson, Bernard C. "Accountability in Inner City Schools Through School-Community Involvement." High School Journal 60(Ja, 1977):158-169.

Weeres, Joseph B. "School-Community Conflict in a Large Urban School System." Administrator's Notebook 19(My, 1971):1-4.

[Weinberg, Meyer] "Effects of Parents on Schooling." Research Review of Equal Education 1(Fall, 1977):29-36.

Weissman, Harold H. Community Councils and Community Control: The Workings of Democratic Mythology. Pittsburgh, PA: U. of Pittsburgh Press, 1970.

Wilcox, Preston. "The Policy Implications of Community Control of Black American Schools." Congressional Record, Ap 18, 1972, E 3900-3903.

Whittier, C. Taylor. "A Look at Decentralization and Community Control." The School Administrator, Ja, 1969.

_____. "School Community Control As a Social Movement." In Opening Opportunities for Disadvantaged Learners, pp. 308-319. Edited by A. Harry Passow. New York: Teachers College Press, 1972.

Willmon, Betty. "Parent Participation as a Factor in the Effectiveness of Head Start Programs." Journal of Educational Research 62(My, 1969):406-410. [Florida]

Wirt, Frederick M. (ed.). Future Directions in Community Power Research: A Colloquium. Berkeley, CA: Institute of Governmental Studies, U. of California, 1971.

Wolf, Eleanor P. "Community Control of Schools as an Ideology and Social Mechanism." Social Science Quarterly 50(D, 1969).

Yin, Robert K., Lucus, William A., Szanton, Peter L., and Spindler, J. Andrew. Citizen Organization: Increasing Client Control Over Services. Santa Monica, CA: Rand, 1973.

Zimmerman, Joseph F. The Federated City: Community Control in Large Cities. New York: St. Martin's Press, 1972.

Zipperer, Dorothy J. "Parent Knowledge and Attitudes Toward ESEA, Title I Programs and Their Ability to Assess Child Achievement." Doctoral disseration, Florida State U., 1978. Univ. Microfilms Order No. 7822217.

Zusman, Richard S. "Parent Involvement in Title I Programs." Integrateducation 12 (S-O, 1974):19.

Other Community Studies

Alinsky, Saul. "A Professional Radical Moves in on Rochester. Conversations with Saul Alinsky, Part II." Harper's, Jl, 1965.

_____. "The Professional Radical. Conversations with Saul Alinsky." Harper's, Je, 1965.

_____. "The War on Poverty--Political Pornography." Journal of Social Issues, Ja, 1965.

_____. "Of Means and Ends." Union Seminary Quarterly Review, Ja, 1967.

_____. "Organizing Low-Income Neighborhoods for Political Action." In Urban School Administration. Edited by Troy V. McKelvey and Austin D. Swanson. Beverly Hills, CA: Sage, 1969.

"Alinsky Says School Quality Stirs Ghetto." Southern Education Report, O, 1967.

Allen, Irving Lewis. "A Retrospective Note on Urban 'Neighborhood School' Ideology." Urban Education 12(Jl, 1977):205-212.

Alsworth, Philip L., and Button, H. Warren. "Mobilization For Youth: A Prototype?" Urban Education, Winter, 1965.

Anderson, Patrick. "Making Trouble is [Saul] Alinsky's Business." New York Times Magazine, O 9, 1966.

Anderson, Theodore R. "Social and Economic Factors Affecting the Location of Residential Neighborhoods." Papers and Proceedings of the Regional Science Association 9(1962).

Baltimore, Estelle. "A Suburban Community and De Facto Segregation." Master's thesis, Southern Connecticut State College, 1970.

Banks, James A. "Liberating the Black Ghetto: Decision-Making and Social Action." National Council for the Social Studies Yearbook, 1972, Vol 42, pp. 159-183.

Baron, Harold M. (ed.). The Racial Aspects of Urban Planning. Chicago: Chicago Urban League, 1968.

"The Battle of the Suburbs." Newsweek, N 15, 1971.

Bell, Daniel, and Held, Virginia. "The Community Revolution." Public Interest, Summer, 1969.

Berry, Brian J. L. and Others. "Attitudes to Integration: The Role of Status in Community Response to Racial Change." In The Changing Face of the Suburbs. Edited by Barry Schwartz. Chicago: U. of Chicago Press, 1976.

Better, Shirley. "The Black Social Worker's Role in the Black Community." Black World 22(N, 1972):4-14.

Biggar, J. C., and Martin, J. H. "Ecological Determinants of White and Black Immigration to Small Areas in Central Cities, 1965 to 1970." Social Forces 55(S, 1976):72-84.

Billingham, Gerald Lee. "A Study of Social Class Differentiation in the Afro-American Community." Doctoral dissertation, New York U., 1963.

Billingsley, Andrew. "Family Functioning in the Low-Income Black Community." Social Casework, D, 1969.

Blackwell, James E. The Black Community: Diversity and Unity. New York: Dodd, Mead, 1975.

Blaut, J. M. "Das Ghetto als Interne Neokolonie." Geographie in Ausbildung und Planung 5(1976).

Bloomberg, Warner, Jr., and Schmandt, Henry J. (eds.). Power, Poverty, and Urban Policy. Beverly Hills, CA: Sage, 1968.

Bowden, Leonard W. "How to Define Neighborhood." Professional Geographer 24(Ag, 1972):227-228.

Bowman, Lewis. "Racial Discrimination and Negro Leadership Problems: The Case of 'Northern Community.'" Social Forces, D, 1965.

Boykin, Junebug and others. "Take a Step Into America." The Movement, D, 1967.

Bradburn, Norman, Sudman, Seymour, and Gockel, Galen L., with Noel, Joseph R. "Integration in the Schools." In Side by Side. Integrated Neighborhoods in America, pp. 135-151. Chicago: Quadrangle, 1971.

Bradford, David F., and Kelejian, Harry H. An Econometric Model of the Flight to the Suburbs, O, 1970. PB 196 060. National Technical Information Service, Springfield, VA 22151.

Brager, George. "New Concepts and Patterns of Service: The Mobilization for Youth Program." In Mental Health of the Poor. Edited by Frank Riessman, Jerome Cohen, and Arthur Pearl. New York: The Free Press of Glencoe, 1964.

Brazer, Marjorie Cahn. "Economic and Social Disparities Between Central Cities and Their Suburbs." Land Economics, Ag, 1967.

Brody, Stanley J. "Maximum Participation of the Poor: Another Holy Grail?" Social Work, Ja, 1970.

Burges, Bill. Good Things Can Happen: Your Community Organization and School Desegregation. Cleveland, OH: Federation for Community Planning, 1978. [1001 Huron Road, Cleveland, OH 44115]

California Elementary School Administrators Association. The Neighborhood and the School: A Study of Socio-economic Status and School Achievement. Burlingame, CA: Author, 1962.

Callahan, John, and Shalala, Donna E. "Some Fiscal Dimensions of Three Hypothetical Decentralization Plans." Education and Urban Society, N, 1969.

Calvo, Robert C. "Issues and Problems in Decentralization." Clearing House 46(My, 1972):549-552.

Campbell, Angus, and Schuman, Howard. "Racial Attitudes in Fifteen American Cities." Supplemental Studies for the National Advisory Commission on Civil Disorders. Survey Research Center, Institute for Social Research, U. of Michigan, Je, 1968. Washington, DC: GPO, 1961.

Candeloro, Dominic. "Recovering the History of a Black Community." History Teacher 7(N, 1973):24-29.

Carey, George W. "Density, Crowding, Stress, and the Ghetto." American Behavioral Scientist 15(Mr-Ap, 1972):495-509.

Chapin, F. Stuart, Jr., Butler, Edgar W., and Patten, Frederick C. Blackways in the Inner City. Chapel Hill, NC: Center for Urban and Regional Studies, U. of North Carolina, Jl, 1972.

Chenault, Jonas. "Special Education and the Black Community." In Restructuring the Educational Process: A Black Perspective. Edited by Lawrence E. Gary and Aaron Favors. Washington, DC: Institute for Urban Affairs and Research, Howard U., 1975.

City of New York Commission on Human Rights. Community Values and Conflict, 1967: A Conference Report. New York: Commission on Human Rights, 1967.

Clark, Terry N. et al. Community Structure, Power, and Decision-Making: Comparative Analyses. Chicago: Science Research Associates, 1968.

Clark, W. A. V. "Patterns of Black Intra-Urban Mobility and Restricted Relocation Opportunities." In Perspectives in Geography 2. Edited by H. Rose and H. McConnell. De Kalb: Northern Illinois U. Press, 1972.

Clary, Phillip L. "The Process of Black Suburbanization." Doctoral dissertation, Massachusetts Institute of Technology, 1975.

Clinard, Marshall B. Slums and Community Development. Experiment in Self-Help. New York: The Free Press, 1966.

Clotfelter, C. T. "Spatial Rearrangement and the Tiebout Hypothesis: The Case of School Desegregation." Southern Economic Journal 42(0, 1975).

Cloward, Richard. "Conflict and Community Organization." Freedom North, Vol I, No. 2, 1964.

_____. "The War on Poverty. Are the Poor Left Out?" Nation, Ag 2, 1965.

Coleman, Peter. "The Perils of Bigness: The Case Against Large School Districts." Education Administration Quarterly 8 (Spring, 1972):58-78.

Coles, Robert. "Looking Back on Chicago." New Society, S 26, 1968.

Colfax, J. David. "Pressure Toward Distortion and Involvement in Studying a Civil Rights Organization." Human Organization, Summer, 1966.

Collins, John N., and Downes, Bryan T. "Support for Public Education in a Racially Changing Suburb." Urban Education 10(0, 1975):221-244.

"Community Politics." Southwestern Social Science Quarterly, D, 1967.

Community Relations Service and National Center for Quality Integrated Education. Desegregation Without Turmoil. The Role of the Multi-Racial Community Coalition in Preparing for Smooth Transition. New York: National Conference of Christians and Jews, 1977.

"Congressional Districts With 15 Per Cent Or More of Families Below Poverty Level." Focus 2(F, 1974):A2-A4.

Connolly, Harold X. "Black Movement into the Suburbs." Urban Affairs Quarterly 9(S, 1973):91-111.

Conway, Jack, and Ginsburg, Woodward. "Extension of Collective Bargaining to New Fields." In Proceedings of the 19th Annual Winter Meeting, Industrial Relations Research Association, 1966.

Coombs, Orde. "Soul in Suburbia." Harper's 244 (Ja, 1972):24-31.

Crain, Robert L. and others. Causes and Effects of School Board Recruitment Patterns, Final Report, Revised. Baltimore, MD: Johns Hopkins U., Dept. of Social Relations, F, 1972, 29 pp. ERIC ED 061 633.

_____. The Politics of School Desegregation. Chicago: Aldine, 1968.

Crain, Robert L., Inger, Morton, McWorter, Gerald A., and Vanecko, James J. School Desegregation in the North. Eight Comparative Case Studies of Community Structure and Policy Making. Chicago: National Opinion Research Center, U. of Chicago, Ap, 1966.

"Crime and the Inner City." Crime and Its Impact--An Assessment. The President's Commission on Law Enforcement and Administration of Justice. Washington, DC: GPO, 1967.

Cunningham, Luvern L. "Decentralization. A Forward Step? Community Control Clouds the Issue." Nation's Schools, My, 1969.

Danzger, Herbert M. "Civil Rights Conflict and Community Power Structure." Doctoral dissertation, Columbia U., 1968.

Davis, George A. "The Neighborhood School: An Elitist Isolationist Concept." In Donald S. Smith Davis and Carlyle Johnson, Black Issues. Patrick Air Force Base, FL: Defense Race Relations Institute, 1975.

Davis, Kingsley. The Modern Urban Resolution. New York: Random House, 1967.

Darden, Clifford E. "Organizational Development in the Black Community." Negro Digest, Je, 1969.

Davidoff, Linda, Gold, Paul, and Gold, Neil N. "The Suburbs Have to Open Their Gates." New York Times Magazine, N 7, 1971.

Davies, J. Clarence III. Neighborhood Groups and Urban Renewal. New York: Columbia U. Press, 1966.

Davis, King E. Fund Raising in the Black Community: History, Feasibility, and Conflict. Metuchen, NJ: Scarecrow Press, 1975.

Dawkins, Mervin. "The Rural Ghetto: An Extension of the Colonial Analogy to a Southern Rural Black Community." Master's thesis, Florida State U., 1973.

Decentralization and Community Involvement: A Status Report. Educational Research Service Circular Number Seven, 1969. Washington, DC: American Association of School Administrators, National Education Association, N, 1969, 60 pp. ERIC ED 041 358.

Delaney, Paul. "Black Middle Class Joining the Exodus to White Suburbia." New York Times, Ja 4, 1976. [Ill., Mass., and N.Y.]

Denton, John. Apartheid American Style. Berkeley, CA: Diablo Press, 1967.

Deskins, Donald R., Jr., Ward, David, and Rose, Harold M. Interaction Patterns and the Spatial Form of the Ghetto. Evanston, IL: Department of Geography, Northwestern U., 1970.

Dodson, Dan W. "The Church, Power, and Alinsky." Religion in Life, Spring, 1967.

Doherty, Neville. Rurality, Poverty, and Health. Medical Problems in Rural Areas. Washington, DC: GPO, F, 1970.

Dorson, Richard. "Is There a Folk in the City?" Journal of American Folklore 83(1970):185-228.

Downs, Anthony. "Alternative Futures for the American Ghetto." Appraisal Journal, O, 1968.

Drake, St. Clair. "The Ghettoization of Negro Life." In Negroes and Jobs, pp. 112-128. Edited by Louis A. Ferman and others. Ann Arbor, MI: U. of Michigan Press, 1968.

_____. The Urban Poor. New York: A. Philip Randolph Educational Fund, 1967.

Dubick, Libby. Racial Employment Patterns in Real Estate Sales. A Survey of Suburban Washington Real Estate Companies, Mr, 1973. Housing Opportunities Council of Metropolitan Washington, Suite 406, 1522 K Street, N.W., Washington, DC 20005.

Duncan, Karen (ed.). Community Action Curriculum Project Compendium. Washington, DC: U.S. National Student Association, 1969.

Durand, Roger. "Some Dynamics of Urban Service Evaluations Among Blacks and Whites." Social Science Quarterly 56(Mr, 1976):698-706.

Erickson, Robert. "Poverty and Race: The Bane of Access to Essential Public Services." Antipode 3(N, 1971):1-8.

Edwards, G. Franklin. "Community and Class Realities: The Ordeal of Change." Daedalus, Winter, 1966.

"Eight Examples of Business Leadership Involvement in School Desegregation Efforts Elsewhere." Bulletin (Citizens' Governmental Research Bureau) 64(Jl 24, 1976). [125 E. Wells St., Milwaukee, WI 53202]

Ellison, Ralph, Young, Whitney, Jr., and Gans, Herbert J. Crisis in the City. New York: A. Philip Randolph Educational Fund, 1967.

Evans, Ronald. "The Lunatic Fringe." African-American Teachers Forum, Mr, 1969.

Fainstein, Norman I., and Fainstein, Susan S. "The Future of Community Control." American Political Science Review 70(S, 1976):905-923.

Fantini, Mario, and Gittell, Marilyn. Decentralization: Achieving Reform. New York: Praeger, 1974.

Farley, Reynolds. "The Changing Distribution of Negroes within Metropolitan Areas: The Emergence of Black Suburbs." American Journal of Sociology 75(1970):512-529.

_____. "Integrating Residential Neighborhoods." Society 14(My-Je, 1977):38-41.

Feagin, Joe R. "A Note on the Friendship Ties of Black Urbanites." Social Forces 49(D, 1970).

Featherstone, Joseph. "The Problem is More than Neighborhood in Urban American Society." Social Work, Jl, 1968.

Fellin, Phillip, and Litwak, Eugene. "The Neighborhood in Urban American Society." Social Work, Jl, 1968.

Fenn, Richard K. "The Community Action Program: An American Gospel?" Science and Society, Spring, 1969.

Ferrer, Terry. The Schools and Urban Renewal. A Case Study from New Haven. New York: Educational Facilities Laboratory, 1964.

Fogelson, Robert M., and Hill, Robert B. "Who Riots? A Study of Participation in the 1967 Riots." Supplemental Studies for the National Advisory Commission on Civil Disorders. Washington, DC: GPO, 1968.

Ford Foundation. The Society of the Streets. New York: The Ford Foundation, 1962.

Foundation for Voluntary Service. Social Participation and Isolation of the Urban Poor, D, 1968. Bureau of Social Science Research, Inc., 1200 Seventeeth Street, N.W., Washigton, DC 20036 [Washington, D.C., N.Y.C., and Bridgeport, Conn.]

Fox, Jeanne. Regionalism and Minority Participation. Washington, DC: Joint Center for Political Studies, 1973.

Frazier, E. Franklin. "A Community School." Southern Workman 54(O, 1925):495-564.

_____. "The Negro Community: A Cultural Phenomenon." Social Forces 7(Mr, 1929):415-420.

Frey, William H. Black Movement to the Suburbs: Potentials and Prospects for Metropolitcan Wide Integration, 1977. ERIC ED 152 933.

Fruchter, Norm, and Kramer, Robert. "An Approach to Community Organizing Prospects." Studies on the Left, Mr-Ap, 1966.

Gaillard, Frye. "White Working-Class Groups Unite." Race Relations Reporter 2(My 3, 1971):8-10. [Baltimore, MD]

Gans, Herbert J. "The Failure of Urban Renewal." Commentary, Ap, 1965.

Garcia, Sandra J. and others. Research in the Black Community: A Need for Self-Determination. Inglewood, CA: Southwest Regional Educational Lab, O, 1969, 8 pp. ERIC ED 055 954.

Gary, Lawrence E. (ed.). Social Research and The Black Community: Selected Issues and Priorities. Washington, DC: Institute for Urban Affairs and Research, Howard U., 1974.

Germenian, L. Wayne. "The Economics of Education in the Urban Ghetto." Doctoral dissertation, U. of Southern California, 1975.

Gibson, James. "Ghetto Economic Development. New Ways of Giving non-Whites the Business?" Civil Rights Digest, Spring, 1969.

Ginzberg, Eli and associates. The Middle-Class Negro in the White Man's World. New York: Columbia U. Press, 1967.

Gitlin, Todd. "Local Pluralism As Theory and Ideology." Studies on the Left, Summer, 1965.

Golin, Sanford, Davis, Eugene, Zuckerman, Edward, and Harrison, Nelson. "Psychology in the Community: Project Self-Esteem." Psychological Reports 26(Je, 1970):735-740.

Gordon, Mitchell. "Saul Alinsky Offers His Radical Methods to Middle-Class Causes." Wall Street Journal, Ap 4, 1969.

Gordon, Sol. "A Guide for Community Groups Evaluating Public Schools." Integrated Education, F-Mr, 1967.

Green, Thomas F. "Schools and Communities: A Look Forward." Harvard Educational Review, Spring, 1969.

Greenberg, Stanley B. Modernization and Response in Five Poor Neighborhoods. New York: Wiley, 1973.

Greening, Thomas C. "Ten Tips on How to Escape from the Ghetto." Ebony 33(Ap, 1978): 97-108.

Greer, Scott. Urban Renewal and American Cities. The Dilemma of Democratic Intervention. Indianapolis: Bobbs-Merrill, 1966.

Greer, Scott, and Greer, Ann L. (eds.). Neighborhood and Ghetto. New York: Basic, 1974.

Grier, Eunice, and Grier, George. Black Suburbanization at the Mid-1970s. The Trends, The New Black Suburbanites. The Policy Implications. Washington, DC: Washington Center for Metropolitan Studes, Ap, 1978.

Grosser, Charles F. Helping Youth. A Study of Six Community Organization Programs. Washington, DC: GPO, 1968.

Grossman, J. S. "Psychological Determinants of Reaction to Neighborhood Racial Change." Doctoral dissertation, Western Reserve U., 1967. Univ. Microfilms Order No. 67-4640.

Guest, Avery M. "Neighborhood Life Cycles and Social Status." Economic Geography 50 (Jl, 1974):228-243.

Guest, Avery M., and Weed, James A. "Ethnic Residential Segregation: Patterns of Change." American Journal of Sociology 81(Mr, 1976): 1088-1111. [Cleveland, Boston and Seattle]

Guseman, Patricia K. and others. "The Measurement of Diversity: Ethnic and Sociometric Mixing in Residential Areas." Social Science Research 5(Mr, 1976):21-34.

Gwaltney, John J. "On Going Home Again--Some Reflections of a Native Anthropologist." Phylon 37(S, 1976):236-242.

Haddad, William F. "Mr. Shriver and the Savage Politics of Poverty." Harper's, D, 1965.

Haggstrom, Warren C. "Poverty and Adult Education." Adult Education, Spring, 1965.

_____. "The Power of the Poor." In Mental Health of the Poor. Edited by Frank Riessman, Jerome Cohen, and Arthur Pearl. New York: The Free Press of Glencoe, 1964.

Haider, Donald. "The Political Economy of Decentralization." American Behavioral Scientist 15(S-O, 1971):108-129.

Hamilton, Charles V. "Urban Economics, Conduit-Colonialism, and Public Policy." Black World 21(O, 1972):40-45.

Hamilton, David L., and Bishop, George D. "Attitudinal and Behavioral Effects of Initial Integration of White Suburban Neighborhoods." In Policy Studies Review Annual, Vol. 1. Edited by S. Nagel. Beverly Hills, CA: Sage, 1977.

Hannerz, Ulf. "Gossip, Networks, and Culture in a Black American Ghetto." Ethnos 32, Nos. 1-4(1967).

Harris, Donald J. "The Black Ghetto as Colony: A Theoretical Critique and Alternative Formulation." Review of Black Political Economy (My-Je, 1972):505-522.

Harris, Theodore. "Political Influence and De
De Facto School Segregation: A Study of
Decisions in Northern Cities." Doctoral
dissertation, Johns Hopkins U., 1972.

Harris, William M., Sr. "Community Development
in Black Ghettoes." Doctoral dissertation,
U. of Washington, 1974. Univ. Microfilms
Order No. 74-29,425.

Harrison, Bennett. "Ghetto Employment and the
Model Cities Program." Journal of Political
Economy 82, Pt. 1(Mr-Ap, 1974):353-371.

_____. "The Intrametropolitan Distribution of
Minority Economic Welfare." Journal of
Regional Science 12(1972):23-43.

_____. Urban Economic Development: Suburban-
ization, Minority Opportunity, and the
Condition of the Central City. Washington,
DC: Urban Institute, 1974.

Harvey, David. Social Justice and the City.
Baltimore, MD: Johns Hopkins U. Press,
1974.

Hauser, Philip M. (ed.). Handbook for Social
Research in Urban Areas. New York: UNESCO,
1966.

Hazard, Leland. "Are We Committing Urban
Suicide?" Harvard Business Review, Jl-Ag,
1964.

Held, Virginia. "Professional Reform or
Participatory Democracy?" Social Policy,
Jl-Ag, 1970.

Hennessey, Gary J. The Neighborhood School
Concept as a Deterrent to Desegregation in
the 1960's and 1970's, 1976. ERIC ED 134
661.

Herbert, Gilbert. "The Neighborhood Unit
Principle and Organic Theory." Sociological
Review [England], Jl, 1963.

Hersey, John. "Our Romance with Poverty."
American Scholar, Autumn, 1964.

Herzog, John D. "The Anthropologist as Broker
in Community Education: A Case Study and
Some General Propositions." Council on
Anthropology and Education Newsletter 3
(N, 1972):9-14.

Hill, Robert. "Occupational and Transportation
Problems of Blacks." Integrateducation 13
(My-Je, 1975):34-37.

Hirsch, Herbert. "Ethnic Identity and Students'
Perceptions of a Community Controlled
School." Social Science Quarterly 55(S,
1974):425-438.

Holland, R. W. School Desegregation and
Community Conflict. School Desegregation
Bulletin Series. Riverside, CA: U. of
California, Riverside Western Regional
School of Desegregation Projects, Je, 1971,
35 pp. ERIC ED 056 407.

Horton, Aimee I. An Analysis of Selected
Programs for the Training of Civil Rights
and Community Leaders in the South. ERIC
ED 011 058.

Hough, John T., Jr. A Peck of Salt. A Year in
the Ghetto. Boston: Little, Brown, 1970.
[Chicago and Detroit]

Hughes, Teresa. "Decentralization: Participatory Education." The Black Politician 2(O,
1970):3, 19.

Iannaccone, Lawrence, and Wiles, David K.
"The Changing Politics of Urban Education."
Education and Urban Society 3(My, 1971):255-
264.

"Interview with Leonard Covello." Urban Review,
Ja, 1969.

Jacobs, Paul. Prelude to Riot: A View of
Urban America from the Bottom. New York:
Random House, 1967.

Jakubs, J. F. "Residential Segregation: The
Taeuber Index Reconsidered." Journal of
Regional Science 17(Ag, 1977).

Jeffers, C. Living Poor: A Participant Observer Study of Choices and Priorities.
Ann Arbor, MI: Ann Arbor Publishers, 1967.

Jeffries, Vincent, and Ransford, H. Edward.
"Interracial Social Contact and Middle-Class
White Reactions to the Watts Riot." Social
Problems, Winter, 1969.

Jibou, Robert M., and Marshall, Harvey H., Jr.
"Urban Structure and the Differentiation
Between Blacks and Whites." American
Sociological Review 36(Ag, 1971):638-649.

Johnson, Norman J., and Sanday, Peggy R. "Sub-
cultural Variations in an Urban Poor
Population." American Anthropologist 73
(F, 1971):128-143. [Pittsburgh, PA]

Joint Task Force on Health, Education, and
Welfare Service and Housing. Strengthening
Community Services in Low-Income Neighbor-
hoods. A Field Guide to Concerted Services.
Washington, DC: GPO, 1967.

Jones, Ruth S. "Community Participation as
Pedagogy: Its Effects on Political Attitudes
of Black Students." Journal of Negro Education 45(Fall, 1976):397-407.

Kain, John, and Persky, Joseph J. Alternatives
to the Gilded Ghetto. Program on Regional
and Urban Economics, Discussion Paper No. 21.
Cambridge, MA: Harvard U., F, 1968.

Kapsis, Robert E. "Black Ghetto Diversity and Anomie: A Sociopolitical View." American Journal of Sociology 83(Mr, 1978):1132-1153.

Katznelson, Ira. "Participation and Political Buffers in Urban America." Race 14(Ap, 1973):465-480.

Kee, Woo Sik. "Suburban Population Growth and Its Implications for Core City Finance." Land Economics, My, 1967.

Kelleher, Daniel T. "Neighborhood Schools and Racial Segregation." Educational Forum 39 (Ja, 1975):209-215.

Keller, Suzanne. Neighbors, Neighboring, and Neighborhoods in Sociological Perspective. Athens, Greece: Athens Technological Institute, 1965.

_____. "Social Class in Physical Planning." International Social Science Journal 18 (1966).

Kirschner Associates, Inc. A National Survey of the Impacts of Head Start Centers on Community Institutions. Summary Report. Washington, DC: GPO, My, 1970.

Kisker, C. V. (ed.). "Demographic Aspects of the Black Community." Milbank Fund Quarterly 48(1970):1-362.

König, René. "The Integration of the Community." In The Community. Tr. Edward Fitzgerald. New York: Schocken Books, 1968.

Kotler, Milton. "Rise of Neighborhood Power." Focus 4(D, 1975).

Kramer, Ralph M. Participation of the Poor: Comparative Case Studies in the War on Poverty. Englewood Cliffs, NJ: Prentice-Hall, 1969.

Krause, Elliot A. "Functions of a Bureaucratic Ideology: 'Citizen Participation.'" Problems, Fall, 1968.

Kristol, Irving. "Decentralization for What?" Public Interest, Spring, 1968.

Krosney, Herbert. Beyond Welfare: Poverty in the Supercity. New York: Holt, Rinehart & Winston, 1966.

Kulski, Julian Eugene. Land of Urban Promise. Notre Dame, IN: U. of Notre Dame Press, 1967.

Kuz, Anthony, and Ziegler, Eugene L. City Space and Schools and Race. A Conceptual Safari Into the Wilds of Urban Public Education and Its Geographic Role in Contemporary Urban Crises. University Park, PA: Department of Geography, Pennsylvania State U., 1971.

Lah, David. "Causes and Consequences of Poverty and Inequality in the Inner City: An In-Depth Study." Doctoral dissertation, U. of Wisconsin, 1976.

Lamb, Curt. Political Power in Poor Neighborhoods. Cambridge, MA: Schenckman, 1975.

Landecker, Werner. "Integration and Group Structure." Social Forces 30(1951-1952).

La Noue, George R., and Smith, Bruce L. R. "The Political Evolution of School Decentralization." American Behavioral Scientist 15(S-O, 1971):73-93.

Lansing, John B., and Marans, Robert W. "Evaluation of Neighborhood Quality." Journal of the American Institute of Planners, My, 1969.

Larson, Calvin J. "Leadership in Three Black Neighborhoods." Phylon 36(Fall, 1975):260-268. [Northwest Indiana]

Leach, Edmund. "What Kind of Community?" New Society, My 8, 1969.

"Leading Black Neighborhoods." Black Enterprise 5(D, 1974):25-33, 61. [Black middle- and upper-middle class areas]

Lemberg Center for the Study of Violence, Brandeis University. "April Aftermath of the King Assassination." Riot Data Review, Ag, 1968.

Lepper, Mark H. and others. "An Approach to Reconciling the Poor and the System." Inquiry, Mr, 1968.

Leslau, Abraham. Sociodemographic Factors and Racial School Desegregation, Jl, 1974. ERIC ED 096 378.

Le Tarte, Clyde, and Minzey, Jack. "Community Education and the Neighborhood School." Community Education Journal 1(F, 1971):26-27.

Levin, Henry M. Decentralization and the Finance of Inner-City Schools. Stanford, CA: Center for Research and Development in Teaching, Stanford U., My, 1969.

Levine, Robert A. "The Silent Majority: Neither Simple Nor Simple-Minded." Public Opinion Quarterly 35(Winter, 1971-1972):571-577. [White views on residential integration]

Ley, D. The Black Inner City as Frontier Outpost. Washington, DC: Association of American Geographers, 1974.

Lincoln, C. Eric. "The Black Ghetto As An Urban Phenomenon." In Sounds of the Struggle. New York: Morrow, 1967.

Lipsitz, Lewis. "'A Better System of Prisons?' On Decentralization and Participation in America." Dissent 18(D, 1971):584-593.

Lipsky, Michael. "Protest As A Political Resource." American Political Science Review, D, 1968.

Little, James T., Nourse, Hugh O., and Phares, Donald. The Neighborhood Succession Process. St. Louis, MO: Institute for Urban and Regional Studies, Washington U., 1975.

Long, Larry H. "How the Racial Composition of Cities Changes." Land Economics 51(Ag, 1975):258-267.

Long, Larry H., and Hansen, Kristin A. "Trends in Return Migration to the South." Demography, N, 1975.

Longstreth, James W. "Knowing Who's Who in 'Power Structure' Can Pay Dividends." American School Board Journal, Ag, 1966.

Lord, J. Dennis. "School Busing and White Abandonment of Public Schools." Southeastern Geographer, N, 1975.

Lundgren, Terry Dennis. "Comparative Study of All Negro Ghettoes in the United States." Doctoral dissertation, Ohio State U., 1976. Univ. Microfilms Order No. 76-24641.

McCoy, Rhody A. "The Formation of a Community-Controlled School District." In Community Control of Schools. Edited by Henry M. Levin. Washington, DC: Brookings, 1970.

McFee, June King. "Children and Cities: An Exploratory Study of Urban-Middle and Low-Income Neighborhood Children's Response in Studying the City." Studies in Art Education 13(F, 1971):50-69.

Major, Geraldyn Hodges, and Saunders, Doris E. Black Society. Chicago: Johnson, 1976.

Marcson, Simon. Decentralization and Community Control in Urban Areas. New Brunswick, NJ: Rutgers U., Ja 15, 1971, 226 pp. ERIC ED 049 330.

Marris, Peter, and Rein, Martin. Dilemmas of Social Reform: Poverty and Community Action in the United States. New York: Atherton, 1967.

Marston, Wilfred G. "Socioeconomic Differentiation Within Negro Areas of American Cities." Social Forces 48(1969):165-176.

Martineau, William H. "Informal Social Ties Among Urban Black Americans: Some New Data and a Review of the Problem." Journal of Black Studies 8(S, 1977):83-104.

Maurer, Robert, and Baxter, James C. "Images of the Neighborhood and City Among Black, Anglo, and Mexican-American Chiildren." Environment and Behavior 4(D, 1972):351-388.

Maxwell, D. W. "Spatial Planning of School Districts." In The Black Urban Community. Edited by Sidney E. Mgbejiofor. Washington, DC: College and University Press, 1975.

Maynard, Robert C. "Black Nationalism and Community Schools." In Community Control of Schools. Edited by Henry M. Levin. Washington, DC: Brookings, 1970.

Meade, Edward J., Jr. Expanding the Community of Education. New York: The Ford Foundation, 1967.

Mercer, Charles. "What Neighbourhood?" New Society, Ja 22, 1976. [What, if anything, is a neighborhood?]

Metcalf, Ralph H., Jr. "Chicago Model Cities and Neocolonization." The Black Scholar, Ap, 1970.

Meyers, Edna O. "Doing Your Own Think: Transmission of Cognitive Skills to Inner City Children." American Journal of Orthopsychiatry 44(Jl, 1974):596-603.

Michener, John. Neighborhoods and Integration, a Guide to Neighborhoods, 1971. Baltimore Neighborhoods, Inc., 32 W. 25th Street, Baltimore, MD 21218.

Midura, Edmund M. (ed.). Blacks and Whites: The Urban Communication Crisis. Washington, DC: Acropolis Books, Ltd., 1975.

Miel, Alice, with Kiester, Edwin, Jr. The Shortchanged Children of Suburbia. New York: Institute of Human Relations Press, American Jewish Committee, 1967. [Analysis of an unnamed East Coast suburb]

Milio, Nancy. The Case of Health in Communities: Access for Outcasts. New York: Macmillan, 1975.

Miller, David Kent. "The Dynamics of Urban Social Boundaries: Attempts at School District Consolidation." Doctoral dissertation, Stanford U., 1974. Univ. Microfilms Order No. 75-6891.

Miller, Henry. "Social Work in the Black Ghetto: The New Colonialism." Social Work, Jl, 1969.

Miller, S. M., and Rein, Martin. "Participation, Poverty, and Administration." Public Administration Review, Ja-F, 1969.

Moffitt, Donald, and Sears, Art, Jr. "Kelly Street Blues." Wall Street Journal, Ja 6, 1969.

Mogulof, Melvin B. "Black Community Development in Five Western Model Cities." Social Work, Ja, 1970.

Morris, David J., and Hess, Karl. Neighborhood Power: The New Localism. Boston: Beacon, 1975.

Morsell, J. A. "Why Minority Groups Want a Say." Palmetto Education Association Journal, Mr, 1967.

Musgrave, P. W. "The Relationship between School and Community: A Reconsideration." Community Development Journal 8(0, 1973): 167-178.

National Center for Quality Integrated Education. Developing the Public Position Statement. The Community's Role in a Peaceful Desegregation Process, Je, 1976. The Center, Room 403, 1201 Sixteenth Street, N.W., Washington, DC. [Collection of local policy statements]

_____. The Role of the Community in the School Desegregation/Integration Process. A Collection of Working Papers, Jl, 1977. Ministries in Public Education, c/o Educational Ministries--ABC, Valley Forge, PA 19481.

National Urban Coalition. Community Action for Desegregation. The Workshop for Citizen Involvement in Community Problem Solving in Public Education. N.p.: N.p., n.d.

Neighborhoods, Where Human Relations Begin. Atlanta: Southern Regional Council, 1967.

Nelson, William E., and Meranto, Philip J. Electing Black Mayors. Political Action in the Black Community. Columbus, OH: Ohio State U. Press, 1977.

Neuwirth, Gertrude. "A Weberian Outline of a Theory of Community: Its Application to the 'Dark Ghetto.'" British Journal of Sociology, Je, 1969.

Nobles, Wade and others. A Formulative and Empirical Study of Black Families, D, 1976. ERIC ED 139 887.

Norman, J. "A Method for Attributing Census Data to School Districts Non-Coterminous With Census Traits." IAR Research Bulletin 10(1969):3-7.

"The NSM [Northern Student Movement] City Projects." Freedom North I, Nos. 4-5, 1965.

Nystrand, Raphael O. "Community Action Programs and School Decision Making." Administrator's Notebook, Ap, 1967.

O'Brien, David J. Neighborhood Organization and Interest-Group Processes. Princeton, NJ: Princeton U. Press, 1976.

O'Connell, G. E. "Zelder's Critique of the Index of Dissimilarity: A Misunderstanding of a Basic Assumption." Journal of Regional Science 17(Ag, 1977).

Office of Program Planning, Community Action Program. Community Action and Urban Housing. Washington, DC: Office of Economic Opportunity, N, 1967.

Ornstein, Allan C. Race and Politics in School/Community Organizations. Pacific Palisades, CA: Goodyear, 1974.

Ozawa, Martha N. "Social Welfare: The Minority Share." Social Work 17(My, 1972): 32-43.

Parelius, R. J. "The Schools and Social Structure of an Economically Depressed Negro Community." Doctoral dissertation, U. of Chicago, 1967.

Parenti, Michael. "Power and Pluralism: A View from the Bottom." Journal of Politics 32(1970). [Newark, NJ, 1967-1969]

Parker, Seymour, and Kleiner, Robert J. "The Culture of Poverty: An Adjustive Dimension." American Anthropologist 72(Je, 1970):516-527.

Parsons, Tim. The Community School Movement. New York: Institute for Community Studies, Queens College, D, 1970.

Pascal, Anthony H. (ed.). Contributions to the Analysis of Urban Problems. Santa Monica, CA: RAND Corporation, Ag, 1968.

Patterson, Ernest. Black City Politics. New York: Dodd, Mead, 1974.

Patterson, Orlando. "The Black Micropolis." In Raising Children in Modern America, pp. 216-236. Edited by Nathan B. Talbot. Boston: Little, Brown, 1976.

Peattie, Lisa. "Reflections on Advocacy Planning." Paper Tiger, Issue 5, 1968.

Pennock, J. Roland, and Chapman, John W. (eds.). Voluntary Associations. New York: Atherton, 1969.

Perlman, Robert, and Jones, David. Neighborhood Service Centers. Washington, DC: GPO, 1967.

Pious, Richard M. "The Phony War on Poverty in the Great Society." Current History 61(N, 1971):266-272.

Piven, Frances Fox. "Cutting Up the City Pie." New Republic, F 5, 1972, pp. 17-22.

Pryor, F. L. "An Empirical Note on the Tipping Point." Land Economics 47(N, 1971).

Rabin, Yale. "Highways as a Barrier to Equal Access." Annals 407(My, 1973):63-77.

"Race Relations and Religious Education." Religious Education, Ja-F, 1964.

Ransford, N. Edward. "Isolation, Powerlessness, and Violence: A Study of Attitudes and Participation in the Watts Riot." American Journal of Sociology, Mr, 1968.

Rasmussen, Karl R. "The Multi-Ordered Urban Area: A Ghetto." Phylon, Fall, 1968.

Record, Wilson, and Cassels, Jane. "The White Social Scientist in the Black Community." Journal of Research and Development in Education 8(Spring, 1975):63-72.

A Relevant War Against Poverty. A Study of Community Action Programs and Observable Social Change. New York: Metropolitan Applied Research Center, 1968.

Riessman, Frank. "The Myth of Saul Alinsky." Dissent, Jl-Ag, 1967.

Robey, John. "The Politics of School Desegregation: A Comparative Analysis of Policy Outcomes in Southern Counties." Doctoral dissertation, U. of Georgia, 1970.

Rogers, David, and Swanson, Bert. "White Citizen Response to the Same Integration Plan: Comparisons of Local School Districts in a Northern City." Sociological Inquiry, Winter, 1965.

Roof, Wade Clark, and Spain, Daphne. "A Research Note on City-Suburban Socioeconomic Differences among American Blacks." Social Forces 56(S, 1977):15-20.

Rose, Harold M. "The All Black Town: Suburban Prototype or Rural Slum?" In People and Politics in Urban Society, pp. 397-431. Edited by Harlan Hahn. Beverly Hills, CA: Sage, 1972.

_____. Black Suburbanization: Improved Access to Quality of Life or Maintenance of the Status Quo? Cambridge, MA: Ballinger, 1976.

_____. Geography of the Ghetto. De Kalb: Northern Illinois U. Press, 1972.

Rose, S. The Betrayal of the Poor: The Transformation of Community Action. Cambridge, MA: Schenkman, 1972.

Rossell, Christine H. "The Effect of School Integration on Community Integration." Journal of Education 160(My, 1978):46-62.

_____. "School Desegregation and White Flight." Political Science Quarterly 90 (Winter, 1975-1976):675-695.

Rossi, Peter H. Community Social Indicators. Baltimore, MD: Center for Social Organization of Schools, Johns Hopkins U., 0, 1970.

Royster, Eugene C. and others. Analyses of Issues of Services to the Black Community. Lincoln University, PA: Department of Sociology, Lincoln U., Je, 1973.

Rubin, Lillian. "Maximum Feasible Participation. The Origins, Implications, and Present Status." Poverty and Human Resources Abstracts, N-D, 1967.

Rubin, Roger H. "Community and Family Violence: Educational Implication for Student Involvement In a Black Community." College Student Journal 7(Ja-F, 1973):97-101.

Ryan, Michael. "News Selection Patterns among Non-White, Urban Slum Residents." Journalism Quarterly 53(Autumn, 1976):441-447.

Saltman, Juliet (ed.). Integrated Neighborhoods in Action. Washington, DC: National Neighbors, 1978.

Sarkissian, W. "The Idea of Social Mix in Town Planning: An Historical Review." Urban Studies 13(0, 1976).

Saunders, Marie Simmons. "The Ghetto: Some Perceptions of a Black Social Worker." Social Work 14(1969):84-88.

Scheibla, Shirley. "Suffer Little Children." Barron's, My 8, 1967.

Schelling, T. C. Models of Segregation. Santa Monica, CA: Rand, My, 1969.

Schindler-Raissman, Eva. "The Poor and the PTA." PTA Magazine, Ap, 1967.

Schnore, Leo F., André, Carolyn D., and Sharp, Harry. "Black Suburbanization, 1930-1970." In The Changing Face of the Suburbs. Edited by Barry Schwartz. Chicago: U. of Chicago Press, 1976.

Schnore, Leo F., and Fagin, Henry (eds.). Urban Research and Policy Planning. Beverly Hills, CA: Sage Publications, 1967.

Schumaker, Paul D., and Getter, Russell W. "The Community Bases of Minority Educational Attainment." Journal of Education 159(N, 1977):4-22.

Scott, Mel. American City Planning Since 1890... Berkeley, CA: U. of California, Berkeley, 1969.

Sharon, Amiel T. "Racial Differences in Newspaper Readership." Public Opinion Quarterly 37(Winter, 1973-1974):611-617.

Shedd, Mark. "Decentralization and Urban Schools." Educational Leadership, 0, 1967.

Shin, Eui-Hang. "Effects of Migration on the Educational Levels of the Black Resident Population at the Origin and Destination, 1955-1960 and 1965-1970." Demography 15(F, 1978).

Simkus, Albert A. "Residential Segregation by Occupation and Race in Ten Urbanized Areas, 1950-1970." American Sociological Review 43 (F, 1978):81-93.

Skeen, Elois M. "A Community-Controlled School. The Effects on Student Perceptions of Locus of Control." Journal of Black Studies 5 (D, 1974):219-224.

Skura, Barry Robert. "The Impact of Collective Racial Violence in Neighborhood Mobilization, 1964-1968." Doctoral dissertation, U. of Chicago, 1975.

Smith, Mildred B., and Brahce, Carl I. "When School and Home Focus on Achievement." Educational Leadership, F, 1963.

Smolensky, Eugene, Becker, Selwyn, and Wilber, Charles K. "The Prisoner's Dilemma and Ghetto Expansion." Land Economics, N, 1968.

Solomon, Barbara Bryant. Black Empowerment. Social Work in Oppressed Communities. New York: Columbia U. Press, 1976.

Solzman, David M. "Some Spatial Effects of School Desegregation in the Inner City." Journal of Social and Behavioral Science 14 (Spring, 1969):3-12.

South Carolina Community Relations Program. "A Guide to Community Leadership on the Discipline/Suspension Issue." Your Schools 7(Ja-F, 1976.

Spencer, D. An Evaluation of Cognitive Mapping Techniques in Neighbourhood Perception. Birmingham, England: Centre for Urban and Regional Studies, 1973.

Spiegel, Hans B. C., and Mittenthal, Stephen D. Neighborhood Power and Control: Implications for Urban Planning, N, 1968. Federal Clearinghouse, U.S. Department of Commerce, Springfield, VA 22151.

Stacey, Margaret. "The Myth of Community Studies." British Journal of Sociology, Je, 1969.

Stack, Carol B. All Our Kin: Strategies for Survival in a Black Community. New York: Harper & Row, 1974.

Staples, Robert E. "Black Ideology and the Search for Community." Liberator, Je, 1969.

Stern, Sol. "The Berkeley City Council Will Never Be the Same." New York Times Magazine, Ag 29, 1971.

Stringfellow, William. "The Eye of the Hurricane." Freedom North, Vol. I, No. 2, 1964.

"Ethnic Minorities: Resistance to Being Researched." Professional Psychology 3(1972): 11-17.

Swanson, Bert E. "The Concern for Community in the Metropolis." Urban Affairs Quarterly, Je, 1966.

_____. The Concern for Community in Urban America. Indianapolis, IN: Bobbs, Merrill, 1971.

_____. "The Political Feasibility of Planning for School Integration." Integrated Education, F-Mr, 1967.

Sweezy, Paul M. "Afterword: The Implications of Community Control." In Schools Against Children. The Case for Community Control. Edited by Annette T. Rubenstein. New York: Monthly Review Press, 1970.

Tabb, William K. The Political Economy of the Black Ghetto. New York: Norton, 1970.

Taeuber, Conrad. "Counting the Invisible Americans: The Inner City and the 1970 Census." In U.S. Bureau of the Census, GE40, No. 5, Papers Presented at the Conference on Small Area Statistics, American Statistical Association, Pittsburgh, Pa. August 23 and Related Paper. Washington, DC: GPO, 1968.

Taeuber, Karl E. Patterns of Negro-White Residential Segregation. Santa Monica, CA: Rand, Ja, 1970.

_____. Race and the Metropolis: A Demographic Perspective on the 1970's, Mr, 1974. ERIC ED 094 050.

Talbert, Carol. "Studying Education in the Ghetto." In To See Ourselves: Anthropology and Modern Social Issues. Edited by Thomas Weaver. Glenview, IL: Scott, Foresman, 1973.

Taylor, Councill. "Clues for the Future: Black Urban Anthropology Reconsidered." In Race, Change, and Urban Setting, pp. 603-618. Edited by Peter Orleans and William Sussell Ellis, Jr. Beverly Hills, CA: Sage, 1971.

Thomas, Robert K. "Colonialism: Classic and Internal." New University Thought, Winter, 1966-1967.

Thomason, George F. "Structural Strains in Changing Urban Communities." Social and Economic Administration (London), Ja, 1967.

Tierney, John T. Sickness and Poverty. A Handbook for Community Workers. Washington, DC: GPO, 1970.

"The Tipping Point." Newsweek, N 27, 1972.

Travis, Dempsey J. "How Whites Are Taking Back Black Neighborhoods." Ebony 33(S, 1978): 72-83.

Tucker, Charles Jackson, and Reid, John Daniel. Urban Growth and Redistribution of the Black Urban American City by Size of City, 1950-1970, O, 1974. ERIC ED 128 473.

Turner, Richard. The Eye of the Needle. An Essay on Participatory Democracy. Johannesburg, South Africa: Special Programme for Christian Action in Society, 1972.

Underhill, Ralph. Youth in Poor Neighborhoods. Chicago: National Opinion Research Center, U. of Chicago, 1967.

U.S. Advisory Commission on Intergovernmental Relations. Intergovernmental Relations in the Poverty Program. Washington, DC: GPO, Ap, 1966.

U.S. Congress, 93rd, 1st session, House of Representatives, Committee on Education and Labor, General Subcommittee on Education. Community Schools. Hearing... Washington, DC: GPO, 1973.

U.S. Congress, 95th, 1st session, Senate, Committee on Human Resources, Subcommittee on Education, Arts, and Humanities. Quality of Education, 1977. Hearings... Washington, DC: GPO, 1977. [Accountability]

U.S. National Commission on Urban Problems. Hearings... Baltimore, New Haven, Boston, and Pittsburgh. May-June, 1967. Washington, DC: GPO, 1968.

Valentine, Charles A. Blackston: Progress Report on a Community Study in Urban Afro-America, F, 1970, 132 pp. ERIC ED 040 229.

_____. Ethnography and Large-scale Complex Sociocultural Fields: Participant Observation from Multiple Perspectives in a Low-Income Urban Afro-American Community, N, 1969, 50 pp. ERIC ED 036 582.

Vance, James E., Jr. "Land Assignment in the Precapitalist, Capitalist, and Postcapitalist City." Economic Geography 47(Ap, 1971): 101-120.

Vanecko, James J., and Kronenfeld, Jennie. "Preferences for Public Expenditures and Ethno-Racial Group Membership: A Test of the Theory of Political Ethos." Ethnicity 4 (D, 1977):311-336.

Vargus, Brian S. "On Sociological Exploitation: Why the Guinea Pig Sometimes Bites." Social Problems 19(Fall, 1971):238-248.

Vernon, Raymond. The Myth and Reality of Our Urban Problems. Cambridge, MA: Harvard U. Press, 1966.

Wallach, I. A. The Police Function in a Negro Community. 2 vols. McLean, VA: Research Analysis Corp., 1971 (NTIS No. PB-196 763).

Warren, Donald I. "Black Neighborhoods." Black World 25(N, 1975):12-26.

_____. Black Neighborhoods: An Assessment of Community Power. Ann Arbor, MI: U. of Michigan Press, 1975. [Detroit]

Wegemann, Robert G. "Neighborhoods and Schools in Racial Transition." Growth and Change 6 (Jl, 1975):3-8.

Wegner, Eldon L., and Mercer, Jane R. "Dynamics of the Desegregation Process: Politics, Policies, and Community Characteristics as Factors in Change." In The Polity of the School, pp. 123-143. Edited by Frederick M. Wirt. Lexington, MA: Lexington Books, 1975.

Wheeler, J. "The Spatial Interaction of Blacks in Metropolitan Areas." Southeastern Geographer 11(1971):101-112.

White, Herbert D., Steinle, Donald R., and Stone, Ronald. "Discussion: Saul Alinsky and the Ethics of Social Change." Union Seminary Quarterly Review, Ja, 1967.

Wilcox, Preston. "From 'Complainant' to 'Spokesman.' Changing Conceptions of Community." Educational Leadership (My, 1972).

Wilder, David et al. Actual and Perceived Consensus on Educational Goals Between School and Community. New York: Bureau of Applied Social Research, Columbia U., 1968.

Wilkerson, Doxey A. How to Make Educational Research Relevant to the Urban Community, F 5, 1971, 8 pp. ERIC ED 048 422.

Willacy, Hazel M. "Men in Poverty Neighborhoods." Monthly Labor Review, F, 1969.

Williams, J. Allen, Jr., and Edwards, Agnes M. "Rehabilitation and the Black Community." Journal of Rehabilitation 37(My-Je, 1971): 43-46.

Williams, Joyce E. Black Community Control: A Study of Transition in a Texas Ghetto. New York: Praeger, 1973.

Williams, Robert L. "The Death of White Research in the Black Community." Journal of Non-White Concerns in Personnel and Guidance 2(Ap, 1974):116-132.

Willie, Charles V. "White Flight from the Cities." Ebony 31(D, 1975):46.

Wilson, James Q. (ed.). Urban Renewal. Cambridge, MA: M.I.T. Press, 1966.

Wilson, Robert A. "Anomie in the Ghetto: A Study of Neighborhood Type, Race and Anomie." American Journal of Sociology 77 (Jl, 1971):66-88.

Winer, M. L. "White Resistance and Negro Insistence: An Ecological Analysis of Urban Desegregation." Honor's thesis, Harvard U., 1964.

Winkel, Gary H., O'Hanlon, Timothy, and
Mussen, Irwin. Black Families in White
Neighborhoods: Experiences and Attitudes.
New York: Environmental Psychology Program,
Graduate Center, City U. of New York, My,
1974.

Winters, Stanley B. "Urban Renewal and Civil
Rights." Studies on the Left, Summer, 1964.

Wirt, Frederick M. "The Urbanization of the
Suburbs." Urban Affairs Annual Review 7,
1973.

Yates, Douglas. Neighborhood Government, Jl,
1971. RAND Corp., 1700 Main Street, Santa
Monica, CA 90401.

Youth Development and Delinquency Prevention
Administration. Volunteers Help Youth.
Washington, DC: GPO, 1971.

Wilson, R. "Psychology and the Black
Community." Newsletter of the Michigan
Black Psychologists, D, 1969.

Wood, Elizabeth. Social Planning. A Primer
for Urbanists. Brooklyn, NY: Planning
Dept., Pratt Institute, 1965.

Young, Whitney. "Minorities and Public School
Decentralization." Journal of Negro
Education, Summer, 1969.

Zelder, R. E. "On the Measurement of Residential Segregation: Reply." Journal of
Regional Science 17(Ag, 1977).

Bibliographies

Barr, Charles W. (comp.). Housing-Health
Relationships: An Annotated Bibliography,
My, 1969. Council of Planning Librarians,
P.O. Box 229, Monticello, IL.

Beach, Mark (comp.). Bibliography on Inter-
racial Neighborhoods, Ag, 1974. Mark and
Oralee Beach, 151 Roslyn Street, Rochester,
NY 14619.

_____ (comp.). Desegregated Housing and In-
terracial Neighborhoods. A Bibliographic
Guide, 1975. National Neighbors, 17
Maplewood Mall, Philadelphia, PA 19144.

Booher, David E. (comp.). Citizen Participation in Planning: Selected Interdisciplinary Bibliography. Monticello, IL:
Council of Planning Libraries, 1975.

Boyce, Byrl N., and Turoff, Sidney (comps.).
Minority Groups and Housing: A Biblio-
graphy, 1950-1970. Morristown, NJ:
General Learning Press, 1972.

Branch, Melville C. (comp.). Comprehensive
Urban Planning. A Selective Annotated
Bibliography with Related Materials.
Beverly Hills, CA: Sage, 1970.

Bureau of Governmental Research and Service.
Issues in the Community. An Annotated
Bibliography of Selected Community Problems
in Oregon. Eugene OR: The Bureau, U. of
Oregon, 1967.

Bureau of Naval Personnel, General Military
Training and Support Division, Library
Services Branch (comp.). Black Heritage--
The American Experience. A Sampling of
Audio-Visual Materials for Use in Libaries.
Washington, DC: GPO, 1972.

Campus/Community Relationships: An Annotated
Bibliography 1971. Exchange Bibliographies,
P.O. Box 229, Monticello, IL 61856.

Clark, Walter E. (comp.). Community Power and
Decision-Making: A Selective Bibliography,
1971. Council of Planning Librarians, P.O.
Box 229, Monticello, IL 61856.

Darden, Joe T. (comp.). The Ghetto: A Bibliography. Monticello, IL: Council of Planning
Librarians, 1977.

Davies, Don, and Zerchykov, Ross (comps.).
Citizen Participation in Education:
Annotated Bibliography. 2nd ed. Boston:
Institute for Responsive Education, 1978.

Davies, Don and others (comps.). Citizen Participation in Education. Annotated Bibliography. New Haven, CT: Institute of
Responsive Education, Yale U., D, 1973.

Davis, Lenwood G. (comp.). Housing in the Black
Community. Monticello, IL: Council of
Planning Librarians, 1975.

Filipovitch, Anthony J., and Reeves, Earl J.
Urban Community: A Guide to Information
Sources. Detroit: Gale, 1978.

Fink, Ira S., and Cooke, Joan (comps.). Campus-
Community Relationships: An Annotated
Bibliography, 1971. Society for College and
University Planning, c/o Columbia U., 616 W.
114th Street, New York, NY 10025.

Geier, Mark, with Bell, Carmen McCoy (comps.).
"Bibliography on School Decentralization and
Community Control." Community Issues 2(Je,
1970):1-32.

Goldsmid, Charles A. and others (comps.).
Programs for Inner-City Communities: An
Annotated Bibliography. Chicago: American
Society of Planning Officials, Ag, 1969.

Greenwald, Meryl A. Parents and Schools: An
Annotated Bibliography, S, 1977. ERIC ED
156 980.

Hawley, Willis D., and Svara, James H. (comps.).
The Study of Community Power: A Bibliographic
Review, 1972. American Bibliographical
Center, Riviera Campus, 2040 A.P.S., Santa
Barbara, CA 93103.

Institute of Governmental Studies. Metropolitan Communities: A Bibliography--1965-1967,
1969. Institute of Governmental Studies,
109 Moses Hall, U. of California, Berkeley,
CA 94720.

Jackson, Kathleen O'Brien (comp.). Annotated
Bibliography on School-Community Relations.
ERIC Clearinghouse on Educational Administration, U. of Oregon, Eugene, OR, Jl,
1969, 25 pp. ERIC ED 030 220.

Mazziotti, Donald F. (comp.). Neighborhoods
and Neighborhood Planning: A Selected
Bibliography. Monticello, IL: Council of
Planning Librarians, 1974.

Parent Involvement in School Programs,
Bibliographies in Education, No. 18.
Canadian Teachers' Federation, Ottawa
Research Division, F, 1971, 33 pp. ERIC
ED 054 270.

Robinson, Lora H., and Shoenfeld, Janet D.
(eds.). Student Participation in Academic
Governance. Washington, DC: ERIC Clearinghouse on Higher Education, George Washington
U., F, 1970.

Rosenberg, Helen (comp.). Displacement and
Relocation of Low-Income Households Due to
Private Market Housing Renovations.
Monticello, IL: Council of Planning
Librarians, 1978.

Sharma, Prokash (comp.). Slum and Ghetto
Studies: A Research Bibliography.
Monticello, IL: Council of Planning
Librarians, 1974.

Siegel, Judith A. (comp.). Racial Discrimination in Housing. Monticello, IL:
Council of Planning Librarians, 1977.

Smith, David H., and Baldwin, Burt R. (comps.).
"Voluntary Associations and Volunteering in
the U.S." In Voluntary Action Research:
1974, pp. 227-305. Edited by David H.
Smith. Lexington, MA: Lexington Books,
1975.

Strand, Sverre (comp.). Urban Geography 1950-
1970: A Comprehensive Bibliography of
Urbanism as Reflected in the Articles and
Book Reviews of 72 American, Canadian,
British, Dutch, and Scandanavian Geographical Periodicals. Monticello, IL: Council
of Planning Librarians, 1973.

Summers, Gene F. et al. (comps.). Community:
Annotated Bibliography of Journal Articles,
1960-1973. Monticello, IL: Council of
Planning Librarians, 1974.

U.S. Congress, 90th, 1st session, Joint
Economic Committee, Subcommittee on Urban
Affairs. A Directory of Urban Research
Study Centers. Washington, DC: GPO, 1967.

U.S. Department of Housing and Urban Development
Library (comp.). Equal Opportunity in
Housing: A Bibliography of Research. 2nd
edition. Washington, DC: GPO, S, 1974.

_____ (comp.). Equal Opportunity. A Bibliography of Research on Equal Opportunity in
Housing. Washington, DC: GPO, Ap, 1969.

_____. New Communities. A Bibliography.
Washington, DC: GPO, 1970.

Where It's At. A Research Guide for Community
Organizing. Ann Arbor, MI: Radical Education Project, 1967.

White, Anthony G. (comp.). Discrimination in
Housing Loans--Redlining: A Selected
Bibliography. Monticello, IL: Council of
Planning Librarians, 1976.

Williams, D. F. (comp.). The Political Economy
of Black Community Development: A Research
Bibliography. Monticello, IL: Council of
Planning Librarians, 1976.

Zikmund, Joseph II, and Dennis, Deborah Ellis
(comps.). Suburbia. A Guide to Information
Sources. Detroit: Gale Research Co., 1979.

20.
HIGHER EDUCATION

Higher Education by State

Alabama

Alexander, Lydia Lewis. "A Study of the Real and Ideal College Environment as Perceived by Black Students in Racially Contrasting Junior Colleges in Alabama." Doctoral dissertation, Auburn U., 1972. Univ. Microfilms Order No. 73-08257.

Alverson, Roy Tilman. "A History of Tuskegee." Master's thesis, Alabama Polytechnic Institute, Auburn, 1929.

Anthony, Paul. "He Conquered Lost Causes: An Epitaph for Lucius Pitts." Southern Voices 1 (My-Je, 1974):71-73.

"Black Instructor Fired for Teaching Malcolm X." African World, Ap 30, 1972. [Miles College, Birmingham]

Butler, Addie L. J. The Distinctive Black College: Talladega, Tuskegee, and Morehouse. Metuchen, NJ: Scarecrow Press, 1977.

_____. "The Distinctive Black College: Talladega, Tuskegee, and Morehouse." Doctoral dissertation, Columbia U., 1976. Univ. Microfilms Order No. 76-27,699.

Chisum, Melvin J. "The Whole Truth About Tuskegee Hospital: Inside Story of Developments, Together with Correspondence between the Principal Parties." Pittsburgh Courier, Je 30, 1923.

Citro, J. F. "Booker T. Washington's Tuskegee Institute: Black School Community, 1900-1915." Doctoral dissertation, U. of Rochester, 1973.

Clift, Eleanor. "A New Look Comes to Miles College." Race Relations Reporter 4(N, 1973):8-9.

Daniel, Pete. "Black Power in the 1920's: The Case of the Tuskegee Veterans Hospital." Journal of Southern History, Ag, 1970.

Du Bois, W. E. B. [Article on Tuskegee Institute] Amsterdam News, Ap 25, 1942.

Egerton, John. "Alabama's Two Per Cent." Southern Education Report, Mr, 1969. [Black students at the U. of Alabama]

_____. "Lucius H. Pitts and U. W. Clemon." New South 25(Summer, 1970):9-20. [Miles College, Birmingham]

Fallows, James M. "ASTA Will Push Fight Against Auburn Center." Southern Courier, Ag 3, 1968. [Proposed Montgomery, AL, Branch of Auburn U.]

Forman, James. Sammy Younge, Jr. The First Black College Student to Die in the Black Liberation Movement. New York: Grove, 1968.

Friedman, Neil. "The Miles College Freshman Social Science Program: Educational Innovation in a Negro College." Journal of Negro Education, Fall, 1969.

Gale, Mary Ellen. "ASTA Sues to Stop New Auburn Branch." Southern Courier, F 24, 1968. [Alabama State Teachers Association suing to stop building of a branch of Auburn U. in Montgomery]

_____. "'Somewhere to go' for Whites?" Southern Courier, My 11, 1968. [Court hearing on proposed Auburn U. branch in Montgomery]

_____. "Texas Murder Suspect Calls Tuskegee 'Dead.'" Southern Courier, N 18, 1967.

Goodenow, Ronald K. "Buell Gallagher As President of Talladega College: An Education Reconstructionist in Action." Cutting Edge: Journal of the Society for Educational Reconstruction 8(Winter, 1977):9-19.

Greenhouse, Linda. "The Reincarnation of John Monro." New York Times Magazine, Mr 15, 1970. [Miles College, Birmingham]

Heggie, Sarah. [Why Negro Teacher Group Opposes New State College in Montgomery, AL] Southern Courier, S 23, 1967

Higgins, Chester A., Jr. "Paper on Student Unrest at Tuskegee Institute." Journal of Social and Behavioral Sciences 16(Fall, 1970):18-26. [1968 events]

Hilliard, Lonnie, Jr. "The New Breed of Black Students: Their Inspiration, Expectations, and Values." Journal of Social and Behavioral Sciences 15(Fall, 1969):51-52. [Sophomore student at Tuskegee Institute]

Howard, Franklin. "Race Relations Group Formed." Southern Courier, N 16, 1968. [Interracial student group at Alexander City Junior College]

Imbriano, Robert J. "Tuskegee and Prichard." Black Enterprise, F, 1973.

Jackson, Reid E. "A Critical Analysis of Curricula for Educating Secondary-School Teachers in Negro Colleges of Alabama." Doctoral dissertation, Ohio State U., 1937.

James, Felix. "The Tuskegee Institute Movable School, 1906-1923." Agricultural History, Jl, 1971.

Jones, Allen W. "The Role of Tuskegee Institute in the Education of Black Farmers." Journal of Negro History 60(Ap, 1975):252-267.

Jones, George W. "The Negro Public College in Alabama." Journal of Negro Education 31 (Summer, 1962):354-361.

Kahn, E. J., Jr. "A Whale of a Difference." New Yorker 47(Ap 10, 1971):43-64. [Prof. John U. Monro, Miles College, Birmingham]

Karriem, Anna. "Islam in Tuskegee." Muhammad Speaks, N 14, 1969.

_____. "Islam in Tuskegee." Muhammad Speaks, Mr 28, 1969. [Tuskegee Institute]

Kimball, Solon T., and Pearsall, Marion. The Talladega Story: A Study in Community Process. University, AL: U. of Alabama Press, 1954.

Larson, Richard F. and others. "Integration Attitudes of College Students at the University of Alabama." Journal of Social Psychology, Ag, 1964.

McClung, Merle. "Miles College: A Chance for Birmingham's Black Students?" American Oxonian 57(Ap, 1970):348-354.

"Claude McKay Describes His Own Life." Pearson's Magazine 39(S, 1918):275-276. [Tuskegee]

"The Man from Harvard." Newsweek, S 24, 1973. [John U. Monro, Miles College, Birmingham]

Marable, Manning. "Tuskegee and the Politics of Illusion in the New South." Black Scholar 8(My, 1977):13-24.

_____. "Tuskegee Institute in the 1920's." Negro History Bulletin 40(N-D, 1977):764-768.

Mines, Stephanie, and Frazier, Phil. "Sammy Younge, Jr. Bringin' It All Down Home." The Movement, Ap, 1969. [Tuskegee Institute]

Muir, Donal E. "The First Years of Desegregation: Patterns of Acceptance of Black Students on a Deep-South Campus, 1963-69." Social Forces 49(Mr, 1971):371-378. [U. of Alabama]

_____. "Six-Year Trends in Integration Attitudes of Deep-South University Students." Integrated Education 9(Ja-F, 1971):21-28.

_____. "Through the School-House Door: Trends in Integration, Attitudes on a Deep-South Campus During the First Decade of Desegregation." Sociology and Social Research 58 (Ja, 1974):113-121. [U. of Alabama]

Muir, Donal E., and McGlamery, C. Donald. "The Evolution of Desegregation Attitudes of Southern University Students." Phylon, Summer, 1968. [U. of Alabama]

"Negro Education at Tuskegee Institute." Journal of Educational Sociology 7(N, 1933): 151-205.

Owens, Otis Holloway. A Study of Black Graduate Students in Alabama, 1976. ERIC ED 125 513.

Phillips, Ollie Reynolds. "Higher Education for Negro Women in Alabama." Master's thesis, Fisk U., 1939.

Prugh, Jeff. "U.S. Could Have Avoided Wallace Confrontation." Los Angeles Times, Je 11, 1978. [In re: U. of Alabama, 1963]

Russakoff, Dale S. "Miles from Harvard: The Black College." Harvard Crimson, F 7, 1973. [John U. Monro, Miles College, Birmingham]

Ryff, Allan W. "The Tuskegee Hospital Controversy, 1921-1924." Master's thesis, U. of Delaware, 1970.

Shannon, Mary Lee Rice. Poverty in Alabama. A Barrier to Postsecondary Education, 1976. ERIC ED 132 911.

Sikes, William Marion. "The Historical Development of Stillman Institute." Master's thesis, U. of Alabama, 1930.

Smith, Gary Vincent. "Daybreak in Alabama--Reflections and Observations on the Black Academic Experience: Alabama State University." Doctoral dissertation, Lehigh U., 1976. Univ. Microfilms Order No. 76-21832.

Stevens, Pat. "'What Is Harvard Doing Here?'" Southern Exposure 7(Summer, 1979):84-88. [John U. Monro, Miles College, Birmingham]

Taylor, Ralph Lee. "A Comparison of the Self-Concept of Negro Students at the University of Alabama and Negro Students at Stillman College." Doctoral dissertation, U. of Alabama, 1970. Univ. Microfilms Order No. 71-09142.

Terry, Paul W., and Lee, L. Tennent (eds.). A Study of Stillman Institute, a Junior College for Negroes. University, AL: U. of Alabama Press, 1947. [Tuscaloosa]

Thrasher, Max Bennett. Tuskegee: Its Story and Its Work. Boston: Small Maynard & Co., 1900.

Turner, Albert L. "Higher Education in Alabama." Quarterly Review of Higher Education Among Negroes 5(0, 1937):153-159.

U.S. Commission on Civil Rights, Alabama Advisory Committee. Agricultural Stabilization and Conservation Service in Alabama Black Belt. Washington, DC: GPO, 1968.

Walker, Anne K. Tuskegee and the Black Belt: A Portrait of a Race. Richmond, VA: Dietz, 1944.

Washington, Booker T. Tuskegee and Its People. New York: Appleton, 1905.

Williams, Roger. "Letter from Tuskegee." South Today, My, 1970.

Willse, James P. "Integration Goes Both Ways in Tuscaloosa." Southern Courier, N 6, 1965. [U. of Alabama]

Alaska

Jacquot, Louis F. "Alaska Natives and Alaska Higher Education, 1960-1972: A Descriptive Study." Doctoral dissertation, U. of Oregon, 1973.

_____. Alaska Natives and Alaska Higher Education, 1960-1972: A Descriptive Study. Fairbanks, AK: Alaska Native Human Resources Development Program, U. of Alaska, 1974.

Kohout, Karen, and Kleinfeld, Judith. Alaska Natives in Higher Education. Fairbanks, AK: Institute of Social, Economic, and Government Research, 1974.

Patty, Ernest. North Country Challenge. New York: McKay, 1969. [U. of Alaska]

Salisbury, Lee H. College Orientation Program for Alaskan Natives, COPAN Program, Education for Survival. College, AK: U. of Alaska, 1968.

Van Dyne, Larry, "New Wealth, Old Anger Among Alaska's 'Natives.'" Chronicle of Higher Education, N 21, 1977. [U. of Alaska]

Watkins, Beverly T. "In the Heart of Alaska's Eskimo Country, Education Tailored to Natives' Needs." Chronicle of Higher Education, N 29, 1976. [Kushokwin Community College, Bethel]

Arizona

Adler, Gail, and Feder, Wendy. "Crisis Hits Navajo College." Navajo Times, Ja 20, 1977. [Navajo Community College]

Arellano, Maria. "Student Organization Continues Action on Discrimination." Summer News, Jl 10, 1975. [Arizona State U.]

Ashe, Robert W. et al. Survey Report: Navajo Community College. Bureau of Educational Research and Services, Arizona State U., Tempe, 1966.

Bielek, Ken. "ASU Arizona Southern University Students Stand by Laundry Workers." La Raza, F 7, 1969. [Phoenix]

Bluehouse, Milton. "The Indian People Have a Story...A Revelation for the Whole World" (an interview by Richard Stafford and Pick Temple). Community 2(My, 1972). [Navajo Community College]

Bradford, Viola. "Letter from Arizona." Southern Courier, Je 24, 1967. [A Negro student from Montgomery, AL, reflects on her first year at the U. of Arizona]

Bryant, Harry L., Sr. [Letter about Navajo Community College] Navajo Times, Ja 22, 1976.

Committee on Indian Education. "Indian Education at Arizona State University." Journal of American Indian Education 1(Ja, 1962):24-27.

Fuchs, Estelle. "The Navajos Build a College." Saturday Review 55(Mr 4, 1972):58-62. [Navajo Community College]

Hamblin, John Ray. "A Study of Some of the Important Factors Which Encourage Indian Students in Apache and Navajo Counties in Arizona to Seek a Higher Education After High School Graduation." Master's thesis, Brigham Young U., 1963.

House, Lloyd Lynn. "The Historical Development of Navajo Community College." Doctoral dissertation, Arizona State U., 1974. Univ. Microfilms Order No. 74-21,532.

Janssen, Peter A. "Navajo C.C.'s Unfulfilled Promise." Change 7(N, 1975):52-53.

Jenkins, Evan. "Literacy Through Socio-linguistics." Change 8(Jl, 1976):38-41. [Navajo Community College]

McCarthy, Colman. "Far from the Madhouse Crowd." Communities in Action, Je, 1969. [Navajo Community College]

MacDonald, Peter. "Navajo Community College Needs a Change." Navajo Times, F 3, 1977.

Navajo Students. "Open Letter to Navajo Nation." Navajo Times, O 2, 1975. [Critique of conditions at Navajo Community College]

"The New NCC." Navajo Times 19(My 4, 1978): 1-7. [Several articles on Navajo Community College]

Nix, L. E. "Promotion of Higher Education Within Arizona Indian Groups." Doctoral dissertation, Arizona State U., 1963.

Pacific Training and Technical Assistance Corp. Evaluation of Navajo Community College, Je, 1970. ERIC ED 135 546.

Parham, Joseph. "Relationships Between Academic Achievement, Attitudes and Attrition of Black Athletes at Arizona State University." Doctoral dissertation, Arizona State U., 1973. Univ. Microfilms Order No. 73-12086.

Patterson, Ann. "Among Arizona Indians... Fewer Red Apples." Indian Historian 8 (Summer, 1975):26. [Arizona State U., Tempe]

Phillips, John C. "A College of, by, and for Navajo Indians." Chronicle of Higher Education, Ja 16, 1978. [Navajo Community College]

Quimby, R. J. "American Indian Students in Arizona Colleges: A Discriminant Analysis of Select Variables that Contribute to Success and Failure." Doctoral dissertation, Arizona State U., 1963.

"Repression in the Southwest." Muhammad Speaks, Ap 17, 1970. [Black athletes at Arizona State U., Tempe]

Steiner, Stan. "Student Activists: the Navajo Way." Progressive, Jl, 1969. [Navajo Community College]

Swift, Peggy. "In-Culture Research at N.C.C." Navajo Times, Jl 3, 1969. [Navajo students study Navajo culture at the Navajo Community College]

Thompson, Hildegard. "A Survey of Factors Contributing to Success or Failure of Indian Students at Northern Arizona University." Indian Education, N 1, 1966.

Tippeconnic, John W. III. "The Center of Indian Education at ASU: A Report by the New Director." Journal of American Indian Education 16(O, 1976):10-12. [Arizona State U.]

Todacheene, Carl L. "NCC Board Disappointed in McCabe." Navajo Times, Ag 10, 1978. [Don McCabe, former president of Navajo Community College]

Van West, Carla. American Indian Students and the Arizona Community College System, Mr 1, 1976. ERIC ED 135 416.

Arkansas

"Arkansas Blacks Fight Threat to Their Colleges." Muhammad Speaks, Mr 17, 1972.

Arkansas State Department of Higher Education. Arkansas College and University Plan for Compliance with Title VI of the Civil Rights Act of 1964. Statewide Plan Implementation Status Report III, Mr, 1976. ERIC ED 124 028.

_____. Arkansas College and University Plan for Compliance with Title VI of the Civil Rights Act of 1964 (Revised 1977). Statewide Plan, 1977. ERIC ED 148 290.

Butler, Martha L. Student Needs Survey Report, Ap, 1977. ERIC ED 146 854. [U. of Arkansas]

Chambers, Fredrick. "Historical Study of Arkansas Agricultural, Mechanical, and Normal College, 1873-1943." Doctoral dissertation, Ball State U., 1970.

Lee, Lurline M. "The Origin, Development, and Present Status of Arkansas' Program of Higher Education for Negroes." Doctoral dissertation, Michigan State U., 1955. Univ. Microfilm Order No. 12151.

Morehead, Qumare A. "A Study of Black Studies in the Social Sciences and Humanities Curricula of Ten Colleges and Universities in Arkansas." Doctoral dissertation, Kansas State U., 1977.

Nam, Tae Y. "A Manifesto of the Black Student Activists in a Southern Black College Under the Integration Order." Journal of Negro Education 46(Spring, 1977):168-185. [U. of Arkansas, Pine Bluff]

Nichols, Guerdon D. "Breaking the Color Barrier at the University of Arkansas." Arkansas Historical Quarterly 27(1968):3-21.

Rothrock, Thomas. "Joseph Carter Corbin and Negro Education in the University of Arkansas." Arkansas Historical Quarterly, Winter, 1971.

"Southern State College (Arkansas)." AAUP Bulletin 57(Spring, 1971):40-49.

Walker, Woodson D. "Schools Must Serve the Struggle." SOBU Newsletter, Mr 6, 1971. [Letter by president of Student Government Association to President Lawrence A. Davis, Arkansas A., M., and N. College]

Wilson, Ralph. The Effects of Special Tutoring and Counseling on the Academic Success of Negro Freshmen at Southern State College. Final Report. Magnolia, AR: Southern State College, S 25, 1970, 107 pp. ERIC ED 043 314.

California

AAUP Investigating Committee. "Academic Freedom and Tenure. The University of California at Los Angeles." AAUP Bulletin 57(S, 1971): 382-420. [The case of Angela Y. Davis]

Academic Characteristics of Negro Students Enrolled at City College of San Francisco, Spring, 1968. San Francisco: City College, My, 1968, 5 pp. ERIC ED 022 436.

Adams, Forrest H. "He'll Make a Good Doctor-- If He Gets In." Los Angeles Times, Ap 30, 1978. [U. of California, Los Angeles]

Allen, Anne G. "Educational Opportunities Programs for Minority and Low-Income Students in California and United States Colleges and Universities." Doctoral dissertation, U. of California, Los Angeles, 1970. Univ. Microfilms Order No. 71-00577.

Alvarado, Roger. [Interview] Guardian, F 1, 1969. [San Francisco State College]

Alvarado, Roger, Crutchfield, Nesbit, and Wong, Mason. [Partial text of radio station KPFA discussion of events at San Francisco State College, D 6, 1968] The Movement, Ja, 1969.

Anderson, Barbara. "Ordeal at San Francisco State College." Library Journal 95(Ap 1, 1970):1275-1280.

Anderson, Wilbert and others. Correlates of Black Clout on Community College Governance and Educational Policy Decisions, D, 1975. ERIC ED 124 239. [Los Angeles]

"Anglo Racism at UCLA." La Raza, Je 7, 1968.

Anthony, Earl. The Time of the Furnaces: A Case Study of Black Student Revolt. New York: Dial, 1971. [San Fernando Valley State College]

Anton, Anatol. "SF State Strike: New Turn in Movement." Guardian, D 28, 1968.

Aptheker, Bettina. "Berkeley's Meddlesome Regents." Nation 211(S 7, 1970):169-173. [U. of California, Berkeley]

"Asian American Students Association. Long Beach State Campus." Gidra 5(D, 1973):21-23.

Barlow, William, and Shapiro, Peter. An End to Silence: The San Francisco State Student Movement. Indianapolis, IN: Bobbs-Merrill, 1971.

Becker, Tamar. "Black Africans and Black Americans on An American Campus: The African View." Sociology and Social Research 57 (Ja, 1973):168-181. [U.C.L.A.]

Belanger, Lawrence L. "Educational Opportunities Program at U.C.L.A." California Education, O, 1965.

Berg, Ernest H., and Axtell, Dayton. Programs for Disadvantaged Students in the California Community Colleges. Oakland, Ca: Peralta Junior College District, 1968, 97 pp. ERIC ED 026 032.

Bergman, Arlene Eisen. "Terrorism and Reform." The Movement, F, 1969. [College of San Mateo]

Bess, Robert O. Annual Report on Educational Opportunity Programs 1970. Prepared for the Joint Legislative Budget Committee. Los Angeles: Office of the Chancellor, California State Colleges, N, 1970.

Billingsley, Andrew, Davidson, Douglas, and Soya, Theresa. "Ethnic Studies at Berkeley." California Monthly 80(Je-Jl, 1970):12-20.

Black Student Union. The Struggle for a School of Black Studies. Los Angeles: B.S.U., California State College at Los Angeles, 1969.

Black Students Union, Merritt College. "A Strike for Self-Determination." Black Panther, F 6, 1971. [Oakland]

Black Students' Union, Stanford University. "Stanford's B.S.U. Exposes University Lackey." Black Panther, Je 12, 1971.

Blake, J. Herman. "The Agony and the Rage." Negro Digest, Mr, 1967. [Racism at the U. of California, Berkeley]

Brann, James. "San Jose: The Bullhorn Message." Nation, N 6, 1967. [Racial discrimination at San Jose State College]

Brown, Rick. "The Limits of Student-Faculty Alliance." Liberation, Je, 1970. [U. of California, Berkeley]

Bruce, Beverly E. "A Comparative Analysis of Graduate Achievement at the University of California, San Diego." Integrateducation 15 (Jl-Ag, 1977).

Bunzel, John H. "Costs of the Politicized College." Educational Record, Spring, 1969. [San Francisco State College]

_____. "Black Studies at San Francisco State College." Public Interest, S, 1968.

_____. "The Faculty Strike at San Francisco State College." AAUP Bulletin 57(S, 1971): 341-351.

_____. "'War of the Flea' at San Francisco State." New York Times Magazine, N 9, 1969.

Cahn, Meyer M. "The 1968-1969 San Francisco State College Crisis: A Minority Report." Phi Delta Kappan, S, 1969.

California Community Colleges. Racial and Ethnic Survey, Fall, 1973..., Jl, 1974. ERIC ED 099 071.

California, Legislature, Assembly, Subcommittee on Post-Secondary Education. Unequal Access to College, Postsecondary Opportunities and Choices of High School Graduates. Sacramento: The Legislature, 1975.

California State Coordinating Council for Higher Education. Through the Open Door: A Study of Persistence and Performance in California's Community Colleges. Report 1: Sources and Selected Characteristics of Students. Report 2: 32,000 Students in 32 Colleges, Je and O, 1973. ERIC ED 086 286-7.

_____. Through the Open Door. A Study of Persistence and Performance in California's Community Colleges. Report 3: The Other Side of Persistence, F, 1974. ERIC ED 121 393.

California State Postsecondary Education Commission. Equal Educational Opportunity in California Postsecondary Education, Part II, Je, 1977. ERIC ED 143 290.

Carter, Thomas B. "Can Colleges Survive a Militant Attack?" Wall Street Journal, N 27, 1968. [San Francisco State College]

_____. "San Francisco State Wonders If Education Can Go On Amid Strife." Wall Street Journal, F 13, 1969.

Chancellor's Minority Affairs Committee. "The Pattern and Practice of Discrimination Against Minorities at the University of California, Irvine--Interim Report." In U.S. Congress, 93rd, 2nd session, House of Representatives, Committee on Education and Labor, Special Subcommittee on Education, Federal Higher Education Programs, Institutional Eligibility. Hearings..., Part 2A, pp. 266-271. Washington, DC: GPO, 1975.

"Chicano Commencement." El Grito, Summer, 1968. [Mexican-American students converge on San Jose State College for their own "commencement."]

"Chicano Liberation Commencement." La Raza, Jl 10, 1968. [Mexican-American protest demonstration on Je 14, 1968, at San Jose College in CA]

Chu, R. Majors of Chinese and Japanese Students at the University of California, Berkeley for the Past 20 Years. Berkeley, CA: Asian Studies Division, U. of California, 1971.

City College of San Francisco. Academic Characteristics of Negro Students Enrolled at City College of San Francisco. San Francisco: City College of San Francisco, 1968.

Clark, James V. "A Study of Male Socio-economically Handicapped Non-High School Graduates and their Performance in Laney and Contra Costa Colleges' Vocational Programs." Doctoral dissertation, U. of California, Berkeley, 1967. Univ. Microfilms Order No. 68-10,263.

Cole, Rick. "New Militancy Rises Among Students." Los Angeles Times, Je 21, 1978. [Occidental College]

"College of Marin...A Kernel of Racist Oppression." Black Panther, N 8, 1969.

Comptroller General of the United States. Financial Difficulties and Funding at D-Q University. Washington, DC: General Accounting Office, O 17, 1977.

"Community Unites to Save College." African World 2(F 19, 1972);12. [Merritt College, Oakland]

"Confrontation at ELAC." Inside Eastside, Ja 13, 1969. [Chicano movement at East Los Angeles College]

"Congress of Mexican-American Unity." La Raza, F 7, 1969. [Chicanos meet to nominate candidates for Los Angeles Junior College board]

Cray, Ed. "The University of Southern California: Avis on the Pacific." Change 9 (My, 1977):23-31.

Daniels, Arlene Kaplan, Kahn-Hut, Rachel and associates. Academics on the Line. The Faculty Strike at San Francisco State [College]. San Francisco: Jossey-Bass, 1970.

Davidson, Douglas. "The Furious Passage of the Black Graduate Student at the University of California, Berkeley ." Berkeley Journal of Sociology 15(1970):192-211. [See comments by Robert Blauner, Andrew Billingsley, and Clement Cottingham.]

De Anda, Jose. [Letter on discrimination in hiring of Mexican-American professors] La Raza, S 3, 1968. [The author is an Assistant Professor, Valley College, Van Nuys, CA.]

Degnan, James P. "Sympathy vs. Standards: Teaching the Underprepared." Change 8(Jl, 1976):16-19. [San Jose State College]

Didion, Joan. "The Revolution Game." Saturday Evening Post, Ja 25, 1969. [San Francisco State College]

"Double Jeopardy for Fresno State Student." African World, Jl 8, 1972. [Fresno State College, Fresno]

Draper, Anne, and Draper, Hal. The Dirt on California. Agribusiness and the University, 1968. Independent Socialist Clubs of America, P.O. Box 910, Berkeley, CA 94701.

Duerr, Edwin C. "Police on the Campus: Crisis at SFSC." Educational Record, Spring, 1969. [San Francisco State College]

DuPree, David. "Tough Black Militant Browbeats Opposition at San Francisco State." Wall Street Journal, My 15, 1969. [Jerry Varnado]

DuPree, David, and McAllister, William. "A Campus Where Black Power Won." Wall Street Journal, N 18, 1969. [Merritt College, Oakland]

Duster, Troy. "T[hird] W[orld] College and the Colonial Analogy." Daily Californian, F 20, 1969. [U. of California, Berkeley]

"East Los Angeles College Strike." La Raza, Vol 1, No. 5(1971):19-21.

"Eleven Busted, Fasting in UC Protest." El Malcriado, O 15, 1968. [Mexican-American protest at U. of California, Berkeley]

"Ethnic Studies in California: Mostly Promises, Plans." Los Angeles Times, Ap 25, 1969.

Faith, Karlene (ed.). Soledad Prison, University of the Poor: An Exchange between Students from the University of California at Santa Cruz and Prisoners at the Soledad Correctional Training Facility. Palo Alto, CA: Science and Behavior Books, 1975.

Fink, Ira Stephen and others. Faculty/Staff Survey. Vol. 3: Demographic Characteristics. Berkeley: Systemwide Administration, U. of California, 1977.

5X (Mason), Melvin. "Community Education Program Sabotaged." Muhammad Speaks, My 15, 1970. [Monterey Peninsula College, Seaside]

Finberg, Howard (ed.). San Francisco State College Crisis. San Francisco: Insight Publications, 1969.

Fleming, Paul. "Merritt College Students Fail to Participate in the Breakfast Program." Black Panther, My 25, 1969. [Oakland]

Forbes, Jack D. Racism, Scholarship and Cultural Pluralism in Higher Education, Mr, 1977. ERIC ED 139 584.

Forbes, Jack D., and Adams, Howard. A Model of "Grass-Roots" Community Development: The D-Q University Native American Language Education Project, F, 1976. ERIC ED 139 582.

Forbes, Jack D. and others. The Establishment of D-Q University: An Example of Successful Indian-Chicano Community Development, D, 1972. ERIC ED 139 581

Freedman, Mervin B. "Urban Campus Prototype." Nation, Ja 13, 1969. [San Francisco State College]

"From the Campus to the Community." Black Panther, S 9, 1972. [Reply to article by J. K. Obatala on the Black Student Unions in southern California]

Garay, Reynaldo and others. Mexican American Community Study, O, 1976. ERIC ED 138 319. [Los Angeles Harbor College]

Gerassi, John. "Revolt at S. F. State." National Guardian, D 23, 1967. [San Francisco State College]

Gitlin, Todd. "S.F. State Strike Brings Tac Squad." The Movement, D, 1968.

_____. "Strike! at S.F. State." Guardian, D 14, 1968.

Gold, Ben K. Survey of Faculty Regarding Campus Incidents of March 10-14 1969, n.d. ERIC ED 030 423. [Los Angeles City College]

Goldman, Ralph M. "Confrontation at S.F. State." Dissent, Mr-Ap, 1969.

Goodman, Mike. "Windsor U.--An Education Bitterness." Los Angeles Times, Mr 19, 1975. [Los Angeles]

Green, Wendell. "Black Students Persecuted at California College." Muhammad Speaks, Ja 9, 1970. [San Fernando Valley State College]

Greenwood, Noel. "Community Colleges: They Open Doors for Thousands." Los Angeles Times, D 9, 1973.

Haight, Maureen. "Community's Unbreakable Spirit Saves Historic Oakland College'." Muhammad Speaks, F 11, 1972. [Grove Street College, Oakland]

Halperin, Irving. "San Francisco State College Diary." Educational Record, Spring, 1969.

Hansen, Donald A., Gold, David, and Labovitz, Eugene. "Socio-Economic Inequities in College Entry: A Critical Specification." American Educational Research Journal 9(Fall, 1972): 573-590. [San Diego]

Hansen, W. L., and Weisbrod, B. A. "The Distribution of Subsidies to Students in California Public Higher Education: Reply." Journal of Human Resources 13(Winter, 1978).

Hare, Nathan. "San Francisco State A.F.T. Sellout." Black Panther, Mr 16, 1969.

Harris, Sheldon. "Meanwhile, Back in the Valley." Commonweal, My 23, 1969. [San Fernando Valley State College]

_____. "San Fernando's Black Revolt." Commonweal, Ja 31, 1969. [San Fernando State College]

Hartman, William T., and Bell, David P. "The Predictive Value of the Stanford University Admissions Rating System." College and University 53(Spring, 1978):280-290.

Haslam, Gerald. "The Young Men of Taft."
Nation, S 13, 1975. [Taft Junior College]

Heath, G. Louis. Berkeley's Educational
Opportunity Program, 1968, 11 pp. ERIC ED
041 986.

_____. "Berkeley's Ethnic Studies College."
Integrated Education, Jl-Ag, 1969.

Hekymara, Kuregiy. "The Third World Movement
and Its History in the San Francisco State
College Strike of 1968-1969." Doctoral
dissertation, U. of California, Berkeley,
1972.

Hendrix, Kathleen. "'No One Told Me I Had
Life Choices.'" Los Angeles Times, My 30,
1975. [Nancy Cohen, black student at
U.C.L.A.]

Horton, Robert E. An Educational Program for a
Junior College Located in South Central Los
Angeles, F 1, 1966. ED 010 948.

Hyde, Stuart. "College in Crisis: The Legacy
of Poor Communications." Educational/
Instructional Broadcasting, Je, 1969.
[San Francisco State College]

"The Judge." "Tam O'Shanter Fascism." The
Movement, D, 1969. [San Francisco State
College]

Karagueuzian, Dikran. Blow It Up! The Black
Student Revolt at San Francisco State
College and the Emergence of Dr. Hayakawa,
1971. Gambit, Inc., 52 Beacon Street,
Boston, MA 02108.

Katz, Jerry Martin. "The Educational
Shibboleth: Equality of Opportunity in a
Democratic Institution, the Public Junior
College." Ph.D. dissertation, Department of
Sociology, UCLA, 1967. Univ. Microfilms
Order No. 68-4461.

Klingelhofer, Edwin L. The College Opportunity
Grant Program... Sacramento, CA: California
State Scholarship and Loan Commission, D,
1970.

Lagos-Franz, Arturo A. "Graduate Admission
Profile, Fall Quarters, 1966-1972. School of
Public Health, University of California,
Los Angeles." In U.S. Congress, 93rd, 1st
session, Senate, Committee on Labor and
Public Welfare, Subcommittee on Education
and Special Subcommittee on Human Resources,
Bilingual Education, Health, and Manpower
Programs, 1973. Joint Hearing..., pp. 62-73.
Washington, DC: GPO, 1973.

Leon, David Jess. "Chicano College Dropouts and
the Educational Opportunity Program: Failure
after High School?" High School Behavioral
Science 3(F, 1975):6-11. [U. of California]

Litwak, Leo, and Wilner, Herbert. College
Drop in Earthquake Country. New York:
Random House, 1972. [San Francisco State
College]

Lopate, Carol. The College Readiness Program:
A Program for Third World Students at the
College of San Mateo, California. The Study
of Collegiate Compensatory Programs for
Minority Group Youth, N, 1969. ERIC ED 035
686.

Lopez-Lee, David. "The Academic Performance and
Attitudes Among Chicanos and Anglos in
College." Journal of Mexican American Studies
1(Spring-Summer, 1971):201-222. [California
State College, Los Angeles]

Lopez-Lee, D. and others. The Cal-State, L.A.
Chicano Student--A Study of Academic Per-
formance of E.O.P. Chicanos, Non-E.O.P.
Chicanos, and Anglos, and the Relationship of
Attitudes to Academic Performance. Los
Angeles: Educational Opportunity Program,
California State U., 1971.

Luethe, Marie. The Status of Women and Ethnic
Minorities Employed in the Libraries of the
California State University and College
System, D, 1974. ERIC ED 127 984.

"Lulacs Demands." Ideal, F 15, 1970. [Demands
that more Chicanos be admitted to state
institutions of higher education in CA]

McGuire, J. W. "The Distribution of Subsidy to
Students in California Public Higher
Education." Journal of Human Resources 11
(Summer, 1976).

Martinez, Juan. [Letter on setting up a Mexican
American Studies Institute at San Francisco
State College] Inside Eastside, O 21, 1968.

Martyn, Kenneth A. Increasing Opportunities for
Disadvantaged Students: A Preliminary
Outline. Sacramento: Joint Committee on
Higher Education, California Legislature, D,
1967.

"MASC-San Jose State College." La Raza, Ap 30,
1969.

Matthews, Connie. "Interview With Angela Davis."
Black Panther, N 1, 1969.

Mauk, Marion. "Black Studies." New Republic,
Mr 15, 1969. [San Francisco State College]

Maxwell, Martha. Remedial Education at Berkeley:
Why Do We Still Require It?, S 15, 1975.
ERIC ED 130 249.

McGuire, J. W. "The Distribution of Subsidies
to Students in California Public Higher
Education: Rejoinder." Journal of Human
Resources 13(Winter, 1978).

McEvoy, William, and Miller, Abraham. "Crisis
at San Francisco State: 'On Strike'--Shut It
Down." Trans-action, Mr, 1969.

McIntyre, Charles, and Smart, John. Financial
Assistance Programs for California College and
University Students. Sacramento: Coordinating
Council for Higher Education, 1967.

McKendall, Benjamin W., Jr. Statewide Seminar on Race and Poverty in Higher Education. Palo Alto, CA: College Entrance Examination Board, 1968.

Melendrez, Gilbert, Spuck, Dennis W., Lowman, Robert P., Doggett, Kathy M., and Banks, Samantha. A Proposed Model for PSDS Admissions, Ja, 1967. Center for Educational Opportxnity, 1009 North College Ave., Claremont, CA 91711. [Program of Special Directed Studies for Transition to College, Claremont Colleges]

Mendel, Ed. "SSU Fails With Minorities." Sacramentao Union, F 7, 1977. [Nurse-training courses in California, especially Sacramento State U.]

Merrill, Preston, and Spears, John. "3rd World Student Drive Accelerating." Muhammad Speaks, F 14, 1969. [U. of California, Berkeley]

Miner, Valerie Jane. Nairobi College: Education for Relevance; One Interpretation of the Community Service Function, D, 1969. ERIC ED 038 131. [East Palo Alto]

Miranda, Tony, Crutchfield, Nesbit, Wong, Mason, and Pifare, Juan. "Strike Over But Struggle Goes On." Movement, My, 1969. [Third World Liberation Front leaders at San Francisco State College]

Miramon, Dan. "MASA Speaks at Garfield." Inside/Eastside, D 23, 1968. [Mexican-American Student Association of East Los Angeles College]

Moellering, Ralph L. "Impasse on California's Academic Scene." Christian Century, F 26, 1969.

Mulherin, Kathy. "California's Academic Fault." Commonweal, My 23, 1969.

Napper, George. Blacker Than Thou: The Struggle for Campus Unity. Grand Rapids, MI: Eerdmans, 1973. [U. of California, Berkeley]

N.A.A.C.P. "The University of California: Impending Lawsuit?" Integrated Education (N-D, 1973):40-43.

Native Americans in Higher Education, 1973. Native American Studies, California State U., Hayward, Hayward, CA 94542.

Negrete, Louis R. Chicano Studies and Rio Hondo College, 1973. ERIC ED 077 483.

"The New Rage at Berkeley." Newsweek, Je 2, 1969. [Student criticism of Professor Arthur Jensen]

Nicolaus, Martin. "S.F. State. History Takes a Leap." The Movement, F, 1969. [San Francisco State College]

"No Seal of Approval." La Raza, N 9, 1969. [California State College at Los Angeles]

Orrick, William H., Jr. Shut It Down! A College in Crisis. Washington, DC: GPO, 1969. [San Francisco State College]

Oskamp, Stuart and others. Effects of a Compensatory College Education Program for the Disadvantaged: A Further Report, Ap 15, 1970. ERIC ED 041 973.

Padilla, Raymond V. "Chicano Studies at the University of California, Berkeley: En Busca del Campus y la Communidad." Doctoral dissertation, U. of California, Berkeley, 1974.

Paris, Richard, and Brown, Janet (eds.). The Sayings of Chairman Hayakawa. San Francisco: American Federation of Labor Local 1928, 1969.

Parker, Mike, and Urquhart, Mike. "The Berkeley Strike." Independent Socialist, Ap, 1969.

Parmalee, Patty Lou. "Legal Terror Tested at Coast College." Guardian, O 11, 1969. [San Fernando Valley State College]

Pearce, Frank C. A Study of Academic Success of College Readiness Students at the College of San Mateo. San Mateo, CA: San Mateo College, 1968, 42 pp. ERIC ED 019 956.

Pechman, Joseph. "The Distributional Effects of Public Higher Education in California." Journal of Human Resources 5(1970):361-370.

Penney, Brooks. "The Battle for S.F. State." The Movement, Ja, 1968.

Pentony, DeVere E. "A Comment on Our Situation at San Francisco State College." College Composition and Communication, D, 1968.

People's Committee for Defense of Merritt. "Merritt Plantation or People's University?" Black Panther, D 5, 1970. [Merritt Community College, Oakland]

Pinkerton, W. Stewart, Jr. "Chancellor of U.C.L.A. Goes to Students When Trouble Appears." Wall Street Journal, Ap 23, 1969.

Pinkus, Mike. "Is Chico Next?" Leviathan, Mr, 1969. [Chico State College]

Pittman, John. "Negroes Challenge the Jackboot in San Francisco." Freedomways, Winter, 1967.

Putnam, Catherine E. "Examination of Equality of Educational Opportunity for Chicanos in California Public Higher Education." Doctoral dissertation, Stanford U., 1978. Univ. Microfilms Order No. 7822561.

"R.D.C. Helps Migrants." Ideal, Mr 1, 1970. [Rural Development Corporation arranges for students at the University of Southern California Dental School to donate services in Indio, CA]

Rawitch, R. "Merrill College's Negro Leader Faces Broad Racial Challenge." Los Angeles Times, S 8, 1968. [President Norvel Smith, Oakland]

Rayford, Deniese D. "Faculty-Student Unrest at San Francisco State College and the Black Studies Issue of 1968-1969." Master's thesis, Atlanta U., 1976.

Reich, Kenneth. "Angela Davis--Is She More Red Than Black?" Black Politician, Ja, 1970.

Reid, Albin Elwell, Jr. "A History of the California Public Junior College Movement." Doctoral dissertation, U. of Southern California, 1970.

"Report on Special Admissions at Boalt Hall After Baake." Journal of Legal Education 28 (1977):363-402. [Law school of the U. of California, Berkeley]

Rogers, Joe. "The California Campus Crisis Underlines Need for Reform." New America, Mr 20, 1969.

Rogers, Ray. "Black Guns on Campus." Nation, My 5, 1969. [U.C.L.A.]

Rose, Clare, and Nyre, Glenn F. Access and Assistance: The Study of EOP/OEPS in California's Institutions of Higher Education, 2 vols., 1977. Evaluation and Training Institute, 1110 Ohio Avenue, Suite 202, Los Angeles, CA 90025.

_____ and _____. "Study of Extended Opportunity Programs and Services in California Community Colleges." Community/ Junior College Research Quarterly 2(Ja-Mr, 1978):139-150.

Rothbart, George S. "The Legitimation of In- equality: Objective Scholarship vs. Black Militancy." Sociology of Education 43 (Spring, 1970):159-174. [San Francisco State College]

Rubenstein, Bonnie. "Coming of Age in Black- ness." Integrated Education, Ja-F, 1969, pp. 59-68. [Merritt College, Oakland]

St. Augustine Community Workers. "An Open Letter to the B.S.U. at Laney College, Oakland." Black Panther, D 14, 1970.

Sable, Alan. "Facing Some Contradictions: My Experience as a White Professor Teaching Minority Students." In Studies in Socialist Pedagogy, pp. 335-350. Edited by Theodore Mills Norton and Bertell Ollman. New York: Monthly Review Press, 1978. [U. of California, Santa Cruz]

Sammon, Peter J. "Semanticist Spreads Dismay at San Francisco State." National Catholic Reporter, Je 25, 1969.

Sammson, Acre X. "Nairobi College President Unsure About Getting Institution Off the Ground." Muhammad Speaks, D 5, 1969. [East Palo Alto]

Sanders, J. Edward, and Palmer, Hans C. The Financial Barriers to Higher Education in California. Claremont, CA: Pomona College, 1965.

Semas, Philip W. "One Year After the Strike, 'Burned-Out' Mood Afflicts San Francisco State." Chronicle of Higher Education, Ja 26, 1970.

Sereseres, César. [Statement on discrimination at the University of California] U.S. Congress, 93rd, 2nd session, House of Representatives, Committee on Education and Labor, Special Subcommittee on Education, Federal Higher Education Programs Institu- tional Eligibility. Hearings..., Part 2A, pp. 255-266. Washington, DC: GPO, 1975.

Shapiro, Peter, and Barlow, Bill. "San Franciso State, Business As Usual." Leviathan, Ap, 1969.

Shired, Carter S. The Formulation, Progress, and Development of Oakland Inner City Project. The Peralta Colleges. Oakland, CA: Peralta Junior College District, O, 1969.

Sievert, William A. "Black Students, White Town: Tense Taft Hunts Solutions." Chronicle of Higher Education, N 24, 1975. [Taft College]

Singleton, Rebecca S., and Myers, Leland W. Educational Opportunity Programs in California Public Higher Education, 1969-70. Sacramento, CA: Coordinating Council for Higher Education, Ap, 1971.

Singleton, Robert, and Dawson, Ralph. Blacks and Public Higher Education in California, 1973. ERIC ED 077 316.

Sklarewitz, Norman. "Stanford Fails to Win Approval of Militants With Pioneer Program." Wall Street Journal, Je 11, 1969.

Smelser, Neil, and Almond, Gabriel (eds.). Public Higher Education in California. Berkeley, CA: U. of California Press, 1974.

Smith, Julie. "A 'Vanishing American' Fights Back." San Francisco Chronicle, Je 10, 1969, Navajo Times, Jl 3, 1969 (reprint). [La Nada Means, a Bannock-Shoshone Indian, a student at the U. of California, Berkeley]

Smith, Robert. "San Francisco State College Experience." In Agony and Promise. Edited by G. Kerry Smith. San Francisco: Jossey- Bass, 1969.

Smith, Robert, Axen, Richard, and Pentony, De Vere. By Any Means Necessary. The Revolutionary Struggle at San Francisco State [College]. San Francisco: Jossey-Bass, 1970.

Spears, Larry. "Nation's First Indian-Chicano School to Open Doors March 1." Oakland (California) Tribune. Reprinted in Akwesasne Notes, Mr, 1971. [Deganawidah-Quetzalcoatl U., Davis, CA]

_____. "New Phase in U.C.'s Black Studies Division." Oakland Tribune, Ag 13, 1972. [U. of California, Berkeley]

Speich, Don. "Dilemma--the Hiring of Angela Davis." Los Angeles Times, N 3, 1975. [Claremont College]

_____. "11 State University-College Officials in Private Clubs." Los Angeles Times, Jl 31, 1978.

Spuck, Dennis W. Environmental Expectations and Perceptions Among College Freshmen, Mr, 1970. Center for Educational Opportunity, 1009 North College Avenue, Claremont, CA 91711.

_____. Pre-Test/Post-Test Analysis for 1968-1969 PSDS Students, F, 1970. Center for Educational Opportunity, 1009 North College Avenue, Claremont, CA 91711. Program of Special Directed Studies for Transition to College, Claremont Colleges

Strike at Frisco State! The Story Behind It, 1969. Research Organizing Cooperative (ROC), 330 Grove Street, San Francisco, CA 94102.

Stringer, Patricia. "White Teacher, Black Campus." Change 6(N, 1974):27-31. [Fort Valley State College]

Summerskill, John. President Seven. New York: World, 1971. [San Francisco State College]

Sung, Susan San-San Chu. "Racial-Ethnic Identity: An Asian Perspective." Doctoral dissertation, U. of California, Berkeley, 1977. Univ. Microfilms Order No. 77-31263. [U. of California, Berkeley]

Telander, Rick. "School of Soft Knocks." Sports Illustrated, Je, 1977. [Pepperdine U.]

Trombley, William. "Medical Dean Aids 'Special Interest' Applicants." Los Angeles Times, Jl 5, 1975. [U. of California, Davis]

_____. "Pepperdine U. Torn by Tragedy, Internal Dissent." Los Angeles Times, Ap 18, 1976.

_____. "Toward an Educated Proletariat: California State Colleges." Change 3(N, 1971):40-43, 46. [California state colleges]

"UMAS-UCLA." La Raza, Ap 30, 1969. [UCLA, CA]

University of California. Beyond High School Graduation: Who Goes to College? A Report on a University of California Survey of the High School Class of '75. Berkeley, CA: Office of Outreach Services, U. of California Systemwide Administration, My, 1978.

_____. U.C. and the Public Schools, 1968. Office of University Relations, 101 University Hall, Berkeley, CA 94720.

University of California, Berkeley. Task Force on Undergraduate Admissions. Final Report, Mr, 1977. ERIC ED 136 648.

Urquhart, Mike. "State of Emergency." Independent Socialist, Mr, 1969. [Protest movements at California colleges and universities]

"La Vida Nueva at ELAC." La Raza, Ja 1, 1969. [List of demands of Chicano students at East Los Angeles College]

Waits, Marilyn. "Soul on Campus." Communities in Action, F, 1969. [About John Buchanan, president, Black Student Union at Los Angeles City College]

Wald, Karen. "SF State In Turmoil." Guardian, Je 1, 1968.

Wallace, Ruby and others. Myth Exposed: Academically Deficient Students Gain 2.3 Grade Equivalents in Only One Semester at a 96% Black Inner-City Community College..., My 11, 1978. ERIC ED 157 570. [Los Angeles Southwest College]

Washington, Kenneth R., and Bess, Robert O. "Minority Group Pressures in a Statewide System." In Donald R. Gerth, James O. Haehn and Associates, An Invisible Giant. The California State Colleges. San Francisco: Jossey-Bass, 1971.

Widmer, Kingsley. "Why the Colleges Blew Up." Nation, F 24, 1969.

Williams, Randy. "A Winding Trail to College." Christian Science Monitor, N 10, 1975. [Tlingit student at California State U., San Jose]

Wilson, Claude E. "Student Describes State Government Attacks on San Francisco State Student Body." Muhammad Speaks, My 16, 1969.

Yoshioka, Robert B. and others. Asian-Americans and Public Higher Education in California, 1973. ERIC ED 077 315.

Colorado

"The Air Force Academy Blows Its Mind." Ebony 27(Mr, 1972):33-42.

Beck, Paul and others. "Recruitment and Retention Program for Minority and Disadvantaged Students." Journal of Medical Education 53 (Ag, 1978):651-657. [U. of Colorado Medical Center]

Boras, Jacqueline. "U.S. Air Force Academy Seeks to Increase Minority Enrollment." LNESC Newsletter 3(My-Je, 1977. [Published by LULAC National Educational Service Centers, Inc.]

Cottle, Thomas J. "Run to Freedom: Chicanos and Higher Education." Change 4(F, 1972): 34-41. [Adams State College]

Gallegos, Samuel, Jr. "Academic Survival and Performance of United Mexican American Students in the Equal Opportunity Program at the University of Colorado in Boulder." Doctoral dissertation, U. of Northern Colorado, 1975. Univ. Microfilms Order No. 75-23,310.

Glenn, Cecil Evans. "A Study of the Self-Concept of Black University Students at the University of Colorado at Denver." Doctoral dissertation, U. of Colorado at Boulder, 1976. Univ. Microfilms Order No. 76-23613.

Guralnick, Elissa S. "The New Segregation: A Recent History of EOP at the University of Colorado, Boulder." College English 39(Ap, 1978):964-974.

Jacobson, Robert L. "The University and the D.A." Chronicle of Higher Education, Mr 7, 1977. [U. of Southern Colorado, Pueblo]

Kinsey, Mary Ann. "Indian Education at Fort Lewis College, Durango, Colorado." Doctoral dissertation, U. of Tennessee, 1975.

McWilliams, Alfred E., Jr. A Follow-Up Study of Academically Talented Black High School Students. U. of Northern Colorado, 1970. [Denver]

Machovec, F. M. "Public Higher Education in Colorado: Who Pays the Costs? Who Receives the Benefits?" Intermountain Economic Review 3(Fall, 1972).

Mason, Peter F. "Some Characteristics of a Youth Ghetto in Boulder, Colorado." Journal of Geography 71(D, 1972):526-540. [U. of Colorado]

Million, Guy P. "Manpower Training Goes to College." American Education 6(N, 1970): 23-25. [Community College of Denver, CO]

Moya, Frank. "Equal Opportunity Plan Change Causes CU Furor." Rocky Mountain News, Mr 20, 1977. [Minority students at the U. of Colorado, Boulder]

Parsons, Paul J. "A Study of Values of Spanish-surname Undergraduate College Students at Five State Colleges in Colorado." Diss. Abstr. Int'l., Vol. 31 (8-A) 3883-4.

Poinsett, Alex. "Colorado University's Chancellor." Ebony 32(Ja, 1977):58-66. [Dr. Mary F. Berry, black woman chancellor of U. of Colorado, Boulder]

Rainer, Ann. "The 'Intercultural Program' at Fort Lewis College." United Scholarship Service News, Jl, 1969. [Durango]

"U.M.A.S.--C.U.D.C." El Gallo, Je-Jl, 1969. [Chicano students at U. of Colorado, Denver Center]

Connecticut

A Group of Faculty Members at the University of Connecticut "Racism Exposed by UConn Faculty." UAG Magazine 1(Summer, 1972):11-26.

Abel, Emily K. Social Equality in Mass Higher Education: Connecticut Community College, N, 1974. ERIC ED 100 427.

Bourne-Vanneck, Richard P. "Toward Another World: A West Indian at Yale." Crisis 81 (F, 1974):43-46.

Brooks, Peter. "Panthers at Yale." Partisan Review 37(1970):420-439.

Brustein, Robert. "When the Panther Came to Yale." New York Times Magazine, Je 21, 1970.

Du Bois, W. E. B. [Article on Yale University] Amsterdam News, My 16, 1942. [See, also, issue of Je 27, 1942]

_____. [On Vassar and Yale] Pittsburgh Courier, My 16, 1942.

Fleming, Macklin, and Pollak, Louis. "The Black Quota at Yale Law School: An Exchange of Letters. Public Interest, Spring, 1970.

"Freedom of Expression at Yale." AAUP Bulletin 62(Ap, 1976):28-42.

Higa, Ellen. "The Half Closed Lotus Blossom." In Asian Women, pp. 60-61, 1971. c/o 3405 Dwinelle Hall, U. of California, Berkeley, CA 94720. [Asian student at Yale]

Lyons, James E. "A Survey of Black Connecticut High School Graduates Attending Out-of-State Colleges and Universities." Journal of Negro Education 43(Fall, 1974):506-511.

Margolis, Richard J. "The Two Nations at Wesleyan University." New York Times Magazine, Ja 18, 1970. [Middletown]

Needs: Socio-Economic, Manpower, Regional;
Report of Task Force I to the Connecticut
Commission for Higher Education. Hartford,
CT: Connecticut Commission for Higher
Education, D, 1970, 92 pp. ERIC ED 048 836.

"On Being Black at Yale." Yale Alumni Magazine,
My, 1969.

Resnick, Ruth. "Black Protest at U-Conn."
Jewish Currents, D, 1969. [U. of
Connecticut]

Ross, Calvin, and Swick, Kevin. "An Explana-
tory Study in the Development of Positive
Changes in Student-Teacher Attitudes toward
Inner-City Teaching." Education and Urban
Society, N, 1969. [U. of Connecticut]

Seals, Ted. "Boola-Boola, or God and the Black
Man At Yale." Chicago Courier, N 3, 1973.

Sharon, Amiel T. Effectiveness of Remediation
in Junior College. Princeton, NJ: Educational Testing Service, S, 1970.

Stetler, Henry G. New Study of College Admission Practices with Respect to Race,
Religion, and National Origin. Hartford,
CT: Connecticut Commission on Civil Rights,
1953. [Connecticut high school graduates]

Synnott, Marcia G. The Half-Opened Door: Discrimination and Admissions at Harvard, Yale,
and Princeton, 1900-1970. Westport, CT:
Greenwood, 1979.

U.S. Congress, 94th, 2nd session, House of
Representatives, Committee on Merchant
Marine and Fisheries. Nondiscriminatory
Appointment of Cadets to the Coast Guard
Academy. Washington, DC: GPO, 1976.

"Yale Men: Historic University Has More than
100 Negro Alumni, Record Total of 33
Colored Students." Ebony, Jl, 1950.

Delaware

Glickstein, Don. "Deseg Pioneer Remembers."
Delaware State News, Ag 1, 1976. [Homer
Minus' attempt to register in the U. of
Delaware, 1950]

Satneck, Walter J. "The History of the
Origins and Development of the Delaware
State College and Its Role in Higher Educa-
tion for Negroes in Delaware." Doctoral
dissertation, New York U., 1962. Univ.
Microfilms Order No. 63-5380.

District of Columbia

Asbury, Charles A. "The Proven Effectiveness
of Black Graduate Schools" (letter).
Chronicle of Higher Education, Ap 25, 1977.
[Howard U.]

Astin, Helen, and Bisconti, Ann. "Higher
Education and the Community: The Role of
Eleven D.C. Area Institutions of Higher
Education in Alleviating Urban Problems,"
Appendix B in The Role of College-Community
Relationships in Urban Higher Education,
Vol. III, A Community Survey of Washington,
D.C., Mr, 1969. ERIC ED 041 570.

Barnes, Andrew. "Howard University."
Washington Post, My 14, 1972.

Bims, Hamilton. "Charles Drew's 'Other'
Medical Revolution." Ebony 29(F, 1974):88-
97. [Medical school, Howard U.]

"Black Student Power." National Review, Ap 9,
1968. [Howard U.]

Bloomfield, Maxwell. "John Mercer Langston and
the Rise of Howard Law School." Records of
the Columbia Historical Society of Washington,
D.C. 1971-1972 48(1973):421-438.

Characteristics of Inner City Students at
American University. Washington, DC:
American U., 1969, 58 pp. ERIC ED 028 737.

Chisholm, Anne. "Howard [University]: Making
Black More Beautiful." Times Higher Education Supplement, S 7, 1973.

Cohn, Victor. "U.S.-Run Medical School Has One
Black." Washington Post, N 1, 1976. [The
military U. of Health Sciences, D.C.]

Cole, Babalola. "Appropriation Politics and
Black Schools: Howard University in the
U.S. Congress, 1879-1928." Journal of Negro
Education 46(Winter, 1977):7-23.

"A College Beset by Black Revolutionaries."
U.S. News and World Report, My 12, 1969.
[Federal City College]

Cummings, Judith. "Return to Howard: The
Turbulent 60's Seem Long Ago." New York
Times, N 16, 1975.

Daniel, A. Mercer. "The Law Library of Howard
University, 1867-1956." Law Library Journal
51(1958).

De Graf, Lawrence B. "Howard: The Evolution of
Black Student Revolt." In Protest: Student
Activism in America. Edited by Julian Foster
and Durward Low. New York: Morrow, 1970.

Delaney, William. "The Big Debate at Howard
U." Washington Evening Star-News, D 6, 1972.

De Witt, Karen. "Big Business Occupies the Ivy
Tower at Howard." Black Enterprise 5(Mr,
1975):49-54.

_____. "The Howard Heritage 1976." Washington
Post, F 22, 1976. [Howard U.]

Dixon, Blase. "The Catholic University of
America and the Racial Question, 1914-1948."
Rec. Am. Cath. Hist. Soc. Philadelphia 84
(D, 1973):221-224.

Dorsey-Young, Flora. "Value Socialization of the Black Physician: The Howard University College of Medicine--A Case Study." Doctoral dissertation, U. of Pennsylvania, 1978. Univ. Microfilms Order No. 7815956.

Dreyfuss, Joel. "Coming Home to Howard." Washington Post, O 26, 1974. [Campus atmosphere at Howard U., 1966 and 1974]

Dyson, Walter. The Founding of Howard University. Washington, DC: Howard U., 1921.

Eboine, Alvin, and Meenes, Max. "Ethnic and Class Preferences Among College Negroes." Journal of Negro Education 29(1960):128-132. [Howard U.]

"Federal City College--History of Struggle." African World 4(My, 1975):5.

Feinberg, Lawrence. "D.C. Public Colleges' Record Spotty." Washington Post, Je 27, 1977.

Fried, Joshua. "A White Face in a Black College." Jewish Currents 25(Ap, 1971): 21-23. [Howard U.]

Hare, Nathan. "Final Reflections on A 'Negro' College: A Case Study." Negro Digest, Mr, 1968. [Howard U.]

Hatter, Henrietta Roberts. "History of Miner Teachers College." Master's thesis, Howard U., 1939.

Hazen, H. H. "Twenty-three Years of Teaching in a Negro Medical School." Social Forces 12(1933):570-575. [Howard U.]

Hinchiff, William E. "Urban Problems and Higher Education: Federal City College." Wilson Library Bulletin, F, 1969.

Hoar, George Frisbie Hoar. The Opportunity of the Colored Leader. An Address to the Law Class of Howard University, 1894. Washington, DC: Howard U. Press, 1894.

Horowitz, Laura Godofsky. "A New College With a City View." Southern Education Report, My, 1969. [Federal City College]

"Howard Law Dean Explains Resignation..." Muhammad Speaks, Mr 14, 1969.

"Howard Students Reject Cutbacks." African World, N 30, 1974.

Hurston, Zora Neal. "The Hue and Cry About Howard University." Messenger 7(S, 1925): 315-319, 338.

Jacoby, Susan. "In Search for a Black Identity." Saturday Review, Ap 20, 1968. [Howard U.]

Jamison, Andrew. "Community College for the Capital." Harvard Crimson, O 19, 1968. [Federal City College]

Jeffery, David. "Up Front at Foggy Bottom." GW (George Washington University Magazine), Ag, 1969. [Student protest at George Washington U., Washington, DC]

Johnson, Mac Arlene. "The Typical College Youth at Howard." Howard Hilltop, Ap 10, 1925.

Kashif, Lonnie. "D.C. City College Begins Community Involvement Test." Muhammad Speaks, O 25, 1968.

_____. "Dental Students Charge 'Black Elitism' at Howard." Muhammad Speaks, F 21, 1975.

_____. "Howard Showdown Spells New Student Dynamics." Muhammad Speaks, My 23, 1969.

_____. "Howard Students Protest Congressional 'Threat.'" Muhammad Speaks, F 22, 1974.

_____. "Howard University Medical School Target of Boycott." Muhammad Speaks, F 21, 1969.

_____. "Howard University Law School Emptied in Wake of Determined Student Protest." Muhammad Speaks, Mr 7, 1969.

_____. "Howard University President Blasts Forced College Integration Scheme." Muhammad Speaks, O 5, 1973.

_____. "New Trends Coming in Black Studies." Muhammad Speaks, Je 27, 1969. [Federal City College]

_____. "Students Continue Thrust Despite Threat by NAACP." Muhammad Speaks, F 7, 1969. [Federal City College and Howard U. in Washington, DC]

_____. "Tony Brown 'Black Journal' Producer Resigns Howard University Position." Muhammad Speaks, D 28, 1973.

_____. "'Unnoticed' Student Protest Plows On at Howard University." Muhammad Speaks, My 9, 1969. [School of Social Work]

_____. "Washington D.C. Muslim Graduates Enter Local Universities, Students Excel." Muhammad Speaks, O 9, 1970.

Lloyd, Sterling M., Jr. and others. "Survey of Graduates of a Traditionally Black College of Medicine." Journal of Medical Education 53(Ag, 1978):640-650. [Howard U. School of Medicine]

Logan, Rayford W. Howard University: The First Hundred Years, 1867-1967. New York: New York U. Press, 1969.

Lowe, Gilbert A., Jr., and McDowell, Sophia F. "Participant-Nonparticipant Differences in the Howard University Student Protest." Journal of Negro Education 40(Winter, 1971): 81-90. [Action of Mr, 1968]

Malson, Robert A. "The Black Power Rebellion at Howard University." Negro Digest, D, 1967.

Mathews, John, and Holsendolph, Ernest. "When Black Students Take Over a Campus." New Republic, Ap 11, 1968. [Howard U.]

McDowell, Sophia F. and   . "Howard University's Student Protest Movement." Public Opinion Quarterly 34(Fall, 1970):383-388.

Miles, Michael. "Colonialism on the Black Campus." New Republic, Ag 5, 1967. [Howard U.]

Miller, Kelly. Address to the Graduating Class of the College Department, Howard University. Washington, DC, 1898.

Miller, Stephen S. "The Emergence of Comprehensive Public Higher Education in the District of Columbia: The Establishment of Federal City College." Doctoral dissertation, Catholic U. of America, 1977.

Mortimer, Kingsley E. "The Melanoblasts of Fate: Aspects and Attitudes at the 'Black Harvard.'" Journal of the National Medical Association 60(S, 1968):357-365. [Howard U.]

Murray, Pauli. "A Blueprint for First Class Citizenship." Crisis, N, 1944. [Howard U.]

Nichols, David C. "Federal City College, a Model for New Urban Universities." In Land-Grant Universities and their Continuing Challenge. Edited by G. Lester Anderson. East Lansing, MI: Michigan State U. Press, 1976.

"'No Haven for Black Elite at Howard U.'" African World 4(My, 1975):4.

Nordlie, Peter G. and others. The Role of College-Community Relationships in Urban Higher Education. Volume II, A Study of Federal City College. Final Report. Washington, DC: Federal City College, Mr, 1969, 271 pp. ERIC ED 041 571.

Office of Institutional Research. Students at Federal City College, Ja, 1976. ERIC ED 124 078.

Poinsett, Alex. "The Metamorphosis of Howard University." Ebony 27(D, 1971):110-122.

Prince, Richard E. "Problems Exceed Solutions." Washington Post, My 16, 1973. [Federal City College]

Randolph, Harland A. and others. The Role of College-Community Relationships in Urban Higher Education. Volume I, Project Summary and Overview. Final Report. Washington, DC: Federal City College, Mr, 1969, 60 pp. ERIC ED 041 569.

Ribsby, Gregory U. "Afro-American Studies at Howard University: One Year Later." Journal of Negro Education 39(Summer, 1970):209-213.

Roberts, Wallace. "Prospects for the Common College." Change, N-D, 1969. [Federal City College]

Rogers, Cornish. "Black Students' Identity Crisis." Christian Century 89(Je 28, 1972): 705-706. [Conference, "Black Spirituality on college campuses," Howard U.]

Scully, Malcolm G. "After a Year of Crises, Federal City College Drops Experiments for Traditional Forms." Chronicle of Higher Education, O 27, 1969.

_____. "Black Studies Plan Sparks Bitter Debate at Federal City College." Chronicle of Higher Education, Mr 24, 1969.

Shackelford, Laurel, and Movitz, Deborah. "High Risk for Higher Education." Civil Rights Digest, Summer, 1969. [George Washington U.]

Sievert, William A. "A New U. in D.C." Chronicle of Higher Education, My 1, 1978. [U. of the District of Columbia]

Stanfiel, James D. "A Profile of the 1972 Freshman Class at Howard University." Journal of Negro Education 45(Winter, 1976): 61-69.

Steif, William. "Federal City College: Will It Become the Prototype for Black Institutions?" College and University Business, F, 1969.

_____. "A New Curriculum for Blacks." Change 2(N-D, 1970):19-22. [Institute for Services to Education]

Sumner, Francis C. "Mental Health Statistics of Negro College Freshmen." School and Society 33(Ap 25, 1931):874-876.

Swanson, David. "First Year at Federal City College." Nation, My 12, 1969.

Taylor, William E. "Howard University Law School. Its History and Present Rating." New York Age, Ag 10, 1935, p. 10.

Thompson, Charles H. "Socio-economic Status of Negro College Students." Journal of Negro Education 2(Ja, 1933):26-37.

Tinker, Irene. "The Unprepared College Student." American Education 6(N, 1970):10-12. [Federal City College]

Trescott, Jacqueline. "Freedmen's: New Home and Name, Continuing Commitment." Washington Post, Mr 2, 1975. [Howard U. Hospital, formerly Freedmen's Hospital, Washington, DC]

Trescott, Jacqueline, and Hendrickson, Paul. "What Happened to the Howard Class of '68?" Washington Post, My 15, 1978.

U.S. Congress, 89th, 2nd session, House of Representatives, Committee on the District of Columbia, Subcommittee No. 4. Authorizing a Public Community College of Arts and Sciences and a Public Vocational Technical College. Washington, DC: GPO, 1966.

U.S. Congress, 90th, 1st session, Senate, Committee on the District of Columbia, Subcommittee on Public Health, Education, Welfare, and Safety. Authorization of Land-Grant College for the District of Columbia. Hearings. Washington, DC: GPO, 1967.

U.S. Congress, 90th, 2nd session, House of Representatives, Committee on the District of Columbia, Subcommittee No. 5. Federal City College as a Land Grant College. Washington, DC: GPO, 1968.

U.S. Congress, 93rd, 2nd session, Senate, Committee on the District of Columbia. University Creation from Existing Institutions. Hearing... Washington, DC: GPO, 1974. [Proposed creation of U. of the District of Columbia]

Wentworth, Eric. "Higher Education: The Reach Exceeds the Grasp." In The Federal Social Dollar in Its Own Back Yard. Edited by Sar A. Levitan, 1973. Bureau of National Affairs, 1231 25th Street, N.W., Washington, DC 20037.

_____. "The Joe Paige Story." Washington Post, Jl 22, 1973.

Whitaker, Joseph D. "Howard Names New Law Dean." Washington Post, D 6, 1977.

"Why a Student Strike?" Baltimore Afro-American, F 28, 1925. [Howard U.]

Florida

Alternatives to the Board of Regents' De-segregation Plan. Tallahassee: United Faculty of Florida, 1976. [Florida A & M U., Tallahassee]

Arocha, Zita. "Study Determines State Schools Still Mostly Segregated." Tampa Times, Ag 9, 1977. [Segregation of public higher education]

Bennett, Sister M., O.S.F. "A Negro University and a Nun." Community, Mr, 1966. [Florida A & M U.]

Bridges, Edgar F. "Consequences of Florida's University Admission Policies on Black and White Entering Freshmen (1975-1976)." Doctoral dissertation, Florida State U., 1978. Univ. Microfilms Order No. 78-15445.

Carelton, William G. "The South's Many Moods." Yale Review, Summer, 1966. [Touches on integration at the U. of Florida]

Cohen, Arthur M. "Miami-Dade Junior College: A Study in Racial Integration." Doctoral dissertation, Florida State U., 1964. Univ. Microfilms Order No. 64-10584.

_____. "Phased Integration in Miami." Integrated Education, D, 1964-Ja, 1965.

Commission on Higher Educational Opportunity. Postsecondary Educational Opportunities for the Negro Student in Florida. Atlanta, GA: Southern Regional Education Board, Ag, 1970.

Curry, George E. Jack Gaither: America's Most Famous Black Coach. New York: Dodd, Mead, 1977. [Florida A & M U.]

Egerton, John. "Black Students Hit UF Policies." Race Relations Reporter 2(Je 7, 1971):6-8. [U. of Florida]

_____. "Merger Predicted for FSU and FAMU." Race Relations Reporter 2(My 17, 1971):4-6.

Evans, Marcia. "FTU Minority Program Aid, But No Cure-all." Orlando Sentinel Star, Mr 5, 1978. [Florida Technological U.]

Ferguson, Paul. "With Vigorous Hand at Helm, University Fights for New Image." Florida Times-Union (Jacksonville), N 4, 1973. [Florida A & M U.]

"FAMU Fights for Life." SOBU Newsletter, My 29, 1971. [Florida A & M U.]

Fisher, Isaac. "Florida Builds Its State Negro College." Southern Workman 58(N, 1929):507-512.

Florida State Department of Education. Report of the Distribution of Financial Assistance to Students in Florida's Community Colleges, Ap, 1977. ERIC ED 139 451.

Jenkins, Jerry, and Patton, Charles. "UNF Battles Anti-Black Image." Jacksonville Journal, Je 26, 1978. [U. of North Florida]

Jenkins, Thomas Miller. "Judicial Discretion in Desegregation: The Hawkins Case." Howard Law Review 4(Je, 1958):192-202.

Kidd, Arthur L. "The Florida Agricultural and Mechanical College." Bulletin of the National Association of Teachers in Colored Schools 11(Ap-My, 1931):13-14, 18.

_____. "Problems Affecting the Higher Education of Negroes in Florida." Quarterly Review of Higher Education Among Negroes 5 (O, 1937):160-170.

Kunerth, Jeff. "White 'Ivory Tower.'" Orlando Sentinel Star, Mr 8, 1977. [Florida Technological U.]

Lassiter, Roy L., Jr. "Affirmative Action at the University of North Florida." Negro Educational Review 23(Ap-Jl, 1972):87-114.

_____. "Affirmative Action at the University of North Florida: A Further Report." Negro Educational Review 25(Ja, 1974):38-50.

Marsh, Georgia. "Junior Colleges and Negroes." Southern Education Report, S, 1968.

Miller, David. "Beneath the Surface of a Pulitzer Winner." Chicago Journalism Review 5(Ja, 1972):10-11. [In re: U. of Florida]

Morganthau, Tom. "Quiet on the Surface, FAMU Fights for Life." Miami Herald, Je 17, 1973.

Neyland, Leedell W. "State-Supported Higher Education Among Negroes in the State of Florida." Florida Historical Quarterly 43 (O, 1964):105-122.

Neyland, Leedell W., and Riley, John W. The History of Florida Agricultural and Mechanical University. Gainesville, FL: U. of Florida Press, 1963.

"160 Black Students Withdraw." SOBU Newsletter, My 15, 1971. [U. of Florida]

Orson, Claire M., and Toomer, Jethro. "Black College Offers National Curriculum Model." International Journal of Continuing Education and Training 2(Winter, 1973):305-308. [Florida Memorial College]

Perry, Benjamin L., Jr. "Black Colleges and Universities in Florida: Past, Present, and Future." Journal of Black Studies 6 (S, 1975):69-78.

Post-Secondary Educational Opportunities and the Negro Student in Florida: A Report to the Select Council on Post-High School Education. Atlanta, GA: Southern Regional Education Board, Institute for Higher Educational Opportunity, Je, 1969. ERIC ED 041 963.

"Racist Assault Sparks Demos." Southern Patriot, N, 1975. [Attacks on black students at Florida State U., Tallahassee]

Ranon, Zita A. "Committee Sees Need for More Black USF Administrators." Tampa Times, Mr 11, 1977. [U. of South Florida]

Sawyer, James A. "The Fulfillment of the Democratization Role of the Community College." Doctoral dissertation, U. of Florida, 1978. Univ. Microfilms Order No. 7900093.

Sessums, Terrell. "A Role for FAMU: Reaching the Disadvantaged." St. Petersburg Times, Jl 29, 1973. [Speaker of the Florida House of Representatives]

Smith, Walter Lee. "A Study of the Black Public Junior Colleges in Florida: 1957-1966." Doctoral dissertation, Florida State U., 1974. Univ. Microfilms Order No. 75-15509.

Stanley, Charles J., Williams, Joshua W., and Barnes, Malcolm Q. "College Desegregation in Florida." Integrateducation 13(S-O, 1975): 14-18.

Stuart, Reginald. Black Perspectives on State-Controlled Higher Education: The Florida Report. New York: John Hay Whitney Foundation, Ap, 1974.

Terhune, Dan Lee. "The Impact of Tuition on Equal Opportunity Equal Access, for Non-white Students in Florida Community Colleges." Doctoral dissertation, U. of Florida, 1976.

Thomas, Jesse O. "A New School in an Old Town." Opportunity 6(Mr, 1928):82-83. [Florida Normal and Collegiate Institute, St. Augustine]

"University of Florida: Black-White Sensitivity Program." NUEA Spectator, Ap-My, 1971, pp. 10-11.

[University of] Florida Students Fight Repression." Southern Patriot, Je, 1968.

University of Miami. "Education." In Psycho-Social Dynamics in Miami. Coral Gables, FL: U. of Miami, Ja, 1969.

Weisman, L. "A Study of Institutional Activities Related to the Special Learning Needs of Educationally Disadvantaged Students in Community Junior Colleges in Florida." Doctoral dissertation, U. of Southern California, 1971.

White, Robert M. "The Tallahassee Sit-ins and CORE: A Non-violent Revolutionary Sub-movement." Doctoral dissertation, Florida State U., 1964. Univ. Microfilms Order No. 65-339.

Windham, Douglas M. Education, Equality and Income Redistribution: A Study of Public Higher Education. Lexington, MA: D. C. Heath, 1970.

_____. "State Financed Higher Education and the Distribution of Income in Florida." Doctoral dissertation, Florida State U., 1969.

Witmer, Stan. "Ben Perry Beat the Odds and Built a Strong Black University." St. Petersburg Times, N 12, 1972. [Florida A & M U.]

Zion, Carol L. "The Desegregation of a Public Junior College: A Case Study of Its Negro Faculty." Doctoral dissertation, Florida State U., 1965. Univ. Microfilms Order No. 66-5462. [Miami-Dade Junior College]

Georgia

Adams, Myron W. A History of Atlanta University. Atlanta, GA: Atlanta U. Press, 1930.

Bacote, Clarence A. The Story of Atlanta University, 1865 to 1965: A Century of Service, 1969. Atlanta University Bookstore, Atlanta U., Atlanta, GA 30314.

Baldwin, Guy. "Students Seek Changes at Atlanta U. Center." Southern Courier, O 19, 1968.

Bellamy, Donnie D. "Henry A. Hunt and Black Agricultural Leadership in the New South." Journal of Negro History 60(O, 1975):464-479.

"Black College Forced to Re-enter Complex." Muhammad Speaks, Jl 13, 1973. [Morris Brown College, Atlanta]

Blake, Elias. "The Negro Public College in Georgia." Journal of Negro Education 31 (Summer, 1962):299-309.

Boger, Dellie L. "The Problems of Morehouse College Students." Doctoral dissertation, Teachers College, 1956.

Bond, Horace Mann. "Education for Production as Conducted at the Fort Valley State College--A Report." Proceedings of the Twentieth and Twenty-First Conference of the Presidents of Negro Land Grant Colleges, pp. 83-87. Twenty-First Conference, Wabash Avenue Y.M.C.A., Chicago, IL, 1943.

_____. "The Education of Teachers for Negro Children at Fort Valley State College." Bulletin, Southern University 29(My, 1943):59-68.

_____. "Ham and Eggs: The Fort Valley Ham and Egg Show." Bulletin 513, Georgia Agricultural Extension Service, Atlanta, GA, Je, 1955.

Braddock, Clayton. "Atlanta U. President Warns Against Separation in Black Studies, Calls for Scholarly Approach." Chronicle of Higher Education, Mr 24, 1969.

Brawley, Benjamin Griffith. History of Morehouse College. Atlanta: Morehouse College, 1917.

Bryant, Roger G. "The Black Student and the Student Affairs Worker at Six Predominantly White Colleges and Universities in Georgia: A Reciprocal Study of their Perceptions." Doctoral dissertation, U. of Georgia, n.d.

"Busing To Hit Black Colleges?" African World 2(Ag 5, 1972). [Fort Valley State College, Fort Valley]

Butler, Addie L. J. "The Distinctive Black College: Talladega, Tuskegee, and Morehouse." Doctoral dissertation, Columbia U., 1976. Univ. Microfilms Order No. 76-27,699.

Calhoun, E. Clayton. "Thoughts I Leave Behind." Integrated Education 8(N-D, 1970):4-7. [Paine College]

Clary, George E. "The Founding of Paine College--A Unique Venture in Inter-racial Cooperation in the New South, 1882-1903." Doctoral dissertation, U. of Georgia, 1965. Univ. Microfilms Order No. 65-10286.

Cocking, Walter Dewey. Report of the Study on Higher Education of Negroes in Georgia. Athens, GA: U. of Georgia, 1938.

Cole, Spurgeon, Steinberg, Jay, and Birkheimer, G. J. "Prejudice and Conservatism in a Recently Integrated Southern College." Psychological Reports, Ag, 1968. [Northern GA]

Colston, James A. "Higher Education in Georgia from 1932 to 1949 with Specific Reference to Higher Education for the Negro." Doctoral dissertation, New York U., 1950. Univ. Microfilms Order No. 2177.

Cook, James F., Jr. "The Eugene Talmadge-Walter Cocking Controversy." Phylon 35(Je, 1974):181-192. [U. of GA]

_____. "Politics and Education in the Talmadge Era: The Controversy Over the University System of Georgia, 1941-42." Doctoral dissertation, U. of Georgia, 1972.

Cowan, Frank. "A Study of the Impact of Participation in Civil Rights Demonstrations on Negro College Students of the Atlanta University Center." Master's thesis, Atlanta U., 1966.

Cutts, Beau. "New Med School Targets Needy Areas." Washington Post, S 11, 1978. [School of Medicine at Morehouse College]

Du Bois, W. E. B. "Atlanta University." In From Servitude to Service; Being the Old South Lectures on the History and Work of Southern Institutions for the Education of the Negro pp. 153-197. Boston: American Unitarian Association, 1905.

_____. "The Cultural Missions of Atlanta University." Phylon 3(1942):105-115.

_____. "The Significance of Henry Hunt." In Founder's and Annual Report Number, Fort Valley [Georgia] State College Bulletin, O, 1940.

Fiske, Edward B. "Black Women's College Competes for Money and Talent." New York Times, Je 1, 1978. [Spelman College]

4X, Harold. "...'Charitable' Ford Foundation..." Muhammad Speaks, O 5, 1973. [Morris Brown College, Atlanta]

"Ga. Black Student Alliance Aims for State-Wide Unity." SOBU Newsletter, Mr 20, 1971.

"Go South Young Grad." Black Enterprise 6(F, 1976). [Master of Business Administration program at Atlanta U.]

Graham, William L. "Patterns of Intergroup Relations in the Cooperative Establishment, Control, and Administration of Paine College (Georgia) by Southern Negro and White People: A Study of Intergroup Process." Doctoral dissertation, New York U., 1955. Univ. Microfilms Order No. 12215.

_____. "The Relation of Paine College to Its Community." Quarterly Review of Higher Education Among Negroes 4(Jl, 1936):129-133.

Hammons, Norma A. "Attitudes of Atlanta University Negro Students Toward Skin Color." Master's thesis, Atlanta U., 1969.

Harber, Randall H. "Georgia: Black Recruitment Lags at University." South Today 3(S, 1971):6. [U. of Georgia]

Hines, Linda O., and Jones, Allen W. "A Voice of Black Protest: The Savannah Men's Sunday Club, 1905-1911." Phylon 35(Je, 1974):193-202.

Holley, Joseph W. You Can't Build a Chimney from the Top. New York: William-Frederick Press, 1948. [President, Georgia Normal College]

Holmes, Hamilton. "My First Year at the University of Georgia." Sepia, My, 1962.

Hunter, Charlayne. "A Homecoming for the First Black Girl at the University of Georgia." New York Times Magazine, Ja 25, 1970.

Jenga, Chimurenga. "Desegregation: What Happens to a Dream Deferred?" Politics and Education 1(Fall, 1978):19-21. [Atlanta Junior College]

Jones, Edward A. A Candle in the Dark: A History of Morehouse College. Valley Forge, PA: Judson Press, 1968.

Kendrick, Edward T. "Community Problems of Off-Campus Non-resident Students at Fort Valley State College." Master's thesis, Fort Valley State College, 1970.

McPheeters, Alphonso A. "The Origin and Development of Clark University and Gammon Theological Seminary, 1869-1944." Doctoral dissertation, U. of Cincinnati, 1944.

Mitchell, W. Grayson, and Stubbs, Frances. "Ala., Ga. College Kids Stage Different Kinds of Protests." Southern Courier, N 16, 1968. [Atlanta, GA and Talledega, AL]

Morgan, John W. The Origin and Distribution of the Graduates of the Negro Colleges of Georgia. Milledgeville, GA: n.p., 1940.

Prugh, Jeff. "Black College in Georgia Told to Integrate" Los Angeles Times, N 23, 1978. [Albany State College]

Ramsey, Berkley Carlyle. "The Public Black College in Georgia: A History of Albany State College, 1903-1965." Doctoral disseration, Florida State U., 1973. Univ. Microfilms Order No. 73-31528.

Range, Willard. The Rise and Progress of Negro Colleges in Georgia, 1865-1949. Athens, GA: U. of Georgia Press, 1951.

Scott, Peter. "New Programs May Lure Whites to Black Colleges." Atlanta Journal, F 11, 1979.

Seligmann, Jean and others. "Wanted: White Students." Newsweek, Ap 9, 1979. [Albany State College]

Stimson, Sandra. "Black Students Combat Racism." Southern Struggle, My-Je, 1978. [Atlanta Junior College]

Taylor, Prince A., Jr. "A History of Gammon Theological Seminary." Doctoral dissertation, New York U., 1948. Univ. Microfilms Order No. 1155.

Terrell, Robert L. "Black Awareness Versus Negro Traditions: Atlanta University Center." New South, Winter, 1969.

Thomas, Jessie C. My Story in Black and White... Autobiography... New York: Exposition Press, 1968. [Founder of the Atlanta U. School of Social Work]

Tift, Rosa. A Preliminary Report on Predicting the Success of College Education Achievement Project Enrollment at Albany State College. Washington, DC: American Educational Research Association, F, 1971, 26 pp. Paper, American Educational Research Association. ERIC ED 049 710.

Trillin, Calvin. An Education in Georgia. The Integration of Charlayne Hunter and Hamilton Holmes. New York: Viking, 1964. [U. of Georgia]

"Two Student Leaders Suspended [at the University of Georgia]." Southern Patriot, Je, 1968.

Ware, Edward Twichell. The Good of It...How It Pays to Give Higher Education to Negroes-- Being Some Account of What Graduates of Atlanta University Are Doing for the Uplifting of Their Race. 3rd ed. Atlanta, GA: n.p., 1905.

White, Anthony G. "A Comparative Study of Academic Performance of White Students and Black Students at the University of Georgia." Doctoral dissertation, U. of Georgia, 1978. Univ. Microfilms Order No. 7822363.

Yancy, Dorothy Cowser. "William Edward Burghardt Du Bois' Atlanta Years: The Human Side--A Study Based Upon Oral Sources." Journal of Negro History 63(Ja, 1978):59-67.

Hawaii

Arkoff, Abe, and Leton, Donald A. "Ethnic and Personality Patterns in College Entrance." Journal of Experimental Education, Fall, 1966.

Facer, Louise. "Friendship Patterns of Mainland Haole Students at the University of Hawaii." Master's thesis, U. of Hawaii, 1961.

Gardner, Kenneth D., and others. "Minority Student Education at the University of Hawaii School of Medicine." Journal of Medical Education 47(J, 1972):467-472.

Kinloch, Graham C. "Racial Prejudice in Highly and Less Racist Societies: Social Distance Preferences Among White College Students in South Africa and Hawaii." Sociology and Social Research 59(O, 1974): 1-13.

Meredith, Gerald M. "Acculturation and Personality Among Japanese-American College Students in Hawaii." Doctoral dissertation, U. of Hawaii, 1969.

_____. "AMAE and Acculturation among Japanese College Students in Hawaii." Journal of Social Psychology 70(1966): 171-180.

Meredith, Gerald M., and Meredith, C. G. W. "Acculturation and Personality among Japanese-American College Students in Hawaii." Journal of Social Psychology 68(1966):175-182.

Peterson, Barbara B., and Baker, John H. "Hawaii's Community Colleges and the Disadvantaged Student." Educational Perspectives 13(My, 1974):28-32.

Shim, Neil, and Dole, Arthur A. "Components of Social Distance Among College Students and their Parents in Hawaii." Journal of Social Psychology, 1967, 73(1): 111-124.

Tong, David. "How Bakke Decision Affects UH: A Survey of Minority Admissions." Honolulu Star Bulletin and Advertiser F 4, 1979. [U. of Hawaii]

Witeck, John. "The East-West Center: An Intercult of Colonialism." Hawaii Pono Journal, 1970. [U. of Hawaii]

Illinois

Askin, Steve, and Gelder, Sharon B. "HEW Flunks on Higher Education Civil Rights Enforcement; Examines University of Chicago, But Little Change Seen." Chicago Reporter 7(Ap, 1978):2-3.

Barlow, R. M. "What Happened at Northwestern?" America, My 18, 1968 [Northwestern U., Evanston]

Barnard, Judith. "If It Works, Stop It." Chicago 25(Ag, 1976). [City Colleges of Chicago]

Biery, James. "Malcolm X: The College that Came Back Black." College and University Business 52(Je, 1972):37-41.

Bindman, Aaron M. "Pre-College Preparation of Negro College Students." Journal of Negro Education, Fall, 1966 [U. of Illinois]

Bowers, John. The Achievement of S.E.O.P. Freshmen in First Year Psychology Courses. Urbana, Illinois: Office of Instructional Resources, U. of Illinois, 1969 [Special Educational Opportunities Program (SEOP)]

_____. "The Comparison of GPA Regression Equations for Regularly Admitted and Disadvantaged Freshmen at the University of Illinois." Journal of Educational Measurement 7(1970):219-225.

Bowie, Maceo T. "Learn Baby Learn. Black Power Awareness and Dead End Programs." Vital Speeches, Jl 15, 1970 [Kennedy-King College, Chicago]

"Bradley U. Blacks Come to Grips With Campus Racism." Muhammad Speaks, My 16, 1969 [Peoria]

Bullard, J. T. "The President of Bantustan U." Muhammad Speaks, O 15, 1971 [Charles Hurst, president, Malcolm X College, Chicago, Illinois]

"C R J Reports on the Incidents in the Union on September 9 [1968]." Laputa Gazette, O, 1968 [Protest movement by Black Students Association at the U. of Illinois]

Carpenter, John N. "The Illini Union Sit-in of September 9-10, 1968, and Why It Happened." Master's thesis, U. of Illinois, Urbana, 1974.

Chan, Betty. "East St. Louis Community College: Problems and Politics." Community College Frontiers 2(Spring, 1974): 17-19.

Check, Joseph M. "Urban-Counterinsurgency and the University of Chicago." Community (Chicago) 33(Fall, 1973):8-13.

Cheverton, Dick. "Learn Baby, Learn." Chicago Today, My 17, 1970 [Dr. Charles Hurst, president, Malcolm X College, Chicago, Illinois]

Concerned Coalition of Faculty and Graduate Students Formed to Oppose the Selection Index. The Selection Index. The Administration's Blind Date With "Quality" Education. Chicago: U. of Illinois, Chicago Circle, Ap, 1977.

Cooke, Benjamin. "Life At the Black Studies Program--Another Day, Another Heartache." Post Prairie Statement, Je 13, 1970. [Prairie State College, Chicago Heights, Illinois]

Corman, Stephen. "Malcolm X College." Equal Opportunity 2(Ja, 1971):9-13.

Cross, Robert. "James Turner: The Face of Black Power at Northwestern." Chicago Tribune Magazine, Jl 14, 1968 [Interview]

Davis, Samuel C., Loeb, Jane W., and Robinson, Lehymann F. "A Comparison of Characteristics of Negro and White College Freshman Classmates." Journal of Negro Education 39(Fall, 1970):359-366 [U. of Illinois, Urbana-Champaign]

Davis, Samuel C., Loeb, Jane W., Robinson, Lehymann F., with Kristjansdottir, Thuridur J. University of Illinois Negro Beginning Freshmen. Confidential. Urbana, Illinois: Univ. Office of School and College Relations, F, 1969.

Division, Paul. "The Blacks, the Radicals, the Reformers." Focus/Midwest, Ja-F, 1969 [U. of Illinois]

DuBois, W. E. B. [Article on the appointment of Allison Davis to the faculty of the University of Chicago] Amsterdam News Je 27, 1942.

Flaherty, Roger. "The Push for Black Doctors Falls Short." Chicago Sun-Times, O 2, 1977 [U. of Illinois medical school]

Freudenheim, Milt. "If Johnny Can't Read, Must College Teach Him?" Chicago Daily News, F 21, 1977 [Chicago colleges and universities]

Friedman, Helen Adams, and Ruck, Sarge. "Why Not Every Man?" Integrateducation 13 (N-D, 1975):33-38. [Dr. Edward Sparling, founder of Roosevelt U.]

George, Zelma. "UC Integration in the 20's (letter). U. of Chicago Magazine, Jl-Ag, 1969.

Heath, G. Louis. "An Inquiry into a University's 'Noble Savage' Program." Integrated Education 8(Jl-Ag, 1970):4-9.

Hill, Freddye. "The Nature and Context of Black Nationalism at Northwestern in 1971." Journal of Black Studies 5(Mr, 1975):320-336.

Hill, Winston. "A Brother Is Dying in the Black Community of the U.S.A. Because of Apathy; It's the Same As If You Were in the Black Community of South Africa." Black Panther, D 19, 1970 [Charge of discrimination against Graylon Whitehead was exercised by the Univ. Health Service, Southern Illinois U., Carbondale, Ill.]

Holleb, Doris B. Higher Education and Urban Poverty: The Role of the Public System in Illinois in Community Service Involvement. 2 vols. Chicago, Ill.: Center for Urban Studies, U. of Chicago, N, 1970.

Holt, Grace Sims. "Speech Communication for the Black American." Bulletin of the National Association of Secondary School Principals 54(D, 1970):100-107 [U. of Illinois, Chicago Circle]

"How Thousands of Students Get Cheated in 'Innovative Education' Swindle." Muhammad Speaks, N 5, 1971 [Malcolm X College, Chicago, Illinois]

Hurst, Charles G., Jr. "Malcolm X: A Community College With a New Perspective." Negro Digest, Mr, 1970.

_____. "Malcolm X College: The Open Door." Essence, S, 1971.

_____. Passport to Freedom. Education, Humanism, and Malcolm X. Hamden, Conn.: Linnet Books, 1972.

"Intellectual Black Power." Time, Ag 16, 1971 [Malcolm X College, Chicago]

Johnson, Norman J., Wyer, Robert, and Gilbert, Neil. "Quality Education and Integration: An Exploratory Study." Phylon, Fall, 1967 [Differential high school preparation of youth who entered the U. of Illinois]

Johnson, Sharon. "The Miracle of Malcolm X [College]." Change 3(My-Je, 1971):18-21.

Kessel, Barbara. "Teachers' Union Local 1600." NUC Newsletter, Ja, 1969 [Student-power issues in the Chicago City College in relation to union policy]

Kornegay, Sharron. "City Colleges: Mostly Black Students; Minority Faculty, One-Third-Growing." Chicago Reporter 5(My, 1976) [City Colleges of Chicago]

_____. "Minority Enrollment, Employment Show Marked Increase At Area's Top Universities Since Last Reporter Study." Chicago Reporter 4(Je, 1975) [Chicago]

Little, Ellis, and Nowell, Gadis. "Integration and Scholastic Performance: A Pilot Study of Chicago Public High School Graduates Attending the University of Illinois, Chicago." Psychological Reports 26(Je, 1970):887-891.

Lumpkin, Beatrice. "Decomposition of Composition." American Teacher, F, 1972 [Malcolm X College, Chicago]

_____. "Where 'Innovation' Equals 120 Students Per Class." American Teacher, D, 1972 [Malcolm X College, Chicago]

McClory, Robert. "Toughness and Loving Care Reshape Chicago State." Change 10(N, 1978): 46-47, 61 [Chicago State U.]

McCrary, J. W. "The Disadvantaged Student in Illinois Public Community Colleges." Doctoral dissertation, Northern Illinois U., 1974.

Mack, Faite R-P. "Educational Opportunity Program Graduates Compared to Educational Opportunity Program Non-Graduates." Journal of Negro Education 43(Winter, 1974): 39-46 [U. of Illinois-Urbana]

Manly, Chesly. "Dr. Hurst's 'Revolution' at Malcolm X." Chicago Tribune, Ja 4, 1970 [Malcolm X College, Chicago]

Mansfield, Ralph. "The Impossible Problems of Two-Year Colleges [in Illinois]." Focus/Midwest, Ja-F, 1969 [Chicago City College]

McClory, Robert J. "Fewer Black Doctors in Chicago." Chicago Reporter 4(My, 1975).

McClory, Robert. "Why Johnny's Teacher Can't Read!" Chicago Defender, Mr 30, 1974 [Chicago State U.]

Meier, Debbie. "Chicago Sit-Ins Attack Jim Crow." New America, F 23, 1962 [U. of Chicago]

Merrick, Jeffries. "Project '500.' An Excellent Plan Poorly Executed." Focus/Midwest, Ja-F, 1969 [U. of Illinois, Urbana]

Monroe, Charles. "A Basic Program in Junior College." Integrated Education, Ja, 1963 [Wilson Junior College, Chicago]

"Monument to Blackness." Newsweek, Ag 2, 1971, pp. 46-47 [Malcolm X College, Chicago]

Moss, Ruth. "Success Is the Key Word at Malcolm X College." Chicago Tribune, Ag 13, 1972 [Chicago]

Northwestern University. "Black Studies and the University." (Chapter 7 of A Community of Scholars. New Approaches to Undergraduate Education at Ill.: Northwestern U. S, 1968), Integrated Education, Mr-Ap, 1969, pp. 27-33.

Penelton, Barbara Spencer. "Perceptions of Black and Non-Black Students Concerning Campus Life at a Predominantly White University." Doctoral dissertation, Indiana U., 1977. Univ. Microfilm Order No. 78-1033 [Bradley U., Peoria]

Pitts, James P. "The Politicization of Black Students: Northwestern University." Journal of Black Studies 5(Mr, 1975): 277-319.

Poinsett, Alex. "Dr. Charles G. Hurst: The Mastermind of Malcolm X College." Ebony 25(1970):29-38.

Pope, Rick. "Blacks Face Cultural Roadblocks at ISU." Bloomington Daily Pantagraph, D 9, 1975.

"Profile: Malcolm X Community College." The Black Collegian 2(N-D, 1971):10-12, 50 [Chicago]

Rawles, Nancy. "NU's Race Relations." Daily Northwestern, F 20-Mr 2, 1978 [Nine articles]

Reilly, Joseph. "U. of I. Blacks. In Trying Times, A Time to Try." Chicago Sun-Times, Mr 16, 1969 [Black students at U. of Illinois, Urbana]

"'Revolutionary' Black College Scene of Conspiracy: Teachers." Muhammad Speaks, My 19, 1972 [Malcolm X College, Chicago]

"Riot in the Union? Law School Report. Conclusion of Fact." Laputa Gazette, Ja 9, 1969 [Black Students Association protest at U. of Illinois, S, 1968]

Rouzan, Brisbane. "A History of Black Educational Leadership at the University of Illinois." Doctoral dissertation, U. of Illinois, 1975.

Schnedler, Jack. "Circle at the 10-Year Mark: Fighting to Flesh Out a Dream." Chicago Daily News, F 22, 1975 [U. of Illinois at Chicago Circle]

Scott, David W. "School District Integration in a Metropolitan Area." Education and Urban Society 4(F, 1972):135-154 [Formation of common junior college districts in Chicago metropolitan area]

Semas, Philip W. "Malcolm X College's Aim: Black Community Self-Determination." Chronicle of Higher Education, My 31, 1971.

17X, Samuel. "Black Thugs Intimidate Black Teachers." Muhammad Speaks, Ja 22, 1971 [Malcolm X College]

Simon, Rita James, McCall, George, and Rosenthal, Evelyn. "A Selective Evaluation of Their University by Negro and White Undergraduates." Phylon, Spring, 1969 [U. of Illinois, Urbana]

Smith, Ralph L. "Rustlings at a Midwest Campus." Focus/Midwest, Ja-F, 1969 [Illinois State U.]

"Some Blacks Choose Fascism." Muhammad Speaks, F 19, 1971 [Malcolm X College, Chicago]

Southern Illinois University System. "No Tuition for State Universities." Integrated Education 12(Ja-Ap, 1974): 23-25.

Spivey, Donald, and Jones, Thomas A. "Intercollegiate Athletic Servitude: A Case Study of the Black Illini Student-Athletes, 1931-1967." Social Science Quarterly 55(Mr, 1975):939-947.

"Statewide Battle on Illinois Jim Crow." Crisis, F, 1937 [U. of Chicago and Northwestern U.]

"The University [of Chicago] and Its Community." Chicago Maroon, My 28, 1968.

University of Illinois at Chicago Circle. Educational Assistance Program Study, n.p., Ap, 1974.

Vega, Paul. "The Academic Performance of a Group of Latin Students Admitted to the University of Illinois, Chicago Circle Campus, Fall, 1969, through the Educational Assistance Program." Master's thesis, Northeastern Illinois U., 1971.

Washington, Betty. "Malcolm X College: The Stigma Lingers." Chicago Daily News, F 25, 1978.

Weintroub, Benjamin. "Edward J. Sparling--Quality in Education." Decalogue Journal 7(F, 1957) [Roosevelt U.]

Ward, Renee. "Black Students Talk About Making It Through Chicago's Major Universities." Chicago Reporter 2 (Je, 1973):1, 4-5.

Indiana

Adams, Donald W. "An Analysis of the Black Undergraduate Student at Indiana University." Doctoral dissertation, Indiana U., 1969. Univ. Microfilms Order No. 70-11676.

Byers, Thomas, and Byers, Jacquelyn. "Practicum in Democratic Living: A Report of Progress from Middletown, U.S.A." Indiana Social Studies Quarterly, Spring, 1964 [Indiana Council of the Social Studies. Ball State Teachers College, Muncie, Indiana]

Burke, Kaaren O. "A Study of Racial Attitudes of Six Freshman Women Involved in Integrated Room Situations in a College Residence Hall." ISSQ, Spring, 1964. Muncie, Ind.: Indiana Council of the Social Studies, Ball State Teachers College.

Cooper, Theodore B. "Adjustment Problems of Undergraduate Negroes Enrolled at Indiana University." Doctoral dissertation, Indiana U., 1952.

Greenwood, Charles Huddie. "Characteristics of Black Freshman Dropouts at Ball State University." Doctoral dissertation, Indiana U., 1972. Univ. Microfilms Order No. 73-10823.

Green Associates. Central Area Revitalization and the Urban University; An Exploratory Study of the Indianapolis Core Area. Beverly Hills, California, 1967.

Hatcher, Harold. Survey of Negro Enrollment at Indiana Colleges. Indianapolis, Ind.: Indiana Civil Rights Commission, 1964.

"Negroes at Notre Dame." Ebony, F, 1950.

Vredeveld, George M. "Income Redistributive Effects of Subsidizing Public Higher Education in Indiana." Doctoral dissertation, Indiana U., 1974.

Warren, Stanley. "An Analysis of the Black Freshman Student at Indiana-Purdue University at Indianapolis." Doctoral dissertation, Indiana U., 1973. Univ. Microfilms Order No. 74-02610.

Iowa

Howe, Trevor G., Byerly, Richard L., and Klitt, John A. Profile of the Disadvantaged in Area XI-1968, Des Moines Area Community College District. Des Moines, Iowa: Department of Public Instruction, 1968.

Jenkins, Herbert C. "The Negro Student at the University of Iowa, A Sociological Study." Master's thesis, U. of Iowa, 1933.

Liu, Annabel. "The Problems Blacks Meet at Iowa State." Des Moines Register, My 5, 1974.

MacKenzie, John P. "Racial Issues Cloud Iowa Athlete's Murder Conviction." Washington Post, Mr 31, 1976 [U. of Iowa, Iowa City]

Kansas

Belisaro, Arevalo. "Latin American Students at the University of Kansas." Master's thesis, U. of Kansas, 1974.

Haldeman-Julius, Marcet. "What the Negro Students Endure in Kansas." Haldeman-Julius Monthly 7(Ja, 1926).

Michaeux, Latioa. "Black Students Hurt by Treatment." Wichita Eagle, F 21, 1978 (letter) [Fort Hays State U.]

Peace, Larry M. "Colored Students and Graduates at the University of Kansas." In The College-Bred Negro American, pp. 34-41. Edited by W. E. B. DuBois and Augustus G. Dill (Atlanta, Ga.: Atlanta U. Press, 1910).

Kentucky

Aprile, Dianne. "Scores of Black Students Leaving U of L." Louisville Times, F 14, 1979 [U. of Louisville]

_____. "Separate Tables." Louisville Times, Mr 16, 1979 [Black and white students at the U. of Louisville]

Bruce, Andrew A. "The Berea College Decision and the Segregation of the Colored Races." Century Law Journal 68(F 19, 1909): 137-142.

Edwards, Austin. "History of the Kentucky State Industrial College for Negroes." Master's thesis, Indiana State Teachers College, 1936. (Abstract in: Teachers College Journal 8(Jl, 1937):66-67.

Coleman, Lena Mae. "A History of Kentucky State College for Negroes." Master's thesis, Indiana U., 1938.

Embree, Edwin R. "A Kentucky Crusader." American Mercury, S, 1931 [John G. Fee, founder of Berea College]

Galloway, Oscar F. "Higher Education for Negroes in Kentucky." Doctoral dissertation, U. of Kentucky, 1932.

Hager, Paul C., and Elton, Charles F. "The Vocational Interests of Black Males." Journal of Vocational Behavior 1(Ap, 1971): 153-158 [Berea College]

Hall, Betty Jean and Heckman, Richard Allen. "Berea's First Decade." Filson Club History Quarterly, O, 1968.

Heckman, Richard Allen and Hall, Betty Jean. "Berea College and the Day Law." Register of the Kentucky Historical Society 66 (1968):35-52.

Landy, Marc, and Landy, Mieko. "Higher Learning in Appalachia: A Model for Change." Journal of Higher Education 42(Mr, 1971):169-174 [Alice Lloyd College, Knott County]

"Municipal College for Negroes." School and Society 32(N 22, 1930):692.

Murrell, Glen. "The Desegregation of Paducah Junior College." Register of the Kentucky Historical Society 67(Ja, 1969):63-79.

Nelson, Paul. "Experiment in Interracial Education at Berea College, 1858-1908." Journal of Negro History 59(Ja, 1974).

Peterson, Bill. "Identity Crisis." Louisville Courier-Journal, Ja 31, 1972 [Kentucky State College, Frankfort]

Runyon, Keith. "U of L: Still a 'Streetcar' College." Louisville Courier-Journal, F 2, 1976 [U. of Louisville]

Yarbrough, Willard. "Berea College: Troubled Monument to Equality." Knoxville (Tenn.) News Sentinel, F 13, 1972.

Louisiana

Attorney General's Special Commission of Inquiry on the Southern University Tragedy of November 16, 1972. Report. Baton Rouge, La.: Attorney General, 1973.

Ball, Millie. "Insight Into SUNO." New Orleans Times-Picayune, Ap 1, 1973-Ap 7, 1973 [A series of seven articles on Southern U. in New Orleans]

Boaga, Walter. "Black Colleges in Crisis: The Issues at Baton Rouge." Southern Patriot, Ja, 1973.

Carter, Doris D. "Charles P. Adams and Grambling State University: The Formative Years (1901-1928)." Louisiana History 17 (Fall, 1976):401-412.

Cassimere, Raphael, Jr. "Crisis of Public Higher Education in Louisiana." Integrateducation 13(S-O, 1975):8-13.

Chriss, Nicholas C. "A Moderate's First Test." Nation, D 18, 1972 [Gov. Edwin W. Edwards and the killing of two students at Southern U. at Baton Rouge]

Clark, Felton G. "Certain Facts Concerning Collegiate and Secondary Education in Louisiana." Quarterly Review of Higher Education Among Negroes 5(O, 1937):171-172.

Daniels, Virginia R. McDonald. "Reading Abilities of Southern University Freshmen." Southern University Bulletin, Mr, 1941.

Egerton, John. "Xavier Tightens Financial Belt." Race Relations Reporter 2(F 16, 1971) [Xavier U., New Orleans]

Elshorst, Hansjorg. "Two Years After Integration: Race Relations at a Deep South University." Phylon, Spring, 1967 [Louisiana State U., Baton Rouge]

4X, George. "Southern Students Demand Revolution." Muhammad Speaks, N 17, 1972 [Southern U.]

"Grambling College (Louisiana).' AAUP Bulletin 57(Spring, 1971):50-52.

Guillory, Ferrel. "Xavier [University] -- Black and Catholic." National Catholic Reporter, Ap 7, 1972 [New Orleans]

Huson, Carolyn F., and Schiltz, Michael E. College, Color, and Employment: Racial Differentials in Postgraduate Employment Among 1964 Graduates of Louisiana Colleges. Chicago, Ill.: National Opinion Research Center, Jl, 1966.

Jabul, Ahmad and others. "Ivory Raps About Grambling's Legendary Shoulders." Muhammad Speaks, N 24, 1972.

Jones, John Sebastian. "History of the Negro College Movement in Louisiana." Louisiana Colored Teachers' Journal 15 (My, 1942).

Lane, Ulysses Simpson. "The History of Southern University, 1879-1960." Doctoral dissertation, Utah State; 1970.

"Legacy of the Southern U. Struggle." African World, N 30, 1974.

Lief, Thomas Parrish. "The Decision to Migrate: Black College Graduates and their Tendency to Leave New Orleans." Doctoral dissertation, Tulane U., 1970. Univ. Microfilms Order No. 71-08067.

McWorter, Gerald. "Tragedy at Southern U: Accident or Political Assassination?" Edcentric 22(Mr, 1973).

Marshall, David C. "A History of the Higher Education of Negroes in the State of Louisiana." Doctoral dissertation, Louisiana State U., 1956. Univ. Microfilms Order No. 17447.

_____. "A History of the Higher Education of Negroes in the State of Louisiana." Doctoral dissertation, Louisiana State U., 1956.

Maxie, Earl. "The Development of Grambling College." Master's thesis, Tuskegee Institute, 1950.

NEA Hearing Panel for Southern University Investigation. Report of An Investigation. A Study of Student Protest Suggestions for University Response. Southern University, Baton Rouge, Louisiana. Washington, DC: National Education Association, S, 1973.

Perkins, Iris Johnson. "Felton Grandison Clark, Louisiana Educator." Doctoral dissertation, Louisiana State U., 1976. Univ. Microfilms Order No. 77-10,391 [Southern U.]

Pope, John. "The Prez: He Played It Cool." Washington Post, Je 5, 1977 [Ralph Waldo Emerson Jones, president of Grambling College]

Reed, Germaine A. "David Boyd, LSU, and Louisiana Reconstruction." La. Stud. 14 (Fall, 1975):259-276.

St. John, Edward P. A Study of Selected Developing Colleges and Universities. Vol. 4. Washington, DC: U.S. Office of Education, D, 1977 [Xavier U., New Orleans]

"Southern University Threatened by H.E.W." SOBU Newsletter, My 1, 1971 [Possible merger of Louisiana State U. and Southern U.]

Terry, Bill. "Blacks Oppose Unification of Louisiana Colleges." Washington Post, Ap 23, 1974.

Thomas, Willie James. "Cincinnati Black Faces Prison for Fighting for Black Studies." Muhammad Speaks, Mr 10, 1972 [Xavier U.]

Thompson, Daniel C. The Dillard Class of 1964: A Study of Employment Patterns. New Orleans: Dillard U., 1967.

Weidlein, Edward R. "Southern U.--Tragedy on a Tortured Campus." Chronicle of Higher Education 7(N 27, 1972).

Maryland

Barbarin, Oscar. Race and Social Climate as Determinants of Effective Adaptation in a University Setting, Mr 30, 1977. ERIC ED 148 940 [U. of Maryland]

Barnes, Bart. "Shutdown of Black College on Eastern Shore Advised." Washington Post, Mr 8, 1977 [U. of Maryland Eastern Shore]

Brooks, Glenwood C., Jr., and Sedlacek, William E. "The Racial Census of College Students." College and University 47 (Winter, 1972):125-127 [U. of Maryland]

Carrington, Christine H., and Sedlacek, William E. Attitudes and Characteristics of Black Graduate Students, 1976. ERIC ED 132 234 [U. of Maryland]

Corpin, Owen D. Development of a Model for Minority Recruitment at the United States Naval Academy. Springfield, Va.: National Technical Information Service, My 21, 1974. Order No. AD-784 111.

Craig, Argentine S., and Cooke, Gwendolyn J. "The Federal Government as a Change Agent in Higher Education and a Black College's Response to that Role." Journal of Negro Education 44(Fall, 1975):468-475 [U. Without Walls, Morgan State U.]

Di Cesare, Anthony C., Sedlacek, Wm. E., and Brooks, Glenwood C., Jr. Non-Intellectual Correlates of Black Student Attrition. College Park, Md.: Cultural Study Center, U. of Maryland, Ap, 1970 [U. of Md.]

Di Cesare, Anthony C., Sedlacek, Wm. E., Brooks, Glenwood C., Jr. and others. Non-Intellectual Correlates of Black Student Attrition: Differences in Black Student Perceptions of the Communication Structure in a Predominantly White University, 1970, p. 35. College Park, Maryland: Cultural Study Center, U. of Maryland. ERIC ED 047 323.

————. Non-Intellectual Correlates of Black Student Attrition, 1970, p. 14. College Park, Maryland: U. of Maryland, Cultural Study Center. ERIC ED 049 714.

Froe, Otis D. "A Comparative Study of a Population of 'Disadvantaged' College Freshmen." Journal of Negro Education, Fall, 1968 [Morgan State College]

Hass, Mark. "Intangibles Afflict U. of Maryland's Recruitment of Blacks." Washington Post, F 18, 1979.

[Holmes, Dwight Oliver Wendel] "Inaugural Address of Dwight Oliver Wendel Holmes as President of Morgan College." Quarterly Review of Higher Education Among Negroes 6(Ja, 1938):38-45.

Hytche, William and others. Toward Equality of Educational Opportunity and Attainment in Higher Education in Maryland, 1977. ERIC ED 140 710.

Knudson, Mary. "Do Blacks Get Into Medical School Easier than Whites?" Baltimore Sun, S 12, 1976.

Kuebler, Edward J. "The Desegregation of the University of Maryland." Md. Hist. Mag. 71 (Spring, 1976):37-49.

Lavender, Abraham D. "Disadvantages of Minority Group Membership: The Perspective of a Nondeprived Minority Group." Ethnicity 2(1975):99-119 [Jewish under-graduates, U. of Maryland]

"'A Lot of Blood Has Been Shed to Get Us Out Here!'" African World, Mr, 1975 [U. of Maryland]

Low, W. A. "Methodism and the Beginning of Higher Education of Negroes in Maryland." Quarterly Review of Higher Education Among Negroes 18(O, 1950):137-149.

Maryland Council for Higher Education. Report to Propose Ways of Enhancing the Role and Image of Predominantly Black Public Colleges in Maryland, Ag 9, 1974. ERIC ED 121 225.

Maryland State Board for Higher Education. Assessment of the Progress Made by the State in Enrolling Black Students, My 9, 1978. ERIC ED 158 684.

Maryland State Board for Higher Education. The Impact of Academic Program Offerings on the Desegregation Process of the Maryland Post-secondary Education Institutions, F, 1977. ERIC ED 158 688.

Maryland State Board for Higher Education. Third Midyear Desegregation Status Report for Public Postsecondary Education Institutions in the State of Maryland, Jl, 1977. ERIC ED 148 912-148 917.

Merritt, Mary Strader and others. Quality of Interracial Interaction Among University Students, 1974. ERIC ED 097 833 [U. of Maryland]

Myers, Samuel L., Jr. "Personal Testimony: The Agony of the Black Scholar in the White World." Phi Delta Kappan (Je, 1977): 746-750 [Deals also with Morgan State College]

Norwell, Merritt J., Jr. "The Desegregation of Higher Education: A Case Study of the Problems and Issues Confronting the Implementation of the Maryland Plan for Completing the Desegregation of Its Public Postsecondary Education Institution." Doctoral dissertation, U. of Wisconsin--Milwaukee, 1976.

Pfeifer, C. Michael, Jr., and Sedlacek, William E. Non-Intellectual Correlates of Black and White Student Grades at the University of Maryland, 1970, p. 36. College Park, Maryland: U. of Maryland, Cultural Study Center. ERIC ED 050 680.

————. "Predicting Black [College] Student Grades with Nonintellectual Measures." Journal of Negro Education 43(Winter, 1974): 67-76 [U. of Maryland]

Pfeifer, C. Michael, and Sedlacek, William E. The Validity of Academic Predictors for Black and White Students at the University of Maryland, 1970, p. 30. College Park, Maryland: U. of Maryland, Cultural Studies Center. ERIC ED 050 681.

Putney, Martha S. "The Formative Years of Maryland's First Black Postsecondary School." Md. Hist. Mag. 72(Je, 1978):168-179.

Rawlings, Howard P., Lee, Ulysses S., Jr., and Neverdon, Cynthia. Position Paper and Recommendations for a Model Financial Aid Grant Program for the State of Maryland. College Park, Md.: Black Coalition of the U. of Maryland Campuses, 1971.

Seawright, Sally. "Desegregation at [the University of] Maryland: The NAACP and the Murray Case in the 1930's." Maryland History 1(Spring, 1970).

Sedlacek, Wm. E., Brooks, Glenwood C., Jr., and Herman, Michele H. Black Student Attitudes Toward a Predominantly White University. College Park, Md.: Cultural Study Center, U. of Maryland, Mr, 1972 [U. of Md.]

Sloan, Jane. "Morgan State College." Integrateducation 15(N-D, 1977):141-142.

Thompson, Vernon C. "Policy Questions Greet New Head of Bowie State College." Washington Post, My 4, 1978 [Rufus L. Barfield]

Tildon, Charles, Bard, Harry, and Wilson, Robert, Jr. "The Black Student: The Community College." Junior College Journal, N, 1969 [Baltimore]

Wennersten, John R., and Ellen, Ruth. "Separate and Unequal: The Evolution of a Black Land Grant College in Maryland, 1890-1930." Md. Hist. Mag. 72(Spring, 1977):110-117.

Wilson, Edward N. The History of Morgan State College. N.Y.: Vantage Press, 1977.

Massachusetts

Abram, Morris B. "The Eleven Days at Brandeis--As Seen from the President's Chair." New York Times Magazine, F 16, 1969 [Black student demonstration, J, 1969]

"Afro-American Studies--What's Going On Here?" Harvard Crimson, Ap 12, 1969 [A documentary account of events at Harvard]

Alexander, Raymond Pace. "Voices from Harvard's Own Negroes." Opportunity 1 (Mr, 1923).

Alverson, Charles. "Howard University's 'Relevance' Throes." Wall Street Journal, Je 17, 1968.

"[Black] Student Sought 'Relevant' Education." Muhammad Speaks, F 28, 1969 [Brandeis U.]

Black Student Union of the Harvard Graduate School of Education. "Black Student Union Statements." Harvard Educational Review, Summer, 1969 [In re: Arthur R. Jensen]

"Black Students at Harvard." New York Times Magazine, O 14, 1973 [An exchange of letters]

"Black Students at Harvard: The Rosovsky Report." Harvard Crimson, F 4, 1969.

"Black Students Fight for Research Institute." African World, Mr, 1975 [Harvard U.]

Bloomfield, Morton W. and others. "No Quotas [at Harvard]." Change 3 (O, 1971) 4 (letter).

Blumenthal, David. "Back to School." Harvard Crimson, S 28, 1968 [Harvard Graduate School of Education]

_____. "The Ed School and Roxbury: Hostile Partnership." Harvard Crimson, My 28, 1968 [The Graduate School of Education, Harvard]

"Brandeis Student Says Blacks Seek Knowledge to Liberate Their People." Muhammad Speaks, F 28, 1969.

Burton, Robert. "CCEBS. Interview with Michael Jackson." Drum (Winter, 1977-1978):10-17 [Executive director of the Committee for the Collegiate Education of Black Students, U. of Massachusetts, Amherst]

Butler, Keith. "Blacks Seek Social Ease; Coercion Is Not a Factor." Harvard Crimson, O 23, 1974 [Harvard U.]

_____. "Harvard's Black Admissions." Harvard Crimson, F 11, 1974.

_____. "The Man With the Fishing Poles." Harvard Crimson, Mr 26, 1974 [David L. Evans, Associate Director, Harvard College Admissions]

Carlson, Elliot. "Two Liberal Schools Decide Campus Turmoil Was Worth the Trouble." Wall Street Journal, Mr 24, 1969 [Brandeis and Swarthmore]

Clinton, Catherine. "Joint Concentrations for Afro?" Harvard Crimson, F 13, 1973. [Afro-American Studies at Harvard U.]

Committee for the Collegiate Education of Black Students. CCEBS, University of Massachusetts at Amherst. Amherst, MA: U. of Masschusetts, 1969.

Concentrators in Afro-American Studies [At Harvard University]. "A Student Self-Interview." Harvard Crimson, Mr 21, 1972.

Contreras, Joseph L. "Recruiting in the Barrios." Harvard Crimson, Ap 19, 1976. [Recruiting Mexican-American students for Harvard U.]

Corazzini, Arthur J. and others. Study of Higher Education, Metropolitan II: An Economic Analysis of the Potential and Realized Demand for Higher Education in Boston SMSA. Draft, 1968. ERIC ED 040 250.

Davis, A. M. "The Indian College at Cambridge." Magazine of American History 24(J1, 1890): 33-39.

Davis, Ron L., and Poyer, Lisa M. "For Black Faculty and Administrators, It's Not an Easy Life." Harvard Crimson, N 25, 1974.

Du Bois, W. E. B. [Article on Wilberforce and Harvard Universities] Amsterdam News, Je 29, 1940.

_____. "A Negro Student at Harvard at the End of the 19th Century." Massachusetts Review I (1960).

_____. "Harvard." Fisk Herald 10(N, 1892): 1-4. [Letter]

_____. "That Outer, White World of Harvard." In The Harvard Book. Edited by W. Bentinck-Smith. Cambridge, MA: Harvard U. Press, 1953.

Evans, David L. "Making It, as a Black, at Harvard and Radcliffe." New York Times, N 24, 1976.

Fitzgerald, John M., and Scruggs, Otey M. "A Note on Marcus Garvey at Harvard, 1922: A Recollection of John M. Fitzgerald." Journal of Negro History 63(Ap, 1978):157-160.

Fletcher, William. "Affirmative Action at Harvard." Harvard Crimson, F 24, 1976.

Foster, J. W. "Race and Truth at Harvard." New Republic, J1 17, 1976. [Case of Dr. Bernard D. Davis' criticism of special admissions program at Harvard Medical School]

Fraser, Leon A., Jr. "Harvard and De Funis." Harvard Crimson (letter), F 14, 1974.

Glassman, James K. "A Report on the Future of the University." Harvard Crimson Supplement, My 7, 1969.

Green, Joseph. "The Pit in Harvard Yard." Boston Globe, Mr 10, 1974. [Black Harvard professors Martin Kilson and Ewart Guinier]

Griffin, Richard B. "Harvard Ablaze." America, My 17, 1969.

Gross, Kenneth G. "Blacks on Campus: Angry and Alone Together." Nation, F 17, 1969. [Brandeis U. and Queens College]

Guinier, Ewart. "Black Studies: Training for Leadership." Freedomways 15(Third Quarter, 1975):196-205. [Harvard U.]

_____. "Harvard U Accused of 'Academic Lynching' of Black Students." Amsterdam News, N 9, 1974.

Hamilton, Charles J., Jr. "The Black Student at Harvard." Harvard Crimson, O 11, 1967.

_____. "New Mood for Harvard Blacks." Harvard Crimson, O 20, 1967.

Hardie, Peter. "Black Roots, White Poison." Harvard Crimson, N 25, 1975. [Harvard]

Hardie, Peter, and Jacobs, Bruce. "On the Brink: Afro-American Studies at Harvard." Harvard Crimson, Ja 18, 1977.

Harris, Seymour E. The Economics of Harvard. New York: McGraw-Hill, 1971.

Harvard University, Faculty of Arts and Sciences. Report of the Faculty Committee on African and Afro-American Studies. Cambridge, MA: Harvard U. Press, Ja 20, 1969.

"Harvard's New Policy." Messenger 5(Mr, 1923): 621. [Segregated housing of black freshmen]

Hayes, Laurie. "Ed Bordley Grapples with Being Blind, Being Black and Being at Harvard." Harvard Crimson, Ja 11, 1978.

How Harvard Rules. Cambridge, MA: A. R. G. and The Old Mole, 1969. The Old Mole, 2 Brookline Street, Cambridge, MA or The New England Free Press, 791 Tremont Street, Boston, MA

Isaacs, Stephen. "What's Happened to Harvard?" Washington Post, N 25, 1973.

Jones, Edward P. "Is It Easier to Get In If You're Colored?" National Catholic Reporter, O 15, 1969. [Black student at Holy Cross College, Worcester]

Kilson, Martin L., Jr. "Black and White in the Ivy: The Ethnic Cul-de-Sac." Harvard Crimson, O 17, 1978. [See response by Gabrielle Nicole Virgo, O 21, 1978.]

_____. "The Black Experience at Harvard." New York Times Magazine, S 2, 1973.

Kozol, Jonathan. "Harvard's Role in Perpetuation of Class-Exploitation." Harvard Crimson, O 31, 1973.

Laing, Mercedes A. "Black Students at Harvard: A Problem of Image." Harvard Crimson, O 10, 1975.

Ledecky, Jonathan J. "Harvard Professor Profiles 'Mini-Mack' Herron." Harvard Crimson, D 12, 1975. [Prof. James McCoy Jones]

Lee, Richard T. "Resolution Causes Enrollment Drop in B-School Blacks." Harvard Crimson, n.d. [Harvard Business School]

Leonard, H. Jeffrey. "Inside Harvard's Brief." Harvard Crimson, F 14, 1974. [In re: amicus curiae brief in De Funis v. Odegaard case]

_____. "The 'Reverse Discrimination' Backlash." Harvard Crimson, F 8, 1974. [De Funis v. Odegaard]

Leonard, Walter J. "Innocence and Ignorance." Harvard Crimson, O 2, 1973. [On equal employment opportunity and affirmative action]

Lipset, Seymour, and Riesman, David. Education and Politics at Harvard. New York: McGraw-Hill, 1975.

Lukas, J. Anthony. "Roy." Esquire 75(Mr, 1971):122. [Roy De Berry, Brandeis U.]

McArthur, John H. Research Project Concerning Students from Minority Groups, Je, 1974. ERIC ED 121 135. [Harvard Business School]

McClendon, Monica. "Riding on the Back of the University's Bus." Harvard Crimson, N 25, 1975. [Harvard]

Markham, Richard B. "Blacks at Wellesley Discover Indifference Swallows Its Own Children." Harvard Crimson, D 19, 1968.

McDouglass, Harold A. "Negro Students' Challenge to Liberalism." Harvard Crimson, My 31, 1967. [The Association of African and Afro-American Students at Harvard University]

McGrady, Mike. "Soc Sci. 5: 'A Place for the Black Man at Harvard?'" Harvard Crimson, N 14, 1968.

Marcus, Lawrence R. Affirmative Action in Science Departments: A Challenge for Higher Education, 1976. ERIC ED 134 110. [U. of Massachusetts]

Massing, Michael A. "Whites Feel Indifferent, But Many Are Uneasy." Harvard Crimson, O 23, 1974. [Harvard U.]

Melnick, Peter R. "Minority Recruitment at Harvard: Still a Ways to Go." Harvard Crimson, Ja 23, 1978. [See, also, letters in issue of Ja 25, 1978.]

Milstein, Tom. "Roots of Campus Black Separation." New America, Ja 30, 1969. [Brandeis U., Waltham]

Monroe, Sylvester. "Guest in a Strange House. A Black at Harvard." Saturday Review of Education, F, 1973.

Muskrat, Jerry. "Indian Enrollment at Harvard Urged." American Anthropologist Newsletter 12(1971).

Myers, Samuel L., Jr. "Personal Testimony: The Agony of the Black Scholars in the White World." Phi Delta Kappan (Je, 1977):746-750. [M.I.T.]

Nelson, Bryce. "Brandeis. How a Liberal University Reacts to a Black Takeover." Science, Mr 28, 1969, pp. 1431-1434.

Osgood, Viola. "New Hope for Roxbury College." Boston Globe, Ag 27, 1978.

Painter, Nell. "Jim Crow at Harvard, 1923." New England Quarterly, D, 1971.

Pan-African Liberation Committee. "Harvard's Investments in Southern Africa." Black Scholar 3(Ja, 1972):25-31.

Patterson, Orlando. "Angola, Gulf, and Harvard." Harvard Crimson, My 2, 1972.

Porter, Horace. "Reflections of a Black Son." Change 9(F, 1977):34-39. [Amherst College]

Portrait of Three Brandeis Students." Muhammad Speaks, F 28, 1969.

"Problems of Race in the Liberal University." Harvard Crimson, Je 12, 1975. [Articles on Harvard U.]

Profit, Wesley. "The Future of Afro-American Studies at Harvard University ." Harvard Crimson, O 25, 1972.

_____. "The Hell You Say." Harvard Crimson, O 8, 1974. [The politics of Afro-American studies at Harvard U.]

Ratner, Jonathan D. "The Gulf Protesters: Changing Harvard?" Harvard Crimson, Ap 21, 1977.

Riesman, David. "Education at Harvard." Change 5(S, 1973):24-37.

Rosenthal, Michael, Ritterman, Pamela, and Sherman, Bob. "Blacks at Brandeis." Commonweal, Mr 14, 1969.

Rosovsky, Henry. "Black Studies at Harvard. Personal Reflections Concerning Recent Events." American Scholar, Autumn, 1969.

Seder, Jeff. "'Fair Harvard'--Who's Here and Why?" Harvard Crimson, D 18, 1968.

Seder, Jeff, and Labaree, David. "Fair Harvard--Where the Money Goes." Harvard Crimson, My 30, 1969.

Shelton, Florence C. "Some Impressions of Fair Harvard's Blacks." Harvard Journal of Negro Affairs, D, 1965.

Survey Report of State-Funded College Programs for "Disadvantaged" Students in Massachusetts, Mr 1, 1972. ERIC ED 060 836.

Synott, Marcia G. The Half-Opened Door: Discrimination and Admissions at Harvard, Yale and Princeton, 1900-1970. Westport, CT: Greenwood Press, 1979.

Takaki, Ronald. "Aesculapius Was a White Man: Antebellum Racism and Male Chauvinism at Harvard Medical School." Phylon 39 (Summer, 1978):128-134.

Task Force on Affirmative Action. "The Task Force on Affirmative Action: Building a Mass Movement." Harvard Crimson, Ja 3, 1977. [Harvard U.]

Vargus, Ione Dugger. "The Revival of Ideology: The Afro-American Society Movement." Doctoral dissertation, Brandeis U., F, 1971. [Tufts and Brandeis Universities]

Wade, Harold, Jr. Black Men of Amherst. Amherst, MA: Amherst College Press, 1976.

Walker, Joe. "Why Blacks Rebelled at Brandeis." Muhammad Speaks, F 28, 1969.

Waroff, Deborah R. "Chester Hartman, City Planning, and the [Harvard] Graduate School of Design. Harvard Crimson, My 27, 1970.

Weiss, Philip. "Finding Blacks in Baltimore." Harvard Crimson, Ap 19, 1976. [Recruiting students for Harvard U.]

"Wellesley Class of '73." Ebony 28(Ag, 1973): 64-70.

West, Cornell. "Black Culture: The Golden Mean." Harvard Crimson, Mr 26, 1974. [Martin Kilson]

West, Emory J. "Black Students At Harvard: 1900-1917." Harvard Crimson, F 9, 1972.

Wexler, Natalie. "Harvard's Indians Are Getting Ahead to Help Their People." Harvard Crimson, Ja 20, 1975.

Williams, Sidney. "A Few Words Before I Go." Harvard Crimson, My 2, 1972. [A black football player-student on racism at Harvard]

Michigan

Anderson, Clarence A. and others. Reading Progress: A Bi-Racial Comparison; A Study of the Reading Achievement of Black and White Students at Flint Community Junior College, My, 1970, 23 pp. ERIC ED 039 878.

Behee, John. Hail to the Victors! Black Athletes at the University of Michigan, 1974. Ulrich's Books, Inc., 549 East University, Ann Arbor, MI 48104.

Biskin, Donald S. Analysis of the 1969-1970 Academic Tutorial Program at Michigan State University. East Lansing, MI: Center for Urban Affairs, Mr, 1971.

"Blacks and the University of Michigan." Integrated Education 8(J1-Ag, 1970):10-12.

Boone, W. H. "Problems of Adjustment of Negro Students at a White School." Journal of Negro Education, 0, 1942. [U. of Michigan]

Brown, Elizabeth Gaspar. "The Initial Admission of Negro Students to the University of Michigan." Michigan Quarterly Review 2 (Autumn, 1963):233-230.

Brown, Noah, Jr. "A Descriptive Research Study of a Developmental Plan for Recruitment and Retention of Minority Students." Doctoral dissertation, Wayne State U., 1976. [Wayne State U.]

Brown, Orchid. "A Comparative Study of Black Freshmen, Special Admit Students and Regular Admit Students at Michigan State University." Doctoral dissertation, Michigan State U., 1971.

Bullard, J. T. "Black Educational Drive Expanding Michigan College." Muhammad Speaks, 0 23, 1970. [Wayne County Community College]

Cassidy, Sally Whelan and others. Impact of a High-Demand College in a Large University of Working Class Youth. 2 vols., Ag, 1968. ERIC ED 025 223. [Monteith College, Wayne State U., Detroit]

Center for Urban Affairs. Survey of Minority Group Participation in the Graduate Programs at MSU. East Lansing, MI: Center for Urban Affairs, Michigan State U., 1970.

Chalmers, W. Ellison. Racial Negotiations: Potentials and Limitations. Ann Arbor, MI: Institute of Labor and Industrial Relations, 1973. [Includes section on U. of Michigan]

Chernoff, P. R. "Negro Students at [the University of] Michigan." Science, 0 13, 1967 (letter).

Clagett, J. C. "The Post-Admission Support Policies of Public Colleges and Universities of Michigan in Relation to Indian Students' Needs." Doctoral dissertation, Michigan State U., 1973.

Clamage, Dena. "Wayne State Strike." Movement, Ag, 1969. [Wayne State U., Detroit]

Coleman, Don E. "The Status of the Black Student Aide Program and the Black Student Movement at Michigan State University." Doctoral dissertation, Michigan State U., 1971.

"College Presidents and Minority Students." Integrated Education 12(Ja-Ap, 1974):41-44.

Cross, Robert. "Let's Win This One for the Private Sector." Chicago Tribune Magazine, My 8, 1977. [Hillsdale College]

Fenstemacher, William Proctor. A Study of the Relationship of Instrumental and Intellectual Orientations to the Educational Experiences of Black Students at the University of Michigan. Final Report, Ap, 1971. ERIC ED 054 732.

_____. "A Study of the Relationship of Instrumental and Intellectual Orientations to the Educational Experiences of Black Students at the University of Michigan." Doctoral dissertation, U. of Michigan, 1971. Univ. Microfilms Order No. 71-23749.

Garner, June Brown. "Desegregation Is Crippling Black Colleges' Vital Role." Detroit News, O 3, 1976. [Detroit Institute of Technology]

Grant, William. "Race Issue in Colleges Subsiding." Detroit Free Press, F 27, 1978.

Green, Robert L., Lezotte, Lawrence, Schweitzer, John, and Biskin, Donald. "The Admission of f Minority Students: A Framework for Action." Integrated Education 9(Mr-Ap, 1971):9-16.

Greider, William. "Black Woman's Bid to Become Dean Stirs Controversy." Washington Post, My 17, 1975. [Prof. Jewel Cobb and U. of Michigan]

Hardy, Dan. "More on Wayne State [University]." The Movement, O, 1969. [Detroit]

Hedegard, J. M. Longitudinal Study of Working-Class College Students [at the University of Michigan]. Ann Arbor, MI: U. of Michigan, 1971.

"'Institute of Black Studies' Opening in Detroit Under Black Student Control." Muhammad Speaks, Mr 28, 1969. [Wayne State U.]

Johnson, Joan Thomasena Jackson. "Affirmative Action Employment Programs: How Blacks Employed at Michigan State University and Vocational Rehabilitation Services Understand the Program and Perceive It as Affecting their Careers." Doctoral dissertation, Michigan State U., 1976. Univ. Microfilms Order No. 76-27115.

Johnson, Oakley C. "The Negro-Caucasian Club." Negro History Bulletin 33(F, 1970):35-41. [U. of Michigan]

Kallingal, A. "The Prediction of Grades for Black and White at Michigan State University." Journal of Educational Measurement 8(1971):263-265.

Kazmann, R. G. "Negroes at [the University of] Michigan." Science, Ag 4, 1967 (letter).

Kinsey, Morris. "Financial Assistance as a Significant Factor in the Educational Survival of Selected Black Students at Michigan State University." Doctoral dissertation, Michigan State U., 1972. Univ. Microfilms Order No. 73-05414.

Lezotte, Lawrence, and Schweitzer, John. A Reanalysis of the Post Secondary Educational Plans of Michigan High School Graduates 1970. East Lansing, MI: Center for Urban Affairs, Ja 21, 1971.

Michigan State Department of Education. Equality of Access to Postsecondary Education, Ap, 1974. ERIC ED 099 017.

Michigan Department of Education. Survey of Post-Secondary Plans of Michigan High School Graduates. Lansing, MI: State Department of Education, Jl, 1970.

Michigan. Senate. Committee to Investigate Campus Disorders and Student Unrest. Final Staff Report. Part 1. Study Findings and Recommendations. Lansing, MI, 1970.

Nelson, Bryce. "Michigan: Ruckus over Race Has Relevance to Other Universities." Science 156(Je 2, 1967):1209-1212. [See also ibid., 157(Ag 4, 1967):190 and 158(O 13, 1967):205-206.]

Newsome, Emanuel. "Michigan Universities Lead Trend in Negro Appointments to Governing Boards." College and University Business, Jl, 1969.

Pollack, Susan R. "Colleges Grapple With Lag in Minority Enrollment." Detroit News, F 18, 1979.

Presidential Commission on Admissions and Student Body Composition. A Report to the President of Michigan State University. East Lansing, MI: Michigan State U., N 1, 1971.

Pulliams, Preston. "Comparison of Self-Perceived Needs Among Black Students Attending Muskegon Community College." Doctoral dissertation, U. of Michigan, 1976.

Ratliffe, Sharon A., and Steil, Lyman K. "Attitudinal Differences between Black and White College Students." Speech Teacher 19 (S, 1970):190-198. [Wayne State U. and Western Michigan U.]

Riesman, David, Gusfield, Joseph, and Gramson, Zelda. Academic Values and Mass Education: The Early Years of Oakland and Montieth. Garden City, NY: Doubleday, 1970.

Sabine, Gordon A. "Michigan State's Search for More Negro Students." College Board Review, Fall, 1968.

Salsinger, Harry. "A Change of Heart." Change 2(N-D, 1970):23-24. [Black students at the Law School of Wayne State U., Detroit]

Schmidt, William H. Survey of Minority Group Participation in the Graduate Programs at Michigan State University. East Lansing, MI: Center for Urban Affairs, Michigan State U., Je 1, 1970.

Scott, James E. "An Investigation of Black and White Student Expectations and Perceptions of a Predominantly White Public Institution." Doctoral dissertation, U. of Michigan, 1978. Univ. Microfilms Order No. 7823004. [Eastern Michigan U.]

Sempliner, Ester. "A History of Jewish Students at the University of Michigan." Master's thesis, U. of Michigan, 1940.

Shapiro, B. J. "The Black Athlete at Michigan State University." Master's thesis, Michigan State U., 1970.

"Students Say Whites Still Dominate Black Studies [at Michigan State University]." Muhammad Speaks, N 7, 1969.

2X, Herman L. "Students Cite Injustices at U. of Detroit." Muhammad Speaks, Ap 16, 1971.

Vice President for University Relations and the Office of Equal Opportunity Programs. Report on Equal Opportunity and Affirmative Action at Michigan State University, 1970-1971. East Lansing, MI: Board of Trustees, Michigan State U., S 9, 1971.

Ward, Francis. "Michigan Colleges Differ in Goals for Blacks." Los Angeles Times, Je 12, 1974. [Michigan State U. and U. of Michigan]

Winston, Eric Von Arthur. "Black Student Activism at Michigan State University, September, 1967 to June 30, 1972: The University's Response." Doctoral dissertation, Michigan State U., 1973. Univ. Microfilms Order No. 73-20424.

Wright, Madeline. "Black Coeds in More than Academic Dilemma at UM?" Michigan Chronicle, D 6, 1975. [U. of Michigan]

Minnesota

Anderson, Brian. "Department of Indian Studies at 'U' Struggles Through Infancy." Minneapolis Tribune, Ja 24, 1971. [U. of Minnesota]

Armstrong, Roberta A., and Hall, William V. A Comparative Study of Martin Luther King Program and Randomly Selected Freshmen Entering the University of Minnesota in Fall, 1970: Entrance Data and Subsequent Performance, Je, 1976. ERIC ED 125 478.

_____ and _____. The Relationship of Course Characteristics to Differential Performance of Martin Luther King Program and Other Students in Selected College of Liberal Arts Courses, Je, 1976. ERIC ED 125 479. [U. of Minnesota]

"Black Students Face Choice: Progress or Racial Isolation." Milwaukee Journal, Ja 10, 1971. [Carleton College, Northfield, MN]

Borreson, B. J., and Williamson, E. G. Learning to Resolve Social Conflicts." Educational Record 31(1950):26-38. [U. of Minnesota]

Britts, Maurice W. Blacks on White College Campuses. Minneapolis, MN: Challenge Productions, Inc., 1976. [Concordia College, St. Paul]

Cavender, Christian C. "A Study of Selected Intellective and Non-Intellective Factors Related to Achievement of Native American Freshmen at the University of Minnesota." Doctoral dissertation, U. of Minnesota, 1974.

Du Bois, W. E. B. [Article on Macelester College and the Universities of Minnesota and Northwestern] Amsterdam News, My 24, 1941.

Minnesota Private College Research Foundation. Indian Students in Minnesota's Private Colleges--Who They Are, Where They Come From, Where They're Going, What They Think of Their Experience in College, Mr 12, 1974. ED 088 633.

Moen, Norman W., and Giese, David L. Martin Luther King Tutorial Program University of Minnesota. Volume Six, Number Four, 1970. ERIC ED 041 321.

Rosales, Francisco. The Chicano Student at the University and College in the Midwest Summer, 1971. Montal Education Associates, Suite 1207, 1700 K Street, N.W., Washington, DC 20006. [U. of Minnesota]

Skinner, Kenneth A., and Hendricks, Glenn L. A New Minority: Indochinese Refugees in Higher Education, D, 1977. ERIC ED 148 274. [U. of Minnesota]

Stone, Doug. "Black Students Harassed in Northfield." Minneapolis Tribune, Ap 25, 1976. [Carleton College, Northfield]

Mississippi

Barrett, Russell H. Integration at Ole Miss. Chicago, IL: Quadrangle, 1965.

"Board of Trustees Sued." Kudzu 2(My, 1970):9. [Board of Trustees of Institutions of Higher Learning]

Buck, James R., Jr. "Some Identifiable Characteristics of Students Entering Negro Senior Colleges in Mississippi." Doctoral dissertation, George Peabody College for Teachers, 1964. Univ. Microfilms Order No. 65-344.

Campbell, Clarice T. "History of Tougaloo College." Doctoral dissertation, U. of Mississippi, 1970.

Clark, Robert, and Doggett, David. [Account of police shooting at Jackson State College, Jackson, Mississippi, May 13 and 14, 1970] Kudzu 2(My, 1970):2.

Coombs, Orde. "Jackson State College." Change 5(O, 1973):34-39.

"Community Response [to police shooting at Jackson State College, Jackson, Mississippi, May 13 and 14, 1970]." Kudzu 2(My, 1970): 4, 15.

Cunningen, Donald. "The Motivations of Black Mississippi Students to Attend Black Colleges." Master's thesis, U. of New Hampshire, 1976.

Dansby, B. Baldwin. A Brief History of Jackson College. New York: American Book Stratford Press, 1953.

Delaney, Joe. "Justice Dept. Suit Threatens Existence of Black Colleges." Muhammad Speaks, Mr 7, 1975.

Doherty, William T. "Confrontation at Ole Miss: A Southern Political Barbecue, 1962." North Dakota Quarterly, Winter, 1973.

Dunham, Melerson Guy. Centennial History of Alcorn A. & M. College. Hattiesburg, MS: University and College Press of Mississippi, 1971.

Holtzclaw, R. Fulton. William Henry Holtzclaw and Utica Junior College. Dillon-Liederbaek, 1976.

Huge, Harry. "Inquest at Jackson State." New South 25(Summer, 1970):65-70.

"Integration at Old Miss." Ebony, My, 1966.

King, Willye M. "Higher Negro Education in the State of Mississippi." Quarterly Review of Higher Education Among Negroes 5(O, 1937): 173-183.

Lesher, Stephan. "Jackson State a Year Ago." New York Times Magazine, Mr 21, 1971.

Love, Sam. "Mississippi College Students Challenge the Courthouse Gang." New South, Spring, 1969.

Meacham, Carl E. "Recruiting, 1971." The Black Collegian 2(N-D, 1971):20-21. [Recruiting in Mississippi high schools for students to attend Mary Holmes College in West Point]

Meredith, James. Three Years in Mississippi. Bloomington, IN: U. of Indiana Press, 1966.

Mississippi Gulf Coast Junior College. Race and Sex Analysis of Students, Ja 26, 1976. ERIC ED 126 959.

"New Misery at Ole Miss [Law School]." Time, Ag 30, 1968.

Parsons, Cynthia. "Two Women With a Vision." Southern Education Report, Ap, 1969. [Jackson State College, Jackson]

President's Commission on Campus Unrest. "Jackson State." In The Report...Campus Unrest, pp. 411-465. Washington, DC: GPO, 1970. [The shootings of My 14, 1970 at Jackson State College]

Rhodes, Lelia G. Jackson State University: The First Hundred Years. Jackson, MS: U. Press of Mississippi, 1978.

Scheips, Paul J. The Role of the Army in the Oxford, Mississippi Incident, 1962-1963. Washington, DC: Office of the Chief of Military History, Department of the Army, 1965.

Sievert, William A., and Adams, Jacqueline J. "Jackson State College, Scene of Killings, Tries to Shake Haunts of Past." Chronicle of Higher Education 6(D 6, 1971):6-7.

Smith, Jay T. "Origin and Development of Industrial Education at Alcorn Agricultural and Mechanical College." Doctoral dissertation, U. of Missouri, 1971.

Spencer, Howard. "White Repression and Black Response in Mississippi." Liberation, Ap, 1969. [Tougaloo College]

Stuart, Reginald. Black Perspectives on State-Controlled Higher Education: The Mississippi Report. New York: John Hay Whitney Foundation, Ja, 1974.

Thompson, Cleopatra D. "The Jackson State College Graduate in American Society, 1944-1953." Doctoral dissertation, Cornell U., 1960.

Tinsley, Sammy Jay. "A History of Mississippi Valley State College." Doctoral dissertation, U. of Mississippi, 1972.

Tucker, Richard D. "State of Miss Education." Kudzu 2(My, 1970):8, 5. [Mississippi Valley State College]

"The University of Mississippi." AAUP Bulletin 56(1970):75-86.

"What Happened in the Alcorn College Student Strike." Crisis, Je-J1, 1957.

"White Repression and Black Response." Black Panther, Mr 9, 1969. [Tougaloo College]

Williams, James W. Black College Alumni Follow-up Study of Graduates from 1971-73, 1974. ERIC ED 125 441. [Alcorn State U.]

Williams, James W., and Bunner, Gary N. Class of 1975: Selected Student Characteristics from a Predominantly Black College, Ap, 1976. ERIC ED 125 415. [Alcorn State U.]

Missouri

Aber, Elaine M. "Reverse Pattern of Integration." Journal of Educational Sociology, F, 1958. [Lincoln U.]

Andrus, Gorden F. "Students Trigger Reform." Focus/Midwest, Ja-F, 1969. [Washington U.]

Bluford, Lucile. "Missouri 'Shows' the Supreme Court." Crisis 46(Ag, 1939):231-232, 242, 246.

Brigham, R. J. "Church-Related Colleges for Negroes in Missouri to 1945." Negro History Bulletin, Ja, 1951.

Collins, William, Jr. "Attitudes of Undergraduate Black Students at Saint Louis University." Doctoral dissertation, Saint Louis U., 1974. Univ. Microfilms Order No. 74-24061.

Davis, Dorothy. "She Knocks at the Door of Missouri University." Crisis 46(My, 1940). [Lucile Bluford, School of Journalism, U. of Missouri]

Davis, Joseph S. A Study of Attitudes Held by Black Students Living in Residence Halls. Columbia, MO: U. of Missouri, College of Education, My 1, 1970, 11 pp. ERIC ED 045 036.

Egerton, John. "Central Missouri's Inner City Project Tells a Near-Parable." Southern Education Report, My, 1967. [The "inner-college" resistance to a program of teacher preparation for inner-city work, Central Missouri State College]

Eliot, Thomas H. "Administrative Response to Campus Turmoil." In The Campus and the Racial Crisis. Washington, DC: American Council on Education, 1969. [Washington U., St. Louis]

Faherty, William B. "Nativism and Midwestern Education: The Experience of Saint Louis University, 1832-1856. The Century of Hope II." History of Education Quarterly, Winter, 1968.

Holtzman, Jo. "Color Caste Changes Among Black College Students." Journal of Black Studies 4(S, 1973):92-101. [Forest Park Community College, St. Louis, MO]

Kelleher, Daniel T. "The Case of Lloyd Lionel Gaines: The Demise of the Separate But Equal Doctrine." Journal of Negro History 56 (O, 1971):262-271.

Levine, Daniel U., Mitchell, Edna S., and Havighurst, Robert J. Opportunities for Higher Education in a Metropolitan Area: A Study of High School Seniors in Kansas City [Mo.] 1967. Bloomington, IN: Phi Delta Kappa, 1970.

McMurdock, Bertha J. "The Development of Higher Education for Negroes in Missouri." Master's thesis, Howard U., 1939.

McWilliams, Carey. "Racial Dialectic: Missouri Style." Nation 160(F 24, 1945):208-209.

Pandey, R. E. "A Comparative Study of Dropout at an Integrated University: The 16 Personality Factor Test." Journal of Negro Education 42(Fall, 1973):447-451. [Lincoln U.]

Perry, Floyd. "Selected Variables Related to Academic Success of Black Freshmen Students at the University of Missouri." Doctoral dissertation, U. of Missouri, 1972.

Sadukai, Owusu. [Text of an address] IFCO News 3(N-D, 1972). [Lincoln U.]

Savage, W. Sherman. The History of Lincoln University. Jefferson City, MO: Lincoln U., 1939.

Sawyer, Robert M. "The Gaines Case: Its Background and Influence on the University of Missouri and Lincoln University, 1936-1950." Doctoral dissertation, U. of Missouri, 1966. Univ. Microfilms Order No. 66-9000.

Wagman, Paul. "Blacks Tell of Rising Frustration at Missouri U." St. Louis Post-Dispatch, J1 21, 1974.

Willson, John P. "Apathy Distinguishes Students, Faculty, and Administration." Focus/Midwest, Ja-F, 1969. [St. Louis U.]

Young, Charles. "Will the Real Lincoln University Please Stand Up?" Focus/Midwest, V, No. 33 (1966).

Montana

Voyich, Daniel L. "A Study of Selected Characteristics of Successful and Unsuccessful American Indian Students Enrolled at Montana State University from September, 1967 to June, 1972." Doctoral dissertation, Montana State U., 1974.

Nebraska

Barnds, William J. "Nebraska College, The Episcopal School at Nebraska City, 1868-1885." Nebraska History 52(Summer, 1971):169-189.

Parrott, Larry. "More Blacks Fulfilling College Degree Quest." Omaha World-Herald, Mr 18, 1979.

Smith, Jeffrey H. "The Omaha De Porres Club." Negro History Bulletin 33(D, 1970):194-199. [Creighton U., Omaha, NE]

New Hampshire

Bureau of Indian Affairs. Evaluation Report of Dartmouth's A Better Chance Program, N, 1976. ERIC ED 147 089. [Indian students]

Conniff, Michael. "Seething Dartmouth Minorities Sound Off." Boston Herald American, Mr 9, 1979.

Kenney, Charles. "Dartmouth Halts Classes for a Day to Discuss Charges of Sexism, Racism." Boston Globe, Mr 9, 1979.

Merton, Andy. "Fraternity Freedom vs. Racism-Sexism." Boston Globe, N 26, 1978. [Dartmouth College]

New Jersey

Alman, Emily. "Desegregation at Rutgers University." In Black Life and Culture in the United States, pp. 210-233. Edited by Rhoda Goldstein. New York: Crowell, 1971.

Baker, Ross K. "Black Student, White School: The Challenge of the Total Environment." Journal of Social and Behavioral Sciences 15 (Fall, 1970):53-60. [Rutgers U.]

"Blacks, Puerto Ricans, Demand 'Decision-Making Participation' at Catholic N.J. University." Muhammad Speaks, My 16, 1975. [Seton Hall U., South Orange]

Bray, Thomas J. "Experimental Programs for Ghetto Students Stirs Hope at Rutgers." Wall Street Journal, My 13, 1970.

Bryan, Louis Marie. "Assessments of Upward Bound Participation and the Black Liberation Movement as Indicated by Data Obtained from a Group of Black Youth in Newark, New Jersey." Doctoral dissertation, Columbia U., 1976. Univ. Microfilms Order No. 76-29578.

Dawson, Charles S. "Black Student Organizations on Predominantly White Campuses." University: A Princeton Quarterly, Winter, 1970-71.

Downing, Margo. "Black Lawyers Plan to Probe Charge of Racism by Rutgers." Philadelphia Bulletin, My 2, 1976. [Rutgers Law School at Camden]

Du Bois, W. E. B. "John Howard [First Negro Graduate of Princeton University]." Chicago Defender, My 10, 1947.

Duhl, Leonard J., with Steetle, Nancy Jo. "Newark: Community or Chaos. A Case Study of the Medical School Controversy." Journal of Applied Behavioral Science 5(1969):537-588.

Engs, Robert F., and Williams, John B. "Integration by Evasion." Nation, N 17, 1969. [Princeton U.]

Farrow, Earl Vann. "A Longitudinal Study: The Long-Term Impact of the Rutgers Upward Bound Program on its Participants." Doctoral dissertation, Rutgers U., 1976. Univ. Microfilms Order No. 76-27,319.

Farrow, Earl Vann and others. A Longitudinal Study: The Long-Term Impact of the Rutgers Upward Bound Program on its Participants, My, 1977. ERIC ED 144 982.

Fields, Carl A. "One University's Response to Today's Negro Student." University (Princeton University), Spring, 1968.

_____. "Princeton University's Response to Today's Negro Student." Journal of the National Association of Women Deans and Counselors, Winter, 1969.

Fishman, George. "Paul Robeson's Student Days and the Fight Against Racism at Rutgers." Freedomways, Summer, 1969.

Franco, Ralph A. "The Influence of the Puerto Rican Family on Its Male College-Bound Youths in Camden, New Jersey." Doctoral dissertation, Pennsylvania State U., 1975. Univ. Microfilms Order No. 76-6487.

Hidalgo, Hilda. "No One Model American: A Collegiate Case in Point." Journal of Teacher Education 24(Winter, 1973):294-301.

Holleman, Edith. "Trials of an Innovative College." Change 3(Summer, 1971):17-20. [Livingston College, Rutgers]

Johnson, Henry C. "Minority and Nonminority Medical Students' Perceptions of the Medical School Environment." Journal of Medical Education 53(F, 1978):135-136. [Rutgers U.]

Koffler, Stephen L. Basic Skills Mastery of New Jersey's College Bound Students, n.d. ERIC ED 146 234.

Ravitch, Diane. "The Dream of Livingston College." Change, My-Je, 1969. [Urban college of Rutgers U.]

Robeson, Paul, Jr. "Rutgers Salutes Paul Robeson." Freedomways 10(Third Quarter, 1970):237-241.

Robinson, Eugene H. "A Distant Image: Paul Robeson and Rutgers' Students Today." Freedomways 11(First Quarter, 1971):64-73.

Rudenstein, Neil L. "Staying the Course at Princeton." New York Times Magazine, S 23, 1973 (letter).

"Rutgers Undergrads Win Major Concessions." Muhammad Speaks, Ap 11, 1969.

"Seizing the Time at Essex." Leviathan, Mr, 1970. [Essex County College, Newark]

Synnott, Marcia G. The Half-Opened Door: Discrimination and Admissions at Harvard, Yale and Princeton, 1900-1970. Westport, CT: Greenwood, 1979.

Walker, Joe. "De-Brainwashing Whitened Mind." Muhammad Speaks, Ap 4, 1969. [About James C. McDonald, Assistant Dean, Livingston College, Rutgers U.]

"White Supremacy at Princeton." Negro Digest, Ja, 1943.

Wiggins, Jefferson. White Cross-Black Crucifixion: Conflict on the College Campus. A Social Commentary. New York: Exposition Press, 1970. [Upsala College, East Orange]

Yeakey, Lamont H. "A Student Without Peer: The Undergraduate College Years of Paul Robeson." Journal of Negro Education 42 (Fall, 1973):489-503. [Rutgers U.]

Young, Hugh Edward. "Comparative Case Study of Two New Jersey Public Predominantly Black Two-Year Colleges." Doctoral dissertation, Rutgers U., 1976. Univ. Microfilms Order No. 76-17324.

New Mexico

American Indian School of Medicine. AISOM, Mr, 1977. ERIC ED 141 026. [Shiprock]

Barney, Robert Knight. Cowboys and Indians: College Football on the American Frontier-- The New Mexico Territory, 1892-1912, Ap, 1975. ERIC ED 129 817.

Carlson, Nils S. "An Investigation of the Self-Concept and Values of Selected Spanish-American Male College Students Enrolled in the University of New Mexico." Doctoral dissertation, U. of New Mexico, 1972.

Goldberg, Dave. "Indian Medical School Snarled in Red Tape." Washington Post, Mr 19, 1978.

Howell, James Oliver. "A Comparison of Academic Chracteristics and Predictability of Academic Success of Mexican American Students with That of Non-Mexican American Students at New Mexico State University." Doctoral dissertation, New Mexico State U., 1971.

Mann, Aubrey E. "The History and Development of Eastern New Mexico University." Doctoral dissertation, Colorado State College, 1959.

Patton, Walter S. "An Investigation of Selected Factors Related to Persistence of American-Indian Students at Two New Mexico Universities." Doctoral dissertation, New Mexico State U., 1972.

Sunseri, Alvin R. "The Angry Chicano." Ethnic and Minority Studies Review 1(Fall-Winter, 1972-1973):2-5. [Mexican-American students at College of Santa Fe and New Mexico Highlands U.]

U.S. Bureau of Indian Affairs. Evaluation Report of the Special Scholarship in Law for American Indians, University of New Mexico Law School. Research and Evaluation Report No. 12. Albuquerque, NM: Office of Indian Education Programs, Indian Education Resources Center, Summer, 1972.

University of New Mexico. Ethnic Minorities at the University of New Mexico, My, 1977. ERIC ED 139 322.

Winther, Sven F. and others. The Invisible Student: A Longitudinal Study of the Beginning Freshman Class of 1963 at the University of New Mexico, My, 1969. ERIC ED 030 532.

New York

A Longitudinal Study of the Barriers Affecting the Pursuit of Higher Education by New York State High School Seniors. Phase II: College and University Enrollment. New York State, Fall, 1970 (Preliminary), Jl, 1970. ERIC ED 046 020.

Abeel, Erica. "John Jay's Pocket Revolution." Change 7(O, 1975):34-38. [John Jay College of Criminal Justice, CUNY]

Adelson, Howard L. "An Answer to Peter Sourian." Nation, Ap 23, 1973. [Open enrollment in CCNY]

_____. "City University--A Jewish Tragedy." American Zionist 62(S, 1971).

Alexander, James, Jr. "Columbia College: A Paradox for the Negro." Columbia Daily Spectator, The Supplement, Ap 26, 1967.

Anderson, Nels. "The Social Antecedents of a Slum: A Development of the East Harlem Area of Manhattan Island." Doctoral dissertation, New York U., 1930.

Andrews, George L. "West Point and the Colored Cadets." International Review 9(N, 1880).

Babbit, Charles E., and Burbach, Harold J. "Perceptions of Social Control Among Black College Students." Journal of Negro Education 48(Winter, 1979):37-42. [New York State]

Bach, William. "Exit John Kneller." Village Voice, Ja 15, 1979. [Brooklyn College]

Bailey, Peter. "Getting It Together At 'The Point.'" Ebony 27(D, 1971):135-144. [U.S. Military Academy]

_____. "New Image in the Ivy League." Negro Digest, J1, 1967. [The Students' Afro-American Society at Columbia U.]

Baird, Charles F. "Attendance of Negroes at U.S. Naval Academy." Integrated Education, Ja-F, 1968.

Ballard, Allen B. "'It Can Mean, God Help Us, the Admission of Everybody!' Open Ad-missions." Chapter 7 in The Education of Black Folk. New York: Harper & Row, 1973. [Open Admissions in City U. of New York]

Bard, Bernard. "College for All: Dream or Disaster?" Phi Delta Kappan 56(F, 1975): 390-395. [C.U.N.Y.]

Baum, Joan. "An Exhortation for Teachers of English in Open-Admissions Programs." College Composition and Communication 25(O, 1974):292-297.

Bazell, Robert J. "City College of New York: Bearing the Brunt of Open Admissions." Science 175(Ja, 1972):38-42.

Benjamin, Jeanette Ann, and Powell, Philip Edward. "Open Admissions: Expanding Educa-tional Opportunity." Journal of the Nation-al Association of Women Deans and Counselors 34(Summer, 1971):146-148. [C.U.N.Y.]

Bentsen, Cheryl. "Training for Human Services." Change 3(O, 1971):11-13. [College for Human Services, NYC]

Berger, Leslie, and Leaf, Jeanette B. "The Promise of Open Admissions: An Evaluation After Four Years at CUNY." Educational Records 57(1977):155-161.

Berkowitz, David S., with Frazier, E. Franklin, and Leigh, Robert D. Inequality of Opportu-nity in Higher Education: A Study of Minority Group and Related Barriers to College Admission. Legislative Document No. 33. 1948. Albany, NY: Williams Press, 1948.

Birenbaum, William M. "From Class to Mass in Higher Education." Higher Education Review 6(Autumn, 1973):3-16. [C.U.N.Y.]

Birnbaum, Robert. "Who Goes to College in New York City?" Integrated Education, S-O, 1972, pp. 69-73.

Birnbaum, Robert, and Goldman, Joseph. The Graduates: A Follow-up Study of New York City High School Graduates of 1970. New York: Center for Social Research, The City U. of New York, My, 1971.

"The Black Student." New Yorker, Mr 26, 1966, pp. 41-42. [Story of the founding of a new magazine, The Black Student, by a group of Columbia U. students]

"Black Students Say No Talking to Grand Jury." African World, J1 8, 1972. [N.Y. State College, Cobbleskill]

Blumberg, Paul. "The New Academic Proletariat." Nation, Ag 14, 197. [Faculty in CUNY]

Board of Regents. Financial Aid for New York State Students. Albany, NY: State Educa-tion Department, Mr, 1974.

Borden, Ruth Weiskopf. "The Psychological Orientation of the Jewish Graduate Student at Columbia University." Master's thesis, Columbia U., 1939.

Bronx Community College. The Academic and Remedial Placement Profile of Students Entering B.C.C. in September 1974 by Curriculum Group, D, 1974. ERIC ED 099 051.

Brown, Roscoe C., Jr. "New York University: The Institute of Afro-American Affairs." Journal of Negro Education 39(Summer, 1970): 214-220.

Burch, M. L. "Columbia University and Inter-racial Relations." Southern Workman 59(Ap, 1930):191-193.

Burlage, Robb, and Pope, Dan. "Building Medical Empires." Liberation, Mr-Ap, 1969. [Columbia U.]

Butler, Barbara. "Columbia University, the Arrogant Giant." Liberator, Je, 1968.

Capeci, Dominic J., Jr. "From Different Liberal Perspectives: Fiorello H. La Guardia, Adam Clayton Powell, Jr., and Civil Rights in New York City, 1941-1943." Journal of Negro History 62(Ap, 1977):160-173. [Touches on racial discrimination in municipal colleges]

Castro, Barry. "Hostos: Report from a Ghetto College." Harvard Educational Review 44 (My, 1974):270-294. [Eugenio María de Hostos Community College]

Chancellor's Advisory Council on SEEK. Report on the SEEK Program at Queens College. Flushing, NY: Queens College, F 3, 1969.

Characteristics of Freshmen Students at the City University of New York. Washington, DC: University Research Corp., S 3, 1971. ERIC ED 055 542.

"Charge Bias at Columbia U." Headlines and Pictures, Ag, 1946.

Chin, Laura, with Holton, Audree B. (eds.). Equal Employment Opportunity at the State University of New York. Washington, DC: U.S. Commission on Civil Rights, 1976.

"City College [of New York] Adjusts to Open Enrollment." Chemical and Engineering News, D 7, 1970.

City University of New York. Proceedings of the Third Annual Conference of the City University of New York (November, 1973), 1974. ERIC ED 100 222. [Third annual conference on Open Admissions]

"The City University of New York (SEEK Center)." AAUP Bulletin 60(Mr, 1974):67-81

Clarity, James F. "Racial and Social Conflict Disrupting Brooklyn College." New York Times, Ap 30, 1978.

Cohen, Irving. Profile of BMCC's First Open Admission Entry Class, Fall, 1970 (City University of New York, Borough of Manhattan Community College), Ap, 1971. ERIC ED 050 716.

Cohen, Edward G. and others. Comparative Data on the Distribution of Grades Before and During the Open Admissions Policy at Queensborough Community College, 1977. ERIC ED 144 652.

Colmen, Joseph G., and Wheeler, Barbara A., with Cartey, Wilfred (eds.). Human Uses of the University. Planning a Curriculum in Urban and Ethnic Affairs at Columbia University. New York: Columbia U. Press, 1970.

"Cornell--Ashes or Blaze." The Movement, Jl, 1969. [Ithaca]

"Cornell Black Students View Kinship of Campus, Community Role As Key Fulcrum for Liberation." Muhammad Speaks, My 30, 1969. [Ithaca]

Crisis at CUNY. New York: Newt Davidson Collective, 1974. [Newt Davidson Collective, P.O. Box 1034, Manhattanville Station, NY, NY 10027]

Daniel, Walter G. "Negro Welfare and Mabel Carney at Teachers College, Columbia University." Journal of Negro Education 11(O, 1942): 560-562.

Davidson, Carl. "Open Admissions: Who Benefits?" Guardian, Je 14, 1969.

"Debate on Open Admissions." New York Times Magazine, Je 6, 1971. [A series of letters]

Decker, Anne Folger, Jody, Rugh, and Brings, Felicia. A Handbook on Open Admissions: Success, Failure, Potential. Boulder, CO: Westview Press, 1977. [CUNY, esp. Hunter College]

Dispenzieri, Angelo, and Kweller, Irving. A Survey of Community Agency Experience with the SEEK Program, Je, 1969. ERIC ED 031 151.

Donadio, Stephen. "Black Power at Columbia." Commentary 46(S, 1968):67-76.

Dowd, Douglas. "Cornell's Uptight Spring." New Politics, Fall, 1968. [O, 1969]

Doyle, Joan. "On Access to Ph.D.'s." New York Times, F 21, 1975. [St. John's U., Queens, NY]

Drescher, Nuala McGann. "Affirmative Action: Outlook Not Sunny at SUNY." Universities 1 (D, 1978):8-12.

Du Bois, W. E. B. [Article on lack of employment of black faculty in New York colleges] Amsterdam News, Mr 7, 1942.

Dudnick, Robert. "Students in Uprising at N.Y. College." Guardian, Ja 18, 1969. [Queens College]

Eagle, Norman. The Academic and Remedial Placement Profile of Students Entering B.C.C. in September, 1976 [and September 1977] by Curriculum Group, D, 1977. ERIC ED 148 434. [Bronx Community College]

Edwards, Harry. "April 1969: Confrontations at Cornell: A Case Study." In Black Students, pp. 138-183. New York: Free Press, 1970.

The Expansion of Equal Educational Opportunities: An Evaluation Study of the New York State Higher Education Opportunity Program. Final Report, Part Two. New York: Human Affairs Research Center, Je, 1970, 49 pp. ERIC ED 051 763.

Fairweather, Malcolm. "Community College Enrollment in New York State." College Student Journal 11(Summer, 1977):105-110.

Farago, John M. "The Decline in CUNY Applications: Who and How Come." Research in Higher Education 8(1978):193-203.

Feron, James. "Integrated West Point Prepares for First Women Cadets." New York Times, S 22, 1975.

Field, R. L. "The Black Midshipman at the U.S. Naval Academy." U.S. Naval Institute Proceedings 99(Ap, 1973):28-36.

Finley, John H. "John H. Finley at CCNY--1903-1913." History of Education Quarterly 10 (Winter, 1971):423-439.

Fiske, Edward B. "City College Is Focus of Debate Over Effects of Open Admissions." New York Times, Je 19, 1978.

_____. "City University Rethinks Goals." New York Times, O 19, 1975.

_____. "How Open Admissions Plan Has Altered City College." New York Times, Je 20, 1978.

_____. "Rigorous High School Courses Attract Fewer in New York City." New York Times, Mr 23, 1978.

Flipper, Henry O. The Colored Cadet at West Point. New York: Arno Press, 1969. [Orig. 1878]

"Follow-Up: Report of Committee on Allegations of Racial Discrimination in the Football Program." Syracuse University Record 1 (D 17, 1970):4-5.

Freedman, Florence B., and Myers, Florence C. "The College Discovery and Development Program: Disadvantaged Youth Prepare for College." Journal of the National Association of Women Deans and Counselors, Winter, 1969. [N.Y.C.]

Friedenberg, Edgar Z. "Report from the Niagara Frontier." New York Review of Books 14 (1970):29-35. [U. of Buffalo]

Friedland, William H., and Edwards, Harry. "Confrontation at Cornell." Trans-action 6 (Je, 1969):29-36, 76.

Furst, Randy. "Armed Self-Defense at Cornell." Guardian, My 3, 1969. [Ithaca]

Gartner, Lloyd P. "The Five Demands at New York City College." Midstream 15(1969):15-35.

Gayle, Addison, Jr. "The Quiet Revolution: The Pre-Baccalaureate Program of the City College." Journal of Human Relations, Third Quarter, 1968.

_____. "White Don Quixotes and Black Sancho Panzas. An Open Letter to Nat Hentoff." Liberator 10(O, 1970):8-9. [The Alamac Ten and the SEEK program, City U. of New York]

Gellhorn, Alfred, and Scheuer, Ruth. "The Experiment in Medical Education at the City College of New York." Journal of Medical Education 53(Jl, 1978):574-582.

Gershman, Carl. "Counter-Revolution at Columbia U." New America, My 25, 1969.

Gershowitz, Mike. "Queens College Retains Its Elitist Requirements." Long Island Press, D 19, 1974.

Gilbert, David, and Hornstein, Alvin. "First Fight." The Movement, Je, 1969. [Protest movement at Queensborough Community College]

Ginzberg, Eli. "Black Power and Student Unrest: Reflections on Columbia University and Harlem." George Washington Law Review 37 (My, 1969):835-847.

Gittell, Marilyn. "A Pilot Study of Negro Middle Class Attitudes Toward Higher Education in New York." Journal of Negro Education, Fall, 1965.

Glantz, Oscar. "Native Sons and Immigrants: Some Beliefs and Values of American-Born and West Indian Blacks at Brooklyn College." Ethnicity 5(Je, 1978):189-202.

Goldstein, Marilyn, and Collins, T. J. "Minority Cutbacks Spur Protest." Newsday, Mr 19, 1976. [State U. College at Old Westbury]

Gordon, Sheila C. "The Transformation of the City University of New York, 1945-1970." Doctoral dissertation, Columbia U., 1975. Univ. Microfilms Order No. 77-27,856.

Groselose, Everett. "The New Mood at Turbulent Columbia." Wall Street Journal, Ap 23, 1969.

Gross, Theodore. "How to Kill a College." Saturday Review, F 4, 1978. [City College of N.Y.]

_____. "Together in Harlem: Some Notes on Hiring in a College Committed to Open Admissions." ADE Bulletin 38(S, 1973):28-34.

Grosso, Anne D. "Hostos Community College: Vehicle for Social Change." Community and Junior College Journal 48(O, 1977):6-9.

Hall, Eleanor. Attitudes of City University of New York Students Towards Open Admissions. Washington, DC: University Research Corp., S 3, 1971, 11 pp. Paper, American Psychological Association. ERIC ED 055 556.

Hamalian, Leo, and Hatch, James V. "The City College Rebellion Revisited." Changing Education 4(1969-1970):15-21. [N.Y.C.]

Harrington, Michael. "Keep Open Admissions Open." New York Times Magazine, N 2, 1975. [C.U.N.Y.]

Harris, Beatrice, and Brody, Lawrence. Discovering and Developing the College Potential of Disadvantaged High School Youth: a Report of the Fourth Year of Longitudinal Study on the College Discovery and Development Program, Je, 1970. ERIC ED 042 824.

Harris, Marvin. "Big Bust on Morningside Heights." Nation, Je 10, 1968. [An analysis of events at Columbia U. in Ap-My, 1968]

Harris, Theodore D. "Henry Ossian Flipper: The First Negro Graduate of West Point." Doctoral dissertation, U. of Minnesota, 1971. Univ. Microfilms Order No. 72-14436.

Hassiz, Tariq Ibn (Hardwick). "On That Black Administrator Sitting in Darkness." Liberation 11(Mr, 1971):10-11. [Columbia U.]

Hatchett, John F. "'The Last To Be Hired, the First To Be Fired.'" Liberation, D, 1968. [New York U.]

Hawkes, Robert A. "An Analysis of Student Opinion of an Equal Opportunity Program." Black Academy Review 1(Summer, 1970):57-70. [SEEK program in State U. of New York]

Healy, Timothy S. "Will Everyman Destroy the University?" Saturday Review, D 20, 1969.

Henderson, R. "Negro Education at Columbia." Southern Workman 61(Jl, 1932):305-309.

Henry, Oliver. "A Negro Student on Campus Turmoil." Columbia Spectator, Connection, Mr 11, 1969. [Reprinted in Dissent, Jl-Ag, 1969]

Higher Education Opportunity Program. Part One. Final Report. Albany, NY: New York State Education Dept., Division of Higher Education, 1970, 71 pp. ERIC ED 043 306.

Hightower, Charles. "Brooklyn College Joins the Movement." Guardian, Je 1, 1968.

Hoffman, Randall W. "Eight Negro Students Come to Hofstra." Improving College and University Teaching, Winter, 1966. [Long Island]

Hood, Wenford L. Higher Education for the Disadvantaged in New York State: A Summary Report of Programs of Higher Education for the Disadvantaged at Colleges and Universities in New York State. State U. of New York, Plattsburgh College at Plattsburgh, Ja, 1969, 36 pp. ERIC ED 031 993.

"Hostos--Who's Really Guilty?" News and Letters, N, 1976. [Hostos Community College]

Hunter-Gault, Charlayne. "Blacks on City U. Faculties Are Filing Bias Charge in Large-Scale Dismissals." New York Times, D 17, 1975. [C.U.N.Y.]

_____. "New York Medical Schools Lag in Attracting Minority Students." New York Times, Ap 28, 1977. [N.Y.C.]

Hyman, Seymour C. [The City University of New York's Open Admissions Program: A Reply to an Article by Rowland Evans and Robert Novak] New York: City U. of New York, Ja 4, 1971, 12 pp. ERIC ED 051 732.

Information Center on Education. Afro-American Studies in Colleges and Universities of New York State 1968-69 and 1969-70. Albany, NY: State Education Department, S, 1969.

"It Can't Happen Here--Can It?" Newsweek, My 5, 1969. [Cornell U., Ithaca]

Johnson, Lloyd A. The Urban University. A Report on the Activities of the Urban Center. September 1, 1967-June 30, 1970. New York: The Urban Center, Columbia U., 1970.

Joseph, Gloria, and Newsom, Barbara. "Cornell's Black Student: A Report from the Inside." Cornell Alumni News, Je, 1968.

Katz, Jeffrey M. "What Price CUNY?" Change 8 (Je, 1976):45-47. [Open Admissions student at Lehman College of CUNY]

Katzenstein, Herbert. "New Gains for the Black Graduate." City Colleges Alumnus, D, 1972. [CCNY and Howard U.]

Kaufman, Barry, and Loveland, Susan A. Academic Progress at the City University of New York: September 1970 to June 1975, N, 1976. ERIC ED 131 813.

Kaufman, Barry, and Terdeman, Robert. Application and Enrollment of CUNY Freshmen: Fall 1975 vs. Fall 1976, N, 1977. ERIC ED 148 209.

Kaufman, Barry and others. Application, Allocation, and Enrollment of CUNY Freshmen: 1970-1974, Jl, 1976. ERIC ED 129 145.

Kaufman, Betsy B. "A Semantic Analysis of Open Admissions." Integrateducation 14(My-Je, 1976):11-13.

Keene, William V. "Minority Students and Placement Services: A Survey of New York State Community Colleges." Master's thesis, Cornell U., 1974.

Kibbee, Robert. "Open Admissions at CUNY." Integrateducation 13(My-Je, 1975):175-179.

Kihss, Peter. "A Bilingual College Paced for the Individual." New York Times, N 16, 1975. [Hostos Community College, NYC]

Kloperman, Gilbert. "The Beginning of Yeshiva University." Doctoral dissertation, Yeshiva U., 1955.

_____. The Story of Yeshiva University: The First Jewish University in America. New York: Macmillan, 1969.

Knoell, Dorothy M. "New York Challenges Its Urban Colleges." Junior College Journal, Mr, 1967.

Konvitz, Milton. "A Letter from Cornell. Why One Professor Changed His Vote." New York Times Magazine, My 18, 1969.

Kramer, Rena, Kaufman, Barry, and Podell, Lawrence. Application, Allocation, and Enrollment of Freshmen by Residential Area, 1969-1972. New York: Office of Program and Policy Research, City U. of New York, Mr, 1974. [C.U.N.Y.]

_____, and _____. Characteristics of Enrollees and Non-Enrollees Among Freshmen, 1972. New York: Office of Programs and Polich Research, City U. of New York, Ap, 1974. [C.U.N.Y.]

_____, _____ and _____. Distribution of Grades: 1972. New York: Office of Program and Policy Research, City U. of New York, S, 1974. [C.U.N.Y.]

Kreuter, Mortimer. "A New College for an Old Ghetto." Urban Review, S, 1969. [A college in Harlem]

_____. Feasibility Study for a Proposed Teachers College in Harlem. New York: Center for Urban Education, S, 1967.

_____. Feasibility Study for Proposed Teachers College in Harlem. Addendum #1. Analysis of Interviews with Community Leaders. New York: Center for Urban Education, O, 1967.

Kriegel, Leonard. "Expendable CUNY." New Republic, O 2, 1976.

_____. "Headstart for College." Nation, F 26, 1968.

_____. "Playing It Black." Change, Mr-Ap, 1969. [C.C.N.Y.]

_____. "When Blue-Collar Students Go To College." Saturday Review 55(Jl 22, 1972): 46-51. [Long Island U.]

_____. Working Through: A Teacher's Journey in the Urban University. New York: Saturday Review Press, 1972.

Lavin, David E. Open Admissions at CUNY: An Overview of Policy and Research. New York: City U. of New York, Herbert Lehman College, S, 1971, 8 pp. Paper, American Psychological Association. ERIC ED 055 544.

_____. Outline for a Research Program on Open Admissions in the City University of New York. New York: Department of Sociology, Lehman College, City U. of New York, D, 1970.

_____. Student Retention and Graduation at the City University of New York: September 1970 Enrollees Through Seven Semesters. New York: Office of Program and Policy Research, City U. of New York, Ag, 1974.

_____. Summary of the Report: Open Admissions at the City University of New York. A Description of Academic Outcomes After Two Years. New York: Office of Program and Policy Research, City U. of New York, Je, 1974.

Lavin, David E., and Silberstein, Richard A. Alternative Admissions Criteria at the City University of New York. Effects Upon Ethnic Composition. New York: City U. of New York, 1976.

_____ and _____. New Admissions Criteria: Some Consequences for CUNY and the City of New York. New York: City U. of New York, 1976.

_____ and _____. Student Retention Under Open Admissions at the City University of New York: September 1970 Enrollees Followed Through Four Semesters. New York: City U. of New York, F, 1974.

_____ and _____. "Student Retention Under Open Admissions at the City University of New York." Integrateducation 12(Jl-Ag, 1974):26-29.

Libo, Kenneth, and Stewart, Edward. "Open Admissions: An Open-and-Shut Case?" Saturday Review, D 9, 1972.

Mabee, Carleton. "Toussaint College: A Proposed Black College for New York State in the 1870's." Afro-American New York Life History 1(Ja, 1977):25-35.

Maeroff, Gene. "City College Policy Stirs History Department Rift." New York Times, F 19, 1974.

_____. "City U. Open Admissions Held a Success." New York Times, Mr 17, 1974. [N.Y.C.]

Mahome, Othello. "Incident at Cornell." Liberator, Je, 1969.

Marshak, Robert E. "Problems and Prospects of an Urban Public University." Daedalus 104 (Winter, 1975):192-201. [C.U.N.Y.]

Marszalek, John F., Jr. Court-Martial: A Black Man in America. New York: Scribner's, 1972. [Black cadet at West Point, 1876-1881]

Martin, Peter B. Ethnic Profile and Place of Residence. Student Body: Spring 1976, Mr 1, 1976. ERIC ED 125 682. [Hostos Community College]

_____. Ethnic Profile, Fall 1977 [and] Enrollment in E.S.L., 1977. ERIC ED 148 413. [Hostos Community College]

Mauer, Eric. "From the Cornell Campus" (letter). Jewish Currents, Je, 1969.

Meister, Morris, and Tauber, Abraham. "Experiments in Expanding Educational Opportunity for the Disadvantaged." Phi Delta Kappan, Mr, 1965. [Bronx Community College]

Migration Division. Puerto Ricans and Other Hispanics in New York City's Public Schools and Universities. New York: Migration Division of the Commonwealth of Puerto Rico, 1975.

Miller, James B. "An Analysis of the Remedial Curriculum for Open Admissions Freshmen Students at Herbert H. Lehman College." Doctoral dissertation, Fordham U., 1972.

Missick, Victoria. "City University Opposes McCoy's Bid for Community College Presidency." African-American Teachers Forum, S, 1969.

Moss, James A. "Utilization of Negro Teachers in the Colleges of New York State." Doctoral dissertation, Columbia U., 1957. Univ. Microfilms Order No. 25148.

_____. "The Utilization of Negro Teachers in the Colleges of New York State." Phylon 21 (1960):63-70.

Moss, James A., and Mercer, Herman A. A Study of the Potential Supply of Negro Teachers for the Colleges of New York State. Schenectady, NY: Union College, My, 1961.

Muravchik, Josh. "CCNY Confrontation Stirs Racial and Ethnic Conflict." New America, My 25, 1969.

Nash, George, and Epstein, Cynthia. Harlem Views Columbia University. New York: Bureau of Applied Social Research, Columbia U., 1968.

Nathan, Otto, and Schappes, Morris U. "Open Admissions at City College." Jewish Currents, D, 1969.

Neiman, Barbara G. "Open Admissions: The First Year Experience." Master's thesis, Bank Street College of Education, 1972.

Nevins, Lawrence. "A Remedial Program for Effective Open Admissions." National Association of College Admission Counselors Journal 15(Ag, 1970):19-22. [SUNY Urban Center in Manhattan]

N.Y. State Board of Regents. Report of the Regents on the City University of New York. Albany, NY: State Education Department, D, 1975.

"Notes and Comment." New Yorker, My 3, 1969. [Student protest movements at New York City colleges]

The Open Admission Story: 1970 at the City University of New York. New York: City U. of New York, Office of University Relations, D 3, 1970, 95 pp. ERIC ED 048 820.

"Open Admissions: A Mixed Report." Time, N 29, 1971. [N.Y.C.]

Ostro, Ernest A. "The Guns of April [at Cornell University]: A Threat or Self-Defense?" National Catholic Reporter, Jl 23, 1969. [Ithaca]

Perry, Deborah L. "Because I am Black." Saturday Review, Je 21, 1969. [Barnard College, Columbia U.]

Persico, Sylvia L., and Wolfe, Helen B. A Longitudinal Study of the Barriers Affecting the Pursuit of Higher Education by New York State High School Seniors. Phase 2. Albany, NY: Office of Planning in Higher Education, 1970.

Piesco, Judith J., and Podell, Lawrence. Retention and Graduation of Disadvantaged Students in the Senior Colleges of CUNY, Mr, 1977. ERIC ED 138 162. [CUNY]

Piesco, Judith L. and others. Review of the Evaluative Literature on Open Admissions at CUNY, O, 1974. ERIC ED 097 816.

Podell, Lawrence. City University Student Survey, N, 1977. ERIC ED 150 926.

Polishook, Irwin. "Open Admissions Assessed: The Example of the City University of New York, 1970-1975." Midstream, Ap, 1976, pp. 16-27.

Powers, Tom. "Autopsy On Old Westbury." Harper's 243(S, 1971):52-61. [State U. at Old Westbury]

The Privileged Many: A Study of the City University's Open Admissions Policy, 1970-1975. New York: Women's City Club of New York, 1975.

Professional Staff Congress, CUNY. "The Administration and Evaluation of Open Admissions at the City University of New York." Integrateducation 12(Jl-Ag, 1974):30-32.

"The Question of Open Admissions." Commentary 55 (My, 1973):4-24. [Letters on open admissions in the City U. of New York]

"Racism Threatens to Divide New CUNY Student Coalition." News and Letters, N, 1975. [Queens College]

Raspberry, William. "Desegregating '7 Brooks.'" Washington Post, Mr 11, 1974. [Brooks Hall, Barnard College, Columbia U.]

Rempson, Joe L. "Minority Access to Higher Education in N.Y. City." City Almanac 7 (Ag, 1972):1-15.

Report and Recommendations to the Board of Higher Education of the City of New York. New York: The City U. of New York, University Commission on Admissions, O 7, 1969. ERIC ED 035 373.

"Report of Trustee, Faculty and Student Committee on Allegations of Racial Discrimination in the Football Program." Syracuse University Record 1(D 10, 1970):3-7.

Resnik, Solomon. "Black Power and Education: The SEEK Experience at Queens College." Community Issues 2(My, 1970):1-11.

_____. "Open Admissions: A Critique."
Community, Ap, 1970. [N.Y.C.]

Resnik, Solomon, and Kaplan, Barbara. "College
Programs for Black Adults." Journal of
Higher Education 42(Mr, 1971):202-218.
[SEEK program at Queens College]

_____ and _____. "Report on Open Admissions:
Remedial Work Recommended." New York Times
Magazine, My 9, 1971. [N.Y.C.]

Richardson, Curtis, and Dentler, Robert A.,
with Woodbeck, Eleanor and Dentler, Deborah.
College Careers Program Evaluation. New
York: Center for Urban bducation, Mr, 1971.
[Westchester County]

Rivera, Emilio, Jr. "New Programs for the Nitty
Gritty College." Black Academy Review 1
(Summer, 1970):28-33. [Cooperative College
Centers, New York State]

Robinson, Jackie. "The SEEK Program: A SEEK
Student's View." Community Issues 2(Jl,
1970):1-16. [Queens College]

Rondinone, Peter J. "Open Admissions and the
Inward 'I.'" Change 9(My, 1977):43-47.
[C.U.N.Y.]

Rosner, Benjamin. Open Admissions at the City
University of New York, D 27, 1970. ERIC
ED 050 676.

Rossmann, Jack E., Astin, Helen S., Astin,
Alexander W., and El-Khawas, Elaine H.
Open Admissions at City University of New
York: An Analysis of the First Year.
Englewood Cliffs, NJ: Prentice-Hall, 1975.

Rowley, Virginia. "SEEK--A New Hope for the
Disadvantaged." New Era, F, 1969.

Ruchkin, Judith P. "The [N.Y.] City College
Dual Admissions Proposal Viewed as a
Contemporary Education Program." Liberal
Education 56(1970).

Rudd, Mark. "Notes on Columbia." The Movement,
Mr, 1969.

Rudy, S. Willis. The College of the City of
New York: A History, 1847-1947. New York:
City College Press, 1949.

Rustin, Bayard. "Cornell Revisted." New
America, Mr 28, 1974.

Salpukas, Agis. "Negroes at Hofstra Asking
Hard Questions." New York Times, Jl 12,
1968. [Long Island]

Sanua, Victor D. "Attitudes of Jewish
Adolescents and College Students in New York
City of Different Ideologies Toward Inter-
marriage." News and Views (Federation of
Jewish Philanthropies of New York) 2(F-Mr,
1969):3-29.

Scheffler, Linda Weingarten. "What 70 SEEK
Kids Taught Their Counselor." New York Times
Magazine, N 16, 1969. [C.C.N.Y.]

Schiavone, James. Effectiveness of Remedial
Reading Courses in Upgrading Skills of Under-
prepared Students Who Entered Manhattan
Community College Under the Open Admissions
Policy, Ja, 1977. ERIC ED 134 284. [N.Y.C.]

Scully, Malcolm G. "Plan to Admit All High
School Graduates Stirs N.Y.[C.] Storm."
Chronicle of Higher Education, N 10, 1969.

Semas, Philip W. "Cornell Is Calm, But Unresolved
Issues Could Trigger a New Crisis."
Chronicle of Higher Education, O 13, 1969.
[Ithaca]

_____. "Drop-Out Rate of 35.8 Pct. Is Reported
for CUNY's Open-Admissions Students."
Chronicle of Higher Education 6(N 29, 1971):3.

17X, Samuel. "Zionist Splinter Group Attacks
Black Students." Muhammad Speaks, My 21,
1971. [Brooklyn College]

Shanker, Albert. "Open Admissions: The Record
Thus Far." New York Times, Ag 5, 1973.
[CUNY]

Stamberg, Margie. "CUNY Offers Pacification
Program." Guardian, Jl 19, 1969.

_____. "Hard Road Ahead for N.Y.U. Movement."
Guardian, O 26, 1968.

_____. "Students Strike at N.Y.U. Strike
Rally." Guardian, O 19, 1968. [The issue
of John F. Hatchett]

Straus, Rebecca S. "Open Admissions 1970: The
Audacious Experiment." Teachers College
Record 72(My, 1971):513-518.

Strout, Cushing, and Grossvogel, David I. (eds.).
Divided We Stand: Reflections on the Crisis
at Cornell. Garden City, NY: Doubleday,
1970.

Tep, Boreysa, Wong, Richard K., and Yonemura,
Jean. "Declaration of Asian American Studies
at City College of New York." Bridge 3(Ap,
1974):36-38.

Tetlow, William L., Jr. Preliminary Investiga-
tions on the Academic Performance of Minority
Group Students of Cornell University,
D 27, 1970. ERIC ED 051 744.

Tobier, Arthur. "A Political Education." Urban
Review, S, 1969. [A college for Bedford-
Stuyvesant, Brooklyn]

Torigoe, Dennis T. "Asian American Studies:
Which Way." Bridge 2(Je, 1973):6-8.
[Program at C.C.N.Y.]

Trimberger, Ellen Kay. "Open Admissions: A New
Form of Tracking?" Insurgent Sociologist 4
(Fall, 1973):29-43.

"Universities in Danger: The United States Office for Civil Rights Contra Columbia University." Minerva 10(Ap, 1972):319-322.

University Commission on Admissions. Report and Recommendations to the Board of Higher Education of the City of New York. New York: The City U. of New York, O 7, 1969.

Van Dyne, Larry. "City University of New York." Atlantic 239(Je, 1977):14-18.

_____. "The New York Tragedy" (Part 1). Chronicle of Higher Education, S 13, 1976. [The City U. of New York]

Vaughn, William P. "West Point and the First Negro Cadet." Military Affairs 35(O, 1971): 100-102. [James Webster Smith, Columbia, S.C.]

Vidal, David. "...While Hostos College Resists Losing Its Identity." New York Times, Mr 6, 1976. [Eugenio Maria de Hostos Community College, Bronx]

Wagner, Geoffrey. The End of Education: The Experience of the City University of New York with Open Enrollment and the Threat to Higher Education in America. Cranbury, NJ: A. S. Barnes and Co., 1977.

Waldinger, Renee. "Foreign Languages under Open Admissions: A Report from City College." Bulletin of the Association of Departments of Foreign Languages 9(My, 1978): 30-32.

Walker, Joe. "Cornell: What Black Students Wanted." Muhammad Speaks, My 16, 1969. [Ithaca]

_____. "Where Black and Puerto Rican Students United." Muhammad Speaks, My 16, 1969. [C.C.N.Y.]

_____. "White Gunmen Stalk Black Students." Muhammad Speaks, Je 20, 1969. [State U. of New York, Stony Brook]

Waller, Kim Kurt. "The College Readiness Program of East Harlem." Saturday Review, Ap 16, 1966.

Wasser, Henry. "An American University and Universal Higher Education: The 'Open Admissions' System at C.U.N.Y." Higher Education 2(My, 1973):151-159.

_____. "Coming to Terms With Lower Standards." Times Higher Education Supplement, Jl 27, 1973. [Open Admissions in C.U.N.Y.]

Wechsler, Harold S. The Qualified Student: A History of Selective College Admission in America. New York: Wiley, 1977. [Columbia U.]

Weisman, Seymour S. "Chinese College Students Perceive their Cultural Identity." Education 92(Ap-My, 1972):116-117. [C.C.N.Y.]

Weiss, Samuel. "SEEK Program Striving to Ride Out Its Troubles." New York Times, My 4, 1975.

"West Point: Braced for Reform." Newsweek, S 24, 1973.

Whitfield, Edward L. "Black Students at Cornell, Part II." Muhammad Speaks, My 23, 1969. [First-hand account of events of Ap 19-20, 1969] [Ithaca]

"Who Killed the Elitism in Higher Education?" College and University Business 49(N, 1970): 60-63, 68-70. [Open Admissions in the City U. of New York]

Wiener, Harvey. "An Open Not a Revolving Door." Times Higher Education Supplement, Jl 13, 1973. [Open enrollment in C.U.N.Y.]

Wingfield, Clyde J. "C.U.N.Y.'s Open Door: A Wise Investment." New York Times, N 16, 1975.

Wolfe, Alan. "Working with the Working Class." Change 4(F, 1972):48-53. [Richmond College, CUNY]

Wolfe, Helen B. A Longitudinal Study of the Barriers Affecting the Pursuit of Higher Education by New York State High School Seniors, Phase I. Albany, NY: State Office of Planning in Higher Education, 1969.

Yarosz, Edward J. Evaluating Report: The City University of New York College Adapter Program. PB-203 524. Springfield, VA: National Technical Information Service, Ag, 1971.

North Carolina

Ackley, Randall. "Pembroke State University." Indian Historian 5(Summer, 1972):43-45.

Alexander, Harold W. "The Academic Skills Center of North Carolina Central University." Black Academy Review 1(Summer, 1970):34-56. [Durham]

Anderson, William, Jr. and others. "Black Survival in White Academe." Journal of Negro Education 48(Winter, 1979):92-102.

"Black Law School 'Shockingly' Underfinanced." African World, Ap, 1974. [North Carolina Central U., Durham]

"Black Students Win Against Klan and Univ." African World, Mr, 1975. [U. of North Carolina]

Board of Governors of the University of North Carolina. The North Carolina State Plan for the Further Elimination of Racial Duality in the Public Post-Secondary Education Systems. Raleigh, NC, 1974.

Boggs, Wade Hamilton III. "State-Supported Higher Education for Blacks in North Carolina, 1877-1945." Doctoral dissertation, Duke U., 1972. Univ. Microfilms Order No. 73-22976.

Canfield, Hubert. "Too Black for a Black College." SOBU Newsletter, My 1, 1971. [North Carolina Central U., Durham]

Chafe, William. "The Greensboro Sit-Ins." Southern Exposure 6(Fall, 1978):78-87.

Christensen, Rob. "UNC Desegregation: The Greensboro Case." Raleigh News and Observer, F 19, 1978.

Colston, Marshall H. "Black Campuses: 'Separate and Unequal.'" Greensboro Daily News, Je 27, 1976.

Council, Kathryn A. Graduation and Attrition of Black Students at North Carolina State University, Ag, 1974. ERIC ED 130 588.

Davis, J. A., and Kerner-Hoeg, S. Validity of Pre-admissions Indices for Blacks and Whites in Six Traditionally White Public Universities in North Carolina. Princeton, NJ: Educational Testing Service, 1971.

Davis, Junius A., and Borders-Patterson, Anne. Black Students in Predominantly White North Carolina Colleges and Universities. New York: College Entrance Examination Board, 1973.

Davis, Willie E. "Malcolm X Liberation University." SOBU Newsletter 1(F 6, 1971):10. [Greensboro]

Evans, Gary. "White Students Getting Education at Black Schools on Minority Grants." Greensboro Record, Ag 16, 1977.

George, Arthur A. "The History of Johnson C. Smith University, 1867 to the Present..." Doctoral dissertation, New York U., 1954.

Grant, Jim. "Malcolm X Liberation University Thrives in North Carolina." Southern Patriot 29(S, 1971). [Greensboro]

Grant, Jim, and Coleman, Milton. "Day of Solidarity to Save Black Schools." African World 2(N 13, 1971):1-4. [Black colleges in North Carolina]

_____ and _____. "Save Black Colleges in North Carolina." Integrated Education (Mr-Ap, 1972):36-40.

Hillman, James E. Survey of Negro Colleges of North Carolina. Raleigh, NC: North Carolina State Department of Public Instruction, 1930.

Hopkins, Chuck. "Malcolm X Liberation University." Negro Digest, Mr, 1970. [Durham]

_____. "Reorganization Plans Would Phase Out Black Colleges [in North Carolina]." SOBU Newsletter, Mr 6, 1971.

Jenkins, Clara B. "An Historical Study of Shaw University, 1865-1963." Doctoral dissertation, U. of Pittsburgh, 1965. Univ. Microfilms Order No. 65-12946.

Jones, Rudolph. "The Development of Negro State Colleges and Normal Schools in North Carolina." Quarterly Review of Higher Education Among Negroes 6(Ap, 1938):132-144.

Kleinbaum, David G., and Kleinbaum, Anna. "The Minority Experience at a Predominantly White University--A Report of a 1972 Survey at the University of North Carolina at Chapel Hill." Journal of Negro Education 45(Summer, 1976): 312-328.

Kramer, Barbara B. "Perceived Effects of Affirmative Action Regulations by Administrators at the University of North Carolina at Chapel Hill: A Case Study (1973-1976)." Doctoral dissertation, U. of North Carolina, 1978. Univ. Microfilms Order No. 7900473.

McCrory, Henry Lawrence. "A Brief History of Johnson C. Smith University." Quarterly Review of Higher Education Among Negroes 1 (Ap, 1933):29-36. [Charlotte]

"Malcolm X Liberation Univ[ersity] Closed." African World, Jl 14, 1973. [Greensboro]

"MXLU: Serious Education for Black Freedom." IFCO News 3, No. 1(1972). [Malcolm X Liberation U., Greensboro, N.C.]

Middleton, Lorenzo. "How the U.S. and N.C. Reached Accord." Chronicle of Higher Education, My 22, 1978. [Desegregation of public higher education]

Mitchell, Joseph Thurman. "Black Music in the University System of North Carolina: 1960-1974." Doctoral dissertation, U. of North Carolina, Greensboro, 1975. Univ. Microfilms Order No. 75-23146.

Murphy, Ella L. "Origin and Development of Fayetteville STate Teachers College, 1867-1959--A Chapter in the History of the Education of Negroes in North Carolina." Doctoral dissertation, New York U., 1960. Univ. Microfilms Order No. 61-341.

"New Breed of Black College Students?" African World 2(O 16, 1971):10. [North Carolina Central U.]

North Carolina Governor's Office. The Revised North Carolina State Plan for the Further Elimination of Racial Duality in the Public Post-Secondary Education Systems, My 31, 1974. Photographic Services Dept., U. of North Carolina, Chapel Hills, NC 27514.

Paddock, Polly. "Smith Shake-Up Has Deep Roots." Charlotte Observer, Ag 17, 1972. [Johnson C. Smith U., Charlotte]

_____. "3 Whites Study Among Blacks." Charlotte (N.C.) Observer, D 5, 1971. [Johnson C. Smith U., Charlotte]

Poindexter, C. C., Jr. "Degrees and Dropouts: A Profile of Student Characteristics in North Carolina Community Colleges." Doctoral dissertation, U. of North Carolina, 1970.

Rentschler, Donald R. "Courts and Politics: Integrated Higher Education in North Carolina." NOLPE School Law Journal 7 (1977):1-20.

Robinson, Isaac Alphonso. "Profiles of Black Students in North Carolina Community Colleges and Technical Institutes." Doctoral dissertation, North Carolina State U., 1978. Univ. Microfilms Order No. 7820050.

Robinson, Isaac A., and Shearon, Ronald W. Black Students in the North Carolina Community College System: Implications for Educational Programming, Jl 19, 1978. ERIC ED 157 576.

"St. Augustine's College." Black Enterprise 3 (S, 1972):29-32. [Raleigh]

St. John, Edward P. A Study of Selected Developing Colleges and Universities, Vol. 5. Washington, DC: U.S. Office of Education, D, 1977. [North Carolina Agricultural and Technical State U., Greensboro]

Shearon, Ronald W. and others. Profile of Students in North Carolina Community Colleges and Technical Institutes, Vol. I, Je, 1976. ERIC ED 136 846.

"Showdown on Black Schools." African World 2 (O 30, 1971):1, 12. [Black colleges in North Carolina]

Student Organization for Black Unity (SOBU). A Report on the Crisis in Black Higher Education in North Carolina, Ap, 1971. SOBU News Service, Box 20826, Greensboro, NC 27420.

Templin, Robert T. and others. "Are Community Colleges Truly the 'People's College'?" Community College Review 4(Spring, 1977):7-14.

Thompson, Cleo F., Jr. "A Comparison of Black and White Institutions of Higher Education in North Carolina." Doctoral dissertation, Duke U., 1977.

Tornquist, Elizabeth. "Tear Gas Blurs the Image As Duke Opts for 'Law and Order.'" New South, Spring, 1969.

Turner, Darwin T. "The Center for African Afro-American Studies at North Carolina Agricultural and Technical State University." Journal of Negro Education 39(Summer, 1970): 221-229.

University of North Carolina. A Comparative Study of the Five Historically Black Constituent Institutions of the University of North Carolina, 1976. ERIC ED 125 498.

_____. The Revised North Carolina State Plan for the Further Elimination of Racial Duality in Public Higher Education Systems, Phase II: 1978-1983, Ag, 1977. ERIC ED 143 297.

White, Jack. "Black University Services in N.C." Race Relations Reporter 2(Jl 6, 1971): 5-6. [Malcolm X Liberation U., Greensboro]

Williams, Elizabeth L. "Racial and Political Attitudes among Appalachian State University Students." Master's thesis, Appalachian State U., 1974.

Williams, Randall. "Unfinished Business at North Carolina." Change 10(D-Ja, 1978/79): 58-59. [U. of North Carolina, Chapel Hill]

Wolff, Miles. Lunch at the Five and Ten: The Greensboro Sit-ins--A Contemporary History. New York: Stein & Day, 19 0.

North Dakota

Ellis, Cheryl. "Campus Minority Picture Changes in F-M." Fargo Forum, Mr 13, 1977. [North Dakota State U., Fargo-Moorhead]

Ohio

"Academic Freedom and Tenure: The Ohio State University." AAUP Bulletin 58(S, 1972):306-321. [The case of David E. Green]

Anderson, Henry. "Letter from Ohio State [University]." Black Panther, Mr 16, 1969.

Bennis, Warren. "Spring of Hope." Cincinnati Enquirer, My 26, 1974. [History of the U. of Cincinnati]

Bigglestone, W. E. "Oberlin College and the Negro Student, 1865-1940." Journal of Negro History 56(Jl, 1971):198-219.

Bowman, Georgiana Hood. "Developmental Services and Cultural Programming for Black Students at the Ohio State University: 1968-1975." Doctoral dissertation, Ohio State U., 1976. Univ. Microfilms Order No. 77-2355.

Burgess, Philip M., and Hofstetter, C. Richard "The 'Student Movement': Ideology and Reality." Midwest Journal of Political Science 15(N, 1971):687-702. [Ohio State U.]

Central State University. *Central State University. Its Unique Role: In Retrospect, In Prospect*, 1974. ERIC ED 098 885.

Clark, Kenneth B. "Letter of Resignation from Board of Directors of Antioch College." In *Black Studies; Myths and Realities*, pp. 32-34. New York: A. Philip Randolph Educational Fund, 1969.

Coughlin, Ellen K. "Antioch [University] Cuts Back Its Sprawling Network of Urban Centers." *Chronicle of Higher Education*, Ag 7, 1978.

Du Bois, W. E. B. [Article on Wilberforce University] *Amsterdam News*, Jl 19, 1941.

_____. "The Future of the Negro State University." *Wilberforce University Quarterly*, Ap, 1941.

_____. "The Future of Wilberforce University." *Journal of Negro Education*, O, 1940.

_____. "Wilberforce College." *Chicago Defender*, Je 7, 1947, p. 19.

Ervin, James Elbert. "Black Students' Perceptions of their Experiences at Kent State University." Doctoral dissertation, Kent State U., 1972. Univ. Microfilms Order No. 73-06619.

Fletcher, Juanita A. "Against the Consensus: Oberlin College and the Education of Negroes 1835-1865." Doctoral dissertation, American U., 1974.

Fletcher, Robert S. "The Students--The Oppressed Race." In *A History of Oberlin College: From Its Foundation Through the Civil War*, chapter 33. 2 vols. Oberlin, OH: Oberlin College, 1943.

Gerber, David A. "Segregation, Separatism, and Sectariansim: Ohio Blacks and Wilberforce University's Effort to Obtain Federal Funds, 1891." *Journal of Negro Education* 45 (Winter, 1976):1-20.

Graham, Jewel. *The Antioch Program for Interracial Education--The First Three Years, 1964-67*. Yellow Springs, OH: Antioch College, 1967, 38 pp. ERIC ED 015 965.

_____. *The Antioch Program for Interracial Education. A Five-Year Report, 1964-1969*, Jl, 1969. ERIC ED 033 416.

Hamps, Shirley. "Campus Racism" (letter). *Ebony* 29(Je, 1974):21. [Defiance College, Defiance]

Hartson, Louis D. "The Occupation of Oberlin's Colored Alumni." *Oberlin Alumni Magazine*, Jl, 1932.

Henry, Diana M. "Probing Antioch College's Novel Psyche." *Harvard Crimson*, F 5, 1969.

Keiser, Edward Charles. "An Analytical Study of the Educational Experiences of Negro Students at the University of Cincinnati with Implications for Institutional Policies and Programs." Doctoral dissertation, U. of Cincinnati, 1969. Univ. Microfilms Order No. 70-04277.

Lawyer, Cyrus Jefferson III. "Attitudes of the University of Toledo as Perceived by a Black Community and a White Community." Doctoral dissertation, U. of Toledo, 1972. Univ. Microfilms Order No. 75-06488.

Lythcott, Stephen. "Black Studies at Antioch." *Antioch Review* 29(Summer, 1969):149-154.

McGinnis, Frederick A. "A History of Wilberforce University." Doctoral dissertation, U. of Cincinnati, 1940.

Meyers, Michael. "Black Education at Antioch College." *Youth and Society* 5(Je, 1974):379-396.

_____. "Black Separatism at Antioch." *Civil Liberties*, Ap, 1971.

Milkereit, John E. "Building Takeover at the University of Akron." *School and Society* 98 (O, 1970):374-375.

Miller, Edmund F. "Big City Elites and Educational Stratification: Business/Upper-Class Power in Creating a Community College for Cleveland, 1950-1970." Doctoral dissertation, Case Western Reserve U., 1975. Univ. Microfilms Order No. 75-19,229.

Moore, William. "An Analysis of Perceived and State Objectives of the Black Studies Department of the Ohio State University." Doctoral dissertation, Ohio State U., 1973.

"Ohio State University Lifts Color Bar." *Wilberforce University Quarterly*, Ap, 1941.

Parzen, Herbert. "The Purge of the Dissidents. Hebrew Union College and Zionism, 1903-1907." *Jewish Social Studies* 37(Summer-Fall, 1975):291-322.

Peters, Maurice, Jr. "Antioch College Black Students' Group Bases Program on Muhammad's Teachings." *Muhammad Speaks*, Mr 14, 1969.

Sanders, Kenneth B. "A Study of Negro Failures in the Ohio State University College of Education." Master's thesis, Ohio State U., 1941.

"Say It Isn't So." *New Republic*, My 24, 1969. [Title IV of the Civil Rights Act of 1964 and Antioch College, Yellow Springs]

"Students Leave Racist College." *Liberator*, My, 1970. [Defiance College, Defiance]

Study of Jewish Youth on the University of Cincinnati Campus. Cincinnati, OH: Jewish Federation of Cincinnati, D 1, 1968

Walker, William O. "Education for Blacks--Or a Sentimental Monument." Clevland Plain Dealer, My 11, 1974. [Central State U.]

White, Shirley. "Social and Academic Alienation among Black and White Students at Bowling Green State University." Master's thesis, Bowling Green State U., 1974.

Wilson, Milton E., Jr. Involvement/2 Years Later. Kent, OH: Human Relations Dept., Kent State U., 1971. [Black students at Kent State U.]

Yinger, J. Milton and others. Middle Start: Supportive Interventions for Higher Education Among Students of Disadvantaged Backgrounds. Final Report, N 24, 1970. ERIC ED 047 659. [Oberlin College]

Oklahoma

"The Desegregated All-White Institution... The University of Oklahoma." Journal of Educational Sociology 32(F, 1959):275-282.

Celarier, Michelle. "A Study of Public Opinion on Desegregation in Oklahoma Higher Education." Chronicles of Oklahoma, Autumn, 1969.

Cross, George Lynn. Blacks in White Colleges: Oklahoma's Landmark Cases. Norman, OK: U. of Oklahoma Press, 1975.

Fierst, E. U. "Constitutionality of Educational Segregation." George Washington Law Review 17(F, 1949):208-225. [Sipuel v. Bd. of Regents of U. of Oklahoma, 68 Superior Court 294]

Henderson, Jim. "Angry OU Black Students Feel Unwanted, Left Out." Tulsa (Oklahoma) Daily World, D 5, 1971. [U. of Oklahoma, Norman]

Hubbell, John T. "The Desegregation of the University of Oklahoma, 1946-1950." Journal of Negro History 57(O, 1972):370-384.

_____. "The Desegregation of the University of Oklahoma, 1946-1950." Master's thesis, U. of Oklahoma, 1961.

_____. "Some Reactions to the Desegregation of the University of Oklahoma, 1946-1950." Phylon 34(Je, 1973):187-196.

Stockton-Hiss, Brenda. "Is [Higher] Education Chance or Right for Indians?" Daily Oklahoman, Je 19, 1977.

"Two Whites at a Black College Find Racial Problems Are Few." New York Times, Ja 31, 1971. [Langston U.]

Zizzo, David. "Rights Pioneer Returns." Oklahoma City Journal, F 2, 1979. [The former Ada Lois Sipuel who had been refused entrance to a law school in 1946]

Oregon

Bonaparte, Lawson G. "Opinions and Characteristics of Portland Community College Black Students." Doctoral dissertation, Oregon State U., 1971.

Casey, Rick. "Funds Shortage Threatens First Private Chicano College." National Catholic Reporter, N 19, 1976. [Colegio Cesar Chavez, Mount Angel]

Green, Miles. "Small-Town College Readied for Blacks." Portland Oregonian, S 25, 1974. [George Fox College, Newberg]

Kersten, Timothy. "Public Higher Education in Oregon: Who Gets It? Who Pays For It?" Doctoral dissertation, U. of Oregon, 1973.

McComb, Marlin R. "Native American Programs as Socio-Cultural Adaptive Mechanisms to the College Environment: A Case Comparison of the University of Oregon and Oregon State University." Doctoral dissertation. Oregon State U., 1975.

"Mexican-Americans Face Loss of School." New York Times, D 5, 1976. [Colegio Cesar Chavez, Mount Angel]

"Minorities at OSU: Strangers in a Strange Land." Portland Oregonian, D 10, 1972. [Oregon State U., Corvallis]

Picotte, Agnes Goes in Center. "An Analysis of Statements Made By Indian College Students Concerning Success or Failure in Four-Year Colleges in Oregon." Doctoral dissertation, U. of Oregon, 1974.

Quaintance, Charles W. "Race, Evolution and Mormonism." Christian Century 88(My 12, 1971):586-589. [Eastern Oregon College]

Romney, Miles C., and Ikedara, Joseph T. A Report on the Programs for the Disadvantaged in the Oregon State System of Higher Education, N 17, 1969. ERIC ED 044 067.

Schultz, Raymond E., andAzure, Pete. "A College Program for Native Americans." Community College Frontiers 6(F, 1977):25-31. [Confederated Tribes of Warm Springs and Central Oregon Community College]

"Si, Se Puede." Agenda (Winter, 1976). [Colegio Cesar Chavez]

Stuart, Reginald. "'Here I Am Exposed to the Real World." New York Times, N 14, 1976. [Portland State U.]

"Teacher Charges Student Harassment."
Navajo Times, Ap 20, 1972. [Leroy Selam,
Yakima, student at Oregon College of
Education]

Pennsylvania

"Black Students at Penn State Charged."
African World, S 16, 1972.

Bond, Horace Mann. Education for Freedom. A
History of Lincoln University, Pennsylvania.
Lincoln U., 1976.

_____. "Lincoln University, A Laboratory of
Leadership." Lincoln University Herald 38
(J1, 1933).

Conyers, Charline F. "A History of the Cheyney
State Teachers College, 1837-1951."
Doctoral dissertation, New York U., 1960.
Univ. Microfilms Order No. 60-3767.

Du Bois, W. E. B. "New Day at Lincoln
University." Chicago Defender, My 18,
1946, p. 15.

Gatheru, R. Mugo. Child of Two Worlds: A
Kikuyu's Story. New York: Praeger, 1964.
[Chapter 14, the author attends Lincoln U.,
Pennsylvania]

Gray, William H. Report on Attendance of
Negroes in Pennsylvania Colleges, 1963.
Harrisburg, PA: State Superintendent of
Public Instruction, 1963.

Griefer, Julian L. Factors Influencing the
Post-High School Plans of Black and White
Pupils. Final Report, Je 15, 1971.
ERIC ED 056 349. [Coatesville, PA]

Grimke, Francis J. "On Lincoln University."
Baltimore Afro-American, J1 17, 1926.

Guinard, Dave. "Cheyney State Boycott
Succeeds." The Heterodoxical Voice, Ja,
1969. [Box 24, Newark, DE 19711]

Higher Education Assistance Agency. State
Higher Education Grant Program Summary
Statistics by Parental Gross Income Levels
and Type of Institution. Harrisburg, PA,
1974.

Hildebrand, Robert. "Academicians and Urban
Social Change: A Study of Academicians' Involvement in Selected Race Relations Programs in Pittsburgh, Pennsylvania."
Doctoral dissertation, U. of Pittsburgh,
1970.

Hill, Leslie P. "The State Teachers College
at Cheyney and Its Relation to Segregation
in the North." Journal of Negro Education
1(O, 1932):408-413.

Hummel, Roger G., and Nunemaker, George.
Fall College Enrollments by Racial/Ethnic
Categories, 1974 and Associate and Higher
Degrees Conferred by Racial/Ethnic
Categories, 1973-74. Harrisburg: Bureau
of Educational Statistics, 1975.

Innerst, Carol. "Do Colleges Care About
Educating Blacks?" Philadelphia Bulletin,
My 2, 1976. [Philadelphia area]

Jackson, Inez L. "The Evolution of State-
Supported Teacher College Education for
Negroes in Pennsylvania." Master's thesis,
Howard U., 1949.

Jameson, John, and Hessler, Richard M. "The
Natives Are Restless: The Ethos and Mythos
of Student Power." Human Organization 29
(Summer, 1970):81-94.

Kashif, Lonnie. "The Fight Against Racism in
the Law." Muhammad Speaks, N 21, 1969.
[U. of Pennsylvania]

Le Berthon, Ted. "Why Jim Crow Won at Webster
College." Pittsburgh Courier, F 5, 1944.

Menchan, William M. "An Evaluation of Cheyney
Training School for Teachers." Doctoral
dissertation, U. of Pennsylvania, 1950.

Nyden, Paul. "Racism in the University."
Black Action Society News (University of
Pittsburgh 1(1976).

Pennsylvania Human Relations Commission.
Affirmative Action Recommendations. For
Pennsylvania State-Owned Institutions of
Higher Education. Harrisburg, PA: The
Commission, Mr, 1973.

_____. "Minorities and Women in Pennsylvania
Colleges." Integrateducation 16(N-D,
1978):45-46.

Powers, Mary F. "End Discrimination To Hold
Onto Federal Funding." College Management 6
(My, 1971):24-26. [U. of Pittsburgh]

"Private Schools Take Positive Action."
Pennsylvania Education 2(Mr-Ap, 1970):27-29.

Simon, Walter A. "Dilemma of Black Students at
Small State Colleges." Crisis 80(N, 1973):
313-314. [Bloomsburg State College]

Stone, Chuck. "Racism and Ideals at Temple."
Philadelphia Daily News, My 6, 1976.

Walls, Jean H. "A Study of the Negro Graduate
of the University of Pittsburgh for the
Decade 1926-1936." Doctoral dissertation,
U. of Pittsburgh, 1938.

Weales, Gerald. "What Were the Blacks Doing
in the Balcony?" New York Times Magazine,
My 4, 1969. [Le Roi Jones at the U. of
Pennsylvania]

Wenckowski, Charlene. "Black-White Attitudes Toward Advisability of Opposite Race Inter-actions." Journal of College Student Personnel 14(Jl, 1973):303-308.

"West Chester State College." AAUP Bulletin 58 (Summer, 1972):126-134.

Winchester, Richard C. "Wanting to Reach Them." Christian Science Monitor, Ja 25, 1969. [Lincoln U., Oxford]

Wodtke, Kenneth H. Desegregation in Higher Education: A Proposal to Recruit Minority Group Students at the Pennsylvania State University. Cambridge, MA: Harvard U. Graduate School of Education, My 8, 1968.

Rhode Island

"Black Students Lead Strike at Brown Uni-versity." News and Letters, My, 1975.

Brudnoy, David. "I Was an 'Affirmative Action' Dropout. Human Events, S 7, 1974. [U. of Rhode Island]

Matthews, Mark D. "The 1975 Student Struggle at Brown University." Monthly Review 28 (Ja, 1977):32-49.

Todd, Richard. "The Missing Middle on Campus." New York Times Magazine, F 1, 1976. [Brown U.]

Wald, Matthew L. "At Brown, Still 2 Communi-ties." New York Times, N 16, 1975.

South Carolina

Bass, Jack. "The Trial of Cleveland Sellers." New South 25(Fall, 1970):18-22. [In relation to police shootings at South Carolina State College, Orangeburg, SC, F, 1968]

"Big Man on Campus." Ebony 26(Ag, 1971):106-112. [Harry Walker, U. of South Carolina]

Clancy, Paul. "The Fight for Quality On Two Negro Campuses." Reporter, Jl 13, 1967. [South Carolina State College and Allen U.]

Douglass, Robert Langham. "Education, The Hope of Democracy." Quarterly Review of Higher Education Among Negroes 6(Ap, 1938):101-107. [By a member of the first faculty of South Carolina State College, Orangeburg]

Fidler, Paul, and Ponder, Eunice. A Compara-tive Study of USC Student Survival Rates by Race, 1973-76, Ja, 1977. ERIC ED 138 221. [U. of South Carolina]

"Former Vorhees Students Honored." African World, Jl 8, 1972. [Vorhees College, Denmark]

4X, Harold. "Ford Foundation Aims For a Black-Finished Product." Muhammad Speaks, N 16, 1973. [Benedict College]

_____. "Orangeburg Revisited: Was It Worth It All?" Muhammad Speaks, N 16, 1973. [South Carolina State College; F, 1968]

Goals for Higher Education to 1980. Volume 1: Discussion and Recommendations and Summary. Columbia, SC: South Carolina Commission on Higher Education, Ja, 1972, 244 pp. ERIC ED 059 678.

Hoaglund, Jim. "Incident at Orangeburg: A Reporter's Notes." Columbia Journal Review, Spring, 1968.

Jabs, Albert E. "On Being a White Professor in a Black College." Negro Educational Review 24(Jl-O, 1973):138-143. [Vorhees College]

_____. "A White Professor's Notes on a Black College in 1972." Negro History Bulletin 39(Ja, 1976):508-510. [Vorhees College]

Leifermann, Henry P. "Not Yet Still Means Never: Orangeburg, South Carolina." New South, Fall, 1969.

McMillan, George. "Integration with Dignity." Saturday Evening Post, Mr 9, 1963. [Clemson U.]

McMillan, Lewis K. Negro Higher Education in the State of South Carolina. Orangeburg, SC: South Carolina State A. & M. College, 1952.

Nelson, Jack, and Bass, Jack. "The F.B.I. and Orangeburg [S.C.]." New South 25(Fall, 1970):2-17. [Includes letter of protest from F.B.I. Director J. Edgar Hoover and reply by authors]

_____ and _____. The Orangeburg Massacre. New York: World, 1970.

"Orangeburg Massacre." New Republic, Mr 9, 1968.

"Plantation Justice Is Real." African World 2 (Ag 5, 1972). [Vorhees College, Denmark]

Platt, Kenneth. "A Year at a Southern Negro College." Journal of the National Associ-ation of Women Deans and Counselors, Winter, 1969. [Benedict College]

Robinson, James Christopher. "South Carolina's Black Colleges: A Strategy for Survival." Doctoral dissertation, U. of Massachusetts, 1973. Univ. Microfilms Order No. 74-03787.

Scott, Cornelius Chapman. "When Negroes Attended the University [of South Carolina]." Columbia (S.C.) State, My 8, 1911.

Sellers, Cleveland L. "Sellers Seeking New Orangeburg Investigation." African World, 0, 1973.

Smith, Arthur G. "Some Problems of Higher Education in South Carolina." Quarterly Review of Higher Eduction Among Negroes 5 (0, 1973):182-185.

"The Voorhees College Boycott." Muhammad Speaks, Mr 13, 1970.

"Voorhees College (South Carolina)." AAUP Bulletin 60(Mr, 1974):82-89.

"Voorhees Students Now Behind Prison Walls." African World, Jl 22, 1972. [Voorhees College, Denmark]

Watters, Pat, and Rougeau, Weldon. Events at Orangeburg. Atlanta, GA: Southern Regional Council, F 25, 1968.

Wilkinson, R. S. The Negro Colleges of South Carolina. State Agricultural and Mechanical College, Orangeburg, SC, 1928.

South Dakota

Art o hocker, John, Jr., and Palmer, Neil M. The Sioux Indian Goes to College. An Analysis of Selected Problems of South Dakota Indian College Students, Mr, 1959. ERIC ED 131 956.

Hanck, W. C. "A Study of American Indian Graduates of Black Hills State College." Doctoral dissertation, U. of South Dakota, 1971.

Tennessee

Akins, B. "The University of Tennessee School of Social Work--Black Student Caucus." National Association of Black Social Workers News 1(0, 1973):9.

Aseltine, Gwendolyn P. Family Socialization Perceptions Among Black and White High School Students in Rutherford County, Tennessee: Comparison and Contrast, 1977. ERIC ED 139 902.

Bennett, William. "Desegregation Earns a Higher Degree." Memphis Commercial Appeal, Ag 14, 1977. [Tennessee State U., Nashville]

Bims, Hamilton. "Business As Usual at Flexible Fisk." Ebony 29(Ap, 1974):66-74.

Black Students [of Fisk University]. "Black University." Liberator, F, 1970.

Bond, Horace Mann. "Education as a Social Process: A Case Study of a Higher Institution as an Incident in the Process of Acculturation." Education and the Cultural Process, pp. 73-82. Papers presented at Symposium commemorating the seventy-fifth anniversary of the founding of Fisk University, reprinted from the American Journal of Sociology, Vol. XLVIII, No. 6, My, 1943.

Bradley, Nolen. "The Negro Undergraduate Student: Factors Relative to Performance in Predominantly White State Colleges and Universities in Tennessee." Journal of Negro Education, Winter, 1967.

Brown, Juanita. "A Unique Southern College." Southern Workman 60(Jl, 1931):291-297.

Clift, Eleanor. "Death of a Neighborhood." South Today 3(My, 1972):3. [University Center, Nashville; in re: Vanderbilt U.]

Cummings, Judith. "Fisk U. Cutting Faculty and Salaries." New York Times, Jl 14, 1975.

Davis, Thomas Edward. "A Study of Fisk Freshmen from 1928 to 1930." Journal of Negro Education 2(0, 1933):477-483.

Donaldson, Robert H., and Pride, Richard A. "Black Students at a White University; Their Attitudes and Behavior in an Era of Confrontation." Journal of Social and Behavioral Sciences 15(Fall, 1969):22-38. [Vanderbilt U., Nashville]

Du Bois, W. E. B. "A Crisis at Fisk." Nation, S 7, 1946.

_____. "Fisk." Crisis, 0, 1924.

Egerton, John. "Suit Unresolved on Dual Colleges." Race Relations Reporter 2(My 3, 1971):4-6.

_____. "Tennessee's Long-Running Desegregation Drama." Chronicle of Higher Education, Ap 4, 1977. [Tennessee State U. and the U. of Tennessee]

Fabio, Sarah Webster. "Going Home." Negro Digest, Mr, 1969. [Shift of teaching from Merritt College to Fisk U.]

Falk, Leslie A. "A Century of Service. Meharry Medical College." Southern Exposure 6(1978): 14-17.

"Fisk Students to Citizens of Nashville." Nashville Banner, F 7, 1925.

4X, Harold. "Meharry: 'Giant' in Teaching Blacks." Muhammad Speaks, Ja 18, 1974. [Nashville]

Gaillard, Frye. "Vanderbilt Adjusts to Black Studies." Race Relations Reporter 2(N 1, 1971):8-10.

Gaither, Gerald and others. "Directives for Decision Making: Attitudinal Diversity Among Black, White, and International Students." Quarterly Review of Higher Education Among Negroes 37(1969):195-197. [U. of Tennessee]

Gore, George W., Jr. "a Brief Survey of Secondary and Higher Education of Negroes in Tennessee." Quarterly Review of Higher Education Among Negroes 5(O, 1937):186-190.

Grigorieff, W. W. 1969-70 Oak Ridge Workshops for Faculty and Administrators of Traditionally Negro Institutions, Je, 1971. ERIC ED 055 545.

[Haywood, John W.] "Inaugural Address of John W. Haywood as President of Morristown College." Quarterly Review of Higher Education Among Negroes 6(Ja, 1938):51-56.

Ivey, Saundra. "A Black Medical School Faces Financial Troubles." Chronicle of Higher Education, O 17, 1977. [Meharry Medical College, Nashville]

Jackson, John S. III. "Alienation and Black Political Participation. Journal of Politics 35(N, 1973):849-885. [College students in Tennessee]

_____. "The Political Behavior and Socio-Economic Backgrounds of Black Students: The Antecedents of Protes." Midwest Journal of Political Science 15(N, 1971):661-686. [Fisk U.; Arkansas A, M, and N College; and Tennessee State U.]

Johnson, Marcia Lynn. "Student Protest at Fisk University in the 1920's." Negro History Bulletin 33(O, 1970):137-140.

Johnson, Thomas A. "Fisk Commencement Hears Alumni Report on Endowment Drain." New York Times, My 11, 1976.

Kennedy, Elizabeth Carolyn. "The Development of Higher Education in Tennessee for Negroes from 1865 to 1900." Master's thesis, Fisk U., 1950.

Lamon, Lester C. "The Black Community in Nashville and the Fisk University Student Strike of 1924-1925." Journal of Southern History 40(My, 1974).

_____. "The Tennessee Agricultural and Industrial Normal School: Public Education for Black Tennesseans." Tennessee Historical Quarterly 32(Spring, 1973).

Larsen, Suzanne W. A Comparison of Black Entering Full-Time Freshmen in the University of Tennessee, Knoxville with Other Groups, Fall, 1973, Ap 19, 1974. ERIC ED 131 816.

Layne, Richard Hollingsworth. "An Investigation of Black Students' Expectations and Perceptions of a Traditionally Black Institution: A Study of the Fisk University Campus Environment." Doctoral dissertation, U. of Houston, 1976. Univ. Microfilms Order No. 76-23374.

Lincoln, C. Eric, and Lincoln, Cecil Eric. "Voices of Fisk '70--." New York Times Magazine, Je 7, 1970.

Lloyd, R. Grann. Tennessee Agricultural and Industrial State University, 1912-1962. Nashville, 1962.

McKenzie, Fayette Avery. Ideals of Fisk. Inaugural Address of Doctor Fayette Avery McKenzie, on the Occasion of His Inauguration as Fourth President of Fisk University, Nashville, Tennessee, November 9, 1915. Nashville, 1915.

Moyer, Donna W. "The Desegregation-Integration Process at a Public University in the South." Doctoral dissertation, U. of Tennessee, 1978. Univ. Microfilms Order No. 7903449. [U. of Tennessee at Martin]

Poinsett, Alex. "Meharry Medical College Celebrates Its 100th Anniversay." Ebony 31 (O, 1976):31-40.

Rhodes, Ernest C. "Family Structure and the Achievement Syndrome Among Students at Tennessee A. and I. State University. Journal of Social and Behavioral Sciences 14 (Spring, 1969):55-59.

Richardson, Joe M. "Fisk University: The First Critical Years." Tennessee Historical Quarterly, Spring, 1970. [1866-1874]

Robinson, Charlotte. "The Changing Face of Fisk: Now It's Afros and Superflies." Detroit Free Press, S 30, 1973.

Roman, Charles Victor. Meharry Medical College, A History. Nashville, TN: Sunday School Publishing Board of the National Baptists Convention, 1934.

"Save Tennessee State University." African World 4(Mr, 1974):6.

"State Desegregation of Higher Education Institutions, Sanders v. Ellington, 288 F. Supp. 937 (M.D. Tenn. 1968). Harvard Law Review, 82(Je, 1969); Howard Law Journal 15 (Winter, 1969); Vanderbilt Law Review 22 (D, 1968).

Steif, William. "Meharry Pioneers in Care for Poor." National Catholic Reporter, O 15, 1969.

Stuart, Reginald. Black Perspectives on State-Controlled Higher Education: The Tennessee Report. New York: John Hay Whitney Foundation, N, 1973.

_____. "Black University: Tradition and Image Hinder Recruitment." South Today 3 (0, 1971):3. [Tennessee State U., Nashville]

_____. "The Dilemma of a Dual System." New South 26(Winter, 1971):39-45. [Desegregation of public higher education in Tennessee]

Stubblefield, Ruth L. "The Education of the Negro in Tennessee During Reconstruction." Master's thesis, Fisk U., 1943.

Terrell, Robert L. "Lane College: The Fires of Discontent." New South, Spring, 1969. [Jackson]

U.S. Congress, 90th, 1st session, Senate, Committee on Government Operations, Permanent Subcommittee on Investigations. Riots, Civil and Criminal Disorders. Hearings... Part 2. Washington, DC: GPO, 1967. [Investigation of disorders at Fisk and Tennessee A & I Universities; and of Nashville Liberation School]

"Violence Erupts at Lane College." African World, Je 16, 1973. [Jackson]

Walker, Joe. "Students Are Trying to Make Fisk a Black University." Muhammad Speaks, Ja 23, 1970.

White, Katie Kinnard. An Analysis of the Process of Dismantling the Dual System of Public Higher Education as Related Specifically to Tennessee State University and the University of Tennessee in Nashville, Tennessee. Doctoral dissertation, Walden U., 1976. ERIC ED 127 896.

Texas

"Academic Freedom and Tenure: Bishop College (Texas)." AAUP Bulletin, Winter, 1969.

Allen, Jewel. "The History of Negro Education at Wiley College." Master's thesis, East Texas State Teachers College, 1940.

Amdur, Neil. "A Different Manner of Integration." New York Times, D 16, 1976. [White woman athlete at Texas Southern U., Houston]

Beeker, Heather, and Mowsesian, Richard. "Examining Engineering Students by Sex and Ethnic Background." Engineering Education 67(N, 1976):162-166. [U. of Texas]

Boyd, Bob. "Administration Cover-Up at Pan Am." Texas Observer, Mr 31, 1972. [Pan American U., Edinburg]

Bryant, Ira B. Texas Southern University. Houston: D. Armstrong Co., 1975.

Bryson, William C. "Texas Southern University: Born in Sin. A College Finally Makes Houston Listen." Harvard Crimson, My 22, 1967.

Casimere, Dwight. "Terror Trial of the Texas Five." Muhammad Speaks, Mr 21, 1969. [Texas Southern U.]

"College and University Government: The University of Texas at El Paso." Bulletin of the A.A.U.P., Summer, 1974, pp. 126-138.

Cooper, Ralph. "Grievances Behind Prairie View College Violence." Muhammad Speaks, Ap 2, 1971.

Dugger, Ronnie. Our Invaded Universities. Form, Reform, and New Starts. New York: Norton, 1974. [U. of Texas]

F., J. "Positively Frank Erwin." Texas Observer, F 15, 1974. [U. of Texas]

Fogartie, Ruth Ann. Texas-Born Spanish-Name Students in Texas Colleges and Universities (1940-1946). Austin, TX: U. of Texas Press, 1948.

Hinton, William H. "A History of Howard Payne College with Emphasis on the Life and Administration of Thomas H. Taylor." Doctoral dissertation, U. of Texas, 1957. [Brownwood]

Hornsby, Alton, Jr. "The 'Colored Branch University' Issue in Texas--Prelude to Sweatt vs. Painter." Journal of Negro History 41 (Ja, 1976):51-60.

Ivins, Molly. "The University Universe." New York Times Magazine, N 10, 1974. [Living in Austin, TX]

Jacobson, Robert L. "The Case of El Paso's Alfredo de los Santos." Chronicle of Higher Education, My 10, 1976. [El Paso Community College]

Jones, William Henry. Tillotson College from 1930-1940. Austin: n.p., 1940.

Lanier, Raphael O. "The History of Higher Education for Negroes in Texas, 1930-1955, with Particular Reference to Texas Southern University." Doctoral dissertation, New York U., 1957. Univ. Microfilms Order No. 58-634.

Levin, Beatrice. "Wanting to Reach Them." Christian Science Monitor, Ja 25, 1969. [Texas Southern U.]

Levine, Harold G. and others. "Six Years of Experience with a Summer Program for Minority Students. Journal of Medical Education 51 (S, 1976):735-742. [U. of Texas Medical Branch, Galveston]

Lincoln, C. Eric. "Equalizing the Opportunity to Learn." Change 8(Jl, 1976):60-63. [Southwest Texas State U., San Marcos]

Martínez, John W. "Individuals and Institutions: Mexican Americans in a Community
College." Doctoral dissertation, U. of
Texas, 1978. Univ. Microfilms Order No.
7817677. [Austin, TX]

Mason, Don. "Seg at SMU." Texas Observer,
O 5, 1973. [Southern Methodist U.]

Mestas, Leonard J. "A Brief History of the
Juarez-Lincoln University." Hojas, 1976,
p. 52. [Austin]

Minority Affairs Committee of Sam Houston State
University Student Senate. "A Proposal for
Ethnic Studies." Texas Observer, Mr 16,
1973, Mr 30, 1973.

Nichols, Floyd. [Interview with a leader of
the black protest at Texas Southern
University] The Movement, My, 1968.

Ornstein, Jacob, and Goodman, Paul W. Bi-
lingualism/Biculturalism Viewed in the
Light of Socio-Educational Correlates, Ag,
1974. ERIC ED 157 397. [U. of Texas, El
Paso]

Phelps, Ralph A., Jr. "The Struggle for Public
Higher Education for Negroes in Texas."
Doctoral dissertation, Southwestern Baptist
Theological Seminary, 1949.

Powell, Ronald. "Huston-Tillotson Faces a
Shortage of Finances." Austin American
Statesman, O 30, 1977.

Pryor, Wanda. "Black Students Describe U.T."
Austin American, Mr 31, 1975. [U. of
Texas]

Smith, Erna. "Blacks Fought To Get Into UT."
Austin American, Mr 30, 1975. [U. of
Texas]

Texas Atlas of Higher Education. Austin:
Lyndon B. Johnson School of Public Affairs,
U. of Texas, 1974.

Thompson, Lloyd Kay. "The Origins and
Development of Black Religious Colleges in
East Texas." Doctoral dissertation, North
Texas State U., 1976. Univ. Microfilms
Order No. 77-11122.

Toles, Caesar F. "The History of Bishop
College." Master's thesis, U. of
Michigan, 1947.

Totten, H. L. "Traditionally Black Texas
Colleges' Libraries and ACRL Standards."
Texas Library Journal 45(Winter, 1969).

U.S. Congress, 90th, 1st session, Senate,
Committee on Government Operation, Permanent
Subcommittee on Investigations. Riots,
Civil and Criminal Disorders. Hearings...
Parts 1 and 3. Washington, DC: GPO, 1967.
[Investigation of disorders at Texas Southern
U.]

Wade, Norma Adams. "The Small Black College:
Can It Survive?" Dallas News, Je 13, 1976.
[Wiley College, Marshall]

Weems, John Edward and others. Black Art in
Houston: The Texas Southern University
Experience. College Station: Texas A & M
U. Press, 1978.

Westbrooks, Johnnie Mae. "The Sweatt Case:
A Study in Minority Strategy in Texas."
Master's thesis, Prairie View A & M College,
1953.

Williams, David A. "The History of Higher
Education for Black Texans, 1872-1977."
Doctoral dissertation, Baylor U., 1978.
Univ. Microfilms No. 7822691.

Woolfolk, George R. Prairie View: A Study in
Public Conscience, 1878-1946. New York:
Pageant Press, 1962.

Utah

Adams, L. La Mar and others. "Academic Success
of American Indian Students at a Large Private
University." College and University 53(F,
1977):100-107. [Brigham Young U.]

Holt, Judith. "A Study of the Relationship
between American College Test Scores and
Achievement of Indian Students at Brigham
Young University." Master's thesis, Brigham
Young U., 1967.

Martinez, Luciano S. Report on the Ethnic
Minority at the University of Utah with a
Specific Look at the Health Sciences, F,
1978. ERIC ED 149 940.

Osborne, Virgis C. "An Appraisal of the Educa-
tion Program for Native Americans at Brigham
Young University 1966-1974 with Curricular
Recommendations." Doctoral dissertation,
U. of Utah, 1975.

Pope, Albert Wallace. "An Exploration of the
University Environment as Perceived by Native
American Freshmen." Doctoral dissertation,
U. of Utah, 1977. Univ. Microfilms Order
No. 77-27,708. [Brigham Young U.]

Steele, Carolyn S. "The Relationship of Cultural
Background to the Academic Success of American
Indian Students at Brigham Young University."
Master's thesis, Brigham Young U., 1967.

Virginia

Adams, David Wallace. "Education in Hues: Red
and Black at Hampton Institute, 1878-1893."
South Atlantic Quarterly 76(Spring, 1977):
159-176.

Anderson, Alvin Frederick. "An Analysis of Job Placement Patterns of Black and Non-Black Male and Female Undergraduates at the University of Virginia and Hampton Institute." Doctoral dissertation, U. of Virginia, 1975. Univ. Microfilms Order No. 75-22811.

Barnes, Bart. "Future of Black Colleges." Washington Post, Jl 7, 1978. [St. Paul's College, Lawrenceville]

Barr, Steve. "Mood Varies in Virginia on 'Reverse Integration.'" Richmond [Va.] Times Dispatch, D 9, 1973. [Whites in predominantly black Virginia colleges]

Brooks, Lynn B. "The Norfolk State College Experiment in Training the Hard-Core Unemployed." Phi Delta Kappan, N, 1964.

Buszek, Beatrice R., and Mitchell, Blythe C. Influence of College Experience on Intelligence Quotients of Negro Students. Hampton, VA: Hampton Institute, 1967, 42 pp. ERIC ED 038 437.

Corey, Charles H. A History of the Richmond Theological Seminary with Reminiscences of Thirty Years' Work Among the Colored People of the South. Richmond, VA: J. W. Randolph Co., 1895.

Craig, William L., Jr., Anthony, Patricia, Austin, Joseph, Bracey, Martha, and Cooper, Angela. Profile of Norfolk State Students (A Pilot Study). PB-200 287. Springfield, VA: National Technical Information Service, My, 1971.

Du Bois, W. E. B. "The Hampton Idea." Voice of the Negro 3(S, 1906):332-336.

_____. "Hampton Strike." Nation, N 2, 1927.

_____. "[On] Hampton [Institute]." Crisis, N, 1917.

Egerton, John. "'A Pervasive Acceptance of Segregation.'" Chronicle of Higher Education, My 15, 1978. [Virgina Polytechnic Institute and State U.]

Gandy, John M. "The Development of Virginia State College." Virginia State College Gazette, D, 1940.

Gavins, Raymond. "Gordon Blaine Hancock: A Black Profile from the New South." Journal of Negro History 59(Jl, 1974):207-227. [Virginia Union U.]

_____. "Gordon Blaine Hancock: Southern Black Leader in a Time of Crisis, 1920-1954." Doctoral dissertation, U. of Virginia, 1970. [Virginia Union U.]

Graham, Edward K. "The Hampton Institute Strike of 1927: A Case Study in Student Protest." American Scholar 38(1969):668-682.

Grundman, Adolph H. "Northern Baptists and the Founding of Virginia Union University: The Perils of Paternalism." Journal of Negro History 63(Ja, 1978):26-41.

Hampton, Va. Normal and Agricultural Institute. Twenty-two Years' Work of the Hampton Normal and Agricultural Institute at Hampton, Virginia. Hampton, VA: Hampton Normal School Press, 1893.

Jackson, Luther P. "The Origin of Hampton Institute." Journal of Negro History 10(Ap, 1925):131-149.

Jeffreys, Richard Langston. "A History of Virginia State College for Negroes, Ettrick, Virginia." Master's thesis, U. of Michigan, 1937.

John, Walton Colcord. Hampton Normal and Agricultural Instiute: Its Evolution and Contribution to Education as a Federal Land-Grant College. Washington, DC: GPO, 1923. U.S. Bureau of Education, Bulletin 1923, No. 27.

Jones, Lance G. E. "An Englishman Sees Hampton." Southern Workman 58(Ag, 1929):370-373.

Knight, Athelia. "Facilities at 2 Va. State Colleges As Different as Black and White." Washington Post, Ja 30, 1978. [Old Dominion U. and Norfolk State College]

_____. "Fears Over Desegregation." Washington Post, Ja 31, 1978. [Higher education in Virginia]

Lake, Marvin Leon. "'Brain Drain' Plagues Black College." Norfolk Virginian-Pilot, Ag 13, 1978. [Hampton Institute]

Lipper, Bob. "U. Va. Acts to Heed Black Voices." Norfolk Virginian-Pilot, F 28, 1977.

Loomis, Peter A. "Blacks Think Racism Affects O.D.U. Grades, Survey Finds." Norfolk Ledger-Star, Ag 30, 1978. [Old Dominion U.]

Mosley, Bill. "UR's Black Student Group Struggles to Remain Visible." Richmond News Leader, F 4, 1977. [U. of Richmond]

Robinson, William H. "The History of Hampton Institute, 1868-1949." Doctoral dissertation, New York U., 1954. Univ. Microfilms Order No. 10646.

Schall, Keith L. (ed.). Stony the Road: Chapters in the History of Hampton Institute. Charlottesville: U. Press of Virginia, 1977.

Schuler, Edgar A., and Green, Robert L. "A Southern Educator and School Integration: An Interview." Phylon, Spring, 1967. [Dean C. S. Gordon Moss, Longwood College, Farmville, Prince Edward County]

Seamans, Geoff. "Ferrum Helps Blacks Find the School in the Blue Ridge." Roanoke Times & World News, Ap 23, 1978. [Ferrum College, Ferrum]

Spellman, C. L. Rough Steps on My Stairway. New York: Exposition Press, 1953. [Hampton Institute]

"The Strike at Hampton." Southern Workman 56 (1927):569-572.

Stuart, Reginald. Black Perspectives on State-Controlled Higher Education: The Virginia Report. New York: John Hay Whitney Foundation, Ja, 1974.

Tillar, Thomas Cato, Jr. Investigation of Racial Discrimination Among National Collegiate Social Fraternities at Virginia Polytechnic Institute and State University. Virginia Polytechnic Institute, F, 1972.

U.S. Commission on Civil Rights, Virginia Advisory Committee. George Mason College-- For All the People? Washington, DC: The Commission, 1971.

University of Virginia Presidential Advisory Committee on Educational and Employment Opportunities, Obligations and Rights. The Black Experience at the University of Virginia. Charlottesville, VA: Office of the President, U. of Virginia, S 17, 1974.

Weymouth, Richard J., and Wergin, Jon F. "Pilot Programs for Minority Students: One School's Experience." Journal of Medical Education 51(Ag, 1976):668-670. [Medical College of Virginia]

White, Ronald D. "A Campus Minority, Whites Fight Right In." Norfolk Virginian Pilot, N 20, 1978. [Norfolk State College]

Wilkerson, Doxey A. "Social Relations of Students at Virginia State College." Southern Workman 63(D, 1934):357-360.

Washington

Du Pree, David. "Clash of Values Catches Black Coach." Wall Street Journal, Ja 6, 1970. [U. of Washington]

Hansson, Robert O. and others. "The Measurement of Racism in College Students." Journal of Social and Behavioral Sciences 20(Summer, 1974):37-48. [U. of Washington]

Swanson, August G. "Black Recruitment at the University of Washington." Journal of the American Medical Association, Ag 18, 1969.

Totenberg, Nina. "Discriminating To End Discrimination." New York Times Magazine, Ap 14, 1974. [De Funis case, U. of Washington]

Weidlein, Edward R. "Judges Approve Rules Favoring Minorities." Chronicle of Higher Education, Mr 26, 1973. [U. of Washington Law School]

West Virginia

Canady, Herman G. "Individual Differences Among Freshmen at West Virginia State College." Journal of Negro Education 4(Ap, 1935):246-258.

Crowell, Suzanne. "Trials of Bluefield Students Being." Southern Patriot, My, 1969.

_____. "Why Bluefield State [College] Students Rebelled." Southern Patriot, Ap, 1968.

Drain, John Robert. "The History of West Virginia State College from 1892-1950." Master's thesis, West Virginia State College, 1958.

Francois, Bill. "A Living Laboratory of Human Relations." Saturday Review, My 21, 1966. [West Virginia State College]

Posey, Thomas E. "Socio-Economic Background of Freshmen at West Virginia State College." Journal of Negro Education 2(O, 1933):466-476.

Wells, Danny. "Social Life Slow for WVU Blacks." Charleston Gazette, Je 1, 1974. [West Virginia U.]

Woodson, Carter Godwin. Early Negro Education in West Virginia Institute, W. Va. West Virginia Collegiate Institute, 1921.

Wisconsin

Abrahams, Paul P. "Black Thursday at Oshkosh." Crisis, N, 1969. [Wisconsin State U.-Oshkosh, N, 1968]

Aukema, Richard L. "Oshkosh: Black Student Revolt in Microcosm." Christian Century, F 12, 1969.

Birnbaum, Robert. The Impact of Open University Access in Wisconsin, N, 1976. ERIC ED 135 325. [U. of Wisconsin-Oshkosh]

_____. "Minority Enrollment Patterns in Wisconsin and the Role of Educational Research." Integrateducation 14(My-Je, 1976):7-10.

Blecha, Mike. "Black Harassment Claimed Here." Green Bay Press Gazette, O 18, 1977. [U. of Wisconsin-Green Bay]

Brown, Dick. "Black Student Union Details Grievances at UW-Whitewater." Janesville Gazette, Ap 29, 1977. [U. of Wisconsin-Whitewater]

Drew, Bill, Hunter, Alan, and Siegle, Paul. "The National Guard Stands Around Her Door." The Movement, Ap, 1969. [U. of Wisconsin]

Hopgood, Andrew. "Academic Performance of Black Students at the University of Wisconsin-Oshkosh." Master's thesis, U. of Wisconsin-Oshkosh, 1973.

Jones, Kirkland C. "The Language of the Black 'In-Crowd': Some Observations on Intra-Group Communication." CLA Journal 15 (S, 1971):80-89. [The 'in-crowd" at the U. of Wisconsin]

Kirkhorn, Michael J. "'Mission' Translates Into Money." Milwaukee Journal, N 12, 13, and 15, 1972. [U. of Wisconsin-Milwaukee]

Lyons, Judith, and Lyons, Morgan. "Black Student Power." In Academic Supermarkets. A Critical Case Study of a Multiversity. Edited by Philip G. Altbach, Robert S. Laufer and Sheila McVey. San Francisco, CA: Jossey-Bass, 1971. [U. of Wisconsin]

Mensah, Anthony J. "Social Commitment: A Study to Determine an Effective Participation for Urban Universities in Poverty Programs in America's Turbulent Cities, with Special Reference to the People of Milwaukee's Inner City-North Negro Community." Doctoral dissertation, Marquette U., 1968.

Olive, Ralph D., and Perry, Clay. "White Males in Command at Colleges." Milwaukee Journal, Ja 14, 1979. [Milwaukee-area colleges and universities]

Olive, Ralph D., and Stone, Debbie. "Races Uneasy at U.W.M." Milwaukee Journal, Mr 28, 1976.

Perry, Clay. "[Black] Professors Face Subtle Bias." Milwaukee Journal, Ja 15, 1979. [Milwaukee-area colleges and universities]

Preis, Julie. "UW: The Unrevolutionary Present." North American Review 6(1969): 16-33, 46-61. [U. of Wisconsin, F, 1969]

Report of the Ad Hoc Committee on Afro-American Studies and Services for Black Students. Milwaukee: U. of Wisconsin-Milwaukee, My, 1977.

Roberts, Ozzie. "Director-Coach On the Spot." Ebony 29(F, 1974):48-54. [Black athletic director at College of Racine]

Sheard, Chester. "Minority Student Center Rip-Off." Muhammad Speaks, O 5, 1973. [U. of Wisconsin]

"Suspend Blacks After Racist 'Frat's' Attacks." Muhammad Speaks, F 13, 1970. [Wisconsin State U., Whitewater]

Tabankin, Margery, and Hanson, Rhonda. A History of Participation by Black Students in the University Structure. Madison, WI: Wisconsin Student Association, F, 1969.

Thomas, Christine and others. "University of Wisconsin Attempts to Attract and Keep Minority Group Students." Bulletin of United States National Student Assistance Center, D, 1967.

Trillin, Calvin. "U.S. Journal: Oshkosh." New Yorker, Ja 4, 1969. [Events growing out of black students' movement at Wisconsin State U.-Oshkosh, especially events of N 21, 1968]

U.S. Commission on Civil Rights, Wisconsin Advisory Committee. The Black Student in the Wisconsin University System. Washington, DC: The Commission, 1971.

University Extension Services to Minority Groups (A Compendium of Divisional Reports), Ap 13, 1967. ERIC ED 027 833.

Historically Black Colleges

Adams, Frank. "Black Colleges Under Attack." Southern Exposure 7(Summer, 1978):129-133.

The Administration of Admissions and Financial Aid in the United Negro College Fund Colleges. New York: College Entrance Examination Board, 1969.

Agnihotri, B. K. "Negro Legal Education and 'Black' Law Schools." Loyola Law Review 17 (1970-71).

Allen, LeRoy B. "The Possibilities of Integration for Public Colleges Founded for Negroes." Journal of Negro Education, Fall, 1966.

Allen, Robert L. "Black Campuses Today." Guardian, Mr 9, 1968.

_____. "Black [College] Studnets Seek Role." Guardian, Mr 2, 1968.

Archer, S. H. "Football in Our Colleges." Voice of the Negro 3(Mr, 1906):199-205.

Badger, Henry G. Statistics of Negro Colleges and Universities: Students, Staff, and Finances, 1900-1950. Washington, DC: Federal Security Agency, 1951.

Baker, Houston A., Jr. "One Black College." Liberator, Ap, 1970.

Bass, Jack, and Clancy, Paul. "The Militant Mood in Negro Colleges." Reporter, My 16, 1968.

Bayer, Alan E. "The New Student in Black Colleges." School Review 81(My, 1973):415-426.

Beaumont, André G., and Goodbolt, Rena D. (eds.). Handbook for Recruiting at the Traditionally Black College (1974-1975 Edition). Elizabeth, PA: College Placement Service, 1975.

Belles, A. Gilbert. "The College Faculty, the Negro Scholar, and the Julius Rosenwald Fund." Journal of Negro History, 1970.

"[Black] Campus Queens." Ebony 30(Ap, 1975): 78-87.

"Black College Football Fights for Survival." Ebony, D, 1972.

Black Colleges in the South; From Tragedy to Promise. An Historical and Statistical Review. Atlanta, GA: Southern Association of Colleges and Schools, Commission on Colleges, 1971. ERIC ED 053 230.

Blake, Elias, Jr. "Background Paper on the Traditionally Negro College." Congressional Record, My 11, 1970, E 4091.

_____. "Future Leadership Roles for Pre-dominantly Black Colleges and Universities in American Higher Education." Daedalus 100 (Summer, 1971):745-771.

Blake, Elias, Jr., and Beckmann, Joseph. [Exchange of letters on the Institute for Services to Education] Change 3(Mr-Ap, 1971):4-6.

Blake, Elias, Jr. and others. Degrees Granted and Enrollment Trends in Historically Black Colleges: An Eight-Year Study [1966-1973], O, 1974. ERIC ED 096 879.

Blake, J. Herman. "The Black University and Its Community." Negro Digest, Mr, 1968.

Bond, Horace Mann. "A Century of Negro Higher Education." In A Century of American Higher Education. Edited by William M. Brickman and Stanley Lehrer. New York: n.p., 1962.

_____. "Education for Political and Social Responsibility: Its Natural History in the American Colege." Journal of Negro Education 16(Spring, 1947):165-171. (Address delivered at the 60th Annual Convention of the Middle States Assocation of Colleges and Secondary Schools, New York City, N 29, 1946.)

_____. "The Evolution and Present Status of Negro Higher and Professional Education in the United States." Journal of Negro Education 17(Summer, 1948):224-235.

_____. "How Beta Kappa Chi Began." Beta Kappa Chi Scientific Society News Letter 2 (Ja, 1944).

_____. "Human Nature and Its Study in the Negro College." Opportunity, F, 1928, pp. 38-40.

_____. "The Liberal Arts College for Negroes--A Social Force." In A Century of Municipal Higher Education. A Collection of Addresses Delivered During the Centennial Observance of the University of Louisville, America's Oldest Municipal University. Chicago: Lincoln Printing Company, 1937.

_____. "The Origin and Development of the Negro Church Related College." Journal of Negro Education, Summer, 1960.

Bonds, A. B. "The President's Commission on Higher Education and Negro Higher Education." Journal of Negro Education 17(1948):426-436.

Bowles, Frank, and De Costa, Frank A. Between Two Worlds. A Profile of Negro High-er Education. New York: McGraw-Hill, 1971.

Boykin, Leander L. Research in Black Colleges and Universities: Administrative Perspectives, Prospectives and Challenges. Tallahassee, Fl. Florida Agricultural and Mechanical U., 1971. ERIC ED 062 906.

Bradley, Dorothy P. "Student Participation in the Governance of Predominantly Negro Colleges and Universities." Doctoral dissertation, U. of Mississippi, 1968. Univ. Microfilms Order 69-3957.

Branch, London G. "Jazz Education in Pre-dominantly Black Colleges" Doctoral disser-tation, Southern Illinois U., 1975. Univ. Microfilms Order No. 76-26,932.

Brawley, Benjamin G. "Hamlet and the Negro." Southern Workman 61(N, 1932):443-448.

Brawley, James P. Two Centuries of Methodist Concern: Bondage, Freedom and Education of Black People. Atlanta, GA: Clark College, n.d. [United Methodist Church's colleges]

Brewer, June H. "In Defense of the Black College." Journal of the National Associ-ation of Women Deans and Counselors, Winter, 1969.

Brimmer, Andrew F. "The Economic Outlook and the Future of the Negro College." Daedalus 100(Summer, 1971):539-572.

Brisbane, Robert H. The Black Vanguard: Origins of the Negro Social Revolution, 1900-1960. Valley Forge, PA: n.p., 1970. [Black higher education]

Brown, Charles I. The White Student on the Black Campus. Atlanta, GA: Institute for Higher Educational Opportunity, Southern Regional Education Board, S, 1973.

Brown, Charles I., and Stein, Phyllis R. "The White Student in Five Predominantly Black Universities." Negro Educational Review 23(O, 1972):148-169.

Brown, Ina Corinne, Blauch, Lloyd E., Jenkins, Martin D., and Caliver, Ambrose. National Survey of the Higher Education of Negroes. 4 vols. U.S. Office of Education Miscellany Bulletin No. 6. Washington, DC: GPO, 1942-1943.

Browne, Robert S. "Financing the Black University." In What Black Educators Are Saying, pp. 85-93. Edited by Nathan Wright, Jr. New York: Hawthorn, 1970.

Buggs, Charles W. Premedical Education for Negroes: Interpretations and Recommendations Based Upon a Survey in Fifteen Selected Negro Colleges, 1949. ERIC ED 150 925.

Bullock, Henry A. "The Black College and the New Black Awareness." Daedalus 100(Summer, 1971):573-602.

_____. "The Black College Must Turn Black." In Effective Use of Resources in State Higher Education, pp. 40-42. Atlanta, GA: Southern Regional Education Board, Ag, 1970.

Bumstead, Horace. Secondary and Higher Education in the South for Whites and Negroes. Publication of the National Association for the Advancement of Colored People, No. 2, 1910.

Burch, Charles Easton. "Freshman Papers in a Negro College." Crisis, S, 1921.

Burke, Arthur E. "Standards in Negro Colleges." Crisis, Ag-S, 1949.

Burnim, Mickey L. "Comparative Rates of Return to Black College Graduates: The Black versus the Nonblack Schools." Doctoral dissertation, U. of Wisconsin, 1976.

Butler, Addie J. "Some Functions of the Black College." Negro Educational Review 26 (O, 1975):167-180.

Butler, Melvin A. "The Implications of Black Dialect for Teaching English in Predominantly Black Colleges." CLA Journal 15 (D, 1971):235-239.

Calbert, Roosevelt, and Nwagbaraocha, Joel. Curriculum Change in Black Colleges. V, D, 1973. ERIC ED 089 569.

Caliver, Ambrose. A Background Study of Negro College Students. Washington, DC: GPO, 1933, 132 pp. (U.S. Department of the Interior, Office of Education, Bulletin 1933, No. 8.)

_____. "Deans and Registrars." Crisis 36(Ap, 1928):304, 322.

_____. "Some Tendencies in Higher Education and Their Application to the Negro College." Opportunity 6(Ja, 1928):6-9.

Campbell, Robert F. "Negro Colleges Have a Job." Southern Education Report, N, 1967.

Carnegie Commission on Higher Education. From Isolation to Mainstream. Problems of the Colleges Founded for Negroes. New York: McGraw-Hill, F, 1971.

Carson, Suzanne. "Samuel Chapman Armstrong: Missionary to the South." Doctoral dissertation, Johns Hopkins U., 1952.

Center for Studies in Vocational and Technical Education. The Encouragement of Research in Predominantly Negro Universities. Madison, WI: U. of Wisconsin, 1967.

Chalk, Ocania. Black College Sport. New York: Dodd Mead, 1976.

Chambers, Frederick. "Histories of Black Colleges Colleges and Universities." Journal of Negro History 57(Jl, 1972).

Chandra, Kananur V. Black Students' Concerns in a Black College. San Francisco, CA: R and E Research Associates, 1976.

Chapman, Oscar J. "A Historical Study of Negro Land-Grant Colleges in Relationship with Their Social, Economic, Political, and Educational Background." Doctoral dissertation, Ohio State U., 1940.

Cheatham, Harold E. "The Black College and University Counseling Center." Journal of College Student Personnel 17(N, 1976):495-498.

Cheatham, Roy Edward. "A Study of Financial Support Provided by Selected Private Foundations to Historically Black Colleges and Universities." Doctoral disseratation, Saint Louis U., 1975. Univ. Microfilms Order No. 76-00856.

Cheek, James E. "Black Institutions and Black Students." Integrated Education 8(N-D, 1970):16-20.

Cheek, King V., Jr. "Black Students, Black Studies, Black Colleges." Chronicle of Higher Education, N 22, 1971.

_____. The Philosophical Justification for Black Colleges in a Multiracial Society. Washington, DC: American Association for Higher Education, Mr 6, 1972, 9 pp. Address, 27th National Conference on Higher Education. ERIC ED 061 871.

Cheek, King V., Jr. and others. Toward a New Liberal Education. Edwardsville, IL: Office of Program Evaluation and Development, Southern Illinos U., 1971.

Church, Zelmera. "The Participation of Negro Land-Grant Colleges and Universities in Federal Emergency and Regular Educational Funds." Master's thesis, Howard U., 1939.

Clement, Rufus E. "The Historical Development of Higher Education for Negro Americans." Journal of Negro Education, Fall, 1966.

Cook, Samuel Du Bois. "Politics and the Future of Black Colleges: A Commentary. Western Journal of Black Studies 2(Fall, 1978):173-181.

Crew, Louie. "Opportunities for White Students in Black Colleges." Colorado Quarterly 21 (Spring, 1973):437-447.

Davis, Gwendolyn R. "Administrative Intern Program Strengthens Black Colleges." South Today 5(O, 1973).

Davis, Arthur P. "The Negro Professor." Crisis, Ap, 1936.

Davis, Jerry S., and Kirschner, Alan H. "United Negro College Fund Research Report." Western Journal of Black Studies 1(S, 1977):217-223.

Davis, John. "The Unrest in Negro Colleges." The New Student, Ja, 1929.

Davis, John Warren. Problems in the Collegiate Education of Negroes. West Virginia: Institute, WV, 1937.

Davis, Ronald. "The Black University: In Peril Before Birth." Negro Digest, Mr, 1970.

Days, Everett A., and Ready, I. E. "The Future of Black Colleges. An Articulation Challenge." Community College Review 2 (Spring, 1974):53-60.

Delaney, Paul. "'Black Schools Are Not as Impersonal.'" New York Times, N 14, 1976.

Dent, Thomas C. "Blues for the Negro College." Freedomways, Fall, 1968.

Derbigny, Irving A. General Education in the Negro College. Palo Alto, CA: Stanford U. Press, 1947.

"Desegregating Black Public Colleges. What Will It Mean?" Civil Rights Digest 7(Winter, 1975):26-35.

Dickerson, J. Edward. "The Failing Student-- an Academic Problem in Negro Colleges." Quarterly Review of Higher Education Among Negroes 18(O, 1950):155-171.

Dickerson, Milton O., Jr. "The External Administration of Negro Land-Grant Colleges and Universities from 1890 to 1920." Doctoral dissertation, Catholic U. of America, 1975. Univ. Microfilms Order No. 75-16829.

Directory of Negro Colleges and Universities, Mr, 1967. Plans for Progress, 1800 G Street, N.W., Washington, DC 20006.

Directory of Predominantly Black Colleges and Universities in the United States of America, 1971. National Alliance of Businessmen, 1730 K Street, N.W., Washington, DC 20006.

Directory of Predominantly Negro Colleges and Universities in the United States of America (Four-Year Institutions Only), Ja, 1969. Plans for Progress, 1800 G Street, N.W., Suite 703, Washington, DC 20006.

Dixon, Robert M., and Taylor, Julius H. "Establishing Physics Programs in Black Colleges." Physics Today 29(Je, 1976).

Dobbins, Cheryl J. Developing the Black Community to Save Black Colleges. Report of the Second Black Colleges and Community Development Conference (Chicago, IL, S 19-21, 1973). ERIC ED 088 388.

Dobbins, Cheryl, and Walker, Dollie R. "The Role of Black Colleges in Public Affairs Education." Public Administration Review 34 (N-D, 1974):540-552.

Document. "Black College Presidents Demand Action." Integrated Education 8(Jl-Ag, 1970): 13-14.

Drake, St. Clair. "The Black University in the American Social Order." Daedalus 100(Summer, 1971):833-897.

Du Bois, W. E. B. "The Field and Function of the American Negro College." Fisk University News 6(Je, 1933).

_____. "The Future and Function of the Private Negro College." Crisis, Ag, 1946.

_____. "Higher Education of the Negro." Talladega College Record, N, 1902.

_____. "The Negro College." Crisis, Ag, 1933.

_____. "Representative Higher Institutions for Negro Education in the South." Boston Globe, F 9, 1905.

Egerton, John. The Black Public Colleges: Integration and Disintegration. Nashville, TN: Race Relations Information Center, Je, 1971.

Easton, William D. "Survey of the Characteristics of the Successful Black Deans in Predominantly Black Four-Year Colleges and Universities in the Southeastern United States." Doctoral dissertation, U. of Montana, 1973. Univ. Microfilms Order No. 74-1631.

Elam, Ada Maria. "Social Attitudes Held and Methods for Change Desired by Black and White Students in a 'Reverse Integration' College Setting." Doctoral dissertation, Pennsylvania State U., 1972. Univ. Micro films Order No. 73-07431.

_____. "Two Sides of the Coin: White Students in Black Institutions." Journal of the NAWDAC 41(Winter, 1978):57-61.

_____. White Students in Black Institutions, 1977. ERIC ED 138 914.

"The Fall 1975 Freshman Class at Black Colleges." Research Report (United Negro College Fund) 1(My, 1976).

"Federal Aid and Black Colleges." Black Enterprise 3(S, 1972):28

Federal Interagency Committee on Education. Federal Agencies and Black Colleges. Fiscal Year 1969. Rev. ed. Washington, DC: FICE, Ja, 1971.

_____. Federal Agencies and Black Colleges. Fiscal Year 1970. Washington, DC: GPO, 1972.

_____. "Federal Aid to Black Colleges." FICE Report 1(N, 1974):1-8.

_____. Federal Agencies and Black Colleges, FY 1974, J1, 1976. ERIC ED 131 770.

_____. Federal Agencies and Black Colleges. 1977. F.I.C.E., Room 3023, 400 Maryland Avenue, S.W., Washington, DC 20202. [For years 1972 and 1973]

Fisher, Franklin G., Jr. Assessment of Job Placement Services in Colleges with Predominantly Black Students. 3 vols., D, 1976. ERIC ED 140-114 to 140-116.

Fisher, Miles Mark IV. "Crusader for the Black College." Civil Rights Digest 3 (Spring, 1970):18-21. [About the National Association for Equal Opportunity in Higher Education]

"FOCUS: Death by Merger. Black Education vs. Integration." The Black Collegian 2 (N-D, 1971):28-30, 42-44. [Black colleges]

Forrest, Leon. "Black Colleges thrown to Wolves." Muhammad Speaks, Mr 24, 1972.

Fosdick, F. "Can Negro Colleges Survive?" Negro Digest, Ja, 1951.

Frazier, E. Franklin. "Graduate Education in Negro Colleges and Universities." Journal of Negro Education 2(J1, 1933):329-341.

Freeman, Ludwig Felix. "Federal Agency Support to Black Colleges and Universities: Patterns and Problems." Doctoral dissertation, U. of Pittsburgh, 1973. Univ. Microfilms Order No. 74-15624.

Friedman, Neil, White, Agatha, and Epps, Edgar G. "Attitudes of Southern Black College Students Toward Black Consciousness and Integration." Afro-American Studies 1 (Ja, 1971):191-202.

_____ (ed.). "Learning in Black Colleges." Wilson Library Bulletin 44(S, 1969):49-74.

Gallagher, Buell G. American Caste and the Negro College. New York: Columbia U. Press, 1938.

George, Preston A. "An Analysis of the Financial Health of Predominantly Black Graduate Institutions of Higher Education." Doctoral dissertation, Kansas State U., 1978. Univ. Microfilms Order No. 7821913.

Gibbs, Warmoth T. "Engineering Education in Negro Land Grant Colleges." Quarterly Review of Higher Education Among Negroes 20(Ap, 1952):81-85.

_____. "Problems in Negro Graduate Schools." Quarterly Review of Higher Education Among Negroes 13(O, 1945):371-376.

Gloster, Hugh M. "The Black College--Its Struggle for Survival and Success." Journal of Negro History 63(Ap, 1978):101-107.

Goodwin, Louis C. "A Historical Study of Accreditation in Negro Public and Private Colleges, 1927-1952, with Special Reference to Colleges in the Southern Association." Doctoral dissertation, New York U., 1956. Univ. Microfilms Order No. 19989.

Gore, George W., Jr. "Honor Societies in Negro Colleges." Quarterly Review of Higher Education Among Negroes 5(J1, 1937):113-117.

Green, Harry W. "Higher Standards for the Negro College." Opportunity, Ja, 1931.

Green, Robert Lee. "Why the Push to 'Upgrade' Negro Colleges?" Southern Education Report, J1-Ag, 1967.

Greene, Harry W. "Negro Colleges in the Southwest." Opportunity 5(N, 1927):322-325.

Greene, John W. "Did Black Colleges Kill Dial Accress?" Journal of Negro Education 45 (Spring, 1976):204-211.

Gupta, Bhaguan Swarup. "A Study of Title III, Higher Education Act of 1965, and an Evaluation of its Impact at Selected Predominantly Black Colleges." Doctoral dissertation, North Texas State U., 1971. Univ. Microfilms Order No. 72-17009.

Gurin, Patricia. "Motivation and Aspirations of Southern Negro College Youth." *American Journal of Sociology* 75(1970), pt. 2, 607-631.

_____. "Social Class Constraints on the Occupational Aspirations of Students Attending Some Predominantly Negro Colleges." *Journal of Negro Education*, Fall, 1966.

Gurin, Patricia, and Epps, Edgar. "Some Characteristics of Students from Poverty Backgrounds Attending Predominantly Negro Colleges in the Deep South." *Social Forces*, S, 1966.

_____ and _____. *Black Consciousness, Identity, and Achievement: A Study of Students in Historically Black Colleges*. New York: Wiley, 1975.

Gurin, Patricia, and Gaylord, C. "Educational and Occupational Goals of Men and Women at Black Colleges." *Monthly Labor Review* 99 (Je, 1976).

Gurin, Patricia, and Katz, Daniel. *Motivation and Aspiration in the Negro College*. Ann Arbor, MI: Institute for Racial Research, U. of Michigan, 1966.

Hackshaw, James O. F. "The Case for a Black University." *New York University Education Quarterly* 3(Summer, 1972):12-19.

Hall, Gwendolyn Midlo. "Rural Black College." *Negro Digest*, Mr, 1969.

Hall, Samuel M., Jr. and others. *Developing Career Counseling Services at a Predominantly Black College: Implications for More Effective Programs for Black Students at "White" Colleges or Universities*. American College Personnel Association (convention, St. Louis, MO), Mr 16, 1970, 25 pp. ERIC ED 041 317.

Hall-Mosley, Myrtis. "A Study of the Self-Perception of the Leadership Behavior of Presidents of Black Four Year Colleges and Universities." Doctoral dissertation, U. of Cincinnati, 1978. Univ. Microfilms Order No. 7821581.

Hamilton, Charles V. "The Place of the Black College in the Human Rights Struggle." *Negro Digest*, S, 1967.

Harding, Vincent. "A Place of Murder." *Soundings*, Winter, 1968.

_____. "Some International Implications of the Black University." *Negro Digest*, Mr, 1968.

_____. "Toward the Black University." *Ebony*, Ag, 1970.

Hare, Nathan. "Conflicting Racial Orientation of Negro College Students and Professors." *Journal of Negro Education*, Fall, 1965.

_____. "War on Black Colleges." *Black Scholar* 9(My/Je, 1978):12-19.

Harper, Conrad K. "The Legal Status of the Black College." *Daedalus* 100(Summer, 1971): 772-782.

Harrington, Eugene M. "Negro Law Schools: The Liberals' Dilemma." *Commonweal*, Ap 12, 1968.

Harris, J. John III and others. "A Historical Perspective of the Emergence of Higher Education in Black Colleges." *Journal of Black Studies* 6(S, 1975):55-68.

Harris, Patricia Roberts. "The Negro College and Its Community." *Daedalus* 100(Summer, 1971):720-731.

Harrison, E. C. "Student Unrest on the Black College Campus." *Journal of Negro Education* 41(Spring, 1972):113-120.

Haynes, Leonard L. III. "An Analysis of the Effects of Desegregation upon Public Black Colleges." Doctoral dissertation, Ohio State U., 1975. Univ. Microfilms Order No. 75-26591.

Hedrick, James. "The Negro in Southern Graduate Education." Doctoral dissertation, North Texas State College, 1954. Univ. Microfilms Order No. 10816.

Henderson, Stephen E. "The Black University: Toward Its Realization." *Negro Digest*, Mr, 1968.

Henderson, Vivian W. "Negro Colleges Face the Future." *Daedalus* 100(Summer, 1971):630-646.

_____. "The Role of the Predominantly Negro Institutions." *Journal of Negro Education*, Summer, 1967.

_____. "Unique Problems of Black Colleges." *Liberal Education* 56(O, 1970):373-383.

High, Juanita J. "Black Colleges as Social Intervention: The Development of Higher Education Within the African Methodist Episcopal Church." Doctoral dissertation, Rutgers U., 1978. Univ. Microfilms Order No. 7810230. [1786-1976]

Hilger, A. F. "Higher Education for the Colored Youth." *Independent* 54, pp. 1500-1502.

Hill, Johnny Ray. *A Contemporary Status Report on the Libraries of Historically Black Public Colleges and Universities*, S 20, 1976. ERIC ED 131 743.

_____. A Study of the Public-Assisted Black College Presidency. New York: Carlton Press, 1957.

_____. "A Study of the Public-Assisted Black College Presidency." Doctoral dissertation, Miami U., 1972. Univ. Microfilms Order No. 73-01325.

_____. The Members of Governing Boards of Historically Black Public Colleges and Universities in Profile, JI, 1977. ERIC ED 142 155.

_____. "Presidential Perception: Administrative Problems and Needs of Public Black Colleges." Journal of Negro Education 44 (Winter, 1975):53-62

Holland, Jerome H. "Educational Implications Behind the Racial Wall." Journal of the Association of College Admissions Counselors, Fall, 1964. [Problems of the Negro college]

Holmes, Dwight O. W. The Evolution of the Negro College. New York: Bureau of Publications, Teachers College, Columbia U., 1934.

Holsendolph, Ernest. "Black Colleges are Worth Saving." Fortune 84 (O, 1971).

_____. "Title III Storm Signals." Change 10 (D-Ja, 1978/79:56-57. [Higher Education Act of 1965 and black colleges]

Hornsby, Alton, Jr. "Historical Overview of Black Colleges in the United States." Western Journal of Black Studies 2(Fall, 1978):162-166.

Houston, G. David. "Weaknesses of the Negro College." Crisis, Jl, 1920.

Howe, Harold II. Black Colleges and the Continuing Dream. New York: Ford Foundation, 1976.

Hrabowski, Freeman Alphonso. "A Comparison of the Graduate Academic Performance of Black Students Who Graduated from Predominantly Black Colleges and from Predominantly White Colleges." Doctoral dissertation, U. of Illinois, 1975. Univ. Microfilms Order No. 75-24322.

Hughes, Langston. "Cowards from the [Negro] Colleges." Crisis, Ag, 1934.

Humphries, Frederick S. Black Colleges--A National Resource for the Training of Minority Scientific and Engineering Manpower, F, 1976. ERIC ED 132 029.

Hunter, Charlayne. "Black Colleges and the Black Mood." Southern Education Report, My 1969.

Institute for Higher Educational Opportunity. Special Financial Need of Traditionally Negro Colleges. A Task Force Report. Atlanta: Southern Regional Education Board, 1969.

Jackson, Jacqueline J. "An Exploration of Attitudes Toward Faculty Desegregation at Negro Colleges." Phylon, Winter, 1967.

_____. "Faculty Desegregation at Negro Colleges." Phylon 27(Winter, 1967):338-352.

Jacobson, Robert L. "Negro Student Editors Want 'Black' Institutions." Chronicle of Higher Education, Je 10, 1968.

Jaffe, A. J., Adams, Walter, and Meyers, Sandra G. Negro Higher Education in the 1960's. New York: Praeger, 1968.

_____, _____ and _____. "The Sharply Stratified World of the Negro Colleges." College Board Review, Winter, 1967-1968.

Jencks, Christopher, and Riesman, David. "The American Negro College." Harvard Educational Review, Summer-Fall, 1967. [See Sekora, below]

Joesting, Joan A. A Comparative Study of Activists and Nonactivists at a Southern Black College." Diss. Abstr. Int'l. 31 (8-A) (F, 1971) 3958.

Joesting, Joan, and Joesting, Robert. "Sex and Social Class Differences in Verbal Aggression in Black College Students." College Student Journal 7(Ja-F, 1973).

Johnson, Charles S. The Negro College Graduate. Chapel Hill, NC: The U. of North Carolina Press, 1938.

Johnson, Howard N. "A Survey of Students' Attitudes Toward Counseling at a Predominantly Black University." Journal of Counseling Psychology 24(Mr, 1977):162-164.

Johnson, James Weldon. Relations of the Negro College to the American Race Question." Southern Workman 62(Jl, 1933):291-298.

Johnson, O. C. "Importance of Black Colleges." Educational Review (Spring, 1971):165-170.

Johnson, Tobe. "The Black College as System." Daedalus 100(Summer, 1971):798-812.

Jones, Ann. Uncle Tom's Campus. New York: Praeger, 1973. [Teaching at a black college]

Jones, Butler A. "The Tradition of Sociology Teaching in Black Colleges: The Unheralded Professional." In Black Sociologists: Historical and Contemporary Perspectives. Edited by James E. Blackwell and Morris Janovitz. Chicago: U. of Chicago Press, 1974.

Jones, Mack H. "The Responsibility of the Black College to the Black Community: Then and Now." Daedalus 100(Summer, 1971):732-744.

_____. "Some Observations on Student Rebellions on Black Campuses." Journal of Social and Behavioral Sciences 16(Fall, 1969):61-65.

Jones, Wendall P. "The Negro Press and the Higher Education of Negroes, 1933-1952: A Study of News and Opinion on Higher Education in the Three Leading Negro Newspapers." Doctoral dissertation, U. of Chicago, 1954.

Jordan, Vernon E., Jr. The Historically Black Public College in an Integrated Society. New York: National Urban League, 1975.

Klein, Arthur J. Survey of Negro Colleges and Universities. Office of Education Bulletin, 1928, No. 7. Washington, DC: GPO, 1929.

Kuritz, Hyman. "Integration on Negro College Campuses." Phylon 27(Summer, 1967):121-130.

_____. "The Intellectual World of the Negro College Student." Journal of Social and Behavioral Sciences 13(Fall, 1968):18-24.

Langer, E. "Negro Colleges." Science 145(Jl 24, 1964):139-144.

Lash, John S. "The Literature of the Negro in Negro Colleges: Its Status and Curricula Accommodation." Quarterly Review of Higher Education Among Negroes 16(Ap, 1948):66-76.

Lawson, James R., Mays, Benjamin E., Proctor, Samuel D., and Payton, Benjamin F. "Educators Respond [to the Black University Concept]." Negro Digest, Mr, 1969.

Lawson, Margaret L. "Black Campuses: Can They Survive Desegregation?" Washington Post, Ap 1, 1979.

Leeson, Jim. "The Short Road Home." Southern Education Report, My, 1969. [Migration survey of black colleges]

Le Francois, Jean. "A White Among Blacks." Integrated Education (Ja-G, 1972):48-52.

Lehfeldt, Martin C. "A Very Mixed Bag: White Teachers at Black Colleges." Soundings 52 (Summer, 1969):128-153.

LeMelle, Tilden J., and Le Melle, Wilbert J. The Black College. A Strategy for Development. New York: Praeger, 1969.

Lewis, Alba M. "Comparisons of Student-Faculty Perceptions of Real and Ideal Environments at Five Negro Colleges, 1967-1968." Diss. Abstr. Int'l., 1969, 30 (2-A) 522-523

Lincoln, C. Eric. "The Negro Colleges and Cultural Change." Daedalus 100(Summer, 1971):603-629.

Little, Monroe Henry, Jr. "The Black Student at the Black College, 1880-1964." Doctoral dissertation, Princeton U., 1977. Univ. Microfilms Order No. 78-286.

Lloyd, R. Grann. "Economics Curricula in Black Colleges." American Journal of Economics and Sociology 30(0, 1971):365-376.

Long, Herman H. "The Future of Private Black Colleges." Philadelphia Inquirer, F 5, 1972.

_____. "Perspectives on the Negro College Teacher's World: Crisis and Redefinition in Racial Perspective." College Language Association Journal, N, 1957.

Lowe, Keith. "Towards a Black University." Liberator, S, 1968.

Lyells, Ruby E. S. "The Library in Negro Land-Grant Colleges." Master's thesis, U. of Chicago, 1942.

Lynch, Acklyn R. "Blueprint for Change." Black Books Bulletin 1 (Winter, 1972):16-20.

Lyons, Charles A., Jr. Toward Equity for Blacks in Higher Education, Ap 1, 1977. ERIC ED 141 455.

Lyons, Charles A., Jr., Curry, Milton K., Jr., and Fisher, Miles Mark. [Testimony on problems of black higher education, representing the National Association for Equal Opportunity in Higher Education] U.S. Congress, 94th, 1st session, Senate, Committee on Labor and Public Welfare, Subcommittee on Education, Higher Education Legislation, 1975. Hearings..., pp. 747-800. Washington, DC: GPO, 1975.

Lyons, James Earl. "The Admission of Non-Black Students as an Indication of a Potential Shift in the Traditional Role of the Black Publicly Supported Colleges and Universities." Doctoral dissertation, U. of Connecticut, 1974. Univ. Microfilms Order No. 74-00014.

_____. "The Black Public College: To Stay Open or to Close?" Integrateducation 12 (Jl-Ag, 1974):22-23.

_____. "The Case for the Black College." Southern Exposure 7(Summer, 1979):134-135.

McAdoo, Douglas Decator. "America's Black Colleges--Survival or Demise: Do They Still Have a Place in Our Present Society?" Doctoral dissertation, U. of Massachusetts, 1974. Univ. Microfilms Order No. 75-16578.

McClain, Edwin W. "Personality Characteristics of Negro College Students in the South--A Recent Appraisal." Journal of Negro Education, Summer, 1967.

McClendon, William H. "Which College--White or Negro?" Crisis, S, 1934.

McGee, Leo, and McAfee, Dalton. "The Predominantly Black Institution of Higher Learning and Adult Education: New Challenge." Adult Leadership 23(My, 1975): 345-347.

_____ and _____. "Role of the Traditionally Black Public Institution of Higher Learning in Extension Education." Journal of Negro Education 46(Winter, 1977):46-52.

McGrath, E. J. "Predominantly Negro Colleges." The Encyclopedia of Education 7(1971): 192-196.

_____. The Predominantly Negro Colleges and Universities. New York: Teachers College, Columbia U., 1965.

McKinney, Theophilus E. Higher Education Among Negroes. Charlotte, NC: Johnson C. Smith U., 1932.

McMillan, Lewis K. "The American Negro in American Higher Education." Crisis, AG, 1947.

McWorter, Gerald A. "The Nature and Needs of the Black University." Negro Digest, Mr, 1968.

_____. "Struggle, Ideology, and the Black University." Negro Digest, Mr, 1969.

Margarell, Jack. "Inequality Threat Grows, Black-College Leaders Say." Chronicle of Higher Education, My 3, 1976.

Mason, Rose L. "Students in Black Colleges Organize To Save Their Schools." South Today 5(N, 1973).

Mayhew, Lewis B. "Neighboring Black and White Colleges: A Study in Waste." Educational Record 52(Spring, 1971):159-164.

Mays, Benjamin E. "Achievements of the Negro Colleges." Atlantic 217(F, 1966):90-92.

_____. "Black Colleges: Past, Present and Future." Black Scholar 6(S, 1974):32-37.

_____. "Future of Negro Colleges." Saturday Review (N 18, 1961):53-54.

_____. "Higher Education and the American Negro." In What Black Educators Are Saying, pp. 104-113. Edited by Nathan Wright, Jr. New York: Hawthorn, 1970.

_____. "A Look at the Black Colleges." Foundations 17(J1-S, 1974):237-246.

Meacham, Carl E. "Separate but Better." New Republic 165(0 9, 1971):10-11.

Meeth, Richard. "The [McGrath] Report on Predominantly Negro Colleges One Year Later." Journal of Negro Education, Summer, 1966.

_____. "The Transition of the Predominantly Negro College." Journal of Negro Educa Fall, 1966.

Meier, August. "Race Relations at Negro Colleges." Crisis, N, 1959.

Melish, I. H. "Attitudes Toward the White Minority on a Black Campus: 1966-1968." Sociol. Quart. 11(1970):321-330.

Middleton, Lorenzo. "Students Organize to Save Public Black Colleges." Chronicle of Higher Education, My 1, 1978.

Miller, Carroll L. Graduate Education in the Predominantly Negro Institution. Washington, DC: Howard U., N 15, 1968. ERIC ED 028 690.

_____. "Issues and Problems in the Higher Education of Negro Americans." Journal of Negro Education, Fall, 1966.

Miller, Kelly. "Education for Manhood." Monographic Magazine, Ap, 1913.

_____. "Function of the Negro College." Dial 32(Ap 16, 1902):267-270.

_____. "The Higher Education of the Negro is at the Crossroads." Educational Review 72 (D, 1926):272-278.

_____. "The Past, Present and Future of the Negro College." Journal of Negro Education 2(J1, 1933):411-422.

_____. "The Reorganization of the Higher Education of the Negro in Light of Changing Conditions." Journal of Negro Education 5 (J1, 1936):484-494.

Minority Institutions Science Improvement Program. Washington, DC: National Science Foundation, 1978.

Mohr, Paul B., Sr. A Cross-Cultural Program for Attitude Modification of White Students on a Predominantly Black University Campus, 1975. ERIC ED 102 153.

Mohr, Paul, and Jones, Adelbert (eds.). Law and the Unitary System of Higher Education--A Discussion of the Impact of Title VI, U.S. Civil Rights Act on Selected Black Public Colleges and Universities, 1975. Nebraska Curriculum Development Center, Andrews Hall, U. of Nebraska, Lincoln NB 68508.

Monro, John U. "The Black College Dilemma." Educational Record 53(Spring, 1972):132-137.

_____. "Black Studies, White Teachers, and Black Colleges." Teaching Forum III(1970): 3-9.

_____. "Escape from the Dark Cave." Nation, O 27, 1969.

_____. "Teaching in a Black College." In New Teaching, New Learning, pp. 27-33. Edited by G. Kerry Smith and Others. San Francisco: Jossey-Bass, 1971.

Montgomery, Barbara and others. Federal Agencies and Black Colleges. Fiscal Years 1972 and 1973, 1976. ERIC ED 131 773.

Morgan, Paul E. "Fostering Development of Negro Engineering Colleges." Engineering Education 60(Je, 1970):967-969.

Moton Consortium on Admissions and Financial Aid. The Moton Guide to American Colleges with a Black Heritage, 1974-75, 1974. ERIC ED 100 270.

_____. Some Highlights of the Astin Study of Dropouts and Implications for the Black Colleges, n.d. ERIC ED 126 806.

Moton, Robert R. "Negro Higher and Professional Education in 1943." Journal of Negro Education 2(Jl, 1933):397-402.

Moynihan, Daniel P. "The Presidency and the Press." Commentary 51(Mr, 1971):41-52. [Touches on the subject of black colleges]

Muhammad, Elijah. "Black Intellectuals." Muhammad Speaks, F 7, 1969.

Murphy, Mary Kay, and Kozell, Charles E. "Black Colleges: They Have a Special Role in Basic Adult Education." South Today 3 (D, 1871):3.

Nabrit, S. M. "Reflections on the Future of Black Colleges." Daedalus 100(Summer, 1971): 660-677.

National Advisory Committee on Black Higher Education and Black Colleges and Universities. Higher Education Equity: The Crisis of Appearance versus Reality, Je, 1978. ERIC ED 157 493.

National Association for Equal Opportunity in Higher Education. A Partnership for Leadership in the Development of a Year 2000 Plan for Parity in Education. The National Goal of Equal Opportunity and the Historically Black Colleges, N 4, 1975. ERIC ED 121 168.

Nelson, Edward A., and Uhl, Norman P. "The Development of Attitudes and Social Characteristics of Students Attending Predominantly Black Colleges: A Longitudinal Study." Research in Higher Education 7(1977):299-314.

_____ and _____. "A Factorial Study of the Attitude Scales on the College Student Questionnaire with Students at a Predominantly Black University." Multivariate Behavioral Research 9(0, 1974):395-405.

Nelson, Edward A., and Johnson, Norman C. Attitude Changes on the College Student Questionnaires: A Study of Students Enrolled in Predominantly Black Colleges and Universities, F, 1971. ERIC ED 049 296.

Nelson, Jac. "Black Colleges." Atlantic 226 (0, 1970):22-27.

Nicholas, Freddie Warren. "The Black Land Grant Colleges: An Assessment of the Major Changes Between 1965-66 and 1970-71." Doctoral dissertation, U. of Virginia, 1973. Univ. Microfilms Order No. 73-31149.

Niles, Lyndrey A. "The Status of Speech Communication Programs at Predominantly Black Four Year Colleges: 1971-1972." Doctoral dissertation, Temple U., 1973.

"Nixon and Co. Still Part of the Problem for Black Colleges." African World, F 9, 1974.

Office for Advancement of Public Negro Colleges. Public Negro Colleges. A Fact Book, Jl, 1969. Office for Advancement of Public Negro Colleges of the National Association of State Universities and Land-Grant Colleges, 805 Peachtree St., N.E., Suite 577, Atlanta, GA 30308.

Orr, C. W. "Evolution of the Admission Practices of Negro Land-Grant Colleges, 1890-1950." Negro Educational Review, Ap, 1959.

Patterson, Joseph M. "A Study of the History of the Contribution of the American Missionary Association to the Higher Education of the Negro." Doctoral dissertation, Cornell U., 1956.

Patterson, Lindsay. "Black Schools of Engineering + Corporate Support = Better Graduates." Black Enterprise 7(My, 1977):45-48.

Payne, Joseph A. "An Analysis of the Role of the Association of Colleges and Secondary Schools for Negroes from 1934 to 1954." Doctoral dissertation, Indiana U., 1957. Univ. Microfilms Order No. 24836.

Payne, William. "The Negro Land-Grant Colleges." Civil Rights Digest 3(Spring, 1970):12-27.

Payton, Benjamin F. "An Interview...A Candid Look At Black Colleges and Where They Are Going." Black Enterprise 3(S, 1972):33-37. [Interviewed by Pat Patterson]

Pettigrew, Thomas F. "The Role of Whites in the Black College of the Future." Daedalus 100 (Summer, 1971):813-832.

_____. "A Social Psychological View of the Predominantly Negro College." Journal of Negro Education, Summer, 1967.

Pfanner, Daniel J. "The Thought of Negro Educators on Negro Higher Education, 1900-1950." Doctoral dissertation, Columbia U. Teachers College, 1958.

Pierce, Donald L. "Report of Committee L, 1973–74." Bulletin of the AAUP (Summer, 1974):244–246. [On predominantly black higher institutions]

Pierce, Ponchitta. "Integration: Negro College's Newest Challenge." Ebony, Mr, 1966.

Posey, Thomas E. "Negro Land Grant Colleges. Opportunity, Ja, 1932.

Proctor, Samuel D. "Land-Grant Universities and the Black Presence." In Land-Grant Universities and their Continuing Challenge. Edited by G. Lester Anderson. East Lansing, MI: Michigan State U. Press, 1976.

Public Negro Colleges: A Fact Book, 1971. Office for the Advancement of Public Negro Colleges, 805 Peachtree Street, N.E., Atlanta, GA 30308.

Raffalovich, George. "Piety Rules a Negro College." Outlook and Independent 160(Ja 13, 1932):45–46.

Rand, Earl W. "An Analysis of the Boards of Control of a Group of Selected Negro Protestant Church-Related Colleges." Doctoral dissertation, Indiana U., 1952.

Redd, George. "An Analysis of Teacher Education Trends in Negro Colleges." Educational Administration and Supervision 35(N, 1949): 461–474.

"Report on the Meeting of the Association of Colleges and Secondary Schools for Negroes Held in Atlanta, Georgia, December 5–6, 1934." Quarterly Review of Higher Education Among Negroes 3(Ja, 1935):18–81. [D, 1934]

Robbins, Richard. Desegregation in the Negro College in the South, and Persistence in College, 1966. ERIC ED 010 603.

_____. "The Future of Negro Colleges." New South Student, Ap, 1966. [Southern Student Organizing Committee, P.O. Box 6403, Nashville, TN 37212.

Sandle, Floyd L. "A History of the Development of the Educational Theatre in Negro Colleges and Universities from 1911 to 1959." Doctoral dissertation, Louisiana State U., 1959. Univ. Microfilms Order No. 59-5527.

Sawyer, Granville M. "A Future for the Black University." Quarterly Review of Higher Education Among Negroes, Ja, 1969.

_____. "Negro Colleges for the Great Society." College and University Journal, Summer, 1965.

_____. "Student Dissent on the Negro College Campus." Quarterly Review of Higher Education Among Negroes, Ap, 1968.

Schuck, Peter H. "Black Land-Grant Colleges. Discrimination as Public Policy." Saturday Review 55(Je 24, 1972):46–48.

Scotford, John R. "The New Negro Edcuation." Christian Century 12(Ja, 1928).

Scott-Heron, Gil. The Nigger Factory. New York: Dial, 1972. [Novel set in all-black college]

Sedlacek, William E., and Brown, Glenwood C., Jr. College Admissions and the Black Student: Results of a National Survey, Mr 17, 1970. ERIC ED 040 230.

Sekora, John. "The Emergence of Negro Higher Education in America, a Review." Race, Jl, 1968.

_____. "Murder Relentless and Impassive: The American Academic Community and the Negro College." Soundings, Fall, 1968.

_____. "On Negro Colleges: A Reply to Jencks and Riesman." Antioch Review, Spring, 1968.

67X, Charles. "Fraternities: Guardians of the Black Bourgeoisie." Muhammad Speaks, O 5, 1973.

Slater, Jack. "Is the Black Public College Dying?" Ebony 27(O, 1972):92–101.

Small Change: A Report on Federal Support for Black College, 1972. Southern Education Foundation, 811 Cypress Street, N.E., Atlanta, GA 30308.

Smith, Bernard S. A Cross-Cultural Program for Attitude Modification of White Students On a Black University Campus, 1973. United Board for College Development, 159 Forrest Avenue, N.E., Suite 514, Atlanta, GA 30303.

Smith, Charles U. "Problems and Possibilities of the Predominantly Negro College." Journal of Social and Behavioral Sciences 13(Fall, 1968): 3–8.

Smith, Estus. "Encroachment." Journal of Higher Education 42(F, 1971):147–150. [Black colleges]

Smith, Herman B., Jr. "New Roles for Black Colleges." In Effective Use of Resources in State Higher Education, pp. 35–39. Atlanta, GA: Southern Regional Education Board, Ag, 1970.

Smith, Jessie Carney. Black Academic Libraries and Research Collections: An Historical Survey. Westport, CT: Greenwood, 1978.

Smith, Stanley H. "Administrators Should Heed Student Views." Southern Education Report, Je, 1969. [Views of students from ten Negro colleges]

Stanfiel, James D. "Education and Outcome of Parents of Students at Predominantly Black Colleges." Journal of Negro Education 41 (Spring, 1972):170-176.

Steinberg, David. "Black Power Roots on Black Campuses." Commonweal, Ap 19, 1967.

Stephens, Ernest. "The Black University in America Today: A Student Viewpoint." Freedomways, Spring, 1967.

Stevens, I. R. "Beliefs of Caucasian Students Enrolled in Selected Negro Higher Education Institutions Concerning Housing and Student Activities." Doctoral dissertation, Southern Illinois U., 1976.

Stevenson, Janet. "Ignorant Armies." Atlantic Monthly, S 19, 1969. [Higher education of the Negro in the South]

Stuart, Reginald. "All-Black Sports World Changing." Race Relations Reporter 2(Ap 19, 1971):8-10.

_____. "Black Colleges: Trying to Get It Together to Prevent Their Being Killed in Efforts to Save Their Lives." South Today 5(S, 1973):5-6.

_____. "Paradoxes of Black Public Colleges." South Today 3(My, 1972):10.

Taylor, Estelle W. "Survival or Surrender: Dilemma in Higher Education." Crisis 82(N, 1975):335-340.

Taylor, Joseph T. "An Analysis of Some Factors Involved in the Changing Function and Objectives of the Negro College." Doctoral dissertation, Indiana U., 1952. Univ. Microfilms Order No. 7427.

[Testimony on the Black colleges by officers and members of the National Association for Equal Opportunity in Higher Education] U.S. Congress, 91st, 2nd session, Senate, Committee on Labor and Public Welfare, Subcommittee on Education, Higher Education Amendments of 1970. Hearings..., Part 2. Washington, DC: GPO, 1971, pp. 1245-1382.

Thompson, Daniel C. Private Black Colleges at the Crossroads. Westport, CT: Greenwood Press, 1973.

Thompson, Theodis. "Black Colleges and Health Program Development." Crisis 84(N, 1977):443-445.

Tollett, Kenneth S. "Black Institutions of Higher Learning: Inadvertent Victims or Necessary Sacrifices." Black Law Journal 3(1973).

Tubbs, Levester. "Changes in Attitudes and Values Associated with a Racially Mixed Student Population in a Historically Black University." Doctoral dissertation, U. of Missouri-Columbia, 1975. Univ. Microfilms Order No. 76-07554.

U.S. Office of Education. Toward the Maintenance of Quality Graduate Education in Historically Black Colleges and Universities, O, 1976. ERIC ED 144 457.

Van Dyne, Larry. "The South's Black Colleges Lose a Football Monopoly." Chronicle of Higher Education, N 15, 1976.

Venson, Louis Augustus. "Trends in Black Colleges: Strategies for Improvement of Educational Opportunities in Selected Areas." Doctoral dissertation, U. of Pittsburgh, 1975. Univ. Microfilms Order No. 76-05484.

Vernón, Carlos H. "A Current History of Black Colleges." Black World 22(F, 1973):26-33.

Votaw, Dow, and Sethi, S. Prakash. "Some Paradoxes in the Support of Predominantly Black Colleges." Journal of Higher Education 41(D, 1970):673-694.

Walker, Walter L. "Defining the Role of Black Colleges." Integrateducation 13(Mr-Ap, 1975): 34-37.

Washington, Booker T. "Observations on Negro Colleges." World's Work, Ap, 1911.

_____. "University Education for Negroes." Independent, Mr 24, 1910.

Watson, J. B. "Football in Southern Negro Colleges." Voice of the Negro 4(My, 1907):165-169.

Weathersby, George B., and Trueheart, William E. Production Function Analysis in Higher Education: General Methodology and Applications to Four Year Black Colleges, Ja, 1977. ERIC ED 148 244.

Weaver, Robert C. "Black Women's Colleges." Crisis 84(N, 1977):435-437.

Wesley, Charles H. "Guiding Principles in the Teaching of Social Sciences in the Negro Colleges." Quarterly Review of Higher Education Among Negroes 3(O, 1935):180-188.

Wheaton, Louis Augustus. "The Black Subculture and the Traditional Black College: The Ideology of Future Black Educators." Doctoral dissertation, Columbia U., 1973. Univ. Microfilms Order No. 75-28931.

White, Jack. "Black Universities Seek Liberation." Race Relations Reporter 2(Je 7, 1971): 5-6.

Wilkerson, Doxey A. "The Curriculum of the Negro Arts College and the Demands of a Bi-Racial Society." Quarterly Review of Higher Education Among Negroes 2(Ap, 1934):109-116.

Wilkinson, Robert Shaw. "Negro Land-Grant Colleges." Messenger 9(My, 1927):145-146.

Williams, Dewitt Stanton. "Policy Boards of Private Predominantly Black Colleges and Universities." Doctoral dissertation, Indiana U., 1975. Univ. Microfilms Order No. 76-06360.

Williams, Juanita Lee. "Federal Legislation in Relation to Negro Land Grant Colleges." Master's thesis, Howard U., 1933.

Williams, Mary Carter. Profile of Enrollments in the Historically Black Colleges. Fall, 1977, 1977. ERIC ED 157 467.

Williams, Wilbur (ed.). Proceedings of the Conference on Research and Training Opportunities for Minority Colleges. Springfield, VA: National Technical Information Service, 1976.

Willie, Charles V., and MacLeish, Marlene Y. "Priorities of Black College Presidents." Educational Record 57(Spring, 1976):92-100.

Wilson, George Dewey. "Developments in Negro Colleges During the Twenty-Year Period 1914-15 to 1933-34." Doctoral dissertation, Ohio State U., 1935.

Wolters, Raymond. The New Negro on Campus. Black College Rebellions of the 1920's. Princeton, NJ: Princeton U. Press, 1974.

Woolfolk, E. O., and Smith, L. S. "Chemical Education in Negro Colleges." Negro History Bulletin, F, 1967.

Working Conference-Meeting of Deans of Black Graduate Schools. Toward the Maintenance of Quality Graduate Education in Historically Black Colleges and Universities. Washington, DC: U.S. Department of Health, Education, and Welfare, 1976.

Wright, Stephen J. "The Dilemma of the Negro College: Transition and the Brain Drain." Journal of Education 153(D, 1970):48-58.

Young, Herman A., and McAnulty, Brenda H. "Traditional Black Colleges: The Role, Social Benefits, and Costs." Western Journal of Black Studies 2(Fall, 1978):167-172.

Zinn, Howard. "A New Direction for Negro Colleges." Harper's, My, 1966.

American Indian Students

Bernstein, Alison. "Aiding Indian Postsecondary Education." Native American (published by Office of Native American Programs, HEW), Ja, 1976.

Bill, Willard E. "Position Paper [on Counseling Indian Students in a Large University]." American Indian Culture Center Journal 3 (Fall-Winter, 1971-72.

Brown, Eddie F. "Guidance and Counseling of the American Indian College Student." American Indian Culture Center Journal 3(Fall-Winter, 1971-72):28-29.

"Bureau of Indian Affairs. Higher Education Scholarship Grant Growth from 1965 to 1975. High School Graduates and Those Entering College for the Past Years." Education Dialogue, Mr, 1975.

Bureau of Indian Affairs, Division of Evaluation and Program Review. Higher Education Evaluation. Student Characteristics. Indian Education Resources Center. P.O. Box 1788, Albuquerque, NM 87103.

Castillo, Ed. "Financial Aid Resources for American Indian College Students." American Indian Culture Center Journal 3(Fall, 1972): 15-21.

Chavers, Dean. "Higher Education for Indians: The Numbers." Wassaja 2(Jl, 1974):14.

Clark, Richard O. "Higher Education Programs for American Indians at Selected Southwestern Colleges and Universities." Doctoral dissertation, U. of Southern California, 1972.

Cohen, Roxane W. "Pathways to College: Urban American Indian Community College Student." Doctoral dissertation, U. of California, Los Angeles, 1973.

Compton, John H. Social Work Education for American Indians, S, 1976. ERIC ED 138 421.

"Dartmouth College Steps Up Service to Native American Students." Navajo Times, N 13, 1975.

Dasbach, Joseph M. "AAAS Project on Native Americans in Science." Science 194(N, 1976): 597-598, 648.

Edington, Everett D. "A Communication System the American Indian in Higher Education." American Indian Culture Center Journal 3(Fall-Winter, 1971-72):22-25.

"Education." Indian Historian 3(Spring, 1970): 54-56. [News about college programs for Indian youth]

Flores Macías, Reynaldo, and Gomez Quiñones, Juan (eds.). National Directory of Chicano Faculty and Research. Los Angeles: Aztlan Publications, 1976.

Forbes, Jack D. "An American Indian University: A Proposal for Survival." Journal of American Indian Education, Ja, 1966.

"For Indians, by Indians." Newsweek, F 13, 1973. [Lakota Higher Education Center and Sinte Gleska College]

Guillerud, Ernest N. "Planning Professional Educational Programs for Ethnic Minority Students: Native American Examples." Journal of Education for Social Work 13 (Winter, 68-75.

Halfmoon, Ronald T. "Position Paper on Financial Aid [to Indian American College Students]," American Indian Culture Center Journal 3(Fall-Winter, 1971-72):26-27.

"Historical Background: Indian Higher Education. American Indian Journal of the Institute for the Development of Indian Law 2 (Je, 1976):2-4.

"Indian College Students' Perspective of Education." Journal of American Indian Education 15(Ja, 1976):18-22.

Jensen, Kenneth D., and Jensen, Shirley. "Factors in College Education for Indian Students." Improving College and University Teaching 18(Winter, 1970):52-54.

Kleinfeld, Judith S., and Kohout, K. L. "Increasing the College Success of Alaska Natives." Journal of American Indian Education 13(My, 1974):27-31.

Kohout, Karen, and Kleinfeld, Judith. Alaska Natives in Higher Education. Fairbanks, AK: Institute of Social, Economic, and Government Research, U. of Alaska, 1974.

Lake, Robert G. "A Sociological Study of Native American Indians in Higher Education." Master's thesis, California State U., Arcata, 1974.

Leitka, E. "A Study of the Effectiveness of Existing Native American Studies Programs in Selected Universities and Colleges." Doctoral dissertation, U. of New Mexico, 1973.

Locke, Patricia. A Survey of College and University Programs for American Indians. Boulder, CO: Western Interstate Commission for Higher Education, 1974.

Ludeman, W. W. "The Indian Student in College." Journal of Educational Sociology 33(Mr, 1960):333-335.

McDonald, Arthur. "Why Do Indian Students Drop Out of College?" In The Schooling of Native America, pp. 73-85. Edited by Thomas Thompson. Washington, DC: American Association of Colleges for Teachers' Education, Ag, 1978.

McGrath, G. D. et al. Higher Education of Southwestern Indians with Reference to Success and Failure. Arizona State U.; 1962.

Magan, Vernon D. "Indian College Students Plan for the Future." South Dakota Farm and Home Research 10(N, 1958):10-15.

Noon, John. The Navajo Way: From High School to College, 1975. DNA-People's Legal Services, P.O. Box 306, Window Rock, AZ 86515.

Oliver, Emmett. "Indians at College--1971." College of Education Record (U. of Washington) 37(My, 1971):81-82.

Parker, Alan "Unmelted Lumps in the Melting Pot." United Scholarship Service News, Jl, 1969. [Report on visits with Indian students on many college campuses in Far West, primarily]

_____. "A Word on Indian Studies Programs." United Scholarship Service News, Jl, 1969.

Peck, David. "The American Indian and Higher Education." Journal of Social and Behavioral Sciences 20(Winter, 1974):17-32.

Ruoff, A. La Vonne. "Freshman Composition and the Urban Native American." ADE Bulletin 37 (My, 1973):3-8.

Sandstrom, Roy H. (ed.). Clash of Cultures. The American Indian Student in Higher Education. Canton, NY: St. Lawrence U., 1973. [Write: Dr. Robert N. Wells, Program Director, St. Lawrence U., Canton, NY 13617.]

Scholarships for American Indian Youth, 1969. Albuquerque, NM: Bureau of Indian Affairs, 1969. ERIC ED 029 738.

Scholarships for American Indian Youth, 1970. Albuquerque, NM: Bureau of Indian Affairs, 1970. ERIC ED 041 649.

Selinger, Alphonse D. The American Indian Graduate: After High School What? Portland, OR: Northwest Regional Educational Lab, N, 1968. ERIC ED 026 165.

Shunatona, Owen. "Indian Goals for Higher Education." Integrateducation 12(S-O, 1974):30.

Smith, Marie H. "Higher Education for the Indians in the American Colonies." Master's thesis, New York U., 1950.

Supporter. "U. of M Native Americans Demand Their Treaty Rights." News and Letters, Je, 1975. [U. of Michigan]

Survey of Services to American Indians Through Institutions of Higher Learning in Seven Northwestern States. Rev. ed. Salt Lake City, UT: Bureau of Indian Services, U. of Utah, My, 1970.

Thornton, Russell. "American Indian Studies As an Academic Discipline." Journal of Ethnic Studies 5(Fall, 1977):1-15.

United Scholarship Service, Inc. "...The Necessity of Education Is Admitted..." Denver, CO: United Scholarship Service, Inc., 1973. [Higher education of American Indians]

U.S. Congress, 94th, 1st session, Senate, Committee on Interior and Insular Affairs, Subcommittee on Indian Affairs. Indian Postsecondary Educational Assistance Act. Hearing... Washington, DC: GPO, 1976.

U.S. Congress, 95th, 1st session, House of Representatives, Committee on Education and Labor, Subcommittee on Postsecondary Education. Indian Education. Hearing... Washington, DC: GPO, 1977.

U.S. Congress, 95th, 1st session, Senate, Select Committee on Indian Affairs. Grants to Indian-Controlled Postsecondary Educational Institutions and the Navajo Community College Act. Hearings... Washington, DC: GPO, 1977.

Whiteman, Henrietta V. "Native American Studies, the University, and the Indian Student." In The Schooling of Native America, pp. 105-116. Edited by Thomas Thompson. Washington, DC: American Association of Colleges for Teacher Education, Ag, 1978.

WICHE. A Survey of College and University Programs for American Indians. Boulder, CO: WICHE, Ag, 1974.

Wright, Carol. "Indian Graduate Programs Threatened." Navajo Times, Ap 17, 1975. [U. of Okalhoma and U. of California, Berkeley]

Wright, Rolland H. "The American Indian College Student: A Study in Marginality." Doctoral dissertation, Brandeis U., 1972.

Mexican-American Students

Alejandro, Franco. "The Chicano and Higher Education." Hojas. A Chicano Journal of Education 1(1976).

Alers-Montalvo, Manuel. Universities and the Chicano Student: An Assessment, Ap 29, 1976. ERIC ED 137 398.

"An Interview with Marciso Aleman." La Raza 11 (1973):30-31. [Colegio Jacinto Trevino]

Arce, Carlos H. "Chicanos in Higher Education." Integrateducation 14(My-Je, 1976):14-18.

Branklin, Mayer J., Martin, Terry, and Sanchez, Corinne. Proceedings of the Conference on Increasing Opportunities for Mexican American Students in Higher Education. Long Beach, CA: Long Beach State College, 1969.

Cabrera, Art uro Y. A Survey of Spanish-Surname Enrolled Students, San Jose State College, 1963-1964. San Jose, CA: San Jose State College, 1964, 10 pp. ERIC ED 020 031.

Calkins, Dick S., and Whitworth, Randolph. Differential Prediction of Freshmen Grade Point Average for Sex and Two Ethnic Classifications at a Southwestern University, 1974. ERIC ED 102 199.

Cardenas, Isaac. "Equality of Educational Opportunity: A Descriptive Study on Mexican American Access to Higher Education." Doctoral dissertation, U. of Massachusetts, 1974. Univ. Microfilms Order No. 74-25,828.

Casso, Henry. "Higher Education and the Mexican-American." In Mexican Americans Tomorrow. Edited by Gus Tyler. Albuquerque, NM: U. of New Mexico Press, 1975.

Casso, Henry J., and Román, Gilbert D. (eds.). Chicanos in Higher Education. Albuquerque: U. of New Mexico Press, 1976.

Chicano Coordinating Council on Higher Education. El Plan de Santa Barbara. A Chicano Plan for Higher Education, O, 1969. La Causa Publications, P.O. Box 4818, Santa Barbara, CA 93103.

Chicano Studies Center. Guide to Chicano Studies Departments, Programs and Centers. Los Angeles: U. of California, 1975.

College Entrance Examination Board. Access to College for Mexican Americans in the Southwest, 1972. Southwestern Regional Office, CEEB, Suite 119, 3818 Medical Parkway, Austin, TX 78756.

De Los Santos, Gilbert. "An Analysis of Strategies Used by Community Junior Colleges to Serve the Educational and Cultural Needs of Their Mexican American Students." Doctoral dissertation, U. of Texas, 1972.

Edington, Everett D., and Angel, Frank. Recruitment of Spanish-Speaking Students into Higher Education. Long Beach: California State College, My, 1969, 23 pp. ERIC ED 031 320.

Esquibel, Antonio. "The Status of Chicano Administrators in Higher Education." In Chicanos in Higher Education, pp. 95-105. Edited by Henry J. Casso and Gilbert D. Román. Albuquerque: U. of New Mexico Press, 1976.

Fry, William Albert. "Instructional Materials for a Community College Course in Chicano Literature." Doctoral dissertation, U. of Maryland, 1976. Univ. Microfilms Order No. 77-9509.

Garza, Roberto Jesus. "Chicano Studies: A New Curricular Dimension for Higher Education in the Southwest." Doctoral dissertation, Oklahoma State U., 1975. Univ. Microfilms Order No. 76-9673.

Gerry, Martin H. "Three Types of Discrimination in Minority Education." In Chicanos in Higher Education, pp. 20-28. Edited by Henry J. Casso and Gilbert D. Román. Albuquerque: U. of New Mexico Press, 1976.

Godoy, Charles Edward. "Variables Differentiating Mexican American College and High School Graduates." Doctoral dissertation, U. of Southern California, 1970.

Goldman, Roy D., and Hewitt, Barbara N. "An Investigation of Test Bias for Mexican American College Students." Journal of Educational Measurement 12(F, 1975):187-196.

Gomez, Angel I. Mexican Americans in Higher Education, 1973. ERIC ED 077 618.

Hernández, John Lawrence. "The Perception of Students and Parents Toward College Advisement with Implications for Mexican Americans." Doctoral dissertation, U. of Southern California, 1973.

Immenhausen, Richard L. "Academic Performance of Chicano EOG Recipients." Journal of Student Financial Aid 5(Mr, 1975):50-56.

Law School Preparatory Program for College Graduates of Spanish-American Descent. Progress Report to the Ford Foundation Denver, CO: Denver U., S 1, 1967, 86 pp. ERIC ED 021 682.

Lee, John B., and Malgoire, Mary A. The Distribution of Student Aid to Mexican American College Students 1972-73, Jl 24, 1975. ERIC ED 149 887.

Longoupe, Kay. "The Identity Crises of 'Harvard's' Chicanos." Boston Globe, My 2, 1971.

López, Richard E. "An Investigation of the Inter-Relationships Between Skin Color, Skin Color Preference, and Acculturation-Assimilation Among Chicano College Students." Doctoral dissertation, U. of California, Davis, 1972.

López, Ronald W., Madrid-Barela, Arturo, and Macías, Reynaldo Flores. Chicanos in Higher Education: Status and Issues. Los Angeles: Chicano Studies Center, U. of California, 1976.

Lowman, Robert P., and Spuck, Dennis W. "Predictors of College Success for the Disadvantaged Mexican-American." Journal of College Student Personnel 16(Ja, 1975):40-47.

McIntyre, Catherine and others. Higher Education for Hispanics: An Evaluation of the LULAC National Education Service Centers, N 10, 1977. ERIC ED 149 804. [League of United Latin American Citizens]

Martinez, Vilma S., and Roos, Peter D. "Statement Against Bakke Decision by The Mexican American Legal and Educational Fund and the National La Raza Lawyers' Association." La Raza 3(Spring, 1977):35-37.

Merrill, Celia. Contrastive Analysis and Chicano Compositions, 1976. ERIC ED 136 291.

Mirocha, Mary F. "Junior Colleges Enroll More Mexican Americans." LNESC Newsletter 3(Jl-Ag, 1977):6.

Myers, Derrel. "Chicano Students Victorious in Struggle at University of Minnesota." El Gallo, D, 1970.

Nieto Gomez, Anna, and Vasquez, J. Anthony. The Needs of the Chicano on the College Campus, My, 1969. ERIC ED 031 323.

"Opening Academic Doors." Agenda (quarterly), Fall, 1973, pp. 7-10. [Mexican Americans in higher education]

Ovando, Carlos Julio. Factors Influencing High School Latino Students' Aspirations to Go to College: The Urban Midwest. San Francisco: R and E Research Associates, 1977.

Pesqueira, Richard E. "Mexican-American Student (Staying) Power in College." College Board Review 90(Winter, 1973-1974):6-9; 26-28.

Reich, Alice Higman. "The Cultural Production of Ethnicity: Chicanos in the Universities." Doctoral dissertation, U. of Colorado, 1977. Univ. Microfilms Order No. 77-29,967.

Rivera, Julius. "The Implementation of Mexican American Studies in Texas College and Universities." Epoca: The National Concilio for Chicano Studies Journal, Winter, 1971.

Román, Gilbert D. "Chicano Alternatives in Higher Education." In Chicanos in Higher Education. Edited by Henry J. Casso and Gilbert D. Román. Albuquerque: U. of New Mexico Press, 1976, pp. 165-177.

Romero, Dan. The Impact and Use of Minority Faculty Within a University, Ag 30, 1977. ERIC ED 146 240.

Sanchez, Corinne J. "Chicano Studies: A Challenge for Colleges and Universities." Civil Rights Digest 3(Fall, 1970):36-39.

Sifuentes, Frank Moreno. "Mexican-Americans and Higher Education in the Golden State." Regeneracion, Ja, 1970. [California]

Sotomayor, Marta, and Ortega y Gasca, Philip D. (eds.). Chicano Content and Social Work Education. New York: Council on Social Work Education, 1975.

Southwestern Committee for Higher Education. Access to College for Mexican Americans in the Southwest. Report of Action Conferences, July 31-August 4, 1972. Princeton, NJ: College Entrance Examination Board, 1972.

Sutherland, Kenton. "Attracting Spanish-Speaking Students." Change 7(S, 1975):51-52. [Cañada College, CA]

Valverde, Leonard A. "Prohibitive Trends in Chicano Faculty Employment." In Chicanos in Higher Education. Edited by Henry J. Casso and Gilbert D. Román. Albuquerque: U. of New Mexico Press, 1976.

Vasquez, Melba J. T. "Chicana and Anglo University Women: Factors Related to Their Performance, Persistence and Attrition." Doctoral dissertation, U. of Texas, 1978. Univ. Microfilms Order No. 7900647.

Watkins, Beverly T. "Graduate Schools: Unfair to Chicanos?" Chronicle of Higher Education, D 16, 1974.

_____. "Mexican Americans Assail Barriers." Chronicle of Higher Education, O 20, 1975.

Weaver, Charles N. and others. What Black and Mexican-American Male College Students Want from Their Future Jobs, Mr 30, 1977. ERIC ED 143 477.

Zelaya, Guillermo. "After First Victory." Edcentric, O-N, 1972. [Chicanos in higher education]

Puerto Rican Students

Betances, Samuel. "Puerto Ricans and Mexican Americans in Higher Education." Rican 1(My, 1974):27-36.

Bonilla, Frank. "Cultural Pluralism and the University: The Case of Puerto Rican Studies." Revista del Instituto de Estudios Puertorriquenos de Brooklyn College 2(O, 1972):5-14.

Final Report on Needs Assessment of the Processes, Programs, and Services Used to Enroll Spanish-Speaking Students in Higher Education in New Jersey, 1974. Puerto Rican Congress of N.J., 222 West State Street, Trenton, NJ 08608.

Migration Division. Puerto Ricans and Other Hispanics in New York City's Public Schools and Universities. New York: Migration Division of the Commonwealth of Puerto Rico, 1975.

Morales-Carrion, Arturo. [Statement on university student aid programs at the University of Puerto Rico] U.S. Congress, 94th, 1st session, Senate, Committee on Labor and Public Welfare, Subcommittee on Education, Higher Education Legislation, 1975. Hearings... Washington, DC: GPO, 1975, pp. 190-204.

Pantoja, Antonia. "Universidad Boricua: A Model for the Implementation of an Alternative University for Puerto Ricans." Doctoral dissertation, Antioch U., 1972.

Rivera, Marie. "Culture Conflicts Among Puerto Rican College Students." New York State Personnel and Guidance Journal 8(1973):19-24.

Rustin, Stanley L., and Del Toro, Maria. "The Two Worlds of the Puerto Rican College Student." New York State Personnel and Guidance Journal 8(1973):25-29.

Asian-American Students

Asian American Law Students Association. "Report of the Boalt Hall Asian American Special Admissions Research Project." Amerasia Journal 5(1978):21-37.

DeGracia, Cesar, and Frial, Paula. "[Discrimination in Employment of Philipinos in] Colleges and Public Schools." In Joseph R. Sanchez (comp.), Asian Americans Reference Book. Patrick Air Force Base, FL: Defense Race Relations Institute, 1975.

Endo, Russell. Asian Americans and Higher Education, Mr, 1974. ErIC ED 089 610.

Nakanishi, Don T., and Leong, Russell. "Toward the Second Decade: A National Survey of Asian American Studies Programs in 1978." Amerasia Journal 5(1978):1-19.

O'Brien, Robert M. The College Nisei. Palo Alto, CA: Pacific Books, 1949.

Sue, Derald Wing, and Kirk. Barbara A. "Asian Americans: Use of Counseling and Psychiatric Services On a College Campus." Journal of Counseling Psychology 22(Ja, 1975):84-86.

_____. "Differential Characteristics of Japanese-American and Chinese-American College Students." Journal of Counseling Psychology 20(Mr, 1973):142-148.

Sue, Derald Wing, and Frank, Austin C. "A Typological Approach to the Psychological Study of Chinese and Japanese American College Males." Journal of Social Issues 29(1973):129-148.

Sun, S. "Cracks in the Flower Drum." San Francisco Magazine 8(1966):36-48. [Chinese in American Colleges]

Takemiya, Fred. "Minority Admissions to Law Schools" What Are the Issues?" Integrateducation 14(My-Je, 1976):24-27.

Tinlay, Marion Y. "Factors Affecting College Enrollment Decisions of Oriental Students." Master's thesis, California State U., Hayward, 1971.

Community Colleges

Andrews, Alice C. "Some Demographic and Geographic Aspects of Community Colleges." Journal of Geography 73(F, 1974):10-16.

Brooks, Lyman Beecher. "A Socio-Economic and Educational Study of Negro High School and Junior College Training." Doctoral dissertation, U. of Michigan, 1943.

Brice, Edward W. "A Study of Junior Colleges for Negroes in the United States." Doctoral dissertation, U. of Pennsylvania, 1950.

Birenbaum, William M. "The More We Change the Worse We Get." Social Policy 2(My-Je, 1971): 10-13.

Bailey, Helen Miller. "Students of Mexican Ancestry in Junior College." Journal of Secondary Education, 1951.

Barron, Jose. "Chicanos in the Community College." Junior College Journal 42(Je-Jl, 1972):23-26.

Black Student League of Community College of Philadelphia. "Open Letter to Frank Rizzo." African World 2(Mr 4, 1972):4.

Bushnell, David S. "Community College: Organizing for Change." In New Teaching New Learning. Edited by G. Kersy Smith and others. San Francisco, CA: Jossey-Bass, 1971.

Carnegie Council on Policy Studies in Higher Education. Low or No Tuition. The Feasibility of a National Policy for the First Two Years of College: An Analytical Report. San Francisco, CA: Jossey-Bass, 1975.

Cheeves, Lyndell. Mexican-American Studies: Guidelines for a Junior College Program, Ag, 1969. ERIC ED 036 286.

Cohen, Arthur M. "The Social Equalization Fantasy." Community College Review 5(F, 1977): 74-82.

_____. "Stretching Pre-College Education." Social Policy 2(My-Je, 1971):5-9.

Colston, James A. Minority Programs in Higher Education: Alternatives to the Revolving Door, Mr 19, 1976. ERIC ED 125 711.

Crawford, Allan. "A Short History of the Public Community Junior College Movement in the United States." Paedagogica Historica 10 (1970):28-48.

Davis, Jerry, and Johns, Kingston, Jr. "Changes in the Family Income Distribution of Freshmen." Community and Junior College Journal 43(D-Ja, 1973).

Deslonde, James L. III. "Beliefs in Internal-External Control of Reinforcements, Racial Ideology, and Militancy of Urban Community College Students." Doctoral dissertation, Case Western Reserve U., 1970. Univ. Microfilms Order No. 71-18984.

Emond, Louis. The Status Remediation in American Junior Colleges, 1976. ERIC ED 122 264.

Farris, Theodore N. "The Community College--For Whom, For What?" Urban Review, S, 1969.

Felton, Gary S. "Black Voices in the Classroom: Who Is Listening?" Education 96(S, 1976): 282-290.

Ferrin, Richard J. Developmental Programs in Midwestern Community Colleges, F, 1971. Midwestern Regional Office, College Entrance Examination Board, 990 Grove Street, Evanston, IL 60201.

Garza, Manuel Ramon. "The Community College and the Chicano Student." Community College Frontiers 2(Fall, 1973):23-24.

Gibson, Walker (ed.). New Students in Two-Year Colleges. Urbana, IL: National Council of Teachers of English, 1979.

Goodrich, Andrew. "Education for the New Student at Community Colleges: A Legacy and a Hope." Peabody Journal of Education 48(Jl, 1971):286-293.

_____. "Minority Group Programs in Community Junior Colleges." Social Education 36(F 1,

_____. "A Survey of Selected Community Services Programs for the Disadvantaged at Inner-City Community Colleges." Doctoral dissertation, Michigan State U., 1969. Univ. Microfilms Order. No. 70-20,462.

Goodrich, Andrew L., Lazotte, Lawrence W., and Welch, James A. "Minorities in Two-Year Colleges: A Survey." Community and Junior College Journal 43(D-Ja, 1973).

Hall, Eleanor R. "Motivation and Achievement in Black and White Junior College Students." Journal of Social Psychology 97(O, 1975):107-113.

Hankin, Joseph N. "Selected Urban Problems and the Public Community College." Doctoral dissertation, Teachers College, Columbia U., 1967. Univ. Microfilms Order No. 68-8980.

Henderson, Romeo C. "The Academic Adaptability of Negro Junior College Graduates to Senior College." Doctoral dissertation, Pennsylvania State U., 1951.

Hunt, Thomas C. and others. "Community Colleges: A Democratizing Influence?' Community College Review 4(Spring, 1977):15-24.

Institute for Higher Educational Opportunity. The Black Community and the Community College. Action Programs for Expanding Opportunity. A Project Report. Atlanta, GA: Southern Regional Education Board, O, 1970.

_____. New Challenges to the Junior Colleges. Their Role in Expanding Opportunity for Negroes. A Progress Report. Atlanta, GA: Southern Regional Education Board, Ap, 1970.

Jacobs, Provergs, Jr. "Persistence Factors in the Academic Success of Low Socio-Economic Status Black Community College Students." Doctoral dissertation, U. of California, Berkeley, 1974.

Jones, William H. "Minority Groups Press Demands for Changes in Junior Colleges." Chronicle of Higher Education, Mr 16, 1970.

Katz, Jerry M., Gold, Donna F., and Jones, Elliott T. "Equality of Opportunity in a Democratic Institution: The Public Junior College." Education and Urban Society 5(My, 1973):261-276.

Kickingbird, Lynn. "A Case for Indian Controlled Community Colleges." American Indian Journal of the Institute for the Development of Indian Law 2(Je, 1976):5-11.

Kimmons, Willie James. Black Administrators in Public Community Colleges. New York: Carlton Press, 1977.

Knoell, Dorothy M. "Are Our Colleges Really Accessible to the Poor?" Junior College Journal 39(1968):9-11.

_____. Black Student Potential. Washington, DC: American Association of Junior Colleges, 1970. [A summary of People Who Need College: A Report on Students We Have Yet to Serve]

_____. People Who Need College: A Report on Students We Have Yet to Serve. Washington, DC: American Association of Junior Colleges, 1970. [Dallas, Fort Worth, Philadelphia, St. Louis, and San Francisco]

Lamer, Aaron L., Jr. "A Black Educator's Perspectives: How the Black Student Perceives the Community College." Community College Review 1(Winter, 1974):41-46.

Lane, David A., Jr. "The Junior College Movement Among Negroes." Journal of Negro Education 2(Jl, 1933):272-283.

Lombardi, John (comp.). Black Student Activists--Position Papers and Reactions to Them from Twelve Colleges, S, 1970. ERIC ED 041 578.

_____. "Faculty Reaction to Black Student Demands: 1968-1969." Junior College Research Review 4(1970):12-15.

_____. "The Myth of the No-Tuition College: An ERIC Review." Community College Review 4 (Summer, 1976):59-64.

_____. No- or Low-Tuition: A Lost Cause, O, 1976. ERIC ED 129 353.

_____. The Position Papers of Black [College] Student Activists, S, 1970. ERIC Clearinghouse for Junior Colleges, Graduate School of Education and the University Library, U. of California, Los Angeles, CA 90024.

_____. The President's Reaction to Black Student Activism. Los Angeles, CA: U. of California, ERIC Clearinghouse for Junior College Information, Ja, 1971. Available from UCLA Students' Store, Mail Out, 308 Westwood Plaza, Los Angeles, CA 90024. ERIC ED 046 390.

_____. Student Activism in Junior Colleges: An Administrator's View. Washington, DC: American Association of Junior Colleges, 1969.

_____. "Unique Problems of the Inner City Colleges." Integrated Education, My-Je, 1969, pp. 62-70.

London, Howard B. "Pursuing Integrity: The Culture of a Working Class Community College." Doctoral dissertation, Boston College, 1976. Univ. Microfilms Order No. 76-18,920.

The Many Doors of the Community College. A Project Summary. Atlanta, GA: Institute for Higher Educational Opportunity, Southern Regional Education Board, Ap, 1974.

Marsh, Georgia. "Junior Colleges and Negroes." Southern Education Report 4(1968):11-17.

Martin, William H. "The Status of the Negro Junior College." Quarterly Review of Higher Education Among Negroes 8(Ja, 1940):1-7.

Mechling, Jerry Eugene. "The Case for a System of Inner City Community Colleges: Equalizing Opportunities for Higher Education." Public and International Affairs Review, Spring, 1968. [Published by the Woodrow Wilson School]

Medsker, Leland,L., and Tillery, Dale. "The Junior College and Urban Life." Breaking the Access Barriers. A Profile of Two-Year Colleges. NY: McGraw-Hill, 1971.

Menefee, Selden (ed). The Low-Income Student in the Community College: Problems and Programs. Washington, D. C.: American Association of Junior Colleges, Program with Developing Institutions, Mr, 1972. ERIC ED 062 972.

Moore, William, Jr. Against the Odds. The High Risk Student in the Community College. San Francisco, CA: Jossey-Bass, 1970.

_____. "Black Knight/White Fortress." Community and Junior College Journal 46 (Ap, 1976):18-20, 40-43.

_____. Blind Man On a Freeway. The Community College Administrator. San Francisco, CA: Jossey-Bass, Inc., 1971.

_____. "The Community College Board of Trustees: A Question of Competency." Journal of Higher Education 44(Mr, 1973):171-190.

Morrison, James L. "The Community College and the Disadvantaged." Research in Higher Education 1(1973):401-413.

Morris, Clarence W., Jr. The Historically Black Two-Year College: A Forgotten Part of American Higher Education, Ja, 1975. ERIC ED 101 801.

Pincus, Fred. "Tracking in Community Colleges." Insurgent Sociologist 4(S, 1974):17-35.

_____. Tracking in the Community Colleges. Research Group One, 2743 Maryland Avenue, Baltimore, MD 21218.

Rawls, Wendell, Jr. "Are 2-Year Colleges Useless for Blacks?" Philadelphia Inquirer, F 5, 1974.

Research and Development Division, American College Testing Program. The Two-Year College and Its Students: An Empirical Report, 1970. ACT Publications, P. O. Box 168, Iowa City, IO 52240.

Santos, Alfredo de Los, Jr. "Congreso Nacional de Asuntos Colegiales and the Chicanos in the Community/Junior Colleges." ERIC/CRESS News Letter 7(Summer, 1972):1-3.

Schafer, Susan, and Wattenbarger, James I. "Tuition and the Open Door." New Directions for Community Colleges 1(Summer, 1973):57-64.

Shea, Brent Mack. "Two-Year Colleges and In-equality." Integrateducation 13(Ja-F, 1975): 38-43.

Sherman, Charles E. "An Investigation of the Interpersonal Values of Negro and White Junior College Students." Journal of Negro Education 40(Fall, 1971):356-360.

Shor, Ira. "Community Colleges: Slightly Higher Education." Liberation 18(My-Je, 1974):32-38.

Smith, Norvel. "AAJC's Black Caucus Goes Into Action." Junior College Journal 42(Mr, 1972): 16-17. [American Association of Junior Colleges]

_____. "The Minority Transfer Problem." College Board Review 87(Spring, 1973):21-22, 28.

Smolich, Robert S. "An Analysis of Influences Affecting the Origin and Early Development of Three Mid-Western Public Junior Colleges--Joliet, Goshen, and Crane." Doctoral dissertation, U. of Texas, 1967. Univ. Microfilms Order No. 68-4241.

Tinto, Vincent. "The Distributive Effects of Public Junior College Availability." Research in Higher Education 3(1975):261-274.

_____. Public Junior Colleges and the Substitution Effect in Higher Education, Ap 16, 1974. ERIC ED 089 808. [Negative effect on attendance of minority students in four-year colleges]

U.S. Bureau of the Census. Undergraduate Enrollment in 2-Year and 4-Year Colleges: October, 1972. Washington, DC: GPO, N, 1973.

Wallace, Rue, Friedman, Warren, and Friedman, Linda. "The Movement at Work: The Community College Scene." Liberation, O, 1969.

Zwerling, L. Steven. "The Community College: Cooling-Out or Heating Up?" Community College Frontiers 3(Spring, 1974):4-8.

_____. "Second-Class Education at the Community College." New Directions for Community Colleges 7(1974):23-37.

Zwerling, L. Steven, and Park, D. "Curriculum Comprehensiveness and Tracking." Community College Review (Spring, 1974):10-20.

General

A Chance to Go To College. A Director of 800 Colleges that Have Special Help for Students from Minorities and Low-income Families. New York: College Entrance Examination Board, 1971.

Abramson, Stephen A., and Nielsen, Robert C. "Human Relations Training for Campus Police." College Management 8(N-D, 1973):21-22.

Ackley, Sheldon. "To Overcome Discrimination Now." Current 129(My, 1971):35-38.

Adams, Walter. "Financial and Non-financial Factors Affecting Post-High School Plans and Eventuations, 1939-1965." Proceedings of the American Statistical Association, 1969.

_____. "Student Grade and Academic Self-Image--Relationships to College Entrance and Retention." New York Statistician 21(N-D, 1969): 3-6.

"Affirmative Duty to Desegregate State Systems of Higher Education Without Eliminating Racially Identifiable Schools." North Carolina Central Law Journal 5(Spring, 1974): 365-370.

"Affirmative Duty to Integrate in Higher Education." Yale Law Journal 79(1970).

Agnew, Spiro. "Toward a 'Middle Way' in College Admissions." Educational Record 51(Spring, 1970):106-111.

Albee, George W. "A Conference on Recruitment of Black and Other Minority Students and Faculty." American Psychologist 24(1969): 720-723.

Albright, Robert L. "College and the Minority Student." Journal of the National Association of College Admissions Counselors 19(Jl, 1974):13-16.

Alexander, Karl L., and Eckland, Bruce K. High School Context, College Quality, and Educational Attainment: Institutional Constraints in Educational Stratification. Baltimore: Center for Social Organization of Schools, Johns Hopkins U., Jl, 1976.

Alexander, Kern, and Solomon, Erwin. "Racial Segregation in Higher Education." College and University Law. Charlottesville, VA: The Michie Company, 1972.

Allen, George Jackson, Jr. "A History of the Commission on Colleges of the Southern Association of Colleges and Schools, 1949-1975." Doctoral dissertation, Georgia State U., 1978. Univ. Microfilms Order No. 7901820.

Alker, Henry A., and Closson, Michael B. "Admission Standards, the Perceived Legitimacy of Grading and Black Student Protest." Cornell Journal of Social Relations 8(Fall, 1978):219-234.

Allen, Arthur Dequest. "A Study of Existing Graduate Public Affairs and Administration Programs in American Universities and their Status in the Training of Black and Minority-Group Students." Doctoral dissertation, U. of Pittsburgh, 1972. Univ. Microfilms Order No. 75-21743.

Allen, Bernadene V. "The Success of the EOP: A Refutation of the Immutability of Scholastic Achievement." Journal of Negro Education 45(Winter, 1976).

Allen, Donald E., and Kinnard, Richmond E. "Academic Aspirations and Financial Preparations for College." Journal of Negro Education 40(Spring, 1971):126-132.

Allmendinger, David F., Jr. "Indigent Students and their Institutions, 1800-1860." Doctoral dissertation, U. of Wisconsin, 1968. Univ. Microfilms Order No. 68-15960.

Alston, Lester. "Minority Students and the College Mental Health Clinic." Journal of the American College Health Association 23 (0, 1974):22-29. [Black psychotherapist]

Althauser, Robert P., Spivack, Sydney S., with Amsel, Beverly M. The Unequal Elites. New York: Wiley, 1975. [Black and white graduates of three eastern U.S. universities]

Altman, Robert A., and Snyder, Patricia O. (eds.). The Minority Student on the Campus: Expectations and Possibilities, N, 1970. Western Interstate Commission for Higher Education, P.O. Drawer "P," Boulder, CO 80302.

"Ameliorative Racial Classification Under the Equal Protection clause: De Funis v. Odegaard." Duke Law Journal, 1973.

American Association of College Registrars and Admissions Officers. "Nontraditional Programs, Including Programs for Special Categories of Students (Including Equal Opportunity Programs)." College and University 52(Summer, 1977):659-679.

American Association of University Professors. "Affirmative Action in Higher Education." AAUP Bulletin 59(Je, 1973):178-183.

American Council on Education. Higher Education for Everybody? Issues and Implications. Washington, DC: American Council on Education, Ag, 1973.

_____. Teaching Faculty in Academe: 1972-73. Washington, DC: American Council on Education, Ag, 1973.

_____ Women and Minorities in Health Fields: A Trend Analysis of College Freshmen. Vol. III: A Comparison of Minority Aspirants to Health Careers. Washington, DC: GPO, 1977.

Anderson, Ernest F., and Hrabowski, Freeman A. "Graduate School Success of Black Students from White Colleges and Black Colleges." Journal of Higher Education 48(My-Je, 1977): 294-303.

Andrulis, Dennis P., Iscoe, Ira, Sikes, Melvin P., and Friedman, Thomas. "Black Professionals in Predominantly White Institutions of Higher Education—An Examination of Some Demographic and Mobility Characteristics." Journal of Negro Education 44(Winter, 1975):6-11.

"The Angry Black Athlete." Newsweek, Jl 15, 1968.

Anzalone, J. S. (ed.). Pre-College Counseling and the Black Student: A Report on the Invitational Workshop for In-Service School Counselors, Jackson State College, 1970, 1970. ERIC ED 045 787.

Appleton, James R. "Survey of Minority Group Persons Employed in Student Affairs Positions at NASPA Member Institutions." NASPA Journal 9(0, 1971):96-105.

Aptheker, Bettina. The Academic Rebellion in the United States. New York: Citadel, 1973.

_____. "Aspects of the Crisis in Higher Education." Political Affairs 46(0, 1967): 9-18.

Arbeiter, Solomon. "The Challenge Is Still There. Public-College Desegregation." Compact 8(S-O, 1974):5-7.

Arce, Carlos Humberto. "Historical, Institutional, and Contextual Determinants of Black Enrollment in Predominantly White Colleges and Universities, 1946 to 1974." Doctoral dissertation, U. of Michigan, 1976. Univ. Microfilms Order No. 76-27,437.

Armor, David. "The Racial Composition of Schools and College Aspirations of Negro Students." Racial Isolation in the Public Schools. (Appendix C2), Vol. II. Washington, DC: GPO, 1967.

Asgill, Amanda. "The Importance of Accreditation: Perceptions of Black and White College Presidents." Journal of Negro Education 45 (Summer, 1976):284-294.

Association of American Colleges. Minority Women and Higher Education, N, 1974. ERIC ED 098 852.

_____. Recruiting Minority Women, N, 1974. ERIC ED 098 851.

_____. Spanish Speaking Women and Higher Education: A Review of their Current Status, Mr, 1975. ERIC ED 149 945.

Astin, Alexander W. "College Admissions: A Systems Perspective." In New Teaching New Learning. Edited by G. Kerry Smith and others. San Francisco, CA: Jossey-Bass, 1971.

_____. College Dropouts: A National Profile. Washington, DC: American Council on Education, F, 1972.

_____. "Equal Access to Postsecondary Education: Myth or Reality?" UCLA Educator 19 (Spring, 1977):8-17.

_____. Four Critical Years. Effects of College on Beliefs, Attitudes, and Knowledge. San Francisco: Jossey-Bass, 1977.

_____. "Minority Enrollments in Higher Education." Integrateducation 13(My-Je, 1975): 173-174.

_____. "The Myth of Equal Access." Educational Research and Methods 9(1976).

_____. "Open Admissions and Programs for the Disadvantaged." Journal of Higher Education 42(N, 1971):629-647.

_____. Preventing Students from Dropping Out. San Francisco, CA: Jossey-Bass, 1975.

_____. "Racial Considerations in Admissions." The Campus and the Racial Crisis. Washington, DC: American Council on Education, 1969.

Astin, Alexander W., and Rossmann, Jack E. "The Case for Open Admissions. A Status Report." Change 5(Summer, 1973):35-37.

Astin, Alexander W., King, Margo R., Light, John M., and Richardson, Gerald T. The American Freshman: National Norms for Fall 1973, 1974. Cooperative Institutional Research Program, Graduate School of Education, U. of California, Los Angeles, 405 Hilgard Ave., Los Angeles, CA 90024.

Astin, Alexander W., Astin, Helen S., Bayer, Alan E., and Bisconti, Ann S. The Power of Protest. San Francisco, CA: Jossey-Bass, 1975. [Campus protest during the 1960's]

Astin, Helen S. Educational Progress of Disadvantaged Students, Ag, 1970. Human Service Press, a division of U. Research Corporation, 4301 Connecticut Ave., N.W., Washington, DC: 20008.

Astin, Helen S., and Bisconti, Ann S. Trends in Academic and Career Plans of College Freshmen, 1972. College Placement Council, P. O. Box 2263, Bethlehem, PA 18018.

Atelsek, Frank J., and Gomberg, Irene L. Bachelor's Degrees Awarded to Minority Students 1973-1974. Washington, DC: American Council on Education, 1977.

Atkins, Glen C. (ed.). The Impact of the Black Experience on Higher Education in New England. Storrs, CT: 1971.

Aulston, Melvin D. "Black Transfer Students in White Colleges." NASPA 12(F, 1974):116-123.

Avery, Anita. "Admission, Yes--Retention, No." Journal of the National Association of College Admissions Counselors 19(Mr, 1975): 17-18.

Babbitt, Charles Edwin. "The Dilemma in American Higher Education: Alienation and Control of Black Students." Doctoral dissertation, State U. of New York-Buffalo, 1971. Univ. Microfilms Order No. 72-10474.

Baber, Buford B., Jr., and Caple, Richard B. "Educational Opportunity Grant Students: Persisters and Nonpersisters." Journal of College Student Personnel 11(Mr, 1970):115-118.

Backner, Burton L., and Beckenstein, Lewis. "A Survey of Disadvantaged Students' Attitudes Towards a Special College Program." Journal of Human Resources 5(1970):117-127.

Baggaley, Andrew R. "Academic Prediction at an Ivy League College, Moderated by Demographic Variables." Measurement and Evaluation in Guidance 6(Ja, 1974):232-235.

Bailey, Harold. "Institutional and Societal Effects on the Black Student Athlete." Doctoral dissertation, U. of New Mexico, 1975. Univ. Microfilms Order No. 76-25652.

Bailey, Robert L., with Hafner, Anne L. Minority Admissions. Lexington, MA: Lexington Books, 1978.

Baird, Leonard L. A Portrait of Blacks in Graduate Studies. Princeton, NJ: Educational Testing Service, 1974.

_____. "Social Class and Entrance to Graduate and Professional School." Integrateducation 15(Jl-Ag, 1977).

Baker, Therese L. "The Weakening of Authoritarianism in Black and White College Students." Sociology and Social Research 60(Jl, 1976): 440-460.

Baldwin, Evanell K. Differential Attitudes and Practices Relative to Minority Groups as Evidenced by College and Community Experiences, Je, 1970. ERIC ED 043 329.

Ballard, Allen B. "Academia's Record of Benign Neglect." Change 5(Mr, 1973):27-33.

_____. The Education of Black Folk. The Afro-American Struggle for Knowledge in White America. New York: Harper & Row, 1973.

Barbarin, Oscar. Survival Skills: Social Climate and the Development of Adaptive Behavior in Black and White College Students, 1976. ERIC ED 151 463.

Barriers to Higher Education. New York: College Entrance Examination Board, 1971.

Barros, Francis J. "Equal Opportunity in Higher Education." Journal of Negro Education, Summer, 1968.

Barzun, Jacques and others. Open Admissions: The Pros and Cons, 1972. Council for Basic Education, 725 Fifteenth Street, N.W., Washington, DC. 20005.

Bayer, Alan E. The Black College Freshman: Characteristics and Recent Trends. Washington, DC: American Council on Education, 1972.

Bayer, Alan E., and Boruch, Robert F. "Black and White Freshmen Entering Four Year Colleges." Educational Record 50(1969): 371-386.

_____. The Black Student in American Colleges. Washington, DC: American Council on Education, 1969.

Bayer, Alan E., and Astin, Alexander W. Campus Disruption During 1968-1969. Washington, DC: American Council on Education, 1969.

Bayer, Alan E., Astin, Alexander W., and Boruch, Robert F. Social Issues and Protest Activity: Recent Student Trends. Washington, DC: American Council on Education, F, 1970.

Beaumont, Andre G., and Godboldt, Rena D. (eds.). Handbook for Recruiting at Minority Colleges. Bethlehem, PA: College Placement Services, Inc., 1978.

Beck, Armin. "Professional Involvement in Cities." In Rethinking Urban Education. Edited by Herbert J. Walberg and Andrew T. Kopan. San Francisco, CA: Jossey-Bass, 1972.

Beckham, Edgar F. "What Do We Mean by 'the Black University'?" College Board Review, Spring, 1969.

Beichman, Arnold. "Will Teacher Be the New Drop-Out?" New York Times Magazine, D 7, 1969. [Colleges and universities]

Belcher, Leon H., and Campbell, Joel T. "An Exploratory Study of Word Associations of Negro College Students." Psychological Reports, Ag, 1968.

Bell, Derrick A., Jr. "In Defense of Minority Admissions Programs: A Response to Professor Graglia." Black Law Journal 3(1974).

Belles, A. Gilbert. "Negroes Are Few on College Faculties." Southern Education Report, Jl-Ag, 1968.

Bennett, Don C. "Interracial Ratios and Proximity in Dormitories: Attitudes of University Students." Environment and Behavior 6(Je, 1974):212-232.

Berls, Robert H. "Higher Education Opportunity and Achievement in the United States." In U.S. Congress, 91st, 1st session, Joint Economic Committee. The Economics and Financing of Higher Education in the United States. Washington, DC: GPO, n.d.

Bertsch, Eilene. "The Small College Opens Its Doors.": Who Runs the High Risk College Programs, S 4, 1970. ERIC ED 044 482.

Beverley, John. "Higher Education and Capitalist Crisis." Socialist Review 8(N-D, 1978):67-91.

Beyond Desegregation: Urgent Issues in the Education of Minorities. Princeton, NJ: College Board, 1978.

Billingsley, Andrew. "The Black Presence in American Higher Education." In What Black Educators Are Saying. Edited by Nathan Wright, Jr. New York: Hawthorn, 1970: 126-149.

Bishop, John. "The Effect of Public Policies on the Demand for Higher Education." Journal of Human Resources 12(Summer, 1977):285-307.

_____. Income, Ability, and the Demand for Higher Education. Madison: Institute for Research on Poverty, U. of Wisconsin, 1975.

"Black Coaches Earn Their Recognition." Chicago Defender, N 9, 1974. [Black workers in colleges and universities]

"Black College Athletic Officials Hit NCAA Drive to Silence Young Athletes." Muhammad Speaks, Ja 31, 1969.

"Black Mood on Campus." Newsweek, F 10, 1969.

Blackburn, Robert T., and Peterson, Marvin W. Administrator and Faculty Responses to Increased Black Enrollment in White Universities, 1976. ERIC ED 123 988.

Blackwell, James E. Access of Black Students to Graduate and Professional Schools. Boston: U. of Massachusetts, Jl, 1975.

_____. In Support of Preferential Admissions and Affirmative Action in Higher Education: Pre- and Post-Bakke Considerations, My, 1977. ERIC ED 139 351.

_____. The Participation of Blacks in Graduate and Professional Schools: An Assessment. Atlanta, GA: Southern Education Foundation, 1977.

Bleich, Maxine. Funding of Minority Programs from the Private Sector; 1966-1976, A Ten-Year Perspective. F, 1976. ERIC ED 133 189 [Medicine and related health professions]

Blumenfeld, Warren S. "College Preferences of Able Negro Students: A Comparison of Those Naming Predominantly Negro Institutions and Those Naming Predominantly White Institutions." College and University, Spring, 1968.

Bode, Elroy. "The Rhetoric of Revenge." Nation, Ap 29, 1968. [Regional Black Student Conference, Ap, 1968, in El Paso, TX]

Boerner, Robert J. "Family Income of Medical School Applicants and Acceptees and of College Students." Journal of Medical Education 52(N, 1977):948-949.

Bohnke, David R. "Attitude Differential Between Negro and Caucasian Intercollegiate Athletes." Dissertation Abstracts International 32(5-A) N, 1971:2797.

Bolden, Wiley S. "The Role of the College Board in the South: Improving Access to College for Black Students." College Board Review 84(Summer, 1972):18-22.

Bond, Horace Mann. "Historical and Socio-Economic Factors in College Persistence Rates." Proceedings, American Educational Research Association, F, 1962. Atlantic City, NJ.

Bond, Julian. "The Black Mind on the American Campus." Black Politician 2(Summer, 1970): 2-5.

Bonham, George W. "Charade of Equality." Change 3(My-Je, 1971):13-15.

Borgen, Fred H. Able Black Americans in College: Entry and Freshman Experience, 1970. ERIC ED 043 285.

_____. "Differential Expectations? Predicting Grades for Black Students in Five Types of Colleges." Measurement and Evaluation in Guidance 4(Ja, 1972):206-212.

Borup, Jerry H. "The Validity of American College Test for Discerning Potential Academic Achievement Levels--Etnnic and Sex Groups." Journal of Educational Research 65 (S, 1971):3-6.

Bowers, John. The Evaluation of a Special Educational Opportunities Program for Disadvantaged College Students. Final Report, Je, 1971. ERIC ED 060 814.

Bowles, Frank. "Access to Higher Education." The Encyclopedia of Education 4 (1971):380-385.

_____. Access to Higher Education, I. New York: UNESCO, 1963.

Bowles, Samuel. "Contradiction in U.S. Higher Education." In Political Economy: Radical vs. Orthodox Approaches. Edited by James Weaver. Boston, MA: Allyn and Bacon, 1972.

_____. "The Integration of Higher Education Into the Wage Labor System." Review of Radical Political Economics 6(Spring, 1974): 100-133.

Bowman, James L. Some Thoughts and Reflections Regarding Parental Ability to Pay for Higher Education, D, 1970. College Scholarship Service, Educational Testing Service, Princeton, NJ 08540.

Boyd, W. M. II. Access and Power for Blacks in Higher Education. New York: Educational Policy Center, 1972.

_____. "Are White Colleges Cooling Blacks Recruitment?" Change 5(Winter, 1973-1974): 56-56,78.

_____. "Black Student, White College." College Board Review 90(Winter, 1973-1974): 18-25.

_____. "Black Undergraduates Succeed in White Colleges." Educational Record 58 (Summer, 1977):309-315. [A Better Chance, Inc.]

_____. Desegregating America's Colleges. A Nationwide Survey of Black Students 1972-73. New York: Praeger, 1974.

Boykin, Leander L. "A Summary of Reading Investigations Among Negro College Students, 1940-1954." Quarterly Review of Higher Education Among Negroes 25(Ap, 1957):94-101.

Braddock, Jomills H. II. Institutional Racism in Higher Education: The Issue of Faculty Tenure." Western Journal of Black Studies 2(Winter, 1978):236-243.

_____. "Radicalism and Alienation Among Black College Students." Negro Educational Review 29(Ja, 1978):4-21.

_____. "Television and College Football: In Black and White." Journal of Black Studies 8(Mr, 1978):369-380.

Brand, Norman. "Minority Writing Problems and Law School Writing Programs." Journal of Legal Education 26(1974):331-337.

Brann, James W. "Negro [College] Students Are Organizing National Groups." The Chronicle of Higher Education, My 6, 1968.

_____. "Students from 84 Campuses Map War on College 'Racism.'" The Chronicle of Higher Education, D 9, 1968.

Branson, Herman R. "Financing Higher Education for Poor People: Fact and Fiction." College Board Review, Fall, 1970.

_____. "Interinstitutional Programs for Pro-
moting Equal Higher Educational Opportunities for Negroes." Journal of Negro
Education, Fall, 1966.

Braskamp, Larry A., and Brown, Robert D.
"Evaluation of [Higher Education] Programs
for Blacks." Educational Record 53
(Winter, 1972):51-58.

Bray, Thomas J. "A Crunch Is Coming in
Higher Education." Wall Street Journal,
Je 25, 1969.

Brazziel, William F. "Black-White Comparability in College Enrollment." Journal of
Human Resources 5(1970):106-116.

_____. Blacks, Whites and College Training:
Manpower Pools and Training Rates, Ap 23,
1976. ERIC ED 127 842.

_____. "Getting Black Kids Into College."
Personnel and Guidance Journal 48(My,
1970):747-751.

_____. "New Urban Colleges for the Seventies."
Journal of Higher Education 41(Mr, 1970):
169-178.

Breivik, Patricia S. Open Admissions and the
Academic Library. Chicago: American
Library Association, 1977.

Bressler, Marvin. "White Colleges and Negro
Higher Education." Journal of Negro
Education, Summer, 1967.

Britts, Maurice W. Blacks on White College
Campuses, D, 1976. Challenge Productions,
Inc., P. O. Box 9624, Minneapolis, MN 55440.

_____. "Blacks on White College Campuses:
1823-Present." Negro History Bulletin 37
(Je-J1, 1974):269-272.

Brodbelt, S. S. "The Democratic Myth--Equality
of Educational Opportunity." College
Student Journal 6(N-D, 1972):93-97.

Brody, Lawrence, and Schenker, Hank. Discover-
ing and Developing the College Potential of
Disadvantaged High School Youth. A Report
of the Fifth Year of a Longitudinal Study
on the College Discovery and Development
Program. New York: City University of
New York, Office of Teacher Education.
Ja, 1972. ERIC ED 061 408.

Bronzhaft, Arline L., and Epstein, Gilda F.
"Test Anxiety, Academic Achievement, and
the Open Admissions Student." Journal of
Social Psychology 92(1974):321-322.

Brough, C. H. "Work of the Commission of
Southern Universities on the Race Question." Annals 49(1913):47-57.

Brown, Anthony Lawer. "Role Conflict of Black
Administrators at Big Ten Universities."
Doctoral dissertation, U. of Wisconsin,
1978. Univ. Microfilms Order No. 7814254.

Brown, Delindus R. Self-Disclosure and
Identification: Dyadic Communications of
the New Assistant Black Professor on a
White Campus, 1974. ERIC ED 102 630.

Brown, Frank, and Stent, Madelon. "Black
College Undergraduates, Enrollment, and
Earned Degrees: Parity or Under Representation?" Journal of Black Studies 6(S,
1975):5-22.

_____. "Black Graduate and Professional
School Enrollment: A Struggle for Equality."
Journal of Black Studies 6(S, 1975):23-24.

_____. Minority Representation in Higher
Education in the United States. New York:
Praeger, 1977.

Browne, Lee F. Developing Skills for Coping.
(For Minority Students at Predominantly
White Institutions; But Maybe for All
Students.) Pasadena, CA: Office of
Secondary School Relations and Spacial
Student Programs, California Institute
of Technology, 1977.

Brown, Nina W. An Investigation of Personality
Characteristics of Negroes Attending a
Predominantly White University and Negroes
Attending a Predominantly Black College,
1973. ERIC ED 102 258.

Brown, Roscoe C., Jr. "The University's
Responsibility to Black Students." Notre
Dame Journal of Education I(Summer, 1970):
149-152.

_____. "The White University Must Respond to
Black Student Needs." Negro Digest, Mr,
1969.

Brown, Warren. "Equal but Separate in College."
Chicago Sun-Times, D 11, 1977. [Race relations on college campuses in the U.S.]

Browning, Jane E. Smith. "The Origins, Development, and Desegregation of the Traditionally
Black Public Colleges and Universities:
1837-1975." Doctoral dissertation, Harvard
U., 1975. Univ. Microfilms Order No. 76-
10557.

Brubacher, John Seiler, and Rudy, Willis.
Higher Education in Transition: A History
of American Colleges and Universities, 1636-
1976. 3rd ed. New York: Harper and Row,
1976.

Brudnow, David. "Black Power and the Campus."
National Review, 0 8, 1968.

Bruhn, John G., and Hrachovy, Richard A. "Black
College Students' Attitudes Toward Opportuni-
ties in the Health Profession." Journal of
Medical Education 52(0, 1977):847-849.

Brustein, Robert. "The Case for Professionalism." New Republic, Ap 26, 1969.

Bryant, James W. A Survey of Black American Doctorates. New York: The Ford Foundation, F, 1970.

Buccieri, Claudia. "Computerized Construction Technic Makes Black Beautiful in Black College Designs." College and University Business 52(Je, 1972):56-58.

Buffkins, Archie. "White Students at Black Schools." Journal of Afro-American Issues 5(Winter, 1977):66-71.

Bunche, Ralph J. "The Role of the University in the Political Orientation of Negro Youth." Journal of Negro Education, O, 1940.

Bunzel, John H. "The Politics of Quotas." Change 4(O, 1972).

Burbach, Harold J., and Thompson, Myron A. "Alienation Among College Freshmen: A Comparison of Puerto Rican, Black, and White Students." Journal of College Student Personnel 12(Jl, 1971):248-252.

Burkheimer, Graham J., Jr. and Others. A National Study of the Upward Bound Program: Analysis, Major Findings and Implications, Ap, 1976. ERIC ED 129 925.

_____. Evaluation of the Upward Bound Program: A First Follow-Up, S, 1977. ERIC ED 148 891.

Burrell, Leon F. "Non-Academic Variables as They Relate to Academic Achievement of Male Black Doctoral Candidates." Doctoral dissertation, Michigan State U., 1971.

Burrows, Rodney A. "The Impact of Desegregation on Black Public Colleges and Blacks in Public Higher Education: Some Views of Black Public College Administrators." Negro Educational Review 28(Ap, 1977):63-74.

Burton, Gene E. "Some Problems of Minority Recruiting." Journal of College Placement 35(Winter, 1975):71-73.

Butler, Oscar P., Jr. "A Comparative Study of the Self Concept of Black and White Freshmen Students from the Midwest and the South." Doctoral dissertation, Michigan State U., 1970.

Byrnes, James C., and Tussing, A. Dale. The "Financial Crisis" in Higher Education: Past, Present, and Future. Rev. edition. Syracuse, NY: Educational Policy Research Center, Syracuse U. Research Corporation, D, 1971.

Cain, Rudolph A. "What's Happening to Black Ph.D. Applicants?" Educational Forum 37 (Ja, 1973):225-228.

Caldwell, Oliver J. "The Need for Intercultural Education in Our Universities." Phi Delta Kappan 52(My, 1971):544-545.

California State Legislature. Report of the Joint Committee on the Master Plan for Higher Education, S, 1973. ERIC ED 086 043.

Calitri, Charles J. "Open Enrollment: Ticket to Reality." Record 72(S, 1970):81-91.

Calvert, Robert, Jr. How to Recruit a Minority Group of College Graduates. Swathmore, PA: The Personnel Journal, 1963.

Campbell, Robert, and Siegel, Barry N. "The Demand for Higher Education in the United States, 1919-1964." American Economic Review, Je, 1967.

The Campus and the Racial Crisis. Washington, DC: American Council on Education, O, 1969.

Campus '70: Agenda for Critical Renewal: Annual Conference of Hillel Directors 1969. Washington, DC: B'nai B'rith Hillel Foundations, 1970.

Cardoso, Jack J. "Ghetto Blacks and College Policy." Liberal Education 55(O, 1969): 363-372.

"Career Counseling and Placement Needs of Black Students at Integrated Colleges." Journal of College Placement, O-N, 1969.

Carey, Phillip. "The Dynamics of Black Higher Education: A Sociological Perspective." Negro Educational Review 27(Jl-O, 1976):241-270.

_____. "The Relationship Between Black Studies, Self-Concept, and Academic Performance of Black Students on White Campuses in the Southwest." Doctoral dissertation, Oklahoma State U., 1975. Univ. Microfilms Order No. 76-9639.

_____. "Selection Without Discrimination: An Analysis of the ASA Minority Fellowship Program." Sociology of Education 42(1977): 144-150.

Carlisle, Donald. The Disadvantaged Student in Graduate School Master's and Doctoral Degree Programs in Predominantly Non-Negro Universities. Los Angeles, CA: U. of California, D, 1968. ERIC ED 026 021.

Carnegie Commission on Higher Education. A Chance to Learn. An Action Agenda for Equal Opportunity in Higher Education. New York: McGraw-Hill, Mr, 1970.

_____. The Open-Door Colleges. Policies for Community Colleges. New York: McGraw-Hill, Je, 1970.

Carnegie Council on Policy Studies in Higher Education. Selective Admissions in Higher Education. San Francisco: Jossey-Bass, 1977.

Carter, Fred M., and Schaefer, Richard T. "Race in the College Classroom: An Exploratory Study." Integrateducation 14(S-0, 1976).

_____. "Racial Consciousness in the College Classroom." Integrateducation 14(My-Je, 1976):41-44.

Carter, Helen R., and Shepherd, Gene D. Locked In--Locked Out. New York: Vantage Press, 1975. [Novel about racial discrimination in higher education]

Carter, Louis H. "The Black Instructor: An Essential Dimension to the Content and Structure of the Social Work Curriculum." Journal of Education for Social Work 14 (Winter, 1978):16-22.

Cass, James. "Can the University Survive the Black Challenge?" Saturday Review, Je 21, 1969.

Cassidy, Sally Wheelan and others. Impact of a High-Demand College in a Large University on Working Class Youth. Volumes I, II. Detroit, MN: Wayne State U., Ag 31, 1968. ERIC ED 025 223.

Castro, Raymond E., and Garcia, John. "Admissions: Who Shall Occupy the Seats of Privilege?" Aztlán 6(Fall, 1975):363-377.

Catlin, Jamie Beth. "The Impact of Interracial Living on the Racial Attitudes and Interaction Patterns of White College Students." 2 vols. Doctoral dissertation, U. of Michigan, 1977. Univ. Microfilms Order No. 7804664.

Center for Applied Linguistics, Washington, DC. Current Social Dialect Research at American Higher Institutions, N 15, 1966. ERIC ED 010 876.

Centra, John A. Black Students at Predominantly White Colleges: A Research Description. Princeton, NJ: Educational Testing Service, 1970.

Centra, John A. and others. "Academic Growth in Predominantly Negro and Predominantly White Colleges." American Education Research Journal 7(Ja, 1970):83-98.

Chait, Richard Paul. "The Desegregation of Higher Education: A Legal History." Doctoral dissertation, U. of Wisconsin, 1972.

Chalk, Ocania. Black College Sport. New York: Dodd Mead, 1976. [History of black athletes in colleges]

Cheatham, Harold S. "Black Americans in White Colleges: A Season of Reassessment." Journal of Non-White Concerns in Personnel and Guidance 1(Ja, 1973):111-119.

Cherdack, A. N. "The Predictive Validity of the Scholastic Aptitude Test for Disadvantaged College Students Enrolled in a Special Education Program." Doctoral dissertation, U. of California, Los Angeles, 1970.

_____. The Predictive Validity of the Scholastic Aptitude Test for Disadvantaged College Students Enrolled in a Special Education Program. Final Report. Los Angeles, CA: U. of California, Ap, 1971. ERIC ED 051 759.

Chunn, Jay. The State of an Projections for Black Professional Education in Human Services, N. 1977. ERIC ED 152 157.

Claerbaut, David Paul. "A Study of Black Student Alienation at Small Private Liberal Arts Colleges." Doctoral dissertation, Loyola U. of Chicago, 1976. Univ. Microfilms Order No. 76-11,711.

_____. "Alienation Among Black Students at Small Liberal Arts Colleges." The Urban Minority Experience." Selected Proceedings of the 4th Annual Conference on Minority Studies. Edited by George E. Carter and James R. Parker. LaCrosse, WI: Institute for Minority Studies, U. of Wisconsin--LaCrosse, 1978.

_____. Black Student Alienation: A Study. Palo Alto, CA: R & E Research Associates, 1978.

_____. Ethnicity in the American University System, 1977. ERIC ED 141 471.

_____. The Liberal Arts College: Desegregation Without Integration, 1976. ERIC ED 141 239. [Eight midwestern liberal arts colleges]

Clark, Burton R. Problems of Access in the Context of Academic Structures. New Haven, CT: Institute for Social and Policy Studies, Yale U., F, 1977.

Clark, Felton G. The Control of State-Supported Teacher Training Programs for Negroes. New York: Teachers College, Columbia U., 1934.

Clark, Hilton. "The Black Ivy League: Some Personal Observations on an Apathetic Negro." The Black Student, Spring, 1966.

Clark, Kenneth B. "The Attitude of Negro College Students Toward Their Parents." Master's thesis, Howard U., 1936.

_____. "A Charade of Power: Black Students at White Colleges." Antioch Review 29 (Summer, 1969):145-148.

_____. "The Governance of Universities in the Cities of Man." American Scholar 39 (Autumn, 1970):566-573.

_____. "Higher Education for Negroes: Challenges and Prospects." Journal of Negro Education, Summer, 1967. [Followed by a "Symposium"]

_____. "Learning from Students." Antioch Notes 46(N, 1968):1-7.

_____. "The Negro College Student: Some Facts and Some Concerns." Journal of the Association of College Admissions Counselors, Winter, 1964.

_____. "The Negro Student in Northern Interracial Colleges: An Overview." The Black Student, Spring, 1966.

_____. "Professor and Student: Moral Inconsistency and the Failure of Nerve." American Scholar 42(Winter, 1972-1973):156-164.

_____. "Response to Julian C. Stanley's Paper." Barriers to Higher Education. New York: College Entrance Examination Board, 1971. [See Stanley, below]

Clark, Kenneth B., and Plotkin, Lawrence. The Negro Student at Integrated Colleges. New York: National Scholarship Service and Fund for Negro Students, 1963.

Clark, Vernon L., and Graham, Frank P. "The Case for Black College Sponsorship of Head Start Programs." Journal of Negro Education 44(Fall, 1975):476-481.

Cleary, T. Anne. "Test Bias: Prediction of Grades of Negro and White Students in Integrated Colleges." Journal of Educational Measurement, Summer, 1968.

Cobb, Jewel P., and McDew, Carolyn (eds.). The Morning After--A Retrospective View of a Select Number of Colleges and Universities with Increased Black Student Enrollment in the Past Five Years, 1974. ERIC ED 101 599.

Cohen, Carl. "Race and the Constitution." Nation, F 8, 1975. [The De Funis case]

Cohn, Elchanan. "Benefits and Costs of Higher Education and Income Redistribution: Three Comments." Journal of Human Resources 5(Spring, 1970):222-236.

Coleman, Don Edwin. "Black Student Aide Program and MSU Black Student Organizations." In "The Status of the Black Student Aide Program and the Black Student Movement at Michigan State University." Doctoral dissertation, Michigan State U., 1971:21-131. Univ. Microfilms Order No. 72-16,404. [Detailed account of campus events, 1967-1970]

The College and Cultural Diversity: The Black Student on Campus. Atlanta, GA: Southern Regional Education Board, 1971.

"[College] Board Will Compile Registries of Six Cities' Ghetto Students." College Board Review, Fall, 1968.

College-Bound Seniors, 1973-74. New York: College Entrance Examination Board, 1974.

The College Choices of Thirty Black Project Opportunity Students. Atlanta, GA: College Entrance Examination Board; Southern Association of Colleges and Schools, 1971. ERIC ED 062 914.

Colvin, Sandra. "Students Seek Black Unity." Southern Courier, My 11, 1968. [Meeting at Shaw U., NC, to form national black students' organization]

Commission for Higher Education. Notes on Comparison of Minority Enrollment, 1970-1972. Hartford, CT: Commission for Higher Education, n.d.

Commission on Higher Educational Opportunity in the South. The Negro and Higher Education in the South. Ag, 1967. Southern Regional Education Board, 130 Sixty Street, N.W., Atlanta, GA 30313.

"The Communiversity." Negro Digest, Mr, 1970.

Comptroller General of the United States. Assessing the Federal Program for Strengthening Developing Institutions of Higher Education. Washington, DC: General Accounting Office, O 31, 1975.

_____. More Assurances Needed That Colleges and Universities With Government Contracts Provide Equal Employment Opportunity. Washington, DC: General Accounting Office, Ag 25, 1975.

Cone, James H. "Black Theologies and the Black College Student." Journal of Afro-American Issues 4(Summer, 1976):420-431.

Conley, Harold C. "An Empirical Strategy for Predicting Academic Success for Disadvantaged Negro Freshmen." Doctoral dissertation, U. of Connecticut, 1968.

Conley, Houston and others. Desegregation Dilemma and Its Impact on the Quality of Life for Black Americans--Year 2000. Ap, 1977. ERIC ED 141 450.

Conyers, James E. "Negro Doctorates in Sociology: A Social Portrait." Phylon, Fall, 1968.

Copeland, Large Lee. "An Exploration of the Causes of Black Attrition at Predominantly White Institutes of Higher Education." Doctoral dissertation, U. of Michigan, 1976. Univ. Microfilms Order No. 76-27469.

Corazzini, A. J., Dugan, D. J., and Grabowski, H. S. "Determinants and Distributional Aspects of Enrollment in U. S. Higher Education." Journal of Human Resources 7(Winter, 1972):39-59.

Corson, William R. Promise or Peril: The Black College Student in America. New York: Norton, 1970.

Cottle, Thomas J. "The Non-Elite Student: I. Billy Kowalski Goes to College." Change 3 (Mr-Ap, 1971):36-42.

Cox, Otha P., Jr. "A Comparative Analysis of Self-Perceived Roles of Black and Non-Black Administrators in Predominantly White Institutions of Higher Education." Doctoral dissertation, Michigan State U., 1971.

Crain, Robert L., and Mahard, R. High School Racial Composition, Achievement and College Attendance. Santa Monica, CA: Rand, 1977.

_____. "School Racial Composition and Black College Attendance and Achievement Test Performance." Sociology of Education 51(Ap, 1978):81-101.

Creager, John A. The American Graduate Student: A Normative Description. Washington, D. C.: American Council on Education, 1971.

Cross, K. Patricia. Beyond the Open Door. New Students to Higher Education. San Francisco, CA: Jossey-Bass, 1971.

Crossland, Fred E. "Heavy Burdens at the Narrow Gate: The American Negro and Higher Education." Journal of the Association of College Admissions Counselors, Mr, 1968.

_____. Minority Access to College. New York: Schocken Books, 1971.

Crowfoot, James E., Bryant, Bunyan I., Jr., and Chesler, Mark A. "Whatever Happened to Affirmative Action?" Integrateducation 14 (N/D, 1976).

Cuthbert, Marion V. Education and Marginality: A Study of the Negro College Graduate. New York: Columbia U. Press, 1942.

Dalomba, Roland F. "The Racial Integration Movement in the State Universities of the South, 1933-1954." Doctoral dissertation, New York U., 1956. Univ. Microfilms Order No. 20279.

Daniel, Jack L. "Black Academic Activism." Black Scholar 4(Ja, 1973):44-52.

Daniel, Jessica Henderson. "A Study of Black Sororities at a University with Marginal Integration." Journal of Non-White Concerns in Personnel and Guidance 4(Jl, 1976): 191-201.

Davidson, Carl. "From the New Left." Guardian, F 8, 1969. [About black students and white radicals on college campuses]

Davis, Howard. "A Comparison of Academic Achievement of Black P[hysical] E[ducation] Majors at Predominantly Black and Predominantly White Institutions." Journal of Physical Education and Recreation 48(Mr, 1977):24-25.

David, Junius A. "The Desegregation/Integration Dilemma in Higher Education: Implications for Research from Minority Student Experiences." Invitational Papers Submitted to the Select Education Subcommittee of the U.S. House of Representatives. Princeton, NJ: Educational Testing Service, Mr, 1971. ERIC ED 051 314.

Davis, Marcheta Z. "The Social Science Curriculum in a Traditionally Black College." Improving College and University Teaching 23(Winter, 1975):24-26.

Days, Drew S. III. Can the Enforcement of Civil Rights Laws Protect Minority Gains in Higher Education During a Period of Retrenchment? My 7, 1977. ERIC ED 140 709.

DeBlassie, Richard R., and Boswell, Katherine. "The Culturally Disadvantaged College Student." Journal of the National Association of Women Deans and Counselors 35 (Spring, 1972):126-132.

Delaney, Paul. "Blacks Say Drive to Spur College Enrollment Ends." New York Times, Mr 26, 1975.

Delgado, Paul A. "Institutional Response to Minorities in Graduate Schools of Social Work." Doctoral dissertation, U. of Michigan, 1978. Univ. Microfilms Order No. 7822882.

Dennis, Lawrence E. "Equalizing Colleges and Universities." Phi Delta Kappan, My, 1964.

"Department Heads in White Colleges." Ebony, My, 1958.

Dillard, Sherman. "A Speck in the Crowd: Black Athletes on White Campuses." Journal of Physical Education and Recreation 48(Ap, 1977):66-68.

Dillingham, Gerald L. "Blacks and the College Experience--Revisited." Integrateducation 14(My - Je, 1976):37-40.

Dillon, James Carroll. "Black College Students' Attitudes and Other Factors Related to Blacks' Participation in the Sciences." Doctoral dissertation, Kansas State U., 1975.

Dillon, James C., and James, Robert K. "Attitudes of Black College Students Toward Science." School Science and Mathematics 77 (N, 1977):592-600.

Dispenzieri, Angelo and others. "College Performance of Disadvantaged Students as a Function of Ability and Personality." Journal of Consulting Psychology 18(Jl, 1971): 298-305.

Dinin, Samuel. "Higher Jewish Education." Jewish Education 10(Ja-Mr, 1938):11-19.

Doermann, Humphrey. "Lack of Money: A Barrier to Higher Education." Barriers to Higher Education. New York: College Entrance Examination Board, 1971.

Donaldson, Leon Matthew. "The Influence of Federal Grants on REsearch and Instruction in the Sciences as Perceived by Selected Predominantly Black Private Institutions." Doctoral dissertation, Rutgers U., 1973. Univ. Microfilms Order No. 74-08864.

Dorsett, Herman W. "Social, Economic, and Essential Problems Anticipated by Graduate School-Bound Negro College Students." Dissertation Abstracts International 31(7A) Ja, 1971:3334.

Drew, David E. A Profile of the Jewish Freshman. Washington, DC: American Council on Education. Je, 1970. ERIC ED 041 338.

DuBois, W. E. B. "A Program for Negro Land Grant Colleges." Proceedings, 19th Annual Conference. Presidents of Negro Land Grant Colleges. N, 1941. Chicago, 1941:42-57.

_____. [Article on college education] Amsterdam News, S 5, 1942.

_____. [Article on the need for black faculty in "white" universities] Amsterdam News, My 29, 1943.

_____. College-Bred Negro Communities: Address of Professor W. E. B. DuBois at Brookline, Mass. Atlanta U. Leaflet No. 23. Atlanta, GA: Atlanta U., 1910.

_____. "Discrimination in Northern Colleges." Crisis, Ag, 1931.

_____. "Diuturni Silenti." Fisk Herald 33 (1924):i-xii.

_____. "Jacob and Esau." The Talladegan 42 (N, 1944):1-6.

_____. [On increasing the number of black faculty in white universities] Pittsburgh Courier, My 29, 1943.

_____. "The Revelation of Saint Orgne the Damned." Fisk News 9(N-D, 1938):3-9.

_____. "The Young Negro Scholar--Colored Colleges Important--Importance is Growing." Amsterdam Star-News [New York City], Je 27, 1942.

Ducey, Walter J. "Equal Employment Opportunity Comes to the Campus." Journal of the College and University Personnel Association 25 (Ja, 1974):1-13.

Dunbar, Ernest. "The Black Revolt Hits the White Campus." Look, O 31, 1967.

Durley, Gerald. "A Center for Black Students on University Campuses." Journal of Higher Education, Je, 1969.

Dworkin, Ronald. "The Bakke Decision: Did It Decide Anything?" New York Review of Books Ag 17, 1978.

Dyer, Henry S. "Toward More Effective Recruitment and Selection of Negroes for College." Journal of Negro Education, Summer, 1967.

Dyer, James S. Assessing the Effects of Changes in the Cost of Higher Education to the Student. Santa Monica, CA: The Rand Corporation, Je, 1970. ERIC ED 045 012.

Eastman, William M. "Mix versus Fit: The Admission Officer's Dilemma." College Board Review, Summer, 1966.

Edley, Christopher F. "Black Education: The Need for Black Support." Crisis 82(D, 1975): 14-16.

Edwards, Harry. The Revolt of the Black Athlete. New York: The Free Press, 1969.

Egerton, John. "Adams v. Richardson: Can Separate Be Equal?" Change 6(D-Ja, 1974-1975):29-36.

_____. "Almost All-White." Southern Education Report, My, 1969. [State universities]

_____. "Black Admissions Officers Organize." Race Relations Reporter, N 16, 1970.

_____. "Black Enrollment [in Colleges] Now 6.5 Per Cent." Race Relations Reporter 2 (Ag 2, 1971):6-7.

_____. Ending Discrimination in Higher Education: A Report from Ten States. Atlanta, GA: Southern Education Foundation, N, 1974.

_____. "High Risk." Parts 1 and 2. Southern Education Report, Mr, 1968 and Ap, 1968. [Disadvantaged students in college]

_____. "Inflated Body Count." Change 2(Jl-Ag, 1970):13-15. [Analysis of statistics relating to numbers of black students in college]

_____. State Universities and Black Americans. An Inquiry Into Desegregation and Equity for Negroes in 100 Public Universities. Atlanta, GA: Southern Education Foundation, My, 1969.

_____. "Still Separate and Unequal." Progressive 40(Ap, 1976):26-29.

_____. "Survey: A Lack of Preparation in the Colleges." Southern Education Report, Ap, 1967. [Training teachers of the disadvantaged]

Eitzen, D. Stanley, and Yetman, Norman R. "Immune from Racism?" Civil Rights Digest 9(Winter, 1977):3-13. [Discrimination against blacks in sports]

Eldridge, H. M. "Is the Negro Male High School, Technical Institute, and College Student Becoming Extinct?" North Carolina Teacher, O, 1967.

El-Khawas, Elaine H., and Kinzer, Joan L. Enrollment of Minority Graduate Students at Ph.D. Granting Institutions, Ag, 1974. ERIC ED 094 620.

Elkind, David. "From Ghetto School to College Campus: Some Discontinuities and Continuities." Journal of School Psychology 9(F, 1971):241-245.

Elton, Charles F. "Black and White Colleges: A Comparative Analysis." Journal of Negro Education 43(Winter, 1974):111-116.

Enarson, Harold L. "Higher Education and Community Services." The Campus and the Racial Crisis. Washington, DC: American Council on Education, 1969.

English, Richard A., and Settle, Theodore J. "Minority Students in Higher Education." Integrateducation 14(My-Je, 1976):3-6.

Enrollment, Housing and Financial Aids of Minority Group Students. Fall, 1968. Central Staff Office of Institutional Research, State U. of New York, Albany, NY, My, 1969. ERIC ED 030 389.

Erwin, James. "The Attitudes of Black 'New Students' and Administrative Response." Journal of Negro Education 45(Spring, 1976): 161-165.

Etzioni, Amitai. "Faculty Response to Racial Tensions." The Campus and the Racial Crisis. Washington, DC: American Council on Education, 1969.

_____. "The Policy of Open Admissions." In New Teaching New Learning. Edited by S. Kerry Smith and Others. San Francisco, CA: Jossey-Bass, 1971.

_____. Towards Higher Education in An Active Society: Three Policy Guidelines, Je, 1970. Center for Policy Research, 432 W. 118th Street, New York, NY 10027.

Etzioni, Amitai, Tinker, Irene, and Atkinson, Carolyn O, with Kalb, Judith. Post-Secondary Education and the Disadvantaged: A Policy Study, 1969. Center for Policy Research, 423 W. 118th Street, New York, NY 10027.

Evans, Charles J. "What Happens to Black Administrators in White Universities." Negro American Literature Forum 5(F, 1971): 98-101.

Evans, D. A. and others. "Traditional Criteria as Predictors of Minority Student Success in Medical School." Journal of Medical Education 50(1975):934-939.

Evans, David L. "On Criticism of Black Students." Ebony 32(Ja, 1977):38.

Evans, Doris A., and Jackson, Edgar B., Jr. "Deans of Minority Student Affairs in Medical Schools." Journal of Medical Education 51(Mr, 1976):197-199.

Expanding Opportunities. Case Studies of Interinstitutional Cooperation, 1969. Atlanta, GA: Southern Regional Education Board, 1969. [Cooperation between and among Negro colleges and/or white colleges in the South]

Exum, William Henry. "Black Student Movements in White Colleges and Universities: A Case Study." Doctoral dissertation, New York U., 1974. Univ. Microfilms Order No. 74-18153.

_____. Black Student Unions, 1965-1975: A Retrospective Look at the Last Decade, Mr, 1976. ERIC ED 124 666.

Fact Book on Higher Education in the South 1971 and 1972. Atlanta, GA: Southern Regional Education Board, 1972.

Faia, Michael A. "The Myth of the Liberal Professor." Sociology of Education 47 (Spring, 1974):171-202.

Fair, Martha H. "The Myth of the 'Free Ride' Through College." Journal of Non-White Concerns in Personnel and Guidance 4(Jl, 1976):174-180.

Fairfax, Jean. "Current Status of the Adams Case: Implications for the Education of Blacks and Other Minorities." Beyond Desegregation. Urgent Issues in the Education of Minorities. New York: College Entrance Examination Board, 1978.

Farley, Frank H. and others. "Predicting Locus of Control in Black and White College Students." Journal of Black Studies 6(Mr, 1976):299-304.

Farver, Albert S. and others. "Longitudinal Predictions of University Grades for Blacks and Whites." Measurement and Evaluation in Guidance 7(Ja, 1975):243-250.

"February 1st Movement." African World 4(F, 1975): ["An anti-imperialist Black student organization" begun in December, 1974]

Fein, Leonard. "Dilemmas of Jewish Identity on the College Campus." Judaism 17(Winter, 1968):10-21.

Feingold, S. Norman, Sexton, Iris, Rose, Karen, and Kaiser, Ronald S. An Analysis of Major Trends in Jewish College Enrollment: A Resource for Education and Vocational Guidance Counselors. Washington, DC: B'nai B'rith Vocational Service, 1969.

Feinstein, Otto, with Melman, Seymour, Merbaum, Richard, Pettengill, Robert, Vann, Carl, and Weiss, John. Higher Education in the United States. Economics, Personalism, Quality. Lexington, MA: Health Lexington Books, 1971.

Fendrich, James M. "A Study of the Association Among Verbal Attitudes, Commitment and Overt Behavior in Different Experimental Situations." Social Forces, Mr, 1967. [Students at a Big Ten university in relation to joining a branch of the NAACP]

Ferrin, Richard J. "An Analysis of the Changes in Free-Access Higher Education in the United States from 1958 to 1968." Unpublished dissertation, Stanford U., 1970.

_____. Barriers to Universal Higher Education. Mr, 1970. Access Research Office, College Entrance Examination Board, Suite 363, 800 Welch Road, Palo Alto, CA: 94304.

_____. A Decade of Change in Free-Access Higher Education. New York: College Entrance Examination Board, 1971.

Fife, Jonathan D., and Leslie, Larry L. "The College Student Grant Study: The Effectiveness of Student Grant and Scholarship Programs in Promoting Equal Educational Opportunity." Research in Higher Education 4(1976):317-333.

Financing Equal Opportunity in Higher Education. New York: College Entrance Examination Board, 1970.

Fink, Jerome S. "Let's Recruit Adult Minority Students Too." College Board Review 80 (Summer, 1971):11-12.

The First National Congress of Black Professionals in Higher Education. Policy Statements. Austin, TX: U. of Texas, 1972.

Fleming, John E. The Lengthening Shadow of Slavery: A Historical Justification for Affirmative Action for Blacks in Higher Education. Washington, DC: Howard U. Press, 1976.

Fleming, John E. and others. The Case for Affirmative Action for Blacks in Higher Education. Washington, DC: Howard U. Press, 1978.

Flynn, Peter F. "A New Approach to the Admissions Dilemma." Orient (Michigan State U.) 6(1971):2-6.

Folger, John K., Astin, Helen S., and Bayer, Alan E. Human Resources and Higher Education: Staff Report of the Commission on Human Resources and Advanced Education. New York: Russell Sage Foundation, 1970.

Forbes, Gordon B., and Gipson, Marilyn. "Political Attitudes and Opinions, Need for Social Approval, Dogmatism and Anxiety in Negro and White College Students." Journal of Negro Education, Winter, 1969.

Ford Foundation Assistance to Minorities in Higher Education. New York: Ford Foundation, Ap, 1971.

Ford Foundation. Four Minorities and the Ph.D. Ford Foundation Graduate Fellowships for Blacks, Chicanos, Puerto Ricans, and American Indians. New York: The Ford Foundation, 0, 1973.

Foreman, Paul B. "Race Confronts Universities: A Preface for Policy." Journal of General Education, Jl, 1968.

Forston, Thomas S. "Black Students and Campus Security Forces." Orient (Michigan State U.) 6(1971):7-16.

Framework for Evaluating Institutional Commitment to Minorities. Washington, DC: American Council on Education, 1976.

Freeman, Richard Barry. Black Elite: The New Market for Highly Educated Black Americans. New York: McGraw-Hill, 1976.

_____. "The New Job Market for Black Academicians." Industrial and Labor Relations Review 30(Ja, 1977):161-174.

_____. The Overeducated American. New York: Academic Press, 1976.

Freeman, Richard, and Hollomon, J. Herbert. "The Declining Value of College Going." Change 7(S, 1975):24-31, 62.

Froe, Otis D. "Educational Planning for Disadvantaged College Youth." Journal of Negro
Education, Summer, 1964.

Froomkin, Joseph. Aspirations, Enrollments,
and Resources. The Challenge to Higher
Education in the Seventies. Washington,
DC: GPO, 1970.

_____. Students and Buildings. An Analysis
of Selected Federal Programs for Higher
Education. Washington, DC: GPO, 1968.

_____. Trends in the Sources of Student Sup-
port for Postsecondary Education. Iowa
City: American College Testing Program,
1978.

Furniss, W. Todd (ed.). Higher Education for
Everybody? Washington, DC: American
Council on Education, 1971.

Gaier, Eugene L., and Watts, William A. "Current Attitudes and Socialization Patterns
of White and Negro Students Entering College." Journal of Negro Education, Fall,
1969.

Gaillard, Frye. "Black Recruiting Increases in
SEC." Race Relations Reporter 2(Mr 1, 1970):
7-8. [Southern Conference]

_____. "Crumbling Segregation in the South-
eastern Conference. The Black Athlete-1970.
Nashville, TN: Race Relations Information
Center, Ag, 1970.

Galambos, Eva C. Black College Graduates and
the Job Market in the South, 1980, 1976.
ERIC ED 129 170.

Galchus, Donna S., and Galabus, Kenneth E.
"Drug Use: Some Comparisons of Black and
White College Students." Drug Forum: The
Journal of Human Issues 6(1977):65-73.

Gallagher, Buell G. Campus in Crisis. New
York: Harper and Row, 1974.

_____. (ed.). College and the Black Student.
NAACP Tract for the Times. New York: NAACP,
1971.

Gappa, Judith M. Improving Equity in Post-
secondary Education. New Directions for
Leadership. Washington, DC: GPO, D, 1977.

Garcia, Sandra A., and Seligsohn, Harriet C.
"Undergraduate Black Student Retention Revisited." Educational Record 59(Spring,
1978):156-165.

Gardner, W. E. "Cracking the College Color Line:
NAACP, Supreme Court Open Southern Colleges
to Negro Students." Our World, Mr, 1951.

Garza, Raymond T., and Nelson, Darwin B. "A
Comparison of Mexican- and Anglo-American
Perceptions of the University Environment."
Journal of College Student Personnel 14(S,
1973):399-401.

Gates, Maurice. "Negro Students Challenge
Social Forces." Crisis, Ag, 1935.

Geiger, Louis G., and Geiger, Helen M. "The
Revolt Against Excellence." AAUP Bulletin
56(Fall, 1970):297-301. [On open admissions
and related subjects]

Geiger, Roger L. "The Case of the Missing Students." Change 10(D-Ja, 1978/79):64-65.

Gibbs, Jewelle Taylor. "Black Students at a
White University: An Exploratory Study."
Master's thesis, U. of California, Berkeley,
1970.

_____. "Black Students at Integrated Colleges:
Problems and Prospects." In Black/Brown/
White Relations. Edited by Charles V. Willie.
New Brunswick, NJ: Transaction, 1977.

_____. "Black Students/White University:
Different Expectations." Personnel and
Guidance Journal 51(Mr, 1973):463-469.

_____. "Use of Mental Health Services by
Black Students at a Predominantly White
University: A Three-Year Study." American
Journal of Orthopsychiatry 45(Ap, 1975).

Gilliam, Reginald E., Jr. "The College-Educa-
ted Black: Another Dead End?" Afro-
American Studies 3(Je, 1972):21-28.

Gittell, Marilyn, and Dollar, Bruce. "Cultural
Pluralism: Traditional And Alternative
Models in Higher Education." In Badges and
Indicia of Slavery: Cultural Pluralism Re-
defined. Edited by Antonia Pantoja, Barbara
Blourock, and James Bowman. Lincoln, NB:
Study Commission on Undergraduate Education
and the Education of Teachers, 1975.

Glazer, Nathan. "Are Academic Standards
Obsolete?" Change 2(N-D, 1970):38-44.

Glickstein, Howard, and Todorovich, Miro.
"Discrimination in Higher Education. A
Debate on Faculty Employment." Civil
Rights Digest 7(Spring, 1975):3-21.

Glover, John A. "Comparative Levels of
Creative Ability in Black and White College
Students." Journal of Genetic Psychology
128 (Mr, 1976):95-99.

Godwin, Winifred L. "A Determined Effort to
Improve Higher Education [in the South]."
Monthly Labor Review, Mr, 1968.

_____. "Southern State Governments and Higher
Education for Negroes." Daedalus 100(Summer,
1971):783-797.

Goins, Alvin, and Meenes, Max. "Ethnic and
Class Preferences Among College Negroes."
Journal of Negro Education 29(1970):128-133.

Goldman, Roy D. "Hidden Opportunities in the Prediction of College Grades for Different Subgroups." Journal of Educational Measurement 10(F, 1973):205-210.

Goldman, Roy D., and Widawski, Mel H. "An Analysis of Types of Errors in the Selection of Minority College Students." Journal of Educational Measurement 13(F, 1976):185-200.

Goldstein, Gloria (ed.). College Bound: A Directory of Special Programs and Financial Aid for Minority Group Students. White Plains, NY: Urban League of Westchester, Inc., S, 1970. ERIC ED 045 776.

Good, Paul. "The American Dream of Cleveland Sellers." New South 28(Spring, 1973):2-23.

Goodman, James A. "The Social Health of Disadvantaged Black College Students." Journal of the American College Health Association 22(Ap, 1974):272-273.

Gordon, Edmund W. "Access to Higher Education." IRCD Bulletin 8(F, 1972):7-10.

_____. "Admissions Policy: Implications and Consequences. I," Liberal Education 56 (My, 1970):270-277.

_____. "Higher Education and the Challenge of Universal Access to Post-Secondary Education." Liberal Education 56(1970).

_____. The Higher Education of the Disadvantaged. New Dimensions in Higher Education, Number 28. Ap, 1967. ERIC ED 013 350.

_____. "Opportunities in Higher Education for Socially Disadvantaged Youth." From High School to College: Readings for Counselors. College Entrance Examination Board. New York: CEEB, 1965.

_____. "Programs and Practices for Minority Group Youth in Higher Education." Barriers to Higher Education. New York: College Entrance Examination Board, 1971.

Gordon, Edmund W., and Thomas, Charles L. Brief: A Study on Compensatory Collegiate Programs for Minority Group Youth. New York: Columbia U. Teachers College, 1969. ERIC ED 028 746.

Gordon, Milton A. "An Analysis of Enrollment Data for Black Students in Institutions of Higher Education, From 1940-1972." Journal of Negro Education 45(Spring, 1976):117-121.

Gordon, Nancy M. and others. "Faculty Salaries: Is There Discrimination by Sex, Race, and Discipline?" American Economic Review 64 (Je, 1974):419-427.

Gordon, Travis L., and Johnson, Davis G. "Study of U.S. Medical School Applicants, 1975-76." Journal of Medical Education 52(S, 1977):707-730.

Gottlieb, David. "College Youth and the Meaning of Work." Vocational Guidance Quarterly 24(D, 1975):116-124.

Graduate and Professional School Opportunities for Minority Students. Fifth edition, 1973-1974. Princeton, NJ: Educational Testing Service, 1973.

Graham, D. Robert. "State Planning for Expanded Opportunity." Effective Use of Resources in State Higher Education. Atlanta, GA: Southern Regional Education Board, Ag, 1970.

Gray, T. S., and Thompson, A. H. "The Ethnic Prejudices of White and Negro College Students." Journal of Abnormal and Social Psychology 48(1953):311-313.

Greeley, Andrew M. "The New Urban Studies—A Work of Caution." Educational Record 51 (Summer, 1970):232-236.

Green, Robert L. "The Black Quest for Higher Education: An Admissions Dilemma." Personnel and Guidance Journal, My, 1969.

_____. "Minority Admissions and Support." Journal of Student Financial Aid 5(Mr, 1975):24-31.

_____. "Minority Admissions and Support: Higher Education and the Quest for Equality." College Board Review 88(Summer, 1973):14-18.

_____. "Minority Group Students at Predominantly White Universities: Needs and Perspectives." Educational Journal (U. of Wisconsin) 92(S-O, 1971).

Green, Robert L., McMillan, Joseph R., and Gunnings, Thomas S. "Blacks in the Big Ten." Integrated Education, My-Je, 1972: 32-39.

Green, Robert L., and others. "Black Athletes: Educational, Economic, and Political Considerations." Journal of Non-White Concerns 3(O, 1974):6-38.

Greene, Thomas W. "After the Explosion, Two Years of Fallout." Southern Education Report, My, 1969.

Greer, C. R. "Returns to Investment in Undergraduate Education by Race and Sex in 1960 and 1970." Review of Business and Economic Research 12(Winter, 1976-77).

Grier, Marian Esther Samuels. "A Comparison of Self-Concept and Interpersonal Relationship Between Black Students on a Predominantly Black College Campus and Black Students on a Predominantly White College Campus." Doctoral dissertation, U. of Oklahoma, 1975. Univ. Microfilms Order No. 76-03100.

Griffin, Ronald C. "Admissions: A Time for Change." Howard Law Journal 20(1977):128-149. [Law schools]

Griggs, Anthony. "Two Sides of a Medical Conference." Race Relations Reporter 5(Ap 29, 1974):4-6. [Student National Medical Association conference, Atlanta, GA, Ap, 1974]

Grimke, Francis J. "Colored Men as Professors in Colored Institutions." A.M.E. Church Review 4(1885):142-149. [In Bracey, Meier, and Rudwick (eds.). Black Nationalism in America, 1970]

Grobman, Arnold B. "Short changing the Disadvantaged Student." Science 177(J1, 1972):297.

Gwartney, James D. "Discrimination, Achievement, and Payoffs of a College Degree." Journal of Human Resources 7(Winter, 1972):60-70.

Habecker, Eugene B. Affirmative Action in the Independent College: A Practical Planning Model. Washington, DC: Council for the Advancement of Small Colleges, 1977.

Haettenschwiller, Dunstan L. "Counseling Black College Students in Special Programs." Personnel and Guidance Journal 50(S, 1971):29-35.

Hale, Frank W., Jr. "A Sprinkle of Pepper: The State of Black Influence in White Colleges and Universities." Journal of Non-White Concerns in Personnel and Guidance 3 (Ja, 1975):45-52.

Hall, Laurence (ed.). New Colleges for New Students. San Francisco, CA: Jossey-Bass, 1974.

Hall, Richard W. "No Room in a Culture of Talents." College Composition and Communication 23(D, 1972):357-364.

Hamilton, Charles V. "Minority Groups [in the Colleges]" Proceedings of the Academy of Political Science 30(1970):15-27.

Hamilton, Ian Bruce, Jr. Graduate School Programs for Minority/Disadvantaged Students: Report of an Initial Survey. Princeton, NJ: Graduate Record Examination Board, 1973.

_____. "Irresistible Force Meets Immovable Object: A Study of American Graduate Schools' Response to the Black Revolution." Doctoral dissertation, Stanford U., 1975. Univ. Microfilms Order No. 75-13533.

Handlin, Oscar, and Handlin, Mary F. The American College and American Culture: Socialization as a Function of Higher Education. New York: McGraw-Hill, 1970.

Hannah, John A. "Civil Rights and the Public Universities." Journal of Higher Education, F, 1966.

Hano, Arnold. "The Black Rebel Who 'Whitelists' the Olympics." New York Times Magazine, My 12, 1968. [Professor Harry Edwards]

Haskell, Paul G. "Legal Education on the Academic Plantation." Journal of the American Bar Association 60(F, 1974).

Hansen, W. Lee, and Lampman, Robert J. "Basic Opportunity Grants for Higher Education: Good Intentions and Mixed Results." Challenge, N-D, 1974.

Harcleroad, Fred F. "Disadvantaged Students and Survival in College." In New Teaching New Learning. Edited by G. Kerry Smith and others. San Francisco, CA: Jossey-Bass, 1971.

Hare, Nathan. "The Battle for Black Studies." Black Scholar 3(My, 1972):32-47.

_____. "Black Invisibility of White Campuses." Negro Digest, Mr, 1969.

_____. [Review of Jaffe, Adams, and Meyers, Negro Higher Education in the 1960's] Journal of Higher Education, O, 1969.

Hargrave, Edythe. "How I Feel as a Negro at a White College." Journal of Negro Education, O, 1942.

Harleston, B. W. "Higher Education for the Negro." Atlantic 216(N, 1965):136-144.

Harper, Frederick D. "Black Student Revolt on the White Campus." Journal of College Student Personnel 10(1969):291-295.

_____. Black Students, White Campus: Implications for Counseling. Washington, DC: American Personnel and Guidance Association Press, 1975.

_____. "Media for Change: Black Students in the White University." Journal of Negro Education 40(Summer, 1971):255-265.

Harris, Ann Sutherland. "The Second Sex in Academe." AAUP Bulletin 56(Fall, 1970):283-296.

Harris, Edward E. "Conforming Deviant Educational Attitudes and Group Position." College Student Survey 4(F, 1970):33-41.

_____. "Personal and Parental Influences on College Attendance: Some Negro-White Differences." Journal of Negro Education 39 (Fall, 1970):305-313.

_____. "Special Working Class Educational Needs: Fact or Myth?" Education 92 (Ap-My, 1972):94-97.

Harris, Major L. Testing and Evaluation in Higher Education and Its Effect on Racial Minorities, 1971. ERIC ED 053 213.

Harris, Seymour E. A Statistical Portrait of Higher Education. New York: McGraw-Hill, 1972.

Harris, William J. "The Militant Separatists in the White Academy." American Scholar 41(Summer, 1972):366-376.

Hartman, Robert W. "Higher Education Subsidies: An Analysis of Selected Programs in Current Legislation. In U.S. Congress, 92nd, 2nd session, Joint Economic Committee, The Economics of Federal Subsidy Programs, Part 4--Higher Education and Manpower Subsidies. Washington, DC: GPO, Ag 28, 1972. [See also appendix by Daniel Sullivan, pp 493-494.]

Hartnett, Rodney T. College and University Trustees: Their Backgrounds, Roles, and Educational Attitudes. Princeton, NJ: Educational Testing Services, 1969.

_____. "Differences in Selected Attitudes and College Orientations Between Black Students Attending Traditionally Negro and Traditionally White Institutions." Sociology of Education 43(Fall, 1970):419-436.

_____. The New College Trustee: Some Predictions for the 1970's. Princeton, NJ: Educational Testing Service, 1970.

Hartnett, Rodney T., and Payton, Benjamin F. Minority Admissions and Performance in Graduate Study. New York: Ford Foundation, 1978.

Hartsough, W. Ross, and Fontana, Alan F. "Persistence of Ethnic Stereotypes and the Relative Importance of Positive and Negative Stereotyping for Association Preferences." Psychological Reports 27(D, 1970):723-731.

Harvey, James. Minorities and Advanced Degrees. Washington, DC: ERIC Clearinghouse on Higher Education, Je 1, 1972. ERIC ED 062 957.

Haurek, Edward W. "The Impact of Socio-Economic Status and Peer and Parental Influences Upon College Aspiration and Attendance." Doctoral dissertation, U. of Illinois, Ag, 1970. [Project TALENT data]

Hayes, Annamarie G. "A Study of Economic Needs of Selected Black and White Students at a Northern University." Journal of Student Financial Aid 5(Mr, 1975):4-16.

Hayes, Edward J., and Franks, Joan. "College Environment: Differential Perceptions of Black Minority Students." Journal of Non-White Concerns in Personnel and Guidance 4 (O, 1975):31-35.

Health Resources Administration. An Exploratory Evaluation...Of U.S. Medical Schools' Efforts to Achieve Equal Representation of Minority Students, D, 1977. ERIC ED 157 441.

Healy, Timothy S. "Open Admissions: Status, Trends, and Implications." Barriers to Higher Education. New York: College Entrance Examination Board, 1971.

Heath, G. Louis. The Hot Campus: The Politics That Impede Change in the Technoversity. Metuchen, NJ: Scarecrow Press, 1973.

Hechinger, Fred M. "Class War Over Tuition." New York Times, F 5, 1974.

Helms, Janet E., and Willis, Cecilia A. "Factors Contributing to the Attrition of Precollege Minority Students Prior to Freshman Year." Journal of College Student Personnel 16(N, 1975):490-492.

Hemingway, Herman W., and Milstein, Tom. "Campus Black Separatism." New America, Ap 22, 1969. [An exchange of views]

Henderson, A. D. "Balm for a Troubled Conscience." Educational Record 35(1954):170-174. [Fraternities]

Henderson, Donald M. "Some Necessary Changes in University Practices for Education of the Disadvantaged." Education 92(S-O, 1971): 21-25.

_____. "Black Student Protest in White Universities." In Black America. Edited by John F. Szwed. New York: Basic Books, 1970:256-270.

Henderson, T. H. and others. "Racial Barriers Affecting the Admission of Qualified Students to Southern Colleges and Universities." Quarterly Review of Higher Education Among 20(O, 1952):150-167.

Hendrickson, Robert M. "'State Action' and Private Higher Education." Journal of Law and Education 2(Ja, 1973):53-75.

Hester, James M. "Some Observations on the Urban Involvement of Universities." Urban Affairs 6(S, 1970):88-93.

Heyne, Clare Del. "Racial Conceptions of College Students About Members of the Black and White Races." Doctoral dissertation, Saint Louis U., 1973. Univ. Microfilms Order No. 74-24090.

Hidgon, Hal. "The Troubled Heart of Sigma Chi." New York Times Magazine, N 14, 1965. [Segregation in fraternities]

"Higher Education for Urban America." Educational Record, Summer, 1965 (Special supplement). [Report of national conference in Detroit, Je 21-23, 1964]

Higher Education Opportunity Program, 1970-71. Interim Report. Albany, New York: New York State Education Dept., Division of Higher Education, Ja 21, 1971. ERIC ED 051 771.

Hight, Joseph E., and Pollock, Richard. "In-come Distribution Effects of Higher Education Expenditures in California, Florida, and Hawaii." Journal of Human Resources 8 (Summer, 1973):318-330.

Hill, Norman. "For Liberty and Equality." Current 129(My, 1971):32-35. [On preference for blacks in colleges]

Hill, Sylvia B. "The School of Education and the Prospects for Equal Educational Opportunity." Journal of Teacher Education 20 (1969):410-417.

Hills, John R., and Stanley, Julian C. "Easier Test Improves Prediction of Black Students' College Grades." Journal of Negro Education 39(Fall, 1970):320-324.

Hinderaker, Ivan. The University and Race Relations. Riverside, CA: U. of California, Ja 14, 1969. ERIC ED 029 558.

Hines, Ralph H. "Social Distance Components in Integration Attitudes of Negro College Students." Journal of Negro Education, Winter, 1968.

Hirsch, Werner Z. and others. Universities and Foundations Search for Relevance. Los Angeles: Institute of Government and Public Affairs, U. of California, 1968.

Hixson, Judson, and Epps, Edgar G. "The Failure of Selection and the Problem of Prediction: Racism vs. Measurement in Higher Education." Journal of Afro-American Issues 3(Winter, 1975).

Hoenack, and Feldman, Paul. Private Demand for Higher Education in the United States. Springfield, VA: Clearinghouse for Federal Scientific and Technical Information, Ag, 1969.

Hogges, Ralph. Perspectives on White Administrators in Higher Education and Affirmative Action, O 29, 1976. ERIC ED 134 082.

Holleb, Doris B. Colleges and the Urban Poor. The Role of Public Higher Education in Community Service. Lexington, MA: D. C. Health, 1972.

Holloway, Lou Emma. "'It's Winter in America' for Black College Students." Encore, O 6, 1975.

Holman, Forest H. C., Jr. "A History of Selected Critical Factors and Barriers in the Development of Black Higher Education." Doctoral dissertation, Michigan State U., 1975. Univ. Microfilms Order No. 75-20,847.

Holmes, George R., and Heckel, Robert V. "Psychotherapy with the First Negro Male on One Southern University Campus: A Case Study." Journal of Consulting and Clinical Psychology 34(Je, 1970):297-301.

Holmes, Robert. "The Ivy League University and the 'Talented Tenth.'" Journal of Social and Behavioral Sciences 18(Fall-Winter, 1971-1972):63-79.

Holsendolph, Ernest. "Black Presence Grows in Higher Education." New York Times, N 14, 1976.

Holtzman, Jo. "Attitudes toward Integration of Segregated and Integrated Students." Integrated Education, My-Je, 1972:52-56.

Horowitz, Irving Louis. "Young Radicals and Professional Critics." Commonweal, Ja 31, 1969.

Howard, Lawrence C. "Black Consciousness," chapter 10 in Identity Crisis in Higher Education. Edited by Harold L. Hodgkinson and Myron B. Bloy, Jr. San Francisco, CA: Jossey-Bass, 1970.

_____ (ed.). Black Consciousness and Higher Education, 1968. The Church Society for College Work, 2 Brewer Street, Cambridge, MA 02138.

_____. Graduate Education for the "Disadvantaged" and Black-Oriented University Graduates. Washington, DC: Council of Graduate Schools in the United States, D 18, 1968. ERIC ED 026 022.

Howe, Harold II. The Negro American and Higher Education, D 3, 1968. ERIC ED 026 036.

Huberman, Michael. "Reflections on Democratization of Secondary and Higher Education." Bulletin of the National Association of Secondary School Principals 55(Ap, 1971):1-16.

Hull, W. Frank IV. Higher Education and the Black Atypical Student. U. Park, PA: Pennsylvania State U., F, 1970. ERIC ED 038 479.

_____. The "Special Admission" Student and the Colleges. University Park, PA: Pennsylvania State U. Center for the Study of Higher Education, N, 1969. ERIC ED 037 487.

Humphreys, Lloyd G. "Racial Differences: Dilemma of College Admissions." (letter) Science 166(O 10, 1969):167.

Hunt, Chester L. "Patterns of Minority Group Adjustment." Educational Forum 39(Ja, 1975): 137-147.

Hurst, Charles G., Jr. "Pluralism and Peace on Campus." In The Minority Student on the Campus: Expectations and Possibilities. Edited by Robert A. Altman and Patricia O. Snyder. N, 1970. Western Interstate Commission for Higher Education, P. O. Drawer "P." Boulder, CO 80302.

Huther, John W. "The Open Door: How Open Is It?" Junior College Journal 41(Ap, 1971): 24-27.

Huyck, Earl E. "Faculty in Predominantly White and Predominantly Negro Higher Institutions." Journal of Negro Education, Fall, 1966.

Identification of Problems and Concerns Regarding Educational Research and Development Activities Involving Black Citizens, 1973. Order: Elementary Education Department, 315 Education Building, Urbana, IL 61801.

Institute for Higher Educational Opportunity. The College and Cultural Diversity. The Black Student on Campus. A Project Report. Atlanta, GA: Southern Regional Education Board, O, 1971.

Institute for the Study of Educational Policy, Howard U. Equal Educational Opportunity for Blacks in U.S. Higher Education. An Assessment. Washington, DC: Howard U. Press, 1976.

"Integrating Higher Education: Defining the Scope of the Affirmative Duty to Integrate," Iowa Law Review 57(1972).

"Integration in Reverse." Look, Ap 21, 1964.

Ivy, James W., and Cannon, Raymond W. "What Good Are College Fraternities? A Debate." Messenger 9(Je, 1927):179-182.

Jackson, Jewell. "Black College Students' Perceptions of Black and White Counselors in a Predominantly White University." Doctoral dissertation, Kansas State U., 1975. Univ. Microfilms Order No. 76-05865.

Jackson, John S. III. "The Political Behavior and Socio-Economic Backgrounds of Black Students: The Antecedents of Protest." Midwest Journal of Political Science 15(N, 1971):661-686.

_____. "Reference Groups and Protest Participation Among Black College Students [1968-1969]." Western Political Quarterly 26(S, 1973).

Jackson, Pamela R. "Self-Conceptions in Black Male and Female College Students." Doctoral dissertation, Michigan State U., 1972.

Jacobson, Robert L. "Black Graduate Schools Caught in Critical Dilemma." Chronicle of Higher Education, F 22, 1977.

_____. "New Negro College Group To Seek More Influence." Chronicle of Higher Education, O 20, 1969. [Association of Negro colleges]

Jaffe, A. J., and Adams, Walter. Academic and Socio-Economic Factors Related to Entrance and Retention at Two- and Four-Year Colleges in the Late 1960's. New York: Columbia U., Bureau of Applied Social Research, 1970. ERIC ED 049 679.

_____. American Higher Education in Transition. New York: Bureau of Applied Social Research, Columbia U., Ap, 1969.

_____. "Open Admissions and Academic Quality." Change 3(Mr-Ap, 1971):11,78.

_____. "Two Models of Open Enrollment." Universal Higher Education. Costs and Benefits. Washington, DC: American Council on Higher Education, 1971.

Jaffe, A. J., and Froomkin, J. "Occupational Opportunities for College--Educated Workers, 1950-75." Monthly Labor Review 101(Je, 1978).

Jefferson, Joseph Levoid. "The Effects of Anxiety on the Achievement of Black Graduate Students Taking Standardized Achievement Tests." Doctoral dissertation, Ohio State U., 1974. Univ. Microfilms Order No. 75-03105.

Jencks, Christopher. "Social Stratification and Higher Education." Harvard Educational Review, Spring, 1968.

Jenkins, Martin D. Guidelines for Institutional Self-Study of Involvement in Urban Affairs. Washington, DC: American Council on Education, My, 1971.

Jensema, Carl J. "A Preliminary Investigation of a Special Education Program for Minority Group University Students." Measurement and Evaluation in Guidance 5(Jl, 1972):326-331.

Joesting, Joan, and Joesting, Robert. "Differences Among Self-Descriptions of Gifted Black College Students and Their Less Intelligent Counterparts." Gifted Child Quarterly 13(1969):175-180.

Joffe, Barbara Maureen. "Current Attitudes Toward the Negro: A Study of American College Faculty Members." Doctoral dissertation, New York U., 1973. Univ. Microfilms Order No. 73-19429.

Johns, Daniel Jay. Correlates of Academic Success in a Predominantly Black, Open-door, Public, Urban Community College, 1970. ERIC ED 039 877.

Johnson, Davis G., and Sedlacek, William E. "Retention by Sex and Race of 1968-1972 Medical School Entrants." Journal of Medical Education 50(O, 1975):925-933.

Johnson, Eldon L. "Race and Reform." From Riot to Reason. Urbana, IL: U. of Illinois Press, 1971.

Johnson, Henry. "Black Students at White Colleges." Today's Education 64(Ja-F, 1975):33-36.

Johnson, James Leroy. "Shop and Typing for the Masses." Los Angeles Times, S 12, 1976. [Elitism in higher education]

Johnson, L. T. B. "The Interaction of Soul, Wind, and Body: A Study of the Role Compatibility, Role Conflict, and Role Resolutions of Black Student Athletes on a Predominantly White University Campus." Master's thesis, Purdue U., 1972.

Johnson, Norman J. "About this Thing Called Ghetto Education." In Black America. Edited by John F. Szwed. New York: Basic Books, 1970.

Johnson, Oscar Clayton. "The Institute for Services to Education: An Effort at Educational Reform to Ameliorate the Status of Black People in America." Doctoral dissertation, Rutgers U., 1974. Univ. Microfilms Order No. 74-27310.

Johnson, Roosevelt C. "Black Administrators and Higher Education." The Black Scholar, N, 1969.

_____. "Black Males and White Females Will Compete, But That's Not The Real Problem." (letter) Chronicle of Higher Education, N 19, 1973.

_____. (ed.). Black Scholars on Higher Education in the 70's, 1974. ECCa Publications, 2425 N. High Street, Columbus, OH 43202.

_____. "Irreparable Cleavages in the Academic Community." NASPA Journal 10(Jl, 1972): 21-25.

Johnson, Sheila K. "It's Action, But Is It Affirmative?" New York Times Magazine, My 11, 1975.

Jolly, Henry Paul, and Larson, Thomas A. Participation of Women and Minorities on U.S. Medical School Faculties. Washington, DC: Association of American Medical Colleges, 1976.

Jones, J. Charles, Harris, Lynn J., and Hauck, William E. "Differences in Perceived Sources of Academic Difficulties: Black Students in Predominantly White Colleges." Journal of Negro Education 44(Fall, 1975):519-529.

Jones, Phillip E. The Changing Profile of Black Administrators in Predominantly White Colleges and Universities, Mr 14, 1977. ERIC ED 138 192.

_____. Educational Opportunity Students: Their Learning Environments and Achievements, Ap 22, 1976. ERIC ED 125 518.

_____. (ed.). Historical Perspectives on the Development of Equal Opportunity in Higher Education. Iowa City, IO: American College Testing Program, 1978.

Jones, Sandra, and Diener, Edward. "Ethnic Preference of College Students for their Own and Other Racial Groups." Social Behavior and Personality 4(1976):225-231.

Jordan, C. L. Black Academic Libraries: An Inventory. Atlanta, GA: Atlanta U., 1970.

Jordan, Vernon E., Jr. "Blacks and Higher Education--Some Reflections." Daedalus 104 (Winter, 1975):160-165.

Jorgensen, Carl. "Countering Past Discrimination Through Affirmative Action." American Sociologist, Ag, 1974:153-157. [See, below, Lords]

Joseph, Gloria I. "Black Students on the Predominantly White Campus." Journal of the National Association of Women Deans and Counselors, Winter, 1969.

Joyner, Nancy Douglas. "'Reverse' Discrimination in Student Financial Aid for Higher Education: The Flanagan Case in Perspective." Journal of Law and Education 6(Jl, 1977):327-348.

Jung, Steven M. and others. A Study of State Oversight in Post-secondary Education. Washington, DC: Department of Health, Education, and Welfare, Office of Planning, Budgeting, and Evaluation, 1977.

Kamens, David. "Colleges and Elite Formation: The Case of Prestigious American Colleges." Sociology of Education 47(Summer, 1974): 354-378.

Kapel, David E. "Attitudes Toward Selected Stimuli. Commonality and Differences in Two Dissimilar High-Risk Black College Groups." Urban Education 8(0, 1973):297-310.

Kapel, David E., and Wexler, Norman. "Conceptual Structures of High Risk Black and Regular Freshmen Toward College Related Stimuli." Journal of Negro Education 41 (Winter, 1972):16-25.

_____. An Investigation of Selected Factors in the Affective Domains of High Risk Black and Regular College Freshmen. Washington, DC: American Educational Research Association, Mr 6, 1970. ERIC ED 045 017.

Kaplan, Barbara. "Open Admissions: A Critique." Liberal Education 58(My, 1972):210-221.

Karabel, Jerome. "Open Admissions: Toward Meritocracy or Equality?" Change, My, 1972.

_____. "Perspectives on Open Admissions." Educational Record 53(Winter, 1972):30-44.

Karabel, Jerome, and Astin, Alexander W. "Social Class, Academic Ability, and College 'Quality.'" Social Forces 53(Mr, 1975): 381-398.

Karweit, Nancy. Patterns of Educational Activities: Discontinuities and Sequences. Baltimore, MD: Center for Social Organization of Schools, Johns Hopkins U. Press, 1977.

Katz, Irwin and others. "Factors Affecting Response to White Intellectual Standards at Two Negro Colleges." Psychological Reports 27(D, 1970):995-1003.

Kaufman, Harold. "Black Engineering Students. Why the Poor Retention Rate?" New Engineer (Ja, 1977):33-38.

Kay, Patricia M. and others. "Selecting Tests to Predict the Need for Remediation in a University Open Admissions Population." Measurement and Evaluation in Guidance 4(O, 1971):154-159.

Kelly, Ernece B. "Black Community and White College." Integrated Education, N-D, 1968: 30-37.

Kelly, William Melvin. "The Ivy League Negro." Esquire Magazine, Ag, 1963.

Kendrick, S. A. "The Coming Segregation of Our Selective Colleges." College Board Review, Winter, 1967-1968.

_____. "Extending Educational Opportunity--Problems of Recruitment, Admissions, High Risk Students." Liberal Education, Mr, 1969.

_____. "Minority Students On Campus." In The Minority Student on the Campus: Expectations and Possibilities. Edited by Robert A. Altman and Patricia O. Snyder. N, 1970. Western Interstate Commission for Higher Education, P.O. Drawer "P," Boulder, CO 80302.

Kendrick, S. A., and Thomas, Charles L. "Transition from School to College." Review of Educational Research 40(F, 1970):151-179.

Keniston, Kenneth, and Lerner, Michael. "The Unholy Alliance Against the Campus." New York Times Magazine, N 8, 1970.

Kerr, Clark. "'The University' Civil Rights and Civic Responsibilities." Congressional Record, Je 23, 1964:14257-14258.

Kilson, Martin, Jr. "Campus Radicalism." New America, S 29, 1969.

_____. "Negro Separation in the Colleges." Harvard Today, Spring, 1968.

Kimbo, Conney Matthew. "The Problems of Black Students in Liberal Arts Colleges: As Perceived by the Black and White College Communities." Doctoral dissertation, U. of Iowa, 1973. Univ. Microfilms Order No. 74-16654.

Kimmons, Willie James. Black Administrators in Public Community Colleges: Self-Perceived Role and Status. New York: Carlton Press, 1977.

King, Kenneth J. "African Students in Negro American Colleges: Notes on the Good African." Phylon 36(1970):16-30.

Kirp, David L., and Yudof, Mark G. "De Funis and Beyond." Change 6(N, 1974):22-26.

Kirschner, Alan H. Annual Statistical Report of the Member Institutions. New York: United Negro College Fund, Ja, 1977.

Klopf, Gordon, and Bowman, Gerda. Teacher Education in a Social Context. Working Copy. New York: Bank Street College of Education, Ja, 1966. ERIC ED 015 881.

Knight, James H. "Counseling Black Students on Integrated Campuses." Journal of College Placement 32(Ap-My, 1972):30-37.

Knighten, Jacqueline J. "Self-Concept: Black Students on a Predominantly White Campus." Doctoral dissertation, U. of Northern Colorado, 1975. Univ. Microfilms Order No. 75-23318.

Knoell, Dorothy M. "Those Not in College." New Directions for Community Colleges 1 (Autumn, 1973):107-122.

Knoll, Erwin. "Colleges: An Imprint Already." Southern Education Report, Jl-Ag, 1968. [Black militancy in colleges]

Koch, James V. "Student Choice of Undergraduate Major Field of Study and Private Internal Rates of Return." Industrial and Labor Relations Review 26(O, 1972):680-685.

Kohen, Andrew I. and others. "Factors Affecting Individual Persistence Rates in Undergraduate College Programs." American Educational Research Journal 15(Spring, 1978):233-252.

Kolstad, Andrew. National Longitudinal Study of the High School Class of 1972. Attrition from College: The Class of 1972 Two and One-Half Years After High School Graduation, 1977. ERIC ED 144 989.

Konheim, Beatrice G. "Report of the Council Committee on Discrimination." AAUP Bulletin 58(Summer, 1972):160-163.

Kuck, Elizabeth. "Providing Equal Employment Opportunities--A Challenge to Personnel Administrators." Journal of the College and University Personnel Association, 1969.

Kurland, Norman D. "More Negroes in College. A Program for Action Now." School and Society, Ja 22, 1966.

LaFarge, John. "The Higher Education of Negroes in the United States." Ecclesiastical Review 91(1934):130-153.

Lane, Ellen A. "Childhood characteristics of Black College Graduates Reared in Poverty" Developmental Psychology 8(Ja, 1973):42-45.

Lane, Hugh W. "Admissions Policy: Implications and Consequences. II." Liberal Education 56(My, 1970):278-285.

_____. "Financing of Higher Education." Congressional Record, Ap 18, 1972. E 3895-3898.

_____. "Response to Winton H. Manning's Paper." Barriers to Higher Education. New York: College Entrance Examination Board, 1971:100-108. [See Manning, below]

_____. "Where Do Black Students Go to College and Why?" Journal of the National Association of College Admissions Counselors 16 (S, 1971):22-24.

Lane, Hugh W. and others. "What Black [College] Students Want from You." College Management, Mr, 1969.

Landberg, George, and Freedman, Philip L. "Self-Selection of Student Teachers." Integrated Education, Ag-N, 1965.

Lao, Rosina C. "Internal-External Control and Competent and Innovative Behavior Among Negro College Students." Journal of Personality and Social Psychology 14(Mr, 1970): 263-270.

Lattimer, Peter B. "Admissions Counseling of Black Students at an Open Door Admissions College." Journal of the National Association of College Admissions Counselors 16 (Jl, 1971):16-17.

Lawson, Cassell A. "A Study of the Differential Effects of Integrated Living Environment on the Black and White College Student." Doctoral dissertation, U. of Notre Dame, 1974.

Lederman, Marie Jean. "Open Admissions and Teaching English: Birds Caged and Uncaged." Educational Forum 37(Mr, 1973):286-292.

Lee, Alfred M. "Can Social Fraternities Be Democratic?" Journal of Higher Education 26 (1955):173-179.

_____. "Discrimination in College Fraternities and Sororities." School and Society 79(1954):199.

Lee, John Robert E. III. "Toward Black Consciousness and Acceptance: A Study of Relevant Attitudes and Practices in Big Eight Football." Doctoral dissertaiton, U. of Kansas, 1973. Univ. Microfilms Order No. 74-12505.

Leeson, Jim. "Colleges and 'Choice.'" Southern Education Report, O, 1968.

_____. "Most Students [in Ten Negro Colleges] See a Strong Future." Southern Education Report, Je, 1969.

Lennon, Frank and others. The Beginning of a Journey--A Report on Minority Programs in Predominantly White Dental Schools, Ap, 1974. ERIC ED 125 383.

Leonard, Walter J. "A Tower of Glass, Not Ivory. A View of Minority Students in Predominantly White Institutions." Harvard Crimson, N 9, 1976.

Lepper, Mary M. Minority Access to Higher Education: Problems, Trends, and Challenges. Washington, DC: Office of Civil Rights, Jl, 1975.

Leslie, Larry L. Higher Education Opportunity: A Decade of Progress. Washington, DC: American Association for Higher Education, 1977.

Lessing, Elise E., and Zagorin, Susan W. "Black Power Ideology and College Students' Attitudes Toward Their Own and Other Racial Groups." Journal of Personality and Social Psychology 21(Ja, 1972):61-73.

Lester, Richard A. Antibias Regulation of Universities: Faculty Problems and Their Solutions. New York: McGraw-Hill, 1973.

Levin, Henry M. "Financing Higher Education and Social Equity: Implications for Lifelong Learning." School Review 86(My, 1978): 327-347.

Levine, Murray, and Levine, David I. "To the Editor." American Historical Review 76(Ap, 1971):581-582. [Comment on McPherson, "White Liberals and Black Power in Negro Education, 1865-1915," below]

Levine, Naomi. "Affirmative Action--Or Equal Opportunity." Congress Bi-Weekly, N 9, 1973.

Levine, Naomi, and Schappes, Morris U. "The DeFunis Issue: More Ado." Jewish Currents O, 1974. [Pro and con on the preferential admission case]

Levinson, Dian S. "How Colleges Practice Bias." Congress Weekly 14(M4 7, 1947):6-8.

Levy, Nissim and others. "Personality Types Among Negro College Students." Educational and Psychological Measurement 32(Autumn, 1972):641-653.

Lewinson, Barbara. "Black Students in Eastern Colleges, 1895-1940." Crisis 81(Mr, 1974): 84-87.

Lichtman, Richard. "The Ideological Function of the University." International Socialist Journal, D, 1967.

Light, Donald, Jr. and others. The Dynamics of University Protest. Chicago: Nelson-Hall, 1977.

Ligon, J. Frank (ed.). Confrontations. Minorities/Majorities. Rights/Responsibilities. Change/Establishment. Corvallis, OR: Oregon State U. Press, 1970.

Linderfelt, Florence Margaret. "A Comparative Study of the Rorschach Protocols of Japanese and Caucasian College Students." Master's thesis, U. of Hawaii, 1949.

Lindsey, Robert. "White/Caucasian--and Rejected." New York Times Magazine, Ap 3, 1977. [Affirmative action in higher education]

Link, C. R. "Graduate Education, School Quality, Experience, Student Ability, and Earnings." Journal of Business 48(O, 1975).

Linowitz, Sol and others. Campus Tensions: Analysis and Recommendations. Washington, DC: American Council on Education, 1970.

Lipsky, Michael (ed.). Synopsis of Edward Bound Winter Conference...January 16-19, 1968. Sponsored by the Office of Economic Opportunity. Educational Associates, Inc., 1717 Massachusetts Avenue, N.W., Washington, DC 20030.

Littig, Lawrence W. A Study of Certain Personality Correlates of Occupational Aspirations of Negro and White College Students, Final Report. Washington, DC: Howard U. ERIC ED 022 419.

Lorch, Barbara D. "Reverse Discrimination in Hiring in Sociology Departments: A Preliminary Report." American Sociologist, Ag, 1973:116-120. [See, above, Jorgensen]

Lounsbury, Jerald E. "An Analysis of the Satisfaction with College Experienced by Special Project Students, Primarily Inner-City and Negro, at a Non-Metropolitan University as Measured by the College Student Questionnaire." Doctoral dissertation, Michigan State U., 1971.

Luetgert, M. J. "The Ethnic Student: Academic and Social Problems." Adolescence 12(F, 1977):321-327.

Lykes, Richard W. "A History of the Division of Higher Education, United States Office of Education, from Its Creation in 1911 until the Establishment of the Department of Health, Education, and Welfare in 1953." Doctoral dissertation, American U., 1960.

Lyons, James E. "The Adjustment of Black Students to Predominantly White Campuses." Journal of Negro Education 42(Fall, 1973): 462-466.

Lyons, Richard D. "Gifts from Parents to 'Buy' Places in Professional Schools on the Rise." New York Times, Ap 23, 1978.

McCarthy, John Rollin. "The Slavery Issue in Selected Colleges and Universities in Illinois, Ohio, Kentucky, and Indiana: 1840-1860." Doctoral dissertation, Florida State U., 1974. Univ. Microfilms Order No. 75-12,656.

McCarthy, Joseph L., and Wolfle, Dael. "Doctorates Granted to Women and Minority Group Members." Science 189(S, 1975):856-859.

McClain, John Dudley, Jr. Political Profiles of Black College Students in the South: Social-Political Attitudes, Preferences, Personality, and Characteristics. Atlanta, GA: Resurgens Publications, 1977.

McClendon, McKee, Jr., and Eitzen, D. Stanley. "Interracial Contact on Collegiate Basketball Teams: A Test of Sherif's Theory of Superordinate Goals." Social Science Quarterly 55(Mr, 1975):926-930.

McCormack, Wayne (ed.). The Bakke Decision: Implications for Higher Education Admissions. Washington, DC: American Council on Education, 1978.

McDaniel, Clyde O., Jr., and Balgopal, Pallassana R. "Patterns of Black Leadership: Implications for Social Work Education." Journal of Education for Social Work 14 (Winter, 1978):87-93.

McDiffett, Kenneth E. Minority Group Involvement in University Life, Mr 17, 1970. ERIC ED 039 604.

McKee, James Willis. "Patterns of Institutional Response to Blacks in Higher Education." Doctoral dissertation, Indiana U., 1971. Univ. Microfilms Order No. 72-05121.

McKenzie, Obie L. "Communicating with Black College Graduates--You Can't Get There From Here." Journal of College Placement 30(Ap-My, 1970):93-96.

McMahon, Walter W. "Influences on Investment by Blacks in Higher Education." American Economic Review 66(My, 1976):320-323.

Mackey, Paul R. "A Survey of Negro Participation in Intercollegiate Athletics in American Co-racial Colleges and Universities." Master's thesis, Ohio State U., 1940.

McNeil, Elaine O. and others. "Have Our Colleges and Universities Provided Adquately for the Special Education Needs of Blacks?" Change 9(Je, 1977):54-56.

McNett, Ian E. "U.S. Asking Colleges in 17 States to Submit Desegregation Plans." Chronicle of Higher Education, Ja 27, 1969.

McPherson, James M. "The New Puritanism: Values and Goals of Freedmen's Education in America." In The University in Society. Edited by Lawrence Stone. 2 vols. Princeton, NJ: Princeton U. Press, 1974.

_____. "White Liberals and Black Power in Negro Education, 1865-1915." American Historical Review 75(Je, 1970):1357-1386.

McSwine, Bartley. "Black Visions, White Realities." Change 3(My-Je, 1971):28-34.

Mack, Faite. "A Study of the Relationship between the Characteristics of Persisters and Nonpersisters in an Educational Opportunity Program." Doctoral dissertation, U. of Illinois, 1972.

Mackey, Elvin. "Some Observations on Coping Styles of Black Students on White Campuses." Journal of the American College Health Association 21(1972):126-130.

Majer, K. Minority Underpresentation in Natural Science Graduate Programs. La Jolla, CA: U. of California, San Diego, 1975.

Maliver, Bruce L. "Anti-Negro Bias Among Negro College Students." Journal of Personality and Social Psychology, N, 1965.

Mann, Peter B. Higher Education in Black and White. A Seminar Report. Washington, DC: American Association for Higher Education, 1972.

Manning, Winton H. "Personal and Institutional Assessment: Alternatives to Tests of Scholastic Aptitude and Achievement in the Admissions Process." Barriers to Higher Education. New York: College Entrance Examination Board, 1971.

Mantovani, Richard E. Medical Student Finances and Personal Characteristics, 1974-75. Hyattsville, MD: Public Health Service, Bureau of Health Manpower, 1977.

Marcuse, F. L. "'Gentlemen's Agreement' in Science." School and Society 74(1951):152-153.

_____. "Some Attitudes toward Employing Negroes as Teachers in a Northern University." Journal of Negro Education 17(1948):18-26.

Mares, Kenneth R., and Levine, Daniel U. "Survey of Academic Programs for Disadvantaged Students in Higher Education." Research in Higher Education 3(Je, 1975):169-176.

Marien, Michael. Public Noneconomic Benefits of Higher Education. Working Draft. Syracuse, NY: Syracuse U. Research Corporation, Educational Policy Research Center, Mr, 1972. ERIC ED 062 616.

Marshall, Thurgood. "The State-Supported University Cases." In The Negro Handbook, 1946-1947. Edited by Florence Murray. New York: Wyn, 1947:50-53.

Mather, Anne D. University-Wide Planning for the Minority Student, Ja, 1975. ERIC ED 149 663.

Maxey, E. James and others. Trends in the Academic Abilities, Background Characteristics, and Educational and Vocational Plans of College-Bound Students: 1970-1 to 1974-5, My, 1976. ERIC ED 141 390.

May, Eugene P. "Type of Housing and Achievement of Disadvantaged University Students." College Student Journal 8(Ap-My, 1974):48-51.

Mayes, Sharon S. "The Increasing Stratification of Higher Education: Ideology and Consequence." Journal of Educational Thought 11(Ap, 1977):16-27.

Mayhew, Lewis B. Reform in Graduate Education. Atlanta, GA: Southern Regional Education Board, 1972.

Maykovich, Minako Kurokawa. "Changes in Racial Stereotypes Among [American] College Students [Since 1932]." British Journal of Social Psychiatry and Community Health 6 (1972).

Medley, Morris L., and Johnse, Kathryn P. "The Economics of College Plans Among Black High School Seniors." Journal of Negro Education 45(Spring, 1976):134-140.

Medsker, Leland L., and Trent, James W. The Influence of Different Types of Public Higher Institutions on College Attendance from Varying Socioeconomic and Ability Levels. Berkeley, CA: U. of California, 1965.

Meeth, L. Richard. "Breaking Racial Barriers: Part I: Inter-racial Student-Exchange Programs; Part II: Inter-Institutional Cooperative Programs between Colleges for Negroes and Colleges for Whites; Part II: Scholarships for Negro Students in Predominantly White Colleges and Universities." Journal of Higher Education, Mr-My, 1966.

Melnick, Murray. Higher Education for the Disadvantaged: Summary, Abstracts and Reviews of Research in Higher Education, Number 12. [Upward Bound students] Ap, 1971. ED 052 695.

_____. Review of Higher Education for the Disadvantaged, S 7, 1971. ERIC ED 054 288.

Menacker, Julius. "Counterproductive High School Requirements for College Admission." Educational Record 54(Winter, 1973):68-73.

_____. "Rivalry Among Minorities in Higher Education." Integrateducation 12(N-D, 1974): 24-27.

Mendenhall, Thomas C. "Admissions Policy: Implications and Consequences." Liberal Education 56(1970).

Menges, Robert J. "Cognitive Bias and College Admission." Integrated Education, Ja-Ap, 1974:30-32.

Merritt, Mary Strader, Sedlacek, William E., and Brooks, Glenwood C., Jr. "Quality of Interracial Interaction Among University Students." Integrateducation 15(My-Je, 1977).

Meyers, Michael. "The New Black Apartheid." Change 4(O, 1972):8-9.

_____. "Voluntary Segregation: One Viewpoint." Crisis 81(Ja, 1974):12-14.

Middleton, Lorenzo. "Black Professors on White Campuses." Chronicle of Higher Education 17(O 2, 1978).

Middleton, Lorenzo, and Sievert, William A. "The Uneasy Undercurrent." Chronicle of Higher Education, My 15, 1978. [Blacks on predominantly white campuses]

Middleton, Russell, and Moland, John. "Humor in Negro and White Subcultures: A Study of Jokes Among University Students." American Sociological Review 24(F, 1959):61-69.

Miller, Albert H. "Problems of the Minority Student on the Campus." Liberal Education, Mr, 1969.

_____. Problems of the Minority Student on the Campus. Washington, DC: Association of American Colleges, Ja 15, 1969. ERIC ED 026 018.

Miller, L. J. "Afro-Americans in American Universities." Voice of the Negro 3(S, 1906):655-657.

Milliken, Robert. "Prejudice and Counseling Effectivenss." Personnel and Guidance Journal, Mr, 1965.

Milliken, Robert, and Clardy, Fay. "Prejudice and Discrimination in College Student Personnel Services." Journal of Negro Education, Winter, 1967.

Mingle, James R. "Faculty and Departmental Response to Increased Black Student Enrollment." Journal of Higher Education 49 (My-Je, 1978):201-217.

Minor, Willie. "The Status of Blacks with Doctoral Degrees in Collegiate Business Education." Doctoral dissertation, Arizona State U., 1976. Univ. Microfilms Order No. 77-08132.

Minority-Awareness: Programming for Success, 1976. ERIC ED 130 689.

Minter, J. John, and Thompson, Ian M. (eds.). Colleges and Universities as Agents of Social Change. Boulder, CO: Western Interstate Commission for Higher Education, 1968.

Mitchell, Clarence. "Harvest of Hate." Crisis 81(D, 1974):343-345.

Mitchell, Horace. "The Black Experience in Higher Education." Counseling Psychologist 2 (1970):30-36.

Mitchell, Oliver C., Jr. "Don't Challenge My Blackness!" Crisis 85(Ag-S, 1978):250.

Mohlenhoff, George, and Scott, Arthur. "Desegregation Progress Noted at State Institutions." Pennsylvania Education 3 (S-O, 1971):31-36. [Higher education]

Mommsen, Kent G. "Black Doctorates in American Higher Education: A Cohort Analysis." Journal of Social and Behavioral Sciences 20(Spring, 1974):101-117.

_____. "Career Patterns of Black American Doctorates." Doctoral dissertation, Florida State U., 1970.

Monlouis, Wilma D. "Higher Education Opportunities for High-Risk Disadvantaged Students: A Review of the Literature." Currents '70, F, 1970.

Monro, John U. "The Case for Special Attention to Black Student Needs in Higher Education." In Beyond Desegregation. Urgent Issues in the Education of Minorities. New York: College Entrance Examination Board, 1978:13-17.

Montayne, Theodore II. "Assessing Prejudice Toward Negroes at Three Universities Using the Lost-Letter Technique." Psychological Reports 29(O, 1971):531-537.

Montgomery, Lee. Black Administrators and Black Faculty at Work in White Institutions. New York: AFRAM Associates, Ja 20, 1971.

Moore, Gilbert. "Blacks and Colleges: 1. The Dot and the Elephant." Change 4(Ap, 1972): 33-41.

Moore, William, Jr. Academic Remediation in Higher Education: Problems and Prospect. Atlanta: Southern Education Foundation, n.d.

Moore, William, Jr., and Wagstaff, Lonnie H. Black Educators in White Colleges. San Francisco, CA: Jossey-Bass, 1974.

Moorman, Elliott Duane. "The Benefit of Anger." Saturday Review, Je 21, 1969. [Blacks in colleges]

Morgan, Gordon D. The Ghetto College Student: A Descriptive Essay on College Youth From the Inner City. Iowa City, IO: American College Testing Program, 1970.

Morris, Ernest R. "Black Admissions Counselors: Whom Must They Serve?" Journal of the National Association of College Admissions Counselors 16(My, 1971):16-17.

Moss, James A. "Programs for the Disadvantaged: Perspectives and Problems." Black Academy Review 1(Summer, 1970):16-21.

Motley, Frank. "Black Dean, White College." Journal of the National Association of College Admissions Counselors 21(Je, 1977):13-14.

Muehl, Siegmar, and Muehl, Lois. "A College-Level Compensatory Program for Educationally Disadvantaged Black Students: Interim Findings and Reflections." Journal of Negro Education 41(Winter, 1972):65-81.

Mundel, DAvid S. "Federal Aid to Higher Education: An Analysis of Federal Subsidies to Undergraduate Education." In U.S. Congress, 92nd, 2nd session, Joint Economic Committee, The Economics of Federal Subsidy Programs, Part 4--Higher Education and Manpower Subsidies. Washington, DC: GPO, Ag 28, 1972:407-463.

Musgrave, Marian E. "Failing Minority Students: Class, Caste, and Racial Bias in American Colleges." College Composition and Communication 22(F, 1971):24-29.

Myers, Edward M., and Sandeen, Arthur. "Survey of Minority and Women Student Affairs Staff Members Employed in NASPA Member Institutions." NASPA Journal 11(Jl, 1973): 2-14.

Myers, Ernest R. The Role of College-Community Relationships in Urban Higher Education Phase II--Exploratory Planning. An Exploratory Study of an Urban University Prototype. Washington, DC: Federal City College Mr, 1971. ERIC ED 059 409.

NAACP Legal Defense and Educational Fund. Dismantling Dual Systems of Public Higher Education: Criteria for a State Plan. New York: NAACP LDF, Je 11, 1973.

Nabrit, Samuel M., and Scott, Julius S., Jr. Inventory of Academic Leadership. An Analysis of the Boards of Trustees of Fifty Predominantly Black Institutions, 1970. The Southern Fellowships Fund, 795 Peachtree Street, N. E., Suite 484, Atlanta, GA 30308.

Nathan, Marvin. "The Attitude of the Jewish Student in the Colleges and Universities Toward His Religion. A Social Study of Religious Changes." Doctoral dissertation, U. of Pennsylvania, 1932.

National Association for Equal Opportunity in Higher Education. Year 2000 Plan for Parity in Higher Education. Washington, DC: The Association, 1975.

NAACP. "Black Educators in Merged Colleges." Crisis 80(N, 1973):293.

National Advisory Council on Extension and Continuing Education. Equity of Access. Continuing Education and the Part-Time Student, Mr 31, 1975. The Council, 425 Thirteenth St., N. W., Washington, DC: 20004.

National Association of State Universities and Land-Grant Colleges. Minority Enrollment at State Universities and Land-Grant Colleges, Fall 1976, O, 1977. ERIC ED 145 748.

National Board on Graduate Education. Minority Group Participation in Graduate Education. Washington, DC: National Academy of Sciences, Je,1976.

Naughton, Ezra A. "Report of the Special Project for Developing Institutions." AAUP Bulletin 58(Summer, 1972):166-167.

Nearing, Scott. "Who's Who Among College Trustees." School and Society 6(S 8, 1917): 297-299.

"Negro and Other Minority Enrollments at 2,350 Colleges." Chronicle of Higher Education, Mr 29, 1971.

"Negroes Who Teach in White Colleges." Our World, Je, 1952.

Nelson, J. E. A Review of Data Available Regarding Family Income and Financial Aid Characteristics of Students. New York: College Entrance Examination Board, 1977.

Newman, Louis Israel. A Jewish University in America? New York: Bloch, 1923.

Nichols, David C. (eds.). Perspectives on Campus Tensions. Washington, DC: American Council on Education, 1970.

Nichols, David C., and Mills, Olive (eds.). The Campus and the Racial Crisis. Washington, DC: American Council on Education, 1970.

Nieves, Luis. The GRE and the Minority Student: A Perspective, S, 1976. ERIC ED 135 827. [Graduate Record Examination]

9X, Robert. "Future Black Scientists 'Schooled.'" Muhammad Speaks, Ja 18, 1974. [Fifth Annual Conference of the National Black Science Students Organization]

Nordheimer, Jon. "Black Fraternities Big on Campus." New York Times, My 26, 1972.

Nordallie, Peter G. and others. The Role of College-Community Relationships in Urban Higher Education. Washington, DC: Bureau of Research, U.S. Office of Education, 1969.

Nowak, W. S. "Black Athlete Under Tender: An Investigation of the Sociological Background of the Negro Football Player at a Midwest University." Senior Honors Thesis, U. of Illinois, 1968.

Obatala, J. K. "Where Did Their Revolution Go?" Nation, O 2, 1972. [Black college students]

O'Daniel, Richard M. "An Exploratory Case Study on the Felt Effect of Race on Job Satisfaction by Black Administrators in White Institutions of Higher Education." Doctoral dissertation, U. of MA, 1978. Univ. Microfilms Order No. 7903817. [Five insitutions in MA]

Office for Civil Rights. Availability Data: Minorities and Women, Je, 1973. ERIC ED 098 883.

_____. Higher Education Guidelines. Executive Order 11246. Washington, DC: U.S. Department of Health, Education, and Welfare, O 1, 1972.

_____. Racial and Ethnic Enrollment Data from Institutions of Higher Education. Washington, DC: HEW [1977?] [Fall 1974 data]

Office of Institutional Research. Minority Group Enrollment, Housing, and Financial Aid Statistics, Fall, 1969-Fall, 1971. Albany, New York: State U. of New York, 1971.

Ogletree, Kathryn Marie. "Internal and External Control Beliefs Among 2 Four Year Cohort of Black Graduates from 2 Selective White University." Doctoral dissertation, Northwestern U., 1976. Univ. Microfilms Order No. 77-01321.

O'Hear, Michael F. "Black Students and White Graduate Schools." Integrated Education 11 (Jl-O, 1973):53-55.

Olive, Helen. "White Professors Grading Black Students." Improving College and University Teaching 23(Winter, 1975):31-32.

Olsen, Henry D. "The Effect of Compensatory Education Upon the Self-Concept of Academic Ability of Black and White Pre-College Students." Dissertation Abstracts International 32(3-A)S, 1971:1302.

_____. The Effect of Compensatory Education upon the Self-Concept-of-Academic Ability, Significant Others and Academic Significant Others of Black and White Pre-College Students. F, 1971. (Paper, Annual Meeting of the American Educational Research Association) ERIC ED 047 075.

Olsen, Jack and others. The Black Athletes: A Shameful Story: The Myth of Integration in American Sport. New York: Time-Life Books, 1968.

On Further Examination. Report of the Advisory Panel on the Scholastic Aptitude Test Score Decline. New York: College Entrance Examination Board, 1977.

Orbell, John M. "Protest Participation Among Southern Negro College Students." American Political Science Review, Je, 1967.

Organization for Social and Technical Innovation. Urban Universities: Rhetoric, Reality, and Conflict. Washington, DC: GPO, 1970.

Ornstein, J. A. "Discrimination in Fraternities." School and Society 81(1951):11.

Orum, Anthony M. "The Class and Status Bases of Negro Student Protest." Social Science Quarterly, D, 1968.

Orwig, M. D. Toward More Equitable Distribution of College Student Aid Funds: Problems in Assessing Student Financial Need, My, 1971. ERIC ED 052 682.

Owen, John D. Toward a More Consistent, Socially Relevant College Scholarships Policy, Ja, 1970. ERIC ED 036 280.

Packard, David. "Business Gifts [to Higher Education] Should Be Selective." Human Events, N 17, 1973.

Padre, David. "The Courting of Tony Branch." Chicago Tribune Magazine, D 12, 1976. [Efforts by colleges to recruit outstanding black athlete]

Pandey, R. E. "Intellectual Characteristics of Successful, Dropout, and Probationary Black and White University Students." Psychological Reports 34(Je, 1974):917-953.

Pantages, Timothy J., and Creedon, Carol F. "Studies of College Attrition: 1950-1975." Review of Educational Research 48(Winter, 1978):49-101.

Parenti, Michael. "Equality and Privilege in Higher Education." New Politics, Summer, 1965.

Parker, Ernest L. "A Comparison of Educational Motivation: Northern Black Students versus Southern Black Students." International Journal of Continuing Education and Training 2(Winter, 1973):299-303.

Parker, Max, and Wittmer, Joe. "The Effects of a Communications Training Program on the Racial Attitudes of Black and White Fraternity Members." Journal of College Student Personnel 17(N, 1976):500-503.

Parsons, Talcott, and Platt, Gerald M. "Age, Social Structure, and Socialization in Higher Education." Sociology of Education 43 (Winter, 1970):1-37.

Patterson, David L, and Smits, Stanley J. "Communication Bias in Black-White Groups." Journal of Psychology 88(S, 1974):9-25.

Paynter, Julie (ed.). Graduate Opportunities for Black Students, 1969-1970, 1969. Graduate Opportunities for Black Students, Care of Julie Paynter, 6753 South Chappel Avenue, Chicago, IL 60649.

Payton, Carolyn R. "Negro College Students." Doctoral dissertation project, Teachers College, Columbia U., 1962.

Peek, V. Lonnie, Jr. "The Black Student in a White University." Counseling Psychologist 2(1970):11-16.

Peng, Samuel S. "Trends in the Entry to Higher Education: 1961-1972." Educational Researcher 6(Ja, 1977):15-19.

Peng, Samuel S., Bailey, J. P., Jr., and Eckland, Bruce K. "Access to Higher Education: Results from the National Longitudinal Study of the High School Class of 1972." Educational Researcher 6(D, 1972):3-7.

Perkins, W. E., and Higginson, J. E. "Black Students: Reformists or Revolutionaries?" In The New American Revolution. Edited by Roderick Aya and Norman Miller. New York: Free Press, 1971.

Peretti, Peter O. "Closest Friendships of Black College Students: Social Intimacy." Adolescence 11(F, 1976):395-403.

Pesqueira, Richard E. "Equal Opportunity in Higher Education: Choice as Well as Access." College Board Review 97(F, 1975):10-13,19.

Peterson, Marvin W. and others. Black Students on White Campus: The Impacts of Increased Black Enrollments. Ann Arbor: Institute for Social Research, U. of Michigan, 1979.

Peterson, Roy P., and Peterson, Juanita Betz. "Southern White Institutions and Black Students: A New Partnership." Educational Record 55(Winter, 1974):13-22.

Pfeifer, C. Michael, and Schneider, Benjamin. "University Climate Perceptions by Black and White Students." Journal of Applied Psychology 59(O, 1974):660-662.

Pfeifer, C. Michael, Jr., and Sedlacek, William E. "The Validity of Academic Predictors for Black and White Students at a Predominantly White University." Journal of Educational Measurement 8(Winter, 1971):253-261.

Phillips, Romeo E. "Contemporary Crisis of the AfraAmerican Faculty in White Academe." Negro History Bulletin 39(Ap, 1976):577-579.

Pickens, William. "Southern Negro in Northern University." Voice of the Negro 2(Ap, 1905):234-236.

Piedmond, Eugene B. "Changing Racial Attitudes at a Southern University: 1947-1964." Journal of Negro Education, Winter, 1967.

Pierce, Richard M., and Norrell, Gwendolyn. "White Tutors for Black Students." Journal of College Student Personnel 11(My, 1970):169-172.

Pifer, Alan. The Higher Education of Blacks in the United States. New York: Carnegie Corporation of New York, 1973.

Theo, James Pinnock. Human Resources Development--An Emerging Role for Black Professionals in Higher Education, Ap, 1972. ERIC ED 061 404.

Pitchell, Robert J. Financing Part-Time Students: The New Majority in Postsecondary Education, Mr 11, 1974. ERIC ED 089 627.

Pitts, James P. "Does Graduation from a White College Make a Difference?" Black Collegian My, 1975.

Plaut, Richard L. "Plans for Assisting Negro Students to Enter and to Remain in College." Journal of Negro Education, Fall, 1966.

_____. "Prospects for the Entrance and Scholastic Advancement of Negroes in Higher Educational Institutions." Journal of Negro Education, Summer, 1967.

_____. Searching and Salvaging Talent Among Socially Disadvantaged Populations, Ap 24, 1963. ERIC ED 013 261.

Poindexter, C. C. "Some Student Experiences." Voice of the Negro 3(My, 1906):335-338. [Blacks in northern colleges]

Poinsett, Alex. "Education and the New Generation." Ebony 33(Ag, 1978):70-74.

Pollard, William B. III. "A Black Student Looks to the Future." Counseling Psychologist 2(1970):38-39.

Porter, Andrew, and Stanley, Julian C. A Comparison of the Predictability of Academic Success of Negro College Students with that of White College Students, 1967. ERIC ED 017 546.

Posner, James Robert. "Income and Occupation of Negro and White College Graduates: 1931-1966." Doctoral dissertation, Princton U., 1970. Univ. Microfilms Order No. 71-14404.

Pottinger, J. Stanley. Affirmative Action and Faculty Policy, My 5, 1970. ERIC ED 062 929.

_____. "The Drive Toward Equality." Change 4(O, 1972).

Poussaint, Alvin. "The Black Administrator in the White University." Black Scholar 6 (S, 1974):8-14.

_____. "The Psychology of Coping with Racism." Black Collegian 4(My-Je, 1974):34-35,39.

President's Commission on Campus Unrest. The Report...Campus Unrest. Washington, DC: GPO, 1970.

Pride, Richard, and Donaldson, Robert. "Black Students at a White University." Journal of the Association of Social and Behavioral Sciences 15(Fall, 1969):22-38.

"Problems at Interracial Colleges." Crisis, Mr, 1952.

Proctor, Samuel. "The College and the Urban Community; Racial Insularity and National Purpose." Liberal Education, Mr, 1969.

_____. "Racial Pressures on Urban Institutions." The Campus and the Racial Crisis. Washington, DC: American Council on Education, 1969.

"Prominent Black Medical Professor Rips Medical Schools Ban on Black Students." Muhammad Speaks, Mr 7, 1969. [Dr. Alfred Haynes, Johns Hopkins]

Proxmire, William. "The Challenge of Equality in Higher Education." Marquette University Education Review 1(Spring, 1970):4-5,12-14.

Pruitt, Anne S. "Black Poor at White Colleges-- Personal Growth Goals." Journal of College Student Personnel 11(1970):3-6.

Public Affairs Committee. Religion and Race: Barriers for College. NY: Public Affairs Committee, 1948.

Puttkammer, Charles. Negroes in the Ivy League, 1962. ERIC ED 150 924.

Rabinove, Samuel. "Law School Minorities: What Price Admission?" America 128(Ap 28, 1973): 387-389.

"Racially Identifiable Dual Systems of Higher Education: The 1971 Affirmative Duty to Desegregate." Wayne Law Review 18(1972).

Radner, R., and Miller, L. S. "Demand and Supply in U.S. Higher Education: A Progress Report." American Economic Review, My, 1970.

Rafky, David M. "Ambiguities in Race Relations: Blacks and Whites in Higher Education." International Journal of Group Tensions 3 (1973):12-27.

_____. "The Black Academic in the Marketplace." Change 3(O, 1971):6,65.

_____. Race Relations in Higher Education. Syracuse, NY: Syracuse U., 1972. ERIC ED 060 773.

_____. "Wit and Racial Conflict among Colleagues." Integrated Education (Ja-F, 1972): 39-43.

Raines, Howell. "Higher Education." My Soul is Rested. Movement Days in the Deep South Remembered. nY: Putnam's, 1977.

Rainsford, George, N. Congress and Higher Education in the Nineteenth Century. Nashville, TN: U. of Tennessee Press, 1972.

Randolph, Harland. "The Northern Student Movement." Educational Record, Fall, 1964.

Raspberry, William. "Fighting Campus Discrimination." Washington Post, Mr 15, 1974. [On Jewish groups and the campaign against affirmative action programs]

Rauh, Joseph L., Jr., and Scheuer, James H. "The Rauh-Scheuer Letters [on Affirmative Action in Medical Schools]." ADA World 30(Je, 1975):9,11.

Ray, Lillian Beatrice. "A Study of the Socioeconomic, Intellectual, and Cultural Status of Negro College Students." Master's thesis, 1939. CO (Abstract in: U. of Colorado Studies, 26:108-109.

Raymond, Richard D. "The Impact of Financial Aid Upon Equality of Opportunity in Higher Education." Journal of Student Financial Aid 6(N, 1976):39-51.

Record, Wilson. "White Sociologist and Black Students in Predominantly White Universities." Sociological Quarterly 15(Spring, 1974):164-182.

Redish, Martin H. "Preferential Law School Admissions and the Equal Protection Clause: An Analysis of the Competing Arguments." UCLA Law Review 22(D, 1974):343-400.

Reed, Rodney J. "Increasing the Opportunities for Black Students in Higher Education." Journal of Negro Education 47(Spring, 1978): 143-150.

Reeves, Alexis Scott and others. [Three variously titled articles on black colleges] Norfolk Ledger-Star, Je 6-8, 1978.

Regents of the State University of New York. "Minorities and Post-Secondary Education." Integrated Education 11(Ja-F, 1973):58-64.

Reid, Robert D. "Curricular Changes in Colleges and Universities for Negroes." Journal of Higher Education, Mr, 1967.

Reid, Susan. "Making Social Work Education More Responsive to the Needs of Black Students." Journal of Education for Social Work 13(F, 1977):70-75.

Reidhaar, Donald L. "Minority Preference in Student Admissions." Journal of College and University Law 2(Spring, 1975):197-209.

Report of the First National Congress of Black Professionals in Higher Education. Austin, TX: Hogg Foundation for Mental Health, 1973.

Report on Higher Education Public Service Responsibilities in the Black Community. Urbana, IL: Institute of Government and Public Affairs, U. of Illinois, 1972.

Resource Group VII. Equal Opportunity, Special Needs of Minorities in Higher Education and Methods of Meeting Needs. Hartford, CT: Commission for Higher Education, 1973.

Rever, Philip R. (ed.). Open admissions and Equal Access. Iowa City, IO: American College Testing Program, 1971.

Rhodes, Barbara A. "Special College Entry Programs for Afro-Americans." School and Society 98(O, 1970):360-362.

Richardson, Elliot L. "HEW, Affirmative Action and the Universities." Commentary 53(My, 1972):10. [letter]

Riccobono, J. A. and others. Money and College: Differences in Ability and SES, S, 1976. ERIC ED 148 280.

Riddick, Melvin Cornelious. "Black students' Preferences for Black and White Counselors." Doctoral dissertation, George Washington U., 1976. Univ. Microfilms Order No. 76-23557.

Riessman, Frank. "The Vocationalization of Higher Education: Duping the Poor." Social Policy 2(My-Je, 1971):3-4.

Rivera, Haydee. "Early College Entrance for Ghetto Young Adults." Report of the Commission on Undergraduate Education. New York: New York U., 1971.

Roark, Anne C. "Business Graduates Find It Helps to Be Female or Black--or Both." Chronicle of Higher Education, Ag 1, 1977.

Robb, Felix C., and Tyler, James W. "The Law and Segregation in Southern Higher Education: A Chronology." Educational Forum 16(My, 1952):475-480.

Roberts, Roy J., and Nichols, Robert C. Participants in the National Achievement Scholarship Program for Negroes. ERIC ED 011 527, n.d.

Roberts, Wallace. "The Coming of the Common College." Saturday Review, Je 21, 1969.

Robinson, Omelia T. "Contributions of Black American Academic Women to American Higher Education." Doctoral dissertation, Wayne State U., 1978. Univ. Microfilms Order No. 7816079.

Robinson, Walter G., Jr. "Blacks in Higher Education Before 1865." Doctoral dissertation, Southern Illinois U., 1976.

Roche, Richard J. Catholic Colleges and the Negro Student. Washington, DC: Catholic U. of America Press, 1948.

Rodriguez, Richard. "Beyond the Minority Myth." Change 10(S, 1978):28-34.

Roizen, Judy. "Black Students in Higher Education." In Teachers and Students: Aspects of American Higher Education. Edited by Martin Trow. New York: McGraw-Hill, 1976.

Rosen, Bruce. "The Use of Potentially Discriminatory Questions on College Applications in the Southern United States." Journal of Negro Education, Spring, 1969.

Rosen, David, Brunner, Seth, and Fowler, Steve. Open Admissions: The Promise and the Lie of Open Access to American Higher Education. Lincoln, NB: Nebraska Curriculum Development Center, Andrews Hall, U. of Nebraska, 1973. [Nebraska, California, and New York City]

Ross, James J. "A Study of Racially Integrated Rooms in Men's Residence Halls at a State University." Master's thesis, Illinois State U., 1970.

Rosser, James. "Higher Education and the Black American: An Overview." Journal of Afro-American Issues 1(F, 1972):189-204.

Rossmann, Jack E. Open Admissions and the College Environment, Ap 8, 1972. ERIC ED 060 818.

Routh, Frederick B., and Waldo, Everett A. Affirmative Action in Employment in Higher Education: A Consultation... Washington, DC: U.S. Commission on Civil Rights, 1977.

Rowe, Cyprian. "Blacker Than Thou: The Struggle for Campus Unity." Black World 23(D, 1973):80-83.

Rowley-Rotunno, Virginia. "Open Admissions: A New Promise for the 'Disadvantaged.'" Freedomways 13(1973):152-156.

Rubin, Dorothy. "Halo Effect in Self-Rated Attitudes of Certain Black College Freshmen." Psychological Reports 26(Je, 1970):940.

Ruchkin, Judith P. "Expanding Opportunities in Higher Education: Some Trends and Counter-trends." IRCD Bulletin 8(F, 1972):3-6.

_____. "Selected Issues in Collegiate Compensatory Education." In Opening Opportunities for Disadvantaged Learners. Edited by A. Harry Passow. New York: Teachers College Press, 1972:243-259.

Ruhe, Ed. "Programs for Blacks at the College Level." TAC' TIC (National Student Association), S-O, 1968.

_____. "Programs for Blacks at the College Level." Part 2. TAC' TIC, N-D, 1968.

Russell, Carlos. "Open Admissions...Where Now?" Amsterdam News, Jl 8, 1972.

Rustin, Bayard. "A Word to Black Students." Dissent 17(N-D, 1970):496, 581-585. [Commencement address, My 31, 1970, at Tuskegee Institute]

Sabine, Gordon. "Encouraging Minority Enrollments: Five Institutions' Efforts." Intellect 106(F, 1978):329-332.

Sampel, David D. A Comparison of Negro and White Students Using the SCAT in Predicting College Grades, 1969. ERIC ED 034 244.

Sampel, David D., and Seymour, Warren R. "The Academic Success of Black Students: A Dilemma." Journal of College Student Personnel 12(Jl, 1971):243-247.

_____. Prediction of Academic Success of Black Students: A Dilemma, 1969. ERIC ED 040 416.

Sampson, Charles. "An Analysis of Administrative Responses to Incidents of Student Rebellion on American College Campuses." Journal of Social and Behavioral Sciences 19(Summer-Fall, 1972):50-58.

Sanders, K. B., and Love, L. L. "Causes of Failures of Negro Students in a Northern University." Journal of Negro Education, O, 1941.

Sandusky, Nancy, and Johnson, Susan. An Evaluation of the Special Services Program for Disadvantaged Students in Post-Secondary Institutions, Ja 31, 1976. ERIC ED 145 743.

Satterwhite, Frank Joseph. "Black Power and Education: A Political Theory and Model of Black Higher Education." Doctoral dissertation, Stanford U., 1977. Univ. Microfilms Order No. 77-12693.

Savage, Lonnie Cole. "A Study of Measures of Black Alienation Among a Selected Group of Black College Students." Doctoral dissertation, New York U., 1975. Univ. Microfilms Order No. 75-22921.

Saylor, Roland I. "An Exploration of Race Prejudice in College Students and Interracial Contact." Dissertation Abstracts International, 1969, 30(6-A):2620.

Scarborough, William Saunders. The Educated Negro and His Mission. Washington, DC: The Negro Academy, 1903.

_____. "Educated Negroes and Menial Pursuits." Forum 26(1899):434.

_____. What Should be the Standard of the University, College, Normal School, Teacher Training and Secondary Schools. Durham, NC: 1916.

Schaap, Dick. "The Revolt of the Black Athletes." Look, Ag 6, 1968.

Schlekat, George A. and others. "Who Really Gets Financial Aid?" Journal of the National Association of College Admission Counselors 14(1970):20-24.

Scott, Patricia Bell. "Two Sides of the Coin: Black Students in White Institutions." Journal of the NAWDAC 41(Winter, 1978):62-66.

Scully, Malcolm G. "Minority Literatures Gain a Slippery Foothold." Chronicle of Higher Education, N 29, 1976.

Sedlacek, William E. "Should Higher Education Students Be Admitted Differentially by Race and Sex: The Evidence." Journal of the National Association of College Admissions Counselors 22(S, 1977):22-23.

Sedlacek, William E. and others. "Black and Other Minority Admissions to Large Universities: A Four-Year National Survey of Policies and Outcomes." Research in Higher Education 2(1974):221-230.

Sedlacek, William E., and Pelham, Judy C. "Minority Admissions to Large Universities: A National Survey." Journal of Non-White Concerns in Personnel and Guidance 4(Ja, 1976):53-62.

Schudson, Michael S. "Organizing the 'Meritocracy': A History of the College Entrance Examination Board." Harvard Educational Review 42(F, 1972):34-69.

Scientific Manpower Commissions. Professional Women and Minorities—A Manpower Data Resource Service, 1975. SMC, 1776 Massachusetts Avenue, N.W., Washington, DC 20036.

Scott, Jack. "The White Olympics." Ramparts 6(My, 1968):54-61.

Scott, John Vincent. The Role of Athletics in Americhan Higher Education, 1970. Center for Educational Reform, 2115 "S" Street, N.W., Washington, DC.

Scott, Peter. "Education Fails to Remove Class Barriers in American Society." Times Higher Education Supplement, S 5, 1975.

Scully, Malcolm G. "Higher Education's Response to Nation's Racial Crisis Is Said to Be More Apparent than Real." Chronicle of Higher Education, O 6, 1969.

_____. "Negro Students Push Demands: Reaction Grows." Chronicle of Higher Education, Ja 27, 1969.

Sedlacek, William E. "Issues in Predicting Black Student Success in Higher Education." Journal of Negro Education 43(Fall, 1974): 512-516.

Sedlacek, William E., and Brooks, Glenwood C., Jr. "Black Freshmen in Large Colleges: A Survey." Personnel and Guidance Journal 49 (D, 1970):307-311.

Sedlacek, William E., Brooks, Glenwood, C., Jr., and Mindus, Lester A. Black and Other Minority Admissions to Large Universities: Three Year National Trends. College Park, MD: Cultural Study Center, U. of Maryland, Mr, 1972.

Sedlacek, William E. and others. Black Admissions to Large Universities: Are Things Changing? College Park, MD: U. of Maryland, Cultural Study Center, 1971. ERIC ED 049 715.

_____. A National Comparison of Universities Successful and Unsuccessful in Enrolling Blacks Over a Five Year Period, 1974. ERIC ED 089 644.

_____. "Racial Attitudes of White University Students and Their Parents." Journal of College Student Personnel 14(N, 1973):517-520.

Segal, David. "'Equity' versus 'Efficiency' in Higher Education." In U.S. Congress, 91st, 1st session, Joint Economic Committee, The Economics and Fianncing of Higher Education in the United States. Washington, DC: GPO, 1969:135-144.

Selby, James E. Relationships Existing among Race, Persistence and Student Financial Aids. Columbia, MI: U. of Missouri, College of Education, 1970. ERIC ED 045 051.

Sells, Lucy Watson. "Sex, Ethnic, and Field Differences in Doctoral Outcomes." Doctoral dissertation, U. of California, Berkeley, 1975. Univ. Microfilms Order No. 76-15,363.

Semas, Philip. "Admissions Officers Say Non-white Students Should Be 10 Pct. of Colleges' Enrollment." Chronicle of Higher Education O 20, 1969.

Sewell, William H. "Inequality of Opportunity for Higher Education." American Sociological Review 36(O, 1971):793-809.

Sewell, William H., and Hauser, Robert M. "Causes and Consequences of Higher Education: Models of the Status Attainment Process." American Journal of Agricultural Economics 54(D, 1972):851-862.

Shea, Brent Mack. "Schooling and Its Antecedents: Substantive and Methodological Issues in the Status Attainment Process." Review of Educational Research 46(Fall, 1976):463-526. [Can "anyone go to college"?]

Shea, John R., and Wilkens, Roger A. Determinants of Educational Attainment and Retention in School. PB-209 625. Springfield, VA: National Technical Information Service, Ap 12, 1972.

Shoemaker, Elwood A., and McKeen, Ronald L. "Affirmative Action and Hiring Practices in Higher Education." Research in Higher Education 3(D, 1975):359-364.

Shulman, Carol H. Recruiting Disadvantaged Students, D, 1970. ERIC Clearinghouse on Higher Education, George Washington U., 1 Dupont Circle, Suite 630, Washington, DC: 20036.

Sievert, William A. "Black Students Organize to Promote Interests." Chronicle of Higher Education, Mr 13, 1978. [Big Eight Council on Black Student Government]

Sikes, Melvin P. (ed.). Black Professionals in Predominantly White Institutions of Higher Education. Directory. Austin, TX: Hogg Foundation for Mental Health, U. of Texas, 1972.

Sill, Geoffrey M. "Channeling and Tracking in Higher Education." Changing Education, American Teacher, Je, 1971.

Silver, George A. "Beyond the Bakke Case." Washington Post, S 18, 1977. [Open admissions to medical schools]

Simpson, Shirley. "Permissive College Admissions Policies and Minority Students' Self-Concepts." School Counselor 17(1970):208-211.

Sims, B. M., and Patrick, J. R. "Attitude Toward the Negro of Northern College Students." Journal of Negro Education 8(1936):192-204.

Smith, Calvert H. "Why Black Administrators 'Fail.'" Black World 24(Ag, 1975):26-29, 53.

Smedley, Joseph W., and Bayton, James A. "Evaluative Race-Class Stereotypes by Race and Perceived Class of Subjects." Journal of Personality and Social Psychology 36(My, 1978):530-535.

Smith, Charles U. "Race Relations and the New Agenda for Higher Education." Phi Delta Kappan, My, 1965.

Smith, Coby Vernon. "The Control Relationship Between Higher Education Policies and Black Politics." Doctoral dissertation, U. of Massachusetts, 1974. Univ. Microfilms Order No. 75-06090.

Smith, Elsie J. "Black Counselor Educator in a Predominantly White Institution." Counselor Education and Supervision 15(D, 1975):84-93.

Smith, Jessie Carney. Black Academic Libraries and Research Collections: An Historical Survey. Westport, CT: Greenwood, 1977.

Smith, Paul M. "Some Implications for Freshmen Orientation Activities with Negro College Students." Journal of College Student Personnel, Mr, 1964.

Smith, Robert E. "HEW, Affirmative Action and the Universities." Commentary 53(My, 1972): 10-11 (letter)

Snell, Joel C., and Wakefield, William O. "Working Class Youth: Academic Participation and Anomie Perception of the World." College Student Survey 5(Spring, 1971): 16-19.

Solmon, Lewis C. "The Definition of College Quality and Its Impact on Earnings." Explorations in Economic Research 2(Fall, 1975):537-587.

_____. The Definition and Impact of College Quality. New York: Center for Economic Analysis of Human Behavior and Social Institutions, National Bureau of Economic Research, Ag, 1973.

Solmon, Lewis C., and Taubman, Paul J. (eds.). Does College Matter? Some Evidence on the Impacts of Higher Education. New York: Academic Press, 1973.

Solmon, Lewis C., and Wachtel, Paul. "The Effects on Income of Type of College Attended." Sociology of Education 48(Winter, 1975):75-90.

Somerville, Bill. "Can Selective Colleges Accommodate the Disadvantaged? Berkeley Says 'Yes.'" College Board Review, Fall, 1967.

Sorkin, Alan L. "A Comparison of Quality Characteristics of Negro and White Private and Church-Related Colleges and Universities in the South." College and University 46(Spring, 1961):199-210.

_____. "A Comparison of Quality Characteristics in Negro and White Public Colleges and Universities in the South." Journal of Negro Education, Spring, 1969.

Sowell, Thomas. "Affirmative Action Reconsidered." Urban League Review 2(Summer, 1977):9-24.

_____. Affirmative Action Reconsidered: Was It Necessary in Academia? Washington, DC: American Enterprise Institute for Public Policy Research, 1975.

_____. "The 'Available' University." University of Chicago Magazine 63(N-D, 1970):2-4.

_____. "Colleges Are Skipping Over Competent Blacks to Admit 'Authentic' Ghetto Types." New York Times Magazine, D 13, 1970.

Sowell, Thomas. "The 'Need' for More 'Education.'" Bulletin of the American Association of University Professors, D, 1966.

_____. "The Plight of Black Students in the United States." Daedalus 103(Spring, 1974): 179-196.

Sowell, Thomas, and Ballard, Allen. "Compensatory Education: Two Views." New York Times, N 14, 1976.

Spady, William G. "Dropouts from Higher Education: An Interdisciplinary Review and Synthesis." Interchange 1(Ap, 1970):64-85.

Spaights, Ernest. "Black Students on White Campuses: Issues and Problems." Journal of Instructional Psychology 2(Winter, 1975): 2-8.

_____ (ed.). Support Services for Disadvantaged College Students: A Symposium, Mr, 1970. ERIC ED 041 972.

Speich, Don. "How Special Admissions Are Working." Los Angeles Times, Ja 15, 1978.

Spence, David S. A Profile of Higher Education in the South in 1985, 1977. ERIC ED 142 104.

Spurlock, Langley A. "Black [College] Student Problem Has Shifted From Recruitment to Retention." New York Times, Ja 16, 1974.

_____. Minorities in White Colleges: A Survey of Opinion from Students, Faculty, and Administrators. Washington, DC: American Council on Education, Ap 11, 1974.

_____. "Still Struggling: Minorities and White Colleges in the Mid-Seventies." Educational Record 57(Summer, 1976):186-193.

Staehr, Thomas E. "College Student Migration to Predominantly Black Institutions of Higher Education in the United States." Review of Public Data Use 4(My, 1976):34-41.

Stanley, Julian C. "Predicting College Success of the Educationally Disadvantaged." Science 171(F 19, 1971):640-647.

_____. Predicting College Success of Educationally Disadvantaged Students, S, 1970. ERIC ED 043 295.

_____. "Predicting College Success of Educationally Disadvantaged Students." Barriers to Higher Education. New York: College Entrance Examination Board, 1971.

Stanley, Julian C., and Porter, Andrew C. "Correlation of Scholastic Aptitude Test Scores With College Grades for Negroes Versus Whites." Journal of Educational Measurement, Winter, 1967.

_____. Predicting College Grades of Negroes versus Whites. Madison, WI: Department of Educational Psychology, U. of Wisconsin, 1966.

State of New Jersey. Second Annual Report of the Educational Opportunity Fund, 1969-1970. Trenton, NJ: Department of Higher Education, Mr 30, 1971.

Statement of the Board of Trustees, National Urban League on Open Admissions in American Colleges and Universities. New York: National Urban League, Inc., F, 1970. ERIC ED 050 682.

Steinberg, Stephen. The Academic Melting Pot: Catholics and Jews in American Higher Education. New York: McGraw-Hill, 1974.

_____. "How Jewish Quotas [in American Higher Education] Began." Commentary 52(S, 1971): 67-76.

Steinbridge, Barbara Penn. "A Student's Appraisal of the Adequacy of Higher Education for Black Americans." Journal of Negro Education, Summer, 1968.

Stent, Madelon D. and others. Minority Enrollment and Representation in Institutions of Higher Education. Commissioned by the Ford Foundation, 1974. Urban Ed, Inc., 277 Broadway, New York, NY 10007.

Steward, Gustavus Adolphus. "The Negro Student Prefers Prejudice." Crisis, Ag, 1935.

Stewart, Dorothy Granberry. "The Social Adjustment of Black Females at a Predominantly White University." Doctoral dissertation, U. of Connecticut, 1971. Univ. Microfilms Order No. 72-14259.

Stewart, Mac A. "The Challenges of Housing." Journal of Afro-American Issues 5(Winter, 1977):43-50. [Residence of black students in mainly white universities]

_____. "Financial Aid Recipients: An Appraisal by Race." Journal of College Student Personnel 16(My, 1975):238-243.

Stewart, Ted. "Separatism vs. Integration at White Colleges." Sepia 21(S, 1972):16-21.

Stone, Richard. "Revolt in Sports. Negro Athletes Push for Better Treatment, Wider Job Opportunity." Wall Street Journal, Je 19, 1968.

Stone, Winifred O. "Mood of the Black Student on Predominantly White Campus." Journal of Afro-American Issues 5(Winter, 1977):4-19.

Strickman, Leonard P. "The Tuition-Poor, the Public University, and Equal Protection." University of Florida Law Review 29(Summer, 1977):595-624.

Stuart, Reginald. "States Slow in Ending Dual School Systems." New York Times, N 28, 1975. [Desegregation of public higher education]

_____. "'We Didn't Have an Approach Before.' Public College Desegregation." Compact 8 (S-O, 1974):2-4.

Styles, Marvalene H. "Personality Characteristics, Self-Concept, Vocational Aspiration and Academic Performance of Negro Freshmen at a Predominantly White University as Compared with Negro Freshmen at a Predominantly Negro University." Dissertation Abstracts International, Je, 1970, 30(12-A): 5249.

Sullivan, Margaret (ed.). Directory of National Sources of Data on Blacks in Higher Education, 1976. ERIC ED 126 166.

Sullivan, Oona. "Black Colleges—Midway Toward a New Era." AGB Reports 17(Mr-Ap, 1975):37-39. [Ford Foundation grants to historically black private colleges]

Summary of Equal Educational Opportunity for Blacks in U.S. Higher Education: An Assessment. Report No. 1 The 1973-74 Academic Year, 1975. ERIC ED 121 226.

Summary of the First National Conference on the Role of Minorities in Urban Management and Related Fields. Washington, DC: Metropolis Washington Council of Governments, 1973.

Swan, Annalyn. "College Entrance Test: Biased and Burdensome Or a Real Opportunity?" Wall Street Journal, S 5, 1972.

Swinton, David H. "Higher Education: A Major Determinant of Economic Well-Being." Black Enterprise 6(Je, 1976).

Swinton, David H., and Gill, Gerald. Affirmative Action for Blacks in Higher Education: A Report. Washington, DC: Institute for the Study of Educational Policy, Howard U., 1978.

Switkin, Linda R., and Gynther, Malcolm D. "Trust, Activism, and Interpersonal Perception in Black and White College Students." Journal of Social Psychology 94(O, 1974):153-154.

Synnott, Marcia Graham. "A Social History of Admissions Policies at Harvard, Yale, and Princeton, 1900-1930." Doctoral dissertation, U. of Massachusetts, 1974. Univ. Microfilms Order No. 74-25,906.

Task Force. Report on Higher Education. Washington, DC: GPO, Mr, 1971. [The Newman Report]

Tatham, Clifford B., and Tatham, Elaine L. "Academic Predictors for Black Students." Educational and Psychological Measurement 34 (Summer, 1974):371-374.

Taubman, P. J., and Wales, T. J. "Higher Education, Mental Ability, and Screening." Journal of Political Economy 81(Ja-F, 1973).

_____. Mental Ability and Higher Educational Attainment in the 20th Century. Berkeley, CA: Carnegie Commission on Higher Education, 1972.

Taylor, Maurice C. "Academic Performance of Blacks on White Campuses." Integrateducation 16(S-O, 1978):28-31.

Temp, George. Test Bias: Validity of the SAT for Blacks and Whites in Thirteen Integrated Institutions. Princeton, NJ: Educational Testing Service, Ja, 1971.

_____. "Validity of the SAT for Blacks and Whites in Thirteen Integrated Institutions." Journal of Educational Measurement 8(Winter, 1971):245-251.

Tennessee General Assembly. Study on College Entrance Tests and Testing Services. Nashville: TN: Legislative Council Committee, 1973.

Terenzini, Patrick T., and Pascarella, Ernest T. "Voluntary Freshman Attrition and Patterns of Social and Academic Integration in a University: A Test of a Conceptual Model." Research in Higher Education 6(1977):25-43.

Thackrey, Russell I. What's Behind the Rising Cost of Education? Washington, DC: National Association of State Universities and Land-Grant Colleges, 1971.

Third Inter-University Conference on the Negro. Blueprint for Action by Universities for Achieving Integration in Education. Milwaukee, WS: Institute for Human Relations, U. of Wisconsin-Milwaukee, 1965.

Thomas, Charles Leo. "Relative Effectiveness of High School Grades for Predicting College Grades: Sex and Ability Level Effects." Journal of Negro Education 48(Winter, 1979):6-13.

Thomas, Charles Leo, and Stanley, Julian C. "Effectiveness of High School Grades for Predicting College Grades of Black Students: A Review and Discussion." Journal of Educational Measurement 6(Winter, 1969):203-221.

Thomas, Charles W. "Black-White Campus and the Function of Counseling." Counseling Psychologist 1(1969):70-73.

Thomas, Gail E. Family Status and Standardized Achievement Tests as Contingencies for Black and White College Entry. Baltimore, MD: Center for Social Organization of Schools, Johns Hopkins U., D, 1977.

_____. Race and Sex Effects on Access to College. Baltimore: Center for Social Organization of Schools, Johns Hopkins U., 1977.

Thomas, Gail E., Alexander, Karl L., and Eckland, Bruce K. Access to Higher Education: How Important Are Race, Sex, Social Class and Academic Credentials for College Access? Baltimore: Center for Social Organization of Schools, Johns Hopkins U., 1977.

Thompson, Charles H. "The Socio-economic Status of Negro College Students." Journal of Negro Education, Ja, 1933.

_____. "Teachers in Negro Colleges (A Sociological Analysis)." Doctoral dissertation, Columbia U., 1956. Univ. Microfilms Order No. 17084.

Thomas, Lucinda E., and Yates, Richard I. "Paraprofessionals in Minority Programs." Personnel and Guidance Journal 53(D, 1974):285-288.

Thorpe, Marion D. "The Future of Black Colleges and Universities in the Desegregation and Integration Process." Journal of Black Studies 6(S, 1975):100-112.

Thresher, B. Alden. "Uses and Abuses of Scholastic Aptitude and Achievement Tests." Barriers to Higher Education. New York: College Entrance Examination Board, 1971.

Tilford, Michael P., and Allen, Donald E. "Science and Non-Science Majors in Three Predominantly Black Colleges." Journal of Negro Education 43(Winter, 1974):117-126.

Tillar, Thomas C., Jr. "The Status of Racial Integration in Men's Social Fraternities at a Select Sample of Southeastern Universities." Master's thesis, Virginia Polytechnic Institute and State U., 1972.

_____. "A Study of Racial Integration in Southeastern Social Fraternities." Journal of College Student Personnel 15(My, 1974):207-212.

Tillery, Dale. Distribution and Differentiation of Youth: A Study of Differential Outcomes of High School Graduates. Cambridge, MA: Ballinger, 1973.

Tinto, Vincent. "Dropout from Higher Education: A Theoretical Synthesis of Recent Research." Review of Educational Research 45(Winter, 1975):89-125.

Tobias, Channing H. "Young Men's Christian Associations in American Negro Colleges." The Student World 16(1923).

Tonigan, Richard F. Prison Education: The College of Santa Fe and the New Mexico Penitentiary Approach, My 21, 1975. ERIC ED 125 722.

Turner, Darwin T. "The Afro-American College in American Higher Education. In What Black Educators Are Saying. Edited by Nathan Wright, Jr. New York: Hawthorn, 1970:94-103.

Totten, Herman L. "A Survey of the Academic Status of Black College and University Librarians." Journal of Negro Education 40(Fall, 1971):342-346.

_____. "They Had a Dream: Black Colleges and Library Standards." Wilson Library Bulletin, S, 1969.

Trahan, Richard George. "University Response to Black Student Protest: The Role of Organizational Characteristics in Structuring Institutional Response." Doctoral dissertation, U. of Wisconsin, 1976. Univ. Microfilms Order No. 76-20, 141.

Trent, William J., Jr. "The Future Role of the Negro College and Its Financing." Daedalus 100(Summer, 1971):647-659.

Trent, William T. College Compensatory Programs for Disadvantaged Students, S, 1970. ERIC Clearinghouse on Higher Education, The George Washington U., 1 Dupont Circle, Suite 630, Washington, DC 20036.

Trow, Martin (ed.). Teachers and Students: Aspects of American Higher Education. New York: McGraw-Hill, 1975. [See chapter by Judy Roizen].

Turner, Darwin T. "The Black University: A Practical Approach." Negro Digest, Mr, 1968.

"The Two Societies." Time, N 27, 1972. [Black and white on college campuses]

"Undergraduate Enrollment of Minorities in U.S. Higher Education." Chronicle of Higher Education, Mr 20, 1978. [Fall, 1976 data]

U.S. Bureau of Education. "The College-Bred Negro." Report of 1902. Washington, DC: GPO, 1903:191-229.

U.S. Bureau of the Census. Characteristics of Students and Their Colleges October 1966. Current Population Reports, Series P-20, No. 183, My 22, 1969. Washington, DC: GPO, 1969.

_____. Major Field of Study of College Students: October 1974. Washington, DC: GPO, F, 1976. [By age, sex, race, and income]

_____. School Enrollment--Social and Economic Characteristics of Students: October 1974. Washington, DC: GPO, N, 1975.

_____. Undergraduate Enrollment in Two-Year and Four-Year Colleges: October, 1970. Washington, DC: GPO, 1972.

_____. Social and Economic Characteristics of [College] Students. October, 1972. Washington, DC: GPO, F, 1974.

_____. Undergraduate Enrollment in Two-Year and Four-Year Colleges: October, 1971. Washington, DC: GPO, Je, 1972.

U.S. Bureau of Labor Statistics. College: Who Needs It?, 1971. Herbert Bienstock, U. S. Department of Labor, Bureau of Labor Statistics, 341 Ninth Avenue, New York, NY 10001.

U.S. Bureau of the Census. College Plans of High School Seniors: October 1973. Washington, DC: GPO, O, 1974.

_____. Income and Expenses Enrolled in Postsecondary Schools: October 1973. Washington, DC: GPO, Je, 1975.

U.S. Civil Service Commission. "Expanding Cooperation With Minority Colleges." Bulletin No. 330-18, Mr 10, 1971.

U.S. Congress, 93rd, 1st session, House of Representatives, Committee on Education and Labor, Special Subcommittee on Education. Student Financial Assistance (Theory and Practice of Need Analysis). Hearings.... Part 1. Washington, DC: GPO, 1974.

U.S. Department of Commerce, Office of Minority Business Enterprise. Higher Education Aid for Minority Business. A Director of Assistance Available to Minorities by Selected Collegiate Schools of Business. Washington, DC: GPO, Ap, 1970.

U.S. Congress, 93rd, 1st session, Senate, Committee on Labor and Public Welfare, Subcommittee on Education. Federal Student Assistance Programs, 1973. Hearing.... Washington, DC: GPO, 1973.

U.S. Congress, 93rd, 1st and 2nd sessions, House of Representatives, Committee on Education and Labor, Special Subcommittee on Education. Basic Educational Opportunity Grant Program. Hearings.... Washington, DC: GPO, 1974.

U.S. Congress, 93rd, 2nd session, House of Representatives, Committee on Education and Labor, Special Subcommittee on Education. Federal Higher Education Programs. Institutional Eligibility (Civil Rights Obligations). Parts 2A and 2B. Washington, DC: GPO, 1975.

U.S. Congress, 93rd, 2nd session, House of Representatives, Committee on Education and Labor, Special Subcommittee on Education. Federal Higher Education Programs Institutional Eligibility. Hearings.... Parts 2A and 2B. Washington, DC: GPO, 1975.

U.S. Congress, 93rd, 2nd session, House of Representatives, Committee on Education and Labor, Special Subcommittee on Education. Student Financial Assistance, Hearings.... Parts 1-10. Washington, DC: GPO, 1975.

U.S. Congress, 93rd, 2nd session, House of Representatives, Committee on Education and Labor, Special Subcommittee on Education. Student Financial Assistance (Seminars). Part 9. Washington, DC: GPO, 1974.

U.S. Congress, 94th, 1st session, House of Representatives, Committee on Education and Labor, Subcommittee on Postsecondary Education. Basic Educational Opportunity Grant Programs. Hearing.... Washington, DC: GPO, 1976.

U.S. Congress, 94th, 1st session, House of Representatives, Committee on Education and Labor, Subcommittee on Postsecondary Education. The Student Financial Aid Act of 1975. Hearings.... Washington, DC: GPO, 1975.

U.S. Congress, 95th, 1st session, House of Representatives, Committee on Education and Labor, Subcommittee on Postsecondary Education. Oversight Hearings on All Forms of Federal Student Financial Assistance. Washington, DC: GPO, 1977.

U.S. Congress, 95th, 2nd session, House of Representatives, Committee on Education and Labor. Middle Income Student Assistance Act: Report.... Washington, DC: GPO, 1978.

U.S. Congress, 95th, 2nd session, Senate, Committee on Human Resources. College Opportunity Act of 1978: Report.... Washington, DC: GPO, 1978.

U.S. Congressional Budget Office. Postsecondary Education. The Current Federal Role and Alternative Approaches. Washington, DC: GPO, 1977.

U.S. Department of Health, Education, and Welfare, Office for Civil Rights. Racial and Ethnic Enrollment Data from Institutions of Higher Education, Fall, 1970. Washington, DC: GPO, 1972.

U.S. Federal Interagency Committee on Education. Federal Agencies and Black Colleges. Washington, DC: GPO, 1970.

U.S. Office for Civil Rights. Racial Ethnic Enrollment Data from Institutions of Higher Education, Fall, 1972.

U.S. Office of Education. "Higher Education of Southwestern Indians with Reference to Success and Failure." Journal of American Indian Education, Ja, 1965.

_____. Selected List of Postsecondary Education Opportunities for Minorities and Women. Washington, DC: Office of Education, 1977.

_____. Statistics of Negro Colleges and Universities, Students, Staff and Finances, 1900-50. Circular No. 293. Washington, DC: GPO, 1951.

U.S. Office of Health Resources Opportunity. An Exploratory Evaluation of U.S. Medical Schools' Efforts to Achieve Equal Representation of Minority Students. Washington, DC: GPO, 1977.

Universal Higher Education, Costs and Benefits. Washington, DC: American Council on Education, 1971.

"Universities. Courting the Negro." Time, Ap 28, 1967.

University Research Corporation. Higher Education and the Disadvantaged Student, 1972. Human Service Press, 4301 Connecticut Avenue, N.W., Washington, DC 20008.

Upward Bound 1965-1969: A History of Synthesis of Data on the Program in the Office of Economic Opportunity, Mr 30, 1970. ERIC ED 046 319.

Useem, Michael, and Miller, S. M. "Privilege and Domination: The Role of the Upper Class in American Higher Education." Social Science Information 14(1975):115-145.

Van Alstyne, Carol, Withers, Julie, and Elliott, Sharon. "Affirmative Inaction. The Bottom Line Tells the Tale." Change 9(Ag, 1977):39-41, 60.

Van Alstyne, Carol and others. Women and Minorities in Administration of Higher Education Institutions: Employment Patterns and Salary Comparisons. Washington, DC: College and University Personnel Association, 1977.

Villard, Oswald Garrison. "Higher Education of Negroes." Nation 74(1902):381.

Vittersen, Lillian K. "Areas of Concern to Negro College Students As Indicated by Their Responses to the Mooney Problem Check List." Journal of Negro Education, Winter, 1967.

Wachman, Marvin. "The Culturally Deprived: Have Urban Universities Discharged Their Responsibility?" Graduate Comment (Wayne State U.), Ap, 1964.

Waldman, Bart. "Economic and Racial Disadvantages as Reflected in Traditional Medical School Selection Factors." Journal of Medical Education 52(D, 1977):961-970.

Walker, Marion E., and Beach, Mark. Making It in College: A Minority Students Guide. New York: Mason/Charter, 1975.

Walster, Elaine and others. The Effect of Race and Sex on College Admission, 1968. ERIC ED 043 893.

Waltz, Garry R. and others. An Investigation to Identify, Describe and Evaluate an Optimal Program of Student Personnel Services for Student from Disadvantaged Background, S, 1971. ERIC ED 063 567.

Warnat, Winifred I. "The Role of White Faculty on the Black College Campus." Journal of Negro Education 45(Summer, 1976):334-338.

Watkins, Beverly T. "Will It Be Blacks vs. Women for Faculty Jobs?" Chronicle of Higher Education, O 23, 1973.

Watley, Donovan J. Black and Nonblack Youth: Characteristics and College Attendance Patterns, 1971. ERIC ED 052 712.

_____. Black and Nonblack Youth: Does Marriage Hinder College Attendance?, 1971. ERIC ED 051 789.

_____. Black and Nonblack Youth: Finance and College Attendance, 1971. ERIC ED 052 713.

_____. Brain Gains and Brain Drains: The Migration of Black and Nonblack Talent, 1971. ERIC ED 051 741.

_____. Bright Black Youth: Their Educational Plans and Career Aspirations, 1971. ERIC ED 053 676.

Watson, Bernard C. The Black Administrator in Higher Education: Current Dilemmas, Problems and Opportunities, Ap, 1972. ERIC ED 063 867.

Wayland, H. L. "Higher Education of Negroes." American Journal of Social Science 34:68.

Weiner, Howard R. "The Instructor and Open Admissions." Urban Education 5(O, 1970): 287-294.

Welch, Eloise T. "The Background and Development of the American Missionary Association's Decision to Educate Freedmen in the South, with Subsequent Repercussions for Higher Education." Doctoral dissertation, Bryn Mawr College.

Wellington, John S., and Montero, Pilar. "Equal Educational Opportunity Programs in American Medical Schools." Journal of Medical Education 53(Ag, 1978):633-639.

Wessman, Alden E. "Scholastic and Psychological Effects of a Compensatory Education Program for Disadvantaged High School Students: Project ABC." American Educational Research Journal 9(Summer, 1972):361-372.

Western Association of Graduate Schools and Western Interstate Commission for Higher Education. Graduate Education and Ethnic Minorities, F, 1970. Western Interstate Commission for Higher Education, P.O. Drawer "P," Boulder, CO 80302.

Westin, A. F. "Segregation and Discrimination in Higher Education." Law Guild Review 10 (Winter, 1950):209-214.

Wharton, Clifton R., Jr. "Black Intellectual Manpower." Integrated Bulletin, Jl-Ag, 1972:65-71.

_____. "Study Now, Pay Later: Threat to a Great Commitment." Chronicle of Higher Education 6(D 6, 1971):12.

Whetstone, Robert D., and Hayles, V. Robert. "The SVIB and Black College Men." Measurement and Evaluation in Guidance 8(Jl, 1975):105-109.

Whiting, Albert N. "Apartheid in American Higher Education." Educational Record 53 (Spring, 1972):128-131.

Whitla, Dean K. and others. "Controversy and Change in Testing." Journal of the National Association of College Admissions Counselors 14(1970):28-32.

Wiggins, Sam P. The Desegregation Era in Higher Education. Berkeley, CA: McCutchan Publishing Co., 1966. [Southeastern colleges and universities]

_____. "Dilemmas in Desegregation in Higher Education." Journal of Negro Education, Fall, 1966.

Williams, Charles H. "Negro Athletes in the Tenth Olympiad." Southern Workman 61(N, 1932):449-460.

_____. "Twenty Years' Work of the C.I.A.A." Southern Workman 61(F, 1932):65-76. [Colored Inter-Collegiate Athletic Association]

Williams, Clarence G. "An Investigation of the Basic 'Affective Dimensions' of the Black Tradition and of Black Studies in Higher Education." Journal of Social and Behavioral Sciences 19(Summer-Fall, 1972):43-49.

Williams, Clarence G., and Lyons, James E. "Black Coeds on a White Campus." Integrated Education, S-O, 1972:61-64.

Williams, Donald T., Jr. Black Higher Education: Whence and Whither?, Mr, 1970. ERIC ED 040 232.

Williams, Franklin H. "The Black Crisis On Campus." In What Black Educators Are Saying. Edited by Nathan Wright, Jr. New York: Hawthorn, 1970.

_____. "The University's Black Crisis." College and University Journal, Spring, 1969.

Williams, James H., and Whitney, Douglas. "Vocational Interest of Minority Disadvantaged Students: Are They Different?" NASPA Journal 15(Spring, 1978):20-26.

Williams, Robert Kenton. "An Exploratory Study of the Adjustment of 49 Male Negro College Students at One Segregated and Two Mixed Colleges." Master's thesis, 1940, Pennsylvania State U.

Williams, Ronald. "The New Sentimentality." Afro-American Studies 3(Je, 1972):55-59.

Willie, Charles V. "Black Is Lonely." Psychology Today, Mr, 1972.

Willingham, Warren W. Accessibility of Higher Education. Palo Alto, CA: College Entrance Examination Board, 1970.

_____. Admission of Minority Students in Midwestern Colleges, My, 1970. College Entrance Examination Board, 625 Colfax Street, Evanston, IL 60201.

_____. "Free-access Colleges: Where They Are and Whom They Serve." College Board Review, Summer, 1970.

_____. Free-Access Higher Education. New York: College Entrance Examination Board, 1970.

Willis, A. Leroy. "Greater Influence by the Black Community." In The Campus and the Racial Crisis. Edited by David C. Nichols and Olive Mills. Washington, DC: American Council on Education, 1970.

Willis, Carl T., and Goldberg, Faye J. Correlates of Attitudes Toward Black Militancy Among Black College Students. Research Report No. 13, F 28, 1969. ERIC ED 035 041.

Wilson, Clint C. II. "What Can Be Done About the Black Journalism Student?" Journalism Educator 32(Ap, 1977):12-15.

Wilson, Kenneth M. Black Students Entering CRC Colleges. Their Characteristics and Their First-Year Academic Performance. Research Memorandum 69-1, Ap 15, 1969. ERIC ED 030 897.

Wilson, Logan, and Mills, Olive (eds.). Universal Higher Education: Costs, Benefits, Options. Washington, DC: American Council on Education, 1972.

Wilson, Ruth Danenhower. "Negroes in Mixed Colleges." Crisis, Mr, 1949.

Wilson, Shirley J. "Survey of Minority and Women Student Affairs Staff Members Employed in NASPA Member Institutions in 1974." NASPA 14(Winter, 1977):57-73.

Wilson, William J. "A Rejoinder to Vincent Harding." Negro Digest, Mr, 1970. [In re: raiding of southern black faculties by northern colleges]

Wilson, Ruth D. "Negro Colleges of Liberal Arts." American Scholar 19(Autumn, 1950).

Windham, Douglas M. "The Efficiency/Equity Quandary and Higher Educational Finance." American Educational Research Association 42(Fall, 1972):541-560.

Winer, Jerry A. and others. "Nonwhite Student Usage of University Mental Health Services." Journal of College Student Personnel 15 (S, 1974):410-412.

Winston, Eric V. A. "Advising Minority Students." Integrateducation, Jl-Ag, 1976.

Winston, Michael R. "Through the Back Door: Academic Racism and the Negro Scholar in Historical Perspective." Daedalus 100 (Summer, 1971):678-719.

Wise, Michael (ed.). "Post Secondary Institutions." Desegregation in Education: A Directory of Reported Federal Decisions. Notre Dame, IN: Center for Civil Rights, U. of Notre Dame Law School, Ap, 1977:201. [1954-1976]

Wolfe, Alan. "Reform Without Reform: The Carnegie Commission on Higher Education." Social Policy 2(My-Je, 1971):18-27.

Woodring, Paul. "The Struggle for Black Identity." Saturday Review, Ja 18, 1969. [College campus movements]

Woods, Gwendolyn Patton. "The Black Student Movement." In Perspectives on Campus Tensions. Edited by David C. Nichols. Washington, DC: American Council on Education, 1970:68-72.

Word, Kenneth M. "Black Problems Through Blue Eyes." Journal of the National Association of Women Deans and Counselors 36(Spring, 1973):133-136. [Blacks on white campuses]

"World War II and Negro Higher Education." Journal of Negro Education 11(Jl, 1942).

Wright, Madeleine Elaine Pate. "Self-Concept and the Coping Process of Black Graduate and Undergraduate Women at a Predominantly White University." Doctoral dissertation, U. of Michigan, 1975. Univ. Microfilms Order No. 75-29351.

Wright, Patricia S., and Huyck, Earl E. "Faculty in White and Negro Colleges." Health, Education and Welfare Indicators, F, 1965.

Wright, Stephen J. "The Use of Socio-Economic Factors and Intelligence Test Scores in the Prediction of Academic Achievement of Negro College Students." Master's thesis, Howard U., 1939.

Wyatt, Gail E. and others. "A Survey of Ethnic and Sociocultural Issues in Medical School Education." Journal of Medical Education 53(Ag, 1978):627-632.

Yates, J. Frank and others. "Some Approaches to Black Academic Motivation in Predominantly White Universities." Journal of Social and Behavioral Sciences 20(Summer, 1974):19-36.

Yehle, Lawrence C. "EEO Compliance Officer--Friend or Foe?" Journal of the College and University Personnel Association 23(Mr, 1972).

Young, Anne M. "The High School Class of 1972: More at Work, Fewer in College." Monthly Labor Review 96(Je, 1973):26-32.

Young, H. A. and others. "Role Models for Blacks in Engineering." Engineering Education 66(Ja, 1976):337-339.

Young, Kenneth E. Access to Higher Education. Washington, DC: American Association of State Colleges and Universities, Ap 20, 1971. ERIC ED 052 710.

_____. Exploring the Case for Low Tuition in Public Higher Education, 1974. ERIC ED 096 929.

Young, Nathan B. "These 'Colored' United States." Messenger 5(N, 1923).

Young, Robert W. "College-Admissions Policies: Index or Enemy of Education?" School Shop 30(N, 1970):45-47.

Zeitlin, Solomon. "Jewish [Higher] Learning in America." Jewish Quarterly Review 45(Ap, 1955):582-616.

Zeller, Belle. "College Education for All?" Today's Education, Mr, 1972.

Bibliographies

Alexander, Norman D. (comp.). Bibliography on Higher Education. A Critical Guide to Literature and Information on Access to Higher Education. 2 vols. Ashland, OR: Library, Southern Oregon College, 1973.

Aptheker, Bettina (comp.). Bibliography of Higher Education and the Student Rebellion in the United States. 1972 edition. New York: American Institute for Marxist Studies, 1972.

_____. Higher Education and the Student Rebellion in the United States, 1960-1969: A Bibliography. New York: American Institute for Marxist Studies, 1969.

Allen, John C. (comp.). Collective Bargaining in Higher Education, 1971-73. New York: National Center for the Study of Collective Bargaining in Higher Education, Baruch College, Ap 12, 1973.

Altbach, Philip (comp.). Student Politics and Higher Education in the U.S., a Select Bibliography. Cambridge, MA: Center for International Affairs, Harvard U., 1968.

Beach, Mark (comp.). A Bibliographic Guide to American Colleges and Universities: From Colonial Times to the Present. Westport CT: Greenwood Press, 1975.

Beale, Andrew V. (comp.). "History of College Admission Requirements: A Selected Bibliography." NASPA Journal 10(Ap, 1973).

Beeler, Kent D. "Source Bibliographies in Higher Education: 1960-1970." Viewpoints 47(Ja, 1971):1-100.

Caldwell, John (comp.). Histories of American Colleges and Universities: A Bibliography, 1976. ERIC ED 129 138.

Chambers, Frederick (comp.). Black Higher Education in the United States: A Selected Bibliography on Negro Higher Education and Historically Black Colleges and Universities. Westport, CT: Greenwood, 1978.

College Placement Council (comp.). A Bibliography of Selected Research and Statistical Studies Pertaining to College-Trained Manpower and Supplement. Bethlehem, PA: College Placement Council, 1969.

Daley, Kenneth (comp.). Institutions of Higher Education and Urban Problems: A Bibliography and Review for Planners, My, 1973. Council of Planning Librarians, P. O. Box 229, Monticello, IL 61856.

Duvall, W. H., and Duvall, V. S. (comps.). An Index to Major Articles in the Chronicle of Higher Education, November, 1966 thru August 30, 1972. Richmond, VA: Virginia Commonwealth U., 1973.

Ebbers, Larry H., Marks, Kenneth E., and Stoner, Kenneth L. (comps.). Residence Halls in U.S. Higher Education: A Bibliography. Ames, IA: The Library, Iowa State U., 1973.

Furniss, W. Todd (comp.). "Colleges and Minority/Poverty Issues. Bibliography and Other Resources." A. C. E. Special Report, N 14, 1969.

Gordon, Edmund W. (comp.). An Annotated Bibliography on Higher Education of the Disadvantaged (Includes addendum by Edwina D. Frank) New York: The Study of Collegiate Compensatory Programs for Minority Group Youth, Teachers College, Columbia U., 1969.

Hillman Library. Financing Higher Education: A Bibliography, 1971. Institute for Higher Education, U. of Pittsburgh, 4000 Fifth Avenue, Pittsburgh, PA 15213.

Hull, W. Frank III (comp.). "The Black Student in Higher Education: A Bibliography." Journal of College Student Personnel 11(N, 1970):423-425.

Hull, W. Frank III, and Davies, Marshall W. (comps.). "The Black Student in Higher Education: A Second Bibliography." Journal of College Student Personnel 14(Jl, 1973):309-312.

Institute for the Study of Educational Policy. Directory of National Sources of Data on Blacks in Higher Education. Washington, DC: The Institute, Howard U., 1976.

Isaacson, Arlene (comp.). College Student Attrition: An Annotated Bibliography, Ja, 1974. ERIC ED 101 633.

Karkhanis, Sharad (comp.). Open Admissions: A Bibliography, 1968-1973, 1974. ERIC ED 089 575.

Kelsey, Roger R. (comp.). A Bibliography on Higher Education. Takoma Park, MD: Higher Education Council, Maryland State Teachers Association, 1970.

Kerstiens, Gene (comp.). Junior-Community College Reading/Study Skills: An Annotated Bibliography, 1971. International Reading Association, 6 Tyre Avenue, Newark, DL 19711.

Lambert, Linda J. (comp.). Concerns of Historically and Developing Black Institutions: A Bibliography, F, 1975. ERIC ED 100 880.

Noel, Lee, and Renter, Lois (comps.). College Student Retention. An Annotated Bibliography of Recent Dissertations (1970-March 1975), 1975. ERIC ED 121 233.

Randolph, Harland A. and others. "Bibliography on College Community Relationships." The Role of College-Community Relationships in Urban Higher Education, Vol. I, Mr, 1969. ERIC ED 041 569.

Regan, Lynda (comp.). Annotated Bibliography, Educational Opportunity Programs. Albany, New York: New York Office of ESC Educational Opportunity Programs, [1975?]

Rosenthal, Carl F. (comp.). Social Conflict and Collective Violence in American Institutions of Higher Learning. Volume II. Bibliography. PB-210 161. Springfield, VA: National Technical Information Service, Ja, 1971.

Shrier, Irene, and Lavin, David E. (comps.). Open Admissions: A Bibliography for Research and Applications, Mr, 1974. ERIC ED 090 840.

Suljak, Nedjelko D. (comp.). Campus Disorder and Cultural Counter-Revolution: A Bibliography. Davis, CA: Institute of Governmental Affairs, U. of California, Davis, 1971.

Wilcox, Preston (comp.). The Black University: A Bibliography. New York: National Association for African American Education, Ag, 1969.

21.
GENERAL

Armed Forces

Air Force. Directorate of Personnel Plans.
Personnel Research and Analysis Division.
A Comparison of Attitudes of Black and
White Cadets in AFROTC. Washington, DC,
My, 1972.

Armenta, Gilbert. Measuring the Effectiveness
of Defense Race Relations Instruction.
Maxwell Air Force Base, Alabama: Air
Command and Staff College, Air U., My,
1973.

Armstrong, Warren B. "Union Chaplains and the
Education of the Freedmen." Journal of
Negro History 52(Ap, 1967):104-115.

Bahney, Robert S. "Generals and Negroes:
Education of Negroes by the Union Army,
1861-65." Doctoral dissertation, U. of
Michigan, 1965. Univ. Microfilms Order No.
66-5035.

Berry, Mary F. Military Necessity and Civil
Rights Policy: Black Citizenship and the
Constitution, 1861-1868. Port Washington,
NY: Kennikat Press, 1977.

Beusse, William E. and others. Perceptions of
Equal Opportunity and Race Relations Among
Military Personnel. Brooks Air Force Base,
TX: Air Force Human Resources Laboratory,
1976.

Black and White Perceptions of the Army's Equal
Opportunity and Treatment Programs. McLean,
VA: Human Sciences Research, Inc., My,
1974.

Blassingame, John W. "The Union Army as an
Educational Institution for Negroes, 1862-
1865." Journal of Negro Education, Spring,
1965.

Bond, Horace Mann. "The Negro in the Armed
Forces of the United States Prior to World
War I." Journal of Negro Education 12
(Summer, 1943):268-287.

Brooks, Harry W., Jr., and Miller, James M.
The Gathering Storm: An Analysis of Racial
Instability Within the Army. Carlisle
Barracks, PA: Army War College, Mr 9, 1970.

Buchanan, A. Russell. Black Americans in World
War II. Santa Barbara, CA: Clio Press,
1977.

Burns, Mervyn J. "The Black United States
Marine: A Challenge for the 1970's." Student
thesis, Naval War College, Ap, 1971.

Burran, James A. III. "Racial Violence in the
South during World War II." Doctoral
dissertation, U. of Tennessee, 1977.

Butler, John Sibley. "Assessing Black Enlisted
Participation in the Army." Social Problems
23(Je, 1976):558-566.

Cardwell, John J., Jr. "Racial Composition in
the All-Volunteer Force." Urban League
Review 1(Fall, 1975).

Collins, Walter A. The Race Problem in the
United States Air Force. Maxwell Air Force
Base, AL: Air Command and Staff College,
Air U., My, 1972.

Comptroller General of the United States.
A Need to Address Illiteracy Problems in the
Military Services. Washington, DC: General
Accounting Office, 1977.

Cressy, Peter H., and Desfosses, Louis R.
"Developing an Alternative Approach to Race
Relations Education: Identifying Military
Middle Management Resistance." Naval War
College Review 27(Jl-Ag, 1974):58-68.

Dalfiume, Richard M. Desegregation of the U.S.
Armed Forces. Fighting on Two Fronts,
1939-1953. Columbia, MO: U. of Missouri
Press, 1971.

Endicott, William, and Williford, Stanley.
"Uptight in the Armed Forces." Nation, N 3,
1969.

Field, R. L. "The Black Midshipman at the U.S. Naval Academy." U.S. Naval Institute Proceedings 99(Ap, 1973):28-36.

Fuller, William T. An Analysis of Racial Discrimination in the U.S. Air Force. Maxwell Air Force Base, AL: Air Command and Staff College, Air U., My, 1972.

Gropman, Alan Louis. "The Air Force Integrates: Blacks in the Air Force from 1945 to 1964." Doctoral dissertation, Tufts U., 1975. Univ. Microfilms Order No. 76-19452.

_____. The Air Force Integrates, 1945-1964. Washington, DC: Department of Defense, Department of the Air Force, Office of Air Force History, 1978.

Hayden, Gaylord V. Discrimination in the United States Air Force. Maxwell Air Force Base, AL: Air Command and Staff College, Air U., My, 1973.

Janowitz, Morris. "The All-Volunteer Military As a 'Socio-political' Problem." Social Problems 22(F, 1975):432-449.

Johnson, Charles. "The Army, the Negro, and the Civilian Conservation Corps: 1933-1942." Military Affairs 36(O, 1972):82-88.

Kuvlesky, William, and Dietrich, Katheryn. "Southern Black Youths' Perceptions of Military Service: A Nonmetroplitan-Metropolitan Comparison of Attitudes, Aspirations and Expectations." Journal of Political and Military Sociology 1(Spring, 1973).

Lane, David A., Jr. "An Army Project in the Duty-Time General Education of Negro Troops in Europe, 1947-1951." Journal of Negro Education, Spring, 1964.

Lee, Ulysses. United States Army in World War II. The Employment of Negro Troops. Washington, DC: GPO, 1966.

MacGregor, Morris J., and Nalty, Bernard C. (eds.). Blacks in the United States Armed Forces: Basic Documents. Vol I: A Time of Slavery. Wilmington, DE: Scholarly Resources, 1977.

Matthews, John J. Racial Equity in Selection in Air Force Officer Training School and Undergraduate Flying Training, My, 1977. ERIC ED 145 029.

Moskos, Charles C., Jr. "Race in the Armed Forces." Annals 406(Mr, 1973):94-106.

_____. "Racial Integration in the Armed Forces." American Journal of Sociology, S, 1966.

_____. "Racial Relations in the Armed Forces." In The American Enlisted Man: The Rank and File in Today's Military, pp. 108-133. New York: Russell Sage, 1970.

Osur, Alan Michael. "Negroes in the Army Air Forces During World War II: The Problem of Race Relations." Doctoral dissertation, U. of Denver, 1974. Univ. Microfilms Order No. 75-2209.

Parks, Robert J. "The Development of Segregation in U.S. Army Hospitals, 1940-1942." Military Affairs 37(D, 1973).

Parrish, Noel F. The Segregation of Negroes in the Army Air Forces. Maxwell Field, AL: The Air University, My, 1947.

Patton, Gerald W. "War and Race: The Black Officer in the American Military 1915-1925." Doctoral dissertation, U. of Iowa, 1978. Univ. Microfilms Order No. 7822439.

Renfroe, Earl W., Jr. "The Commander and the Minority Mental Process." Air University Review 23(N-D, 1971):39-46.

Swint, Henry L. (ed.). Dear Ones at Home. Letters from Contraband Camps. Nashville, TN: Vanderbilt U. Press, 1966.

Taggart, John H. Free Military School for Applicants for Command of Colored Troops. Philadelphia: King and Baird, 1864.

Thomas, James A. Changes in Black and White Perceptions of the Army's Race Relations/Equal Opportunity Programs—1972 to 1974. Arlington, VA: Army Research Institute for the Behavioral and Social Sciences, 1976.

Trautsch, Rolf A. "Recruitment of Minority Students at the U.S. Air Force Academy." Air University Review 25(My-Je, 1974):66-74.

23X, Leroy. "Farrakhan Brings Wisdom of Muhammad to West Point." Muhammad Speaks, N 24, 1972.

U.S. Bureau of Naval Personnel. Black Americans in the Navy. Washington, DC: GPO, 1977.

U.S. Bureau of the Budget. A Survey of Socially and Economically Disadvantaged Vietnam Era Veterans. Washington, DC: The Bureau, N, 1969.

Walker, Elvoid, Jr. "Race Relations (Black-White) in the United States Army." Doctoral dissertation, United States International U., 1978. Univ. Microfilms Order No. 7906219.

White, William Bruce. "The Military and the Melting Post: The American Army and Minority Groups, 1865-1924." Doctoral dissertation, U. of Wisconsin, 1968.

Wilson, George C. "Blacks in Army: Staying and Advancing." Washington Post, Jl 10, 1978.

Wilson, Joseph T. "The Phalanx at School." In The Black Phalanx: A History of the Negro Soldiers of the United States in the Wars of 1775-1812, 1861-1865. Hartford, CT: American Publishing Co., 1890.

Wynn, Neil A. The Afro-American and the Second World War. London: Paul Elek, 1976.

Busing

Armor, David J. "The Dangers of Forced Integration." Society 14(My-Je, 1977):41-44.

_____. Sociology and School Busing Policy, S, 1976. ERIC ED 134 668.

Aronson, Elliot. "Busing and Racial Tension: The Jigsaw Route to Learning and Liking." Psychology Today, F, 1975.

Arulanandam, Saleth J. "School Busing: Solution or Evasion--A Critical Analysis of the Literature from 1960 to 1972." Master's thesis, Loyola U., Chicago, 1973.

Beckler, John. "Busing Controversy Results in Another Look at Title I." School Management 16(My, 1972):4-6.

Bell, Dean. "Busing as Related to Desegregation of Schools in the Rural South." Master's thesis, U. of Cincinnati, 1974.

Bell, Terrel H. "Is School Busing At a Dead End?" U.S. News and World Report, S 16, 1974, pp. 41-44. [U.S. Commissioner of Education]

Berk, Laura E., and Berson, Minnie P. "The School Bus as a Developmental Experience for Young Children." Illinois Schools Research 11(Spring, 1975):1-14.

Blake, Clarence E. "The Consolidation of Schools and the Conveyance of Children." Forum, Mr, 1902.

Blumenberg, Eleanor. "The New 'Yellow Peril' (Facts and Fictions About School Busing)." Journal of Intergroup Relations 2(Summer, 1973):33-45.

Bosco, James J., and Robin, Stanley S. "White Flight from Busing? A Second Longer Look." Urban Education 11(O, 1976):263-274.

Braden, Anne. "Busing Hysteria: Road to Tyranny." Southern Patriot, O, 1972.

Brown, Warner. "Busing: Bigots Battle to Keep Blacks Separate and Unequal." Jet 42(My 18, 1972):22-25, 28-31.

Bryant, Spurgeon Q., Sr. Why I Do Not Like Busing. New York: Vantage Press, 1974. [Dean, School of Education, Alabama A & M U., Normal]

Buncher, Judith F. (ed.). The School Busing Controversy, 1970-75. New York: Facts on File, 1975.

Caplan, Marvin. "Truth--and Shame--about Busing." Dissent 23(Fall, 1976):383-391.

Carrison, Muriel P. "Beyond Busing." Journal of Education 160(My, 1978):63-74.

_____. Beyond Busing: A Societal and Generic View, Ag 30, 1977. ERIC ED 147 412.

_____. "On Busing: Legitimacy and Public Opinion." School and Society 100(Ap, 1972): 224-226.

Carter, David G., Sr. Anti-Busing Legislation and Society: Reflections During the Bicentennial, 1977. ERIC ED 143 089.

Clarke, S., and Surkis, J. "An Operations Research Approach to Racial Desegregation of School Systems." Socio-Economic Planning Sciences 1(1968):259-272.

Clindry, Evans, and Cody, Elisabeth A. It Is Time to Put Something at the End of the Bus Ride. Boston: Educational Planning Associates, D, 1975.

Coleman, James S. "Can We Integrate Our Public Schools Without Busing?" Chicago Tribune, S 17, 1978.

_____. "Population Stability and Equal Rights." Society 14(My-Je, 1977):34-36.

Coles, Robert. "Does Busing Harm Children?" Inequality in Education 11(Mr, 1972):25.

Collins, Clinton. "An Equalitarian's Case Against School Busing." Intellect 101(O, 1972):27-30.

Cooper, Charles R. "An Educator Looks at Busing." National Elementary Principal 50 (Ap, 1971):26-31.

Cottle, Thomas J. "Big City Busing and the Golden Opportunity." Urban Review 6(S-O, 1972):26-30.

_____. Busing. Boston: Beacon, 1976.

De Mont, Roger, Hillman, Larry, and Mansergh, Gerald (eds.). Busing, Taxes, and Desegregation. Danville, IL: Interstate Printers and Publishers, 1973.

Dobson, Russell and others. "Comparison of Achievement, Self-Concept, Perceived Environment, and Attendance of Bused and Non-bused, White, Fifth- and Sixth-Grade Children." Humanist Educator 15(Mr, 1977): 140-147.

Durham, Joseph T. "Sense and Nonsense About Busing." Journal of Negro Education 42 (Summer, 1973):322-335.

Edmonds, Ron. "You Can Get Hurt Waiting for the Bus." Journal of Intergroup Relations 2(0, 1972):13-23.

Erbe, Brigitte Mach. "On 'The Politics of School Busing.'" Public Opinion Quarterly 41(1977):113-117. [On racism and anti-busing attitudes]

ERIC Clearinghouse on Educational Management. Busing for Desegregation, 1977. ERIC ED 136 344.

Fact Book on Pupil Transportation, Ap, 1972. Metropolitan Applied Research Center, 60 East 86th Street, New York, NY 10028.

The Facts About Busing, 1972. Leadership Conference on Civil Rights, 2027 Massachusetts Avenue, N.W., Washington, DC 20036.

Farrell, Claude H. III. "Forced Busing and the Demand for Schooling." Doctoral dissertation, North Carolina State U., 1974.

Farrell, C. H. and others. "Forced Busing and the Demand for Private Schooling." Journal of Legal Studies 6(Je, 1977):363-372.

Felice, L., and Richardson, R. "The Effects of Busing and School Desegregation on Minority Student Dropout Rates." Journal of Educational Research 70(My-Je, 1977): 242-246.

Ferns, Maryann H., and Bergsma, Harold M. Thoughts on Busing and Integration in the Seventies, 1977. ERIC ED 159 236.

Finger, John A., Jr. "Why Busing Plans Work." School Review 84(My, 1976):364-372.

Fleming, Thomas. Rulers of the City. Garden City, NY: Doubleday, 1977. [A novel about busing]

Fogel, Barbara. "Is Busing Evil?" Educate 4 (Ap, 1971):24-26, 36.

Gaston, George W., Jr. "Busing: Excuse or Challenge?" Clearing House 46(Mr, 1972): 434-439.

Giles, Michael W. "Racial Stability and Urban School Desegregation." Urban Affairs Quarterly 12(Je, 1977):499-510.

Giles, Michael W., Gatlin, Douglas S., and Cataldo, Everett F. Determinants of Resegregation: Compliance/Rejection Behavior and Policy Alternatives. Washington, DC: National Science Foundation, Division of Advanced Productivity Research and Technology, Research Applied to National Needs, Ap 29, 1976.

Glass, Robert L. "Computers Enter the Busing Controversy." Computers and Automation 20 (Jl, 1971):18-23.

Glass, Thomas E. "Analysis and Effects of School Busing." Western Journal of Black Studies 1(S, 1977):204-216.

Glazer, Nathan, Green, Robert L., Morgan, Charles, Jr., and Patterson, Orlando. Busing: Constructive or Divisive? Washington, DC: American Enterprise Institute for Public Policy Research, 1976.

Goley, Beatrice T., Brown, Geraldine, and Samson, Elizabeth. Household Travel in the United States. Washington, DC: U.S. Department of Transportation, D, 1972.

Goodwin, P. B., and Hutchinson, T. P. "The Risk of Walking." Transportation 6(1977):217-230.

Graham, Robert A. "Bus the Children?" America, F 1, 1964.

Graves, Curtis M. "Lines of Least Resistance: A Case Against Busing" (letter). Harper's 245(S, 1972):92-93.

Gunn, Gerald. "Economic Aspects of Desegregation." Doctoral dissertation, Colorado State U., 1973.

Gunning, Rosemary R. "Busing Versus the Neighborhood School." Urban Review 6(S-O, 1972): 2-5.

Guthrie, James W. "Schoolbusing: The Fear Issue of 1972." Baltimore Sun, My 7, 1972.

Lardy, Clifford A. "Student Attitudes: A Study of Social Class." Improving College and University Teaching 24(Summer, 1976):151-152, 1954. [Items on busing]

Harshman, Ronald. "School Bussing: A Moral Development Viewpoint." Educational Leadership 34(Ja, 1977):293-297.

Hartsell, John E. "The Relationship of Authoritarianism, Education, and Income to Resistance to School Busing." Master's thesis, East Texas State U., Commerce, 1973.

Harzenski, S. S. "Jurisdictional Limitations and Suspicious Motives: Why Congress Cannot Forbid Court-Ordered Busing." Temple Law Quarterly 50(1976):14-57.

Hayes, Edward J., and Rayburn, Wendell G. "Black-White Dilemmas: Counselors, Busing, Desegregation." School Counselor 23(N, 1975): 99-102.

Henderson, Ronald D. Busing: Implications for Social Change in Urban and Rural Areas, Ap, 1976. ERIC ED 124 616.

Herbers, John. "Fear of Busing Exceeds Impact." New York Times, My 28, 1972.

Janssen, Peter. "Busing." Saturday Review of Education 55(0, 1972):68.

Jenkins, Ray. "The Bus." South Today 3(O, 1971):7-8. [Busing for segregation a generation ago]

Jordan, K. Forbis, and Hanes, Carol E. "A Survey of State Pupil Transportation Programs." School Business Affairs 44(My, 1978):133-134, 136.

Kancewick, Mary. "Busing Changed My Life." Integrateducation 15(Ja-F, 1977).

Karimi, Mohammed, and Hicks, Louise Day. "NSCAR vs. ROAR: A Debate on Busing." Militant, Je 4, 1976. [Debate of Ap 21, 1976, at Georgia State U.]

Kelley, Jonathan. "The Politics of School Busing." Public Opinion Quarterly 38 (Spring, 1974):23-39.

Kohl, Herb and others. "Busing: A Symposium." Ramparts 13(D, 1974-Ja, 1975):38-48.

Kramer, Shelley. Black Liberation: Integration and Busing, N, 1976. Revolutionary Marxist Committee, P.O. Box 134, Detroit, MI 48221.

Lambda Corporation. "School Desegregation with Minimum Busing." In U.S. Congress, 92nd, 2nd session, House of Representatives, Committee on Education and Labor, Equal Educational Opportunities Act. Hearings... Washington, DC: GPO, 1972.

Leeson, Jim. "Busing and Desegregation." Southern Education Report, N, 1968.

_____. "Busing and Desegregation--II." Southern Education Report, D, 1968.

Leavy, Robert L. "This Business of Busing." Massachusetts Teacher, S, 1965.

Leibman, Malvina W. "Busing is Irrelevant: The Need is More Fundamental." Intellect 101(D, 1972):160-163.

Levine, Leonard, and Griffith, Kitty. "The Busing Myth: Seg[regated] Academies Bus More Children, and Further." South Today, My, 1970.

Little, Arthur D., Inc. The State of the Art of Traffic Safety: A Comprehensive Review of Existing Information. New York: Praeger, 1970.

_____. The State of the Art of Traffic Safety. Cambridge, MA, Je, 1966. [Prepared for the Automobile Manufacturers Association]

Lord, J. Dennis. "School Busing and White Abandonment of Public Schools." Southeastern Geographer 15(1975):81-92.

Lord, J. Dennis, and Catan, John C. "School Desegregation, Busing, and Suburban Migration." Urban Education 11(O, 1976): 275-294. [Charlotte, NC]

_____. Spatial Perspectives on School Desegregation and Busing. Washington, DC: Association of American Geographers, 1977.

Lu, Y.-C., and Tweeten, L. "The Impact of Busing on Student Achievement: Reply." Growth and Change 7(Jl, 1976).

McConahay, John B., and Hawley, Willis D. Is It the Buses or the Blacks? Self-Interest Versus Symbolic Racism as Predictors of Opposition to Busing in Louisville. Durham, NC: Institute of Policy Sciences, Duke U., 1977.

McDaniel, R. Dale. "Case Study of the Use of the Transportation Algorithm for School Districting Under Federal Integration Guidelines." Socio-Economic Planning Sciences 9 (D, 1975):271-272. [Milwaukee]

MacGee, Jane. "Politico-Geographic Implications of School Busing." Doctoral dissertation, U. of Kansas, 1974.

McGovern, George. "Busing: The Issue Is Us." Integrateducation 14(Mr-Ap, 1976):15-18.

Marzolf, Charlotte. "Busing as a Cost." Master's thesis, U. of Illinois, Chicago, 1976.

Mazzarella, Jo Ann. Making Your Busing Plan Work: A Guide to Desegregation, 1977. ERIC 149 414.

Miah, Malik. Busing and the Black Struggle. New York: Pathfinder Press, N, 1976.

Miller, James Nathan. "What Happens After Busing Starts." Reader's Digest, O, 1971.

Mills, Nicholaus (ed.). The Great School Bus Controversy. New York: Teachers College Press, 1973.

Myers, Albert E. Factors Relating to the Acceptance of Negro Children in a Busing Integration Program (Paper based on a talk given at the meeting of the American Educational Research Association), 1968, 21 pp. ERIC ED 021 925.

National Commission on Safety Education, National Education Association. Study of School Bus Safety (Final Report), D, 1967. Clearinghouse for Federal Scientific and Technical Information, Springfield, VA 22151.

"Nearly 3 of 4 [Administrators] Frown on Busing for Desegregation." Nation's Schools, My, 1968.

Nelson, L. D. "Attitudes Toward Objects and Situations in Opinion Formation: An Inquiry into the School Transportation Issue." Journal of Afro-American Issues 2(1974): 291-302.

Nicoletti, John A., and Patterson, Tom W. "Attitudes Toward Busing as a Means of Desegregation." Psychological Reports 35, part 2(Ag, 1974):371-376.

Novak, Michael. "Busing: The Four Regions." Columbia Journalism Review, Mr-Ap, 1976.

_____. "Busing Won't Always Work." Commonweal, S 22, 1972.

Olitt, Ray, and Malmstrom, Dorothy. School Desegregation and Busing: Guidelines for Transportation Administrators. Riverside, CA: Center for the Study of Intergroup Relations, U. of California, Riverside, Mr, 1970.

Orfield, Gary. Must We Bus?--Segregated Schools and National Policy. Washington, DC: Brookings Institution, 1978.

Ozmon, Howard, and Craver, Sam. Busing: A Moral Issue. Bloomington, IN: Phi Delta Kappa, 1972.

Peterson, Paul E. "The School Busing Controversy: Redistributive or Pluralist Politics?" Administrator's Notebook 20 (1972):1-4.

Pettigrew, Thomas F. "On Busing and Race Relations." Today's Education 63(N-D, 1973).

_____. "School Research and the Busing Issue." Urban Review 6(S-O, 1972):24-25.

Pettigrew, Thomas F. and others. "Busing: a Review of the 'Evidence.'" Public Interest 30(Winter, 1973):88-118.

Planz, Charles A. "It Can Work: Busing Inner City Pupils to Suburban Schools." Clearing House 46(N, 1971):158-162.

Ploeger, Ouida. "A Comparison of Academic Performance and Selected School-Related Attitudes of Bused and Non-Bused White Students in Urban Elementary Schools." Doctoral dissertation, North Texas State U., 1978. Univ. Microfilms Order No. 7816731.

Pugh, George E., and Killalea, J. Neil. A Survey of Urban School Desegregation: Summary Report ["Lambda Report"], My 9, 1974. ERIC ED 094 047.

Rand Corporation. The Costs of School Desegregation: Data from a Sample of School Districts. Santa Monica, CA: Rand Corporation, 1976. [Busing costs]

Randill, Alice, Greenhalgh, Helen, and Samson, Elizabeth. Mode of Transportation and Personal Characteristics of Tripmakers. Washington, DC: U.S. Department of Transportation, N, 1973.

Raspberry, William. "Forget About Busing--Concentrate on Education." Integrateducation 12(S-O, 1974):32. [See Meyers, above.]

Ravitch, Diane. "Busing: The Solution That Has Failed to Solve." New York Times, D 21, 1975.

Samuels, Joseph M. "Busing: One Alternative for Some Children." Contemporary Education 44(O, 1972):7-9.

Scherer, Jacqueline, and Slawski, Edward J. The Social Context of Desegregation: Busing and Scapegoat, 1978. ERIC ED 154 069. [Pontiac]

School Bus Task Force. Pupil Transportation Safety Program Plan. Washington, DC: GPO, My, 1973.

"The 'School Busing' Controversy in the Current Congress." Congressional Digest 53(Ap, 1974):99-107.

Scott, Ralph [Edward P. Langerton, pseud.] The Busing Coverup. Cape Canaveral, FL: Howard Allen, 1975.

Severy, Derwyn M., Brink, Harrison M., and Baird, Jack D. School Bus Passenger Protection, 1967. Society of Automotive Engineers, 485 Lexington Avenue, New York, NY 10017.

Shannon, Randy. "The Busing Issue: New Smokescreen." Southern Patriot, My, 1972.

"Should Your City Or Town Try To Integrate Its Public Schools Through Redistricting and Busing?" Transcript of two telecasts in "The Advocates" program, Ap 12, 19, 1970. Reprinted in U.S. Congress, 91st, 2nd session, Senate, Select Committee on Equal Educational Opportunity, Equal Educational Opportunity. Hearings... Part 3E, pp. 2361-2388. Washington, DC: GPO, 1970.

Smith, Paul V. "Pupil Transportation: A Brief History." Inequality in Education 11(Mr, 1972):6-21.

Solstad, Karl Johan. "Pupils' Views on School Transportation." Scandanavian Journal of Educational Research 19(1975):27-43.

Spence, Ralph B. "Best Education for All Children Includes Busing." Phi Delta Kappan (My, 1972):539, 573.

Stimson, David H., and Thompson, Ronald P. "The Importance of 'Weltanschauung' in Operations Research: The Case of the School Busing Problem." Management Science 21(Je, 1975):1123-1132.

Stockton, Ronald R., and Wayman, Francis W. "The Busing Issue: Race and Social Change." Michigan Academician 8(Spring, 1976).

Straley, Harry G. "A Comparative Study of the Academic Achievement and Social Adjustment of Transported and Non-Transported High School Seniors." Doctoral dissertation, U. of Virginia, 1956.

"The Talk of the Town. Notes and Comment." New Yorker, Mr 11, 1972. [Public debate over busing]

Taylor, William L. "Busing: Realities and Evasions." Dissent (Fall, 1972):586-594.

Thibeault, Robert J. and others. "The Achievement of Bus Transported Students." Journal of Teaching and Learning 2(Ja, 1977):17-22.

Thompson, Ronald P., and Stimson, David H. Operations Research and the School Busing Problem. Berkeley, CA: Institute of Urban and Regional Development, U. of California, Berkeley, Ag, 1972.

U.S. Commission on Civil Rights. Your Child and Busing. Washington, DC: GPO, My, 1972.

U.S. Congress, 92nd, 2nd session, House of Representatives, Committee on the Judiciary, Subcommittee No. 5. School Busing. Hearings... 3 parts. Washington, DC: GPO, 1972.

U.S. Congress, 93rd, 2nd session, Senate, Committee on the Judiciary, Subcommittee on Constitutional Rights. Busing of Schoolchildren. Hearings... Washington, DC: GPO, 1974.

U.S. Congress, 95th, 1st session, Senate, Committee on the Judiciary. Busing of Schoolchildren. Hearings... Washington, DC: GPO, 1977.

U.S. Congress, 95th, 1st session, Senate, Committee on the Judiciary. Transportation as a Remedy in School Desegregation. Washington, DC: GPO, 1977.

U.S. Department of Transportation. Report on School Busing, Mr 10, 1972. Submitted to U.S. Commission on Civil Rights.

U.S. Department of Transportation. School Bus Vehicle Safety Report. Washington, DC: Department of Transportation, 1977.

Van Fleet, Alanson A. "Student Transportation Costs Following Desegregation." Integrat-education 15(N-D, 1977):75-77.

Vaughn, S. C. "Congressional Power to Eliminate Busing in School Desegregation Cases." Arkansas Law Review 31(Summer, 1977):251-253.

Wasserman, Miriam. "The Contradictions of Antibusing and the Politics of Busing." Liberation 17(S, 1972):14-21.

Watters, Pat. "That Big Old Yellow Busing Bamboozle." South Today 3(Ap, 1972):2.

Weidman, John C. "Resistance of White Adults to the Busing of School Children." Journal of Research and Development in Education 9(F, 1975):123-129.

White, Dan S. "Does Busing Harm Urban Elementary Pupils?" Phi Delta Kappan 53(N, 1971): 192-193.

Whiting, Frank Sheldon. "Selected Effects of Busing on Black Students." Doctoral Dissertation, n.p., 1974, Univ. Microfilm Order No. 75-5583.

Wise, Michael (ed.). "Busing." In Desegregation in Education: A Directory of Reported Federal Decisions, p. 202. Notre Dame, IN: Center for Civil Rights, U. of Notre Dame Law School, Ap, 1977. [1954-1976]

Woodard, James D. "Busing Plans, Media Agendas, and Patterns of White Flight: Nashville, Tennessee and Louisville, Kentucky." Doctoral dissertation, Vanderbilt U., 1978. Univ. Microfilms Order No. 7819545. [White Flight]

Zoloth, Barbara S. The Impact of Busing on Student Achievement: A Reanalysis. Madison, WI: Institute for Research on Poverty, U. of Wisconsin, n.d.

_____. "The Impact of Busing on Student Achievement: Reanalysis." Growth and Change 7(Jl, 1976).

_____. "The Impact of Busing on Student Achievement: Rejoinder." Growth and Change 7(Jl, 1976).

Libraries

American Library Association. "Library Service to Educational Institutions Established to Circumvent Desegregation Laws." ALA Intellectual Freedom News 18(Mr, 1970): 17.

Bell, B. L. "Library Integration in Thirteen Southern States. Library Journal, D, 1963.

Berman, Sanford. Prejudices and Antipathies: A Tract on the LC Subject Heads Concerning People. Metuchen, NJ: Scarecrow Press, 1971.

Braverman, Miriam. "In Touch: Connecting the Library's Resources to the Ghetto." Wilson Library Bulletin, My, 1969.

Cabello-Argandona, Roberto. "Recruiting Spanish-Speaking Library Students." Library
Journal 101(My, 1976):1177-1179.

Cabello-Argandona, Roberto, and Haro, Roberto
Peter. System Analysis of Library and
Information Services to the Spanish Speaking
Community of the United States, 1977. ERIC
ED 143 368.

Carter, Jane Robbins. "Multi-cultural Graduate
Library Education." Journal of Education
for Librarianship 18(Spring, 1978):295-314.

Clark, A. A. "Black Parent Looks at Service
from a Large Urban Library System." Pennsylvania Library Association Bulletin 24
(N, 1969):321-323.

Clark, Kenneth B. "A Role for Librarians in
the Relevant War Against Poverty." Wilson
Library Bulletin, S, 1965.

Childers, Thomas, and Adams, Kathlyn. "Recruitment of Minorities." American Libraries 3(Je, 1972):612-621.

Clack, Doris H. "The Adequacy of Library of
Congress Subject Headings for Black Liter-
ature Resources." Library Resources and
Technical Services 22(Spring, 1978):137-144.

Curtis, Florence Rising. "Colored Libraries
in Conference." Library Journal 52(Ap,
1927):408.

Davila, Daniel. Library Service for the Spanish-Speaking User: Source Guide for Librarians, 1976. ERIC ED 135 400.

DuBois, W. E. B. "The Opening of the Library."
Independent, Ap, 1902.

Estes, R. "Segregated Libraries." Library
Journal, D, 1960.

Franklin, Hardy Rogers. "The Relationship Be-
tween Adult Communication Practices and
Public Library Use in a Northern, Urban,
Black Ghetto." Doctoral dissertation,
Rutgers U., 1971. Univ. Microfilms Order
No. 72-09621.

Garrison, Dee. Apostles of Culture: The
Public Librarian and American Society,
1876-1920. New York: Macmillan Information,
1979.

Gleason, Elizabeth A. The Southern Library
and the Negro. N.p., n.p.: 1939.

Higgins, Norman, and Smith, Lotsee. Recommendations for Improving Library Media Training
and Services in Rural Indian Communities,
Ap, 1977. ERIC ED 142 183.

Hinchcliff, William. "Ivory Tower Ghettoes."
Library Journal, N, 1969, pp. 3971-3974.

Hughes, Langston. Books and the Negro Child."
In American Library Association. Committee
on Library Work with Children, Children's
Library Yearbook. No. 4, pp. 108-110.
Chicago, IL: American Library Association,
1932.

"In Search of Soul." Library Journal 95(Ag,
1970):2632-2634.

International Research Associates. Access to
Public Libraries. Chicago, IL: American
Library Association, 1963.

Jackson, Wallace Van. "Some Pioneer Negro
Library Workers." Library Journal 44(Mr,
1939):216-217.

Jordan, C. L. "Library Service to Black Americans." Library Trends 20(O, 1971):271-
279.

_____. "Can Library Affirmative Action
Succeed?" Library Journal 100(Ja, 1975):
28-31.

Josey, E. J. "Coddling Segregation: The Case
for ALA Action." Library Journal 96(My,
1971):1778-1779.

_____. "The Future of the Black College
Library." Library Journal, S, 1969.

_____. "Libraries, Reading and the Liberation
of Black People." Library Scene 1(Winter,
1972):4-7.

_____. "Mouthful of Civil Rights and an
Empty Stomach." Library Journal, Ja, 1965.

_____. "Statement of the IFC Report." School
Library Journal 18(S, 1971):26-29. [On
library service to segregated academies]

Josey, E. J. (ed.). The Black Librarian in
America. Metuchen, NJ: Scarecrow Press,
1970.

Josey, E. J., and Peeples, Kenneth E. (eds.).
Opportunities for Minorities in Librarianship. Metuchen, NJ: Scarecrow Press, 1977.

Josey, E. J., and Shockley, Ann Allen (eds.).
Handbook of Black Librarianship. Littleton,
CO: Libraries Unlimited, 1978.

Library Administration Division, American
Library Association. "Library Employment of
Minority Group Personnel." ALA Bulletin,
Jl-Ag, 1969.

Monroe, M. E. "Reader Services to the Disadvantaged in Inner Cities." In Advances in
Librarianship 2, pp. 253-274. Seminar Press,
1971.

Moon, Eric. "A Survey of Segregation."
Library Journal, Mr, 1961.

Moore, Ray Nicholas. "Mollie Huston Lee: A Profile." Wilson Library Bulletin 49(F, 1975):432-439.

"Negro Research Libraries Needs Identified." Library Journal 95(My, 1970).

Obeler, E. M. "Attitudes on Segregation, How American Library Association Compares with Other Professional Associations." Library Journal, D, 1961.

Office for Library Service to the Disadvantaged. Directory of Ethnic Study Librarians. Chicago, IL: American Library Association, 1977.

Orange, N.J. Public Library. "Subject Headings from Negro to Black." ALA Bulletin, Je, 1969.

Perry, Margaret. "Race and Education." American Libraries 2(N, 1971):1051-1054.

"Personality Plus: Profiles of Contemporary Black Librarians." American Libraries 9 (F, 1978):81-86.

Peterson, Anita R. and others. Library Service to the Spanish Speaking. Inglewood, CA: Inglewood Public Library, 1977.

Pierce, Sydney. Public Libraries and Affirmative Action: Exploiting the Resources of ALA, Jl, 1976. ERIC ED 127 963.

Rayford, V. A. "Black Librarian Takes a Look at Discrimination: By a Law School Library Survey." Law Library Journal 65(My, 1972): 183-189.

Rhodes, Lelia Gaston. "A Critical Analysis of the Career Backgrounds of Selected Black Female Librarians." Doctoral dissertation, Florida State U., 1975. Univ. Microfilms Order No. 75-26810.

Richardson, B. E. "QuoJure?" American Libraries 2(Mr, 1971):304-305. [On advertising for black librarians]

Rockwood, Ruth H. (ed.). Urban Change and Public Library Development: Selected Papers. Tallahassee, FL: School of Library Science, Florida State U., 1972.

Rose, Ernestine and others. "Work with Negroes." Library Journal, Ag, 1922.

Rouselle, W., and Ireland, J. "Public Libraries and Black People." Louisiana Library Association Bulletin 33(Spring, 1970):6-10.

Schuman, Patricia. "Southern Integration: Writing Off the Black Librarian." School Library Journal, My, 1971, pp. 37-39.

Scott, S. L. "Integration of Public Library Facilities in the South: Attitudes and Actions of the Library Profession." Southeastern Librarian, Fall, 1968.

"Segregation in Libraries: Negro Librarians Give Their Views." Wilson Library Bulletin, My, 1961.

Shaughnessy, Thomas W. "Library Services to Educationally Disadvantaged Students." College and Research Libraries 36(N, 1975): 443-448.

Shockley, Ann Allen. "Black Book Reviewing: A Case for Library Action." College and Research Libraries 35(Ja, 1974):16-20.

Shores, Louis. "Public Library Service to Negroes." Library Journal 55(F, 1930):150-154.

South, J. A. and others. "Panel on Negro Research Libraries." In Conference on Federal Information Resources. Washington, DC: Federal City College Press, 1971.

"Southern Segregationism Echoed in Library Patterns." Library Journal 95(My, 1970): 1883. [Comment, O, 1970 by A. Powell]

Totten, Herman L. "A Survey and Evaluation of Minority Programs in Selected Graduate Library Schools." Journal of Education for Librarianship 18(Summer, 1977):18-34.

Urzua, Roberto and others (eds.). Library Services to Mexican Americans: Policies, Practices and Prospects, Ja, 1978. ERIC ED 151 110.

White, Lorenzo C. "The Negro Organization Society Library Work." Southern Workman 8(Ag, 1927):363-372.

Wilkins, John. "Blue's 'Colored Branch: A Second Plan' that Became a First in Librarianship." American Libraries 7(My, 1976): 256-257. [Louisville, KY]

Wright, J. R. "Staffing Inner-City Libraries: Black or White, or Black and White." Wilson Library Journal 45(Je, 1971):987.

Racism

Adam, Barry. "Social Psychology of Inferiorized Peoples." Doctoral dissertation, U. of Toronto, 1978.

Adams, Paul L. "Dealing with Racism in Biracial Psychiatry." Journal of the American Academy of Child Psychiatry 9(1970):33-43.

Addlestone, David F., and Sherer, Susan. "Race in Viet Nam." Civil Liberties, F, 1973.

Adedeji, Moses. "Crossing the Colorline: Three Decades of the United Packinghouse Workers of America's Crusade Against Racism in the Trans-Mississippi West, 1936-1968." Doctoral dissertation, North Texas State U., 1978. Univ. Microfilms Order No. 7824626. [Texas, Oklahoma, Louisiana, Arkansas, New Mexico, and south Kansas]

Alatas, Syed Hussein. The Myth of the Lazy Native. Edinburgh: Edinburgh U. Press, 1977.

Aldrich, Mark. "Capital Theory and Racism: From Laissez-Faire to the Eugenics Movement in the Career of Irving Fisher." Review of Radical Political Economics 7 (Fall, 1975):33-42.

Alexander, George W. "Racism and the Chaplaincy." Military Chaplains' Review 2 (Ag, 1973):45-51.

Alexander, Rae. "What is a Racist Book?" Interracial Books for Children 3(Autumn, 1970).

Allen, Ben P. "Implications of Social Reaction Research for Racism." Psychological Reports 29(D, 1971):883-891.

Allen, Robert L. Black Awakening in Capitalist America. Garden City, NY: Doubleday, 1969.

_____. "Racism and the Black Nation Thesis." Socialist Revolution 6(Ja-Mr, 1976):145-150.

_____. "Rap Brown Raps: Racism and Revolution." Guardian, Je, 1968.

_____. Relectant Reformers: The Impact of Racism on American Social Reform Movements. Washington, DC: Howard U. Press, 1974.

Allen, Sheila. "The Institutionalization of Racism." Race 15(Jl, 1973):99-106.

Allen, Theodore. "'...They Would Have Destroyed me': Slavery and the Origins of Racism." Radical America 9(My-Je, 1975).

American Library Association. "Resolution on Racism and Sexism Awareness." Integrateducation 15(Ja-F, 1977).

Anderson, Glenn B., and Bowe, Frank G. "Racism Within the Deaf Community." American Annals of the Deaf 117(D, 1972):617-619.

Aptheker, Herbert. "The History of Anti-Racism in the United States." Black Scholar 6(Ja-F, 1975):16-22.

_____. "Racism and Historiography." Political Affairs, My, 1970.

_____. "US Imperialism and Racism: A History." Political Affairs 52(Jl, 1973):75-85.

Ashmore, Richard D., and Del Boca, Frances K. "Psychological Approaches to Understanding Intergroup Conflicts." In Towards the Elimination of Racism, pp. 73-123. Edited by Phyllis A. Katz. New York: Pergamon, 1976.

Bagley, Christopher. "Racialism and Pluralism: A Dimensional Analysis of Forty-Eight Countries." Race 13(Ja, 1972):347-354.

Banton, Michael. "What Do We Mean by Racism?" New Society, Ap, 1969.

_____. "Race As A Social Category." Race, Jl, 1966.

Baran, Paul, and Sweezy, Paul M. "Monopoly Capitalism and Race Relations." Monopoly Capital. New York: Monthly Review Press, 1966.

Baron, Harold M. "Racial Domination in Advanced Capitalism: A Theory of Nationalism and Division in the Labor Market." In R. C. Edwards and others, Labor Market Segmentation. Lexington: Heath, 1975.

_____. "Web of Urban Racism." Appendix to Institutional Racism in America. Edited by Kenneth Prewitt and Louis Knowles. Englewood Cliffs, NJ: Prentice-Hall, 1969.

Baxter, Paul, and Sansom, Basil (eds.). Race and Social Difference. Selected Readings. Baltimore MD: Penguin, 1972.

Beardsley, Edward H. "The American Scientist as Social Adctivist. Franz Boas, Burt G. Wilder, and the Cause of Racial Justice, 1900-1915." Isis 64(Mr, 1973):50-66.

Beasley, Lou. "A Beginning Attempt to Eradicate Racist Attitudes." Social Casework 53(Ja, 1972):9-13.

Beaver, Gene Marvin. "The Beliefs of the Citizens' Councils: A Study in Segregationist Thought." Master's thesis, California State College at Fullerton, 1968. Univ. Microfilms Order No. M-1669.

Becker, Jorg. "Racism in Children's and Young People's Literature in the Western World." Journal of Peace Research, 1973.

Bell, Derrick A., Jr. "Black Faith in a Racist Land." Journal of Public Law 20(1971).

_____. "Racism in American Courts." California Law Review 61(1973).

Belli, Robert E. Racism: Problem for the Officer. Maxwell Air Force Base, AL: Air War College, Air U., Ap, 1973.

Ben-Tovin, Gideon. "The Struggle Against Racism: Theoretical and Strategic Perspectives." Marxism Today 22(Jl, 1978).

Bennett, Lerone, Jr. "System. Internal Colonialism Structures Black, White Relations in America." Ebony 27(Ap, 1972):33-42.

Benokraitis, Nijole, and Feagin, Joe. "Institutional Racism: A Perspective in Search of Clarity and Research." In Black/Brown/White Relations. Edited by Charles V. Willie. New Brunswick, NJ: Transaction, 1977.

Berlowitz, Marvin J. "Institutional Racism and School Staffing in an Urban Area." Journal of Negro Education 43(Winter, 1974):25-29.

Berman, Sanford. "Racism and Library Science." Library Journal, F, 1969.

Berreman, Gerald D. "Race, Caste, and Other Invidious Distinctions in Social Stratification." Race 13(Ap, 1972):385-414.

Biddiss, Michael D. "Fascism and the Race Question: A Review of Recent Historiography." Race, Ja, 1969.

Bidol, Patricia M. "'A Rap on Race'--A Mini-Lecture on Racism Awareness." Interracial Books for Children 5(1974):9-10.

Billings, Charles. Racism and Prejudice. N.p.: Hayden, 1977.

"Black Revolution and White Backlash." National Guardian, Jl, 1964. [Verbatim transcript of forum; participants included Lorraine Hansberry, David Susskind, Paule Marshall, Leroi Jones, Ossie Davis, Ruby Dee, Charles E. Silberman, John Killens, and James Wechsler.]

"Black, Isabella. "Race and Unreason: Anti-Negro Opinion in Professional and Scientific Literature Since 1954." Phylon, Spring, 1965.

"Black Psychiatrists: How Racism is Reflected in Referrals." Frontier of Clinical Psychiatry (Roche Report), Jl, 1969.

Black Racism Project. Critique of the Black Nation Thesis, 1975. P.O. Box 3026, South Berkeley Station, Berkeley, CA 94703.

Blackwell, Ed. "Challenging the Establishment: A Black Reporter Looks at the Press." Communication: Journalism Education Today 8(F, 1974):10-11.

Blauner, Robert. Racial Oppression in America. New York: Harper and Row, 1972.

Bloom, Jack. "Racism and Higher Education." Independent Socialist, Ap, 1969.

Blumer, Herbert. "The Future of the Color Line." In The South in Continuity and Change. Edited by John C. McKinney and Edgar T. Thompson. Durham, NC: Duke U. Press, 1965.

Boggs, James, and Boggs, Grace Lee. "Uprooting Racists and Racism in the U.S." Negro Digest 19(Ja, 1970):20-22.

Bond, Julian. "The Roots of Racism and War." Black Scholar(N, 1970):20-24.

"Books, Libraries and Racism." Race Today 5 (O-N, 1973).

Braddock, Jomills Henry II. "Colonialism, Education, and Black Students: A Social-Psychological Analysis." Doctoral dissertation, Florida State U., 1973. Univ. Microfilms Order No. 74-09479.

_____. "Internal Colonialism and Black American Education." Western Journal of Black Studies 2(Spring, 1978):24-33.

Bresnahan, James F. "White Racism." America, Mr, 1969.

Brodbelt, Samuel. "Disguised Racism in Public Schools." Educational Leadership 29(My, 1972):699-702.

Bromley, Stephanie and others. Black and White Racism: An Unobtrusive Experimental Assessment, Ap, 1977. ERIC ED 151 626.

Brophy, Michael C. and others. Advocacy and Institutional Racism, S, 1976. ERIC ED 141 649.

Brown, Bertram S. "Racism and Our Ethnic Minorities." In White Working Class Culture. Compiled by Frank F. Montalvo. Patrick Air Force Base, FL: Defense Race Relations Institute, 1975.

Brown, H. Rap. Die, Nigger, Die. New York: Dial, 1969.

Brown, Roy. "Racism: The Worst Tool of Cruelty." Integrated Education (My-Je, 1972):3-10.

Bruening, William H. "Racism: A Philosophical Analysis of a Concept." Journal of Black Studies 5(S, 1974):3-17.

Bullock, Charles S. III, and Rodgers, Harrell R., Jr. "Institutional Racism: Prerequisites, Freezing, and Mapping." Phylon 37(S, 1976):212-223.

Burgest. David R. "Language, Culture and White Supremacy." Doctoral dissertation, Syracuse U., 1974. Univ. Microfilms Order No. 76-7886.

Butler, John Sibley. "Inequality in the Military: An Examination of Promotion Time for Black and White Enlisted Men." American Sociological Review 41(1976):807-818.

_____. "Unsanctioned Institutional Racism in the U.S. Army." Doctoral dissertation, Northwestern U., 1974.

Butts, Hugh F. "Psychoanalysis and Unconscious Racism." Journal of Contemporary Psychotherapy 3(Spring, 1971):67-81.

_____. "Psychoanalysis, the Black Community and Mental Health." Contemporary Psychoanalysis 7(Spring, 1971):147-152.

_____. "White Racism: Its Origin, Institution, and the Implication for Professional Practice in Mental Health." International Journal of Psychiatry 8(1969):914-944.

CIBC Racism and Sexism Resource Center for Educators. Human and Anti-Human Values in Children's Books, 1976. Racism and Sexism Resource Center for Educators, 1841 Broadway,

Camejo, Peter. Racism, Revolution, Reaction, 1861-1877. The Rise and Fall of Radical Reconstruction. New York: Monad Press, 1976.

Campbell, Angus. White Attitudes Toward Black People. Ann Arbor, MI: Institute for Social Research, U. of Michigan, 1971.

Campbell, Ernest L. (ed.). Racial Tensions and National Identity. Nashville, TN: Vanderbilt U. Press, 1972.

Campbell, Mavis. "Aristotle and Black Slavery: A Study in Race Prejudice." Race 15(Ja, 1974):283-301.

Carew, Jan. "The Origins of Racism in the Americas." Bim (Christ Church, Barbados)15 (D, 1975):222-242.

Carnoy, Martin. Education as Cultural Imperialism. New York: David McKay, 1974.

Carpenter, Joseph. "Racism in American Education." Marquette University Education Review 6(Spring, 1975):5-19.

Carruthers, Iva Elayne Johnson Wells. "Black Power and Integration: A Reformulation of the Theory of Race Relations." Doctoral dissertation, Northwestern U., 1972. Univ. Microfilms Order No. 72-32400.

Casserly, Michael D., and Garrett, John R. "Beyond the Victim: New Avenues for Research on Racism in Education." Educational Theory 27(Summer, 1977):196-204.

Castro, Rudolph and others. "The Problem of Racism: An Attitudinal Study of the Spanish Surname." Master's thesis, U. of Denver, 1972.

Cauthen, Nelson R. and others. "Stereotypes: A Review of the Literature, 1926-1968." Journal of Social Psychology 84(Je, 1971): 103-125. [Ethnic group stereotypes]

Chambers, Bradford. "Book Publishing: A Racist Club?" Publishers Weekly, F, 1971.

Chapman, T. H. "Simulation Game Effects on Attitudes Regarding Racism and Sexism." Doctoral dissertation, U. of Maryland, 1974.

Chase, Allan. The Legacy of Malthus. The Social Cost of the New Scientific Racism. New York: Knopf, 1977.

Cherry, R. "Racial Thought and the Early Economics Profession." Review of Social Economy 34(O, 1976).

Chesler, Mark S. "Contemporary Sociological Theories of Racism." In Towards the Elimination of Racism, pp. 21-71. Edited by Phyllis A. Katz. New York: Pergamon, 1976.

Chisholm, Shirley. "The Black As a Colonized Man." Afro-American Studies I(My, 1970): 1-10.

Chrisman, Robert. "Blacks, Racism, and Bourgeois Culture." Black Scholar 7(Ja-F, 1976):2-10.

_____. "Blacks, Racism and Bourgeois Culture." College English 38(Ap, 1977).

Clark, Cedric C. "On Racism and Racist Systems." Negro Digest, Ag, 1969.

Clark, Kenneth B. "'Any Kind of Racism Is a Constriction of the Mind" (interview). This Week, Je, 1969.

_____. "As Old as Human Cruelty." New York Times Book Review, S, 1968.

_____. "Beyond the Dilemma." In Representative American Speeches: 1969-1970, pp. 168-178. Edited by Lester Thoussen. New York: Wilson, 1970. [Effect of racism on whites]

_____. "Intelligence, the University, and the Society." American Scholar, Winter, 1966-1967.

Clark, Robert, and Ward, C. G. (eds.). Racism and the Desegregating Process. Jackson, MS: Educational Resources Center, 1970.

Coffin, Gregory C. "Combating Racism in the Junior High School." Middle School/Junior High Principal's Service, F, 1971.

_____. "Desegregation-Integration-Racism." School Board Policies (Croft Educational Services) No. 7(F, 1972).

Coggs, Pauline R., and Johnson, Betty S. "Re-flections on Five Continuing Education Pro-grams on Race and Social Work Practice." In "The Urban Minority Experience," Selected Proceedings of the 4th Annual Con-ference on Minority Studies, pp. 41-47. Edited by George E. Carter and James R. Parker. La Crosse, WI: Institute for Minority Studies, U. of Wisconson-La Crosse, 1978.

Coles, Robert. "Understanding White Racists." New York Review of Books 18(D, 1971):12-15.

_____. "The White Northerner. Pride and Prejudice." Atlantic Monthly, Je, 1966.

Collier, Betty. "Economics, Psychology, and Racism: An Analysis of Oppression." Journal of Black Psychology 3(F, 1977):50-60.

Colman, Andrew M. "'Scientific' Racism and the Evidence on Race and Intelligence." Race 14(O, 1972):137-153.

Comarmond, Patrice de, and Duchet, Claude. Racisme et Societe. Paris: N.p., 1969.

Comer, James P., and Coleman, James E., Jr. "Quotas, Race, and Justice." New York Times, Mr 17, 1974. [Two articles]

Comer, James P. "White Racism: Its Roots, Form, and Function." American Journal of Psychiatry 120(1969):802-806.

Conlen, Paul. "The Historical Genesis and Material Basis of Racial Endogamy in Racist Societies." Doctoral dissertation, U. of Lund, Sweden, 1974. [Nazi Germany, South Africa, and the United States]

Cooper, David I., Jr. "Race in the Military: The Tarnished Sword." Retired Officer, F, 1971.

Cooper, Mark N. "Racialism and Pluralism as Dimensions of Nations: A Further Investi-gation." Race 15(Ja, 1974):370-381.

Cox, Uri. "Goose Father." Human Behavior 3 (Mr, 1974):17-22. [Includes discussion of early racist writings by Nobel Laureate Karl Lorenz]

Crockett, George W., Jr. "Racism in the Law." Muhammad Speaks, N, 1969.

Crosby, Edward W. "The Nigger and the Nar-cissus (or Self-Awareness in Black Educa-tion)." In Black America, pp. 271-285. Edited by John F. Szwed. New York: Basic Books, 1970.

Cross, Malcolm. "On Conflict, Race Relations, and the Theory of the Plural Society." Race 12(Ap, 1971):477-494.

Culver, Thomas. "Race at German Bases." Civil Liberties (A.C.L.U.), Ja, 1972.

da Costa, G. A. "Orphans and Outlaws: Some Impacts of Racism." Multiculturalism 2 (1978):4-7.

Daniels, Roger, and Kitano, Harry H. L. "Racism in Practice: 1769-1942." In American Racism: Exploration of the Nature of Prejudice, pp. 29-72. Englewood Cliffs, NJ: Prentice-Hall, 1970.

Davis, Angela Y. "Racism and Contemporary Literature on Rape." Freedomways 16(1976): 25-33.

Delany, Lloyd T. "Racism and Strategy for Change." Psychology Today, Ag, 1968.

Della-Sora, Delmo. "The Schools Can Overcome Racism" Educational Leadership 29(F, 1972):443-449.

Dewey, John. "Racial Prejudice and Friction." Chinese Social and Political Science Review 6(1921):1-17.

Daams, Gerrit. "Summary of Segregation, Dis-crimination, and Open Housing." Citizen, My, 1965. [A segregationist statement by a professor of philosophy at Kent State U.]

Daniels, O. C. Bobby. Racism: Awareness, Tolerance and Evaluation. A Research Re-port on the Level of Interracial Appercep-tion and Ideology in the Residential Areas of the University. Amherst, MA: U. of Massachusetts, 1974.

Danzig, David. "Rightists, Racists, and Sep-aratists: A White Block in the Making?" Commentary, Ag, 1964.

Davis, George A. "The Hypocricies of White Racism." In George A. Davis, Donald S. Smith, and Carlyle Johnson, Black Issues. Patrick Air Force Base, FL: Defense Race Relations Institute, 1975.

Denantes, F. "Racisme et 'Classe Ouvriere'." Project 80(D, 1973):1233-1240.

Dhondy, Farrukh. "Overtly Political Focus." Times Educational Supplement, N 2, 1973. [The missing political element in race relations instruction]

Dickeman, Mildred. "Racism in the Library: A Model from the Public Schools." School Library Journal, F, 1973.

_____. "Thoughts on the Dominant American." Massachusetts Review 15(Summer, 1974):405-418.

Dieterich. Daniel. "Racism, Sexism in Child-ren's Literature." Reading Teacher 28 (D, 1974):346-349.

Division of Legal Information and Community Service. It's Not the Distance, "It's the Niggers". Comments on the Controversy Over School Busing, My, 1972. NAACP Legal Defense and Educational Fund, 10 Columbus Circle, New York, NY 10019.

Dodson, Dan W. "Institutionalized Racism in Social Welfare Agencies." In The Social Welfare Forum, 1970, pp. 88-98. New York: Columbia U. Press, 1970.

_____. "Perspectives on Institutional Racism." In New Challenge to Social Agency Leadership. Edited by Arnold H. Grossman, 1979. Groupwork Today, Inc., P.O. Box 258, South Plainfield, NJ 07080.

Donaldson, O. Fred. "To Keep Them in Their Place - A Socio-Spatial Perspective on Race Relations in America." Doctoral dissertation, U. of Washington, 1974.

Downs, Anthony. Racism in America and How to Combat It. U.S. Commission on Civil Rights Clearinghouse Publication. Washington, DC: GPO, 1970.

"Draft Programme for 10 Years of Action Against Racialism. A UNESCO Memoransum." Patterns of Prejudice 6(S-O, 1972):21-24.

Dressler, John. "Racism: A New Analytical Tool in Recent American Historiography." Journal of Social and Behavioral Sciences 18 (Fall-Winter, 1971-1972):42-49.

Drewry, Henry N. "U.S. Rationalized Slavery and Produced Racism." University (Princeton U.), Summer, 1969.

Dreyfus, Joel. "The New Racism." Black Enterprise 8(Ja, 1978):41-44, 54.

Drimmer, Melvin. "Thoughts on the Persistence of American Racism." Afro-American Studies 1(Ap, 1971):309-313.

Duchet, C., and de Comarmond, P. (eds.). Racisme et Societe. Paris: Maspero, 1969.

Duster, Troy. "The Structure of Privilege and Its Universe of Discourse." American Sociologist 11(My, 1976):73-78.

Edler, James M. "White on White: An Anti-Racism Manual for White Educators in the Process of Becoming." Doctoral dissertation, U. of Massachusetts, 1974. Univ. Microfilms Order No. 74-15008.

Edmondson, Locksley. "Trans-Atlantic Slavery and the Internationalization of Race." Caribbean Quarterly 22(Je-S, 1976):5-25.

Education and Racism. An Action Manual. Washington, DC: National Education Associates, 1973.

Edwards, Daniel W. "Blacks versus Whites: When Is Race a Relevant Variable?" Journal of Personality and Social Psychology 29 (Ja, 1974):39-49.

Edwards, Herbert O., Jr. "Christian Ethics and Racism." Doctoral dissertation, Brown U., 1974.

Ehrlich, Howard J. Some Criteria for Radical Social Research. Research Group One, 2743 Maryland Ave., Baltimore, MD 21218.

_____. The Social Psychology of Prejudice: A Systematic Theoretical Review and Propositional Inventory of the American Social Psychological Study of Prejudice. New York: Wiley, 1973.

Eidson, Bettye. "Institutional Racism: Minority Group Manpower Policies of Major Urban Employers." Doctoral dissertation, Johns Hopkins U., 1971.

Erving, Lee. "It Can Happen Here." Family, Supplement of Army Times, Ag, 1971. [Racial conflict at Travis Air Force Base, My 22-24, 1971]

Faris, J. C., Kroch, A. S., and Newcomer, P. "On the Continuing Revival of Scientific Racism." Newsletter of the American Anthropological Association 13(1972):10-11.

Feagin, Joe R. "White Separatists and Black Separatists: A Comparative Analysis." Social Problems 19(Fall, 1971):167-180.

Fein, Helen. "Toleration of Genocide." Patters of Prejudice 7(S-O, 1973):22-28. [Attitudes in U.S., 1933-1945]

Feldstein, Stanley (ed.). The Poisoned Tongue. A Documentary History of American Racism and Prejudice. New York: Morrow, 1972.

Field, Geoffrey G. "H. S. Chamberlain: Prophet of Bayreuth." Doctoral dissertation, Columbia U., 1972.

_____. "Nordic Racism." Journal of the History of Ideas 38(Jl-S, 1977):523-540.

Forman, James. "The Indivisible Struggle Against Racism, Apartheid and Colonialism. Position Paper of SNCC delivered at the International Seminar...in Lusaka, Zambia, July 24-August 4, 1967." List Mailing, Jl, 1967.

Franklin, Raymond S., and Resnik, Solomon. The Political Economy of Racism. New York: Holt, Rinehart, and Winston, 1973.

Frazier, E. Franklin. "My Most Humiliating Jim Crow Experience." Negro Digest 4(N, 1945).

Fuentes, Luis. The Fight Against Racism in Our Schools. New York: Pathfinder Press, 1974.

Gagala, Kenneth L. "Racism in the Building Trade." Doctoral dissertation, Michigan State U., 1970. [Detroit and Chicago]

Garrett, Henry E. Children: Black and White. 1968. Patrick Henry Press, Box 355, Kilmarnock, VA 22482 [A revision of How Classroom Desegregation Will Work]

_____. "Garrett's Stuff." Integrated Education (Mr-Ap, 1968):42.

_____. How Classroom Desegregation Will Work. Richmond, VA: Patrick Henry Press, 1965.

"Dr. [Henry E.] Garrett Teaches School Superintendent Neil V. Sullivan." Citizen, O, 1967.

Gay, Geneva. "Racism in America: Imperatives for Teaching Ethnic Studies." In Teaching Ethnic Studies: Concepts and Strategies. Edited by James A. Banks. Washington, DC: National Council for the School Studies, 1973.

Gayle, Addison, Jr. "Black Power or Black Fascism?" Liberator, My, 1968.

Gilbert, Neil, and Specht, Harry. "Institutional Racism." Urban and Social Change Review 6(F, 1972):2-6.

Giles, Michael W., Gatlin, Douglas S., and Cataldo, Everett F. "Racial and Class Prejudice: Their Relative Effects on Protest Against School Desegregation." American Sociological Review 41(Ap, 1976): 280-288.

Gillam, Richard. "White Racism and the Civil Rights Movement." Yale Review 62(Je, 1973): 520-543.

Ginger, Ann Fagan. "Combating Racism in U.S. Law Schools." Lawyers Guild Practitioner 31(1974).

_____. "The Use of the Law Against Racism in the United States." Review of Contemporary Law 2(1976):43-47.

Glott, Charles S., and King, George D. "Institutional Racism and White Racists: A Socio-Psychological View of Race and Educational Development." In Race and Education Across Cultures. Edited by G. H. Verma and Christopher Bagley. Stamford, CT: Greylock Publishers, 1975.

Gobetz, Giles Edward. "'Race' Differences in Attitude and Ability Among the Geriatric Blind." Journal of Negro Education 41(Winter, 1972):57-61.

Goldschmid, Marcel L. (ed.). Black Americans and White Racism: Theory and Research. New York: Holt, Rinehart and Winston, 1970.

Good, Paul. "The Bricks and Mortar of Racism." New York Times Magazine, My 21, 1972. [N.Y.C. building crafts]

Goodman, James (ed.). Dynamics of Racism in Social Work Practice. Washington, DC: National Association of Social Workers, 1973.

Goodman, Paul. "Reflections on Racism, Spite, Guilt, and Violence." New York Review of Books, My, 1968.

Goodrich, Linda Sharon. "A Historical Survey of Cultural Racism and Its Subsequent Impact on the Education of Black Americans." Doctoral dissertation, Ohio State U., 1976. Univ. Microfilms Order No. 76-24651.

Gould, Stuart H., and Van Den Berghe, Pierre L. "Particularism in Sociology Departments' Hiring Practices." Race 15(Jl, 1973):106-111.

Gould, William Stuart. "Radical Conflict in the U.S. Army." Race 15(Jl, 1973):1-24.

Grabener, Jurgen. Klassengesellschaft und Rassismus. Dusseldorf, West Germany: Bertelsmann Universitätsverlag, 1971.

Grant, Carl S. "Racism in School and Society." Educational Leadership 33(D, 1975):184-188.

Greeley, Andrew M., and Sheatsley, Paul B. "Attitudes Toward Racial Integration." Scientific American 225(D, 1971):13-19.

Green, Philip. "Can It [Fascism] Happen Here?" New York Times Magazine, S 20, 1970.

Green, Robert Lee. "Racism in American Education." Phi Delta Kappan 53(Ja, 1972):274-276.

Greenberg, Bradley S., and Hanneman, Gerhard J. "Racial Attitudes and the Impact of TV Blacks." Educational Broadcasting Review 4(Ap, 1970):27-34.

Greer, Edward. "Racism and U.S. Steel, 1906-1976." Radical America 10(S-O, 1976):54-71.

Gross, Peter W. "[White Racism]. Making Up For It." Civil Rights Digest, Summer, 1969.

Grubbs, Donald H., and Landers, Clifford E. "Racism: From Irrational Anachronism to Functional Social Condition." Review of Black Political Economy 6(Fall, 1975).

Gruber, Jacob. "Racism and the Idea of Progress in the 19th Century." In Anthropology: Ancestors and Heirs. Edited by Stanley Diamond. The Hague: Mouton, 1979.

Guillaumin, Colette. "Caracteres specifiques de l'ideologie raciste." Cahiers Internationaux de Sociologie 53(1972):247-274.

_____. L'ideologie raciste, genese et langage actuel. The Hague: Mouton, 1972.

Guillaumin, Colette, and Poliakov, Leon. "Max Weber et les Theories Bioraciales du XXe Siecle." Cahiers International de Sociologie 56, pp. 115-126.

Guthrie, Robert V. "White Racism and Its Impact on Black and White Behavior." Journal of Non-White Concerns in Personnel and Guidance 1(Ap, 1973):144-149.

Harmon, Rosemary. "The Measurement of Racism and Sexism Through the Select-a-Face Inventory." Doctoral dissertation, U. of Virginia, 1977. Univ. Microfilms Order No. 79-01138.

Harper, Frederick D. The Student Personnel Worker's Commitment to Eliminating Racism, F, 1970. ERIC ED 043 910.

Harris, Edward E. "Prejudice and Other Social Factors in School Segregation." Journal of Negro Education, Fall, 1968.

Harris, Robert L., Jr. "The Free Black Response to American Racism, 1790-1863." Doctoral dissertation, Northwestern U., 1974. Univ. Microfilms Order No. 74-28639.

Harwood, Vic, and Shalom, Steve. "Racism and the Campus." Paper Tiger, Je, 1968.

Hayashi, Wayne. "Decolonization Within and Without." Hawaii Pono Journal 1(Ap, 1971): 2-5.

Height, Dorothy I. The YWCA's One Imperative: Eliminate Racism, 1971. National Board, YWCA, 600 Lexington Ave., New York, NY 10022.

Heiligman, Avron C. "Racism in United States: Drug Legislation and the Trade-off Behind It." Drug Forum: The Journal of Human Issues 7(1978-1979):19-25.

Hernton, Calvin C. Sex and Racism in America. Garden City, NY: Doubleday, 1965.

Higginbotham, A. Leon, Jr. "Racism and the Early American Legal Process, 1619-1896." Annals 407(My, 1973):1-17.

Hill, Robert B. Benign Neglect Revisited: The Illusions of Black Progress. Washington, DC: National Urban League, 1973.

Hixson, Judson, and Epps, Edgar G. "The Failure of Selection and the Problem of Prediction: Racism vs. Measurement in Higher Education." Journal of Afro-American Issues 3(Winter, 1975):117-128.

Hodge, John L. Cultural Bases of Racism and Group Oppression. Berkeley, CA: Two Riders Press, 1975.

Howie, Don. "The Origins of Racism." Negro Digest, F, 1970.

Hunter, John M. "Teaching to Eliminate Black-White Racism: An Educational Systems Approach." Journal of Geography 71(F, 1972): 87-95.

Hutchings, Phil. "What Program for Black Liberation Movement?" Guardian, Je, 1974. [Conference on Racism and Imperialism, Howard U., My 23-24, 1974]

The Institute of the Black World (ed.). Education and Black Struggle: Notes from the Colonized World. Cambridge, MA: Harvard Educational Review, 1973.

Institutional Racism Awareness Seminar. Evanston, IL: National School Boards Association, 1973.

"Institutional Racism in the Military." Congressional Record 118(Mr, 1972):E1902-E1910.

Isaacs, Charles. "Racism, Reaction, and Repression." Edcentric 36(O, 1975):4-8, 33-34.

Isgar, Tom, and Susan (eds.). Racism and Higher Education. Washington, DC: U.S. National Student Association, 1969.

Jackson, Agnes Moreland. "Challenge to All White Americans or, White Ethnicity from a Black Perspective." Sounding, Spring, 1973.

Jerrems, Raymond L. "Racism: Vector of Ghetto Education." Integrated Education (Jl-Ag, 1970):40-47.

Johnston, Robert L. "Church on Racism? 'Disinterest Deafening.'" National Catholic Reporter, S, 1975.

Jones, James M. Prejudice and Racism. Reading, MA: Addison-Wesley, 1972.

Jones, Reginald L. "Racism, Mental Health, and the Schools." In Racism and Mental Health, pp. 319-352. Edited by Charles V. Willie, Bernard M. Kramer and Bertram S. Brown. Pittsburgh: U. of Pittsburgh Press, 1973.

Jones, Terry. "Institutional Racism in the United States." Social Work 19(Mr, 1974): 218-225.

Jordan, Winthrop D. White Over Black. The Development of American Attitudes toward the Negro, 1550-1812. Chapel Hill, NC: U. of North Carolina Press, 1968.

Josey, E. J. "Black Aspirations, White Racism, and Libraries." Wilson Library Bulletin, S, 1969.

Jordan, Winthrop D. The White Man's Burden: Historical Origins of Racism. New York: Oxford U. Press, 1974. [Condensation of author's White Over Black]

Joyce, Frank. "Racism: History and Definition." Tailorbird (2 parts), Mr, 1969 and Ap, 1969. [Published by Tutorial Assistance Center, U.S. National Student Assembly]

_____. "What Is Racism?" Paper Tiger, Je, 1968.

Karcher, Carolyn L. "Melville's 'The 'Gees': A Forgotten Satire on Scientific Racism." American Quarterly 27(O, 1975):421-442.

Katz, Judy Helen. "A Systematic Handbook of Exercises for the Re-education of White People with Respect to Racist Attitudes and Behaviors." Doctoral dissertation, U. of Massachusetts, 1976. Univ. Microfilms Order No. 76-14695.

_____. White Awareness: A Handbook for Anti-Racism Training. Norman, OK: U. of Oklahoma Press, 1978.

Katz, Judy H., and Ivey, Allen. "White Awareness: The Frontier of Racism Awareness Training." Personnel and Guidance Journal 55(Ap, 1977):485-489.

Katz, Maude White. "End Racism in Education: A Concerned Parent Speaks." Freedomways, Fall, 1968.

Katz, Phyllis S. "Racism and Social Science: Towards a New Commitment." In Towards the Elimination of Racism, pp. 3-18. Edited by Phyllis S. Katz. New York: Pergamon, 1976.

Kelly, Ernece B. (ed.). Searching for America. Urbana, IL: National Council of Teachers of English, 1972. [Report of the Task Force on Racism and Bias in the Teaching of English and Textbook Review Committee

Kelly, M. E., and McConnochie, K. R. "Compensatory Education: A Subtle Form of Racism?" Australian Journal of Education 18(Mr, 1974): 30-49.

Kelly, Walter J. "Historical Perspectives on Racism." History Teacher 2(1969):27-30.

Key, Richard Charles. "A Critical Analysis of Racism and Socialization in the Sociological Enterprise: The Sociology of Black Sociologists." Doctoral dissertation, U. of Missouri, 1975. Univ. Microfilms Order No. 76-7513.

King, Larry L. "Confessions of a White Racist." Harper's Magazine, Ja, 1970.

_____. Confessions of a White Racist. New York: Viking, 1971.

_____. "The Traveling Carnival of Racism." New Times 1(D, 1973):36-40. [Debate at Princeton U. between William B. Shockley and Ashley Montagu on racial factors in intelligence]

Kline, Hayes K. "An Exploration of Racism in Ego Ideal Formation." Smith College Studies in Social Work 40(Je, 1970):211-235.

Klitgaard, R. E. "Institutional Racism: An Analytic Approach." J. Peace Res. 1(1972): 41-49.

Knowles, Louis, and Prewitt, Kenneth (eds.). Institutional Racism in America. Englewood Cliffs, NJ: Prentice-Hall, 1969.

Knuth, Helen. "The Climax of American Anglo-Saxonism, 1898-1905." Doctoral dissertation, Northwestern U., 1958.

Kranz, Peter L. "Confronting Bigotry Brings It Home." Civil Rights Digest 5(Summer, 1973):37-38.

Kroch, Anthony. "Racist Ideology in Recent Social Science." The UAG Magazine 2(Winter, 1973):5-14.

Kurokawa, Minako (ed.). Minority Responses: Comparative Views of Reactions to Subordination. New York: Random House, 1970.

Lacy, Leslie Alexander. The Rise and Fall of a Proper Negro. An Autobiography. New York: Macmillan, 1970.

Lapides, L. R., and Burrows, D. Racism: A Casebook. 1971.

Larson, R. G. "Racism in Kindergarten?" Elementary School Journal 69(1969):180-185.

Larrick, Nancy. "The All-White World of Children's Books." Saturday Review, S, 1965.

Lattimer, Bettye I. "Children's Books and Racism." Black Scholar 4(My-Je, 1973):21-27.

La Vega, M. I. de. El racismo en los Estados Unidos una vision latino-americana del problema. Bogota: Ediciones Centro de Estudios Colombianos, 1970.

Lawrence, Ken. Thirty Years of Selective Service Racism, 1971. National Black Draft Counselors, 711 North Dearborn St., Chicago, IL 60605.

Lawton, John H. "'Alternative': Student Dialogue Attacks Racism." Catholic Educational Review, N, 1968.

Lecky, Robert B., and Wright, H. Elliott (eds.). Black Manifesto: Religion, Racism, and Reparations. New York: Sheed and Ward, 1969.

Leeke, John Frederic. "Project Demonstrating Excellence." Doctoral dissertation, Union Graduate School, 1977. Univ. Microfilms Order No. 77-29889. [On combating racism]

Leeper, Robert R. (ed.). Dare to Care/Dare to Act. Racism and Education. Washington, DC: Association for Supervision and Curriculum Development, 1971.

Le Vine, Robert A., and Campbell, Donald T. Ethnocentrism: Theories of Conflict, Ethnic Attitudes and Group Behavior. New York: Wiley, 1972.

Levi-Strauss, Claude. Rasse und Geschichte. Tr. Traugott Konig. Frankfurt: Suhrkamp, 1972.

Levy, Burton. "The Racial Bureaucracy, 1941-1971: From Prejudice to Discrimination to Racism." Journal of Intergroup Relations 2 (J1, 1972):3-32.

Lewis, Hylan. "Race, the Polity, and the Professions." Education for Social Work 5 (1969):19-30.

Lieberman, Leonard and Reynolds, Larry T. "The Debate Over Race Revisited: An Empirical Investigation." Phylon 39(D, 1978):333-343.

Lightfoot, Claude. "Racism in U.S. School Textbooks." Political Affairs 52(Je, 1973): 17-29.

Lindsay, Ouida. Breaking the Bonds of Racism. 1974. ETC Publications, Dept. L, 18512 Pierce Terrace, Homewood, IL 60430.

Loewenberg, Peter. "Racism and Tolerance in Historical Perspective." In Race, Change and Urban Setting, pp. 561-576. Edited by Peter Orleans and William Russell Ellis, Jr. Beverly Hills, CA: Sage, 1971.

Longres, John. "The Impact of Racism on Social Work Education." Journal of Education for Social Work 8(Winter, 1974).

Lopez, Richard E., and Cheek, Donald. "The Prevention of Institutional Racism: Training Couseling Psychologists as Agents for Change." Counseling Psychologist 7(1977): 64-68.

Lundsgaarde, H. P. "Racial and Ethnic Classifications: An Appraisal of the Role of Anthropology in the Lawmaking Process." Houston Law Review 10(1973):641-654.

Lyman, Phillip C. Race Relations Seminars. Handbook for Moderators, Coordinators, and Commanders. Fort Benning, GA: Race Relations Coordinating Group, Ag, 1971.

MacCann, D., and Woodard, G. The Black American in Books for Children: Readings in Racism. Metuchen, NJ: Scarecrow Press, 1972.

McCarthy, John D., and Yancey, William L. "Uncle Tom and Mr. Charlie: Metaphysical Pathos in the Study of Racism and Personal Disorganization." American Journal of Sociology 76(Ja, 1971):648-672.

McConahay, John B., and Hough, Joseph C., Jr. "Symbolic Racism." Journal of Social Issues 32(1976):23-45.

_____. Value Roots of Symbolic Racism. Durham, NC: Institute of Policy Sciences, Duke U., O, 1975.

McCree, Wade H., Jr. "Completing Emancipation: A Commencement Address." Integrateducation 15(S-O, 1977).

McCrory, John B. "White Racism, Freedom from It." Civil Rights Digest, Summer, 1969.

MacDonnell, Joan Benson. Cross Cultural Impact, 1972. Division of Youth Activities, United States Catholic Conference, 1312 Massachusetts Ave., N.W., Washington, DC 20005. [Holding workshops on racism]

McGuire, Phillip. "Black Civilian Aides and the Problems of Racism and Segregation in the United States Armed Forces: 1940-1950." Doctoral dissertation, Howard U., 1975.

_____. "Judge Hastie, World War II, and Army Racism." Journal of Negro History 62(O, 1977):351-362.

McLean, Deckle. "Education Bears the Burden of Eliminating Racism." Boston Globe, O 19, 1971.

Malcolm X. The End of White World Supremacy. Four Speeches. New York: Monthly Review Press, 1971.

Malpass, Elizabeth Deanne. "Organized Southern Racism Since 1954." Master's thesis, U. of Miami, 1963.

March, Carl C., Jr. "Old Assumptions and New Packages: Racism, Educational Models, and Black Children." Young Children 33(S, 1978): 45-51.

Marshment, Margaret. "Racist Ideology and Popular Fiction." Race and Class 19(Spring, 1978):331-344.

Martin, Tony. "C.L.R. James and the Race/Class Question." Race 14(O, 1972):183-193.

Martin, W. "On the Social Mechanism of White Supremacy." Pacific Sociological Review 15(1972):203-224.

Marx, Gary T. "Perspectives on Racism." In Confrontation Psychology and the Problems of Today. Edited by Michael Wertheimer and others. Glenview, IL: Scott, Foreman, 1970.

_____. *Protest and Prejudice*. New York: Harper and Row, 1967. 2nd edition, 1969.

Massaquoi, Hans J. "A Battle the Army Can't Afford to Lose." *Ebony* 29(F, 1974):116-124. [Racism in U.S. Army in Germany]

Massey, Grace C., Scott, Mona V., and Dornbusch, Sanford M. "Racism Without Racists: Institutional Racism in Urban Schools." *Black Scholar* 7(N, 1975):2-11.

Merriam, Allen H. "Racism in the Expansionist Controversy of 1898-1900." *Phylon* 39(D, 1978):369-380.

Metress, James. "The Scientific Misuse of the Biological Concept of Race." *Social Studies* 66(My-Je, 1975):114-116.

Miller, Kelly. *An Appeal to Reason: An Open Letter to John Temple Graves*. Washington, DC: Hayworth Publishing House, 1906.

_____. *As to the Leopard's Spots: An Open Letter to Thomas Dixon, Jr.* Washington, DC: K. Miller, 1905.

Miller, William Lee. "Analysis of the 'White Backlash.'" *New York Times Magazine*, Ag 23, 1964. [Deals, in part, with New Haven, CT]

Mintz, Sidney W. (ed.). *Slavery, Colonialism, and Racism*. New York: Norton, 1975.

Moore, Carlos. *Were Marx and Engels White Racists? The Proletaryan Outlook of Marx and Engels*, 1973. Black Peoples' Information Centre, 301 Portobello Rd., London, W.10, England.

_____. "Were Marx and Engels White Racists?" *Berkeley Journal of Sociology* 19(1974-1975).

Moore, Howard, Jr. "Racism as Justice." *Black Law Journal* 3(Spring, 1973):54-66.

_____. "Racism as Justice." *Rhythm* 1(1970):30-34.

Moore, Robert B. *Racism in the English Language. A Lesson Plan and Study Essay*, 1976. Racism and Sexism Resource Center for Educators, 1841 Broadway, New York, NY 10023.

Morales, Armando. "The Collective Preconscious and Racism." *Social Casework* 52(My, 1971):285-293.

Moreland, Lois B. *White Racism and the Law*. Columbus, OH: Merrill, 1971.

Morris, Frank L. "The Jensen Hypothesis: Was It the White Perspective or White Racism?" *Journal of Black Studies* 2(Mr, 1972):371-386.

Morrison, Iris. "White Studies." *Forum for the Discussion of New Trends in Education* 20(Ap, 1977):5-8.

Moyer, Charles R. "Concerning the Cant of 'White Racism.'" *Dissent*, Ja-F, 1969.

Moynihan, Daniel P. "The New Racialism." *Atlantic*, Ag, 1968.

Muhammad, W. D. "The Dravidian Roots of Aryan White Supremacy and Diabolic Consciousness." *Muhammad Speaks*, Ag, 1975.

Murray, Paul Thom, Jr. "Blacks and the Draft: An Analysis of Institutional Racism, 1917-1971." Doctoral dissertation, Florida State U., 1972. Univ. Microfilms Order No. 72-31420.

Nash, Gary B. "Red, White, and Black: The Origins of Racism in Colonial America." In *The Great Fear. Race in the Mind of America*, pp. 1-26. Edited by Gary B. Nash and Richard Weiss. New York: Holt, Rinehart and Winston, 1970.

Nash, Gary B., and Weiss, Richard (eds.). *The Great Fear. Race in the Mind of America*. New York: Holt, Rinehart and Winston, 1970.

Nash, Manning. "Race and the Ideology of Race." *Current Anthropology*, Je, 1962.

Nesteby, James R. "The Tarzan Series of Edgar Rice Burroughs: Lost Races and Racism in American Popular Culture." Doctoral dissertation, Bowling Green State U., 1978. Univ. Microfilms Order No. 79-01450.

Newby, I. A. *Challenge to the Court: Social Scientists and the Defense of Segregation, 1954-1966*. 2nd edition. Baton Rouge, LA: Louisiana State U. Press, 1969.

Newby, I. A. *Jim Crow's Defense: Anti-Negro Thought in America, 1900-1930*. Baton Rouge, LA: Louisiana State U. Press, 1965.

Newby, I. A. (ed.). *The Development of Segregationist Thought*. Homewood, IL: Dorsey, 1968.

Newton, Huey. *Revolutionary Suicide*. New York: Harcourt Brace Jovanovich, 1973.

Ney, James W. *Elitism, Racism and Some Contemporary Views of English Spelling*, 1974. ERIC ED 097 731.

Nickel, James W. "Discrimination and Morally Relevant Characteristics." *Analysis* 32(1972):113-114.

Nikolinakos, Marios. "Notes on an Economic Theory of Racism." *Race* 14(Ap, 1973):365-381.

Noel, Joseph R. "White Anti-Black Prejudice in the United States." *International Journal of Group Tensions* 1(Ja, 1971):59-76.

Nordlie, Peter G. Measuring Changes in Institutional Racial Discrimination in the Army. McLean, VA: Champion Press, 1974.

Nordlie, Peter G., Friedman, C. G., and Marbury, G. R. Race Relations in the Army: Policies, Problems, Programs. McLean, VA: Human Sciences Research, 1972.

Norfleet, Marvin B. Forced School Integration in the U.S.A. New York: Carlton Press, 1961.

"Not All Of It Was Noble---or Funny." American School Board Journal 163(Ag, 1976):13-14. [Self-critical review of racism in this journal in past years]

Nyerere, Julius K. "Under Racism, Man Either Becomes Less Than a Man, or He Must Fight." Objective: Justice 3(Ja-Mr, 1972):26-27, 50.

Oatis, Bobbie N. Racism: How Shall We as Administrators Work for a Smooth Transition? 1978. ERIC ED 157 966. [Higher education]

Obudho, Constance E. (comp.). Black-White Racial Attitudes: An Annotated Bibliography. Westport, CT: Greenwood Press, 1976.

O'Callaghan, M. G., and Guillaumin, C. "Race et race...la mode 'naturelle' en sciences humaines." L'Homme et la societe 31-32 (1974):195-210.

Oden, Chester W., Jr., and MacDonald, W. Scott. "Human Relations Training in School Settings." In School Crime and Disruption: Prevention Models, pp. 103-114. Washington, DC: GPO, Je, 1978.

Olsen, Edward G. "What Shall We Teach About Race and Racism?" Kansas Teacher, D, 1968.

Omvedt, Gail. "Towards a Theory of Colonialism." Insurgent Sociologist 3(Spring, 1973): 1-24.

Padfield, Harland, and Young, John A. The Institutional Processing of Human Resources: A Theory of Social Marginalization. Corvallis, OR: Western Rural Development Center, Oregon State U., 1974.

Paige, Jeffery M. "Changing Patterns of Anti-White Attitudes Among Blacks." Journal of Social Issues 26(Fall, 1970):69-86.

Palmore, Erdman, and Whittington, Frank J. "Differential Trends Toward Equality Between Whites and Nonwhites." Social Forces 49(S, 1970):108-117.

Paraf, P. Le racisme dans le monde. 3rd ed. Paris: Payot, 1969.

Parker, Glenn M., and O'Connor, William. "Racism in the Schools." Training and Development Journal 24(N, 1970):27-32.

Parker, James R. "Paternalism and Racism: Senator John C. Spooner and American Minorities, 1897-1907." Wisconson Magazine of History 57(Spring, 1974):195-200.

Pearl, Arthur. "Can the Cause be the Cure?" Journal of Teacher Education 20(1969):427-434. [Racism and teacher-training]

Peirson, Gwynne Walker. "An Introductory Study of Institutional Racism in Police Law Enforcement." Doctoral dissertation, U. of California, Berkeley, 1977. Univ. Microfilms Order No. 78-12452. [Oakland, California]

Perlo, Victor. Economics of Racism USA: Roots of Black Inequality. New York: International, 1975.

Pettigrew, Thomas F. Racially Separate or Together? New York: McGraw-Hill, 1971.

Pierce, Chester M. "Poverty and Racism as They Affect Children." In Advocacy for Child Mental Health. Edited by I. N. Berlin. New York: Brunner/Mazel, 1975.

Pillsbury, Peter W. Some Thoughts on White Supremacy and the Church, Ag, 1968. People Against Racism, 2631 Woodward Ave., Detroit, MI 48201.

Pines, Jim. "The Study of Racial Images: A Structural Approach." Screen Education 23 (Summer, 1977):24-32.

Poliakov, Leon and others. Le Racisme. Paris: Seghers, 1976.

Popkin, Richard H. "The Philosophical Basis of Eighteenth Century Racism." In Racism in the Eighteenth Century. Edited by Harold E. Pagliaro, Cleveland, OH: Press of Case Western Reserve U., 1973.

Prager, Jeffrey. "White Racial Privilege and Social Change: An Examination of Theories of Racism." Berkeley Journal of Sociology 17(1972-1973).

Pratt, Solomon A. J., and Krishuaswami, Arcot. Seminar on the Elimination of All Forms of Racial Discrimination. U.N. Document ST/RAD/HR/34. New York: United Nations, 1968.

Prudhomme, Charles and Musto, David F. "Historical Perspectives on Mental Health and Racism in the United States." In Racism and Mental Health, pp. 25-57. Edited by Charles V. Willie, Bernard M. Kramer, and Bertram S. Brown. Pittsburgh, PA: U. of Pittsburgh Press, 1973.

Prunty, Howard E., Singer, Terry L., and Thomas, Lindsay A. "Confronting Racism in Inner-City Schools." Social Work 22(My, 1977):190-194. [Pittsburgh]

Punke, Harold H. "Racism and Inferior Education." _Alabama Lawyer_ 32(1971).

"Race, Sex and Class: A Statement from England." _Interracial Books for Children_ 5 (1974):6.

Racial Integration Is a Vicious Crime. Jefferson-Lincoln Americans, Inc., 1967. P.O. Box 51912, New Orleans, LA.

"Racism: An American Ideology." _Akwesasne Notes_ 9(Autumn, 1977):6-7.

"Racism in the Law: A Symposium." _Guild Practitioner_ 27(Fall, 1968):169.

"Racism in the Military: A New System for Rewards and Punishment." _Congressional Record_ 118, Part 2(O, 14, 1972):E 8674-E 8688. [Congressional Black Caucus Report]

"Racism in the YMCA." _Southern Courier_, Jl, 1968.

"Radical Racists' International." _Patterns of Prejudice_ 10(S-O, 1976):18-21.

Rainville, Raymond E., and McCormick, Edward. "Extent of Covert Racial Prejudice in Pro-Football Announcers' Speech." _Journalism Quarterly_ (Spring, 1977):20-26.

Reeves, Don. "Supplements for Campus Racism." _Ebony_ 29(Mr, 1974):114.

Reich, Michael. "Economic Theories of Racism." In _Schooling in a Corporate Society. The Political Economy of Education in America_, pp. 67-79. Edited by Martin Carnoy. New York: McKay, 1972.

Reich, Michael. "The Economics of Racism." In _Problems in Political Economy_, pp. 107-113. Edited by David M. Gordon. Lexington: Lexington Books, 1971.

Rex, John. _Race, Colonialism and the City._ London: Routledge and Kegan Paul, 1973.

_____. _Race Relations in Sociological Theory._ London: Weidenfeld and Nicolson, 1970.

_____. "Racism" (letter). _New Society_, Ap, 1969. [Comment on Banton, "What Do We Mean by 'Racism'?"]

Rodgers, Harrell R., Jr. (ed.). _Racism and Racial Inequality: The Policy Alternatives._ San Francisco: Freeman, 1975.

Rogin, Michael. "Wallace and the Middle Class: The White Backlash in Wisconsin." _Public Opinion Quarterly_, Spring, 1966.

Rose, Steven, Hambley, John, and Haywood, Jeff. "Science, Racism, and Ideology." _Socialist Register_, 1973.

Rosenberg, Neil Vandraegen. "Stereotype and Tradition: White Folklore about Blacks (Volumes 1 and 2)." Doctoral dissertation, Indiana U., 1970.

Roucek, Joseph. "Roots of Racism of American Social Scientists." _Indian Sociological Bulletin_, Ap, 1969.

Rubin, Lillian. "The Racism of Liberals." _Trans-action_, S, 1968.

Ruchames, Louis (ed.). _Racial Thought in America. From the Puritans to Abraham Lincoln._ Amherst, MA: U. of Massachusetts Press, 1969.

Sabshin, Melvin, Diesenhaus, Herman, and Wilkerson, Raymond. "Dimensions of Institutional Racism in Psychiatry." _American Journal of Psychiatry_ 127(D, 1970):787-793.

Sacks, Karen. "The New Rassenscience. The Racism of the Jensens and Shockleys." _Jewish Currents_ 32(F, 1978):4-12.

Sales, William, Jr. "Capitalism Without Racism: Science or Fantasy." _Black Scholar_ 9(Mr, 1978):23-34.

Sanders, Charles. "A Typology of Racism in Bureaucratic Systems." In National Association of Black Social Workers, _Diversity: Cohesion or Chaos- Mobilization for Survival_, pp. 252-268. Proceedings of the Fourth Annual Conference of N.A.B.S.W. Nashville, TN: Fisk U., 1973.

_____. _Black Professionals' Perceptions of Institutional Racism in Health and Welfare Organizations._ Fair Lawn, NJ: R. E. Burdick, 1974.

Sanders, Ronald. _Lost Tribes and Promised Lands: The Origins of American Racism._ Boston: Little Brown, 1978.

Santa Cruz, Hernan. _Special Study of Racial Discrimination in the Political, Economic, Social and Cultural Spheres._ U.N. Document E/CN.4/Sub.2/301. New York: United Nations, Je, 1969.

Sawyer, Jack, and Senn, David J. "Institutional Racism and the American Psychological Association." _Journal of Social Issues_ 29 (1973):67-79.

Schneiderman, Leonard. "Racism and Revenue-Sharing." _Social Work_ 17(My, 1972):44-49.

Schnexider, Alvin J. "The Development of Racial Solidarity in the Armed Forces." _Journal of Black Studies_ (Je, 1975):415-435.

Schniedewind, Nancy. _Confronting Racism and Sexism: A Practical Handbook for Educators._ New Paltz, NY: Commonground Press, 1977.

Scott, James F. "White-Racism: Explanation or Anathema?" Journal of Social and Behavioral Sciences 18(Fall-Winter, 1971-1972):27-34.

Schuman, Howard. "Sociological Racism." Transaction 7(1969):44-48.

Scott, James A. "Racism, the Church, and Educational Strategies." Foundations 17(Jl-S, 1974):268-280.

Sedlacek, William E. "Test Bias and the Elimination of Racism." Journal of College Student Personnel 18(Ja, 1977):16-19.

Sedlacek, William E., and Brooks, Glenwood C., Jr. A Procedure for Eliminating Racism in Our Schools, Ag, 1973. ERIC ED 085 649.

_____. Racism in American Education: A Model for Change. Chicago: Nelson-Hall, 1976.

_____. "Racism in the Public Schools: A Model for Change." Journal of Non-White Concerns in Personnel and Guidance 1(Ap, 1973):133-143.

Sedlacek, William E. and others. Racism and Sexism: A Comparison and Contrast, 1974. ERIC ED 098 133.

"Sexism and Racism: Different Issues?" Interracial Books for Children 5(1974):11.

Sexism and Racism in Popular Basal Readers 1964-1976, 1976. Racism and Sexism Resource Center for Educators, 1841 Broadway, New York, NY 10023.

Shannon, Barbara E. "The Impact of Racism on Personality Development." Social Casework 54(N, 1973):519-525.

_____. "Implications of White Racism for Social Work Practice." Social Casework 51 (1970):270-276.

Shapiro, Richard. "Discrimination and Community Mental Health. Challenging Institutional Racism." Civil Rights Digest 8(Fall, 1975):19-23.

Shaw, Van B. "The Concept of Institutional Racism." Journal of Intergroup Relations 5(N, 1976):3-12.

Shute, Gary. "The Natural History of American Black-White Relations: A Question of Structural Persistence." 15 p. paper, 1971. Annual Meeting of the Southern Anthropological Society. ERIC ED 049 336.

Simmons, Arthur, Jr. "Charlie and His Polls." Liberator, Je, 1969.

Simon, Pierre-J. "Ethnisme et racisme ou 'l'ecole de 1492.'" Cahiers internationaux de sociologie 48(1970):119-152.

Simon, Yves R. "Secret Source of the Success of the Racist Ideology." In Community of the Free. New York: Holt, 1948.

Singleton, Royce, Jr., and Turner, Jonathan H. "Racism: White Oppression of Blacks in America." In Understanding Social Problems, pp. 130-160. Edited by D. H. Zimmerman, D. L. Wieder, and S. Zimmerman. New York: Praeger, 1976.

"Sisters Desert 'Racist Institution.'" America, F, 1971. [St. Raymond's Elementary School, Detroit, MI]

Sivanandan, A. "Culture and Identity." Liberator, Je, 1970.

_____. Race and Resistance: The IRR Story, 1974. Race Today Publications 1974, 184 King's Cross Rd., London W.C.1, 01-8370041 England. [In re: Institute of Race Relations]

_____. "Race, Class and Power: An Outline for Study." Race 14(Ap, 1973):383-391.

Skinner, Howard. "Citizen Participation and Racism." Public Administration Review 32 (My-Je, 1972):210-211.

Smith, Carroll Ann. "Anglo-Saxon Science: The Scientific Rationale for Immigration Restriction." Master's thesis, Columbia U., 1958.

Smith, H. Shelton. In His Image, But...Racism in Southern Religion, 1780-1910. Durham, NC: Duke U. Press, 1972.

Snyder, Louis L. The Idea of Racialism. Its Meaning and History. Princeton, NJ: D. Van Nostrand, 1968.

Sparrow, Floyd. "Definitional Racism and Public Education." Forum, N-D, 1972.

Spears, Arthur K. "Institutionalized Racism and the Education of Blacks." Anthropology and Education Quarterly 9(Summer, 1978):127-136.

American Journal of Psychiatry 127(1970):787-814. [Special section on racism]

Spurlock, Jeanne. "Some Consequences of Racism for Children." In Racism and Mental Health, pp. 147-163. Edited by Charles V. Willie, Bernard M. Kramer, and Bertram S. Brown. Pittsburgh, PA: U. of Pittsburgh Press, 1973.

Stafford, Walter, and Ladner, Joyce. "Comprehensive Planning and Racism." Journal of the American Institute of Planners, Mr, 1969.

Staples, Robert. "Race and Colonialism: The Domestic Case in Theory and Practice." Black Scholar 7(Je, 1976):37-49.

_____. "White Racism, Black Crime and American Justice: An Application of the Colonial Model to Explain Crime and Race." Phylon 36(Mr, 1975):14-22.

Stein, Annie. "Educational Equality in the U.S.: The Emperor's Clothes." Science and Society 36(Winter, 1972):469-476.

Stein, Judith. "'Of Mr. Booker T. Washington and Others': The Political Economy of Racism in the United States." Science and Society 38(Winter, 1974-1975):422-463.

Stember, Charles Herbert. Racial Sexism. The Emotional Barrier to an Integrated Society. New York: Elsevier, 1976. [Racism]

Sternhell, Zeev. "Fascist Ideology." In Fascism, A Reader's Guide: Analyses, Interpretations, Bibliography. Edited by Walter Laquer. Berkeley, CA: U. of California Press, 1976.

Stevens, John D. "Color" in the Comic Strips: Racial Stereotyping Trends in Black and in White Newspapers, 1976. ERIC ED 157 081.

Stringfellow, William. My People Is The Enemy. New York: Holt, Rinehart, and Winston, 1964.

Strom, Robert D. "The Mythology of Racism." International Education 1(Spring, 1972): 37-45.

Szymanski, Albert. "Racial Discrimination and White Gain." American Sociological Review 41(Je, 1976):403-414.

Tabb, William K. "Capitalism, Colonialism, and Racism." Review of Radical Political Economy 3(Summer, 1971).

_____. "Race Relations Models and Social Change." Social Problems 18(Spring, 1971): 431-444.

Tajfel, Henri. "Racism" (letter). New Society, My 29, 1969. [Reply to Banton, New Society, Ap 10, 1969]

Takagi, Paul. "Tracing Racism in U.S. National Policies." Journal of Intergroup Relations 3(S, 1974):14-30.

Taking Racism Personally: White Anti-racism at the Crossroads. London: Peace News, 1978.

Tate, Binnie. "LAPL Racism Workshop Reaction to SLJ Feature." Library Journal 96(My, 1971):1752+.

Taylor, Howard F. "Quantitative Racism: A Partial Documentation." Journal of Afro-American Issues 3(Winter, 1975):19-42.

Taylor, Jerome. "Proposal for a Taxonomy of Racialism." Bulletin of the Menninger Clinic 35(N, 1971):421-428.

Teague, Bob. "Charlie Doesn't Even Know His Daily Racism Is a Sick Joke." New York Times Magazine, S 15, 1968.

Terry, Robert W. For Whites Only. Rev. ed. Grand Rapids, MI: Eerdmans, 1975.

Thalberg, Irving. "Justification of Institutional Racism." Philosophical Forum 3 (Winter, 1971-1972).

_____. "Visceral Racism." Monist 56(Ja, 1972).

Thomas, Alexander, and Sillen, Samuel. Racism and Psychiatry. New York: Brunner/Mazel, 1972.

Tillman, James A., Jr. "Why America Needs Racism." 2 parts. Liberator, Je, Jl, 1968.

Tillman, James A., Jr., and Tillman, Mary Norman. What Is Your Racism Quotient? A Laymen's Guide for Detecting and Treating Racism." Syracuse, NY: Tillman Associates, 1968.

Tillman, N. P. "The National Council of Teachers of English and Racial Discrimination." Quarterly Review of Higher Education Among Negroes 10(O, 1942):218-222.

Tomlinson, Tommy M. "White Racism and the Common Man." The Integrator, Fall, 1968.

Tourgee, Albion W. "Shall White Minorities Rule?" Forum 7:143.

Towle, Joseph, and Turnbull, Colin. "The White Problem in America." Natural History, Je, 1968.

Triandis, Harry C. "The Future of Pluralism." Journal of Social Issues 32, No. 4(1976): 179-208.

Turner, James. "Black America: 'Colonial Economy Under Siege.'" First World 1(Mr-Ap, 1977):7-9.

Turner, Jonathan H., and Singleton, Royce, Jr. "A Theory of Ethnic Oppression: Toward a Reintegration of Cultural and Structural Concepts in Ethnic Relations Theory." Social Forces 56(Je, 1978):1001-1018.

UNESCO. Race, Science and Society. New York: Columbia U. Press, 1975.

UNESCO. "Statement on Race and Racial Prejudice." International Social Service Bulletin XX, No. 1(1968). [Adopted in Paris, S, 1967]

United Nations. "A Program Against Racism." Integrateducation 12(N-D, 1974):32-35.

_____. "Program for a Decade for Action to Combat Racism and Racial Discrimination." Objective: Justice 5(O-D, 1973):21-25.

United Nations, Division of Human Rights. Seminar on the Dangers of a Recrudescence of Intolerance in All its Forms and the Search for Ways of Preventing and Combating It. UN document ST/TAO/HR/44. [Ag-24-S 6, 1971]

Valentine, Charles A. "Voluntary Ethnicity and Social Change: Classism, Racism, Marginality, Mobility, and Revolution with Special Reference to Afro-American and Other Third World People." Journal of Ethnic Studies 3(Spring, 1975):1-27.

Valentine, Charles A., and Valentine, Bettylou. "Brain Damage and the Intellectual Defense of Inequality." Current Anthropology 16 (Mr, 1975):117-150.

Van Den Berghe, Pierre L. Race and Racism. A Comparative Perspective. New York: Wiley, 1967.

Varet, G. Racisme et philosophie. Essai sur une limite de la pensée. Paris: Denoel-Gonthier, 1973.

Walton, Eugene. "Will the Supreme Court Revert to Racism?" Black World 21(O, 1972):46-48.

Washington Task Force on African Affairs. A Black Paper. Institutional Racism in African Studies and U.S.-African Relations. 1969. The Washington Task Force on African Affairs, P.O. Box 13033, Washington, DC 20009.

Wasserman, Miriam. "Busing as a 'Cover Issue'-A Radical View." Urban Review 6(S-O, 1972): 6-11.

Watford, Ben A. "Racism in Suburban Schools." Changing Education, Spring, 1969.

Wayson, William W. "White Racists in America: We Have Met Them and They Are Us." In Race and Education Across Cultures. Edited by G. K. Verma and Christopher Bagley. Stamford, CT: Greylock Publishers, 1975.

Weiss, Philip, and Cramer, James. "Shockley's Racism Circus Comes to Yale." Harvard Crimson, Ap, 1975.

Weiss, Richard. "Racism in the Era of Industrialization." In The Great Fear. Race in the Mind of America, pp. 121-143. Edited by Gary B. Nash and Richard Weiss. New York: Holt, Rinehart and Winston, 1970.

Welsing, Frances L. Cress. "Build A World Without Racism." Integrateducation 13(Ja-F, 1975):20-26.

_____. "On 'Black Genetic Inferiority.'" Ebony 29(Jl, 1974):104-105.

West, Hollie I. "Telling a Black Child About Racism." Washington Post, S 9, 1973.

West, Louis Jolyon. "The Psychobiology of Racial Violence." Archives of General Psychiatry, Je, 1967.

Weston, Rubin F. Racism in U.S. Imperialism: The Influence of Racial Assumptions on American Foreign Policy, 1893-1946. Columbia, SC: U. of South Carolina Press, 1972.

Whitaker, Ben. "Minority Conflicts in Present-Day Societies: A Sociopsychological Analysis." In Selected Proceedings of the 3rd Annual Conference on Minority Studies, April, 1975, pp. 5-10. Edited by George E. Carter, James R. Parker, and Carol Sweeney. La Crosse, WI: Institute for Minority Studies, U. of Wisconsin, La Crosse, 1976.

White, J., and Frideres, J. S. "Race, Prejudice and Racism: A Distinction." Canadian Review of Sociology and Anthropology 14(F, 1977).

White and Negro Attitudes Towards Race Related Issues and Activities. A CBS News Public Opinion Survey. Research Park, Princeton, NJ: Opinion Research Corporation, Jl, 1968.

["White Racism]. Strategies Against It." Civil Rights Digest, Summer, 1969.

Wilcox, Preston. "Humanness In a Racist Society." Black Caucus 3(Fall, 1970):50-59.

_____. "Social Policy and White Racism." Social Policy, My-Je, 1970.

Wilkie, Mary E. "Colonials, Marginals and Immigrants: Contributions to a Theory of Ethnic Stratification." Comparative Studies in Society and History 19(Ja, 1977): 67-95.

Willhelm, Sidney. "Black Man, Red Man, and White America: The Constitutional Approach to Genocide." Catalyst, Spring, 1969.

_____. The Demise of Black People in a White America: The Perpetuation of Economic Racism, 1977. ERIC ED 139 891.

_____. "Equality: America's Racist Ideology." In Radical Sociology, pp. 246-262. Edited by J. David Colfax and Jack L. Roach. New York: Basic Books, 1971.

_____. "A Sociological Perspective of Racism and the Supreme Court." The Catholic Lawyer 16(Spring, 1970).

_____. Who Needs the Negro? Cambridge, MA: Schenkman, 1971.

Wilkerson, Cathy. "The False Privilege." New Left Notes, O, 1968. [White racism]

Willie, Charles V. Oreo: A Perspective on Race and Marginal Men and Women. Wakefield, MA: Parameter Press, 1975.

Willie, Charles V., Kramer, Bernard M., and Brown, Bertram S. Racism and Mental Health: Essays. Pittsburgh, PA: U. of Pittsburgh Press, 1972.

Wilson, C. E. "Black Power and the Myth of Black Racism." Liberation, S, 1966.

_____. "On Watching Race Riots." Jewish Currents, Je, 1967.

Wilson, Charles. "Racism in Education: A Black Position Paper." Community, Mr-Ap, 1969. [Presented at Mr 19, 1969, annual conference of the Association for Supervision and Curriculum Development]

Wilson, Maggie. White Student Black World: A Handbook for Action Against Racism. Oxford: Third World First, 1978.

Wilson, Reginald. "The Educational Establishment." People Against Racism in Education 1(Je, 1973).

Wilson, William J. Power, Racism, and Privilege. Race Relations in Theoretical and Sociohistorical Perspective. New York: Macmillan, 1973.

Wittlin, Curt J. "Synchronic Etymologies of Ethnonyms as Cause of the Traditional Belief in Monstrous Races." In Second Language Teaching 1975. Edited by Hector Hammerly and Isabel Sawyer. ERIC ED 138 042.

Wobogo, V. "Diop's Two Cradle Theory and the Origin of White Racism." Black Books Bulletin 4(Winter, 1976):20-29.

Woodson, Carter G. Miseducation of the Negro. Washington, DC: Associated Publishers, Inc., 1932.

Wright, Bobby. "The Psychopathic Radical Personality." Black Books Bulletin 2(F, 1974): 24-32.

Wright, G. C., Jr. "Racism and Welfare Policy in America." Social Science Quarterly 44 (Mr, 1977).

Yergin, Peter. "'I'm Not a Racist. I'm a Raceologist.'" Times Higher Education Supplement, My, 1974. [Interview with William Schockley]

Yette, Samuel F. The Choice: The Issue of Black Survival in America. New York: Putnam's, 1971.

York, Everett L. "Ethnocentrism or Racism: Some Thoughts on the Nature of Early Indian-White Relations." American Indian Quarterly 1(Winter, 1974-1975):281-291.

Young, Whitney M. Beyond Racism: Building an Open Society. New York: McGraw Hill, 1969.

Yuill, Phyllis. "Little Black Sambo: The Continuing Controversy." School Library Journal 22(Mr, 1976):71-75.

Zubaida, Sami (ed.). Race and Racialism. New York: Barnes and Noble, 1970.

White Flight

Ayres, B. Drummond, Jr. "South's 'Seg' Schools Are Now Part of the System." New York Times, Je 27, 1976. [The "segregation academies"]

Becker, Henry Jay. The Impact of Racial Composition and Public School Desegregation on Changes in Non-Public Enrollment by White Pupils. Baltimore, MD: Center for Social Organization of Schools, Johns Hopkins U., Je, 1978.

Boykin, Arsene O. "Coleman's Grievous Error." Phi Delta Kappan 57(D, 1975), letter. [Research on desegregation and white flight]

_____. "The Racial Balance Policy: An Appeal to the Common Good." Journal of Negro Education 45(Spring, 1976):141-149.

Brooke, Edward W., and Javits, Jacob. "Desegregation and the Cities." 19 parts. Congressional Record, My, 4-5, 11-13, 20-21, 25-27, Je, 3, 9-10, 18, 22, 26, and 29, 1976.

Cataldo, Everett F., and Giles, Michael W. School Desegregation Policy. Compliance, Avoidance, and the Metropolitan Remedy. Lexington, MA: Lexington Books, 1978.

Cataldo, Everett F., Giles, Michael W., Athos, Deborah, and Gatlin, Douglas. "Desegregation and White Flight." Integrateducation 13(Ja-F, 1975):3-5.

Cataldo, Everett F., Giles, Michael W., and Gatlin, Douglas S. "Metropolitan School Desegregation: Practical Remedy or Impractical Ideal?" Annals 422(N, 1975):97-104.

Coleman, James S. "A Reply to Green and Pettigrew." Phi Delta Kappan 57(Mr, 1976):454-455.

_____. "Coleman Replies to the Times" (letter). Phi Delta Kappan 57(Mr, 1976).

_____. "Liberty and Equality in School Desegregation." Social Policy 6(Ja-F, 1976): 9-13.

_____. Presentation on School Desegregation and White Flight, S, 1976. ERIC ED 135 894.

_____. "Recent Trends in School Integration." Educational Researcher 4(Jl-Ag, 1975):3-12.

_____. "Response to Professors Petigrew and Green." Harvard Educational Review 46(My, 1976):217-225.

_____. "School Desegregation and Loss of Whites from Large Central-City School Districts." In School Desegregation: The Courts and Suburban Migration. N.p.: U.S. Commission on Civil Rights, n.d.

Cunningham, George K. and others. "The Impact of Court-Ordered Desegregation on Student Enrollment and Residential Patterns (White Flight)." Journal of Education 160 (My, 1978):36-45. [Jefferson County, KY]

Farley, Reynolds. "Is Coleman Right [About Desegregation and White Flight]?" Social Policy 6(Ja-F, 1976):14-23.

_____. "Racial Integration in the Public Schools, 1967 to 1972: Assessing the Effect of Governmental Policies." Sociological Focus 8(Ja, 1975):3-26.

Fitzgerald, Michael R., and Morgan, David R. "School Desegregation and White Flight: North and South." Integrateducation 15(N-D, 1977):78-81.

Frey, William H. Central City White Flight: Racial and Nonracial Causes, S, 1977. ERIC ED 146 248.

_____. White Flight and Central City Loss: Application of an Analytic Migration Framework, Ag, 1977. ERIC ED 152 932.

Giles, Micheal W. School Desegregation and White Withdrawal: A Test of the Tipping Point Model. Boca Raton, FL: Department of Political Science, Florida Atlantic U., 1977.

_____. White Flight and Black Concentrations in American Schools, 1978. ERIC ED 159 293.

Giles, Michael W. and others. "White Flight and Percent Black: The Tipping Point Reexamined." Social Science Quarterly 56(Je, 1975):85-92.

Green, Robert L., and Pettigrew, Thomas F. "Public School Desegregation and White Flight: A Reply to Professor Coleman." In School Desegregation: The Courts and Suburban Migration. N.p.: U.S. Commission on Civil Rights, n.d.

_____. "Urban Desegregation and White Flight: A Response to Coleman." Phi Delta Kappan 57(F, 1976):399-402.

Griffith, Katherine S. "Segregation Academies' Flourish in the South." South Today, O, 1969. [Private academies]

Harris, Joan R. "Stopping White Flight." Society 14(My-Je, 1977):44-46.

Jackson, Gregg. "Reanalysis of Coleman's 'Recent Trends in School Integration.'" Educational Researcher 4(N, 1975):21-25.

_____. "Some Limitations in Coleman's Recent Segregation Research." Phi Delta Kappan 57 (D, 1975):274-275.

Kantrowitz, Nathan. School Segregation, Residential Segregation: Some Speculation, Je, 1976. ERIC ED 139 870. [On "white flight"]

Lord, J. Dennis, and Catau, John C. "School Desegregation Policy and Intra-School District Migration." Social Science Quarterly 57(1977):787-796.

Mader, Frederick H., and Mader, Paul Douglas. Direct Experience as a Factor in the Development of Public School Superintendents' Attitudes Toward the Private School Movement, N, 1976. ERIC ED 135 086.

_____. Private Schools and Public School Officials: An Attitudinal Study of Social Impact and Decline in the Deep South, F, 1976. ERIC ED 122 402.

_____. Private Schools in the Deep South: An Examination of Public School Officials' Attitudes Toward Their Social Impact, Growth, and Decline, N, 1975. ERIC ED 135 085.

Munford, Luther. "Desegregation and Private Schools." Social Policy 6(Ja-F, 1976):42-45.

NAACP Legal Defense Fund. The Status of Private Academies in Eleven Southern States. New York: NAACP Legal Defense Fund, S, 1972.

National Institute of Education. School Desegregation in Metropolitan Areas: Choices and Prospects. Washington, DC: National Institute of Education, 1977.

Nevin, David, and Bills, Robert E. The Schools That Fear Built. Segregationist Academies in the South. Washington, DC: Acropolis Books, Ltd., 1976.

Orfield, Gary. [Is Coleman Right About Desegregation and White Flight?] Social Policy 6(Ja-F, 1976):24-29.

Orfield, Gary (ed.). Symposium on School Desegregation and White Flight. Washington, DC: Center for National Policy Review, Catholic U., Ag, 1975.

Palmer, James M. The Impact of Private Education on the Rural South. F, 1974. National Educational Laboratory Publishers, 813 Airport Blvd., Austin, TX 78702. ["Segregation academies"]

_____. "Resegregation and the Private School Movement." Integrated Education 9(My-Je, 1971):4-10.

Parvin, J. "The Effect on Race on the Flight to the Suburbs." Journal of Political Economy 83(Ag, 1975).

Pettigrew, Thomas F., and Green, Robert L. "A Reply to Professor Coleman." Harvard Educational Review 46(My, 1976):225-233. [On white flight]

Ravitch, Diane. "The 'White Flight' Controversy." Public Interest 51(Spring, 1978):135-149.

Rist, Ray C., and Orfield, Gary. "School Desegregation and White Flight." Social Policy 6(Ja-F, 1976):6-8.

Robin, Stanley S., and Bosco, James J. "Coleman's Desegregation Research and Policy Recommendations." School Review 84(My, 1976):352-363.

Rossell, Christine H. "School Desegregation and White Flight." Political Science Quarterly 90(Winter, 1975-1976):675-695.

Rossell, Christine H., Ravitch, Diane, and Armor, David J. "Social Science and Social Policy." Public Interest 53(Fall, 1978):109-115. [On the "white flight" phenomenon]

Schwartz, Janice (comp.). Resegregation: An Annotated Bibliography. Ann Arbor, MI: Program for Educational Opportunity, School of Education, U. of Michigan, 1976.

Sly, David F., and Pol, Louis G. "The Demographic Context of School Segregation and Desegregation." Social Forces 56(Je, 1978): 1072-1086.

_____. "White Flight, School Segregation and Demographic Change." In Three Myths: An Exposure of Popular Misconceptions About School Desegregation, pp. 57-66. Edited by Meyer Weinberg and others. Atlanta: Southern Regional Council, S, 1976.

Stinchcombe, Arthur L., McDill, Mary S., and Walker, Dollie. "Is There A Racial Tipping Point in Changing Schools?" Journal of Social Issues, Ja, 1969.

Taeuber, Karl E., and Wilson, Franklin D. The Demographic Impact of School Desegregation Policy, Ja, 1978. ERIC ED 155 289.

Terjen, Kitty. "Close-Up on Segregation Academies." New South 27(Fall, 1972):50-58.

_____. "The Segregation Academy Movement." In The South and Her Children: School Desegregation, 1970-1971, pp. 69-79. Edited by Robert E. Anderson, Jr. Atlanta: Southern Regional Council, Mr, 1971.

Wegmann, Robert G. "Desegregation and Resegregation: A Review of the Research on White Flight in Urban Areas." In The Future of Big-City Schools. Edited by Daniel U. Levine and Robert J. Havighurst. Berkeley, CA: McCutchan, 1977.

_____. "White Flight and School Resegregation: Some Hypotheses." Phi Delta Kappan 58(Ja, 1977):389-393.

_____. White Flight: Some Hypotheses, Ap, 1976. ERIC ED 121 924.

Weinberg, Meyer. "A Critique of Coleman." Integrateducation 13(S-O, 1975):3-7. [See Coleman, 1975, above.]

_____. "Desegregation and the Movement of People." Research Review of Equal Education 1(Summer, 1977):18-33.

Miscellaneous

A.C.L.U. "Discrimination Where It Hurts." Integrated Education 12(Ja-Ap, 1974):38. [Fluoridation of water in Los Angeles]

Abbey, Brian, and Ashenden, Dean. Society and Experience with Particular Reference to Class and Education, 1976. ERIC ED 141 313.

Abbott, Simon. "Defining Racial Discrimination." Race 11(1970):477-480.

Abrahams, Roger D. "Cultural Differences and the Melting Pot Ideology." Educational Leadership 29(N, 1971):118-121.

_____. Positively Black. Englewood Cliffs, NJ: Prentice-Hall, 1969.

Abrams, Charles. The City Is the Frontier. New York: Harper and Row, 1965.

Ackerman, Donald. A Study of School Activities Intended to Effect Racial, Economic, or Social Balance. Final Report, Ag, 1969. ERIC ED 041 096.

Adam, Barry D. The Survival of Domination: Inferiorization and Everyday Life. New York: Elsevier, 1978.

Addams, Jane. "Rise of Negro Education." School Life 18(Ja, 1933):98.

Africa Research Group. African Studies in America: The Extended Family, 1969. Africa Research Group, P.O. Box 213, Cambridge, MA 02138.

After School Integration---What? Proceedings of the Third Annual Invitational Conference on Urban Education. Graduate School of Education, Yeshiva U., 110 W. 87th St., New York, N.Y. 10010.

Agger, Robert E., and Goldstein, Marshall N. Who Will Rule the Schools: A Cultural Class Crisis. Belmont, CA: Wadsworth, 1971.

Agricultural Stabilization and Conservation Service. Report on Participation in ASCS County Programs and Operations by Racial Groups 1974. Washington, DC: U.S. Dept. of Agriculture, S, 1975.

Aguirre Beltran, Gonzalo. El Processo de Aculturacion. Mexico City: UNAM, 1957.

Aigner, D. J. "A Comment on Problems in Making Inferences from the Coleman Report." American Sociological Review 35(1970):249-252.

Alatie, James E. (ed.). Report of the Twenty-First Annual Round Table Meeting on Linguistics and Languages Studies/Bilingualism and Language Contact: Anthropological, Linguistic, Psychological, and Sociological Aspects, 1970. ERIC ED 043 885.

Albert, June T. "The Sexual Basis of White Resistance to Racial Integration." Doctoral dissertation, Rutgers U., 1971. Univ. Microfilms Order No. 72-17828. [Interracial dating and marriage]

Aldridge, Delores P. "Teaching About Black Families." Social Education 41(O, 1977): 484-487.

Allen, James E., Jr. "School Integration and Civil Rights" (a letter to teachers). School and Society, N, 1964.

_____. "A Talk to School Board Members." Integrated Education, O-N, 1964.

_____. "Urban Education Crisis---The Need for Agreement on Procedure." Community, Summer, 1969.

Allen, Richard S. "The White Administrator: The Dangers of a Perspective Non-examined." MSU Orient (Michigan State University), Spring-Summer, 1969.

Alsop, Stewart. "The Tragic Failure [of School Integration]." Newsweek, F, 1970.

Alston, Jon P., and Crouch, Ben M. "White Acceptance of Three Degrees of School Desegregation, 1974." Phylon 39(Fall, 1978): 216-224.

Alston, Jon P., and Knapp, Melvin J. "Acceptance of School Integration: 1965-1969." Integrated Education 9(Ja-F, 1971):11-15.

Althusser, Louis. "Ideology and the Ideological State Apparatus." In Lenin and Philosophy and Other Essays, pp. 127-186. New York: Monthly Review Press, 1971.

American Academy of Arts and Sciences. Working Papers of the Commission on the Year 2,000. 6 vols. Boston: The Academy, 1966.

American Federation of Teachers. "A Resolution on School Integration." Integrated Education, D, 1964-Ja, 1965.

_____. Toward Equal Opportunity. New Directions for AFT Civil Rights Committees. Washington, DC: American Federation of Teachers, 1965.

American Foundation for the Blind. Discrimination Against Minority Groups. Policy Statement, O, 1968. ERIC ED 087 172.

Amerman, Helen. "Perspective for Evaluating Intergroup Relations in a Public School System." Journal of Negro Education, Spring, 1957.

An Inquiry Into Unique Costs of Operations for Urban School Districts. Austin, TX: Governor's Office of Educational Research and Planning, 1975.

Anderson, C. Arnold. "Inequalities in Schooling in the South." American Journal of Sociology, My, 1955.

_____. "Southern Education: A New Research Frontier." In Perspectives on the South: Agenda for Research. Durham, NC: Duke U. Press, 1967.

Anderson, C. Arnold, and Foster, Philip J. "Discrimination and Inequality in Education." Sociology of Education, Fall, 1964.

Anderson, Harold M., Mapes, Joseph L., and Good, Carter V. (comps.). Research Studies in Education, 1968. Itasca, IL: F. E. Peacock, 1970.

Anderson, Monroe. "Young, Middle Class and Very Black." Ebony 28(Ag, 1973):123-127.

Anderson, William A. "Role Salience and Social Research: The Black Sociologist and Field Work Among Black Groups." American Sociologist 5(Ag, 1970):236-239.

Anker, Irving. "Our Northern Cities: Toward Integration---or Segregation?" Strenthening Democracy (Board of Education of New York City), F, 1965.

Anrig, Gregory R. "What's Needed for Quality Integrated Education? Planning for the Future - 5." School Management 16(Mr, 1972): 24-26.

Approaches to Desegregation: The Superintendents' Perspective: A Dialogue on April 27-29, 1969, University of California Conference Center, Lake Arrowhead, Ap, 1969. ERIC ED 047 023.

Aptheker, Herbert. "Integration Education Requires Integrated Texts." Political Affairs, Je, 1964.

Arnez, Nancy L. "A Thoughtful Look at [Teacher] Placement Policies in a New Era." Journal of Negro Education, Winter, 1966.

Asante, Molefi, and Anderson, Peter A. "Transracial Communication and the Changing Image of Black Americans." Journal of Black Studies 4(S, 1973):69-80.

Ashmead, John, Jr. "Class and Race in Humanities Teaching and Criticism." College English 32(Ap, 1971):778-782.

Askew, Reubin. "Temporary Hardship or Continuing Injustice?" Integrated Education (Ja-F, 1972):3-6.

Astin, Alexander W. "Folklore of [College] Selectivity." Saturday Review, D, 1969.

Astor, Gerald. Minorities and the Media. New York: Ford Foundation, N, 1974.

Athey, Louis L. "Florence Kelley and the Quest for Negro Equality." Journal of Negro History 56(O, 1971):249-261.

Bacchus, M. "Education, Social Change, and Cultural Pluralism." Sociology of Education 42(1969):368-385.

Back, Kurt W. "Sociology Encounters the Protest Movement for Desegregation." Phylon, Fall, 1963.

Bagnall, Robert W. "Why Separate Schools Should be Opposed." Messenger 4(S, 1922): 485-487. [Director of Branches, NAACP]

Bailey, Stephen K. Disruption in Urban Public Secondary Schools. Washington, DC: National Association of Secondary School Principals, 1971.

_____. Disruption in Urban Public Secondary Schools, Ag, 1970. Syracuse U. Research Corporation, Merrill Lane, University Heights, Syracuse, NY 13210.

Bailey, Thomas P. Race Orthodoxy in the South, and Other Aspects of the Negro Question. New York: N.p., 1914.

Bain, Helen. "What Do You Want from NEA?" Today's Education, Ja, 1971. [Discussion with three members of minority groups]

Bain, Karen S. "Center on School Desegregation Breaks Communication Barriers." Public Education in Virginia 6(Summer, 1970):19, 24.

Baird, Keith E. "Semantics and Afro-American Liberation." Social Casework 51(1970):265-269.

Baird, Leonard. The Elite Schools: A Profile of Prestigious Independent Preparatory Schools. Lexington, MA: Lexington Books, 1977.

Baker, Donald G. "Race and Power: Comparative Approaches to the Analysis of Race Relations." Ethnic and Racial Studies 1(Jl, 1978):316-335.

Balbo, L. "La scuola di massa nei paesi a capitalismo avanzato." In La scuola del capitale. Classi sociali e scuola di massa. Edited by L. Balbo and G. Chiaretti. Padova, Italy: Marsilio, 1973.

Baldwin, James. "Negroes Are Anti-Semitic Because They're Anti-White." New York Times Magazine, Ap 9, 1967.

_____. "A Talk to Teachers." Saturday Review, D, 1963.

_____. "The White Man's Guilt." Ebony, Ag, 1965.

Balk, Alfred. "The Builder Who Makes Integration Pay." Harper's, Jl, 1965. [About Morris Milgram]

Banks, James A. "A Response to Philip Freedman." Phi Delta Kappan 58(My, 1977). [On multicultural education]

_____. "Cultural Pluralism: Implications for Contemporary Schools." Integrateducation 14 (Ja-F, 1976).

_____. "Imperatives in Ethnic Minority Education." Phi Delta Kappan 53(Ja, 1972):266-269.

Banner, Warren M. Research to Answer What Blacks Ought to Have. Ardmore, PA: Dorrance, 1978.

Banton, Michael. The Idea of Race. London: Tavistock, 1977.

_____. "1960: A Turning Point in the Study of Race Relations." Daedalus 103(Spring, 1974):31-44.

_____. Racial Minorities. London: Fontana, 1972.

_____. "Social Aspects of the Race Question." Objective: Justice 3(Ja-Mr, 1971):20-23.

Banton, Michael, and Harwood, Jonathan. The Race Concept. New York: Praeger, 1975.

Barbaro, Fred. "Ethnic Resentment." Society 11(Mr-Ap, 1974):67-75. [Rivalries among minorities]

Bard, Bernard. The School Lunchroom: Time of Trial. New York: Wiley, 1968.

Baron, Harold. "A Highly Important Book." Integrated Education (Ap-My, 1964):18. [NAIRO Report on segregation]

Barry, Thomas E., and Sheikh, Anees A. "Race as a Dimension in Children's TV Advertising: The Need for More Research." Journal of Advertising 6(Summer, 1977):5-10.

Barta, Russell. "Are the Rules Changing?" America 125(O, 1971):341-345. [From an ethic of equal opportunity to one of assuring equal results]

Barth, Ernest A. T., and Noel, Donald L. "Conceptual Frameworks for the Analysis of Race Relations: An Evaluation." Social Forces 50(Mr, 1972):333-348.

Barth, Fredrik (ed.). Ethnic Groups and Boundaries---The Social Organization of Cultural Difference. London: Allen and Unwin, 1969.

Baskin, Jane A. and others. Race Related Civil Disorders, 1967-1969. Waltham, MA: Lemberg Center for the Study of Violence, Brandeis U., 1972.

Bass, Floyd L. "Impact of the Black Experience on Attitudes toward Continuing Education." Adult Education 22(Spring, 1972):207-217.

Battle, Haron J. "State Involvement in the Urban Education Crisis." Journal of Negro Education 42(Summer, 1973):315-321.

Battle, Mark. "The White Man Can't Help the Black Ghetto." Saturday Evening Post, Ja 29, 1966.

Baty, Roger M. Education for Cultural Awareness. Riverside, CA: Western Regional School Desegregation Projects, U. of California, Je, 1971.

Baughman, E. Earl. Black Americans. A Psychological Analysis. New York: Academic Press, 1971.

Beard, Eugene. "Notes on the Role of the Black Researcher in Restructuring Public Education." In Restructuring the Educational Process: A Black Perspective. Edited by Lawrence E. Gary and Aaron Favors. Washington, DC: Institute for Urban Affairs and Research, Howard U., 1975.

Beaupre, Lee. "White Showmen See Black Life 'All Babes, Needles, and Jive'; Black Intellectuals Hate It." Variety, My, 1974. [First Black Entertainers Symposium]

Beck, Armin, Krumbein, Eliezer, and Erickson, F. D. "Strategies for Change: Conditions for School Desegregation." Phi Delta Kappan, Ja, 1969.

Beckham, Edgar F. "Problems of 'Place,' Personnel, and Practicality." Negro Digest, Mr, 1969.

Beckler, John. "Has School Integration in the South Gone as Far as It Can Go?" School Management 15(O, 1971):2-3.

Belford, P. C., and Ratliff, H. D. "A Network Flow Model for Racially Balancing Schools." Operations Research 20(1972):619-628.

Beggs, David W. III, and Alexander, S. Kern (eds.). Integration and Education. Chicago: Rand, McNally, 1969.

Bell, Daniel. "On Equality: I. Meritocracy and Equality." Public Interest 29(Fall, 1972):29-68.

_____. "Plea for a 'New Phase in Negro Leadership.'" New York Times Magazine, My 31, 1964.

Bell, Terrel H. "Federal Role in Education." New York Teachers Magazine, D, 1974. [Interview]

Bell, Thomas J. "Does the Colored Man Have a Change in the North." Bulletin of Atlanta University, Ja, 1894.

Bendiner, Robert. The Politics of Schools: A Crisis in Self-Government. New York: Harper and Row, 1969.

Bennett, Lerone, Jr. Confrontation: Black and White. Chicago: Johnson, 1965.

_____. The Negro Mood. Chicago: Johnson, 1964.

Benson, Ronald E. "Defining Equality in Education." Educational Studies 8(Summer, 1977):105-112.

Bentley, Robert J. "The Challenge of Pluralism." Journal of Negro Education 40(Fall, 1971):337-341.

Bereiter, Carl. "Are Preschool Programs Built the Wrong Way?" Nation's Schools, Je, 1966.

Bergman, Carol. "Education: Asking the Right Questions." Race Today 4(Ag, 1972):274. [On the broader consequences of educational policy]

Berk, R. A. "Intradistrict Distribution of School Inputs to the Disadvantaged: Evidence for the Courts; Comment." Journal of Human Resources 12(Summer, 1977).

Berkman, Dave. "ESAA-TV." Audiovisual Instruction 19(Ap, 1974):34-36.

Bernard, William. "The Integration of Immigrants in the U.S." International Migration Review, Spring, 1967.

Bernstein, Abraham. The Education of Urban Populations. New York: Random House, 1967.

Bernstein, Basil. "Elaborated and Restricted Codes: Their Social Origins and Some Consequences." American Anthropologist, Part 2, D, 1964.

Berry, Gordon L. "Education in Inner-City Schools. The Community Challenge." Journal of Black Studies 3(Mr, 1973):315-327.

Berube, Maurice R. "Education and the Poor." Commonweal, Mr, 1967.

Besag, Frank P. Alienation and Education: An Empirical Approach, 1966. Hertivilon Press, Box 1677, Buffalo, NY 14216.

Bettelheim, Bruno. "Segregation: New Style." School Review 66(1958):251-272.

"Better Schools Are the Real Goal of Integration." Life, F, 1964.

Beyond Desegregation. Urgent Issues in the Education of Minorities. New York: College Entrance Examination Board, 1978.

Billings, Thomas A. "Education's Stake in the Civil Rights Movement." Phi Delta Kappan, My, 1966.

Binderman, Murray B. "The Failure of Freedom of Choice: Decision-Making in a Southern Black Community." Social Forces 50(Je, 1972):487-498.

Birley, D., and Dufton, A. An Equal Chance: Equalities and Inequalities of Educational Opportunity. London: Routledge and Kegan Paul, 1971.

Black, Brown, and Red. The Movement for Freedom Among Black, Chicano, and Indian, 1972. News and Letters Committees, 1900 East Jefferson, Detroit, MI 48207. Seventy-five cents.

Black, Earl. "The Militant Segregationist Vote in the Post-Brown South: A Comparative Analysis." Social Science Quarterly 54(Je, 1973).

_____. Southern Governors and Civil Rights: Racial Segregation as a Campaign Issue in the Second Reconstruction. Cambridge, MA: Harvard U. Press, 1976.

Black Elected Officials in the South. February 3, 1972. Voter Education Project, Inc., 52 Fairlie St., Atlanta, GA 30303.

"Black Schools that Work." Newsweek (Ja, 1973): 57-58.

"The Black Teachers Speak Out." Instructor, Ag-S, 1969.

Blake, Elias, Jr. "Color Prejudice and the Education of Low Income Negroes in the North and West." Journal of Negro Education, Summer, 1965.

Blackford, Staige D. "Free Choice and Tuition Grants in Five Southern States." New South, Ap, 1964.

Blackman, Allan. "Planning and the Neighborhood School." Integrated Education, Ag-S, 1964.

_____. The Role of City Planning in Child Pedestrian Safety. Berkeley, CA: Center for Planning and Development Research, Institute of Urban and Regional Development, U. of California, Berkeley, Jl, 1966.

Blair, George E. "Educate the Black One, Too." New York State Education, Mr, 1966.

Blalock, Hubert M., Jr. Toward a Theory of Minority-Group Relations. New York: Wiley, 1967.

Block, James H. (ed.). Schools, Society and Mastering Learning. New York: Holt, Rinehart and Winston, 1974.

Block, James H. (ed.), with Airasian, Peter W., Bloom, Benjamin S., and Carroll, John B. Mastering Learning. Theory and Practice. New York: Holt, Rinehart and Winston, 1971.

Bloom, Benjamin S. Stability and Change in Human Characteristics. New York: Wiley, 1964.

Bloom, Leonard. The Social Psychology of Race Relations. London: Allen and Unwin, 1971.

Bloomberg, Warner, Jr. "Making the Urban Schools of Education Relevant." Graduate Comment 9(1966).

Blount, Roy, Jr. "Sports Integration." South Today 1(1970):1, 10-11.

Board of Education, Human Relations Committee. The Interpersonal Plane. A Human Relations Handbook. Houston, TX: Board of Education, 1974.

Boas, Franz. "Race and Progress." Science 74 (Jl, 1931):1-8.

_____. "Race Problems in America." Science 29(My, 1909):845-846.

Boesel, David and Associates. "White Institutions and Black Rage." Transaction, Mr, 1969.

Bogart, Leo (ed.). Social Research and the Desegregation of the U.S. Army. Chicago: Markham, 1969.

Boggs, Grace. "Education for Survival." Foresight, Vol. 1, No. 1(1968).

_____. "Education: The Great Obsession." Foresight, Ja, 1970.

_____. Towards a New System of Education, 1969. Foresight Publications Center, P.O. Box 494, N.W. Station, Detroit, MI 48204.

_____. "Toward a New System of Education." In What Black Educators Are Saying, pp. 186-197. Edited by Nathan Wright, Jr. New York: Hawthorn, 1970.

Bogue, Grant. "Integrated Education in a Small Northern City." Integrated Education, Ag-N, 1965.

Bohmer, Peter and others. Sozialisation und Probleme d. Emanzipation am Beispiel d. Afroamerikaner. Two volumes. Frankfurt a. M./Germany: Europaische Verlag, Anst., 1972.

Bond, Horace Mann. Education for Production. A Textbook on How To Be Healthy, Wealthy, and Wise. Athens, GA: U. of Georgia Press for Fort Valley State College, 1944.

_____. "Education in the South." The Journal of Educational Sociology 12(Ja, 1939).

_____. The Education of the Negro in the American Social Order. New York: Octagon Books, 1966.

_____. "The Educational and Other Social Implications of the Impact of the Present Crisis upon Racial Minorities." Journal of Negro Education 10(Jl, 1941):617-622.

_____. "The Extent and Character of Separate Schools in the United States." Journal of Negro Education 4(Jl, 1935):321-338.

_____. "Factors Involved in School Desegregation." In Proceedings, Conference on Education. United States Commission on Education, United States Commission on Civil Rights, May 3, 1962, Washington, DC.

_____. "Faith in the Death Chamber." Phylon 1(1940):112-125.

_____. "Free Ballots for the Bulgars" (poem). New York Herald Tribune, S 4, 1945. Also in Kappa Alpha Psi Journal 31(O, 1954

_____. How and Isaacs in the Bush: The Ram in the Thicket. Atlanta: Atlanta U. School of Education, 1961.

_____. "Investigation of the Non-intellectual Traits of a Group of Negro Adults." Journal of Abnormal and Social Psychology 21(O, 1926):267-276.

_____. "The Langston Plan." School and Society 20(D, 1924):820-821.

_____. "Let's Be Honest about Nullification." Plain Talk (O, 1929(:392-398.

_____. "Main Currents in the Educational Crisis Affecting Afro-Americans." Freedomways, Fall, 1968.

_____. "The Negro Elementary School and the Cultural Pattern." Journal of Educational Sociology 13(Ap, 1940):479-490.

_____. "A Negro Looks at His South." Harpers 163(Je, 1931):98-108. [Also in The Negro Caravan, pp. 1027-1048, New York: The Dryden Press, 1943]

_____. "Planning in a War-torn World: The Task of Formal Education." In Proceedings, 17th Annual Session, National Association of Deans and Registrars, pp. 65-68. Held at Fisk U., Mr 23-25, 1943.

_____. "Present Status of Racial Integration in the United States with Special Reference to Education." Journal of Negro Education 21(1952):241-250.

_____. "The Role of Negro Education in the Post War World." North Carolina Teachers Record 15(My, 1944):8.

_____. "Talent---and Toilets." Journal of Negro Education, Winter, 1959.

_____. "What Lies Behind Lynching." The Nation 128(Mr, 1929):370-371.

_____. "What the San Francisco Conference Means to the Negro." Journal of Negro Education 14(Fall, 1945). [Address delivered over radio station WMAZ, Macon, GA, Ap 18, 1945]

_____. "Will We Ever Be Like That?" Greater Fisk Herald 4(F, 1929):10-13.

Bond, Horace Mann with Puner, Norton. "Jim Crow in Education." Nation 173(N, 1951): 446-449.

Bond, James. "The Education of the Bond Family." Crisis 34(Ap, 1927):41, 60.

Bonilla, Frank, and Girling, Robert. Structures of Dependency, 1973. Nairobi Bookstore, 1621 Bay Road, East Palo Alto, CA.

Boocock, Sarance S. "Toward a Sociology of Learning: A Selective Review of Existing Research." Sociology of Education, Winter, 1966.

Booms, B. H., and Hu, T. "Economic and Social Factors in the Provision of Urban Public Education." American Journal of Economics and Sociology 32(Ja, 1973).

Boom, Kathleen W. "The Julius Rosenwald's Fund Aid to Education in the South." Doctoral dissertation, U. of Chicago, 1950.

Bosma, Boyd. "Force-Outs. Their Plight Studied At Meeting." South Today 3(Mr, 1972).

Bottomly, Forbes. "The Professional Educator in the Desegregation Suit." In Limits of Justice. The Courts' Role in School Desegregation, pp. 621-639. Edited by Howard I. Kalodner and James J. Fishman. Cambridge, MA: Ballinger, 1978.

Bottomly, Forbes, and Kitfield, Allison (eds.). *Exploring Metropolitan Ways Toward Reducing Isolation: Prospects for Progress*. Denver, CO: Education Commission of the States, 1978.

Boudon, Raymond. *Education, Opportunity and Social Inequality*. London: Wiley, 1974.

Boulding, Kenneth E. "Publicly Supported, Universally Available Education and Equality." *Phi Delta Kappan* 58(S, 1976):36-41.

Bouma, Donald H., and Hoffman, James. *The Dynamics of School Integration: Problems and Approaches in a Northern City*. Grand Rapids, MI: Eerdmans, 1968.

Boutwell, W. C. "What's Happening in Education? Neighborhood-School Policy." *PTA Magazine*, S, 1963.

Bouvier, Leon F. *Educational Change in the Black Population of the United States and the South*, O, 1974. ERIC ED 126 224.

Bowe, Frank G. "Educational, Psychological, and Occupational Aspects of the Nonwhite Deaf Population." *Journal of Rehabilitation of the Deaf* 5(Ja, 1972):33-39.

Bowen, Raymond C. "The New Black Student and the White Liberal Educator." *National Association of Student Personnel Administrators* 6(1969):187-189.

Bowles, Frank. "Two School Systems Within One Society." In *Qualitative Aspects of Educational Planning*." Edited by C. E. Beeby. Paris: UNESCO International Institute for Educational Planning, 1969.

Bowles, Gladys K. *Net Migration of the Population, 1960-1970: By Age, Sex, and Color*. 6 vols. Washington, DC: Economic Research Service, U.S. Dept. of Agriculture, 1975.

Bowles, Samuel. *Educational Production Function. Final Report*, F, 1969. ERIC ED 037 590.

_____. "Getting Nowhere: Programmed Class Stagnation." *Society* 9(Je, 1972):42-49.

_____. "Towards Equality of Educational Opportunity?" *Harvard Educational Review*, Mr, 1968.

_____. "Understanding Unequal Economic Opportunity." *American Economic Review* 63(My, 1973):346-356.

_____. "Unequal Education and the Reproduction of the Social Division of Labor." In *Schooling in a Corporate Society. The Political Economy of Education in America*, pp. 36-64. Edited by Martin Carnoy. New York: McKay, 1972.

Bowles, Samuel, and Gintis, Herbert. "The Contradiction of Liberal Education Reform." In *Work, Technology and Education: Essays in the Intellectual Foundations of Education*. Edited by Henry Rosemont and Walter Feinberg. Urbana, IL: U. of Illinois Press, 1974.

_____. "If John Dewey Calls, Tell Him Things Didn't Work Out." *Journal of Open Education* 2(Winter, 1974):1-17.

_____. *Schooling in Capitalist America: Education and the Contradictions of Economic Life*. New York: Basic Books, 1976.

Bowles, Samuel, and Levin, Henry. "The Determinants of Scholastic Achievement---An Appraisal of Some Recent Evidence." *Journal of Human Resources*, Winter, 1968.

_____. *Equality of Educational Equality---A Critical Appraisal*. Dept. of Economics, Harvard U.: Brookings Institution, 1967. [A severe critique of the Coleman Report]

_____. "More on Multicollinearity and the Effectiveness of Schools." *Journal of Human Resources*, Summer, 1968. [On the Coleman Report]

Boyer, James, and Hill, Howard. "Desegregating the Curriculum." *Educational Leadership* 30 (My, 1973):759-760.

Bradbury, William C. "Evaluation of Research in Race Relations." *Inventory of Research in Racial and Cultural Relations* (Winter-Spring, 1953):99-133.

Brameld, Theodore. "Illusions and Disillusions in American Education." *Phi Delta Kappan*, D, 1968.

_____. *Minority Problems in the Public Schools. A Study of Administrative Policies and Practices in Seven School Systems*. New York: Harper, 1946.

Brawley, Benjamin G. *Doctor Dillard of the Jeanes Fund*. New York: Fleming H. Revell Company, 1930.

Brazziel, William F. "Civic Groups and Compensatory Education." *Integrated Education*, Je-Jl, 1965.

_____. "Head Start: Assessment of Two Programs." *Integrated Education*, Ag-S, 1966.

_____. *Quality Education for All Americans*. Washington, DC: Howard U. Press, 1974.

Bresnick, David and others. *Black/White/Green/Red: The Politics of Education in Ethnic America*. New York: Longman, 1978.

Brickman, William W. "NEA and School Racial Segregation." *School and Society* 87(S, 1959):364.

_____. "Racial Desegregation in Education." School and Society, O, 1969.

Brickman, William W., and Lehrer, Stanley (eds.). The Countdown on Segregated Education. New York: Society for the Advancement of Education, 1960.

Bridges, Lee. "Race Relations Research: From Colonialism to Neo-Colonialism? Some Random Thoughts." Race 14(Ja, 1973):331-341.

Brigham, John C. "Ethnic Stereotypes." Psychological Bulletin 76(Jl, 1971):15-38.

Bright, Hazel V. "TV Versus Black Survival." Black World 23(D, 1973):30-42.

Brink, William. The Negro Revolution in America. New York: Simon and Schuster, 1964.

Brink, William, and Harris, Louis. Black and White. New York: Simon and Schuster, 1967.

Broder, David S. "Blacks Still 'On Fringe' Despite Political Gains." Washington Post, Je 22, 1975.

Broderick, Carfred B. "Social Heterosexual Development Among Urban Negroes and Whites." Journal of Marriage and the Family, My, 1965.

Brody, R. S. "W.E.B. DuBois' Educational Ideas." Doctoral dissertation, Rutgers U., 1972.

Brooke, Edward W. Primises to Keep." New Jersey Education Association Review, Ap, 1968.

Brooks, D. A. "Integration: The Chief Aim of Education." Journal of Human Relations, 2 parts, Spring, Autumn, 1952.

Brooks, J. Clarice. "The Student Personnel of the Negro Elementary School." Journal of Negro Education 1(Jl, 1932):256-276.

Broom, Leonard, and Glenn, Norval D. Transformation of the Negro American. New York: Harper and Row, 1965.

Brousseau, Kate. L'education des Negres aux Etats-Unis. Paris: F. Alcan, 1904.

Brown, Avis. "The Colony of the Colonized: Notes on Race, Class and Sex." Race Today 5(Je, 1973):169-170.

Brown, B. "Minorities and Public Education: An Economic Analysis of the Children of Minority Groups." American Journal of Economics and Sociology 30(Ja, 1971):1-13.

Brown, Frank. "Education and the Black Community." Educational Forum 38(N, 1973):13-18.

Brown, George H. "The New South." U.S. Department of Commerce News, O, 1970.

Brown, Les. "Integration on Network TV Shows: Fall, 1966." Integrated Education, O-N, 1966.

Brown, Roscoe E., Jr. Institute for Training Minority Group Research and Evaluation Specialists. Final Report, S, 1971. ERIC ED 062 960.

Bryant, James W. A Survey of Black American Doctorates. New York: Ford Foundation, F, 1970.

Buggs, John. "School Desegregation, North and South." Integrateducation 13(My-Je, 1975):116-121.

Bulham, Hussein Abdilahi. "Black Psyches in Captivity and Crises." Race and Class 20 (Winter, 1979):243-261.

Bullock, Charles S. III, and Rodgers, Harrell R., Jr. "Impediments to Policy Evaluation: Perceptual Distortion and Agency Loyalty." Social Science Quarterly 57(D, 1976):506-519.

_____. Racial Equality in America: In Search of an Unfulfilled Goal. Pacific Palisades, CA: Goodyear, 1975.

Bullock, H. A. "A Comparison of the Academic Achievements of White and Negro High School Graduates." Journal of Educational Research 44(1950):179-192.

Bullough, Bonnie, and Vern, L. Poverty, Ethnic Identity, and Health Care. New York: Appleton-Century-Crofts, 1972.

Bundy, McGeorge. "An Interview With McGeorge Bundy." Black Enterprise 6(S, 1975):27-32. [President, Ford Foundation]

_____. "The Struggle for Negro Equality." Integrated Education (Mr-Ap, 1968):22.

Bunge, William W. "The Geography of Human Survival." Annals of the Association of American Geographers 63(S, 1973):275-295.

Burd, Gene. "School Press Must Not Ignore Urban Problems: Minority Access." Communication: Journalism Education Today 7(F, 1973):9-11.

Burger, Henry S. Ethnic Live-In. A Guide for Penetrating and Understanding a Cultural Minority, 1969. ERIC ED 045 583.

Burgess, M. Elaine. "The Resurgence of Ethnicity: Myth or Reality?" Ethnic and Racial Studies 1(Jl, 1978):265-285.

Burket, George R., and Flanagan, John C. Project Talent, Identification, Development, and Utilization of Human Talents---Selected Pupil and School Characteristics in Relation to Percentage of Negroes in School Enrollment. Final Report, 1963. ERIC ED 016 719.

Bush, James A. (ed.). Suicide and Blacks: A Monograph for Continuing Education in Suicide Prevention. New York: MSS Information Corp., 1975.

"The Business of Education." Black Enterprise 3(S, 1972):17-20, 54.

Button, James W. Black Violence. Political Impact of the 1960's Riots. Princeton, NJ: Princeton U. Press, 1979.

Cabral, Amilcar. "The Role of Culture in the Struggle for Independence." Objective: Justice 6(Ja-F, 1974):9-12.

Caditz, Judith. "Ambivalence Toward Integration: The Sequence of Response to Six Interracial Situations." Sociological Quarterly 16(Winter, 1975):16-32.

_____. White Liberals in Transition. New York: Halsted Press, 1976.

Cagley, James W., and Cardozo, Richard N. "White Response to Integrated Advertising." Journal of Advertising Research 10(Ap, 1970).

Cahill, Edward E., and Pieper, Hanns. "Closing the Educational Gap: The South Versus the United States." Phylon 35(Mr, 1974):45-53.

Cain, Glen G., and Watts, Harold W. "The Controversy About the Coleman Report: Comment." Journal of Human Resources, Summer, 1968.

_____. "Problems in Making Policy Inferences from the Coleman Report." American Sociological Review 35(1970):228-242.

Caldwell, Catherine. "Social Science as Ammunition." Psychology Today 4(S, 1970):38-41+. [Coleman Report]

Caldwell, Dista H. The Education of the Negro Child. New York: Carleton Press, 1961.

Caliguri, Joseph P. and others. Black Power Attitudes among Students in a Black Junior High School, F, 1970. ERIC ED 045 773.

_____. Suburban Interracial Education Projects. A Resource Booklet, 1970. ERIC ED 051 035.

Caliver, Ambrose. Availability of Educational Facilities to Negroes in Rural Communities. Washington, DC: GPO, 1935. (U.S. Department of the Interior, Office of Education, Bulletin, 1935, No. 12.)

_____. Education of Negro Leaders. Washington, DC: Federal Security Agency, Office of Education, 1949.

_____. Education of Negro Teachers in the United States. Washington, DC: GPO, 1933. (U.S. Department of the Interior, Office of Education, Bulletin, 1933, No. 10, Vol. IV.)

_____. Education of Teachers for Improving Majority-Minority Relationships. Washington, DC: GPO, 1944.

_____. Fundamental Education, the What, How, Where, and Why of It. Washington, DC: U.S. Office of Education, Dept. of Health, Education, and Welfare, 1958.

_____. Literacy Education; National Statistics and Other Related Data. Washington, DC: U.S. Dept. of Health, Education, and Welfare, Office of Education, 1953.

_____. "Outcomes of the National Conference on Fundamental Problems in the Education of Negroes." Quarterly Review of Higher Education Among Negroes 2(Jl, 1934):228-237. [May 1933]

_____. Secondary Education for Negroes. Washington, DC: GPO, 1933. (U.S. Dept. of the Interior, Office of Education. Bulletin, 1932, No. 17; National Survey of Secondary Education, Monograph No. 7)

_____. "Segregation in American Education: An Overview." Annals 304(1956):17-25.

Campbell, Bruce A. "Racial Differences in the Reaction to Watergate: Some Implications for Political Support." Youth and Society 7(Je, 1976):347-366.

Campbell, David, and Feagin, Joe R. "Black Politics in the South: A Descriptive Analysis." Journal of Politics 37(F, 1975):129-162.

Campbell, Ena Keith. "Urban Minorities and Cultural Pluralism: The Perimeters of Program Planning." Doctoral dissertation, Indiana U., 1971.

Campbell, Ernest Q. "Negroes, Education, and the Southern States." Social Forces, Mr, 1969.

Campbell, George E. "The Divergence of the Social and Biological Sciences Over Evolutionary Theory as Illustrated in Studies of Race." Doctoral dissertation, U. of Georgia, 1973. Univ. Microfilms Order No. 73-31865.

Campbell, Leslie R. "The Difference." Negro Teachers Forum, D, 1966. [How to bridge the gap between Negro Professionals and masses]

Campbell, R. R., Johnson, D. M., and Stangler, G. J. "Return Migration of Black People to the South." Rural Sociology 39(1974).

Campbell, Roald F., Marx, Lucy Ann, and Nystrand, Raphael O. (eds.). Education and Urban Renaissance. New York: Wiley, 1969.

Capaert, L. "Desegregation to What?" Michigan Education, My, 1964.

Caplan, Nathan. "The New Ghetto Man: A Review of Recent Empirical Studies." Journal of Social Issues 26(Winter, 1970):59-73.

Carlson, Kenneth. Equalizing Educational Opportunity, Ap, 1972. ERIC ED 063 421.

Carmen, Sister Joann, C.S.F. Study of Race Relations. A Teaching Unit. National Catholic Conference for Interracial Justice, 1307 S. Wabash Ave., Chicago, IL. [Junior high school level]

Carmichael, Peter A. The South and Segregation. Washington, DC: Public Affairs Press, 1965.

Carnes, G. D. "Difficulties in the Recruitment of Black Students." Rehabilitation Counseling Bulletin 16(S, 1972):41-45.

Carson, Clayborne. "The Hollow Prize: Black Power After Ten Years." Nation, Ag, 1976.

Carson, Robert B. "Youthful Labor Surplus in Disaccumulationist Capitalism." Socialist Revolution 9(My-Je, 1972):15-44.

Carter, George E., and Parker, James R. (eds.). Essays on Minority Folklore. Selected Proceedings of the 3rd Annual Conference on Minority Studies: April 1975. Vol. III. La Crosse, WI: Institute for Minority Studies, U. of Wisconsin, 1977.

Carter, George E., Parker, James R., and Sweeney, Carol (eds.). Selected Proceedings of the 3rd Annual Conference on Minority Studies, April, 1975. La Crosse, WI: Institute for Minority Studies, U. of Wisconsin-La Crosse, 1976.

Carter, James Tate. "What Adjustment or Adaptations, If Any, Should Be Made in the Application of Standards to Negro Schools?" Quarterly Review of Higher Education Among Negroes 4(Ja, 1936):14-16.

Carter, R. E., Jr. "Segregation and the News: A Regional Content Study." Journalism Quarterly 34(Winter, 1957):3-18.

Cass, James. "Do We Really Want Equality?" Saturday Review, D, 1966.

Castaneda, Alfredo. "Persisting Ideologies of Assimilation in America: Implications for Psychology and Education." Stisbos 1(Summer 1975):79-91.

"Center for Black Education." Negro Digest, Mr, 1970. [1453 Fairmont St., N.W., Washington, DC]

Cervantes, Lucius F. The Dropout: Causes and Cures. Ann Arbor, MI: U. of Michigan Press, 1965.

Chadima, Steven, and Wabnick, Richard. Inequalities in the Educational Experiences of Black and White Americans. Washington, DC: GPO, 1977.

Chalmers, W. Ellison, and Cormick, Gerald W. (eds.). Racial Conflict and Negotiations. Perspectives and First Case Studies. Ann Arbor, MI: Institute of Labor and Industrial Relations, U. of Michigan, 1971.

Chambliss, W. J., and Nagasawa, R. H. "On the Validity of Official Statistics---A Comparative Study of White, Black, and Japanese High School Boys." Journal of Research in Crime and Delinquency 71(Ja, 1969).

Champagne, David W. "A White Supervisor in a Black School." Phi Delta Kappan, O, 1969.

Chapin, F. Stuart. Education and the Mores. New York: Columbia U. Press, 1911.

Chapman, Colin. "A Briton Views American Schools." American Education, Je, 1967.

Chapman, Frank E., Jr. "A Black Prisoner Speaks Out." Integrateducation 1?(S-O, 1974):17-18.

Chase, Francis S. "A Talk on Equal Opportunity." Integrated Education, Je-Jl, 1964.

"Checkerboard Communities---Patterns for Living." Newsweek, Ap, 1966. [Housing Integration]

Cheng, Charles W. "Civil Rights in the [Collective Bargaining] Contract." American Teacher, Je, 1966.

_____. "Rebop: Unity and Diversity." Integrateducation 14(S-O, 1976). [Television program]

Cherry, Frank T. "Black American Contributions to Western Civilization in Philosophy and Social Science." In The Negro Impact on Western Civilization. Edited by Joseph S. Roucek and Thomas Kiernan. New York: Philosophical Library, 1970.

Chesler, Mark A. "Desegregation and School Crisis." Integrated Education 10(N-D, 1972): 54-63.

Chesler, Mark A., and Arnstein, Fred. "The School Consultant: Change Agent or Defender of the Status Quo?" Integrated Education 8(Jl-Ag, 1970):19-25.

Children's Television Workshop. A Report of Three Studies on the Role and Penetration of Sesame Street in Ghetto Communities (Bedford Stuyvesant, East Harlem, and Washington, DC), 1970 and 1971. ERIC ED 122 819 and 122 820.

Children's Television Workshop. A Report on
the Role and Penetration of Sesame Street
in Ghetto Communities (Bedford Stuyvesant,
East Harlem, Chicago and Washington, DC),
Ap, 1973, ERIC ED 122 821.

Chimezie, Amuzie. "Theorizing on Black Behavior. The Role of the Black Psychologist."
Journal of Black Studies 4(S, 1973):15-28.

Chisholm, Shirley. "Desegregation and National
Policy." Integrateducation 13(My-Je, 1975):
122-126.

Chiswick, B. R. "Generating Inequality: Ab-
solute or Relative Schooling Inequality?"
Journal of Human Resources 13(Winter, 1978).

Citizen Guide to Desegregation. Cleveland:
Citizens' Council for Ohio Schools, 1976.

Clarana, Jose. "The Schooling of the Negro."
Crisis, Jl, 1913.

Clark, Chris, and Rush, Sheila. How To Get
Along With Black People. A Handbook for
White Folks. New York: The Third Press,
1971.

Clark, Kenneth B. "American Education Today."
Integrated Education, D, 1965-Ja, 1966.

_____. The American Revolution: Democratic
Politics and Popular Education. Washington,
DC: American Enterprise Institute for Pub-
lic Policy Research, 1974.

_____. "At This Stage of My Life." Journal
of Current Social Issues 12(Summer, 1975):
24-29.

_____. Autobiographical Sketch [In James
Moss], "Utilization of Negro Teachers in
Colleges in New York State," pp. 106-142.
Doctoral dissertation, Columbia U., 1957.

_____. "Clash of Cultures in the Classroom."
Integrated Education, Ag, 1963.

_____. "Conclusions." Social Problems, Ap,
1955. [Special issue devoted to problems
of desegregation]

_____. "Contemporary Educational Emergency
in America." Journal of the Association
of Deans and Administrators of Student
Affairs, O, 1967.

_____. "Desegregation: An Appraisal of the
Evidence." Journal of Social Issues, O,
1953.

_____. "Desegregation and the Role of the
Social Sciences." Teachers College Record,
O, 1960.

_____. "Discrimination and the Disadvantaged."
In College Entrance Examination Board, The
Search for Talent: College Admissions #7.
New York: CEEB, 1960.

_____. "Education in the Ghetto." Christian-
ity and Crisis, My, 1965.

_____. "Eighteen Years After Brown." Inte-
grated Education 10(N-D, 1972):7-15.

_____. "Implications of Adlerian Theory for
an Understanding of Civil Rights Problems
and Actions." Journal of Individual Psychology 23(N, 1967):181-190.

_____. "Interracial Justice, Our Common
Task." Interracial Review, D, 1961.

_____. "The Negro and the Urban Crisis." In
Agenda for the Nation. Edited by Kermit
Gordon. Washington, DC: Brookings, 1968.

_____. "The Present Dilemma of the Negro."
Journal of Negro History, Ja, 1968.

_____. "Public School Desegregation---18
Years After Brown." Congressional Record,
Ap, 1972, E3566-3569.

_____. "Social and Economic Implications of
Integration in the Public Schools." Semi-
nar on Manpower Policy and Program, N, 1965.
Office of Manpower, Automation and Training,
U.S. Dept. of Labor, Washington, DC
20210.

_____. "Some Principles Related to the Prob-
lem of Desegregation." Journal of Negro
Education 23(Summer, 1954):339-347.

_____. "Too Much Talk." Educate 4(Ja, 1971):
16-21.

_____. "Toward a Defense of 'Non-Relevant'
Education." Amherst Alumni News (Jl, 1969):
10-13.

_____. "The Wonder Is There Have Been So Few
Riots." New York Times Magazine, S, 1965.

Clark, Kenneth B. and others. School Integration. Proceedings of a Symposium on School
Integration, n.d. ERIC ED 011 265.

Clarke, Austin C. "Cultural-Political Origins
of Black Student Anti-Intellectualism."
Studies in Black Literature 1(Spring, 1970):
69-82.

Clarke, Stevens H. Application of Electronic
Computer Techniques to Racial Integration
in School Systems. New York: Bureau of
Applied Social Research, Columbia U., 1967.

Cleghorn, Reese. "The View from Maddox
Country." Nation, Ap, 1970. [Desegregation
in the South]

Clement, Carlton. "Some Processes Through
Which Middle Class Oriented Schools Fail
Students of Lower Class Background." Mas-
ter's thesis, Keene State College, 1971.

Clift, Virgil. "Factors Relating to the Education of Culturally Deprived Negro Youth." Educational Theory, Ap, 1964.

_____. "Higher Education of Minority Groups in the United States." Journal of Negro Education, Summer, 1969.

Clift, Virgil and others. (eds.). Negro Education in America: Its Adequacy, Problems, and Needs. New York: N.p., 1935.

Cobern, Morris, Salem, Claude, and Mushkin, Selma. Indicators of Educational Outcome, Fall, 1972. Washington, DC: GPO, 1973.

Coffin, E. W. "On the Education of Backward Races." Pedagogical Seminary 15(1908):1-62.

Coffin, Gregory C. "Educational Relevance. Environment, Teachers, and Curriculum." Education and Urban Society, Ag, 1969.

_____. "Toward a Single Nation." Educational Leadership, N, 1968.

Cohen, David K. "Desegregation Now---Black, White, and Brown." New Republic, Je, 1974.

_____. "Education and Race." History of Education Quarterly 9(1969):281-286.

_____. "Education and Race: Myths and Truths." New York State Education, My, 1968.

_____. "Hope of Equality." New Jersey Education Association Review, O, 1967.

_____. "Politics and Research: Evaluation of Social Action Programs in Education." Review of Educational Research 40(Ap, 1970): 213-238.

_____. "School Resources and Racial Equality." Education and Urban Society, F, 1969.

_____. "School Segregation and Desegregation: Some Misconceptions." In Urban School Administration. Edited by Troy V. McKelvey and Austin D. Swanson. Beverly Hills, CA: Sage, 1969.

_____. "Social Accounting in Education: Reflections on Supply and Demand." In Proceedings of the 1970 Invitational Conference on Testing Problems - The Promise and Perils of Educational Information Systems. Princeton, NJ: Educational Testing Service, 1971.

Cohen, David K., and Weiss, Janet A. "Science and Social Policy." Educational Forum 41 (My, 1977):393-413.

_____. "Social Science and Social Policy: Schools and Race." In Education, Social Science and the Judicial Process, pp. 55-70. Washington, DC: National Institute of Education, Je, 1976.

Cohen, Marshall, Nagel, Thomas, and Scanlon, Thomas (eds.). Equality and Preferential Treatment. Princeton, NJ: Princeton U. Press, 1977.

Cohen, Percy. "Race Relations as a Sociological Issue." In Race and Ethnic Relations. Edited by Gordon Bowker and John Carrier. London: Hutchinson, 1976.

Cole, Robert W. "Black Moses: Jesse Jackson's PUSH for Excellence." Phi Delta Kappan, Ja, 1977.

Coleman, A. Lee. "Social Scientists' Predictions about Desegregation, 1950-1955." Social Forces, Mr, 1960.

Coleman, James S. "The Concept of Equality of Educational Opportunity." Harvard Educational Review, Winter, 1968.

_____. "Equal Schools or Equal Students?" Public Interest, Summer, 1966.

_____. "Equality and Inequality." New York University Education Quarterly 4(Summer, 1973):2-8.

_____. "Equality of Educational Equality: Reply to Bowles and Levin." Journal of Human Resources, Spring, 1967.

_____. Equality of Educational Opportunity, Reconsidered. Baltimore, MD: Johns Hopkins U., 1967. ERIC ED 015 893.

_____. The Evaluation of Equality of Educational Opportunity. Baltimore, MD: Johns Hopkins U., Center for the Study of Social Organization of Schools, Ag, 1968. ERIC ED 026 721.

_____. "Rawls, Nozick, and Educational Equality." Public Interest 43(Spring, 1976):121-128.

_____. "Reply to Cain and Watts." American Sociological Review 35(1970):242-249.

_____. Resources For Social Change: Race in the United States. New York: Wiley, 1971.

_____. Responsibility of Schools in Provision of Equal Educational Opportunity. Invited Paper. Baltimore, MD: Johns Hopkins U., F, 1968. ERIC ED 023 729.

Coleman, James S., and Karweit, Nancy L. Measures of School Performance. Santa Monica, CA: Rand, 1970.

Coleman, James S. and others. Equality of Educational Opportunity. Washington, DC: GPO, 1966.

Coleman, Milton R. "A Cultural Approach to Education." Negro Digest, Mr, 1969.

Coles, Robert. "A Compelling Summons." Reporter, O, 1965. [Review of Kenneth B. Clark, Dark Ghetto]

_____. "The Gunman Needs a Climate of Hate." New York Times Magazine, Ap, 1968.

_____. "A House of Truth." American Scholar, Autumn, 1965.

_____. "Is There a Mind of the South?" New South, Winter, 1966.

_____. "The Kind of Man You Don't Forget." New Society, Je, 1968. [Robert F. Kennedy]

_____. "Maybe God Will Come and Clean Up This Mess." Atlantic Monthly, O, 1967.

_____. The Migrant Farmer. A Psychiatric Study. Atlanta, GA: Southern Regional Council, 1965.

_____. "The Poor Don't Want to be Middle-Class." New York Times Magazine, D 19, 1965.

_____. "Psychiatry in America." New Society, Ag, 1968.

_____. "Public Evil and Private Problems of Segregation and Psychiatry." Yale Review, Summer, 1965.

_____. "Some Very Old People." Integrated Education (S-O, 1971):65-68.

_____. "The South That Is Man's Destiny." Massachusetts Review, Winter, 1965.

_____. "The Two American Lefts." New Society, Jl, 1968.

_____. "Two Minds About [Stokely] Carmichael." New Republic, N, 1966.

_____. Uprooted Children. The Early Life of Migrant Farm Workers. Pittsburgh, PA: U. of Pittsburgh Press, 1970.

_____. "What Migrant Farm Children Learn." Saturday Review, My, 1965.

_____. "When I Draw the Lord He'll Be a Real Big Man." Atlantic Monthly, My, 1966.

_____. "When Northern Schools Desegregate." Integrated Education, F-Mr, 1966.

_____. "When the Southern Negro Moves North." New York Times Magazine, S 17, 1967.

_____. "White Pieties and Black Reality." Saturday Review, D, 1967.

_____. "Whose Strengths, Whose Weaknesses." American Scholar, Autumn, 1968. [Mississippi Delta]

Coles, Robert, and Brenner, Joseph. "American Youth in a Social Struggle: The Mississippi Summer Project." American Journal of Orthopsychiatry, O, 1965.

"Collective Bargaining for School Integration" (documents). Integrated Education, Ap-My, 1967.

Colton, David L. Urban School Desegregation Costs. Part I. Case Studies ERIC ED 147 972.

Columbia Human Rights Law Review Staff. Legal Rights of Children: Status, Progress, and Proposals. Fair Lawn, NJ: R. E. Burdick, 1973.

Combessie, Jean-Claude. "Education et valeurs de classe dans la sociologie americaine." Revue francaise de sociologie 10(1969):12-36.

Commission on Professional Rights and Responsibilities. Report of [Teacher] Displacement in Seventeen States. Washington, DC: National Education Association, D, 1965.

Commission on School Integration. Public School Segregation and Integration in the North. Washington, DC: National Association of Intergroup Relations Officials, N, 1963.

Committee on Civil and Human Rights of Educators. Faculty Desegregation, Spring, 1966 Conferences. Washington, DC: National Education Association, Jl, 1966.

Committee on School Lunch Participation. Their Daily Bread. A Study of the National School Lunch Program. Atlanta, GA: McNelley-Rudd Printing Service, 1968.

Community Values and Conflict, 1967. A Conference Report. New York: City of New York Commission on Human Rights, 1968. [The National Conference on Community Values and Conflict]

Comptroller General of the United States. The National School Lunch Program---Is It Working? Washington, DC: General Accounting Office, Jl, 1977.

Conant, James B. The Comprehensive High School: A Second Report to Interested Citizens. New York: McGraw-Hill, 1967.

Conant, Ralph and others. "Mass Polarizations: Negro and White Attitudes on the Pace of Integration." American Behavioral Scientist 13(N, 1969):247-263.

Congressional Budget Office. Inequalities in the Educational Experiences of Black and White Americans. Washington, DC: GPO, 1977.

Conley, Elizabeth G. Integration from the Bottom Up. New York: Exposition, 1966.

Cooke, Paul Phillips. "Equal Educational Opportunity: Some Findings and Conclusions." Journal of Negro Education, Summer, 1968.

Cooper, Barbara. 1972 Lifetime Earnings by Age, Sex, Race and Education Level. Washington, DC: Social Security Administration, 1975.

Cormican, M. Alma, and Shanker, Albert. [Exchange of letters] New York Teacher, F, 1974. [On quotas and related issues]

Corrigan, Dean C. "Integration: The Profession's Greatest Challenge." New York State Education, My, 1968.

Cotton, Dorothy F. "CEP: Challenge to the 'New Education.'" Freedomways, Winter, 1969. [The Citizenship Education Program of the Southern Christian Leadership Conference]

Counts, George. The Selective Character of American Education. Chicago, IL: 1922.

Courlander, Harold. "'Roots,' 'The African,' and the Whiskey Jug Case." Village Voice, Ap, 1979. [In the matter of plagiarism in Haley's Roots.]

Coveyou, Michael R., and Pfeiffer, David G. "Education and Voting Turnout of Blacks in the 1968 Presidential Election." Journal of Politics 35(N, 1973):995-1001.

Cowan, J. L. "Inverse Discrimination." Analysis 33(1972):10-12.

Cox, Keith K. "Social Effects of Integrated Advertising." Journal of Advertising Research 10(Ap, 1970).

Cox, Oliver Cromwell. Caste, Class, and Race. A Study in Social Dynamics. New York: Monthly Review Press, 1959.

_____. "The Question of Pluralism." Race 12(Ap, 1971):385-400.

_____. Race Relations: Elements and Social Dynamics. Detroit, MI: Wayne State U. Press, 1976.

Cox, Peter R. and others (eds.). Equalities and Inequalities in Education. New York: Academic Press, 1975.

Crain, Robert L., and Street, C. "School Desegregation and School Decision-Making." In The School in Society: Studies in the Sociology of Education. Edited by S. D. Sieber and D. E. Wilder. New York: Free Press, 1973.

"This Crisis in Our Cities." Howard University Magazine, Jl, 1963.

"Crisis of Color, '66." Newsweek, Ag, 1966. [Results of national survey of attitudes toward civil rights movement; repeats 1963 survey]

Cronbach, L. J., and Snow, R. E. Individual Differences in Learning Ability as a Function of Instructional Variables. Stanford, CA: School of Education, Stanford U., 1969.

Cronin, Joseph M. The Control of Urban Schools: Perspective on the Power of Educational Reformers. New York: Free Press, 1973.

Cross, Dolores E. "Pluralism and the Oppressed." California Journal of Teacher Education 2 (Spring, 1975):120-131.

Cross, Malcolm. "Colonialism and Ethnicity: A Theory and Comparative Case Study." Ethnic and Racial Studies 1(Ja, 1978):37-59.

_____. "Cultural Pluralism and Sociological Theory: A Critique and Re-Evaluation." Social and Economic Studies 17(D, 1968).

Crowe, C. Lawson. "Rights and Differences: Some Notes for Liberals." Christian Century, N, 1964.

Culley, James D., and Bennett, Rex. The Use of Stereotypes in Mass Media Advertising: Blacks in Magazine, Newspaper and Television Ads, 1975. ERIC ED 148 320.

Cunard, Nancy (ed.). Negro: An Anthology. Abridged edition. New York: Ungar, 1970 (orig. 1934).

Cunningham, Luvern L. "Equality of Opportunity: Is It Possible in Education?" Administrator's Notebook, N, 1967.

_____. "Hey, Man, You Our Principal? Urban Education as I Saw It." Phi Delta Kappan, N, 1969.

Curry, Jabez Lamar Monroe. A Brief Sketch of George Peabody and a History of the Peabody Education Fund Through Thirty Years. Cambridge, MA: University Press, 1898.

_____. "Difficulties, Complications and Limitations Connected with the Education of the Negro." Occasional Papers of the Trustees of the John F. Slater Fund, V (1895).

Dandridge, William L. "The Role of Independent Schools." Civil Rights Digest 5(Ag, 1972): 3-7.

Daniel, Jack L. "The Facilitation of White-Black Communication." Journal of Communication 20(Je, 1970):134-141.

Daniel, Walter G. "Problems of Disadvantaged Youth, Urban and Rural." Journal of Negro Education, Summer, 1964.

Daniels, Deborah K. (ed.). Education By, For and About African Americans: A Profile of Several Black Community Schools, 1973. The Nebraska Curriculum Development Center, Andrews Hall, U. of Nebraska, Lincoln, NB 68508.

David, Allen. "NEA: Like an Ostrich." Guardian, Jl, 1969.

Davidoff, Paul. "Integrated Integration." Integrated Education, D, 1966–Ja, 1967.

Davidson, Edmonia W. "Education and Black Cities: Demographic Background." Journal of Negro Education 42(Summer, 1973):233–260.

Davin, Eric. "Christopher Jencks: Does He Lack the Courage of His Convictions?" Harvard Crimson, N, 1974.

Davis, Allison. "Black Leadership and Anger." School Review 81(My, 1973):451–459.

_____. Du Bois and the Problems of the Black Masses. Atlanta, GA: W. E. B. Du Bois Institute, Atlanta U.

Angela Davis. An Autobiography. New York: Random House, 1974.

Davis, Arthur. Racial Crisis in Public Education: A Quest for Social Order. New York: Vantage, 1975.

Davis, Gerald N. "Making the Independent School Relevant to Blacks." Independent School Bulletin 33(O, 1973):25–27.

Davis, John P. (ed.). The American Negro Reference Book. Englewood Cliffs, NJ: Prentice-Hall, 1965.

Davis, John W. "Negro Education versus the Education of the Negro." Negro History Bulletin, Ap, 1946.

Davis, Marianna W. "Black Scholars/White Professional Organizations." Negro American Literature Forum 5(F, 1971):102–107.

Davison, Hugh M. Equality of Educational Opportunity (in the North). A Review of Some Pertinent Data, n.d. ERIC ED 011 140.

Day, Noel A., Ayers, William, Sullivan, Neil V., Kohl, Herbert, and Fantini, Mario D. "Implementing Equal Educational Opportunity." Harvard Educational Review, Winter, 1968.

d"Azevedo, Warren L. "Race and the Negro." Liberator, D, 1968.

"De Facto Segregation: A New Storm Over the Public Schools Divides the Opinion of Educators." Johns Hopkins Magazine, O, 1963.

De Marco, Joseph P. "The Concept of Race in the Social Thought of W. E. B. DuBois." Philosophical Forum 3(Winter, 1972).

De Muth, Jerry. "Ghetto Education in White and Black." Trends, Ap, 1969.

_____. "Public School Turnovers in the South." America 123(N, 1970):377–379.

"The Deepening Crisis." Journal of the New York State School Boards Association, D, 1963. [The text of part of a symposium on racial imbalance in public schools. Among the participants were: Otis E. Finley, Jr., Dr. John H. Fischer, and Theron A. Johnson]

Delaney, Anita M. Black Task Force Report: Project on Ethnicity. New York: Family Service Association of North America, 1978. [Mental health services]

Denby, Charles. "Black Caucuses in the Unions." New Politics, Summer, 1968. [June, 1969]

Denby, Robert V. "Literature By and About Negroes for the Elementary Level." Elementary English 66(1969):909–1913.

Dentler, Robert A. "Barriers to Northern School Desegregation." Daedalus, Winter, 1966.

_____. "Community Behavior and Northern School Desegregation." Journal of Negro Education, Summer, 1965.

_____. "Dropouts, Automation, and the Cities." Teachers College Record, Mr, 1964.

_____. "Equality of Educational Opportunity - A Special Review." Urban Review, D, 1966. [Discussion of the Coleman Report]

_____. "Eulogy On a Laboratory: The Center for Urban Education." Urban Review 6(1973):3–7, 69.

_____. "Is There a Crisis in Urban Education?" The Urban Review, My, 1966.

_____. "Solving Problems in Urban Education." Social Action, S, 1968.

_____. "Urban Crisis in Public Education." United Church Herald, Ja, 1966.

Dentler, Robert A., and Elsbery, James. "Big City School Desegregation: Trends and Methods." In U.S. Commission on Civil Rights, Papers Prepared for National Conference on Equal Educational Opportunity in America's Cities. Washington, DC: GPO, 1968.

Dentler, Robert A., Mackler, Bernard and Warshauer, Mary Ellen (eds.). The Urban R's. Race Relations as the Problem in Urban Education. New York: Praeger, 1967.

Dentler, Robert A., and Warshauer, Mary Ellen. Big City Dropouts and Illiterates. New York: Center for Urban Education, 1966.

"Desegregation [in the South]." Southern Education Report, N–D, 1965.

Deutsch, Martin and others. The Role of the Social Sciences in Desegregation: A Symposium. New York: Anti-Defamation League, 1958.

Deutsch, Martin and Jensen, A. R. (eds.). Social Class, Race, and Psychological Development. New York: Holt, Rinehart and Winston, 1967.

Deutschberger, Paul. "Interaction Patterns in Changing Neighborhoods: New York and Pittsburgh." Sociometry, N, 1946.

DeVos, George. "Social Stratification and Ethnic Pluralism: An Overview from the Perspective of Psychological Anthropology." Race 13(Ap, 1972):435-460.

Dewey, John. "Highly-Colored White Lies." New Republic 42(Ap, 1925):229-230.

Dewing, Rolland. "Desegregation of State NEA Affiliates in the South." Journal of Negro Education, Fall, 1969.

_____. "The Disadvantaged Child and the Learning Process" (a review). Integrated Education, Ja, 1963.

_____. "The National Education Association and Desegregation." Phylon, Summer, 1969.

_____. "Teacher Organizations and Desegregation." Phi Delta Kappan, Ja, 1968.

Diamond, William J., Martin, Charles F., Sr., and Miller, Richard I. Methodology for Assessing the Quality of Public Education. Lexington, KY: Bureau of School Service, U. of Kentucky, 1969.

Dickie-Clarke, Hamish. "Some Issues in the Sociology of Race Relations." Race 15(O, 1973):241-247.

Dietsch, Robert W. "The New, New South: Some Progress, More Myth." Nation 212(My, 1971):615-618.

Dillingham, William P. "The Economics of Segregation." In The Negro in American Society. Edited by James Preu. Tallahassee, FL: Florida State U., 1958.

Dinnerstein, Leonard and Koppel, Gene. Nathan Glazer: A Different Kind of Liberal. Tucson, AZ: U. of Arizona, 1973.

Dixon, Norman R., and Barnes, Edward J. "Liberal Education for the Black Student." Notre Dame Journal of Education I(Summer, 1970):128-131.

Dixon, Vernon J., and Foster, Badi (eds.). Beyond Black or White: An Alternate America. Boston, MA: Little, Brown, 1971.

Dixon, Vernon J., and Lewis, M. R. "Black Consciousness, Societal Values, and Educational Institutions: A Statement of Linkages." Journal of Conflict Resolution, S, 1968.

Dodd, Stuart C., and Christopher, Stefan C. "Poll-Guided Desegregating. A Strategy for Massive Social Change by Fiat." Journal of Human Relations, First Quarter, 1969.

Dodson, Dan W. "Developments in Race Relations and Their Implications for the Education of Negroes in the United States, 1950-1960." Negro Educational Review, Jl-0, 1959.

_____. "Does School Integration Conflict with Quality Education?" Integrated Education, Ap-My, 1966.

_____. "The Dynamic City." Christianity and Crisis, S, 1969.

_____. "The Metropolitan Racial Shift and Three Questions for Inquiry." National Council for the Social Studies Yearbook, 1972. Vol. 42, pp. 75-85.

_____. "What Is Quality Education?" Negro Educational Review 25(Ja, 1974):5-17.

"Does High School Integration Really Work?" Seventeen, N, 1967.

Dolce, Carl J. "Multicultural Education--Some Issues." Journal of Teacher Education 24 (Winter, 1973):282-284.

Dole, Arthur A., and Passons, William R. Black and White Perspectives on the Future, Mr, 1970. ERIC ED 039 305.

Doll, Russell C. Variations Among Inner City Elementary Schools. An Investigation into the Nature and Causes of Their Differences. Kansas City, MO: Center for the Study of Metropolitan Problems in Education, U. of Missouri, Kansas City, Je, 1969.

Dolmatch, Theodore B. "Color Me Brown--I'm Integrated." Saturday Review, S, 1965. [On integrated textbooks]

Dominick, Joseph R., and Greenberg, Bradley S. "Three Seasons of Blacks on Television." Journal of Advertising Research 10(Ap, 1970).

Donaldson, Jeff. "The Role We Want for Black Art." College Board Review, Spring, 1969.

Donovan, Bernard E. "The Role of a School System in a Changing Society." Integrated Education, Ag-S, 1967.

Dooley, W. H. The Education of the Ne'er-do-Well. Boston, MA: 1916.

Doornbos, M. R. "Some Conceptual Problems Concerning Ethnicity in Integration Analysis." Civilisations 22(1972):263-284.

Dore, R. P. "Human Capital Theory, the Diversity of Societies and the Problem of Quality of Education." Higher Education 4(F, 1976):79-102.

Dorfman, William, and Ferrara, Lynette. Social and Economic Characteristics of U.S. School Districts, 1970. Washington, DC: GPO, 1976.

Dorr, Robin. "Ordeal by Desegregation." Integrated Education 10(Jl-Ag, 1972):34-39.

Downing, S. T. To the Friends of Equal School Rights. Providence, RI: 1859.

Drake, St. Clair. Race Relations in a Time of Rapid Social Change, 1966. National Federations of Settlements and Neighborhood Centers, 232 Madison Ave., New York, NY.

_____. "The Social and Economic Status of the Negro in the United States." Daedalus, Fall, 1965.

Dreyfuss, Joel. "Public Television: Toward a Redefinition of Minority Roles." Washington Post, Ja 4, 1976.

Drinan, Robert F. "Racial Balance in Schools." America, F, 1964.

Drinan, Robert F. (ed.). The Right to be Educated. Washington, DC: Corpus Publications, 1968.

Dubey, Sumati N. "Powerlessness and the Predominant Forms of Adaptation Responses of Lower Class Negroes." Doctoral dissertation, Case Western Reserve U., 1969.

Dubey, Sumati N., and Grant, Morris L. "Powerlessness Among Disadvantaged Blacks." Social Casework 51(1970):285-290.

DuBois, W. E. B. [Article on education] Amsterdam News, Jl, 1942.

_____. "A Philosophy of Race Segregation." Quarterly Review of Higher Education Among Negroes 3(O, 1935):189-194.

_____. "A Youth Creed." Chicago Defender (D, 1946):15.

_____. "The Burden of Negro Schooling." Independent, Jl, 1901.

_____. "A Report to the General Education Board 1943." I Report of the First Conference of Negro Land-Grant Colleges for Coordinating a Program of Social Studies. Edited by W. E. B. DuBois. Atlanta, GA: Atlanta U., 1943.

_____. [Editorial on philanthropy and black institutions] Fisk Herald, N, 1887.

_____. "Godfrey of Bouillon." Horizon, Je, 1910. [Address to a high school graduation]

_____. The Immortal Child--Background on Crisis in Education. Chicago: Af-Am Books, 1964.

_____. "The Joy of Living." Political Affairs 44(F, 1965):35-44. [Written 1904]

_____. "The Negro and the Northern Public Schools." Crisis, Mr and Ap, 1923.

_____. "The Negro and the YMCA." Horizon, Mr, 1910.

_____. The Negro Common School. Atlanta, GA: Atlanta U. Press, 1901. Atlanta Study No. 6.

_____. "The Negro Common School." Crisis, D, 1926.

_____. "Negro Education." Crisis, F, 1918.

_____. "The Negro Public School." Crisis, Mr, 1916.

_____. "The Negro Schoolmaster in the New South." Atlantic, Ja, 1899.

_____. "News [about E. Franklin Frazier]." Chicago Defender, My, 1948.

_____. "Of the Training of Black Men." Atlantic, S, 1902.

_____. "Pechstein and Pecksniff." Crisis, S, 1929.

_____. "[Philanthropic] Gifts and Education." Crisis, F, 1925.

_____. "A Pilgrimage to the Negro Schools." Crisis, F, 1929.

_____. Possibilities of the Negro: The Advance Guard of Race. Philadelphia, PA: Library Publications, 1903.

_____. "Problemes de l'integration des races aux U.S.A." Presence Africaine No. 23(D, 1958-Ja 1959):73-80.

_____. "St. Francis of Assisi." Voice of the Negro 3(O, 1906):419-426.

_____. "A Scientist [Charles H. Turner]." Chicago Defender (My, 1947):19.

_____. "No Second Class Citizenship." Progressive Education 25(Ja, 1948):14, 21.

_____. "Sociology and Industry in Southern Education." Voice of the Negro 4(My, 1907): 170-175.

_____. "The Souls of Black Folk and My Larger Education." Journal of Negro Education, Fall, 1961.

_____. "Summer Schools, Devil's Device." Chicago Defender (Je, 1946):17.

_____. "The Talented Tenth." In The Negro Problem. Edited by Booker T. Washington. New York: James Pott Co., 1903.

_____. [Testimony] in U.S. Congress, 75th, 1st session, House of Representatives, Hearings on Federal Aid for the Support of Public Schools, pp. 284-295. Washington, DC: GPO, 1937.

_____. Testimony in U.S., The Industrial Commission, Immigration and Education, Vol. 15, pp. 159-175. Washington, DC: GPO, 1901.

_____. "What Intellectual Training Is Doing for the Negro." Missionary Review of the World, Ag, 1904.

_____. "What Is the Meaning of 'All Deliberate Speed'?" National Guardian, N, 1957.

_____. "Whither Now and Why." Quarterly Review of Higher Education Among Negroes 28(Jl, 1960):135-141.

DuBois, W. E. B. (ed.). College Bred Negro: Report of a Social Study Made by Atlanta University under the Patronage of the Trustees of the John F. Slater Fund. Atlanta, GA: Atlanta U. Press, 1900. Atlanta U. Publications, No. 5.

DuBois, W. E. B., and Dill, A. G. (eds.). The College Bred Negro American. Atlanta, GA: Atlanta U. Press, 1910. Atlanta Study No. 15.

_____. The Common School and the Negro American. Atlanta, GA: Atlanta U. Press, 1911. Atlanta Study No. 16.

Dudley, Bishop Thomas U. "How Shall We Help the Negro?" Century Magazine 30(Je, 1885): 273-280. [Segregation incompatible with white paternalism]

Dunaway, David King. "Desegregation and City Hall: The Mayor's Role in the Schools." Integrateducation 15(Ja-F, 1977).

Dunbar, Leslie W. "Middle-Age Thoughts." New South 25(1970):2-19.

Dunbar, Tony. Our Land Too. New York: Pantheon, 1971.

Duncan, Beverly. "Trends in Output and Distribution of Schooling." In Indicators of Social Change. Edited by E. B. Sheldon and Wilbert E. Moore. New York: Russell Sage Foundation, 1968.

Dunfee, Maxine. Ethnic Modification of the Curriculum. Washington, DC: Association for Supervision and Curriculum Development, 1970.

Dunn, Theodore F. "Assumed Racial Similarity as Related to Attitudes Toward Integration." Doctoral dissertation, American U., 1958. Dissertation Abstracts, XIX. 1959, p. 2533. [Washington, DC]

Dunning, Eric. "Dynamics of Racial Stratification: Some Preliminary Observations." Race 13(Ap, 1972):415-434.

Dyckman, John W. "Civic Order in an Urbanized World." Daedalus, Summer, 1966.

Dye, Thomas R. "Urban School Segregation: A Comparative Analysis." Urban Affairs, D, 1968.

Dyer, Henry S. "Summary and Evaluation of Contributions to the Yearbook: Race and Equality in American Education." Journal of Negro Education, Summer, 1968.

Eddy, Elizabeth M. (ed.). Urban Anthropology: Research, Perspectives and Strategies. Athens, GA: U. of Georgia Press, 1969.

Eddy, Elizabeth M. Walk the White Line: A Profile of Urban Education. New York: Doubleday Anchor, 1967.

Edington, Everett D. "Disadvantaged Rural Youth." Review of Educational Research 40(F, 1970):69-85.

Editors of Ebony. The Negro Handbook. Chicago: Johnson, 1966.

Edmonds, Ronald R. and others. "Desegregation Planning and Educational Equity." Theory Into Practice 17(F, 1978):12-16.

Educating All Our Children. New York: Public Education Association; United Federation of Teachers; and United Parents Association, 1965.

The Education and Training of Racial Minorities. Proceedings of a Conference. Madison, WI: Center for Studies in Vocational and Technical Education, U. of Wisconsin, 1968.

"Education in the News." Education News, O, 1968. [Dr. Neil V. Sullivan]

Education, Invitational Conference on Urban Education, 1964. New York: Graduate School of Education, Yeshiva U., n.d.

"The Education of the Mind of the Negro Child." School and Society, pp. 357-360.

Edwards, T. Bentley, and Wirt, Frederick M. (eds.). School Desegregation in the North. The Challenge and the Experience. San Francisco: Chandler, 1967.

Egerton, John. "IRCD; Its Specialty is Answers." Southern Education Report, Jl-Ag,
1967. [The Information Retrieval Center on
the Disadvantaged, at Teachers College,
Columbia U.]

_____. A Mind to Stay Here. New York:
MacMillan, 1970.

_____. "Report Card on Southern School Deseg-
regation." Saturday Review, Ap, 1972.

_____. "Seg Academies, With Much Church Aid,
Flourish in South, As Other Private Schools
Wane." South Today 5(S, 1973):1, 6.

Ehrlich, Howard J. Selected Differences in the
Life Chances of Black and White in the
United States. Research Group One, 2743
Maryland Ave., Baltimore, MD 21218.

Eisenberg, Leon. "The Sins of the Fathers."
Jewish Currents, F, 1969. ["Blunt words on
the challenge of the Negro question"]

Eisenger, Peter K. "Racial Differences in Protest Participation." American Political
Science Review 68(Je, 1974):592-606.

Eko, Ewa U. "Consortium Approach to Developing
African and Afro-American Studies: An
Assessment." Journal of Afro-American
Issues 2(F, 1974):35-48.

Elam, Stanley (ed.). The Gallup Polls of Attitudes Toward Education, 1969-1973.
Bloomington, IN: Phi Delta Kappa, 1973.

Elgie, Robert A. "Racial Inequality Within a
Socio-spatial System: The Southeastern
U.S., 1950-1970." Doctoral dissertation,
U. of California, Berkeley, 1976.

Elifoglu, Hilmi. "The Distribution of Educational Resources in Large American Cities,
1965-1971." Doctoral dissertation, New
School for Social Research, 1976.

Ellis, Dean S. "Speech and Social Status in
America." Social Forces, Mr, 1967.

Ellis, Richard S. "The Feasibility of Public
School Desegregation." School and Society
99(N, 1971):433-436.

Elsbery, James W. "Educational Reform: Change
the Premise." Urban Review, Ap, 1969.

Engelberg, Morton. "Our Children, Seedlings
for a Great Society." I.U.D. Agenda, Jl,
1965. [Published by the Industrial Union
Department of the A.F.L.-C.I.O.]

Engelhardt, N. L., Jr., and Boyd, James B.
"How to Determine Attendance Area
Boundaries." Nation's Schools, My, 1967.

Engelmann, Hugo O. "The Problem of Dialect in
the American School." Journal of Human Relations, Fourth Quarter, 1968. [Compara-
tive treatment]

Enloe, Cynthia. Ethnic Conflict and Political
Development. Boston, MA: Little, Brown,
1973.

Entin, David. "Standard Planning Techniques
for Desegregation." Integrated Education
11(Mr-Ap, 1973):43-53.

Entwisle, Doris R. "Developmental Sociolinguistics: Inner-City Children." American
Journal of Sociology, Jl, 1968.

Epps, Edgar G. (ed.). Cultural Pluralism.
Berkeley, CA: McCutchan, 1975.

Epps, Edgar G. "Education for Black Americans:
Outlook for the Future." School Review 81
(My, 1973):315-330.

Equal Educational Opportunities in a Changing
Society. Conference Report, 1965. Sacra-
mento, CA: California Commission on Equal
Opportunities in Education, 1965.

Equal Educational Opportunity Workshop for
Human Rights Workers at the Annual Meeting
of the National Association of Human Rights
Workers. New York: National Center for
Research and Information on Equal Educational
Opportunity, Teacher's College, Columbia
U., 1972.

Equality and Quality in the Public Schools.
Report of a Conference, My, 1966. ERIC ED
019 352.

Equality of Educational Opportunity: A Conference, S, 1967. New York State U., Buffalo.
ERIC ED 021 937.

Erickson, Edsel L. "Differences Between Economically Disadvantaged Students Who Volunteer and Who Do Not Volunteer for Economic
Opportunity Programs." Journal of Human
Resources, Winter, 1969.

Erickson, Edsel L., Bryan, Clifford E., and
Walker, Lewis. "The Educability of Dominant
Groups." Phi Delta Kappan 53(Ja, 1972):319-
321.

Erikson, Erik H. "The Concept of Identity in
Race Relations: Notes and Queries."
Daedalus, Winter, 1966.

Erskine, Hazel G. "The Polls: Negro
Philosophies of Life." Public Opinion
Quarterly, Spring, 1969.

_____. "The Polls: Race Relations."
Public Opinion Quarterly 26(1962):137-148.

_____. "The Polls: Recent Opinion on Racial
Problems." Public Opinion Quarterly, Winter,
1968-1969. [From data gathered during My-
Je, 1968]

_____. "The Polls: Speed of Racial Integration." Public Opinion Quarterly, Fall, 1968. [1961-1968]

Ertel, Rachel, Fabre, Genevieve, and Marienstras, Elise. En Marge. Sur les minorites aux Etats-Unis. Paris: Editions Maspero, 1971.

Ethridge, Samuel B. "The Challenge of Quality Integrated Education." Integrated Education 11(Mr-Ap, 1973):22-28.

Eubanks, Eugene E., and Levine, Daniel U. "Big-City Desegregation Since Detroit." Phi Delta Kappan 56(Ap, 1975):521-522, 550.

_____. "The PUSH Program for Excellence in Big-City Schools." Phi Delta Kappan, Ja, 1977.

Evans, Dorothy A., and Alexander, Sheldon. "Some Psychological Correlates of Civil Rights Activity." Psychological Reports 26(Je, 1970):899-906.

Evans, Melvin I. "Minority Groups and the AAHPER." Journal of Health, Physical Education, and Recreation 42(N-D, 1971):22-23. [American Association of Health, Physical Education and Recreation]

Evans, Virden. "The Black Physical Educator's Involvement Is Needed." Journal of Health, Physical Education and Recreation 41(Je, 1970):31.

Evertts, Eldonna L. (ed.). Dimensions of Dialect. Champaign, IL: National Council of Teachers of English, 1967.

Evetts, Julia. "Equality of Educational Opportunity: The Recent History of a Concept." British Journal of Sociology 21(D, 1970): 425-430.

Fagget, H. L. "The Negroes Who Do Not Want to End Segregation." Quarterly Review of Higher Education Among Negroes 23(Jl, 1955): 120-122.

Fairchild, Halford H., and Gurin, Patricia. "Traditions in the Social-Psychological Analysis of Race Relations." American Behavioral Scientist 21(My-Je, 1978):757-778.

Fallers, Lloyd A. Inequality. Social Stratification Reconsidered. Chicago, IL: U. of Chicago Press, 1973.

Farber, Lillian (ed.). Conference on Tensions of Change: Suburban Schools During the Next Decade. Bronxville, NY: Institute for Community Studies, F, 1967.

Farley, Reynolds. Growth of the Black Population. Chicago, IL: Markham, 1970.

_____. "Migration Trends Among Blacks." Southern Regional Demographic Newsletter No. 17(Je, 1974):3-24.

_____. "Trends in Racial Inequalities: Have the Gains of the 1960s Disappeared in the 1970s?" American Sociological Review 42 (Ap, 1977):189-208.

Farley, Reynolds, and Hermalin, Albert. "The 1960's: A Decade of Progress for Blacks?" Demography 9(Ag, 1972).

Farley, Reynolds, and Wurdock, Clarence. Integrating Schools in the Nation's Largest Cities: What Has Been Accomplished and What Is Yet to Be Done, 1977. ERIC ED 146 278.

Farmer, James. "Education is the Answer." Today's Education, Ap, 1969.

_____. Freedom---When? New York: Random House, 1966.

Favrot, Leo M. "Some Facts about Negro High Schools and Their Distribution and Development in 14 Southern States." High-School Quarterly 17(Ap, 1929):139-154.

Feagin, Joe R. "A Note on the Friendship Ties of Black Urbanites." Social Forces 49 (D, 1970):303-308.

Feagin, Joe R., and Hahn, Harlan. Ghetto Revolts. The Politics of Violence in American Cities. New York: Macmillan, 1973.

Fearn, R. M. "Neighborhood Schools and Integration." Review of Regional Studies 1(Spring, 1971-1972).

Fedler, Fred. "The Media and Minority Groups: A Study of Adequacy of Access." Journalism Quarterly 50(Spring, 1973):109-117.

Feinberg, Walter (ed.). Equality and Social Policy. Urbana, IL: U. of Illinois Press, 1977.

Ferguson, Harold A., and Plaut, Richard L. "Talent: To Develop or to Lose." Educational Record, Ap, 1954. [11 non-southern states]

Fidler, William P. "Academic Freedom in the South Today." AAUP Bulletin, D, 1965 [Includes discussion of desegregation]

Fielder, Marie, and Dyckman, Louise M. Leadership Training Institute in Problems of School Desegregation, 1967. ERIC ED 056 121.

Fielding, Byron. "De Facto Segregation." NEA Journal, My, 1964.

Finch, M. M. "Wanted Reliable Information on the Black Man." D.C. Libraries 41 (Spring, 1970):36-38.

Findley, Warren G., and Bryan, Miriam M. "Ability Grouping: Do's and Don'ts." Integrated Education (S-O, 1971):31-36.

Finger, John A., Jr. "School Desegregation Plans for Cities." In Catholic Schools and Racial Integration: Perspectives, Directions, Models, pp. 76-81. Washington, DC: National Catholic Conference for Interracial Justice, 1977.

Fischer, Ann. "The Personality and Subculture of Anthropologists and their Study of U.S. Negroes." In Concepts and Assumptions in in Contemporary Anthropology, pp. 12-17. Edited by Stephen A. Tyler. Athens, GA: U. of Georgia Press, 1969.

Fischer, John H. "Boycotts and Bargaining." Senior Scholastic, Mr, 1964.

_____. "Can Administrators Justify Neighborhood Schools--- If Those Schools Have the Effect of Creating or Continuing Segregation?" Nation's Schools, F, 1964.

_____. "De Facto Issue: Notes on the Broader Context." Teachers College Record, Mr, 1964.

_____. "Desegregating City Schools." Integrated Education, D, 1966-Ja, 1967.

_____. "Desegregating City Schools." PTA Magazine, D, 1964.

_____. "The Inclusive School." Teachers College Record, O, 1964.

_____. "Our Schools: Battleground of Conflicting Interests." Saturday Review, Mr, 1964.

_____. "Race and Reconciliation: The Role of the School." Daedalus, Winter, 1966.

_____. "Urban Schools for an Open Society." In U.S. Commission on Civil Rights, Papers Prepared for National Conference on Equal Educational Opportunity in America's Cities. Washington, DC: Government Printing Office, 1968.

Fisher, Berenice M. "Education in the Big Picture." Sociology of Education 45(Summer, 1972):233-257.

Fisher, Isaac. "School Problems of the Southern Negro." Fisk University News, O, 1922.

Fisher, James S. "Negro Farm Ownership in the South." Annals of the Association of American Geographers 63(D, 1973):478-489. [1900-1969]

Fishman, Joshua A. Language Problems and Types of Political and Socio-Cultural Integration: A Conceptual Postscript, Ap, 1968. ERIC ED 025 739.

Fishman, Joshua A., and Nahirny, Vladimir C. "The Ethnic Group School and Mother Tongue Maintenance in the United States." Sociology of Education, Summer, 1964.

Fiske, Edward B. "Jesse Jackson Builds Up Support in a Drive for Student Discipline." New York Times, Mr 4, 1979.

Flax, Michael J. Blacks and Whites: An Experiment in Racial Indicators, 1971. ERIC ED 054 252.

Fleck, Stephen. "'Interracial Riots' in School and Community Indifference." School Review 79(Ag, 1971):614-623.

Fogelson, Robert M. "From Resentment to Confrontation: The Police, the Negroes, and the Outbreak of the Nineteen-Sixties Riots." Political Science Quarterly, Je, 1968.

Foley, Eugene P. The Achieving Ghetto. Washington, DC: The National Press, Inc., 1968.

Folger, John K., and Nam, Charles B. Education of the American Population. Washington, DC: Government Printing Office, 1967.

Footlick, Jerrold K. "The South and Desegregation," and "The North and Segregation." In Education---A New Era. Silver Spring, MD: The National Observer, 1966.

Forbes, Jack D. "Segregation and Integration: The Multi-Ethnic or Uni-Ethnic School." Phylon, Spring, 1969.

Ford, Hamilton. "A Legal, Psychosocial, and Historic Background of School Desegregation: Deliberate, De Facto, Discordant." Psychiatry Digest, D, 1968.

Ford, Nick Aaron. "Cultural Integration Through Literature." Teachers College Record, Ja, 1965.

Formley, John P. "An Economic Analysis of Black Separatism." Negro Educational Review 24 (Ja-Ap, 1973):14-41.

Forrest, Leon R. "Blacks Meet in Atlanta to 'Make Education Relevant.'" Muhammad Speaks, S, 1969. [Conference of the National Association for African American Education, Ag 20-24, 1969]

Forsythe, Dennis (ed.). Black Alienation, Black Rebellion. Falls Church, VA: College and U. Press, 1975.

Fort, Edward B. "Desegregation and the Belgian Congo Syndrome." Teachers College Record, Mr, 1968.

Foster, Gordon. "Desegregating Urban Schools: A Review of Techniques." Harvard Educational Review 43(F, 1973):5-36.

_____. "School Desegregation: Problem or Opportunity for Urban Education?" Urban Review 6(S-O, 1972):12-17.

Frank, Libby. "My Weekly Reader, 1967-1968." Women's International League for Peace and Freedom, 167 Oakdene Ave., Teaneck, NJ 07666.

Frankel, Charles. "Equality of Opportunity." Ethics 81(Ap, 1971):191-211.

Franklin, Anderson J. "The Apathy of Psychology Toward Social Issues." Afro-American Studies 1(Ap, 1971):323-331.

Franklin, Clara. "Should the Negro Teacher Consider a Transfer?" Negro Teachers Forum, D, 1966.

Franklin, H. R. "Relationship between Adult Communication Practices and Public Library Use in a Northern Urban Black Ghetto." Doctoral dissertation, Rutgers U., 1971.

Franklin, John Hope. "A Talk to Teachers." Integrated Education (D, 1964-Ja, 1965):8.

Franklin, Lewis Glenn. "Desegregation and the Rise of Private Education." Doctoral dissertation, n.p., 1975. Univ. Microfilms Order No. 75-23141.

Fraser, James. "Black Publishing for Black Children. The Experience of the Sixties and the Seventies." School Library Journal (N, 1973):3421-3426.

Frazier, E. Franklin. "Desegregation as an Object of Sociological Research." In Human Behavior and Social Processes: An Interactionist Approach, pp. 608-624, 1961.

_____. Negro Youth at the Crossways. Washington, DC: 1940.

_____. "A Note on Negro Education." Opportunity 2(Mr, 1924):75-77.

_____. "The Present State of Knowledge Concerning Race Relations." Transactions of the Fourth World Congress of Sociology, II. London: International Sociological Association, 1959.

_____. "The Role of the Negro in the Post-War World." Journal of Negro Education 13(Fall, 1944):464-473.

Frazier, Levi. "Advertising A Token Product." Integrateducation 14(Mr-Ap, 1976):32.

Frederick, Peter. "In Fear of Academic Backlash." AAUP Bulletin, Winter, 1969.

Freedman, Philip I. "Race as a Factor in Persuasion." Journal of Experimental Education, Spring, 1967.

Freischlag, Jerry. "Ethnic Minorities in Physical Education: Assimilation or Cultural Pluralism." Physical Educator 35(Mr, 1978):30-35.

Frelow, Robert D. "A Comparative Study of Resource Allocation: Compensatory Education and School Desegregation." Doctoral dissertation, U. of California, Berkeley, 1971.

Friedenberg, E. Z. "The Function of the School in Social Homeostasis." Canadian Review of Sociology and Anthropology 7(F, 1970).

_____. "Integrity and Integration: Social Class and Education." In Coming of Age in America. Growth and Acquiescence. New York: Random House, 1965.

Friedman, Neil. "Has Black Come Back to Dixie?" Society 9(My, 1972):47-53.

Froomkin, Joseph. Goals and Alternatives for the Education of Minority Group Students in Elementary and Secondary Schools. U.S. Congress, 92nd, 2nd session, Senate, Select Committee on Equal Educational Opportunity, Washington, DC: GPO, 1972.

Frossard, Robert T. Attitudes Related to a Citizens Committee Study of Equality of Educational Opportunity Diss. Abstr. Intl., 1969, 30(I-A):85-86.

Fuchs, Estelle. "Education and the Culture of Poverty." In Poverty: New Interdisciplinary Perspectives, pp. 162-179. Edited by Thomas Weaver and Alvin Magid. San Francisco: Chandler, 1969.

Furlong, William Barry. "Interracial Marriage Is a Sometime Thing." New York Times Magazine, Je 9, 1968.

"Further Discrimination Against Negro Schools." Outlook (D, 1900):912-913.

Galamison, Milton. "Toward a Definition of Education." Renewal, O-N, 1966.

Galbraith, John Kenneth. "An Attack on Poverty." Harper's, Mr, 1964.

Gall, Peter. Desegregation. How Schools Are Meeting Historic Challenge, 1973. National School Public Relations Association, 1801 North Moore St., Arlington, VA 22209.

Gallup, George. How the Nation Views the Public Schools. A CFK Ltd. Report. Princeton, NJ: Gallup International, Fall, 1969.

Gans, Herbert J. People and Plans. Essays on Urban Problems and Solutions. New York: Basic Books, 1968.

_____. "The White Exodus to Suburbia Steps Up." New York Times Magazine, Ja 7, 1968.

1026 / GENERAL

Garber, Alex. "Working Class and Elite Youth Don't Have Much in Common." New America, Ja, 1969.

Gary, Lawrence E. and others. Social Intervention in the Public School System, F, 1976. ERIC ED 126 205. [Social work intervention]

Gaston, Paul. "The South: Goal Still Distant, But Many Schools Go Well." South Today 2 (D, 1970):3.

Gentry, Stron and others. Urban Education: The Hope Factor. Philadelphia, PA: Saunders, 1972.

Gerbner, George, with Eleey, Michael F., and Tedesco, Nancy. "The Violence Index. A Rating of Various Aspects of Dramatic Violence on Prime-Time Network Television 1967 through 1970." In U.S. Congress, 92nd, 2nd session, Senate, Committee on Commerce, Subcommittee on Communications, Surgeon General's Report by the Scientific Advisory Committee on Television and Social Behavior, Appendix A. Hearings..., pp. 307-526. Washington, DC: GPO, 1972.

Gertler, Diane B. Directory. Public Elementary and Secondary Schools in Large School Districts with Enrollment and Instructional Staff. By Race: Fall, 1967. Washington, DC: GPO, 1969.

_____. Nonpublic Schools in Large Cities. 1970-1971 Edition. Washington, DC: GPO, 1974. [Includes racial data]

Geschwender, James A. "Desegregation, the Educated Negro, and the Future of Social Protest in the South." Sociological Inquiry, Winter, 1965.

_____. "Negro Education: The False Faith." Phylon, Winter, 1968.

_____. "Social Structure and the Negro Revolt: An Examination of Some Hypotheses." Social Forces, D, 1964.

Gibson, Donald B. "The Negro: An Essay on Definition." Yale Review, Spring, 1968.

Gibson, John S. Citizenship. San Rafael, CA: Dimensions Publishing Company, 1969.

_____. "Intergroup Relations in Education: A Force for Change." NASSP Bulletin, D, 1969.

Gibson, Morgan. "Freedom Now for Education." Liberation, Ag, 1964. [A civil rights leader who, during Milwaukee's school boycott of May 18, 1964, served as principal of the James Baldwin Senior High Freedom School]

Gilbert, Albin R., and Sessions, Robert Paul (eds.). Updating Intergroup Education in Public Schools: A Study-Action Manual, Jl, 1969. ERIC ED 041 081.

Giles, Michael W. "Measuring School Desegregation." Journal of Negro Education 43 (Fall, 1974):517-523.

Giles, Michael W., Gatlin, Douglas S., and Cataldo, Everett F. "Parental Support for School Referenda." Journal of Politics 38 (My, 1976):442-451. [Desegregation and school referenda]

Gillin, John P. "Some Principles of Sociocultural Integration." Current Anthropology 12 (F, 1971):63-71.

Gintis, Herbert. "Towards a Political Economy of Education: A Radical Critique of Ivan Illich's Deschooling Society." Harvard Educational Review 42(F, 1972):70-96.

Ginzberg, Eli and others. The Middle-Class Negro in the White Man's World. New York: Columbia U. Press, 1967.

Gittell, Marilyn. "Saving City Schools." National Civic Review, Ja, 1968.

_____. "Urban School Reform." Compact, Ap, 1969.

_____. "Urban School Reform in the 1970's." Education and Urban Society, N, 1968.

Gittell, Marilyn, and Hevesi, Alan C. (eds.). The Politics of Urban Education. New York: Praeger, 1969.

Gladney, Mildred R., and Leaverton, Lloyd. A Model for Teaching Standard English to Non-Standard English Speakers, F, 1968. ERIC ED 016 232.

Glatt, Charles S., and Gaines, William A. "School Desegregation: A Look at Some Common Impediments and Solutions." National Elementary Principal 49(1970):34-39.

Glazer, Nathan. Affirmative Discrimination: Ethnic Inequality and Public Policy. New York: Basic Books, 1976.

_____. "Ethnic Groups and Education: Towards the Tolerance of Difference." Journal of Negro Education, Summer, 1969.

_____. "Interethnic Conflict." Social Work 17(My, 1972):3-9.

_____. "Negroes and Jews: The New Challenge to Pluralism." Commentary, D, 1964.

_____. "The Real Task in America's Cities." New Society, Mr, 1968. [On the Kerner Report]

_____. "The School as an Instrument in Planning." Journal of the American Institute of Planners, 1950-1960. [See also "Comment on Glazer's School Proposals," by John W. Dyckman.]

Glazer, Nathan, and Moynihan, Daniel P. "Why Ethnicity?" Commentary 58(0, 1974):33-39.

Glazer, Nathan and others. "School Integration Policies in Northern Cities." Journal of the American Institute of Planners, Ag, 1964.

Glenn, Norval D. "Recent Trends in White-Non-white Attitudinal Differences." Public Opinion Quarterly 38(Winter, 1974-1975): 596-604.

Glenn, Norval D., and Gotard, Erin. "The Religion of Blacks in the United States: Some Recent Trends and Current Characteristics." American Journal of Sociology 83(S, 1977): 443-451.

Glenn, Vernon L. "Increasing Minority Participation in State Rehabilitation Programs." Rehabilitation Research and Practice Review 2(F, 1971):59-64.

Goldhammer, Keith. The Politics of De Facto Segregation. A Case Study. Eugene, OR: Center for the Advanced Study of Educational Administration, U. of Oregon, 1969.

Goldman, Louis. "Varieties of Alienation and Their Educational Response." Teachers College Record, Ja, 1968.

Goldman, Peter. Report from Black America. New York: Simon and Schuster, 1970.

Goldman, R. J., and Taylor, Francine M. "Colored Immigrant Children: A Survey of Research Studies and Literature on Their Education U.S.A." Educational Research (England), N, 1966.

Goldman, Ralph M. "The Politics of Political Integration." Journal of Negro Education, Winter, 1964.

Goldstein, Bernard. Low Income Youth in Urban Areas. New York: Holt, Rinehart and Winston, 1967.

Gollnick, Donna M., Klassen, Frank H., and Yff, Joost (comps.). Multicultural Education and Ethnic Studies in the United States. An Analysis and Annotated Bibliography of Selected ERIC Documents. Washington, DC: American Association of Colleges for Teacher Education, F, 1976.

Gonzalez, Gilbert G. The Relationship Between Progressive Educational Theory and Practice and Monopoly Capital. Irvine, CA: Program in Comparative Culture, U. of California, Irvine, Ap, 1976.

Good, Paul. The Trouble I've Seen, White Journalist/Black Movement, 1964-1974. Washington, DC: Howard U. Press, 1975.

Goodlad, John I. "Desegregating the Integrated School." In Racial Isolation in the Public Schools. vol. II, Appendix D2.2. Washington, DC: Government Printing Office, 1967.

Goodman, Paul. Growing Up Absurd. New York: Random House, 1960.

Goodman, Walter. "Ebony: Biggest Negro Magazine." Dissent, S-O, 1968.

Gordon, A. H. "Some Disadvantages of Being White." Messenger 10(Ap, 1928):79.

Gordon, Edmund W. Building a Socially Supportive Environment. ERIC Information Retrieval Center on the Disadvantaged. New York: Teachers College, Columbia U., Je, 1970.

_____. "Equalizing Educational Opportunity in the Public School." IRCD Bulletin, N, 1967. [Assessment of the Coleman Report]

_____. "Relevance and Pluralism in Curriculum Development." IRCD Bulletin, Summer, 1969.

_____. "Social Status Differences: "Counseling and Guidance for Disadvantaged Youth." In Schreiber (ed.) below.

_____. "Toward Defining Equality of Educational Opportunity." NCRIEED Newsletter 2(Ja, 1971):3-10.

Gordon, Edmund W., and Green, Robert L. Conference Proceedings: Research Conference on Racial Desegregation and Integration in Public Education; Invitational Conference on Social Change and the Role of Behavioral Scientists. New York: Yeshiva U. Ferkauf Graduate School of Humanities and Social Sciences, 1966. ERIC ED 021 908.

Gordon, Milton M. Assimilation in American Life. New York: Oxford U. Press, 1964.

Gordon, Sol. "The Bankruptcy of Ghetto School Education." Integrated Education, O-N, 1966.

_____. Compensation, Remediation, Innovating and Integrating: Illusions of Educating the Poor, 1972. ERIC ED 062 482.

Gordon, Thomas. "Notes on White and Black Psychology." Journal of Social Issues 29 (1973):87-95.

Goslin, David A. "The School in a Changing Society. Notes on the Development of Strategies for Solving Educational Problems." American Journal of Orthopsychiatry 9, 1967.

Gosnell, Harold F., and Martin, Robert E. "The Negro as Voter and Office-holder." Journal of Negro Education, Fall, 1963.

Gottesfeld, Harry, and Gordon, Sol. "Academic Excellence: Parents and Teachers. The Education of the Ghetto Child." United Teacher, N, 1966 (special supplement).

Gottlieb, Benjamin H., and Gottlieb, Lois J. "An Expanded Role for the School Social Worker." Social Work 16(0, 1971):12-21.

Gottlieb, David. *The American Adolescent*. IL: Dorsey Press, 1964.

_____. "The Americanization of Willis Wardell." *Communities in Action* (O.E.O.), Ag, 1966. [Educational aspects of the Job Corps]

_____. "Teaching and Students: The Views of Negro and White Teachers." *Sociology of Education*, Summer, 1964.

Gottlieb, David (ed.). *Youth in Contemporary Society*. Beverly Hills, CA: Sage, 1973.

Gottschalk, Earl C., Jr. "Despite High Tuition, Private Schools Enjoy a Surge in Enrollment." *Wall Street Journal*, Ap 13, 1977.

Grambs, Jean. *A Guide to School Integration*. Public Affairs Pamphlet No. 255.

_____. *Inter-Group Education: Methods and Materials*. Englewood Cliffs, NJ: Prentice-Hall, 1968.

Grambs, Jean (ed.). *Report of the Leadership Conferences on Institutes* [on School Desegregation]. Baltimore, MD: College of Education, U. of Maryland, 1965.

Grannis, Joseph C. "The School as a Model of Society." *Harvard Graduate School of Education Association Bulletin*, Fall, 1967.

Grant, Donald L., and Bricker, Mildred. "Some Notes on the Capital 'N'." *Phylon* 36(D, 1975):435-443.

Grant, William R. "The Media and School Desegregation." *Integrateducation* 14(N/D, 1976).

_____. "The Media and School Desegregation." In *School Desegregation: Making It Work*, pp. 71-89. East Lansing, MI: College of Urban Development, Michigan State U., 1976.

_____. "Northern Integration." *Race Relation Reporter* 5(My, 1974):23-25.

"Father Greeley Answers and Roth Rebuts." *Integrateducation* 13(Ja-F, 1975):13. [See Roth, below.]

Green, Robert Lee. "Poverty, Race, and the Pursuit of Excellence." *Phi Delta Kappan* (N, 1978):1985-2005.

Greene, Lawrence S., Desor, J. A., and Maller, Owen. "Heredity and Experience: Their Relative Importance in the Development of Taste Preference in Man." *Journal of Comparative and Physiological Psychology* 89 (My, 1975):279-284. [Racial differences]

Green, Max, and Maurer, Hank. "AFT--Mandate for Progress." *New America*, O, 1974. [Election of Albert Shanker as president of the American Federation of Teachers]

Green, Robert Lee. "After School Integration--- What? Problems in Social Learning." *Personnel and Guidance Journal*, Mr, 1966.

_____. "Crisis in American Education: A Racial Dilemma." In U.S. Commission on Civil Rights, *Papers Prepared for National Conference on Equal Educational Opportunity in America's Cities*. Washington, DC: GPO, 1968.

Green, Winifred. "The Struggle for Freedom: Public Education in the South." *New South* 25(Fall, 1970):86-90.

Greenberg, Bradley S., and Mazingo, Sherrie L. "Racial Issues in Mass Media Institutions." In *Towards the Elimination of Racism*, pp. 309-339. Edited by Phyllis A. Katz. New York: Pergamon, 1976.

Greer, Scott and others (eds.). *Accountability in Urban Society: Public Agencies Under Fire*. Beverly Hills, CA: Sage, 1978.

Gregory, Dick. "And I Ain't Just Whistlin' Dixie." *Ebony* 26(Ag, 1971):149-150.

_____. *Nigger: An Autobiography*. New York: Dutton, 1964.

_____. *The Shadow that Scares Me*. Garden City, NY: Doubleday, 1968.

Gregory, Francis A., Hansen, Carl F., and Hypps, Irene C. "From Desegregation to Integration in Education." *Journal of Intergroup Relations*, Winter, 1962-1963.

Grier, George. "Equality and Beyond: Housing Segregation in the Great Society." *Daedalus*, Winter, 1966.

_____. "Human Needs and Public Policy in Urban Development." *American Journal of Orthopsychiatry*, Jl, 1964.

_____. "Obstacles in Desegregation in America's Urban Areas." *Race* (England), Jl, 1964.

Grier, George, and Grier, Eunice. *Equality and Beyond*. Chicago: Quadrangle, 1966.

Griffin, John A. "Biracial Education in the South: A Study in Social Change." Doctoral dissertation, U. of Wisconsin, 1956. Univ. Microfilms Order No. 16168.

Griffiths, Andre, and Winterbottom, John. *A Guide to ETS Activities Related to Minority and Disadvantaged Groups, 1970-1977*, 1978. ERIC ED 159 303. [Educational Testing Service]

Grimes, Alan P. *Equality in America. Religion, Race and the Urban Majority*. New York: Oxford U. Press, 1964.

Grindstaff, Carl. "The Negro, Urbanization, and Relative Deprivation in the Deep South." Social Problems, Winter, 1968.

Grodzins, Morton. The Metropolitan Area as a Racial Problem. Pittsburgh, PA: U. of Pittsburgh Press, 1958.

Grove, John. "Differential Political and Economic Patterns of Ethnic and Race Relations: A Cross-National Analysis." Race 15(Ja, 1974):303-328.

"'Guidelines' Point to Words of Bias." Catholic School Editor 35(Je, 1975):1-7.

Gula, Martin. Quest for Equality. Washington, DC: Government Printing Office, 1966. [Desegregation of treatment centers for emotionally disturbed children in Washington, DC, Baltimore, Detroit, Austin, TX, Louisville, and Charlotte, NC]

Gumperz, J., and Hymes, D. (eds.). Directions in Sociolinguistics. New York: Holt, Rinehart and Winston, 1970.

Gunsky, Frederick R. "Problems and Opportunities in Intergroup Relations." California Journal for Instructional Improvement, O, 1966.

_____. "Questions and Answers About School Integration." California School Administrator, Je, 1969.

Guzman, Jessie P. Race Relations in the South-- 1963. Tuskegee, AL: Tuskegee Institute, Mr, 1964.

Hall, Bob, and Williams, Bob. "Case Study: Who's Getting Rich in the New South." Southern Exposure 6(Fall, 1978):92-95.

Hall, Harry O., and Adams, Mark. "Roadblocks to Desegregation." Educational Leadership, O, 1966.

Hall, Joseph C. Role and Responsibility of the Black Reading Specialist, My, 1972. ERIC ED 063 584.

Hall, Morrill M. and others. "Educational Improvement in Majority Negro School Districts in Seventeen Southern and Border States." (AERA Symposium, Los Angeles, 1969), 1969. ERIC ED 031 353.

Halliburton, Warren J. "Inner City Education--- Studying the Studies." Perspectives on Education 6(Spring, 1973):14-19.

Halverson, Claire, and Pressman, Harvey. "Some Dimensions of a Community School." Bulletin of the Massachusetts Elementary School Principals' Association, Fall, 1968.

Hamilton, Charles V. "Black Students Want Relevancy!" Essence, My, 1970.

_____. "Conflict, Race, and System-Transformation in the United States." Journal of International Affairs, Winter, 1969.

_____. "A Year for the Racial Soft Sell." Newsday, Ap, 1976.

Hammer, Max. "Suicide and White Reformatory Girls' Preference for Negro Men." Corrective Psychiatry and Journal of Social Therapy 15 (1969):99-102.

Hammond, John L. "Race and Electoral Mobilization: White Southerners, 1952-1968." Public Opinion Quarterly 41(1977):13-27.

Handley, Theresa B. Models for the Evaluation of Bias Content in Instructional Materials. Olympia, WA: Equal Educational Opportunities Section, 1975.

Hansberry, Lorraine. The Movement. Documentary of a Struggle for Equality. New York: Simon and Schuster, 1964.

Harding, Vincent. "Fighting the 'Mainstream' Seen for 'Black Decade.'" New York Times, Ja 12, 1970.

_____. "The Vocation of the Black Scholar and the Struggles of the Black Community." In Education and Black Struggle: Notes from the Colonized World. Edited by Institute of the Black World. Cambridge, MA: Harvard Educational Review, 1974.

_____. "When Stokely [Carmichael] met the Presidents: Black Power and Negro Education." Motive, Ja, 1967.

Hare, Nathan. The Black Anglo-Saxons. New York: Marzani and Munsell, 1965.

Harrington, Charles. "Schools and Peers in the Political Socialization of the Urban Poor." Equal Opportunity Review, Ag, 1976.

Harris, Elizabeth, and Stith, Marjorie. Opinions and Attitudes of Head Start Trainees Toward Poverty and Prejudice, 1971. ERIC ED 066 652.

Harris, Helena. Development of Moral Attitudes and the Influence of Ethnic Group Membership, Socio-economic Status, and Intelligence. Final Report, O, 1967. ERIC ED 016 260.

Harris, J. John and others. "Desegregation Since Brown v. Board of Education: A Critical Assessment." Journal of Thought 12 (Jl, 1977):217-227.

Harris, Louis and Associates, Inc. Survival Literacy Study Conducted for the National Reading Council. New York: S, 1970.

_____. "What People Think About Their High Schools." Life, My, 1969.

Harris, Norene, Jackson, Nathaniel, Rydingsword, Carl E. and others. The Integration of American Schools. Problems, Experiences, Solutions. Boston, MA: Allyn and Bacon, 1975.

Harris, Patricia Roberts. "Blacks and Poverty: Roots Run Deep." Los Angeles Times, My 24, 1978. [Interview by Robert Scheer]

Harris, Ron. "The Myth of the 'New South.'" Ebony 34(F, 1979):54-62.

Harrison, Charles H. "The Negro in America." Education News, O, 1968.

Hartocollis, Anemona. "Robert Coles: Humbly Undermining." Harvard Crimson, D 1, 1975.

Haskins, James (ed.). Black Manifesto for Education. New York: Morrow, 1973.

Haskins, James. "New Black Images in the Mass Media. How Educational Is Educational TV?" Freedomways 14(Third Quarter, 1974):200-208.

Haskins, Kenneth W. "Implications: New Conceptions of Relevancy." Educational Leadership 29(My, 1972):687-689.

Haubrich, Vernon. "Ending the Concentration Camps of Segregated Schools." Integrated Education, Ag-S, 1966.

Hauser, Philip M. "Demographic Factors in the Integration of the Negro." Daedalus, Fall, 1965.

Hauser, Robert M. "Educational Stratification in the United States." Sociological Inquiry 40(Spring, 1970):102-129.

Havighurst, Robert J. "Big-City Education: A Cooperative Endeavor." Phi Delta Kappan, Mr, 1967.

_____. Education in Metropolitan Areas. Boston, MA: Allyn and Bacon, 1966.

_____. "Educational Policy for the Large Cities." Social Problems 24(D, 1976): 271-271.

_____. "Metropolitanism and the Schools." Urban Review, N, 1968.

_____. Schools Face New Desegregation Phase." Nation's Schools, Mr, 1966.

_____. "Social Urban Renewal and the Schools." Integrated Education, Ap, 1963.

Havighurst, Robert J., Graham, Richard A., and Eberly, Donald. "American Youth in the Mid-Seventies." NASSP Bulletin 56(N, 1972): 1-13.

Havighurst, Robert J., Smith, Frank L., and Wilder, David E. A Profile of the Large-City High School. Washington, DC: National Association of wecondary School Principals, N, 1970.

Havighurst, Robert J. and others. Growing Up in River City. New York: Wiley, 1962.

Hawkins, Mason A. "Colored High Schools." Crisis, Je, 1911.

Hayden, J. Carleton. "The Congress of African Peoples (Atlanta, Georgia, September 3-7, 1970)." Black Academy Review 1(Winter, 1970):59-62.

Hayes, Charles L. "Institutional Appraisal and Planning for Equal Educational Opportunity." Journal of Negro Education, Summer, 1968.

Haygood, Atticus G. Our Brother in Black: His Freedom and His Future. New York: N.p., 1881.

Heald, James E. "In Defense of Middle-Class Values." Phi Delta Kappan, O, 1964.

Hearn, Robert Wesley. "Foundations and Equal Opportunity." Grantsmanship Center News 2 (F-Mr, 1975):30. [Executive Director of Association of Black Foundation Executives]

Hechinger, Fred M., and Hechinger, Grace. Growing Up in America. New York: McGraw-Hill, 1975.

Heckman, L. B. "School Redistricting." Master's thesis, Cornell U., 1968.

Heckman, L. B., and Taylor, H. M. "School Rezoning to Achieve Racial Balance: A Linear Programming Approach." Socio-Economic Planning Sciences 3(1969):127-133.

Hedgepeth, William. "The American South. Rise of a New Confederacy." Look, N, 1970.

Heer, David M. (ed.). Conference on Social Statistics and the City. Cambridge, MA: Harvard U. Press, 1969.

Heineman, Robert B., and Bernstein, Marilyn. A Return to Learning for Sidetracked Adolescents. Boston, MA: Beacon, 1967.

Henderson, George. "Negroes Into Americans: A Dialectical Development." Journal of Human Relations 14(1966).

_____. "Pupil Integration in Public Schools: Some Reflections." Teachers College Record, Ja, 1966.

Henderson, Vivian W. "Challenges in American Education." Congressional Record, Ap, 1972, E3531-3533.

Henig, Peter. "Up Against the Urban Frontier." Guardian, D, 1968.

Henry, Jules. "A Cross Cultural Index of Education." Current Anthropology 1(Jl, 1960):267-305.

_____. "Is Education Possible? Are We Qualified to Enlighten Dissenters?" In Public Controls for Non-Public Schools, pp. 83-102. Edited by Donald A. Erickson. Chicago: U. of Chicago, 1969.

Hentoff, Nat. "Educators as Dropouts." Evergreen Review, N, 1966.

Herbers, John. The Last Priority. New York: Funk and Wagnalls, 1970.

Hernton, Calvin C. White Papers for White Americans. Garden City, NY: Doubleday, 1966.

Herriott, Robert E., and Hodgkins, Benjamin J. The Environment of Schooling: Formal Education As An Open Social System. Englewood Cliffs, NJ: Prentice-Hall, 1973.

Herriott, Robert E., and St. John, Nancy H. Social Class and the Urban School. New York: Wiley, 1966.

Herzog, Elizabeth. "Social Stereotypes and Social Research." Journal of Social Issues 26(Summer, 1970):109-125.

Hesburgh, Theodore M. "The Challenge to Education." Journal of Negro Education 40 (Summer, 1971):290-296.

_____. "Old Victories, New Battles." Nation, S, 1974.

Hewitt, Alden. "A Comparative Study of White and Colored Pupils in a Southern School System." Elementary School Journal 31 (1930):111-119.

Hewitt, E. L. "Ethnic Factors in Education." American Anthropologist 8(1905):1-16.

Hickerson, Nathaniel. "Physical Integration Alone Is Not Enough." Journal of Negro Education, Spring, 1966.

Hicks, Alexander and others. "Class Power and State Policy: The Case of Large Business Corporations, Labor Unions and Governmental Redistribution in the American States." American Sociological Review 43(Je, 1978): 302-315.

High Schools in the South. Nashville, TN: Center for Southern Education Studies, George Peabody College, 1966.

Higham, John (ed.). Ethnic Leadership in America. Baltimore, MD: Johns Hopkins U. Press, 1978.

Hill, Leslie Pinckney. "The Association of Negro Secondary and Industrial Schools." Crisis, Mr, 1914.

Hill, W. B. "Negro Education in the South." Annals 22(1903):320-329.

Hilliard, Asa G. III. "Equal Educational Opportunity and Quality Education." Anthropology and Education Quarterly 9(Summer, 1978):110-126.

Hines, Paul D., and Wood, Leslie. A Guide to Human Rights Education. Washington, DC: National Education Association, 1969.

Hinton, James L. and others. "Tokenism and Improving Imagery of Blacks in TV Drama and Comedy: 1973." Journal of Broadcasting 18(F, 1974):423-432.

Hobart, Thomas Y. "What Price Quotas?" New York Teachers Magazine, F, 1975.

Hobson, Carol Joy. Statistics of Public Elementary and Secondary Education of Negroes in the Southern States: 1951-1952. U.S. Office of Education Circular No. 444. Washington, DC: GPO, 1955.

Hodge, Patricia Leavey, and Hauser, Philip M. The Challenge of America's Metropolitan Population Outlook---1960 to 1985. Research Report No. 3. Prepared for the Consideration of the National Commission on Urban Problems. Washington, DC: U.S. Dept. of Housing and Urban Development, 1968.

Hodge, Robert W., and Preiman, Donald J. "Class Identification in the United States." American Journal of Sociology, Mr, 1968.

Hodgson, Godfrey. "Do Schools Make a Difference?" Atlantic 231(Mr, 1973):35-46.

Hoffman, Lois W., and Hoffman, Martin L. (eds.). Review of Child Development Research, volume II. New York: Russell Sage Foundation, 1967.

Hogan, Dennis P., and Featherman, David L. Racial Stratification and Socioeconomic Change in the American North and South, D, 1976. ERIC ED 141 454.

Holden, Matthew, Jr. The Divisible Republic. New York: Abelard-Schuman, 1973.

Holland, Jerome H. Black Opportunity. New York: Weybright and Talley, 1969.

Holland, R. W. School Desegregation and Community Conflict. Riverside, CA: Western Regional School Desegregation Projects, U. of California, Je, 1971.

Hollander, T. Edward, and Gittell, Marilyn. Six Urban School Districts: A Comparative Study of Institutional Response. New York: Praeger, 1968.

Holley, Joseph W. Education and the Segregation Issue. New York: William Frederick Press, 1955.

Hollings, Ernest F. The Case Against Hunger: A Demand for a National Policy. New York: Cowles, 1970.

Holman, Ben. "Desegregation and the Community Relations Service." Integrateducation 13 (Ja-F, 1975):27-29.

Holmes, Eugene C. "A Philosophical Approach to the Study of Minority Problems." Journal of Negro Education, Summer, 1969.

Holton, Betty Gene. Program on Problems of School Desegregation. Final Technical Report. Washington, DC: District of Columbia Public Schools, 1967. ERIC ED 016 735.

Holton, Samuel M. "Education in the Changing South." High School Journal 54(0, 1970): 41-54.

Honte, Glenn. Special Training Institute on Problems of School Desegregation, Ag, 1967. ERIC ED 027 242.

Hopkins, Jeannette. Racial Justice and the Press. Mutual Suspicion or "The Saving Remnant?" MARC Paper No. 1. New York: Metropolitan Applied Research Center, S, 1968.

Hornby, D. Brock, and Holmes, George W. III. "Equalization of Resources Within School Districts." Virginia Law Review 58(1972): 1119-1156.

Horton, Billy Dean. "The Ideology of Equal Opportunity and the Sociological Study of Race and Ethnic Relations: A Critique of the Relationship between Liberal Ideology and Social Science." Doctoral dissertation, U. of Kentucky, 1977. Univ. Microfilms Order No. 7815742.

House, James S., and Fischer, Robert D. "Authoritarianism, Age, and Black Militancy." Sociometry 34(Je, 1971):174-197.

Howe, Harold II. "Blueprint for Education." Parents' Magazine, 0, 1966.

_____. "National Ideals and Educational Policy." In U.S. Commission on Civil Rights, Papers Prepared for National Conference on Equal Educational Opportunity in America's Cities. Washington, DC: GPO, 1968.

Hsia, Jayjia, and Strand, Thersa. WTTW-TSAA Television Pilot, "TCR '77,": Formative Evaluation. Evanston, IL: Educational Testing Service, Jl, 1975. [Television pilot on desegregation problems in high schools]

Hubbard, Louise J. "Foreign Language Study and the Black Student." CLA Journal 18 (Je, 1975):563-569.

Human Interaction Research Institute. A Study of Successful Persons from Seriously Disadvantaged Backgrounds. Springfield, VA: National Technical Information Service, Mr, 1970.

Hume, Ellen. "[Black] Panthers Decimated by Violence, Strife." Los Angeles Times, S 22, 1975.

Hummel, Raymond C., and Nagle, John M. Urban Education in America. Problems and Prospects. New York: Oxford U. Press, 1973.

Humphrey, Hubert H. (ed.). School Desegregation. Documents and Commentaries. New York: Crowell, 1964.

Humphries, Kenneth W. "Making the Decision to Desegregate: Case Studies and Analysis of Desegregation in the Public Schools of Five Northern Suburbs." Doctoral dissertation, Columbia U., 1967.

Hunnicutt, C. W. (ed.). Urban Education and Cultural Deprivation. Syracuse, New York: U. Division of Summer Sessions, Syracuse U., 1964.

Hunter, David R. The Slums. Challenge and Response. New York: Free Press of Glencoe, 1964.

Hunter, Guy (ed.). Industrialization and Race Relations, A Symposium. London: Oxford U. Press, 1965. [Contains title essay by Herbert Blumer]

Husen, Torsten. "Does Broader Educational Opportunity Mean Lower Standards?" International Review of Education 17(1971):77-89.

Hutchins, Robert M. Education. New York: Praeger, Ja, 1968.

_____. "Manhood and the Liberal Arts." Urban Review 4(1970):3-6.

Hyde, Rosel. "Racial Coverage Can Heal Wounds." Broadcasting, Ap, 1968. [By the chairman of the Federal Communications Commission]

Hyman, Herbert H., and Sheatsley, Paul B. "Attitudes Toward Desegregation." Scientific American, Jl, 1964.

Ianni, Francis A. J. "Anthropology and Educational Research: A Report on Federal Agency Programs, Policies and Issues." Anthropology and Education Quarterly 7(Ag, 1976):3-11.

Ibom, Godfrey Gamili. "A Dynamic Quasi-Stochastic Model for Forecasting Population Distribution of Residential Black Pupils in Suburbia." Doctoral dissertation, Ohio State U., 1973.

Ickes, Harold L. "The Education of Negroes in the United States." Journal of Negro Education 3(Ja, 1934):5-7.

In the Balance. A Review of Equal Educational Opportunity. Lansing, MI: State Department of Education, 1969. [Addresses by Thomas F. Pettigrew, Mark Chesler, Robert L. Green, Gregory Coffin and others]

Inger, Morton, and Stout, Robert T. "School Desegregation: The Need to Govern." Urban Review, N, 1968.

Ingle, Dwight J. "Aids to Negro Advancement." Journal of Human Relations, First Quarter, 1965.

_____. "Individuality as a Factor in Integration." School Review, Winter, 1965.

_____. "Inequality de Facto: Educate or Integrate?" Economist, F, 1964.

Institute of Community Studies. Programs Relevant to Urban Problems. Interim Phase I Report of the Citizens Committee, Voluntarism and Urban Life Project. New York: The Institute, 1968.

"Integrating the Texts." Newsweek, Mr, 1966.

"Integration: Desirable and Possible." Christian Century, Ap, 1967.

"Integration With and Without Busing." Federal Aid Planner: A Guide for School District Administrators, Winter, 1972.

Invitational Conference on Equal Opportunities in the Cities. Equal Educational Opportunities in the Cities, 1967. The Hartford Public Schools, 249 High School, Hartford, CT 06103.

Internationales Symposium über Paul Robeson und den Kampf der Arbeiterklasse und der Afro-Amerikaner in den USA, Berlin, 1971. Protokoll des Symposium Paul Robeson und der Kampf de Arbeiterklasse und der Schwarzen Amerikaner den USA gegen den Imperialismus, Berlin, am 13, und 14, April 1971. Berlin: Deutsche Akademie der Kunste, Henschelverlag Kunst und Gesellschaft, 1972.

"Interview: John Hope Franklin." Black Collegian 3(My-Je, 1973):24, 26, 49.

Isaacs, Harold R. "The One and the Many." American Educator 2(Spring, 1978):4-14.

Isaacs, Reginald. "Are Urban Neighborhoods Possible?" and "The Neighborhood Unit As An Instrument for Segregation." Journal of Housing, Jl and Ag, 1948.

Isaacs, William. "Dissenting Thoughts on School Integration." High Points, My, 1965.

It's Not Over In the South. School Desegregation in Forty-three Southern Cities Eighteen Years After Brown. A Report by the Alabama Council on Human Relations, American Friends Service Committee, Delta Ministry of the National Council of Churches, NAACP Legal Defense and Educational Fund, Inc., Southern Regional Council, and Washington Research Project, My, 1972.

Itzkoff, Seymour W. "Cultural Pluralism in Urban Education." School and Society, N, 1966.

Jackson, Barbara L. A Re-Definition of Black Folk: Implications for Education. Atlanta, GA: W.E.B. DuBois Institute, Atlanta U.

Jackson, Jesse. "Black Struggle for Silver Rights." Baltimore Sun, Ag 1, 1976.

Jackson, Reid E. "Education for Integration: A Magna Carta." Crisis, Ag, 1942.

Jacob, Herbert. "Problems of Scale Equivalency in Measuring Attitudes in American Subcultures." Social Science Quarterly 52(Je, 1971):61-75.

Jacobs, Glenn. "The Reification of the Notion of Subculture in Public Welfare." Social Casework, N, 1968.

Jaffee, Cabot L., and Whitacre, Robert. "An Unobtrusive Measure of Prejudice Toward Negroes Under Differing Durations of Speech." Psychological Reports 27(D, 1970):823-828.

James, H. Thomas. The New Cult of Efficiency and Education. Pittsburgh, PA: U. of Pittsburgh Press, 1969.

Jameson, Robert U. "Intercultural Education and the Independent Schools." Common Ground 8 (Winter, 1948):37-44.

Janssen, Peter. "AFT: The Union Response to Mass Production." Saturday Review, O, 1967.

_____. "NEA: The Reluctant Dragon." Saturday Review, Je, 1967.

_____. "The Next Step: Teacher Integration." Reporter, N, 1966.

_____. "The School Crisis: Any Way Out?" Newsweek, S, 1967.

Jefferson, Nevers L. "Prediction of Dropouts and Adult Functional Illiteracy Rates in Large Cities with a Black Population of 100,000 or More in 1970." Master's thesis, Howard U., 1974.

Jefferson, Ruth B. "Some Obstacles to Racial Integration." Journal of Negro Education, 1957.

Jencks, Christopher et al. Education and In-
equality: A Preliminary Report to the
Carnegie Corporation of New York. Cambridge,
MA: Center for Educational Policy Research,
Harvard U., 1970.

Jencks, Christopher [An Interview]. Phi
Delta Kappan 54(D, 1972):255-257.

_____. "Is the Public School Obsolete?"
Public Interest, Winter, 1966.

_____. "The Public Schools Are Failing."
Saturday Evening Post, Ap, 1966.

Jenkins, Evan. "School Conflict in South Is
Intensifying As Academies Challenge Public
System." New York Times, Ag 19, 1973
[Segregation academies]

Jennings, M. Kent. "Parental Grievances and
School Politics." Public Opinion
Quarterly, Fall, 1968.

"Jesse Jackson: He Spells Discipline With Five
A's." Creative Discipline 1(Ap-Je, 1978):
4-5. [Interview]

John, Vera P. "A Brief Survey of Research on
the Characteristics of Children from Low-
Income Backgrounds." Urban Education,
I, 4(1965).

Johns, Thomas L., and Magers, Dexter A. "Measuring the Equity of State School Finance
Programs." Journal of Education Finance
3(Spring, 1978):373-385.

Johnson, Carroll F., and Usdan, Michael D.
(eds.). Equality of Educational Opportun-
ity in the Large Cities of America: The
Relationship Between Decentralization and
Racial Integration. New York: Teachers
College Press, 1969.

Johnson, Charles D. "Relation of the Negro
Problem to Education in the South." Doctoral dissertation, U. of Iowa, 1921.

Johnson, Charles Spurgeon. Education and the
Cultural Crisis. New York: Macmillan, 1951.

_____. Into the Main Stream. A Survey of
Best Practices in Race Relations in the
South. Chapel Hill, NC: The U. of North
Carolina Press, 1947.

_____. "[Negro Education]." In The Negro in
American Civilization. New York: Henry
Holt, 1930.

_____. Next Steps in Education in the South.
[Published by the Association of Colleges
and Secondary Schools for Negroes, 1953]

_____. Patterns of Negro Segregation.
New York: Harper and Brothers, 1943.

_____. Shadow of the Plantation. Chicago:
The U. of Chicago Press, 1934.

_____. "The Social Setting of Negro Educa-
tion." Journal of Educational Sociology
12(Ja, 1939):274-287.

Johnson, Edwina Chavers. "Integration Is Not
the Issue." Integrated Education, F-Mr,
1965.

Johnson, Harold T. "Integration: An Assessment." Educational Leadership, N, 1968.

Johnson, Jesse J. "The Black Psychologist:
Pawn or Professional?" In What Black Educa-
tors Are Saying, pp. 31-35. Edited by
Nathan Wright. New York: Hawthorn, 1970.

Johnson, John L. "Special Education and the
Inner City: A Challenge for the Future or
Another Means for Cooling the Mark Out?"
Journal of Special Education 3(1969):241-
251.

Johnson, Nicholas. "'White' Media Must Meet
Challenge of Negro Antipathy and Disbelief."
Variety, Ja, 1968. [By a member of the
Federal Communication Commission]

Johnson, Norman C. "An Analysis of Certain
Problems Related to Integration of Negro
Students Into Interracial Schools." Doc-
toral dissertation, U. of Indiana, 1954.
Dissertation Abstracts, XVI. 1954, p.632.

Johnston, A. Montgomery. "Intellectual
Segregation." Elementary School Journal,
Ja, 1967.

Jones, Ernest M. Systems Approaches to Multi-
Variable Socioeconomic Problems: An
Appraisal. Washington, DC: Program of
Policy Studies in Science and Technology,
George Washington U., Ag, 1968.

Jones, Faustine C. "Ironies of School
Desegregation." Journal of Negro Education
47(Winter, 1978):2-27.

Jones, Lance G. E. Negro Schools in the Southern States. New York: Oxford U. Press,
1928.

Jones, Leon. "School Desegregation in Retrospect and Prospect." Journal of Negro
Education 47(Winter, 1978):46-57.

Jones, Lewis W. "Negro Youth in the South."
In The Nation's Children. Edited by Eli
Ginzberg. New York: Columbia U. Press,
1960.

_____. "The New World View of Negro Youth."
In Problems of Youth. Transition to Adult-
hood in a Changing World. Edited by M. and
C. W. Sherif. Chicago: Aldine, 1965.

Jones, Lewis W., and Lee, Everett S. Rural
Blacks -- A Vanishing Population, O, 1974.
ERIC ED 126 219.

Jones, Mack H. "Scientific Method as a Tool for Improving the Quality of Value Judgements with Particular Concern for the Black Predicament in U.S." Endarch 1(Winter, 1976):37-55.

Jones, Reginald L. (ed.). Black Psychology. New York: Harper and Row, 1972.

Jones, Wendell P. "Education of the Black Man in the U.S." School and Society 98(D, 1970):467-470.

Jordan, June. "White English: The Politics of Language." Black World 22(Ag, 1973):4-10.

Jordan, Vernon E., Jr. The Black Presence in Education, Ap, 1977. ERIC ED 142-608.

_____. "School Integration Still An Issue Despite Quiet Progress." New York Times, Ja 16, 1974.

_____. "The Unfinished Agenda." Integrateducation 13(My-Je, 1975):18-20.

Jorgenson, Lloyd P. "Social and Economic Orientation of the National Education Association." Progressive Education 34(Jl, 1957): 100.

Joyce, William W. "Minority Groups in American Society: Imperatives for Educators." Social Education, Ap, 1969.

Joye, Harlon E. "Dixie's New Left." Transaction 7(S, 1970):50-56, 62.

Kain, John F., and Hanushek, Eric A. On the Value of Equality of Educational Opportunity As a Guide to Policy. Program on Regional and Urban Economics. Cambridge, MA: Harvard U., 1968.

Kapel, David E. Project TALENT. Effects of Negro Density on Student Variables and the Post-High-School Adjustment of Male Negroes. Palo Alto, CA: Project Talent Office, 1968. [PROJECT TALENT, American Institutes for Research, P.O. Box 1113, Palo Alto, CA 94302]

Kaplan, Howard M. "The Black Muslims and the Negro American's Quest for Communion." British Journal of Sociology, Je, 1969.

Kaplan, Sidney J., and Coleman, A. Lee. "The Strategy of Change: Contrasting Approaches to Teacher Integration." Social Science, O, 1963.

Karon, Bertram P. Black Scars: A Rigorous Investigation of Discrimination, with an Appendix on the Southern White. New York: Springer, 1975.

Karweit, Nancy. Patterns of Educational Activities: Discontinuities and Sequences. Baltimore, MD: Center for Social Organization of Schools, Johns Hopkins U., Ja, 1977. [Black and white men, 14-30 years of age]

Kashif, Lonnie. "Black Students Rip White-Geared Psychology Training." Muhammad Speaks, S, 1969. [Annual meeting of the American Psychological Association]

_____. "No Substitute for Academic Excellence, Dr. Shabazz Tells Group." Muhammad Speaks, My, 1971.

Kassarjian, Harold H. "The Negro and American Advertising: 1946-1965." Journal of Marketing Research, F, 1969.

Katz, Bennett D. "Equal Opportunity---Do We Really Mean It?" Compact 5(O, 1971):6-7.

Katz, Daniel. "Group Process and Social Integration." Journal of Social Issues, Ja, 1967.

Katz, Irwin, and Gurin, Patricia (eds.). Race and the Social Sciences. New York: Basic Books, 1969.

Katzman, Martin T. "Ethnic Geography and Regional Economics, 1880-1960." Economic Geography 45(1969):45-52.

Katznelson, Ira. "White Social Science and the Black Man's World. The Case of Urban Ethnography." Race Today 2(1970):47-48.

Kavka, Gregory S. "Equality in Education." In Indeterminacy in Education, pp. 211-252. Edited by John E. McDermott. Berkeley, CA: McCutchan, 1976.

Keeler, Emmett. Planning School Desegregation. A Working Note. Santa Monica, CA: Rand, 1972.

"Keep Neighborhood School. School Administrators' Opinion Poll." Nation's Schools, O, 1963.

Kendrick, S. A. Verbal Ability: An Obsolete Measure!, Mr, 1968. ERIC ED 021 929.

Kennedy, Robert F., Clark, Kenneth B., Lewis, Oscar, Sullivan, Neil V., Hutchins, Robert M., and Ashmore, Harry S. "Ghetto Education." The Center Magazine, N, 1968.

Kent, James K. "The Coleman Report: Opening Pandora's Box." Phi Delta Kappan, Ja, 1968.

Keppel, Francis. "Fundamentals in the Battle for Desegregation." Phi Delta Kappan, S, 1964.

_____. The Necessary Revolution in American Education. New York: Harper and Row, 1966.

Kerchkhoff, Richard K. "The Problem of the City School." Journal of Marriage and the Family, N, 1964.

_____. "Race and Social Class as Opportunities for Early Childhood Education." Young Children, S, 1965.

Keridt, Leonard. "The Schools and the People Must Work for Integration." *California Teachers Association Journal*, Mr, 1964.

Kerlinger, Fred N., and Carroll, John B. (eds.). *Review of Research in Education 2*. Itasca, IL: Peacock, 1974.

Kerner, Otto. "The Current Crisis in Urban Education." *Illinois Schools Journal*, Spring, 1969.

Kerr, Walter. "The Negro Actor Asks Himself: 'Am I a Negro or Am I an Actor.'" *New York Times Magazine*, 0, 1967.

Khleif, Bud B. "A Socio-Cultural Framework for Understanding Race and Ethnic Relations in Schools and Society of the USA." *Sociologus* 28(1978):54-69.

Kiesling, Herbert J. *Multivariate Analysis of Schools and Educational Policy*. Santa Monica, CA: Rand, Mr, 1971.

Killalea, J. Neil. *The Sources of Metropolitan School Segregation. An Analysis of Seventeen Large Urban Areas*. Arlington, VA: Killalea Associates, 0, 1977.

Killens, John O. "The Artist and the Black University." *The Black Scholar*, N, 1969.

Killian, Lewis M. *The Impossible Revolution, Phase II: Black Power and the American Dream*. New York: Random House, 1975.

_____. "School Desegregation: Past, Present, Future." *Integrated Education* (S-O, 1972): 3-10.

Kilpatrick, James Jackson. *The Southern Case for School Segregation*. New York: Crowell-Collier Press, 1962.

Kilson, Martin. "Whither Integration?" *American Scholar* 45(Summer, 1976):360-373.

Kimball, Penn T. *The Disconnected*. New York: Columbia U. Press, 1972. [The minority poor and politics]

Kimbrough, Marvin. *Black Magazines: An Exploratory Study*. Austin, TX: Center for Communication Research, U. of Texas, Ja, 1973.

Kindsvatter, Richard, and Willen, William. "The Dilemma of Racial Imbalance in the Schools." *American Secondary Education* 4(S, 1974): 29-33.

King, Albion Roy. "A White Philosopher in a Southern Ghetto." *Journal of Human Relations*, Third Quarter, 1968.

King, Martin Luther, Jr. "Education and Equality." *Integrated Education*, Je-Jl, 1964.

_____. "The Role of the Behavioral Scientist in the Civil Rights Movement." *American Psychologist*, Mr, 1968.

King, Ruth E. G. "Highlights in the Development of A B Psi." *Journal of Black Psychology* 4(Ag, 1977/F, 1978):9-24. [Association of Black Psychologists]

Kinnick, B. Jo. "De Facto." *Clearing House*, 0, 1967. [A poem about de facto segregation]

Kirby, David J. and others. *School Desegregation in the North: A Preliminary Report*, 0, 1970. ERIC ED 043 714.

Klein, Woody. *Let in the Sun*. New York: Macmillan, 1964.

_____. "News Media and Race Relations: A Self-Portrait." *Columbia Journalism Review*, Fall, 1968.

_____. "The Racial Crisis in America. The News Media Respond to the New Challenge." *Quill*, Ja, 1969.

Kleinberger, Aharon Fritz. "Reflections on Equality in Education." *Studies in Philosophy and Education*, Summer, 1967. [Critique by John R. Perry in the Fall, 1967 issue]

Klemerman, Gerald and others. "Sex Education in a Ghetto School." *Journal of School Health* 41(Ja, 1971):29-33.

Kling, Martin. *Reading and Basic Subject Matter Achievement of Job Corps Urban Center Trainees*. ERIC ED 011 228.

Klitgaard, Robert E., and Hall, George R. "Are There Unusually Effective Schools?" *Journal of Human Resources* 10(Winter, 1975):90-106.

Klopf, Gordon J., and Laster, Israel A. (eds.). *Integrating the Urban School*. New York: Teachers College, Columbia U., 1963.

Knoll, Erwin. "Desegregation Is Facing Some Stunning Setbacks." *Nation's Schools*, N, 1966.

_____. "Ten Years of Deliberate Speed." *American Education*, D, 1964-Ja, 1965.

Koenigsberg, Ernest. *Mathematical Analysis Applied to School Attendance Areas*. Paper presented at the U.S. Office of Education Symposium. Washington, DC: Operations Analysis of Education, N, 1967.

Komisar, B. Paul. "The Paradox of Equality in Schooling." *Teachers College Record*, D, 1966.

Koponen, Niilo E. "The Myth of a 'Tipping Point.'" *Integrated Education*, Ag-S, 1966.

Kornhauser, Stanley H. Planning for the Achievement of Quality Integrated Education in Desegregated Schools: A Composite Report on the Recommendations of Workshop Participants, Je, 1968. ERIC ED 030 702.

Kotler, Milton. "...And What Does He Get?" Liberation, N, 1964. [On color and cruelty]

Kozol, Jonathan. "Halls of Darkness: In the Ghetto Schools." Harvard Educational Review, Summer, 1967.

_____. "Moving On--to Nowhere." Saturday Review, D, 1972.

Kozoll, Charles E. "The Meek Will Inherit Nothing." Integrated Education (N-D, 1973): 35-38.

Kraft, Ivor. "The Classroom Struggle." Nation, Jl, 1967.

_____. "The Coming Crisis in Secondary Education." Bulletin of the National Association of Secondary-School Principals, F. [Followed by a series of commentaries]

_____. "Head Start to What?" Nation, S, 1966.

Kraft, Ivor, and Chilman, Catherine S. Helping Low-Income Families Through Parent Education. Washington, DC: Children's Bureau, U.S. Dept. of Health, Education, and Welfare, 1966.

Kranz, Peter L. "Racial Involvement: Is It Worth the Risk?" Integrated Education 11 (J1-O, 1973):60-61.

Kraus, Richard. Public Recreation and the Negro. A Study of Participation and Administrative Practices. New York: Center for Urban Education, 1968.

Kraushaar, Otto F. American Nonpublic Schools. Patterns of Diversity. Baltimore, MD: Johns Hopkins U. Press, 1972.

Kreuter, Mortimer. "The Teacher in the Brown Paper Bag." The Urban Review, My, 1966.

Kristol, Irving. "A Few Kind Words for Uncle Tom." Harper's Magazine, F, 1965.

Krosney, Herbert. Beyond Welfare: Poverty in the Supercity. New York: Holt, Rinehart and Winston, 1966.

Krumbein, Eliezer and others. Institute of Administrative Leadership in School Desegregation and Equal Education Opportunity. Final Report, Mr, 1969. ERIC ED 056 114.

Krystall, Eric R., Chesler, Mark A., and White, Agatha E. Voting Behavior and Attitudes Toward School Desegregation: A Study of Southern Negroes. Tuskegee, AL: Dept. of Social Science Research, Tuskegee Institute, Mr, 1967.

Kuvlesky, William P. "Rural Youth, Current Status and Prognosis." In Youth in Contemporary Society, pp. 321-345. Edited by David Gottlieb. Beverly Hills, CA: Sage, 1973.

Kvaraceus, William C. "Alienated Youth Here and Abroad." Phi Delta Kappan, N, 1963.

Labov, William. "The Logic of Non-Standard English." In Linguistics and the Teaching of Standard English to Speakers of Other Languages or Dialects, pp. 1-43. Edited by James E. Slatis. Washington, DC: Georgetown U., 1969.

_____. "Phonological Correlates of Social Stratification." American Anthropologist, Part 2, D, 1964. [Based on a study of the Lower East Side of New York City]

Ladd, Everett C., Jr. "The Negro as 'Cause.'" Nation, F, 1965.

Lakin, Martin. "Human Relations Training and Interracial Social Action: Problems in Self and Client." Behavioral Science, Ap-Je, 1966. [Commentary by Robert F. Allen]

Laporte, Robert and others. The Evolution of Public Educational Policy--School Desegregation in a Northern City, 1966. ERIC ED 016 689.

Lasser, Michael L. "The Independent Schools and the Multiracial World. An Interview with Elliott Shapiro." Independent School Bulletin, F, 1968.

Laveman, Gary S. "Conducting a School Ethnic Survey." Social Science Record 14(Spring, 1977):24-25. [Student project]

Lawson, Simpson F. Above Property Rights. Prepared for the U.S. Commission on Civil Rights. Washington, DC: GPO, D, 1972.

Layng, Anthony. "Voluntary Associations and Black Ethnic Identity." Phylon 39 (Summer, 1978):171-179.

Leacock, Eleanor B. Class and Color in City Schools. A Comparative Study. New York: Basic Books, 1969.

_____. "The Concept of Culture and Its Significance for School Counselors." Personnel and Guidance Journal, My, 1968.

_____. "Distortions of Working Class Reality in American Social Science." Science and Society, Winter, 1967.

_____. Teaching and Learning in City Schools. New York: Basic Books, 1969.

League of Women Voters of San Diego, California. Perspectives on School Integration. San Diego, CA: League of Women Voters, 1972.

League of Women Voters of the U.S. "School Desegregation, North and South." Facts and Issues, Je, 1969.

Lear, Elmer N. "On Educational Philosophy, Civil Rights, and the Schools." Journal of Educational Thought, Ap, 1968.

Leavell, Ullin Whitney. Philanthropy in Negro Education. Nashville, TN: George Peabody College for Teachers, 1930.

Lebeaux, Charles. "Life on ADC: Budgets of Despair." New University Thought 3, 4 (1964).

Lee, Eugene C. (ed.). School Desegregation: Retrospect and Prospect. 1970. Southern Newspapers Publishers Association Foundation, P.O. Box 11606, Atlanta, GA 30305.

Lerman, Robert I. "Some Determinants of Youth School Activity." Journal of Human Resources 7(Summer, 1972):366-383.

Leeson, Jim. "Desegregation Faculties." Southern Education Report, My, 1968.

_____. "Desegregation [in the South]: Faster Pace, Scarcer Records." Southern Education Report, Ja-F, 1966.

_____. "How Southern States Are Desegregating." Nation's Schools, N, 1966.

_____. "The Matter of ['Free] Choice.'" Southern Education Report, S, 1968.

_____. "The Pace [of Desegregation] Quickens in the South." Southern Education Report, Ap, 1967.

_____. "Private Schools Continue to Increase in the South." Southern Education Report, N, 1966. [Private schools as response to legal responsibility to desegregate public schools]

_____. "Private Schools for Whites Face Some Hurdles." Southern Education Report, O, 1967.

_____. "Records by Race: To Keep or Not." Southern Education Report, S, 1966.

_____. "Theme and Variations." Southern Education Report, Jl-Ag, 1968. [On black militancy in education]

_____. "They Came Right Out and Said It." Southern Education Report, Mr-Ap, 1966. [Desegregation centers financed under Title IV, Civil Rights Act]

Leonard, Walter J. "Leonard's Speech." Harvard Crimson, Ja, 1977. [Memorial Oration honoring the birthday of Dr. Martin Luther King]

Levenson, William B. "Educational Implications of De Facto School Segregation." Western Reserve Law Review, Ap, 1965.

_____. The Spiral Pendulum: The Urban School in Transition. New York: Rand McNally, 1968. [By the former school superintendent of Cleveland, Ohio]

Levin, Henry M. (ed.). Community Control of Schools. Washington, DC: Brookings, 1970.

Levin, Henry M. Frontier Functions: An Econometric Approach to the Evaluation of Educational Effectiveness. Stanford, CA: School of Education, Stanford U., 1971.

_____. "What Differences Do Schools Make?" Saturday Review, Ja, 1968. [Critique of the Coleman Report]

_____. "Why Ghetto Schools Fail." Saturday Review, Mr, 1970.

Levine, Daniel U. "Can In-Service Training Save the Inner City Schools?" Journal of Secondary Education, Ja, 1968.

_____. "The Community School in Contemporary Perspective." Elementary School Journal, D, 1968.

_____. "Crisis in the Administration of Inner City Schools." School and Society, O, 1966.

_____. "Defaulting in the Schools and Rioting in the Streets." Clearing House, Ja, 1968.

_____. "Differences Between Segregated and Desegregated Settings." Journal of Negro Education 39(1970):139-147.

_____. "From Model to Practice: Guidelines for the Effective Implimentation of Interracial Programs." In Models for Integrated Education, pp. 109-115. Edited by Daniel U. Levine. Worthington, OH: Jones, 1971.

_____. "Integration in Metropolitan Schools: Issues and Prospects." Phi Delta Kappan 54 (Je, 1973).

_____. "Integration: Reconstructing Academic Values of Youth in Deprived Areas." Clearing House, N, 1964.

Levine, Daniel U. (ed.). Models for Integrated Education. Alternative Programs of Integrated Education in Metropolitan Areas. Worthington, OH: Jones, 1971.

Levine, Daniel U., and Clavner, Jerry B. Multi-Jurisdictional Metropolitan Agencies and Education. Kansas City, MO: Center for the Study of Metropolitan Problems in Education, U. of Missouri, 1967.

_____. "The Need for Activist Roles Among Teachers in Big City School Districts." Journal of Secondary Education, Mr, 1969.

_____. "Organizing for Reform in Big-City Schools." Phi Delta Kappan, Mr, 1967.

_____. Raising Standards in the Inner-city Schools. Washington, DC: Council for Basic Education, 1966.

_____. "The Segregated Society: What Must Be Done." Phi Delta Kappan, Ja, 1969.

_____. "Unequal Opportunities in the Large Inner-City High School." Bulletin of the National Association of Secondary School Principals, N, 1968.

_____. "Whatever Happened to the Ideal of the Comprehensive School?" Phi Delta Kappan, O, 1966.

Levine, Daniel U., and Havighurst, Robert J. "Are You Overprojecting Negro Enrollment Growth?" Nation's Schools, Ap, 1968.

Levine, Daniel U., and Havighurst, Robert J. (eds.). The Future of Big-City Schools: Desegregation Policies and Magnet Alternatives. Berkeley, CA: McCutchan, 1977.

Levine, Donald, and Bane, Mary Jo. The "Inequality" Controversy: Schooling and Distributive Justice. New York: Basic Books, 1975.

Levinsohn, Florence H. "TV's Deadly Inadvertent Bias." In School Desegregation. Shadow and Substance. Edited by Florence H. Levinsohn and Benajmin D. Wright. Chicago: U. of Chicago Press, 1976.

Levitan, Sar A., Johnston, William B., and Taggart, Robert (eds.). Minorities in the United States. Washington, DC: Public Affairs Press, 1975.

Levy, Mark. "Upward Bound: A Summer Romance." Reporter, O, 1966.

Lewis, Alphonse (ed.). How To Achieve Quality-Integrated Education in the 1970's, 1972. Quality-Integrated Study Group Organization, San Jose Teachers Association, 2476 Almaden Expressway, San Jose, CA 95125.

Lewis, Hylan. Black Families: Sociological Profiles. 1974. ERIC ED 126 227.

Lewis, James O. "Education and the Two Nation Drift." CTA Journal, My, 1968.

Lewis, Michael. The Culture of Inequality. Amherst, MA: U. of Massachusetts Press, 1978.

Lewis, Reginald. "Educational Institutions in a Plural Society." Journal of Conflict Resolution, S, 1968.

Ley, John W., and McElvogue, Joseph F. "Racial Segregation in American Sports." International Review of Sport Sociology 5(1970):5-24.

Lieberman, Myron. "Civil Rights and the NEA." School and Society 85(My, 1957):166-168.

_____. "Segregation's Challenge to the NEA." School and Society 81(My, 1955):167-168.

Lieberman, Stanley, and Wilkinson, Christy A. "A Comparison Between Northern and Southern Blacks Residing in the North." Demography 13(My, 1976).

Liggett, Robin Segerblom. "The Application of an Implicit Enumeration Algorithm to the School Desegregation Problem." Management Science 20(0, 1973):159-168. [Revising school attendance boundaries]

Light a Fire. National Committee for Support of the Public Schools, 1424 16th St., N.W., Washington, DC, 1964.

Lightfoote-Wilson, Thomasyne. "Institutional Access: The Road to National Integration." Journal of Human Relations, Third Quarter, 1968.

Lincoln, C. Eric. "Anxiety, Fear, and Integration." Phylon, 1960.

_____. "Color and Group Identity in the United States." Daedalus, Spring, 1967.

_____. My Face Is Black. Boston: Beacon, 1964.

_____. "The Relevance of Education for Black Americans." Journal of Negro Education, Summer, 1969.

_____. Sounds of Struggle: Persons and Perspectives in Civil Rights. New York: Morrow, 1967.

Lindsay, Leon. "The Views of Benjamin Mays." Integrated Education: Race and Schools 8 (My-Je, 1970):50-53.

Link, Charles R., and Ratledge, Edward C. "Social Returns to Quantity and Quality of Education: A Further Statement." Journal of Human Resources 10(Winter, 1975):78-89.

Link, William R. "Black Youth, Black Nationalism, and White Independent Youth." Independent School Bulletin, O, 1969.

Lipset, Seymour Martin. Group Life in America. A Task Force Report. New York: American Jewish Committee, 1972.

Lipset, Seymour Martin, and Schneider, William. "Racial Equality in America." New Society, Ap, 1978. [Public opinion polls]

Liston, Hardy. "Work of the Jeanes Supervising Teachers for Negro Rural Schools." Master's thesis, The U. of Chicago, 1928.

Little, Roger W. "Basic Education and Youth Socialization in the Armed Forces." American Journal of Orthopsychiatry, 0, 1968. [See Pilisuk, below]

Lloyd, R. Grann. "Defining the Situation." Negro Educational Review, Jl-0, 1964.

Loewen, James W. "Is Segregation OK If Social Scientists Approve?" Integrated Education (S-0, 1972):65-68.

Logan, Rayford W. "Educational Segregation in the North." Journal of Negro Education 2 (Ja, 1933):65-67.

Lohman, Joseph D. "Expose--Don't Impose." NEA Journal, Ja, 1966.

Long, Larry. "The Migration Experience of Blacks." Integrateducation 13(My-Je, 1975): 28-31.

Long, Larry, and Hansen, Kristin A. "Return Migration to the South." Integrateducation 14(Ja-F, 1976).

_____. "Selectivity of Black Return Migration to the South." Rural Sociology 42(F, 1977): 317-331.

Lopez, Thomas R., Jr. "Cultural Pluralism: Political Hoax? Educational Need?" Journal of Teacher Education 24(Winter, 1973):277-281.

Lottman, Herbert. "'The Action Is Everywhere the Black Man Goes'" New York Times Book Review, Ap, 1968. [Black expatriate writers in Paris]

Lowe, Jim. "However, If You Happen To Be Black..." New Generation 52(Summer, 1970):41-45.

Lowell, Stanley H. "Equality in Our Time." Jewish Currents, S, 1964.

Loy, John W., and Elvogue, Joseph F. "Racial Segregation in American Sport." International Review of Sport Sociology 5(1970): 5-24. (UNIPUB, Inc., P.O. Box 433, N.Y., N.Y. 10016).

Lubell, Samuel H. White and Black. Test of a Nation. New York: Harper and Row, 1964.

Luchterhand, Elmer, and Weller, Leonard. "Social Class and the Desegregation Movement: A Study of Parents' Decisions in a Negro Ghetto." Social Problems, Summer, 1964.

Lutz, R. P. and others. "An Application of Operations Research to School Desegregation." Management Science 19(D, 1972):100-109.

Lyford, Joseph P. "An Unpopular Essay on Civil Rights." Phi Delta Kappan, My, 1964.

Lyle, Jerolyn R. Research on Achievement Determinants in Educational Systems: A Survey. Technical Note No. 56. Washington, DC: Division of Operations Analysis, National Center for Educational Statistics, U.S. Office of Education, Ja, 1968.

McAdams, John. "Can Open Enrollment Work?" Public Interest 37(Fall, 1974):69-88.

McAteer, J. Eugene. "Equality of Opportunity Must Be Real." California Teachers Association Journal, Mr, 1964.

McCauley, Patrick, and Bell, Edward D. (eds.). Southern Schools: Progress and Problems. Nashville, TN: Southern Education Reporting Service, 1959.

McClurkin, W. D. Rural Education in the United States, 1970. ERIC ED 043 408.

McDavid, Raven I., Jr. "American Social Dialects." College English, Ja, 1965.

_____. "Dialectology and the Teaching of Reading." Reading Teacher, D, 1964.

McCune, Shirley, and Matthews, Martha. Programs for Educational Equity: Schools and Affirmative Action. Washington, DC: GPO, 1975.

McDonagh, Paula. "The People and the Schools: A Confrontation." HGSEA (Harvard Graduate School of Education Association) Bulletin, Winter-Spring, 1968. [Conference sponsored by Harvard, November 3-4, 1967]

McDonald, J. C. "Equal Opportunity--An Adequate Goal?" Minnesota Journal of Education, S, 1964.

McElligott, Catherine V. De Facto Segregation in Public Schools in the Northeast. Urban Studies Center, Rutgers, The State U.

McFarland, Valerie. Data on Selected Racial Groups: Available from the Bureau of the Census. Rev. May 1977. Washington, DC: Subscriber Services Section, Bureau of the Census, 1977.

McGee, Cherry A. "A Content Analysis of the Treatment of Black Americans on Television." Social Education 41(Ap, 1977):336-344.

McGee, Leo. "Twenty Years of Education for the Black Adult: Implications for Teachers and Administrators." Adult Leadership 21(Mr, 1973):291-294.

McKenney, Nampeo D. R. and others. The Social and Economic Status of the Black Population in the United States, 1972. Washington, DC: G.P.O., 1973.

_____. The Social and Economic Status of the Black Population in the United States, 1971. Special Studies. Washington, DC: GPO, 1972.

McLean, Linda. "The Black Student in the White Independent School." Independent School Bulletin, F, 1969.

McManus, Luther M., Jr., and Cunningham, James J. The New Breed. Black Activists, 1969. ERIC ED 044 077.

McNeil, Albert J. "The Social Foundations of the Music of Black Americans." Music Education Journal 60(F, 1974):43-46, 81-82.

McPartland, James. "Should We Give Up School Desegregation?" Johns Hopkins Magazine 21 (Ap, 1970):20,25.

McPartland, James M., and Karweit, Nancy L. Methodological Issues in School Effects Research. Baltimore, MD: Center for Social Organization of Schools, Johns Hopkins U., F. 1978.

MacPhee, Barbara Campbell. Emergency School Assistance Program Community Grants. A Preliminary Report. Atlanta, GA: Southern Education Foundation, N, 1971.

McWilliams, Wilson Carey. The Idea of Fraternity in America. Berkeley, CA: U. of California Press, 1973.

Maddox, James G., with Liebhafsky, E. E., Henderson, Vivian W., and Hamlin, Herbert M. "Education and Southern Economic Growth." In The Advancing South: Manpower Prospects and Problems. New York: Twentieth Century Fund, 1967.

"Major [Northern] Cities Face School-Race Problems." Southern School News, N, 1963.

Maliver, Bernard L. "Education in the Ghetto: American vs. German." Integrated Education, Ag-S, 1966.

Mallery, David. Negro Students in Independent Schools. Boston: National Association of Independent Schools, 4 Liberty Square, 1964.

Manella, Raymond L. "Racially Integrating a State's Training Schools." Children, Mr-Ap, 1964.

Marable, Manning. "The Black Movement: A Psychopolitical Analysis." State and Mind 6(Spring, 1978).

_____. "The Post-Movement Reaction. Thoughts on Black Politics." Southern Exposure 7 (Spring, 1979):60-64.

Marburger, Carl L. "School and Community Roles in Effective Planning." Journal of Negro Education, Summer, 1964.

Marker, G. A. "Some Aspects of Educational Park Planning." Socio-Economic Planning Sciences 2(1969):155-166.

Marks, Russell. "Trackers, Testers, and Trustees." Doctoral dissertation, Harvard U., 1974.

Marland, Sidney P. "Ferment in the Schools." Children, Mr-Ap, 1965.

Marshall, Kim. Law and Order in Grade 6-E: A Story of Chaos and Innovation in a Ghetto School. Boston, MA: Little, Brown, 1972.

Martin, Donald F. "Adult Education: Implications for the Black Community." Adult Leadership 24(My, 1976):286-289.

Martin, James G. "Political Power and Discrimination in Education." Integrated Education, O-N, 1963.

_____. The Tolerant Personality. Detroit, MI: Wayne State U. Press, 1964.

Martin, William C. "Sociological Strategies in Urban Society: Intergroup Relations and Social Conflict." Journal of Social and Behavioral Sciences 18(Spring, 1972):2-13.

Martin Luther King, Jr. Washington, DC: National Education Association, 1969. [A memorial record]

Martin Luther King Memorial. 1968. Metropolitan Urban Service Training Facility (MUST), 235 East 49th St., N.Y., N.Y. 10017.

Marx, Gary T. "Status Insecurity and the Negro Intellectual." Berkeley Journal of Sociology, Spring, 1962.

_____. "Tolerance in Militancy." Nation, F, 1968.

_____. "The White Negro and the Negro White." Phylon, Summer, 1967.

Marx, Robert J. "For the Purpose of Racial Integration." Reform Judaism, O, 1972.

Mason, Major A. The Educational Programs and Activities of the Black Panther Party. Pittsburgh, PA: International and Development Education Program, 1976.

Mason, Philip. "A Democratic Dilemma: Consensus and Leadership." Race, Ap, 1969.

_____. "A Theory for Urban Education." Educational Theory, Ja, 1967.

_____. "Decline and Crisis in Big-City Education." Phi Delta Kappan, Mr, 1967.

_____. "Race Relations and Human Rights." Race, Jl, 1968.

Masters, Stanley H. "Are Black Migrants from the South to the Northern Cities Worse Off than Blacks Already There?" Journal of Human Resources 7(N, 1972):411-423.

Masurofsky, Mark. "The Title I Migrant Program: Passivity Perpetuates a Non-System of Education for Migrant Children." Inequality in Education 21(Je, 1976):11-24.

Matthews, Donald R., and Prothro, James W. Negroes and the New Southern Politics. New York: Harcourt, Brace and World, 1966.

Maxfield, Donald W. "School Desegregation and Overcrowding: A Mathematically Based Solution." Bulletin of the Georgia Academy of Science 28(1970).

_____. "Spatial Planning of School Districts." Annals of the Association of American Geographers 62(D, 1972):582-590.

May, Susan. "Civil Rights and Human Liberation." Integrateducation 12(S-O, 1974):15.

Mayer, Martin. "Stop Waiting for Miracles." PTA Magazine, N, 1966.

Mayeske, George W., Weinfeld, Frederic D., Tabler, Kenneth A., Cohen, Wallace M., Proshek, John M., and Beaton, Albert E., Jr. Correlational and Factorial Analyses of Items from the Educational Opportunities Survey Principal Questionnaire. Technical Note No. 62. Washington, DC: National Center for Educational Statistics, Mr, 1968.

Mayeske, George W., Tabler, Kenneth A., Weinfeld, Frederic D., and Beaton, Albert E., Jr. Correlational and Factorial Analyses of Items from the Ninth Grade Questionnaire of the Educational Opportunities Survey. Technical Note No. 59. Washington, DC: National Center for Educational Statistics, Mr, 1968.

Mayeske, George W., Tabler, Kenneth A., Proshek, John M., and Cohen, Wallace M. Correlational and Factorial Analyses of Items from the Twelfth Grade Student Questionnaire of the Educational Opportunities Survey. Technical Note No. 60. Washington, DC: National Center for Educational Statistics, Mr, 1968.

Mayeske, George W., Tabler, Kenneth A., Weinfeld, Frederic D., Beaton, Albert E., Jr., and Proshek, John M. Correlational and Regression Analyses of Differences Between the Achievement Levels of Ninth Grade Schools from the Educational Opportunities Survey. Technical Note No. 61. Washington, DC: National Center for Educational Statistics, Mr, 1968.

Mayeske, George W. and others. Item Response Analyses of the Educational Opportunities Survey. Principal Questionnaire. Technical Note No. 58. Washington, DC: National Center for Educational Statistics, Mr, 1968.

Mayeske, George W., Weinfeld, Frederic D., Beaton, Albert E., Jr., Davis, Walter, Fetters, William B., and Hixson, Eugene E. Item Response Analyses of the Educational Opportunities Survey Student Questionnaires. Technical Note No. 64. Washington, DC: National Center for Educational Statistics, Ap, 1968.

Mayeske, George W., Weinfeld, Frederic D., and Beaton, Albert E., Jr. Item Response Analyses of the Educational Opportunities Survey Teacher Questionnaire. Analytical Note No. 59. Washington, DC: Division of Operations Analysis, National Center for Educational Statistics, U.S. Office of Education, My, 1967.

Mayeske, George W., Wisler, Carl E., Beaton, Albert E., Jr., Weinfeld, Frederic D., Cohen, Wallace M., Okada, Tetsuo, Proshek, John M., and Tabler, Kenneth A. A Study of Our Nation's Schools. Washington, DC: U.S. Dept. of Health, Education and Welfare, Office of Education, n.d.

Mayeske, George W. and others. A Study of Our Nation's Schools. Washington, DC: GPO, 1972.

Mayo, A. D. "The Negro of the South. How Shall He Be Educated?" New England Magazine, n.s., 17:213.

Mays, Benjamin E. "The Role of the Schools in a Social Revolution." Teachers College Record, My, 1964.

Mboya, Tom. "The American Negro Cannot Look to Africa for an Escape." New York Times Magazine, Jl 13, 1969.

Meier, Deborah W. "The Coleman Report." Integrated Education, D, 1967-Ja, 1968.

Mercedes, Sister Maria. "Integration: Contrast in Freedom." Liberal Education, O, 1964.

Mercer, Walter A. Humanizing the Desegregated School. New York: Vantage Press, 1974.

Merelman, Richard M. "Social Mobility and Equal Opportunity." American Journal of Political Science 17(My, 1973):213-236.

Merrill, Charles. "Negroes in the Private Schools." Atlantic Monthly, Jl, 1967.

Meyers, Michael. "A Response to Raspberry." Integrateducation 12(S-O, 1974):33-34.

Michael, Donald N. The Next Generation. The Prospects Ahead for the Youth of Today and Tomorrow. New York: Random House, 1965.

Miller, Arthur H. "Political Issues and Trust in Government: 1964-1970." American Political Science Review 68(S, 1974):951-972. [See comment by Citrin and rejoinder by Miller, pp. 973-100]

Miller, Arthur H., Brown, Thad, and Raine, Alden. Social Conflict and Political Estrangement, 1958-1972. Ann Arbor, MI: Institute for Social Research, U. of Michigan, 1973.

Miller, Carroll L. "Educational Opportunities and the Negro Child in the South." Harvard Educational Review, Summer, 1960.

Miller, Carroll L., and Gregg, Howard D. "The Teaching Staff of the Negro Elementary School." Journal of Negro Education 1(J1, 1932):196-223.

Miller, Herman P., and Newman, Dorothy K. Social and Economic Conditions of Negroes in the United States. BLS Report No. 332. Current Population Reports, Series P-23, No. 24. Washington, DC: Government Printing Office, O, 1967.

Miller, Kelly. An Appeal to Conscience; America's Code of Caste a Disgrace to Democracy. New York: The Macmillan Company, 1918.

_____. "Education of the City Negro." Southern Workman 32(Ja, 1903):10.

_____. "The Education of the Negro." Journal of Social Science 39(N, 1901).

_____. The Education of the Negro. Washington, DC: Government Printing Office, 1902.

_____. The Everlasting Stain. Washington, DC: The Associated Publishers, 1924.

_____. The Primary Needs of the Negro Race. Washington, DC: Howard U. Press, 1899.

_____. Race Adjustment. New York and Washington, DC: The Neale Publishing Company, 1908.

Miller, La Mar P. "Integration and Ethnic Studies in Elementary and Secondary Schools." In Equality of Educational Opportunity, pp. 250-265. Edited by La Mar P. Miller and Edmund W. Gordon. New York: AMS Press, 1974.

Miller, La Mar P., and Sommerfeld, Donald A. The Black and White of Educational Research. Mr, 1970. ERIC ED 041 057.

Miller, Margaret L. "Your Homework Assignment for Tonight...Compassion, Empathy, and Understanding." Integrated Education 9 (My-Je, 1971):11-15.

Miller, S. M. "The American Lower Class: A Typological Approach." Social Research, Spring, 1964.

_____. "Dropouts: A Political Problem." Integrated Education, Ag, 1963.

_____. "The Politics of Poverty." Dissent, Spring, 1964.

Miller, S. M. "The Search for an Educational Revolution." In Hunnicutt (ed.), above.

_____. "Types of Equality: Sorting, Rewarding, Performing." In Education, Inequality and National Policy, pp. 15-43. Edited by Nelson F. Ashline, Thomas R. Pezzullo, and Charles I. Norris. Lexington, MA: Lexington Books, 1976.

Miller, S. M., and Rein, Martin. "Poverty and Social Change." American Child, Mr, 1964.

Miller, S. M., Rein, Martin, Roby, Pamela, and Gross, Bertram M. "Poverty, Inequality, and Conflict." Annals, S, 1967.

Milner, Murray, Jr. The Illusion of Equality: The Effects of Education on Opportunity, Inequality, and Social Conflict. San Francisco: Jossey-Bass, 1972.

Minard, George C. "Negro Education in the Northern States." Master's thesis, New York U., 1929.

Minor, Michael J., and Bradburn, Norman M. The Effects of Viewing "Feeling Good": Results from a Field Experiment in a Low-Income Community, Ap, 1976. ERIC ED 125 646.

Mirelowitz, Seymour, and Grossman, Leona. "Ethnicity: An Intervening Variable in Social Work Education." Journal of Education for Social Work 11(F, 1975):76-83.

Mitchell, Terence R., Dossett, Dennis L., and Fiedler, Fred E. Culture Training: Validation Evidence for the Culture Assimilator. AD-731 082. Springfield, VA: National Technical Information Service, Ag, 1971.

Mizell, M. Hayes, and Jenkins, H. Harrison. "A Divisive Issue: Freedom of Choice." Southern Education Report, Ja-F, 1968. [Pro and con]

Mochelmann, Jurgen. "Die Bildungs-chancen der Amerikanischen Neger und die Ueberwindung der Rassendiskriminierung in den U.S.A." Bildung und Erziehung, N-D, 1965.

Modiano, Nancy. Educational Anthropology: An Overview, 1970. ERIC ED 039 294.

Monroe, Paul. "Influence of the Growing Perception of Human Interrelationship on Education." American Journal of Sociology 18(1913):622-640.

Montagu, Ashley. "Just What is 'Equal Opportunity'?" Vista 6(1970):23-25, 56.

Monti, Daniel J., Jr. "Intervening in School
Desegregation: Some Political and Ethical
Considerations." Social Change 8(My, 1978):
1-6.

Moock, Peter R. "Education and the Transfer of
Inequality from Generation to Generation."
Teachers College Record 79(My, 1978):737-748.

Moore, Charles A. (ed.). The Status of the
Individual in East and West. Honolulu,
HI: U. of Hawaii Press, 1971.

Moore, Dan Emery. "School Segregation in
Southern Cities." Doctoral dissertation,
U. of Wisconsin, 1973. Univ. Microfilms
Order No. 73-21169. [1968 data]

Moore, G. Alexander, Jr. "An Ahtropological
View of Urban Education." Education and
Urban Society, Ag, 1969.

_____. Realities of the Urban Classroom:
Observations in Elementary Schools. New
York: Doubleday Anchor, 1967.

Moore, Jane Ann. "Review of Crain and Weisman,
Discrimination, Personality and Achievement-
A Survey of Northern Blacks." Contemporary
Sociology 3(My, 1974):257-259.

Moore, Ronnie M. 1967 School Board Seminar for
Newly Elected Members of Southern School
Boards. New York: Scholarship, Education,
and Defense Fund for Racial Equality, 1967.
ERIC ED 029 857.

Moore, Samuel A. II, and Woodard, Samuel L.
"School Desegregation: Localism and
Metropolitanism." School and Society,
Summer, 1966.

Moreno, Dan and others (eds.). The Political
Economy of Institutional Change: Proceed-
ings of the Ethnic Studies Symposium. 1977.
ERIC ED 148 537.

Morland, J. Kenneth (ed.). The Not So Solid
South: Anthropological Studies in a
Regional Subculture. Athens, GA: U. of
Georgia Press, 1971.

_____. School Desegregation---Help Needed?
Washington, DC: The Potomac Institute, 1962.

_____. Study of Desegregation Based on South-
ern Administrators' Reports. Washington,
DC: Potomac Institute, F, 1963.

Morlock, Laura L. "Black Power and Black Influence in 91 Northern Cities." Doctoral
dissertation, Johns Hopkins U., 1973.

Mornell, Eugene S., and Payne, Joseph F.
Resources for Planning and Implementing
School Desegregation. Riverside, CA:
Western Regional School Desegregation
Projects, U. of California, Riverside, Ap,
1971.

Morris, Joseph. "Personal Adjustment of the
High Achieving Negro Student." Doctoral
dissertation, U. of Michigan, 1968.

Morrison, Toni. "The Black Experience. A Slow
Walk of Trees (As Grandmother Would Say)
Hopeless (As Grandfather Would Say)."
New York Times Magazine, Jl, 1976.

_____. "On to Disneyland and the Real Un-
reality." New York Times, O 20, 1973.

Morsell, John A. "Racial Desegregation and
Integration in Public Education." Journal
of Negro Education, Summer, 1969.

Moseley, Francis S. "The Urban Secondary
School: Too Late for Mere Change." Phi
Delta Kappan (My, 1972):559-564.

Mosley, Doris Y. Nursing Students' Perceptions
of the Urban Poor. New York: National
League for Nursing, 1977.

Moskow, Michael H., and McLennan, Kenneth.
"Teacher Negotiations and School Decen-
tralization." In Community Control of
Schools. Edited by Henry M. Levin.
Washington, DC: Brookings, 1970.

Mouat, Lucia. "Desegregated Schools Tested."
Christian Science Monitor, N, 1968.

_____. "North Inches Toward Desegregation."
Christian Science Monitor, D, 1966.

Muhammad, Elijah. "Destruction of America's
Education." Muhammad Speaks, Je, 1970.

_____. "Messenger Muhammad Speaks on Educa-
tion." Muhammad Speaks, O, 1969.

_____. "Qualification Is a Must." Muhammad
Speaks, N, 1969.

Mullen, David J. Desegregation Questionnaire.
S, 1971. ERIC ED 057 098.

Mumford, Joy, Johnson, Scott and Toomsen, Amy.
"How I Would Integrate the Public Schools."
Integrateducation 14(Jl-Ag, 1976):20-21.

Munford, C. J. "Structure sociale et revolution noire en Amerique." L'homme et la
societe, F-Mr, 1971.

Murphy, Edgar Gardner. Problems of the
Present South. New York: 1904.

Murray, Albert. The Omni-Americans: New
Perspectives on Black Experience and
American Culture. New York: Outerbridge
and Dienstfrey, 1970.

Muse, Benjamin. The American Negro Revolution: From Nonviolence to Black Power, 1963-1967. Bloomington, IN: U. of Indiana Press, 1968.

Myers, David G., and Bishop, George D. "Discussion Effects on Racial Attitudes." Science 169(Ag, 1970):778-779.

Myers, Miles. "The Role of the AFT in School Desegregation." Changing Education, Fall, 1966.

Myers, Robert B. Problems in School Desegregation: Three Institutes for Public School, Junior College, and Professional Organization Leaders. Gainesville, FL: Florida U., 1960. ERIC ED 028 229.

Myrdal, Gunnar. "The American Dilemma: 1967." (An interview by Donald McDonald) Center Magazine, O-N, 1967.

_____. "How Scientific are the Social Sciences?" Journal of Social Issues 28 (1972):151-170.

NAACP. NAACP Report on Quality Education for Black Americans: An Imperative. New York: NAACP, S, 1977.

NAACP. Racial Inequalities in Education. New York: NAACP, 1938.

National Academy of Sciences. America's Uncounted People. My, 1972. Washington, DC: Printing and Publishing Office, National Academy of Sciences, 2101 Constitution Ave., N.W., Washington, DC 20418.

National Advisory Council. Schools for an Open Society." Integrated Education, Mr-Ap, 1968.

National Center for Education Statistics. The Condition of Education. A Statistical Report on the Condition of Education in the United States. Washington, DC: GPO, Mr, 1976.

National Commission on Urban Problems. Building the American City. Washington, DC: Government Printing Office, 1969. U.S. Congress, 91st, 1st session, House Document 91-34.

_____. Hearings. Vol. 5. Washington, DC: Government Printing Office. [Detroit, East St. Louis, St. Louis, Washington, DC]

National Committee for Support of the Public Schools. Education and Social Change. Proceedings of the 4th Annual Conference...1966. Washington, DC: The Committee, 1424 16th St., N.W., Washington, DC 20036.

National Conference of Christians and Jews. National Conference on Quality Integrated Education. Reports of Conference Discussion Groups--Resolutions. New York: NCCJ, 1973.

National Education Association. "Desegregation in the Public Schools." Integrated Education, Ag-S, 1966.

NEA Committee on Professional Ethics. "Discrimination and Professional Ethics." Today's Education, Mr, 1971.

NEA. Local Associations Speak on Reducing Racial Barriers. Washington, DC: National Education Association, 1965.

"NEA Sidesteps the Real Issue." America, Jl, 1956.

National Goals Research Staff. Toward Balanced Growth: Quantity With Quality. Washington, DC: Government Printing Office, Jl, 1970.

National Institute of Education. Demonstration Studies of Funds Allocation within Districts. Washington, DC: NIE, 1977.

National Institute of Mental Health. The Mental Health of Urban America. The Urban Programs of the National Institute of Mental Health. Washington, DC: Government Printing Office, 1969.

National Study of Secondary School Evaluation. Evaluative Criteria For the Evaluation of Secondary Schools. 4th edition. Washington, DC: The Study, 1969.

National Urban League, Inc. The State of Black America 1977. New York: National Urban League, Inc., 1977.

Neff, Ted. "What Do We Know About Desegregation?" California Education, Mr, 1965.

"The Negro Common Schools." Outlook (Jl, 1902):676-677.

"Negro Public Schools." Independent 73(Jl, 1912):217-219.

"'Neighborhood' School Systems in Danger? Story Back of School Boycotts." U.S. News and World Report, Mr, 1964.

Neighborhood Schools vs. Integration---Questions and Answers. New York State Conference of the NAACP, 2 Croydon Rd., Amityville, NY 11701.

Nelson, Harold A. "Charity, Poverty, and Race." Phylon, Fall, 1968.

Nelson, Lester W. "Educational Opportunity and the Small Secondary School." Bulletin of the National Association of Secondary School Principals, Ap, 1964.

Nestingen, Ivan A. "Challenge to the Schools." Integrated Education, D, 1963-Ja, 1964.

Neufville, Richard De, and Connor, Caryl. "How Good Are Our Schools? Armed Forces Qualification Test Provides a Clue." American Education, O, 1966.

"New Principles of School Site Selection." American School Board Journal, Jl, 1966.

Newman, Dorothy K. and others. The Negroes in the United States: Their Economic and Social Situation. Washington, DC: Government Printing Office, Je, 1966. [A 241-page handbook]

Newman, Dorothy K. "The Negro's Journey to the City - Part I." Monthly Labor Review, My, 1966.

Newman, G. R. "A Sociological Approach to the Problem of Educational Segregation." Slow Learning Child, #1, 1969.

Newman, Jeremiah. Race: Migration and Integration. New York: Taplinger, 1967.

Newton, Eunice Shaed. "Planning for the Language Development of Disadvantaged Children and Youth." Journal of Negro Education, Summer, 1964.

Newton, Eunice Shaed, and West, Earle H. "The Progress of the Negro in Elementary and Secondary Education." Journal of Negro Education, Fall, 1963.

Nickel, James W. "Classification by Race in Compensatory Programs." Ethics 84(Ja, 1974): 146-150.

Nicolas, Guy. "Fait 'ethnique' et usages du concept d' 'ethnie.'" Cahiers internationaux de sociologie 54(1973):95-126.

Nielsen, Margaret O. "Enforcing Desegregation Policy: Changing Racial Segregation in Urban School Districts, 1967-1972." Doctoral dissertation, U. of Michigan, 1977. Univ. Microfilms Order No. 78-04783.

Nielsen, Waldeman S. "Big Philanthropy and the Race Question: A Case Study of Performance." In The Big Foundations, ch. 18. New York: Twentieth Century Fund, 1972.

Niemeyer, John H. "The Bank Street Readers: Support for Movement Toward an Integrated Society." Reading Teacher, Ap, 1965.

Nishioka, Gail A. "Ethnic Studies: Educations for Integration." Master's thesis, U. of California, Davis, 1972.

Nixon, John W. "To Live and Die in Dixie." In The Rising South, II, pp. 95-116. Edited by Robert H. McKenzie. University of Alabama Press, 1976.

Noel, Donald. "Group Identification among Negroes: An Empirical Analysis." Journal of Social Issues 20(Ap, 1964):71-84.

_____. "A Theory of the Origin of Ethnic Stratification." Social Problems, Fall, 1968.

Noland, James R., and Rand, E. W. Special Training Institute on Problems of School Desegregation. Final Report. Houston, TX: Saint Thomas U., Je, 1968. ERIC ED 026 433.

Norisett, Lloyd N. "Preschool Education: Report on a Conference." Items (Social Science Research Council), Je, 1966.

Northcott, Herbert C. and others. "Trends in TV Portrayal of Blacks and Women." Journalism Quarterly 52(Winter, 1975):741-744.

Novak, Benjamin J. "Problems and Dilemmas in Urban School Integration." Education, F-Mr, 1968.

Obadele, Imari Abubakari, I. "On the Matter of Black Survival." Ebony 29(My, 1974):84-85. [President of the Provisional Government of The Republic of Africa]

O'Brien, Richard J. A Model for the Determination of School Attendance Areas Under Specified Objectives and Constraints. Technical Note No. 55. Washington, DC: Divisions of Operations Analysis. National Center for Educational Statistics, U.S. Office of Education, Ja, 1968.

O'Brien, Richard J., and Lyle, Jerolyn R. Outline of an Urban Educational Model. Technical Note No. 57. Washington, DC: Division of Operations Analysis. National Center for Educational Statistics, U.S. Office of Education, Ja, 1968.

O'Dell, J. H. "On the Transition from Civil Rights to Civil Equality." (Part 1) Freedomways 18(2nd Quarter, 1978):56-69.

Office of Child Development. Toward Reflective Analysis of Black Families, N, 1976. ERIC ED 133 416.

Office for Civil Rights, U.S. Dept. of H.E.W. [Tables on the extent of Interracial schooling in the United States] Integrated Education 9(Mr-Ap, 1971):40-43.

Ogbu, John. Minority Education and Caste: The American System in Cross-Cultural Perspective.

_____. "School Desegregation in Racially Stratified Communities---A Problem of Congruence." Anthropology and Education Quarterly 9(Winter, 1978):290-292.

O'Gorman, Hubert J. "Pluralistic Ignorance and White Estimates of White Support for Racial Segregation." Public Opinion Quarterly 39 (Fall, 1975):313-330.

Ohio Education Association. Desegregation: Its Impact on Quality Education, Je, 1977. ERIC ED 150 219.

Okada, Tetsuo, Stoller, David S., and Weinfeld, Frederic D. Dynamics of Achievement. Differential Growth of Achievement for Negro and White Students by S.M.S.A./Non-S.M.S.A. and Region. Technical Note No. 54. Washington, DC: Division of Operations Analysis, National Center for Educational Statistics, U.S. Office of Education, Ja, 1968.

_____, _____ and _____. Dynamics of Achievement: Differential Growth of Achievement for Negro and White Students by SMSA/Non-SMSA and Region. Washington, DC: National Center for Educational Statistics (HEW), Divisions of Operations Analysis, 1968. ERIC ED 021 940.

_____, _____ and _____. Dynamics of Achievement: A Study of Differential Growth of Achievement Over Time. Technical Note No. 53. Washington, DC: Division of Operations, Analysis, National Center for Educational Statistics, U.S. Office of Education, Ja, 1968.

Okia, Martha Gray. A Programmed Foundation for an Adult Education Program in Black Identity for the Congress of Racial Equality, Je, 1969. ERIC ED 037 661.

Olbert, K. "Quality Through Racial Balance: It Isn't That Easy." Ohio Schools, Ja, 1967.

Olkinuora, Erkki. "On the Problems of Developing Educational Indicators." Acta Sociologica 16(1973):284-302. [See commentary by Lena Johansson, pp. 303-304.]

"Open Letter to U.S. President Jimmy Carter from RNA President Imari Abubakari Obadele, 1." Black Scholar 10(O, 1978):53-67.

Ordway, John S. "What Is Violence?" Psychiatry Digest, Ap, 1972.

O'Reilly, Robert C. "Racially Integrated Schools and the Future of Public Education." Educational Leadership 27(My, 1970):837-840.

Orfield, Gary. Desegregation and the Cities-- The Trends and Policy Choices. Washington, DC: GPO, 1977. [U.S. Congress, 95th, 1st session, Senate Committee on Human Resources, Committee Print]

_____. Must We Bus? Washington, DC: Brookings Institution, 1978.

_____. "School Integration and Its Academic Critics." Civil Rights Digest 5(Summer, 1973):2-10.

_____. "Will Separate Be More Equal?" Integrateducation 14(Ja-F, 1976).

Ornstein, Allan C. "The Myths of Liberalism and School Integration." School and Society 99 (N, 1971):436-439.

Orshansky, Mollie. "Children of the Poor." Social Security Bulletin, Jl, 1963.

Orun, Anthony M. "A Reappraisal of the Social and Political Participation of Negroes." American Journal of Sociology, Jl, 1966.

O'Shea, David W. (ed.). Sociology of the School and Schooling. Proceedings of the Second Annual Conference of the Sociology of Education Association. Washington, DC: National Institute of Education, 1974.

Ovington, Mary White. "Closing the Little Black School House." Survey 24(My, 1910):343-345.

Owen, Chandler. "Mistakes of Kelly Miller. Reply to Kelly Miller on Segregation in Education." Messenger 4(Je, 1922):422-424; 443-445.

Owen, John D. Educational Opportunity, Democratic Theory, and the Economics of Educational Subsidy. Baltimore, MD: Johns Hopkins U., Center for the Study of Social Organization of Schools, 1968. ERIC ED 026 722.

Palen, J. John, and Schnore, Leo F. "Color Composition and City-Suburban Status Differences: A Replication and Extension." Land Economics, F, 1965.

Panel on Educational Research and Development. "The Deprived and the Segregated." In Innovation and Experiment in Education, Progress Report, pp. 29-38. Washington, DC: GPO, 1964.

Parenti, Michael. Power and the Powerless. New York: St. Martin's Press, 1978.

Parson, Talcott, and Clark, Kenneth B. (eds.). The Negro American. Boston: Houghton Mifflin, 1966.

Pascal, Anthony H. Racial Discrimination in Organized Baseball. Santa Monica, CA: Rand, 1970.

Pasnick, Ray. "School Segregation--North and West." American Federationist, Jl, 1963.

Passi, Michael. "The Irony of Ethnic Studeis in America." Doctoral dissertation, U. of Minnesota, 1972.

Passonneau, Joseph R., and Wurman, Richard S. An Urban Atlas of 20 American Cities. Cambridge, MA: M.I.T. Press, 1966.

Passow, S. Harry. American Secondary Education. The Conant Influence. Reston, VA: National Association of Secondary School Principals, 1977.

_____. "Compensatory Instructional Interven-
tion." In Review of Research in Education 2,
pp. 145-175. Edited by Fred N. Kerlinger
and John B. Carroll. Itasca, IL: Peacock,
1974.

_____. "Urban Education in the 1970's."
Interchange 1(1970):28-43.

Patterson, Orlando. "The Essays of James
Baldwin." New Left Review 26(Summer, 1964):
31-38.

_____. Ethnic Chauvinism: The Reactionary
Impulse. New York: Stein and Day, 1977.

_____. "Ethnicity and the Pluralist Fallacy."
Change 7(Mr, 1975):10-11.

_____. "The Moral Crisis of the Black Ameri-
can." Public Interest 32(Summer, 1973):43-
69.

Pattison, Rose Mary (ed.). Counseling Educationally Disadvantaged Adults. Proceedings
of Intstitute Series. Indianapolis, IN:
Indiana State Dept. of Public Instruction,
1968. ERIC ED 023 015.

Pauker, C. J. Black Nationalism and Prospects
for Violence in the Ghetto. Santa Monica,
CA: Rand, 1969.

Payne, E. George. An Estimate of Our Negro
Schools. New York: American Church
Institute for Negroes, 1930.

_____. "Negroes in the Public Elementary
Schools of the North." Annals 140(N, 1928):
244-253.

Peck, Sidney, and Cohen, David K. "The Social
Context of De Facto School Segregation."
Western Reserve Law Review, Ap, 1965.

Pennock, J. Roland, and Chapman, John W. (eds.).
Equality: Nomos IX. New York: Atherton,
1967.

Perlman, Leonard. "The Neighborhood School and
School Integration in the North." Contem-
porary Issues, Spring, 1965. P.O. Box 2357,
Church Street Station, New York, NY 10008.

Perlmutter, Philip. "Prejudice and Discrimination." Massachusetts Teacher 50(Ja, 1971):
12-14.

_____. "Suburbia and Human Rights." New York
State Education, Mr, 1969.

Perry, George. "The Burden of Integration."
Independent School Bulletin 33(My, 1974):
41-44.

Persell, Caroline H. Education and Inequality:
A Theoretical and Empirical Synthesis.
New York: Free Press, 1977.

Pettigrew, Thomas F. "A Sociological View of
the Post-Bradley Era." Wayne Law Review 21
(Mr, 1975):813-832.

_____. A Study of School Integration. Final
Report, Ag, 1970. ERIC ED 044 468.

_____. The Case for School Integration, 1968.
ERIC ED 030 695.

_____. "Continuing Barriers to Desegregated
Education in the South." Sociology of Education, Ja, 1965.

_____. "The Cold Structural Inducements to
Integration." Urban Review 8(Summer, 1975):
137-144.

_____. "Desegregation and Its Chances for
Success: Northern and Southern Views."
Social Forces 35(1957):339-344.

_____. "De Facto Segregation, Southern Style."
Integrated Education, O-N, 1963.

_____. "For Desegregation, a Broader Game
Plan." Los Angeles Times, N 19, 1978.
[Metropolitan desegregation]

_____. "The Negro and Education: Problems
and Proposals." In Race and the Social
Sciences. Edited by Irwin Katz and Patricia
Gurin. New York: Basic Books, 1969.

_____. Profile of the Negro American.
Princeton, NJ: Van Nostrand, 1964.

_____. "Public Policy and Desegregation Re-
search." Integrated Education (Ja-F, 1972):
18-22.

_____. "Racially Separate or Together?"
Integrated Education (Ja-F, 1969):36-56.

_____. Racially Separate or Together? New
York: Anti-Defamation League, Ap, 1969.

_____. "School Desegreation." Consultants'
Papers. The White House Conference on Educa-
tion, Vol. II, July 20-21, 1965. Washington,
DC: GPO, 1965.

_____. "School Desegregation: Expanding Edu-
cational Opportunities to All Americans."
In Guidance in American Education III: Needs
and Influencing Forces. Cambridge, MA:
Harvard U. Press, 1966.

_____. "School Integration in Current Perspec-
tive." Urban Review, Ja, 1969.

Pettigrew, Thomas F., and Cramer, M. Richard.
"The Demography of Desegregation."
Journal of Social Issues, XV, 4(1959).

Pettigrew, Thomas F., and Back, Kurt W. "Soc-
iology in the Desegregation Process: Its
Use and Disuse." In The Uses of Sociology,
pp. 692-722. Edited by Paul F. Lazarsfeld,
William H. Sewell and Harold L. Wilensky.
New York: Basic Books, 1967.

Pettigrew, Thomas F., and Pajonas, Patricia J.
"Social Psychological Considerations of
Racially Imblanced Schools." [Paper presented at New York Education Department Conference, March, 1964, and included as reference material in Report of the Advisory
Committee on Racial Imbalance and Education
of the Massachusetts State Board of Education, April, 1965.]

Pfautz, Harold W. "The American Dilemma: Per-
spectives and Proposals for White Americans."
In Urban Violence. Edited by Charles U.
Daly. Chicago: U. of Chicago Press, 1969.

"Phi Delta Kappa Repeals 'White Clause.'"
Quarterly Review of Higher Education Among
Negroes, Jl, 1942.

Pickens, William. "Types of Southern Schools."
Crisis, My, 1937.

Pierce, David H. "Use the Public School."
Crisis, O, 1924.

Pierce, Truman M. and others. White and Negro
Schools in the South. An Analysis of Bi-
racial Education. New York: Prentice-Hall,
1955.

Pilisuk, Marc. "Basic Educatin and Youth
Socialization." American Journal of Orthopsychiatry, O, 1968. [Reply to Little,
above]

Pinkney, Alphonse. Black Americans.
Englewood Cliffs, NJ: Prentice-Hall, 1969.

Piper, Henry Dan. Frederick Douglass and
Colloquial American Prose Style: A Study in
Language Proficiency and Cultural Dominance,
1977. ERIC ED 157 055.

Pitts, James P. "Black High School Students: A
Generation of Change." Doctoral dissertation, Northwestern U., 1971.

_____ (ed.). "Working Papers in the Study of
Race Consciousness." Journal of Black
Studies 5(Mr, 1975).

Piven, Frances Fox, and Cloward, Richard A.
Poor People's Movements. Why They Succeed,
How They Failed. New York: Pantheon, 1977.

Plattor, Stanton D. Preliminary Findings from
a Longitudinal Educational Improvement
Project Being Conducted for Instructionally
Improverished Pupils in Intact Schools in the
Urban South. Southern Association of Col-
leges and Schools. New Orleans, LA: New
Orleans Education Improvement Project, n.d.
ERIC ED 020 021.

Plaut, Richard L. "A Second Front in the Fight
on Segregated Education." Crisis, Jl, 1950.

_____. "Variables Affecting the Scholastic
Achievement of Negro Children in Non-Segre-
gated Schools." Social Problems, Ap, 1955.

Ploughman, T., Darnton, W., and Heuser, W. "An
Assignment Program to Establish School
Attendance Boundaries and Forecast Construction Needs." Socio-Economic Planning Sciences
1(1968):243-258.

Plumpp, Sterling D. Black Rituals. Chicago,
IL: Third World Press, 1972.

Podhoretz, Norman. "School Integration and
Liberal Opinion." Commentary 53(Mr, 1972):7.

Poinsett, Alex. "The Dixie Schools Charade."
Ebony 26(Ag, 1971):144-148.

_____. "Push for Excellence." Ebony 32
(F, 1977):104-111.

Pollard, Diane S. "Educational Achievement and
Ethnic Group Membership." Comparative Education Review 17(O, 1973):362-374.

Polley, John W. and others. Problems Connected
with Equalization of Educational Opportunity,
Jl, 1970. ERIC ED 046 098.

Popkewitz, Thomas S. "Educational Reform and
the Problem of Institutional Life." Educational Researcher 8(Mr, 1979):3-8.

Porter, Jennie D. "The Problem of Negro Education in Northern and Border Cities." Doctoral
dissertation, U. of Cincinnati, 1928.

Porter, John. "Equality and Education--Part 1."
Integrateducation 13(Jl-Ag, 1975):17-20.

Porter, Lyman W., and Dubin, Robert. Communication in Racially Integrated Organizations.
Springfield, VA: Clearinghouse for Federal
Scientific and Technical Information, Je 15,
1970.

Powledge, Fred. "Black Power, White Resistance."
Notes on the New Civil War. Cleveland, OH:
World, 1967.

_____. "Segregation, Northern Style."
American Education, D, 1966-Ja, 1967.

Preserving the Right to an Education for All
Children, Ap 5, 1967. Citizens Committee
for Children of New York, 112 East 19th
Street, New York, NY 10010. [On suspending
children from school]

President's Commission on Income Maintenance
Programs. Background Papers. Washington,
DC: GPO, 1970.

President's Task Force on Manpower Conservation. One-third of a Nation. A Report on Young Men Found Unqualified for Military Service. Washington, DC: GPO, 1964.

Price, Daniel O. Changing Characteristics of the Negro Population. Washington, DC: GPO, 1969.

Price, Richard A., and Clarke, Daniel H. "Race Relations in Television News: A Content Analysis of the Networks." Journal Quarterly 50(Summer, 1973):319-328.

Problems in Planning Urban School Facilities. Washington, DC: GPO, 1964.

Proceeding of the First National Association of African American Education Conference. Lincoln University, PA, Je, 1968.

Proctor, Samuel. Racial Insularity and the National Purpose. Washington, DC: Association of American Colleges, Ja 15, 1969. ERIC ED 026 957.

_____. The Young Negro in America: 1960-1980. New York: Association Press, 1966.

Profit, Wesley E. "Self Definition of Blackness." Harvard Crimson, My 21, 1974.

Project NECESSITIES: Phase I Report. Cambridge, MA: Abt Associates, Inc., Salt Lake City, Utah: U. of Utah, 1969. ERIC ED 049 846.

Project NECESSITIES: Phase II. Volume I: Summary and Recommendations, Liaison Network, Appendices. Cambridge, MA: Abt Associates, Inc., 1969. ERIC ED 049 847.

Project NECESSITIES: Phase II, Vol. II, People, Places and Things. Cambridge, MA: Abt Associates, Inc., D, 1969. ERIC ED 049 848.

Project NECESSITIES: Phase II, Vol. III: Communication Skills--Fact and Opinion. Cambridge, MA: Abt Associates, Inc, D, 1969. ERIC ED 049 849

Project NECESSITIES: Phase II. Vol. IV: Economics--The Science of Survival. Cambridge, MA: Abt Associates, Inc., D, 1969. ERIC ED 049 850.

Project NECESSITIES: Phase III. Vol. V: Teaching Materials for Second and Third Grades. Cambridge, MA: Abt Associates, Inc., Jl, 1969.

"Public Schools in Southern Cities." Southern Workman 34(N, 1905):615.

Purdon, Eric. Black Company: The Story of Subchaser 1264. New York: McKay, 1972. [World War II]

"Quality Education: The Goal of the NEA." Georgia Education Journal 27(S, 1960):16.

Rafky, David M. "Blue-Collar Power." The Social Impact of Urban School Custodians", Part II." Urban Education 7(Ap, 1972):5-32.

Rainwater, Lee. "The Problem of Lower Class Culture." Journal of Social Issues 26(Spring, 1970):133-148.

Raitz, Karl B. "Ethnic Maps of North America." Geographical Review, 68(Jl, 1978):335-350.

Ramirez, Antonio. "The Open Society on Ethnic Quotas." New York Teacher, Mr 10, 1974, [Ethnic quotas in governance of NEA]

Ramsoy, Matalie Rogoff. "On the Flow of Talent in Society." Acta Sociologia 9(1965).

Randolph, A. Philip. "Segregation in the Public Schools. A Promise or Menace." Messenger 6(Je, 1924):185-188.

Ransford, Edward H. Race and Class in American Society: Black, Chicano, Anglo. Cambridge, MA.: Schenkman, 1977.

Raskin, A. H. "Shanker's Great Leap." New York Times Magazine, S 9, 1973.

Raths, L. E., and Schweickert, E. F. "Social Acceptance with Interracial School Groups." Education Research Bulletin, Ap, 1946.

Ravitch, Diane. "Integration, Segregation, Pluralism." American Scholar 45(Spring, 1976):206-217.

_____. The Revisionists Revised. A Critique of the Radical Attack on the Schools. New York: Basic Books, 1978.

"Reading Programs: A Look as Distar." Interracial Books for Children 5(1974).

Wilson Record. "Changing Attitudes of School Personnel." Integrated Education, O-N, 1964.

Redclay, Edward E. County Training Schools and Public Secondary Education of the Negro in the South. Washington, DC: John F. Slater Fund, 1935.

_____. Public Secondary Schools for Negroes in the Southern States of the United States. Washington, DC: Trustees of the John F. Slater Fund, 1935.

Redl, Fritz. "The Nature and Nuture of Prejudice." Childhood Education, Ja, 1969.

Redl, Fritz, Polier, Justine Wise, Saltzman, Henry, Black, Algeron, and Danzig, David. "Education and the National Conscience." Conference, 1964. New York: Bank Street College of Education, 1964.

Reece, Ray, Jr. "Racial Intellectuals Form Organizations." Guardian, Ap 6, 1968.

Reed, Harold J. "Guidance and Counseling." Journal of Negro Education, Summer, 1964.

Rees, T. B. "Accommodation, Integration, Cultural Pluralism, and Assimilation: Their Place in Equilibrium Theories of Society." Race 11(1970):481-490.

Reid, Ira De Augustine. Adult Education Among Negroes. Washington, DC: The Associates in Negro Folk Education, 1936.

_____. The Negro Immigrant, His Background, Characteristics and Social Adjustment, 1899-1937. New York: N.p., 1939.

Reid, John D. "Black Urbanization of the South." Phylon 35(S, 1974):259-267.

Rein, Martin, and Miller, S. M. "The Demonstration Project as a Strategy." In Organizing for Community Welfare. Edited by Mayer N. Zald. Chicago, IL: Quadrangle, 1967.

Rentsch, George. "Open Enrollment: An Appraisal." Doctoral dissertation, State University of New York at Buffalo, 1966.

"Research and Reference Service." Desegregation in Education, 1964-1965. Washington, DC: U.S. Information Agency, Ag, 1965.

Reynolds, Barbara. "Patricia Harris, the No-Nonsense Chief of HUD." Chicago Tribune Magazine, Ja 14, 1979.

Reynolds, V. "Human Racial Variation: Current Knowledge and Future Trends." New Community 3(Winter-Spring, 1974):31-35.

Ribich, Thomas I. "The Case for Equal Educational Opportunity." In Schooling a Corporate Society. The Political Economy of Education in America. Edited by Martin Carnoy. New York: McKay, 1972, pp. 123-139.

Rice, Arthur H. "Rigid Integration Policy Ignores Community Values." Nation's Schools 85(Mr, 1970).

Rich, Cynthia Jo. "The Civil Right Decision Process." Race Relations Reporter 4(S, 1973):30-34.

Richmond, Anthony H. "Migration, Ethnicity and Race Relations." Ethnic and Racial Studies 1(Ja, 1978):1-18.

Riedesel, Paul L., and Blocker, Jean T. "Race Prejudice, Status Prejudice, Socioeconomic Status." Sociology and Social Research 62(J1, 1968):558-571.

Riga, Peter L. "How to Integrate Public Schools." National Catholic Reporter, Ja 12, 1973.

Riggan, Will. "Education for Indoctrination and Social Control." Integrateducation 16(N-D, 1978):2-8.

Riley, Clayton. "Civil War at CORE." Village Voice, S 4, 1978.

Rilling, Paul M. "Desegregation: The South Is Different." New Republic, My 16, 1970.

Rist, Ray. "Imperatives of Integration." Society 14(My-Je, 1977):32-34.

_____. "Why Public Schools Don't Change: An Assessment of Current Attempts at Educational Reform in the United States." Australian and New Zealand Journal of Sociology 10(F, 1974): 26-30.

Ritterband, Paul. Education, Employment, and Immigration. Israel in Comparative Perspective. New York: Cambridge U. Press, 1978. [Israeli students in the U.S.]

Rivlin, Alice M., and Martin, Ruby G. Equal Opportunity Goal Setting, Ja 17, 1969. [Memorandum of Assistant Secretary for Planning and Evaluation and Director, Office of Civil Rights, HEW to Secretary, HEW]

Robert, Charles E. Negro Civilization in the South. Nashville, TN: N.p., 1880.

Roberts, Albert R. Sourcebook on Prison Education: Past, Present, and Future. Springfield, IL: Charles C. Thomas, 1971.

Roberts, Churchill. "The Presentation of Blacks in Television Network Newscasts." Journalism Quarterly 52(1975).

Robey, John S. "The Politics of School Segregaton: A Comparative Analysis of Policy Outcome in Southern Counties." Doctoral disseration, U. of Georgia, 1970.

Robinson, John P., and Shaver, Phillip R. Measure of Social Psychological Attitudes. Ann Arbor, MI: Institute for Social Research, U. of Michigan, 1969.

Robinson, Robert V., and Bell, Wendell. "Equality, Success, and Social Justice in England and the United States." American Sociological Review 43(Ap, 1978):125-143.

Rodgers, Harrell R., Jr., and Bullock, Charles III. "School Desegregation: A Policy Analysis." Journal of Black Studies 2(Je, 1972): 409-437.

Roessler, Richard. (ed.). The 1970's--Decade for Survival. Riverside, California: Western Regional School Desegregation Projects, University of California, Riverside, 1971. [Transcript of a conference]

Rokeach, Milton. "Change and Stability in American Value Systems, 1968-1971." Public Opinion Quarterly 37(Summer, 1974):222-238.

Rooney, Robert C. (ed.). Equal Opportunity in the United States. A Symposium on Civil Rights. Austin, TX: Lyndon B. Johnson School of Public Affairs, U. of Texas, 1973.

Roosevelt, Eleanor. "Segregation." Educational Forum 24(N, 1959):5-6.

Rose, David. Establishment of Agency Equal Opportunity Objectives and Accompanying Report System, Jl 5, 1968. [Memorandum from Special Assistant to the U.S. Attorney General for Title VI of the Civil Rights Act of 1964 to the Attorney General]

Rosen, Bernard C. "Attitude Changes Within the Negro Press Toward Segregation Discrimination." Journal of Social Psychology 62(F, 1964):77-84.

Rosenberg, Mae R. Early Childhood Education: Perspectives on the Federal and Office of Education Roles. Menlo Park, CA: Stanford Research Institute, Jl, 1972.

Ross, E. Lamar. Cluster Analysis in Minority Group Poverty Studies. Paper, Annual Meeting of the American Anthropological Association, San Diego, CA, 1970. ERIC ED 045 796.

Rossell, Christine. "The Mayor's Role in School Desegregation Implementation." Urban Education 12(O, 1977):247-269.

Rossi, Peter H. "The Future of Race Relations in the U.S.: Some Progress and Directions for Research." Negro Educational Review 22 (Ja, 1971):3-23.

_____. "New Directions for Race Relations Research in the Sixties." Review of Religious Research 5(Spring, 1964):125-132.

Rossi, Peter H. and others. "The Theory and Practice of Applied Social Research." Evaluation Quarterly 2(My, 1978):171-191.

Roth, Maury. "Those Ethnicity Commercials." Integrateducation 2(Ja-F, 1975):12.

Rothbart, Myron. "Achieving Racial Equality: An Analysis of Resistance to Social Reform." In Towards the Elimination of Racism, pp. 341-375. Edited by Phyllis A. Katz. New York: Pergamon, 1976.

Rothman, David J., and Rothman, Shelia M. (eds.). On Their Own: The Poor in Modern America. Reading, MA: Addison-Wesley, 1972.

Rousseve, Ronald J. "Social Hypocrisy and the Promise of Integrated Education." Integrated Education 7(N-D, 1968):42-50.

Rubin, Israel. "Ethnicity and Cultural Pluralism." Phylon 36(Summer, 1975):140-148.

Rubin, Lillian. "An Interview," by Carl E. Rydingsword, pp. 132-141. In Norene Harris, Nathaniel Jackson, and Carl Rydingsword and contributors, The Integration of American Schools: Problems, Experiences, Solutions. Boston, MA: Allyn and Bacon, 1975.

Rubin, Samuel S., and Porciotto, Alice. Racial Integration in School and Society. New York: Vantage Press, 1974.

Ruffer, William A. "Symposium on the Problems of the Black Athlete." Journal of Health, Physical Education and Recreation 42(F, 1971): 11-12, 15.

Ruke, John, and Eatman, John. "Effects of Racial Composition on Small Work Groups." Small Group Behavior 8(N, 1977):479-489.

Runciman, W. G. "Race and Social Stratification." Race 13(Ap, 1972):497-509.

Rungeling, Brian. Employment, Income and Welfare in the Rural South. New York: Praeger Special Studies, 1977.

Russell, Dorothy S., and Rogers, Joseph F. "Exploring Desegregation through a Case Study Approach." Social Studies 69(Ja-F, 1978):25-30.

Russell, Michele. "Erased, Debased, and Encased: The Dynamics of Africa Educational Colonization in America." College English 31(Ap, 1970):671-681.

Rustin, Bayard. "Is Affirmative Action Reverse Discrimination?" Community (Chicago) 34 (Spring, 1975):10-15.

_____. "Man, One in Beauty and in Depravity." Integrated Education 9(Ja-F, 1971):16-20.

Sadezsky, H. "The Geographical Pattern of School Desegregation in the Soth." Master's thesis, Michigan State U., 1958.

St. John, Nancy Hoyt. "De Facto Segregation and Interracial Association in High School." Sociology of Education, Summer, 1964.

_____. "Desegregation: Voluntary or Mandatory?" Integrated Education (Ja-F, 1972):7-16.

_____. "Negro Children in Our Northern Schools." Unpublished paper, My, 1960, Boston.

Salamon, Lester M., and Van Evera, Stephen. "Fear, Apthy, and Discrimination: A Text of Explanations of Political Participation. Aurenean Political Science Review 67(D, 1973): 1288-1306; also 1319-1326.

Saltman, Juliet Z. "Integration Attitude Differentials and the Social Situation." Phylon 32(Fall, 1971):312-325.

Sampson, William A., and Milam, Vera. "The Intraracial Attitudes of the Black Middle Class: Have They Changed?" Social Problems 23(D, 1975):153-165. [Chicago and Evanston, IL]

Sampson, William A., and Williams, Ben. "School Desegregation: The Non-Traditional Sociological Perspective." Journal of Negro Education 47(Winter, 1978):72-80.

Sanchy, George I. "The Equalization of Educational Opportunity--Some Issues and Problems." University of New Mexico Bulletin, Educational series 10(1939):1-47.

Sanchez, Ramon. "Scenario for a Ghetto School System." Urban Review 6(My, 1973): 8-11.

Sanday, Peggy Reeves. "Cultural and Structural Pluralism in the United States." Edited by Sanday. Anthropology and the Public Interest. New York: Academic Press, 1976.

Sanders, Charles L. (ed.). Black Agenda for Social Work Education in the 70's. Afram Associates, 68-72 East 131st Street, Harlem, NY 10037.

_____. "A Frank Interview with Roy Wilkins." Ebony 29(Ap, 1974):35-42.

_____. "Growth of the Association of Black Social Workers." Social Casework 51(1970): 277-284.

Schafer, Walter E., and Polk, Kenneth. "Delinquency and the Schools." Appendix M in the President's Commission on Law Enforcement and Administration of Justice, Juvenile Delinquency and Youth Crime. Washington, DC: GPO, 1967.

Scharf, Richard K. "Pupil Placement and Public School Desegregation." Doctoral dissertation, U. of Chicago, 1963.

Schermer, George. Guidelines: A Manual for Bi-Racial Committees. New York: Anti-Defamation League, 1964.

Schermerhorn, R. A. Comparative Ethnic Relations. New York: Random House, 1969.

Schmuck, Richard A., and Luszki, M. B. "Black and White Students in Veveral Small Communities." Journal of Applied Behavioral Science, Ap-Je, 1969.

The School and the Migrant Child. National Committee on the Education of Migrant Children, 145 East 32nd Street, New York, NY 10016, n.d.

School Desegregation. An NCAEW Background Paper, F, 1972. National Council for the Advancement of Education Writing, PO Box 233, McLean, VA 22101.

School Desegregation: Making It Work. East Lansing, MI: College of Urban Development, Michigan State U., 1976.

Schrag, Peter. "The Circle of Futility. Integrating the Schools." Commonweal, Mr 6, 1964.

_____. "A Hesitant New South. Fragile Promise on the Last Frontier." Saturday Review 55(F 12, 1972):51-58.

_____. "Why Our Schools Have Failed." Commentary, Mr, 1968.

Schreiber, Danield and others. Dropout Studies. Design and Conduct. Washington, DC: National Education Association, 1965.

_____. Holding Power, Large City School Systems. Washington, DC: National Education Association, 1964.

_____. Profile of the School Dropout. New York: Random House, 1967.

Schultz, Michael J. "The Desegregation Effort of the National Education Association." Integrated Education 8(Mr-Ap, 1970):37-44.

Schuman, Howard, and Gruenberg, Barry. "The Impact of City on Racial Attitudes." American Journal of Sociology 76(S, 1970).

Schuman, Howard, and Hatchett, Shirley. Black Racial Attitudes, Trends and Complexities. Ann Arbor, MI: Institute for Racial Research, U. of Michigan, 1974.

Schuyler, George S., and Lewis, Theophilus. "A Page of Calumny and Satire." Messenger 6 (O, 1974):315, 323. [On the Caucasian Problem]

Schwab, John J. and others. "Social Psychiatric Impairment: Racial Companions." American Journal of Psychiatry 130 (F, 1973):183-187.

Schwartz, Robert and others. "Desegregation: Assessing the Alternatives." Nation's Schools, Mr, 1968.

Scott, Hugh J. "Reflections on Issues and Conditions Related to Public Education for Black Students." Journal of Negro Education 42(Summer, 1973):414-426.

Scott, John Finley. The Soul Brother, Mr 26, 1970. ERIC ED 040 256.

Scott, John Finley, and Scott, Lois Heyman. "They Are Not So Much Anti Negro as Pro- Middle-Class." New York Times Magazine, Mr 24, 1968.

Scott, Joseph W. The Black Revolts: Racial Stratification in the USA. Cambridge, MA.: Schenkman, 1976.

Scott, Marvin B. "Playing at Affirmative Action." Integrateducation 13(S-O, 1975):37-38.

Sears, Barnas. "Education in Mixed Schools." Atlantic Monthly, 34(1874).

Sedlacek, William, and Brooks, Glenwood C., Jr. "Measuring Racial Attitudes in a Situational Context." Psychological Reports 27(D, 1970):971-980.

_____ and _____. The Measurement of Attitudes of Whites Toward Blacks with Certain Beliefs, 1970. ERIC ED 045 768.

Segre, M. L. Tanguy, and Zortic, M. F. "A New Ideology of Education." Social Forces 50 (Mr, 1972).

"A Segregated Professional Association." Social Service Review, D, 1967. [The Association of Black Social Workers]

"Segregation South--and North." Time, F 23, 1970.

"Segregation: Story Is Refuted by AFT." American Teacher, Mr, 1971. [Reference to a charge that the American Federation of Teachers (AFT) is appealing to segregation-minded teachers in the South]

Selden, David. "Desegregating Northern Schools." American Teacher, My, 1971.

Sellers, Cleveland, with Terrell, Robert. The River of No Return. New York: Morrow, 1973.

Semone, Ronald Cecil. The Negro Middle Class in the South: A Study of Race, Class, and Political Behavior." Doctoral dissertation, U. of North Carolina, 1969. Univ. Microfilms Order No. 70-12, 105.

Senior, Clarence, and Bernard, William S. (eds.). Toward Cultural Democracy. New York: Associated Educational Services Corporation, 1968.

Sewell, William H., Marascuilo, Leonard A., and Pfautz, Harold W. Review Symposium [on the Coleman Report]. American Sociological Review, Je, 1967.

Sexton, Patricia Cayo. The American School: A Sociological Analysis. Englewood Cliffs, NJ: Prentice-Hall, 1967.

_____. "City of Schools." Annals, Mr, 1964.

_____. "Class Education and Struggle in the Schools." New America, My, 1964.

_____. "A Letter to Paul Goodman." New America, Mr 24, 1965. [On prescribing for dropouts]

_____. "Negro Career Expectations." Merrill-Palmer Quarterly, O, 1963.

_____. School Adjustment and Maladjustment of Boys of Lower Socioeconomic Status. New York: New York U., 1968.

Sexton, Patricia Cayo and others. The Urban School Crisis. New York: League for Industrial Democracy, 1966.

Seymour, Bill. "Blacks, Whites and Browns on Blacks and White Film." Photolith ScM, 26 (Ja, 1976):18-21.

Shaftel, Fannie R., and Robinson, John T. Intergroup Workshop for Special Training on Problems of School Desegregation, Interim Report, Final Report and Follow-up in Participating School Districts, 1965. ERIC ED 056 127.

Shagaloff, June. "Progress Report on Northern Desegregation." Integrated Education, O-N, 1966.

Shaheen, Thomas. "Desegregation - in a Community's Best Interest." California Journal of Teacher Education 1(N, 1972):37-44.

Shanker, Albert. "The Quota Principle: Dangerous Arithmetic." New York Times, D 9, 1973.

"Shanker: NEA Uses NEA Forum for Attack on Shanker." New York Teacher, Jl, 1973.

Shannon, Albert. "An Interview with Rev. James Groppi." Marquette University Education Review 1(Spring, 1970):8-9, 15-22.

Shapiro, Beth J. (comp.). Directory of Ethnic Publishers and Resource Organizations. Chicago: American Library Association, 1977.

Shapiro, Elliot. "The Dynamics of Self-Deception." Phi Delta Kappan, Mr, 1967.

Shapiro, Michael J. "Social Control Ideologies and the Politics of American Education." International Review of Education 20(1974):17-35.

Shaw, Frederick. "Major Urban Problem: Educating Disadvantaged Youth." Journal of the National Association of Women Deans and Counselors, Winter, 1974.

Shaw, William Burns. "Education as a Human Right: The Analysis of an Emerging Concept." Doctoral dissertation, Northwestern U., 1967.

Sheatsley, Paul B. "White Attitudes Toward the Negro." Daedalus, Winter, 1966.

Shedd, Mark. "Problems in Northern Suburbs." Bulletin of the Harvard Graduate School of Education Association, Winter, 1964.

Shepard, Samuel, Jr. (ed.) Working with Parents of Disadvantaged Children, in Hunnicutt, above.

Shepard, Samuel, Jr., and Hunnicutt, C. W. Urban Elementary School Desegregation. Summary Report, Jl, 1965-My, 1966. Syracuse, NY: Syracuse U., 1966, 111 pp. ERIC ED 016 691.

Sher, Jonathan P. Public Education in Sparsely Populated Areas of the United States. Washington, DC: National Institute of Education, 1977.

Sherif, Muzafer, and Sherif, Carol. "Black Unrest as a Social Movement Toward an Emerging Self Identity." Journal of Social and Behavioral Sciences 15(Spring, 1970):41-52.

_____ and _____. The Black Unrest, Part of a Social Movement Toward Human Rights, F 10, 1968. ERIC ED 017 602.

Sherriffs, Alex C., and Clark, Kenneth B. How Relevant Is Education in America Today? Washington, DC: American Enterprise Institute for Public Policy Research, 1970.

Sherrill, Robert. "It Isn't True That Nobody Starves in America." New York Times Magazine, Je 4, 1967.

Shimkin, Dimitri B., and Shimkin, Edith M. The Extended Family in U.S. Black Societies: Findings and Problems, 1974. ERIC ED 102 467.

Shin, E. "Effects of Immigration on the Educational Levels of the Black Resident Population at the Origin and Destination, 1955-1960 and 1965-1970." Demography 15(F, 1978): 41-56.

Shon, Donald. "Assimilation of Migrants Into Urban Centers." President's National Advisory Commission on Rural Poverty, Rural Poverty in the United States. Washington, DC: GPO, My, 1968.

Shorter, Rufus. "Points of View." Bridges to Understanding, Ja, 1966. [Reply to William Isaacs, " Dissenting Thoughts on School Integration," High Prints, My, 1965]

Shulman, Lee S. (ed.). Review of Research in Education 4, 1976. Itasca, IL: Peacock, 1977.

Shuy, Roger W. "Dialectology and Usage." Baltimore Bulletin of Education 43(1966-1967).

Siegel, Jerome M. "A Brief Review of the Effects of Race in Clinical Service Interaction." American Journal of Orthopsychiatry 44(Jl, 1974):555-562.

Siegel, Sol. "Prejudice and Plain Talk--The Risks and the Gains." Integrated Education 9 (My-Je, 1971):43-45.

Siegel, Irving E., and Perry, Cereta. "Psycholinguistic Diversity Among Culturally Deprived Children." American Journal of Orthopsychiatry, Ja, 1968.

Silberman, Charles E. Crisis in Black and White. New York: Random House, 1964.

_____. "Give Slum Children a Chance." A Radical Proposal. Harper's, My, 1964.

_____. "Murder in the Schoolroom. Part II." Atlantic, Jl, 1970.

_____. "The Yearning for a Better Life. Freedom North 1(1965), Nos. 7-8.

Simey, T. S. Social Science and Social Purpose. London: Constable, 1968.

Simms, Richard L. "Bias in Textbooks: Not Yet Corrected." Phi Delta Kappan 57(N, 1975): 201-202.

Simpson, Elizabeth L. "Moral Development Research --A Case Study of Scientific Cultural Bias." Human Development 17(1974):81-106.

Sims, Patsy. The Klan. New York: Stein and Day, 1978.

Stinger, L. "Ethnogenesis and Negro Americans Today." Social Research 29(Winter, 1969): 419-432.

Singh, P. "City Centre Schools and Community Relations." Trends in Education 33(1974):27-30.

Singleton, John. "Education and Ethnicity." Comparative Education Review 21(Je-O, 1977): 329-344.

Sipple, Peter W. "Separatism, Assimilation, Interaction: The Case of the Urban School." Journal of General Education 22(O, 1970):193-204.

Sizemore, Barbara A. "Education for Liberation." School Review 81(My, 1973):389-404.

_____. [Testimony] U.S. Congress, 92nd, 1st session, Senate, Select Committee on Equal Education Opportunity, Equal Educational Opportunity Hearings...Part 13--Quality and Control of Urban Schools. Washington, DC: GPO, 1971.

Sizer, Theodore R. "Education and Assimilation: A Fresh Plea for Pluralism." Phi Delta Kappan 58(S, 1976):31-35.

_____. "The Schools in the City." In J.Q. Wilson (ed.), The Metropolitan Enigma. Washington, DC: U.S. Chamber of Commerce, 1967.

Sjöstrand, Wilhelm. Freedom and Equality on Fundamental Education Principles in Western Democracy from John Locke to Edmund Burke. Tr. A. Ljunggren. Stockholm, Sweden: Foreningen för Svensk Undervisningshistoria, 1974.

Skinner, Vincent. "The Verbal Aptitude Test: Flagrant Discrimination for College Admission." Changing Education, Winter, 1969.

Slaiman, Donald. Civil Rights in the Urban Crisis. Seminar on Manpower Policy and Program, U.S. Dept. of Labor, Washington, DC: GPO, 1968.

Slayton, William L. "The Influence of Urban Renewal on Education." School Life, Je, 1962.

Smith Barbara Lee, and Hughes, Anita L. "'Spillover' Effect of the Black Educated. Catalysts for Equality." Journal of Black Studies 4(S, 1973):52-68.

Smith, Cynthia J. (ed.). Advancing Equality of Opportunity: A Matter of Justice. Washington, DC: Institute for the Study of Educational Policy, Howard U., 1978.

Smith, Donald H. "Changing Controls in Ghetto Schools." Phi Delta Kappan, Ap, 1968.

Smith, Edward C. "The Coming of the Black Ghetto-State." Yale Review 61(D, 1971):161-182.

Smith, Linda. "Literature for the Negro Student." High Points, O, 1965.

Smith, Linwood. "Work-Study Program and Black Deaf People." Journal of Rehabilitation of the Deaf 6(O, 1972):116-119.

Smith, Marshall S. "The Equality of Educational Opportunity Report--A Reply to Bowles and Levin." Journal of Human Resources, Summer, 1968. [On the Coleman Report]

Smith, Marzell, and Dziuban, Charles D. "The Gap Between Desegregation Research and Remedy." Integrateducation 15(N-D, 1977): 51-55.

Smith, Ralph Lee. "New Tools for School Integration." Progressive, My, 1966.

Smith, S. L. "Negro Public Schools In The South." Southern Workman 57(N, 1928):444-461.

Smith, Sidonie. Where I'm Bound: Patterns of Slavery and Freedom in Black American Autobiography. Westport, CT: Greenwood Press, 1974.

Smith, Wilfred R. "A Normative Study of Desegregation in Public Education--A Crisis of Meanings in Culture." Doctoral Dissertation. Wayne State University, 1959. Univ. Microfilms Order No. 59-4706.

Smith, Wm. David. "Which Way Black Psychologists: Tradition, Modification, or Verification--Innovation?" Journal of Black Studies 4(S, 1973):3-14.

Smyth, John Henry. "Negro Criminality." Southern Workman 29(1900). [Reform schools for Negro youth]

Smythe, Hugh H., and Moss, James A. "The Cultural Atmosphere of Depressed Areas." Journal of Human Relations, Second Quarter, 1965.

Smythe, Hugh H., and Murray, W. I. "Human Relations Perspective on Integration in the U.S.A." Journal of Human Relations, Second Quarter, 1965.

Smythe, Mabel M. (ed.). The Black American Reference Book. Englewood Cliffs, NJ: Prentice-Hall, 1976.

Snyder, Ben and others. Minority Affairs Report 1969-1978. Boston: National Association of Independent Schools, My, 1978.

Sobel, Morton J. "What's Really Blocking School Desegregation?" Journal of Intergroup Relations 2(O, 1972):3-12.

Solomon, Benjamin. "Educators and the Racial Issue in Education." Illinois Schools Journal, Spring, 1968.

_____. "Integration and the Educators." Integrated Education, Ag, 1963.

_____. "A Perspective for Educators on the Racial Issue in Education." Phi Delta Kappan, My, 1966.

Sorensen, Aage Bottger. Organizational Differentiation of Students and Educational Opportunity, D, 1969. ERIC ED 041 361.

Southern Economics Association. Papers on Rural Poverty Presented at the Annual Conference..., November, 1968. Raleigh, NC: Agricultural Policy Institute, North Carolina State U., 1969.

Sowell, Thomas. "Affirmative Action Reconsidered." Public Interest 42(Winter, 1976): 47-65.

_____. Black Education. Myths and Tragedies. Philadelphia: McKay, 1972.

Spears, Harold. "Kappans Ponder Racial Issues in Education." Phi Delta Kappan 1972):244-246.

Spears, Harold, and Pivnick, Isadore. "How an Urban School System Identifies Its Disadvantaged." Journal of Negro Education, Summer, 1964.

Spearks, Mack J. "Improving Educational Opportunities for Minority Group.s" Bulletin of NAASP 55(My, 1971):98-105.

"Special Issue Busing." NCRIEEO Newsletter 3 (My, 1972).

"Special Program for Black Art Students." Communication Arts Magazine 10, No. 2, 1968.

Special Task Force Report. Graduation Requirements. Preston, VA: National Association of Secondary School Principals, 1975.

Special Training Institute on Problems of School Desegregation, June 20, 1966-August 31, 1967. Chapel Hill: North Carolina U., Rougemont: Learning Institute of North Carolina; Washington, DC: Office of Education (DHEW), 196b, 23 pp. ERIC ED 019 347.

Spencer, Lyle M. "The Flight from Experience." Integrated Education, D, 1967-Ja, 1968.

Spindler, G. D. (ed.). Education and Cultural Process: Toward an Anthropology of Education. New York: Holt, Rinehart and Winston, 1974.

_____. "Our Changing Culture, Creativity and the Schools." California Journal for Instructional Improvement, My, 1966.

Stafford, James, Birdwell, Al, and Van Tassel, Charles. "Integrated Advertising--White Backlash?" Journal of Advertising Research 10(Ap, 1970).

Stage 7. Toward a Black Perspective in Education. Collective Monologues 1, 1976. ERIC ED 147 373.

Stahl, Ben. "The A.F.T. and School Integration." Integrated Education, Ag-N, 1965.

Staples, Robert. "Land of Promise, Cities of Despair: Blacks in Urban America." Black Scholar 10(O, 1978):2-11.

_____. "Violence and Black America." Black World 23(My, 1974):17-34.

"State of the Southern States." New Spring, 1969.

Steinkamp, Egon W. Sport und Rasse: Der Schwarze Sportler in den U.S.A. Ahrensburg bei Hamburg: Czwalina, 1976.

Stephens, Lenora C. "Telecommunications and the Urban Black Community: An Interdisciplinary Study of Public Television, 1952-1975." Doctoral dissertation, Emory U., 1976. Univ. Microfilms Order No. 77-983. [Public television in N.Y.C., Washington, D.C. and Atlanta]

Stewart, Barbara H. "'Sesame Street': A Linguistic Detour for Black-Language Speakers." Black World 22(Ag, 1973):12-20.

Stewart, James B., and Scott, Joseph W. "The Institutional Decimation of Black American Males." Western Journal of Black Studies (Summer, 1978):82-92.

Stewart, William A. "Sociolinguistic Factors in the History of American Negro Dialects." Florida F N Reporter, Spring, 1967.

Sterling, Dorothy. "The Soul of Learning," Feb., 1968, 15 pp. Speech given at the NDEA Institute in English, U. of Wisconsin, Milwaukee: Summer, 1967. English Journal 57, No. 2, pp. 166-80, F, 1968.

Stern, Sol. "When the Black G.I. Comes Back from Vietnam." New York Times Magazine, Mr 24, 1968.

Stillman, Richard J. II. Integration of the Negro in the U.S. Armed Forces. New York: Praeger, 1968.

_____. "Negroes in the Armed Forces." Phylon, Summer, 1969.

Stout, Robert, and Sroufe, Gerald. "Outside New York City Schools Desegregation Is Alive and Living." Center Forum, D 23, 1968.

Straton, John Roach. "Will Education Solve the Race Problem." North American Review 170 (Je, 1900).

Strickland, William. "American and Civil Rights." Freedom North, II, No. 1, 1966.

Strickman, Leonard P. "Desegregation: The Metropolitan Concept." Urban Review 6(S-O, 1972):18-23.

Strodtbeck, Fred (ed.). "The Hidden Curriculum of the Middle Class Home." Hunnicutt.

Study Group on Urban Education. Urban Education: Problems and Priorities, Mr 18, 1968. Republican Coordinating Committee, Republican National Committee, Washington, DC

A Study of the Country Training Schools for Negroes in the South. The trustees of the John F. Slater Fund. Occasional papers, No. 23. Charlottesville, VA, 1923.

Suchman, Edward A. and others. Desegregation: Some Propositions and Research Suggestions. New York: Anti-Defamation League, 1958.

Sue, Derald Wing, and Sue, David. "Ethnic Minorities: Failures and Responsbilities of the Social Sciences." Journal of Non-White Concerns in Personnel and Guidance 5(Ap, 1977):99-105.

Taylor, D. Garth and others. "Attitudes toward Racial Integration." *Scientific American* 238)Je, 1978):42-49.

Teague, Bob. *Letters to a Black Boy.* New York: Walker, 1968.

Teahan, John E. "A Longitudinal Study of Attitude Shifts Among Black and White Police Officers." *Journal of Social Issues* 31(1975): 47-56.

_____. "Role Playing and Group Experience to Facilitate Attitude and Value Changes among Black and White Police Officers." *Journal of Social Issues* 31(1975): 35-45.

Tedesco, John L. "The White Character in Black Drama, 1955-1970: Description and Rhetorical Function." *Communication Monographs* 45(Mr, 1978):64-74.

Teele, James E., and Mayo, Clara. "School Integration: Tumult and Shame." *Journal of Social Issues*, Ja, 1969.

Terjen, Kitty. "Camping: Admission Bias Under Attack." *South Today* 2(N, 1970):3.

Terry, Wallace III. "Bringing the War Home..." *Harvard Crimson*, O 8 and 9, 1970.

Tesconi, Charles A., Jr., and Hurwitz, Emanuel, Jr. *Education for Whom? The Question of Educational Opportunity.* New York: Dodd, Mead, 1974.

"Textbooks, Civil Rights and the Education of the American Negro." *Publishers Weekly*, My 10, 1965.

Thernstorm, Stephan. "Is There Really A New Poor?" *Dissent*, Ja-F, 1968.

Thomas, C. A. "Dimensions of Democracy in Education." *Vital Speeches*, N 15, 1964.

Thomas, Claudewell S., and Lindenthal, Jacob J. "Depression of the Oppressed." *MH* 59(Summer):12-14.

Thomas, George, assisted by Stewart, Merrilee. *Poverty in the Non-Metropolitan South.* Athens, GA: Regional Institute for Social Welfare Research, U. of Georgia, 1972.

Thomas, Ida Bell X. "Forced Integration." *Muhammad Speaks*, S 15, 1972.

Thomas, Pearl. "Reforming the English Curriculum in Secondary Schools." *Changing Education*, Fall, 1966.

Thomas, Tony (ed.). *Black Liberation and Socialism: An Anthology.* New York: Pathfinder Press, 1974.

Thompkins, Rachel, and Kaeser, Susan (eds.). *Citizens' Guide to Quality Education.* Cleveland: Citizens' Council for Ohio Schools, 1978.

Thompson, Bryan, and Agocs, Carol. "Ethnic Studies: Teaching and Research Needs." *Journal of Geography* 72(Ap, 1973):13-23.

Thompson, Charles H. "The Negro Separate School." *Crisis*, Ag, 1935.

_____. "Race, Equality of Educational Opportunity: Defining the Problem." *Journal of Negro Education*, Summer, 1968.

Thompson, Charles H. and others. "A Critical Survey of the Negro Elementary School." *Journal of Negro Education*, Jl, 1932.

Thompson, Daniel C. "Evaluation as a Factor in Planning Programs for the Culturally-Disadvantaged." *Journal of Negro Education*, Summer, 1964.

_____. "Our Wasted Potential," in Klopf and Laster, above.

_____. *The Role of Leadership in School Desegregation*, N, 1971. ERIC ED 064 432.

_____. *Sociology of the Black Experience.* Westport, CT: Greenwood Press, 1974.

Toepfer, Conrad F., Jr. "Integration...A Curricular Concern." *Educational Leadership*, D, 1968.

Tolo, Kenneth W. (ed.). *Educating a Nation: The Changing American Commitment...* Austin, TX: Lyndon B. Johnson School of Public Affairs, U. of Texas, 1973.

Tomasi, Lydio F. *The Ethnic Factor in the Future of Inquality.* Staten Island, NY: Center for Migration Studies, 1973.

Tompkins, Rachel B. (ed.). *The Media and School Desegregation*, 1977. ERIC ED 148-964.

Torrance, E. Paul. "Differences Are Not Deficits." *Teachers College Record* 75(My, 1974): 471-487.

Tourgee, Albion W. *Appeal to Caesar*, 1884.

"Transcript of the American Academy [of Arts and Sciences] Conferences on the Negro-American, May 14-15, 1965. *Daedalus*, Winter, 1966.

Trends in Black School Segregation, 1970-1974. Vol I. Washington, DC: Center for National Policy Review, The Law School, Catholic University of America, Ja, 1977.

Trenholm, Councill J. "The Accreditation of Negro High Schools." *Journal of Negro Education* 1(Ap, 1932):34-43.

Triandis, Harry C., Loh, Wallace D., and Levin, Leslie Ann. "Race, Status, Quality of Spoken English, and Opinions About Civil Rights, as Determinants of Interpersonal Attitudes." Journal of Personality and Social Psychology, Ap, 1966.

Trillin, Calvin. "Remembrance of Moderates Past." New Yorker 53(Mr 21, 1977):85-97. [White racial moderates in the South]

Trotman, C. James. "The Posture of the Black Student in America." Pennsylvania School Journal 8, 1969.

Tumin, Melvin. Comparative Perspectives on Race Relations. Boston: Little, Brown, 1969.

_____. "The Emerging Social Policy in the Education of Young Children." Young Children, Ja, 1968.

_____. The Progress of Integration." National-al Elementary Principal 45(F, 1966):7-14.

_____ (ed.). Research Annual on Intergroup Relations--1972. Chicago, IL: Quadrangle, 1972.

_____. "Some Social Consequences of Research on Racial Tensions." American Sociologist 3 (1968):117-124.

Tumin, Melvin, and Bressler, Marvin (eds.). Conference on "Quality and Equality in Education," Proceedings. Princeton, NJ" Princeton U. Press, 1966.

Tumin, Melvin, and Greenblat, Cathy S. (eds.). Research Annual on Intergroup Relations--1966. New York: Praeger, 1967.

Tumin, Melvin, and Ploch, Walter (eds.). Pluralism in a Democratic Society. New York: Praeger, 1977.

Turner, Castellano B., and Wilson, William J. "Dimensions of Racial Ideology: A Study of Urban Black Attitudes." Journal of Social Issues 32(1976):139-152.

Turner, Jasper. "Glossary for Desegregation." Quarterly Review of Higher Education Among Negroes, Ja, 1969.

Tutorial Assistance Center. Directory of Tutorial Projects. Washington, DC: National Student Association, 1968.

Tyler, Stephen A. (ed.). Cognitive Anthropology. N.p.: N.p., 1969.

Underwood, Willard, and Ferguson. Ralph E. Black Americans in the Southwest, F 24, 1977. ERIC ED 145 994.

UNESCO. "Biological Aspects of Race: Proposals." Integrated Education, Ag-N, 1965-

UNESCO. Cultural Rights As Human Rights. Paris: UNESCO, 1970.

U.S. Advisory Commission on Intergovernmental Relations. Urban and Rural America: Policies for Future Growth. Washington, DC: GPO, Ap, 1968.

U.S. Bureau of the Census. Coverage of Population in the 1970 Census and Some Implications for Public Programs. Washington, DC: GPO, Ag, 1975.

_____. "Characteristics of American Youth: 1971." Current Population Reports, Series P-23, No. 40. Washington, DC: GPO, 1972.

_____. "Characteristics of American Youth." Current Population Reports, Series P-23, No. 30. Washington, DC: GPO, 1970.

_____. "Educational Attainment: March, 1971." Current Population Reports, Series P-20, No. 229. Washington, DC: GPO, 1971.

_____. "Selected Characteristics of Persons and Families: March 1970. Income, Poverty, Education, Mobility, Family and Household Composition." Current Population Reports, Series P-20, No. 204, Jl 13, 1970.

_____. "School Enrollment: October 1968 and 1967." Current Population Reports, Series P-20, No. 190. Washington, DC: GPO, 1969.

_____. Data on Selected Racial Groups Available from the Bureau of the Census. Washington, DC: Bureau of the Census, My, 1975.

_____. Language Minority, Illiteracy, and Voting Data Used in Making Determinations for the Voting Rights Acts Amendments of 1975 (Public Law 94-73). Washington, DC: GPO, Je, 1976.

_____. Population of the United States. Trends and Prospects: 1950-1990. Washington, DC: GPO, My, 1974.

_____. School Enrollment--Social and Economic Characteristics of Students: October, 1974. Washington, DC: GPO, F, 1975.

_____. School Enrollment, Social and Economic Characteristics of Students, October, 1977. Washington, DC: GPO, 1977.

_____. Social and Economic Characteristics of Students: October, 1971. Washington, DC: GPO, Oc, 1972.

_____. The Social and Economic Status of Negroes in the United States, 1970. Washington, DC: GPO, Jl, 1971.

U.S. Bureau of the Census. The Social and Economic Status of the Black Population in the United States, 1973. Washington, DC: GPO, 1974.

_____. Social Indicators, 1976: Selected Data on Social Conditions and Trends in the United States. Washington, DC: GPO, D, 1977.

_____. Papers Prepared for National Conference on Equal Educational Opportunity in America's Cities. Washington, DC: GPO, 1968.

_____. Political Participation: A Study of the Participation by Negroes in the Electoral and Political Processes in 10 Southern States Since Passage of the Voting Rights Act of 1965. Washington, DC: GPO, 1968.

_____. Reviewing a Decade of School Desegregation 1966-1975. Report of a National Survey of School Superintendents. Washington, DC: The Commission, Ja, 1977.

_____. Social Indicators of Equality for Minorities and Women. Washington, DC: The Commission, Ag, 1978.

_____. The State of Civil Rights: 1976. Washington, DC: The Commission, F 15, 1977.

_____. Statement on Metropolitan School Desegreation. Washington, DC: The Commission, F, 1977.

_____. Toward a More Cooperative and Productive Relationship Among Civil Rights Agencies and Officials. Washington, DC: The Commission, 1975.

_____. Understanding School Desegregation. Washington, DC: GPO, 1971.

_____. "Urban Renewal and Segregation." Integrated Education, F-Mr, 1964.

_____. The Voting Rights Act: Ten Years After. Washington, DC: The Commission, Ja, 1975.

_____. Window Dressing On the Set: Women and Minorities in Television. Washington, DC: The Commission, Ag, 1977.

_____. Women and Poverty. Washington, DC: The Commission, Je, 1974.

U.S. Commission on Civil Rights, and The State Advisory Committee. Unfinished Business. Twenty Years Later... Washington, DC: The Commission, S, 1977.

U.S. Congress, 90th, 1st session, House of Representatives. Committee on Government Operations, Research and Technical Programs Subcommittee. The Use of Social Research in Federal Domestic Programs, 4 parts, Committee Print. Washington, DC: GPO, Ap, 1967.

U.S. Congress, and House of Representatives. Committee on Education and Labor, General Subcommittee on Education. The Juvenile Delinquency Prevention Act of 1967. Hearings. Washington, DC: GPO, 1967.

U.S. Congress, and Joint Economic Committee. Employment and Manpower Problems in the Cities: Implications of the Report of the National Advisory Commission on Civil Disorders... Report. Washington, DC: GPO, S, 1968.

U.S. Congress, 87th, 2nd Session, House of Representatives. Committee on Education and Labor, Subcommittee on Integration in Federally Assisted Public Education Programs. Integration in Public Education Programs, Hearings... Washington, DC: GPO, 1962. G. Watson Algire (Maryland), Carl F. Hansen (Washington, D.C.), John Niemeyer (New York City), and Guy B. Johnson (South).

U.S. Congress, 88th, 2nd Session, Senate, Committee on Labor and Public Welfare, Subcommittee on Employment and Manpower: Problems of Youth. A Fact Book. Washington, DC: GPO, 1964.

U.S. Congress, 89th, 2nd Session, House of Representatives, Committee on Education and Labor, Ad Hoc Subcommittee on De Factor School Segregation Hearings... Books for Schools and the Treatment of Minorities. Washington, DC: GPO, 1966.

U.S. Congress, 90th, 1st Session, Join Economic Committee, Subcommittee on Urban Affairs, Urban America: Goals and Problems, Hearings ... Washington, DC: GPO, 1967.

U.S. Congress, 91st Session, House of Representatives, Committee on Education and Labor, Special Subcommittee on Education. Hearings ... Campus Unrest. Washington, DC: GPO, 1969.

U.S. Congress, 90th, 1st Session, Senate Committee on Government Operations, Subcommittee on Government Research. Full Opportunity and Social Accounting Act...Hearings, 3 parts. Washington, DC: GPO, 1968.

U.S. Congress, 91st, 1st and 2nd Sessions, Senate Committee on Labor and Public Welfare. Subcommittee on Migratory Labor. Migrant and Seasonal Farmworker Powerlessness. Hearings ...on the Migrant Subculture. Part 2. Washington, DC: GPO, 1970.

U.S. Congress, 91st, 2nd Session, Senate, Committee on the Judiciary, Subcommittee to Investigate the Administration of the Internal Security Act and Other Internal Security Laws. Testimony of Robert F. Williams. Hearings... 2 parts. Washington, DC: GPO, 1971.

U.S. Congress, 92nd, 1st Session, Senate, Committee on Government Operations. The Economic and Social Condition of Rural America in the 1970's. Washington, DC: GPO, My, 1971.

U.S. Congress, 91st, 2nd Session, House of Representatives, Committee on Banking and Currency. Investigation and Hearing of Abuse in Federal Low- and Moderate-Income Housing Programs. Staff Report and Recommendations. Washington, DC: GPO, D, 1970.

U.S. Congress, 92nd, 2nd Session, Senate, Committee on Labor and Public Welfare, Subcommittee on Education. Equal Educational Opportunities Act of 1972. Hearings... Washington, DC: GPO, 1972.

U.S. Congress, 93rd, ist Session, Senate Committee on Government Operations, Subcommittee on Intergovernmental Relations. Confidence and Concern: Citizens View American Government. A Survey of Public Attitides Part 1. (A study by Louis Harris and Associates.) Washington, DC: GPO, 1973.

U.S. Congress, 93rd, 1st Session, Senate, Committee on Government Operation Subcommittee on Intergovernmental Relations. Confidence and Concern: Citizens View American Government. Hearings... Washington, DC: GPO, 1974.

U.S. Congress, 93rd, ist Session, Senate Committee on Labor and Public Welfare, Subcommittee on Education. Reading Emphasis Program, 1973. Hearings... Washington, DC: GPO, 1973.

U.S. Congress, 94th 1st, Session, House of Representatives, Committee on Education and Labor, Subcommittee on Manpower, Compensation, and Health and Safety. Young Adult Conservation Corps.: Hearings... Washington, DC: GPO, 1976.

U.S. Congress, 94th, 1st Session, House of Representatives, Committee on the Judiciary, Subcommittee on Civil and Constitutional Rights. Extension of the Voting Rights Act. Hearings... Serial No. 1. Part 1. Washington, DC: GPO, 1975.

U.S. Congress, 94th, 1st Session, House of Representatives, Committee on Education and Labor, Subcommittee on Elementary, Secondary, and Vocational Education. National Education Opportunities Act of 1975: Hearings... Washington, DC: GPO, 1976.

U.S. Congress, 94th, 2nd Session, House of Representatives, Committee on Interstate and Foreign Commerce, Subcommittee on Communications. Enforcement of Equal Opportunity and Antidiscrimination Laws in Public Broadcasting. Hearings... Washington, DC: GPO, 1977.

U.S. Congress, 94th, 1st Session, Senate Committee on Finance. Nomination of Forrest David Mathews. Hearings... Washington, DC: GPO, 1975.

U.S. Congress, 94th, 1st Session, Senate, Committee on the Judiciary, Subcommittee to Investigate Juvenile Delinquency. Our Nation's Schools--A Report Card: "A" in School Violence and Vandalism. Washington, DC: GPO, Ap, 1975.

U.S. Congress, 94th, 1st Session, Senate, Committee on Rules and Adminstration. Nomination of Daniel J. Boorstin of the District of Columbia to be Librarian of Congress. Hearings ... Washington, DC: GPO, 1975.

U.S. Congress, 94th, 2nd Session, Senate Committee on Appropriations, Subcommittee. Emergency School Aid Hearings. Washington, DC: GPO, 1976.

U.S. Congress, 94th, 2nd Session, Senate, Committee on the Judiciary, Subcommittee on Constitutional Rights. Civil Rights: A Staff Report. Washington, DC: GPO, 1976.

U.S. Congress, 95th, 1st Session, Senate, Committee on Human Resources. Desegregation and the Cities, the Trends and Policy Changes. Washington, DC: GPO, 1977.

U.S. Congress, 95th, 1st and 2nd Sessions, Senate, Committee on the Judiciary, Subcommittee on the Constitution. Civil Rights Commission Authorization Act of 1978: Hearings... Washington, DC: GPO, 1978.

U.S. Department of Agriculture. Human Resources in the Ozarks Region...With Emphasis On the Poor. Washington, DC: GPO, My, 1970.

U.S. Department of Commerce, Bureau of the Census. Public School Systems in 1966-67. (Census of Governments, 1967.) Washington, DC: Bureau of the Census, N, 1967.

U.S. Department of Commerce, Bureau of the Census. Social and Economic Characteristics of the Population in Metropolitan and Non-Metropolitan Areas: 1970 and 1960. Washington, DC: GPO, Je, 1971.

U.S. Department of Health, Education, and Welfare. Educational Research and Development in the United States. Washington, DC: GPO, 1970.

_____. A Measure of Poverty. Washington, DC: GPO, 1976.

_____. Planning Educational Change: Vol. 1: Technical Aspects of School Desegregation. Washington, DC: GPO, 1969.

U.S. Department of Justice. Report of the Department of Justice Task Force to Review the FBI Martin Luther King Jr., Security and Assassination Investigations. Washington, DC: Department of Justice, Ja 11, 1977.

U.S. Department of Labor. "Educational Deprivation in Three Minorities." Integrated Education, Je-Jl, 1964.

U.S. Marine Corps., 2nd Division. Document Relative to the Racial Situation in the Marine Corps, O 31, 1969. [Army War College]

U.S. National Commission on the Causes and Prevention of Violence. Progress Report...to President Lyndon B. Johnson, Ja 9, 1969. Washington, DC: GPO, 1969.

U.S. National Commission on Urban Problems. Hearings, Vols. 2 and 3. Washington, DC: GPO, 1968.

U.S. Office of Economic Opportunity. Community Education: Tutorial Programs. Washington, DC: GPO, O, 1967.

U.S. Office of Education. Education '65, A Report to the Profession. Washington, DC: GPO, 1966.

U.S. Office of Education. Education of the Gifted and Talented. Volume 1. Report to the Congress of the United States by the U.S. Commissioner of Education. Washington, DC: GPO, Ag, 1971.

U.S. Office of Education. Federal Assistance to Desegregation School Districts. A Report on Activities from S, 1973 to Mr, 1974, Mr 30, 1974. ERIC ED 094 067.

U.S. Office of Education. James E. Allen, Jr. On Education. Washington, DC: Office of Education, My, 1969.

U.S. Office of Education. School Social Work: A Service of Schools. Washington, DC: GPO, 1964.

Urban America, Inc. and the Urban Coalition. One Year Later: An Assessment of the Nation's Response to the Crisis Described by The National Advisory Commission On Civil Disorders. New York: Prager, 1969.

Usdan, Michael D. and others. "Reflections on Recent Studies in Race and Education: A Symposium." Law and Society Review, N, 1967.

Van Egmond, E. "Social Policy and Education: Quality of Segregated Education." Review of Educational Research, F, 1964.

Vander Zanden, James W. "Sociological Studies of American Blacks." Sociological Quarterly 14(Winter, 1973):32-52.

Vanfossen, Beth E. "Variables Related to Resistance to Desegregation in the South." Social Forces 47(1968):39-44.

Vanneman, Reeve D., and Pettigrew, Thomas F. "Race and Relative Deprivation in the Urban United States." Race 13(Ap, 1972):461-486.

Van Til, Wm. "Going the Second Mile." Phi Delta Kappan 56(N, 1974):220-221. [Personal narrative of participation in intergroup tions and desegregation movements]

Vasquez, Hector. "Civil Rights at the Crossroads." Integrateducation 13(My-Je, 1975): 168-70.

Verba, Sidney, Ahmed, Bashiruddin, and Bhatt, Anil. Caste, Race and Politics: A Comparative Study of India and the United States Beverly Hills, CA: Sage, 1971.

Vickery, William Edward. The Economics of the Negro Mitigation, 1900-1960. New York: Arno Press, 1977.

Vontress, Clemmont E. "Our Demoralizing Slum Schools." Phi Delta Kappan, N, 1963.

_____. "There is Too Much Apathy in the Negro Campus." Negro Digest, Je, 1977.

Vose, Clement, "School Desegregation. A Political Scientist's View." Law & Society Review, N, 1967.

Voter Education Project. "Southside Conference of Black Elected Officials, D 11-14, 1968." Conference Proceedings, Atlanta, GA: Southern Regional Council, 1969.

Wagoner, David S. "Where School Desegregation Isn't Happening." American School Board Journal, 159(S, 1971):31-34.

Waite, Richard R. "Further Attempts to Integrate and Urbanize First Grade Reading Textbooks: A Research Study." Journal of Negro Education, Winter, 1968.

Walberg, Herbert J., and Kopan, Andrew T. (eds.). Rethinking Urban Education. A Sourcebook of Contemporary Issues, San Francisco, CA: Jossey-Bass, 1972.

Walsh, John E. Education and Political Power. New York: Center for Applied Research in Education, 1964.

Walzer, Michael. "A Case for Quotas." Dissent, Fall, 1973, reprinted in Integrated Education, (N-D, 1973):5.

_____. "Thoughts on Democratic Schools." Dissent, 23(Winter, 1976):57-64. [See, also, "The Discussion," pp. 65-71.]

Warner, Keith Q. "Negritude: A New Dimension in the French Classroom." Journal of Negro History 43(Winter, 1974):77-81.

Warren, Robert Penn. Who Speaks for the Negro? New York: Random House, 1965.

Warshauer, Mary Ellen, and Dentler, Robert A. "A New Definition of School Segregation." In The Urban R's. Edited by Robert A. Dentler and others. New York: Praeger, 1967.

Washington, Alethea H. "The Supervision of Instruction in the Negro Elementary School." Journal of Negro Education 1(Jl, 1932):224-255.

Washington, Booker T. "Destitute Colored Children of the South", pp. 114-117. Proceedings of the Conference on the Care of Dependent Children Held at Washington, D.C., Ja, 25, 26, 1909. Washington, DC, 1909.

_____. "Educate Six Million Negro Children." World's Work 20(Je, 1910):87-88.

_____. "Education Will Solve the Race Problem. A Reply." North American Review 171(1900).

Wasserman, M. Demystifying School. Writings and Experiences. New York: Praeger, 1974.

Watkins, Mel. "White Skins, Dark Skins, Thin Skins." New York Times Magazine, D 3, 1967. [Negroes in suburbia]

Watson, Bernard C. Current Issues and the Future of Education in the Black Community, Mr 31, 1977. ERIC ED 141 456.

_____. In Spite of the System: The Individual and Educational Reform. Cambridge, MA: Ballinger Publ. Co., 1974.

_____. (ed.). National Policy Conference on Education for Blacks. Proceedings, 1972. The Congressional Black Caucus, U.S. House of Representatives, Washington, DC 20515.

Watson, Goodwin. "A Critical Evaluation of the Yearbook, 1964 (on 'Educational Planning for Socially Disadvantaged Children and Youth')." Journal of Negro Education, Summer, 1964.

Watson, Peter. "Psychology's Contribution to Race Relations." IRR Newsletter, Je, 1968. [A review of research]

Watters, Pat. Down to Now: Reflections on the Southern Civil Rights Movement. New York: Pantheon, 1972.

_____. "It's been 20 Long Years." Southern Voices 1(My-Je, 1974):5-8. [Twenty years of Brown]

_____. "A Region of Contrasts. South's Old and New Live Side-By-Side." South Today 3(S, 1971):1,7.

Wax, Murray L., Diamond, Stanley, and Gearing, Fred O. (eds.). Anthropological Perspectives on Education. New York: Basic Books, 1971.

Wayson, William W. "Expressed Motives of Teachers in Slum Schools." Urban Education 1, 1965.

_____. "Source of Teacher Satisfaction in Slum Schools." Administrator's Notebook, My, 1966.

_____. "Twenty-two Arguments on Integration." Integrated Education, Mr-Ap, 1972, pp. 46-50.

Weaver, Edward K. "The New Literature on Education of the Black Child." Freedomways, Fall, 1968.

Weaver, Robert C. Dilemmas of Urban America. Cambridge: Harvard U. Press, 1965.

_____. "The Urban Crisis." PTA Magazine, O, 1964.

Weber, Robert J., and Custer, Carson. Youth Involvement. Washington, DC: GPO, 1970.

Webster, Staten W. The Education of Black Americans. New York: Intext Educational Publishers, 1974.

Webster, Staten W., and Lund, S. E. Torstein. "Defectors and Persisters: Teachers of Disadvantaged Students." Integrated Education, Mr-Ap, 1969, pp. 48-55.

Weiler, David M. "Urban Education." Edited by Anthony J. Pascal. Cities in Trouble: An Agenda for Urban Research. Santa Monica, CA: Rand Corporation, Ag, 1968.

Weinberg, Meyer. "Civil Rights and the Schoolmen." Phi Delta Kappan, My, 1964.

_____. "Commentary on the St. John Article." Integrated Education, 55(Ja-F, 1972): pp. 16, 17. [See St. John, above.]

_____. "Conant's New Book." Integrated Education, D, 1964-Je, 1965.

_____. "Desegregation: Question and Answers." Intergroup, 1, 2(1970):4-5.

_____. "Educational Bureaucracy and Educational Change." Integrated Education 7(S-O, 1969):39-48.

_____. (ed.). Integrated Education: A Reader. Beverly Hills, CA: Glencoe Press, 1968.

_____. "Introduction: Race and Educational Opportunity," pp. 1-6. Edited by Daniel U. Levine. Models for Integrated Education. Worthington, OH: Jones, 1971.

_____. "Issues in American Education." Edited by Mathew Ahmann and Margaret Roach. The Church and the Urban Racial Crisis. Techny, IL: Divine Word Publications, 1968.

_____. (ed.). Learning Together. A Book on Integrated Education. Chicago: Integrated Associates, 1964.

_____. "Research on Race and Schools." Intergroup 1(1970):2-3.

_____. "School Integration--or Else." Commonweal, Ap 17, 1964.

_____. "The Status of Desegregation in American Cities: Implications for the State Role." Research Review of Equal Education 1(Fall, 1977):3-12.

_____. "Token Man." Integrated Education, Je-Jl, 1966.

_____. (ed.). W.E.B. DuBois: A Reader. New York: Harper & Row, 1970.

Weinfeld, Frederick D. "Educational Quality: Definitions and Measurement." Analytical Note No. 21. Washington, DC: Division of Operations Analysis, National Center for Educational Statistics, U.S. Office of Education, S 2, 1966.

Weinstein, Eugene A. "The Negro's Family's Decision to Desegregate." Southern School News, O, 1960.

Weinstein, Eugene A., and Geisel, P. N. "Family Decision Making over Desegregation." Sociometry, vol. 25, 1961.

Weir, Edward C. "The ASCD in Chicago: An Experiment in Planned Black-White Confrontation." Phi Delta Kappan, My, 1969.

Weitzel, Tony. "A Walk in the Zoo." Integrated Education, D, 1964-Je, 1965, p. 43.

Welsh, James. "A Long Range Look at School Desegregation." Education Researcher 1973):17-18. [Projected study by U.S. Commission on Civil Rights]

West, Earle H. "Toward Equality of Opportunity in Elementry and Secondard Education." Journal of Negro Education, Summer, 1968.

West Virginia Human Rights Commission. The Myths of Racial Integration, 1966.

Westby, Daniel L. "The Civic Sphere in the American City." Social Forces, D, 1966.

Whaley, Ruth Whitehead. "Closed Doors. A Study in Segregation." Messenger 5(Jl, 1923):771-772.

"What America Think of Itself." Newsweek, D 10, 1973.

"When the Negro Faces North." Look, D 17, 1962.

White, George Abbot. "Psychiatry and Belief. A Conversation with Robert Coles." Commonweal 97(O 27, 1972):78-82.

White, Helen., and Redding, S. Sugg, Jr. (eds.). From the Mountain. An Anthology from Psedopodia, South Today, and the North Georgia Review. Memphis, TN: Memphis State U. Press, 1972. [Magazines edited by Lillian Smith and Paula Snelling]

The White House Conference on Child Health and Protection, Committee on the School Child, Section III-C, Thomas D. Wood, chairman, Report of Subcommittee on the Negro School Child. Washington, DC: The Conference, 1930.

White House Conference on Children 1970. Report to the President. White House Conference on Children. Washington, DC: GPO, 1971.

White House Conference on Food, Nutrition, and Health. Summary Report. Washington, DC: GPO, D, 1970.

White House Conference on Youth, 1971. Profiles of Youth. Washington, DC: GPO, 1972.

White, Jack. "The Angry Black Soldiers." Progressive, Mr, 1970.

White, Maomi Rosh. "Ethnicity, Culture and Culture Pluralism." Ethnic and Racial Studies 1(Ap, 1978):139-153.

_____. "The Unchanged South." Ebony 26(Ag, 1971):126-133A.

White, Walter. "Negro Segregation Comes North." Nation, O, 21 1925.

Whiteman, Maxwell. "Black Genealogy." RQ 11 (Summer, 1972):311-319.

"Whites Say Integration Has Gone Too Far, Blacks Not Far Enough." Newsday, Je, 1976. [National sample survey]

Whitlock, James W. "Changing Elementary and Secondary Education in the South." Monthly Labor Review, Mr, 1968.

Wiggins, Sam P. "Cues for the New South." Integrated Education, Ag-S, 1966.

Wilkerson, Doxey Alphonse. "American Caste and the Social Studies Curriculum." Quarterly Review of Higher Education Among Negroes 5 (Ap, 1937):67-74.

_____. The People versus Segregated Schools. New York: N.p., 1955.

_____. "School Integration, Compensatory Education and the Civil Rights Movement in the North." Journal of Negro Education, Summer 1965.

_____. Special Problems of Negro Education. Washington, DC: GPO, 1939.

Wilkins, Roger. "A Black at the Gridiron Dinner." Integrated Education 8(S-O, 1970): 56-58.

Wilkins, Roy. "Discrimination in Education." Yale Political, Ag, 1963.

Willey, Darrell S. An Interdisciplinary Institute for the In-Service Training of Teachers and Other School Personnel to Accelerate the School Acceptance of Indian, Negro, and Spanish-speaking Pupils of Southwest, Mr, 1967. ERIC ED 015 795.

Williams, Charles T. Cultural Pluralism, a Step Beyond School Desegregation. Lansing, MI: Michigan Education Association, 1975.

Williams, Eddie. "Blacks and the Political Process." Integrateducation 13(My-Je, 1975): 14-15.

William, Franklin. "Progress Towards Civil Rights." Integrateducation 13(My-Je, 1975): 60-62.

Williams, George W. Do Negroes Really Believe Black is Beautiful? New York: Vantage Press, 1975.

Williams, J. Sherwood, and Acock, A. C. "Poverty and Color: Their Interrelation." L.S.U. Journal of Sociology 3(Spring, 1973):86-96.

Williams, J. Sherwood and others. "Blacks and Southern Poverty." Journal of Social and Behavioral Sciences 20(Winter, 1974):62-71.

Williams, James D. "Blacks and Public T.V." Black Enterprise 4(Ja, 1974):31-33.

Williams, James D. (ed.). When the Machinery Stopped. An Analysis of Black Issues in the '70's." New York: Nat'l Urban League, 1974.

Williams, John A. This is My Country, Too. New York: New American Library, 1965.

Williams, John B. III. "Desegregating Private Secondary Schools. A Southern Example." Doctoral dissertation, Harvard University, 1977. Univ. Microfilms Order No. 77-30705. [The Anne C. Stouffer Scholarship Program]

Williams, John E. "Connotations of Racial Concepts and Color Names." Journal of Personality and Social Psychology, My, 1966.

Williams, Louis N., and El-Khawas, Mohamed. "A Philosophy of Black Education." Journal of Negro Education 47(Spring, 1978):177-191.

Williams, Robert L. The Changing Image of the Black American: A Socio-psychological Appraisal, 1969. ERIC ED 035 681.

_____. Education Alternatives for Colonized People: Models for Liberation. Cambridge: MA: Dunellen, 1974.

Williams, Robert L., Cormier, William H., Sapp, Gary L., and Andrews, Henry B. "The Utility of Behavior Management Techniques in Changing Interracial Behaviors." Journal of Psychology 77(Ja, 1971):127-138.

Williams, Robin M., Jr. "Social Change and Social Conflict: Race Relations in the United States, 1944-1964." Sociological Inquiry 35(1965):8-25.

Williams, Robin M., Jr., Fisher, Burton R., and Janis, Irving L. "Educational Desegregation as a Context for Basic Social Science Research." American Sociological Review, O, 1956.

Willie, Charles V. "Anti-Social Behavior Among Disadvantaged Youth: Some Observations on Prevention for Teachers." Journal of Negro Education, Spring, 1964.

_____. "The Inclining Significance of Race." Society 15(Jl-Ag, 1978):10,12-15. [See William J. Wilson, below]

_____. "New Perspectives in School-Community Relations." Journal of Negro Education, Summer, 1968.

_____. "Racial Balance or Quality Education?" School Review 84(My, 1976):313-325.

_____. "The Relative Contribution of Family Status and Economic Status to Juvenile Delinquency." Social Problems, Winter, 1967.

_____. "Researchers, to Work!" Integrated Education 7(S-O, 1969):32-38.

_____. (ed.). Black/Brown/White Relations. Race Relations in the 1970s. New Brunswick, NJ: Transaction, 1977.

Wills, Gary. The Second Civil War, Arming for Armageddon. New York: New American Library, 1968.

Wilson, Jacques M. P. "Needed: An 'Operation Bootstrap': Adult Education...for the Undereducated Poor." Texas Observer, Mr 20, 1964.

Wilson, Robert L. "Northern Race Patterns Move to the South." Christian Century, Ja 18, 1967.

Wilson, Thomasyne Lightfoote. "Notes Toward a Process of Afro-American Education." Harvard Educational Review 42(Ag, 1972):374-389.

Wilson, William Julius. "The Declining Significance of Race." Society 15(Ja-F, 1978):56-62.

_____. "The Declining Significance of Race: Revisited but Not Revised." Society 11(Jl-Ag, 1978):11,16-21. [See Charles V. Willie, above]

Wilson, William Julius and others. "Racial Solidarity and Separate Education." School Review 81(My, 1973):365-373.

Winecoff, H. Larry, and Kelly, Eugene W., Jr. "Problems in School Desegregation: Real or Imaginary?" Integrated Education 9(Ja-F, 1971):3-10.

Winn, William. "School Integration: What Worked In Recent Weeks Across the South." South Today, Mr, 1970.

_____. "The South After Thirty Years: A Talk With Gunnar Myrdal." New South 26 (Winter, 1971):2-5.

Wirt, Frederick M. "School Policy Culture and State Centralization." In Yearbook on the Politics of Education. Edited by Jay Scribner. Chicago: National Society for the Study of Education, 1977.

Wirt, Frederick M., and Kirst, Michael W. The Political Web of American Schools. Boston, MA: Little, Brown, 1972.

Wittes, Simon. People and Power. A Study of Crisis in Secondary Schools. Ann Arbor, MI: Institute for Social Research, U. of Michigan, 1970. [Seven northern and western states]

Wohl, Anorzej. "Competitive Sport and Its Social Functions." International Review of Sport Sociology 5(1970):117-130.

Wolf, Eleanor P. "Civil Rights and Social Science Data." Race 14(O, 1972):155-182.

_____. "The Tipping Point in Racially Changing Neighborhoods." American Institute of Planners Journal, Ag, 1963.

Wolfgang, Aaron. "The Silent Language in the Multicultural Classroom." Theory Into Practice 16(Je, 1977):145-152.

Wolk, Anthy. "Linguistic and Social Bias in 'The American Heritage Dictionary.'" College English 33(My, 1972):930-935.

Woloshin, Renee. "Public Opinion and School Desegregation." Equal Opportunity Review, Ag, 1973.

Woock, Roger R. "Social Perspectives on Desegregation Policy and Research." Education and Urban Society 9(My, 1977):385-394.

Woodmansee, John H., and Turker, Richard D. "A Scale of Black Separation." Psychological Reports 27(D, 1970):855-858.

Woodring, Paul. "No Easy Solution." Saturday Review, F 19, 1966.

Woodside, A. G. "Credibility of Advertising Themes Among Blacks and Whites." Marquette Business Review 19(Fall, 1975).

Woodson, Carter G. "The Miseducation of the Negro." Crisis, Ag, 1931.

_____. The Rural Negro. Washington, DC: The Association for the Study of Negro Life and History, Inc., 1930.

Woofter, Thomas J. (ed.). Negro Problems in Cities. Garden City, NY: Doubleday, Doran, 1928.

Wortham, Jacob. "Closing Doors at the Money Stores." Black Enterprise 6(S, 1975):15-20. [Minority-related grants from foundations]

Wright, Arthur D. Negro rural school fund incorporated. Anna T. Jeanes Foundation 1907-1933. Washington, DC: Negro Rural School Fund, Incorporated, 1933.

Wright, Nathan, Jr. (ed.). What Black Educators Are Saying. New York: Hawthorne Books, 1970.

Wynne, Edward. "School Output Measures as Tools For Change." Education and Urban Society, N, 1969.

4X, Harold. "Black Psychologist Team Explores New Directions." Muhammad Speaks, S 27, 1974. [Seventh Annual Convention of National Association of Black Psychologists]

Yaari, Arieh. "Assimilation versus differenciation. Le phénomène national aux etats-unis d'Amerique." l'homme et la société 37-38(1975):117-141.

Yancey, William L., Ericksen, Eugene P., and Juliani, Richard N. "Emergent Ethnicity: A Review and Reformulation." American Sociological Review 41(Je, 1976):391-403.

Yeates, John W. "Private Schools and Public Confusion." New South 25(Fall, 1970):83-85.

Yetman, Norman R., and Eitzen, D. Stanley. "Black Americans in Sports: Unequal Opportunity for Equal Ability." Civil Rights Digest 5(Ag, 1972):21-34.

Yinger, J. M. "Desegregation in American Society: the Record of a Generation of Change." Sociology and Social Research, Jl, 1963.

_____. A Minority Group in American Society. New York: McGraw-Hill, 1965. [Negro Americans]

_____. "Sociological Guidelines for Research in Intergroup Relations Education." Journal of Intergroup Relations, Summer, 1965.

Young, Andrew J., Jr. "Resegregation and Inflation: New Challenges to Education." American Teacher, S, 1973.

Young, Biloine Whiting, and Bress, Grace Billings. "A New Educational Decision: Is Detroit the End of the School Bus Line?" Phi Delta Kappan 56(Ap, 1975):515-520.

Young, Whitney M., Jr. "A Cry from the Dispossessed." Christian Century, D 9, 1964.

_____. "Text of...Keynote Speech at Council for Exceptional Children Convention." Exceptional Children 36(Summer, 1970):727-734.

_____. To Be Equal. New York: McGraw-Hill, 1964.

_____. "Why We Should Suspend the Studies of Negroes." National Observer, Ap 1, 1968. A letter]

Zeluck, Steve. "What Chance for Educational Reform?" Changing Education, Winter, 1969.

Ziegler, Earle F. "The Black Athlete's Non-Athletic Problems." Educational Theory 22 (F, 1972):420-426.

Zimmer, Basil G, and Hawley, Amos H. "Factors Associated with Resistance to the Organization of Metropolitan Area Schools." Sociology of Education, Fall, 1967.

Zinn, Howard. "The Southern Mystique." American Scholar, Winter, 1963-64.

Zoloth, Barbara S. "Alternative Measures of School Segregation." Land Economics (Ag, 1976):278-298.

_____. An Investigation of Alternative Measures of School Segregation, N, 1974. ERIC ED 101 024.

Bibliographies

Albright, John B. (comp.). "A Bibliography of Community Analyses for Libraries." Library Trends 24(Ja, 1976):619-643.

Altus, David M. (comp.). Migrant Education. A Selected Bibliography. Supplement No. 2. Washington, DC: GPO, Ag, 1971.

_____. Rural Education and Small Schools. A Selected Bibliography. Supplement No. 1. University Park, NM: New Mexico State U., Jl, 1971. ERIC ED 055 695.

An Annotated Bibliography of Migrant Related Materials. Florida Atlanta U., Boca Raton, Mr, 1969. ERIC ED 030 523. [For a microfiche copy, send 75 cents to EDRS, The National Cash Register Company, Box 2206, Rockville, MD 20852]

Beal, George M. and others (comps.). Social Indicators: Bibliography I. Ames, IA: Department of Sociology and Anthropology, Iowa State U., 1971.

Bibliographies in Non-Formal Education: No. 1- Non-Formal Education in Anthropological Perspective. East Lansing, MI: Institute for International Studies in Education, Michigan State U., 1971.

Bibliography for Migrant Education Programs. Educational Systems Corp., Washington, DC, 1968. ERIC ED 030 052. [For a microfiche copy send 50 cents to EDRS, The National Cash Register Company, Box 2206, Rockville, MD 20852]

Bobson, Sarah (comp.). Nonstandard Dialects: An Annotated Bibliography..., Ag, 1974. ERIC ED 095 227.

Brasch, Ila Wales, and Brasch, Walter Milton (comps.). A Comprehensive Annotated Bibliography of American Black English. Baton Rouge: Louisiana State U., 1974.

Brignano, Russell C. (comp.). Black Americans in Autobiography. An Annotated Bibliography of Autobiographies and Autobiographical Books Written Since the Civil War. Durham, NC: Duke U. Press, 1974.

Brode, John (comp.). The Process of Modernization. Cambridge, MA: Harvard U. Press, 1969.

Brucker, Joan W. (comp.). An Annotated Bibliography of White Racism in Public School Education Today: Sources for Awareness and Action. 1972. Joan W. Brucker, 445 W. S. College Street, Yellow Springs, OH 45387. Fifty cents. [23 books and 25 articles]

Burnett, Jacquetta H., with Gordon, Sally W., and Gormley, Carol J. (comps.). Anthropology and Education. An Annotated Bibliographic Guide. New Haven, CT: Human Relations Area Files Press, 1974.

Buser, Robert L., and Humm, William L. (comps.). State Education Agencies: A Bibliography, 1969. ERIC ED 034 297.

Cardenas, Jose A. (comp.). Multicultural Education: An Annotated Bibliography, Ap, 1976. ERIC ED 151 430.

Childers, Thomas, and Post, Joyce A. (comps.). The Information-Poor in America. Metuchen, NJ: Scarecrow, 1975.

Christiansen, Dorothy (comp.). Busing and Education. New York: Center for Urban Education, F, 1969.

_____. Busing. Third Edition. A Center for Urban Education Bibliography. New York: Center for Urban Education, O, 1971. ERIC ED 061 378.

_____. "Busing Bibliography." Urban Review 6(S-O, 1972):35-38.

Coelho, George V., Hamburg, David A., Moor, Rudolph, and Randolph, Peter (comps.). Coping and Adaptation. A Behavioral Sciences Bibliography. Washington, DC: GPO, 1970.

Cohen, David (comp.). Multi-Ethnic Media: Selected Bibliographies in Print. Chicago: Office for Library Service to the Disadvantaged, American Library Association, 1975.

Coller, Alan R., and Guthrie, P. D. Self-Concept Measures: An Annotated Bibliography. Princeton, NJ: Educational Testing Service, Head Start Test Collection, Ap, 1971. ERIC ED 051 305.

Comas, Juan (comp.). Bibliographia selectiva de las culturas indigenas de America. Mexico: Pan American Institute of Geography and History, 1953.

Cordasco, Francesco, Hillson, Maurie, and Bucchioni, Eugene (comps.). The Equality of Educational Opportunity. Totowa, NJ: Littlefield, Adams & Co., 1973.

"Current Bibliographic Sources in Education." Educational Documentation and Information 203(2nd Quarter, 1977):9-60.

d'Arc, Helene Riviere, and Kayser, Bernard (comps.). International Migration of Man-power--Bibliography. Paris: Organization for Economic Cooperation and Development, 1969.

Davis, E. E. (ed.). Attitude Change: A Review and Bibliography of Selected Research. Paris: UNESCO, 1953.

Davis, Lenwood G. (comp.). The Black Family in Urban Areas in the United States. 2nd ed., Je, 1975. ERIC ED 126 184.

_____. The Black Family in the United States. A Selected Bibliography of Annotated Books, Articles, and Dissertations on Black Families in America. Westport, CT: Greenwood, 1978.

DeBoer, Peter P., and McCaul, Robert L. (comps.). "Annotated List of 'Chicago Tribune Editorials' on Elementary and Secondary Education in the U.S.," Part III. History of Education Quarterly 13(Winter, 1973):457-485.

Diamond, Stanley and others. Culture of Schools. 4 vols. Washington, DC: Office of Education, 1966.

Directory for Reaching Minority Groups. Washington, DC: Manpower Administration (DOL), Bureau of Apprenticeship and Training, 1970. Available from Supt. of Documents. ERIC ED 052 356.

Dixon, Johanne C. (comp.). A Selected Annotated Bibliography on Black Families. Vol. I. New York: National Urban League, 1977.

Domyahn, Roger A. (comp.). "Annotated Bibliography on Accountability." Audiovisual Instruction 16(My, 1971):93-101.

Dorko, Kathryn. Compensation and Equalization in Education: Selected Annotated References in Periodical Literature, 1968-1971. Washington, DC: Library of Congress, Congressional Research Service, F 11, 1972. ERIC ED 064 453.

Dvorkin, Bettifae E. (comp.). Blacks and Mental Health in the United States, 1963-1973... Washington, DC: Medical-Dental Library, Howard U., 1974.

ERIC. Educational Documents Index, 1966-1969. 2 vols. New York: CCM Information Corporation, 1970.

ERIC. Clearinghouse on Educational Administration (comp.). Human Relations in Educational Administration. Washington, DC: American Association of School Administrators, 1970.

ERIC. Clearinghouse on Rural Education and Small Schools (comp.). Public Libraries and Mexican Americans, My, 1977. ERIC ED 152 473.

Foster, Robert J. (comp.). Human Factors in Civic Action: A Selected Annotated Bibliography. Alexandria, VA: Human Resources Research Office, George Washington U., n.d.

Gilissen, John. Introduction bibliographique a' l'histoire du droit et a l'ethnologie juridique. Bruxelles: Les Éditions de l'institut de Sociologie-Université Libre de Bruxelles, 1970.

Glenn, Norval, Alston, Jon P., and Weiner, David (comps.). Social Stratification: A Research Bibliography, 1970. The Glendessary Press, 2512 Grove Street, Berkeley, CA 94704.

Goldstaub, Jesse (ed.). Manpower and Educational Planning: An Annotated Bibliography of Currently Available Materials. School of Education, Pittsburgh U., Jl, 1968. ERIC ED 030 195.

Hall, Jo Anne (comp.). "Busing Bibliography." RQ 11(Summer, 1972):320-327.

Handler, June. "Books for Loving." Elementary English 47(My, 1970):687-692.

Heathman, James E., and Nafziger, Alyce J. (comps.). Migrant Education, A Selected Bibliography. Supplement No. 1. University Park, NM: New Mexico State U., Je, 1970. Available from Manager, Duplicating Service, New Mexico State U., PO Box 3-CB, Las Cruces, NM.

Hillyer, Mildred. Bibliography of Spanish and Southwestern Indian Cultures Library Books. Grants, NM: Grants Municipal Schools, My 20, 1969. ERIC ED 047 846.

HUD Clearinghouse Service. Recent Research in Public Administration. A Reference. 1969. Washington, DC: GPO, Je, 1969.

_____. Selected Abstracts of Planning Reports. Washington, DC: GPO, Je, 1969.

_____. Selected Information Sources for Urban Specialists. Washington, DC: GPO, Je, 1969.

Institute for Rural America. Poverty, Rural Poverty, and Minority Groups Living in Rural Poverty: An Annotated Bibliography, 1969. Spindletop Research, Inc., PO Box 481, Iron Works Road, Lexington, KY 40501.

Jablonsky, Adelaide (comp.). Curriculum and Instruction for Minority Groups: An Annotated Bibliography of Doctoral Dissertations. ERIC ED 086 748.

_____. School Dropout Programs. A Review of the ERIC Literature. New York: ERIC, Teachers College, Columbia U., Mr, 1970.

_____. The School Dropout and the World of Work. A Review of the ERIC Literature. New York: ERIC, Teachers College, Columbia U., 1970.

Jackson, Clara O. (comp.). Bibliography of Afro-American and Other Minorities Represented in Library Listings, 1971. American Institute for Marxist Studies, 20 East 30th Street, New York, NY 10016.

Jenkins, Betty Lanier, and Phillis, Susan (comps.). Black Separatism: A Bibliography. Westport, CT: Greenwood Press, 1976.

Johnson, Harry A. (ed.). Ethnic American Minorities: A Guide to Media and Materials. New York: Bowker, 1976.

Johnson, Leanor Boulin (comp.). "Relevant Literature in the Study of the Black Family: An Annotated Bibliography." Journal of Social and Behavioral Sciences 20(Spring, 1974):79-100.

Kleve, John A. (comp.), and Smith Stuart C. Selected Bibliography on Educational Parks. Bibliography Series, No. 15. ERIC Clearinghouse on Educational Administration, U. of Oregon, Jl, 1969.

Kniefel, David R., and Kniefel, Tanya S. Annotated Bibliography and Descriptive Summary of Dissertations and Theses on Rurality and Small Schools. University Park, NM: New Mexico State U. ERIC Clearinghouse on Rural Education and Small Schools, My, 1970. ERIC ED 039 962.

Kolm, Richard (comp.). Bibliography of Ethnicity and Ethnic Groups. Washington, DC: GPO, 1973.

Leffall, Dolores C., and Johnson, James P. (comps.). Black English: An Annotated Bibliography. Washington, DC: Minority Research Center, 1973.

Lewis, Spencer H. (comp.). The Minority Group Workers. Urbana, IL: Institute of Labor and Industrial Relations, U. of Illinos, S, 1969.

Linking Schools to State Education Departments. Eugene, OR: ERIC Clearinghouse on Educational Administration, U. of Oregon, S, 1970.

Lockwood, William G. (comp.). Toward a Theory of Ethnicity: A Working Bibliography on Ethnic Groups and Interethnic Relations in Cross-Cultural Perspective, with Supplemental References to Caste, Nationalism, "Tribe" and "Race." Monticello, IL: Council of Planning Librarians, 1977.

Lystod, Mary H. (comp.). Social Aspects of Alienation. An Annotated Bibliography. Public Health Service Pub. No. 1978. Washington, DC: GPO, 1969.

Maguire, Lucas M. and others. An Annotated Bibliography on Administering for Change. Philadelphia, PA: Research for Better Schools, Inc., O, 1971. ERIC ED 056 246.

Mangione, Anthony Roy (comp.). "Literature on the White Ethnic Experience." English Journal 63(Ja, 1974):42-51.

Marien, Michael (comp.). Essential Reading for the Future of Education. A Selected and Critically Annotated Bibliography. Syracuse, NY: Syracuse U. Research Corp., New York Educational Policy Research Center, 1970. ERIC ED 047 406.

Marshall, John F., Morris, Susan, and Polgar, Steven (comps.). "Culture and Notability: A Preliminary Classified Bibliography." Current Anthropology 13(Ap, 1972):268-278.

Master Annotated Bibliography of the Papers of Mobilization for Youth. New York: Mobilization for Youth, 1965.

MARC: A Selected Bibliography, 1967-1971. New York: Metropolitan Applied Research Center, 1972.

Michigan-Ohio Regional Educational Laboratory. Racism and Education: A Review of Selected Literature Related to Segregation, Discrimination, and Other Implications of Racism for Education. Detroit: The Laboratory, 1969.

Miller, Wayne C. (comp.). A Comprehensive Bibliography for the Study of American Minorities. New York: New York U. Press, 1976.

Minority Groups: A Bibliography and Supplement. Salt Lake City, UT: Utah State Board of Education, 1968. ERIC ED 042 767.

Murphy, Sharon (comp.). Other Voices: Black, Chicano, and American Indian Press. Pflaum/Standard, 38 W. 5th Street, Dayton, OH 45402.

National Directory of Black School Board Members: Elected and Appointed. New York: Scholarship, Education and Defense Fund for Racial Equality, N, 1971.

National Institute of Mental Health, National Clearinghouse for Mental Health Information (comp.). Bibliography on Racism. Washington, DC: GPO, 1972.

Nichols, Margaret S., and O'Neill, Peggy (comps.). Multicultural Resources for Children. A Bibliography of Materials for Preschool Through Elementary School in the Areas of Black, Spanish-speaking, Asian-Americans, Native American, and Pacific Island Cultures. Stanford, CA: Multicultural Resources, 1977.

Office of Human Resources and Minority Affairs. Human Resources for U.S. School Boards. A Compendium of Individuals with Expertise in the Area of Human Relations. Evanston, IL: National School Boards Association, 1971.

Office of Personnel and Training. Directory of Organizations Serving Minority Communities. Washington, DC: U.S. Department of Justice, 1970.

Piele, Philip K., and Smith, Stuart C. (comps.). Directory of Organizations and Personnel in Educational Management. 3rd edition: 1971-1972. Eugene, OR: ERIC Clearinghouse on Educational Management, U. of Oregon, D, 1971.

Pilcher, William W. (comp.). Urban Anthropology: A Research Bibliography. Monticello, IL: Council of Planning Librarians, 1975.

Population Index Bibliography, Cumulated 1935-1968. 8 vols. Boston, MA: G. K. Hall & Co., 1971.

Poverty, Rural Poverty and Minority Groups Living in Rural Poverty: An Annotated Bibliography. Lexington, KY: Institute for Rural America, Spindletop Research Center, Je, 1969. ERIC ED 041 679.

Price, Daniel O., and Sikes, Melanie M. (comps.). Rural-Urban Migration Research in the United States. Annoted Bibliography and Sythesis. Washington, DC: GPO, 1975.

Programs for Inner-City Communities: An Annotated Bibliography. American Society of Planning Officials Advisory Service Report No. 249, Ag, 1969 (entire issue).

Quay, Richard H. (comp.). In Pursuit of Equality of Education Opportunity. A Selected Bibliography and Guide to the Research Literature. New York: Garland, 1977.

Racism and Education: A Review of Selected Literature Related to Segregation, Discrimination, and Other Aspects of Racism in Education. Detroit, MI: Michigan-Ohio Regional Education Lab., Inc., My, 1969. ERIC ED 034 836.

Reference List of Private and Denominational Southern Colored Schools. 3rd edition. Charlottesville, VA: Surber-Arundale Company, 1925.

Regnell, John B. (comp.). United States Urban Revolution: Cities in Crisis. A Selected and Subject-Classified Bibliography of Books Relating to Cities, 1960-1969. Reno, NV: Bureau of Governmental Research, U. of Nevada, 1969.

Resegregation: An Annotated Bibliography. Ann Arbor: Program for Educational Opportunity, U. of Michigan, n.d.

Rose Bibliography (Project). Analytical Guide and Indexes to: Alexander's Magazine, 1905-1909. The Colored American Magazine, 1900-1909. 2 vols. The Voice of the Negro, 1904-1907. Westport, CT: Greenwood Press, 1974.

Rosenthal, Annette (comp.). Education and Anthropology. An Annotated Bibliography. New York: Garland, 1977.

Rural Poverty: An Annotated and Referenced Bibliography, 1966. ERIC ED 032 163.

Sanders, Charles L., and McLean, Linda (comps.). Directory: National Black Organizations. New York: AFRAM Associates, 1972.

Spencer, Richard E., and Awe, Ruth (comps.). International Educational Exchange: A Bibliography. 1970. Institute of International Education, 809 United States Plaza, New York, NY 10017.

State Board of Education. Minority Groups. A Bibliography. Salt Lake City, UT: The Board, 1968.

Storey, Edward (comp.). Anthropology and Education: A General Bibliography. Altanta, GA Department of Anthropology, Georgia State U., 1971.

Suhor, Charles. "Pater's Sibling Thomas." Media & Methods, O, 1969.

Sullivan, Marjorie, and Goodell, John S. "Media Use in the Study of Minorities." Emporia State Res. Stud. 24(Fall, 1975):5-63.

Sullivan, Neil V. "Desegregation Techniques," Racial Isolation in the Public Schools. Vol. II, Appendix D2.5. Washington, DC: GPO, 1967.

_____. "The Eye of the Hurricane." Integrated Education, Ag-N, 1965.

_____. "Ghetto Schools? Close 'Em!" Nation, My 27, 1968.

_____. "Make Freedom Live." Integrated Education, Ag-S, 1966.

_____. "Myths and Gaps in School Integration." Today's Education, S, 1968.

_____. The New Three R's of Education: Refunding, Regional Cooperation, Racial Balance. Boston, MA: Department of Education, Bureau of Educational Information Services, Ja 20, 1972.

_____. "Speeding School Integretation in the South." Bulletin of the Harvard Graduate School of Education, Winter, 1964-1965.

"Summary of Proceedings of Research Conference." Integrated Education, Ag-S, 1966.

Stuart, Surlin H., and Turner, Phillip M. The Persuasibility of a White or Black Source upon High and Low Racially Prejudiced White Individuals, Ap, 1972. ERIC ED 060 660.

Suval, Elizabeth M., and Hamilton, Horace. "Some New Evidence on Educational Selectivity in Migration to and from the South." Social Forces, My, 1965.

Swanson, Austin D. "An International Perspective on Social Science Research and School Integration." Journal of Negro Education (Winter, 1979):57-66.

Swartz, Darlene J. "School Discontenter." Integrateducation 13(Mr-Ap, 1975):33 [Verse]

Swearingen, Mildren E. and others. Institute Training Programs on Problems of School Desegregation: Interim Report. Final Report, and Followup Conference, 1966. ERIC ED 056 106.

Sweet, James A. Indicators of Family and Household Structure of Racial and Ethnic Minorities in the U.S., O, 1977. ERIC ED 155 235.

Swenson, Esther J. "Education for A New Generation." In The Rising South, II, pp. 141-161. Edited by Robert H. McKenzie. University, AL: U. of Alabama Press, 1976.

"Symposium on Desegregation." NEA Journal, D, 1963.

"Symposium on Negro Education." NEA Proceedings, 1890, pp. 254-285.

Syrkin, Marie. "Jim Crow in the Classroom." Common Ground, Summer, 1944.

Szasz, Thomas S. "Blackness and Madness." Yale Review 59(1970):333-341.

Szilak, Dennis. "AFRO a.m.: Renaissance in the Revolution." College English 31(Ap, 1970): 685-694.

Taeuber, Irene B. "Change and Transition in the Black Population of the United States." Population Index 34(Ap-Je, 1968):121-151.

Taeuber, Karl L. "Race Age, and School Enrollment in Large Metropolitan Areas." Preliminary. Washington, DC: U.S. Commission on Civil Rights, Ja 19, 1967, unpublished.

Taeuber, Karl E., and Taeuber, Alma F. "The Changing Character of Negro Migration." American Journal of Sociology, Ja, 1965.

_____ and _____. "Is the Negro an Immigrant Group." Integrated Education, Je, 1963.

_____ and _____. "The Negro As An Immigrant Group: Recent Trends in Racial and Ethnic Segregation in Chicago." American Journal of Sociology, Ja, 1964.

_____ and _____. Negroes in Cities: Residential Segregation and Neighborhood Change. Chicago: Aldine, 1965.

_____ and _____. "White Migration and Socio-Economic Differences between Cities and Suburbs." American Sociological Review, O, 1964.

Takahashi, Herb. "Mental Illness and Pooressed People." Hawaii Pono Journal, 1(Ap, 1971): 72-85.

Tangman, Jack. "The Fully Integrated Curriculum in Secondary Schools." Changing Education, Fall, 1966.

Tanner, Daniel, and Tanner, Laurel N. "Parent Education and Cultural Inheritance." School and Society 99(Ja, 1971):21-24.

Task Force on Urban Education. Schools of the Urban Crisis. Washington, DC: National Education Association, 1969.

Taylor, Bryan P. "The School Cafeteria and Equal Treatment." Integrated Education, 10(N-D, 1972):73-75.

Taylor, Charles. "Politics and Policies. Or Are the Public Schools Equal Opportunity Employers?" Black Enterprise 31(S, 1972):22-23.

U.S. Commission on Civil Rights. Civil Rights Directory. Revised edition. Washington, DC: GPO, 1970.

U.S. Department of Commerce. Directory of Minority Media. Washington, DC: GPO, Je, 1973.

U.S. Department of Health, Education, and Welfare, Office for Civil Rights. Directory of Public Elementary and Secondary Schools in Selected Districts. Enrollment and Staff by Racial/Ethnic Group. Fall, 1972. Washington, DC: GPO, 1974.

_____. Directory of Public Elementary and Secondary Schools in Selected Districts. Enrollment and Staff by Racial/Ethnic Group. Fall, 1970. Washington, DC: GPO, 1972.

_____. Directory of Public Elementary and Secondary Schools in Selected Districts. Enrollment and Staff by Racial/Ethnic Group. Fall, 1968. Washington, DC: GPO, 1970.

U.S. Department of Labor, Bureau of Labor Statistics. Black Americans. A Handbook. Washington, DC: GPO, 1971.

U.S. Department of Labor. Directory for Reaching Minority Groups. Washington, DC: GPO, 1973.

U.S. Department of Labor, Manpower Administration. Manpower Research Projects Sponsored by the U.S. Department of Labor, Manpower Administration through June 30, 1970. Washington, DC: GPO, 1970.

U.S. Social Security Administration (comp.). Poverty Studies in the Sixties. A Selected, Annotated Bibliography. Washington, DC: GPO, 1970.

Utah. State Board of Education. Minority Groups. A Bibliography. Salt Lake City, UT: The Board, 1968.

Webster, Maureen and others. Educational Planning and Policy: An International Bibliography. Working Draft. Parts I-VI. Syracuse, NY: Syracuse U. Research Corp. Je, 1969. ERIC ED 042 238.

Zachariasen, Ellen (comp.). Poverty in the United States, 1969-1970: Selected References. Washington, DC: Library of Congress, Legislative Reference Service, N 18, 1970. ERIC ED 064 454.

Zusman, Jack, Hannon, Virginia, Locke, Ben Z., and Geller, Miriam (comps.). Bibliography on Epidemiology of Mental Disorders. Washington: DC: GPO, 1970.

22.
WORLD SCENE

Education Studies by Country

Afghanistan

Halliday, Fred. "Revolution in Afghanistan."
New Left Review 112(N-D, 1978):3-44.

Poullada, Leon B. Reform and Rebellion in
Afghanistan, 1919-1929: King Amanullah's
Failure to Modernize a Tribal Society.
Ithaca, NY: Cornell U. Press, 1973.

Sullivan, Michael G. "Schooling and National
Integration in Afghanistan: A Study of
Students in the Faculty of Education, Kabul
University." Doctoral dissertation, U. of
Pittsburgh, 1973. Univ. Microfilms Order No.
74-16,539.

Algeria

Ageron, Charles-Robert. Les Musulmans
Algeriens et la France (1871-1919). 2 vols.
Paris: Presses Universitaires de Frances,
1968.

Bourdieu, Pierre. Algeria 1960. New York:
Cambridge U. Press, 1979.

_____. "The Algerian Subproletariat." In
Man, State, and Society in the Contemporary
Maghrib. Edited by William Zartman. New
York: n.p., 1973.

_____. Travail et Travailleurs en Algérie.
Paris: Mouton, 1962.

Briggs, L. C., and Guele, M. L. No More For
Ever: A Saharan Jewish Town. Cambridge, MA:
Harvard U. Press, 1964.

Chaib, Mohamed. Bilingualism and the Choice of
a Teaching Language. A Survey of the Algerian
Case. Lund, Sweden: Pedagogiska
institutionen, U. of Lund, 1972.

Chemoulli, Henri. Une Diaspora meconnue:
Les juifs d'Algérie. Paris: Imp, 1976.

Colonna, Fanny. "Cultural Resistance and
Religious Legitimacy in Colonial Algeria."
Economy and Society 3(1974):233-252.

_____. Instituteurs algériens, 1883-1939.
Paris: Presses de la fondation nationale
des sciences politiques, 1975.

_____. "Le système d'enseignement de l'Algérie
coloniale." Archives Européannes de
Sociologie 13(1972):195-220.

_____. "Verdict scolaire et position de classe
sous l'Algérie coloniale." Revue francaise
de Sociologie 14(1973):180-201.

De Gramont, Sanche. "Our Other Man in Algiers."
New York Times Magazine, N 1, 1970.
[Eldridge Cleaver and revolutionary movements
of Africa and Asia]

Firestone, Ya'akov. "The Doctrine of Integration
with France Among the Europeans of Algeria,
1955-1960." Comparative Political Studies,
J1, 1971.

Fitzgerald, E. Peter. [Native Schoolteachers as
a Mediating Elite in Colonial Algeria: the
"Association des Instituteurs d'origine
indigene" and La Voix de Humbles during the
1920's] Proc. Fr. Colonial Hist. Soc. 2(1977):
155-168.

Gallissot, René. "Precolonial Algeria." Economy
and Society 4(N, 1975):418-445.

Gellner, Ernest, and Micaud, Charles (eds.).
Arabs and Berbers: from Tribes to Nation in
North Africa. London: Duckworth, 1973.

Heggoy, Alf Andrew. "Arab Education in Colonial
Algeria." J. Afric. Studies 2(Summer, 1975):
149-160.

_____. "Education in French Algeria: An Essay
on Cultural Conflict." Comparative Education
Review 17(Je, 1973):180-197.

_____. "Kepi and Chalkboards: French Soldiers and Education in Revolutionary Algeria." Military Affairs 37(D, 1973).

Kuper, Leo. The Pity of It All: Polarisation of Racial and Ethnic Relations. London: Duckworth, 1977.

_____. "Race, Class and Power: Some Comments on Revolutionary Change." Comparative Studies in Society and History 14(S, 1972): 400-421. [South Africa and Algeria]

Lacheraf, Mostefa. L'Algérie: Nation et Société. Paris: Maspers, 1965.

Lazreg, Marnia. The Emergence of Classes in Algeria. Boulder, CO: Westview Press, 1976.

Meymé, Georges. L'Algerie juive. Paris: Nouvelle Librairie Parisienne, 1887.

Morel, Jacques. "L'école et la formation des élites en Algérie de 1919 à 1939." Bull. Inst. hist. Pays Outre-Mer 3(1968-1969).

M'Quidech. "Une minorité berbère d'Algérie: les Kabyles." Partisans, My-Ag, 1971.

Murphy, Dermot F. "Colonial and Post-Colonial Language Policy in the Maghreb." Maghreb Review 2(Mr-Ap, 1977):1-9.

Nora, Pierre. Les Français d'Algerie. Paris: Julliard, 1961.

Nouschi, André. La Naissance du Nationalisme Algérien, 1914-1954. Paris: Editions de Minuit, 1962.

Peters, Philip. "Algeria After Independence." New Society, Ap 6, 1972.

Simmons, Charles. "Algerians Correct French Lies About 'Benefits' of Colonization." Muhammad Speaks, Ap 23, 1971.

Smith, T. "Muslim Impoverishment in Colonial Algeria." R. Occident musulman Meditérr. 17 (1974):139-162.

"Thunder in Marseilles." Patterns of Prejudice 7(S-O, 1973):16-18. [Anti-Algerian movement]

Trebous, Madeleine. Migration and Development-- The Case of Algeria. Paris: Development Centre Studies, 1970. [France, Belgium, and Germany]

Turin, Yvonne. Affrontements culturels dans l'Algérie coloniale: Écoles, médecines, religion, 1830-1880. Paris: Maspero, 1971.

Vatin, Jean Claude. "Conditions et formes de la domination coloniale en Algérie (1919-1945)." Revue algérienne des sciences juridiques, politiques et économiques 9(D, 1972):873-906.

Angola

António, Mário. Luanda "Ilha" Crioula. Lisbon: Agencia-Geral Do Ultramar, 1969. [Luanda Creole Island]

Bender, Gerald Jacob. Angola Under the Portuguese. The Myth and the Reality. Berkeley, CA: U. of California Press, 1978.

_____. "The Myth and Reality of Portuguese Rule in Angola: A Study of Racial Domination." Doctoral dissertation, U. of California, Los Angeles, 1975. Univ. Microfilms Order No. 76-05117.

Boavida, Américo. Angola: Five Centuries of Portuguese Exploitation, O, 1972. LSM Information Center, Box 338, Richmond, B.C., Canada.

Bustin, Edouard. Lunda Under Belgian Rule: The Politics of Ethnicity. Cambridge, MA: Harvard U. Press, 1975. [Angola]

Dash, Leon. "A Long March in Angola." Washington Post, Ag 13, 1977. [Seven articles on the UNITA forces]

Davidson, Basil. In the Eye of the Storm. London: Longman, 1972. [The revolt in Angola]

"Education: A Strategy Factor of Liberation." Angola in Arms 1(F, 1971).

Heimer, Franz-Wilhelm. Social Change in Angola. Munich: Weltforum Verlag, 1973.

"MPLA: Against Racism, Tribalism." Race and Class 18(Winter, 1977):293-298.

Pelissier, Rene. La Colonie du Minotaure: Nationalismes et Revoltes en Angola (1926-1961). Montamets, France: Pelissier, 1978.

_____. Les Guerres Grises: Resistance et Revoltes en Angola (1845-1941). Montamets, France: Pelissier, 1977.

Samuels, Michael A. Education in Angola, 1878-1914: A History of Culture Transfer and Administration. New York: Teachers College Press, 1970.

_____. "Educaçāo or Instruçāo? A History of Education in Angola, 1878-1914." Doctoral dissertation, Columbia U., 1969.

Argentina

Abou, Selim. Immigrés dans l'autre Amerique: Autobiographies de quatre Argentins d'origine libanaise. Paris: Plon, 1972.

Andress, George Reid. "Forgotten But Not Gone: The Afro-Argentines of Buenos Aires, 1800-1900." Doctoral dissertation, U. of Wisconsin, 1978. Univ. Microfilms Order No. 7817090

Ansel, Bernard D. "The Beginnings of the Modern Jewish Community in Argentina, 1852-1891." Doctoral dissertation, U. of Kansas, 1969. Univ. Microfilms Order No. 70-10,993.

Ansel, B. D. "Discord Among Western and Eastern European Jews in Argentina." American Jewish Historical Quarterly 60(D, 1970):151-158.

"Chronicle: Education." Jewish Journal of Sociology 11(Je, 1969). [Buenos Aires]

Goldberg, M. B. "La poblacíon negra y mulata de la ciudad de Buenos Aires, 1810-1840." Desarrollo Económico 16(Ap-Je, 1976).

Lanuza, José Luis. Morenada. Buenos Aires: Emecé, 1946.

Mirelman, Victor A. "Attitudes towards Jews in Argentina." Jewish Social Studies 37 (Summer-Fall, 1975):205-220.

Perlman, Janice E. The Myth of Marginality. Urban Poverty and Politics in Rio de Janeiro. Berkeley, CA: U. of California Press, 1977.

Rodriguez, Nemesio J. Oppression in Argentina: The Mataco Case. Copenhagen: International Work Group for Indigenous Affairs, 1975.

Schwartz, Kessel. "Antisemitism in Modern Argentine Fiction." Jewish Social Studies 40(Spring, 1978):131-140.

Spratlin, V. B. "Latin America and the Negro." Quarterly Review of Higher Education Among Negroes 10(O, 1942):201-204.

Tedesco, Juan Carlos. "Oligarquía, clase media y Educacíon en la Argentina (1900-1930). Aportes 21(1971). [See, also, "Crítica" by Aldo E. Solari.]

_____. "Universidad y clases sociales: el caso argentino." R. latinoamer. Cienc. polit. 3(1972):197-227.

Thompson, Era Bell. "Argentina: Land of the Vanishing Blacks." Ebony, O, 1973.

Weisbrot, Robert. "Anti-Semitism in Argentina." Midstream 24(My, 1978):12-23.

Australia

Aborigines

Abbie, Andrew A. The Original Australians. New York: American Elsevier, 1969.

Aboriginal Children at School. Special Problems and Special Needs. Sydney, Australia: New South Wales Teachers Federation, 1971.

"Aboriginal Education: Quo Vadis?" Northian 11(Summer, 1975):5-9.

"The Aborigines: White Australia's Anaomaly." Race Today 4(N, 1972):362-363.

Aborigines in the '70's. Seminars 1972-73. Centre for Research into Aboriginal Affairs, 1974.

"Advance for Australia's Aborigines." Institute of Race Relations Newsletter, O-N, 1967.

Altman, Jon C., and Nieuwenhuysen, John P. The Economic Status of Australian Aborigines. New York: Cambridge U. Press, 1979.

"Are Aborigines Australians?" Education (Australia), Je 18, 1969.

Australia, Commonweath of. The Australian Aborigines. Halstead, 1973.

Australian Advisory Group on Teaching in Aboriginal Languages in Schools in Aboriginal Communities in the Northern Territory. Bilingual Education in Schools in Aboriginal Communities in the Northern Territory. Canberra: Department of Education, 1973.

Australian Government Commission Into Poverty. "Aboriginals and Education." In Poverty and Education in Australia, chapter 9. Canberra: Australian Government Publishing Service, 1976.

Australian Institute of Aboriginal Studies Catalogue of Tape Archive No. 6, My, 1970. ERIC ED 040 400.

Baglin, D., and Mullins, B. The Aborigines of Australia. Sydney, Australia: Horwitz, 1969.

Bailey, Jean. "An Experiment in Human Relations." Education (New South Wales Federation of Teachers), 2 parts, Je 14, 28, 1967. [An aborigine boy lives with an Australian white family in Newcastle.]

Baldwin, E. "A Mandate Ignored by Governments." Education (New South Wales Federation of Teachers), N 20, 1968. [Education of Australian Aborigines]

Barker, Jimmie, as told to Matthews, Janet. The Two Worlds of Jimmie Barker: The Life of an Australian Aboriginal, 1900-1972. Canberra: Australian Institute of Aboriginal Studies, 1977.

Bates, Daisy. The Passing of the Aborigines. A Lifetime Spent Among the Natives of Australia. Melbourne, Australia, 1966.

Beckett, Jeremy R. "Kinship, Mobility and Community among Part-Aborigines in Rural Australia." International Journal of Comparative Sociology 6(1965):7-23.

Beddle, E. H. "The Assimilation of Aborigines in Brisbane." Doctoral dissertation, U. of Missouri, 1965.

Berndt, R. M. (ed.). Aborigines and Change: Australia in the 70's. Atlantic Highlands, NJ: Humanities, 1978.

_____ (ed.). Australian Aboriginal Anthropology: Modern Studies in the Social Anthropology of the Australian Aborigines. Nedlands, Australia: U. of Western Australia Press, 1970.

_____. "Problems of Assimilation in Australia." Sociologus 11(1961):34-51.

Berndt, R. M., and Berndt, C. The World of First Australians. Sydney, Australia: Ure Smith, 1964.

Berry, John W. "Marginality, Stress, and Ethnic Identification in an Acculturated Aboriginal Community." Journal of Cross Cultural Psychology 1(S, 1970):239-252.

Biddle, Ellen, and Smith, Hazel. "Educational Standard of People of Aboriginal Descent Living in the Brisbane Metropolitan Area." Australian Journal of Social Issues 3(1968): 13-25.

Biskup, Peter. "Native Administration and Welfare in Western Australia, 1897-1954. Master's thesis, U. of Western Australia, 1965.

_____. Not Slaves Not Citizens: The Aboriginal Problem in Western Australia 1898-1954. New York: Crane, Russak & Co., 1973.

_____. "White Aboriginal Relations in Western Australia: An Overview." Comparative Studies in Society & History, J1, 1968.

Blainey, Geoffrey. Triumph of the Nomads. A History of Ancient Australia. London: Macmillan, 1976.

Blundell, Valda Jean. "Aboriginal Adaptation in Northwest Australia." Doctoral dissertation, U. of Wisconsin, 1975. Univ. Microfilms Order No. 76-8571.

"Bobbi Sykes Talks to Leila Hassan." Race Today 4(D, 1972):388. [Black Australians]

Bochner, Stephen. "An Unobtrusive Approach to the Study of Housing Discrimination against Aborigines." Australian Journal of Psychology 24(D, 1972):335-337.

Bridges, Barry. "Considerations for an Educational Policy for the Part Aborigines of New South Wales." Australian Journal of Social Issues 3(1969):3-32.

_____. "Educational Policy for Aborigines." Australian Journal of Social Issues 3(1968): 26-32.

Broom, L. "Educational Status of Aborigines." Australian and New Zealand Journal of Sociology 6(O, 1970):150-156.

Broom, Leonard. "Workforce and Occupational Statuses of Aborigines." Australian and New Zealand Journal of Sociology 7(Ap, 1971): 21-34.

Broster, Peter. "Out in the Real Australia." Times Educational Supplement, S 3, 1976. [Aboriginal education]

Bruce, D. W., Hengeveld, M., and Radford, W. C. Some Cognitive Skills in Aboriginal Children in Victorian Primary Schools. Hawthorn, Victoria: Australian Council for Educational Programs, 1971.

Burridge, Kenelm. Encountering Aborigines. Anthropology and the Australian Aboriginal (A Case Study). London: Pergamon, 1973.

Cawte, John. Cruel, Poor and Brutal Nations: The Assessment of Mental Health in an Australian Aboriginal Community by Short-Stay Psychiatric Field Team Methods. Honolulu: U. Press of Hawaii, 1972.

Centre for Research into Aboriginal Affairs. Seminars 1971. Monash U., 1972.

Chaples, Ernest A. and others. Racial Attitudes of Australian Tertiary Students, 1976. ERIC ED 142 887. [Attitudes toward Aborigines]

Clark, H. M. "Aboriginal Assimilation in Two Communities." Master's thesis, U. of Newcastle, 1971.

Clyne, M. (ed.). Australia Talks: Essays on the Sociology of Australian Immigrant and Aboriginal Languages. Canberra: Australian National U., 1976.

Coe, Paul. The Australian Aborigine Black Power Movement 1972. Native Struggles Support Group, 100 St. George Street, Room 1037, Toronto 181, Canada.

Coombs, H. C. "A Programme for Aboriginal Progress." Education (New South Wales Federation of Teachers), My 1, 1968.

Coombs, H. C. Australia's Policy Towards Aborigines 1967-1977. London: Minority Rights Group, Mr, 1978.

Coppell, W. G., and Mitchell, Jan S. "Teaching About Aborigines in Australian Teachers' Colleges." Race 14(J1, 1972):77-81.

Corris, Peter. Aborigines and Europeans in Western Victoria. Canberra: Australian Institute of Aboriginal Studies, 1968.

Dasen, Pierre. "The Development of Conservation in Aboriginal Children: A Replication Study." International Journal of Psychology 7(1972):75-85. [See De Lemos, below.]

Davidson, G. S. and others. Education of Isolated School Children, S, 1976. ERIC ED 153 748.

Davies, B. "Aboriginal Pygmalion in Australia: An Open and Closed Case." Multiculturalism 2, No. 2(1978):15-17.

_____. "The Part-Aboriginal Child in the Australian Classroom." Doctoral dissertation, U. of New England, 1974.

Dawson, John L. M. A Comparative Analysis of the Origin and Structure of Certain Aboriginal Attitudes Towards Education and Integration. Canberra: University Press, 1970.

_____. "Aboriginal Attitudes Towards Education and Integration." In R. Taft and Others, Attitudes and Social Conditions. Canberra: Australian National U., 1970

_____. "Attitude, Change, and Conflict Among Australian Aborigines." Australian Journal of Psychiatry 21(1969).

_____. "Exchange Theory and Comparison Level Changes Among Australian Aborigines." British Journal of Social and Clinical Psychology 8(1969):133-140.

De Lacey, Philip R. "A Cross-Cultural Study of Classificatory Ability in Australia." Journal of Cross Cultural Psychology 1(D, 1970):293-304.

_____. "An Index of Contact for Aboriginal Communities." Australian Journal of Social Issues 5(1970):219-223.

_____. So Many Lessons to Learn: Failure in Australian Education. Ringwood, Victoria, Australia: Penguin, 1974.

_____. "Verbal Intelligence, Operational Thinking and Environment in Part-Aboriginal Children." Australian Journal of Psychology 23(1971):145-149.

De Lacey, Philip R. and others. "Effects of Enrichment Preschooling: An Australian Followup Study." Exceptional Children 40 (N, 1973):171-176.

De Lemos, Marion M. "The Development of Conservation in Aboriginal Children." International Journal of Psychology 4(1969):255-269. [See Dasen, above.]

_____. "The Development of the Concept of Conservation in Australian Children." Ph.D. dissertation, U. of Western Australian, 1966.

Denoon, D. "Guilt and the Gurrindji." Meanjin Quarterly 29(1970):253-268. [Aborigines]

Duguid, Charles. Doctor and the Aborigines. Rigby, 1973. [Autobiography of defender of Aboriginal rights]

Duncan, A. T. "Aboriginal Education in Australia," Integrated Education, D, 1966-Jan, 1967.

_____. "Strategies in Aboriginal Adult Education." Australian Journal of Adult Education 13(N, 1973):115-120.

Duncan, A. T., and Skelton, J. J. Consultative Committee on Aboriginal Education Submissions to the Legislative Council and Legislative Assembly Upon Aborigines Welfare, Mr, 1966. Department of Adult Education, U. of Sydney, Sydney, Australia.

Dunn, S. S., and Tatz, C. Aborigines and Education. Melbourne, Australia: Sun Books, 1969.

Dwyer, L. J. "A Language Program for Aboriginal Children." Exceptional Child 23(Mr, 1976):8-24.

Edwards, N. R. Native Education in the Northern Territory: A Critical Account of Its Aims, Development and Present Position. Sydney, Australia: Fisher Library, U. of Sydney, 1963.

Elkin, Adolphus P. Aboriginal Men of High Degree. 2nd ed. New York: St. Martin's Press, 1978.

_____. "Native Education with Special Reference to the Australian Aborigines." Oceania 7(1937):459-500.

Ellis, S. "Racism in Australia: A Contribution to the Debate." Australian Quarterly (S, 1972):58-66.

Einfeld, Marcus R. "Prejudice Down Under." Patterns of Prejudice 6(Jl-Ag, 1972):16-18.

Epstein, Charlotte. "Intergroup Education in Australia." Integrated Education 11(Jl-O, 1973):38-41.

Evans, Raymond, Saunders, Kay, and Cronin, Kathryn. Exclusion Exploitation and Extermination: Race Relations in Colonial Queensland. Sydney: Australia and New Zealand Book Co., 1975.

Fleming, J. "Using a Language Experience Program for Teaching Reading to Aboriginal Children." Exceptional Child 28(Mr, 1976):25-30.

Fowler, H. L. "Report on Psychological Tests on Natives in the Northwest of Western Australia." Australian Journal of Science 2 (1940):124-127.

Gale, Fay. A Study of Assimilation: Part-Aborigines in South Australia. Adelaide, Australia: Libraries Board of South Australia, 1964.

_____. Urban Aborigines. Canberra, Australia: National U. Press, 1973.

_____ (ed.). Woman's Role in Aboriginal Society. Canberra: Australian Institute of Aboriginal Studies, 1970.

Gale, G. Fay. "The Role of Education." In A Study of Assimilation: Part-Aborigines in South Australia, pp. 235-274. Adelaide: Libraries Board of South Australia, 1964.

Gale, Fay, and Brookman, Alison (eds.). Race Relations in Australia: The Aborigines. Sydney: McGraw-Hill, 1975.

Gale, Fay, and Binnion, Joan. Poverty Among Aboriginal Families in Adelaide. Canberra: AGPS, 1975.

Gale, Jim. "Australian Aborigines: Myth and Reality." Interracial Books for Children Bulletin 9(1978):8-12. [Analysis of Olga Hoyt's Aborigines of Australia, 1969]

Gilbert, Kevin. Because a White Man'll Never Do It. Sydney, Australia: Angus & Robertson, 1974.

_____. Living Black: Blacks Talking to Kevin Gilbert. London: Allen Lane, 1978.

Gordon, Harry. "How the Daughter of an Ancient Race Made It Out of the Australian Outback By Hitting a Tennis Ball Sweetly and Hard." New York Times Magazine, Ag 29, 1971.

Gregor, A. James. "Ethnocentrism Among the Australian Aborigines: Some Preliminary Notes." Sociological Quarterly 4(1963):162-167.

Grey, A. "Aboriginal Family Education Centres," Part 1. Australian Journal of Adult Education 10(Ap, 1970):25-31.

_____. "Aboriginal Family Education Centres." Australian Journal of Adult Education 10(Jl, 1970):66-71.

Guthrie, Gerard. Cherbourg: A Queensland Aboriginal Reserve. Armidale, Australia: Department of Geography, U. of New England, 1977.

_____. "Attitudes of Queensland Reserve Aborigines to Cities." Australian Geographical Studies 14(1976):43-48.

Harrison, Barbara. Aboriginal Issues--Racism in Australia, n.d. World Council of Churches, 475 Riverside Drive, New York, NY 10027.

_____. "Aborigines in White Australia." Race Today 3(Ag, 1971):261-263.

_____. "Aborigines in White Australia." Part 2. Race Today 3(S, 1971):300-302.

_____. Outside Down Under: The History, Conditions and Struggle of the Australian Aborigines. Denver, CO: Center on International Race Relations, U. of Denver, 1971.

Hart, J. A. "A Study of the Cognitive Capacity of a Group of Australian Aboriginal Children." Master's thesis, U. of Brisbane, 1965.

Hart, Max. Kulila: On Aboriginal Education. N.p.: n.p., 1974

Hasluck, P. Black Australia: A Survey of Native Policy in Western Australia, 1829-1897. Melbourne, Australia: Oxford U. Press, 1942.

Hassel, Kathleen. The Relations between the Settlers and Aborigines in South Australia, 1836-1860. Adelaide, Australia: N.p., 1966.

Hausfield, R. G. "The Expanding Universe of the Aboriginal Child." Australian Pre-School Quarterly, My, 1965.

Herbert, Xavier. Poor Fellow, My Country. London: Pan Books, 1977. [Novel]

Hetzel, B. S. and others. Better Help for Aborigines? Brisbane: Queensland U. Press, 1974.

Hiatt, L. R. "Aborigines in the Australian Community." In Australian Society. Edited by A. F. Davies and S. Encel. New York: Atherton, 1965.

Hill, Barry. "Australia's New Citizens." Times Educational Supplement, Ap 13, 1973. [Aboriginal children]

Hill, Ernestine. Kabbarli: A Personal Memoir. N.p.: n.p., 1973.

Hillard, Winifred M. The People in Between: The Pitjantjatjara People of Ernabella. New York: Funk & Wagnalls, 1968. [Western Australia]

Horner, Jack. "Apartheid Divides Australia." Race Today 4(Ja, 1972):19-20.

_____. "Canberra's Embassy Extraordinary." Race Today 4(N, 1972):366-367.

_____. "White Australia Thinks Again." Race Today 3(Je, 1971):200.

Howard, Michael C. (ed.). "Whitefella Business": Aborigines in Australian Politics. Philadelphia: Institute for the Study of Human Issues, 1978.

Hunt, Albert. "The Black Theatre." New Society, N 13, 1975. [Redfern, Sydney]

Huttenback, Robert A. Racism and Empire. White Settlers and Colored Immigrants in the British Self-Governing Colonies, 1830-1910. Ithaca: Cornell U. Press, 1976.

Jernudd, Björn H. "Social Change and Aboriginal Speech Variation in Australia." Anthropological Linguistics 13(1971):16-32.

Jones, F. Lancaster. The Structure and Growth of Australia's Aboriginal Population. Canberra, Australia: Australian National U. Press, 1970.

Kamien, M. "Housing and Health in an Ab- orginal Community in Bourke, New South Wales." Australian Journal of Social Issues 11(1976).

Kearney, G. E. "Some Aspects of the General Cognitive Ability of Various Groups of Aboriginal Australians as Assessed by the Queensland Test." Doctoral dissertation, Brisbane: U. of Queensland Library, 1966.

Kearney, G. E., De Lacey, P. R., and Davidson, G. R. The Psychology of Aboriginal Australians. New York: Wiley, 1974.

Kearney, G. E., and McElivain, D. W. (eds.). Aboriginal Cognition: Retrospect and Prospect. Atlantic Highlands, NJ: Hamanities, 1976.

Lickiss, J. Norelle. "Health Problems of Sydney Aboriginal Children." Med. J. Aust. 2(N 28, 1970).

Lindstrom, Deanne R. "Some Perceptual Aspects of Aboriginal Education." Master's thesis, U. of Sydney, 1965.

Lippman, Lorna. A Survey of Race Relations in Selected Country Towns. Centre for Research into Aboriginal Affairs, Monash U., F, 1970.

_____. "Australia's Aborigines." Patterns of Prejudice 9(S-O, 1975):23-27.

_____. "The Invisible People of Australian History." Interracial Books for Children Bulletin 10, Nos. 1-2(1979):14-15.

_____. "Literacy and Ethnic Minorities in Australia." Literacy Discussion 7(Summer, 1976):23-35.

_____. To Achieve Our Country: Australia and Aborigines. Melbourne, Australia: Cheshire Group Publishers, 1970.

_____. "'White Australia' and the Aborigines." Patterns of Prejudice 5(Ja-F, 1971):11-15.

_____. Words or Blows: Racial Attitudes in Australia. Victoria, Australia: Penguin Books Australia Ltd., 1973.

Litvin, Joel. The Importance of Developing Intercultural Communication Curricula in Australia, D, 1976. ERIC ED 150 644.

Lommel, Andreas. Fortschritt ins Nichts: Die Modernisierung der Primitiven Australiens: Beschreibung und Definition eines psychischen Verfalls. Zurich, Switzerland: Atlantis, 1969.

Le Sueur, E. M. "Aboriginal Assimilation: An Evaluation of Some Ambiguities in Policy and Service." In Australian Social Issues of the '70's. Edited by P. R. Wilson. Sydney: Butterworths, 1972.

Long, J. P. M. Aboriginal Settlements: A Survey of Institutional Communities in Eastern Australia. Canberra, Australia: Australian National U. Press, 1970.

Lovegrove, Malcolm, and Poole, Millicent. "Groping Towards Tolerance: the Australian Experience." In Race and Education Across Cultures. Edited by G. K. Verma and Christopher Bagley. Stamford, CT: Greylock Publishers, 1975.

McBryde, Isabel (ed.). Records of Times Past: Ethnohistorical Essays on the Culture and Ecology of the New England Tribes. Canberra: Australian Institute of Aboriginal Studies, 1978.

McConnochie, Keith R. Realities of Race. An Analysis of the Concepts of Race and Racism and their Relevance to Australian Society. Brookvale, Australia: Australia and New Zealand Book Co., 1973.

McDonald, Cathy. "Aborigines Suffer Inequali- ties." Education, O 13, 1971. [Published by New South Wales Federation of Teachers]

McElwain, D. W. "The Cognitive Ability of Australian Aborigines." Proceedings of the Australian Institute of Aboriginal Studies Conference. Canberra, Australia: A.I.A.S., 1966.

McQueen, Humphrey. Australia Connexions-- Aborigines, Race and Racism. Ringwood, Victoria: Penguin Books Australia, 1974.

_____. "The Sustenance of Silence: Racism in Twentieth Century Australia." Meanjin Quarterly 30(Je, 1971).

Maddock, Kenneth. The Australian Aborigines: A Portrait of their Society. Hammondsworth, England: Penguin, 1974.

Marshall, Eric. It Pays to Be White. Sydney, Australia: Alpha Books, 1973. [The story of Elizabeth Marshall and a movement against racism in Australia and elsewhere]

Massola, A. The Aboriginal People. Melbourne, Australia: Cypress, 1969.

Middleton, Margaret R., and Francis, Sarah H. Yuendumu and Its Children: Life and Health on an Aboriginal Settlement. Canberra: Australian Government Publishing Service, 1976.

Moffitt, P., Nurcombe, B., Passmore, M., and McNeilly, A. "Intervention in Cultural Deprivation: The Comparative Success of Preschool Techniques for Rural Aborigines and Europeans." Australian Psychologist 6 (Mr, 1971):51-61.

Moodie, P. M. Aboriginal Health. ANU Press, 1973.

_____. "Mortality and Morbidity in Australian Aboriginal Children." Medical Journal of Australia 1(1969):180-184.

Morrell, W. P. "Colonists and Aborigines in the Early Australian Settlements." New Zealand Journal of History 12(Ap, 1978):50-61.

Mountford, Charles P. Nomads of the Australian Desert. Kent Town, South Australia: Rigby, 1976.

Muller, Mike. More Facts and Figures. Aboriginal Issues. Racism in Australia, D, 1971. World Council of Churches, 475 Riverside Drive, New York, NY 10027.

Mulvaney, D. J. The Prehistory of Australia. New York: Praeger, 1969.

Mulvaney, D. J., and Golson, J. (eds.). Aboriginal Man and Environment in Australia. Canberra: Australian National U. Press, 1971.

National Seminar on Aboriginal Antiquities in Australia. The Preservation of Australia's Aboriginal Heritage. Canberra: Australian Institute of Aboriginal Studes, 1975.

Nettheim, Garth (ed.). Aborigines Human Rights and the Law. Sydney, Australia: Australia and New Zealand Press, 1974.

Neville, A. O. Australia's Coloured Minority: His Place in the Community. Sydney, Australia: Currawong Publishing Co., 1974.

New South Wales Federation of Teachers. "Black Moratorium in Australia." Integrated Education 11(Mr-Ap, 1973):60-63.

Nurcombe, Barry. Children of the Dispossessed. Honolulu: U. Press of Hawaii, 1975. [Aborigines]

_____. "Deprivation: An Essay in Deprivation with Special Reference to Australian Aborigines." Medical Journal of Australia 2 (1970):87-92.

Paterson, Jennifer I. "Native Administration and Welfare in Western Australia, 1905-1936." Bachelor's honors thesis, U. of Western Australia, 1957.

Perkins, Charles. Black Power in Australia. Armidale, N.S.W., Australia: Department of University Extension, U. of New England, 1968.

Perkins, Charles, and Smith, Ure. A Bastard Like Me. Sydney: Dee Why West, 1975. [Aborigine autobiography]

Peterson, Nicolas (ed.). Tribes and Boundaries in Australia. Canberra: Australian Institute of Aboriginal Studes, 1976.

Phelan, Gloria. "Aboriginal Children in New South Wales Schools." Integrated Education, Je-Jl, 1965.

Pierson, James C. "Aboriginality in Adelaide: An Urban Context of Australian Aboriginal Ethnicity." Urban Anthropology 6(Winter, 1977):307-327.

_____. "Voluntary Organizations and Australian Aboriginal Urban Adaptations in Adelaide." Oceania 48(S, 1977):46-58.

Pilling, Arnold. Diprotodon to Detribalization. Studies of Change Among Australian Aborigines. East Lansing, MI: Michigan State U. Press, 1970.

Pittock, A. B. Towards a Multi Racial Society. North Melbourne, Victoria: National Union of Australian University Students, 1969.

Porteus, S. D. "Mental Capacity" In Aboriginal Man in South and Central Australia. Edited by B. C. Cotton. Adelaide: Government Printer, 1966.

Prideaux, David. "The South Australian Prohibition of Discrimination Act and Racism." Australian Journal of Social Issues 10(N, 1975):315-321.

Pryor, R. J. "The Aboriginal Population of North Queensland: A Demographic Profile." Newsletter. Australian Institute of Aboriginal Studies 2(1974):13-19.

Reay, M. (ed.). Aborigines Now: New Perspectives in the Study of Aboriginal Communities. Sydney, Australia: Argus & Robertson, 1964.

Reece, R. H. W. Aborigines and Colonists. Aborigines and Colonial Society in New South Wales in the 1830's and 1840's. Sydney, Australia: Sydney U. Press, 1975.

Reiger, K., and Thompson, F. (comps.). Youth Studies in Australia: An Annotated Bibliography. Bundoora, Victoria, Australia: La Trobe U., 1974.

Reynolds, Henry. "The Other Side of the Frontier: Early Aboriginal Reactions to Pastoral Settlement in Queensland and Northern New South Wales." Hist. Stud. 17 (Ap, 1976):50-63.

_____ (ed.). Aborigines and Settlers: The Australian Experience, 1788-1939. N.p.: n.p., 1973.

Reynolds, Henry, and Loos, Noel. "Aboriginal Resistance in Queensland." Australian Journal of Political History 22(Ag, 1976): 214-226.

Roberts, Janine. From Massacres to Mining: The Colonization of Aboriginal Australia. London: CIMRA and War on Want, 1978.

Roberts, J. P. (ed.). The Mapoon Story by the Mapoon People. Victoria, Australia: International Development Action, 1975.

Roberts, J. P., and McLean, D. The Cape York Aluminium Companies and the Native Peoples. Camalco, R.T.Z., Kaiser, C.R.A., Alcan, Billiton, Pechiney, Tipperary. Victoria, Australia: International Development Action, 1976.

Roberts, J. P., Parsons, M., and Russell, B. The Mapoon Story According to the Invaders. Church Mission, Queensland Government and Mining Company. Victoria, Australia: International Development Action, 1975.

Roper, Thomas W. "Aboriginal Education and Teacher Training." Education (Australia), N 29, 1967.

_____ (ed.). Aboriginal Education. The Teacher's Role. North Melbourne, Victoria: National Union of Australian University Students, 1969.

Rose, F. Australia Revisited. Berlin, Germany: Seven Seas Books, 1968.

_____. Winds of Change in Central Australia. Berlin, Germany: Akademie Verlag, 1965.

Rowley, C. D. A Matter of Justice: The Aborigines in Australian Politics. London: Australian National U. Press, 1979.

_____. The Destruction of Aboriginal Society. Canberra, Australia: National U. Press, 1970.

_____. Outcasts in White Australia: Aboriginal Policy and Practice. Vol. II. Canberra, Australia: Australian National U. Press, 1971.

_____. Outcasts in White Australia. Middlesex: Penguin Books, 1972.

_____. The Remote Aborigines: Aboriginal Policy and Practice. Vol. III. Canberra, Australia: Australian National U. Press, 1971.

Roy, P. K. "Part Aborigines of Moora: Factors Hindering Assimilation and Integration." Oceania 39(1969):275-280. [Western Australia]

Schapper, Henry P. Aboriginal Advancement to Integration: Conditions and Plans for Western Australia. Canberra, Australia: Australian National U. Press, 1970.

_____. "Administration and Welfare as Threats to Aboriginal Assimilation." Australian Journal of Social Issues 3(0, 1968).

Schoenheimer, Henry (ed.). Good Australian Schools. Victoria, Australia: Technical Teachers Association of Victoria, 1973. [Includes discussion of Aboriginal family education centers]

Schonell, F. J. School Attainments and Home Backgrounds of Aboriginal Children in Queensland. Brisbane: U. of Queensland Press, 1960.

Schools Commission. "Education for Aborigines." Report for the Triennium 1974-1976. Canberra, Australia: Australian Government Publishing Service, 1975.

Scott, Phyllis M., and Darbyshire, Margaret. Early Education Programs and Aboriginal Families in Victoria. Monash U., 1973.

Sharp, I. G., and Tatz, C. M. (eds.). Aborigines in the Economy. Brisbane, Australia: Jacaranda, in association with Centre for Research into Aboriginal Affairs, Monash U., 1966.

Sheehan, Peter W. "The Variability of Eidetic Imagery among Australian Aboriginal Children." Journal of Social Psychology 91 (0, 1973):29-36.

Smith, Hazel M., and Biddle, Ellen H. Look Forward Not Back: Aborigines in Metropolitan Brisbane 1965-1966. Canberra: Australian National U. Press, 1975.

Sommer, Bruce A. "Aboriginal Non-standard English." English in Australia 26(F, 1974): 39-46.

_____. "For the Aborigines: A Vernacular Education?" English in Australia 25(N, 1973):5-12.

Sommerlad, C. Duke, and Sommerlad, Elizabeth. Design for Diversity: Further Education for Tribal Aborigines in the North. Canberra: Australian National U. Press, 1977.

Sommerlad, Elizabeth Ann. "The Impact of Formal Education on the Personal Identity of the Australian Aboriginal Adolescents." Doctoral dissertation, Australian National U., 1972.

_____. Kormilda, the Way to Tomorrow? Canberra: Australian National U. Press, 1976. [Kormilda College]

Sommerlad, Elizabeth A., and Bellingham, W. P. "Cooperation-Competition: A Comparison of Australian European and Aboriginal School Children." Journal of Cross-Cultural Psychology 3(Je, 1972):149-158.

Spalding, I. "Elements in the Australian Racist Syndrome." Historian 25(O, 1973).

Stanley, Gordon. "Australian Students' Attitudes to Negroes and Aborigines on the Multifactor Racial Attitude Inventory (MRAI)." Journal of Social Psychology 77 (1969):281-282.

Stanley, O. "Aboriginal Communities on Cattle Stations in Central Australia." Australian Economic Papers 15(D, 1976).

Stanner, W. E. H. "The Aborigine: Our Children's Brother." Education (New South Wales Federation of Teachers), Jl 15, 1970.

_____. After the Dreaming. Australian Broadcasting Commission, 1969.

Stevens, F. "Aborigines." In Australian Society: A Sociological Introduction, pp. 362-412. Second edition. Edited by A. F. Davies and S. Encel. Melbourne: F. W. Cheshire, 1970.

Stevens, F. S. (ed.). Racism: The Australian Experience. A Study of Race Prejudice in Australia. 3 vols. Sydney, Australia: Australia and New Zealand Book Co., 1971-1972. (In U.S.: New York: Taplinger, 1971-1972.)

Stone, Sharman S. (ed.). Aborigines in White Australia. London: Heinemann, 1975.

Strehlow, T. G. H. Assimilation Problems: The Aboriginal Viewpoint. Adelaide, Australia: n.p., 1964.

_____. Dark and White Australia. Port Melbourne, Australia: Riall Brothers, 1957.

Taft, Ronald, Dawson, John L., and Beasley, Pamela. Aborigines in Australian Society: Attitudes and Social Conditions. Canberra: Australian National U. Press, 1970.

Tatz, C. M. "Aborigines—Equality or Inequality?" Australian Quarterly, Mr, 1966.

_____. "Health Status of Australian Aborigines." Medical Journal of Australia, Jl 25, 1970.

Tatz, Colin (ed.). Black Viewpoints: The Aboriginal Experience. Sydney: Australia and New Zealand Book Co., 1975.

Teasdale, G. R. "Language Disabilities of Children from Lower Socio-Economic and Part-Aboriginal Backgrounds." Australian Journal of Mental Retardation 2(S, 1972):69-74.

Teasdale, G. R., and Katz, F. M. "Psycholinguistic Abilities of Children from Different Ethnic and Socio-economic Backgrounds." Australian Journal of Psychology, D, 1968.

Thompson, Era Bell. "Australia: Its White Policy and the Negro." Ebony, Jl, 1966.

Tindale, Norman B. Aboriginal Tribes of Australia. 2 vols. Berkeley, CA: U. of California Press, 1974.

Trumbull, Robert. "Australian Aborigines Get a Push Upward." New York Times, Je 24, 1969.

Tugby, D. (ed.). Aboriginal Identity in Contemporary Australian Society. N.p.: Jacaranda Press, 1973.

Turnbull, Clive. Black War: The Extermination of the Tasmanian Aborigines. Melbourne: F. W. Cheshire, 1948.

Twomey, A., and de Lacey, P. R. "Piaget, Pre-Schools and Aboriginal Children." Australian Journal of Early Childhood 2(D, 1977):28-33.

Unrau, William E. "An International Perspective on American Indian Policy: The South Australian Protector and Aborigines Protection Society." Pacific Historical Review 45(N, 1976):519-538.

Walker, Je. "Black Australians Fight Genocide." Muhammad Speaks, N 6, 1970.

Watts, B. "Some Determinants of the Academic Success of Australian Aboriginal Adolescent Girls." Doctoral dissertation, U. of Queensland, 1970.

Watts, Betty H. (ed.). Report of the National Workshop on Aboriginal Education: Priorities for Action and Research. Brisbane: Department of Education, U. of Queensland, 1971.

White, Doug. "Aboriginal Cultures: The New Welfare." Arena (Australia) 36(1974).

_____. "Aboriginal Education." Arena 37 (1975).

Williams, J. R. "Conference on Aboriginal Affairs." Education (New South Wales Federation of Teachers), My 1, 1968. [11th Annual Conference of the Federal Council for the Advancement of Aborigines and Torres Straits Islanders, Ap 12-14, 1968]

Wilton, Rob. "The Law and Discrimination." Aboriginal Quarterly 2(1969).

Wolman, Marianne. "Visit to a Mission School for Aboriginal Children." Elementary School Journal 70(1970):261-264.

Wongar, B. The Track to Bralgu. Boston: Little, Brown, 1978. [Stories by an Aborigine]

General

Abbey, Brian, and Ashenden, Dean. What Is To Be Done in Teacher Education?, 1974. ERIC ED 141 315.

Adam, R. S. "Equal Opportunities for University Education." Vestes (Australia), D, 1963. [A comparative view]

_____. "Full Stature for the Under-privileged." Education (New South Wales Federation of Teachers), O 20, 1965.

Anderson, Don and others. Students in Australian Higher Education: A Study of their Social Composition Since the Abolition of Fees. N.p.: Australian Government Printer, 1978.

Australian College of Education. Priorities in Australian Education, 1972. ERIC ED 133 806.

Australian Council of Trade Unions. Survey of Young Workers. Canberra: AGPS, 1975.

Bassett, G. W. "The Occupational Background of Teachers." Australian Journal of Education 2(Jl, 1958):79-90.

_____. "The Occupational Background of Teachers--Some Recent Data." Australian Journal of Education 15(Je, 1971):211-214.

Beck, Christopher. "White Australia May Face Guerilla War." Akwesasne Notes 3(S, 1971): 29.

Beswick, D. G., and Hills, M. D. "An Australian Ethnocentrism Scale." Australian Journal of Psychology 21(D, 1969):211-225.

_____ and _____. "A Survey of Ethnocentrism in Australia." Australian Journal of Psychology 24(1972):153-163.

Bottomley, Gillian. "Ethnic Diversity in Australia." Patterns of Prejudice 10(N-D, 1976):30-35.

Bourke, J. E. "Educational Attainment and Migration." Australian Journal of Education 15(Mr, 1971):1-15. [By ethnic group]

Broom, Leonard, and Jones, F. Lancaster. Opportunity and Attainment in Australia. Stanford: Stanford U. Press, 1977.

Browne, Ronald K., Simkins, William S., and Foster, Lois E. A Guide to the Sociology of Australian Education. South Melbourne, Victoria: Macmillan of Australia, 1974.

Bryson, Lois. "Poverty Research in Australia in the Seventies: Unmasking Noble Terms." Australian and New Zealand Journal of Sociology 13(O, 1977):196-202.

Burnley, I. H. "Ethnic Factors in Social Segregation and Residential Stratification in Australia's Large Cities." Australian and New Zealand Journal of Sociology, F, 1975.

Carroll, Margaret. "The Teaching of Greek in Australia." Greek-Australian Review, Ap, 1974.

Claydon, Leslie, Knight, Tony, and Rado, Marta. Curriculum and Culture. Schooling in a Pluralist Society. Winchester, MA: Allen & Unwin, 1978.

Cleverby, John F. The First Generation: School and Society in Early Australia. Sydney: Sydney U. Press, 1971.

Connell, R. W. Ruling Class. Ruling Culture. Studies in Conflict, Power and Hegemony in Australian Life. New York: Cambridge U. Press, 1977.

Crittenden, Brian. "Equality and Education." Australian Journal of Education 21(Je, 1977): 113-126.

Cronin, Constance. The Sting of Change. Sicilians in Sicily and in Australia. Chicago, IL: U. of Chicago Press, 1970.

Cronin, Kathryn. "The Chinese Community in Queensland, 1874-1900." Queensland Heritage 2(My, 1973):3-13.

Crowley, F. K. (ed.). Modern Australia in Documents. Vol. I: 1901-1939. Vol. II: 1939-1970. London: Wren, 1974.

Doczy, A. G. "Life Problems of Young Adolescent Immigrant Boys in Australia." International Migration 6(1968):12-19.

_____. "The Social Assimilation of Adolescent Boys of European Parentage in the Metropolitan Area of Western Australia." Doctoral dissertation, U. of Western Australia, 1967.

Edgar, Donald E. (ed.). Sociology of Australian Education. Sydney, Australia: Angus & Robertson, 1974.

Encel, S. Equality and Authority: A Study of Class, Status and Power in Australia. New York: Barnes and Noble, 1970.

Encel, S. and others. Australian Society. A Sociological Introduction. 3rd ed. London: Longman, 1978.

Fensham, P. J. (ed.). Rights and Inequality in Australian Education. Melbourne: Cheshire Ltd., 1970.

Gale, Fay. Race Relations in Australia. N.p.: McGraw-Hill, 1975.

Getzler, Israel. *Neither Toleration Nor Favour. Australian Chapter of Jewish Emancipation.* Melbourne, Australia: U. Press, 1970.

Glynn, Sean. *Urbanisation in Australian History 1788-1900.* Melbourne: Thomas Nelson (Australia) Limited, 1970.

Goyen, Judith D. "Incidence of Adult Illiteracy in Sydney Metropolitan Area." *Literacy Discussion* 7(F, 1976):63-71.

Halladay, Allan. "The Significance of Poverty Definition to Australians." *Australian Journal of Social Issues* 10(F, 1975):46-50.

Henderson, Ronald. *Poverty in Australia.* Canberra: AGPS, 1975.

Henderson, Ronald F. and others. *People in Poverty: A Melbourne Survey.* Enlarged edition. N.p.: Cheshire, 1976.

Hodgkin, Mary C. *Australian Training and Asian Living.* Nedlands, Western Australia: U. of Western Australia Press, 1966. [Malaysian students in Western Australia]

Hollingworth, P. G. *The Powerless Poor.* North Melbourne, Australia: Stockland Press, 1972.

Hunt, F. J. (ed.). *Socialization in Australia.* Sydney, Australia: Argus & Robertson, 1972.

Inglis, Christine. "Chinese in Australia." *International Migration Review* 6(Fall, 1972):266-281.

_____. "Some Recent Australian Writing on Immigration and Assimilation." *International Migration Review* 9(Fall, 1975): 335-344.

Isaacs, Eva. "Ethnic Groups in Urban Education." *Australian Journal of Social Issues* 9(N, 1974):298-305.

Johnston, Ruth. "Factors in the Assimilation of Selected Groups of Polish Post-War Immigrants in Western Australia." Doctoral dissertation, U. of Western Australia, 1963.

_____. *Future Australians. Immigrant Children in Perth, Western Australia.* Canberra: Australian National U. Press, 1972.

Jones, F. Lancaster. "Social Stratification in Australia..." *Social Science Information* 13(1974):99-118.

Kaim-Caundle, P. R. "More About Poverty in Australia." *Journal of Social Policy* 6 (J1, 1977):317-334.

Kerr, R. H., and Woolford, J. A. "The Education of Migrant Adults and Children." *Feedback* 1(D, 1973). [New South Wales Federation of Teachers]

London, Herbert I. "Liberalizing the White Australia Policy: Integration, Assimilation, or Cultural Pluralism?" *Australian Outlook*, D, 1967.

_____. *Non-White Immigration and the 'White Australia' Policy.* New York: New York U. Press, 1970.

McMillan, A. N. "The Migrant Child in Australia." *Education* (New South Wales Federation of Teachers), D 4, 1968.

McQueen, Humphrey. *A New Britannia.* Melbourne, Australia: Penguin, 1970.

Manning, Ian. "The Geographic Distribution of Povery in Australia." *Australian Geographical Studies* 14(1976):133-147.

Mansfield, B. C. "The Origins of White Australia." *Australian Quarterly*, D, 1954.

Medding, P. (ed.). *Jews in Australian Society.* Melbourne: MacMillan and Monash U., 1973.

Northern Territory Department of Education. *Second Progress Report on the Bilingual Education Program in Schools in the Northern Territory*, D, 1974. ERIC ED 126 683.

O'Byrne, Vera de R. "L'enseignement des langues des groupes des ethniques en Australie." *Canadian and International Education* 7(Je, 1978):37-41.

O'Neill, J., and Paterson, J. *The Cost of Free Education: Schools and Low Income Families.* Melbourne, Australia: Cheshire, 1968.

Palfreeman, A. C. "Non-White Immigration to Australia." *Pacific Affairs* 47(Fall, 1974): 344-357.

Penny, Ronald. "Nationality and Social Choice among School Children." *Australian Journal of Education* 15(O, 1971):269-277. Adelaide

Poverty and Education in Australia. Canberra: Australian Government Publishing Service, 1976.

Price, Charles A. "Australian Immigration: 1947-73." *International Migration Review* 9(Fall, 1975):304-318.

_____. "Immigration and Ethnic Studies in Australia." *Immigration History Newsletter* 9(N, 1977):5-9.

_____. *Southern Europeans in Australia.* Melbourne: Oxford U. Press, 1963.

Rada, Marta (ed.). Bilingual Education. Melbourne: Centre for the Study of Teaching, La Trobe U. School of Education, N.D.

Rahnema, Majid. "Education and Equality: Intentions and Consequences." Australian Journal of Adult Education 16(N, 1977): 97-106.

Ray, John J. "Antisemitic Types in Australia." Patterns of Prejudice 7(Ja-F, 1973):6-16.

_____. "Is Antisemitism a Cognitive Simplification? Some Observations on Australian Neo-Nazis." Jewish Journal of Sociology 14(D, 1972).

Richardson, Penelope, and Van Der Veur, Karol. "Community-School Relations in Urban Areas of the Territory of Papua and New Guinea." Australian Journal of Education, Mr, 1968.

Rivett, Kenneth. "Non-White Immigration: An Australian Turning Point." Population Review 18(Ja-D, 1974).

_____ (ed.). Australia and the Non-White Migrant. Carlton South, Victoria: Melbourne U. Press, 1975.

Rosier, Malcolm J. Early School Leavers in Australia. Stockholm: Almquist & Wiksell, 1978.

Smolicz, J. J., and Secombe, M. J. "A Study of Attitudes to the Introduction of Ethnic Languages and Cultures in Australian Schools." Australian Journal of Education 21 (Mr, 1977):1-24.

Storer, Des (ed.). Ethnic Rights, Power and Participation: Toward a Multicultural Australia. Richmond, Victoria: Clearing House on Migration Issues, Ecumenical Migration Centre, and Centre for Urban Research and Action, 1976.

Stricker, P., and Sheehan, P. "Youth Unemployment in Australia: A Survey." Australian Economic Review, 1978.

Taft, Ronald. From Stranger to Citizen. A Survey of Studies of Immigrant Assimilation in Western Australia. London: Tavistock, 1967.

Taft, Ronald, Dawson, John L. M., and Beasley, Pamela. Attitudes and Social Conflicts. Canberra, Australia: Australian National U. Press, 1970.

Teo, Siew Eng. "A Preliminary Study of the Chinese Community in Sydney: A Basis for the Study of Social Change." Australian Geographer 11(1971):579-592.

Throssell, H. (ed.). Ethnic Minorities in Australia. Sydney: Australian Council of Social Services, 1968.

Ts'ai, Cheng-jen [Choi, C. Y.] Chinese Migration and Settlement in Australia. Sydney: Sydney U. Press, 1975.

Tsounis, M. P. Greek Ethnic Schools in Australia. Canberra: Australian National U., 1975.

_____. "Greek Ethnic Schools in Australia." International Migration Review 9(Fall, 1975):345-359.

Wild, Ronald Arthur. Social Stratification in Australia. Boston: G. Allen & Unwin, 1978.

Windt, U., Berdarkas, A., Einstein, S., King, M., Lake, G., Lamb, R., Ryan, P., and Smith, M. Content Analysis of N.S.W. Primary School Social Studies Text Books with Respect to the Development of Racial Attitudes in Children. Sydney, Australia: Movement Research, 1970.

Wiseman, R. "Integration and Attainment of Immigrant Secondary School Students in Adelaide." Australian Journal of Education 15(O, 1971):253-268.

Wynne, Edward C. "Racial Discrimination in the Attitude of Australia towards the Japanese." 2 vols. Doctoral dissertation, Harvard U., 1927.

Yarwood, A. T. (ed.). Attitudes to Non-European Immigration. Melbourne, Australia: Cassell, 1968.

Yong, C. F. The New Gold Mountain: The Chinese in Australia 1901-1921. Richmond, Australia: Raphael Arts, 1977.

Zubrzycki, Jerzy. "Ethnic Segregation in Australian Cities." International Population Conference, Vienna, Austria, 1959.

Austria

Adler, Philip J. "Hapsburg School Reform Among the Orthodox Minorities, 1770-1780." Slavic Review 33(Mr, 1974):23-45.

"Antisemites in Austria." Patterns of Prejudice 11(My-Je, 1977):13-15.

[Articles on Austrian-Slav minority problems] Neues Forum 268(Ap, 1976).

Carsten, Francis L. Fascist Movements in Austria: From Schönerer to Hitler. Beverly Hills, CA: Sage, 1977.

Chlebowczyk, Józef. "Die Madjarisierungs-und die Germanisierungspolitik in 18.-19. Jahrhundert und um die Jahrhundertwende." Acta Poloniae Hist. 30(1974):163–186.

Faustini, Gianni. "Il Trentino e l'Università italiana in Austria." Stud. trentini sci. stor. 54(1975):289–318.

Fraenkel, Josef (ed.). The Jews of Austria. London: Vallentine, Mitchell, 1967.

Gal, Susan. Language Shift: Social Determinants of Linguistic Change in Bilingual Austria. New York: Academic Press, 1978.

Gehmacher, Ernst. Gastarbeiter-Wirtschaftsfaktor und soziale Herausforderung. Wien: Europaverlag, 1973.

Grzynowicz, S. "Workers Immigration in Austria." Biuletyn IGS (Warsaw) 18 (1975):6–26.

Hackler, James. "The Viennese School System: Social Mobility and Its Implications." International Journal of Comparative Sociology 2(1961):65–69.

Musharbash, Jutta. "Die Gasamtschulentwicklung in Österreich von 1918–1962." Doctoral dissertation, U. of Vienna, 1975.

Neugelbauer, Wolfgang. "Rumblings on the Austrian Right-wing." Patterns of Prejudice 11(Ja-F, 1977):14–16.

_____ (ed.). Widerstand und Verfolgung in Wien 1934–1945. Vols. 2 and 3: 1938–1945 Eine Dokumentation. Wien: Österreichischer Bundesverlag für Unterricht, Wissensc haft und Kunst, 1975. [Jews]

Pflergerl, Siegfried. Gastarbeiter: Zwischen Integration and Abstrossung. Vienna: Jugend und Volk, 1977.

Rohn, Aryeh. "Jewish Education in Vienna Between the Two World Wars." Doctoral dissertation, Dropsie College, 1965.

Rosenaft, Menachem Z. "Jews and Antisemites in Austria at the End of the Nineteen Century." Leo Baeck Inst. Yrbk. 21 (1976):57–86.

Simon, Maria, Tajfel, Henri, and Johnson, Nicolas. "Eine Untersuchung über Vorurteile bei Wiener Kindern." Kölner Zeitschrift für Soziologie und Soziolpsychologie 19(1967):511–537.

Sugar, Peter F. "The Nature of Non-Germanic Societies under Hapsburg Rule." Slavic Review 20(Mr, 1963).

Thiele, Peter W. "Untersuchungen zur Akkulturation bei den Kroaten des österreichischen Burgenlandes." Doctoral dissertation, U. of Berlin, 1968.

Van Arkel, Dirk. "Antisemitism in Austria." Doctoral dissertation, U. of Leiden, 1966.

Bahrain

Al Hamer, A. M. Development of Education in Bahrain 1940–1965. Bahrain, 1969.

Khalaf, Alhadi. "The Influence of Education on Ethnic Relations in Bahrain." In Socio-Economic Changes and their Impact on Inter-Ethnic Relations in Bahrain, pp. 126–149. Lund, Sweden: Department of Sociology, U. of Lund, 1972.

Bangladesh

Alamgir, M. "Some Analysis of Distribution of Income, Consumption, Saving and Poverty in Bangladesh." Bangladesh Development Studies 2(O, 1974).

Blair, H. W. "Rural Development, Class Structure and Bureaucracy in Bangladesh." World Development 6(Ja, 1978).

Cain, M. T. "The Economic Activities of Children in a Village in Bangladesh." Population and Development Review 2(S, 1977).

Mukherjce, R. "Nation-building and State Formation in Bangladesh. A Retrospective Study." South Asian Studies 7(Jl, 1972): 137–162.

Stepanek, Joseph F. Bangladesh, Equitable Growth? New York: Pergamon Press, 1978.

Belgium

Baton, Pierre. Coeducation D'Enfants Belges Et Etrangers. Problemes Qu'elle Engendre Dans Les Ecole Et Classes Primaires Francophones A Population Fortement Heterogene. Brussels: Universite Libre de Bruxelle, 1968.

Braeckman, C. Les Étrangers en Belgique. Brussels: Les Editions Vie Ouvière, 1973.

Centre de Recherches et d'Information Sociopolitique. "L'affaire de Louvain." Courrier Hebdomadaire (Brussels), S 16, 1966. Louvain U. in the ethnic struggle inside Belgium

Clemens, Rene and others. L'Assimilation culturelle des Immigrants en Belgique (Italiens et Polonais dans la région liegeoise). Liège: Faculte de Droit de Liège, 1953.

Couper, Kristin. "Stateless." Race Today 5 (Ja, 1973):18–19. [Uganda Asian refugees in Belgium]

Curtis, Arthur E. "New Perspectives on the History of the Language Problem in Belgium." Doctoral dissertation, U. of Oregon, 1971.

Czeslaw, Jesman. "Winds of Change in Belgium." Institute of Race Relations Newsletter, F, 1968.

De Coster, S. L'integration des enfants grecs dans les ecole Bruxelloises. Bruxelles, Belgium: Institut de Sociologie, 1974.

De Lannoy, W. "Residential Segregation of Foreigners in Brussels." Bulletin de la Societe Belge d'Etudes Geographiques 44 (1975):215-238.

Dunn, James A., Jr. "The Constitutional Protection of Minorities in Belgium." In Politics 1973: Minorities in Politics. Edited by Twisley E. Yarbrough, John P. East and Sandra Hough. East Carolina U. Publications, P.O. Box 2771, Greenville, NC 27834, n.d.

Du Roy, Albert. La Guerre des Belges. Paris: Seuil, 1968. [Flemish-Walloon conflict]

Graffar, M. Conditions de vie et santé de migrants et de leur familles. Brussels: Universite Libre de Bruxelles, 1969.

Heisler, Martin. "Managing Ethnic Conflict in Belgium." Annals of the American Academy of Political and Social Sciences, S, 1977, pp. 32-46.

Kabambi, Justin-Ntanda. "L'Adaptation des étudiants Africains a l'enseignement universitaire Belge." Doctoral dissertation, U. of Louvain (U.C.L.), 1974.

Kabugubugu, Amedee, and Nuttin, Joseph R. "Changement d'attitude envers la Belgique chez des étudiants Flamands: Comparaison de groupes équivalents a douze années d'intervalle." Psychologica Belgica 11(1971):23-44.

Kanitkar, Helen. "The Education of Immigrant Children in Belgium." New Community 2 (Summer, 1973):254-256.

Lange, Wilfried. "Die Umbildung des belgischen Staates auf der Grundlage der sprachlich-ethnischen Gegebenheit en." Doctoral dissertation, U. of Munich, 1972.

Liebman, Marcel. Né Juif. Une enfance juive pendant la guerre. Paris: Ed Duculot, 1978.

Mallinson, Vernon. Power and Politics in Belgian Education. London: Heinemann, 1963.

Mandel, Ernest. "The Dialectic of Class and Region in Belgium." New Left Review 20 (1963):5-31.

Mughan, Anthony. "Modernisation, Deprivation and the Distribution of Power Resources: Towards a Theory of Ethnic Conflict." New Community 5(Spring-Summer, 1977):360-370. [Belgium, Canada, Great Britain]

Pichault, C. "La Condition des Immigres en Belgique." Journal des Tribunaux, N 30, 1968.

"Pour une societé ouverte aux étrangers." Revue de l'institut de sociologie (Belgium) 1(1972):9-158.

Ruys, Manu. The Flemings. A People on the Move. A Nation in Being. Tr. Henri Schoup. Launoo, Tielt, and Utrecht, 1973.

Schmidt, Detlef. "Die Beteiligung der Nationalitaeten an der politischen Elite in Belgien, 1944-1968. Ein Beitrag zum Verständnis der belgischen Nationalentaetenfrage." Doctoral dissertation, U. of Kiel, 1970.

Segers, J., and van Den Broeck, J. "Bilingual Education Program for the Children of Migrant Workers in the Belgian Province of Limburg." International Journal of the Sociology of Language 15.

Swing, Elizabeth Sherman. "Separate But Equal: An Inquiry into the Impact of the Language Controversy on Education in Belgium." Western European Education 5(Winter, 1974):6-33.

Thomas, David. "Immigrants in Belgium and Luxembourg." New Community 1(0, 1971): 11-15.

Universite Libre de Bruxelles. Multilingual Contacts in Brussels, Ag, 1974. ERIC ED 101 576.

Zolberg, Aristide R. "The Making of Flemings and Walloons: Belgium, 1830-1914." Journal of Interdisciplinary History 5 (Autumn, 1974).

Belize

Bolland, O. Nigel. The Formation of a Colonial Society: Belize, from Conquest to Crown Colony. Baltimore: Johns Hopkins U. Press, 1977.

Young, Colville Norbert. "Belize Creole: A Study of the Creolized English Spoken in the City of Belize in its Cultural and Social Setting." Doctoral dissertation, U. of York, 1973.

Bolivia

Comitas, Lambros. "Education y Estrafication Social En Bolivia." America Indigena, Jl, 1968.

_____. "Education and Social Stratification in Bolivia." Transactions of the New York Academy of Sciences 29(1967):935-948.

_____. "Education and Social Stratification in Contemporary Bolivia." In Cultural Relevance and Educational Issues. Edited by Francis A. J. Ianni and Edward Storey. Boston: Little, Brown, 1967.

Kelley, Jonathan, and Klein, Herbert S. Revolution and the Re-birth of Inequality: The Bolivian National Revolution, 1977. ERIC ED 155 073.

Kehn, Heinz. "Indios, Blancos und Cambas in Oriente Boliviens." Sociologus 17(1967): 146-162. [English summary, p. 162]

Kubler, George. "The Quechua in the Colonial World." In Handbook of South American Indians. Vol. II, pp. 331-410. Edited by Julian H. Steward. Washington, DC: Smithsonian Institutution, 1946.

Massing, Michael. "Bolivia." Part 1. Harvard Crimson, F 22, 1974.

Ovando, Jorge. Sobre el Problema Nacional y Colonial de Bolivia. Cochabamb, Bolivia: Canelos, 1961.

Reinaga, Fausto. El indio y el cholaje boliviano. La Paz, Bolivia: The author, 1964.

_____. El indio y los escritores de América. La Paz, Bolivia: The author, 1969.

_____. La "intelligentsia" del cholaje boliviano. La Paz, Bolivia: The author, 1967.

_____. La revolucíon indio. La Paz, Bolivia: The author, 1970.

Riester, Jürgen. "Camba-Paico. Zur Integration der ostbolivianischen Indianer." Sociologus 20(1970):172-185.

_____. Indians of Eastern Bolivia: Aspects of Their Present Situation. Copenhagen: International Work Group for Indigenous Affairs, 1975.

UNESCO. Race and Class in Post-Colonial Society: A Study of Ethnic Group Relations in the English-speaking Caribbean, Bolivia, Chile and Mexico. Paris: UNESCO, 1977.

Brazil

Aborigines Protection Society. Tribes of the Amazon Basin in Brazil, 1972. London: Charles Knight & Co., 1973.

Akerren, Bo, Bakker, Sjouke, and Habersang, Rolf. Report of the ICRC Medical Mission to the Brazilian Amazon Region (May-August, 1978). Geneva, Switzerland: International Committee of the Red Cross, O, 1970.

"A Policy of Genocide." Akwesasne Notes 6 (Early Winter, 1975):8-10. [Indians in Brazil]

Azevedo, Thales de. Cultura e situacao racial no Brazil. Rio de Janeiro: Editora Civilizacao-Brasileira, 1966.

_____. Les Elites de Coleur dans une Vile Brasiliene. Paris: UNESCO, 1953.

Bastani, Tannus J. O Libano, e os libaneses no Brasil. Rio de Janeiro, n.p., 1945. [Lebanese in Brazil]

Bastide, Roger. The African Religions of Brazil: Toward a Sociology of the Interpretation of Civilizations. Tr. Helen Sebba. Baltimore, MD: Johns Hopkins U. Press, 1978.

_____. "Race Relations in Brazil." International Social Science Bulletin 4(1957): 495-512.

Bastide, Roger, and Fernandes, Florestan. Brancos e Negros ein São Paulo. São Paulo, Brazil: Companhia Editoria Nacional, 1959.

Bicudo, Virginia Leone. "Relacões raciais entre negros e brancos en São Paulo. Attitudes dos alunos dos grupos escolares em relacão com dos sens colegos." Anheimbi 12(O, 1953):234-259. [See, also, three following issues of journal.]

Blanco, Merida H. "Race and Face Among the Poor: The Language of Color in a Brazilian Bairro." Doctoral dissertation, Stanford U., 1978. Univ. Microfilms Order No. 7808766.

Bodard, Lucien. Green Hell, Massacre of the Brazilian Indians. Tr. by Jennifer Monaghan. New York: Outerbridge & Dienstfrey, 1971.

"Brazilian Indians Hold First National Assembly." Indígena, Summer, 1977.

Brooks, Edwin. "The Brazilian Road to Ethnicide." Contemporary Review, My, 1974.

_____. "The Indians of Brazil." Patterns of Prejudice 7(Mr-Ap, 1973):23-28.

Brooks, Edwin, Fuerst, René, Hemming, John, and Huxley, Francis. Tribes of the Amazon Basin in Brazil 1972: Report for the Aborigines Protection Society. London: Charles Knight, 1973.

Burajiru Nikkeijn Jittai Chose Iinkai. Burajiru No Nihoa Imin (The Japanese Immigrant in Brazil). 2 vols. Tokyo: Tokyo Daigaku Shuppan Kai Hatubai, 1964.

Cardoso, Fernando Herriques, and Ianni, Octavio. Cor e mobiladade social em Florianopolis. Aspectos dos relacoes entre negros e brancos numa comunidade do Brasil meriodinal. Sao Paulo, Brazil: Companhia Editora Nacional, 1960.

Cardoso de Oliveira, Roberto. "Indigenous Peoples and Sociocultural Change in the Amazon." In Man in the Amazon. Edited by Charles Wagley. Gainesville, FL: U. of Florida Press, 1974.

Chaves, L. G. M. "Minorias e seu estudo no Brasil." Revista de Ciências Sociales 2 (1971):149-168.

Conrad, Robert. The Destruction of Brazilian Slavery, 1850-1888. Berkeley, CA: U. of California Press, 1972.

_____. "Nineteenth-Century Brazilian Slavery." In Slavery and Race Relations in Latin America, pp. 146-175. Edited by Robert B. Toplin. Westport, CT: Greenwood Press, 1974.

Corwin, Arthur F. "Afro-Brazilians: Myths and Realities." In Slavery and Race Relations in Latin America, pp. 385-437. Edited by Robert B. Toplin. Westport, CT: Greenwood Press, 1974.

Da Costa Eduardo, Octavio. The Negro in Northern Brazil. A Study in Acculturation. Seattle, WA: U. of Washington, Press, 1948.

Dalbey, R. O. "The German Private School of Southern Brazil during the Vargas Years, 1930-1945: German Nationalism v. Brazilian Nationalization." Doctoral dissertation, Indiana U., 1970.

Davis, Shelton. "Custer Is Alive and He Lives in Brazil." Indian Historian 6(Winter, 1973):11-18.

De Compos, Murillo. O Indio no Brasil. O problema de seu adjustamento a communidade nacional. Rio de Janeiro: G.B., 1964.

Degler, Carl N. Neither Black Nor White. Slavery and Race Relations in Brazil and the United States. New York: Macmillan, 1971.

_____. "Slavery in Brazil and the United States: An Essay in Comparative History." American Historical Review 75(Ap, 1970): 1004-1028.

De Oliveira Torres, Joao Camillo. Estratifiaaas Social No Brazil. São Paulo: Difusao Europeia Do Livro, 1965.

Donald, Cleveland, Jr. "Equality in Brazil: Confronting Reality." Black World 22(N, 1972):23-34.

Doria, Carlos Alberto, and Ricardo, Carlos Alberto. Populations Indigènes du Brésil: Perspectives de Survie dans la Région dite Amazonie Légale. Geneva, Switzerland: Societé Suisse des Americanistes, 1972.

Dzidzienyo, Anani. The Position of Blacks in Brazilian Society, D, 1971. Minority Rights Group, 36 Craven Street, London WC2N5NG, England.

_____. "Race in Brazil." Race Today 3(O, 1971):333-335.

Fernandes, Florestan. A Integracao de Negro a Sociedade de Classes. Boletin No. 301, Sociologia I, No. 12. Sao Paulo, Brasil, 1964.

_____. "Beyond Poverty: The Negro and the Mulatto in Brazil." In Slavery and Race Relations in Latin America, pp. 277-297. Edited by Robert B. Toplin. Westport, CT: Greenwood Press, 1974.

_____. The Negro in Brazilian Society. New York: Columbia U. Press, 1969.

_____. "The Weight of the Past." Daedalus, Spring, 1967. [The Negro in Brazil]

Filho, Mario. O Negro no Futebol Brasileiro. 2nd ed. Rio de Janeiro: Editora .Civilzacao Brasileira, 1964. [How soccer became racially integrated in Brazil]

Flory, Thomas. "Race and Social Control in Independent Brazil." Journal of Latin American Studies 9(N, 1977):199-224.

Forgione, Pascal D. and others. Race and Reason: A Comparison of Racial Attitudes in the United States and Brazil, Ag 8, 1969. ERIC ED 044 342.

Forman, Shepard. The Brazilian Peasantry. New York: Columbia U. Press, 1975.

Frazier, E. Franklin. "Brazil Has No Race Problem." Common Sense 11(N, 1942):363-365.

_____. "A Comparison of Negro-White Relations in Brazil and in the United States." Transactions of the New York Academy of Sciences, Series 2, 6, 7 (My, 1944):251-269.

_____. "Some Aspects of Race Relations in Brazil." Phylon 3(Third Quarter, 1942).

Fujii, Yukio, and Smith, T. Lynn. The Acculturation of the Japanese Immigrants in Brazil. Gainesville, FL: U. of Florida Press, 1959.

Garcia-Zamor, Jean-Claude. "Social Mobility of Negroes in Brazil." Journal of Inter-American Studies and World Affairs 12(1970): 242-254.

Hanbury-Tenison, Robin. A Question of Survival for the Indians of Brazil. New York: Scribner's, 1973.

Harris, Marvin. "Referential Ambiguity in the Calculus of Brazilian Racial Identity." Southwestern Journal of Anthropology 26 (1970):1-14.

Hasting, Donald. "Japanese Emigration and Assimilation in Brazil." International Migration Review, Spring, 1969.

Havighurst, Robert J., and Moreira, J. Roberto. Society and Education in Brazil. Pittsburgh, PA: U. of Pittsburgh Press, 1965.

Hemming, John. Red Gold: The Conquest of the Brazilian Indians, 1500-1760. Cambridge, MA: Harvard U. Press, 1978.

Hewlitt, Sylvia-Ann. "Educational Investment in Brazil." Doctoral dissertation, Cambridge U., n.d.

Hopper, Janice (ed.). Indians of Brazil in the Twentieth Century. Washington, DC: Heldref Publications, 1973.

Ianni, Octavio. "Political Process and Economic Development in Brazil" (2 parts). New Left Review 25 and 26(My-Je and Summer, 1964):42-52 and 50-68.

_____. Racas E Classes Socialis No Brasil. Rio de Janiero: n.p., 1966.

Jallade, Jean-Pierre. Basic Education and In-come Inequality in Brazil: The Long-Term View, Je, 1977. ERIC ED 154 478.

Kanko, Iinkai. A History of the Japanese Immigrants in Brazil (in Japanese). 2 vols. N.p.: n.p., 1941 and 1953.

Karasch, Mary C. "Slave Life in Rio de Janeiro, 1808-1850." Doctoral disserta-tion, U. of Wisconsin, 1972.

Kietzman, Dale Walter. "Indian Survival in Brazil." Doctoral dissertation, U. of Southern California, 1972. Univ. Microfilms Order No. 72-27,669.

Klein, Herbert S. "Nineteenth-Century Brazil." In Neither Slave Nor Free. The Freedmen of African Descent in the Slave Societies of the New World, pp. 309-334. Edited by David W. Cohen and Jack P. Greene. Balti-more, MD: Johns Hopkins U. Press, 1972.

Koyama, Rokuro. A Forty-Year History of [Japanese] Immigrants. Sao Paulo, privately printed, 1949.

Leitman, Spencer L. "The Black Ragamuffins: Racial Hypocrisy in Nineteenth Century Southern Brazil." Americas 33(Ja, 1977): 504-518.

Levine, Robert M. "The First Afro-Brazilian Congress: Opportunities for the Study of Race in the Brazilian Northeast." Race 15 (O, 1973):185-193.

MacLachlan, Colin M. "The Indian Directorate: Forced Acculturation in Portuguese America (1757-1799)." Americas 28(Ap, 1972):357-387.

_____. "The Indian Labor Structure in the Portuguese Amazon, 1700-1800." In Colonial Roots of Modern Brazil: Papers of the Newberry Library Conference. Edited by Dauril Alden. Berkeley, CA: U. of California Press, 1973.

McNeill, Malvina Rosat. Guidelines to Problems of Education in Brazil: A Review and Selected Bibliography. New York: Teachers College Press, 1970.

Marginalization of Peoples. Racial Oppression in Japan, Political Repression in South Korea, Economic Slavery in Brazil. New York: Idoc/North America, 1974.

Martins, Wilson. Um Brasil diferente: ensaio sobre fenomenos de aculturacao no Parana. Sao Paulo: Editora Anhembi, 1955.

Medina, Cecelia. "The Legal Status of Indians in Brazil." American Indian Journal 3 (S, 1977):12-24.

Melatti, Julio Cezar. Indios do Brasil. Brasilia: n.p., 1960.

Metall, R. A., and Paranhos, M. "Equality of Opportunity in Multiracial Society: Brazil." International Labor Review, My, 1966.

Neiva, A. H., and Diégues, M., Jr. "The Cultural Assimilation of Immigrants in Brazil." In W. D. Borrie and others, The Cultural Integation of Immigrants, pp. 181-233. Paris: UNESCO, 1959.

Nogueira, Oracy. "Skin Color and Social Class." In Plantation Systems of the New World: Papers and Discussion Summaries of the Seminar Held in San Juan, Puerto Rico. Washington, DC: Pan America Union, 1959.

Oliveira, Roberto Cardoso de. A Sociologia do Brasil Indígena. Rio de Janeiro, Brazil: Tempo Brasileiro, 1972.

Peixoto, Afranio and others. Os judeus na historia do Brasil. Rio de Janeiro: n.p., 1936. [Jews in Brazilian history]

Pereira de Queriroz, Maria-Isaura. "Les classes sociales dans le Brésil actual." Cahiers interationaux de sociologie 39 (1965):137-169.

Pettinati, Francesco. O elemento italiano na formacao do Brasil. Sao Paulo: n.p., 1939. [Italians in Brazil]

Pierson, Donald. "The Educational Process and the Brazilian Negro." American Journal of Sociology 48(My, 1943).

Pietraszek, Bernadine. "The Poles in Brazil, 1889-1910" Polish American Studies 31 (Autumn, 1974):5-19.

Pinto, L. A. da Costa. O Negro no Rio de Janeiro. Sao Paulo, Brazil: Companhia Editora Nacional, 1953.

Price, Paul H. "The Polish Immigrants in Brazil: A Study of Immigration, Assimilation, and Acculturation." Doctoral dissertation, Vanderbilt U., 1950.

"The Progress of Genocide in Brazil." Akwesasne Notes 7(Late Summer, 1975):26-28.

Reeve, Richard Penn. "Black Economic Mobility in a Brazilian Town." Plural Societies 6 (Autumn, 1975):45-50.

_____. "Race and Social Mobility in a Brazilian Industrial Town." Luzo-Braz. Rev. 14(Winter, 1977):236-253.

_____. "Race and Socio-Economic Mobility in a Brazilian Town." Doctoral dissertation, Washington U., 1974. [Near Belo Horizonte, state capital of Minas Gerais]

Ribeiro, Darcy. The Indians and Civilization: The Process of Integration of Indigenous Populations in Modern Brazil. New York: Columbia U. Press, 1970.

_____. Os Indios e a Civilizacão: A Integracão das Populacões Indígenas no Brasil Moderno. Rio de Janeiro, Brazil: Civilizacão Brasileira, 1970.

_____. "The Social Integration of Indigenous Populations in Brazil." International Labor Review 85(Ap, 1962):325-346, and 85(My, 1962):459-477.

Rout, Leslie B., Jr. "Brazil: Study in Black, Brown and Beige." Negro Digest, F, 1970.

_____. "Race and Slavery in Brazil." Wilson Quarterly 1(Autumn, 1976):73-89.

_____. "Sleight of Hand: Brazilian and American Authors Manipulate the Brazilian Racial Situation, 1910-1951." Americas 29 (Ap, 1973):471-488.

Russell-Wood, A. J. R. "Colonial Brazil." In Neither Slave Nor Free. The Freedmen of African Descent in the Slave Societies of the New World, pp. 84-133. Edited by David W. Cohen and Jack P. Greene. Baltimore, MD: Johns Hopkins U. Press, 1972.

Saffioti, Heleieth I. B. Women in Class Society. Tr. Michael Vale. New York: Monthly Review Press, 1978.

Salzano, Francisco M., and Freiremaia, Newton. Problems in Human Biology: A Study of Brazilian Populations. Detroit, MI: Wayne State U. Press, 1970.

Sanjek, Roger. "Brazilian Racial Terms: Some Aspects of Meaning and Learning." American Anthropologist 73(O, 1971):1126-1143.

Sao Paulo Justice and Peace Commission. Sao Paulo--Growth and Poverty. London: Bowerdean Press, 1978.

Sardina, Abel. "Brazilian Indians Perennial Victims." Muhammad Speaks, Ja 17, 1975.

Saunders, John. "Class, Color, and Prejudice: A Brazilian Counterpoint." In Racial Tensions and National Identity. Edited by Ernest Q. Campbell. Nashville, TN: n.p., 1972.

_____ (ed.). Modern Brazil: New Patterns and Development. Gainesville, FL: U. of Florida Press, 1971.

Schwartz, Stuart B. "Elite Politics and the Growth of a Peasantry." In From Colony to Nation, pp. 133-154. Edited by A. J. R. Russell-Wood. Baltimore, MD: Johns Hopkins U. Press, 1975.

_____. "Indian Labor and New World Plantations: European Demands and Indian Responses in Northeastern Brazil." American Historical Review 83(F, 1978):43-79.

Shoumatoff, Alex. "Ranchers and Indians." Washington Post, O 17, 1976.

Silva, Nelson do Valle. "Black-White Income Differentials: Brazil, 1960." Doctoral dissertation, U. of Michigan, 1978. Univ. Microfilms Order No. 7823008.

Sims, Harold D. "Japanese Postwar Migration to Brazil: An Analysis of Data Presently Available." International Migration Review 6(Fall, 1972):246-265.

Skidmore, Thomas E. Black Into White. Race and Nationality in Brazilian Thought. New York: Oxford U. Press, 1974.

_____. "Toward a Comparative Analysis of Race Relations since Abolition in Brazil and the United States." Journal of Latin American Studies, My, 1972.

Smith, Donald B. "Recent Interpretations of Race Relations in Brazil." _Anthropologica_ 12(1970):241-252.

Staniford, Philip. "The Japanese in Brazil: Contemporary Pioneers." _New Society_, Jl 3, 1975.

_____. _Pioneers in the Tropics_. London: Athlone Press, 1973. [Japanese in Brazil]

Supysáua. _A Documentary Report on the Conditions of Indian Peoples_. Berkeley, CA: Indigena and American Friends of Brazil, N, 1974.

Thomas, Georg. _Die portugiesische Indianerpolitik in Bresilien, 1500-1640_. Berlin: .p., 1968.

Toplin, Robert B. "Abolition and the Issue of the Black Freedmen's Future in Brazil." In _Slavery and Race Relations in Latin America_, pp. 253-276. Edited by Robert B. Toplin. Westport, CT: Greenwood Press, 1974.

_____. "Brazil: Racial Polarization in the Developing Giant." _Black World_ 22(N, 1972): 15-22.

_____. "From Slavery to Fettered Freedom: Attitudes toward the Negro in Brazil." _Luso-Brazilian Review_, Summer, 1970, pp. 3-12.

_____. "The Problem of Double Identity: Black Brazilians on the Issue of Racial Consciousness." _Journal of Human Relations_ 20(1972): 205-214.

_____. "Reinterpreting Comparative Race Relations: The United States and Brazil." _Journal of Black Studies_ 2(D, 1971):135-155.

Vidal, David. "Many Blacks Shut Out of Brazil's Racial 'Paradise.'" _New York Times_, Je 5, 1978.

Wagley, Charles. "The Road of the Brazilian Indians." _Focus_, Spring, 1974.

_____. _Welcome of Tears. The Tapirapé Indians of Central Brazil_. New York: Oxford, 1977.

Willems, Emilio. _Aspectos da aculturacao de japoneses no Estado de São Paulo_. São Paulo: U. of São Paulo, 1948.

Wiznitzer, Arnold. _Jews in Colonial Brazil_. New York: Columbia U. Press, 1960.

Bulgaria

Chary, Frederick B. "Bulgaria and the Jews: The Final Solution, 1940 to 1944." Doctoral dissertation, U. of Pittsburgh, 1968. Univ. Microfilms Order No. 69-12,825.

_____. _The Bulgarian Jews and the Final Solution, 1940-1944_. Pittsburgh, PA: U. of Pittsburgh Press, 1973.

Terzioski, Rastislav. _The Denationalizing Activity of Bulgarian Cultural-Educational Institutions of Macedonia (Skopje and Bitola Occupation District)_ [in Bulgarian]. Skopje: Institut za natoionalna istorija, 1974.

Burma

Chakravarti, Nalini R. _The Indian Minority in Burma: The Rise and Decline of an Immigrant Community_. New York: Oxford U. Press, 1971.

Lieberman, Victor B. "Ethnic Politics in Eighteenth Century Burma." _Mod. Asian Stud._ 12(Jl, 1978):455-482.

Mahajani, Usha Ganesh. _The Role of Indian Minorities in Burma and Malaya_. Bombay: Vora, 1960.

Maung, I. "A Survey of the History of Education in Burma before the British Conquest and After." Doctoral dissertation, U. of London, 1929.

Theodorson, George A. "Minority Peoples in the Union of Burma." _Journal of Southeast Asian History_ 5(1964):1-16.

Burundi

Connen, Bernard. "L'enfant dans la societé contemporaine au Burundi." _R. jur. pol._ 31 (Ap-Je, 1977):213-224.

Greenland, Jeremy. "The Reform of Education in Burundi: Enlightened Theory Faced with Political Reality." _Comparative Education_ 10 (Mr, 1974):57-63.

Kuper, Leo. _The Pity of It All: Polarisation of Racial and Ethnic Relations_. London: Ducksworth, 1977.

Lemarchand, René. "Ethnic Genocide." _Society_ 12(Ja-F, 1975):50-60.

_____. "Ethnic Genocide in Burundi." _Bull. S. Assoc. Africanists_ 4(F, 1976):15-26.

Lemarchand, René, and Martin, David. _Selective Genocide in Burundi_. London: Minority Rights Group, Jl, 1974.

Weinstein, Warren. "Ethnicity and Conflict Regulation: The 1972 Burundi Revolt." Afrika Spectrum 9(1974):42-49.

Weinstein, Warren, and Schrire, Robert. Political Conflict and Ethnic Strategies: A Case Study of Burundi. New York: Maxwell School of Citizenship and Public Affairs, Syracuse U., 1976.

Cambodia

Wilmott, W. E. The Chinese in Cambodia. Vancouver, Canada: U. of British Columbia, 1967.

_____. The Political Structure of the Chinese Community in Cambodia. Athlone Press, 1970.

Cameroon

Booth, B. R. "A Comparative Study of Mission and Government Influence in Educational Development in W. Cameroon, 1922-69." Doctoral dissertation, U. of California, Los Angeles, 1973.

Clignet, Remi. "Educational and Occupational Differentiation in Cameroun." EDCC 25 (1977):731-745.

_____. "The Role of Schools in the Rise of Camerounian Nationalism." Education and Urban Society 10(F, 1978):177-208.

Constable, D. "Bilingualism in the United Republic of Cameroon." English Language Teaching Journal 31(Ap, 1977):249-253.

_____. "Bilingualism in the United Republic of Cameroon: Proficiency and Distribution." Comparative Education 10(O, 1974):233-246.

Haupt, W. Norman. "The Secondary School As An Agent of Ethnic Integration in West Cameroon." Doctoral dissertation, Michigan State U., 1968.

Marchand, C. "Apercu sur le contenu de l'enseignement au Cameroun, 1921-1939." Annales de la Faculté des lettres et sciences humaines de Yaounda 1(1972):45-55.

Martin, Jean-Yves. "Inégalités régionales et inégalités sociales: l'enseignement secondaire au Cameroun septentrional." Rev Revue francaise de Sociologie 16(1975): 317-334.

Nyima, Barthelmy Moondo. "L'enseignement dans la la politique coloniale française au Cameroun de 1916 à 1938." Ét. Hist. afric. 8(1976):199-216.

Quinn, Frederick. "German and French Rule in the Cameroon." Tarikh 4(1974):55-69.

Shu, S. N. "The Collaboration Policy in Cameroun Education, 1910-1931." Doctoral dissertation, Institute of Education, London, 1972.

Stoecker, H. Kamerun unter Deutscher Kolonialherrschaft, I. Berlin: n.p., 1960.

Canada

French-Canadians

Allnutt, Peter, and Chodos, Robert. "Quebec: Into the Streets." Radical America 6(S-O, 1972):29-52. [Reprinted from Last Post, vol. I, No. 1]

Basham, Richard D. Crisis in Blanc and White: Urbanization and Ethnic Identity in French Canada. Cambridge, MA: Schenekman, 1977.

Beattie, Christopher. Minority Men in Majority Setting: Middle-Level Francophones in the Canadian Public Service. Toronto: McClelland and Stewart, 1975.

Beaudoin, Gérald-A. "Le bilinguisme et la constitution." Revue générale de droit 4 (1973):321.

Belanger, Paul G., Paquet, Pierre, and Valois, Jocelyne. "Formation des adulte et contradictions sociales." Sociologie et Sociétés 5(My, 1973):59-90.

Bélanger, Pierre W., and Juneau, Andre. "Les maître de l'enseignement primaise: étude socio-culturelle." Recherches Sociographiques 1(Ja-Mr, 1961):55-68.

Bélanger, Pierre W., and Rocher, Guy. École et Société au Québec: Eléments d'une sociologie de l'education. Montreal, Canada: Editions HMH, Ltée, 1970.

Bourassa, Guy. "La structure du pouvoir a Montréal: le domaine de l'éducation." Recherches sociographiques 8(1967):125-149.

Bourque, Gilles. Classes sociales et question nationale au Québec, 1760-1840. Montréal, Canada: Editions Parti Pris, 1970.

_____. L'État capitaliste et la question nationale. Montréal: Les Presses de l'Université de Montréal, 1977.

Bousquet, Marie E. "Les maîtres au Canada français: Valeur et formation, 1608-1856." Doctoral dissertation, Montréal U., 1970.

Brochu, Michel. "L'Heure du Nouveau Quebec." Action Nationale 56(1967):681-689, 909-913. [Labrador Eskimo]

Brutus, Merlaine (Chrispin). "Adaptation de l'enfant haitien à Montréal. Étude réalisée auprès de 27 familles haitiennes à Montréal." Master's thesis, Montréal U., 1970.

Bryant, William. "French Canadian Literature and the Teacher of French." Canadian Modern Language Review 30(0, 1973):6-10.

Bryant, William H. "Marxist Blueprints for Quebec Schools." Social Science Journal 15 (Ja, 1978):81-102.

Cappon, P. Conflit entre les Néo-Canadiens et les francophones de Montréal. Québec: Les Presses de l'Université Laval, 1974.

Carter, G. E. The Catholic Public Schools of Quebec. Toronto: Gage, 1957.

Chabot-Robitaille, Louise. De l'eau chaude, de l'espace et un peu de justice. Des citoyens de quartier ouvrier analysent leur situation. Montréal, Canada: Conseil de Développement social, 1970.

Chaput, Marcel. Why I Am a Separatist. Trans. Robert A. Taylor. Westport, CT: Greenwood Press, 1975.

Choquette, R. Language and Religion: A History of English-French Conflict in Ontario. Ottawa: U. of Ottawa Press, 1975.

Churchill, Stacy. "National Linguistic Minorities: The Franco-Ontarian Educational Renaissance." Prospects 6(1976):439-449.

Cook, Ramsay (ed.). French-Canadian National-ism: An Anthology. Toronto: Macmillan, 1969.

Corbeil, Jean Claude. "Origine Historique de la Situation Linguistique Quebecoise." Langue Francaise 31(S, 1976):6-19.

Corriveau, Arthur. "The Struggle for Français in Manitoba." Multiculturalism 1(1978): 19-25.

Crestwohl, Leon D. Jewish School Problem in the Province of Quebec From Its Origin to the Present Day. Montreal: n.p., 1926.

Cuneo, Carl J., and Curtis, James E. "Quebec Separatism: An Analysis of Determinants within Social-Class Levels." Canadian Review of Sociology and Anthropology 11 (F, 1974).

Dofny, Jacques, and Arnaud, Nicole. Natural-ism and the National Question. Montreal: Black Rose Books, 1978. [Quebec]

Dofny, Jacques, and Rioux, Marcel. "Les classes sociales au Canada francais." Revue francaise de sociologie 3(1962): 290-300.

Dufournaud, C. "Les aspects écologiques de l'assimilation des Canadiens français a l'extérieur du Québec." Master's thesis, Université Laval, 1973.

Dumont, J., Hamelin, J., Harvey, F., and Montiminy, J. P. Idéologies au Canada francais 1900-1929. Quebec: Les Presses de L'Université Laval, 1974.

Dumont, Fernand, and Montiminy, J. (eds.). Le pouvoir dans la societé canadienne-francaise. Montreal, Canada: Presses de l'Université Laval, 1966.

Dumont, Fernand, and Martin, Yves (eds.). Situation de la recherche sur le Canada francais. Montréal, Canada: Presses de l'Université Laval, 1962.

Dunton, A. Davidson, and Laurendeau, André. Report of the Royal Commission on Bi-lingualism and Biculturalism. Vol. II: Education. Ottawa, Canada: Queen's Printer, 1970.

Farine, Avigdor. "La Politique de la Langue et de L'Enseignement au Québec." Canadian and International Education 1(1972).

Fournier, Pierre. "Language and Education." In The Quebec Establishment. The Ruling Class and the State, pp. 116-142. Montréal: Black Rose Books, 1976.

_____. "The Politics of School Reorganization in Montreal." Master's thesis, McGill U., 1971.

Gagnon, L. "The Economics of the Quebec Independentist Movement." Canadian Dimen-sions 7(D, 1970):55-60.

Gendron, Jean-Denis. "La situation du francais comme langue d'usage au Quebec." Langue Francaise 31(S, 1976):20-39.

Gill, Robert M. Quebec's French-Language Universities and the Politics of Develop-ment, Ap, 1977. ERIC ED 146 783.

Girard, Ghislaine. "Training of Native Teachers in Quebec." In Education in the North, pp. 275-281. Edited by Frank Darnell. Arctic Institute of North America, U. of Alaska, 1972.

Godbout, Arthur. "Les Ecoles franco-ontariennes d'avant 1800." Canadian Historial Association Report, 1953.

_____. "Les Franco-Ontariens et leurs ecoles de 1791 a 1844." Revue de l'universite d'Ottawa. Vol. 33, 1963, pp. 245-268; Vol. 36, 1966, pp. 462-479, 678-697; Vol. 37, 1967, pp. 80-100.

_____. "Les Francophones du Haut-Canada et leurs écoles avant l'acte d'union." Doctoral dissertation, Ottawa U., 1969.

_____. "The History of Franco-Ontarian Schools." Orbit 2(Ap, 1971).

_____. L'origine des écoles françaises dans l'Ontario. Ottawa: Les Editions de l' Université d'Ottawa, 1972.

Gold, Gerald L. St. Pascal. Toronto: Holt, Rinehart and Winston of Canada Limited, 1975. [Quebec]

Gray, Stan. "Schools, Language and the National Liberation Struggle." This Magazine Is for Schools 4(Spring, 1970):77-100.

Groupe de Recherches Sociales. La Situation des Immigrants a Montreal. Etude sur L' Adaptation Occupationnelle, les Conditions Residentielles et les Relations Sociales. Montreal, 1959.

Hache, Jean-Baptiste. "Language and Religious Factors in Canadian Ethnic Politices of Education: A Case Study in Power Mobilization." Doctoral dissertation, U. of Toronto, 1976. [Toronto: Franco-Ontarians]

Hart, Edward J. "The History of the French-Speaking Community of Education, 1795-1935." Master's thesis, Alberta U., 1971.

Hebert, Raymond. "L'Evolution de l'education francaise au Manitoba." Canadian Modern Language Review 34(F, 1978):348-362.

Henchey, Norman. "Quebec Education: The Unfinished Revolution." McGill Journal of Education 7(Fall, 1972):95-118.

Henripin, J., Charbonneau, H., and Legare, J. "La situation démographique des francophones au Québec et à Montreal d'ici l'an 2000." Le Devoir, N 4, 1969.

Jadotte, Herard. "Haitian Immigration to Quebec." Journal of Black Studies 7(Je, 1977):485-500.

Jaenen, Cornelius J. "Minority Group Schooling and Canadian National Unity." Journal of Educational Thought 7(Ag, 1973):81-93.

_____. "Problems of Assimilation in New France, 1603-1645." French Historical Studies 4(Spring, 1966):265-289.

Katz, Joseph. "Bilingualism and Biculturalism in Canada." Comparative Education, Mr, 1966.

Lambert, Pierre D. "Contemporary Pattern of French-Canadian Education in the Province of Quebec." Doctoral dissertation, U. of Iowa, 1956.

Lambert, W. E., Yackley, A., and Hein, R. N. "Child Training Values of English Canadian and French Canadian Parents." Canadian Journal of Behavioral Science 3(1971):217-236.

Lambert, W. E., and McNamara, J. "Some Cognitive Consequences of Following a First-Grade Curriculum in a Second Language." Journal of Educational Psychology 60(1969):86-96.

Lanphier, C. M., and Morris, R. N. "Structural Aspects of Differences in Income between Anglophones and Francophones." Canadian Review of Sociology and Anthropology 11(F, 1974).

Latif, G., and Tanguay, B. "Pour Contrabalances le Prestige de l'Anglais les Quebecois Mettent au Point Pedagogie Attractive Destinee aux Enfants Immigres." Migrants Formation 19(N-D, 1976).

Laurin, Camille. "Nationalism, Diversity and Quebec." Multiculturalism 1(1978):10-14.

Lauzon, Adèle. "The New Left in Québec." Our Generation 7(1970):14-30.

Lavoie-Roux, Therese. "A Program for Action in Disadvantaged Areas." Education Canada 11(D, 1971):65-68.

Lazures, Jacques. La Jeunesse du Quebec en Revolution. Montreal: Presses de l'Université du Quebec, 1971.

Leblanc, Paul-Emile. "L'enseigement francais au Manitoba, 1916-1968." Master's thesis, U. of Ottawa, 1969.

Le Gresley, Omer. "L'Enseignement du francais en Acadie, 1604-1926." Doctoral dissertation, U. of Paris, 1925.

Lieberson, Stanley. Language and Ethnic Relations in Canada. New York: Wiley, 1970.

_____. Linguistic and Ethnic Segregation in Montreal. Ottawa: Royal Commission on Bilingualism and Biculturalism, Commission Royale d'Enquete Sur Le Bilinguisme and Le Biculturalisme, 1966.

Little, Jack. "French Canadian Colonization of the Eastern Townships, 1850-1893." Doctoral dissertation, U. of Ottawa, 1976.

Mackey, William F. (ed.). Le Bilinguisme Canadien: bibliographie analytique et guide du chercheur. Quebec: Centre international de recherche sur le bilinguisme, 1978.

McLeod, Keith Alwyn. A History of the Status of the French Language in the Schools of the North-West Territories 1870-1905 and in Saskatchewan 1905-1934. Saskatoon, Sask.: n.p., 1966.

Magnuson, Roger. "Education and Society in Quebec in the 1970's." Journal of Educational Thought 7(Ag, 1973):94-104.

_____. Education in the Province of Quebec. Washington, DC: GPO, 1969.

Mallea, John (ed.). Quebec's Language Policies: Background and Response. Quebec: Les Presses de l'Université Laval, 1977.

Maxwell, Thomas R. "French Canadians in Toronto." Doctoral dissertation, U. of Toronto, 1968.

_____. The Invisible French: The French in Metropolitan Toronto. Waterloo, Ontario: Wilfred Laurier U. Press, 1977.

Milner, Sheilagh Hodgins, and Milner, Henry. The Decolonization of Quebec. Toronto, Canada: McClelland and Stewart, 1973.

Morris, Lorenzo. "The Politics of Education and Language in Quebec: A Comparative Perspective." Canadian and International Education 5(D, 1976):1-37.

Nock, David. "History and Evolution of French Canadian Sociology." Insurgent Sociologist 4(Summer, 1974):15-27.

Richert, Jean Pierre. "The Impact of Ethnicity on the Perception of Heroes and Historical Symbols." Canadian Review of Sociology and Anthropology 11(My, 1974):156-163.

Richmond A. H. "Perspectives on French Canada." Canadian Review of Sociology and Anthropology 10(Ag, 1973).

Rioux, Marcel, and Martin, Yves (eds.). French-Canadian Society. 2 vols. Toronto: McClelland and Stewart, 1965.

_____ and _____ (eds.). La société canadienne-francaise. Vol. 1. Montréal, Canada: Editions H.M.H., 1971.

Rocher, Guy, and Belanger, Pierre W. Ecole et Société au Québec: Éléments d'une sociologie de l'éducation. Montréal, Canada: Editions HMH, 1970.

Roussopoulos, Dimitrios. "Social Classes and Nationalism in Québec." Our Generation 8 (Ap, 1972):37-57.

Royal Commission on Bilingualism and Biculturalism. A Preliminary Report. Ottawa, Canada: The Queen's Printer, 1965.

_____. Report....General Introduction. Book I. The Official Languages. Ottawa: Queen's Printer, O 8, 1967.

Sissons, C. B. Bi-Lingual Schools in Canada. Toronto: Dent, 1917.

Stratford, Philip (comp.). Bibliography of Canadian Books in Translation: French to English and English to French. Ottawa: Humanities Research Counceil of Canada, 1977.

Szpakowska, Janina-Klara, and Laplante, Marc. Profils Culturels des Jeunes Montrealais. Montreal: Universite de Montreal, 1970.

Taylor, D. M., Bassili, J. N., and Aboud, F. E. "Dimensions of Ethnic Identity: An Example from Quebec." Journal of Social Psychology 89(1973).

Teeple, Gary (ed.). Capitalism and the National Question in Canada. Toronto, Canada: U. of Toronto Press, 1972.

Vallières, Pierre. White Niggers of America. The Precocious Autobiography of a Quebec "Terrorist." Tr. Joan Pinkham. New York: Monthly Review Press, 1971.

Blacks in Canada

Ages, Arnold. "A Racial Problem in Canada?" Christian Century, Ap 30, 1969. [Black student protest at Sir George Williams U., Montreal, Quebec]

Arnott, Hilary. "West Indians in the Classroom." Race Today 2(1970):126-127.

Arthurs, H. W. "Civil Liberties-Public Schools-Segregation of Negro Students." Canadian Bar Review 41(1963):453

Bargen, Peter F. "Separate Schools for Negroes in Ontario." In The Legal Status of the Canadian Public School Pupil, pp. 33-36. Toronto: n.p., 1961.

Bell, D. and others (comps.). Canadian Black Studies Bibliography. London, Ontario: Office of International Education, U. of Western Ontario, 1971.

Beserve, C. A. "West Indian Immigrant Children: A Study of Some Problems of Adjustment." Master's thesis, U. of Toronto, 1973.

Betcherman, Lita-Rose. "Canada's Human Rights After the Quebec Elections." Patterns of Prejudice 11(My-Je, 1977):23-27.

"Black Students in Canada Stage Sit-In at University, Present Demands List." Muhammad Speaks, F 14, 1969. [Sir George Williams U.]

"Blacks Convicted in Takeover." SOBU Newsletter, My 29, 1971. [Aftermath of events of F, 1969 at Sir George Williams U., Montreal]

Bogner, Carl J. "West Indians, IQ, and Special Education Placement." Orbit 7(Ap, 1976):18-20.

Bowden, Ted. "Questions on Black Power [in England]." Black Liberation 1(1972):67-73.

Brand, G. Survey of Negro Population of Halifax County... Halifax, Nova Scotia: Social Development Division, Nova Scotia Department of Public Welfare, 1964.

Brooksbank, C. R. "Afro-Canadian Communities in Halifax County, Nova Scotia." Master's thesis, U. of Toronto, 1949.

Brown, William Wells. "The Colored People of Canada." Pine and Palm, S 7, 14, 21, and 28; O 19; N 30; and D 7, 1861. [Seven articles]

Calderwood, William. "The Rise and Fall of the Ku Klux Klan in Saskatchewan." Master's thesis, U. of Saskatchewan (Regina), 1968.

"Canadian Blacks Form New Organization." SOBU Newsletter, Ap 3, 1971.

Clairmont, Donald H., and Magill, Dennis W. Africville: The Life and Death of a Canadian Black Community. Toronto: McClelland and Stewart, 1974. [Bedford Basin, near Halifax]

_____ and _____. Nova Scotian Blacks: An Historical and Structural Overview. Halifax, Nova Scotia: Institute of Public Affairs, Dalhousie U., 1970.

Clairmont, Donald H., and Wien, Fred. "Blacks and Whites: The Nova Scotia Race Relations Experience." In Banked Fires--The Ethnics of Nova Scotia. Edited by Douglas F. Campbell. The Scribblers' Press, 1978.

Clarke, Austin C. "The Meaning of Immigration--Some Psychological Speculation about the Immigration of Black West Indians in Toronto and in Canada." Black Lines 1 (Winter, 1970):9-16.

Coelho, Liz. "West Indian Students in the Secondary School." TESL Talk 7(S, 1976): 37-46.

Collins, Sydney. "Social Processes Integrating Coloured People in Britain." British Journal of Sociology 3(1952):20-29.

Cooper, William M. A Proposed Program for the Nova Scotia Association for the Advancement of Colored People. Halifax, Nova Scotia: Adult Education Division, Nova Scotia Department of Education, 1954.

Cottle, Thomas J. "A Question of Fault." Progressive 41(0, 1977):34-36. [Brixton, London]

_____. "A Wasted Death?" New Society, S 29, 1977. [A Jamaican in London]

Dalhousie University Library (comp.). Blacks in Canada: Representative Source Materials. Halifax: Dalhousie U. Library, 1970.

Davis, Morris. "Results of Personality Tests Given to Negroes in the Northern and Southern United States and in Halifax, Canada." Phylon, Winter, 1964.

Derevensky, Jeffrey L., and Lusthaus, Charles. Black and Immigrant Children in Montreal: A Curricula Comparison, Ap, 1976. ERIC ED 126 167.

Dexter, Susan. "Black Ghetto that Fears Integration." Maclean's Magazine, Jl 24, 1965. [Africville]

Dillard, J. L. "The History of Black English in Nova Scotia." Revista/Review Inter-americana 2(1972).

D'Oyley, Vincent. "Another Note on the Education of Urban West Indian Black Canadians." Interchange 7(1976-77):23-26.

_____. "Symposium on Multiculturalism and the Black Presence in the Canadian Mosaic: A Summary Note." Multiculturalism 1(1977): 22-23.

D'Oyley, Vincent, and Silverman, Harry (eds.). Black Students in Urban Canada. Toronto: Citizenship Branch, Ministry of Culture and Recreation, 1976.

Driver, Geoffrey. "Cultural Competence, Social Power and School Achievement: West Indian Secondary School Pupils in the West Midlands." New Community 5(Spring-Summer, 1977):353-359.

_____. "Ethnicity, Cultural Competence and School Achievement: A Case Study of West Indian Pupils Attending a British Secondary Modern School." Doctoral dissertation, U. of Illinois, 1976.

Eber, Dorothy. The Computer Centre Party. Montreal, Canada: Tundra Books, 1969.

"Education Funds for Black Students." Education (Nova Scotia) 6(Je 16, 1976).

Eltis, David. "Dr. Stephen Lushington: Liberal Reformer and Radical Advocate of Negro Rights." Master's thesis, U. of Alberta, 1969.

Farrell, John K. A. "The History of the Negro Community in Chatham, Ontario, 1787-1865." Doctoral dissertation, U. of Ottawa, 1955.

Feinberg, A. L. "Uncle Tom's Tomb in Jim Crow's Cradle." Negro Digest, My, 1950.

Fergusson, C. B. A Documentary Study of the Establishment of the Negroes in Nova Scotia between the War of 1812 and the Winning of Responsible Government. Halifax, N.S.: Public Archives, 1948.

Figueroa, Peter M. E. "The Employment Prospects of West Indian School-Leavers in London, England." Social and Economic Studies 25(S, 1976):216-233.

Fitzherbert, K. "West Indian Children in London." Occasional Papers on Social Administration, No. 19. London: Bell, 1967.

Foner, Nancy. "The Meaning of Education to Jamaicans at Home and in London." New Community 4(Summer, 1975):195-202.

Foner, Philip S. "The Colored Inhabitants of Vancouver Island." B.C. Studies (Winter, 1970-1971):29-33.

Forsythe, Dennis (ed.). Let the Niggers Burn! The Sir George Williams University Affair and Its Caribbean Aftermath, 1971. Black Rose Books, 3934 rue St. Urbain, Montreal, Quebec, Canada

Gannon, Roger. "The English Language Education of West Indian Migrants to Canada." English Quarterly 8(Winter, 1975-76): 33-42.

Gillis, John S., and Kinsella, Noel A. "Some Personality Factors of Matched Groups of New Brunswick, Blacks and Whites." Canadian Journal of Behavioral Science 3 (1971):66-71. [High school students]

Greaves, Ida. The Negro in Canada. No. 16, Economic Studies in the National Problems of Canada. Montreal: McGill U., 1930.

Greene, J. E. "Political Perspectives on the Assimilation of Immigrants: A Case Study of West Indians in Vancouver." Social and Economic Studies 19(S, 1970):406-423.

Grow, Stewart. "The Blacks of Amber Valley." Canadian Ethnic Studies 6(1975).

Harker, Mary. "The Nightgown Brigade." Multiculturalism 2(1978):23-24. [Suburb of Toronto]

Head, Wilson A. "The Blacks in Canada: A Revised Edition." Multiculturalism 1(1978): 17-19.

_____. The Black Presence in the Canadian Mosaic--A Study of Perception and the Practice of Discrimination Against Blacks in Metropolitan Toronto. Toronto: Ontario Human Rights Commission, 1975.

Helling, Rudolph A. The Position of Negroes, Chinese and Italians in the Social Structure of Windsor, Ontario. Ontario Human Rights Commission, Toronto, D, 1965.

Hendelman, Don. "West Indian Associations in Montreal." Master's thesis, McGill U., 1964.

Henry, Frances. The Dynamics of Racism in Toronto: A Preliminary Report. Downsview, Ontario: Department of Anthropology, York U., 1977.

_____. "West Indians in Canada: A Reply." Social and Economic Studies, D, 1968.

Henry, Frances, and Mills, Don. Forgotten Canadians: The Blacks of Nova Scotia. Ontario, Canada: Longman Canada, Ltd., 1973.

Henry, Franklin J. The Experience of Discrimination: A Case Study Approach. San Francisco, CA: R and E Research Associates, 1974.

_____. Perception of Discrimination Among Negroes and Japanese-Canadians in Hamilton. Ontario Human Rights Commission, Toronto, N, 1965.

Hill, Daniel Grafton. "Black History in Early Toronto." Multiculturalism 2(1978):11-16.

_____. "Negroes in Toronto: A Sociological Study of a Minority Group." Doctoral dissertation, U. of Toronto, 1960.

Hinds, Barbara. "Black Power: Has Halifax Found the Answer?" Atlantic Advocate (Fredericton, New Brunswick), Ja, 1969.

Institute of Public Affairs. The Condition of the Negroes of Halifax City. Halifax, Nova Scotia: Dalhousie U., 1962.

_____. Poverty in Nova Scotia. Halifax, Canada: Dalhousie U., 1971.

Irby, Charles C. "The Black Settlers on Saltspring Island in the Nineteenth Century." Phylon 35(D, 1974):368-374. [British Columbia]

Israel, Wilfred Emmerson. "The Montreal Negro Community." Master's thesis, McGill U., 1928.

Johnson, Thomas. "Color Prejudice in Canada." Anthropological Journal of Canada 16 (1978):2-11.

Killian, Crawford. Go Do Some Great Thing: The Black Pioneers of British Columbia. Vancouver: Douglas & McIntyre, 1978.

Landon, Fred C. "Negro Colonization in Upper Canada Before 1860." Proceedings and Transactions of the Royal Society of Canada, 3rd series (1929):73-80.

_____. "The Work of the American Missionary Association among the Negro Refugees in Canada West, 1848-1864." Ontario Historical Society, Papers and Records 31(1924).

Mac Lennon, Phyllis M. "a Study of the Coloured Community." Master's thesis, Maritime School of Social Work, 1959.

Martin, G. "British Officials and Their Attitudes to the Negro Community in Canada, 1833-1861." Ontario Hist. 66(Je, 1974): 79-88.

Oliver, Jules Ramon. "Nova Scotia Association for the Advancement of Colored People. An Historical Evaluation of the NSAACP and the Role it Has Played in the Area of Employment." Master's thesis, U. of Acadia, 1969.

Oliver, W. P. A Brief Summary of Nova Scotia Negro Communities. Halifax, Nova Scotia: Adult Education Division, Nova Scotia Department of Education, Mr, 1964.

_____. The Advancement of Negroes in Nova Scotia. Halifax, Nova Scotia: Adult Education Division, Nova Scotia Department of Education, 1949.

_____. "The Cultural Progress of the Negro in Nova Scotia." Dalhousie Review 29 (1949).

_____. "The Negro in Nova Scotia." Journal of Education, D, 1949. [Published by the Nova Scotia Department of Education]

Perry, Charlotte Bronte. The Long Road. The History of the Coloured Canadian in Windsor, Ontario. Windsor: Summer, 1969.

Pilton, J. W. "Negro Settlement in British Columbia: 1858-1871." Master's thesis, U. of British Columbia, 1951.

Potter, Harold Herbert. "The Occupational Adjustments of Montreal Negroes, 1941-1948." Master's thesis, McGill U., 1949.

Potter, Harold H., and Hill, D. H. Negro Settlement in Canada, 1628-1965: A Survey. Royal Commission on Bilingualism & Biculturalism, 1966.

Rawlyk, G. A. "The Guysborough Negroes--A Study in Isolation." Dalhousie Review, Spring, 1968.

Richmond, Anthony H. "Black and Asian Immigrants in Britain and Canada: Some Comparisons." New Community 4(Winter-Spring, 1975-76):501-516.

Rock, Robert E. "The Story of the Emerging Visibility of the Community of Black People, North Preston, Nova Scotia." Master's thesis, Waterloo Lutheran, 1970.

Ross, Jean B. "Negroes of Halifax." Master's thesis, Maritime School of Social Work, 1959.

Roth, J. West Indians in Toronto: The Students and the Schools. Toronto: Board of Education for the Borough of York, 1973.

Sargeant, A. J. "Participation of West Indian Boys in English Schools' Sports Teams." Educational Research 14(Je, 1972): 225-230.

Schreiber, Jon. In the Course of Discovery. West Indian Immigrants in Toronto Schools. Toronto, Canada: Research Dept., Board of Education, 1970.

Schweinger, Loren. "A Fugitive Negro in the Promised Land: James Rapier in Canada, 1856-1864." Ontario History 67(Je, 1975): 91-104.

Schand, Gwendolyn V. Adult Education Among the Negroes of Nova Scotia. Halifax, Nova Scotia's Institute of Public Affairs, Dalhousie U., 1961.

Simpson, Donald G. "Negroes in Ontario from Early Times to 1870." Doctoral dissertation, Western U., 1971.

Soutar-Hynes, Mary Lou. "West Indian Realities in the Intermediate Grades--The Emerging Role of the ESD Teacher." TESL Talk 7(S, 1976):31-36.

Spray, W. A. The Blacks in New Brunswick. St. Thomas U., Brunswick Press, 1972.

Stasiuk, Pamela. "West Indian Students in the High School." Orbit 33(Je, 1976):8-11.

Tarlo, Jenne M. "Racial Antipathy in an Urban Environment." Master's thesis, Dalhousie U., 1969.

Taylor, Edward. "Conflict, Group Affiliation and Social Adjustment: The Case of West Indians in Toronto." Master's thesis, U. of Guelph, 1969.

Teach-In Report. The Black Man in Nova Scotia. Antigonish, Nova Scotia: Saint Francis Xavier U., Ja, 1969.

Thompson, Alford Wingrove. "Assimilation of West Indians in London and Hamilton, Ontario." Master's thesis, Western U., 1970.

Thomson, Colin Argyle. "The Historical and Social Background to Nova Scotian Negro Education." Master's thesis, U. of Saskatchewan (Saskatoon), 1968.

Troper, Harold Martin. "The Creek-Negroes of Oklahoma and Canadian Immigration, 1909-11." Canadian Historical Review 53(S, 1972): 272-288.

Trudel, Marcel. L'Esclavage au Canada Français. Québec: Presses Universitaires Laval, 1960.

Tulloch, Headley. Black Canadians. Toronto: NC Press, 1975.

Tunteng, P. Kiven. "Racism and the Montreal Computer Incident of 1969." Race 14 (Ja, 1973):229-240.

Vuorinen, Saara Sofia. "Ethnic Identification of Caribbean Immigrants in the Kitchener-Waterloo Area." Doctoral dissertation, Waterloo U., 1974.

Walker, James W. St. G. The Black Loyalists. The Search for a Promised Land in Nova Scotia and Sierra Leone 1783-1870. New York: Holmes and Meier, 1976.

_____. "The Establishment of a Free Black Community in Nova Scotia, 1783-1840." In The African Diaspora. Edited by Martin L. Kilson and Robert I. Rotberg. Cambridge, MA: Harvard U. Press, 1976.

Wilson, Elden Gibson. The Loyal Blacks. New York: Putnam's, 1976.

Wilson, R. D. "Note on Negro-White Relations in Canada." Social Forces 28(1949):77-78.

Winks, Robin. The Blacks in Canada. A History. New Haven, CT: Yale U. Press, 1971.

_____. "Canadian Negro: A Historical Assessment." Journal of Negro History, vol. 53, O, 1968, pp. 283-300.

_____. "The Canadian Negro: A Historical Assessment. Part II: The Problem of Identity." Journal of Negro History, Ja, 1969.

_____. Canadian West-Indian Union. A Forty-Year Minuet. New York: Oxford U. Press, 1969.

_____. "A History of Negro School Segregation in Nova Scotia and Ontario." Canadian Historical Review 52(1969):64-191.

_____. "Negroes in the Maritimes: An Introductory Survey." Dalhousie Review 48(1968-69).

Yeadon, Marjorie. "Stress of Adolescence in a Colored Community." Master's thesis, Maritime School of Social Work, 1959.

Indians in Canada

About Indians: A Listing of Books. 2nd ed. Ottawa, Canada: Information Canada, 1973.

Abu-Laban, Baha. "In-Group Orientation and Self-Conceptions of Indian and Non-Indian Students in an Integrated School." Alberta Journal of Educational Research, S, 1965. [Desegregated high school outside Edmonton, Alberta]

Adams, Howard. "The Cree as a Colonial People." Western Canadian Journal of Anthropology 1 (1969).

_____. The Outsiders: An Educational Survey of Metis and Non-Treaty Indians. Regina, Saskatchewan: Metis Society of Saskatchewan, Je, 1972.

_____. Prison of Grass: Canada from the Native Point of View. Toronto: New Press, 1975.

_____. "The Revolutionary Movement of the Indians and Metis." Our Generation 8(Ap, 1972):91-95.

Ahenakew, Dave. "Report from the Federation of Saskatchewan Indians." Journal of the Canadian College of Teachers 14(1971).

Alilkatuktuk, Jeela. "Canada: Stranger in My Own Land." Ms. 2(F, 1974):8-10. [Inuit people]

Anderson, Francis G. "Contact Between City and Indian Children." Master's thesis, U. of Calgary, 1969.

Aoki, T. "Toward Devolution in the Control of Education on a Native Reserve in Alberta. The Hobbeina Curriculum Story." Council on Anthropology and Education Newsletter 4(N, 1973).

Association of Iroquois and Allied Indians. "Proposal on Education for the Canadian Indian." Northian 9(Winter, 1972):28-34.

The Attitude of Toronto Students Towards the Canadian Indians. Toronto, Canada: Indian-Eskimo Association of Canada, Ja, 1970, 29 pp. ERIC ED 041 660.

"B.C. Native People Choose Freedom." Akwesasne Notes 7(Early Summer, 1975).

Bailey, A. G. The Conflict of European and Eastern Algonkian Cultures, 1504-1700. 2nd ed. Toronto: U. of Toronto Press, 1969.

Baker, Donald G. "Color, Culture and Power: Indian-White Relations in Canada and America." Canadian Review of American Studies 3(Spring, 1972):3-20.

Balfour, Margaret. The Problems of Post-Secondary Education for Manitoba Indians and Metis, Ja, 1973. ERIC ED 138 426.

Band, Richard W. "Decision Making among the Squamish." Master's thesis, Simon Fraser U., 1969.

Barger, Kenneth, and Earl, Daphne. "Differential Adaptation to Northern Town Life by the Eskimos and Indians of Great Whale River." Human Organization 30(Spring, 1971):25-30.

Bean, Raymond E. "An Exploratory Comparison of Indian and Non-Indian Secondary School Students." Master's thesis, U. of Alberta, 1966.

Belkin, Cheryl. "Indian and Eskimo Poetry." English Quarterly 10(Summer, 1977):15-32.

Berger, Allen. "The Education of Canadian Indians: An In-Depth Study of Nine Families." Alberta Journal of Educational Research 19(D, 1973):334-342.

Berger, Allen, and Das, J. P. A Report on Indian Education: (A) In-Depth Study of Nine Indian Families (Berger); (B) Memory and Reasoning in Native Children: An Effort at Improvement Through the Teaching of Cognitive Strategies. Edmonton, Alberta: U. of Alberta, 1972.

Berger, Yves. "Canada's Indians: Quest for Self-Respect." Guardian, F 6, 1977.

Blackbird, William. "Native Perspectives on Native Education." History and Social Science Teacher 10(Summer, 1975):31-38.

Bowd, A. D. "Some Determinants of School Achievement in Several Indian Groups." Alberta Journal of Educational Research 18 (Je, 1972):69-81.

_____. "Ten Years After the Hawthorn Report: Changing Psychological Implications for the Education of Native People." Canadian Psychological Review 18(O, 1977):332-346.

Bowles, R. B., Hanley, J. L., Hodgins, B. W., and Rawlyk, G. A. The Indian: Assimilation, Integration or Separation? Prentice-Hall of Canada, Ltd., 1973.

Braroe, Niels W. Indian and White: Self-Image and Interaction in a Canadian Plains Community. Stanford, CA: Stanford U. Press, 1975. [Cree Indians]

Briggs, Jean L. Never in Anger. Portrait of an Eskimo Family. Cambridge, MA: Harvard U. Press, 1970.

Brody, Hugh. "Eskimo Politics: the Threat from the South." New Left Review 79(My-Je, 1973): 60-68.

_____. The People's Land. Eskimos and Whites in the Eastern Arctic. New York: Penguin, 1977.

Brooks, I. R. Why They Leave: A Selected Review of the Literature on Native Student Drop-Outs. Calgary: Indian Students University Program Services, U. of Calgary, 1975.

Brun, H. "Les droits des Indians sur le territoire de Quebec." Cahiers de Droit 10 (1969).

Bryce, P. H. Report on the Indian Schools of Manitoba and the North-West Territories. Ottawa, Ontario: Queen's Printer, 1907.

Buck, Ruth M. "Little Pine: An Indian Day School." Saskatchewan History 18(1965): 55-62. [Little Pine Reserve]

Buckley, Helen and others. The Indians and Metis of Northern Saskatchewan. A Report on Economic and Social Development. Saskatchewan, Canada: Canadian Center for Community Studies, 1963, 121 pp. ERIC ED 026 197. Available from Centre for Community Studies, Saskatoon, Saskatchewan, Canada.

Bullen, Edward Lester. "An Historical Study of the Education of the Indians of Teslin, Yukon Territory." Master's thesis, U. of Alberta, 1968.

Cairns, H. A. C. and others. A Survey of the Contemporary Indians of Canada: A Report on Economic, Political, Educational Needs and Policies. Vol. I. Ottawa, Canada: Department of Indian Affairs and Northern Development, O, 1966, 409 pp. ERIC ED052 530.

Caldwell, George. "An Island Between Two Cultures: The Residential Indian School." Canadian Welfare 43(1967):12-17.

Caloren, Fred. "The Revolutionary Struggle of the Native People in the Northwest." Our Generation 12(1970):43-56.

Cameron, A., and Storm, T. "Achievement Motivation in Canadian Indian, Middle and Working-Class Children." Psychological Reports 16 (1965):459-463.

Campbell, Maria. Halfbreed. New York: Saturday Review Press, 1973. [Autobiography; northwestern Saskatchewan]

Canada. Department of Indian Affairs and Northern Development. Indian Education in Canada, 1973. ERIC ED 143 486.

Canadian Association of School Superintendents and Inspectors. Indian Education in Canada. Toronto, Canada: Ryerson Press, 1965.

The Canadian Indian. An Outline. Ottawa: Information Canada, 1973.

The Canadian Indian in Ontario's School Texts. A Study of Social Studies Textbooks Grades 1 through 8. Toronto: Indian-Eskimo Association of Canada, F, 1970, 43 pp. ERIC ED 041 656.

Cardinal, Harold. "Canadian Indians and the Federal Government." Western Canadian Journal of Anthropology 1(1969).

_____. The Rebirth of Canada's Indians. Edmonton: Hurtig, 1977.

_____. The Unjust Society: The Tragedy of Canada's Indians. Edmonton, Alberta: M. G. Hurtig, 1969.

Cargill, I. "An Investigation of Cognitive Development Among Infants on a Canadian Indian Reservation." Master's thesis, Ontario Institute for Studies in Education, 1970.

Carr, Kevin James. "A Historical Survey of Education in Early Blackfoot Indian Culture and its Implication for Indian Schools." Master's thesis, U. of Alberta, 1968.

Cauthers, Janet (ed.). "My Own Native Land. Some Reflections on the Lives of Native People in British Columbia." Sound Heritage 4(1976):12-37.

Cerbeland-Salagnac, Georges. "Louis Riel, le fondateur du Manitoba, la révolte des Métis dans l'ouest canadien." C. R. Trimestriels Acad. Sci. Outre-Mer 36(No. 1, 1976):49-60.

Chalmers, John W. "Schools for Our Other Indians: Education of Western Canadian Metis Children." In The Canadian West, 1977. Edited by Henry C. Klassen. Comprint Publishing Co., Box 4642, Postal Station C, Calgary, Alberta.

Chamberlain, J. E. The Harrowing of Eden--White Attitudes Toward North American Natives. Toronto: Fitzhenry and Whiteside, 1975.

Chretien, Jean. "A Progress Report on Indian Education." Northian 8(D, 1971):34-38.

Clairmont, Donald H. J. Deviance Among Indians and Eskimos in Aklavik, N.W.T. Ottawa, Canada: Canadian Dept. of Northern Affairs and National Resources, O, 1963, 95 pp. ERIC Ed 039 073. Available from Northern Co-ordination and Research Centre, Dept. of Northern Affairs and National Resources, Ottawa, Canada.

Con, Ronald Jonathan. "Government and Ethnic Minority Groups: A Case Study of the Relationships between Federal Adult-Oriented Programs and Citizen Organizations of the Chinese in Canada." Doctoral dissertation, Boston U., 1974. Univ. Microfilms Order No. 74-20,425.

Concerns of Indians in British Columbia. Theme: "Equal Opportunity in Our Land." Toronto: Canada: Indian-Eskimo Association of Canada, D 4, 1966, 33 pp. ERIC ED041 659.

Connelly, Bob. "What's Lacking in the Integration Kit?" The Saskatchewan Bulletin, My, 1964. [Indian children]

Cook, Thelma L. S. "Producing Equal Status Interaction Between Indian and White Boys in British Columbia: An Application of Expectation Training." Doctoral dissertation, Stanford U., 1975.

Couture, Joseph E. "Alberta Indian Youth: A Study in Cree and Blood Student Conflict." Doctoral dissertation, U. of Alberta, 1972.

Cowan, Susan. We Don't Live in Snow Houses Now: Reflections of Arctic Bay. Ottawa: Hurtig Publishers, 1976.

Cox, Bruce (ed.). Cultural Ecology: Readings on the Canadian Indians and Eskimos. Toronto, Canada: McClelland and Stewart, 1973.

Crowe, Keith J. A History of the Original Peoples of Northern Canada. Montreal: McGill-Queen's U. Press, 1974.

Cruikshank, Julia M. "The Role of Northern Canadian Indian Women in Social Change." Master's thesis, U. of British Columbia, 1969.

Cumming, Peter A. Canada: Native Land Rights and Northern Development. Copenhagen: International Work Group for Indigenous Affairs, 1977.

Cumming, Peter A., and Mickenberg, Neil H. (eds.). Native Rights in Canada. 2nd ed. Toronto, Canada: General Publishing Co., Ltd., 1972.

Daniels, E. R. "The Legal Context of Indian Education in Canada." Doctoral dissertation, U. of Alberta, 1973.

Davey, R. F. and others. The Education of Indian Children in Canada. A Symposium Written by Members of Indian Affairs Education Division, with Comments by the Indian Peoples. The Canadian Superintendent 1965. Ottawa: Canadian Association of School Superintendents and Inspectors, 1965, 143 pp. ERIC ED 027 988.

Davis, Arthur K. "Urban Indians in Western Canada: Implications for Social Theory and Social Policy." Mémoires de la Société Royale du Canada, 1968, pp. 217-228.

Davis, M. "Indian Housing Statistics." Bulletin (of the Canadian Association in Support of the Native Peoples) 17(1976):10-11.

Davis, Robert, and Zannis, Mark. The Genocide Machine in Canada. The Pacification of the North. Montreal, Canada: Black Rose Books, 1973.

Day, David, and Bowering, Marilyn (eds.). Many Voices: An Anthology of Contemporary Canadian Indian Poetry. Vancouver: J. J. Douglas, 1978.

Dempsey, Hugh. "The Centennial of Treaty Seven--And Why Indians Think Whites Are Knaves." Canadian Geographical Journal 95 (O/N, 1977):10-20.

Denton, Trevor D. "Canadian Indian Migrants and Impression Management of Ethnic Stigma." Canadian Review of Sociology and Anthropology 12(F, 1975):65-71.

_____. "Strangers in their Land. A Study of Migration from a Canadian Indian Reserve." Doctoral dissertation, Toronto U., 1970.

Devrome, R. "The Métis: Colonialism, Culture Change, and the Saskatchewan Rebellion of 1885." Master's thesis, U. of Alberta, 1976.

Dilling, Harold John. "Educational Achievement and Social Acceptance of Indian Pupils Integrated in Non-Indian Schools of Southern Ontario." Ontario Journal of Educational Research, Autumn, 1965.

_____. "Integration of the Indian in and through Schools with Emphasis on the St. Clair Reserve in Somia." Master's thesis, U. of Toronto, 1962.

"Discussion Paper for Indian Act Revision." Indian News 19(N, 1978):1-10.

Dosman, Edgar J. Indians: The Urban Dilemma. Toronto, Canada: McClelland and Stewart, 1972.

_____. "The Urban Dimension of the Indian Problem in Canada." Doctoral dissertation, Harvard U., 1971.

Douville, R., and Casanova, J. D. La Vie quotidienne des Indiens du Canada à l'époque de la colonisation francaise. Montréal: n.p., 1967.

Driben, Paul. "We Are Metis: The Ethnography of a Halfbreed Community in Northern Alberta." Doctoral dissertation, U. of Minnesota, 1975.

Drummond, William J. "Government Concern Halts the Eskimos' Slide Into the Twilight." Los Angeles Times, Je 19, 1977.

Duran, James A., Jr. "Candian Indian Policy: A Year of Debate." Indian Historian 4(Fall, 1971):34-36.

_____. "Why Canadian Indians Demonstrate." NCAI Sentinel, Winter-Spring, 1969.

Education Division, Indian Affairs Branch. The Education of Indian Children in Canada: A Symposium. Toronto: Ryerson Press, 1965.

The Education of Indian Children in Canada: A Symposium Written by Members of the Indian Affairs Education Division with Comments by the Indian Peoples. Toronto: Ryerson Press, 1965.

Eisenberg, John, and Troper, Harold. Native Survival. Toronto: Ontario Institute for Studies in Education, 1973.

Elliott, Jean Leonard. "Native Minorities and Ethnic Conflict in Canada." Current History 66(Ap, 1974).

Embree, Jesse. Let Us Live: The Native Peoples of Canada. Toronto: Dent, 1977.

Evard, Evelyn, Mitchell, George C., Weaver, Yvonne J., and Weaver, Robert R., Jr. "A New Concept on the Navajo." Journal of American Indian Education, D, 1966. [The Alberta Indian]

Fisher, A. D. "The Dialectic of Indian Life in Canada." Canadian Review of Sociology and Anthropology 13(N, 1976):458-464.

Fogg, Pat. "Old Sun, New Hope for Canada's Native People." Community and Junior College Journal 43(S, 1972):21-23.

Foster, Douglas Ray. "The Canadian Indian: A Study of the Education of a Minority Group and Its Social Problems." Master's thesis, U. of Wisconsin, 1963.

Foy, P. E. "Les Indiens au Canada." Doctoral dissertation, Université de Montréal, 1960.

Franklyn, Gaston J. "Alienation and Achievement among Indian-Metis and Non-Indians in the Mackenzie District of the Northwest Territories." Northian 10(Spring, 1974): 28-39.

French, Doris. Indian Residential Schools. A Research Study of the Child Care Programs of Nine Residential Schools in Saskatchewan. Ottawa, Ja 31, 1967. ERIC ED 027 989.

Frideres, James. Canada's Indians: Contemporary Conflicts. Scarborough, Ontario: Prentice-Hall of Canada, 1974.

Frideres, J. S. "Education for Indians vs. Indian Education in Canada." Indian Historian 11(Winter, 1978):29-35.

Friesen, J. W. "Education and Values in an Indian Community." Alberta Journal of Educational Research 20(Je, 1974):146-156. [Blackfoot band near Calgary, Alberta]

Friesen, John W. "The Preparation of Teachers for Native Students." Yearbook, Canadian Society for the Study of Education 1(1974): 56-64.

Friesen, John W., and Lyon, Louise C. "Progress of Southern Alberta Native Peoples." Journal of American Indian Education 9(My, 1970):15-23.

Frisch, Jack A. "Conflict, Confrontation, and Social Change on the St. Regis Indian Reserve." Northian 8(D, 1971):11-15. [Mohawks]

Fumoleau, René. As Long As This Land Shall Last: A History of Treaty 8 and Treaty 11, 1870-1939. Toronto: McClelland and Stewart, 1975. [Northwest Territories]

Galloway, Charles G., and Nickelson, Norma I. "Changes in Personal-Social Distance of Teachers of Indian Children." American Journal of Orthopsychiatry 40(Jl, 1970): 681-683. [Vancouver Island, British Columbia]

Gambill, Jerry T. "On the Art of Stealing Human Rights." Native Youth News, Je, 1972. [Native Youth Association, Ottawa]

Getty, I. A. L. "The Church Missionary Society Among the Blackfoot Indians of Southern Alberta, 1880-1895." Master's thesis, U. of Calgary, 1971.

Gibbins, R., and Ponting, J. R. "Contemporary Prairie Perceptions of Canada's Native People." Prairie Forum 2(My, 1977): 57-81.

Gibbins, R., and Pointing, J. Rick. "Public Opinion and Canadian Indians: A Preliminary Probe." Canadian Ethnic Studies 8, No. 2(1976): 1-17.

Gibson, George D. "Jesuit Education Among the Indians in New France, 1611-1758." Doctoral dissertation, U. of California, 1940.

Giraud, Marcel. Le Metis Canadien: Son Role dan l'Histoire des Province de l'Ouest. Paris: Travaux et Memoires de l'Institut d'Ethnologie, 1945.

Gladstone, James. "Indian School Days." Alberta Historical Review 15(1967): 18-24. [St. Paul's Missions schools, Blood Reservation, Calgary Industrial School]

Gleason, Aileen M. "A Study of the Relationship that Exists Between the Deceleration in Academic Achievement of the Indian Children Integrated in the Separate Schools of Fort Frances, Ontario and their Social Acceptance and Personality Structure." Master's thesis, U. of Manitoba, 1970.

Goldenson, K. "Cognitive Development of Indian Elementary School Children on a Southern Ontario Reserve." Master's thesis, Ontario Institute for Studies in Education, 1970.

Gooderham, G. K. (ed.). I Am an Indian. Toronto: Dent, 1969.

Goucher, A. C. The Dropout Problem Among Indian and Metis Students. Calgary, Canada: Dome Petroleum, Ltd., 1967, 52 pp. ERIC ED 042 528.

Green, L. C. "Canada's Indians: Federal Policy, International and Constitutional Law." Ottawa Law Review, Summer, 1970.

_____. "Trusteeship and Canada's Indians." Dalhousie Law Journal 3(1976): 104-135.

Gresko, J. "White 'Rites' and Indian 'Rites': Indian Education and Native Responses in the West, 1870-1910." In Western Canada Past and Present. Edited by A. W. Rasporich. Calgary: McClelland and Stewart West, 1975.

Grindstaff, Carl F., Galloway, Wilda, and Nixon, Joanne. "Racial and Cultural Identification Among Canadian Indian Children." Phylon 34(D, 1973): 368-377.

Gue, Leslie R. "Patterns in Native Education in Canada." Yearbook, Canadian Society for the Study of Education 1(1974): 7-20.

_____. "Some Forces Impinging on the Education of Indians." Indian-Education 1(1973): 3-4.

_____. "Value Orientations in an Indian Community." Alberta Journal of Educational Research 17(Mr, 1971): 19-31.

Guillemin, Jeanne. "The Politics of National Integration: A Comparison of United States and Canadian Indian Administrators." Social Problems 25(F, 1978): 319-332.

Hammersmith, Jerome A. "The Indian in Saskatchewan Elementary School Studies Textbooks: A Content Analysis." Master's thesis, U. of Saskatchewan, 1971.

_____. "The New Breed--Interview with Dr. Howard Adams" (2 parts). Northian 6, 7 (Winter, Spring, 1970): 3-5, 2-7.

Harrison, William G. "A Survey of Indian Education in Five Selected Alberta Community Colleges: Some Models and Recommendations." Doctoral dissertation, Washington State U., 1977.

Hatt, Fred K. "The Canadian Metis: Recent Interpretations." Canadian Ethnic Studies 3 (Je, 1971): 1-16.

Hatt, Judith Keever. "The Rights and Duties of the Metis Preschool Child." Master's thesis, U. of Alberta, 1969.

Haugen, Maureen M. "Attitudes Toward Indian Education: Implications for Counselling." Master's thesis, Victoria U., British Columbia, 1971.

Hawthorne, Harry B. (ed.). A Survey of the Contemporary Indians of Canada... 2 vols. Ottawa: Department of Indian Affairs and Northern Development, 1966-1967.

Hawthorn, Harry, Belshaw, C. S., and Jamieson, S. M. "Schools and Education." Chapter 23 in The Indians of British Columbia. Berkeley, CA: U. of California Press, 1960.

Haythorne, Owen, Layton, Carol, and La Roque, Emma (comps.). Natives of North America: A Selected Bibliography to Improve Resources Availability in Native Studies Programs. Edmonton: Curriculum Branch, Department of Education, Government of Alberta, 1975.

Henderson, Rob, and Wilman, David. "Development of Culturally Relevant Programs in Broughton Island." Northian 11(Spring, 1975): 1-3. [Eskimos]

Hibbard, Dale. "Integration Poses Biggest Problem for Indian Student Residents." Indian News, F-Mr, 1975.

Hirbour, Rene. "L'enseignement des cultures amerindiennes en milieu pre-universitaire." Recherches Amérindindiennes au Quebec 4 (Je, 1974).

Hobart, Charles W. "Eskimo Education in the Canadian Arctic." Canadian Review of Sociology and Anthropology 7(1970):49-70.

_____. "Some Consequences of Residential Schooling of Eskimos in the Canadian Arctic." Arctic Anthropology 6(1970):123-135.

Hobart, C. W., and Brant, C. S. "Eskimo Education, Danish and Canadian: A Comparison." Canadian Review of Sociology and Anthropology, My, 1966.

Hodgkinson, C. J. "Socio-Cultural Change and Continuing Education Among Eskimo in Frobisher Bay, N.W.T." Master's thesis, U. of Alberta, 1972.

Holmgren, Donald H. "Experiences of Indian Students Undergoing Acculturation in Urban High Schools: An Exploratory Study." Master's thesis, U. of Alberta, 1971.

Honigmann, John J., and Honigmann, Irma. Arctic Townsmen: Ethnic Backgrounds and Modernization. Ottawa, Canada: Canadian Research Centre for Anthropology, Saint Paul U., 1970.

Hopkins, Thomas R. "Secondary Education of Native North Americans." Northian 7 (Summer, 1970):5-9.

Houghton, Vincent P. "Educational Provision for Canadian Eskimo Children." Race Today, S, 1969.

Howard, Joseph K. Strange Empire. New York: Morrow, 1952. [On the Metis]

Howe, Shirley Ann. "Pre-European Conditions of Micmac People." Tawow 5(1976):12-17.

Hubert, Kenneth W. "A Study of Attitudes of Non-Indian Children Toward Indian Children in an Integrated Urban Elementary School." Master's thesis, U. of Calgary, 1969.

Hunsberger, B. "Racial Awareness and Preference of White and Indian Children." Canadian Journal of Behavioural Science 10 (April, 1978):176-180.

"'I Believe in Apartheid,' Says Spokeswoman." Montreal Gazette, Je 4, 1971. [Kahn-Tineta Horn, Iroquois]

Indian Affairs Branch. Choosing a Path. A Discussion Handbook for the Indian People. Ottawa, Canada: Department of Indian Affairs and Northern Development, 1968.

Indian Association of Alberta. Proposals for the Future Education of Treaty Indians in Alberta, Brief. Educational Planning Commission, Indian Association of Alberta, Ja, 1971.

"Indian Control of Indian Education." Northian 10(Spring, 1974):11-25.

"Indian Education in the Dryden Area." Indian News 18, No. 1(1977). [Ontario]

Indian-Eskimo Association of Canada. The Canadian Indian in Ontario's School Texts: A Study of Social Studies Textbooks Grades 1 through 8. Toronto, F, 1970.

Indian, Metis and Eskimo Leaders in Contemporary Canada. Saskatoon: Curriculum Resources Centre, U. of Saskatchewan, 1971.

"Indian Students Against Canadian Integration." Indian Voices, O, 1965.

Inglis, Gordon B. "The Canadian Indian Reserve: Community Population and Social System." Doctoral dissertation, U. of British Columbia, 1970.

"L'Inuit et 'Votre' Systeme d'Education." Action Pedagogique 24(1972):35-47.

Jaenen, Cornelius J. "Amerindian Views of French Culture in the Seventeenth Century." Canadian Historical Review 55(S, 1974):261-291.

Jaenen, Cornelius J. Friend and Foe. Aspects of French-Amerindian Cultural Contact in the Sixteenth and Seventeenth Centuries. New York: Columbia U. Press, 1976.

Jamieson, Elmer. "Indian Education in Canada." Master's thesis, McMaster U., 1922.

Jamieson, Elmer, and Sandiford, Peter. "The Mental Capacity of Southern Ontario Indians." Journal of Educational Psychology 19(1928): 313-328 and 536-551.

Jamieson, Kathleen. Indian Women and the Law in Canada: Citizens Minus, Ap, 1978. ERIC ED 158 913.

Jenness, Diamond. "Canada's Indians Yesterday. What of Today?" _Canadian Journal of Economics and Political Science_, F, 1954.

_____. _Indians of Canada_. 7th ed. Toronto: U. of Toronto Press, 1977.

Joblin, Elgin E. M. "The Education of the Indians of Western Ontario." Master's thesis, U. of Western Ontario, 1946. [Also, in _Bulletin_ 13, Ontario College of Education, Department of Educational Research, 1947]

Kabayama, J. E. "Educational Retardation Among Non-Roman Catholic Indians at Oka." Master's thesis, McGill U., 1959.

Kassirer, E. _Programs of Interest to Indians and Metis Administered by the Department of Regional Economic Expansion_. Ottawa, Canada: Canadian Department of Regional Economic Expansion, Je, 1970. ERIC ED 041 223.

Keenleyside, David. "The Fallacy of Freedom: Education for the Adult Eskimo." _Northian_, Summer, 1969.

Kehoe, Alice B. "Dakota Indian Ethnicity in Saskatchewan." _Journal of Ethnic Studies_ 3 (Summer, 1975):37-42.

Kelly, Reg. _Indian Education Programs in British Columbia_, My, 1974. ERIC ED 094 926.

Kennedy, Dan (Ochankugahe). _Recollections of an Assiniboine Chief_. Toronto, Canada: McClelland and Stewart, 1972. [Saskatchewan]

Kennedy, Jacqueline Judith. "'Lic' Appelle Industrial School: White 'Rites' for the Indians of the Old Northwest." Master's thesis, Carleton U., 1970.

Kerri, James Nwannukwu. "The Economic Adjustment of Indians in Winnipeg, Canada." _Urban Anthropology_ 5(Winter, 1976):351-366.

_____. "Indians in a Canadian City: Analyses of Social Adaptive Strategies." _Urban Anthropology_ 5(Summer, 1976):143-156.

Kew, Mike. "100 Years of Making Indians in BC." _Canadian Dimension_ 18(N, 1971).

Kidd, J. Roby. "Education of the Canadian Indian and Eskimo." _Integrated Education_, D, 1966-Ja, 1967.

King, A. R. "The Native Indian 'Paraprofessional' in British Columbia." _Northian_ 11(F, 1975):22-27.

_____. _Native Indians and Schooling in British Columbia: A Handbook for Teachers_. Victoria, Canada: Faculty of Education, U. of Victoria, 1978.

_____. _The School at Mopass. A Problem of Identity_. New York: Holt, Rinehart & Winston, 1967. [Yukon Territory]

King, R. "On the Intellectual Character of the Esquimaux." _Journal of the Ethnological Society of London_ 1(1848):127-153.

Kirkness, Verna J. _Education For and About Children of Native Ancestry_. Winnipeg: Manitoba Indian Brotherhood, Jl, 1971.

_____. "Prejudice about Indians in Textbooks." _Journal of Reading_ 20(Ap, 1977):595-600.

_____. "Programs for Native People by Native People." _Education Canada_ 16(Winter, 1976): 32-35.

Knowles, Donald W. "A Comparative Study of Mediational-Task Performance of Indian and Middle-Clan Children." Doctoral dissertation, U. of Alberta, 1968.

Knowles, Donald W., and Boersma, Frederick J. "Optional Shift Performance of Culturally-Different Children to Concrete and Abstract Stimuli." _Alberta Journal of Educational Research_, S, 1968. [Suburban white and Indian American children in Western Canada]

Koolage, William W. "Adaptation of Chippewan Indians and Other Persons of Native Background in Churchill, Manitoba." Doctoral dissertation, U. of North Carolina, 1971. Univ. Microfilms Order No. 71-20,978.

Kozak, Kathryn. "Education and the Blackfoot, 1870-1900." Master's Thesis, U. of Alberta, 1970.

Krywaniuk, L, and Das, J. "Cognitive Strategies in Native Children: Analysis and Intervention." _Alberta Journal of Educational Research_ 22(D, 1976):271-280.

Kuo, C-Y. "The Effect of Education on the Earnings of Indian, Eskimo, Metis, and White Workers in the Mackenzie District of Northern Canada." _Economic Development and Cultural Change_ 24(Ja, 1976).

Laforce, Marguerite M. "Moral Judgments Among Indian and White Children." Master's thesis, U. of Alberta, 1967.

Lagasse, Jean-Henry. _The People of Indian Ancestry in Manitoba: A Social and Economic Study. Main Report_. Winnipeg: Department of Agriculture and Immigration, 1959.

Lambert, Carmen. "Ethnic Identification and Integration in a Northern Urban Center. Whitehorse, Yukon." Doctoral dissertation, McGill U., 1974. [Order from National Library of Canada, Ottawa]

Lane, Robert B. "Canadian Indians." _Canadian Psychologist_ 13(O, 1972):350-359.

LaRoque, Emma. Defeathering the Indian, 1975. Book Society of Canada, Ltd., 4386 Sheppard Avenue, Agincourt, Ontario, Canada.

LaVallee, Mary Anne (ed.). National Conference on Indian and Northern Education. (Saskatoon, Canada, 1967). Saskatoon, Canada: Saskatchewan U. Extension Division: Society for Indian and Northern Education, 1967. ERIC ED 028 861.

Lavigne, Solange D. "Canada's Indian Heritage. A Northern Instructional Project." Saskatchewan Journal of Educational Research and Development 2(Fall, 1971):17-23.

LaViolette, F. E. The Struggle for Survival: Indian Cultures and the Protestant Ethic in B.C. Toronto: U. of Toronto Press, 1973.

Lawton, Ernest P. "A Study of the Attitudes of Indian Parents Toward Education in Fort Rae." Master's thesis, Saskatchewan U., Saskatoon, 1970.

Lazure, Denis. "Indian Children of Canada: Educational Services and Mental Health." Child Psychiatry and Human Development 4 (Fall, 1973):44-52.

Levaque, J. E. Y. "A Look at the Parliamentary Report on Indian Education." Northian 8(D, 1971):6-10.

Ledgewood, C. D. (ed.). Native Education in the Province of Alberta, Je, 1972. ERIC ED 087 603.

Lewis, Brian W. "The Teaching of English to Canadian Eskimos." Master's thesis, Toronto U., 1971.

Lewis, Claudia L. "A Study of the Impact of Modern Life in a Canadian Indian Band." Doctoral dissertation, Columbia U., 1959.

Littlejohn, Catherine I. "The Indian Oral Tradition: A Model for Teachers." Master's thesis, U. of Sasketchewan, 1975.

Lysyke, Ken. "Human Rights and the Native Peoples in Canada." Canadian Bar Review 46 (1968):695.

_____. "The Unique Constitutional Position of the Canadian Indian." Canadian Bar Review 45(1967):513-533.

MacArthur, R. S. "Assessing Intellectual Potential of Native Canadian Pupils: A Summary." Alberta Journal of Educational Research. Je, 1968.

_____. Educational Potential of Northern Canadian Native Pupils, Ag, 1968. ERIC ED 028 889.

_____. Longitudinal Predictions of School Achievement for Metis and Eskimo Pupils. Winnipeg, Canada: Conference of the Canadian Council of Research on Education, 1967.

McCarthy, William Charles. "Indian Dropouts and Graduates in Northern Alberta." Master's thesis, U. of Alberta, 1971.

McCaskill, Don M. "Migration, Adjustment, and Integration of the Indian into the Urban Environment." Master's thesis, Carleton U., 1970. [Winnipeg]

McConkey, W. G. "The Canadian Association in Support of the Native Peoples." Northian 11(Spring, 1975):20-22.

McDiarmid, Garnet. The Challenge of a Differential Curriculum: Ontario's Indian Children. Toronto, Ontario Institute for Studies in Education, 1971.

_____. "The Politics of Inclusion and Exclusion: Ontario's Indian Students as a Special Case." In Canadian Society for the Study of Education, The Politics of Canadian Education. Fourth Yearbook 1977. Canadian Society for the Study of Education, PO Box 1000, Faculty of Education, U. of Alberta, Canada, 1977.

MacDonald, A. A. Community Resources and Dimensions of Alienation on Indian Reserves. Antigonish, Nova Scotia: Extension Department, Saint Francis Xavier U., My, 1967.

Macdonald, Ronald St. John, with Lysyk, Kenneth, and Hooper, Anthony. Native Rights in Canada. Toronto: Indian-Eskimo Association of Canada, 1970.

McEwen, E. R. Community Development Services for Canadian Indian and Metis Communities. Toronto, Canada: Indian-Eskimo Association of Canada, 1968.

McGee, Harold F., Jr. "Ethnic Boundaries and Strategies of Ethnic Interaction: A History of Micmac-White Relations in Nova Scotia." Doctoral dissertation, Southern Illinois U., 1974.

MacLean, Hope. A Review of Indian Education in North America. Toronto: Ontario Teacher's Federation, 1972.

MacLeod, J. M. "Indian Education in Canada: A Study of Indian Education with Special Reference to the Briefs Presented to the Joint Committee of the Senate and the House of Commons on Indian Affairs." Master's thesis, U. of New Brunswick, 1964.

MacNeill, Don. "The Arab East and the Eastern Arctic: A Comparison of Approaches taken with Inuit with those taken with Arab Peoples." Literacy Discussion 5(Summer, 1974):267-274.

Malaurie, Jean (ed.). The Eskimo People Today and Tomorrow. The Hague: Mouton, 1973.

Manuel, George. The Fourth World: An Indian Reality. Don Mills, Ontario: Collier-Macmillan Canada, 1974.

Maracle, Carmen. "Maori and [Canadian] Indian People Share Common Problems and Aspirations." Indian News (Ottawa, Canada) 16 (O, 1973):5.

Maranda, Elli K. "British Columbian Indian Myth and Education: A Review Article." B. C. Studies 25(Spring, 1975):125-134.

Marshall, John. Library Services for Native People: A Brief to the Ontario Task Force on the Education of Native Peoples, N 20, 1975. ERIC ED 136 768.

Mear-Crive, A. "Systemes d'Education Bilinque pour les Indiens du Canada." Revue des Langues Vivantes 41(1975):528-533.

Melling, John. Right to a Future: The Native Peoples of Canada. Ontario: The Anglican Church of Canada and the United Church of Canada, 1967.

The Memramcook Conference of North American Indian Young People. Memramcook, New Brunswick: Teaching and Research in Bicultural Education, 1969.

Miller, Anthony G., and Thomas, Ron. "Cooperation and Competition Among Blackfoot Indian and Urban Canadian Children." Child Development 43(S, 1972):1104-1110.

Milton Freeman Research Limited. Inuit Land Use and Occupancy Project. Vol. Two: Supporting Studies. New York: Unipub, 1977.

Mitsuru, Shimpo. "The Advantages and the Limitations of the Residential School for the 'Integration' of Canadian Indians." Minzokugaku-Kenkyu (The Japanese Journal of Ethnology), 32(1967).

"Mohawks Reject Quebec Authority." Akwesasne Notes 10(S, 1978):19. [Kahnawake Survival School, Caughnawaga Reserve]

Molgat, Paul, and MacMillan, J. A. Education in Area Economic Development, Je, 1972. Center for Settlement Studies, U. of Manitoba, Box 5, Winnepeg, Maintoba R3T 2N2.

Morrison, Kenneth M. "The People of the Dawn: The Abnaki and Their Relations with New England and New France, 1602-1727." Doctoral dissertation, U. of Maine, 1975.

_____. "Sebastien Rale vs. New England: A Case Study of Frontier Conflict." Master's thesis, U. of Maine, 1970.

Mortimer, G. E. "Sorting and Cooling: The Politics of Development on a Canadian Indian Reserve." In Perceptions of Development. Edited by Sandra Wallman. New York: Cambridge U. Press, 1977.

Mortimer, Molly. "Canada: Indians on the 'Peace Path.'" Institute Race Relations Newsletter, Ja, 1969.

Moss-Davies, Anthony. "The Educator Who Went Out in the Cold." Phi Delta Kappan, D, 1973. [Fired for marrying Eskimo women]

Murdock, John S. "Amerindianization [of Schools]: The Institution and the Happening." Northian 12(F, 1976):19-25.

Murphy, H. B. Psychological Test Performance of Children on the Caughnawaga Reserve: A Pilot Study. Montreal: McGill U., 1965.

Nagler, Mark. Indians in the City: A Study of the Urbanization of Indians in Toronto. Ottawa, Canada: Canadian Research Centre for Anthropology, Saint Paul U., 1970.

_____. Natives without a Home: The Canadian Indian. Don Mills, Ontario: Longman Canada Ltd., 1975.

_____. "Status and Identification Grouping Amongst Urban Indians." Northian 7(Summer, 1970):22-25.

Nash, Lynn D. "Drop-Out Among Senior High School Inuit Students in Frobisher Bay." Multiculturalism 2, No. 2 (1978):11-14.

Masser-Bush, Merun Hussein. "Differential Adjustment between Two Indian Immigrant Communities in Toronto: Sikhs and Ismailies." Doctoral dissertation, U. of Colorado, 1974. Univ. Microfilms Order No. 74-22,376.

National Indian Brotherhood. Indian Control of Indian Education, 1972. National Indian Brotherhood, 130 Albert Street, Suite 1610, Ottawa K1P 564, Canada.

_____. "On Integration of Canadian Indian Schools." Integrated Education (N-D, 1973): 13.

Native Council of Canada. "Metis and Non-Status Indians in Canada." Integrated Education 10(N-D, 1972):64-72.

Ontario Ministry of Colleges and Universities. Native Studies in Colleges and Universities: A Guide to Courses in Native Studies Offered in Ontario Beyond the Secondary School Level, D, 1977. ERIC ED 154 954.

Ornstein, Toby E. The First People in Quebec. A Reference Work on the History, Environment, Economic, and Legal Positions of the Indians and Inuit of Quebec. 3 vols. Montreal, Canada: Indians of Quebec Association, 1973.

Osborne, Ralph (ed.). Who Is the Chairman of this Meeting? A Collection of Essays. Toronto: Neewin Publishing Co., 1972.

Paine, Robert (ed.). The White Arctic. Anthropological Essays on Tutelage and Ethnicity. St. John's, Newfoundland: ISER Publications, Queen's College, Memorial U., 1978.

Patterson, E. Palmer. The Canadian Indian: A History Since 1500. Don Mills, Ontario, Collier-Macmillan, 1972.

Parker, Douglas V. Language Policy and Indian Education, Ap, 1975. ERIC ED 128 113.

Patterson, R. S. and Urion, C. (eds.). Canadian Native Schools in Transition. Edmonton: Canadian Society for the Study of Education, 1974.

Paul, P. "Regina--A Native Urban Tragedy." Indian News 18, No. 2(1977):9.

Peitchinis, Stephen G. "Equality and Inequality of Opportunity: The Financing of Post-Secondary Education in Canada." Australian Journal of Higher Education 5(D, 1973):64-75.

Pelletier, Wilfred. "Childhood in an Indian Village." This Magazine Is About Schools, Spring, 1969. [Odawa Indian recalls life in village of Wikwemikong on Manitoulin Island, Ontario.]

_____. "Childhood in an Indian Village." Northian 7(Spring, 1970):20-23.

Penfold, Douglas J. "A Study of the Scholastic Aptitude of the Indian Children of the Caradoc Reserve." Master's thesis, U. of Western Ontario, 1951.

Persson, Diane. "Report of the Northland School Division Study Group of the Minister of Education. Alberta, July, 1975." Indian-Ed 3(Fall, 1975):1-2.

Peterson, Lester Ray. "Indian Education in British Columbia." Master's thesis, U. of British Columbia, 1959.

Piepenburg, Roy L. "Indian Education in Alberta as I Viewed It." (Eight articles) The Native People (Edmonton), S, 1969-F, 1971.

Presentation to Special Senate Committee on Mass Media. Winnipeg, Canada: Canadian Metis Society, Toronto: Indian-Eskimo Association of Canada; Winnipeg: National Indian Brotherhood of Canada, D 17, 1969. ERIC ED 041 654.

Price, John A. "An Ethnographic Approach to U.S. and Canadian Indian Education." Canadian and International Education 3(D, 1974):99-115.

_____. Native Studies: American and Canadian Indians. Toronto: McGraw-Hill Ryerson, 1978.

_____. "U.S. and Canadian Indian Urban Ethnic Institutions." Urban Anthropology 4 (Spring, 1975):35-52.

Pyne, Garry H. "The Pre-Reserve Blackfoot: Cultural Persistence and Change." Master's thesis, Senior Fraser U., 1971.

The Queen v. Louis Riel. Toronto: U. of Toronto Press, 1974.

Raboy, Marc. "Classes Spurned at Caughnawaga." Montreal Star, Mr 20, 1971. [Howard S. Billings Regional High School]

Radulovich, Mary Lou. "Indians Must Be Indians: Education on Manitoulin Island." Northian 11(Spring, 1975):13-14.

Ramcharan, Subhas. "Adaptation of West Indians in Canada." Doctoral dissertation, York U., Toronto, 1974.

_____. "The Economic Adaptation of West Indians in Toronto." Canadian Review of Sociology and Anthropology 13(1976).

Ratten, Mohindar S. "Predictive Validity and Stability of Measures of Intellectual Potential for Two Samples of Indian-Metis and Eskimo Children." Master's thesis, U. of Alberta, 1966.

Rattan, M. S., and MacArthur, R. S. "Longitudinal Prediction of School Achievement for Metis and Eskimo Pupils." Alberta Journal of Educational Research, Mr, 1968.

Renaud, Andre. Education from Within, an Experiment in Curriculum Development with Children of Indian Background in Saskatchewan, N, 1964. Paper presented at the Ontario Conference on Indian Affairs, N, 1964, London, Ontario, Canada. ERIC ED 026 179.

_____. The Indians of Canada as an Ethnic Minority. Ottawa: Indian and Eskimo Welfare Association, 1960.

Renaud, Andre, and Adams, Howard (eds.). National Conference on Indian and Northern Education. Saskatoon, Mr 28-30, 1967.

"Report by David Ahenakew, Chief of the Federation of Saskatchewan Indians and Mr. Rodney Soomias, President of the Canadian Association for Indian-Eskimo Education." In Standing Committee on Indian Affairs and Northern Development. Minutes of Proceedings and Evidence, No. 6, F 24, 1970.

"Response to the House Standing Committee's Recommendations for Indian Education (Watson Report)." Northian 10(Winter, 1974):1-7. [Canada]

Richardson, Boyce. "Indians Move to Control Own Education." Montreal Star, Ja 2, 1971. [Alberta]

Robertson, Heather. Reservations are for Indians. Toronto: James Lewis & Samuel, 1970.

Robinson, Paul. "Curriculum Development." Yearbook, Canadian Society for the Study of Education 1(1974):35-46. [Indian education]

Robinson, Reva Leah. "The Children of Opasquia: A Study of Socialization and Society on a Contemporary Indian Reserve." Master's thesis, U. of British Columbia, 1970.

Rogers, Helen (comp.). Indian-Inuit Authors: An Annotated Bibliography. 1974. Ottawa: Publishing Centre, Supply and Services Canada, 1974.

Rohner, Ronald P. "Factors Influencing the Academic Performance of Kwakiutl Children in Canada." Comparative Education Review 9 (O, 1964):331-340.

Rosset, A. M. "Government Policy With Respect to Canadian Indians." Doctoral dissertation, U. of Toronto, 1969.

St. Pierre, Paul. "Apartheid and the Indian." 7th Annual Conference of the Canada Association for Indian and Eskimo Education. Ottawa, My 28, 1969.

Sanders, Douglas Esmond. "The Bill of Rights and Indian Status." University of British Columbia Law Review 7(1972):81-105.

_____. "No Question Indians Have Special Status." Indian News 19, No. 2(1978):6-8.

_____ (ed.). Native Rights in Canada... Toronto: Indian Eskimo Association of Canada, 1969.

Schalm, Philip. "School Administrators' Perception of Problems Arising from the Integration of Indian and Non-Indian Children in Publicly Supported Schools in Saskatchewan." Master's thesis, U. of Saskatchewan, 1968.

Schubert, Josef, and Cropley, A. J. "Verbal Regulation of Behavior and IQ in Canadian Indian and White Children." Developmental Psychology 7(N, 1972):295-301.

Schotte, Frederik. "Native Education in Northwestern Ontario: The Ontario Northern Corps and Formal Schooling in Isolated Ojibway Communities." Doctoral dissertation, U. of Toronto, 1977.

Sealey, D. Bruce. "Indians and Metis: Canadians Plus or Minus?" English Quarterly 3 (Spring, 1970):29-35.

_____. "The Metis: A Unique Canadian Ethnic Group." Multiculturalism 1(1977):8-10.

Sealy, D. Bruce and Lussier, Antoine S. The Metis: Canada's Forgotten People. Winnipeg: Manitoba Metis Federation Press, 1975.

Selinger, Alphonse D. "Toward Local Autonomy in Indian Education." Yearbook, Canadian Society for the Study of Education 1(1974): 47-55.

Salter, Michael A. The Indian Athlete: Exploiting or Exploited?, Je, 1976. ERIC ED 129 828. [Lacrosse in Canada]

Sikand, Jack. Native Studies Programs in Canada and the United States, ERIC ED 138 427.

_____ (comp.). Indian Education in Saskatchewan. A Report by the Federation of Saskatchewan Indians. 2 Vols., 1973. ERIC ED 087 600 and 087 601.

Sikand, Jack and others (comps.). Indians of Saskatchewan. Vol. III., 1973. Federation of Saskatchewan Indians, 1402 Quebec Avenue, Saskatoon, Saskatchewan 47K 1V4, Canada.

Silver, Arthur. "French Quebec and the Metis Question, 1869-1885." In The West and the Nation. Edited by Carl Berger and Ramsay Cook. Toronto: McClelland and Stewart, 1976.

Sim, R. Alexander. The Education of Indians in Ontario. A Report to the Provincial Committee on Aims and Objectives of Education in the Schools of Ontario. North Gower, Ontario, 1967. Mimeographed.

_____. "Indian Schools for Indian Children." Canadian Welfare 45(Mr-Ap, 1969):11-16.

Simonson, David A. "A Multi-variate Analysis of Indian and Non-Indian Student Alienation." Doctoral dissertation, U. of Alberta, 1973.

Sinclair, Will. "The Indian Drop-out." Northian, Spring, 1969.

Siperko, Gloria M. Burima. A Study of Native Youth in Edmonton, Je, 1971. ERIC ED 094 901.

Slavin, Suzy M. Indians and Eskimos of Canada: A Student's Guide to Reference Resources, 1975. ERIC ED 124 358.

Slobodin, Richard. Metis of the MacKenzie District. Candian REsearch Centre for Anthropology, Saint-Paul U., Ottawa, 1966.

Smallboy, R. "Decision to Leave Hobbema." Western Canadian Journal of Anthropology 1 (1969). [Indian chief]

Smith, Derek G. (comp.). Canadian Indians and the Law: Selected Documents, 1663-1972. Toronto: McClelland and Stewart, 1975.

Smith, Donald Boyd. "French-Canadian Historians' Images of the Indian in the 'Heroic Period' of New France, 1534-1663." Master's thesis, U. of Laval, 1969.

"Social Change in the North." Akwesasne Notes 6(Late Spring, 1974):31. [Native student demonstrations at high school in Balcarres high school/Saskatchewan]

Soonias, Rodney. Selected Findings of the Federation of Saskatchewan Indian Education Task Force, 1970-1972, a Preliminary Report. Regina, Ap 11, 1972.

Stanbury, W. T. B.C. Living Off Reserve: Some Economic Aspects, N 8, 1972. ERIC ED 087 604. [British Columbia]

_____. "The Education Gap: Urban Indians in British Columbia." British Columbia Studies 19(Autumn, 1973):21-49.

_____. "Indians in British Columbia: Level of Income Welfare Dependency and Poverty Rate." British Columbia Studies 20(Winter, 1973-1974):66-78.

_____. "Reserve and Urban Indians in British Columbia: A Social and Economic Profile." British Columbia Studies 26 (1975):39-64.

_____. Success and Failure: Indians in Urban Society. Vancouver: U. of British Columbia Press, 1975.

Stanley, George F. C. "The Indian Background of Canadian History." Annual Report of the Canadian Historical Association, 1952: 14-21.

_____. "The Policy of 'Francisation' as Applied to the Indians During the Ancien Regime." Revue d'histoire de l'Amerique francais 3(1949).

Stocken, H. W. Gibbon. Among the Blackfoot and Sacree. Calgary: Glenbow-Alberta Institute, 1977.

Stuart, Jacqueline E. "The Indians of Canada." Patterns of Prejudice 4(N-D, 1970).

Stymeist, David H. Ethnics and Indians: Social Relations in a Northwestern Ontario Town. Toronto: Peter Martin Associates, 1975.

Taylor, L. J. and Skanes, G. R. "Cognitive Abilities in Inuit and White Children from Similar Environments." Canadian Journal of Behavioural Science 8(Ja, 1976):1-9.

Thomson, Colin A. "The Emergence of Native American Education at the University of Lethbridge." Canadian and International Education 6(D, 1977):34-48.

_____. "Indian Education in Canada." Integreducation 15(S-O, 1977).

"Transition." Canadian Broadcasting Corporation, Audiotape, Catalog No. 302L. [Eskimos in white man's schools]

Trant, W. "Treatment of the Canadian Indians." Westminster Review, N, 1895:506-527.

Tremblay, Marc-Adelard (ed.). Les facettes de l'identite amerindienne/The Patterns of "Amerindian Identity." Quebec: Les Presses de l'Universite Laval, 1976.

Tremblay, Marc-Adelard and others. A Survey of the Contemporary Indians of Canada: Economic, Political, Educational Needs and Policies, Vol. II., O, 1967. ERIC ED 035 466.

Trussler, N. E. "Educational Programs for Indian Adults in Southern Alberta." Master's thesis, U. of Calgary, 1971.

Turner, G. H., and Penfold, D. J. "The Scholastic Aptitude of Indian Children of the Caradoc Reserve." Canadian Journal of Psychology 6(1952):31-44.

Valentine, Victor F., and Vallee, Frank G. (eds.). Eskimo of the Canadian Artic. Princeton, NJ: D. Van Nostrand, 1968.

Vallee, Frank G. Eskimos of Canada as a Minority Group: Social and Cultural Perspectives, Ag, 1969. Available from the Arctic Institute of North America, 3458 Redpath Street, Montreal 25, P.Q. Canada.

Vallery, H. J. "A History of Indian Education in Canada." Master's thesis, Queen's U., 1942.

Vernon, Philip E. "Educational and Intellectual Development among Canadian Indians and Eskimos." Educational Review, England, Vol. 1, 1966.

_____. "Education and Intellectual Development Among Canadian Indians and Eskimos-II." Educational Review, Je, 1966.

Voget, Fred. "Acculturation at Caughnawaga: A Note on the Native-Modified Group." American Anthropologist 53(1951):220-231.

Wahbung: Our Tomorrows. The Indian Tribes of Manitoba, O, 1971.

Walker, Joe. "Indian Teach-In at McGill University." Muhammad Speaks, Ap 3, 1970.

Waller, L. G. P. (ed.). The Education of Indian Children in Canada. Toronto, Canada: Ryerson Press, 1965.

Walter, Theodore R. "A Comparison of Value Orientations of Indian and Non-Indian High School Students." Master's thesis, U. of Alberta, 1971.

Watkins, Mel (ed.). The Dene Nation, Colony Within. Buffalo: U. of Toronto Press, 1977.

Wattie, D. K. F. "Education in the Canadian Arctic." Polar Record (Great Britain) 14 (1968):293-304.

Waubageshig [Dr. Harvey McCue]. The Only Good Indian. Essays by Canadian Indians. Toronto: New Press, n.d.

Wells, Robert N., Jr. and others. Community Mobilization and Leadership Development on the St. Regis (Akwesasne) Mohawk Reservation, Mr 24, 1974. ERIC ED 088 625.

West, L. W., and MacArthur, R. S. "An Evaluation of Selected Intelligence Tests for Two Samples of Metis and Indian Children." Alberta Journal of Educational Research 10 (Mr, 1964):17-27.

Whelan, Mary E. "Reading Achievement and Intelligence Scores of Indian Children." Master's Thesis, U. of Ottawa, 1956.

Whiteside (Sin-a-Paw), Don. "Legislative Discrimination: Civil Rights and the Registered Indian." Northian 13(Spring, 1978):29-32.

_____ (comp.). Aboriginal People. A Selected Bibliography Concerning Canada's First People. Ottawa: National Indian Brotherhood, 1973.

Who Am I? The Poetry of Indian Children. Toronto, Canada: Canadian Department of Indian Affairs and Northern Development, Jl, 1969. ERIC ED 037 268.

Whyte, John D. "The Lavell Case and Equality in Canada." Queen's Quarterly 81(1974):28-42.

Wichern, P. A., Jr. and others. Political Development on Canadian Reserves, Jl, 1972. Center for Settlement Studies, U. of Manitoba R3T 2N2.

Wiedel, Janine. "Keeping Up With the Past." Times Educational Supplement, D 28, 1973. [Eskimos of the Canadian Arctic]

Williamson, Robert G. Eskimo Underground: Socio-Cultural Change in the Canadian Central Arctic. Uppsala, Sweden: Institutionen för allmän och jämförande etnografi vid Uppsala Universitet, 1974.

Wilmott, Jill A. Indians of British Columbia: A Study Discussion Text. Vancouver: U. of British Columbia Press, 1963.

Wilson, James. "A Report on the Conditions of the Native People of Canada." Akwesasne Notes 6(Early Winter, 1975):23.

_____. Canada's Indians. London: Minority Rights Group, Ag, 1974.

Wilson, Lolita. "Canadian Indian Children Who Had Never Attended School." Alberta Journal of Educational Research 19(D, 1973):309-313.

Winkless, P. B. "A Survey of Indian Education in Canada and of Teacher Preparation for Teaching in a Cross-Cultural Situation, Specifically in Frontier School Division No. 48 in Manitoba." Master's thesis, U. of Wales, 1976.

Wintrob, Ronald M. and Sindell, Peter S. Education and Identity Conflict Among Cree Indian Youth: A Preliminary Report, Annex 3. Montreal, Canada: McGill U., O, 1968. ERIC ED 039-063.

Wolcott, Harry Fletcher. "Acculturation Among the Indian Children of Western Canada: A Case Study." Doctoral dissertation, Stanford U., 1963.

Wolfleg, Rose. "Indian Students Suffer from Discrimination in Saskatoon." Involvement (Newmarket, Ontario) 4(Fall, 1971):34-38.

Woodcock, George. Gabriel Dumont, the Metis Chief and His Lost World. Edmonton: Hurtig, 1975.

Wuttunee, William J. C. "Integration--the Best Solution." Manitoba Teacher 46(1968):6-8.

_____. Ruffled Feathers: Indians in Canadian Society. Calgary, Alberta: Bell Books, 1971.

Wutzke, Richard, and Tanaka, David. Education and the Native Students: A Study of the Difficulties Encountered by Native Youth in Relation to Education. U. of Lethbridge, 1969.

Wyatt, June. "Native Teacher Education in a Community Setting: The Mt. Currie Program." Canadian Journal of Education 2, No. 3(1977): 1-14. [Near Vancouver, B. C.]

_____. "Self-Determination Through Education: A Canadian Indian Example." Phi Delta Kappan 58(Ja, 1977):405-408.

Young, John. "How Our Schools Are Teaching Indians to Become Failures." Vancouver Sun, Mr 17, 1973.

Yukon Native Brotherhood. "The Education of Yukon Indians: A Position Paper." Northian 8(Mr, 1972):6-14.

Zeeh, Thecla. "The Indian and the Ph.D., A Run-Down on a Kind of Education." Northian, Spring, 1969.

Zeleny, Carolyn. "Governmental Treatment of the Indian. Problem in Canada. Master's thesis, Yale U., 1939.

Zentner, Henry. "Cultural Assimilation Between Indians and Non-Indians in Southern Alberta." Alberta Journal of Educational Research 9(Je, 1963):79-86.

_____. "Parental Behavior and Student Attitudes Toward High School Graduation Among Indian and Non-Indian Students in Oregon and Alberta." Alberta Journal of Educational Research, D, 1962.

_____. "Value Congruence Among Indian and Non-Indian High School Students in Southern Alberta." Alberta Journal of Educational Research 9(S, 1963):168-178.

Zuk, William M. "A Descriptive Study of Motivational Themes on the Drawings of Indian, Metis and Eskimo Students." Master's thesis, U. of Alberta, 1970.

_____. "A Study of Attitudes of Indian and Metis Students Toward Euro-Canadians in Northern Manitoba." Manitoba Journal of Education 7(N, 1971):69-80.

Asians in Canada

Adachi, Ken. The Enemy That Never Was: A History of the Japanese Canadians. Toronto: McClelland and Stewart, 1976.

Ames, Michael M., and Inglis, Joy. "Conflict and Change in British Columbia Sikh Family Life." B.C. Studies 20(Winter, 1973):15-49.

Andracki, Stanislaw. "The Immigration of Orientals into Canada with Special Reference to Chinese." Doctoral dissertation, McGill U., 1958.

Angus, H. F. "Asian Minorities in Canada." United Asia 5(1953):281-285.

Anonymous. "From Chapathies to Hamburgers." Asianadian 1(Fall-Winter, 1978):9-13. [Indian background]

Aoki, T. Ted. "On Being and Becoming a Teacher in Alberta: A Japanese-Canadian Experience." In The Japanese Experience in North America, pp. 88-103. Edited by N. Brian Winchester and others. Lethbridge, Alberta, Canada: Department of Political Science, U. of Lethbridge, n.d.

Ashworth, Mary. "The Segregation of Immigrant Children in B. C. Schools." Working Teacher 1(Winter, 1978):7-10.

Awan, Sadiq Noor Alaw. The People of Pakistani Origin in Canada: The First Quarter Century, 1978. Canada-Pakistani Association of Ohawa-Hull, P.O. Box 458, Station B, Ottawa, Ontario K1P5P6 Canada.

Ban, Seng Hoc. Structural Changes of Two Chinese Communities in Alberta. Ottawa: National Museums of Canada, Canadian Centre for Folk Culture, 1976.

Baureiss, Gunter. "The Chinese Community of Calgary." Canadian Ethnic Studies 3(Je, 1971):43-55.

Berwick, Richard and others. "Beyond Chinatown: The English Language Needs of Vancouver's Chinese Community." TESLTalk 9(Winter, 1978): 13-20.

Bhatti, F. M. "East Indian Immigration into Canada, 1905-1973." Doctoral dissertation, U. of Surrey, 1974.

Bo, Lao. "Hostages in Canada: Toronto's Chinese (1880-1947)." Asianadian 1(Summer, 1978):11-13.

Broadfoot, Barry. Years of Sorrow, Years of Shame. Toronto: Doubleday Canada, 1977. [Evacuation of Japanese Canadians during Work War II]

Buckignani, Norm. "A Review of the Historical and Sociological Literature on East Indians in Canada." Canadian Ethnic Studies 9(1977): 86-108.

_____. "Immigration, Adaptation, and the Management of Ethnic Identity: An Examination of Fijian East Indians in British Columbia." Doctoral dissertation, Simon Fraser U., 1977.

Chadney, James Gaylord. "Demography, Ethnic Identity, and Decision-Making: The Case of Vancouver Sikhs." Urban Anthropology 6(F, 1977):187-204.

_____. "The Vancouver Sikhs: An Ethnic Community in Canada." Doctoral dissertation, Michigan State U., 1976. Univ. Microfilm Order No. 77-5777.

Chan, Anthony B. "The Chinese Community in Canada: Background and Teaching Resources." Asianadian 1(Spring, 1978):13-16.

Chan, Anthony. "Neither French nor British: The Rise of the Asianadian Culture." *Canadian Ethnic Studies* 10(1978):114-117.

Chan, Ivy. "The Chinese Immigrant: Language and Cultural Concerns." *TESLTalk* 7(Je, 1976):9-19.

_____. "The Problems of Language Learning by Chinese Immigrants." *Papers on the Chinese Community.* Toronto: Ministry of Culture and Recreation, 1976:9-29.

Chan, Lilian Y. O. "The Adolescent Chinese Immigrant Student in Canada." *TESLTalk* 8 (F, 1977):3-10.

Chandra, Kananur V. *Racial Discrimination in Canada. Asian Minorities.* San Francisco, CA: R and E Research Associates, 1973.

Cheng, Tien-fang. "Oriental Immigration to Canada." Doctoral dissertation, U. of Toronto, 1926.

Chiang, Frances S-C. "Occupational Mobility and Achievements of Post-War Chinese Immigrants in Montreal." Master's thesis, McGill U., 1978.

Cho, George. "Residential Patterns of the Chinese in Vancouver, B. C." Master's thesis, U. of British Columbia, 1970.

Coward, Harold, and Kawamura, Leslie (eds.). *Religion and Ethnicity.* Waterloo, Ontario: Wilfrid Lawier U. Press, 1978. [Japanese in Canada]

Dahlie, Jorgen. "The Japanese Challenge to Public Schools in Society in British Columbia." *Journal of Ethnic Studies* 2 (Spring, 1974):10-23.

_____. "Some Aspects of the Education of Minorities: The Japanese in B. C., Lost Opportunity?" *B. C. Studies* 8(Winter, 1970-1971):3-16.

Daniels, Roger. "The Japanese Experience in North America." *Canadian Ethnic Studies* 9(1977):91-100.

_____. "Japanese in the United States and Canada: An Essay in Comparative Racism." In *The Japanese Experience in North America.* Edited by N. Brian Winchester and others. Lethbridge, Alberta, Canada: Department of Political Science, U. of Lethbridge, n.d., pp. 85-87.

Deosaran, Ramesh A., and Gershman, Janis S. *An Evaluation of the 1975-76 Chinese-Canadian Bi-Cultural Program,* Je, 1976. ERIC ED 131 718.

"Face to Face With Jag Bhadauria." *Asianadian* 1(Summer, 1978):19-22. [Executive director, Canadian Council for Racial Harmony]

"Face to Face with Shizuye Takashima." *Asianadian* 1(Fall-Winter 1978):26-30. [Japanese background]

Ferguson, Ted. *A White Man's Country: An Exercise in Canadian Prejudice.* Garden City, NY: Doubleday, 1975. [Asians in Vancouver]

Foraie, Judy, and Dear, Michael. "The Politics of Discontent Among Canadian Indians." *Antipode* 10(Mr, 1978):34-45.

Glynn-Ward, H. *The Writing on the Wall: Chinese and Japanese Immigration to 1920.* Toronto: U. of Toronto Press, 1974.

Henry, Franklin J. *The Experience of Discrimination: A Case Study Approach.* San Francisco: R and E Research Associates, 1974. [Anti-Japanese discrimination in Canada]

Hirabayaski, Gordon K. "The Japanese Canadian Identity: How We Perceive Ourselves." In *The Japanese Experience in North America.* Edited by N. Brian Winchester and others. Lethbridge, Alberta, Canada: Department of Political Science, U. of Lethbridge, n.d., pp. 26-42.

Hoe, Ban Seng. "Structural Changes of Two Chinese Communities in Alberta, Canada." Doctoral dissertation, Vanderbilt U., 1974.

_____. *Structural Changes of Two Chinese Communities in Alberta.* Ottawa: National Museum of Man, 1976.

Huot, John. "In Defense of Toronto's Asians." *Race Today* 10(F, 1978):33-38.

Hutchinson, H. K. "Dimensions of Ethnic Education: The Japanese in British Columbia, 1880-1940." Master's thesis, U. of British Columbia, 1973.

Irwin, Jane (ed.). "Stevetson: The Japanese-Canadian Experience." *Sound Heritage* 3 (No. 3, 1974):5-16.

Ito, Roy. *The Japanese Canadians.* Toronto: Van Nostrand Reinhold Ltd., 1978.

Iwaasa, David B. "The Japanese in Southern Alberta, 1941-45." *Alberta History* 24 (1976):5-19.

_____. "Relocation and Integration, A Southern Alberta Experience." In *The Japanese Experience in North America.* Edited by N. Brian Winchester and others. Lethbridge, Alberta, Canada: Department of Political Science, U. of Lethbridge, n.d., pp. 43-64.

Jain, Sushil Kumar. *East Indians in Canada.* Je, 1971. P. H. Klop, P. O. Box 6040, The Hague, Netherlands.

Khattob, Abdelmoneim M. "The Assimilation of Arab Muslims in Alberta." Master's thesis, U. of Alberta, 1969.

Knight, Rolf and Koizumi, Maya (eds.). A Man of Our Times: The Life-Story of a Japanese-Canadian-Fisherman. Vancouver: New Star Books, 1976. [Ryuichi Yoshida]

Kobayashi, Cassandra. "Sexual Slavery in Canada: Our Herstory." Asianadian 1(Fall-Winter, 1978):4-8. [Japanese background]

Lai, Vivien. "The Assimilation of Chinese Immigrants in Toronto." Master's thesis, York U., 1970.

Lal, Brij. "East Indians in British Columbia, 1904-1914: A Historical Study in Growth and Integration." Master's thesis, U. of British Columbia, 1976.

Lamoureux, Pierre. "La population chinoise au Canada." Master's thesis, U. of Montreal, 1953.

Le, P. "The Vietnamese: An Often-Overlooked Minority." Multiculturalism 2, No. 2(1978): 3-6. [Reprinted from Emergency Librarian]

Lee, Carol F. "The Road to Enfranchisement: Chinese and Japanese in British Columbia." B.C. Studies 30(1976):44-76.

Lee, R. "Sources of Information and Education Used by Korean Adults in Vancouver." Master's thesis, U. of British Columbia, 1972.

Macdonald, Elizabeth. "Japanese Canadians in Edmonton 1969: An Exploratory Search for Patterns of Assimilation." Master's thesis, Alberta U., 1970.

Makabe, Tomoko. "Ethnic Group Identity-Canadian-Born Japanese in Metropolitan Toronto." Doctoral dissertation, U. of Toronto, 1976.

Mao, T. T. (pseud.). "How to Make a Buck in the Canadian Ethnic Industry and Not Be Called a Racist or Uncle Tong." Asianadian 1 (Spring, 1978):29.

Meyer, Adrian C. A Report on the East Indian Community in Vancouver. Vancouver: Institute of Social & Economic Research, U. of British Columbia, D, 1959.

Minai, Keiko. "The Japanese in Montreal: Socio-Economic Integration and Ethnic Identification of an Immigrant Group." Master's thesis, McGill U., 1977.

Morah, Benson C. "The Assimilation of Ugandan Asians in Calgary." Master's thesis, U. of Calgary, 1974.

Morton, James. In the Sea of Sterile Mountains: The Chinese in British Columbia. Vancouver: J. J. Douglas, 1974.

Moudgil, Ranvir. "From Stranger to Refugee. A Study of the Integration of Ugandan Asians in Canada." Doctoral dissertation, State U. of New York at Buffalo, 1977.

Muthanna, I. M. People of India in North America. Vancouver: Vancouver Globe Spices, Ltd., 1975. [East Indians]

Nizamuddin, K. "Some Behavioural Characteristics of Migrants from India and Pakistan in Windsor Ontario--A Case Study." Master's thesis, U. of Windsor, 1976.

Ono, Dawn Kiyoye. "White Male Supremacy and the 'Oriental Doll.'" Asianadian 1(Fall-Winter, 1978):24-25.

Pannu, R. S. "A Sociological Survey of Teachers from India Teaching in Alberta, 1958-65." Master's thesis, U. of Alberta, 1966.

Paupst, K. "A Note on Anti-Chinese Sentiment in Toronto Before the First World War." Canadian Ethnic Studies 9(1977):54-59.

Pereira, Cecil P. "East Indians in Winnipeg: A Study of the Consequences of Immigration for an Ethnic Group in Canada." Master's thesis, Manitoba U., 1971.

Pereira, Cecil P. and others. "Canadian Beliefs and Policy Regarding the Admission of Ugandan Asians to Canada." Ethnic and Racial Studies 1(Jl, 1978):352-364.

Ramcharan, Subhas. "East Indian Immigration to Canada." Multiculturalism 2, No. 3(1979): 14-16.

Roy, Patricia E. "The Oriental 'Menace' in British Columbia." In Historical Essays on British Columbia. Edited by J. Friesen and H. K. Ralaton. Toronto: McClelland and Stewart, 1976.

Sampat-Mehta, R. Aliens, Immigration and Citizenship in Canada. Canada Research Bureau, 1972. [Restrictions on Chinese, pp., 23-124]

Sandhu, Ker mal Singh. "Indian Immigration and Racial Prejudice in British Columbia: Some Preliminary Observations." In Peoples of the Living Land: Geography of Cultural Diversity in British Columbia. Edited by Julian V. Minghi. Vancouver: Tantalus Research Ltd., 1972.

Saniford, Peter, and Ken, Ruby. "Intelligence of Chinese and Japanese Children." Journal of Educational Psychology 17(1927):361-369. [Vancouver, B.C.]

Shibata, Yuko and others. The Forgotten History of the Japanese Canadians. Vancouver: New Sun Books for the Japanese-Canadian History Group, 1977.

Shimizu, Ron. "The Centennial Youth Conference of Japanese Canadians." Multiculturalism 1 (1978):21-23.

Siddique, C. "Structural Separation and Family Change: An Exploratory Study of the Immigrant Indian and Pakitani Community of Saskatoon, Canada." International Review of Modern Sociology 7(Ja-Je, 1977): 13-35.

Sien, Foon. The Chinese in Canada. Royal Commission on Biblingualism and Biculturalism, Ja, 1967. [Ottawa]

Subramaniam, Indira A. "Identity-Shift: Post-Migration Changes in Identity Among First-Generation East Indian Immigrants in Toronto." Doctoral dissertation, U. of Toronto, 1978.

Sugimoto, Howard H. Japanese Immigration, the Vancouver Riots, and Canadian Diplomacy. New York: Arno, 1979.

Suzuki, David T. "On Being Japanese in Canada." In The Japanese Experience in North America. Edited by N. Brian Winchester and others. Lethbridge, Alberta, Canada: Department of Political Science, U. of Lethbridge, n.d., pp. 1-25.

Takashima, Shizuye. A Child in Prison Camp. New York: Morrow, 1974. [Internment of Japanese-Canadians during World War II]

Takata, Toyo. "1977: A Centennial for Forty Thousand." Multiculturalism 1(1977):6-8. [Japanese in Canada]

Taylor, Gordon R. "Chinese Schools in Canada." Master's thesis, McGill U., 1933.

Trumbull, Robert. "Japanese-Canadians Honored in Ottawa." New York Times, J1 9, 1978.

Ubale, Bhausaheb. Equal Opportunity and Public Policy, 1978. Indian Immigrant Aid Services, 9 Boon Avenue, Toronto, Ontario M6E3Z2. [South Asians in Canada]

Ujimoto, K. Victor. "Contrasts in the Prewar and Postwar Japanese Community in B. C.: Conflict and Change." Canadian Review of Sociology and Anthropology 13(1976):80-89.

UNESCO. Ethnicity and the Media. London: HMSO, 1978. [Punjabi issue in Canada]

Voisey, Paul L. "Two Chinese Communities in Alberta: An Historical Perspective." Canadian Ethnic Studies 2(D, 1970):15-29.

Walker, Lilly S. "University Success for Canadian Indians." Canadian Journal of Behavioral Science 9(Ap, 1977):169-175.

Wang, Stephen Shen-Yin. "The Teaching of English in Chinese Schools." Master's thesis, U. of Toronto, 1948.

Ward, W. Peter. "British Columbia and the Japanese Evacuation." Canadian Historical Review 57(S, 1976):289-308.

_____. "White Canada Forever: British Columbia's Response to Orientals, 1858-1914." Doctoral dissertation, Queens' U., Kingston, Ontario, 1972.

Wenxiong, Gao. "Hamilton [Ontario]: The Chinatown That Died." Asianadian 1(Summer, 1978):15-17.

Winchester, N. Brian, Fujimagari, Laurel H., and Ichikawa, Akira (eds.). The Japanese Experience in North America. Lethbridge, Alberta, Canada: Department of Political Science, U. of Lethbridge, n.d.

Witzel, A. Chinese Immigrants and China. Toronto: Board of Education, 1969.

Wolfgang, Aaron, and Josefowitz, Nina. "Chinese Immigrant Value Changes with Length of Time in Canada and Value Differences Compared to Canadian Students." Canadian Ethnic Studies 10(1978):130-135.

Wynne, Robert E. "Reaction to the Chinese in the Pacific Northwest and British Columbia, 1850 to 1910." Doctoral dissertation, U. of Washington, 1964.

Young, Charles H., and Reidd, Helen R. Y. The Japanese Canadians. With a second part on Oriental Standards of Living, by W. A. Carruthers and H. A. Innis (eds.). Toronto: U. of Toronto Press, 1938.

Young, Charles H. The Japanese Canadians. Toronto: N.p., 1939.

Yiu, Esther Kan Yu. "Youth in Need: A Study of the Need for After-School Programs Geared to the Acculturation of Chinese Immigrant Youth from Downtown Toronto." Master's thesis, U. of Toronto, 1968.

Europeans in Canada

Anderson, Grace. Networks of Contact: The Portuguese in Toronto. Waterloo: Wilfred Lawier Press, 1974.

Anderson, Grace, and Higgs, David. A Future to Inherit: Portuguese Communities in Canada. Toronto: McClelland & Stewart, 1976.

Bercuson, Leonard. "Education in the Block Settlements of Western Canada." Master's thesis, McGill U., 1941. [German Canadians]

Bilash, Borislaw N. "Bilingual [German] Public School in Manitoba, 1897-1916." Master's thesis, U. of Manitoba, 1960.

Boissevain, Jeremy. The Italians of Montreal: Social Adjustment in a Plural Society. Ottawa, Canada: Royal Commission on Bilingualism and Biculturalism, 1970.

Borhek, J. T. "Ethnic-Group Cohesion." American Journal of Sociology 76(J1, 1970): 33-46.

Chimbos, Peter D. "A Comparison of the Social Adaptation of Dutch, Greek and Slovak Immigrants in a Canadian Community." International Migration Review 6(Fall, 1972):230-244.

_____. "Immigrants' Attitudes toward their Children's Inter-ethnic Marriages in a Canadian Community." International Migration Review 5(Fall, 1970).

Chu, Godwin C. Communication and Assimilation of Polish Immigrants in British Columbia: An Exploration in Culture Learning, Ap, 1972. ERIC ED 062 768.

Cipywnyk, Sonia V. "Educational Implications of Ukranian-English Childhood Bilingualism in Saskatchewan." Master's thesis, U. of Saskatchewan, 1968.

Crooks, William R. "The Effectiveness of Culture-Free Tests in Measuring the Intellectual Characteristics of German Immigrants in Canada." Doctoral dissertation, Oregon State U., 1956.

Darcovich, William. Ukranians in Canada: The Struggle to Retain Their Identity. Ottawa: Ukranian Self-Reliance Association, 1967.

Deverell, Jessie M. "The Ukranian Teacher as an Agent of Cultural Assimilation." Master's thesis, U. of Toronto, 1941.

Doerksen, John G. "History of Education of the Mennonite Brethern of Canada." Master's thesis, U. of Manitoba, 1963.

Friesen, Isaac I. "The Mennonites of Western Canada with Special Reference to Education." Master's thesis, U. of Saskatchewan, 1934.

Gaida, Pr. The Lithuanians in Canada. UVAN Book Service, P.O. Box 3597, Winnipeg 4, Manitoba, Canada, n.d.

Gaida, Pr. and others. Lithuanians in Canada. Toronto, Canada: Lights Publishing Co., 1967.

Jansen, Clifford J. "Leadership in a Toronto Ethnic Group: A Study of Italian Immigrants." International Migration Review 4 (1969).

Kirschbaum, Joseph. Slovaks in Canada. Middletown, PA: Jednota Press, 1967.

Klassen, P. G. "A History of Mennonite Education in Manitoba." Master's thesis, U. of Manitoba, 1959.

Kott, Teresa, and Wojciechwski, Jerzy A. (eds.). Polonia of Tomorrow. Toronto: Canadian Polish Congress, 1978.

Krychowski, T. W. (ed.). Polish Canadians. Toronto: Polish Alliance Press, 1969.

Lindal, Walter Jacobson. The Icelanders in Canada. Ottawa-Winnipeg: Canada Ethnics, 1967.

Lupul, Manoly R. (ed.). Ukranian Canadians, Multiculturalism, and Separatism: An Assessment. Edmonton, Alberta: U. of Alberta Press, 1978.

Lyons, John. "The (Almost) Quiet Evolution: Doukhobor Schooling in Saskatchewan." Canadian Ethnic Studies 8(1976):23-37.

Makowski, W. B. History and Integration of Poles in Canada. Lindsay, Ontario: John Deyell, Ltd., 1967.

Matejko, Alexander. "Multiculturalism. The Polish-Canadian Case." Polish Review 21 (1976):177-194.

Nagata, Judith A. "Adaptation and Integration of Greek Working Class Immigrants to the City of Toronto: A Situational Approach." International Migration Review 4(1969).

Okulevich, Grigorii. Russkie v Kanade. Toronto: Federation of Russian Canadians, 1952.

Petroff, L. "Macedonians: From Village to City." Canadian Ethnic Studies 9(1977):29-41.

Potrebenko, Helen. No Streets of Gold: A Social History of Ukranians in Alberta. Vancouver: New Star Books, 1977.

Quinn, George William. "Impact of European Immigrants Upon the Elementary Schools of Central Toronto, 1815-1915." Master's thesis, U. of Toronto, 1968.

Rees-Powell, Alan. "Differentials in the Integration Process of Dutch and Italian Immigrants in Edmonton, Canada." International Migration 4(1966):100-120.

Saruk, Alec. "Academic Performance of the Students of Ukranian Descent and the Cultural Orientation of Their Parents." Master's thesis, U. of Alberta, 1966.

Skwarok, Josaphat. "The Ukranian Settlers and Their Schools With Reference to Government, French Canadian, and Ukranian Missionary Influence, 1891-192." Master's thesis, U. of Alberta, 1958. [Published in 1959 by Basiban Press, in Edmonton, Canada]

_____. The Ukranian Settlers in Canada and Their Schools. Toronto: N.p., 1959.

Szyrnski, Victor. "Social Preferences in School Children and Adolescents: A Comparative Study of English and Polish Children." Doctoral dissertation, U. of Ottawa, 1949.

Tagashire, K., and Lozowchuk, Y. W. "A Preliminary Report on Ethnicity and University Education in Saskatchewan, 1910-1962." Slavs In Canada, vol. 3, 217-246. Toronto: N.p., 1971.

Trumbull, Robert. "Upsurge of Racism in Toronto Afflicts South Asian Immigrants." New York Times, F 27, 1977.

Turek, Witkor (ed.). The Polish Past in Canada. Toronto: Polish Alliance Press, 1960.

Woycenko. Ol'ha. The Ukranians in Canada. UVAN Book Service, P. O. Box 3597, Winnipeg 4, Manitoba, Canada, n.d.

Zubkowski, A. K. R. The Poles in Canada. UVAN Book Service, P. O. Box 3597, Winnipeg 4, Manitoba, Canada, n.d.

Zubek, John P. "A Study of the Local Attitudes of High School Students and Adults Towards the Doukhobors of Southern British Columbia." Master's thesis, U. of Toronto, 1948.

Yuzyk, Paul. The Ukranians in Manitoba: A Social History. Toronto: N.p., 1953.

Jews in Canada

Becker, Lavy M., and Rosenberg, Louis. "Jewish Education in Montreal." Jewish Education 22(Winter-Spring, 1950-1951):63-71.

Belkin, Simon. Through Narrow Gates. Montreal: Eagle Publishing Co., 1966. [Jews in Canada, 1840's-1940]

Feldbrill, Zeld. "The Adjustment of European Youth in the Toronto Jewish Community." Master's thesis, U. of Toronto, 1952.

Godfrey, M. "A Study of the Academic Achievement and Personal and Social Adjustment of Jewish Moroccan Immigrant Students in the English High Schools of Montreal." Master's thesis, McGill U., 1970.

Herstein, Harvey H. "The Growth of the Winnipeg Jewish Community and the Evolution of Its Educational Institutions." Master's thesis, U. of Manitoba, 1964.

Kage, Joseph. "The Initial Organizational Efforts Among the Jewish Newcomers from North Africa." JIAS News (Jewish Immigrant Aid Services, Montreal) 25(Summer, 1978). [1957-1966]

Lewin, S. "Jewish Education in Montreal." Jewish Education 38(Je, 1968):24-29.

Munro, P. F. "An Experimental Investigation of the Mentality of the Jew in Ryerson Public School, Toronto." Doctoral dissertation, U. of Toronto, 1926.

Pirie, Margaret C. "Patterns of Mobility and Assimilation: A Study of the Toronto Jewish Community." Doctoral dissertation, Yale U., 1957.

Rome, David. Clouds in the Thirties. On Antisemitism in Canada, 1929-1939. A Chapter on Canadian Jewish History. Montreal: Canadian Jewish Congress, 1977.

Rosenberg, Louis. Canada's Jews: A Social and Economic Study of the Jews in Canada. Montreal: Bureau of Social and Economic Research, Canadian Jewish Congress, 1939.

Rosenberg, Stuart E. The Jewish Community in Canada. Two vols. Toronto: McClelland and Stewart, 1970-1971.

Sack, Benjamin G. History of the Jews in Canada. Tr. Ralph Novek. Montreal: Harvest House, 1968.

Shaffir, William. "The Organization of Secular Education in a Chassidic Jewish Community." Canadian Ethnic Studies 8(1976):38-51. [Montreal]

Yam, Joseph. "Selected Data on the Canadian Population Whose Mother Tongue is Yiddish." Canadian Jewish Population Studies, D, 1973.

General

A National Understanding: The Official Languages of Canada. Ottawa: Publishing Centre Supply and Services, 1977.

Adams, Ian. The Poverty Wall. Toronto: McClelland & Stewart, 1970.

Adelman, Howard, and Lee, Dennis (eds.). The University Game. Toronto: Anasi, 1968.

Allen, G. P. "Ethnic Organization in Canadian Society." International Migration Review, Spring, 1969.

Anderson, Grace M. Spanish-speaking Immigrants in Selected Canadian Cities. Burnaby, B.C.: Department of Sociology and Anthropology and the Latin American Studies Program, Simon Fraser U., 1977.

Ashworth, Mary. "The Education of Immigrant Children." English Quarterly 7(Winter, 1974-1975):9-20.

_____. "Multiculturalism and Canadian Schools." New Community 4(Summer, 1975): 203-210.

Attwell, Arthur, and Linton, T. E. "Problems Inherent in Ability Groupings." Alberta Journal of Educational Research, Mr, 1964.

Bacchus, M. K. Education and Socio-Cultural Integration in a "Plural" Society. Montreal: Centre for Developing-Area Studies, McGill U., 1970.

Barclay, Harold B. "An Arab Community in the Canadian Northwest: A Preliminary Discussion of the Lebanese Community in Lac Lo Biche, Alberta." Anthropologica 10 (1968):143-156.

Berezowecki, Anthony R. "Liberation or Domestication: Adult Education in Canada." Literacy Discussion 5(Winter, 1974):607-621.

Berry, John W. and others. Multiculturalism and Ethnic Attitudes in Canada: A Summary of a National Survey, Je 11, 1976. ERIC ED 129 942.

Betcherman, Lita-Rose. "The Early History of Canada's Anti-Discrimination Law." Patterns of Prejudice 7(N-D, 1973):19-23.

_____. The Swastika and the Maple Leaf: Fascist Movement in Canada in the Thirties. Toronto: Fitzhenry and Whiteside, 1975.

Bhatnagar, Joti. "Education of Immigrant Children." Canadian Ethnic Studies 8(1976): 52-70.

Bibby, Reginald W. "Prejudice and Education." School Guidance Worker 32(Ja, 1977):1679.

Boyd, Monica. "The Status of Immigrant Women in Canada." Canadian Review of Sociology and Anthropology 12(N, 1975).

Bradshaw, Marvi. "The University of Toronto, Multiculturalism, and Ethnic Relations." Multiculturalism 1(1978):6-9.

Breton, Raymond. "Academic Stratification in Secondary Schools and Educational Plans of Students." Canadian Review of Sociology and Anthropology 7(F, 1970):17-34.

_____. The Canadian Condition: A Guide to Research in Public Policy. Montreal: Institute for Research in Public Policy, 1977.

_____. "Class Bias in Toronto Schools." This Magazine is About Schools 5(Fall-Winter, 1971):7-35.

Breton, Raymond and others. "Research Issues on Canadian Cultures and Ethnic Groups: An Analysis of a Conference." Canadian Review of Sociology and Anthropology 12(F, 1975).

Breton, Raymond, with McDonald John, and Richer, Stephen. Social and Academic Factors in the Career Decisions of Canadian Youth. Ottawa: Department of Manpower and Immigration, 1972.

Brown, W. J. "Interprovincial Educational Differences in Canada: Alternative Measures of Their Underlying Causes and Their Alleviation." Master's thesis, U. of Toronto, 1969.

Bunge, William W., and Bordessa, R. The Canadian Alternative. Survival, Expeditions and Urban Change. Downsview, Ontario: York U., 1975.

Burnet, Jean R. Ethnic Groups in Upper Canada. Toronto: Ontario Historical Society, 1972.

_____. "Ethnic Relations and Ethnic Policies in Canadian Society." In Ethnicity in the Americas. Edited by F. Henry. The Hague: Mouton, 1976.

_____. "The Policy of Multiculturalism Within a Bilingual Framework: A Stock-taking." Canadian Ethnic Studies 10(1978):107-113.

Byrne, Niall, and Quarter, Jack. Must Schools Fail? The Growing Debate in Canadian Education. Toronto, Canada: McClelland & Stewart, 1972.

Cairns, J. C. "Adult Functional Illiteracy in Canada." Convergence 10(1977):43-52.

Caldewood, William. "Pulpit, Press, and Political Reactions to the Ku Klux Klan in Saskatchewan." In The Twenties in Western Canada: Papers of the Western Canadian Studies Conference. Edited by S. M. Trofiurenkoff. Ottawa: History Division, National Museum of Man, 1972.

Canada. Royal Commission on Bilingualism and Biculturalism. The Cultural Contribution of the Other Ethnic Groups. Ottawa: Queen's Printer, 1970.

The Canadian Family Tree. Centennial ed. Prepared by Canadian Citizenship Branch, Dept. of the Secretary of State and published in cooperation with the Centennial Commission, Ottawa. Queen's Printer, 1967.

Card, B. Y., and Nixon, Mary. "Poverty and Education in Canada." Education for the Disadvantaged Child 1(Spring, 1973):12-17.

Carlton, R. A., Colley, L. A., and MacKinnon, N. J. (eds.). Education, Change, and Society: A Sociology of Canadian Education. Toronto: Gage, 1977.

Carney, Robert J. "Relations in Education Between the Federal and Territorial Governments and the Roman Catholic Church in the Mackenzie District, Northwest Territories, 1867-1961." Doctoral dissertation, U. of Alberta, 1971.

Chabassol, D. "Prejudice and Personality in Adolescents." Alberta Journal of Educational Research 16(1970):3-12.

Chalmers, John W. and others. The Poor at School in Canada; Observational Studies of Canadian Schools, Classrooms and Pupils. Ottawa, Canada: Canadian Teachers' Federation. Available from Canadian Teachers' Federation, 320 Queen Street, Ottawa 4, Canada. ERIC ED 046 598.

Colls, Robert. "'Oh Happy English Children': Coal, Class and Education in the North-East." Past and Present 73(N, 1976):75-99.

Curreo, Carl J., and Curtis, James E. "Social Ascription in the Educational and Occupational Status Attainment of Urban Canadians." Canadian Review of Sociology and Anthropology 12(F, 1975).

Curtis, J., and Scott, W. (eds.). Social Stratification, Canada. Scarborough, Canada: Prentice-Hall, 1973.

Czerny, Robert E. "New Citizenship Act." TESLTalk 8(Ja, 1977):22-24.

Darroch, A. Gordon, and Marston, Wilfred G. "The Social Class Basis of Ethnic Residential Segregation: The Canadian Case." American Journal of Sociology 77(N, 1971): 491-510. [Toronto]

Das, J. P. and others. "Performance of Canadian Native, Black and White Children on Some Cognitive and Personality Tests." Alberta Journal of Educational Research 21 (S, 1975):183-195.

Dawson, C. A. Group Settlement: Ethnic Communities in Western Canada. Toronto: Macmillan, 1936.

Depatie, Raymond and others. Identification of the Disadvantaged Areas on the Island of Montreal with a View to Intervention Programmes Being Initiated by the School Community, D 27, 1974. ERIC ED 121 888.

_____. Identification of the Schools in Which a Considerable Proportion of the Students Come from Disadvantaged Areas, D, 1975. ERIC ED 129 953. [Island of Montreal]

Dewar, Ken. "The Road to Happiness: Canadian History in Public Schools." This Magazine Is About Schools 7(Fall, 1972):102-127.

Downes, Walter Edward. "The Influence of British Colonial Policy on Education in Upper Canada, 1738-1840." Doctoral dissertation, U. of Ottawa, 1975.

D'Oyley, Vincent R. "Schooling and Ethnic Rights." Interchange 8(1977-1978):101-108.

_____ (ed.). The Impact of Multi-Ethnicity on Canadian Education. Toronto: Urban Alliance on Race Relations, 1977.

Driedger, Leo, and Church, Glenn. "Residential Segregation & Institutional Completeness: A Comparison of Ethnic Minorities." Canadian Review of Sociology and Anthropology 11(F, 1974).

Dumont, Fred J. Report of an Assessment of the Educational Needs of Northern Albertans, 1976, N, 1976. ERIC ED 140 998.

Education Support Branch. Some Characteristics of Post-Secondary Students in Canada. Ottawa: Department of the Secretary of State, 1976.

Elliott, Jean Leonard (ed.). Minority Canadians. 2 vols. Scarborough, Ontario, Canada: Prentice-Hall of Canada, Ltd., 1971.

Ellis, E. N. Survey of Pupils in Vancouver Schools for Whom English is a Second Language, Ja, 1975. ERIC ED 132 847.

Elliston, Inez. "Is Racism Increasing in the Schools? A Survey of the Opinion of School Personnel." Multiculturalism 2(1978). [Metropolitan Toronto]

Epp, I. H. Mennonites in Canada, 1786-1920: The History of a Separate People. Toronto: Macmillan, 1974.

Ferguson, Ted. A White Man's Country. An Exercise in Canadian Prejudice. Garden City, NY: Doubleday, 1976. [The Komagata Maru incident of 1914]

Fitzpatrick, Thomas and others. "A New Intelligence Test With a Canadian Identity." Orbit 2(Ap, 1971):16-19.

Francis, E. K. "The Manitoba School Problem." Mennonite Quarterly Review 27(1953).

"The Friction at Jarvis Isn't Racial." Toronto Daily Star, Je 14, 1976. [Jarvis Collegiate High School, Toronto]

Frideres, J. S. "British Canadian Attitudes Toward Minority Ethnic Groups in Canada." Ethnicity 5(Mr, 1978):20-32.

_____. "Discrimination in Western Canada." Race 15(O, 1973):213-222.

_____. "Prejudice in Western Canada." Patterns of Prejudice 7(Ja-F, 1973):17-22.

_____. "Prejudice Towards Minority Groups: Ethnicity or Class." Ethnicity 2(1975): 34-42.

Friesen, John W. People Culture and Learning. Calgary: Detselig, 1977.

_____. "Teacher Preparation and Intercultural Education." Journal of Educational Thought 10(D, 1976):179-187.

Fromson, Ronald D. "Acculturation or Assimilation: A Geographic Analysis of Residential Segregation of Selected Ethnic Groups: Metropolitan Winnipeg, 1951-1961." Master's thesis, U. of Manitoba, 1965.

Gulustan, Metro, and Saruk, Alec. "Academic Performance of Students and the Cultural Orientation of their Parents." Alberta Journal of Educational Research 16(S, 1970).

Gardner, R. C., Taylor, D. M., and Feenstra, H. J. "Ethnic Stereotypes: Attitudes or Beliefs?" Canadian Journal of Psychology 24(O, 1970):321-334.

Genesee, F., Tucker, G. R., and Lambert, W. E. "Communicational Effectiveness of English Children in Franch Schools." Canadian Journal of Education 2, No. 3 (1977):15-24.

George, P. M. Social Factors and Educational Aspirations of Canadian High School Students, O, 1970. ERIC ED 043 899.

Godfrey, Marvin J. "A Study of the Academic Achievement and Personal and Social Adjustment of Jewish Moroccan Immigrant Students in the English High Schools of Montreal." Master's thesis, McGill U., 1970.

Gossage, Carolyn. A Question of Privilege: Canada's Independent Schools. Toronto: Peter Martin, 1977.

Hache, Jean-Baptiste. "Language and Religious Factors in Canadian Ethnic Politics of Education: A Case Study in Power Mobilization." Doctoral dissertation, U. of Toronto, 1976.

Haller, Emil J., and Anderson, Barry D. "Contexual Effects on Educational Aspirations: Some Canadian Evidence." Administrator's Notebook, Mr, 1969.

Harasym, Carolyn R. "Cultural Orientation of Rural Ukranian High School Students." Master's thesis, U. of Calgary, 1969.

Harp, John, and Hofley, John R. (eds.). Poverty in Canada. Scarborough, Ontario, Canada: Prentice-Hall, Ltd., 1971.

Harris, Robin S. A History of Higher Education in Canada, 1663-1960. Toronto: U. of Toronto Press, 1976.

Harvey, Edward B. Educational Systems and the Labour Market. Toronto: Longman Canada, 1974.

Hawkins, Freda. "Canada's Immigration Policy Re-examined." Race Today 3(N, 1971):369-371.

Heap, James L. (ed.). Everybody's Canada: The Vertical Mosaic Reviewed and Re-examined. Toronto: Burns and MacEachern, 1974.

Henry, Franklin J. "The Measurement of Perceived Discrimination: A Canadian Case Study." Race, Ap, 1969. [Hamilton, Ontario]

Herberg, Edward N. "Fighting Racial Discrimination in Toronto: The Urban Alliance on Race Relations." Multiculturalism 2(1978): 20-23.

Hody, Maud. "The Development of the Bilingual Schools of New Brunswick." Doctoral dissertation, U. of Toronto, 1960.

Houston, Susan E. "Politics, Schools, and Social Change in Upper Canada." Canadian Historical Review 53(S, 1972).

Hoy, C. H. "Education and Minority Groups in the United Kingdom and Canada: A Comparative Study of Policies and Objectives." Doctoral dissertation, U. of London, Institute of Education, 1975.

Hughes, David R., and Kallen, Evelyn. The Anatomy of Racism: Canadian Dimensions. Montreal: Harvest House, 1974.

Humphreys, Edward H. "Equality? The Rural-Urban Disparity in Ontario Elementary Schools." Education Canada 11(Mr, 1971):34-39.

Hunnius, Gerry (ed.). Participating Democracy for Canada. Workers' Control and Community Control. Montreal, Canada: Black Rose Books, 1971.

Huttenback, Robert A. Racism and Empire. White Settlers and Colored Immigrants in the British Self-Governing Colonies, 1830-1910. Ithaca, NY: Cornell U. Press, 1976.

Ingram, John C. L. "Social Class Based Educational Deficit and the Social Class Environment of the School." Master's thesis, Alberta U., 1971.

Isajiw, Wsevolod (ed.). Identities: The Impact of Ethnicity on Canadian Society. Toronto: Peter Martin Associates, 1976.

Issalys, Pierre Francois. "Ethnic Pluralism and Public Law in Selected Commonwealth Countries." Doctoral dissertation, U. of London, 1972.

Johnson, F. Henry. A Brief History of Canadian Education. Toronto: McGraw-Hill, 1968.

Johnson, Leo. "The Development of Class in Canada in the 20th Century." In Capitalism and the National Question in Canada. Edited by Gary Teeple. Toronto: U. of Toronto Press, 1972.

Johnstone, John C., Willig, Jean-Claude, and Spina, Joseph M. Young People's Images of Canadian Society. Ottawa: Royal Commission on Bilingualism and Biculturalism, 1969.

Kalbach, Warren E., and McVey, Wayne W. The Demographic Bases of Canadian Society. Toronto: McGraw-Hill Co. of Canada, 1971.

Katz, Joseph. "Multicultural Curricula." Education Canada 14(S, 1974):43-47.

_____. Society, Schools and Progress in Canada. Oxford: Pergamon, 1969.

Kealy, Jean, and McLeod, John. "Learning Disability and Socioeconomic Status." Journal of Learning Disabilities 9(N, 1976):596-599.

Kernaghan, W. D. K. "Civil Liberties in the Canadian Community." In Law and Justice: Essays in Honor of Robert S. Rankin. Edited by Carl Beck. Durham, NC: Duke U. Press, 1970, pp. 323-345.

Kindrachuk, M. J. "Some Thoughts on Multiculturalism." Education Canada 15(Winter, 1975):59-61. [Saskatoon Public Schools]

King, A. J. C. "Ethnicity and School Adjustment." Canadian Review of Sociology and Anthropology, My, 1968.

Kirby, D. M. and Gardner, R. C. "Ethnic Stereotypes: Determinants in Children & Their Parents." Canadian Journal of Psychology 27(Je, 1973):127-143.

Knill, William K. "Occupational Aspirations of Northern Saskatchewan Students." Alberta Journal of Educational Research, Mr, 1964.

Knill, W. D., and Davis, A. K. "Provincial Education in Northern Saskatchewan: Progress and Bogdown, 1944-1962." In A Northern Dilemma: Reference Papers. Edited by A. K. Davis and others. Bellingham, WN, Western WN State College, 1967.

Kovacs, Martin L. Ethnic Canadians: Culture and Education. Regina, Canada: Canadian Plains Research Center, 1978.

Kralt, John. Ethnic Origins of Canadians. Ottawa: N.p., 1977.

Krashinsky, Michael. Day Care and Public Policy in Ontario. Toronto: U. of Toronto Press, 1977.

Krauter, Joseph F. "Civil Liberties and the Canadian Minorities." Doctoral dissertation, U. of Illinois, 1968.

Krauter, Joseph F., and Davis, Morris. Minority Canadians: Ethnic Groups. Agincourt, Ontario, Canada: Methuen Publication, 1978.

Krukowski, T. "Canadian Private Ethnic Schools." Comparative Education, Je, 1968.

Labovitz, Sanford. "Some Evidence of Canadian Ethnic, Racial, and Sexual, Antagonism." Canadian Review of Sociology and Anthropology 2(Ag, 1974).

Lawless, D. J. "Attitudes of Leaders of Immigrant and Ethnic Societies in Vancouver Towards Integration Into Canadian Life." International Migration 2(1964):201-211.

Lawton, S. B., and O'Neill, G. P. "Ethnic Segregation in Toronto's Elementary Schools." Alberta Journal of Educational Research 19 (S, 1973):195-201.

Lewis, Maurice H. "The Anglican Church and Its Mission School Dispute." Alberta Historical Review 14(1966):7-13.

Lind, Loren Jay. The Learning Machine: A Hard Look at Toronto Schools. N.p: The House of Anansi, 1975.

_____. "New Canadianism: Melting the Ethnics in Toronto Schools." This Magazine Is About Schools (1973):6-10.

Lipsius, Frank. "And the Parents Ask: 'Can We Learn Too?'?" Times Educational Supplement, Ag 30, 1974. [Education of Gypsy children]

Lovey, Martin. "Canada's Immigration Policy." Race Today 3(S, 1971):303-304.

_____. "A Consumer Perspective on Canadian Immigration Policy." Race Today 4(Ap, 1972):117-119.

Lotz, James R. "Socio-Economic Development in the Canadian North: Some Perspectives and Problems." In Education in the North. Edited by Frank Darnell. Arctic Institute of North America, U. of Alaska, 1972, pp. 229-239.

Love, R., and Oja, G. "Low Income in Canada." *Review of Income and Wealth* 23(Mr, 1977).

Lupul, M. R. "The Portrayal of Canada's 'Other' Peoples in Senior High School History and Social Studies Textbooks in Alberta, 1905 to the Present." *Alberta Journal of Educational Research* 22(Mr, 1976):1-33.

McDiarmid, Garnet, and Pratt, David. *Teaching Prejudice: A Content Analysis of Social Studies Textbooks Authorized for Use in Ontario.* Toronto: Ontario Institute for Studies in Education, 1971.

MacDonald, Norman. *Canada: Immigration and Colonization (1841-1903).* Toronto: Macmillan, 1966.

MacDonald, P. V. "Race Relations and Canadian Law." *University of Toronto Faculty of Law Review* 18(Ap, 1960):115-127.

MacKay, W. A. "Equality of Opportunity: Recent Developments in the Field of Human Rights in Nova Scotia." *University of Toronto Law Journal* 17(1967)

McLeod, Norman R. *Need, Culture and Curriculum. Educating Immigrants and Ethnic Minorities (A Survey of Literature)*, O, 1968. ERIC ED 064 443.

Malik, Mukhtar A. *School Performance of Children in Families Receiving Public Assistance in Canada.* The Canadian Welfare Council, S, 1966.

Manley-Casimir, M., and Housego, I. E. "Equality of Educational Opportunity: A Canadian Perspective." *Alberta Journal of Educational Research* 16(Je, 1970):79-87.

Mann, W. E. (ed.). *Canada: A Sociological Profile.* Toronto: Copp Clark Publishing Co., 1968.

Marsden, L. R. "Canadian Economic and Sociological Trends: Implications for Counseling." *School Guidance Worker* 30 (Je, 1975):5-11.

Marshall, L. G. "The Development of Education in Northern Saskatchewan." Master's thesis, U. of Saskatchewan, 1966.

Marston, Wilfred G. "Social Class Segregation Within Ethnic Groups in Toronto." *Canadian Review of Sociology and Anthropology* 6 (1969):65-79.

Martell, George. "Community Control of the Schools: In New York and Toronto." *This Magazine is About Schools* 4(Summer, 1970).

Martin, Wilfred B. W. "Neglected Aspects in the Sociology of Education in Canada." *Canadian Journal of Education* 3, No. 4 (1978):15-30.

Martin, Wilfred B. W., and Macdonnel, Allan J. *Canadian Education: A Sociological Analysis.* Toronto: Prentice-Hall, 1978.

Mason, G. A. "Ability Grouping: An Ethnographic Study of a Structural Feature of Schools." *Australian and New Zealand Journal of Sociology* 10(F, 1974):53-56.

Means, John E. "Human Rights and Canadian Federalism." *Phylon*, Winter, 1969.

Medd, G., Hayball, H., and Dilling, H. J. *A Description of Foreign Born Students in One Scarborough Collegiate.* Scarborough: Board of Education for the Borough of Scarborough, 1972.

Migus, Paul M. (ed.). *Sounds Canadian: Languages and Cultures in Multi-Ethnic Society.* Toronto: P. Martin Associates, 1975.

Mordan, John, and Arthurs, Harry. "Racial Discrimination: A Legal Problem." *Obiter Dicta* (1960):30.

Morton, W. L. "Manitoba Schools and Canadian Nationality 1890-1923." *Canadian Historical Association Report*, 1951:51-59.

Nash, Paul. "Quality and Equality in Canadian Education." *Comparative Education Review* 5(1961):118-129.

Neatby, Hilda. "Racism in the Old Province of Quebec." In *Racism in the Eighteenth Century.* Edited by Harold E. Pagliaro. Cleveland, Ohio: Press of Case Western Reserve U., 1973.

O'Bryan, K. S. and others. *Non-Official Languages: A Study in Canadian Multiculturalism.* Ottawa: Minister of Supply and Services, 1976.

"Official Languages in Canada: A Review of the Constitutional Issues." *University of New Brunswick Law Journal* 26(N, 1977):47-63.

Ogmundson, Rich. "Man-Elite Linkages and Class Issues in Canada." *Canadian Review of Sociology and Anthropology* 13(F, 1976).

Organization for Economic Cooperation and Development. *Educational Policy and Planning.* Canada. Parts I-VI, 1975. ERIC ED 125 133-138.

_____. *External Examiners' Report on Educational Policy in Canada.* Paris: OECD, 1975.

d'Oyley, Vincent. Canada's Visible Minorities: Selected Dimensions in their Education. Toronto: Ontario Institute for Studies in Education, 1977.

Palmer, Howard. "Canada: Multicultural or Bicultural?" Canadian Ethnic Studies 3 (Je, 1971):109-118.

_____. "History and Present State of Ethnic Studies in Canada." Immigration History Newsletter 6(My, 1974):1-9.

_____. Land of the Second Chance. 1972 The Lethbridge Herald, P. O. Box 670, Lethbridge, Alberta T1J 3Z7, Canada. [Minorities in southern Alberta]

_____. "Mosaic versus Melting Pot? Immigration and Ethnicity in Canada and the U.S." International Journal 31(Summer, 1976): 488-528.

Palmer, Howard, and Troper, Harold. "Canadian Ethnic Studies: Historical Perspectives and Contemporary Implications." Interchange 4(1973):15-23.

Paton, L., and Deverell, J. (eds.). Prejudice in Social Studies Textbooks: A Content Analysis of Social Studies Textbooks Used in Saskatchewan Schools. Saskatoon: Saskatchewan Human Rights Commission, 1974.

Payne, Geoffrey. "Some Problems of Academic Success for Working Class Students in a Public School." Master's thesis, McMaster U., 1968.

Pike, Robert M. Who Doesn't Get to University- and Why: A Study on Accessibility to Higher Education in Canada. Ottawa, Canada: Association of Universities and Colleges of Canada, 1970.

Pineo, Peter C. "The Social Standing of Ethnic and Racial Groupings." Canadian Review of Sociology and Anthropology 14 (1977).

Pitman, Walter. Now Is Not Too Late. Toronto: Task Force on Human Relations, Council of Metropolitan Toronto, N, 1977.

Podmore, C. J. "Private Schooling in English Canada." Doctoral dissertation, McMaster U., 1976.

Porter, John. "The Democratization of the Canadian Universities and the Need for a National System." Minerva 8(J1, 1970).

_____. "Ethnic Pluralism in Canada Perspective." In Ethnicity: Theory and Experience." Edited by Nathan Glazer and Daniel P. Moynihan. Cambridge, MA: Harvard U. Press, 1975.

_____. "Educational and Occupational Opportunity in the Canadian Mosaic." Canadian Counsellor 8(Ap, 1974):90-105.

_____. "Equality and Education: Part II." Integrateducation 13(S-O, 1975):41-43.

_____. "Social Change and the Aims and Problems of Education in Canada." McGill Journal of Education, Fall, 1966.

_____. "Social Class and Educational Opportunity." The Vertical Mosaic. An Analysis of Social Class and Power in Canada. Toronto: U. of Toronto Press, 1965.

Porter, Marion R., Porter, John, and Blishen, Bernard R. Does Money Matter? Prospects for Higher Education. Toronto, Canada: Institute for Behavioural Research, 1973.

Powers, Mary G. "Socioeconomic Heterogeneity of Urban Residential Areas." Canadian Review of Sociology and Anthropology. Ag, 1964.

Prentice, Alison. The School Promoters: Education and Social Class in Mid-Nineteenth Century Upper Canada. Toronto: McClelland and Stewart, 1977.

Proceedings of a Symposium on the Educational Process and Social Change in a Specialized Environmental Milieu, 1968. ERIC ED 035 502.

Raby, S., and Richards T. Residential Areas in Regina and Saskatoon. In Atlas of Saskatchewan. Edited by J. H. Richards and K. J. Fung. Saskatoon: U. of Saskatchewan, 1969.

Raitz, Karl B. "Ethnic Maps of North America." Geographical Review 68(1978):335-350.

Ramsey, C. A., and Ramsey, E. N. Language Backgrounds and Achievements in Toronto Schools. Toronto, Canada: Research Department, Board of Education, 1970.

Rea, K. J. "Public Investment in Educational, Health, and Public Welfare Facilities in the North." The Political Economy of the Canadian North. Toronto: U. of Toronto Press, 1968.

Richmond, Anthony H. Ethnic Residential Segregation in Metropolitan Toronto. Toronto: Ethnic Research Programme, Institute for Behavioural Research, York U., F, 1972.

_____. "Immigration and Cultural Pluralism in Canada." International Migration Review, 4 1969.

_____. Immigrants and Ethnic Groups in Metropolitan Toronto. Toronto: Institute for Behavioral Research, York U., 1967.

Robbins, J. E. "The Home and Family Background of Ottawa Public School Children in Relation to their IQ's." Canadian Journal of Psychology 2(1948):35-41.

Ryan, Thomas J. "Poverty and Early Education in Canada." Interchange 2(1971):1-11.

_____ (ed.). Poverty and the Child: A Canadian Study. Toronto, Canada: McGraw-Hill Ryerson, 1972.

Sabey, Ralph H. "The Preparation of Culturally Sensitive Curriculum Material for Canadian Schools: An Overview." Council on Anthropology and Education Newsletter 4(N, 1973).

Saruk, Alec, and Gulutsan, Metro. "Academic Performance of Students and the Cultural Orientation of their Parents." Alberta Journal of Educational Research 16(S, 1970): 189-195.

Sealy, D. Bruce. "Race, Culture and Education." Manitoba Journal of Education 10 (1975):3-10.

Seastone, Donald. Economic and Demographic Futures in Education in Alberta. Edmonton, Alberta: Human Resources Research Council, 1971.

Semas, Philip W. "It's Business As Usual—Almost—for the Province of Quebec's English-Language Universities." Chronicle of Higher Education, S 12, 1977.

Smith, Allan. "The Myth of the Self-Made Man in English Canada, 1850-1914." Canadian Historical Review 59(Je, 1978):189-219.

Smollett, Eleanor. "Differential Enculturation and Social Class in Canadian Schools." In Socialization and Communication in Primary Groups. Edited by Thomas R. Williams. Chicago, IL: Aldine, 1975.

Social Development in Rural Manitoba. Winnipeg, Canada: Manitoba Cabinet Secretariat, D 15, 1971. ERIC ED 049 873.

Spinks, Sarah. "Notes on McGill and Sir George [Williams University]." This Magazine is About Schools, Spring, 1969.

Stevenson, Hugh A., and Wilson, J. Donald (eds.). Precepts, Policy and Process: Perspectives on Contemporary Canadian Education. London, Ontario: Alexander, Blake, 1977.

Stibble, Hugo L. P. "The Distribution of Ethnic Groups in Alberta, Canada, According to the 1961 Census." Master's thesis, U. of Alberta, 1967.

Strayer, B. L. "Blitner v. Regina Public School Board and the Constitutional Right to Segregate." Saskatchewan Bar Review 31 (1966):225.

Sutherland, J. Neil. Children in English Canadian Society: 1880-1920. Toronto: U. of Toronto Press, 1976.

Swain, Merrill. "Bilingualism: Some Non-Political Issues." Multiculturalism 1 (1977):13-16.

_____ (ed.). Yearbook: Bilingualism in Canadian Education: Issues and Research. Vol. III. Edmonton, Alberta, Canada: Western Industrial Research Centre, 1976.

Swain, Merrill, and Barik, H. C. "The Role of Curricular Approach, Rural-Urban Background and Socioeconomic Status in Second Language Learning: The Cornwall Area Study." Alberta Journal of Educational Research 24 (Mr, 1978):1-16. [Kindergarten children in bilingual program]

Tarnopolsky, W. S. "Le controle de la discrimination raciale au Canada." Les Cahiers de Droit 18(D, 1977):663-689.

Taylor, Lorne J., and Skanes, Graham R. "Big Bird Flies to Labrador." Integrateducation 15(S-O, 1977).

Thomas, Barbara. "Lost in the Jungles of Multi-Culturalism: Immigrant Children and Canadian Schools: A Review." This Magazine 10(F-Mr, 1976):8-10.

Trent, Faith Helen Elly. Cultural Differences in Spatial Perception of the Environment among Children 10-17 Years Old in the Whitehorse Area, D, 1971. ERIC ED 063 998.

Troper, Harold Martin. "Alternative Approaches for the Education of Minorities in Canada." Manitoba Journal of Education 10(1975):14-17.

Troper, Harold Martin, and Palmer, L. (eds.). Issues in Cultural Diversity. Toronto: OISE, 1976.

UNESCO. Ethnicity and the Media: An Analysis of Media Reporting in the United Kingdom, Canada, and Ireland. Paris: UNESCO, 1978.

Vallee, Brian. "Immigrant Pupils Straining Schools." Toronto Daily Star, Je 14, 1976. [Toronto metropolitan area]

Vallee, Frank G., Schwartz, Mildred, and Darkwell, Frank. "Ethnic Assimilation & Differentiation in Canada." Canadian Journal of Economics and Political Science 23 (1957):540-549.

Vincent. C. Spatial Variations of Educational Opportunity in the Publicly Supported High Schools of Ontario, Ap 1, 1969. Available on Interlibrary loan from the U. of Waterloo, Ontario, Canada. ERIC ED 040 811.

Walhouse, Freda. "The Influence of Minority Ethnic Groups on the Cultural Geography of Vancouver." Master's thesis, U. of British Columbia, 1961.

Wassef, Nadia. "The Egyptians in Montreal: A New Colour in the Canadian Ethnic Mosaic." Master's thesis, McGill U., 1978.

Webb, B. M. "Canada's Sub-Literate Adults: Can They, or Should They, REturn to School." Continuous Learning 9(1970):5-16.

Weiermair, Klaus. "The Economic Effects of Language Training to Immigrants: A Case Study." International Migration Review 10(Summer, 1976):205-219. [Toronto]

Wolfgang, A. Education of Immigrant Students: Issues and Answers. Toronto: Ontario Institute for Studies in Education, 1975.

Wright, E. N., and Ramsey, C. A. Students of Non-Canadian Origin: Age on Arrival, Academic Achievement and Ability. Toronto, Canada: Research Department, Board of Education, 1970.

York Borough Board of Education, Toronto. A Draft Report of the Work Group on Multiculturalism, Ja 31, 1977. ERIC ED 146 060.

Young, Bert. "Canadian Society: Social Justice or Social Control?" Our Generation 11(Winter, 1976).

Chad

Amady, Nathe. "La condition de l'enfant au Tchad." R. jur. pol. 31(Ap-Je, 1977):427-442.

Chile

Bucknam, Ronald Bruce. "Equality of Educational Opportunity in the Chilean Middle School: A Study of Participation and Representation." Doctoral dissertation, Syracuse U., 1971. Univ. Microfilm Order No. 72-11,827.

Caniuqueo, Antonio Millape. "Chilean War Games." Akwesasne Notes 6(Early Spring, 1974):30-31. [By the president of the National Mapuche Confederation]

Ellis, Herbert Lee. "The Indian Policy of the Republic of Chile." Doctoral dissertation, Columbia U., 1956. Univ. Microfilm Order No. 16,278.

Farrell, J. P. and Schiefelbein, E. "Expanding the Scope of Educational Planning: The Experience of Chile." Interchange 5(1974): 18-30.

Hakim, Peter, and Solimano, Giorgia. Development, Reform, and Malnutrition in Chile. Cambridge, MA: MIT Press, 1978.

"Mapuches Continue Their Struggle." Akwesasne Notes 7(Early Winter, 1975):38-39. [Chile]

Raczynski, Dagmar. "Oportunidades ocupacionales: Origen socio-economico versus educacion en Chile." Revista Latinoamericana de Sociologia 1(1974):18-22.

Sankueza A., Guillermo. "La Educacion y la Oferta de Mano de Obra en Chile." Revista del Centro de Estudios Educativos 4(1974): 31-41.

Sater, William F. "The Black Experience in Chile." In Slavery and Race Relations in Latin America. Edited by Robert B. Toplin. Westport, CT: Greenwood Press, 1974:13-50.

Schiefelbein, Ernesto, and Farrell, Joseph P. "Social and Pedagogical Factors Influencing Survival in the Schools of Chile." Canadian and International Education 7(Je, 1978):59-87.

Selowsky, Marcelo, and Taylor, Lance. "The Economics of Malnourished Children: An Example of Disinvestment in Human Capital." Economic Development and Cultural Change 22(O, 1973):17-30. [Santiago]

Silvert, Kalman H., and Reissman, Leonard. Education, Class and Nation: The Experiences of Chile and Venezuela. N.p: Elsevier, 1978.

"Testimony of a Chilean Woman Who Left Chile September 29, 1973." Akwesasne Notes 6 (Early Spring, 1974):31. [Conditions of the Mapuche people in the zone of Cantin]

UNESCO. Race and Class in Post-Colonial Society: A Study of Ethnic Group Relations in the English-speaking Caribbean, Bolivia, Chile and Mexico. Paris: UNESCO, 1977.

Young, George F. W. The Germans in Chile. Immigration and Colonization (1849-1914). New York: Center for Migration Studies, 1974.

China

National Minorities

"A College to Train National Minority Cadres."
China Reconstructs 22(D, 1973):23-25, 48.
[Central Institute of Nationalities, Peking]

"A National Minority County." *Peking Review* 20
(D 2, 1977):31-32. [Yuku people in
southern Kansu Province, northwest China]

Beauclair, Inez de. "Culture Traits of Non-
Chinese Tribes in Kweichow Province,
Southwest China." *Sinologica* 5(1958):20-35.

_____. "Present Day Conditions Among the
Aborigines of Formosa (Stayal and Brunun)."
Sociologus 6(1956):153-169.

Birnbaum, Norman. "Communist China's Policy
Toward Her Minority Nationalities: 1950-
1965." Doctoral dissertation, St. John's
U., 1970. Univ. Microfilms Order No. 70-
25,590.

Bogoslovskij, V. A. *Essai sur l'histoire du
peuple tibétain: ou la naissance d'une
société de classes.* Paris: Librarie C.
Klincksieck, 1972.

Brennan, Walter J., Jr. "The Chinese Communist
Party Model for Culture Change Among Its
Ethnic Minority Groups: The Case of the
Pastoralists." Master's thesis, U. of
California, Los Angeles, 1973.

Brod, Raymond M. "Second Order Boundaries and
Political Stability in the Sinkiang Uighur
Autonomous Region, People's Republic of
China." *Geographical Survey, Blue Earth
County Geographical Society* 4(1975):83-100.

Broder, David B. "Tibet Under Peking's Control." *Washington Post*, O 20, 1977.

Burchett, Wilfred, with Alley, Rewi. "Minorities Stand Up." *China: The Quality of
Life.* Baltimore: Penguin, 1976, pp. 264-
281.

Burns, John. "China Strives to Integrate Her
Minorities." *New York Times*, Jl 31, 1972.

Carthew, M. "The History of the Thai in
Yunnan: 2205 BC-1253 AD." *Journal of the
Siam Society* 40(1952):1-38.

[Central Intelligence Agency] "Ethnolinguistic
Groups in China." *Integrateducation* 12
(N-D, 1974):22-23.

"Chairman Mao Led Us to a Bright Future."
Peking Review 20(N 25, 1977):19-21.
[Tibet]

"Chairman Mao's Nationality Policy Guies Us
Forward." *Peking Review*, Je 3, 1977.

Chang, Chi Jen. "The Minority Groups of
Yunnan and Chinese Political Expansion into
Southeast Asia." Doctoral dissertation, U.
of Michigan, 1956.

Chang, Ching-Wu. "The Victory of Democratic
Reform in Tibet." *Peking Review*, Mr 29,
1960.

Chaudhuri, Sibadas (comp.). *Bibliography of
Tibetan Studies Being a Record of Printed
Publications Mainly in European Languages.*
Calcutta: The Asiatic Society, 1971.

Chien, Po-tsan. *A Compendium of the History of
All Nationalities in Successive Dynasties.*
(in Chinese) Peking: N.p., 1958.

Chin, Chen-wu. *Education of the Nationalities
in Lungsheng Autonomous Hsien.* Joint
Publications Research Service. *IPRS Reports* 15540(O 2, 1962).

China's Minority Nationalities. Selected
Articles from Chinese Sources. San Francisco: Red Sun Publishers, 1977.

Chinese Nationalities. Hong Kong: Chien Chu
Publishing Co., 1972.

Ching-hsin, Jung. "Minority Nationals Study
Medicine." *China Pictorial*, F, 1955.

Chou K' un-t'ien. *A Short History of Chinese
Border Nationalities.* (in Chinese) Taipei:
N.p., 1962.

Chu Wen-djang. *The Moslem Rebellion in
Northwestern China, 1862-1878.* The Hague:
Mouton, 1966.

Chung, In Teak. "The Korean Minority in
Manchuria (1900-1937)." Doctoral disserta-
tion, American U., 1966. Univ. Microfilm
Order No. 66-13,586.

Clarke, Samuel R. *Among the Tribes in South-
West China.* London: Morgan & Scott, 1911.

Cohen, Myron. "The Hakka or Guest People:
Dialect as a Sociocultural Variable in
Southeastern China." *Ethnohistory* 15(1968):
237-292.

Cony, Ed, and Kann, Peter R. "Sinkiang Area
Differs in Culture, Traditions from Rest
of Country." *Wall Street Journal*, N 3, 1977.

Cordier, Henri. "Islam in China." *Brunei
Museum Journal* 4(1977):97-111.

Cushman, Richard. "Rebel Haunts and Lotus
Huts: Problems in the Ethnohistory of the
Yao." Doctoral dissertation, Cornell U.,
1970. [Kwangsi Province]

Davis, Horace B. "Nationalism and the Chinese Revolution." Toward a Marxist Theory of Nationalism. New York: Monthly Review Press, 1978, pp. 165-181.

Deal, David Michael. "National Minority Policy in Southwest China, 1911-1965." Doctoral dissertation, U. of Washington, 1971.

Deshpande, G. P. "Towards Integration: Tibet Since the Revolt." International Studies [New Delhi] Ap, 1969.

Diao, Richard. "The National Minorities of China and their Relation with the Chinese Communist Regime." In Southeast Asian Tribes, Minorites, and Nations. Edited by Peter Kunstadter. Princeton: Princeton U. Press, 1967.

Dolfin, John III. "The Process of Reincorporation and Integration in the Tibetan Nationality Areas of China, 1950-1955." Master's thesis, Columbia U., 1969.

Dreyer, June T. China's Forty Millions: Minority Nationalities and National Integration in the People's Republic of China. Cambridge: Harvard U. Press, 1976.

_____. "China's Minority Nationalities: Traditional and Party Elites." Pacific Affairs 43(1970-1971):506-530.

_____. "Go West Young Han: The Hsia Fang Movement to China's Minority Areas." Pacific Affairs 48(Fall, 1975):353-369.

Eberhard, Wolfram. Kultur und Siedlung der Randvolker Chinas. Leiden: E. J. Brill, 1942.

Ekvall, Robert. Cultural Relations on the Kansu-Tibetan Border. Chicago: U. of Chicago Press, 1939.

Ferguson, Charles A. "Applied Linguistics in China." Linguistic Reporter 17(Ap, 1975). [Includes teaching of minority languages]

"First Medical College in Tibet." Peking Review, Ag 4, 1978.

Forman, Harrison. "China's Moslems." Canadian Geographic Journal 27(S, 1948): 134-143.

Freeberne, Michael. "Changing Population Characteristics in Tibet, 1959 to 1965." Population Studies 19(Mr, 1966):317-320.

_____. "Demographic and Economic Changes in the Sinkiang Uighur Autonomous Region." Population Studies 20(Jl, 1966):103-124.

Gjessing, Guttorm. "Chinese Anthropology and New China's Policy Towards Her Minorities." Acta Sociologica 2(1957):45-68.

Goldstein, Melvyn C. "Serfdom and Mobility: An Examination of the Institution of 'Human Lease' in Traditional Tibetan Society." Journal of Asian Studies 30(My, 1971).

Goldwasser, Janet, and Dowty, Stuart. "National Minorities: Equality, Autonomy, and Unity." In Huang-Ying: Workers' China. New York: Monthly Review Press, 1975.

Great Changes in Tibet. Peking: Foreign Languages Press, 1973.

Grunfeld, Tom. "Tibet: Myths and Realities." New China 1(Fall, 1975):17-20.

Han-seng, Chen. "Sibang: Serfdom to Freedom." China Reconstructs, S-O, 1954.

Hasiotis, Arthur C., Jr. "A Comparative Study of the Political and Economic Policies Pursued by the USSR and Communist China in their Attempt to Consolidate their Respective Positions Within Russian Central Asia (1917-1934) and Sinkiang (1949-late 1957)." Master's thesis, Columbia U., 1968. [USSR]

Hayit, Baymirza. Turkestan zwischen Russland und China. Amsterdam: Philo Press, 1971.

Heaton, William. "Inner Mongolia: Aftermath of the Revolution." Current Scene 9(Ap, 1971):6-16.

Heaton, William R., Jr. "The Minorities and the Military in China." Armed Forces and Society 3(Winter, 1977):325-346.

Heckel, Benno. "The Yao Tribe: Their Culture and Education." University of London Institute of Education Studies and Report 4(1935):9-53.

Henderson, Gay (comp.). Traditional Tibet. A Selected and Annotated Bibliography of European Language Materials on the Pre-Communist Period. New York: Garland, 1977.

Hsi Chang-hao, and Kao Yuan-mei. Tibet Leaps Forward. Peking: Foreign Languages Press, 1977.

Hsiao-pang, Wu. "Songs and Dances of National Minorities in Southwest China." China Pictorial, Jl, 1954.

Hsiao-tung, Fei. "China's Multi-National Family." China Reconstructs 3(1952).

Hsieh, Pei-chih. "Changes and Continuity in Southwestern Yunnan: The Xishuangbanna Tai Autonomous Prefecture." Bulletin of Concerned Asian Scholars 10(Jl-S, 1978).

Hsin Hua-li. "Big Increase in Tibetan Population." Peking Review 21(Jl 7, 1978):36-37.

Hu, C. T. The Education of National Minorities in Communist China. Washington, DC: GPO, 1970.

Hung-mao Tien. "Sinicization of National Minorities in China." Current Scene (N, 1974):1-14.

"Interview With Artists of the Tibetan Song and Dance Troupe." Peking Review 21(Ag 18, 1978):20-24.

Jacob, Alain. "Ethnic Diversity in Southern China: Cultural Rape or Cultural Revolution?" Guardian, Ag 15, 1976.

Jordan, David K. "Language Choice and Interethnic Relations in Taiwan." Monda Lingvo-Problemo 5(1973):35-44.

Kao Yun, and Hsiang Jung. "Driving Back the Deserts." Peking Review 20(O 28, 1977): 14-18.

_____. "Mongolian Population: From Sharp Decline to Steady Increase." Peking Review 20(N 18, 1977):14-18.

Karan, Pradyumma, P. The Changing Face of Tibet. Lexington: The U. Press of Kentucky, 1976.

Kolmas, Josef. "The Minority Nationalities." In Contemporary China. Edited by Ruth Adams. New York: Vantage Books, 1968.

Kotov, K. F. Autonomy of Local Nationalites in the Chinese People's Republic. New York: Joint Publications Research Service, 1960.

Krader, Ruth S. "Ch'ih-ya. An Account of Non-Chinese Peoples of Southern China." Doctoral dissertation, Yale U., 1946.

"Kwangai County Trains Minority Teachers in Rural Areas." Daily Report 1(N 3, 1971).

Lal, Awrit. "Sinification of Ethnic Minorities in China." Current Scene 8(F 15, 1970):1-25.

Lattimore, Owen. "The Historical Setting of Inner Mongolian Nationalism." Pacific Affairs 18(Fall, 1936):388-408.

Lee, Fu-hsiang. "The Turkic-Moslem Problem in Sinkiang: A Case Study of the Chinese Communists' Nationality Policy." Doctoral dissertation, Putgers U., 1973. Univ. Microfilm Order No. 74-8801.

"Literacy Histories of National Minorities." Peking Review, Je 23, 1961.

Liu L'-t'ang. A History of the Border Peoples of China (in Chinese). Taipei: N.p., 1969.

Llata, Richard, and Barrera, Mario. "The Chinese National Minorities Policy." Aztlan 6(Fall, 1975):379-408.

Loh, Pichon P. Y. "The Institute of Modern History, Peita, and the Central Institute of Nationalities." China Quarterly 70 (Je, 1977):383-389.

Lu Chen-yu. A Short History of China's Nationalities (in Chinese). Shanghai: N.p., 1950.

Lu Ting-Yi. "Cultural Revolution of China's National Minorities." Peking Review, D 4, 1964.

Lum, John B. "Bilingual Policies in the Peoples Republic of China." Studies in Comparative International Development 11 (Spring, 1976).

Ma Hsueh-Liang. "Minority Languages of China." China Reconstructs 3(My-Je, 1954): 37-41.

"Mao Tsetung Thought Guides the Revolution in Tibet." Peking Review 20(N 25, 1977)·14-19.

Maxwell, Neville. "Monks, Who Dominated Tibetan Society, Vanishing Under Communist Rule." New York Times, Ag 19, 1976.

_____. "Tibet Schools Stress Politics and Manual Labor." New York Times, Jl 11, 1976.

Ming, Yin. United and Equal. The Progress of China's Minority Nationalities. Peking: Foreign Languages Press, 1977.

"Minority Nationalities." Geography of China. Peking: Foreign Languages Press, 1972:14-21.

Morrock, Richard. "Minority Nationalities in China." Journal of Contemporary Asia Quarterly 2(1972):181-191.

Moseley, George VanHorn III. A Sino-Soviet Cultural Frontier: The Ili Kazakh Autonomous Chou. Cambridge, MA: Harvard U. Press, 1966.

_____. "China's Fresh Approach to the Minority Question." China Quarterly 24(O-D, 1965): 15-27.

_____. The Consolidation of the South China Frontier. Berkeley, CA: U. of California Press, 1973.

_____. "Policy Toward Ethnic Minorities on the Southern Frontier of the People's Republic of China." Doctoral dissertation, Oxford U., 1970.

_____ (ed.). The Party and the National Question in China. Cambridge, MA: MIT Press, 1966.

Nai-min, Liang (ed.). Tibet, 1950-1969. Hong Kong: Union Research Institute, 1968.

"National Minorities in China." Interracial Books for Children 5(1974):8.

"New Scheme for the Yi Written Language." Peking Review 20(Jl 1, 1977):31-32.

Norins, Martin. "The New Sinkiang: China's Link with the Middle East." Pacific Affairs 15(D, 1942):457-470.

Onon, Urgunge. My Childhood in Mongolia. New York: Oxford U. Press, 1973.

"Panchen Erdeni Interviewed." Peking Review 21(Mr 17, 1978):41-42.

Pasternak, Burton. "Continuity and Discontinuity in Chinese Policy toward the Southwestern Tribes Since 1911." Master's thesis, Columbia U., 1962.

Pillsbury, Barbara L. K. "Cohesion and Cleavage in a Chinese Muslim Minority." Doctoral dissertation, Columbia U., 1973. [Taipei, Taiwan]

Prybyla, J. S. "Hsia-fang: The Economics and Politics of Rustication in China." Pacific Affairs 48(Summer, 1975):153-172.

Pye, Lucien. "China: Ethnic Minorities and National Security." In Ethnicity. Edited by Nathan Glazer and Patrick Daniel Moynihan. Cambridge, MA: Harvard U. Press, 1975.

"Reminiscences of Premier Chou En-lai." Peking Review, Ap 1, 1977. [Touches on national minorities]

Robinson, Joan. "In the Deep Southwest. The Thai People of Yunnan Before and After Liberation." New China 1(Fall, 1975):21-23.

Rupen, Robert A. "Peking and National Minorities." In Communist China, 1949-1969. Edited by Frank N. Trager and William Henderson. New York: New York U. Press, n.d.

Sa Kung-Liao. "The Great Success of China's Policy for Nationalities." Peking Review, S 28, 1962.

Schwarz, Henry G. Chinese Policies Towards Minorities. An Essay and Documents. Bellingham, WN: Program in East Asian Studies, Western Washington State College, 1971.

_____. "The Treatment of Minorities." In Developmental Experience. Edited by Michael Oksenberg. New York: Praeger, 1973.

Shu, Li. "The Hiu Peoples' Academy." China Reconstructs, My, 1955.

"Sinkiang's Highways." Peking Review 21(Jl 14, 1978).

Snow, Sian. "Equal--But Not the Same. How Does the Revolution Affect Minority Cultures?" New China 1(Fall, 1975):12-17. [Inner Mongolia]

Solinger, Dorothy J. "Minority Nationalities in China's Yunnan Province: Assimilation, Power, and Policy in a Socialist State." World Pol. 2. 30(O, 1977):1-23.

_____. Regional Government and Political Integration. Southwest China, 1949-1954. Berkeley: U. of California Press, 1977.

Stein, R. A. Tibetan Civilization. Tr. by J. E. Stapleton Driver. Stanford: Stanford U. Press, 1972.

Stockwell, Rhoda. "National Minorities in China." Integrateducation 12(N-D, 1974): 20-21.

Stubel, Hans. "Die nichtchinesischen Völker Chinas." Sociologus 2(1952):84-117. [English summary, pp 115-117]

Tomson, Edgar (ed.). Dokumente: die Volksrepublik China und das Recht nationaler Minderheiten. Frankfurt: Alfred Metzner, 1963.

"30th Anniversary of the Inner Mongolian Autonomous Region." Peking Review 20(Ag 12, 1977): 33-35.

Tien, San-sung, and Kuo Pi-hung. "Minority Nationality Cadres Come of Age." Peking Review 19(D 10, 1976):19-22. [Sinkiang]

To, Cho-Yee. "Education of the Aborigines in Taiwan..." Journal of Negro Education 41(Summer, 1972):183-194.

Tsao Hsueh. "Ningsia Hui Autonomous Region: 20th Anniversary." Peking Review, D 29, 1978.

Tsing Yuan. "Yakub Beg (1820-1877) and the Moslem Rebellion in Chinese Turkestan." Central Asiatic Journal 6(1961):134-167.

"Unveiling the Mysteries of the 'Roof of the World.'" Peking Review, Jl 15, 1977. [Tibet]

"Volume V of 'Selected Works of Mao Tsetung' in Minority Languages Distributed." Peking Review, Jl 8, 1977. [Korean, Mongolian, Tibetan, Uighur, and Kazabh].

Walker, A. R. "The Laku of the Yunnan-Indochina Borderlands. Ethnic Group and Village Community." Doctoral dissertation, U. of Oxford, 1973.

Wang, Shu-tang. China: Land of Many Nationalities. Peking: Foreign Languages Press, 1955.

Wang, Wei-Hsun. "The Yis Leap from Slavery to Socialism." Peking Review, Ag 2, 1960. [Yi people in Szechuan]

Wei, Alice B. G. "The Moslem Rebellion in Yunnan, 1855-1873." Doctoral dissertation, U. of Chicago, 1974.

Wen-tsao, Wu. "Facts on National Minorities." China Reconstructs, Mr, 1955.

Xueliang, Ma. "The Relationship Between the Plan for the Phonetic Spelling of Chinese and National Minority Written Languages." Chinese Education 10(Fall-Winter, 1977-1978):149-155.

Yang, Chao. "Workers, Peasants and Soldiers of Tibet Go to College." Great Changes in Tibet. Peking: Foreign Languages Press, 1972:19-21.

Yu Tai-Chung. "The Party's Nationality Policy Shines Over Inner Mongolia." Peking Review 20(O 21, 1977):15-19.

General

Allen, Geoffrey. "Combining Manual and Mental Labour." Times Higher Education Supplement, Jl 27, 1973. [Higher education]

Alley, Rewi. Travels in China, 1966-1971. Peking: New World Press, 1973.

Appleton, Sheldon. "Taiwanese and Mainlanders on Taiwan: A Survey of Student Attitudes." China Quarterly, O-D, 1970.

Bady, Paul. "La revolution dans l'enseignement en Chine." Esprit 399(Ja, 1971):73-88.

Barendsen, Robert D. The Educational Revolution in China. Washington, DC: GPO, 1973.

Benn, Caroline. "'All Our Children Can Be Bright'" Part 1. Times Educational Supplement, N 5, 1971.

_____. "'All Who Wish May Come'" Times Educational Supplement, Part 2, N 12, 1971. [Secondary schools]

_____. "Children of Workers Come First." Times Educational Supplement, N 19, 1971. [Higher education]

Bonavia, David. "Workers Make Up Half of Wuta Students." Times Higher Education Supplement, F 23, 1973. [University of Wuhan]

Cary, William H., Jr. "'Criticism Made Us Professors Uncomfortable, But...'" Harvard Crimson, Ja 5, 1973. [Nanking U.]

Casella, Alexander. "Recent Developments in China's University Recruitman System." China Quarterly 62(Je, 1975).

Chen, I-te. "Japanese Colonialism in Korea and Formosa: A Comparison of Its Effects Upon the Development of Nationalism." Doctoral dissertation, U. of Pennsylvania, 1968.

Chen, Jack. A Year in Upper Felicity: Life in a Chinese Village During the Cultural Revolution. New York: Macmillan, 1973.

Chen, Theodore Hsi-en. "Education in Communist China." In Communist China, 1949-1969: A Twenty-Year Appraisal. Edited by Frank N. Trager and William Henderson. York U. Press, 1970.

"[College] Enrolment System. A Meaningful Discussion." Peking Review, Jl 28, 1978.

Collier, John, and Collier, Elsie. China's Socialist Revolution. London: Stage One, 1974. [1966-1968]

Culter, Maurice. "Impact of China's Cultural Revolution on University Elitism & the Masses." Canadian University and College 7 (Mr-Ap, 1972):29-30.

Eberstadt, Nick. "Women and Education in China: How Much Progress?" New York Review of Books, Ap 19, 1979.

Fenson, Melvin. "A Jew of Kaifeng Fu?" Jerusalem Post, F 20, 1979.

Fitzgerald, Stephen. "China and the Overseas Chinese: Perceptions and Policies." China Quarterly, O-D, 1970.

_____. China & the Overseas Chinese: A Study of Peking's Changing Policy, 1949-1970. London: Cambridge U. Press, 1972.

Fraser, Stewart E. (ed.). Education & Communism in China: An Anthology of Commentary and Documents. London: Pall Mall Press, 1971.

Fraser, Stewart E., and Hawkins, John N. "Chinese Education: Revolution & Development." Phi Delta Kappan 53(Ap, 1972):487-500.

_____. Glimpses of China: School and Society. Nashville, TN: Surora Publishers, 1972.

Frolic, B. Michael. "What the Cultural Revolution Was All About." New York Times Magazine, O 24, 1971. [Peking U.]

Galston, Arthur W. "The Chinese University." Natural History 81(Ag-S, 1972):18-23.

Galston, Arthur W., with Savage, Jean S. Daily Life in People's China. New York: Crowell, 1973.

Gardner, J. "Educated Youth and Urban-Rural Inequalities, 1958-1966." In The City in Communist China. Edited by J. W. Lewis. Stanford, CA: Stanford U. Press, 1971, pp. 235-286.

Going Back. Los Angeles, CA: Asian American Studies Center, U. of CA, Los Angeles, 1973. [Overseas Chinese Americans visit relatives in China.]

Hook, Brian. "China Revamps Its Education." New Society, Jl 1, 1971.

Howard, Roger. "'Bourgeois Staff' Under Attack." Times Educational Supplement, O 26, 1973. [Peking U.]

Hsu, Wen-hsiung. "Chinese Colonization of Taiwan." Doctoral dissertation, U. of Chicago, 1975.

Hu, C. T. "Education in China--Redness versus Expertness." Perspectives on Education 6 (Spring, 1973):20-29.

Hu, Shi Ming. Education in the People's Republic of China (Mainland) from 1949 to 1969. Occasional Paper 7, 1972. ERIC ED 063 212.

Hunter, Neale. "Chinese Education for Total Class Integration." New York University Education Quarterly 3(Spring, 1972):13-18.

Joly, Roxee W. "A First Look at Education, Schools in the People's Republic of China." NASSP Bulletin 57(D, 1973):66-85.

Kessen, William (ed.). Childhood in China. New Haven: Yale U. Press, 1975.

Kranzler, David H. "The History of the Jewish Refugee Community of Shanghai, 1938-1945." Doctoral dissertation, Yeshiva U., 1971.

_____. Japanese, Nazis and Jews: The Jewish Refugee Community of Shanghai, 1938-1945. New York: Yeshiva U. Press, 1976.

_____. "The Jewish Refugee Community of Shanghai, 1938-1945." Wiener Library Bulletin 2 (1972-1973):28-37.

Kublin, Hyman (ed.). Studies of the Chinese Jews. New York: Paragon, 1971.

Lamley, Harry Jerome. "The Taiwan Literati and Early Japanese Rule, 1895-1915: A Study of their Reactions to the Japanese Occupation and Subsequent Responses to Colonial Rule and Modernization." Doctoral dissertation, U. of Washington, 1964.

Lampton, David M. "Performance and the Chinese Political System: A Preliminary Assessment of Education and Health Policies." China Quarterly (S, 1978).

Mendel, Douglas. The Politics of Formosan Nationalism. Berkeley, CA: U. of California Press, 1970.

Mumo, Donald J. "The Malleability of Man in Chinese Marxism." China Quarterly 48 (O-D, 1971):609-640.

Nee, Victor, with Layman, Don. "The Cultural Revolution at Peking University." Monthly Review, Jl-Ag, 1969.

Needham, Joseph. "Skin-Color in Chinese Thought: An Extract from a letter to the Editor." Race, O, 1967.

Orleans, Leo A. Every Fifth Child. The Population of China. Stanford, CA: Stanford U. Press, 1972.

Penfield, Wilder. "Oriental Renaissance in Education and Medicine." Science 141(S 20, 1963):1153-1161.

Price, R. F. Education in Communist China. London: Routledge & Kegan Paul, 1970.

Printz, Peggy. "The Chen Family Still Has Class." New York Times Magazine, O 14, 1973.

Rawski, Evelyn S. Education and Popular Literacy in Ch'ing China. Ann Arbor: U. of Michigan Press, 1979.

Reid, Jean. "'Friendship First, Competition Second.'" Times Educational Supplement, Ja 4, 1974.

Saloff, Janet. "Youth, Family, and Political Power in Communist China." Doctoral dissertation, U. of CA, Berkeley, 1972.

Salo, Matt T., and Sheila, M. G. The Kalderas in Eastern Canada. Ottawa: National Museum of Man, 1977. [Gypsies]

Schram, Stuart R. (ed.). Authority, Participation and Cultural Change in China. New York: Cambridge U. Press, 1973.

Seyboldt, Peter J. (ed.). Revolutionary Education in China: Documents and Commentary. White Plains, NY: International Arts and Sciences Press, 1973.

_____. "The Yenan Revolution in Mass Education." China Quarterly 48(O-D, 1971):641-669.

Shanghai Revolutionary Mass Criticism Writing Group. "Who Transforms Whom? A Comment on Kairov's Pedagogy." Peking Review, Mr 6, 1970.

Shirk, Susan. "The 1963 Temporary Work Regulations for Full-Time Middle & Primary Schools: Commentary and Translation." China Quarterly 55(Jl-S, 1973).

Sidel, Ruth. Women and Child Care in China: A Firsthand Report. New York: Hill & Wang, 1972.

Snow, Lois Wheeler. "Education in China After the Cultural Revolution." National Elementary Principal 52(Ja, 1972):6-14.

Stein, Annie. "Middle School No. 26, Peking, China." Integrated Education 11(Mr-Ap, 1973):15-21.

Strive to Build a Socialist University of Science and Engineering. Peking: Foreign Languages Press, 1972.

"Student Admission Policies and Procedures: Insist on the Unity of Politics and Vocational Work, Comprehensively Group Conditions for Enrollment." Chinese Education 6 (Summer, 1973):6-11.

Taylor, Robert I. D. "Policies Governing University Enrolment in the People's Republic of China since 1949." Doctoral dissertation, U. of London, 1974.

Teng, S. Y. "The Predispositions of Westerners in Treating Chinese History and Civilization." Historian 19(1957).

Tien, H. Yuan. China's Population Struggle: Demographic Decisions of the People's Republic, 1949-1969. Columbus, OH: Ohio State U. Press, 1973.

Tokayer, Marvin, and Swartz, Mary. The Fugu Plan: The Untold Story of the Japanese and the Jews in World War II. New York: Paddington Press, 1979. [Shanghai]

Tsang, Chiu-Sam. Society, Schools and Progress in China. London: Pergamon, 1973.

Tsurumi, Elizabeth Patricia. "Attempting to Create a Colonial Mentality: Japanese Elementary Education in Taiwan, 1895-1945." Canadian and International Education 5(Je, 1976):29-45.

_____. Japanese Colonial Education in Taiwan, 1895-1945. Cambridge, MA: Harvard U. Press, 1977.

_____. "Japanese Colonial Education in Taiwan, 1895-1945." Doctoral dissertation, Harvard U., 1971.

Whitehead, Rhea Menzel. "How the Young Are Taught in Mao's China." Saturday Review 55 (Mr 4, 1972).

Whyte, Martin King. "Educational Reform: China in the 1970's and Russia in the 1920's." Comparative Education Review 18 (F, 1974):112-128.

_____. "Inequality and Stratification in China." China Quarterly 64(D, 1975): 684-711.

Yang, Pen-hua Lee, and Yang, Kuo-shu. "National-Ethnic Stereotypes of 240 Chinese Students at the National Taiwan University." Acta Psychologica Taiwanica 12 (Mr, 1970):7-23.

Yee, Albert H. "China Revisited." International Educational and Cultural Exchange 9(Summer, 1973):1-18.

_____. "Schools and Progress in the People's Republic of China." Educational Researcher 2(Jl, 1973):5-15.

Yee, Albert H., and Croft, Doreen. "Education in the Land of Mao." Learning 2(N, 1973): 22-27.

Yen, Chu. "Why the University Enrolling System Should be Reformed" (Part 1). Peking Review 16(S 21, 1973):19-21.

Young, Marilyn B. (ed.). Women in China. Studies in Social Change and Feminism. Ann Arbor, MI: Center for Chinese Studies, U. of Michigan, 1973.

Colombia

Arboleda, José Rafaél. "La Historia y la antropología del Negro en Colombia." Universidad 41(Ap-Je, 1964):233-248.

Arcand, Bernard. The Urgent Situation of the Cuivá Indians of Colombia. Copenhagen, Denmark: International Work Group for Indigenous Affairs, 1972.

Bonilla, Victor Daniel. Servants of God or Masters of Men? The Story of a Capuchin Mission in Amazonia. Tr. by Rosemary Sheed. Baltimore, MD: Penguin, 1972.

Community Systems Foundation. Community Experiments in the Reducation of Malnourishment in Colombia; First Year Progress Report, June 30, 1974-June 30, 1975. Ann Arbor, MI: Community Systems Foundation, 1975.

Escalante, Aquíles. El Negro en Colombia. Bogota, Colombia: Universidad Nacional de Colombia, 1964.

Havens, Eugene, and Flinn, William (eds.). Internal Colonialism and Structural Change in Colombia. New York: Praeger, 1970.

Helguera, J. León. Indigenismo in Colombia: A Facet of the National Identity Search, 1821-1973. Buffalo, NY: Council on International Studies, State U. of New York at Buffalo, 1974.

Mina, Mateo (pseud. for M. Taussig and A. Rubbo). Esclavitud y Libertad en el Valle de Rio Cauca. Bogotá, Colombia: La Rosca, 1975.

Pavy, Paul David III. "The Negro in Western Colombia." Doctoral dissertation, Tulane U., 1967. Univ. Microfilms Order No. 67-17,936.

Renner, Richard R. Education for a New Colombia. Washington, DC: GPO, 1971.

Rocca, Marie L. "The Negro in Colombia: An Historical Geography." In Columbia Essays in International Affairs, Vol. 7, The Dean's Papers, 1971. Edited by Andrew W. Cordier. New York: Columbia U. Press, 1972.

Sharp, William F. "Manumission Libres, and Black Resistance: The Colombian Choco 1680-1810." In Slavery and Race Relations in Latin America, pp. 89-111. Edited by Robert B. Toplin. Westport, CT: Greenwood Press, 1974.

Smith, John Kenneth. "Jewish Education in Colombia: Group Survival versus Assimilation." Doctoral dissertation, U. of Wisconsin, 1972. Univ. Microfilms Order No. 72-19,005.

Taussig, Michael. "Rural Proletarianization: A Social and Historical Enquiry into the Commercialization of the Southern Canca Valley, Colombia." Doctoral dissertation, U. of London, 1974.

Urrutia, M. "Income Distribution in Colombia." Internation Labour Review 113(Mr-Ap, 1976).

Walter, John P. Deprived Urban Youth: An Economic and Cross-Cultural Analysis of the United States, Colombia, and Peru. New York: Praeger, 1975.

Zschock, Dieter K. "Inequality in Colombia." Current History 72(F, 1977):68-72.

Congo

Georis, Pol, and Agbiano, Baudouin. Evolution de l'enseignement en République Démocratique due Congo depuis l'Indépendence. Brussels: CEMUBAC, 1965.

Costa Rica

"A Forgotten People--The Indians of Costa Rica." Indigena, Summer, 1977.

Aguilar Bulgarelli, Oscar R. "La esclavitud en Costa Rica durante el período colonial. (Hipótesis de trabajo)." Estudios Sociales Centroamericanos 2(1973):187-199.

Koch, C. W. "Jamaican Blacks and their Descendants in Costa Rica." Social and Economic Studies 26(S, 1977).

Meléndez, Carlos, and Duncan, Quince (eds.). El Negro en Costa Rica. San Jose: Editorial Costa Rica, 1972.

Olien, Michael David. "The Negro in Costa Rica: The Ethnohistory of an Ethnic Minority in a Complex Society." Doctoral dissertation, U. of Oregon, 1967. Univ. Microfilms Order No. 68-10,011.

Wignal, Guillermo Joseph. "Black Liberation Struggle in Costa Rica." Militant, O 14, 1977. Interview

Cuba

"A Black Expatriate in Cuba." Black Scholar 4 (F, 1973):49-55.

Aguirre, Bergio. "De nacionalidad a nación en Cuba." Universidad de La Habana, Nos. 196-197 (1972):30-60.

Aguirre, Benigno E. "Differential Migration of Cuban Social Races: A Review and Interpretation of the Problem." Latin American Research Review 11(1976):103-124. [Emigration from Cuba]

Aimes, Hubert H. S. A History of Slavery in Cuba, 1511-1868. New York: Octagon, 1967, reprint (orig. 1907).

Allen, Garland E. "Education in Revolutionary Cuba." American Biology Teacher 36(My, 1974): 267-274.

Amaro, Nelson, and Mesa-Lago, Carmelo. "Inequality and Classes." In Revolutionary Change in Cuba, pp. 347-353. Edited by C. Mesa-Lago. Pittsburgh: n.p., 1971.

Arrendondo, Alberto. El Negro en Cuba. Havana: Editorial "Alfa," 1939.

Barreda, Pedro. "La caracterizacion del protagonista negro en la novela cubana." Doctoral dissertation, State U. of New York,

Bergman, Arlene Eisen. "Red and Black in Cuba." The Movement, Ja, 1969. [The racial factor in Cuban life]

Booth, David. "Cuba, Color and the Revolution." Science and Society 40(Summer, 1976):129-172.

Bowles, Samuel. "Cuban Education and the Revolutionary Ideology." Harvard Educational Review 41(N, 1971):472-500.

Carneado, J. F. "La discriminación racial en Cuba no volverá jamás." Cuba Socialista 2 (Ja, 1963):54-56.

Carneado, Jose F. "La discriminación racial en Cuba no volverá." Cuba Socialista 2(Ja, 1962):54-67.

Chadwick, Lee. Cuba Today. New York: Lawrence Hill, 1976.

_____. "Cuba: Schooling the Whole Man." Times Educational Supplement, Ag 18, 1972.

Chaka, Malik. "Lessons from Cuba for African Revolution." African World, S 16, 1972.

Chrisman, Robert, and Allen, Robert L. "The Cuban Revolution: Lessons for the Third World." Black Scholar 4(F, 1973):2-14.

Clytus, John. Black Man in Cuba. Coral Gables, FL: U. of Miami Press, 1970.

Corbitt, Duvon C. A Study of the Chinese in Cuba, 1847-1947. Wilmore, KY: Asbury College, 1971.

Cuba. "The Educational Movement: Cuba, 1969-1970." School and Society 99(O, 1971): 382-385.

Cuban National Committee to UNESCO. "First National Congress on Education and Culture." UNESCO Bulletin, Jl, 1972.

Dahlman, Carl J. The National Learning System of Cuba. Princeton, NJ: Research Program in Economic Development, Woodrow Wilson School, Princeton U., Jl, 1973.

Depestre, René. "Carta de Cuba sobre el imperialismo de la mala fe." In Por la Revolución, Por la Poesia, pp. 71-130. Havana: N.p., 1969.

Deschamps-Chapeaux, Pedro. El Negro en la economía habanera del siglo XIX. Habana, Cuba: Unión Nacional de Escritores y Artistas de Cuba, 1971.

Epstein, Erwin H. Education and American Colonialism in Cuba, 1898-1901. National Institute of Education Project No. 1-0518. Washington, DC: U.S. Dept. of Health, Education, and Welfare, Ag 1, 1974.

Fermoselle-Lopez, Rafael. "Black Politics in Cuba: The Race War of 1912." Doctoral dissertation, American U., 1972.

_____. Politica y color en Cuba: La Guerrita de 1912. Montivideo, Uruguay: Ediciones Geminis, 1974.

Fernandez de Castro, José Antonio. Tema Negro las Letras de Cuba (1608-1935). Havana: Mirador, 1943.

Fitchen, Edward D. "Primary Education in Colonial Cuba: Spanish Tool for Retaining 'La Isla Siempre Leal'?" Caribbean Studies 14(Ap, 1974).

_____. "The United States Military Government: Alexis E. Frye and Cuban Education, 1898-1902." Revista/Review Interamericana 2 (Summer, 1972):123-149.

Foner, Philip S. Antonio Maceo. The "Bronze Titan" of Cuba's Struggle for Independence. New York: Monthly Review Press, 1977.

Fox, Geoffrey E. "Cuban Racism." In Cuban Communism, pp. 21-30, 2nd. ed. Edited by Irving Louis Horowitz. Edison, NJ: Transaction Books, 1972.

García, Calixto. "El negro en la narrativa cubana." Doctoral dissertation, City U. of New York, 1973.

García Montes, Jorge, and Alonso Aguilar, Antonio. Historia del Partido Comunista de Cuba. Miami: N.p., 1970.

Garmendia, Teresa. "La socialización del negro en Cuba." Nuevos Rumbos (Gainesvilla, FL) 2(1974):20-31.

Garnier, Jean-Pierre. "Les Problemes urbaine à la Havane et la construction du socialisme à Cuba, 1959-1971." Doctoral dissertation, U. of Toulouse II, 1972.

Gillette, Arthur. Cuba's Educational Revolution. London: Fabian Society, Je, 1972.

_____. "New Education for New Man." Times Higher Education Supplement, Jl 14, 1972.

Green, Gil. Revolution Cuba Style. New York: International, 1970.

Grillo Saez, David. El Problema del Negro Cubano. Havana: N.p., 1953.

Guardado, Elisa. "Interview with a Cuban Educator." Edcentric, Ja, 1973. [Interview by Larry Magid]

Hall, Gwendolyn Midlo. Social Control in Slave Plantation Societies: A Comparison of St. Domingue and Cuba. Baltimore, MD: Johns Hopkins Press, 1971.

Henderson, James D. "Mariana Grajales: Black Progenitress of Cuban Independence." Journal of Negro History 63(Ap, 1978):135-148.

Hochschild, Arlie. "Student Power in Action." Trans-action, Ap, 1969.

Hopkins, Dwight N. "A Black Student's Journal: Trip to Communist Cuba." Harvard Crimson, Ja 13, 1975.

Horne, Gerald C. "Black Youth in Cuba." Freedomways 15(Third Quarter, 1975):215-220.

Huberman, Leo, and Sweezy, Paul M. "Education." Socialism in Cuba. New York: Monthly Review Press, 1969.

Johnson, Herschel. "Inside Report on Black Congressman's Visit to Castro's Cuba." Jet, Jl 7, 1977. [Rep. Ronald V. Dellums]

Kashif, Lonnie. "Cuba Tackles Problem of Wiping Out Effects of Imperialist Racism." Muhammad Speaks, Ap 9, 1971.

Katzin, Donna. "The Jews of Cuba." Nation 218 (My 25, 1974):658-660.

Kiple, Kenneth F. Blacks in Colonial Cuba, 1774-1899. Gainesville, FL: University Presses of Florida, 1975.

Knight, Franklin W. "Cuba." In Neither Slave Nor Free. The Freedmen of African Descent in the Slave Societies of the New World, pp. 278-308. Edited by David W. Cohen and Jack P. Greene. Baltimore, MD: Johns Hopkins U. Press, 1972.

_____. Slave Society in Cuba During the Nineteenth Century. Madison, WI: U. of Wisconsin Press, 1970.

_____. "Slavery, Race, and Social Structure in Cuba During the Nineteenth Century." In Slavery and Race Relations in Latin America, pp. 204-227. Edited by Robert B. Toplin. Westport, CT: Greenwood Press, 1974.

Kozol, Jonathan. Children of the Revolution: A Yankee Teacher in the Cuban Schools. New York: Delacorte Press, 1978.

Lachantañere, Romulo. "Some Aspects of the Color Problem in Cuba." Negro Quarterly 2 (Summer, 1942):145-154.

Laska-Mierzejewska, T. "Morphological and Developmental Difference between Negro and White Cuban Youths." Human Biology 42(1970): 581-597.

Leiner, Marvin. Children Are the Revolution. Day Care in Cuba. New York: Viking, 1974.

Lewis, Oscar and others. Four Men: Living the Revolution, an Oral History of Contemporary Cuba, Vol I. Urban: U. of Illinois Press, 1977.

Lewis, Oscar, Lewis, Ruth M., and Rigdon, Susan M. Four Women: An Oral History of Contemporary Cuba. Urbana: U. of Illinos Press, 1977.

Loney, Martin. "Social Control in Cuba." In Politics and Deviance. Edited by Ian Taylor and Laurie Taylor. Harmondsworth, 1973.

Lopez Valdes, Rafael. Racial Discrimination from Colonial Times to the Revolution. Havana: Instituto Cubano de Amistad con los Pueblos, 1971.

_____. " Racial Discrimination in Cuba." Cuba Resource Center Newsletter (NYC) 2 (Ja, 1973):6-14.

Malinowski, Bronislaw. "Intruccion, educacion y trans-culturacion de los Negros." Revista Bimestre Cubana, Mr-Ap, 1944.

Marcos Vequeri, Pascual. El Negro en Cuba. Havana: N.p., 1955.

Martin, Lionel. "La Revolucion en Camaguey-- The Building of a New Society." Guardian, Jl 26, 1969.

Martinez-Alier, Verena. "Colour As a Symbol of Social Classification." Renaissance 2, Issue 3 [1973]:36-45.

_____. Marriage, Class and Color in Nineteenth Century Cuba. A Study of Racial Attitudes and Sexual Values in a Slave Society. New York: Cambridge U. Press, 1974.

Masferrer, Marianne, and Mesa-Lago, Carmelo. "The Gradual Integration of the Black in Cuba: Under the Colony, the Republic, and the Revolution." In Slavery and Race Relations in Latin America, pp. 348-384. Edited by Robert B. Toplin. Westport, CT: Greenwood Press, 1974.

Mesa-Lago, Carmelo (ed.). Revolutionary Change in Cuba: Polity, Economy, and Society. Pittsburgh, PA: U. of Pittsburgh Press, 1971.

More, Carlos. "Le peuple noir a-t-il sa place dans la révolution cubaine?" Presence Africaine 52(1964):177-230.

Moreno Fraginals, Manuel. The Sugarmill. The Socioeconomic Complex of Sugar in Cuba. Tr. Cedric Belfrage. New York: Monthly Review Press, 1976.

Morrell, Marta F. "The Chinese in Cuba." Master's thesis, Columbia U., 1946.

Nelson, Lowry. Cuba: The Measure of a Revolution. Minneapolis, MN: U. of Minnesota Press, 1972.

_____. "The School Dropout Problem in Cuba." School and Society 99(Ap, 1971):234-235.

Ortiz, Fernando. Hampa afrocubana: Los negros brujos. 2nd ed. Miami: Ediciones Universal, 1973.

_____. "Por la Integracion Cubana de Blancos y Negros." Revista Bimestre Cubana, Mr-Ap, 1943.

Packard, Robert Lawrence. Education in Cuba, Porto Rico, and the Philippines. Washington, DC: GPO, 1899. [Reprinted from Report of the Commissioner of Education for 1897-98, chapter 20]

Paulton, Rolland G. "Cambios en la Educacion cubana." Aportes 21 (1971).

_____. "Changes in Cuban Education." In Educational Innovations in Latin America, pp. 150-177. Edited by Richard L. Cummings and Donald A. Lemke. Metuchen, NJ: Scarecrow Press, 1973.

_____. Cuban Rural Education: A New Strategy for Revolutionary Development. N.p.: n.p., n.d. ERIC ED 071 808.

_____. "Cultural Revitalization and Educational Change in Cuba." Comparative Education Review 16(O, 1972):121-144.

_____. "Revitalización cultural y cambio educativo en Cuba." Aportes 26(O, 1972).

_____. "Revolutionizing Educational Policy in Cuba." School and Society 99(N, 1971): 452-453.

Perez de la Riva, Juan. "La contradicción fundamental de la sociedad colonial cubana: trabajo esclavo contra trabajo libre." Economía y Desarrollo, Ap-Je, 1970, pp. 144-154.

_____. "Desaparición de la población indigena cubana." Universidad de La Habana 196-197 (1972):61-814

Pichardo, Hortensia. "El gobierno colonial contra los estudios superiores en Cuba." Universidad de La Habana 195(Ja, 1972):10-21.

Powers, Marshall Kent. "Chinese Coolie Migration to Cuba." Doctoral dissertation, U. of Florida, 1953.

Purcell, Susan. "Educating Women for a Modern Society." In Female and Male in Latin America. Edited by Ann Pescatello. Pittsburgh, PA: U. of Pittsburgh Press, 1973.

Randall, Margaret (ed.). Cuban Women Now: Interviews with Cuban Women. Toronto: Canadian Women's Educational Press, 1974.

Read, Gerald H. "The Cuban Revolutionary Offensive in Education." Comparative Education Review 14(Je, 1970):131-143.

_____. "Persisting Problems in Cuban Education." Phi Delta Kappan 53(F, 1972): 352-357.

Reckord, Mary. "Chinese Contract Labour in Cuba 1847-1874." Caribbean Studies 14(Jl, 1974).

Ring, Harry. How Cuba Uprooted Race Discrimination. 2nd ed. New York: N.p., 1969.

Rivero, Manuel de la Calle. Las culturas aborigenes de Cuba. Habana: Editorial Universitaria, 1969.

Roller, Arnold. "The Jews of Cuba." Menorah Journal 17(D, 1929).

Roucek, Joseph S. "Changes in Cuban Education Since Castro." Phi Delta Kappan 45(Ja, 1964):193-197.

Sánchez, Juan. "Aspectos de la discriminación racial: Un mal del pasado." Bohemia 65 (My 25, 1973):100-106.

Siegel, Judy. "Remnant of a Community." Jerusalem Post, S 1, 1978. [Jews in Cuba]

Sutherland, Elizabeth. "Colony Within the Colony." In The Youngest Revolution: A Personal Report on Cuba. New York: Dial, 1969. [Blacks in Cuban life]

Thomas, Hugh. "Black Cuba." In Cuba: The Pursuit of Freedom, ch. 91. New York: Harper & Row, 1971.

Valdés-Cruz, Rosa. "The Black Man's Contribution to Cuban Culture." Americas 34(O, 1977):244-251.

Zeitlin, Maurice. "Economic Insecurity and Political Attitudes of Cuban Workers." American Sociological Review 31(F, 1966):35-51.

Cyprus

Kitromilides, P. M., and Couloumbis, T. A. "Ethnic Conflict in a Strategic Area: The Case of Cyprus." Greek Review of Social Research (Athens) 24(1975):270-291.

Patrick, Richard. "Intercommunal Conflict in Cyprus--Some Demographic and Geopolitical Consequences. New Community 2(Spring, 1973): 137-144.

Czechoslovakia

Brock, Peter. The Slovak National Awakening. Toronto: U. of Toronto Press, 1976.

Bruegel, J. W. Czechoslovakia Before Munich: The German Minority Problem and British Appeasement Policy. New York: Cambridge U. Press, 1973.

Cohen, Gary B. "Jews in German Society: Prague, 1860-1914." Central European History 10 (Mr, 1977):28-54.

Davidová, Eva, and Guy, D. E. "Czechoslovakia Solves Its Gypsy Problem." Race Today 4 (Mr, 1972):82-84.

Glejdura, S. "Eslovaquia en erupción revolucionaria (1945-1975)." R. Polit. int. (Madrid) 143(1976):115-137.

Haufler, Vlastislav. The Ethnographic Map of the Czech Lands, 1880-1970. Prague: Ahademie Ved., 1973.

Janics, Kalman. "Czechoslovakia's Magyar
Minority: An Example of Diaspora Nationalism." Can. R. Stud. Nationalism 3(Fall,
1975):34–44.

Jelinek, Yeshayahu. "The Jews in Slovakia,
1945–1949." Soviet Jewish Affairs 8(Autumn,
1978).

_____. The Pariah Republic: Hlinka's
Slovak People's Party, 1939–1945. New York:
Columbia U. Press, 1976.

Kirschbaum, Joseph M. (ed.). Slovakia in the
19th and 20th Centuries... Toronto:
Slovak World Congress, 1973.

Kaiser, Johann. "Die Politik des dritten
Reiches gegenüber der Slowakei 1939–1945."
Doctoral dissertation, U. of Bochum, 1969.

Kirschbaum, S. J. "Le nationalisme minori-
taire: le cas de la Tchecoslovaquie." R.
Canad. Sci. polit. 7(Je, 1974);248–267.
[Slovaks]

Krejci, Jaroslav. "Classes and Elites in
Socialist Czechoslovakia." In The Social
Structure of Eastern Europe, pp. 143–165.
Edited by Bernard Lewis Faber. New York:
Praeger, 1976.

Kwasnik-Rabinowicz, Kurt A. M. "Die juedische
Minderheit in der Tschechoslovakei. Eine
recht sgeschichtliche Analyse, 1918–1939."
Doctoral dissertation, U. of Amsterdam,
1966.

Musil, Jiri. "The Development of Prague's
Ecological Structure." In Readings in Urban
Sociology. Edited by R. E. Pahl. London:
Pergamon, 1968.

Odlozilik, Otakar. "Education, Religion, and
Politics in Bohemia, 1526–1621." Journal of
World History 13(1971):172–203.

Riff, M. A. "The Assimilation of the Jews of
Bohemia and the Rise of Political Anti-
Semitism, 1848–1918." Doctoral disserta-
tion, U. of London, School of Slavonic and
East European Studies, n.d.

Skinner, Donald. "Streaming in a Communist
Country: The Case of Czechoslovakia."
Scottish Educational Studies 5(1973):103–
112.

Steiner, Eugen. The Slovak Dilemma. New York:
Cambridge U. Press, 1973.

Vysny, P. Neo-Slavism and the Czechs, 1898–
1914. New York: Cambridge U. Press, 1976.

Weiss, John. "Fascism in Czechoslovakia, 1919–
39." E. Central Eur. 4(No. 1, 1977):35–43.

Dahomey

Asiwaju, A. I. "The Colonial Education Heritage
and the Problem of Nation-Building in
Dahomey." Bull. I.F.A.N. 37(Ap, 1975):340–
357. [Benin]

Baldus, Bernd. "Social Structure and Ideology:
Cognitive and Behavioral Responses to
Servitude among the machube of Northern
Dahomey." Canadian Journal of African
Studies 8(1974):355–384.

Ronen, Dov. "The Colonial Elite in Dahomey."
African Studies Review 17, pp. 55–76.

Denmark

Bamberger, Ib Nathan. "Jews in Denmark, 1913–
1943." Master's thesis, Yeshiva U., 1967.

Borchsensius, Poul. "Aspects of the Rescue of
Danish Jews." Wiener Library Bulletin 22
(Autumn, 1968):36–40.

Brooks, Glenwood C. and others. "A Cross-
Cultural Comparison of Danish and U.S.
Attitudes Toward Minority Groups."
Research in Higher Education 2(1974):
207–220.

Frazier, E. Franklin. "The Cooperative Movement
in Denmark." Southern Workman 52(O, 1923).

_____. "Danish People's High Schools and
America." Southern Workman 9(S, 1922).

_____. "The Folk High School at Roskiede."
Southern Workman 51(Jl, 1922):325–328.

Geiger, Theodor. "Intelligentsia." Acta
Sociologica 1(1956):49–61

_____. "Recruitment of University Students."
Acta Sociologica 1(1956):39–48.

Hansen, Erik Jorgen. "The Problem of Equality
in the Danish Educational Structure." Acta
Sociologica 16(1973):258–278. [See commentary
by Boel Berner, pp. 279–283.]

Hobart, C. W., and Brant, C. S. "Eskimo
Education-Danish and Canadian: A Comparison."
Canadian Review of Sociology and Anthropology,
My, 1966.

"The Immigrant Worker and the Danish Public
Library System." UNESCO Bulletin for
Libraries 32(Ja-F, 1978):23–32.

McGuire, Brian Patrick. "The Danish Applecart."
Nation, F 23, 1974.

Orum, Bente, and Fridberg, Torben. "Boys and
Girls in the Danish Secondary School in this
Century." Scandanavian Journal of Education-
al Research 17(1973).

Rasmussen, Victor. "Towards a Freer School."
The Danish Journal 69(1970):2-6.
[Gladsaxe Municipality]

Sorensen, Aage Bottger. Equality of Educational Opportunity in an Expanding Educational System, N, 1969. ERIC ED 041 360.

_____. Organizational Differentiation of
Students and Occupational Opportunity.
Baltimore, MD: Center for Social Organization of Schools, Johns Hopkins U., D,
1969.

Yahil, Leni. The Rescue of Danish Jewry:
Test of a Democracy. Tr. Morris Gradel.
Philadelphia: Jewish Publication Society
of America, 1969.

                        Ecuador

Brandi, John (ed.). Chimborazo: Life on the
Haciendas of Highland Ecuador. Roosevelt,
NY: Akwesasne Notes, 1976.

Casagrande, Joseph. "Strategies for Survival:
The Indians of Highland Ecuador." In Contemporary Cultures and Societies of Latin
America: A Reader in the Social Anthropology of Middle and South America.
2nd ed. Edited by Dwight B. Heath.
New York: Random House, 1974.

Rodriguez-Abad, Luis Alberto. "Social
Structure, Opportunity and Institutional
Change. The Universities of Ecuador."
Doctoral dissertation, Syracuse U., 1969.
Univ. Microfilms Order No. 70-10,389.

Salazar, Ernesto. An Indian Federation in Lowland Ecuador. Copenhagen: International
Work Group in Lowland Ecuador, Je, 1977.

Schmitz, H. Walter. "Interethnic Relations
in Saraguro (Ecuador) from the Point of View
of an Anthropology of Communication."
Sociologus 27(1977):64-84.

Stutzman, Ronald. "Black Highlanders:
Recession and Ethnic Stratification in the
Ecuadorian Sierra." Doctoral dissertation,
Washington U., 1974.

Whitten, Norman E., Jr. Class, Kinship, and
Power in an Ecuadorian Town: The Negroes
of San Lorenzo. Stanford, CA: Stanford U.
Press, 1965.

_____. "Ecuadorian Ethnocide and Indigenous
Ethnogenesis: Amazonian Resurgence Amidst
Andean Colonialism." Journal of Ethnic
Studies 4(Summer, 1976):1-22.

_____. Sacha Runa: Ethnicity and Adaptation
of Ecuadorian Jungle Quichua. Urbana, IL:
U. of Illinois Press, 1975. [Canelo
Indians]

                        Egypt

Allman, T. D. "Poor Get Poorer in Sadat's
Egypt." In These Times, Jl 12, 1978.

Ammar, H. M. "An Enquiry into Inequalities of
Educational Opportunities in Egypt."
Doctoral dissertation, U. of London,
Institute of Education, 1949.

Awak' Ayom. "Cheikh Anta Diop et l'origine
nègre de la civilisation égyptienne."
Zaïre-Afrique (Ag-S, 1977):419-434.

Bowie, Leland. "The Copts, Wafd, and Religious
Issues in Egyptian Politics." Muslim World
67(Ap, 1977):106-126.

Deeb, Marius. "The Socioeconomic Role of the
Local Foreign Minorities in Modern Egypt,
1805-1961." Inst. J. Mid. E. Stud. 9(F,
1978):11-22.

Diop, Cheikh Anta. "Pigmentation des anciens
Égyptiens. Text par la melanine." Bull.
IFAN 35(Jl, 1973):515-531.

el Erian, Mohammad. "A Suggested Plan to
Democratize the Educational Enterprise in
Egypt." Doctoral dissertation, Columbia U.,
1953.

El-Nofely, Aly A. "Anthropometric Study of
Growth of Egyptian Nubian Children." Human
Biology 50(1978):183-208.

Eskandaramy, Ya'acoub Daoud. "Egyptian Jewry--
Why It Declined." Khamsin 5(1978).

"Ethnic and Religious Minorities in Egypt:
A Table." Mid. E. R. 9(Fall, 1976):60.

Faksh, M. A. "An Historical Survey of the
Educational System in Egypt." International
Review of Education 22(1976):234-244.

Faksh, Mahmud A. "The Chimera of Education for
Development in Egypt: The Socio-Economic
Roles of University Graduates." Middle E.
Stud. 13(My, 1977):229-240.

Holt, A. E. "The Non-Muslim Communities in
Cairo, 969-1517 A.D." Master's thesis, U.
of Heil, 1974.

Holter, Age. "The Copts in the Egypt of Today.
A Camouflaged Minority Problem." Norsk Tids.
Misjon 27(1973):129-146.

Hyde, Georgie D. M. Education in Modern Egypt:
Ideals and Realities. Boston: Routledge &
Kegan Paul, 1978.

John, Robert. "In Search of Milk and Honey."
Times Educational Supplement, N 5, 1976.
[Palestinian children]

Koning, Karen L. "Some Political Effects of
British Educational Policy in Egypt."
Makerere Hist. Journal 1(1975):129-136.

Landau, Jacob M. Jews in Nineteenth-Century Egypt. New York: New York U. Press, 1969.

Lippman, Thomas W. "Egypt's Christian Minority." Washington Post, My 16, 1976.

Mesriya, Yahudiya. Les juifs en Egypte. Aperçu sur 3,000 ans d'histoire. Genève: Les Editions de L'Avenir, 1971.

Mikhail, Kyriakos. Copts and Moslems Under British Control. London: Smith, Elder, 1911.

Mizrahi, Maurice. L'Egypte et ses Juifs. Le Temps revolu (XIXe et XXe siecles). Lausanne: The author, 1977.

Murphy, Robert Thomas. "The Minorities of Egypt." Doctoral dissertation, Harvard U., 1959.

Perconel-Hugoz, Jean-Pierre. "The Copts: Egypt's Second-Class Citizens." Guardian, D 11, 1977.

Reid, Donald M. "Educational and Career Choices of Egyptian Students, 1881-1922." International Journal of Middle East Studies 8 (1977):349-378.

Reid, Donald M. "The Rise of Professions and Professional Organization in Modern Egypt." Comparative Studies in Society and History 16(Ja, 1974):24-57.

Saif, Philip Saber. "Public Education in Egypt: Practice and Theory." Doctoral dissertation, U. of Connecticut, 1959. Univ. Microfilms Order No. 59-3866.

Shaltout, Ali F. M. "The Relation Between Socio-economic Status and Intelligence of Egyptian Pupils in Alexandria." Doctoral dissertation, Wayne State U., 1955. Univ. Microfilms Order No. 15,415.

Strong, John. "Egypt and the Rule of Kush-- Racism and Historiography: A Case Study." Journal of Afro-American Issues, Winter, 1973, pp. 397-408, F, 1974, pp. 59-71.

Ye'Or, B. "Zionism in Islamic Lands: The Case of Egypt." Wiener Library Bulletin 30 (1977):16-29.

Zuroff, Abraham N. "The Responsa of Maimonides." Doctoral dissertation, Yeshiva U., 1966. Univ. Microfilms Order No. 67-9938. [Jews in Egypt, second half of the 12th century]

Ethiopia

Abir, Mordechai. "Education and National Unity in Ethiopia." African Affairs 69(Ja, 1970): 44-59.

Adelman, Kenneth Lee. "Black Jews of Ethiopia." Christian Century 92(1975):38-41.

Berger, Graenum. "The Plight of the Falashas." Congress Bi-Weekly 41(O 25, 1974):5-7

Corlett, J. "Despised Occupational Groups in Ethiopia." B. Litt. thesis, Oxford U., n.d.

Fishbein, J. I. "The Plight of Ethiopia's Black Jews." Chicago Tribune Magazine, D 1, 1968.

Grey, R. "Determinants of National Identifications in Ethiopia. A Research Note." Afric. R. 3(1973):501-517.

Kessler, David. "Falashas: A Pattern of Prejudice?" Patterns of Prejudice 9(Ja-F, 1975):2-6.

Krempel, Veronika. "Eine Berufskaste in Nordwest-Aethiopen-die Kayla (Falascha)." Sociologus 24(1974):37-55. English summary, p. 55

Lencho, Tumtu. "The Question of Nationalities and Class Struggle in Ethiopia." Challenge 11(Jl, 19 1):1-66.

Leslau, Wolf. "The Black Jews of Ethiopia." Commentary(Mr, 1949).

Levin, Meyer. "Filming a Truly Lost Tribe of Israel." Variety, Ja 6, 1971. [The Falashas]

Levine, Donald N. Greater Etheopia. The Evolution of a Multiethnic Society. Chicago: U. of Chicago Press, 1974.

Markakis, John. Ethiopia: Anatomy of a Traditional Polity. Oxford: Clarendon Press, 1974.

Markakis, John, and Ayele, Nega. Class and Revolution in Ethiopia. Nottingham, England: Spokesman, 1978.

Milkias, Paulos. "Traditional Institutions and Traditional Elites: The Role of Education in the Ethiopian Body-Politic." Afric. Stud. R. 19(D, 1976):79-94.

Pankhurst, Richard. "Education in Etheopia during the Italian Fascist Occupation (1936-1941)." International Journal of African Historical Studies 3(1972).

_____. "The Secret History of Italian Fascist Occupation of Ethiopia." Africa Quarterly 16(Ap, 1977):35-86.

Payne, Eric. Etheopian Jews. The Story of a Mission. London: Olive Press, 1972.

Quinn, James A. "The Beta Israel (Felasha) in
Etheopian History: Caste Formation and
Culture Change, 1270-1868." Doctoral
dissertation, U. of Minnesota, 1977. Univ.
Microfilms Order No. 7802709.

Rapoport, Louis. "A Bitter History."
Jerusalem Post Magazine, Ja 19, 1979.
[Falashas]

_____. "Falasha Means Stranger." Jerusalem
Post Magazine, Ja 12, 1979.

Sbacchi, Alberto. "Italian Colonialism in
Ethiopia, 1936-1940." Doctoral disserta-
tion, U. of Illinois, Chicago Circle, 1975.
Univ. Microfilms Order No. 75-23364.

Schoenberger, M. A. "The Falashas of
Etheopia: An Ethnographic Study." Master's
thesis, Cambridge U., 1976.

Soen, Dan. "The Falashas--The Black Jews of
Ethiopia." International Committee on Ur-
gent Anthropological and Ethnological
Research Bulletin 10(1968):67-74.

Finland

Allardt, Erik. "Finns and Swedes as Minorities in Sweden and Finland." Scandanavian
Review 66(Mr, 1978):17-23.

Asp, Erkki. The Finnicization of the Lapps.
Turku, Finland: Turku U., 1966.

Butzin, Bernhard. Die Entwicklung Finnisch-
Lapplands. Bochumer Geographische
Arbeiten 30(1977).

Eidheim, Harald. Aspects of the Lappish
Minority Situation, Oslo, Norway:
Universitetsforlaget, 1971.

Forsius, H. "The Finnish Skolt Lapp Children:
A Child Psychiatric Study." Acta
Paediatrica Scandinavica Supplement, 239
(1973).

Hamalainen, Pekka K. In Time of Storm: Revo-
lution, Civil War, and the Ethnolinguistic
Issue in Finland. Albany: State U. of New
York Press, 1979.

_____. "The Nationality Struggle Between the
Finns and the Swedish-Speaking Minority in
Finland, 1917-1939." Doctoral dissertation,
Indiana U., 1966. Univ. Microfilms Order
No. 67-3671.

Hill, R. G. P. (ed.). The Lapps Today in
Finland, Norway and Sweden, I. Paris:
Mouton, 1960.

Hill, R. G. P., and Nickul, K. (eds.). The
Lapps Today in Finland, Norway and Sweden,
II. Oslo-Bergen-Tromso, Norway:
Universitetsvorlaget, 1969.

Ingold, Tim. The Skolt Lapps Today.
New York: Cambridge U. Press, 1976.

_____. "Social and Economic Problems of
Finnish Lapland." Polar Record 16(1973):
809-826.

Kangasniemi, Erkki. A Review of Research Into
Comprehensive Education in Finland, 1977.
ERIC ED 139 757.

Müller-Wille, Ludger. Lappen und Finnen in
Utsjoki (Ohcijohka), Finnland: Eine
Studie zur Identität ethnischer Gruppen im
Kulturkontakt. Münster: Institut für
Geographie und Länderkunde, 1974.

_____. "The 'Lappish Movement' and 'Lappish
Affairs' in Finland and their Relations
to Nordic and International Ethnic Politics."
Arctic and Alpine Research 9(1977):235-247.

Nickul, Kar. The Sámi as People and Citizens.
Helsinki: Society of Finnish Literature,
1970.

Niskanen, Erkki A. School Achievement and
Personality. Description of School Achievement in Terms of Ability, Trait, Situational
and Background Variables. I: Design and
Hypotheses: VI: Results and Discussion.
Helsinki, Finland: U. of Helsinki, Institute
of Education, n.d.

Paulston, Rolland G. "Separate Education as an
Ethnic Survival Strategy: The Finlandssvenka
Case." Anthropology and Education Quarterly
8(Ag, 1977).

Seitamo, L. "Intellectual Functions in Skolt
and Northern Finnish Children with Special
Reference to Cultural Factors." Inter-Nord
12(1972):338-343.

Thors, Carl Eric. "The Swedish School System
in Finland." Adult Education in Finland 11
(1974):25-26.

de Vries, John. "Net Effects of Language Shift
in Finland, 1951-1960: A Demographic
Analysis." Acta Sociologica 17(1974-1975):
140-149.

_____. "A Transition Model of Language Shift
in Nine Finnish Cities, 1920-1930." Acta
Sociologica 16(1973):121-135.

Willis, Richard H. "Finnish Images of the
Northern Lands and Peoples." Acta
Sociologica 7(1964):73-88.

France

Adams, Adrian. "Prisoners in Exile: Senegalese
Workers in France." Race and Class 16(O,
1974):157-179.

_____. "The Racism in Marseilles." Race Today
5(D, 1973):328.

Adler, S. Migration and International Relations: The Case of France and Algeria. Cambridge, MA: Migration and Development Study Group, 1977.

Ageron, Charles A. Les Algériens Musulmans et la France, 1871-1919. 2 vols. Paris: N.p., n.d.

Aiach, Pierre, and Willmott, Peter. "Inequality and Education in the East End of Paris." New Society, O 9, 1975. [Folie Méricourt]

Albert, Phyllis Cohen. The Modernization of French Jewry. Consistory and Community in the Nineteenth Century. Hanover, NH: U. Press of New England, 1977.

Allies, Paul. L'occitanie et la lutte des classes. Montpellier: Librairie F. Maspéro, 1972.

Amoroux, Henri. Les beaux jours des collabos, Juin 1941-Juin 1942. Paris: Laffont, 1978. [Collaborators in France]

Anderson, R. D. Education in France, 1848-1870. New York: Oxford, 1975.

Anderson, Robert. "The Conflict in Education." In Conflicts in French Society: Anticlericalism, Education and Morals in the Nineteenth Century. Edited by Theodore Zeldin. New York: Humanities Press, 1970.

"Apprendre le Portugais à l'école." Le Monde, S 26, 1973.

Aymeric, G. "Une tâche ardue et de longue haleine: l'alphabétisation des étrangers à Marseilles." Vivre en France 2(Mr, 1969).

Azzouz, Wahid ben. "Le racisme centre l'émigration algérienne en France." Révolution Africaine 365-306(F 19-25, 26 - Mr 4, 1971).

Baillet, Pierre. Les Rapatries d'Algerie en France. Paris: Documentation Francaise, Notes et Etudes Documentaires, Mr, 1976.

Bakunin, Jack. "National Socialists and Socialist Anti-semites." Patterns of Prejudice 11(Mr-Ap, 1977):29-33.

Bankowitz, Philip C. F. Alsatian Autonomist Leaders, 1919-1947. Lawrence, KS: Regents Press of Kansas, 1978.

Barou, Jacques. "La répartition géographique des travailleurs immigres d'Afrique Noire à Paris et à Lyon." Cahiers d'Outre-Mer 28 (1975):362-375.

Baudelot, Christian, and Establet, Roger. L'École Capitaliste en France. Paris: Maspero, 1971.

Bastide, Roger. "Les études et les recherches interethniques en France de 1945 à 1968." In Centre for Multiracial Studies and le Centre d'Etudes des Relations Interethnique de Nice, Ethnies. Anglo-French Conference on Race Relations in France and Great Britain, pp. 37-54. Paris: Mouton, 1972.

Beattie, Nicholas. "Parent Participation in French Education, 1968-1975." British Journal of Educational Studies 26(F, 1978): 40-53.

Belloula, Tayeb. Les Algériens en France. Algiers: N.p., 1965.

Benisti, S., Castellet, H., and Molinier, G. Etude comparative de quelque aspects de l'acculturation des immigrés algériens et senegalais de la Seine-Saint Denis. Paris: Université René-Descartes, 1973.

Bennoune, Mahfoud. "The Maghribin Migrant Workers in France." Race and Class 17 (Summer, 1975):39-56.

Benouis, Mustapha K. Langue et Culture: Cliches et Racisme en France. In Second Language Teaching 75, 1975. Edited by Hector Hammerly and Isabel Sayer. ERIC ED 138 042.

Bensimon, Doris. "La perception de l'identité juive par les Juifs nord-africains installé en France." Revue francaise de Sociologie 11 (O-D, 1970).

Bensimon-Donath, Doris. "L'Integration des juifs nordafricains en France." Doctoral dissertation, U. of Paris, 1971.

Bergues, M. "L'immigration des travailleurs Africains Noirs en France et particulièrment dans la région Parisienne." Population (Paris) 28(J-F, 1973):59-79.

Bernardi, François-Noel and others. Les dossiers noirs du racisme dans le Midi de la France. Paris: Seuil, 1976. [Anti-Algerian racism]

Bernheim, Nicole. "Les enfants de travailleurs migrants restent souvent en Marg de la communauté francaise." Le Monde, Ja 1, 1969.

_____. "Les enfants des soutiers." Le Monde, N 21-24, 1970.

_____. "La scolarisation des enfants de travailleurs migrants: difficultes dans les écoles de la cité de transit de Gennevilliers." Le Monde, N 14, 1970.

Berrigan, Frances. "What the Children Are Missing." Times Educational Supplement, N 2, 1973. Children of immigrant workers

Berthoz Proux, M. "Les enfants étrangers à l'école francaise." Petite enfance, Je, 1973.

Betts, Raymond F. Assimilation and Association in French Colonial Theory, 1890-1941. New York: N.p., 1961.

Bisseret, Noëlle. "La 'naissance' et le diplôme. Les processus de sélection au début des études universitaires." Revue française de sociologie 9(1968):185-207.

Blumenkranz, Bernhard. "How Holocaust History is (Not) Taught. Shortcomings of French Textbooks." Patterns of Prejudice 9(My-Je, 1975):8-12.

_____ (ed.). Histoire des Juifs en France. Toulouse, France: Edouard Privat, 1972.

Boudon, Raymond. "La Crise universitaire francaise: Essai de diagnotic socio-logique." Annales 24(My-Je, 1969):738-764.

Bouhouche, Ammar. "Conditions and Attitudes of Migrant Algerian Workers in France: A Survey Analysis." Doctoral dissertation, U. of Missouri, 1971. Univ. Microfilmes Order No. 71-22,896.

_____. "Conditions et attitudes des travailleurs algériens émigrés en France." R. algérienne sci. jur. éc. pol. 10(Je, 1973):511-526.

Bourdarias-Mons, F. Les conditions de vie des travailleurs algériens à Tours. Tour: Université de Tour, 1972.

Bourdieu, P., Grignon, C., and Passeron, J. "L'évolution des chances d'accès à l'enseignement supérieur en France, 1962-1966." Higher Education 2(1973):407-421.

Bourdieu, Pierre, and Passeron, Jean-Claude. "L'examen d'une illusion." Revue francaise de sociologie 9(1968):227-253.

_____ and _____. Les Héritiers: Les étudients et la culture. Paris: Editions de Minuit, 1964.

_____ and _____. La Reproduction: Elements pour une Théorie du Système d'Enseignement. Paris: Editions de Minuit, 1970.

Bouquet, Marie-Noelle. "Race et folklore l'image officielle de la France en 1800." Annales: Economies, Sociétés, Civilisations 31(1976):802-823.

Brasseur, Paule. "Le mot 'Nègre' dans les dictionnaires encyclopédiques francais due XIXe siècle." Cult. Dév. 8, No. 4(1976): 57.

Brettell, C. B. "Portuguese Emigration to France, 1950-1974: A Brief Demographic Report." European Demographic Information Bulletin 7(1976):85-91

Buiron, M. "L'accueil et l'intégration des enfants étrangers dans les écoles primaires de l'Ain." Bulletin de la societe Alfred Binet et Théodore Simon 492(Mr, 1966): 210-223.

Busi, Frederick. "The Impact of Fascism [on French Treatment of Jews]." Patterns of Prejudice 8(Ja-F, 1974):9-16.

Calame, Paulette, and Calame, Pierre. Les Travailleurs Etrangers en France. Paris: Ouvrieres (Les Editions), 1972.

Camilleri, Carmel. "L'Image dans la cohabitation de groupes étrangers en relation inegalitaire." Cahiers internationaux de sociologie 59(1975):239-254.

Castles, Godula. "Racial Prejudice in France." Race Today, Ja, 1970.

Castles, Godula, and Castles, Stephen. "Immigrant Workers and Class Structure in France." Race 12(Ja, 1971):303-315.

Catanii, Maurice. "L'Alphabétisation des travailleurs étrangers, une relation 'dominant-dominé.'" 2 vols. Doctoral dissertation, U. of Paris, V, 1972.

_____. "L'enseignement de l'ecriture a des travailleurs etrangers en France." Francais dans le Monde 109(D, 1974):68-79.

_____. Journal de Mohamed. Un Algérien en France parmi huit cent mille autres. Témoigner/Stock 2, 1973.

Centre Africain des Sciences Humaines Appliquees. Connaissance de l'Immigration Nord-africaine en France: Essai de Synthese Documentaire. Aix-en-Provence: N.p., 1964.

Chapoulie, Jean-Michel, and Merllie, Dominique. "Les Classes Sociales et l'École." Cahiers Pédagogiques 102(Ja, 1972):41-48.

Charlot, Martine. "L'enseignement aupres des travailleurs etrangers en France." Francais dans le Monde 134(Ja, 1978):47-52.

de Charnace, Francoise (comp.). "Pour Enfant, Francais Langue Etrangere." Francais dans le Monde 117(N-D, 1975):8-9.

Chartier, Roger and others. L'education en France du XVIe au XVIIIe siècle. Paris: Société d'Édition d'Enseignement Supérieur, 1976.

Clerc, P. "Nouvelles données sur l'orientation scolaire au moment de l'entrée en sixième." In Institut National d'Etudes Démographiques, Population et l'enseignement, pp. 189-232. Paris: P.U.F., 1970

Club de Pédiatrie sociale. Les enfants de travailleurs migrants. Paris: Centre Internationale de l'Enfance, 1972.

Cohen, William B. "Literature and Race: Nineteenth Century French Fiction, Blacks and Africa 1800-1800." Race and Class 16(O, 1974):181-205.

Colson, William N. "The Social Experience of the Negro Soldier Abroad." Messenger 2(O, 1919):26-27.

Confer, Vincent. "French Colonial Ideas Before 1789." French Historical Studies 3(Spring, 1964):338-359.

Cotler, Julio. "L'adaptation des immigrants espagnols en France." Doctoral dissertation, U. of Bordeaux, 1960.

Coulon, Christian. "French Political Science and Regional Diversity: A Strategy of Silence." Ethnic and Racial Studies 1(Ja, 1978):80-99.

Courault, B., Rouragnan, B., and Chenut, N. Rapport de recherche sur l'immigration des travailleurs étrangers en France. 2 vols. Paris: Cordes, 1972.

Crepon, Y., and Oppe, A. M. Enfants étrangers dans une école primaire de Paris 9° arrondissement. Paris: Mémoire de Maîtrise, 1972.

Darnton, Robert. "The High Enlightenment and the Low Life of Literature in Pre-Revolutionary France." Past and Present 51(1971): 81-115.

Davies, Alan T. "Religion and Racism: The Case of French Anti-Semitism." Journal of Church and State 20(Spring, 1978):273-286.

De Comarmond, P., and Duchet, C. (eds.). Racisme et Société. Paris: Maspéro, 1969.

De la Presle, Anne. "Immigrant and Minority Groups in France." New Community 1(O, 1971): 16-20.

_____. "Language Instruction and Education of Migrants in France." New Community 2(Summer, 1973):249-253.

Delerm, Robert. "L'immigration noire en France. Perspectives, consequences." Hommes et Migrations, 1971.

_____. "La population noire en France." Population 19(1964).

Delesalle, Simone, and Valensi, Lucette. "Le mot 'negre' dans les dictionnaires francais d'Ancien regime: histoire et lexicographie." Langue Francaise 15 (S, 1972):79-104.

Delpech, F. "Les Juifs en Frances 1780-1840." An. hist. Rév. fr. 48(Ja-Mr, 1976):3-46.

Descloitres, R. L'Adaptation des travailleurs étrangers. Paris: n.p., 1967.

Development et a l'organisation des etudes interethniques en France. Nice: Centre d'Etude des Relations Interethniques de Nice, Universite de Nice, O, 1968.

Devyver, M. A. Le sang épuré. Les préjugés de race chez les gentilshommes francais l'Ancien Régime, 1560-1720. N.p.: n.p., n.d.

Dofny, Jacques, and Arnaud, Nicole. Nationalism and the National Question. Montreal: Black Rose Books, 1978. [Occitanie]

Dricot-d'Ans, Christiane. "Croissance de métis eurasiens transplantés en France." Doctoral dissertation, U. of Paris, VII, 1972.

Dubois, R. "Les écoliers des bidonvilles." Droit et liberté 297(N, 1970):17-24.

Dubresson, Alain. "Les travailleurs Soninké et Toucouleur dans l'Ouest Parisien." Cahiers O.R.S.T.O.M. Série Sciences Humaines 12(1975): 189-208.

Dulong, Renaud. La question bretonne. Paris: Presses de la Fondation nationale des Sciences Politiques, 1975.

Edmond-Smith, Joyce. "Report from France." New Community 2(Summer, 1973):286-295.

_____. "Report from France--1973." New Community 3(Winter-Spring, 1974):140-143.

_____. "West Indian Workers in France." New Community 1(Autumn, 1972):444-450.

_____. "West Indian Workers in France--II." New Community 2(Winter, 1972-1973):74-79.

_____. "West Indian Workers in France--III." New Community 2(Summer, 1973):306-314.

Ehrlich, Monique, and Zirotti, Jean-Pierre. "Scolarisation et destructuration des groupes minoritaires." In Les travailleurs étrangers en Europe occidentale, pp. 241-259. Edited by Bernard J. Philippe. Paris: Mouton, 1976. [Gypsies in France]

"Enfants d'ethnies différentes: difficultés d'insertion sociale." Interéducation 27 (My-Je, 1972):21-28; 28(Jl-Ag, 1972):28-40; 29(S-O, 1972):20-39.

"Les enfants etrangers en France." Hommes et Migrations: Documents 15(F, 1974):1-25.

Englehardt, Klaus. The Occitan Movement in Southern France. In Second Language Teaching 75, 1975. Edited by Hector Hammerly and Isabel Sawyer. ERIC ED 138 042.

"Esquisse d'une méthodologie interculturelle pour la formation des enseignants et des opérateurs sociaux intervenant dans le milieu des travailleurs migrants." Le Service Sociale 55(Ag-S, 1977):201-248.

Ettori, F. "L'enseignement de la langue corse." Langue Francaise 25(F, 1975):104-111.

Fabre, Michel. "Rene Maran, The New Negro and Negritude." Phylon 36(S, 1975):340-351.

Fanoudh-Siefer, Leon. Le Mythe du nègre et de l'Afrique noire dans la littérature francaise (de 1800 à la 2e guerre mondiale). Paris: N.p., 1968.

Farinaux, Martine. "L'accueil des étudiants." Esprit 348(Ap, 1966):610-630. (Special issue: "Les Étrangers en France")

Farr, William. "'Clean Sweep' Policy Faces Strong Criticism." Times Educational Supplement, Ja 25, 1974.

Fauret, J. "Le traditionalisme par excès de modernité." Archives européennes de Sociologie 40(1967):5-42.

Ferenczi, Victor. "Les besoin languagiers comme representation des pratiques sociales d'intercommunication. Revue de Phonetique Appliquee 38(1976):81-94. [Paris region]

"Fighting Racism in France." Race Today 6(F, 1974):55.

Franzblau, Daniel M. "The Impact of French Educational Reforms (1959-1972) on Access of Disadvantaged Students to Secondary and Higher Education in a Retreating Elitist Society." Doctoral dissertation, Miami U., 1972.

_____. "Secondary Education Reforms in France." International Education 4(1975):20-26.

Freeman, Gary P. Immigrant Labor and Racial Conflict in Industrial Societies: The French and British Experience, 1945-1975. Princeton, NJ: Princeton U. Press, 1979.

Frijhoff, Willem, and Julia, Dominique. École et société dans la France d'Ancien Régime: Quatre exemples Auch, Avallon, Condom et Gisors. Paris: Colin, 1975.

Fritsch, Philippe, and de Montlibert, Christian. "Le cumul des desavantages: les élèves des centre ménagers. Revue francaise de sociologie 13(1972):80-93.

Furet, F., and Ozouf, J. "Literacy and Industrialization: The Case of the Departement du Nord in France." Journal of European Economic History 5(Spring, 1975).

Furet, Francois, and Sachs, Wladimir. "La croissance de l'alphabetisation en France (XVIIIe - XIXe siècle)." Annales 29(My-Je, 1974).

Gani, Leon. "L'attitude des syndicate ouvriers à l'égard de l'immigration en France 1945-1968." Doctoral dissertation, U. of Paris, 1969.

Gardin, B. "Loi Deixonne et langues regionales: representation de la nature et de la fonction de leur enseignement." Langue Francaise 25(F, 1975):29-36. [Breton, Basque, Catalan, and Occitan]

Gayet, Denis. "Le racisme en Guyane française." Les Temps Modernes 23(1968):1671-1700.

Georges, G. "L'enseignement des enfants etrangers. Les classes d'initiation." L'école libératrice 29(Ap 30, 1971):1455-1464.

Giacomo, Mathee. "La politique a propos des langues regionales: cadre historique." Langue Francaise 25(F, 1975):12-28.

Gil, Jose. "La Corse et les impasses du pouvoir." Les temps modernes 366(Ja, 1977).

Giordan, Henri. "Occitan vs. Langues d'oc. Cultures subalternes et culture dominante." Annals de l'Institut d'Estudis occitans 5 (1977).

_____. "Occitanie: langue, culture, lutte des classes." l'homme et la société 28(1973).

Girard, Alain. "Les immigrés du Maghreb. Etudes sur l'adaptation en milieu urbain." Population 32(1977):405-410.

Girard, A., and Bastide, H. "La stratification sociale et la démocratisation de l'enseignement." Population (Paris) 18(Jl-S, 1963):435-472.

Giarard, A., Bastide, H., and Purcher, G. "Enquête nationale sur l'entrée en sixième et la démocratisation de l'enseignement." Population (Paris) 18(Ja-Mr, 1963):9-48.

Girard, A., Charbit, Y., and Lamy, M. "Attitudes des Francais a l'égard de l'immigration étrangère." Population (Paris) 29(N-D, 1974):1015-1064.

Girard, Patrick. Les Juifs de France de 1789 à 1860: de l'émancipation à l'égalité. Paris: Calmann Levy, 1976.

Goyheneche, Eugene. "Medieval French Basque Economic and Political Institutions." Proc. W. Soc. Fr. Hist. 4(1976):1-13.

Grange, P. "Les problèmes scolaires posés en France par les enfants de travailleurs immigrés." Orientation 47(Jl, 1973):87-100.

Granotier, Bernard. Les Travailleurs Immigrés en France. Paris: Maspero, 1970.

Gras, Christian, and Livet, Georges (eds.). Régions et régionalisme en France du XVIIIe siècle à nos jours. Paris: Presses Universitaires de France, 1977.

Gratiot-Alphandesy, H., and Lambiotte, B. Le retard scolaire des enfants de travailleurs migrants. Paris: Centre Internationale de l'enfance, 1973.

"Grave Deterioration in Race Relations in France." Runnymede Trust Bulletin, European Supplement 9(0, 1973):1.

Greenhough, R. "Pourquoi les enfants de travailleurs réussissent moins bien a l'école." Education et développment 71 (0, 1971):56-60.

Griffin, Christopher C. "Italians into South-East France." Doctoral dissertation, U. of Sussex, 1973.

Guillaumin, Collette. "The Popular Press and Ethnic Pluralism: The Situation in France." International Social Science Journal 23(1971).

Harrigan, Patrick J. "Elites, Education, and Social Mobility in France during the Second Empire." Proc. W. Soc. Fr. Hist. 4(1976): 334-344.

Hermet, Guy. Les Espagnols en France. Paris: Les editions ouvrières, 1967.

Hufton, Olwen. The Poor of 18th Century France 1750-1789. London: Oxford U. Press, 1974.

Hyman, Paula. "Challenge to Assimilation: French Jewish Youth Movements Between the Wars." Jewish Journal of Sociology 18(D, 1976).

"Immigrant Children School Integrated." France Actuelle 21(0, 1972).

Immigration et le Système de Prestations Sociales. Grenoble: Université des Sciences Sociales de Grenoble, N, 1973.

Inbar, Michael, and Adler, Chaim. "The Vulnerable Age: A Serendipitous Finding." Sociology of Education 49(Jl, 1976):193-200. [Children of Moroccan immigrants in Israel and France]

ben Jalloun, Tahar. La plus haute des solitudes. Paris: Editions du Sevil, 1978. [North Africans in France]

Jeanne, B. "Les Algériens dans l'agglomération rouennaise." Et. normandes 82(1972):1-16.

Jessua, C. "Travailleurs migrants et la discrimination raciale." Revue des Droits de l'Homme 5(1972). [Discussion in following issues]

Join-Lambert, P. "Discriminations raciales et tsiganes." Revue des Droits de l'Homme 5(1972).

Jouanna, Arlette. L'idée de race en France au XVIème sièecle et au début du XVIIème siècle (1498-1614). 3 vols. Paris: Librairie Honoré Champion, 1976.

"Juifs, en France, Aujourd'hui. Esprit 36 (Ap, 1968):577-624.

Kamm, Thomas. "Swastikas Reappear in Paris." Jerusalem Post, Ap 5, 1979.

Karady, V. "L'expansion universitaire et l'evolution des inégalities devant la carrière d'enseignant au début de la IIIe Republique." Revue française de sociologie 14(1973):443-470.

Kessler, Jane Sargent. "Educating the Black Frenchmen." Doctoral dissertation, Harvard U., 1958.

Korenchandler, Ch. Yidn in Paris. Les Juifs à Paris. Paris: The Author, 1970.

Ladurie, Emmanuel Le Roy. "Occitania in Historical Perspective." Review 1(Summer, 1977).

Laffey, John F. "Racism and Imperialism: French Views of the Yellow Peril, 1894-1914." Third Republic 1(My, 1976):1-52.

Lagarde, J.-P., and Vigier, C. Alphabetisation et Insertion Linguistique des Travailleurs Etrangers, 1974. ERIC ED 148 114. [Portuguese workers in France]

Lambiotte-Fekkar, B. "Le problème de l'adaptation scolaire des enfants algériens de la région parisienne." Enfance 4-5(0, 1966): 129-136.

Lauran, Annie. "Les enfants de nulle part. Entretien avec des enfants de travailleurs migrants." Terre entière 54(Jl-Ag, 1972).

Le Calloc'h, Bernard. "La diaspora chinoise en France." Acta Geographica (Paris) 30 (1977):7-14.

Legendre, Bernard. "La vie d'un prolétariat: les ouvriers de Fougères au début du XXe siecle." Mouvement soc. 98(Ja-Mr, 1977):3-42.

"Living Standard of African Immigrants at Issue in Wave of French Protests." Muhammad Speaks, Jl 10, 1970.

Lynch, James, and Plunkett, H. Dudley.
Teacher Education and Cultural Change.
London: George Allen & Unwin, 1973.
[England, France, and West Germany]

McCloy, Shelby T. The Negro in France.
Lexington, KY: N.p., 1961.

McDonald, James R. "Labor Immigration in
France, 1946-1965." Annals of the Association of American Geographers 59(Mr, 1969):
116-134.

Malino, Frances. The Sephardic Jews of
Bordeaux: Assimilation and Emancipation in
Revolutionary and Napoleonic France.
University, AL: U. of Alabama Press, 1977.

Mangin, Stanislas. "Problèmes de l'immigration étrangère en France. L'immigration et
l'enseignement." Revue des travaux de l'
Académie des sciences morales et politiques
1(1971).

Marceau, Jane. Class and Status in France.
Economic Change and Social Immobility, 1945-
1975. New York: Oxford U. Press, 1977.

Mangue, Pierre. "La Particularisme alsacien,
1918-1967." Doctoral dissertation, U. of
Paris, 1967.

Mancorps, P. H., Memmi, Albert, and Held, J.-F.
Les Francais et le racisme. Paris: Payot,
1965.

Mayo, Patricia Elton. The Roots of Identity:
Three National Movements in Contemporary
European Politics. London: Allen Lane,
1974. [Bretons]

Memmi, A. "Jewish Students and the Paris
Rebellion" (interview). Jewish Digest 15
(My, 1969):57-65.

Merimée, J. P. Les Travailleurs Antillais en
France--Aspects economiques. Memoire pour
le Diplome d'Etudes superieures de Science
Economique, Paris, 1971.

Mesnil, Jacques. "Quelques attitudes et
opinions des Francais a l'égard des
travailleurs africains." Esprit 34(Ap,
1966):744-757.

Meynier, G. "Les Algériens en France, 1914-
1918." R. hist. Maghrébine (Ja, 1976):
49-58.

Michel, Andree. "Mate Selection in Various
Ethnic Groups in France." Acta Sociologica
8(1965):163-176. [Spaniards, Italians, and
North African Muslims]

_____. The Modernization of North African
Families in the Paris Area. The Hague:
Mouton, 1974.

_____. Les Travailleurs Algériens en France.
Paris: N.p., 1956.

"Les Migrants: des hommes à part." Project
(Paris) 70(D, 1972):1188-1248.

"La migration algerienne." Hommes et Migration
116(1970):1-168 (entire issue).
[Algerian migration]

Mili, Ali. "Deux groupes d'immigrants tunisiens
en Frances, groupes ethniques et adaptation."
Doctoral dissertation, U. of Paris, VII,
1972.

Le Milieu social des eleves et leurs chances de
success a l'ecole (The Social Background of
Students and Their Chances of Success at
School), S, 1971. ERIC ED 060 278.

Minces, Juliette. Les Travailleurs Etrangers
en France. Paris: N.p., 1974.

Moreau-Defarges, Philippe. "L'immigration des
Africains en France." R. jur. pol. 31
(J1-S, 1977):967-974.

Morin, Francoise, and Raveau, Francois. "Les
Häitiens en France: étude preliminaire."
In Ethnies. Anglo-French Conference on Race
Relations in France and Great Britain, pp.
157-166. Paris: Mouton, 1972.

Morokvasic, Miriana. "Les Yougoslaves en
France--recherche des liens entre l'identité
nationale et l'acculturation." Doctoral
dissertation, U. of Paris, 1971.

Mouvaux, J.-P. "Les Etrangers Chez Nous."
Esprit (1973):753-770. [North Africans
in Denain]

Munoz, Marie-Claude. "Aspects psychologiques
de l'adaptation des enfants de travailleurs
immigres." In Les travailleurs étrangers
en Europe occidentale, pp. 163-171. Edited
by Philippe J. Bernard. Paris: Mouton,
1976.

_____. "Le developpement stéréotypé ethnique
chez l'enfant, approche psycho-sociologique."
Doctoral dissertation, U. of Paris, 1973.

_____. "Les enfants de migrants." Droit et
Liberté 322(J1, 1973).

N'diaye, Jean-Pierre. Enquete sur les
Etudiants Noirs en France. Paris: Editions
Realities Africaines, 1962.

_____. Négriers modernes: les travailleurs
noirs en France. Paris: Presence
Africaine, 1970.

N'Dongo, Sally. "From Senegal to France. An
Immigrant's Journey" (interview). Race
Today, F, 1975.

_____. "Nous ne venons pas manger votre pain."
Nouvel Observateur, Ag, 1973.

Niang, M. M. "Condition juridique des
Sénégalais en France." Revue Sénégalais de
Droit 5(Mr, 1971).

Odile, Rabut. "Les Étrangers en France." Population (1974):147-160.

"L'Offensive de haine contre les Algériens émigrés en France." El Moudjahid, Je 1, 1971.

Ogden, Philip E. Foreigners in Paris: A Residential Segregation in the Nineteenth and Twentieth Centuries. London: Department of Geography, Queen Mary College, 1977.

Ollivier, Francoise. "Vingt-quatre nationalités." Droit et Liberté 297(N, 1970).

Palmer, R. R. "Free Secondary Education in France Before and After the Revolution." History of Education Quarterly 14(Winter, 1974).

Papyle, H. "Les travailleurs étrangers en France, essai d'une bibliographie en langue française." Hommes et migrations 120(1972).

Patterson, Michelle. "Governmental Policy and Equality in Higher Education: The Junior Collegization of the French University." Social Problems 24(D, 1976):173-183.

Person, Yves (ed.). Minorités nationales en France. Paris: Les Temps Modernes, 1973.

"Les petits enfants étrangers de l'école maternelle." L'école maternelle francaise 6(F, 1969):9-24.

"La peur des 'Autres.'" L'Express 1037(My 24-30, 1971):28-31. [Algerians]

Pignon, Leila Sebbar. "Le mythe du bon nègre ou l'ideologie coloniale dans la production romanesque due XIIIIe siècle." Les Temps Modernes 337-338(1974).

Pike, David W. "L'immigration espagnole en France (1945-1952)." R. hist. mod. contemp. 24(Ap-Je, 1977):286-300.

Poinard, M. "Les Portugais dans le département du Rhone entre 1960 et 1970." R. Géogr. Lyon 47(1972):35-58.

"Problèmes de l'immigration étrangère en France." R. Trav. Acad. Sci. mor. polit. 124(1971):59-124.

Proctor, Carole. "The Jewish Policy of Vichy France." Master's thesis, U. of San Francisco, 1972.

Rager, J. J. L'émigration en France des Musulmans d'Algériens en France et dans les pays islamiques. Paris: Les Belles Lettres, 1950.

Rash, Yehoshua. "French, Foreigners and Jews." Patterns of Prejudice 10(Ja-F, 1976):6-13.

Raveau, Francois. "An Outline of the Role of Color in Adaptation Phenomena." Daedalus, Spring, 1967. [Africans in France]

Raveau, François, and Morin, Françoise. "Couleur et adaptation." In Ethnies. Anglo-French Conference on Race Relations in France and Great Britain, pp. 179-190. Paris: Mouton, 1972. [Blacks]

Ray, Joanny. "Les Marocains en France." Doctoral dissertation, U. of Paris, 1937.

Reece, Jack E. The Bretons Against France. Ethnic Minority Nationalism in Twentieth-Century Brittany. Chapel Hill: U. of North Carolina Press, 1977.

Rogers, J. A. "The American Negro in France." American Mercury 20(My, 1930):1-10.

Rosen, Dan. "France's Fed-Up Students." Nation 214(F 14, 1972):209-211.

Sauvel, J. "Accord franco-algérien du 27 decembre 1968 relatif à la circulation, au séjour et a l'emploi en France des ressortissants algériens et de leurs familles." Revue Juridique et Politique, Indépendence et Coopération 23(Ap-Je, 1969).

Sayad, Abdel Malek. "Les trois 'âges' de l'émigration algérienne en France." Actes de la Recherche en Sciences Sociales 15 (Je, 1977).

Schwarzfuchs, S. Les Juifs de France. Paris: Albin Michel, 1975.

Servier, J. Les enfants des travailleurs migrants. Communication presentée au colloque sur les travailleurs étrangers en Europe Occidentale. Paris 5, 6 et 7 juin 1974.

Servier, Jean. "A propos d'une enquête sociologique sur les gitans et nomades de France--Méthodes et prospective." In Ethnies. Anglo-French Conference on Race Relations in France and Great Britain, pp. 203-209. Paris: Mouton, 1972.

Sheehan, Edward R. F. "Europe's Hired Poor." New York Times Magazine, D 9, 1973.

Simon, P. J. "Un village franco-indochinois en Bourbonnais: aspects de la colonisation et le décolonisation de l'Indochine orientale." Doctoral dissertation, U. of Paris V, 1973.

Singer, Barnett. "France and Its Jews in World War II." Contemp. Fr. Civil. 2 (Fall, 1977):1-24.

Sofres. "Quel Raciste Etes-Vous?" Le Nouvel Observateur, N 7, 1967. [Ethnic attitudes of professional men in Paris]

Spillmann, Georges. "L'anticolonialisme en France due XVIIe siècle à nos jours." Afrique et Asie 2(1974):3-20.

Sternberg, Zeev. La Droite Revolutionnaire 1885-1914: les origines françaises du facisme. Paris: n.p., 1978.

Stevens, Auriol. "French Notebook." Times Educational Supplement, Mr 5, 1976.

Szajkowski, Zosa. Analytical Franco-Jewish Gazetteer, 1939-1945. New York: The Author, 1971.

_____. Jews and the French Foreign Legion. New York: Ktav Publ. House, 1975.

Talha, Larbi. "L'évolution du mouvement migratoire entre la Maghreb et la France." Maghreb-Machrek, Ja-F, 1974, pp. 17-34.

Tallard, M. "Les conditions de logement des travailleurs migrants en France." Consommation 14(Ja-Mr, 1977). [English summary]

Tapia, Claude. "Contacts inter-culturels dans un quartier de Paris." Cahiers internationaux de sociologie 54(1973):127-158.

_____. "North African Jews in Belleville." Jewish Journal of Sociology 16(Je, 1974): 5-23.

Tapinos, Georges. L'immigration Etrangere en France 1946-1973. Paris: Presses Universitaires de France, 1975.

Tilly, Charles. "Population and Pedagogy in France." History of Education Quarterly 13 (Summer, 1973):113-128.

"Les travailleurs immigres et le formation professionnelle." Migrants Formation (Paris) 17-18(O, 1976):1-136.

"Les travailleurs migrants et leur famille en France." Informations sociales (France) (N, 1971):4-93.

Trebous, Madeleine. "North and West African Workers in Roubaix" (France). Institute Race Relations Newsletter, Mr, 1968 supplement.

_____. Vie et Travail des Algériens en France. Paris: Editions du Jour, 1974.

Trindade, Maria B. R. Immigrés Portugais: Observation psycho-sociologique d'un groupe de Portugais dans la bonlieve Parisienne (Orsay). Lisbon: Instituto superior de ciencias sociais e politica ultra-marina, 1973.

Union Géneral des Travailleurs Sénégalais en France. Le Livre des Travailleurs Africains en France. Paris: Francois Maspero, 1970.

UNESCO Commission of France. Alphabetisation et Promotion des Migrants Étrangers en France. Paris: UNESCO, 1971.

Valabregue, C. "Les enfants de travailleurs étrangers." In L'homme déraciné, pp. 155-175. Paris: Mercuse de France, 1973.

Vaughn, Michalina, and Archer, Margaret Scotford. Social Conflict and Educational Change in England and France, 1789-1848. London: Cambridge U. Press, 1972.

Verbunt, Gilles. "Intégration et desintégration de la famille." Hommes et Migrations Documents 771(Jl 15, 1969).

Verbunt, G. "Travailleurs étrangers: L'integration personnelle." Cahiers d'action religieuse et sociale 517(My, 1970):273-276.

_____. "Travailleurs étrangers: problèmes de l'integration." Cahiers d'action religieuse et sociale 523(S, 1970):453-458.

Verdes-Leroux, Jeannine. "Pouvoir et assistance: cinquante ans de service social." Actes de la Recherche en Sciences Sociales 2(Je, 1976).

Vidal, C. "Colonisation et decolonisation du Rwanda la question tutsi-luitu." Revue Francaise d'Etudes Politiques Africaines 91 (1973):32-47.

Vignery, Robert J. The French Revolution and the Schools: Educational Policies of the Mountain, 1792-1794. Madison, WI: State Historical Society of Wisconsin, 1966.

Viguier, Marie-Claire. "France's Portuguese Workers." Race Today 2(1970):78-80/

_____. Un Modelle pour l'Étude de la Mobilité Professionelle des Travailleurs Immigres. Toulouse, France: Centre Nationale de la Recherche Scientifique et Université de Toulouse le Mirail, 1973. [Immigrant workers in Haute-Garonne]

van den Burg-Porte, Denise. La Tête de l'Autre. N.p.: n.p., 1977. [Racism in a Burgundy town]

Vouin, R. "Répression de la discrimination raciale en France." Revue des Droits de l' Homme 5(1972).

Wanner, Raymond E. Some French Initiatives in Educating the Socially and Culturally Disadvantaged. Washington, DC: GPO, 1973.

Webster, Mark. "Open Admissions--Oui ou Non." Change 9(Mr, 1977):16-19.

Weinberg, David H. A Community on Trial.
The Jews of Paris in the 1930's. Chicago:
U. of Chicago Press, 1977.

Wilson, Stephen. "Antisemitism in France
during the Belle Epoque." Wiener Library
Bulletin 29(1976-1977):9-18.

_____. "Le Monument Henry: la structure de
l'antisémitisme en France, 1898-1899."
An. éc. soc. civil. 32(Mr-Ap, 1977):
265-291.

Yansane, Ibrahima. "An African in Paris:
Rhapsody in Black." New York Times, S 4,
1976.

Zehraoui, Ahsène. Les travailleurs algériens
en France. Paris: Francois Maspero, 1971.

Zolberg, Aristide R., and Zolberg, Vera L.
"The Regimentation of Bourgeois Culture:
Public Secondary Schools in Modern France."
Comparative Education Review 15(O, 1971):
330-345.

The Germanies

Abdullah Muhammad S., and Mildenberger,
Michael. Moslems Unter Uns. Stuttgart:
Quell, 1974. Muslims in Western Germany

Adam, H. "Nachhilfeunterricht als pädaogagi-
scher und soziologischer Index." Die
Sammlung 15(1960).

Adam, Uwe Dietrich. Hochschule und National-
sozialismus. Die Universität in Dritten
Reich. Tübingen: J. C. B. Mohr, 1977.
[Tübingen U.]

_____. Judenpolitik in Dritten Reich.
Düsseldorf: Droste Verlag, 1972.

Adler-Rudel, Solomon. Jüdische Selbsthilfe
unter dem Naziregime 1933-1939. Tübingen:
J. C. B. Mohr (P. Siebeck), 1974.

Adler-Rudel, S. Ostjuden in Deutschland,
1880-1940. Tübingen: N.p., 1959.

Aich, Prodosch. "Asian and African Students
in the West German University." Minerva
(1963):439-452.

_____. Farbige unter Weissen. Köln:
Kiepenheuer und Witsch, 1962. [A study
of Negroes and Africans in West German
institutions of higher learning]

_____. "The Problems of Colored Students in
Germany." Social Sciences Information
(Paris) 1(1962).

Akpinar, U. and others. Pädagogische Arbeit
mit ausländischen Kinder und Jugendlichen.
Munich: Juventa Verlag, 1977.

Amir, Amnon. "Euthanasia in Nazi Germany."
Doctoral dissertation, State U. of New York
at Albany, 1977. Univ. Microfilms Order No.
77-32,241.

Ansay, Tugrul, and Gessner, Volkmer (eds.).
Gastarbeiter in Gesellschaft und Recht.
Munich: Beck'sche Verlagsbuchhandlung,
1974.

Arnold, Wilhelm. Begabung und Bildungswilling-
keit. München, Germany: Ernst Reinhardt
Verlag, 1968.

Aronsfeld, C. C. "'Perish Judah.' Nazi
Extermination Propaganda, 1920-1945."
Patterns of Prejudice 12(S-O, 1978):17-26.

Aurin, K. et al. Gleiche Chancen in
Bildungsgang.... Villingen, West Germany:
Neckar-Verlag, 1968.

Baker, Leonard. Days of Sorrow and Pain: Leo
Baeck and the Berlin Jews. New York:
Macmillan, 1978.

Boll-Kaduri, K. J. "Zum Leben der Juden in
Deutschland während des Zweiten Weltkrieges."
Z. Gesch. Juden 10(1973):33-38.

Beck, Earl R. "German Views of Negro Life in
the United States, 1919-1933." Journal of
Negro History 48(Ja, 1963).

Becker, Jorg. "Anti-Semitism in German Children's Materials." Interracial Books for
Children Bulletin 10, Nos. 1-2(1979):11-12.

_____. "Racism in West German Children's
Books." Interracial Books for Children 4
(Winter, 1972-1973):3.

Ben Elissar, Eliahu. "Le Facteur juif dans la
politique etrangere du IIIe Reich, 1933-
1939." Doctoral dissertation, U. of Geneva,
1969.

Bermann, Dagmar T. "Produktivierungsmythen
und Anti-semitisms. Assimilatorische und
zionistische Berufsumschichtungsbe-
strebungen unter den Juden Deutschlands
und Oesterreichs bis 1938." Doctoral
dissertation, Ludwig-Maximilian Universität,
1971.

Berman, Russell and others. "Jews and Germans
at the Turn of the Century." Telos 28
(Summer, 1976):167-173.

Bernstein, Reiner. "Zwischen Emanzipation und
Antisemitismus--Die Publizistik der deutschen
Juden am Beispiel der C. V. Zeitung... 1924-
1933." Doctoral dissertation, U. of Berlin,
1969.

Bettelheim. Bruno. "Reflections. Surviving."
New Yorker (Ag 2, 1976):31-52. [Concentra-
tion camps]

Bildungsprobleme und Zukunftserwartungen der
Kinder Türkischer Gastarbeiter. Munich:
Südosteuropagesellschaft, 1976.

Bingemer, Karl, Meistermann-Seeger, Edeltrud,
and Neubert, Edgar. Leben Als Gastarbeiter-
Geglückte und Missglückte Integration.
Köln: Westdeutscher Verlag, 1970.
[Köln]

Böhning, W. R. "Germany's Foreign Workers."
Race Today 2(O, 1970):350-352.

Bolkosky, Sidney M. The Distorted Image.
German Jewish Perceptions of Germans and
Germany, 1918-1935. Amsterdam: Elsevier,
1975.

Bracher, Karl Dietrich. "Stages of Totalitarian Integration." In Republic to Reich:
The Making of the Nazi Revolution. Edited
by Hajo Holborn. New York: Pantheon,
1972.

Brankačk, Jan, and Metsk, Frido. Geschichte
der Sorben. Vol. I: Von den Anfängen
1789. Bautzen, German Democratic Republic:
VEB Domowina-Verlag, 1977.

Brayne, Mark. "Sorbs Clinging to Identity in
[East] Germany." Los Angeles Times, D 1,
1977.

Brie, Alfred. Geschandete deutsche Frauen:
Wie die farbigen Franzosen in den besetzten
Gebieten wüten. Leipzig: N.p., 1921.

Buchhofer, Bernd, Friedrichs, Jürgen, and
Lundtke, Hartmut. "Entgangene Bildungschancen. Eine Empirische Analyse der Reak-
tionsmuster bei jungen Erwachsenen."
Zeitschrift für Soziologie 2(1973);239-253.

Buhl, W. L. "Schulaufbau und Verteilung der
Bildungschancen in der Bundesrepublik
Deutschland (1925-1960)." Doctoral disser-
tation, U. of Munster, 1965.

Cahnman, Werner J. Völker und Rassen im
Urteil der Jugend. Munich: Günter Olzog,
1965. [Intergroup attitudes of students
in Munich public schools]

Carmon, Arye. "The Impact of the Nazi Racial
Decrees on the University of Heidelberg:
A Case Study." In Yad Vashem Studies XI.
Jerusalem: Yad Vashem, 1976.

Castles, Stephen, and Kosack, Godula. "How
the Trade Unions Try to Control and Integrate Immigrant Workers in the German Federal Republic." Race 15(Ap, 1974):497-514.

Cecil, Robert. Alfred Rosenberg and Nazi
Ideology. New York: Dodd, Mead, 1972.

Clark, John Rosslyn. "Turkish Cologne: The
Mental Maps of Migrant Workers in a German
City." Doctoral dissertation, U. of
Michigan, 1974. Univ. Microfilms Order No.
75-658.

Colodner, Solomon. Jewish Education in
Germany under the Nazis. New York: Jewish
Education Committee Press, 1964.

Crew, David. "Definitions of Modernity: Social
Mobility in a German Town, 1880-1901."
Journal of Social History 7(F 11, 1973):51-74.
[Bochum]

Cyž, Jan. "Zum Ringen Jan Skalas für die Rechte
der Sorben in den Jahren 1926 bis 1930."
Letopis, Ser. B, 23(No. 2, 1976):183-188.

Dahrendorf, Rolf. Arbeiterkinder an deutschen
Universitäten. Tübingen: N.p., 1965.

_____. Bildung ist Buergerrecht. Hamburg:
Die Zeit Buecher, 1965.

_____. "The Crisis in German Education."
In Education and Social Structure in the
Twentieth Century. Edited by Walter Laqueur
and George L. Mosse. New York: Harper &
Row, 1967.

Dahrendorf, Rolf, and Peisert, H. (eds.).
Der vorzeitige Abgang von Gymnasium:
Studien und Materialien zum Schulerfolg.
Uillingen: Necker-Verlag, 1967.

Deutsch für ausländische Gastarbeiter, 1973.
Internationale Sozialistische Publikationen,
2000 Hamburg 13, Hochallee 21, Germany.

Diamont, Doris. "Ausländische Arbeiterkinder
in der deutschen Schule." In Gastarbeiter.
Analysen und Berichte. Frankfurt am Main:
Suhrkamp, 1972.

Dippmann, Klaus J. "The Legal Position of the
Lusatian Sorbs Since the Second World War."
Slavonic and East European Review 53(Ja,
1975):62-77.

Dirickx, Yvo, and Kudat, Ayse. Ghettos:
Individual or Systemic Choice? Berlin:
International Institute of Comparative Social
Studies, S, 1975. [Housing segregation for
Turks and Yugoslavs in West Berlin]

Dorn, Anne. Mein Vater arbeitet in der
Mültonne. Gastarbeiterkinder erzählen ihre
Geschichten. Frankfurt: N.p., 1972.

Drettakis, E. G. Yugoslav Migration to and
from West Germany, 1962-1973. Zagreb:
Centre for Migration Studies, 1975.

Drobisch, Klaus, Goguel, Rudi, Muller, Werner,
and Dohle, Horst. Juden unterm Hakenkreuz.
Verfolgung und Austrottung der deutschen
Juden, 1933-1945. Frankfurt/M: Roderberg-
Verlag, 1973.

Dungworth, David. "'Inconclusive' Migrant
Language Experiment." Times Educational
Supplement, Ap 22, 1977. [Language-teaching
of children of immigrant workers in Bavaria]

_____. "Programme Set Up to Help Immigrant Children." Times Educational Supplement, O 6, 1978. [West Germany]

Ebert, Hans. "The Expulsion of the Jews from the Berlin-Charlottenburg Technische Hochschule." Leo Baeck Institute Yearbook 19(1974):155-171.

Edelstein, W., and Raschert, J. "Dürchlässigkeit und Differenzierung in der Gesamtschule." In A. Rang and W. Schulz, Die differenzierte Gesamtschule. München: Piper, 1969.

"Eine verlorene Generation ausländischen Kinder?" Frankfurter Rundschau, O 4, 1975.

Eisenstadt, G. Michael, and Kaltefleiter, Werner (eds.). "Minorities in the Metropolis: A German American Comparison." Sozialwissenchaftliche Studien zur Politik 6(1975).

Elkar, Rainer S. "Jakob Wassermann, ein deutscher Jude zwischen Assimilation und Antisemitismus." In Jahrbuch des Instituts für Deutsche Geschichte, Vol. III. Edited by Walter Grab. Tel Aviv: Institut für Deutsche Geschichte, 1974.

Engelsing, Rolf. Analphabetentum und Lektüre: Zur Sozialgeschichte des Lesens in Deutschland zwischen feudaler und industrieller Gesellschaft. Stuttgart: J. B. Metzlersche Verlag, 1973.

_____. Zur Sozialgeschichte deutscher Mittel- und Unterschichten. Göttingen: Vandenhoeck und Ruprecht, 1973.

Evangelische Akademikerschaft in Deutschland, Katholischer Akademikerverband. Die Kinder der Gastarbeiter. Stuttgart/Bonn, 1971.

Eyferth, K. "Leistunger verschiedener Gruppen von Besatzungskindern in Hamburg-Wechsler Intelligenztest für Kinder (HAWIK)." Archiv. für die gesamte Psychologie 113 (1961):222-241.

_____. "A Study of Mulatto Children in West Germany." Vita Hum. 2(1959):112-114.

Eyferth, K., Brandt, U., and Hawel, W. Farbige Kinder in Deutschland. Munich: Juventa Verlag, 1960.

Feuser, Willfried. "The Image of the Black in the Writings of Johann Gottfried Herder." Jr. Eur. Stud. 8(Je, 1978):108-128.

Fink, Carole K. "Defender of Minorities: Germany in the League of Nations, 1926-1933." Central European History, D, 1972.

_____. "The Weimar Republic as a Defender of Minorities, 1919-1933..." Doctoral dissertation, Yale U., 1968. Univ. Microfilms Order No. 69-13,104.

FitzHerbert, Katrin. "Authoritarianism in German Schools." New Society, My 9, 1974.

Flessau, Kurt-Ingo. Schule der Diktatur. Schule der Diktatur. Lehrpläne und Schulbücher des Nationalsozialismus. Munich: Ehrenwirth Verlag, 1977.

"Foreign Workers." Patterns of Prejudice 11 (Mr-Ap, 1977):16. [Turkish workers in Germany]

Fuhr, Christoph, Ubish, Gisela, and Halls, W. D. (eds.). Educational Reform in the Federal Republic of Germany. Initiatives and Trends. Hamburg: UNESCO Institute for Education, 1970.

Gardei, Christa. Zur Frage der Integration türkischer Gastarbeiterkinder in Weddinger Grundschulen. Examenarbeit zur Zweiten Staatsprügung, Berlin, 1971.

Geiselberger, Siegmar (ed.). Schwarzbuch: Auslaendische Arbeiter. Frankfurt, West Germany: Fischer, 1972.

Gelles, R. "Polish Issues in German School-books in the 1930's in the Evaluation of Polish Historians." Polish W. Aff. 16, No. 2(1976):204-221.

Gerstenmaier, J., and Hamburger, F. "Bildungswünsche ausländischer Arbeitkinder. Ergebnisse einer Befraagung von Eltern und Kindern." Soziale Welt 3(1974):279-293.

Getler, Michael. "Hitler's Grandchildren." Washington Post, Ap 22, 1979. [Young neo-Nazis in West Germany]

Gewerkschaft Erziehung und Wissenschaft. "Tagungsbericht: Kinder ausländischer Arbeiter." Berliner Lehrerzeitung, Mr 15, 1974.

Geyer, H. "Gibt es Bildungsprivilegien in der Bunderrespublik?" Heidelberger Blätter 9-10(1966-1967).

Giles, Geoffrey J. "The Structure of Higher Education in the German Democratic Republic." Higher Education 7(My 1978):131-156.

Gilman, Sander L. "The Image of the Black in the German Colonial Novel." Jr. Eur. Stud. 8(Mr, 1978):1-11.

Ginat, Jochanan. "The Jewish Teacher in Germany." Leo Baeck Institute Yearbook 19 (1974):71-76.

Glatzer, W. "Besoins et déficits éducatifs des enfants de travailleurs étrangers en R.F.A." In R. Lendesdorff and H. Zillessen, Gastarbeiter-Mitbürger, pp. 61-68. Gelnhausen and Berlin, 1971.

Goldberger, Erich. "Obsession and Realpolitik in the 'Final Solution.'" Patterns of Prejudice 12(Ja-F, 1978):1-16.

Goldschmidt, Dietrich, and Sommerkorn, Ingrid. "Deprivation and Disadvantage: Federal Republic of Germany." In Deprivation and Disadvantage. Nature and Manifestations, pp. 119-169. Edited by A. Harry Passow. Hamburg, Germany: UNESCO Institute for Education, 1970.

Goldschmidt, Dietrich, and Jenne, Michael. "Educational Sociology in the Federal Republic of Germany." Social Science Information, Ag, 1969.

Goshko, John M. "The Jews in Germany." Washington Post, D 1, 1974.

Graham, Loren R. "Science and Values: The Eugenics Movement in Germany and Russia in the 1920's." American Historical Review 82(D, 1977):1133-1164.

Grieswelle, Detlef. "Antisemitismus in deutschen Studentenverbindungen des 19. Jahrhunderts." Stud. Wandel Ges. Bilding im 19. Jh. 12(1975):366-379.

Gross, Eberhard. "Gastarbeiterkinder an deutschen Schulen." Pädagogische Rundschau 23(1969):537-551.

Grossmann, Wilma. "Die Situation der Kinder ausländischer Arbeiter." In Schwarzbuch: Ausländische Arbeiter, pp. 133-146. Fischer Taschenbuch Verlag, 1972.

Habermas, Jürgen. "Pädagogischer 'Optimismus' von Gericht einer pessimistischen Anthropologie: Schelskys Bedanken zur Schulreform." Neue Sammlung 1(1961).

Hafner, H. "Psychological Disturbances Following Prolonged Persecution." Social Psychiatry 3(1968):79-88.

Hagen, William W. "Poles, Germans and Jews: The Nationality Conflict in Prussian Poland in the Nineteenth and Early Twentieth Century." Doctoral dissertation, U. of Chicago, 1971.

Hahn, Walter. "Extending Equal Opportunity in West German Higher Education." Educational Record 58(F, 1977):403-417.

Hamburger, E. "Jews in Public Service under the German Monarchy." Leo Baeck Yearbook 9 (1964):206-238. [Includes teaching]

Hammam, Hassan. "Die arabischen Studenten in der Bundesrepublik Deutschland mit besondere Beruecksichtigung der Studierenden aus Aegypten." Doctoral dissertation, U. of Saarbruecken, 1972.

Harant, S. "Schulprobleme von Gastarbeiter-kinder." In Gastarbeiter, pp. 149-168. Edited by H. Reimann and H. Reimann. Munich: William Goldmann, 1976.

Hardach, Gerd. "Klassen und Schichten in Deutschland 1848-1970." Gesch. Gesellschaft 3(No. 4, 1977):503-524.

Hartmann, H. E. O. "Probleme des Polentums in Preussen zwischen 1815 und 1871." Doctoral dissertation, U. of Erlangen-Nuremberg, 1973.

Hearnden, Arthur. Education, Culture and Politics in West Germany. Oxford: Pergamon Press, 1976.

Hegmann, Franz. "Fundamental Issues and Present Trends in West-German Secondary Education." Canadian and International Education 6(D, 1977):49-59.

Hermann, Klaus Jacob. "Jews and Judaism in East Germany." Reform Judaism, N, 1973.

Hillel, Marc, and Henry, Clarissa. Lebenborn E. V. Im Namen der Rasse. Wien: Zsolnay, 1975. [Nazi institution for breeding]

Hilsberg, Raul. "Prologue to Assimilation: A Study of the Identification, Impoverishment, and Isolation of the Jewish Victims of Nazi Policy." Doctoral dissertation, Columbia U., 1955. Univ. Microfilms Order No. 11,457.

Hohmann, M. "Spanische Gastarbeiter in Niederrheinischen Industriestadten, Materialien und Analysen." Zeitschrift für Jugendhilfe in Wissenschaft und Praxis 23(1971):493-511.

Hohmann, M. (ed.). Unterricht mit ausländischen Kindern. Düsseldorf: Pädagogischer Verlag Schwann, 1976.

Hopf, W., and Preuss-Lausitz, U. "Probleme der Gesamtschule." Blätter für deutsche und internationale Politik 15(1970).

Horn, Daniel. "Youth Resistance in the Third Reich: A Social Portrait." Journal of Social History 7(Fall, 1973):26-50.

Jacobmeyer, Wolfgang. "Polnische Juden in der amerikanischen Besatzungszone Deutschlands." Vierteljahrsch Zeitgesch. 25(Ja, 1977):120-135.

Jungk, D. "Probleme des sozialen Aufsteigs berufstätiger Jugendlicher." Doctoral dissertation, Hanover Technischer Hochschule, 1966.

Kaelble, Hartmut. "Chancenungleicheit und akademische Ausbildung in Deutschland 1910-1960." Geschichte und Gesellschaft 1 (No. 1, 1975):121-149.

Kaelble, Hartmut. "Social Stratification in Germany in the 19th and 20th Centuries: A Survey of Research since 1945." Journal of Social History 10(Winter, 1976):144-165.

Kardamakis, Matthaeus K. "Zur sozialen Kommunikation der auslaendischen Arbeitnehmer in Deutschland untersucht am Beispiel der griechischen Gastarbeiter." Doctoral dissertation, U. of Munich, 1971.

Kasper, Martin. "Neue Merkmale in der sorbischen nationalen Bewegung nach dem ersten Weltkrieg (1919-1932)." Letopis, Series B., 23(No. 2, 1976):140-150.

Kater, Michael H. "Die Artamanen-Völkische Jugend in der Weimarer Republik." Historische Zeitschrift, D, 1971.

Kath, G. Das soziale Bild der Stundentenschaft in der Bundesrepublik Deutschland. Bonn: Deutsches Studentenwerk, 1969.

Kaupen-Haas, H. Some Problems of Integration of Foreign Workers in Cologne. Paris: OECD Manpower and Social Affairs Directorate, 1969.

Kisch, Guido. The Jews in Medieval Germany. Chicago: U. of Chicago Press, 1949.

Klee, Ernst (ed.). Gastarbeiter, Analysen und Berichte. Frankfurt a. M., Germany: Suhsckamp, 1972.

Klein, Helmut. Education in a Socialist Country. Berlin: Panorama PDR, 1974.

Kleine Westendpresse von der Elsa-Brändström-Schule. Gastarbeiterkinder am unserer Schule. Frankfurt: Sommer, 1971.

Kleming, Gerhard. "Soziale Mobilität in der Bundesrepublik Deutschland. I: Klassenmobilität." Kölner Zeitschrift für Soziologie und Sozialpsychologie 27(1975): 97-121.

_____. "Soziale Mobilität in der Bundesrepublik Deutschland. II: Status-Oder Prestige-Mobilität." Kölner Zeitschrift für Soziologie und Sozialpsychologie 27(Ag, 1975):273-292.

Klessmann, Christoph. "Polen in deutschen Geschichtsbüchern." Geschichte in Wissenschaft und Unterricht, D, 1972.

Knauss, Erwin. "Dokumentation über das Schicksal der Giessener Juden von 1933 bis 1945." Mitt. Oberhess. Geschichtsver 59 (1974):3-166.

Koch, Herbert R. Gastarbeiterkindern in deutschen Schulen. Königswinter am Rhein: Verlag für Sprachmethodik, 1970.

Kohler, H. Daten zur Situation der Hauptschulen in Berlin (West). Berlin: Max Planck Institut für Bildungsforehung, 1976.

Koehn, Ilse. Mischling, Second Degree. My Childhood in Nazi Germany. N.p: Greenwillow, 1977.

Köhler, Roland and others. Higher Education in the G.D.R. Berlin: Institut für Hochschulbildung, 1973.

Kolinsky, Eva. "Nazi Shadows Are Lengthening Over Germany. Patterns of Prejudice 12 (N-D, 1978):25-32.

Konieczny, Alfred. "Bemerkungen über die Anfänge des Konzentrationslagers Auschwitz." Hefte Auschwitz 12(1970):5-44.

Krane, R. E. "Effects of Cyclical International Composition Migration Upon Socio-Economic Mobility." International Migration Review 7(Winter, 1973):427-436. [Turkish workers return from Germany]

_____. (ed.). Manpower Mobility Across Cultural Boundaries. Social, Economic, and Legal Aspects: The Case of Turkey and West Germany. Leiden, Netherlands: E. J. Brill, 1975.

Krohn, Helga. Die Juden in Hamburg: Die politische, soziale und kulturelle Entwicklung einer jüdischen Grossstadtgemeinde nach der Emanzipation, 1848-1918. Hamburg: Hans Christian Verlag, 1974.

Kulak, Zbigniew. "Polen und die deutschpolnischen Beziehungen in den neuesten Schul-geschichtsbüchern der Bundesrepublik Deutschland." Polish Western Aff. 16 (Nos. 1-2, 1976):173-189.

Kulczycki, John J. "The School Strike of 1906-1907 in the Province of Poznán." In American Contributions to the Seventh International Congress of Slavists, III. The Hague: Mouton, 1973.

_____. "Social Change in the Polish National Movement in Prussia Before World War I." Nationalities Papers 4(Spring, 1976):17-53.

Lamberti, Marjorie. Jewish Activism in Imperial Germany: The Struggle for Civil Equality. New Haven, CT: Yale U. Press, 1978.

Lammich, Maria. "Das Bild der Slaven in deutschen Zeitschriften der Jahre 1860-1880: Ein Beitrag zur Erforschung nationaler Vorurteile." Beitr. Konfliktforsch No. 4(1976):63-93.

Lattimore, Bertram G., Jr. The Assimilation of German Expellees Into the West German Polity and Society Since 1945. A Case Study of Eutin, Schleswig-Holstein. The Hague: Martinus Nijhoff, 1974.

Lea, Charlene A. Emancipation, Assimilation and Stereotype: The Image of the Jew in German and Austrian Drama, 1800-1850. Bonn: Bouvier, 1978.

Levine, Herbert S. "Educating Jewish Children in Weimar and Nazi Germany." Integrateducation 13(S-O, 1975):33-36.

Levy, Richard S. The Downfall of the Anti-Semitic Political Parties in Imperial Germany. New Haven, CT: Yale U. Press, 1975.

Lightfoot, Claude. Racism and Human Survival. New York: International, 1972.

Littlewood, William T. "'Gastarbeiterdeutsch' and Its Significance for German Teaching." Audio-Visual Language Journal 14(Winter, 1976-77):155-158.

Lohmann, Joachim. "Entwicklung und Stand der Gesamtschulplanung in der Bundesrepublik Deutschland." International Review of Education 17(1971):50-56.

Lowenfeld, David. "A Futile Defense: Jewish Responses to German Anti-Semitism 1879-1914." Olam (Spring, 1976).

Luczak, Czeslaw (ed.). The Position of Polish Forced Laborers in the Reich, 1939-1945 (In Polish with an English introduction). Poznan: Institut Zachodni, 1975.

Lüpke, Rolf. "Third World Stereotypes in FRG Religious Materials." Interracial Books for Children Bulletin 10, Nos. 1-2(1979):15-17.

Lundgreen, Peter. "Industrialization and the Educational Formation of Manpower in Germany." Journal of Social History 9(Fall, 1975):64-80.

Lutz, Hartmut. "The Image of the American Indian in German Literature." Interracial Books for Children Bulletin 10, Nos. 1-2 (1979):17-18.

Lynch, James, and Plunkett, H. Dudley. Teacher Education and Cultural Change. London: George Allen & Unwin, 1973. [England, France, and West Germany]

McKale, Donald M. "Hitlerism for Export! The Nazi Attempt to Control Schools and Youth Clubs Outside Germany." J. Eur. Stud. 5 (S, 1975):239-253.

Malhotra, M. K. "Die Soziale Integration der Gastarbeiterkinder in die Deutsche Schulkorse." Kölner Zeitschrift für Soziologie 25(1973):104-121. [Düsseldorf and Krefeld]

Margoshes, Samuel. "The Curriculum of the Jewish Schools in Germany from the Middle of the Seventeenth to the Middle of the Nineteenth Century." Doctoral dissertation, Jewish Theological Seminary of America, 1917.

Massaquoi, Hans J. "Integration--Germany's New Way of Life." Ebony, Mr, 1966. Children of Negro-American soldiers

Mehrlander, Ursula. "Problèmes formation professionelle des travailleurs étrangers et de leurs enfants en République fédérale d'Allemagne." In Les travailleurs étrangers en Europe occidentale, pp. 193-202. Edited by Philippe J. Bernard. Paris: Mouton, 1976.

_____. Soziale Aspekte der Auslaenderbeschaeftigung. Bonn-Bad Godesberg: Verlag Neue Gesellschaft, 1974.

Merritt, Richard L. "Democratizing West German Education." Comparative Education 7(D, 1971):121-136.

Merritt, Richard L. and others. "Political Man in Postwar West German Education." Comparative Education Review 15(O, 1971): 346-361.

Metall, I. G. Zur schulischen Integration der Kinder ausländischer Arbeitnehmer. Frankfurt a. Main, Germany: I. G. Metall, 1970.

Meyer, Michael A. The Origins of the Modern Jew: Jewish Identity and European Culture in Germany, 1749-1824. Detroit, MI: Wayne State U. Press, 1967.

Mohrmann, Walter. Antisemitismus: Ideologie und Geschichte im Kaiserreich und in der Weimarer Republik. Berlin: N.p., 1972.

Mork, Gordon R. "Out of the Ghetto: German Jews and American Blacks." Integrated Education 12(My-Je, 1974):46-48.

Mosse, W. E., and Paucker, A. (eds.). Deutsches Judentum in Krieg und Revolution 1916-1923. Tübingen: N.p., 1971.

_____ and _____ (eds.). Juden in Wilhelminischen Deutschland. Tübingen: N.p., 1976.

Müller, Detlef. "Sozialstruktur und Schulsystem. Forschungsbericht über eine mehrdimensionale Analyse des Schulwesens im 19. Jahrhundert, Modellfall Berlin." Annales cisalpines d'histoire sociale, Ser. 1, No. 2(1971):31-60.

Müller, Hermann. Gutachten zur Schul-und Berufsausbildung der Gastarbeiterkinder. Bochum: Verbrand Bildung und Erzielrung, 1971.

_____. Rassen und Völker in Denken der Jugend. Stuttgart, Germany: Ernst Klett Verlag, 1967. [Frankfurt/Main]

Müller, Walter. "Bildung und Mobilitätsprozess--Eine Anwendung der Pfadanalyse." Zeitschrift für Soziologie 1(1972):65-84.

Nast, Manfred. "The Planning of Higher Education in the German Democratic Republic." Higher Education 3(1974):201-212.

Nebe, Michael. "Regionale und soziale Unterschiede der 'Lebensqualität' in Bundesgebiet." Geographische Rundschau 28 (1976):178-185.

Nelson, Keith L. "The 'Black Horror on the Rhine': Race as a Factor in Post-World War I Diplomacy." Journal of Modern History 42(D, 1970):606-627.

Niethammer, Lutz. Entnazifizierung in Bayern: Saüberung und Rehabilitierung unter amerikanischer Besatzung. Frankfurt am Main, Germany: S. Fischer, 1972.

Niewyk, Donald L. "The Economic and Cultural Role of the Jews in the Weimar Republic." Leo Baeck Institute Yearbook 16(1971).

Nikolinakos, Marios. "Economic Foundations of Discrimination in the Federal Republic of Germany." In Foreigners in Our Community, pp. 78-97. Edited by Hans von Houte and Willy Melgert. Amsterdam, The Netherlands: Keesing, 1972.

_____. Politische Ökonomie der Gestarbeiterfrage Migration und Kapitalismus. Hamburg: Rowolt, 1973.

Nixdorff, Peter W. "The Pace of West German Educational Reform as Affected by State Politics." Doctoral dissertation, U. of Florida, 1970.

Norden, Günther von. Das Dritte Reich im Unterricht. Frankfurt am Main: Hirschgraben Taschenbücher Verlag, 1970.

Olenhusen, Albrecht Gotz von. "Die 'nicht-arischen' Studenten an den deutschen Hochschulen" 1933-1945. Vierteljahrhefte für Zeitgeschichte 14(Ap, 1966):175-206.

Paetzold, Kurt. Faschismus, Rassenwahn, Judenverfolg. Eine Studie zur politischen Strategie und Taktik des faschistischen deutschen Imperialismus (1933-1945). Berlin: VEB Deutscher Verlag der Wissenschaften, 1975.

Pancker, Arnold. "Jewish Defence Against Nazism in the Weimar Republic." Wiener Library Bulletin 26(1972):21-31.

Picht, G. Die deutsche Bildungskatastrophe. Freiburg: N.p., 1964.

Pieper, Helmut. Die Minderheitenfrage und des Deutsche Reich 1919-1933/34. Frankfurt a/M: Metzner, für Internationale Angelegenenheiten der Univ. Hamburg, 1974.

Pierson, Ruth. "German-Jewish Identity in the Weimar Republic." Doctoral dissertation, Yale U., 1970.

Pollack, Herman. Jewish Folkways in Germanic Lands (1648-1806): Studies in Aspects of Daily Life. Cambridge, MA: MIT Press, 1971.

Poppel, Stephen M. "German Zionism and Jewish Identity." Jewish Journal of Sociology 18 (D, 1976).

_____. "Nationalism and Identity: German Zionism, 1897-1933." Doctoral dissertation, Harvard U., 1973.

_____. "New Views on Jewish Integration in Germany." Central European History 9(Mr, 1976):86-108.

Preston, David L. "The German Jews in Secular Education, University Teaching, and Science: A Preliminary Inquiry." Jewish Social Studies 38(Spring, 1976):99-116.

Ramirez, H. J. Spanische Gastarbeiterkinder in der Bundesrepublik Deutschland. Vergleichsuntersuchung zur Frage der Akkulturation. Bonn: N.p., 1972.

Reimann, Helga, and Reimann, Horst (eds.). "Gastarbeiter." In Das wissenschaftliche Tagebuch, Abteilung Soziologie-Soziale Probleme 4. München: Wilhem Goldmann Verlag GmbH, 1976.

Reinharz, Jehuda. "Deutschtum and Judentum: Jewish Liberalism and Zionism in Germany, 1893-1914." Doctoral dissertation, Brandeis U., 1972.

_____. Fatherland or Promised Land. The Dilemma of the German Jew, 1893-1914. Ann Arbor: U. of Michigan Press, 1975.

Rheins, Carl J. "German Jewish Patriotism, 1918-1935." Doctoral dissertation, State U. of New York, Stony Brook, 1977.

Renner, E. Enziehungs und Sozialisationsbedingungen türkischer Kinder. Ein Vergleich zwischen Deutschland und der Turkei. Rheinstetten: Neuburgweier, 1975.

Rhoades, Robert Edward. "Guest Workers and Germans: A Study in the Anthropology of Migration." Doctoral dissertation, U. of Oklahoma, 1976. Univ. Microfilms Order No. 76-24,390.

Richarz, Monika. Der Eintritt der Juden in die akademischen Berufe. Jüdische in Akademiker in Deutschland, 1677-1848. Tübingen: Mohr, 1974.

_____. "Jewish Social Mobility in Germany during the Time of Emancipation (1790-1871)." Leo Baeck Institute Yearbook 20(1975):69-77.

_____ (ed.). Jüdisches Leben in Deutschland: Selbstzengnisse zur Sozialgeschichte, 1780-1871. Stuttgart: Deutsche Verlags-Anstalt, 1976.

Richter, Ingo. Bildungsverfassungsrecht--
studien zum Verfassungswandel in
Bildungswesen. Stuttgart: Ernst Klett-
Verlag, 1973.

_____. "Educational Innovation and the
Constitution." Education and Urban Society
6(N, 1973):5-21.

Ringer, Fritz K. "Higher Education in Germany
in the Nineteenth Century." In Education
and Social Structure in the Twentieth
Century. Edited by Walter Laqueur and
George L. Mosse. New York: Harper & Row,
1967.

Rinott, Chanoch. "Jüdische Jugendbewegung in
Deutschland (1912-1942)." Neue Sammlung 17
(Ja-F, 1977):75-94.

Rist, Ray C. Guestworkers in Germany: The
Prospects for Pluralism. New York:
Praeger, 1978.

_____. On the Education of Guestworker
Children in Germany: A Comparative Study
of Policies and Programs in Bavaria and
Berlin, Mr, 1978. ERIC ED 153 913.

Roeder, P. M., Pasczierny, A., and Wolf, W.
Sozialstatus und Schulerfolg...
Heidelberg, Germany: Quelle & Meyer, 1965.

Roeder, P. M. and others. Sprache und
Sozialstatus. Heidelberg: Quelle und
Meyer, 1965.

Ronneberg, F. (ed.). Zukunftserwartungen der
Kinder türkischer Arbeitnehmer. Türkische
Kinder in Deutschland. Nürnberg: Verlag
der Nürnberger Forschungvereinigung, 1977.

Rosdolsky, R. "Friedrich Engels und das
Problem der 'Geschichtlosen Völker.'"
Archiv für Sozialgeschichte 4(1964).

Rosenthal, Ludwig. How Was It Possible? The
History of the Persecution of the Jews in
Germany from the Earliest Times to 1933,
as Forerunner of Hitler's "Final Solution"
to the Jewish Problem. Tr. Regina Eis.
Berkeley, CA: Judah L. Magnes Memorial
Museum, 1971.

Roskies, Diane K. Teaching the Holocaust to
Children: A Review and Bibliography. New
York: Ktav Publishing House, 1975.

Rürüp, Reinhard. Emanzipation und Antisemitismus. Göttingen: N.p., 1976.

_____. "Emanzipation und Krise--zur
Geschichte der 'Judenfrage' in Deutschland
vor 1890." In Juden in Wilhelminischen
Deutschland, 1890-1914. Edited by Werner E.
Mosse. Tübingen: J. C. B. Mohr, 1976.

Schallenberger, E. Horst, and Stein, Gerd.
"Jewish History in German Textbooks."
Patterns of Prejudice 10(S-O, 1976):15-17,
21.

Schenda, Rudolf. Volk ohne Buch: Studien zur
Sozialgeschichte der populären Lesestoffe
1770-1910. Frankfurt am Main: Vittorio
Klostermann, 1970.

Schenk, Wolfgang. "Ausländer, inbesonders
ausländische Arbeitnehmer, in der Altstadt
von Nürnberg." Nürnberger Wirtschafts-und
Sozialgeographische Arbeiten 24(1975):221-
234.

Schleunes, Karl. A. "Nazi Policy toward German
Jews, 1933-1938." Doctoral dissertation, U.
of Minnesota, 1966. Univ. Microfilms Order
No. 68-1619.

_____. The Twisted Road to Auschwitz. Nazi
Policy Toward German Jews, 1933-1939.
Urbana, IL: U. of Illinois Press, 1971.

Schneider, Hagen. "Die Darstellung Polens in
Schulgeschichtsbüchern des Kaiserreiches."
Int. Jb. Geschichtsunter 16(1975):164-241.

Schneider, W. "Die soziale Bedingtheit der
Ausbildungschancen." In F. Hess and
others, Die Ungleichheit der Bildungschancen.
Freiburg, Germany: Olten, 1966.

Schochat, A. "German Jews' Integration." Zion
2-3(1956):207-235.

Schofer, Lawrence. The Formation of a Modern
Labor Force. Upper Silesia, 1865-1914.
Berkeley: U. of California Press, 1975.

Schorsch, Ismar. Jewish Reactions to German
Anti-Semitism, 1870-1914. New York:
Columbia U. Press, 1972.

Schrader, A. and others. Die Zweite Generation:
Ausländischer Kinder in der Bundesrepublik.
Darmstadt: Athenäuns Verlag, 1976.

Schwab, Herman. The History of Orthodox Jewry
in Germany. Tr. Irene R. Birnbaum. London:
Mitre, 1950.

Schwarzweller, Harry K. "Educational Aspirations
and Life Chances of German Young People."
Comparative Education 4(N, 1967):35-49.

Selke, Welf. Die Ausländerwanderung als Problem
der Raumordnungspolitik in der Bundesrepublik
Deutschland. Bonner Geographische
Abhandlungen, 1977.

Selmeier, Franz. "Das nationalsozialistische
Geschichtsbild und der Geschichtsunterricht
1933-1945." Doctoral dissertation, U. of
Munich, 1969.

Sigg, Marianne. "Das Rassestrafrecht in Deutsch-
land in den Jahren 1933-1945, unter besonderer
Berücksichtigung des Blutschutzgesetzes."
Doctoral dissertation, U. of Aarau, 1951.

Silkes, Gerna. Ghetto: The Jewish School
System in the Ghetto (in Hebrew). New York:
N.p., 1959. [Illegal Jewish schools under
the Nazis]

Simon, Ernst. "Jewish Adult Education in Nazi Germany as Spiritual Resistance." Leo Baeck Institute Yearbook 1(1956).

Sontz, Ann L. "Neighbors and Strangers: Factory and Community in a West German Immigrant Zone." Doctoral dissertation, Columbia U., 1978. Univ. Microfilms Order No. 7904125. [Italian workers near Nordstadt, the Rhine]

Spidle, Jake W. "Colonial Studies in Imperial Germany." History of Education Quarterly 13(F, 1973):231-248.

Spira, Thomas. "Connections between Trianon Hungary and National Socialist Germany, and the Minority Swabian School Problem." Int. Jb. Geschichtsunter 15(1974):240-258.

Stern, Heinemann. Warum hassen sie uns eigentlich? Jüdische Leben zwischen den Kriegen. Edited by Hans Ch. Meyer. Düsseldorf, Germany: Droste Verlag, 1970.

Stiegnitz, Peter. "Wirtschaftspolitische Aspekte der Beschäftigung von Gastarbeitern." Wirtschaftspolitische Blätter 18 (1971).

Stone, Gerald. The Smallest Slavonic Nation: The Sorbs of Lusatia. New York: Oxford U. Press, 1972. [Slavic minority in East Germany]

Tal, Uriel. Christians and Jews in Germany: Religion, Politics, and Ideology in the Second Reich, 1870-1914. Tr. Noah Jonathan Jacobs. Ithaca: Cornell U. Press, 1975.

Tansk, Walter. Breslauer Tagebuch 1933-1940. East Berlin: Aufbau, 1975. [Diary of a Jew]

"Travailleurs immigrés: realitiés et problèmes." Materialen zur politschen Bildung (Bonn), Vol. 2, pp. 5-104. [West Germany]

Ulrich, E. "Gastarbeiterkinder an deutschen Volkschulen." Pädagogische Welt 24(1970): 345-363.

Vogt, Hartmut. "Das System der Schulvorbereitung in der DDR." Deutschland-Archiv, Mr, 1971.

von Carnap, R., and Edding, F. Der Relativ Schulbesuch in den Ländern der Bundesrepublik 1952-1960. Frankfurt: N.p., 1962.

von Weizsacker, Carl C. "Problems in the Planning of Higher Education." Higher Education (Amsterdam) 1(N, 1972):391-408.

Weingartner, James J. "The SS Race and Settlement. Main Office: Towards an Order of Blood and Soil." Historian 34(N, 1971): 63-77.

Weinreich, Max. Hitler's Professors: The Part of Scholarship in Germany's Crimes Against the Jewish People. New York: Yiddish Scientific Institute-YIVO, 1946.

Weiss, F. J. Entwicklungstendenzen des Besuchs allgemeinbildender Schulen in den Ländern der Bundesrepublik Deutschland. Frankfurt: N.p., 1964.

Wertheimer, Jack L. "German Policy and Jewish Politics: The Absorption of East European Jews in Germany (1868-1914)." Doctoral dissertation, Columbia U., 1978. Univ. Microfilms Order No. 7819463.

Whiting, Charles. "Immigrant Children Get Own Grammar School." Times Education Supplement, Ag 13, 1971. [Bad Driberg, Germany, school for children of foreign workers]

Whitney, Craig R. "Turkish Ghetto in West Berlin Plagued by Unemployment." New York Times, Mr 4, 1977.

Wickham, James. "Germany's Apprenticed Youth." New Society 19(Mr 2, 1972):437-440.

Williamson, W. "Patterns of Educational Inequality in West Germany." Comparative Education 13(Mr, 1977):29-44.

Willke, I. "Schooling of Immigrant Children in West Germany, Sweden, and England." International Review of Education 21(1975): 357-382.

Wilpert, Czarina. Akkulturation Türkischen Arbeiterkinder. Unpublished Magisterarbeit, 1974.

_____. "Children of Foreign Workers in the Federal Republic of Germany." International Migration Review 11(Winter, 1977):473-485.

_____. The Socialization of the Children of Migrant Labourers. Turkish Children in Berlin. Berlin: International Institute of Comparative Social Studies, D, 1974.

Yates, Dora. "Hitler and the Gypsies." Commentary, 1949.

Zimmermann, Hildegard. "Sozialstatus und schulische Leistung. Eine empirische Untersuchung an Realschulen und Gymnasien." Doctoral dissertation, U. of Cologne, 1973.

Zneimer, Richard. "The Nazis and the Professors: Social Origin, Professional Mobility, and Political Involvement of the Frankfurt University Faculty, 1933-1939." Journal of Social History 12(Fall, 1978): 147-158.

Zorn, W. "Hochschule und höhere Schule in der deutschen Sozialgeschichte der Neuzeit." In Spiegel der Geschichte. Edited by K. Repgen and S. Sklaweit. Münster: N.p., 1964.

Ghana

Awudetsey, S. A. "The Problem of Africanization of Education." Ghana Journal of Education 4(Ja, 1978):14-19.

Barkan, Joel D. An African Dilemma: University Students, Development and Politics
in Ghana, Tanzania and Uganda. New York:
Oxford U. Press, 1976.

Bening, R. B. "Colonial Policy on Education
in Northern Ghana, 1908-1951." Universitas
5(My-N, 1976):58-99.

Bibby, John. "The Social Base of Ghanaian
Education: Is It Still Broadening?"
British Journal of Sociology 24(1973):365-
374.

Bibby, John, and Peil, Margaret. "Secondary
Education in Ghana: Private Enterprise and
Social Selection." Sociology of Education
47(Summer, 1974):399-418.

Braimah, B. A. R. "Islamic Education in
Ghana." Ghana Bull. Theol. 4(1973):1-16.

Brokensha, David. Social Change at Larteh,
Ghana. London: Oxford U. Press, n.d.

Chazan, N. "The Manipulation of Youth Politics
in Ghana and the Ivory Coast." Genève-Afr.
15(1976):38-63.

Chinebuah, Isaac K. "The National Language
Issue in Africa: The Case for Akan in
Ghana." Afric. Lang. 3(1977):60-77.

Dogbe, Samuel Kwashi. "Ideological Conflict in
Contemporary Ghanaian Education: 1957-1971."
Doctoral dissertation, U. of Southern
California, 1973. Univ. Microfilms Order
No. 73-14399.

Foster, Philip J. "Ethnicity and the Schools
in Ghana." Comparative Education Review 6
(1962):127-135.

Graham, C. K. The History of Education in
Ghana. London: Frank Cass, 1971.

Humphreys, John. "The Image of the Educated
African: British Attitudes toward the Gold
Coast Educated Community, 1843-1914."
Doctoral dissertation, Harvard U., 1976.

Jahoda, G. White Man: A Study of the Attitudes
of Africans to Europeans in Ghana before
Independence. New York: Oxford U. Press,
1961.

Kanfert, J. M. "Impact of Multiple Ethnic
Loyalties and Linkages on Integration Poten-
tial Among Student Elites in Ghana."
Doctoral dissertation, Northwestern U., 1973.

Kwamena-Poh, Michael A. "The Traditional
Informal System of Education in Pre-Colonial
Ghana." Présence afric. 3(1975):269-283.

McKown, R. E., and Finlay, David J. "Ghana's
Status Systems: Reflections on University
and Society." J. Asian Afric. Studies 11
(Jl-O, 1976):166-179.

Osei-Hwedie, Kwaku. "Education System and
National Development in Ghana: Comparison,
Critique, and Analysis of the Relationship
between Education and National Development
in Colonial and Post-Colonial Ghana."
Doctoral dissertation, Brandeis U., 1978.
Univ. Microfilms Order No. 7821711.

Prah, Kwesi. Essays on African History and
Society. Accra: Ghana Universities Press,
1976.

Rhoda, Richard. "Migration of Educated Youth
from Rural Areas in Ghana." Doctoral
dissertation, U. of Iowa, 1978.

Robertson, Claire. "The Nature and Effects of
Differential Access to Education in Ga
Society." Africa (London) 47(No. 2, 1977):
208-219.

Sackey, J. A. "Language, Education and European
Contact in Ghana Since 1471." Master's
thesis, London External, 1972.

Great Britain

Asians

Akram, Mohammed. "Pakistani Migrants in
Britain--A Note." New Community 4(Winter/
Spring, 1974-5):116-118.

_____. Where Do You Keep Your String Beds?
London: Runnymede Trust, 1974.
[Bureaucracy of immigrant entry]

Ali, Ameer. "The Asian Press in Britain."
Patterns of Prejudice 10(N-D, 1976):6-8.

Allen, Sheila. New Minorities, Old Conflicts:
Asian and West Indian Migrants in Britain.
New York: Random House, 1971.

Anwar, Muhammad. "Young Asians Between Two
Cultures." New Society, D 16, 1976.

Ashby, B. E. "Cultural Background of Education-
al Response: An Investigation Into the
Differences of Ability and Attainment of
Asian Immigrant Pupils and Native Scots in
Glasgow Schools." Master's thesis, U. of
Edinburgh, 1967.

Aurora, Gundip Singh. "Indian Workers in
England: A Socio-Historical Survey of
Indian Workers in England." Master's
thesis, U. of London, 1960.

_____. The New Frontiersmen--A Sociological
Study of Indian Immigrants in the United
Kingdom. Bombay: Popular Prakashan, 1967.

Azim, Tariq. "Race and Repatriation--An Asian Viewpoint." Race Today 3(My, 1971):149.

Bagley, Christopher. "A Survey of Problems Reported by Indian and Pakistani Immigrants in Britain." Race, Jl, 1969.

Ballard, Roger. "Family Organisation among the Sikhs in Britain." New Community 2 (Winter, 1972-1973):12-24.

Ballard, Roger, and Ballard, Catherine. "The Sikhs: The Development of South Asian Settlements in Britain." In Between Two Cultures. Migrants and Minorities in Britain, pp. 21-56. Edited by James L. Watson. Oxford: Basil Blackwell, 1977.

Bandan, Sabir. Small Accidents, 1977. ILEA English Centre, Ebury Teacher's Centre, Sutherland Street, London, SW1, England. [Autobiography of young Ugandan Asian immigrant in London]

Bari, A. F. M. A. "A Comparative Study of Attitude and Reasoning Ability of a Group of East Pakistani Immigrant Children in Britain, and East Pakistani Children in East Pakistan in the Age Group 13-14 Years." Master's thesis, U. of London, Institute of Education, n.d.

Bell, R. "The Grammar of the English Spoken by Indian Immigrants in Smethwick." Master's thesis, U. of Birmingham, 1966.

Bell, Roger T. "The English of an Indian Immigrant: An Essay in Error Analysis." ITL Review of Applied Linguistics 22(1973): 11-61.

Bentley, Stuart. "Intergroup Relations in Local Politics: Pakistanis and Bangladeshis." New Community 2(Winter, 1972-1973):44-48.

Between Two Cultures: A Study of Relationships between Generations in the Asian Community in Britain. London: Community Relations Commission, D, 1976.

Bhatti, F. M. "Language Difficulties and Social Isolation: (The Case of South Asian Women in Britain)." New Community 5(Summer, 1976):115-117.

_____. "Young Pakistanis in Britain: Educational Needs and Problems." New Community 6(Summer, 1978):243-247.

Birmingham Community Development Project. Divided Families, 1974. The Project, 186 St. Savior's Road, Birmingham, England. [Pakistani families in Britain and Pakistan]

Blood on the Streets. London: Bethnal Green and Stepney Trades Council, 1978. [Violence against Bengalee community in London's East End]

Brah, Avtar K. "Age, Race and Power Relations: The Case of South Asian Youth in Britain." In Black Kids, White Kids--What Hope? RTCU, Brunel U., 1978.

_____. "South Asian Teenagers in Southall: Their Perceptions of Marriage, Family and Ethnic Identity." New Community 6(Summer, 1978):197-206.

Brand, Jeanne. "Development of a Special Course for Immigrant Teachers." Education Review 24(F, 1972):145-154. [Asian teachers]

Bristow, Mike. "Britain's Response to the Uganda Asian Crisis: Government Myths versus Political and Resettlement Realities." New Community 5(Autumn, 1976):265-279.

Bristow, Mike, and Adams, Bert N. "Uganda Asians and the Housing Market in Britain." New Community 6(Winter, 1977/78):65-77.

Bristow, Mike, Adams, Bert N., and Pereira, Cecil. "Ugandan Asians in Britain, Canada, and India: Some Characteristics and Resources." New Community 4(Summer, 1975): 155-166.

Broady, Maurice. "The Chinese in Great Britain." In Colloquium on Overseas Chinese. Edited by Morton H. Fried. New York: Institute of Pacific Relations, 1958.

_____. "The Social Adjustment of Chinese Immigrants in Liverpool." Sociological Review 3(1955):65-75.

Brooks, Dennis, and Brooks, Karamjit. "Ethnic Commitment versus Structural Reality: South Asian Immigrant Workers in Britain." New Community 7(Winter, 1978/9):19-30/

Buchanan, Keith. "Economic Growth and Cultural Liquidation: The Case of the Celtic Nations." In Radical Geography: Alternative Viewpoints on Contemporary Social Issues, pp. 125-142. Edited by Richard Peet. Chicago: Maaroufa Press, 1977.

Butterworth, Eric, and Kinnibrugh, Donald. Handbook I, The Social Background of Immigrant Children from India, Pakistan and Cyprus. London: School Council Books for Schools, Ltd., 1970.

Byrne, David. "The 1930 'Arab Riot' in South Shields: A Race Riot that Never Was." Race and Class 18(Winter, 1977):261-277.

Company, Richard C., Jr. "The Pakistani Community in London: A Cultural Geography." Master's thesis, U. of Utah, 1972.

Choo, Ng Kwee. The Chinese in London. London: Oxford U. Press, 1968.

Choonara, I. "Lifting the Veil of Islam." Times Educational Supplement, F 1, 1974. [On Islam and the mixing of the sexes in school]

Clark, David. "The Harijans of Britain." New Society, Je 26, 1975.

Cole, W. Owen. Education of Muslim Girls: A Discussion Paper. Leeds: Yorkshire Committee for Community Relations, O, 1975.

_____ (ed.). Religion in the Multi-Faith School--A Tool for Teachers. Leeds: Yorkshire Committee for Community Relations, 1973.

Corbett, Anne. "Bradford Gambles On Its Coeducational Policy." Times Educational Supplement, Ja 25, 1974. [The issue of Muslim girls and coeducation]

Cowgill, F. "A Study of the Integration of a Group of Indian Children into the School Community in Southall." Diploma in Child Development, U. of London, 1966.

Crishna, Satha. Girls of Asian Origin in Britain. London: YWCA, 1975.

Dahya, B. "The Nature of Pakistani Ethnicity in Industrial Cities in Britain." In Urban Ethnicity, pp. 77-118. Edited by A. Cohen. London: Tavistock, 1974.

_____. "Pakistani Ethnicity in Industrial Cities in Britain." In Urban Ethnicity, pp. 77-118. Edited by Abner Cohen. London: Tavistock, 1974.

_____. "Pakistanis in Britain: Transients or Settlers?" Race 14(Ja, 1973):241-277.

_____. "Pakistanis in England." New Community 2(Winter, 1972-1973):25-33.

Desai, Rashmi H. Indian Immigrants in Britain. London: N.p., 1963.

De Witt, John, Jr. Indian Workers' Associations in Great Britain. London: Oxford U. Press, 1969.

Dhanjal, Beryl. "Asian Housing in Southall: Some Impressions." New Community 6 (Winter, 1977/78):88-93.

_____. "Sikh Women in Southall (some impressions)." New Community 5(Summer, 1976): 109-114.

Dickinson, L., Hobbs, A., Kleinberg, S. M., and Martin, P. J. The Immigrant School Learner. Windsor Berks: NFER Publ. Co., 1975. [Pakistani pupils in Glasgow]

Dosanjh, J. S. "A Study of the Problems in Educational and Social Adjustment of Immigrant Children from the Punjab in Nottingham and Derby." Master's thesis, U. of Nottingham, 1967.

_____. Punjabi Immigrant Children: Their Social and Educational Problems in Adjustment. Nottingham, England: Institute of Education, 1969.

Ealing Community Relations Council. Dispersal of Asian School Children. Ealing: The Council, D, 1975.

Easton, E. G. "A Sociolinguistic Survey of the Chinese Community in Aberdeen." Master's thesis, U. of Aberdeen, 1971.

English and Punjabi Grammar and Syntax: A Comparison. London: National Association for Multiracial Education, 1976.

Ewan, John. Understanding Your Hindu Neighbour. London: Lutterworth Press, 1977.

Feinmann, Jane. "Inscrutable and Tidy--But Scared." Times Educational Supplement, Je 25, 1976. [Chinese children in London] schools

Fenton, Mike. "Asian Households in Owner-Occupation: A Study of the Pattern, Costs and Experiences of Households in Greater Manchester." Working Papers on Ethnic Relations. Bristol: SSRC Research Unit on Ethnic Relations, 1977.

Fitchett, Norman. Chinese Children in Derby. London: National Association for Multi Racial Education, 1976.

Folliot, Michel G. "L'emigration et l'implantation des Indo-Pakistanais en Grande-Bretagne." Doctoral dissertation, U. of Paris II (Cujas), 1971.

Forester, Tom. "Asians in Business." New Society, F 23, 1978.

Fowler, Bridget, Littlewood, Barbara, and Madigan, Ruth. "Sorry, the Job Has Been Taken." New Society, Ap 28, 1977. [Asians in Glasgow]

Garvey, Anne. "'They're Not Black So They Can't Be in Our Gang. And They're Certainly Not White Now, Are They?'" Times Educational Supplement, O 4, 1974. [Chinese in Britain]

Garvey, Anne, and Jackson, Brian. Chinese Children [in Great Britain]. London: National Educational Research and Development Trust, 1974.

Ghuman, Paul Avtar Singh. "A Cross-Cultural Study on the Basic Thinking Processes of English, 'British' Punjabi, and Indigenous Punjabi Boys." Doctoral dissertation, U. of Birmingham, 1974.

_____. The Cultural Context of Thinking. Windsor, Berkshire: NFER Publishing Co., 1975.

Guidelines and Syllabus on Islamic Education. London: Union of Muslim Organisations of U.K. and Eire, Mr, 1976.

Gupta, Y. P. "The Educational and Vocational Aspirations of Asian Immigrant and English School-Leavers: A Comparative Study." British Journal of Sociology 28(Je, 1977): 185-198.

Hallam, Roger. "The Ismailis in Britain." New Community 1(Autumn, 1972):383-388.

Hardy, Allan F. "Language, Truth and the Immigrant Worker." Training Officer 11 (O-N, 1975):260-261.

Haynes, J. M. "The Abilities of Immigrant Children: A Study of the Educational Progress of 7-9 Year Old Indian Children." Doctoral dissertation, U. of London, Institute of Education, 1970.

Hedayatullah, M. "Muslim Migrants and Islam." New Community 5(Spring-Summer, 1977):392-396.

Helweg, Arthur W. "A Punjabi Community in an English Town: A Study in Migrant Adaptation." Doctoral dissertation, Michigan State U., 1977. Univ. Microfilms Order No. 7810061.

Herman, D. L. S. "Asian Girls Are the Best Behaved." Times Educational Supplement, My 12, 1972. [London area]

Hill, Barry. "Daughters of the Temple." Times Educational Supplement, S 1, 1972. [Asian girls]

Hinchcliffe, Margaret. "Teaching English to Asian Men and Women." New Community 4 (Autumn, 1975):342-343.

Hiro, Dilip. "Indians and Pakistanis [in England]." New Society, Mr 13, 1969.

_____. "The Young Asians of Britain." New Society, Je 1, 1967.

Holroyde, Peggy, with Iqbal, Mohammed and Vohra, Dharam Kumar. East Comes West. A Background to Some Asian Faiths. London: Community Relations Commission, 1970.

Hossain, A. B. Md. A. "Fators Influencing Satisfaction with Life in Britain Among Pakistani Immigrants in Leeds and Bradford." Master's thesis, U. of Leeds, 1968.

Hui-lin, Liu. Overseas Chinese Children in Great Britain and the Problems of Chinese Education. Taiwan: Sinological Monthly, Yang Ming Shan, 1975.

Hunter, Kathleen. History of Pakistanis in Britain. London: Page, n.d.

Iqbal, Mohammed. "East is East?" Times Educational Supplement, Ap 21, 1978. [Separate education of Muslim children]

_____. "Education and Islam in Britain--A Muslim View." New Community 5(Spring-Summer, 1977):397-404.

_____. Islamic Education and Single Sex Schools. London: Union of Muslim Organisations in U.K. and Eire, 1975.

Iqbal, Muhammad, and Iqbal, Maryam. Understanding Your Muslim Neighbour. Guilford, England: Lutterworth Press, 1976.

Islam, M. M. "Bengali Migrant Workers in Britain: A Study of their Position in the Class Structure." Doctoral dissertation, U. of Leeds, 1977.

Jackson, Brian, and Garvey, Anne. "The Chinese Children of Britain." New Society 30(O 13, 1974):9-12.

Jackson R. "A Comparative Study of Political Socialisation, with Special Reference to English and Asian Children in English Secondary Schools." Doctoral dissertation, U. of London, Institute of Education, 1971.

Jahoda, Gustav, Thomson, Susan S., and Bhatt, Satindra. "Ethnic Identity and Preferences among Asian Immigrant Children in Glasgow: A Replicated Study." European Journal of Social Psychology 2 (1972):19-32.

James, Alan G. Sikh Children in Britain. New York: Oxford U. Press, 1974.

Jayawardena, Chandra. "Migrants, Networks, and Identities." New Community 2(Autumn, 1973):353-357. [Indian and Pakistani emigration and situation in England]

Jeffery, Patricia. Migrants and Refugees. Muslim and Christian Pakistani Families in Bristol. New York: Cambridge U. Press, 1976.

_____. "Pakistani Families in Bristol." New Community 1(Autumn, 1972):364-369.

Jennings, Loretta. "A Closure of a Ghetto School." Race Today 10(F, 1978):28-29. [Robert Montefiori Secondary School, Spitalfields, 43 percent Bengali enrollment]

Kallarckal, A. M., and Herbert, Martin. "The Happiness of Indian Immigrant Children." New Society, F 26, 1976.

Kanitkar, Helen. "The Social Organisation of Indian Students in the London Area." Doctoral dissertation, S.O.A.S., London U., 1972.

Karn, Valerie. "Property Values Amongst Indians and Pakistanis in a Yorkshire Town." Race, Ja, 1969.

_____. Some Aspects of Owner-Occupation Amongst Indian and Pakistanis in a West Riding Town. Third Annual Race Relations Conference. London, S 19, 1968.

Kanitkar, H. A. "An Indian Elite in Britain." New Community 1(Autumn, 1972):378-382.

Kearsley, Geoffrey W., and Srivastava, S. R. "The Spatial Evolution of Glasgow's Asian Community." Scottish Geog. Mag. 90(S, (1974):110-124.

Khan, Verity Sailfullah. "The Pakistani: Mirpuri Villagers at Home and in Bradford." In Between Two Cultures. Migrants and Minorities in Britain, pp. 57-89. Edited by James L. Watson. Oxford: Basil Blackwell, 1971.

_____. "Pakistani Villagers in a British City." Doctoral dissertation, Bradford U., 1974.

_____. "Pakistani Women in Britain." New Community 5(Summer, 1976):99-108.

_____. "Pakistanis in Britain; Perceptions of a Population." New Community 5(Autumn, 1976):222-229.

Kogan, Maurice. Dispersal in the Ealing Local Education Authority Schools System. London: Race Relations Board, Jl, 1976.

Kramer, Jane. "The Uganda Asians [in London]." New Yorker 50(Ap 8, 1974):47-93.

Lai, Linda Yeuk-lin. "Chinese Families in London: A Study Into Their Social Needs." Master's thesis, Brunel U., 1975.

Leech, Kenneth. "The History of a Trouble Zone." New Society, D 21, 1978. [Asians in the East End, London]

Levine, Ned, and Nayar, Tripta. "Modes of Adaptation by Asian Immigrants in Slough." New Community 4(Autumn, 1975):356-365.

Little, Alan, and Toynbee, Josephine. "The Asians: A Threat or an Asset?" New Society, O 26, 1972. [Kenyan Asians]

Lyon, Michael H. "Ethnicity in Britain: the Gujarati Tradition." New Community 2 (Winter, 1972-1973):1-11.

Mace, Jane, and Harding, Kate. "Unreasonable Demands." Times Educational Supplment, Jl 15, 1977. [BBC program to encourage Asians to learn English]

Mack, Joanna. "a Working Language." New Society, Ag 4, 1977.

_____. "Girls' Schools." New Society, O 23, 1975. [Education of Muslim girls]

Mandani, Mahwood. From Citizen to Refugee. London: Frances Pinter, 1973. [Ugandan in Britain]

Markham, E. A., and Kingston, Arnold (eds.). Merely a Matter of Color: The Ugandan Asian Anthology, 1973. Q Books, 16 Hillersdon Avenue, Edgeware, Middlesex, England.

Martell, B. "Asian Children in English Secondary Schools: An Enquiry Into Some Aspects of Their Background, Adjustment, Social and Educational Problems." Master's thesis, U. of Reading, n.d.

Meredith, Patricia. "'Here Comes Old "Arry Krishna"': Paki-Bashing as Depicted in the Press." Bachelor's thesis, Birmingham U., 1972.

Ng Kwee-choo. The Chinese in London. London: Oxford U. Press, 1968.

Nossiter, Bernard D. "London's 'Little India' Boils." Washington Post, Je 21, 1976. [Southall]

Nowikowski, Susan, and Ward, Robin. "Middle Class and British? An Analysis of South Asians in Suburbia." New Community 7 (Winter, 1978/9):1-10.

O'Brien, Justin. Brown Britons: The Crisis of the Ugandan Asians. London: Runnymede Trust, 1972.

O'Neill, J. A. "The Role of Family and Community in the Social Adjustment of the Chinese in Liverpool." Master's thesis, Liverpool U., 1972.

Pettigrew, Joyce. "Some Notes on the Social System of the Sikh Jats." New Community 1 (Autumn, 1972):354-363.

Pirani, M. "A Study of Indo-Pakistani Immigrants in Britain." Bachelor's thesis, Bath U., 1967.

"Problems of Assimilation Among Muslims in Great Britain." Patterns of Prejudice 9(My-Je, 1975):5-7.

Rahman, Afzal. Problems and Rights of Muslim Parents Regarding Education of Their Children. London: Muslim Educational Trust, 1974.

Rai, Usha. "Between Cultures and Languages in 'Little India.'" Times Educational Supplement, O 6, 1978. [Southall]

_____. "First Taste of Town for Children Up From Another Country." Times Educational Supplement, O 20, 1978. [Asian children in Tudor First School, central Southall]

_____. "How Bradford College Became a Place of Hope for the 'Indian Englishman.'" Times Educational Supplement, N 3, 1978.

_____. "Immigrant Teachers Who Find It's Temp Work or Nothing." Times Educational Supplement, O 13, 1978. [Discrimination in employment of immigrant teachers]

Reed, P. A. "Moslem Adolescent Boys in Batley." Master's thesis, U. of York, n.d.

Rovaretti, June. "Minorities and Underachievement." Times Educational Supplement, O 13, 1978. [West Indian and Asian school children in Newport junior schools]

Saifullah-Khan, V. J. M. "Pakistani Villagers in a British City: The World of the Mirapuri Villager in Bradford and in His Village of Origin." Doctoral dissertation, U. of Bradford, 1974.

Saint, C. K. "The Scholastic and Sociological Adjustment Problems of the Punjabi-Speaking Children in Smethwick." Master's thesis, Birmingham U., 1963.

Schools Council Project in English for Immigrant Children. Scope Handbook 1: The Social Background of Immigrant Children from India, Pakistan and Cyprus. London: Schools Council, 1971.

Scott, Duncan. "West Pakistanis in Huddersfield. Aspects of Race Relations in Local Politics." New Community 2(Winter, 1972-1973):38-43.

Seabrook, Jeremy. "A Change in Atmosphere: Race in One Town." New Society, S 2, 1976. [Blackburn]

Shamsher, Jogindar. "Panjabi Poetry in Britain." New Community 6(Summer, 1978): 291-305.

Shamsher, Jogindar, and Russell, Ralph. "Punjabi Journalism in Britain: A Background." New Community 5(Autumn, 1976): 211-221.

Sharma, Ursula. Rampal and His Family. The Story of an Immigrant. London: Collins, 1971.

Singh, A. K. Indian Students in Britain. London: Asia Publishing House, 1963.

Solanki, Ramniklal. "A View of the Asian Press in Britain." New Community 4(Winter-Spring, 1975-76):471-472.

Sookhdeo, Patrick. The Asian in Britain, 1972. The Community and Race Relations Unit, The British Council of Churches, 10 Eaton Gate, London SW1W9BT, England.

Surridge, Owen. "The Moon of Islam: Rising or Waning?" Times Educational Supplement, D 10, 1976. [Muslim religious education in British schools]

Swinerton, E. Nelson and others. Ugandan Asians in Great Britain. London: Croom Helm, 1975.

Tambs-Lyche, Harald. "A Comparison of Gujarati Communities in London and the Midlands New Community 4(Autumn, 1975):349-355.

_____. "London Patidars." Magistergrad thesis, Bergen U., 1972.

Taylor, J. H. "A Tradition of Respect." New Society 22(O 5, 1972):26-28. [Young Asians]

_____. The Half-Way Generation: A Study of Asian Youths in Newcastle upon Tyne. Windsor, Berks: N.F.E.R., 1976.

_____. "Newcastle upon Tyne: Asian Pupils Do Better Than Whites." British Journal of Sociology 54(1973).

Taylor, Laurie. "The Perfect Victims." New Society, Je 24, 1976.

Thakur, Manab, and Williams, Roger. "Hopeful Travellers: A Study of Asian Graduates Working in Britain." New Community 4(Winter-Spring, 1975-76):476-492.

Thompson, Marcus. "A Study of Generation Differences Amongst Sikhs." M. Phil. thesis, U. of London, 1970.

_____. "The Second Generation--Punjabi or English?" New Community 3(Summer, 1974):242-248.

Tibawi, A. L. Islamic Education. London: Luzac, 1973.

Tinker, Hugh. The Banyan Tree: Overseas Emigrants from India, Pakistan and Bangladesh. New York: Oxford U. Press, 1977.

Twaddle, Michael (ed.). Expulsion of a Minority. Essays on Ugandan Asians. London: Athlone Press, 1978.

Uganda Resettlement Unit. Ugandan Asians in Wandsworth, 1973. Wandsworth CCR, 57 Trinity Road, London SW17 7SO, England.

Wainwright, David. Resettlement: The Educational, Industrial and Social Background of the Uganda Asians. London: Runnymede Trust, 1972.

Walker, Kanta. "Finding Their Own Salvation." Times Educational Supplement, Jl 28, 1978. [Asian children in Manchester]

Wallis, Susan. "The Asians' Arrival." New Society, My 27, 1976. [Kenyan and Ugandan Asians in Britain]

_____. "Pakistanis in Britain." New Community 4(Winter-Spring, 1974-5):105-115.

Walsall Council for Community Relations and Leicester Community Relations Council. Aspirations versus Opportunities. Leicester: Leicester Community Relations Council, 1978.

Ward, Robin H. "What Future for the Uganda Asians?" New Community 2(Fall, 1973):372-378.

Watson, James L. "The Chinese: Hong Kong Villages in the British Catering Trade." In Between Two Cultures. Migrants and Minorities in Britain, pp. 181-213. Edited by James L. Watson. Oxford: Basil Blackwell, 1977.

_____. "Chinese Emigrant Ties to the Home Community." New Community 5(Spring-Summer, 1977):343-352.

_____. "Restaurants and Remittances: Chinese Emigrant Workers in London." In Anthropologists in Cities. Edited by G. M. Foster and R. V. Kemper. Boston: Little, Brown, 1974.

Whitfield, Sylvia. "Pakistanis or Citizens?" New Society, Jl 3, 1975.

Widlake, Paul, and Bell, Lorna. The Education of the Socially Handicapped Child. London: Nelson, 1975. [Asian children in a Midland town school]

Wilkinson, Tony. "Uganda Asians in Leicester: Initial Resettlement." New Community 3 (Winter-Spring, 1974):147-149.

Wilson, Amrit. "A Burning Fever: The Isolation of Asian Women in Britain." Race and Class 20(Autumn, 1978):129-142.

Yorkshire Committee for Community Relations. The Education of Muslim Girls--A Discussion Paper, 1975. The Committee, Charlton House, Hunslet Road, Leeds, England.

Blacks

Abdee, Nino. "Black in Butetown." Race Today 4(N, 1972):364-365.

Allen, Sheila. "Black Workers in Great Britain." In Foreigners in Our Community, pp. 43-49. Edited by Hans van Houst and Willy Melgert. Amsterdam, The Netherlands: Keesing, 1972.

_____. "White Migrants: Black Workers." New Community 7(Winter, 1978/9):11-18.

Atkinson, A. M. "Coloured Immigrants and their Families: A Study of Assimilation in an Inner Urban Area of Newcastle upon Tyle." Master's thesis, U. of Newcastle upon Tyne, 1971.

Bagley, Christopher. "A Comparative Study of Social Environment and Intelligence in West Indian and English Children in London." Social and Economic Studies, D, 1971.

_____. "The Background of Deviance in Black Children in London." In Race and Education Across Cultures. Edited by G. K. Verma and Christopher Bagley. Stamford, Ct: Greylock Publishers, 1975.

_____. "Coloured Neighbours." New Society, Ag 7, 1969.

Bagley, Christopher, and Coard, Bernard. "Cultural Knowledge and Rejection of Ethnic Identity in West Indian Children in London." In Race and Education Across Cultures. Edited by G. K. Verma and Christopher Bagley. Stamford, CT: Greylock Publishers, 1975.

Ballard, Roger, and Holden, Bronwen. "Racial Discrimination: No Room at the Top." New Society, Ap 17, 1975, pp. 133-135. [Children of colored immigrant parents]

Banton, Michael. "The Adjective 'Black'. A Discussion Note." New Community 5(Spring-Summer, 1977):480-482.

Banton, Michael. The Coloured Quarter. London: Cape, 1955.

Barker, A. J. "British Attitudes to the Negro in the Seventeenth and Eighteenth Centuries." Doctoral dissertation, King's College, 1973.

Beauchamp, Kay. Black Citizens, 1973. London District Communist Party, 75 Farringdon Road, London EC1, England.

Beetham, David. "Those Unrealistic Aspirations." Race Today, O, 1969. [Colored school leavers in England]

Bell, Robert R. "The Lower-class Negro Family in the United States and Great Britain: Some Comparison." Race, O, 1969.

Bergman, Jim, and Coard, Bernard. "Trials and Tribulations of a Self-Help Group." Race Today 4(Ap, 1972):112-114. [Afro-Caribbean Self-Help Organization, Birmingham]

Berry, James (ed.). Bluefoot Traveller: An Anthology of Westindian Poets in Britain. London: Limestone Publications, 1976.

"Birmingham. Developments on Dispersal." Race Today, My, 1969. [Dispersing colored children so as to avoid concentrations in a few schools]

"The Black Scholar Interviews: Darcus Howe. Part One." Black Scholar 9(My/Je, 1978):49-55.

"Black Students Protest." Race Today 5(Jl, 1973):196. [Cowper Street Middle School, Chapeltown, Leeds]

"The Black Youth Speak." Race Today, Ap, 1975.

Boutelle, Paul. "Black Power in England" (an interview). Young Socialist, S, 1968.

Bowker, Gordon. Education of Colored Immigrants. London: Longmans, Green, 1968.

_____. "Focus Immigration." New Education, England, Mr, 1966. [How immigrant 'colored' children are faring in the schools of London, Birmingham, Liverpool, Manchester, and Nottingham]

Braithwaite, E. R. "The Colored Immigrant in Britain." Daedalus, Spring, 1967.

Bulgin, Stephen. "The Free University of Black Studies." Race Today, Je, 1970. [London]

Butterworth, A. E. "An Anthropological Critique of Sociological Studies of Coloured Commonwealth Immigrants in Britain, with Special Reference to West Indians." Master's thesis, U. of Manchester, 1974.

Cambridge, A. X. "Education and the West Indian Child--A Criticism of the ESN School System." The Black Liberator 1(S/O, 1971): 8-19.

Cause for Concern: West Indian Pupils in Redbridge. Ilford: Black Peoples Progressive Association and Redbridge Community Relations Council, 1978.

Chase, Louis. "Shades of Black, White and Grey: A View of the West Indian Press." New Community 4(Winter-Spring, 1975-76): 473-475.

Christopher, Lancelot. "West Indian Education in Crisis?" Race Today 4(Je, 1972): 205-206.

Coard, Bernard. How the West Indian Child is Made Educationally Subnormal in the British School System. The Scandal of the Black Child in Schools in Britain, 1971. New Beacon Books, Ltd., 2 Albert Road, London N4, England. [See Leon, below.]

_____. "Making Children Subnormal." Times Educational Supplement, My 7, 1971. [Interview by Carol Bergman with author of How the West Indian Child Is Made Educationally Subnormal in the British School System]

_____. "Making Black Children Subnormal in Britain." Integrated Education (S-O, 1971):49-52. [Reprint of preceding article]

Coard, Bernard, and Coard, Phyllis. Getting to Know Ourselves, 1972. Bogle L'Ouverture Publications, 141 Coldershaw Road, Ealing, London W13, England. [A first book for young black children in England]

_____ and _____. "A West Indian Child's Real Problems." Guardian, Mr 10, 1971.

Collins, Sidney. Coloured Minorities in Britain: Studies in British Race Relations based on African, West Indian and Asiatic Immigrants. London: Lutterworth, 1957.

Community Relations Council and the Black People's Progressive Association. Cause for Concern: West Indian Pupils in Redbridge, 1978. CRC, Methodist Church Hall, Ilford Lane, Ilford, Essex, England.

Cottle, Thomas J. "A Black Teacher in Search of a Job." New Society, Mr 2, 1978.

_____. "At 13, He's Out to Teach Britain History." Los Angeles Times, Ja 11, 1977. [Young black in Britain]

_____. Black Testimony. London: Wildwood House, 1978.

_____. "But a Black Teacher Also Struggles to Find a Place." Los Angeles Times, N 27, 1977. [Employment discrimination in London]

_____. "Working for the Man." Urban Education 13(Jl, 1978):203-211.

Crabbe, Pauline. "The First Fifty Years." New Community 2(Winter, 1972-1973):62-66. [Jamaican family in England since 1919]

Craven, Anna. West Africans in London. London: Institute of Race Relations, 1969.

Davison, R. B. Black British. London: Oxford U. Press, 1967.

Day, Alison. "The Library in the Multi-Racial Secondary School: a Caribbean Book List." The School Librarian (London) 19(S, 1971): 197-203.

Dex, Shirley. "British Black and White Youth Employment Differentials." Doctoral dissertation, U. of Keele, 1977.

Dhavan, Rajeev. Black People in Britain: The Way Forward: A Conference by and for Black People in This Society. London: Post-Conference Constituent Committee, 1976.

Dhondy, Farrukh. "The Black Explosion in Schools." Race Today 6(F, 1974):44-47.

_____. "Teaching Young Blacks." Race Today 10(My-Je, 1978):80-86. [London]

Drake, St. Clair. "The Colour Problem in Britain." Sociological Review 3(D, 1955): 197-217.

Driver, Geoffrey. "Ethnicity, Cultural Competence and School Achievement: A Case Study of West Indian Pupils Attending a British Secondary Modern School." Doctoral dissertation, U. of Illinois, 1977. Univ. Microfilms Order No. 7803977.

Du Bois, W. E. B. " Negro Soldier's Children [in Britain]." Chicago Defender, N 1, 1947, p. 19.

Edwards, Paul, and Walvin, James. "Africans in Britain, 1500-1800." In The African Diaspora. Edited by Martin L. Kilson and Robert I. Rotberg. Cambridge, MA: Harvard U. Press, 1976.

Edwards, Vivienne K. "Can Dialect Cause Comprehension Problems for West Indian Children?" Multiracial School 4(Winter, 1975):1-7.

_____. "Language Attitudes and Underperformance in West Indian Children." Educational Review 30(F, 1978):51-58.

_____. West Indian Language: Attitudes and the School. London: National Association for Multiracial Education, 1976.

_____. The West Indian Language Issue in British Schools. London: Routledge & Kegan Paul, 1979.

Edwards, Vivienne K., and Sutcliffe, Dave. "Broodly Speaking." Times Educational Supplement, O 13, 1978. [Creole in British classrooms]

_____ and _____. "When Creole Can Be King." Times Educational Supplement, Mr 18, 1977. [Black children in Bedfordshire]

Egbuna, Obi. "The 'Contradictions' of Black Power." Race Today 3(S, 1971):298-299.

_____. Destroy This Temple. The Voice of Black Power in Britain. New York: Morrow, 1971.

Ellis, June (ed.). West African Families in Britain. A Meeting of Two Cultures. London: Routledge & Kegan Paul, 1978.

Evans, P. C. C., and LePage, R. B. The Education of West Indian Immigrant Children. London: National Committee for Commonwealth Immigrants, 1967.

Faggett, Harry Lee. Black and Other Minorities in Shakespeare's England. N.p: Prairie View Press, 1973.

Faulkner, R. A. "Some Socio-Psychological Concomitants of Interracial Contact in an English Primary School: A Comparative Study." Master's thesis, U. of Bristol, 1971.

Ferron, O. "The Test Performance of 'Colored' Children." Educational Research, N, 1965.

Figueroa, P. M. E. "The Employment Prospects of West Indian School-Leavers in London, England." Social and Economic Studies 25 (Je, 1976).

_____. "West Indian School-leavers in London: A Sociological Study in Ten Schools in a London Borough, 1966-1967." Doctoral dissertation, London School of Economics, 1975.

Fiscion, C. E. "Minority Group Prejudice: A Study of Some Sociological and Psychological Correlates of Anti-English Prejudice Among West Indian Immigrants in London." Doctoral dissertation, London School of Economics, 1959.

FitzHerbert, Katrin. "Immigrant Self-Help: The West Indians." New Society, Mr 13, 1969.

_____. West Indian Children in London. London: Bell, 1967.

Foner, Nancy. Jamaica Farewell. Jamaican Migrants in London. Berkeley, CA: U. of California Press, 1978.

_____. "The Jamaicans: Cultural and Social Change among Migrants in Britain." In Between Two Cultures. Migrants and Minorities in Britain, pp. 120-150. Edited by James L. Watson. Oxford: Basil Blackwell, 1977.

_____. "Women, Work and Migration: Jamaicans in London." Urban Anthropology 4(Fall, 1975):229-249.

_____. "Women, Work, and Migration: Jamaicans in London." New Community 5 (Summer, 1976):85-98. [Reprinted from Urban Anthropology]

Forge, Ken. "Some Notes on Black Studies." Forum for the Discussion of New Trends in Education 16(Summer, 1974):93-96.

Frey, Sylvia R. "The British and the Black: A New Perspective." Historian 38(F, 1976): 225-238.

Gaitskell, Julia and others. "The Colored School Leaver." Race, Ap, 1969.

Giles, Howard, and Bourhis, Richard Y. "Linguistic Assimilation: West Indians in Cardiff." Language Sciences 38(D, 1975): 9-12.

Giles, Raymond H. The West Indian Experience in British Schools. Multi-Racial Education and Social Disadvantage in London. London: Heinemann, 1977.

Giles, Raymond H., Jr. Black Studies Programs in Public Schools. London: Pall Mall Press, 1975.

Gilroy, Beryl. Black Teacher. London: Cassell, 1976.

_____. "Ever So Coloured." Times Educational Supplement, Jl 16, 1976. [Black teacher in English schools]

_____. "Then and Now. A Headmistress Reports." Community (England), Ap, 1970. [A one-time Guyanese immigrant describes changes in her classrooms over the years]

Glass, Ruth. Newcomers: The West Indians in London. London: Allen and Unwin, 1960.

Grace, A. M. "Attainments and Home Background of West Indian Immigrant Children." Master's thesis, Nottingham U., 1972.

Price, John Rea. "Grassroots Voices." New Society, Je 15, 1978. [West Indians in Islington]

Great Britain. The West Indian Community: Observations on the Report of the Select Committee on Race Relations and Immigration. Command Paper 7186. London: HMSO, 1978.

Green, P. A. "Attitudes of Teachers of West Indian Immigrant Children." Master's thesis, U. of Nottingham, 1971.

Griffin-Beale, Christopher. "Unearthing a Black Tradition." Times Educational Supplement, F 24, 1978. [World history course at Tulse Hill Comprehensive school, South London]

Gullick, Mary. "The Educational Background of Vincentian Immigrants to Britain." New Community 5(Spring-Summer, 1977):405-410.

Hachey, Thomas. "Walter White and the American Negro Soldier in World War II: A Diplomatic Dilemma for Britain." Phylon 39(S, 1978):241-249.

Hall, Stuart. "Black Britons. Some Problems of Adjustment. Part 1." Community (England), Ap, 1970.

_____. "Black Britons. Some Teenage Problems." Community (England) 1(Jl, 1970): 12-14.

Hanna, Max. "The Black Press [in Britain]." New Society, Ag 28, 1975.

Hartmann, Paul, and Husband, Charles. "A British Scale for Measuring White Attitudes to Coloured People." Race 14(O, 1972): 195-204.

Hatch, Stephen. "Colored People in School Textbooks." Race, N, 1962.

Haydon, Caroline. "Labels and Damned Labels-- The Thorny Question of Race Statistics." Times Educational Supplement, N 24, 1978. [Black children]

Hill, Barry. "Too Many Coloured Children Still Dubbed ESN." Times Educational Supplement, Ap 28, 1972.

Hill, Clifford, Immigration and Integration: A Study of the Settlement of Coloured Minorities in Britain. New York: Pergamon Press, 1969.

Hill, D. "The Attitudes of West Indian and English Adolescents in Britain." Master's thesis, U. of Manchester, 1967.

Hinds, Donald. Journey to an Illusion: The West Indian Comes to Britain. London: Heinemann, 1966.

Hines, Vince. Black Youth and the Survival Game. London: Zulu Publications, 1973. 139 Ledbury Road, London W11 1HR, England

_____. Britain, the Black Man and the Future. London: Zulu Publications, Ja, 1972.

Hiro, Dilip. Black British, White British. Rev. ed. New York: Monthly Review Press, 1974.

_____. "The Colored Man's View of the British." New Society, F 22, 1968.

_____. "Three Generations of Tiger Bay." New Society, S 21, 1967. [The historic Negro ghetto in Cardiff, Wales]

Hodkinson, Raymond. "The Negro in Britain." Negro History Bulletin, Ja, 1966.

Holmes, Carolyn. "Please Adjust Your Approach." Times Educational Supplement, S 1, 1978 [West Indian students]

Hood, Catriona, Oppé, T. E., Pless, I. B., and Apte, Evelyn. Children of West Indian Immigrants. A Study of One-Year-Olds in Paddington. London: Research Publications Services, 1970.

Hopkins, B. "Considerations of Comparability of Measures of Cross-Cultural Studies of Early Infancy from a Study on the Development of Black and White Infants in Britain." In Basic Problems in Cross-Cultural Psychology, pp. 36-46. Amsterdam: Swets and Zeitlinger, 1977.

Howe, Darcus. "The Black Scholar Interviews Darcus Howe. Part Two." Black Scholar 9 (Jl-Ag, 1978):37-44.

_____. "Enter Mrs. Thatcher." Race Today 10 (Mr, 1978):57-62.

Humphry, Derek, and John, Gus. Because They're Black. N.p.: Penguin, 1971.

Humphry, Derek, and Tindall, David. False Messiah: The Story of Michael X. London: Hart-Davis, MacGibbon, 1977.

Husband, Charles (ed.). White Media and Black Britain. London: Arrow Books, 1975.

Inner London Education Authority. Black Studies, 1972. Inner London Education Authority, Media Resources Centre, Highway Station Road, London N.1, England.

Jackson, Ray. "Jacob's Ladder." Education and Training 12(D, 1970):462-466. [West Indian children in Britain]

Jackson, Sonia. The Illegal Child-Minders. A Report on the Growth of Unregistered Child-Minding and the West Indian Community, 1971. Priority Area Children, 32 Trumpington Street, Cambridge CB2 1QY, England

Jacobson, P. "Integration or Pluralism? Social Relationships Between White and Coloured Teenagers in a Midland Town." Undergraduate dissertation, Edinburgh U., 1969.

James, Carl. "Language Factors in the Education of 'Coloured' Peoples in Britain." Modern Language Journal 54(O, 1970):420-423.

Jerrome, Dorothy. "Ibos in London: A Case Study in Social Accommodation." New Community 3(Winter-Spring, 1974):79-86.

John, Gus. "West Indians and the Youth Service." Race Today 3(Ap, 1971):130-131.

Jones, Eldred. Othello's Countrymen: The African in English Renaissance Drama. London: N.p., 1965.

Jones, P. N. "Some Aspects of the Changing Population of Colored Immigrants in Birmingham, 1961-1966." Transaction of the Institute of British Geographers 50(1970): 199-219.

Kapo, Remi. "It Couldn't Happen Here." New Society, Je 9, 1977.

Karadia, Chhotu. "The Black People's Alliance." Institute Race Relations Newsletter, Je, 1968. [A black militant confederation in England]

Kareh, Diana. Adoption and the Coloured Child. London: Methodist Book Room, 1970.

Kitzinger, S. "West Indian Children With Problems." Therapeutic Education, Spring, 1972.

Kuya, Dorothy. "Racism in Great Britain: A Black Briton's Perspective." Interracial Books for Children Bulletin 10, Nos. 1-2 (1979):12, 14.

Lawrence, D. "Black Migrants: White Natives: A Study of Race Relations in Nottingham." Doctoral dissertation, U. of Nottingham, n.d.

Leach, Bridget. Youth and Spatial Poverty: Activity Space Patterns of Black and White Young People in Leeds. Bristol: SSRC Research Unit on Ethnic Relations, 1978.

Lee, Frank F. "A Comparative Analysis of Colored Grade School Children: Negroes in the United States and West Indians in Britain." Journal of Educational Sociology, N, 1960.

Leon, R. H. "Critical Remarks on Bernard Coard's Book. How the West Indian Child Is Made Educationally Sub-Normal in the British School System." The Black Liberator 1 (S/O, 1971):21-31. [See Coard, above]

Little, Alan, and Kohler, David. "Do We Hate Blacks?" New Society, Ja 27, 1977.

Little, Kenneth. Negroes in Britain. A Study of Racial Relations in English Society. Rev. ed. London: Routledge, 1972.

Lomas, G. B. Gillian. The Coloured Population of Great Britain. London: Runnymede Trust, 1974.

Longmate, Norman. The GI's: The Americans in Britain 1942-1945. London: Hutchison, 1975.

Lorimer, Douglas A. Class, Colour and the Victorians: A Study of English Attitudes toward the Negro in the Mid-Nineteenth Century. New York: Holmes & Meier, 1978.

Louden, Delroy M. "Conflict and Change Among West Indian Parents and Their Adolescents." Educational Research 20(N, 1977):44-53.

Loughton, Mary, and Walcott, Rex. "These Most Vulnerable of Immigrants." Times Educational Supplement, Jl 30, 1971. [Adolescent West Indians]

Lyons, Charles. "'To Wash an Aethiop White': British Ideas About Black African Educability, 1530-1865." Doctoral dissertation, Columbia U., 1970.

McGee, Henry W. "To Be Young, British, and Black." Harvard Crimson, O 29, 1973.

Mack, Joanna. "West Indians and School." New Society, D 8, 1977.

Maxwell, Marina. "Violence in the Toilets. The Experiences of a Black Teacher in Brent Schools." Race Today, S, 1969.

"Mental Ability--A Comparative Study in the West Midlands." Race Today, D, 1969. [West Indian and British children]

Midgett, Douglas K. "West Indian Ethnicity in Great Britain." In Migration and Development. Edited by Helen I. Safa and Brian M. Du Toit. Chicago, IL: Aldine, 1975.

Mildon, Iva Wallis. "West Indian Home Owners in Croydon." New Community 6(Winter, 1977/78):94-98.

Miles, Robert. Between Two Cultures? The Case of Rastafarianism. Bristol: SSRC Research Unit on Ethnic Relations, 1978.

Miles, Robert, and Phizacklea, A. "The T.U.C. and Black Workers, 1974-1976." British Journal of Industrial Relations 16(J1, 1978).

Miller, Pauline. [On placing black children in separate schools] Journal of the Association of Educational Psychologists (England), Winter, 1973.

Milner, David. "Racial Identification and Preference in 'Black' British Children." European Journal of Social Psychology 3 (1973).

Milson, Fred, and Parr, John. The Colored Teenager in Birmingham. Westhill Occasional Paper No. 13, Operation Integration Two, Supplement to Institute Race Relations Newsletter, S, 1967.

Mohipp, Tony, and Duheal, Ranny. "On the Metro Saga: Interview...at the Black People's Information Centre." [Interview by A. X. Cambridge] Black Liberator 1 (1972):155-169.

Moore, Robert. Racism and Black Resistance in Britain. London: Pluto Press, 1975.

Morris, B. S. International Community. London: National Union of Students and Scottish Union of Students, 1967. [Touches on racism in treatment of colored foreign students]

Morris, Mervyn. "A West Indian Student in England." Caribbean Quarterly 8(D, 1962).

Morris, Sam. "Black Studies in Britain." New Community 2(Summer, 1973):245-248.

Morrison, Lionel. "A Black Journalist's Experience of British Journalism." New Community 4(Autumn, 1975):317-322.

_____. A Race Relations Study of Three Areas from a Black Viewpoint. London: Community Relations Commission, 1976. Huddersfield, Wandsworth, and Brent

_____. "Planning for Britain's Black Community." Race Today, D, 1969.

_____. "Training for Black Youth." New Society, Je 13, 1974.

Muir, Christine, and Goody, Esther. "Student Parents: West African Families in London." Race 13(Ja, 1972):329-326.

Mullard, Chris. Black Britain. London: George Allen & Unwin, 1973.

Munn, G. H. "Thought on Race as Part of the Ideology of British Imperialism, 1894-1904." B. Litt. thesis, Oxford U., 1976.

Nandy, Dipak. "Unrealistic Aspirations [of colored school-leavers]." Race Today, My, 1969.

N'Dem, E. "Negro Immigration in Manchester." Master's thesis, University College, London, 1953.

Nicol, A. R. "Psychiatric Disorder in the Children of Caribbean Immigrants." Journal of Child Psychology and Psychiatry 12(D, 1971):273-287.

_____. "Psychiatric Disorder in West Indian Schoolchildren." Race Today 3(Ja, 1971): 14-15. [London]

Nwosu, S. N. "The British Idea of the Educability of the African: 1840-1939." Ét. hist. afric. 8(1976):149-172.

Ogbu, John U. "West Indians in Britain." In Minority Education and Caste, pp. 241-263. New York: Academic Press, 1978.

Operation Integration Two. The Colored Teenager in Birmingham. Occasional Paper, No. 13. Westhill College of Education, Birmingham.

Oppé, T. T. et al. Children of West Indian Immigrants: A Study of One-Year Olds in Paddington. London: Institute of Race Relations, 1969.

"Our E.S.N. Children." Race Today 5(Ap, 1973): 109-116.

"Our ESN Children." Race Today 5(J1, 1973): 200.

"Our ESN Children." Race Today 5(Ag, 1973): 234.

Payne, J. F. "A Comparative Study of the Mental Abilities of Seven and Eight Year Old British and West Indian Children in a West Midland Town." Master's thesis, U. of Keele, 1967.

_____. "Mental Ability of Two Racial Groups-- A Comparative Study of English and West Indian Children in a West Midlands Town." British Journal of Educational Psychology, N, 1969.

Peach, Ceri. "British Unemployment Cycles and West Indian Immigration--1955-1974." New Community 7(Winter, 1978/9):40-43.

_____. West Indian Migration to Britain: A Social Geography. London: Oxford U. Press, 1968.

Pearson, David G. "West Indian Communal Associations in Britain: Some Observations." New Community 5(Spring-Summer, 1977):371-380.

_____. "West Indians in Easton: A Study of Their Social Organisation with Particular Reference to Participation in Formal and Informal Associations." Doctoral dissertation, Leicester U., 1975.

Phillips, Mike. "Black Actors in Britain." New Society, Mr 9, 1978.

_____. "West Indian Businessmen." New Society, My 18, 1978.

_____. "West Indian Clubland." New Society, Je 15, 1978.

Philips, R. E. K. "Problems of Settlement from the Immigrants' Point of View." In Ethnies. Anglo-French Conference on Race Relations in France and Great Britain, pp. 167-177. Paris: Mouton, 1972. Jamaicans in Britain

_____. "The Black Experience: The 'Liberal' Tradition." Race Today 4(Ag, 1972):262-264.

_____. "The Black Masses and the Political Economy of Manchester." Black Liberator 2 (Ja, 1976-Ag, 1976):291-300.

_____. "The Death of One Lame Darkie." Race Today 4(Ja, 1972):16-18. [Leeds]

Phillips, Melanie. "Brixton and Crime." New Society, Jl 8, 1976. [Blacks in south London area]

Philpott, Stuart B. "The Montserratians: Migration Dependency and the Maintenance of Island Ties in England." In Between Two Cultures. Migrants and Minorities in Britain, pp. 90-119. Edited by James L. Watson. Oxford: Basil Blackwell, 1977.

Phizacklea, A.-M. "The Political Socialisation of Black Adolescents in Britain." Doctoral dissertation, U. of Exeter, 1975.

Plant, Martin A. "The Attitudes of Coloured Immigrants in Two Areas of Birmingham to the Concept of Dispersal." Race 12(Fall, 1970): 323-328.

Pollard, Paul. "Jamaicans and Trinidadians in North London." New Community 1(Autumn, 1972):370-377.

Pryce, Kenneth. "Differing Life Styles amongst West Indian Immigrants in Bristol." Master's thesis, U. of Bristol.

_____. "The Life-Styles of West Indians in Britain: A Study of Bristol." New Community 6(Summer, 1978):207-217.

_____. "West Indian Life-Styles in Bristol: Study of a Black Toiling-Class in an English City." Doctoral dissertation, U. of Bristol, 1974.

Pye, Michael. "Pidgins Come Home to Roost." Times Educational Supplement, S 10, 1976. [Black English in Britain]

Rai, Usha. "Life and Slow Progress of Black Teachers Chasing Career Success." Times Educational Supplement, N 17, 1978.

Richardson, S. A., and Green, A. "When Is Black Beautiful?" British Journal of Educational Psychology, 1971. [London]

Richmond, Anthony H. "Adjustment of a Group of West Indian Negroes in England." Midwest Journal, Summer, 1953.

_____. "Black and Asian Immigrants in Britain and Canada: Some Comparisons." New Community 4(Winter-Spring, 1975-76):501-516.

_____. Colour Prejudice in Britain: A Study of West Indian Workers in Liverpool, 1942-51. London: Routledge, 1954.

Ruck, S. K. (ed.). The West Indian Comes to England. London: Routledge & Kegan Paul, 1960.

Rushton, James, and Turner, John (eds.). Education and Deprivation. Manchester: Manchester U. Press, 1976. [Includes material on black children in Britain]

Rutter, Michael, Yule, William, and Berger, Michael. "The Children of West Indian Migrants." New Society, Mr 14, 1974.

Rutter, Michael, Yule, William, Yule, B., Morton, J., and Bagley, C. "Children of West Indian Immigrants: Home Circumstances and Family Patterns." Journal of Child Psychology and Psychiatry, 1974.

Rutter, Michael, Yule, William, Berger, Michael, Yule, B., Morton, J., and Bagley, C. "Children of West Indian Immigrants: Rates of Behavioral Deviance and of Psychiatric Disorder." Journal of Child Psychology and Psychiatry, 1974.

Scobie, Edward. Black Brittania. A History of Blacks in Britain. Chicago, IL: Johnson, 1973.

Searle, Chris. The Black Man of Shadwell. London: Writers and Readers Publishing Cooperative, 1976. [Four stories set in the context of race relations in Britain]

Select Committee on Race Relations and Immigration, Session 1976-7. The West Indian Community. Vol. I. London: HMSO, 1977.

Shyllon, Folarin. Black People in Britain, 1555-1833. New York: Oxford U. Press, 1977.

Shyllon, F. O. Black Slaves in Britain. London: Oxford U. Press, 1974.

Sivanandan, A. "Race, Class and the State: The Black Experience in Britain." Race and Class 17(Spring, 1976):347-368.

Spittles, Brian. "Black is English." New Society, O 10, 1974.

Stadlen, Frances. "The Carnival Is Over.... Fire Next Time?" Times Educational Supplement, N 26, 1976. [Blacks in Notting Hill]

_____. "Unity or Separatism: The Dilemma of Notting Hill." Times Educational Supplement, D 3, 1976.

Stanworth, J. L. "Culture Conflict and the West Indian Child." Dissertation for Postgraduate Diploma in Social and Administrative Studies, U. of Oxford, 1969.

Sukedo, Fred, and Eversley, David. The Dependents of the Colored Commonwealth Population of England and Wales. London: Institute of Race Relations, Mr, 1969.

Sweeney, Carlton. Flight: West Indians Sojourning in Britain. Leicester: The Author, 1978.

Taifel, Henri, and Dawson, John L. (eds.). Disappointed Guests. Essays by African, Asian and West Indian Students. London: Oxford U. Press, 1966.

Teachers Against Racism. "The Question of Black Studies." TAR Journal 1(1972).

Thorne, Christopher. "Britain and the Black GI's: Racial Issues and Anglo-American Relations in 1942." New Community 3 (Summer, 1974):262-271.

Tobias, P. M. "Differential Adaptation of Grenadian Emigrant Communities in London and New York." Social and Economic Studies 25(Mr, 1976).

Tomlinson, Sally. "West Indian Children and ESN Schooling." New Community 6(Summer, 1978):235-242.

Troyna, Barry S. "Race and Streaming: A Case Study." Educational Review 30(F, 1978):59-65.

Turner, Barry. "Focus Immigration." New Education, England, S, 1965. [Colored immigrants in Birmingham, England]

Vaniak, Achin. "The Free University for Black Studies." Race Today 4(Jl, 1972):239. London

Vaughn, J. "The Negro Problem in Reading." B. Litt. thesis, Oxford U., St. Anthony's, 1959.

Walrond, Eric. "The Negro in London." The Black Man 1(Mr, 1936):9-10.

Walvin, James. Black and White: The Negro and English Society, 1555-1945. London: Allen Lane, 1973.

_____. "Much More Than a Side Show." Times Educational Supplement, O 6, 1978. [British black history in the curriculum]

_____ (ed.). The Black Presence. London: Orbach & Chambers, 1971.

Watson, G. Llewellyn. "The Sociology of Black Nationalism: Identity, Protest, and the Concept of 'Black Power' Among West Indian Immigrants in Britain." Doctoral dissertation, U. of York, England, 1972.

"Who's Educating Who? The Black Education Movement and the Struggle for Power." Race Today 7(Ag, 1975):180-186.

Wight, Jim. "How Much Interference?" Times Educational Supplement, My 14, 1976. [Dialect and West Indian academic achievement]

Wilkins, Geoff. "Race and Homes." New Society, S 18, 1975. [Birmingham]

Wood, Christopher. "Life Styles Among West Indians and Social Work Problems." New Community 3(Summer, 1974):249-254.

Woodroffe, Bev. "Black Identity and Curriculum Change." Dialogue 16(Spring, 1974):9-11. [Tulse Hill School, London]

Working Party on Britain as a Multi-Racial Society. The New Black Presence in Britain: a Christian Scrutiny. London: British Council of Churches, 1976.

Worrell, Keith. "All-Black Schools... An Answer to Underperformance?" Race Today 4(Ja, 1972):7-9.

Yule, William, Berger, Michael, Rutter, Michael, and Yule, B. "Children of West Indian Immigrants: Intellectual Performance and Reading Attainment." Journal of Child Psychology and Psychiatry, 1974.

Northern Ireland

Akenson, Donald H. Education and Ethnicity: The Control of Schooling in Northern Ireland, 1920-50. New York: Barnes and Noble, 1973.

Aunger, Edmund A. "Religion and Occupational Class in Northern Ireland." Economic and Social Review 7(1975):1-18.

Austin, Sue. To Be Called Stupid. An Experimental Approach to the Education of Non-Examination Pupils in Four Belfast Secondary Schools. Belfast: Schools Curriculum Project, Northern Ireland Polytechnic, S, 1975.

Bailey, Anthony. "Matthew and Marie." New Yorker, My 8, 1978.

Bill, John M. "Environmental Stress and Educational Outcomes." Northern Teacher (Belfast) 1(Winter, 1973):31-38.

Boal, F. W. "Territoriality and Class: A Study of Two Residential Areas in Belfast." Irish Geography 6(1971):229-248.

Boyle, Joseph F. "Educational Attainment, Occupational Achievement and Religion in Northern Ireland." Economic and Social Review 8(1977):79-100.

Calvert, Harry. Constitutional Law in Northern Ireland: A Study in Regional Government. London: Stevens and Sons, 1968.

Campbell, J. J. Catholic Schools: A Survey of a Northern Ireland Problem. Belfast: Fallons Educational Supply Co., 1964.

Compton, Paul A. Northern Ireland: A Census Atlas. London: Gill and Macmillan, 1978.

Compton, Paul A. "Religious Affiliation and Demographic Variability in Northern Ireland." Trans. Inst. Brit. Geographers 1, No. 4(1976):433-452.

Darby, John P. Conflict in Northern Ireland: The Development of a Polarised Community. New York: Barnes and Noble, 1976.

_____. "Divisiveness in Education [in Northern Ireland]." Integrated Education (Belfast), Winter, 1973.

_____. "Divisiveness of Education in Northern Ireland." Integrated Education 12(Ja-Ap, 1974):3-11. [Glossary added]

_____ (ed.). Register of Research into the Irish Conflict. Belfast: Northern Ireland Community Relations Commission, N, 1972.

Darby, John, and Morris, Geoffrey. "Community Groups and Research in Northern Ireland." Community Development Journal 10(Ap, 1975): 113-119.

Darby, John, and Williamson, Arthur (eds.). Violence and the Social Services in Northern Ireland. London: Heinemann Educational, 1978.

Darby, John and others. Education and Community in Northern Ireland. Schools Apart? Ulster: New U. of Ulster, N, 1977.

Davies, R. and others. "The Northern Ireland Economy: Progress (1968-75) and Prospects." Regional Studies 11(1977).

Dent, George I. "The Law of Education in Northern Ireland and the Influence of English Law." Doctoral dissertation, U. of London, 1965.

Deutsch, Richard (comp.). Northern Ireland, 1921-1974: A Select Bibliography. New York: Garland, 1975.

Evason, Eileen. Poverty: The Facts in Northern Ireland. London: Child Poverty Action Group, 1976.

Ferguson, John. "Community Relations in Schools in Northern Ireland." Trends in Education 29(Ja, 1973);15-19.

Gonzalez, Arturo F., Jr. "Teaching in War-Torn Belfast: Reading, Writing, Rioting." Learning 2(0, 1973):72-78.

Jones, Emrys. A Social Geography of Belfast. London: Oxford U. Press, 1960.

Knox, H. M. "Religious Segregation in the Schools of Northern Ireland." British Journal of Educational Studies 21(0, 1973): 307-312.

McGill, Paul. "Catholic Bias to Arts Found in Ulster." Times Educational Supplement, 0 13, 1978.

_____. "Discrimination dans l'enseignement en Irlande du Nord." DE. Revue de l'Union des Etudiants sur la Démocratisation et la Réforme de Enseignement (Prague) 1(1973):13-24.

McKeown, M. "Integrated Education: The Debate Surveyed." Furrow 28(Ja, 1977).

McKinnie, Olivia. "Aspects of Religious Segregation in Schools in Northern Ireland." Compare 7(0, 1977).

Magee, Jack. The Teaching of Irish History in Irish Schools, 1970. Northern Ireland Community Relations Commission, Bedford House, Bedford Street, Belfast, Northern Ireland BT2 7FD.

Malone, John. "Schools and Community Relations [in Northern Ireland]." Northern Teacher (Belfast), Winter, 1973.

Murphy, Dervla. A Place Apart. London: John Murray, 1978.

Murray, Russell, and Osborne, Robert. "Segregation on Horn Drive--A Cautionary Tale." New Society, Ap 21, 1977. [Belfast]

O'Donnell, E. E. Northern Irish Stereotypes. Dublin: College of Industrial Relations, 1977.

Poole, M., and Boal, F. W. Religious Residential Segregation in Belfast in Mid-1969: A Multi-Level Analysis. London: Institute of British Geographers, 1973.

Rose, Richard. Governing without Consensus. An Irish Perspective. London: Faber & Faber, 1971.

Russell, James L. Some Aspects of the Civic Education of Secondary Schoolboys in Northern Ireland. Belfast, Northern Ireland: Northern Ireland Community Relations Commission, 1973.

Salters, John. "Attitudes towards Society in Protestant and Roman Catholic School-Children in Belfast." Master's thesis, Queen's U., Belfast, 1970.

Taylor, Laurie, and Nelson, Sarah (eds.). Young People and Civil Conflict in Northern Ireland. N.p.: N.p., Je 1, 1977.

Trew, Karen (ed.). Register of Research in Education: Northern Ireland. Vol. 3: 1972-1975, 1976. ERIC ED 139 674.

Williamson, A. "Community Integration in a West Belfast Housing Estate." Master's thesis, Queen's U., Belfast, 1971.

Scotland

Aberdeen College of Education. International Conference on Education in Sparsely Populated Rural Areas, 1974. ERIC ED 101 913.

Baird, G. "The Effects of Social and Economic Change on the Schools in Central Scotland, 1803-1872." Master's thesis, Glasgow U., 1972.

Baker, Peter. Attitudes to Coloured People in Glasgow. Glasgow: Survey Research Centre, U. of Strathclyde, 1969.

Brand, Jack. The National Movement in Scotland. London: Routledge & Kegan Paul, 1978.

Brown, Gordon (ed.). The Red Paper on Scotland. Edinburgh: Edinburgh U. Student Publication Board, 1975.

Bullough, Vern L. An Historical Case Study of the Effect of Educational Reform On An Underdeveloped Area: Scotland in the Eighteenth Century. Northridge, CA: San Fernando Valley State College, 1969.

Bullough, Vern, and Bullough, Bonnie. "Historical Sociology: Intellectual Achievement in Eighteenth-Century Scotland." British Journal of Sociology 24 (D, 1973):418-430.

Cook, R. "Poverty and Education in the Highlands and Islands." Master's thesis, Glasgow U., 1972.

Cruickshank, Marjorie. "Education in the Highlands and Islands of Scotland: An Historical Retrospect." Paedagogica Historica 7(1967): 361-377.

Daly, Lawrence. "Scotland on the Dole." New Left Review 17(Winter, 1962):17-23.

Dixon, Edward. "The American Negro in Nineteenth Century Scotland." Master's thesis, Edinburgh U., 1969.

Handley, James E. Irish in Scotland, 1798-1845. 2nd ed. Cork: Cork U. Press, 1945.

Hanley, Eric. "Scotland: Avoiding English Mistakes." Race Today, My, 1969.

Harvie, Christopher. Scotland and Nationalism: Scottish Society and Politics, 1707-1977. London: George Allen & Unwin, 1977.

Hutchison, Dongal, and McPherson, Andrew. "Competing Inequalities: The Sex and Social Class Structure of the First Year Scottish University Student Population, 1962-1972." Sociology 10(Ja, 1976):111-116.

Jackson, R. N. "Self-Fulfilling Stigma." Times Educational Supplement, O 22, 1971. [Educationally sub-normal children in Scotland]

Jahoda, G., Thomson, S. T., and Bhatt, S. "Ethnic Identity and Preferences Among Asian Immigrant Children in Glasgow: A Replicated Study." European Journal of Social Psychology 2(1972):19-32.

Kelly, Alison. "Family Background, Subject Specialization and Occupational Recruitment of Scottish University Students: Some Patterns and Trends." Higher Education 5 (My, 1976):177-188.

Lenman, Bruce P. "The Teaching of Scottish History in the Scottish Universities." Scottish Historical Review 52(O, 1973):165-190.

Macaulay, R. K. S., with Trevelyan, G. D. Language, Social Class, and Education: A Glasgow Study. Totowa, NJ: Biblio Distribution Center, 1978.

MacInnes, Colin. "Scotland: A Nation Reviving." New Society, Jl 11, 1974.

MacKinnon, Kenneth M. Language, Education and Social Process in a Gaelic Community. London: Routledge & Kegan Paul, 1976.

_____. "Language Shift and Education: Conversation of Ethnolinguistic Culture amongst Schoolchildren of a Gaelic Community." Linguistics 198(O, 1977):31-55.

MacLaren, A. Allen (ed.). Social Class in Scotland: Past and Present. London: John Donald, 1976.

Maclean, Colin. "Aberdeen: Spoiled Child of Scotland." Times Educational Supplement, D 6, 1974.

McPherson, Andrew, and Neave, Guy. The Scottish Sixth: A Sociological Evaluation of Sixth Year Studies and the Changing Relationship between School and University in Scotland. Atlantic Highlands, NJ: Humanities Press, 1976.

Maxwell, James. "Intelligence, Education, and Fertility: A Comparison Between the 1932 and 1947 Scottish Surveys." Journal of Biosocial Science, 1969.

May, David. "Who Are the Truants?" Times Educational Supplement, My 14, 1976, Aberdeen

Millar, C. J., and Osborne, G. S. "Friendships in an Unstreamed School." Scottish Educational Review 10(My, 1978):47-49.

Morrison, C., with Watts, Joyce and Lee, T. (eds.). EPA: A Scottish Study. London: HMSO, 1974.

Morton, Jane. "Two Scotlands." New Society, Ap 10, 1975.

Myers, Philip. "Class Law in Scotland." New Society, Jl 20, 1978. [Law students at the University of Glasgow]

Nairn, Tom. "Scotland and Europe." New Left Review 83(Ja-F, 1974):57-82.

Nisbet, John. "Deprivation and Disadvantage: Scotland." In Deprivation and Disadvantage. Nature and Manifestions, pp. 170-178. Edited by A. Harry Passow. Hamburg, Germany: UNESCO Institute for Education, 1970.

Norris, Geoff. Poverty: The Facts in Scotland. London: Child Poverty Action Group, 1977.

Payne, G., and Ford, G. "Religion, Class and Educational Policy." Scottish Educational Studies 9(N, 1977):83-99.

Phillips, Melanie. "The Scottish Lion Gets Some Teeth." New Society, D 9, 1976. [Oil and nationalism]

Raffe, D. "Social Class and Entry to Further Education." Scottish Educational Studies 9(N, 1977):100-111.

Smout, T. C. "The Historical Separateness of the Scots." New Society, Jl 1, 1976.

Weir, Jan, and Weir, David. "Scotland: The Houses that Last 1,000 Years." New Left Review 13-14(Ja-Ap, 1962):71-80.

Wales

Baum, Thomas. "A Benefit of Welsh?" New Society, N 24, 1977. [Absenteeism and cultural background in Wales]

Bourhis, Richard, and Giles, Howard. "Welsh Is Beautiful." New Society, Ap 4, 1974.

Bowen, E. G., and Carter H. "The Distribution of the Welsh Language in 1971: An Analysis." Geography 60(Ja, 1975):1-15.

"Breathing Fire into the Red Dragon." Guardian, S 20, 1975. [The Welsh language in the schools]

Central Advisory Council for Education (Wales). Primary Education in Wales. London: HMSO, 1967. [The parallel volume to the Plowden Report]

Chernaik, Judith. "A Year in a Welsh School." Atlantis 229(Jl, 1972):17-25. [Beaumaris Primary School, Anglesey]

Corrado, Raymond R. "Nationalism and Communism in Wales." Ethnicity 2(D, 1975):360-381.

Fishlock, Trevor. Wales and the Welsh. London: Cassell, 1972.

Heath, Tony. "Wales: A Nation Gives Tongue." New Society, N 20, 1975.

Hechter, Michael. Internal Colonialism. The Celtic Fringe in British National Development, 1536-1966. Berkeley, CA: U. of California Press, 1974.

Her Majesty's Inspectors. Comprehensive Schools of Wales: Years One, Two and Three. London: HMSO, 1978.

Hickey, J. "The Origin and Growth of the Irish Community in Cardiff." Master's thesis, U. of Wales, n.d.

Hopkins, Adam. "Beware, Welsh War Zone." Times Educational Supplement, D 1, 1978. [Gwynedd and Llandudno]

Howell, David W. Land and People in Nineteenth-Century Wales. London: Routledge & Kegan Paul, 1978.

Jenkins, Geraint H. Literature, Religion and Society in Wales, 1660-1730. Cardiff: U. of Wales Press, 1978.

Jones, R. Brinely (ed.). Anatomy of Wales. Glamorgan: Peterson-Super-Ely, 1972.

Jones, W. R. Bilingualism in Welsh Education. Cardiff: U. of Wales Press, 1966.

Khleif, Bud B. "Cultural Regeneration and the School: An Anthropological Study of Welsh-Medium Schools in Wales." International Review of Education 22(1976):177-192.

Lewis, E. Glyn. "Attitude to Language among Bilingual Children and Adults in Wales." Linguistics 158(Ag 15, 1975):103-126.

_____. "Bilingualism in Wales." New Society, Ag 10, 1967.

Little, A., and Westergaard, J. "The Trend of Class Differentials in Educational Opportunity in England and Wales." British Journal of Sociology 15(1964):301-316.

Macintyre, Don, and Brannen, Jim. "Equality--or Complacency?" Race Today 3(O, 1971): 350-352. [Cardiff]

Mayo, Patricia Elton. The Roots of Identity: Three National Movements in Contemporary European Politics. London: Allen Lane, 1974.

Morgan, K. O. "Welsh Nationalism: The Historical Background." Journal of Contemporary History 6(1971):153-172.

Morris, Tudor. "Understanding the Welsh." English 10(1975):32-33. [Anti-Welsh prejudice of English children]

Osmond, John. Creative Conflict. The Politics of Welsh Devolution. London: Routledge & Kegan Paul, 1977.

Philip, Alan Butt. The Welsh Question--Nationalism in Welsh Politics 1945-1970. Cardiff: U. of Wales Press, 1975.

Pill, Roisin M. "Education and Social Mobility in Wales, 1938-1968." Doctoral dissertation, U. of Wales, Cardiff, 1970.

_____. "Social Implications of a Bilingual Policy, with Particular Reference to Wales." British Journal of Sociology 25 (1974):94-107.

Randall, Peter J. "The Origins and Establishment of the Welsh Department of Education." Welsh Historical Review 7(D, 1975):450-471.

Roberts, Hywel. "The Welsh Struggle for Survival." Race Today 4(Ap, 1972):115-116.

Sharp, Derrick. "English in Wales." Educational Review 28(Je, 1976):220-228.

Stead, Peter. "Welsh Nationalism: The Language and The People." Institute Race Relations Newsletter, F, 1969.

_____. "Welshness and Welsh Nationalism." New Community 1(Autumn, 1972):393-399.

Sturt, Mary. The Education of the People. History of Primary education in England and Wales in the Nineteenth Century. London: Routledge & Kegal Paul, 1967.

Thomas, Colin J., and Williams, Colin H. "Language and Nationalism in Wales: A Case Study." Ethnic and Racial Studies 1(Ap, 1978):234-258.

Thomas, E. R. "The Foundations of Welsh Education: A Study of the Relationship of an Educational System to its Social Environment." Doctoral dissertation, U. of Birmingham, 1943.

Thomas, Ned. The Welsh Extremists: A Culture in Crisis. London: Gollancz, 1971.

Williams, Glyn (ed.). Social and Cultural Change in Contemporary Wales. London: Routledge and Kegan Paul, 1978.

Williams, H. L. and others. An Experiment in Nursery Education: Report of the NFER Pre-School Project. Windsor: NFER, 1977.

Williams, J. L. "The Welsh Language in Education." In The Welsh Language Today. Edited by M. Stephens. Llandyssul: N.p., 1973.

Williams, L. J., and Boyns, T. "Occupation in Wales, 1851-1971." Brookings Papers on Economic Activity 1(1978).

Hong Kong

Cheung, C.-H. W. "The Chinese Way: A Social Study of the Hong Kong Chinese Community in a Yorkshire City." Master's thesis, U. of York, n.d.

Djao, Angela W. "Social Control in a Colonial Society: A Case Study of Working Class Consciousness in Hong Kong." Doctoral dissertation, U. of Toronto, 1976.

Dwyer, D. J. (ed.). Asian Urbanization: A Hong Kong Case Study. Hong Kong: Hong Kong U. Press, 1971.

Easey, Walter. "Notes on Child Labour in Hong Kong." Race and Class 18(Spring, 1977): 377-387.

"Even 'Learning Shops' Must Have Standards." Bridge 5(Winter, 1977):13-14.

Halliday, Jon. "Hong Kong: Britain's Chinese Colony." New Left Review 87-88(S-D, 1974): 91-112.

Hsia, Ronald, and Chau, Larry. "Industrialisation and Income Distribution in Hong Kong." International Labour Review 117(Jl-Ag, 1978):465-479.

_____ and _____. Industrialisation, Employment and Income Distribution: The Case of
Hong Kong. London: Croom Helm, 1978.

Jarvie, I. C., with Agassi, Joseph (eds.).
Hong Kong: A Society in Transition.
London: N.p., 1969.

Kanwit, Elizabeth. "Chinese Without a Country."
Times Educational Supplement, Ag 23, 1974.

Leeming, Frank. Street Studies in Hong Kong.
London: Oxford U. Press, 1978.

Morland, J. Kenneth. "Race Awareness among
American and Hong Kong Chinese Children."
American Journal of Sociology, N, 1969.

Osgood, Cornelius. The Chinese: A Study of a
Hong Kong Community. 3 vols. Tucson:
U. of Arizona Press, 1975.

Porter, Robin. Child Labour in Hong Kong.
Nottingham, England: The Bertrand Russell
Peace Foundation for the Hong Kong Research
Project and the Spokesman, 1975.

_____. "Child Labour in Hong Kong and Related
Problems: A Brief Review." International
Labour Review 111(Ap, 1975).

Ross, Mark J. M. "Competition for Education in
Hong Kong: The Schools, the Entrance
Examinations, and the Strategies of Chinese
Families." Doctoral dissertation, U. of
Texas, 1976. Univ. Microfilms Order No.
76-26,698.

Travers, Lawrence H. "Cognitive Images of Hong
Kong Youth: A Study of Chinese Urban Perception." Doctoral dissertation, U. of Hawaii,
1976.

Higher Education

Abbott, Joan. Student Life in a Class Society.
Oxford: Pergamon, 1971. [Edinburgh, Durham,
and Newcastle Universities]

"Anti-Zionism at British Universities."
Patterns of Prejudice 11(Jl-Ag, 1977):1-3.

Brockington, Fraser, and Stein, Zena. "Admission, Achievement, and Social Class."
Universities Quarterly, D, 1963.

Burgess, Tyrrell. "The Open University."
New Society 20(Ap 27, 1972):176-178.

Conference of University Administrators.
Conference of University Administrators'
Group on Forecasting and University Ex-
pansion. Norwich: The Registry, U. of East
Anglia, 1978,

Crouch, Colin, and Mennell, Stephen. The
Universities: Pressures and Prospects.
London: Fabian Society, 1972.

Cruickshank, Kennedy, and McManus, Chris.
"Getting into Medicine." New Society, Ja 15,
1976. [Class factors in enrollment in
medical schools]

Draffan, Robert A. "Working Class Students
Still Too Rare." Times Higher Education
Supplement, F 23, 1973.

Eurich, Nell, and Schwenkmeyer, Barry. Great
Britain's Open University: First Chance,
Second Chance, or Last Chance? New York:
Academy for Educational Development, Ag,
1971.

Halsey, A. H. "Students' Comings and Goings."
Times Higher Education Supplement, S 13,
1974. [Origins and destinations of British
university students]

Hasan, Ruqaiya. "Socialization and Cross-
Cultural Education." Linguistics 175(Jl,
1976):7-25. [Asians in British universities]

Kelsall, R. K., Poole, Anne, and Kuhn, Annette.
"University--A Chance to Succeed?"
Times Higher Education Supplement, F 25,
1972.

McDonald, Ian J. "Untapped Reservoirs of
Talent? Social Class and Opportunities
in Scottish Higher Education, 1910-1960."
Scottish Educational Studies, Je, 1967.

McIntosh, Naomi E., and Woodley, Alan.
"Excellence for All at the OU But Some Still
Find More Equality than Others." Times
Higher Education Supplement, D 19, 1975.

_____ and _____. "The Open University and
Second Chance Education. An Analysis of the
Social and Educational Background of Open
University Students." Auszug aus Paedogogica
Europaea 2(1974):85-100.

Maclure, Stuart. One Hundred Years of London
Education 1870-1970. London: Allen Lane,
The Penguin Press, 1970.

Mace, John. "Mythology in the Making: Is the
Open University Really Cost Effective?"
Higher Education 7(1978).

Mack, Joanna. "Anti-Semitism at Essex?" New
Society, F 1, 1979. [Essex U.]

Reid, W. A. "Choice and Selection: the Social
Process of Transfer to Higher Education."
Journal of Social Policy 3(O, 1974):327-340.

Roth, Cecil. "The Jews in the English Universities." In Essays Presented to E. N. Adler
--I, pp. 102-115. Jewish Historical Society
of England, Miscell series, Part 4, 1942.

Scott, Peter and others. "More Room at Top
in Britain than Elsewhere in Europe."
Times Higher Education Supplement, Ja 20,
1978. [Working class and higher education]

Stevens, Auriol, Jackson, Mark, Venning, Philip, and O'Grady, Carolyn. "The Open University: Revolution, Evolution, or Stagnation?" Times Educational Supplement, Ja 25, 1974.

Stockton, C. R. "The Integration of Cambridge: Alexander Crummell As Undergraduate, 1849-1853." Integrateducation 15(Mr-Ap, 1977).

Wasserstein, Bernard. "Jewish Identification Among Students at Oxford." Jewish Journal of Sociology 13(D, 1971).

West, Vera. "The Influence of Parental Background on Jewish University Students." Jewish Journal of Sociology, D, 1968.

General

Abbott, Simon (ed.). The Prevention of Racial Discrimination in Britain. London: Institute of Race Relations, 1971.

Acland, Henry. "Streaming in English Primary Schools." British Journal of Educational Psychology 43(Je, 1973), part 2, 151-160.

_____. "What Is a 'Bad' School?" New Society, S 9, 1971. [Review of educational priorities area concept of the Plowden Report]

Acton, Thomas A. Gypsy Politics and Social Change. London: Routledge & Kegan Paul, 1974.

_____. "True Gypsies--Myth and Reality." New Society, Je 6, 1974.

Acton, T. A. "A Sociological Analysis of the Development of Attitudes Toward the Changing Place of Gypsies in the Social and Cultural Structure in England and Wales from the Moveable Dwellings Act Agitation to the Romanestan Controversy." Doctoral dissertation, Oxford U., 1974.

Adams, Barbara and others. Gypsies and Government Policy in England. London: Heinemann, 1975.

Adams, Barbara, with others. "Gypsies: Current Policies and Practices." Journal of Social Policy 4(Ap, 1975):129-150.

Adams, F. J. Problems of the Education of Immigrants From the Standpoint of the Local Education Authority. Third Annual Race Relations Conference. London, S 19, 1969.

Adeney, Martin. Community Action. Four Examples. London: Runnymede Trust, My, 1971.

Allaun, Frank. No Place Like Home. Britain's Housing Tragedy (from the Victims' View) and How to Overcome It. London: Andre Deutsch, 1972.

Allen, Sheila. "School Leavers and the Labour Market." London Educational Review 4(Autumn, 1975).

_____. "School Leavers: Problems of Method and Explanation." Race Today, D, 1969.

Allen, Sheila, and Smith, Christopher. "From School to Work: Minority Group Experience." In The Entry into Work: Some Sociological Perspectives. Edited by P. Brannen. London: HMSO, 1975.

Alleyne, M. H. "The Teaching of Bilingual Children: Intelligence and Attainment of Children in London, Wales and Trinidad Whose Mother Tongue is Not English." Master's thesis, U. of London, 1962.

"Analysis of an Uncritical Path." Times Educational Supplement, My 24, 1974. [Small size of government expenditures on educational research]

Andrew, Herbert. "Education of Immigrants in England." Integrated Education, Ag-N, 1965.

Ankrah-Dove, L. "Social and Political Orientation of Adolescents in London Secondary Schools with Special Reference to Immigrants." Doctoral dissertation, U. of London, 1973.

Anon. "Inbuilt Prejudice." Times Educational Supplement, S 29, 1978. [Multiracial school in Birmingham]

Armytage, W. H. G. "The 1870 Education Act." British Journal of Educational Studies 18 (Je, 1970):121-133.

_____. Four Hundred Years of English Education. Cambridge, England: Cambridge U. Press, 1964. 2nd ed., 1970.

Arnott, Hilary. "School of the Streets." Race Today 3(Mr, 1971):94-95. [Malcolm X Montessori Programme, London]

"Aspects of Integration." News and Ideas (entire issue). [London] Scout and Guide Graduate Association, Ja, 1966.

Association of Directors of Social Services and the Commission for Racial Equality. Multi-Racial Britain: The Social Services Response. London: Commission for Racial Equality, Jl, 1978.

Babler, Alan M. "Education of the Destitute: A Study of London Ragged Schools, 1844-1874." Doctoral dissertation, Northern Illinois U., 1978. Univ. Microfilms Order No. 7902437.

Bacon, William. Public Accountability and the Schooling System. A Sociology of School Board Democracy. New York: Harper & Row, 1978.

Bagley, Christopher. "Behavioural Deviance in Ethnic Minority Children. A Review of Published Studies." New Community 5(Autumn, 1976):230-238.

_____. "The Educational Performance of Immigrant Children." Race, Jl, 1968.

_____. "Immigrant Children: A Review of Problems and Policy in Education." Journal of Social Policy 2(0, 1973).

_____. "Race Relations and the Press: An Empirical Analysis." Race 15(Jl, 1973): 59-89.

_____. Social Structure and Prejudice in Five English Boroughs. London: Institute of Race Relations, 1970.

Bagley, Christopher, and Verma, Gajendra K. "Inter-ethnic Attitudes and Behavior in British Multi-racial Schools." In Race and Education Across Cultures. Edited by G. K. Verma and Christopher Bagley. Stamford, CT: Greylock Publishers, 1975.

Ballard, Roger E. H., and Holden, Bronwen M. "The Employment of Coloured Graduates in Britain." New Community 4(Autumn, 1975): 325-336.

Ballard, Roger, and Driver, Geoffrey. "The Ethnic Approach." New Society, Je 16, 1977.

Banton, Michael. "The Future of Race Relations Research in Britain: The Establishment of a Multi-Disciplinary Research Unit." Race 15(0, 1973):223-229.

_____. "Integration Into What Society?" New Society, N 9, 1967.

Barker, Rodney. Education and Politics, 1900-1951: A Study of the Labour Party. London: Oxford U. Press, 1972.

Bateman, Jack. "Gypsy Intake." Trends in Education 1(Spring, 1977):9-15.

Beales, A. C. F. "The Beginning of Catholic Elementary Education." Dublin Review, 0, 1939, pp. 284-389.

Beck, G. A. (ed.). The English Catholics 1850-1950. N.p.: N.p., 1950.

Beechey, F. E. "The Irish in York, 1840-1875." Doctoral dissertation, U. of York, 1977.

Beetham, David. Immigrant School Leavers and the Youth Employment Service in Birmingham. London: Institute of Race Relations, 1968.

Bell, Robert R. Immigrant Children in Smethwick Schools 1960-1970. Third Annual Race Relations Conference, London, S 19, 1968.

Benn, Caroline. Comprehensive Schools in 1972. Reorganization Plans to 1975. London, England: The Comprehensive Schools Committee for the Campaign for Comprehensive Education, 1972.

_____. "School Style and Staying On." New Society, Je 24, 1971.

Benn, Caroline, and Simon, Brian. Half Way There: Report on the British Comprehensive School Reform. London: McGraw-Hill, 1970.

Benewick, Robert. The Fascist Movement in Britain. London: Allen Lane, Penguin Press, 1973.

Bennet, Neville, and Jarman, Christopher. "Plowden's Progress." Times Educational Supplement, 0 18, 1974.

Bentley, Stuart. "Harmony: Multi-racial Families in Britain." New Community 5 (Spring-Summer, 1977):495-497.

_____. "Identity and Community Cooperation: A Note on Terminology." Race 14(Jl, 1972): 69-76.

_____. "Politics, Ethnicity and Education: Some Contemporary Issues." New Community 5 (Autumn, 1976):189-195.

Bergman, Carol. "The Self-Fulfilling Prophecy." Community (England), Ja, 1970. [Racism in English schools]

Berk, Ferit. "A Study of the Turkish-Cypriot Community in Haringey, with Particular Reference to Its Background, Its Structure, and Changes Taking Place Within It." Doctoral dissertation, York U., 1972.

Bermant, Chaim. Point of Arrival: A Study of London's East End. London: Eyre Methuen, 1975.

Bernstein, Basil. "Open Schools, Open Society?" New Society, S 14, 1967. [An analysis of schools in terms of Durkheim's concepts of social integration]

Bernstein, Basil, and Davies, Brian. "Some Sociological Comments on Plowden." In Perspectives on Plowden. Edited by R. S. Peters. London: Routledge & Kegan Paul, 1969.

Beswick, W. A. "The Relationship of the Ethnic Background of Secondary Schoolboys to Their Participation in and Attitudes Towards Physical Activity." Research Papers in Physical Education 3(D, 1976):19-21.

Betty, Charles. "EPA Action Research in Educational Priority Areas." Urban Education 6 (Jl-0, 1971):175-195.

_____. EPA's--Reports and Relfections. 1. London--Community Education in the EPA's." Adult Education (London) 43(Ja, 1971): 283-287.

_____. "Race, Community and Schools." Race Today, Je, 1969.

Bhatnagar, Joti K. "a Study of Adjustment of Immigrant Children in a London School." Doctoral dissertation, U. of London, Institute of Education, 1968.

_____. Immigrants at School. London: Cornmarket Press, 1970.

_____. "Teaching Racial Tolerance." Race Today, Je, 1970.

Bidwell, Sidney. Red, White and Black: Race Relations in Britain. London: Gordon and Cremonesi, 1976.

Bilingualism and British Education: The Dimensions of Diversity. London: Centre for Information on Language Teaching and Research, 1976.

Billig, Michael. Fascists: A Social Psychological View of the National Front. London: Academic Press, 1978.

_____. "Patterns of Racism: Interviews with National Front Members." Race and Class 20 (Autumn, 1978):161-179.

Bilski, Raphaella. "Ideology and the Comprehensive Schools." Political Quarterly 44 (Ap-Je, 1973):197-211.

Bindman, Geoffrey. "Restraint On Incitement. The New British Law." Patterns of Prejudice 11(Mr-Ap, 1977):5-9.

Birley, Derek, and Dufton, Anne. An Equal Chance. London: Routledge & Kegan Paul, 1971.

Bishop, A. S. The Rise of a Central Authority for English Education. Cambridge, England: Cambridge U. Press, 1971.

Blackburn, Robin. "Inequality and Exploitation." New Left Review 42(Mr-Ap, 1967):3-24.

Blackett, Richard. "British Groups Against Racism." Study Encounter 7(1971):1-16. [Publications office, World Council of Churches, 150 route de Ferney, CH-1211, Geneva 20, Switzerland]

Blackstone, Tessa. A Fair Start: The Provision of Preschool Education in England London: Penguin Press, 1971.

_____. "The Plowden Report." British Journal of Sociology, S, 1967.

Blair, Carol. "Immigrant Education and Social Class." Race Today 3(Ag, 1971):259-260.

Blake, Kate. "Non English Speakers: The Need for Special Provision." Race Today 4 (O, 1972):330-333.

Blishen, Edward. "Conference on Non-Streaming." Forum, Spring, 1963.

Blume, H. "A History of Anti-Semtic Groups in Britain 1918-1940." M. Phil. thesis, U. of Sussex, 1971.

Blyth, W. A. English Primary Education. A Sociological Description. 2 vols. London: Routledge & Kegan Paul, 1965.

Board for Social Responsibility, Church Assembly. Race Relations in Britain. London: Society for Promoting Christian Knowledge, 1968.

Bolt, Christine. Victorian Attitudes to Race. London: Routledge & Kegan Paul, 1971.

Bolton, Felicity, and Laishley, Jennie. Education for a Multiracial Britain. London: Fabian Society, 1972.

Bossy, John. The English Catholic Community 1570-1850. London: Darton, Longman & Todd, 1976.

Bourne, Richard. "The Snakes and Ladders of the British Class System." New Society, F 8, 1979.

Bowker, Gordon. Education of Coloured Immigrants. London: Longmans, 1968.

Boyd, David. Elites and their Education. Windsor, Berks: NFER, 1973.

Boyle, Edward. "Race Relations: The Limits of Voluntary Action." Race, Ja, 1968.

_____. "School Integration in England." Integrated Education, Je-Jl, 1964.

_____. Race Relations and Education. Liverpool, England: Liverpool U. Press, 1970.

Brake, Mike. "The Skinheads: An English Working Class Subculture." Youth and Society 6(D, 1974):179-200.

Brandon, David. Not Proven. Some Questions About Homelessness and Young Immigrants. London: Runnymede Trust, Ja, 1973.

Brazil, D. E. "The Effect of the Community School on Parental Attitudes to a Multiracial School in an Educational Priority Area." Master's thesis, U. of Birmingham, 1976.

Brennan, Mary, and Stoten, Bryan. "Children, Poverty and Illness." New Society, Je 24, 1976. [Coventry]

Bridgeman, Tessa, and Fox, Irene. "Why People Choose Private Schools." New Society, Je 29, 1978.

"Bright Immigrants in ESN Schools a Blunder." Times Educational Supplement, Mr 26, 1971.

"Britain Faces the Race Problem." Ebony, N, 1951.

"British and U.S. Responses to Minority Demands --A Comparison." Race Today 3(Ap, 1971): 115-126.

British Broadcasting Company. Non-Whites on British Television. London: BBC, 1972.

Brittain, Elaine M. "All Friends Together?" Times Educational Supplement, Jl 16, 1976.

_____. "Multiracial Education. 2. Teacher Opinion on Aspects of School Life. Part 2: Pupils and Teachers." Educational Research 18(Je, 1976):182-191.

Brown, G. A. "An Exploratory Study of Inter- action amongst British and Immigrant Children." British Journal of Social and Clinical Psychology 12(Je, 1973).

Brown, John. The Un-Melting Pot: An English Town and Its Immigrants. London: Macmillan, 1970. Bedford

Buckland, D. G. "Education of Travelling Children." Trends in Education 1(Spring, 1977):3-8.

Burghes, Louie. "More People Poor Now." New Society, O 5, 1978.

Burgin, Trevor, and Edson, Patricia. Spring Grove--The Education of Immigrant Children. London: Oxford U. Press, 1967.

Burke, Elizabeth. "Standards of Reading: A Critical Review of Some Recent Studies." Educational Research 7(Je, 1975):163-174.

Burn, James Dawson. The Autobiography of a Beggar Boy. London: Europa, 1978, reprint. Orig. 1855.

Butterworth, Eric. "A Hardening Color Bar? The School." New Society, Mr 16, 1967.

_____. Immigrants in West Yorkshire, 1968. London: Research Publications, 1968.

Byles, P. G. "Educational Needs and Opport- unities in English Villages, 1870-1902." B. Litt. thesis, Oxford U., 1925.

Byrns, D. S., and Williamson, W. "Some Intra- regional Variations in Educational Provision and their Bearing upon educational Attain- ment--the Case of the North East." Sociology 6(Ja, 1972):71-87. [See, below, Pyle.]

Byrne, David, Williamson, Bill, and Fletcher, Barbara. The Poverty of Education. A Study in the Politics of Opportunity. London: Martin Robertson & Co., 1975. [England and Wales]

Cambridge Poverty Action Group. "Inflation and Means-Tested Benefits. A Survey of Educa- tional Welfare Benefits in Cambridgeshire and the Isle of Ely." Cambridge Poverty, Autumn, 1972.

Cameron, Sue. "Can Church Schools Fit Into a Multiracial Society?" Times Educational Supplement, F 2, 1973.

_____. "Ealing Accused 'Bussing Racist.'" Times Education Supplement, My 25, 1973. [Charge by West Middlesex District Committee of the Communist Party]

Cannon, Miles. "Education in Wolverhampton." Race Today, Jl, 1969.

Caradon, Lord. Race Relations in the British Commonwealth and the United Nations. New York: Cambridge U. Press, 1967.

Carley, Keith, and Thakur, Manab. No Problems Here? London: Institute of Personnel Management, 1977. [Racial discrimination in employment in England]

Carey, A. T. Colonial Students. London: Secker & Warburg, 1956.

Carnie, J. M. "Meeting the Immigrants in Our Schools." New Era, My, 1967.

Carson, John. "A Matter of Policy: The Lessons of Recent British Race Relations Legisla- tion." Albion 8(Summer, 1976):154-177.

Carter, Mark Bonham. "Integration in Britain." Patterns of Prejudice 5(Ja-F, 1971):7-9.

_____. "The Race Relations Board." Race Today, My, 1969.

Cazden, Courtney B. "Language Programs for Young Children: Notes from England and Wales." In Language Training in Early Childhood Education, pp. 119-153. Edited by Celia S. Lavatelli. Urbana, IL: U. of Illinois Press, 1971.

Challinor, Raymond. "Behind Racial Prejudice in England." New Politics, Summer, 1968. [Je, 1969]

Charlot, M. (ed.). Naissance d'un problème racial. Minorities de couleur en Grande- Bretagne. Paris: Colin, 1972.

Chater, A. Race Relations in Britain. London: Lawrence & Wishart, 1966.

Chazan, B. "Models of Ethnic Education. The Case of Jewish Education in Great Britain." British Journal of Educational Studies 26 (F, 1978):54-72.

Chazan, Maurice and others. Studies in Infant School Children. Vol. I: Deprivation and School Progress. Oxford: Basil Blackwell, 1977.

Chaudri, Joyce, and Dhesi, Autar. "Caste in Immigrant Politics." Race Today, My, 1969.

Chazan, Maurice, and Williams, Phillip. Studies of Infant School Children. Vol. I: Deprivation and School Progress. Vol. II: Deprivation and Development. Vol. III: Deprivation and the Bilingual Child. Vol. IV: Deprivation and the Infant School. Oxford: Basil Blackwell, 1978.

Cheetham, Juliet. Social Work with Immigrants. London: Routledge & Kegan Paul, 1972.

Claiborne, Louis F. "Law and Race in Britain." Annals 407(My, 1973):167-178.

Clark, David. Immigrant Responses to the British Housing Market: A Case Study in the West Midlands Conurbation. Bristol: SSRC Research Unit on Ethnic Relations, 1978.

_____. "Leeds." Race Today 5(S, 1973): 267-268.

Clark, George. Community Action in an Area of Special Need. Third Annual Race Relations Conference, London, S 20, 1969. [Notting Hill Summer Project]

Clegg, Alec. "How Reorganization Hits the Deprived Areas." Times Educational Supplement, Ap 2, 1971.

Clegg, Alec, and Megson, B. Children in Distress. Harmondsworth: Penguin, 1968.

Clough, Eric, and Quarmby, Jacqueline. A Public Library Service for Ethnic Minorities in Great Britain. Westport, CT: Greenwood, 1978.

Clyne, P. The Disadvantaged Adult: Educational and Social Needs of Minority Groups. London: Longman, 1973.

Coard, Bernard. "Educational Policies and the 'Socially Deprived.'" Race Today 4(Ap, 1972):124.

Coates, K., and Silburn, R. "Education in Poverty." In Education for Democracy. Edited by David Rubenstein and Colin Stoneman. N.p.: Penguin, 1970.

Colbenson, Peter D. "Socialist Anti-Semitism in Britain, 1884-1914." Doctoral dissertation, Georgia State U., 1977.

Cole, W. Owen. "Education in Multi-racial and Mini-cultural Britain." Patterns of Prejudice 6(Ja-F, 1972):17-21.

_____. "Multi-racial Into Multi-cultural." Patterns of Prejudice 6(N-D, 1972):9-12

_____. "Prejudice and the Denominational School." Patterns of Prejudice 9(Mr-Ap, 1975):17-19.

_____. "Prejudice and the Denominational School." Patterns of Prejudice 9(Mr-Ap, 1975):17-19.

Collins, B. A. N. "Racial Imbalance in Public Services and Security Forces." Race, Ja, 1966.

Collins, Sydney. Coloured Minorities in Britain... London: Lutterworth Press, 1957.

_____. "Social Processes Integrating Coloured People in Britain." British Journal of Sociology 3(Mr, 1952):20-29

Collison, Peter. "Immigrants and Residence." Sociology 1(1967):277-292. [Segregation in Oxford]

Colls, Robert. "Oh Happy English Children!: Coal, Class and Education in the North-East." Past and Present 73(N, 1976)

Colour and Immigration in the United Kingdom, 1969. London: Institute of Race Relations, 1969.

Commission for Racial Equality. Who Tunes in to What? London: Commission for Racial Equality, 1978.

Commission Two--The Teaching of English in Multi Racial Britain. The Challenge of Teachers in Multicultural Britain. London: N.A.T.E., Ap, 1975.

The Community Attitudes Survey 1. England. London: HMSO, 1969. [Social meanings of neighborhood]

Community Relations Commission. A Second Chance: Further Education in Multi-Racial Areas. London: CRC, 1976.

_____. Caring for Under-Fives in a Multi-Racial Society. London: Community Relations Commission, 1977.

_____. Education for a Multi-Cultural Society. 1. Syllabuses. London: Community Relations Commission, 1970.

_____. The Educational Needs of Children from Minority Groups. London: The Commission, 1974.

_____. Ethnic Minorities--Statistical Data. London: C.R.C., D, 1974.

_____. Housing in Multi-Racial Areas. London: CRC, 1976.

_____. Meeting Their Needs: An Account of Language Tuition Schemes for Ethnic Minority Women. London: The Commission, 1977.

_____. Unemployment and Homelessness: A Report. London: HMSO, 1974.

_____. Urban Deprivation, Racial Inequality, and Social Policy. A Report. London: HMSO, 1977.

Cooper, A. R. Review of Current Research on Education of Immigrant Children and Adult Project. London: English Teaching Information Centre, British Council, 1955-1966.

Corbett, Anne. "Aggrieved Areas." New Society, Ja 14, 1971. [Educational priority areas]

_____. "Coloured Schoolbooks." New Society, O 28, 1971.

_____. "Community School." New Society, F 27, 1969. [Wyndham School, Egremont, Cumberland]

_____. "Comprehensives: the Tally." New Society, F 12, 1970.

_____. "The EPA's Judged." New Society 22 (O 5, 1972):31-32.

_____. "How To Tackle Race Relations." Times Educational Supplement, F 8, 1974.

_____. "Immigrant Education." New Society, S 12, 1968.

_____. "No More Kid Catchers." New Society, Mr 4, 1971. [School attendance officers]

_____. "One-Class Schools?" New Society, Jl 6, 1967. [The problem of neighborhood schools]

_____. "Priority Schools." New Society, My 30, 1968.

_____. "A Report that Worked." New Society, Ja 9, 1969. [Plowden Report, two years after]

_____. "Top Priority." Times Educational Supplement, Jl 12, 1974. [First of the articles on educational priority areas]

Corbett, E. W. "The Development of Education in the Isle of Man." Master's thesis, U. of Manchester, 1931.

Cottle, Thomas J. "Young Man from Lancaster Gate." Integrateducation 15(Jl-Ag, 1977).

Council for Educational Advance. Obstacles to Opportunity. London: The Council, 1965.

Cousins, Frank. "Discrimination or Integration?" Community (England), Ap, 1970.

Cox, Theodore. "The Association between Cultural and Material Deprivation in the Home Background and Certain Aspects of Infant School Children's Development." Doctoral dissertation, U. of Wales, 1974.

Cox, T., and Waite, C. A. (eds.). Teaching Disadvantaged Children in the Infant School. Swansea, Wales: Dept. of Education, Wales U., 1970. ERIC Ed 042 840.

Cressy, David. "Educational Opportunity in Tudor and Stuart England." History of Education Quarterly 16(Fall, 1976):301-320.

_____. "Levels of Illiteracy in England, 1530-1730." Historical Journal 20(Mr, 1977): 1-23.

_____. "Literacy in Seventeenth-Century England: More Evidence." Journal of Interdisciplinary History 8(Summer, 1977):141-150.

Crewe, Ivor (ed.). The Politics of Race. British Political Sociology Yearbook, Vol. 2. London: Croom Helm, 1975.

Critcher, Charles and others. Race in the West Midlands Press. Birmingham: Centre for Contemporary Cultural Studies, U. of Birmingham, 1975.

Cross, Crispin P. Ethnic Minorities in the Inner City. London: Commission for Racial Equality, 1978.

_____. "Youth Clubs and Coloured Youths." New Community 5(Spring-Summer, 1977):489-494.

Cross, Malcolm. "Pluralism, Equality and Social Justice." New Community 1(Summer, 1972): 243-249.

_____. "Teaching Race as Social Policy." New Community 5(Spring-Summer, 1977):473-479.

Crouch, Colin. "Class, Status, Party and Education." Oxford Review of Education 2 (1976):59-70.

Cruickshank, Marjorie. Church and State in English Education 1870 to the Present Day. London: St. Martin's Press, 1963.

Curtis, L. Perry, Jr. Apes and Angels. The Irishman in Victorian Caricature. Washington, DC: N.p., 1971.

Curtis, L. P., Jr. Anglo-Saxon and Celts. New York: N.p., 1968. [Anti-Irish prejudice in 19th century Britain]

Curtis, Sarah. "When Black Is White." New Society, D 18, 1975. [Black characters in booklet on sex education]

Curtis, Stanley J. History of Education in Great Britain. 3rd ed. N.p.: N.p., 1953.

Dale, R. R. Mixed or Single-Sex School? London: Routledge & Kegan Paul, 1969.

Dale, R. R., and Griffith, S. Down Stream. Failure in the Grammar School. London: Routledge & Kegan Paul, 1965.

Dale, Roger and others (eds.). Schooling and Capitalism. A Sociological Reader. London: Routledge & Kegan Paul, 1976.

Dalton, M., and Seamen, J. M. "The Distribution of New Commonwealth Immigrants in London Borough of Ealing--1961-1966." Transactions of the Institute of British Geographers 58(1973).

Daniel, W. W. Racial Discrimination in England. N.p.: Penguin, 1968.

David, John. "Strangers in a Strange Land." Jerusalem Post, F 24, 1978. [Jews in Britain]

Davie, Ronald, Butler, Neville, and Goldstein, Harvey. From Birth to Seven: A Report of the National Child Development Study (1958 Cohort). London: Longmans, 1972.

Davies, John D. "The Impact of the Racial Problem on British Education." World and the School 24(F, 1972):18-22.

Davis, John. "The Genteel Patriots." Race Today 5(F, 1973):41. [Interview with chairman of the National Independent Party, a British anti-black group]

Davison, R. B. Commonwealth Immigrants. London: Oxford U. Press, 1964.

_____. "The Distribution of Immigrant Groups in London." Race 5(O, 1963).

Deakin, Nicholas. "Citizens and Immigrants in Britain." The Round Table 242(Ap, 1971): 283-292.

_____. "The Immigration Issue in British Politics (1948-1964), with Special Reference to Three Selected Areas." Doctoral dissertation, U. of Sussex, 1972.

_____. "Race and Human Rights in the City." Urban Studies, N, 1969

_____. "Residential Segregation in Britain: A Comparative Note." Race, England, Jl, 1964.

_____. Whitehall and Integration. London: Institute of Race Relations, 1968.

_____ (ed.). Colour and the British Electorate, 1964: Six Case Studies. London: Pall Mall Press, 1965.

_____ (ed.). Colour, Citizenship, and British Society. London: Panther Books, 1970.

Deakin, Nicholas, and Cohen, B. G. "Dispersal and Choice: Towards a Strategy for Ethnic Minorities in Britain." Environment and Planning 2(1970):193-201

Deakin, Nicholas D., and Mason, P. "Racial Adjustment in Britain." African Forum 2 (1967):98-111.

Deakin, Nicholas, and Ungerson, Clare. "Beyond the Ghetto: The Illusion of Choice." In London: Urban Patterns, Problems, and Policies, pp. 215-247. Edited by Donald Donnison and David Eversley. London: Heinemann, 1973.

Deming, Angus. "How Busing Works in Britain." Saturday Review: The Society 55(O, 1972): 14-16.

Dench, Geoff. "The Maltese in Britain." New Society, Ap 17, 1975, pp. 135-137.

_____. Maltese in London: A Case Study in the Erosion of Ethnic Consciousness. London: Routledge & Kegan Paul, 1975.

Department of Education and Science. Mixed Ability Work in Comprehensive Schools. London: HMSO, 1978.

Derrick, June. Immigrant Children: Teaching of English Report. London: U. of Leeds, Institute of Education, School Council, 1966.

_____. Language Needs of Minority Group Children. Windsor, Berks: NFER Publishing Co., 1977.

Dex, Shirley. "Job Search Methods and Ethnic Discrimination." New Community 7(Winter, 1978/9):31-39. [Bradford and Sheffield]

Dhondy, Farrukh. "The Black Explosion in Schools" (letter). Race Today 6(Ap, 1974): 123.

"Dialectics of Freedom." Patterns of Prejudice 8(My-Je, 1974):12-16, 28. [National Union of Students resolution against racialist or fascist groups]

Dines, Mary. "Pluralism: Promise or Threat?" Race Today 3(D, 1971):408-409.

Dixon, Annabelle. "How Unstreamed Are Infant Schools?" Forum for the Discussion of New Trends in Education 20(Spring, 1978):43-45.

Dodd, David. "Police and Thieves on the Streets of Brixton." New Society, Mr 16, 1978.

Doherty, Joe. "The Distribution and Concentration of Immigrants in London." Race Today, D, 1969.

_____. "Immigrants in London: A Study of the Relationship Between Spatial Structure and Social Structure." Doctoral dissertation, U. of London, 1973.

_____. "Race, Class and Residential Segregation in Britain." Antipode 5(1973):45-52.

Domnitz, Myer. _Judaism and Intergroup Relations-Information Notes_. London: Jewish Board of Deputies, 1967.

_____. _Immigration and Integration--Experiences of the Anglo-Jewish Community_. London: Council of Christians and Jews, 1968.

Donnan, S. P. B. "British Medical Undergraduates in 1975: A Student Survey in 1975 Compared with 1966." _Medical Education_ 10 (S, 1976):341-347.

Donnison, David V. "What We Think About Secondary Schools." _New Society_, Je 25, 1970. [In re: comprehensives and grammar schools]

_____. "Education and Opinion." _New Society_, O 26, 1976. A public opinion study of a national sample of the British population.

Douglas, James W. B. _The Home and the School. A Study of Ability and Attainment in the Primary School_. London: MacGibbon and Kee, 1964.

Douglas, James W. B., and Ross, J. M. "The Later Educational Progress and Emotional Adjustment of Children who Went to Nursery Schools or Classes." _Educational Research_, England, N, 1964.

Dove, Linda A. "Heads Buried in the Sand." _Times Educational Supplement_, Ag 9, 1974. [The issue of race in the schools]

_____. "The Hopes of Immigrant School children." _New Society_, Ap 10, 1975, pp. 63-65. [London]

_____. "Racial Awareness Among Adolescents in London Comprehensive Schools." _New Community_ 3(Summer, 1974):255-261.

Downing, John. "Britain's Race Industry: Harmony Without Justice." _Race Today_ 4(O, 1972):326-329.

Drake, St. Clair. "The 'Colour-Problem' in Britain: A Study in Social Definitions." _Sociological Review_ 3(1955):197-217.

_____. "Report on the Brown Britishers." _Crisis_ 56(1949):188-189.

_____. "Value Systems, Social Structures, and Race Relations in the British Isles." Doctoral dissertation, U. of Chicago, 1954.

Dryland, Ann, and Gumbert, Edgar B. "Education in England: Selected Problems and Issues: A Recent History." _Paedagogica Historica_ 11 (1971):18-30. [Comprehensive schools]

Duff, J. F., and Thomson, G. H. "Social and Geographical Distribution of Intelligence in Northumberland." _British Journal of Psychology_ 14(1923):192-198.

Duke, F. "The Education of Pauper Children: Policy and Administration, 1834-1855." Master's thesis, U. of Manchester, 1968.

Dummett, Ann. "Area Reports on Cities and Boroughs with Substantial Immigrant Settlement." _I.R.R. Newsletter_, Supplement, Je-Jl, 1967. Report on Oxford, England by the Community Liaison Officer of the Oxford Committee for Racial Integration

_____. _A Portrait of English Racism_. N.p.: Pelican, 1973.

_____. _Citizenship and Nationality_. London: Runnemede Trust, 1976.

_____. "What to Do [to Transform Britain from a Racist Society]?" _Race Today_, Jl, 1969.

Dummett, Ann, and Dummett, Michael. _Justice First_. London: Sheed and Ward, 1969. [Chapter on politics of race relations]

Dummett, Ann, and Hollings, Michael. _Restoring the Streets_, 1974. Catholic Committee for Racial Justice, British Council of Churches, 10 Eaton Gate, London SW1, England. [Catholics and racial justice]

Dummett, Michael. "CARD Reconsidered." _Race Today_ 5(F, 1973):42-44.

_____. _Immigrant Organizations_. Third Annual Race Relations Conference, London, S 20, 1969.

Dummett, Michael, and Dummett, Ann. "The Role of Government in Britain's Racial Crisis." In _Justice First_. Edited by Lewis Donnelly. London: Sheed and Ward, 1969.

Duncan, M. "Our ESN Children. Another Point of View." _Race Today_ 5(S, 1973):265-266.

Dunojaiye, M. O. A. "The Attitudes of Teachers of ESN and Normal Pupils." _Educational Research_ 13(F, 1971):125-129.

_____. "Patterns of Friendship and Leadership Choices in a Mixed Ethnic Junior School--A Sociometric Analysis." _British Journal of Educational Psychology_, F, 1969.

_____. "Patterns of Friendship Choices in an Ethnically-Mixed Junior School." _Race_ 12 (O, 1970):189-200.

Durojaiye, S. M. "Social Context of Immigrant Pupils Learning English." _Educational Reserach_ 13(Je, 1971).

"E.S.N.: Government Draft." _Race Today_ 5 (S, 1973):262.

"Ealing School Rumpus." _Race Today_ 6(Ap, 1974)" 101.

Edgar, David. "Racism, Fascism and the Politics of the National Front." _Race and Class_ 19 (Autumn, 1977):111-131.

Edgley, Roy. "Education for Industry." Radical Philosophy 19(Spring, 1968).

Edmondson, D. L. "Working in a Multi-Cultural School: Some Early Impressions." Multiracial School 5(Summer, 1977):10-15. [Birmingham]

Edson, P. "East and West Meetings." In Education for Integration Institute of Race Relations Newsletter. London: Institute of Race Relations, 1966.

"Education." New Community 1(Autumn, 1972): 455-456. [Account of a conference, "Training Teachers for a Multi-Cultural Society," Nottingham College of Education, S, 1972]

"Education and Race." Race Today, O, 1961.

Education and the Immigrants. London: National Association of Schoolmasters, 1969.

Education Committee. The Education of the Immigrant Child in the London Borough of Ealing. London: Ealing International Friendship Council, 1968.

"Education in a Multi-racial Britain." House of Lords. Official Report, Wednesday, 15 D, 1971. Vol. 326, No. 23, Cols. 1137-1253.

Educational Needs of Children from Minority Groups. London: Information Department, Community Relations Department, 1974.

"Educational Policy and Secondary School Reform in England." Western European Education 9 (Winter, 1977-1978):5-107.

Eggleston, S. John. The Social Context of the School. London: Routledge, 1967.

Elder, Glen H., Jr. "Life Opportunity and Personality: Some Consequences of Stratified Secondary Education in Great Britain." Sociology of Education, Ap, 1965.

Ellis, D. "Integration, Attitudes, and Social Distance in the East Midlands." Institute Race Relations Newsletter, Mr, 1969.

Engel, Madeline H. "Case Studies in British Immigration." International Migration Review, Spring, 1969.

Entwistle, Harold. Class, Culture and Education. London: Methuen, 1978.

Essen, Juliet and others. "Long-Term Changes in the School Attainment of a National Sample of Children." Educational Research 20(F, 1978):143-151.

Ethnic Minorities in Britain. London: Runnymede Trust, 1977. [Bibliography]

Evans, Anne. "Parental Involvement in Schools." Race Today 4(Ja, 1972):25. [London's East End]

Evans, Kate. "A Touch of Control in the Classroom." New Society, Ja 25, 1979. [Black and white in open-plan and traditional buildings]

Evans, Peter. The Attitudes of Young Immigrants. London: Runnymede Trust, 1971.

_____. Publish and Be Damned. London: Runnymede Trust, 1976. Race and immigration in 1976 as covered by British press

Everett, H. O. The Catholic Schools of England. N.p: N.p., 1944.

Eversley, David. "How Many Immigrants [in England]." New Society, Mr 13, 1969.

Everesley, D. E. C., and Sukdeo, F. The Dependants of the Coloured Population of England and Wales. London: Institute of Race Relations, 1969.

Featherstone, Joseph. "Schools for Children, What's Happening in British Classrooms"; "How Children Learn"; "Teaching Children to Think." New Republic, Ag 19, 1967; S 2, 1976; and S 9, 1967.

_____. Schools Where Children Learn. New York: Liveright, 1971. [British primary schools]

Feeley, M. "An Investigation of the Social Integration of Coloured Immigrant Children in Selected Secondary Schools." Master's thesis, U. of Liverpool, 1965.

Feeley, Michael. "The Schools Council Project in English for Immigrant Children." Institute Race Relations Newsletter, F, 1969.

Ferguson, Neil. "The Perceptual Motor and Language Skills of School Entrants in Deprived Areas." Doctoral dissertation, U. of Wales, 1972.

Ferguson, Neil and others. "The Plowden Report's Recommendations for Identifying Children in Need of Extra Help." Educational Research 13(Je, 1971):210-213.

Ferri, Elsa. Streaming: Two Years Later. A Follow-Up of a Group of Pupils Who Attended Streamed and Non-Streamed Junior Schools. London: National Foundation for Educational Research in England and Wales, 1971.

Fethney, Valine. "ESN Children: What the Teachers Say." Race Today 4(D, 1972):400-401.

Fiegehen, G. C., Lansley, P. S., and Smith, A. D. Poverty and Progress in Britain 1953-73. New York: Cambridge U. Press, 1977.

Field, A. M. and others. 1971 Census Data on London's Overseas-Born Population and Their Children. London: Department of Planning and Transportation Intelligence Unit, GLC, 1974.

Field, Frank. Free School Meals: The Humiliation Continues. London: Child Poverty Action Group, 1977.

_____. Unequal Britain. A Report on the Cycle of Inequality. London: Arrow Books, 1974.

_____. "Unequal Helpings." New Society, S 14, 1978. [Child benefits]

_____. "What Is Poverty?" New Society, S 25, 1975.

Fielding, Nigel. "Front Line in Schools." New Society, F 23, 1978. [The National Front and the schools]

"Firsthand Report: Birmingham." Race Today 5(My, 1973):144-145.

Five Views on Multi-racial Britain. London: Commission for Racial Equality, 1978.

Flude, Michael, and Ahier, John (eds.). Educability, Schools and Ideology. London: Croom Helm, 1974.

Fogelman, Ken and others. "Ability Grouping in Secondary Schools and Attainment." Educational Studies 4(1978).

Foot, Paul. Immigration and Race in British Politics. Baltimore: Penguin, 1965.

Ford, Julienne. "Comprehensive Schools as Social Dividers." New Society, O 10, 1968.

_____. Social Class and the Comprehensive School. London: Routledge & Kegan Paul, 1969.

Foren, Robert, and Batta, I. D. "'Colour' as a Variable in the Use Mode of a Local Authority Child Care Department." Social Work 27(Jl, 1970).

Fowler, Bridget and others. "Immigrant School Leavers and the Search for Work." Sociology 11(Ja, 1977):65-85.

Freeman, Gary P. Immigrant Labor and Racial Conflict in Industrial Societies: The French and British Experience, 1945-1975. Princeton, NJ: Princeton U. Press, 1979.

Freeman, James, and M.Comisky. "Systematic Trends in First Impression Ratings of Contrasting Racial Groups." Educational Sciences, O, 1966.

Friedman, Harold, and Friedman, Helen. "Four Exceptional Women in British Education." Integrateducation 15(Jl-Ag, 1977).

Fuller, Mary. "Experiences of Adolescents from Ethnic Minorities in the British State Education System." In Les travailleurs étrangers en Europe occidentale, pp. 173-192. Edited by Philippe J. Bernard. Paris: Mouton, 1976.

Gale, Fay. "The Universality of Racism: Minority Groups in the United Kingdom." Proceedings of the Royal Geographical Society of Australasia, South Australian Branch (1974):17-27.

Garner, J. F. "Racial Restrictive Covenants in England and the United States." Mod. Law R. 35(1972):478-488.

Garrard, John A. The English and Immigration. A Comparative Study of the Jewish Influx, 1880-1910. London: Oxford U. Press, 1971.

_____. "Parallels of Protest: English Reactions to Jewish and Commonwealth Immigration." Race, Jl, 1967.

Gartner, Lloyd P. The Jewish Immigrant in England, 1870-1914. London: N.p., 1960.

Garvey, Anne. "A Parents' Centre." New Society, Jl 8, 1976. [Newham]

Gerald, John Bart. "Color in England." Commonweal, D 10, 1965.

Gerner, L., and Steinberg, B. "A Survey of Jewish Education in Great Britain." Jewish Education 38(Ja, 1968):34-44.

Gilbert, Tony. Only One Died. London: Kay Beauchamp, 1976. [Death of Kevin Gately in demonstration against racism, Je 15, 1974]

Glassar, Terry. "Jewburbia: A Portable Community." New Society, O 8, 1970.

Glassman, Bernard. Anti-Semitic Stereotypes Without Jews: Images of the Jews in England, 1290-1700. Detroit: Wayne State U. Press, 1975.

Glean, Marion. "Whatever Happened to CARD?" Race Today 5(Ja, 1973):13-15.

Glendenning, Frank. "Racial Stereotypes in History Textbooks." Race Today 3(F, 1971): 52-54.

Glennerster, Howard. "Education and Inequality." In Labour and Inequality, pp. 82-107. Edited by Peter Townsend and Nicholas Bosanquet. London: Fabian Society, F, 1972.

Glennerster, Howard, and Hatch, Stephen (eds.). Positive Discrimination and Inequality. London: Fabian Society, Mr, 1974.

Goldman, Ronald. Research and the Teaching of Immigrant Children. London: National Committee for Commonwealth Children, 1967.

Goldstrom, J. M. The Social Content of Education, 1808-1870: A Study of the Working Class Reader in England and Ireland. London: Irish Universities Press, 1972.

Gomez, F. G. "The Endowed Schools Act, 1869-- A Middle-Class Conspiracy? The South-West Lancashire Evidence." Journal of Educational Administration and History 6(Ja, 1974): 9-18.

Goodman, George W. "The Englishman Meets the Negro [American Soldier]." Common Ground 5(Autumn, 1944):3-11.

Goody, Joan. "Classroom Interaction in the Multi-racial School." English in Education 11(Spring, 1977):2-10.

Grauman, R. A. "Methods of Studying the Cultural Assimilation of Immigrants." Master's thesis, London School of Economics, 1951.

Great Britain. Board of Education. Educational Systems of the Chief Crown Colonies and Possessions of the British Empire, Including Reports on the Training of Native Races... London: HMSO, 1905. 3 vols.

Great Britain. Department of Education and Science. Bilingualism in Education. London: HMSO, 1965.

_____. Educational Arrangements for Immigrant Children Who May Need Special Education. London: HMSO, 1973.

_____. Potential and Progress in a Second Culture. London: HMSO, 1971.

_____. School Transport. Report of the Working Party... London: HMSO, 1973.

Great Britain. Home Office. Second Report by Commonwealth Immigrants Advisory Council, Cmmd. 2266. London: HMSO, F, 1964.

Great Britain. Report of the Race Relations Board for 1966-1967. London: HMSO, 1967.

Great Britain. Ministry of Education. English for Immigrants. Ministry of Education Pamphlet No. 43. London: HMSO, 1963.

Great Britain. Select Committee on Race Relations and Immigration. Housing. 3 vols. House of Commons Paper 508. London: HMSO, 1971.

Great Britain. Youth Service Development Council. Immigrants and the Youth Service. London: HMSO, 1967.

Greater London Council. Colour and the Allocation of GLC Housing. London: Greater London Council, 1977.

Green, Lawrence. Parents and Teachers: Partners or Rivals? London: Allen & Unwin, 1968.

Gretton, John. "The Race Industry [in England]." New Society, Mr 11, 1971.

_____. "What It's All For." Times Education Supplement, Jl 20, 1973. [Education and income]

Griffiths, J. A. G. The Politics of the Judiciary. London: Fontana, 1978.

Grubb, Martyn. "Ealing: Goodbye to Busing?" Race Today 4(Je, 1972):206-207.

Gruson, Kerry. "Britain's Race Problems: Quick Rewrite of an American Tradition." Harvard Crimson, N 1, 1967.

_____. "Race Problem Looms in Great Britain..." Southern Courier, N 18, 1967.

Gundara, Jagdish. "Tomorrow May Be Too Late." Times Educational Supplement, Ap 29, 1977. [Education of minority children]

Gypsies and Other Travelers. London: HMSO, 1967.

H.M. Inspectors. Mixed Ability Work in Comprehensive Schools. London: HSMO, 1978.

Hakken, David James. "Workers' Education: The Reproduction of Working Class Culture in Sheffield, England and 'Really Useful Knowledge.'" Doctoral dissertation, American U., 1988. Univ. Microfilms Order No. 7822613.

Hall, Oswald, and Carlton, Richard. Basic Skills at School and Work: The Study of Albertown. Toronto: Ontario Economic Council, 1977. [Southern Ontario city]

Hall, Stuart. The Young Englanders. London: Community Relations Commission, 1967.

Hall, Stuart and others. Policing the Crisis: Mugging, the State, and Law and Order. London: Macmillan, 1978.

Halls, W. D. "Cultural Ideals and Elitist Education in England." Comparative Education Review 15(O, 1971):317-329.

Halsall, Elizabeth. The Comprehensive School. London: Pergamon, 1973.

Halsey, A. H. (ed.). Educational Priority. Vol. I: E.P.A. Problems and Policies. London: HMSO, 1972.

_____. "The Public Schools Debacle." New Society, Jl 25, 1968. [The Newsom Report on The English Public Schools]

_____. "Race Relations: The Lines to Think On." New Society, Mr 19, 1970.

_____ (ed.). Trends in British Society Since 1900. London: Macmillan, 1972.

_____. "Whatever Happened to Positive Dis-crimination?" Times Educational Supplement, Ja 21, 1977.

Halsey, A. H., and Trow, Martin. The British Academics. London: Faber & Faber, 1971.

Hamnett, C. "Social Change and Social Segrega-tion in Inner London, 1961-71." Urban Studies 13(0, 1976).

Hanawalt, Barbara A. "Childrearing Among the Lower Classes of Late Medieval England." Journal of Interdisciplinary History 8 (Summer, 1977):1-22.

Hancock, Neil W. "The Role of the English Educational System in Socialisation Theory. A Class Conflict Analysis." Doctoral dis-sertation, U. of Lancaster, 1971.

Hancox, Anthony. "Mr. Rhoden's Revolution." Sunday Mercury and Weekly Post, O 18, 1970. [Mr. Ernest L. Rhoden, headmaster, Grove Junior School, Wolverhampton]

Hanks, B. C. "The Multiracial School." Trends in Education 3(S, 1975):10-14. [Mount Pleasant school, Birmingham]

Hannam, Charles and others. "Serving Out Their Time." Times Educational Supplement, O 20, 1978. [Working-class children in British schools]

Hanson, Caroline. "The Rowntree Communica-tion in Schools Project." Race Today 3 (Jl, 1971):243-244.

Hargreaves, P. H. Social Relations in a Secondary School. London: Routledge & Kegan Paul, 1967.

"Haringey Banding Scheme." Race Relations Bulletin, Ag, 1969. [Ability grouping]

Harris, Marshall. "Teachers Against Racism." Patterns of Prejudice 6(Jl-Ag, 1972):14-15.

Harrison, Paul. "Culture and Migration: The Irish English." New Society, S 20, 1973.

Harrop, M., and Zimmerman, G. "Anatomy of the National Front." Patterns of Prejudice 11 (Jl-Ag, 1977):12-13, 18.

Hart, Jeffrey. "Enoch Powell Tells Some Home Truths." National Catholic Reporter, Ja 8, 1969.

Hartcup, Adeline. "Learning on Site." Times Educational Supplement, D 26, 1975. [Adult literacy class at Gypsy site, Bear, Kent]

Hashmi, Farrukh. "Psychiatric Problems of Immigrants." World Medicine 4(1969).

_____. Psychology of Racial Prejudice. London: Community Relations Commission, n.d.

Hassan, Leila. "Liverpool." Race Today 5 (S, 1973):269-271.

Hatch, Stephen, and Reich, Dennis. "Unsuccess-ful Sandwiches?" New Society, My 14, 1970. Social class factors in access to poly-technics and technological universities

Hawkes, N. Immigrant Children in British Schools. London: Institute of Race Relations, Oxford U. Press, 1966.

Hawkins, E. (ed.). "The Education of Minori-ties [in Britain]." London Educational Review 2(1973) entire issue.

Haynes, Judith M. Educational Assessment of Immigrant Pupils. London: NFER Book Publishing Division, 1971.

_____. "Immigrant Ability." Race Today, My, 1969.

Headley, Dave. "Keeping the Travellers On the Move." Race Today 2(D, 1970):451-454. [Gypsies in England]

Heginbotham, H. "Young Immigrants and Work." Newsletter (of Institute of Race Relations), My, 1967.

Heineman, Benjamin W. The Politics of the Power-less. A Study of the Campaign Aginst Racial Discrimination. London: Oxford U. Press, 1972.

Herbert, Geoffrey. The Classroom Behaviour of Socially-Handicapped Boys, Ap, 1972. The Secretary, Muffield Teacher Enquiry, U. of York, York YO1 5DD, England

Herbert, D. T. "Urban Education: Problems and Policies." In Social Areas in Cities, II, pp. 123-158. Edited by D. T. Herbert and R. J. Johnston. New York: Wiley, 1976.

Hershon, C. "Jewish Elementary Education in England, 1840-1957." Doctoral dissertation, Sheffield U., 1972.

Hill, Barry. "Barbados or Balham--IQ Tests Are Unreliable." Times Educational Supplement, Ap 9, 1971. [Schools for educationally submnormal students (E.S.N.)]

Hill, Barry, and Moorehead, Caroline. "The Making of Adult Illiterates." Times Educa-tional Supplement, O 1, 1971.

Hill, Christopher. Transfer at Eleven. Nation-al Foundation for Educational Research, 1972.

Hill, Clifford. How Colour Prejudiced is Britain? London: Gollancz, 1965.

Hill, David. "The Attitudes of Ethnic Minorities in Britain Among Adolescents." Doctoral dissertation, U. of Birmingham, 1973.

_____. "Personality Factors Amongst Adolescents in Minority Ethnic Groups." Educational Studies 1(Mr, 1975):43-54.

_____. Teaching in Multi-Racial Schools. A Guidebook. London: Methuen, 1976.

Hill, Michael J. Community Action and Race Relations: A Study of Community Relations Committees in Britain. London: Oxford U. Press, 1971,

Hilton, Jennifer. "The Ambitions of School Children." Race Today 4(Mr, 1972):79-81.

Himmelweit, Hilde, and Swift, Betty. "Continuities and Discontinuities in Media Usage and Taste: A Longitudinal Study." Journal of Social Issues 32, No. 4(1976): 133-156.

Hinds, Harvey. "Education in Inner London." Race Today (letter) 4(O, 1972):339-340. [See reply by "Backlash."]

Hipkin, John. "Outsiders Inside the Public Schools." New Society, Jl 18, 1968. [A study of attempted social integration]

Hiro, Dilip. "A Stepchild of Empire." New Society, F 29, 1968. [Immigrants in England]

_____. "Arresting Changes." New Society, S 1, 1977. [Notting Hill carnival]

Hoare, Quintin. "Education: Programmes and Men." New Left Review 32(Jl-Ag, 1965): 40-52.

_____. "Streaming and Its Supporters." New Left Review 29(1965):84-88.

Hobbs, Maurice. Teaching in a Multiracial Society. London: Association of Christian Teachers, 1976.

Hogg, Quintin. "Race Relations and Parliament." Race 12(Jl, 1970):1-13.

Holman, R. (ed.). Socially Deprived Families in Britain. London: Bedford Square Press, 1970.

Holmes, Brian (ed.). Educational Policy and the Mission Schools: Case Studies from the British Empire. New York: Humanities Press, 1967.

Holmes, Colin. "The Protocols of 'The Britons.'" Patterns of Prejudice 12(N-D, 1978):13-18. [Anti-semitism in England]

_____. "Violence and Race Relations in Britain, 1953-1968." Phylon 36(Summer, 1975):113-124.

Hughes, Catherine R. "No British Blueprint for a Nightmare." America, Mr 14, 1970. [Interview with E. J. B. Rose]

Hughes, John. "Employ the Young." New Society, O 14, 1976.

Humble, Stephen. "Neighbourhood Councils and Race Relations." New Community 7(Winter, 1978/9):85-91.

Humble, Stephen, and Talbot, Jennifer. Neighbourhood Councils in England: A Report to the Department of the Environment. Birmingham: Institute of Local Government Studies, U. of Birmingham, N, 1977.

Hunter, Guy K. "Othello and Colour Prejudice." Proceedings of the British Academy 53 (1967).

Hurt, John. Education in Evolution: Church, State, Society and Popular Education 1800-1870. London: Rupert Hart-Davis, 1971.

Huttenback, Robert A. "No Strangers within the Gates: Attitudes and Policies towards the Non-White Residents of the British Empire of Settlement." Journal of Imperial and Commonwealth History 1(My, 1973):271-302.

Huxley, Elspeth. Back Street New Worlds: A Look at Immigration in Britain. New York: Morrow, 1965.

_____. "The Silent Italian." Punch 246(F 12, 1964). [Italian immigrants in English schools]

The Immigrant Child and the Teacher, 1974. The Information Dept., LCSS, 68 Charlton Street, London, NW 1 1JR, England.

Immigrant Children in Infant Schools. London: Evans/Methuen Educational, 1970.

The Immigrant Community in Southall. London: Economist Intelligence Unit, 1965.

Inequality in Child Care, 1976. Child Poverty Action Group, 1 Macklin Street, Drury Lane, London WC2B5NH, England.

Inner London Education Authority. The Education of Immigrant Pupils in Primary Schools, 1967. The County Hall, London, SE 1, England.

_____. "Immigrants and Attainment." New Society, D 14, 1967.

_____. Literary Survey: Summary of Interium Results of the Study of Pupil's Reading Standards, 1969. The County Hall, London, SE 1, England

Institute of Race Relations. Facts Paper: Colour and Immigration in the U.K. 1968. Research Publications, London, SE 10, England.

_____. Facts Paper on the United Kingdom 1970-71. Research Publications, Ltd., 11 Nelson Road, London SE 10, England

Irvine, Elizabeth. "The York Family Project." Race Today 2(O, 1970):357-358.

Isaacson, W. "The Attitude to Jews and Judaism in Textbooks Used in English Secondary Schools for English and European History from the End of Antiquity to the French Revolution." London: World Jewish Congress, unpublished.

Israel, W. H. Colour and Community: A Study of Coloured Immigrants and Race Relations in an Industrial Town. Slough: Slough Council of Social Service, 1966.

"Is the [British] Working Class Really Racialist?" New Society, My 2, 1968.

Isherwood, H. B. Racial Integration. London: Britons Publishers, 1966.

Ivatts, Arthur. Catch '22' Gypsies, 1975. Advisory Committee for the Education of Romany and other Travellers, 204 Church Road, Hanwell, London W7, England

_____. Problems of Educational Policy Design and Implementation for a Cultural Minority--Gypsies, Ap, 1972. The Secretary, Nuffield Teacher Enquiry, U. of York, York YO1 5DD, England

"JCWI: Support on a Shoestring." Race Today 4(J1, 1972):221. [Joint Council for the Welfare of Immigrants]

Jackson, Barbara. Adopting a Black Child. Cambridge: Association of British Adoption Agencies, 1975.

_____. Family Experiences of Inter-racial Adoption. London: Association of Adoption and Fostering Agencies, 1976.

Jackson, Brian. "The Childminders." New Society, N 29, 1973. [Illegal child-minding]

_____. "How the Poorest Live: Education." New Society, F 1, 1973.

_____. Streaming. An Educational System in Miniature. London: Routledge and Kegan Paul, 1964. [A critique of the track system]

Jackson, Brian, and Rae, Ruby. Priority. How We Can Help Young Children in Educational Priority Areas, 1970. Association of Multi-Racial Playgroups, 32 Trumpington Street, Cambridge CB2 1QY, England.

Jackson, Brian and others. What Did Lord Butler Say in 1944? A Discussion Paper On a National Pre-School Policy, 1972. Priority Area Children, 32 Trumpington Street, Cambridge CB2 1QY, England.

Jackson, J. A. "The Irish in London: A Study in Migration and Settlement in the Last Hundred Years." Master's thesis, U. of London, 1958.

Jackson, John Archer. The Irish in Britain. Cleveland: Western Reserve U. Press, 1963.

_____. "The Irish in Britain." The Socio-logical Review, 1962, pp. 5-16.

Jackson, Keith, and Ashcroft, Bob. Adult Education, Deprivation and Community Development--A Critique, Ap, 1972. The Secretary, Nuffield Teacher Enquiry, U. of York, York YO1 5DD, England

Jacoby, Susan. "The Black Political Football." Nation, Je 10, 1978. [Immigration in Great Britain]

Jahoda, Gustav, Veness, Thelma, and Pushkin, I. "Awareness of Ethnic Differences in Young Children: Proposals for a British Study." Race, J1, 1966.

James, Alan. "Creating a Philosophy." Times Educational Supplement, N 26, 1976. [Advanced Diploma in Education in a Multi-racial Society at Lonsdale College]

Jarrett-Yaskey, Daphne, and Phillips, Michael. "Our ESN Children." Race Today 5(O-N, 1973.

Jeffcoate, Robert. "Children's Racial Ideas and Feelings." English in Education 11 (Spring, 1977):31-46.

_____. "Curriculum Planning in Multiracial Education." Educational Research 18(Je, 1976):192-200.

_____. "Where Examiners Fail." Times Educational Supplement, O 13, 1978. [Absence of Third World works in British literature curriculum]

Jelinek, Milena M. "Multiracial Education--3. Pupils' Attitudes to the Multiracial School." Educational Research 19(F, 1977):129-141.

Jelinek, Melina, and Brittan, Elaine. "Multiracial Education." Educational Research 18(November, 1975). [Friendship in multi-racial schools]

Jenkins, Robin. The Production of Knowledge at the Institute of Race Relations, n.d. ILP Pamphlet, 197 King's Cross Road, London WC1, England

Jenkins, Simon, and Randall, Victoria. Here to Live. A Study of Race Relations in an English Town. London: Runnymede Trust, 1971. [Leamington Spa]

John, Gus. "Blaming the Victim?" Times Educa-tional Supplement, J1 1, 1977. ["Youth and Race in the Inner City," a project of the National Association of Youth Clubs]

John, Augustine. Race in the Inner City. A Report from Handsworth, Birmingham. 2nd ed. London: Runnymede Trust, 1972.

Johnson, Linton Kwesi. "Education?" (letter). Race Today 6(Mr, 1974):81. [Comment on Dhondy, "The Black Explosion in Schools," above]

Joint Working Party. Teacher Education for a Multi-Cultural Society. London: Community Relations Commission and Association of Teachers in Colleges and Departments of Education, Je, 1974.

Jones, Catherine. Immigration and Social Policy in Britain. London: Tavistock, 1977.

Jones, Clement and others. Race and the Press. London: Runnymede Trust, 1971.

Jones, Jack. "Learning the Hard Way." Times Educational Supplement, Ja 4, 1974. [Growing up poor in Liverpool after World War I]

Jones, K,, and Smith, A. D. The Economic Impact of Commonwealth Immigration. Cambridge: Cambridge U. Press, 1970.

Jones, Philip N. "Colored Minorities in Birmingham, England." Annals of the Association of American Geographers 66(Mr, 1976):89-103.

_____. The Segregation of Immigrant Communities in the City of Birmingham, 1961. Hull: U. of Hull, 1967.

_____. "Some Aspects of the Changing Distribution of Coloured Immigrants in Birmingham, 1961-1966." Transactions of the Institute of British Geographers 50(1970).

Jones, W. R., Morrison, J. R., Rogers, J., and Saer, H. The Educational Attainments of Bilingual Children in Relation to their Intelligence and Linguistic Background. U. of Wales Press, 1957.

Journes, Claude. "Le Problème racial en Grand Bretagne." R. fr. sci. pol. 26(D, 1976):1080-1100.

Judge, Harry. "Exams for School-Leavers: Chaos and Change." New Society, Jl 11, 1974.

Kawwa, Taysir. "The Ethnic Prejudice and Choice of Friends Among English and Non-English Adolescents." Master's thesis, U. of London, 1963.

_____. "A Study of the Interaction Between Native and Immigrant Children in English Schools with Special Reference to Ethnic Prejudice." Doctoral dissertation, U. of London, 1965.

_____, "A Survey of Ethnic Attitudes of Some British Secondary School Pupils." British Journal of Social and Clinical Psychology 7 (1968):161-168.

_____. "Three Sociometric Studies of Ethnic Relations in London Schools." Race, O, 1968.

Kazamias, Andreas M. Politics, Society and Secondary Education in England. Philadelphia: U. of Pennsyvlania Press, 1966.

Kent County Council. Educational Vouchers in Kent. Maidstone, Kent: County Education Officer, 1978.

Kerckhoff, Alan C. "Stratification Processes and Outcomes in England and the U.S." American Sociological Review 39(D, 1974): 789-801.

Kerr, B. M. "Irish Immigration into Great Britain, 1798-1838." B. Litt. thesis, U. of Oxford, 1938.

The Keys. The Official Organ of the League of Coloured Peoples, 1933-1939. Republished in one volume. Milwood, NJ: Kraus-Thomson Organization Ltd., 1976.

Khan, Naseem. The Arts Britain Ignores: The Arts of Ethnic Minorities in Britain. London: Community Relations Commission, 1976.

Kiddle, Catherin. "A School for Gypsies." New Society, J 27, 1978.

Killian, Lewis M. "The Symbolism of School Busing in Britain and the U.S." In The Chancellor's Lecture Series, 1976-1977, pp. 9-24. Amherst: U. of Massachusetts, 1977.

King, R. A. All Things Bright and Beautiful? A Sociological Study of Infants' Classrooms. New York: Wiley, 1978.

Kirby, David Anthony. Slum Housing and Residential Renewal: The Case in Urban Britain. New York: Longman, 1978.

Kirk, Robert N. "Educating Slum Children in London." School and Society, Mr 20, 1965.

Klein, Gillian. "Racism in Books." Times Educational Supplement, Ap 8, 1977.

Klyhn, Joan. "On the Integration into School of Young Immigrant Children." English Language Teaching, My, 1969.

Kohler, David. "A Ballot on Race Laws." New Society, D 19, 1974.

_____. "Commonwealth Coloured Immigrants and the 1971 Census." New Community 2(Winter, 1972-1973):80-84.

Krausz, Ernest. "The Economic and Social Struc-
ture of Anglo-Jewry." In Jewish Life in
Modern Britain. Edited by Julius Gould and
Shaul Esh. London: Routledge and Kegan
Paul, 1964.

_____. Ethnic Minorities in Britain. London:
MacGibbon & Kee, 1971.

_____. "Factors of Social Mobility in British
Minority Groups." British Journal of Sociology 23(S, 1972):275-286.

_____. "The Jews in Britain: The Sociography
of an Old Minority Group." New Community 2
(Spring, 1973):132-136.

Kravitz, Seth. "London Jokes and Ethnic
Stereotypes." W. Folklore 36(O, 1977):
275-301.

Kushnick, Louis. "Anti-Discrimination Law--
Enforcement and Effectiveness." Institute
of Race Relations Newsletter, Mr, 1968.

Kuya, Dorothy. "The Unacceptable Face of
Publishing." Times Educational Supplement,
Jl 22, 1977. [Racism in textbooks]

_____. "What Did You Learn in School Today?"
Race Today 5(Jl, 1973):210. [Racial bias
in English textbooks]

Lacey, Colin. "Some Sociological Concomitants
of Academic Streaming in a Grammar School."
British Journal of Sociology, S, 1966.

Laishley, Jennie. "Can Comics Join the Multi-
racial Society?" Times Educational
Supplement, N 24, 1972.

_____. "Skin Colour Awareness and Preference
in London Nursery-School Children." Race 13
(Jl, 1971):47-64.

Lambert, J. R. "The Management of Minorities."
New Atlantis, Autumn, 1970.

Lambert, Royston, Hipin, John, and Stagg,
Susan. New Wine in Old Bottles? London:
G. Bell & Sons, 1968. [Social class inte-
gration of the English public schools]

Lambert, Royston. "What Dartington Will Do."
New Society, Ja 30, 1969. [Social integra-
tion at an independent boarding school in
Devon]

Larder, David, Roberts, Barrie W. "Travelling
School." Times Educational Supplement,
Jl 20, 1973. [Gypsies in England]

Last, Mercia. Race Relations in Britain.
London: Longman Group Ltd., 1978.

Lawrence, Daniel. Black Migrants: White
Natives. A Study of Race Relations in
Nottingham. London: Cambridge U. Press,
1974.

_____. "How Prejudiced Are We?" Race Today,
O, 1969.

_____. "Prejudice, Politics and Race." New
Community 7(Winter, 1978/9):44-55.

Lawson, John, and Silver, Harold. A Social
History of Education in England. London:
Methuen, 1973.

Lawton, Denis. Social Class, Language, and
Education. London: Routledge & Kegan Paul,
1968.

Layton-Henry, Zig. "Race, Electoral Strategy
and the Major Parties." Parliamentary
Affairs 31(Summer, 1978):268-281.

Layton-Henry, Zig, and Taylor, Stan. "Immigration and Race Relations: Political
Aspects." New Community 7(Winter, 1978/9):
67-71.

_____ and _____. "Race and Politics in
Ladywood." New Community 6(Winter, 1977/78):
130-142.

Lazonick, William. "Marxian Theory and the
Development of the Labour Force in England."
Doctoral dissertation, Harvard U., 1975.

_____. "The Subjection of Labour to Capital:
The Rise of the Capitalist System."
Review of Radical Political Economics 10
(Spring, 1978):1-31.

LeGrand, Julian. "Who Benefits From Public
Expenditure?" New Society, S 21, 1978.

Le Lohe, M. J. "The National Front and the
General Elections of 1974." New Community
5(Autum, 1976):292-301.

Leach, B. "Postal Screening for a Minority
Group: Young West Indians in Leeds."
Urban Studies 12(Je, 1975).

Lebzelter, Gisela C. Political Anti-Semitism
in England, 1918-1939. New York: Holmes
& Meier, 1978.

Lederman, S. "Factors Relevant to the Social
Acceptance of Immigrant Boys in Secondary
Schools." Master's thesis, Institute of
Education, U. of London, 1968.

_____. "The Social Acceptance [in Secondary
Schools] of Immigrants." Race Today, Je,
1969.

Lee, Rosemary. "The Education of Immigrant
Children in England." Race 7(O, 1965):131-
145.

Lee, T. "On the Relation Between the School
Journal and Social and Emotional Adjustment
in Rural Infant Children." British Journal
of Educational Psychology 26(1957).

Lee, Trevor R. "Immigrants in London: Trends in Distribution and Concentration 1961-71." New Community 2(Spring, 1973):145-158.

_____. Race and Residence: The Concentration and Dispersal of Immigrants in London. London: Oxford U. Press, 1977.

Lees, Lynn H. Exiles of Erin. Irish Migrants in Victorian London. Manchester: Manchester: Manchester U. Press, 1978.

Lees, Ray, and McGrath, Morag. "Community Work With Immigrants." British Journal of Social Work 4(1974):175-186.

Leeson, Jim. "High Priority for Low Levels." Southern Education Report, Jl-Ag, 1967. The Plowden Report

_____. "In Britain, Class and Race." Southern Education Report, O, 1967.

_____. "Race Relations in Britain: One Eye is on America." Southern Education Report, S, 1967.

Leighton, Jeremy. "Needles in the Haystack." Community (England), Ja, 1970. [Integration in Milton Keynes New City]

Lester, Anthony, and Bindman, Geoffrey. Race and Law. London: Longmans, 1972.

Lester, Anthony, and Deakin, Nicolas (eds.). Policies for Racial Equality. Rev. ed. London: The Fabian Society, 1970.

Lestor, Joan. "Multiracial Means All of Us." Multiracial Schools 2(Autumn, 1972):3-5.

Levin, P. H. "The Location of Primary Schools: Some Planning Implications." Journal of the Town Planning Institute, England. F, 1968.

Lewis, Gordon. "Race Relations in Britain. A View from the Caribbean." Race Today, Jl, 1969.

_____. "An Introductory Note to the Study of Race Relations in Britain." Caribbean Studies 11(Ap, 1971).

_____. "Protest Among the Immigrants." Political Quarterly 40(1969):426-435.

Lewis, H. "Jewish Education in London." Jewish Education 10(Ap-Je, 1938):70-76.

Lincoln, C. Eric. "The British Say They Aren't Prejudiced." New York Times Magazine, N 14, 1965.

Lindsay, Kenneth. Social Progress and Educational Waste, Being a Study of the "Free Place" and Scholarship System. N.p.: N.p., 1926.

Lipman, V. D. "The Rise of Jewish Suburbia." Transactions of the Jewish Historical Society of England 21(1968):78-103. [London area]

Little, Alan. "The Educational Achievement of Ethnic Minority Children in London Schools." In Race and Education Across Cultures. Edited by G. K. Verma and Christopher Bagley. Stamford, CT: Greylock Publishers, 1975.

_____. "A Sociological Portrait: Education." New Society 18(D 23, 1971):1245-1248.

_____. "New to this Society." Times Educational Supplement, Jl 23, 1976. ["Colored" immigrants and school services]

_____. "Performance of Children from Ethnic Minority Backgrounds in Primary Schools." Oxford Review of Education 1(1975).

Little, Alan, and Mabey, Christine. "An Index for Designation of Education Priority Areas." In Social Indicators and Social Policy. Edited by Andrew Shonfield and Stella Shaw. London: Heinemann, 1972.

_____ and _____. "Reading Attainment and Social and Ethnic Mix of London Primary Schools." In London: Urban Patterns, Problems, and Policies, pp. 274-312, 443-446. Edited by Donald Donnison and David Eversley. London: Heinemann, 1973.

Little, Alan, and Stern, Vivien. "Immigrants: Facts Hidden by Figures." Times Educational Supplement, O 5, 1973.

Little, Alan, Mabey, Christine, and Whitaker, Graham. "The Education of Immigrant Pupils in Inner London Primary Schools." Race, Ap, 1968.

Little, A., and Westergaard, J. "The Trend of Class Differentials in Educational Opportunity in England and Wales." British Journal of Sociology 15(1964):301-316.

Little, Kenneth L. "Some Aspects of Color, Class, and Culture in Britain." Daedalus, Spring, 1967.

Liu, W. H. "The Evolution of Commonwealth Citizenship and U.K. Statutory Control Over Commonwealth Immigrants." New Community 5 (Spring-Summer, 1977):426-447.

Lobo, Edwin de H. Children of Immigrants to Britain. Their Health and Social Problems. Dunton Green, Sevenoaks, Kent: Hodder & Stoughton, 1978.

Local Government, Schools and Parents, 1971. Confederation for the Advancement of State Education, 17 Jacksons Lane, Billericay, Essex, England.

Lomas, G. B. Gillian. "Colour in the Census." New Society, Ja 24, 1974.

Lomas, Graham. The Inner City. A Preliminary Investigation of the Dynamics of Current Labour and Housing Markets with Special Reference to Minority Groups in Inner London. London: London Council of Social Services, 1975.

London Head Teachers Association. Memorandum on Immigrant Children in London Schools. London: Pegg and Sons, Ltd., 1965.

Lovett, T. O. "EPA's--Reports and Reflections. 2. Liverpool--An Interim Report." Adult Education (England) 43(Ja, 1971):287-293.

Lunn, J. Barker. Streaming in the Primary School. London: National Foundation for Educational Research, 1970.

Lynch, James, and Plunkett, H. Dudley. Teacher Education and Cultural Change. London: George Allen & Unwin, 1973. [England, France, and West Germany]

Lyon, Michael. "Race and Ethnicity in Pluralistic Societies: A Comparison of Minorities in the U.K. and U.S.A." New Community 1(Summer, 1972):256-262.

Lyttle, John. "Anti-discrimination Law in New Zealand and Britain." New Community 1 (Autumn, 1972):451-452.

Mabey, Christine. Social and Ethnic Mix in Schools. London: Centre for Environmental Studies, 1974.

McCarty, Nick, and Christoudoulou, Philip. "Children Without Roots." Times Educational Supplement, Ap 15, 1977. [Cypriot refugee children in England]

McCallum, D. I. "The Middle Classes Still Rise to the Top Even Among Technicians." Times Higher Education Supplement, Jl 28, 1978.

McClelland, V. A. "Roman Catholics and Higher Education in England, 1830-1903." Doctoral dissertation, U. of Sheffield, 1967.

McCreery, Kathleen. "Proltet: Yiddish Theatre in the 1930's." Race and Class 20 (Winter, 1979):293-305.

McCulloch, J. Wallace and others. "Colour as a Variable in the Children's Section of a Local Authority Social Services Department." New Community 7(Winter, 1978/9):78-84. [Bradford]

Macdonald, Ian. Race Relations: The New Law. London: Butterworth, 1977.

Macdonald, K. I. "The Public Elementary-School Pupil Within the Secondary-School System of the 1890's." Journal of Educational Administration and History 6(Ja, 1974):19-26.

McDowell, D. "Some Organizational Issues in the Education of Minorities." London Educational Review 2(Spring, 1973):37-42.

McEwen, E. C., Gipps, C. V., and Sumner, R. Language Proficiency in the Multi-Racial Junior School: A Comparative Study. Windsor: NFER Publishing Co., 1975.

McFie, J., and Thompson, J. "Intellectual Abilities of Immigrant Children." British Journal of Educational Psychology 40(1970).

McGrath, Morag. "The Economic Position of Immigrants in Batley." New Community 5 (Autumn, 1976):239-249. [Yorkshire]

MacInnes, Colin. "That Other Culture." Times Educational Supplement, O 5, 1973. [Working-class culture; see Vaizey, below.]

McIntosh, Neil, and Smith, David J. The Extent of Racial Discrimination. London: PEP, S, 1974. [Jobs and housing]

McKay, David H. Housing and Race in Industrial Society: Civil Rights and Urban Policy in Britain and the United States. Totowa, NJ: Rowman and Littlefield, 1977.

MacKinnon, Kenneth. Language, Education and Social Processes in a Gaelic Community. London: Routledge and Kegan Paul, 1977.

McNeal, Julia. "Education." In The Prevention of Racial Discrimination in Britain. Edited by Simon Abbott. London: Oxford U. Press, 1971.

McNeal, Julia, and Rogers, Margaret (eds.). The Multi-Racial School. A Professional Perspective. Harmondsworth, Middlesex, England: Penguin Books, 1971.

Mack, Joanna. "The School Non-Leavers." New Society, O 2, 1975.

_____. "Schools for Privilege." New Society, Jl 7, 1977. [Fee-paying schools]

_____. "What Makes a Good School?" New Society, Mr 22, 1979. [The Rutter research]

Maizels, Joan. Adolescent Needs and the Transition from School to Work. London: The Athlone Press, U. of London, 1970. [School leavers in North London, 1965]

_____. "How School-Leavers Rate Teachers." New Society 16(S 24, 1970):535-537.

Malcolmson, Patricia E. "Getting a Living in the Slums of Victorian Kensington." London Journal 1(1975):28-55.

Male, George A. "Central Control of Education in England." Education and Urban Society, My, 1969.

Mandle, W. F. Antisemitism and the British Union of Facists. London: N.p., 1968.

Manyoni, J. R. "Ethnic and Cultural Minorities in Reading: A Study of Social Relations and Status of Minority Groups in an English Town." Bachelor's thesis, Oxford U., 1968.

Marcham, A. J. "Educating Our Masters: Political Parties and Elementary Education, 1867-1870." British Journal of Educational Studies 21(Je, 1973):180-191.

Marland, Michael, and Ray, Sarah. The Minority Experience. Harlow, Essex: Longman Thames, 1978.

Marriott, George. "Designation for Outlaws." Race Today 4(Jl, 1972):218. [Gypsies in England]

Marsden, Dennis. "Politicians, Equality and Comprehensives." In Labour and Inequality, pp. 108-142. Edited by Peter Townsend and Nicholas Bosanquet. London: Fabian Society, F, 1972.

Marsh, Alan. "Race, Community and Anxiety." New Society, F 22, 1973.

_____. "Tolerance and Pluralism in Britain: Perspectives in Social Psychology." New Community 1(Summer, 1971):282-289.

_____. "Who Hates the Blacks?" New Society, S 23, 1976.

Mason, A. E. (ed.). The Education of the Socially Handicapped. London: U. of London Goldsmith's College, 1966.

Mason, Philip. "Race Relations in Britain." Christian Century, Je 9, 1965.

_____. "Race Resistance and the IRR." New Community 3(Summer, 1974):285-288.

_____. "Seventeen Years of Race Relations." Race Today, Ja, 1970.

May, Roy, and Cohen, Robin. "The Interaction Between Race and Colonialism: A Case Study of the Liverpool Race Riots of 1919." Race and Class 16(O, 1974):111-126.

Mays, John Barron. "Dole Schools [in England]." New Society, Ja 11, 1973.

_____. Education and the Urban Child. Liverpool, England: Liverpool U. Press, 1962.

Meacham, Standish. A Life Apart: The English Working Class 1890 to 1914. London: Thames and Hudson, 1977.

Medlicott, Pau. "ESN Pupils." New Society, S 6, 1973.

_____. "The Hidden 11 Plus." New Society, Jl 4, 1974.

_____. "Special Teaching for Special Children." New Society, Mr 21, 1974.

Merson, Elizabeth. The Village School. New York: Paul Cave, 1979. [Bramshaw village school, Hampshire, 1812-1977]

Middleton, Nigel. "The Education Act of 1870 as the Start of the Modern Concept of the Child." British Journal of Educational Studies 18(Je, 1970):166-179.

Midwinter, E. C. Education: A Priority Area. London: National Union of Teachers, 1970.

Miles, R., and Phizacklea, A. "The TUC and Black Workers 1974-1976." British Journal of Industrial Relations 16(1978):195-207.

_____ and _____ (eds.). Racism and Political Action in Britain. London: Routledge & Kegan Paul, 1978.

Miller, Gordon W. "Factors in School Achievement and Social Class." Journal of Educational Psychology 61(Ag, 1970):260-269.

_____. "Moves for Equal Opportunity." Times Educational Supplement, O 8, 1971.

Miller, Henry. "Race Relations and the Schools in Great Britain." Phylon, Fall, 1966.

Mills, Roger. A Comprehensive Education. London: Centerprise, 1979. [Effingham Road school, late 1960's]

Milner, David. "The Effects of Prejudice." Race Today, Ag, 1969.

_____. "Ethnic Identity and Preference in Minority Group Children." Doctoral dissertation, Bristol U., 1971.

_____. "The Future of Race Relations Research in Britain: A Social Psychologist's View." Race 15(Jl, 1973):91-99.

_____. "Prejudice and the Immigrant Child." New Society, S 23, 1971.

Mitchell, W. E. "Proximity Patterns of the Urban Jewish Kindred." Man, S-O, 1965.

Monck, Elizabeth, and Lomas, G. B. Gillian. The Employment and Socio-Economic Conditions of the Coloured Population. London: Centre for Environmental Studies, S, 1975.

Moore, Robert S. "Immigration Policy and the Death of Liberal Britain." Times Higher Education Supplement, My 12, 1978.

_____. Race Relations--Britain Today. London: SCM Press, Ltd., 1971.

_____. Racial Justice in Britain? Glasgow: Iona Community, 1969.

Moores, K. "Differential Development of Spatial Ability in Immigrant and English Children." Master's thesis, U. of Manchester, n.d.

Morgan, Barrie S. "The Bases of Family Status Segregation: A Case Study in Exeter." Trans. Inst. Brit. Geographers 1, No. 1 (1976):83-107.

Morris, R. J. "The First Urban Immigrant: The Irish in England: 1830-50." Institute Race Relations Newsletter, Mr, 1969.

Morrish, Ivor. The Background of Immigrant Children. London: Unwin Educational Books, 1971.

Morton, David, and Goldman, Ronald. The Formal Institutions of Pre-School Education in Britain and the Sociological Context of their Emergence. Didsbury College of Education, 1969.

Mullard, Chris. "'Community' Relations: A Non-Starter." Race Today 5(Ap, 1973):105-107.

Murphy, James. The Religious Problem in English Education. The Crucial Experiment. N.p.: N.p., 1959.

Musgrave, P. W. "The Relationship between the Family and Education in England: A Sociological Account." British Journal of Educational Studies 19(F, 1971):17-31.

_____. Society and Education in England Since 1800. London: Methuen, 1968.

Nairn, Tom. The Break-Up of Britain: Crisis and Neo-Nationalism. London: NLB, 1977.

_____. "The Modern Janus." New Left Review 94(N-D, 1975):3-29. [Nationalism]

Nandoo, F. G. "Open Letter--A Reply to Sir William Houghton of ILEA." The Black Liberator 1(S/O, 1971):32-34.

National Association of Schoolmasters. Education and the Immigrants. Hemel Hempstead, England: Educare, 1969.

National Union of Teachers. The N.U.T. View on the Education of Immigrants. London: National Union and Teachers, Ja, 1967.

Neave, Guy. "Comprehensives Help Tap Talents of 11+ Failures." Times Higher Education Supplement, N 10, 1972.

Newbold, David. Ability Grouping--The Banbury Enquiry. Windsor, Berks: NFER Publishing Co., 1977.

Newby, Howard and others. Property, Paternalism and Power: Class and Control in Rural England. London: Hutchinson, 1979.

Noble, Trevor. "Social Mobility and Class Relations in Britain." British Journal of Sociology, D, 1972.

"Non-Streaming. Evidence Submitted by the Editorial Board of FORUM to the Plowden Committee." Forum, England, Autumn, 1964.

Nutik-Idem, Moses. "Brixton--An Informal Education Project." Race Today 4(Mr, 1972):77.

_____. "A Schooling in Alienation." Race Today 4(Jl, 1972):244. [Inner London Borough school]

Nugent, Neill. "The Anti-Immigration Groups." New Community 5(Autumn, 1976):302-310.

Nyahoe, B. "Liverpool and Community Action Group." Race Today 4(D, 1972):395.

Oakley, Robin (ed.). New Backgrounds: The Immigrant Child at Home and at School. London: Oxford U. Press, 1968.

Okley, Judith. "An Economy on Wheels." New Society, Ag 28, 1975. [Gypsy life in Britain]

Okley, Judith, Adams, Barbara, Morgan, David, and Smith, David. Gypsies and Government Policy in England. London: Heinemann Educational Books, 1975.

O'Malley, Jan. The Politics of Community Action: A Decade of Struggle in Notting Hill. London: Spokesman, 1977.

Omar, Barbara. "ESN Children--Labelled for Life." Race Today 3(Ja, 1971):2 [Misclassification of immigrant children as educationally subnormal children in London schools]

"Only One of 53 Race Complaints Upheld by [Race Relations] Board." Times Educational Supplement, Jl 9, 1971.

PEP. Racial Minorities and Public Housing. London: Research Publications Ltd., 1975.

"Packaged Racism from 'Publishers Row.'" International Books for Children 5(1974):1-2, 14, 16.

Pahl, R. H. "Poverty and the Urban System." In Spatial Policy Problems of the British Economy. Edited by M. Chisholm and G. Manners. London: Cambridge U. Press, 1971.

_____. Processes and Patterns of Urban Growth and Change. Third Annual Race Relations Conference, London, S 19, 1968.

Parekh, Bhikhu (ed.). Colour, Culture and Consciousness--Immigrant Intellectuals in Britain. London: Allen and Unwin, 1974.

Parkinson, J. P., and Macdonald, Barry. "Teaching Race Neutrally." Race 13(Ja, 1972):299-313.

Parsons, R. J. S. "Now You See Them, Now You Don't." New Community 7(Winter, 1978/9): 92-98. [Race reporting in the Leicester Mercury]

Partington, J. A. "Parents, Zoning and the Choice of School." Journal of Educational Administration and History 2(Je, 1970):39-45.

Patterson, Sheila. Immigration and Race Relations in Britain, 1960-1967. New York: Oxford U. Press, 1969.

Payne, Joan. Educational Priority. Vol. 2. E.P.A. Surveys and Statistics. London: HMSO, 1974.

Peaker, G. F. The Plowden Children Four Years Later. Berks, England: National Foundation for Educational Research in England and Wales, 1971.

Pearl, David. "Legal Decisions Relating to Ethnic Minorities and Discrimination." New Community 7(Winter, 1978/9):104-110.

Pearson, Karl, and Moul, M. "The Problem of Alien Immigration Into Great Britain, Illustrated by an Examination of Russian and Polish Jewish Children." Annals of Eugenics 1(1925):5-127.

Perkin, Harold. "The Recruitment of Elites in British Society Since 1800." Journal of Social History 12(Winter, 1978):222-234.

Petch, J. A. (ed.). Statistical Supplement to the Seventh Report, 1968-9, N, 1970. The Universities Central Council on Admissions, P.O. Box 28, Cheltenham, Glos. GL50 1 HY, England. [Includes data on social background of applicants for university places]

Peters, R. J. (ed.). Perspectives on Plowden. London: Routledge & Kegan Paul, 1969.

Philpott, S. B. "Remittance Obligations, Special Networks and Choice Among Montserration Migrants in Britain." Man, S, 1968.

Piachaud, David. "Inequality and Social Policy." New Society, Mr 22, 1979.

Pinchbeck, Ivry, and Hewitt, Margaret. Children in English Society. Vol. 2: From the Eighteenth Century to the Children Act 1948. London: Routledge & Kegan Paul, 1973.

Pinder, Ray. "Non-Streaming in Comprehensive Schools, Conference Report." Forum, Ag, 1966.

Pirani, M. "Aspirations and Expectations of English and Immigrant Youth." New Community 3(Winter-Spring, 1974):73-78.

Plender, Richard O. "Race Relations and the Law in Britain." Doctoral dissertation, U. of Illinois, 1972. Univ. Microfilms Order No. 72-19906.

Plowden, Bridget. "Primaries for Democracy." Times Education Supplement, Ag 25, 1972.

Plowden, Lady. "The Education of Gypsy Children." London Educational Review 2(Spring, 1973):31-36.

Polack, A. I. "Education: Children and Adults." In Colour in Britain. Edited by Richard Hooper. London: BBC, 1965.

Pollak, Margaret. Today's 3-Year Olds in London. London: William Heinemann Medical Books, 1972. [Brixton]

Pool, O. "The Needs of Immigrant Communities in Adult Education." Master's thesis, U. of Nottingham, n.d.

Postlethwaite, Keith, and Denton, Cliff. Streams for the Future? Banbury, Oxfordshire: Banbury School, Ruskin Road, Oxfordshire, England, 1978.

Powell, J. Enoch. "Population Figures in the United Kingdom." Mankind Quarterly 11(1970): 87-95.

_____. Still to Decide. London: Batsford, 1972.

Power, Anne. Racial Minorities and Council Housing in Islington, 1977. North Islington Housing Rights Project, 129 St. John's Way, London N 19, England.

Power, J. Immigrants in School: A Survey of Administrative Policies. London: Councils and Education Press, 1967.

Power, M. J., Benn, R. T., and Morris, J. N. "Neighborhood, School and Juveniles before the Courts." British Journal of Criminology, Ap, 1972.

Practical Suggestions for Teachers of Immigrant Children. 3rd ed. London: Community Relations Commission, Je, 1970.

Prais, S. J. "A Sample Survey on Jewish Education in London, 1972-73." Jewish Journal of Sociology 16(D, 1974).

Prandy, Kenneth. "Ethnic Discrimination in Employment and Housing: Evidence from the 1966 British Census." Ethnic and Racial Studies 2(Ja, 1979):66-79.

Preece, P. F. W. "The Laissez-Faire Finance of Education." British Journal of Educational Studies 19(Je, 1971):154-162.

Prem, Dhani R. The Parliamentary Leper: A History of Color Prejudice in Britain. Aligorh, India: Metric Publication, 1965.

Preston, Maurice. "The Profits of Learning." New Education, Jl, 1965.

Pringle, M. L. Kellmer. Deprivation and Education. London: Longmans, Green & Co., 1965.

Pringle, Marjorie. Home Economics for Multi-cultural Britain. London: National Association for Multiracial Education, 1975.

Pryce, Kenneth. "Problems in Minority Fostering." New Community 3(Autumn, 1974):379-385.

Psacharopoulos, George. "Family Background, Education and Achievement: A Path Model of Earnings Determinants in the U.K. and Some Alternatives." British Journal of Sociology 28(S, 1977):321-335.

The Public Schools Commission. "Integration." First Report, Vol. I. London: HMSO, 1968.

Public Libraries in a Multi-Cultural Britain. London: The Library Association, 1977.

Purvis, June. "Equality and Excellence in Adult Education: A Sociological Viewpoint." Studies in Adult Education 5(O, 1973):143-163.

Pushkin, I. "Ethnic Choice in the Play of Young Children." New Era 48, 1967.

_____. "A Study of Ethnic Choice in the Play of Young Children in Three London Districts." Doctoral dissertation, U. of London, 1967.

Puxon, Grattan. "British Romanies on the Move." New Community 1(Autumn, 1972):400-405.

Pyle, D. J. "Intra-regional Variations in Educational Provision... Some Comments on Byrne and Williamson." Sociology 9(S, 1975): 491-493.

Quick, P. "Education and Industrialisation." Doctoral dissertation, Harvard U., 1974. [19th-Century England]

Quinn, Peter Louis Sylvanus. "The Jewish Schooling Systems of London, 1656-1956." Doctoral dissertation, U. of London, 1958.

"Race Complaint Upheld." Times Educational Supplement, Ap 2, 1971, p. 5. [Racial discrimination against teacher by Walsall Education Authority]

Race in Britain. The Facts. London: Labour Research Department, 1976. 78 Blackfriars Road, London SE1 8HF

"Race in Promotion." Education (England) 143 (1974):382. [Employment discrimination]

Race in the Curriculum. A Report of the Conference of Teachers in Liberal Studies. World Studies Bulletin, Je, 1967.

"Racialists in Britain." Wiener Library Bulletin 19(Autumn, 1965):9-14.

Radcliffe, Lord. "Immigration and Settlement-- Some General Considerations." Institute Race Relations Newsletter, F, 1969.

_____. "Immigration and Settlement: Some General Considerations." Race, Jl, 1969.

Rai, Usha. "British Diary." Times Educational Supplement, N 17, 1978. [Racism in British schools and society]

Raynor, Lois. The Adoption of Non-White Children. London: Allen & Unwin, 197.

Rees, Philip (comp.). Fascism in Britain. A Complete Annotated Bibliography. London: Harvester Press, 1978.

Reference Division. Some of My Best Friends... A Report on Race Relations Attitudes. London: Community Relations Commission, 1976.

Reference and Technical Services Division. A Second Chance: Further Education in Multi-Racial Areas. London: Community Relations Commission, Mr, 1976.

Reid, Ivan. Social Class Differences in Britain: A Sourcebook. London: Open Books Publishing Ltd., 1977.

Reid, Ivan, and Franklin, Michael. "Comprehensive Parents." New Society, My 31, 1973.

Reid, Margaret. "Mixed Feelings." Times Educational Supplement, Je 10, 1977. [Mixed ability grouping]

Research Services Limited. Racial Discrimination. Sponsored by Race Relations Board and the National Committee for Commonwealth Immigrants. London: Political and Economic Planning, 1967.

Reubens, Edwin P. "Our Urban Ghettos in British Perspective." Urban Affairs Quarterly 6 (Mr, 1971):319-340.

Rex, John. "The Formation of Ghettoes in Britain's Cities." Political Quarterly, Ja-Mr, 1968.

Rex, John and others. "Housing, Employment, Education and Race Relations in Birmingham." New Community 6(Winter, 1977/78):123-126.

Rex, John. "The Sociology of a Zone of Transition." In Readings in Urban Sociology. Edited by R. E. Pahl. Oxford, England: Pergamon Press, 1968.

Reynolds, David, Jones, Dee, and St. Leger, Selwyn. "Schools Do Make a Difference." New Society, Jl 29, 1976.

Reynolds, Philip Graham. "Imperial-Racial Thought in Mid-Victorian England, 1857-1869." Master's thesis, Queens U. (Canada), 1971.

Rhoden, Ernest L. "A Multi-Racial School in England." Integrated Education (N-D, 1971):43-47.

Rhodes, Gerald. The Government of London: The Struggle for Reform. London: Widenfeld & Nicolson, 1970.

Richardson, C. "Irish Settlement in Mid-nineteenth Century Bradford." Yorkshire Bulletin of Economic and Social Research, 1968.

Richardson, Elizabeth. The Teacher, the School, and the Task of Management. London: Heinemann, 1973. [How Nailsea School in Somerset, England, became a comprehensive school]

Richmond, Anthony H. "Housing and Racial Attitudes in Bristol." Race 12(Jl, 1970): 49-58.

_____. "Immigration as a Social Process: The Case of the Coloured Colonials in the United Kingdom." Social and Economic Studies 1956, pp. 5, 185-201.

_____. Migration and Race Relations in an English City. A Study in Bristol. London: Oxford U. Press, 1973.

_____. "Race Relations in England." Midwest Journal, Summer, 1951.

Rim, Y., and Johnson, N. B. "The Devaluation by Children of Their Own National and Ethnic Group: Two Case Studies." British Journal of Social and Clinical Psychology 11(S, 1972):235-243.

Roberts, C. D. "Education in a Multi-Cultural Society." New Community 2(Summer, 1973): 230-236.

Roberts, Robert. A Ragged Schooling: Growing Up in the Classic Slum. Manchester: Manchester U. Press, 1976. [Salford]

Roberts-Holmes, Jay. "Culture Shock: Remedial Teaching and the Immigrant Child." London Educational Review 2(Summer, 1973):72-79.

Robertson, T. S. "Social Class and Educational Research." Educational Research 16(Je, 1974):189-197.

Robertson, T. S., and Kawwa, T. "Ethnic Relations in a Girls' Comprehensive School." Educational Research 13(Je, 1971).

Robinson, Philip. Education and Poverty. London: Methuen, 1976.

Robson, A. H. "The Education of Children Engaged in Industry in England, 1833-76." Doctoral dissertation, U. of London, King's College, 1930.

Roche, T. W. E. Key in the Locke: A History of Immigration in England from 1066 to the Present Day. London: Johnn Murray, 1969.

Rogers, Margaret. "Education in a Multi-ethnic Britain: A Teacher's Eye View." New Community 2(Summer, 1973):221-229.

_____. "The Education of Children of Immigrants in Britain." Journal of Negro Education 41(Summer, 1972):255-265.

Rolls, Eric F. "Changes in Religious Education." New Community 2(Summer, 1973):241-244.

Rose, E. J. B., in association with Deakin, Nicholas, and Abrams, Mark, Jackson, Valerie, Pester, Maurice, Vanags, A. H., Cohen, Brian, Gaitskell, Julia, and Ward, Paul. Colour and Citizenship. A Report on British Race Relations (published for the Institute of Race Relations, London). London: Oxford U. Press, 1969.

Rose, Hannan. "The Politics of Immigration After the 1971 Act." Political Quarterly 44(Ap-Je, 1973):183-196.

Rosen, Bruce. "Education and Social Control of the Lower Classes in England in the Second Half of the Eighteenth Century." Paedagogica Historica 14(1974):92-105.

Rosen, Harold. "Speaking from Experience." Times Educational Supplement, My 10, 1974.

Ross, J. M. "Does School Size Matter?--the Research." New Society 20(Je 15, 1972):557-558.

Roth, Norman D. "Social and Intellectual Currents in England in the Century Preceding the Jew Bill of 1753." Doctoral dissertation, Cornell U., 1978. Univ. Microfilms Order No. 7902359.

Rowan, M. Writing on the Blackboard: British Schools in Working Class Urban Areas Today. London: T. Stacey, 1972.

Rowland, V. L. "Race, Class, and Occupational Choice." New Community 4(Winter/Spring, 1974-5):46-54.

Rubenstein, David. School Attendance in London, 1870-1904. A Social History. New York: N.p., 1969.

Rubenstein, W. D. "Wealth, Elites and the Class Structure of Modern Britain." Past and Present 76(Ag, 1977):99-126.

Rumyaneck, J. "Social and Economic Development of the Jews in England." Doctoral dissertation, U. of London, 1933.

Runciman, W. G., and Bagley, C. R. "Status Consistency, Relative Deprivation, and Attitudes to Immigrants." Sociology 3(1969): 359-375.

Rushton, J. "A Sociometric Study of Some Immigrant Children in Manchester Schools." Durham Research Journal, S, 1969.

Rutter, Michael. Helping Troubled Children. Harmondsworth: Penguin, 1976.

Rutter, Michael, and Madge, Nicola. Cycles of Disadvantage: A Review of Research. London: Heinemann, 1976.

Rutter, Michael and others. Fifteen Thousand Hours. London: Open Books, 1979. [What makes a good school?]

Sanders, Charles L. "Race Problem in Great Britain." Ebony, N, 1965.

Sanderson, Michael. "Literacy and Social Mobility in the Industrial Revolution in England." Past & Present, Ag, 1972.

Schaefer, Richard T. "Contacts Between Immigrants and Englishmen: Road to Tolerance or Intolerance?" New Community 2(Fall, 1973):358-371.

_____. "The Dynamics of British Racial Prejudice." Patterns of Prejudice 8(N-D, 1974):1-5.

_____. "The Extent and Content of Racial Prejudice in Great Britain." Doctoral dissertatin, U. of Chicago, 1972.

A Schizoid Report--Comments on the First Report of the Select Committee on Race Relations and Immigration. London: Runnymede Trust, Mr, 1978.

_____. The Extent and Content of Racial Prejudice in Great Britain. San Francisco: R and E Research Associates, 1976.

Schoen, Douglas E. Enoch Powell and the Powellites. London: Macmillan, 1977.

Schofield, Michael. Society and the Young School Leaver. A Humanities Programme in Preparation for the Raising of the School Leaving Age. London: HMSO, 1967.

Schofield, R. S. "Dimensions of Illiteracy, 1750-1850." Explorations in Economic History 10(Summer, 1973):437-454.

Schools Council. "Cross'd with Adversity": The Education of Socially Disadvantaged Children in Secondary Schools. London: Evans/Methuen Educational, 1970.

_____. Multiracial Education: Need and Innovation. London: Evans/Methuen, 1973.

Scott, Duncan W. "A Political Sociology of Minorities: The Impact of Coloured Immigrants on Local Politics." Doctoral dissertation, U. of Bristol, 1972.

Scott, Phyllis M., and Darbyshire, Margaret. Early Education Programs and Aboriginal Families in Victoria, S, 1973. ERIC ED 093 466.

Scott, Rachel. A Wedding Man Is Nicer Than Cats, Miss: A Teacher at Work With Immigrant Children. New York: St. Martin's, 1972.

Seabrook, Jeremy. "Dead English." Integrated Education (Jl-Ag, 1972):60-64 (reprinted from New Society).

Searle, Chris (ed.). The World in a Classroom. London: Winters and Readers Publishing Cooperative, 1977.

Secretary of State for Education and Science. Educational Disadvantage and the Educational Needs of Immigrants. Cmnd. 5720. London: HMSO, Ag, 1974.

Select Committee on Race Relations and Immigration. Education, Vol. I: Report; Vol. II: Evidence; Vol. III: Evidence and Appendices. London: HMSO, 1973.

_____. The Problem of Coloured School-Leavers Vol. I. London: HMSO, 1969.

Sevard, J., and Vigneault, R. (eds.). Les États Multilingues, Problèmes et Solutions. Quebec: Les Presses de L'Université Laval, 1975.

Shankland/Cox and Institute of Community Studies. Poverty and Multiple Deprivation, 1975. Department of the Environment, Room P2/127, 2 Marsham Street, London SW1, England.

Shays, Rachel, and Green, Anthony, with Lewis, Jacqueline. Education and Social Control: A Study in Progressive Primary Education. London: Routledge & Kegan Paul, 1975.

Shepherd, John and others. A Social Atlas of London. London: Oxford U. Press, 1976.

Sherman, A. J. Island Refuge: Britain and Refugees from the Third Reich, 1933-9. London: Paul Elek, 1973.

Shillan, David. "A Diploma in 'Education for a Multicultural Society.'" New Community 4 (Autumn, 1975):345-348.

Shipley, Peter. The National Front: Racialism and Neo-fascism in Britain. London: Institute for the Study of Conflict, 1978.

Silk, Andrew. "'The Permanent Immigrants.'" Nation, D 25, 1976.

Silver, Pamela, and Silver, Harold. The Education of the Poor: The History of a National School 1824-1974. London: Routledge & Kegan Paul, 1974. [St. Mark's School, Kennington]

Silver, Harold (ed.). Equal Opportunity in Education. A Reader in Social Class and Educational Opportunity. London: Methuen, 1973.

Simon, Brian. Studies in the History of Education 1780-1870. London: Lawrence & Wishart, 1960.

_____. "Why Unstreaming?" Forum for the Discussion of New Trends in Education 20 (Spring, 1978):34-35.

_____ (ed.). The Radical Tradition in Education in Britain. London: Lawrence & Wishart, 1972.

Simon, Brian, and Rubinstein, David. The Evolution of the Comprehensive School. London: Routledge & Kegan Paul, 1968.

Singh, P. "City Centre Schools and Community Relations." Trends in Education 33(My, 1974):27-30.

Sivanandan, A. "Anatomy of Racism. The British Variant." Race Today 4(Jl, 1972): 223-225.

_____. "From Immigration Control to 'Induced Repatriation.'" Race and Class 20(Summer, 1978):75-82.

_____. "The Institute Story: The Unacceptable Face..." Race Today 6(Mr, 1974): 73-75. Institute of Race Relations, London

Skidelsky, Robert and others. "The National Front and the Young." New Society, My 4, 1978.

Slatter, Stuart, with Wilson, A., and Simmons, K. Some Aspects of Employing non-English Speaking Immigrants in British Industry, 1973. London Business School, Sussex Place, London NW1 4SA, England

Smith, David J. The Facts of Racial Disadvantage: A National Survey. London: PEP, 1976.

_____. Racial Disadvantage in Britain. Harmondsworth: Penguin, 1977.

_____. "The Nature of White Workers' Resistance." New Society, Je 20, 1974.

Smith, J. R. Migration in Post-War Birmingham. Birmingham, England: Birmingham U., 1970.

Smith, Mike. The Underground and Education. London: Methuen, 1977.

Smith, Robert W. "Edmund Burke's Negro Code." History Today 26(N, 1976):715-723.

Smithies, Bill, and Fiddick, Peter (eds.). Enoch Powell on Immigration. London: Sphere, 1969.

Social Background of Students and Their Chance of Success at School, S, 1971 (United Kingdom). ERIC ED 060 280.

Social Issues Committee. Jewish Students: A Question of Identity, 1974. Union of Liberal and Progressive Synagogues, 109 Whitfield Street, London W1P 5RP, England

Sowing the Dragon's Teeth. Bias in Books We Teach, 1973. Liverpool Community Relations Council, 64 Mount Pleasant, Liverpool 3, England.

Spencer, A. E. C. W. "The Catholic Community as a British Melting Pot." New Community 2 (Spring, 1973):125-131.

Stadlen, Frances. "Race Discrimination: Another Uncertain Move?" Times Educational Supplement, F 27, 1976. [Inclusion of education in Race Relations Bill]

Stafford Clark, David. Prejudice in the Community. London: Community Relations Commission, 1970 reprint.

Start, K. B. "Thirty Years of Reading Standards in England." Educational Researcher 1(N, 1972):8-9.

Start, K. B., and Wells, B. K. The Trend of Reading Standards. The Mere, Upton Park, Slough, Buckinghamshire, England: National Foundation for Research, 1972.

Stedman Jones, Gareth. Outcast London. A Study in the Relationship between Classes in Victorian Society. Clarendon Press, 1971.

Steele, E. D. "The Irish Presence in the North of England, 1850-1914." N. Hist. 12(1976): 220-241.

Steele, J. J. D. "A Study of the Education of the Working Class in Stockport During the Nineteenth Century." Master's thesis, U. of Sheffield, 1967.

Steinberg, Bernard. "Jewish Schooling in Great Britain." Jewish Journal of Sociology, Jl, 1964.

Steinberg, M. B. D. "Provisions for Jewish Schooling in Great Britain, 1939-1960." Master's thesis, U. of London, Institute of Education, 1962.

Stephens, E. D. "Some Are More Equal Than Others." Times Educational Supplement, Ap 12, 1974. [Parental choice of school in Britain]

Stephens, Leslie. Human Rights and Race in the UK, 1970. The UNA Trust, 93 Albert Embankment, London SE 1, England.

Stephens, W. B. "Illiteracy in Devon During the Industrial Revolution, 1754-1844." Journal of Educational Administration and History 8 (Ja, 1976):1-5.

Stewart, Ian. "Readers As A Source of Prejudice?" Race Today, Ja, 1970.

Stock, Arthur, and Howell, David (eds.). Education for Adult Immigrants. London: National Institute of Adult Education, 1976.

Stoker, Diana. Immigrant Children in Infant Schools. London: Evans Methuen, 1970.

Stone, Lawrence. "The Educational Revolution in England, 1560-1640." Past & Present 28 (1964):41-80.

_____. "Literacy and Education in England, 1640-1900." Past & Present 42(F, 1969): 69-139.

Studlar, Donley T. "British Public Opinion, Color Issues, and Enoch Powell: A Longitudinal Analysis." British Journal of Political Science 4(Jl, 1974).

_____. "Policy Voting in Britain: The Colored Immigration Issue in the 1964, 1966, and 1970 General Elections." American Political Science Review 72(Mr, 1978):46-64.

_____. "Political Culture and Racial Policy in Britain." Patterns of Prejudice 8(My-Je, 1974):7-12.

_____. "Religion and White Racial Attitudes in Britain." Ethnic and Racial Studies 1 (Jl, 1978):306-315.

St. Romaine, C. "The Social Relations and Adjustment Problems of Coloured Immigrant Pupils in the Primary Schools of Newcastle upon Tyne." Master's thesis, Newcastle upon Tyne U., 1972.

Suelzle, Marijean and others. Early Childhood Socialization in Great Britain: Bradford Field Study Program, 1977. ERIC ED 156 991.

Sugarman, Barry. "Social Norms in Teenage Boys' Peer Groups: A Study of Their Implications for Achievement and Conduct in Four London Schools." Human Relations, F, 1968.

Sutherland, Gillian. "The Magic of Measurement: Mental Testing and English Education, 1900-40." Transactions of the Royal Historical Society 27(1977):135-153.

Swift, D. F. "Educational Psychology, Sociology and the Environment: A Controversy at Cross-Purposes." British Journal of Sociology, D, 1965.

_____. "Social Class and Achievement Motivation." Educational Research, England, N, 1965.

Tanner, Julian. "New Directions for Subcultural Theory: An Analysis of British Working-Class Youth Culture." Youth and Society 9(Je, 1978):343-372.

Tapper, Ted, and Salter, Brian. Education and the Political Order: Changing Patterns of Class Control. London: Macmillan, 1978.

Taylor, Francine. Race, School and Community. A Study of Research and Literature on Education in Multi-racial Britain. New York: Humanities Press, 1974.

Taylor, G., and Ayres, N. Born and Bred Unequal. London: Longmans, 1969.

Taylor, George. "North and South [England]: The Education Split." New Society, Mr, 1971.

Taylor, J. H. "High Unemployment and Coloured Leavers: the Tyneside Pattern." New Community 2(Winter, 1972-1973):85-89.

Taylor, Stan. The National Front: A Contemporary Evaluation. University of Warwick Occasional Paper No. 16, Ap, 1978.

_____. "Race, Extremism and Violence in Contemporary British Politics." New Community 7(Winter, 1978/9):56-66.

Teacher Training for a Multi-Cultural Society: A Report on Courses in Colleges and Departments of Education in Manchester, 1973. Manchester Council for Community Relations, 44 Brazennose Street, Manchester ML5 AP, England.

"Teaching the Children of Working People in London--And Who Decides What to Teach." Educational Courier, Toronto, N, 1966.

"Teaching the New Britons." London Economist, Mr 20, 1963. [School integration in the Midlands]

Thomas, Graham. "The Integration of Immigrants: A Note on the Views of Some Local Government Officials." Race, O, 1967.

Thomas, Ken. "Black and White Tests." New Society, Mr 23, 1978.

Thompson, D. "Toward an Unstreamed Comprehensive School." Forum, England, Summer, 1965.

Thompson, L. A. "Africans in Roman Britain." Mus. Afric. 1(1972):28-38.

Thornberry, Cedric. "Commitment or Withdrawal? The Place of Law in Race Relations in Britain." Race, Jl, 1965.

_____. "A Note on the Legal Position of Commonwealth Immigrants and the White Paper Proposals." Race, O, 1965.

Thornberry, Robert. "Dealing With the Demographic Landslide." Times Educational Supplement, O 25, 1974. [Social class segregation in housing and education]

_____. "Teachers' Centres." New Society, Je 27, 1974.

Thurlow, Richard C. "National Front Ideology. The Witches' Brew." Patterns of Prejudice 12(My-Je, 1978):1-9.

_____. "Political Witchcraft. Roots of Racism." Patterns of Prejudice 11(My-Je, 1977):17-22.

_____. "Racial Populism in England." Patterns of Prejudice 10(Jl-Ag, 1976):27-33.

Tibbenham, A. and others. "Ability Grouping and School Characteristics." British Journal of Educational Studies 26(F, 1978): 8-23.

Townsend, H. E. R., and Brittan, E. M. Multi-racial Education: Need and Innovation. London: Evans/Methuen Educational, 1973.

Townsend, Peter, and Bosanquet, Nicholas (eds.). Labour and Inequality. Sixteen Fabian Essays. London: Fabian Society, F, 1972.

"Trade Unions and Immigrant Workers." New Community 4(Winter/Spring, 1974-5):19-36.

Treiman, Donald J., and Terrell, Kermit. "The Process of Status Attainment in the United States and Great Britain." American Journal of Sociology 81(N, 1975):563-583.

Triselotis, J. P. (ed.). Social Work With Coloured Immigrants and their Families. London: Oxford U. Press, 1972.

Trudgill, Peter. Accent, Dialect and the School. London: Edward Arnold, 1976.

_____ (ed.). Sociolinguistic Patterns in British English. London: Edward Arnold, 1978.

Truman, A. Roy. "School." In Colour in Britain. Edited by Richard Hooper. London: N.p., 1965.

Tuck, Mary G. "The Effect of Different Factors on the Level of Academic Achievement in England and Wales." Social Science Research 3(1974):141-149.

UNESCO. Ethnicity and the Media: An Analysis of Media Reporting in the United Kingdom, Canada, and Ireland. Paris: UNESCO, 1978.

Ungoed-Thomas, J. R. "Race Relations and Moral Education." Race Today 2(O, 1970):353-355.

Vaizey, John. "It's Much More Complicated Than Class." Times Educational Supplement, O 12, 1973. [See, above, MacInnes.]

Van Der Eyken, Willem. "Compensatory Education in Britain: A Review of Research." London Educational Review 3(Autumn, 1974): 19-24.

_____ (ed.). Education, the Child and Society: A Documentary History, 1900-1973. N.p.: Penguin, 1973.

Vaughn, Michalina, and Archer, Margaret Scotford. Social Conflict and Educational Change in England and France, 1789-1848. London: Cambridge U. Press, 1972.

Venning, Philip. "Deafness a Problem Among Immigrants." Times Educational Supplement, O 29, 1971.

Verma. Gajendra K., and MacDonald, Barry. "Teaching Race in Schools: Some Effects on the Attitudinal and Sociometric Patterns of Adolescents." Race 13(O, 1971):187-202.

Verma, Gajendra K., and Bagley, Christopher (eds.). Race, Education and Identity. London: Macmillan, 1979.

Wakefield, Bernard, and Bainbridge, Dennis. "Immigrants in School." New Society, D 5, 1974.

Walker, David. "The Value of a Cool Academic Look at Race Relations." Times Higher Education Supplement, N 7, 1975. [Ethnic Relations Research Unit of the Social Science Research Council]

Walker, Marin. The National Front. 2nd ed. London: Fontana, 1978.

Wallis, M. R. and others. "Phytic Acid and Nutritional Rickets in Immigrants." Lancet, Ap 8, 1972, pp. 771-773.

Wallman, Sandra. "The Boundaries of 'Race': Processes of Ethnicity in England." Man (Je, 1978).

Walston, Lord. "Repatriation: Why It is Wrong." Race Today, My, 1969.

Ward, Bernard. The Dawn of the Catholic Revival in England (1781-1803). 2 vols. N.p.: N.p., 1909.

Ward, David. "The Public Schools and Industry in Britain After 1870." In Education and Social Structure in the Twentieth Century. Edited by Walter Laqueur and George L. Mosse. New York: Harper & Row, 1967.

Ward, G. "The Education of Factory Child Workers, 1833-1850." Economic Journal (Economic History Supplement) 3(1934-1937).

Ward, J. B. "An Observational Approach to the Study of Classroom Affiliation for the Immigrant Child." Doctoral dissertation, U. of London, Institute of Education, 1971.

_____. "An Observational Study of Interaction and Progress for the Immigrant in School." Educational Studies 4(Je, 1978):91-97.

Ward, Robin H. "The Decision to Admit: A Note on Governmental Attitudes to Immigration." New Community 1(Autumn, 1972):428-434.

_____. "How 'Plural' Is Britain?" New Community 1(Summer, 1972):263-270.

_____. "Residential Succession and Race Relations in Moss Side, Manchester." Doctoral dissertation, U. of Manchester, 1975.

_____. "Race Relations in Britain." British Journal of Sociology 29(D, 1978): 464-480. [Followed by a comment by Robert Moore, pp. 480-482]

Wardle, David. English Popular Education, 1780-1970. London: Cambridge U. Press, 1971.

Watkin, E. I. Catholicism in England. From the Reformation to 1950. N.p.: N.p., 1957.

Watson, G. Llewellyn. "The Sociological Relevance of the Concept of Half-Caste in British Society." Phylon 36(Fall, 1975): 309-320.

Watson, James L. (ed.). Between Two Cultures: Migrants and Minorities in Britain. London: Blackwell, 1977.

Watson, Peter. "Colouring Children's Attitudes." New Society, Ag 12, 1971.

Webster, Derek Herbert. "The Ragged School Movement and the Education of the Poor in the Nineteenth Century." Doctoral dissertation, U. of Leicester, 1973.

Wedderburn, Dorothy (ed.). Poverty, Inequality, and Class Structure. London: Cambridge U. Press, 1974.

Wedge, Peter, and Prosser, Hilary. Born to Fail? London: Arrow Books, 1973.

Weightman Gavin. "Flogging Anti-Racism." New Society, My 11, 1978. [Anti-Nazi League]

Weightman, Gavin, and Weir, Stuart. "The National Front and the Young: A Special Survey." New Society, Ap 27, 1978.

Weinberg, Ian. "What Do We Want of the Public Schools?" New Society, F 22, 1968.

_____. The English Public Schools: The Sociology of Elite Education. New York: Atherton Press, 1966.

Weller, M. F. "Immigrants: Some Problems of Integration." Health Visitor (England), Ap, 1970.

West, E. G. "Educational Slowdown and Public Intervention in 19th-Century England: A Study in the Economics of Bureaucracy." Explorations in Economic History 12(Ja, 1975):61-87.

"What the NUS's Controversial Motion on Racialism Really Said." Times Higher Education Supplement, My 10, 1974. [National Union of Students, England]

White, David. "Newham: An Example of Urban Decline." New Society, O 23, 1975.

White, David J. Racial Disadvantage in Employment. London: PEP, 1974.

White, Lydia. "School Textbooks and the Third World." Impact. World Development in British Education, S, 1971. Voluntary Committee on Overseas Aid and Development, 69 Victoria Street, London SW 1, England.

Whiteley, Winifred M. "Coloured Immigrants in Schools." In The Uneducated English. London: Methuen, 1969.

"Who's Afraid of Ghetto Schools? Busing in Ealing." Race Today, Ja, 1975.

Wiles, Sylvaine. "Children from Overseas" (2). Institute Race Relations Newsletter, Je, 1968.

Wilkinson, R. K., with Gulliver, S. "The Impact of Non-White on House Prices." Race 13(Jl, 1971):21-36. [Leeds]

Willey, Richard. "Teacher Education for a Multi-Cultural Society in the U.K." International Review of Education 21(1975).

Williams, Michael. "A Place for Gipsies to Live." New Society, Mr 15, 1979.

Williams, S. "Race Relations in Educational Theory: A Study Based on Observations Made in Two Schools." Master's thesis, U. of Surrey, n.d.

Willis, Paul. Learning to Labour: How Working Class Kids Get Working Class Jobs. Farnborough: Saxon House, 1977.

Willke, I. "Schooling of Immigrant Children in West Germany, Sweden, England." International Review of Education 21(1975):357-382.

Wilmington, S. M. "The Activities of the Aborigines Protection Society as a Pressure Group on the Formulation of Colonial Policy, 1868-1880." Doctoral dissertation, U. of Wales, n.d.

Wilson, F. L. "The Irish in Great Britain during the First Half of the Nineteenth Century," 2 vols. Master's thesis, U. of Manchester, 1946.

Wilson, Harriett, and Herbert, G. W.
Parents and Children in the Inner City.
London: Routledge & Kegan Paul, 1978.

Winchester, S. W. C. "Immigrant Areas in
Coventry in 1971." New Community 4(Winter/
Spring, 1974-5):97-104.

_____. "The Segregation of Social Groups in
Oxford." Geographical Studies in Oxford
and the Oxford Region, 1974.

Wiseman, Stephen, and Goldman, Ronald.
"Deprivation and Disadvantage: England and
Wales." In Deprivation and Disadvantage.
Nature and Manifestations, pp. 94-118.
Edited by A. Harry Passow. Hamburg,
Germany: UNESCO Institute for Education,
1970.

Wolfgang, Aaron (ed.). Education of Immigrant
Students: Issues and Answers. Toronto:
Ontario Institute for Studies in Education,
1975.

Wolverhampton Borough Treasurer's Office.
"Wolverhampton and Immigrant Education."
Race Today, F, 1970.

Wood, Wilford, and Downing, John. Vicious
Circle. London: Society for Promoting
Christian Knowledge, 1968.

Woodhall, Maureen, and Blaug, Mark. "Productivity Trends in British Secondary Education, 1950-63." Sociology of Education,
Winter, 1968.

Woodhead, Martin. Intervening in Disadvantage: A Challenge for Nursery Education.
Windsor, Berks: NFER Publishing Co., 1977.

Woods, Robert. "Aspects of the Scale Problem
in the Calculation of Segregation Indices:
London and Birmingham, 1961 and 1971."
Tijdschrift voor Economische en Sociale
Geografie 67(1976):169-174. [Immigrants]

Woolf, Myrna. Local Authority Services and
the Characteristics of Administrative
Areas. London: HMSO, 1968.

Worrall, Mary. "Curriculum Strategies for
Multiracial Education." Multiracial School
4(Summer, 1976):17-28.

Wright, Derek. "The Changed Morality of Race
Discrimination." New Society 17(My 27,
1971):905-906.

Wulf, Melvin. "Civil Liberties [and Civil
Rights] in Great Britain." Civil Liberties
(A.C.L.U.), S, 1967.

Yates, Alfred. "The Development of Comprehensive Education in England." International
Review of Education 17(1971):58-64.

Young, Michael, and McGeeney, Patrick. Learning Begins at Home: A Study of A Junior
School London: Routledge & Kegan Paul,
1968.

_____ and _____. "Parent Power. Ideas for
England." New Society, Jl 4, 1968.

Youth Service Development Council. Immigrants
and the Youth Service. London: HMSO, 1967.
Problems of the colored immigrant

Zammit, E. L. "The Behaviour Patterns of
Maltese Migrants in London with Reference
to Maltese Social Institutions." Bachelor's
thesis, Oxford U., 1970.

Zurick, Elia. "The Relationship Between the
School System and the Emergence of
Political Attitudes Among English Children."
Where, N, 1969.

Greece

Angel, Marc. The Jews of Rhodes: The History
of a Sephardic Community. New York:
Sepher-Hermon Press, 1978.

Molho, Michael, and Nelhama, Joseph. The
Destruction of Greek Jewry 1941-1944.
Jerusalem: Yad Vashem, 1965.

_____ (ed.). Hommage aux victimes juives des
Nazis en Grèce. 2nd ed. revised by Joseph
Nehama. Thessalonique, Greece: Communauté
israélite de Thessalonique, 1973.
[Salonika]

Pessah, Joseph. "Jewish Education in Greece
After World War II." Jewish Education 39
(Jl, 1969):23-26.

Greenland

Bornemann, Claus. "Economic Development in
Greenland and its Relationship to Education."
In Education in the North, pp. 213-226.
Edited by Frank Darnell. Arctic Institute
of North America, U. of Alaska, 1972.

Duckenfield, Mike. "Out in the Cold." Times
Educational Supplement, My 27, 1977.

Gad, Finn. The History of Greenland. Vol. I:
Earliest Times to 1700. Tr. Ernst Dupont.
Montreal, Canada: McGill-Queens U. Press,
1971.

Gunther, Bent. "The Pedagogical Situation in
Greenland." In Education in the North, pp.
243-267. Edited by Frank Darnell. Arctic
Institute of North America, U. of Alaska,
1972.

Hobart, Charles W. "The Influence of the
School on Acculturation with Special Refer-
ence to Greenland." Journal of Educational
Thought, Ag, 1968.

Jenness, Diamond. Eskimo Administration in Greenland. Montreal: Arctic Institute of North America, 1968.

Kleivan, I. "Language and Ethnic Identity: Language Policy and Debate in Greenland." Folk 11-12(1969-1970):235-286.

Rogers, George W. "Cross-Cultural Education and the Economic Situation: The Greenland and Alaska Cases." In Education in the North, pp. 125-174. Edited by Frank Darnell. Arctic Institute of North America, U. of Alaska, 1972.

Schurman, H. J. C. A Preliminary Survey of Greenland's Social History. Ottawa: Northern Science Research Group, Department of Indian Affairs and Northern Development, Ap, 1970.

Guatemala

Adams, Richard N. (ed.). Political Change in Guatemala Indian Communities. New Orleans, LA: N.p., 1957.

Barreiro, José. "Where the Strong Trees Grow." Akwesasne Notes 8(Midwinter, 1975-1976):20-22. [Todos Santos]

Contreras, J. Daniel. Una Rebelión Indigena en el Partido de Totonicapan en 1920. Guatemala: N.p., 1968.

De Young, Karen. "Guatemalan Indians Gingerly Take Up Politics." Washington Post, Je 21, 1977.

Hirshberg, Richard Irwin. "The Process of Latinization in the Guatemalan Highlands." Doctoral dissertation, Syracuse U., 1958. Univ. Microfilms Order No. 58-7221.

Irwin, Marc and others. "The Relationship of Prior Ability and Family Characteristics to School Attendance and School Achievement in Rural Guatemala." Child Development 49 (Je, 1978):415-427.

Johnson, Francis F. and others. "The Effects of Genetic and Environment[al] Factors upon the Growth of Children in Guatemala City." In Biosocial Interrelationships in Population Adaptation. Edited by Elizabeth Watts and others. Chicago, IL: Aldine, 1975.

Klein, R. E. and others. "Malnutrition and Mental Development in Rural Guatemala." In Studies in Cross-Cultural Psychology, Vol. 1. New York: Academic Press, 1977.

Manz, Beatriz L. "Peasants and Rural Proletariat Ethnicity and Social Class in Guatemala." Doctoral dissertation, State U. of New York at Buffalo, 1977.

Meisler, Stanley. "Guatemalan Co-ops Attract 'Red' Label." Los Angeles Times, F 1, 1976. [Indians]

Moore, Alexander. Life Cycles in Atchalán. The Diverse Careers of Certain Guatemalans. New York: Teachers College Press, 1973.

Pop Caal, Antonio. The Situation of Indian Peoples in Guatemala. Indigena, P.O. Box 4073, Berkeley, CA 94704. [Translated from La Semena, Mr] 1973]

Riding, Alan. "Mayas of Guatemala Live a Bleak Life as Migrant Workers." New York Times, Mr 27, 1978.

Roberts, Bryan R. Organizing Strangers: Poor Families in Guatemala City. Austin, TX: U. of Texas Press, 1973.

Saint-Lu, André. Condition coloniale et conscience créole au Guatemala (1524-1821). Paris: Presses Universitaires de France, 1970.

Seminario de Integración Social Guatemalteca. Integración Socialen Guatemala. ? vols. Guatemala, 1959.

Spronk, Barbara Jane. "The Indian in Guatemala Society." Master's thesis, Alberta U., 1971.

Warren, Kay B. The Symbolism of Subordination: Indian Identity in a Guatemalan Town. Austin: U. of Texas Press, 1973.

Guyana

Apple, Arnold. Son of Guyana. New York: Oxford, 1973.

Bacus, M. Kazim. "The Primary School Curriculum in a Colonial Society." Journal of Curriculum Studies 6(My, 1974):15-29.

Bynoe, Jacob Galton. "Social Change and High School Opportunity in Guyana and Jamaica: 1957-1967." Doctoral dissertation, U. of British Columbia, 1972.

Chamoiseau, Miguel. "Les élèves des classes terminales de lycée." Cahiers de Centre d'Études Régionales Antilles-Guyane 18 (1969):97-112.

Clementi, Cecil. The Chinese in British Guiana. Georgetown: Argosy Press, 1915.

Dennington, G. L. "Race Relations Between Africans and East Indians in British Guiana." Master's thesis, London U., 1965.

Despres, Leo A. Cultural Pluralism and Nationalist Politics in British Guiana. Chicago: Rand McNally, 1967.

_____. Ethnicity and Resource Competition in Guyanese Society. IXth International Congress of Anthropological and Ethnological Sciences, Ag-S, 1973.

Duggal, Ved P. "Relations Between Indians and Africans in Guyana." Revista/Review Interamericana 3(1973).

Fenty, Allan. "New Reading for a New Nation." Interracial Books for Children 4(Winter, 1972-1973):1, 13.

Fried, Morton H. "Some Observations on the Chinese of British Guiana." Social and Economic Studies 5(1956).

Glasgow, Roy Arthur. Guyana: Race and Politics Among Africans and East Indians. The Hague: Martinus Nijhoff, 1970.

Irvine, D. H. "The University and National Development: Case History Guyana." Higher Education and Research in the Netherlands 22(Winter/Spring, 1978):29-38.

Landis, Joseph B. "Race Relations and Politics in Guyana." Doctoral dissertation, Yale U., 1971. Univ. Microfilms Order No. 72-17,137.

Lutchman, Harold A. "Administrative Change in an Ex-Colonial Setting: A Study of Education Administration in Guyana, 1961-1964." Social and Economic Studies 19(1970):26-56.

Menezes, M. N. "British Policy Towards the Amerindians in British Guyana, 1803-1873." Doctoral dissertation, London U. College, 1972.

Menezes, Mary Noel. British Policy Towards the Amerindians in British Guiana, 1803-1873. New York: Oxford U. Press, 1977.

_____ (ed.). Amerindians in Guyana 1803-73: A Documentary History. London: Frank Cass, 1977.

Milne, R. S. "Politics, Ethnicity and Class in Guyana and Malaysia." Social and Economic Studies 26(Mr, 1977):18-37.

Moore, R. J. "East Indians and Negroes in British Guiana, 1838-1880." Doctoral dissertation, Sussex U., 1971.

Nath, Dwarka. A History of Indians in British Guiana. London: Thomas Nelson, 1950.

Omoruyi, Omo. "Exploring Pattern of Alignment in a Plural Society: Guyana Case." Sociologus 27(1977):35-63.

Prescod, Colin. "Guyana's Socialism: An Interview with Walter Rodney." Race and Class 18(Autumn, 1976):109-128.

Sanders, Andrew. "Amerindians in Guyana: A Minority Group in a Multi-Ethnic Society." Caribbean Studies, Jl, 1972

Seymour, Arthur J. Cultural Policy in Guyana. Paris: UNESCO, 1978.

Smith, Raymond T. "Race and Political Conflict in Guyana." Race 12(Ap, 1971):415-427.

Sparer, Joyce L. "Attitudes towards 'Race' in Guyanese Literature." Caribbean Studies 8 (Jl, 1968):23-63.

Sukdeo, I. D. "Racial Integration, With Special Reference to Guyana." Doctoral dissertation, U. of Sussex, 1968.

Vatuk, Ved Prakash. "Craving for a Child in the Folksongs of East Indians in British Guiana." Journal of the Folklore Institute 2(1965):55-77.

Guinea

Laye, Camara. The African Child. Tr. James Kirkup. London: Collins, 1965.

Rivere, Claude. "Genèse d'inégalite dans l'organisation sociale malinké." Cultures et developpement 5(1973):279-314.

Guinea-Bissau

Freire, Paulo. Pedagogy in Process. The Letters to Guinea-Bissau. London: Writers and Readers Publishing Cooperative, 1978.

Haiti

Bastien, Remy. "Haiti: clases y prejudicio de color." Aportes (Paris), Numero 9, 1968.

Nicholls, David. "Race, couleur et independance en Haiti (1804-1825)." R. hist. mod. contemp. 25(Ap-Je, 1978):1-212.

Rotberg, Robert I., with Clague, Christopher K. Haiti: The Politics of Squalor. Boston, MA: Hougton Mifflin, 1971.

Schmidt, Hans. The United States Occupation of Haiti, 1915-1934. New Brunswick, NJ: Rutgers U. Press, 1970.

Honduras

Coelho, Ruy G. de A. "The Black Carib of Honduras: A Study in Acculturation." Doctoral dissertation, Northwestern U., 1955. Univ. Microfilms Order No. 13,076.

White, Leland Ross. "The Development of More Open Racial and Ethnic Relations in British Honduras During the Nineteenth Century." Doctoral dissertation, U. of Missouri, 1969. Univ. Microfilms Order No. 69-16109.

Hungary

Adler, Philip J. "The Introduction of Public Schooling for the Jews of Hungary (1849-1860)." Jewish Social Studies 36(1975):118-133.

Andorka, Rudolf. "Mobilité sociale, développment economique et transformations socio-professionelles de la population active en Hongrie. Vue d'ensemble (1930-1970)." Revue francaise de sociologie 13(1972): 607-629.

Barany, George. "'Magyar Jew or: Jewish Magyar'? (To the Question of Jewish Assimilation in Hungary)." Can.-Am. Slavic Stud. 8(Spring, 1974):1-44.

Braham, Randolph L. The Hungarian Labor Service System, 1939-1945. New York: Columbia U. Press, 1977. [Jews]

Fekete, J. "Public Education in Hungary in the Last 25 Years." New Hungary Quarterly 11 (1970):94-106.

Furst, A. The Liquidation of Jewish Education in Hungary (in Hebrew). New York: N.p., 1960.

Hegedüs, Andras. The Structure of Socialist Society. London: Constable, 1977.

Juhász, Júlia. "Secondary Education of Working Class Children." New Hungarian Quarterly 11 (Autumn, 1970).

Klement, Tomás. Three Decades in the History of Hungarian Higher Education. Tr. by János Rapcsak. Budapest: National Pedagogic Library and Museum, 1976. [1945-1975]

"Limits to Mobility in Hungary." New Society 20(Je 22, 1972):629-630.

McCagg, William O., Jr. Jewish Nobles and Geniuses in Modern Hungary. New York: Columbia U. Press, 1972.

_____. "Jews in Revolutions: The Hungarian Experience." Journal of Social History 6 (Fall, 1972):78-105.

Magocsi, Paul Robert. The Shaping of a National Identity. Subcarpathian Rus', 1848-1948. Cambridge, MA: Harvard U. Press, 1977.

Miles, Margaret. "Truly the People's Schools?" Times Educational Supplement, O 15, 1976.

Moskovits, Aaron. "History of Jewish Education in Hungary from 1781 to 1918." Doctoral dissertation, Dropsie College, 1959.

_____. Jewish Education in Hungary (1848-1948). New York: Bloch, 1964.

Murray, Elinor. "Higher Education in Communist Hungary." Slavic and East European Review 19(1960).

The Social Background of Pupils and Their Prospect for Success at School. Institut Pedagogique National (Hungary), My, 1971. ERIC ED 060 277.

Spira, Thomas. "Connections Between Trianon Hungary and Weimar Republic, and the Swabian Minority School Problem." Internationale Jahrbuch Geschichte und Geographieunterricht 13(1970-1971).

_____. German-Hungarian Relations and the Swabian Problem. New York: Columbia U. Press, 1977.

Szell, Joseph. "Jewish Neurosis in Hungary: A Personal Account." Olam (Spring, 1976).

Iceland

Bjarnason, D. "An Intergenerational Study of Perceptions of Social Stratification and Change in Urban Iceland." Master's thesis, U. of Keele, 1974.

Bjornsson, Sigurjon and others. Explorations in Social Inequality Stratification Dynamics in Social and Individual Development in Iceland, 1977. ERIC ED 158 424.

Broddason, Thorbjorn, and Webb, Keith. "On the Myth of Social Equality in Iceland." Acta Sociologica 18(1975):49-61.

Grimsson, Olafur Ragnar. "The Icelandic Power Structure, 1800-2000." Scandinavian Political Studies 11(1976):9-50.

_____. "Political Power in Iceland Prior to the Period of Class Politics, 1845-1918." Doctoral dissertation, U. of Manchester, 1970.

Josephson, Bragi S. "Education in Iceland: Its Rise and Growth with Respect to Social, Political, and Economic Determinants." Doctoral dissertation, George Peabody College for Teachers, 1968.

Toasson, Richard. "The Literacy of Icelanders." Scandanavian Studies 47(Winter, 1975):66-93.

India

Adams, Nancy L., and Adams, Dennis M. "An Examination of Some Forces Affecting English Educational Policies in India: 1780-1850." History of Education Quarterly, Summer, 1971.

Adamson, Ronald E. "Scheduled Caste Members of India's Parliament: Attitudes, Problems and Programs." Doctoral dissertation, U. of Missouri, 1975.

Addy, Premen, and Azad, Ibne. "Politics and Culture in Bengal." New Left Review 79 (My-Je, 1973):71-112.

Agarwala, B. B. "Emotional Integration and History Textbooks." The Progress of Education (India), Jl, 1965

Aggarwal, Partap C. "Widening Integration and Islamization of a North Indian Muslim Caste." In Themes in Culture (Essays in Honor of Morris E. Opler). Edited by Mario D. Zamora and others. Quezon City: Kayumanggi Publishers, 1975.

Ahmed, Akbar S. Social and Economic Change in the Tribal Areas, 1972-1976. New York: Oxford U. Press, 1977.

Aich, Prodosh. "Wer hat Zugang zur indischen Universität? Eine soziologische Erhebung." Zeitschrift für Soziologie 3(1974):111-137.

Aiyappan, A. Report on the Socio-economic Conditions of the Tribes and Backward Castes of Madras Province. Madras: Madras Museum Publishers, 1948.

Alam, M. A. "Level of Living of Agricultural Labour in Bihar: Case Study." Economic Affairs 21(D, 1976).

Alexander, K. C. Social Mobility in Kerala. Poona, India: Deccan College Postgraduate and Research Institute, 1968.

Ambedkar, B. R. The Untouchables. New Delhi, India: Amrit Book Co., 1968.

Anant, Santokh Singh. "Caste Hindu Attitudes: The Harijans' Perception." Asian Survey 11 (1971):271-278.

_____. "Harijans' Perception of Their Status: A Study in Andra Pradesh (India)." Psychologia: An International Journal of Psychology in the Orient 16(S, 1973): 147-163.

Arles, J.-P. "The Economic and Social Promotion of the Scheduled Castes and Tribes in India." International Labour Review 103 (Ja, 1971):29-64.

Arnaud, Michel-Jacques. "Contribution à l'étude de la ségrégation sociale a travers le systeme scolaire indien: les Brahmanes et les autres castes dominantes face aux castes defavorisees." Doctoral dissertation, U. of Paris, VIII, Vincennes, 1972.

Arora, Balveer. "Specificité ethnique conscience regionale et developpement national: langues et fédéralisme en Inde." Doctoral dissertation, U. of Paris, I, Pantheon-Sorbonne, 1972.

Baig, M. R. A. The Muslim Dilemma in India. Delhi: Vikas Publishing House, 1975.

Barnett, Marguerite Ross. The Politics of Cultural Nationalism in South India. Princeton: Princeton U. Press, 1976.

Basu, Aparna. The Growth of Education and Political Development in India, 1898-1920. Delhi: Oxford U. Press, 1974.

_____. "Policy and Conflict in India: The Reality and Perception of Education." In Education and Colonialism, pp. 53-68. Edited by Philip G. Altbach and Gail P. Kelly. New York: Longman, 1978.

Benegal, Nira. "Children's Books in India, Yesterday and Today: A Letter." Interracial Books for Children 5(1974):15.

Beteille, Andre. "The Future of the Backward Classes: The Competing Demands of Status and Power." In India and Ceylon: Unity and Diversity, pp. 83-120. Edited by Philip Mason. New York: Oxford U. Press, 1967.

_____. "Race and Descent as Social Categories in India." Daedalus, Spring, 1967.

Beteille, Andre, and Srinvas, M. N. "The Harijans of India." In Castes Old and New. Edited by Andre Beteille. Bombay: Asia Publishing House, 1969.

Beyer, H. "Indiens postkoloniale Bildungssystem zwischen Reform und struktureller Stagnation." Doctoral dissertation, Erlangen U., 1975.

Bhagwati, Jagdish. "Education, Class Structure and Income Equality." World Development 1 (My, 1973).

Bhatia, C. M. Performance Tests of Intelligence under Indian Conditions. London: Oxford U. Press, 1955.

Bhatt, R. S. "Some Social Aspects of the Minority Problem in India." Master's thesis, London School of Economics, 1936.

Bhattacharya, D. K. "The Anglo-Indians in Bombay: An Introduction to Their Socio-Economic and Cultural Life." Race, 0, 1968.

Bhattacharyya, Kalyani. "Historical Survey of the Language Problems in Bengal from the Muslim Period to the End of the British Period." Master's thesis, U. of London, 1959.

Bhirud, G. L. "The Most Vexing Problem: The Language One." The Progress of Education (India), Mr, 1968.

Bhowmik, K. L. and others. Tribal India. A Profile in Indian Ethnology. Calcutta: World Press, 1971.

Bhutani, V. C. "Curzon's Educational Reform
in India." Journal of Indian History 51
(Ap, 1973):65-92.

Borale, P. T. Segregation and Desegregation in
India. Bombay, India: Manaktlas, 1968.

Bose, A. B. "Educational Development among
Scheduled Castes." Man in India 50(1970):
209-239.

_____. "Problems of Educational Development
of Scheduled Tribes." Man in India 50
(1970):26-50.

Bose, Mihir. "One Corner of an Indian Slum
That is Forever England." New Society,
Ja 4, 1979. [Anglo-Indians in Calcutta]

Breton, Roland J. Atlas géographique des
langues et ethnies de l'Inde et du subcontinent. Québec: Les Presses de l'
Université Laval, 1976.

Cassen, R. H. India: Population, Economy,
Society. London: Macmillan, 1979.

Chakraborty, A. K. "The Causes of Educated
Unemployment in India." Economic Affairs
20(Jl, 1975).

Chattopadhay, G. "An Anthropologist Looks at
the Problem of National Integration of
India." Journal of the Indian Anthropological Society, Mr, 1966.

Chauhan, Brij Raj. "Special Problems of the
Education of the Scheduled Castes." In
Papers in the Sociology of Education in
India, pp. 228-249. Edited by S. M. Gore
and I. P. Desai. New Delhi: National
Council of Educational Research and Train-
ing, 1967.

Chekki, Danesh A. (comp.). The Social System
and Culture of Modern India: A Research
Bibliography. New York: Garland, 1975.

Chetsingh, Ranjit M. "Early History of Adult
Education in India." Indian Journal of
Adult Education 31(O, 1971):3-10.

Chitra, M. N. "Higher Education and Society
in Mysore under British Rule." Sociol. B.
(Bombay) 21(1972):152-175.

Chopra, Sukhendra Lal. "Cultural Deprivation
and Academic Achievement." Journal of
Educational Research, Jl-Ag, 1969.

_____. "Relationship of Caste System With
Measured Intelligence and Academic Achieve-
ment of Students in India." Social Forces,
Je, 1966.

Cohn, Bernard S. "The Changing Status of a Depressed Caste." In Village India: Studies
in the Little Community, pp. 53-77. Edited
by Marriott McKim. Chicago: U. of Chicago
Press, 1955.

Cormack, Margaret L. "Education and the Poor
in India." In Education and the Many Faces
of the Disadvantaged: Cultural and
Historical Perspectives, pp. 377-385.
Edited by William W. Brickman and Stanley
Lehrer. New York: Wiley, 1972.

Cannan, Crescy. "India: The Problem of the
Graduate Bus Conductor." Times Educational
Supplement, N 17, 1972.

Danda, Kumar Ajit (ed.). Tribal Situation in
Northeast Surguja. Calcutta: Pooran Press,
1977.

Dandekar, V. M., and Rath, N. "Poverty in
India: I." Economic and Political Weekly,
Ja 2, 1971, pp. 25-48.

Das, Amal Kumar. "Comparative Assessment of
Levels of Literacy amongst Scheduled Tribes,
Scheduled Castes and Total Population in
the Districts of West Bengal." Bulletin
of the Cultural Research Institute (Calcutta)
8(1969):57-63.

_____. "Comparative Assessment of Progress
in the Field of Education of the Scheduled
Tribes and Scheduled Castes of West Bengal."
Bulletin of the Cultural Research Institute
(Calcutta)7(1968):13-20.

Das, Amal Kumar, and Saha, Ramendra Nath.
"Post-Matric Education among the Scheduled
Tribes of West Bengal." Bulletin of the
Cultural Research Insitute (Calcutta) 7
(1968):11-23.

D'Costa, Anthony. "The History of the Demand
for Fundamental Rights in India." Indica
10(S, 1973):81-98.

Dewey, C. J. "The Education of a Ruling Caste:
The Indian Civil Service in the Era of Com-
petitive Examination." Educational History
Review 88(Ap, 1973):262-285.

Dholakia, B. H. "Report on Income Distribution
in India." Indian Economic Journal 25(O-D,
1977).

Dhondy, Farrukh. "The Tribals of India. A
Nation in Change." Race Today 6(D, 1974):
323-327.

Djurfeldt, Göran, and Lindberg, Steffan.
Behind Poverty: The Social Formation in a
Tamil Village. London: Curzon, 1975.

D'Souza, Austin A. Anglo-Indian Education:
A Study of Its Origins and Growth in Bengal
up to 1960. Delhi: Oxford U. Press, 1976.

Dube, S. C. Contemporary India and Its
Modernization. Delhi: Vikas, 1974.

_____ (ed.). India Since Independence:
Social Report on India, 1947-1972. New
Delhi: Vikas Pub. House, 1977.

_____ (ed.). Tribal Heritage of India.
Vol. 1. New Delhi: Vikas Pub. House,
1977.

Eapen, P. C. "Education for Emotional
Integration." The Progress of Education,
My-Je, 1965.

Elder, Joseph W. "The Decolonization of
Educational Culture: The Case of India."
Comparative Education Review 15(1971):288-
295. [Lucknow and Madurai]

Embree, Ainslie T. "Pluralism and National
Integration: The Indian Experience."
Journal of International Affairs 27(1973):
41-52.

Freeman, James M. Untouchable. An Indian
Life History. Stanford, CA: Stanford U.
Press, 1978.

Fuchs, Stephen. The Aboriginal Tribes of
India. New York: St. Martin's Prss, 1977.

Gaikwad, V. S. R. R. The Anglo-Indians: A
Study in the Problems and Processes Involved in Emotional and Cultural Integration. Bombay, India: Asia Publishing
House, 1967.

George, Grace. "The Syrian Christians of
Kerala and their Education." Master's
thesis, U. of London, 1959.

Ghosh, Samir K. "Education and Social Change:
NEFA." Ethnos 34(1969):118-129.

_____. "Understanding a Minority Community:
The Chinese of Calcutta." Calcutta.
Cultural Research Institute Bulletin 7
(1968):49-57.

Ghurye, G. S. Caste and Race in India.
Bombay: Popular Prakashan, 1969.

Gist, Noel P. "Conditions of Inter-Group
Relations: The Anglo-Indians." International Journal of Comparative Sociology
8(1967):199-208.

Gist, Noel P., and Wright, Roy Dean. Marginal-
ity and Identity: Anglo-Indians as a
Racially-Mixed Minority in India. Leiden,
Netherlands: E. J. Brill, 1973.

Gordon, Leonard A. Bengal: The Nationalist
Movement, 1876-1940. New York: Columbia
U. Press, 1974.

Gough, Kathleen. "Indian Nationalism and
Ethnic Freedom." In The Concept of Freedom
in Anthropology, pp. 170-207. Edited by
David Bidney. The Hague: Mouton, 1963.

Gregory, Robert G. India and East Africa:
A History of Race Relations within the
British Empire, 1890-1939. Oxford, England:
Clarendon Press, 1972.

Gupta, Giri Raj (ed.). Cohesion and Conflict
in Modern India. Durham, NC: Carolina
Academic Press, 1978.

_____ (ed.). Contemporary India. Some
Sociological Perspectives. Durham, NC:
Carolina Academic Press, 1976.

Haque, S. A. "The Education of the Depressed
Classes in India." Master's thesis, U. of
Leeds, 1938.

Hardy, Peter. The Muslims of British India.
New York: Cambridge U. Press, 1973.

Harman, S. Plight of Muslims in India, 1976.
D. L. Publications, 89 Polesworth House,
Alfred Road, London W2 5EU, England

Hashmi, B. A. "Development of Muslim Education
in India under British Rule." Master's
thesis, U. of Leeds, 1927.

Henson, Harlan Neil. "Elites, Language Policy
and Political Integration in Hyderabad."
Doctoral dissertation, U. of Illinois, 1974.
Univ. Microfilms Order No. 74-14,554.

Hingorani, R. C. "Minorities in India and Their
Rights." Revue des Droits de l'Homme 5
(1972):479-489.

Hiro, Dilip. The Untouchables of India.
London: Minority Rights Group, N, 1975.

Hooja, Rakesh. "Polyvalent Education for the
Tribals?" Indian Journal of Adult Education
36(O, 1975):16-17.

Iman, Mohammed (ed.). Minorities and the Law.
New Delhi: N. M. Tripathi Private, 1972.

Imam, Zafar (ed.). Muslims in India. New
Delhi: Orient Longman, 1975.

Iqbal, Afzal. The Life and Times of Mohamed
Ali: An Analysis of the Hopes, Fears, and
Aspirations of Muslim India from 1778-1931.
Lahore: Institute of Islamic Culture, 1974.

Ishaq, Mohammed. "Islamic Religious Instruction in the Schools of the Punjab and Bengal
in the British Period." Master's thesis,
U. of London, 1956.

Israel, Samuel. "The Colonial Heritage in
Indian Publishing." Library Trends 26
(Spring, 1978):539-552.

Jain, S. P. "Religion, Caste, Class, and
Education in a North Indian Community."
Sociology and Social Research, Jl, 1969.

Joshi, Barbara R. "Democracy in Search of
Equality: Untouchable Politics and Indian
Social Change." Doctoral dissertation,
U. of Chicago, 1975.

Juergensmeyer, Mark Karl. "Political Hope: The Quest for Political Identity and Strategy in the Social Movements of North India's Untouchables, 1900-1970." Doctoral dissertation, U. of California, Berkeley, 1974.

Kalota, R. S. "A History of the Education of the Shudra Untouchables Before and Under the British Rule in India, c. 2000 B.C. to 1947." Master's thesis, U. of Durham, 1950.

Kattackal, Joseph A. "Education in India's Five Year Plans: A Historical Review (1951-1976) and Critical Appraisal." Canadian and International Education 7(Je, 1978):5-25.

Katzenstein, M. F. "Preferential Treatment and Ethnic Conflict in Bombay." Public Policy 25(Summer, 1977).

Kaul, J. N. Higher Education in India: 1951-1971. Two Decades of Planned Drift. Simla, India: Indian Institute of Advanced Study, 1974.

Khanna, Balraj. The Punjab and the Punjabi Way of Life, 1973. Commonwealth Institute, Kensington High Street, London W8 6NQ, England.

Khubchandani, Lachman. "Language Ideology and Language Development: An Appraisal of Indian Education Policy." Linguistics 193(Je 2, 1977):33-51.

Kidwai, M. A. "Protection of Minorities in India." Doctoral dissertation, U. of Lucknow, 1947.

Kolenda, Pauline. Caste in Contemporary India: Beyond Organic Solidarity. Menlo Park, CA: Benjamin/Cummings, 1978.

Kumar, D. "Changes in Income Distribution and Poverty in India: A Review of the Literature." World Development 2(Ja, 1974):31-41.

Kurialacherry, A. J. "The Financing of Private Education in Certain Democratic Countries..." Doctoral dissertation, Loyola U., 1962. [India]

Kurian, K. Mathew (ed.). India, State and Society: A Marxian Approach. Bombay: Orient Longman, 1975.

Le Bihan, Adrien. "Castes et classes au Kérala: essai de géographie sociale." Doctoral dissertation, U. of Nice, 1973.

Lelyveld, David Simon. "Aligarh's First Generation: Muslim Solidarity and English Education in Northern India, 1875-1900." Doctoral dissertation, U. of Chicago, 1975.

_____. Aligarh's First Generation. Muslim Solidarity in British India. Princeton, NJ: Princeton U. Press, 1978. [Aligarh College]

Leopold, Joan. "British Applications of the Aryan Theory of Race in India." Economic History Review 89(Jl, 1974):578-603.

Lindsey, J. K. "Social Class and Primary School Age in Bombay: The Role of Education in the Transition to Capitalism." Canadian and International Education 6(D, 1977):75-97.

Lord, J. H. The Jews in India. Kolhapur, India: N.p., 1907.

Lynch, Owen M. "The Politics of Untouchability: A Case from Agra, India." In Structure and Change in Indian Society, pp. 209-240. Edited by Milton Singer and Bernard Cohn. Chicago: Aldine, 1958.

_____. The Politics of Untouchability: Social Mobility and Social Change in a City in India. New York: Columbia U. Press, 1969.

McDonald, Ellen E., and Stark, Craig M. (eds.). English Education, Nationalist Politics and Elite Groups in Maharashtra, 1885-1915. Berkeley: Center for South and Southeast Asia Studies, U. of California, 1969.

McLevy, Catherine. "Education of Drop-Outs—A Case Study." Literacy Discussion 6(Summer, 1975):63-78.

Nafziger, E. W. "Class, Caste and Community of South Indian Industrialists: An Examination of the Horatio Alger Model." Journal of Developing Areas 9(Jl, 1975).

Mahadevan, Meera. "Face to Face with Poverty: The Mobile Creches in India." Prospects 7 (1977): 570-579.

Mahar, J. Michael (ed.). The Untouchables of Contemporary India. Tucson, AZ: U. of Arizona Press, 1972.

Mahmood, Syed. A History of English Education in India. Aligarh: A.A.-O. College, 1895.

Moffatt, Michael. An Untouchable Community in South India. Structure and Consensus. Princeton, NJ: Princeton U. Press, 1979.

Naik, J. P. Equality, Quality, and Quantity: The Elusive Triangle in Indian Education. Bombay: Allied Publishers, 1975.

_____. Policy and Performance in Indian Education 1947-74. New Delhi: Orient Longman, 1975.

Nair, P. Thankappan. "Jews of Cenaaman galam and Paravur." Journal of Kerala Studies 2 (D, 1975):477-508.

Majumdar, Dhirendra Nath. "Acculturation among the Hajong of Meghalaya." Man in India, Ja-Mr, 1972.

_____. Races and Cultures of India. 4th ed. Bombay: Asia Publishing House, 1961.

Malikail, J. S. "The Public School System in India." Canadian and International Education 4, n.d.

Mallick, A. R. "The Development of the Muslims of Bengal and Bihar, 1813-1856, With especial Reference to Their Education." Doctoral dissertation, London U., School of Oriental and African Studies, 1952.

Mandal, Archana. "The Ideology and the Interests of the Bengali Intelligentsia: Sir George Campbell's Education Policy, 1871-74." Indian Ec. Soc. Hist. Review 12 (Ja-Mr, 1975):81-98.

Manndorff, Hans. "Zum Stand der Forschungen über Akkulturation und Integration der Eingeborenenstämme Indiens." Sociologus 11(1961):20-34. [English summary, pp. 33-34]

Mahaptra, L. K. "Social Movements Among Tribes in Eastern India with Special Reference to Orissa." Sociologus 18(1968):46-63.

Mayhew, Arthur I. The Education of India. London: Faber and Gwyer, Ltd., 1926.

Mazumdar, Vina. "The Economic Scene and Its Implications for Higher Education." New Frontiers in Education 3(Ap, 1973):11-20.

Mehrotra, R. R. "English in India: The Current Scene." English Language Teaching Journal 31(Ja, 1977):163-170.

Mehta, Rama. The Western Educated Hindu Woman. New York: Asia Publishing House, 1970.

Mencher, Joan P. "Group and Self-Identification: The View from the Bottom." Indian Council of Social Science Research Quarterly, Je, 1974.

_____. "Viewing Hierachy from the Bottom Up." In Encounter and Experience. Edited by André Béteille and T. N. Madan. Honolulu: U. Press of Hawaii, 1975. [Untouchables]

Menon, P. M. "Toward Equality of Opportunity in India." International Labour Review, 0, 1966.

Michaelson, Karen Lee. "Class, Caste and Network in Suburban Bombay: Adaptive Strategies among the Middle Class." Doctoral dissertation, U. of Wisconsin, 1973. Univ. Microfilms, Order No. 73-32,133.

Miller, D. B. From Hierarchy to Stratification: Changing Patterns of Social Inequality in a North Indian Village. New York: Oxford, 1975.

Miller, Roladn Eric. "The Mappila Muslims of Southwest India: A Study in Islamic Trends." Doctoral dissertation, Hartford Seminary Foundation, 1973. Univ. Microfilms Order No. 74-18,830.

Minault, Gail, and Lelyveld, David. "The Campaign for a Muslim University, 1898-1920." Mod. Asian Stud. 8(Ap, 1974):145-189.

Mines, Mattison. "Islamization and Muslim Ethnicity in South India." Man 10(1975).

Ministry of Information and Broadcasting. The Tribal People of India. New Delhi: The Ministry, 1973.

Misra, B. B. The Indian Middle Classes: Their Growth in Modern Times. London: Oxford U. Press, 1961.

Misra, R. P. "Nutrition and Health in India: 1950-2000 A.D." Journal of Human Evolution 7(1978):85-93.

Moffatt, Michael. An Untouchable Community in South India. Structure and Consensus. Princeton, NJ: Princeton U. Press, 1979.

Muralidharan, R., and Banerji, Uma. "Effect of Preschool Education on the School Readiness of Underprivileged Children of Delhi." International Journal of Early Childhood 7 (1975):188-192.

Murshid, Ghulam. "Coexistence in a Plural Society under Colonial Rule: Hindu-Muslim Relations in Bengal 1757-1912." J. Inst. Bangladesh Stud. 1(1976):116-144.

Murty, Kambhampaty, R. "An Analysis of the Post-High School Undergraduate Educational Opportunities in India." Doctoral dissertation, Columbia U., 1973. Univ. Microfilms Order No. 75-6470.

Musleah, Ezekiel N. On the Banks of the Ganga. The Sojourn of the Jews in Calcutta. North Quincy, MA: Christopher, 1975.

Naik, T. B. Impact of Education on the Bhils: Cultural Change in the Tribal Life of Madhya Pradesh. New Delhi: Research Programmes Committee, Planning Commission, 1969.

National Seminar on Tribal Education in India. Tribal Education in India. New Delhi: National Council of Educational Research & Training, 1967.

Newman, Robert S. "Caste and the Indian Jews." Eastern Anthropologist 28(Ap-Je, 1975); 28(Jl-S, 1975).

Nijhawan, I. P. "Distribution of Income and Saving Rates in Less Developed Countries: A Caste Study of India." Economic Affairs 22 (Ja-F, 1977).

Ogbu, John U. "Scheduled Castes in India."
In Minority Education and Caste, pp. 287-305.
New York: Academic Press, 1978.

Olcott, Mason. Village Schools in India.
Calcutta, India: Association Press, 1926.

Omvedt, Gail. Cultural Revolt in a Colonial
Society: The Nonbrahaman Movement in
Western India. Poona: Scientific Socialist
Education Trust, 1976.

_____. Women and Rural Revolt in India.
Irvine: Program in Comparative Culture,
U. of California, Irvine, Ja, 1978.

Oren, Stephen. "Linguistic Nationalism and
Sectarian Advantage: Strategies in the
Reorganization of Mysore and Punjab States,
India." Monda Lingvo Problemo 5(1973):1-17.

Pal, N. K. "An Assessment of Progress of Post-
Matric Education Among the Scheduled Tribes
and Scheduled Castes of West Bengal."
(West Bengal) Cultural Research Institute
Bulletin 12(1976):160-170.

Panchanadikar, K. C., and Panchanadikar, J.
Social Stratification and Mobility in a
Rural Community (Mahi) in Gujarat, India,
Ag, 1976. ERIC ED 131 973.

Quinn, M. J. "A Critique of British Educational Policies in India, 1854-1921." Master's
thesis, U. of London, Instiute of Education,
1967.

Qureshi, Ishtisq Hussain. The Muslim Community
of the Indo-Pakistan Subcontinent (610-1947).
The Hague: Mouton, 1962.

Rahman, H. "Muslim Education in 19th Century
Bengal." Quest, My-Je, 1972.

Rahman, M. F. "The Bengali Muslims and
English Education, 1765-1835." Master's
thesis, U. of London, 1948.

Rajaraman, I. "Poverty, Inequality and
Economic Growth: Rural Punjab, 1960/61-
1979/71." Journal of Developmental Studies
11(Jl, 1975).

Ramanathan, Gopalakrishnan. Educational
Planning and National Integration. London:
Asia Publishing House, 1965.

Ramu, G. N., and Wiebe, Paul D. "Occupational
and Educational Mobility in Relation to Caste
in Urban India." Sociology and Social
Research 58(0, 1973):84-94.

Rao, Vasant. "African Dynasty in India."
Black World 24(Ag, 1975):78-80. [The Siddis]

Rege, K. B. Magnitude of Illiteracy in India
(1961-1981), N, 1971. ERIC ED 060 431.

Roberts, A. J. "Education and Society in
the Bombay Presidency, 1840-58." Doctoral
dissertation, U. of London, School of
Oriental and African Studies, n.d.

Robinson, Francis. Separatism Among Indian
Muslims. The Politics of the United
Provinces' Muslims 1860-1923. New York:
Cambridge U. Press, 1975.

Rudolph, Susanne H., and Rudolph, Lloyd I.
(eds.). Education and Politics in India.
Studies in Organization, Society, and
Policy. Cambridge, MA: Harvard U. Press,
1972.

Sachchidananda. The Harijan Elite: A Study
of their Status, Networks, Mobility and
Role in Social Transformation. Faribadad,
Haryana, India: Thomson, 1977.

Sain, K., and Bagchi, B. "Illiteracy and
Development of Rural Economy." Economic
Affairs 21(N, 1976).

Sanyal, S. Social Mobility Movements among
Scheduled Castes and Scheduled Tribes of
India. Delhi: n.p., 1970.

Sapra, C. J. "Common School System and Neighborhood School." NEI Journal (New Delhi),
Jl, 1967.

Savarimuthu, Savarimuthu. "Education and Social
Mobility in Tamil Nadu, India: An Empirical
Study of Intergenerational Occupational
Mobility and Occupational Aspiration."
Doctoral dissertation, Loyola U. (Chicago),
1978. Univ. Microfilms Order No. 7807080.

Saxena, Shakuntala. Sociological Perspectives
in Indian Education. New Delhi: Ashajanak
Publications, 1975.

Schermerhorn, R. A. Ethnic Plurality in India.
Tucson: U. of Arizona Press, 1978.

Schmitt, Erika. "'Sonrat Santal Sanraj':
Eine soziale Bewegung der Santals in Dhanbad-
Distrikt, Bihar, Indien." Sociologus 23
(1973):3-21, 97-115. [Tribal protest against
Hindu discrimination. English summary, p.
115]

Schuth, Katarina. "Literacy in Rural India:
A Geographical Analysis." Doctoral disser-
tation, Syracuse U., 1973. Univ. Microfilms
Order No. 74-17,628.

Schwartz, Barton M. Caste in Overseas Indian
Communities. San Francisco: Chandler, 1967.

Selbourne, David. An Eye to India: The Unmasking of a Tyranny. Harmondsworth:
Penguin, 1977.

Sen, Asoka Kumar. "The Educated Middle
Class of Bengal, 1800-1885: Origin, Traits
and Tendencies." Journal of Indian History
54(D, 1976):731-752.

Sen, Sukowal. *Working Class of India: History of Emergence and Movement, 1830-1970.* Calcutta: K. P. Bagchi, 1977.

Seshadri, C. "Equality of Educational Opportunity--Some Issues in Indian Education." *Comparative Education* 12(O, 1976):219-230.

Sha, B. V. "Inequality of Educational Opportunities." *Economic Weekly*, Ag 20, 1960.

Shah, S. A. "A Statistical Estimate of the Class Structure of Contemporary India." *Science and Society* 28(1964):275-285.

Sharma, Miriam. *The Politics of Inequality: Competition and Control in an Indian Village.* Honolulu: U. Press of Hawaii, 1978.

Simmons, Ruth. " The Berwas of Delhi: School and Political Mobility in a Caste of Ex-Untouchables." Doctoral dissertation, U. of California, Berkeley, 1971.

Singh, Amick. "Indian Education Since 1947: An Assessment." *Prospects* 5(1975):312-322.

Singh, Bhupinder. "Tribal Development at Cross-Roads: A Critique and a Plea." *Man in India* 57(1977):229-243.

Singh, R. P. "Economic Condition of Rural Labour in India." *Economic Affairs* 22(Ag, 1977).

Sirkin, Gerald, and Sirkin, Nathalie Robinson. "John Stuart Mill and Disutilitarianism in Indian Education." *Journal of General Education* 24(Ja, 1973):231-285.

Srinwasan, T. N., and Bardhan, P. K. (eds.). *Poverty and Income Distribution in India.* Calcutta: Statistical Publishing Society, 1974.

Srivastava, L. R. N. "Plans and Programmes of Social Education for the Tribal People." *Calcutta. Cultural Research Institute. Bulletin* 7(1968):39-50.

Strizower, Shifra. *The Children of Israel. The Bene Israel of Bombay.* Oxford, England: Blackwell, 1971.

Tewari, D. D. "Dencentralization in Education." *Indian Education*, Mr, 1968.

Thorpe, C. Lloyd. *Education and the Development of Muslim Nationalism in Pre-Partition India.* Karachi: Pakistan Historical Society, 1965.

Thusu, Kidar Nath. *The Pengo Porajas of Koraput.* Calcutta: Tripti Kumar Mitra, 1977,

Timberg, Thomas Arnold. "The Jews of Calcutta." *Bengal Past and Present* 93(Ja-Ap, 1974):7-22.

Tinker, Hugh. *Separate and Unequal: India and the Indians in the British Commonwealth, 1920-1950.* Vancouver: U. of British Columbia Press, 1976.

Tiwari, Rosalind. "The Social and Political Significance of Anglo-Indian Schools in India." Master's thesis, U. of London, 1965.

Übleis, Franz. "Armut in Südindien: Lebensverhältnisse und Mobilität der armen Schichten des Ballungsraumes Madras." *Sociologus* 28(1978):70-93.

United Nations, Department of Economic and Social Affairs. *Poverty, Unemployment, and Development Policy: A Case Study of Selected Issues with Reference to Kerala.* New York: UN, 1975.

Vagiswari, A. *Income Earning Trends and Social Status of the Harijan Community of Tamilnadu.* Madras, India: Institute of Development Studies, 1972.

Valenti, Jasper J., and Gutek, Gerald L. *Education and Society in India and Thailand.* Washington: U. Press of America, 1977.

Veena, D. R. "Education and Land Utilisation in a Developing Region: A Study of Gujarat." *Bangladesh Development Studies* 3(Ja, 1975).

Verba, Sidney, Ahmed, Bashiruddin, and Bhatt, Anil. *Caste, Race, and Politics: A Comparative Study of India and the United States.* Beverly Hills, CA: Sage, 1971.

Verma, Aditya K. "The Problem of Minorities in India, 1900-1950." Doctoral dissertation, Allahabad U., 1954.

Weisskopf, Thomas E. "The Persistence of Poverty in India: A Political Economic Analysis." *Bulletin of Concerned Asian Scholars* 9(Ja-Mr, 1977):28-44.

Wright, Theodore P., Jr. "Muslim Education in India at the Crossroads: The Case of the Aligarh." *Pacific Affairs*, Spring-Summer, 1966.

Zachariah, Mathew. "Positive Discrimination in Education for India's Scheduled Castes: A Review of the Problem, 1950-1970." *Comparative Education Review* 16(F, 1972).

Zaman, Mukhtar. "The Origins of the All India Muslim Students Federation." *Journal of Pakistan Hist. Soc.* 24(O-D, 1976):211-230.

Indonesia

Abdullah, Taufik. "Schools and Politics: The 'Kaum Muda' Movement in West Sumatra (1927-1933)." Doctoral dissertation, Cornell U., 1970. Univ. Microfilms Order No. 71-07347.

Alatas, Hussein S. The Myth of the Lazy Native: A Study of the Image of the Malays, Filipinos and Javanese from the 16th to the 20th Century and Its Function in the Ideology of Colonial Capitalism. London: Cass, 1977.

Aziz, M. A. Japan's Colonialism and Indonesia. The Hague: Martinus Nyhoff, 1955.

Boland, Bernard Johan. "The Struggle of Islam in Modern Indonesia." Doctoral dissertation, U. of Leiden, 1971.

Clark, Marilyn W. Overseas Chinese Education in Indonesia. Minority Group Schooling in an Asian Context. Washington, DC: U.S. Office of Education, 1965.

Earnest, Keith I. "Dutch Educational Policy in the Netherlands Indies, 1818-1940." Master's thesis, U. of Illinois, Urbana, 1969.

Elley, Warwick B. "National Assessment of the Quality of Indonesian Education." Studies in Educational Evaluation 2(Winter, 1975): 151-166.

Fidler, Richard Calvin. "Kanowit: An Overseas Chinese Community in Borneo." Doctoral dissertation, U. of Pennsylvania, 1973. Univ. Microfilms Order No. SEA 73-24143.

Fischer, Joseph. "The Student Population of a Southeast Asian University: An Indonesia Example." International Journal of Comparative Sociology 2(1961):224-233.

Fletcher, B. A. "Education as a Factor in Colonial Development, with Special Reference to Java." Master's thesis, U. of Bristol, 1934.

Halim, Amran. "Multilingualism in Relation to the Development of Bahasa Indonesia." Regional English Language Centre Journal 2 (D, 1971):4-19.

Hanbury-Tenison, Robin. A Pattern of Peoples: A Journey Among the Tribes of Indonesia's Outer Islands. New York: Scribner, 1975.

Hoay, Kwee Tek. The Origins of the Modern Chinese Movement in Indonesia. Ithaca, NY: Modern Indonesia Project, Cornell U., 1969.

Jacob, T. Some Problems Pertaining to the Racial History of the Indonesian Region. Utrecht: Drukkerij Neerlandia, 1967.

Jaspan, M. A. Social Stratification and Social Mobility in Indonesia. Djakarta, Indonesia: Sunung Agung, 1959.

Jolliffe, Jill. East Timor: Nationalism and Colonialism. St. Lucia, Q.: U. of Queensland Press, 1978.

Jones, Gavin W. "Religion and Education in Indonesia." Indonesia 22(0, 1976):19-56.

Kahn, Joel S. "Ideology and Social Structure in Indonesia." Comparative Studies in Society and History 20(Ja, 1978):103-122.

Krausse, Gerald Hans. "The Kampungs of Jakarta, Indonesia: A Study of Spatial Patterns in Urban Poverty." Doctoral dissertation, U. of Pittsburgh, 1975.

Kroeskamp, H. Early Schoolmasters in a Developing Country. A History of Experiments in School Education in 19th Century Indonesia. Assen, The Netherlands: Van Gorcum, 1974.

Le bar, Frank M. (ed.). Ethnic Groups of Insular Southeast Asia. Vol. I: Indonesia. New Haven, CT: Human Relations Area Files, 1972.

Lee, Kam Hing. "Schooling in Indonesia: Trends in Development and Issues of Controversy, 1945-1965." Doctoral dissertation, Monash U., 1974.

Liem, Tjong Tiat. "Ethnicity and Modernization in Indonesian Education: A Comparative Study of Pre-Independence and Post-Independence Periods." Doctoral dissertation, U. of Wisconsin, 1968.

Mackie, J. A. C. (ed.). The Chinese in Indonesia: Five Essays. Honolulu: U. Press of Hawaii, 1976.

Mauldin, Lloyd Wesley. "The Colonial Influences on Indonesian Education." Doctoral dissertation, George Peabody College, 1961.

Nasution, Sorimuda. "The Development of a Public School System in Indonesia: 1892-1920." Doctoral dissertation, U. of Wisconsin, 1967.

Nawawi, Mohd A. "Punitive Colonialism: The Dutch and the Indonesian National Integration." Journal of South Eastern Asian Studies, S, 1971.

Noesjirwan, Jennifer. "Permanency of Literacy in Indonesia." American Educational Research Journal 11(Winter, 1974):93-99.

Palmier, Leslie H. "Occupational Distribution of Parents of Pupils in Certain Indonesian Institutions." Indonesie 1(1957).

Pearse, R. "The Role of Selection Based on Academic Criteria in the Recruitment Process at an Indonesian Government University." Higher Education 7(My, 1978):157-176.

Penders, Chr. L. M. (ed.). Indonesia: Selected Documents on Colonialism and Nationalism, 1830-1942. St. Lucia: U. of Queensland Press, 1977.

Poerwanto, Hari. "The Problem of Chinese Assimilation and Integration in Indonesia." Philippines Sociological Review 24(1976):51-55.

Rakindo, Adil. "Chinese Scapegoat Politics in Suharto's 'New Order.'" In Ten Years' Military Terror in Indonesia, pp. 135-138. Nottingham: Spokesman Books, 1975.

Schrieke, B. Indonesian Sociological Studies (Part I). The Hague: W. van Hoeve, 1955.

Sharp, Nonie. The Rule of the Sword: The Story of West Irian, 1977. Kibble Books, Box 210, P.O. Malmsbury, 3446, Victoria, Australia.

Skinner, G. William. "Change and Persistence in Chinese Culture Overseas: a Comparison of Thailand and Java." Journal of the South Seas Society (1960):86-100.

Somers, Mary F. "Peranakan Chinese Politics in Indonesia." Doctoral dissertation, Cornell U., 1965.

Suryadinata, Leo. "Ethnicity and National Integration in Indonesia: An Analysis." Asia Quarterly 3(1976):209-234.

_____. "Indonesian Policies Toward the Chinese Minority Under the New Order." Asian Survey 16(Ag, 1976):770-787.

_____. "Three Major Streams in Peranakan Chinese Politics in Java (1971-1942)." Master's thesis, Monash U., 1970.

Sutherland, Heather Amanda. "Pangreh Pradja: Java's Indigenous Administrative Corps and Its Role in the Last Decades of Dutch Colonial Rule." Doctoral dissertation, Yale U., 1973. Univ. Microfilms Order 73-29487.

Taylor, Jean (tr.). "'Educate the Javanese!' A 1903 Memorial by Raden Ajeng Kartini." Indonesia 17(Ap, 1974): 83-98.

Thomas, R. Murray. "Who Shall Be Educated? The Indonesian Case." in The Social Sciences and the Comparative Study of Educational Systems, pp. 277-346. Edited by Joseph Fischer. Scranton, PA: International Textbook, 1970. [1940-1966]

Timmer, Maarten. "Child Mortality and Population Pressure in the D.I. Jogjakarta, Java, Indonesia. A Social-Medical Study." Doctoral dissertation, The Free U. of Amsterdam, 1961.

Van der Veur, Paul W. Education and Social Change in Colonial Indonesia. Tr. by Lian The. Athens, OH: Center for International Studies, Ohio U., 1969.

_____. "Race and Color in Colonial Society: Biographical Sketches by a Eurasian Woman Concerning Pre-World War II Indonesia." Indonesia, 0, 1969.

Wardhana, Goenawan Ardi. "The Effects of Politics on Educational Development in Indonesia: From the Colonial Period to the Present (1511-1971)." Doctoral dissertation, U. of California, Berkeley, 1973.

Weldon, Peter D. "Indonesian and Chinese Status and Language Difference in Urban Java." J.S.E. Asian Stud. 5(Mr, 1974):37-54.

Wertheim, William F. Indonesian Society in Transition. 2nd rev. ed. Westport, CT: Hyperion Press, 1979.

_____. "Islam in Indonesia--A House Divided." In Ten Years' Military Terror in Indonesia, pp. 75-94. Edited by Malcolm Caldwell. Nottingham: Spokesman Books, 1975.

White, Benjamin. "The Economic Importance of Children in a Javanese Village." In Population and Social Organization. Edited by Moni Nag. Chicago, IL: Aldine, 1975.

Williams, Lea E. Overseas Chinese Nationalism: The Genesis of the Pan-Chinese Movement in Indonesia, 1900-1916. Glencoe, IL: Free Press, 1960.

Willmott, William E. The National Status of the Chinese in Indonesia, 1900-1958. Ithaca, NY: Modern Indonesia Project, Cornell U., 1961.

Wilson, Greta. "Dutch Educational Policy in Indonesia, 1850-1900." Asian Profile 3 (F, 1975):59-72.

Iran

Barnes, Ezra. "Seminar on Iranian Jewry." Challenge 3(F, 1979):12-13.

Loeb, Laurence D. Outcaste: Jewish Life in Iran. New York: Gordon and Beach, 1978.

Moorehead, Caroline. "'Our School Is a Moving School.'" Times Educational Supplement, Je 14, 1974.

Paydarfar, Ali A. Social Change in a Southern Province of Iran: A Comparative Analysis of Social, Cultural, and Demographic Characteristics of the Tribal, Rural, and Urban Populations of the Fars Ostan. Chapel Hill, NC: U. of North Carolina Press, 1974.

Rezai, S.-Y. "Studien zur Bekämpfung des Analphabetentums im Iran." Doctoral dissertation, U. of Cologne, 1975.

Rosenfeld, Leonard. "Jewish Education in Iran." Jewish Education 31(Winter, 1961): 18-30.

Salzman, Philip C. "National Integration of the Tribes in Modern Iran." Mid Eastern Studies, Ja, 1970.

Tomkins, Richard. "Esfahan's Jews--'Such a Dirty People.'" Jerusalem Post, O 19, 1978.

Windfuhr, Gernot L. "European Gypsy in Iran: A First Report." Anthropological Linguistics 12(1970):271-292.

Iraq

Al-Rubaiy, Abdul A. "The Failure of Political Integration in Iraq: The Education of the Kurdish Minority." Intellect 102(Ap, 1974): 440-444.

Attar, Kerim Abdul-Razzak. "The Minorities of Iraq During the Period of the Mandate, 1920-1932." Doctoral dissertation, Columbia U., 1967. Univ. Microfilms Order No. 68-12,928.

Batatu, Hanna. The Old Social Classes and the Revolutionary Movements of Iraq. Princeton, NJ: Princeton U. Press, 1979.

Benoit, Yves. "Dans le cadre de la question des minorités: le problème kurde en Irak." Doctoral dissertation, U. of Toulouse, 1972.

Cohen, Hayyim J. "University Education Among Iraqui-born Jews." Jewish Journal of Sociology, Je, 1969.

Edmonds, Cecil John. "The Kurdish National Struggle in Iraq." Asian Affairs 58(1971).

_____. "Kurdish Nationalism." Journal of Contemporary History 6(1971):87-107.

Feitelson, Dina. "Aspects of the Social Life of Kurdish Jews." Jewish Journal of Sociology 1(1959):201-216.

Head, Simon. "The Kurdish Tragedy." New York Review of Books, Jl 18, 1974.

Ivy, Jean. Une minorité musulmane, Les Kurdes. Geneva: Centre d'Information et de Documentation sur le Moyen-Orient, 1973.

Jamali, M. F. "The New Iraq: Its Problems of Bedouin Education." Doctoral dissertation, Teachers College, Columbia U., 1934.

Kedourie, E. "The Jews of Baghdad in 1910." Middle East Studies 3(1971).

Khadduri, W. "The Jews of Iraq in the Nineteenth Century." Journal of the Social Sciences 5(Ja, 1978):208-218.

Luks, H. P. "Iraqi Jews During World War II." Wiener Library Bulletin 30(1977):30-39.

Lytle, Elizabeth E. (comp.). A Bibliography of the Kurds, Kurdistan, and the Kurdish Question. Monticello, IL: Council of Planning Librarians, 1977.

Murray, Andrew [pseud.] "The Kurdish Struggle." Patterns of Prejudice 9(Jl-Ag, 1975):31-36.

O'Ballance, E. The Kurdish Revolt, 1961-70. London: N.p., 1973.

Rudolph, Wolfgang. "Einige hypothetische Ausführungen zur Kultur der Kurden." Sociologus 9(1959):150-162. [English summary, pp. 161-162.]

Santucci, R. "Irak: Une solution a-t-elle été trouvée au problème kurde?" Afrique et Asie (Paris) 104(1975):3-121.

Sarguis, Francis, and Beit-Ishoo, Benedict. "Assyrians on the Millstone." Nation, My 31, 1975.

Sawdayee, Max. All Waiting To Be Hanged. Iraq Post-Six-Day War Diary. Edited by S. Benjamin. Tel-Aviv: Levanda P., 1974. Jews in Iraq

Short, Martin, and McDermott, Anthony. The Kurds. New rev. ed. London: Minority rights Group, Je, 1975.

Vanly, Ismet Cheriff. "La Question nationale du Kurdistan irakien. Etude de la revolution de 1961." Doctoral dissertation, U. of Lausanne, 1970.

Varlet, Henri, and Massoumian, Jessik. "Education for Tribal Populations in Iran." Prospects 5(1975):275-281.

Ireland

Akenson, Donald. The Irish Education Experiment: The National System of Education in the Nineteenth Century. Toronto: U. of Toronto Press, 1970.

Auchmuty, James Johnston. Irish Education: A Historical Survey. Dublin: Hodges Figgis, 1937.

Ellis, P. Berresford. A History of the Irish Working Class. London: Gollancz, 1972.

Gordon, J. E. "The Disadvantaged Pupil." Irish Journal of Education 2(1968):69-105.

Hallak, Jacques, and McCabe, James. Planning the Location of Schools: Case Studies 1. County Sligo, Ireland. Paris: UNESCO, International Institute for Educational Planning, 1973.

Hennessy, Maurice. "Sad Fate of an Irish Dream." Times Educational Supplement, Ag 16, 1974. [Irish-language schools]

Hutchinson, B. Social Status and Inter-
generational Social Mobility in Dublin.
Dublin: Economic and Social Research
Institute, 1969.

Hyman, Louis. The Jews of Ireland. From
Earliest Times to the Year 1970. London:
Jewish Historical Society of England, 1972.

Kellaghan, Thomas. "Deprivation and Disadvantage: Ireland." In Deprivation and Disadvantage. Nature and Manifestations, pp.
179-186. Edited by A. Harry Passow.
Hamburg, Germany: UNESCO Institute for
Education, 1970.

_____. The Evaluation of An Intervention
Programme for Disadvantaged Children.
Windsor: NFER, 1977. Dublin

_____. "Relationships between Home Environ-
ment and Scholastic Behavior in a Disadvantaged Population." Journal of Educational Psychology 69(D, 1977):754-760.

Macnamara, John. Bilingualism and Primary
Education: A Study of Irish Experience.
Chicago: Aldine, 1966.

Moore, Robert. "Race Relations in the Six
Counties: Colonialism, Industrialization,
and Stratification in Ireland." Race 14
(Jly, 1972):20-42.

Murphy, Michael W. "Measured Steps Toward
Equality for Women in Ireland: Education
and Legislation." Convergence 8(1975):
91-98.

Nevin, M. A Better Chance. A Study of the
Educational Aspirations of Parents.
Dublin: University College, 1970.

_____. "A Study of the Social Background of
Students in the Irish Universities."
Journal of the Statistical and Social
Inquiry Society of Ireland 21(1968):201-
255.

Peck, Bryan T. "Protestant Schools in the
Republic of Ireland." International Review
of Education 13(1967):212-223.

UNESCO. Ethnicity and the Media: An Analysis
of Media Reporting in the United Kingdom,
Canada, and Ireland. Paris: UNESCO, 1978.

Israel

Arabs in Israel

Abassi, Mahmoud. "Encounter Between Arab and
Jewish Culture in Israel." Integrated
Education 11(Jl-O, 1973):3-8.

Abboushi, W. F. "The Road to Rebellion: Arab
Palestine in the 1930's." Journal of
Palestine Studies 6(Spring, 1977).

Abu Ghazaleh, Adnan Mohammad. "Arab Cultural
Nationalism in Palestine, 1919-1948."
Doctoral dissertation, New York U., 1967.
Univ. Microfilms Order No. 68-6037.

Abu Ghazaleh, Adnan. Arab Cultural Nationalism
in Palestine During the British Mandate,
1973. Oxford, PA: Institute for Palestine
Studies, 1973.

Abu-Ghosh, Subhi. "The Politics of an Arab
Village in Israel." Doctoral dissertation,
Princeton U., 1965. Univ. Microfilms Order
No. 66-1331.

Abu Hanna, Anis. "Arabs at the Hebrew University." New Outlook (Jl-Ag, 1958):54-56.

Abu-Lughod, Ibrahim (ed.). The Transformation
of Palestine. Evanston, IL: Northwestern
U., 1971.

Abu Shilbaya, Mohammad. "For a Modern,
Democratic [Palestine] State." New Outlook
20(D, 1977-Ja, 1978):30-44.

Adams, Michael. "Israel's Treatment of Arabs
in the Occupied Territories." Journal of
Palestine Studies 6(Winter, 1977).

Al-Zazzag, Ayad (comp.). Women in the Middle
East and North Africa: An Annotated Bibliography. Austin: Center for Middle Eastern
Studies, U. of Texas, 1977. [Arab women
in Israel]

Amad, Adnan (ed.). Documents and Reports on
Israeli Violations of Human and Civil Rights.
Rights. Beirut: Palestine Research
Center, 1975.

Amad, A. (ed.). The Israeli League for Human
and Civil Rights (The Shahak Papers).
Beirut: Near East Ecumenical Bureau for
Information and Interpretation, 1973.

Amittay, Y. "Be'ayot hinnukh we-tarbut shel
'Araviyyet Yisrael" (Problems of the Arabs
of Israel in Education and Culture).
Ba-Sha'ar, May, 1960, pp. 13-20.

"An Arab Voice: Sabri Jiryis" (interview).
Middle East Newsletter 5(Ja, 1971):1-5.
[Israeli Arab]

Arenstein, Zvi. "A Case for the Beduin."
Jerusalem Post, My 31, 1978.

_____. "Correcting Ms.-conceptions."
Jerusalem Post, Je 30, 1978. [Beduin women]

Aronson, Geoffrey. "Israel's Policy of Military
Occupation." Journal of Palestine Studies
7(Summer, 1978):79-98.

Ashrawi, Hanan Mikhail. "The Contemporary
Palestinian Poetry of Occupation." Journal
of Palestine Studies 7(Spring, 1978):77-101.
[West Bank and Gaza]

Aruri, Naseer H. "Resistance and Repression. Political Prisoners in Israeli Occupied Territories." Journal of Palestine Studies 7(Summer, 1978):48-66.

_____ (ed.). The Palestinian Resistance to Israeli Occupation. Wilmette, IL: Medina Press, 1970.

Asad, Talal. "Anthropological Texts and Ideological Problems: An Analysis of Cohen on Arab Villages in Israel." Economy and Society 4(1975).

Aziz Zu'bi, Abdul. "Discontent of Arab Youth." New Outlook (Ja, 1958):12-17.

Bailey, Yitzhak. "Contrary to Our Ideals." Jerusalem Post, Je 6, 1978. [On the Beduin in Israel]

Barakat, Halim I. "The Palestinian Refugees: An Uprooted Community Seeking Repatriation." International Migration Review 7(Summer, 1973):147-161.

Ben-Dor, Gabriel. "The Politics of Innovation and Integration: A Political Study of the Druze Community in Israel." Doctoral dissertation, Princeton U., 1972. Univ. Microfilms Order No. 72-24,667.

_____. "Intellectuals in Israeli Druze Society." Middle E. Studies 12(My, 1976): 133-158.

Ben-Yona, Amity. "What Does Israel Do to Its Palestinians? A Letter from Israel to Jews of the American Left." Arab American University Graduate Bulletin 2, n.d.

Benor, J. L. "Arab Education in Israel." Middle Eastern Affairs, Ag-S, 1950, pp. 224-229.

_____. "Some Problems of Arab Education." New Outlook, O, 1957, pp. 24-27.

_____. "Ten Years of Arab Education in Israel." Jewish Education 28(Spring, 1958): 35-42.

Be'or, H. "Integrating Arabs in Israeli Life." New Outlook 19(D, 1976):21-22.

"Better Education for Israel's Arabs." Israel Digest 6(O 11, 1963):7.

Biadsi, Mahmud. "The Arab Local Authorities: Achievements and Problems." New Outlook 18 (1975).

Bierman, John. "A Thorn in Israel's Side." Boston Globe, Ap 8, 1979. [Bir Zeit U.]

Black, Ian. "A Palestinian Woman Writes on Nationalism and Feminism." Jerusalem Post, Ja 21, 1979. [Raymonda Tawil]

Booth, Marilyn L. "Dissidence in the Promised Land. An Israeli Professor Fights for Human Rights." Harvard Crimson, S 29, 1977. [Israel Shahak]

Borsten, Joan. "The Case of the Druse." Jerusalem Post, Mr 1, 1979.

Bowden, Tom. "The Politics of the Arab Rebellion in Palestine, 1936-39." Mid. E. Stud. 11(My, 1975):147-174.

Bregman, Arie. The Economy of the Administered Areas, 1974-1975. Jerusalem: The Bank of Israel, 1976.

Buehrig, Edward H. The U.N. and the Palestinian Refugees. Bloomington, IN: Indiana U. Press, 1971.

Chomsky, Noam. "The Arabs in Israel." Monthly Review 27(Ap, 1976):20-30.

_____. "Israel and the Palestinians." Socialist Revolution 5(Je, 1975):45-86, 133-141.

Claiborne, William. "Israeli Military Said to Harass Palestinian School." Washington Post, Je 24, 1978. [Bir Zeit U., West Bank]

Cohen, Amnon. "The West Bank--Gaza Connection." Jerusalem Post, F 17, 1978.

Cohen, Avner. Arab Border Villages in Israel. Manchester, England: Manchester U. Press, 1965.

Cohen, Erik. "Arab Boys and Tourist Girls in a Mixed Jewish-Arab Community." International Journal of Comparative Sociology 12 (1971):217-233.

_____. Integration vs. Separation in the Planning of a Mixed Jewish-Arab City in Israel. Jerusalem: Levi Eshkol Institute of Economic, Social and Political Research, Hebrew U., 1973.

_____. Bibliography of Arabs and Other Minorities in Israel. Givat Heviva, Israel: Center for Arab and Afro-Asian Studies, 1974.

Cohen, Florence Chanock. "Tell Them in Jerusalem." Chicago 27(Je, 1978):166-171. [Hittin, Israel, an Arab village]

Davis, Uri. "Stranger in His Own Land." Journal of Palestine Studies 8(Winter, 1979):133-143. [Arabs in Israel]

Dib, G., and Jaber, F. Israel's Violations of Human Rights in the Occupied Territories, n.d. Institute for Palestine Studies, Box 329A, Rd. No. 1, Oxford, PA 19363.

Drummond, William J. "Israeli Arab Village Grows...and Grows." Los Angeles Times, Je 25, 1976. [Sakhnin, Galilee]

_____. "'Red' Nazareth Puts Tel Aviv on Notice." Los Angeles Times, D 18, 1975.

_____. "Stereotyped Image Shackles Israeli Arab." Los Angeles Times, N 29, 1974.

Eisenstadt, S. N., and Peres, Y. Some Problems of Educating a National Minority: A Study of Israeli Education for Arabs. Jerusalem: Hebrew U., S 30, 1968. ERIC ED 033 967.

El-Asmar, Fouzi. "Israel Revisted." Journal of Palestine Studies 6(Spring, 1977):47-65.

_____. To Be An Arab in Israel. 2nd ed. Washington, DC: Institute for Palestine Studies, 1978.

el-Yacovbi, Hassan H. S. S. "The Evolution of Palestinian Consciousness." Doctoral dissertation, U. of Colorado, 1973. Univ. Microfilms Order No. 74-12,370.

Eliav, Arieh Luva. Land of the Deer. Tel Aviv: Am Oved Publishers, 1972. [Arabs]

Elrazik, Adnan Abed and others. "Problems of Palestinians in Israel." Journal of Palestine Studies 7(Spring, 1978):31-54.

Erskine, Beatrice. Palestine of the Arabs. Westport, CT: Hyperion Press, 1975, reprint of 1935 edition.

Evanari, M. and others. "The Case for the Black Goat" (letter). Jerusalem Post, Je 15, 1978. [On grazing practices of Beduins]

Fahri, D. "The West Bank--1948-1971: The Sociological Basis of Israel Occupation Attitudes." New Middle East 38(N, 1971): 33-36.

Falah, Salman H. "Druze Communal Organization in Israel." New Outlook (Mr-Ap, 1967):40-44.

Farrell, William E. "Israeli Housing for Gaza Refugees Spurs Friction With U.N." New York Times, N 24, 1976.

_____. "Unease is Deepening in Israel Over the Arab Minority." New York Times, N 2, 1976.

"Felicia Langer: With Her Own Eyes." MERIP Reports 57(My, 1977):14-16.

Flapan, Simha. "National Inequality in Israel." New Outlook (N-D, 1964):24-36.

The Fourth Conference of the Academy of Islamic Research. Al Azhar. Academy of Islamic Research. Cairo, Egypt: General Organization for Government Printing Offices, Rajab 1388, S, 1968. Published 1970.

"Freedom in Universities." Journal of Palestine Studies 7(Autumn, 1977):171-174. [Arab students in Haifa U.]

Fried, M. "Israels Besatsungspolitik 1967-1972. Eine Fallstudie über Politik, Wirtschaft und Verwaltung in militärisch besetzten Gebieten." Doctoral dissertation, U. of Tübingen, 1975.

Gavron, Daniel. "Education for the Bedouin." New Outlook, S, 1965. pp. 24-28.

Geffner, Ellen Joyce Kuberslay. "Attitudes of Arab Editorialists in Israel, 1948-67..." Doctoral dissertation, U. of Michigan, 1973. Univ. Microfilms Order No. 73-24,576.

Geraisy, Sami Farah. "Arab Village Youth in Jewish Urban Centers: A Study of Youth from Um el Fahm Working in the Tel Aviv Metropolitan Area." Doctoral dissertation, Brandeis U., 1971. Univ. Microfilms Order No. 1 22,689.

Geries, Sabri, and Lobel, Eli. Die Araber in Israel. München: Verlagskooperative Trikont, 1970.

Gillon, Philip. "The Beduin Come to Town." Jerusalem Post, My 19, 1978.

Giora, Z., Esformes, Y., and Barak, A. "Dreams in Cross-Cultural Research." Comprehensive Psychiatry 13(Mr, 1972):105-114. [Israeli and Arab high school students in Israel]

Goell, Yosef. "Integrating Arab Citizens." Jerusalem Post, Ja 22, 1976.

_____. "Thorny Problem in the Negev." Jerusalem Post, Je 2, 1978. [Beduin]

Goitein, S. D. "The Arab Schools in Israel Revisted." Middle Eastern Affairs, O, 1952, pp. 272-275.

Goldberg, A. "Le Changement Social dans un Village Musulman d'Israël." Doctoral dissertation, Paris V, 3ème Cycle, 1974.

Gorni, Y. "Zionist Socialism and the Arab Question, 1918-1930." Middle Eastern Studies 13(Ja, 1977):50-70.

Granquist, Hilma. Birth and Childhood Among the Arabs: Studies in a Muhamedan Village in Palestine. Helsingfors, Finland: Soderstrom, 1947.

Green, Barbara D. "The Status of the Arab Minority in Israel." Master's thesis, Columbia U., 1966.

Greenough, Richard. "Where the Bible is a Baedeker." Times Educational Supplement, My 21, 1971. [Schooling of Palestine refugee children]

Greenspan, Morris. "Human Rights in The Territories Occupied by Israel." Santa Clara Lawyer 12(1973):377-402.

Greenway, H. D. S. "Arabs Jailed in Israel: A Curious Limbo." Washington Post, Mr 20, 1977.

_____. "Galilee Arabs Issue Embroils Israelis." Washington Post, S 10, 1976.

_____. "Israel as Occupier: 'Excessive Force' or Strict Security?" Washington Post, Mr 20, 1977.

Gruen, George. The Arab Minority in Israel. New York: American Jewish Committee, Mr, 1965.

Halpern, B. "The Arabs of Israel: A Test of Jewishness." Judaism 26(Fall, 1977):413-417.

Harari, Yeghiel (ed.). The Arabs in Israel: Statistics and Facts. Givat Haviva, Israel: Center for Arab and Afro-Asian Studies, 1972.

Harkabi, Yehoshafat. Arab Attitudes to Israel. Jerusalem, Israel: Israel Universities Press, 1971.

_____. "Liberation or Genocide?" Transaction 7(Jl-Ag, 1970):62-67, 83.

Herzfeld, Caryl R. "Arab Knesset Members and Israel's Muslim Community. The Reaction of Arab Knesset Members to Legislation Affecting Israel's Muslim Community in Matters Pertaining to the Institution of Shari's Courts, Waqf, and Matters of Personal Status." Master's thesis, Columbia U., 1966.

Hilal, Jamil. The West Bank: Its Social and Economic Structure, 1948-1974. Beirut: Palestine Liberation Organization, 1976.

Hoffnitz, L. "Dynamite on the Campus: Jewish-Arab Relations in the Israeli Universities." Jewish Frontier 43(Mr, 1976):15-18.

Hofman, John. Identity and Inter-Group Perception in Israel: Jews and Arabs. Occasional Papers on the Middle East, No. 7. Haifa: Jewish-Arab Centre, U. of Haifa, 1976.

Hofman, John E. "Readiness for Social Relations Between Arabs and Jews in Israel." Journal of Conflict Resolution 16(1972).

Jiryis, Sabri. The Arabs in Israel. Tr. Inea Bushnaq. New York: Monthly Review Press, 1976.

_____. The Arabs in Israel, 1948-1966. Tr. Meric Dobson. Beirut, Lebananon: The Institute for Palestine Studies, 1968.

_____. Democratic Freedom in Israel. Beirut: Institute for Palestine Studies, 1972.

_____. "Recent Knesset Legislation and the Arabs in Israel." Journal of Palestine Studies (Autumn, 1971):53-67.

Kadi, Leila S. (ed.). Basic Political Documents of the Armed Palestinian Resistance Movement. Beirut, Lebanon: Research Center, Palestine Liberation Organization, D, 1969.

Kahane, M. "The Arab Problem in Israel: Emigration is the Only Solution." Judaism 26(Fall, 1977):393-404.

Kampf, H. A. "On Palestinian Arab Self-Determination." American Zionist 68(My, 1978):8-12.

Kanaana, Sharif. Socio-Cultural and Psychological Adjustment of the Arab Minority in Israel. San Francisco: R and E Research Associates, 1976. [Al-Karya, Israel]

_____. "Survival Strategies of Arabs in Israel." MERIP Reports 41(0, 1975). [Published by Middle East Research and Information Project, Inc.]

Kapeliouk, A. "L'état social, économique, culturel et juridique des Arabes chrétiens en Israël." Asian Afr. Stud. (1969):51-95.

Kaplan, Robert D. "View from the East." Jerusalem Post, N 22, 1978. [Arab newspapers in East Jerusalem and the West Bank]

Kashti, Yitzak. "Socially Disadvantaged Youth in Residential Education in Israel." Doctoral dissertation, U. of Sussex, 1974.

Kayyali, A. W. "Palestinian Arab Reactions to Zionism and the British Mandate, 1917-1939." Doctoral dissertation, U. of London, 1970.

Khouri, Fred J. "Arabs in Exile." Transaction 7(Jl-Ag, 1970):52-60.

Kipnis, Baruch A., and Schnell, Izhak. "Changes in the Distribution of Arabs in Mixed Jewish-Arab Cities in Israel." Economic Geography 54(Ap, 1978):168-180. [Haifa, Akko, and Tel-Aviv]

Krivine, David. "Work of Charlatans." Jerusalem Post, F 21, 1979. [Critique of U.S. National Lawyers Guild report on treatment of Arabs]

Kugelmass, Sol and others. "Patterns of Intellectual Ability in Jewish and Arab Children in Israel." Journal of Cross-Cultural Psychology 5(Je, 1974):184-198.

Lakin, M., Lomranz, J., and Lieberman, M. A. Arab and Jew in Israel. Washington, DC: NTL-Institute for Applied Behavioral Science, 1969.

Langer, Felicia. "10 Years of Palestinian Children's Resistance." Palestine 3(Je 1, 1977):25-28.

_____. With My Own Eyes: Israel and the Occupied Territories. London: Ithaca Press, 1975.

Layish, Aharon. "Qadis and Sharia in Israel." Asian and African Studies 7(1972):237-272.

_____. Women and Islamic Law in a Non-Muslim State. New York: Halsted Press, 1975.

Lesch, Ann M. "Israeli Deportation of Palestinians from the West Bank and the Gaza Strip, 1967-1978." Journal of Palestine Studies 8(Winter, 1979):101-131.

_____. "Politicization of the Occupied Palestinians." New Outlook 20(D, 1977-Ja, 1978):48-51.

Lieblich, Amia and others. "Developmental Trends in Directionality of Drawing in Jewish and Arab Israeli Children." Journal of Cross-Cultural Psychology 6(D, 1975): 504-511.

Lustick, Ian. "Arabs in the Jewish State: A Study in the Effective Control of a National Minority." Doctoral dissertation, U. of California, Berkeley, 1976.

_____. "Israeli Arabs: Built-in Inequality." New Outlook (Tel Aviv), Jl, 1974.

Mandel, Neville J. The Arabs and Zionism Before World War I. Berkeley: U. of California Press, 1976.

Mansour, Atallah. Waiting for the Dawn. London: Seeker and Warburg, 1965. [An Arab in Israel]

Mansur, G. The Arab Worker under Palestinian Mandate. Jerusalem: 1936.

Mar'i, Sami Khalil. Arab Education in Israel. Syracuse, NY: Syracuse U. Press, 1978.

_____. Creative and Critical Thinking Abilities of Arab Youth in Israel and on the West-Bank. Haifa: Institute for Research and Development, U. of Haifa, 1977.

_____. "The Education of Minorities in Israel." Journal of Christian Education 14 (1971):95-104.

_____. Scholastic Achievement of Arab High School Pupils in Israel. Haifa: Institute for Research and Development of Arab Education, U. of Haifa, 1977.

_____. Scholastic Achievement of Arab Secondary School Students in Israel and on the West Bank. Haifa: Institute for Reasearch and Development of Arab Education, U. of Haifa, 1976.

Mar'i, Sami Khalil, and Benjamin, A. The Attitude of Arab Society Towards Vocational Education. Haifa: Institute for Research and Development of Arab Education, U. of Haifa, 1976.

Migdal, Joel S. "Urbanization and Political Change: The Impact of Foreign Rule." Comparative Studies in Society and History 19(Jl, 1977):328-349. [Palestinian Arabs during the British Mandate]

Miller, Judith. "Israel's Own Arabs: A Crisis of Identity." Progressive 40(Ag, 1976): 35-38.

Mishal, Shaul. West Bank/East Bank. The Palestinians in Jordan, 1949-1967. New Haven, CT: Yale U. Press, 1978.

Morris, Benny. "A Radical Education." Jerusalem Post Magazine, O 27, 1978. [Bir Zeit U.]

_____. "The Conflict in Education." Jerusalem Post Magazine, Ja 26, 1979. [How Israeli schools teach about the Arab-Jewish conflict]

Morris, Benny and others. "Israel's Arabs." Jerusalem Post, F 23-Mr 2, 1979. [Series of seven articles]

Mushkatel, Alvin, and Nakhleh, Khalil. "Eminent Domain: Land-Use Planning and the Powerless in the United States and Israel." Social Problems 26(D, 1978): 147-159.

Nahas, Dunia. The Israeli Communist Party. London: Croom Helm, 1976.

Nakhleh, Khalil Abdullah. "Anthropological and Sociological Studies on the Arabs in Israel: A Critique." Journal of Palestine Studies 6(Summer, 1977):41-70.

_____. Arab Villages in Israel: A Study in Conflict Interaction. The Hague, Netherlands: Mouton, 1974.

_____. "Cultural Determinants of Palestinian Collective Identity: The Case of the Arabs in Israel." New Outlook, O-N, 1975.

_____. "The Direction of Local-Level Conflict in Two Arab Villages in Israel." American Ethnologist 2(1975):497-516.

_____. "The Goals of Education for Arabs in Israel." New Outlook 20(Ap-My, 1977):29-35.

_____. "Israeli Arabists." Journal of Palestine Studies 8(Autumn, 1978):124-126.

_____. "Shifting Patterns of Conflict in Selected Arab Villages in Israel." Doctoral dissertation, Indiana U., 1973. Univ. Microfilms Order No. 73-16,551.

Nashef, Salim. Education on the West Bank. Tul-Karm: College of Agriculture, 1973.

Nasser, Munir K. Along Freedom's Double Edge: The Arab Press Under Israeli Occupation, Ag, 1974. ERIC ED 097685.

Nazzal, Nafez. "The Flight of the Palestinian Arabs from the Galilee, 1948." Doctoral dissertation, Georgetown U., 1976.

_____. The Palestinian Exodus from Galilee 1948. Beirut, Lebanon: Institute for Palestine Studies, 1978.

Nissan, Mordechai. Israel and the Territories: A Study in Control. Ramat Gan: Turtledove Publishing, 1978.

Oppenheimer, Jonathan. "The Druze in Israel, as Arabs and non-Arabs." Cambridge Anthropology 4(1978):23-44.

Orr, David B. "Arab Education." In Impressions of Education in Israel, pp. 41-47. Edited by Judith Reed. Washington, DC: Educational Staff Seminar, Institute for Educational Leadership, George Washington U., F, 1976.

Palestine Book Project. Our Roots Are Still Alive. The Story of the Palestinian People. N.p.: Peoples Press, 1977.

Pelled, Elad. "Israel's Arab Schools: Comments on Abassi Article." Integreducation 12(Jl-Ag, 1974):21.

Peled, Mattityahu. "The Cure for Nazareth." New Outlook 19(Ja, 1976):35-38.

Peres, Yohanan. Aspects of Arab Education in Israel. Jerusalem: Department of Sociology, Hebrew U., 1970.

Peres, Yochanan. "Modernization and Nationalism in the Identity of the Israeli Arab." Middle East Journal (1970):479-492.

Peres, Y., and Davis, N. Yuval. "Some Observations on the National Identity of Israeli Arabs." Human Relations 22(1969):219-233.

Peres, Yochanan, and Levy, Zipporah. "Jews and Arabs: Ethnic Group Stereotypes in Israel." Race, Ap, 1969.

Peres, Yochanan, Ehrlich, Avishai, and Yuval-Davis, Nira. "National Education for Arab Youth in Israel: A Comparative Analysis of Curricula." Jewish Journal of Sociology 12(D, 1970):147-163.

Peretz, Don. "The Arab Minority of Israel." Middle East Journal 8(Spring, 1954):139-154.

_____. Israel and the Palestine Arabs. Washington, DC: N.p., 1958.

_____. "Palestine's Arabs." Trans-action 7 (Jl-Ag, 1970):43-49.

_____. "Palestinian Social Stratification: The Political Implications." Journal of Palestine Studies 7(Autumn, 1977):48-74.

Porath, Yehoshua. The Emergence of the Palestinian-Arab National Movement, 1918-1929. London: Cass, 1974.

Pundik, Herbert. "Israel's Arabs Establish Their Identity." New Middle East, Ag, 1969.

Qahwaji, Habib. The Arabs in the Shadow of Israeli Occupation Since 1948. Beirut: Palestine Liberation Organization Research Center, 1972.

Reich, Yaffa-Nicole. "Arabs on Campus." Israeli Magazine 4(1972):16-24.

Rejwan, N. "Palestinians under Israeli Occupation: The Search for Identity." Midstream 17(F, 1971):43-52.

Robins, Edward Alan. "Pluralism in Israel: Relations Between Arabs and Jews." Doctoral dissertation, Tulane U., 1972. Univ. Microfilms Order No. 73-2211.

Rosenfeld, Henry. "The Arab Village Proletariat." In S. N. Eisenstadt and others, Revadim Be' Israel. Jerusalem: Akadmon, 1968.

_____. "The Class Situation of the Arab National Minority in Israel." Comparative Studies in Society and History 20(Jl, 1978):374-407.

_____. They Were Peasants. Israel: Hakibbutz Hamenchad, 1964.

Rubenstein, Danny. "Double Standard." Journal of Palestine Studies 8(Autumn, 1978):132-134. [Censorship of Arab newspapers in East Jerusalem; translated from Davar]

_____. "Israel Arabs." Moment 1(My-Je, 1976):21-26.

_____. "Reform in Educational Objectives for the Arab Sector." New Outlook 19(F-Mr, 1976).

Samuelson, Arthur H. "There Is Another Way." Judaism 26(Fall, 1977):404-412. [Israeli Arabs]

Saudi, Mona (ed.). In Time of War: Children Testify. Beirut, Lebanon: Mawakif, P.O. Box 1489, 1970. [Palestinian children in refugee camps]

Sayegh, Fayez, A. Discrimination in Education against Arabs in Israel. Beirut:
Palestine Liberation Organiation, 1966.

Schiff, Ze'ev. "Arab Secondary Education in
Israel." New Outlook, My, 1960, pp. 32-34.

Schwarz, Walter. The Arabs in Israel.
London: Faber and Faber, 1959.

_____. "Israel's Arab Minority." Commentary
25(Ja, 1958):23-27.

Segal, J. B. "The Arab Image in Israeli
Fiction." Jewish Quarterly 21(1973):45-54.

Segal, Mark. "The Arab Village Vote."
Jerusalem Post, N 28, 1978. [Interview with
Eli Reches]

_____. "Arabist Says Too Little Attention
Being Paid to Radicalization Here."
Jerusalem Post, F 24, 1978. [Eli Reches
on Arabs in Israel]

_____. "Radical Threat." Jerusalem Post,
Ag 7, 1978. [Interview with Eli Reches
on growing radicalization of Israeli Arabs]

Sereni, Enzo, and Ashery, R. E. (eds.).
Jews and Arabs in Palestine: Studies
in a National and Colonial Problem. Westport, CT: Hyperion Press, 1976, orig.
1936.

Shahak, Israel. "No Change in Zion" (interview). Journal of Palestine Studies 7
(Spring, 1978):3-30.

Shahak, Israel. Le racisme de l'Etat d'
Israel. Paris: Guy Authier, 1975.
[Founder, Israeli League for Human and
Citizens' Rights]

_____. "The Racist Nature of Zionism and
of the Zionist State of Israel." Link 8
(Winter, 1975-1976):10-13.

_____ (ed.). The Non-Jew in the Jewish
State. A Collection of Documents. London:
CAABU, 1977.

Shaicovitch, B. "Dialetical Paternalism:
Marx on the West Bank." New Middle East 55
(1973).

Shamir, S. and others. The Professional Elite
in Samaria: Summary of Findings. Tel
Aviv: The Shiloah Center Surveys, Tel Aviv
U., Mr, 1976. [West Bank]

Shapira, Ariella, and Lomranz, Jacob.
"Cooperative and Cognitive Behavior of
Rural Arab Children in Israel." Journal
of Cross-Cultural Psychology 3 (D, 1972):
353-360.

Shapiro, Allan E. "Jewish Imperatives."
Jerusalem Post, Ja 10, 1979.
[Discrimination against Arabs in welfare
legislation]

_____. "Jewish Quarter Case Revisited."
Jerusalem Post, Ag 9, 1978. [Ethnic
aspects of Arab legal rights]

Sherrow, Fred S. "The Arabs of Palestine as
Seen through Jewish Eyes: A Newspaper
Study, 1925-1929." Master's thesis,
Columbia U., 1965.

Shimoni, Yaacov. Arvei Erets-Yisrael
[Arabs of Palestine]. Tel Aviv: Am Oved,
1947.

Shumueli, Avshalom. "Bedouin Rural Settlement
in Eretz-Israel." In Geography in
Israel, pp. 308-326. Edited by D. H. K.
Amran and Y. Ben-Arieh. Jerusalem:
International Georgraphical Union, 1976.

Shokeid, M. "Israeli Arab Vote in Transition:
Observations on Campaign Strategies in a
Mixed Town." Middle Eastern Studies 14
(Ja. 1978):76-90.

Sider, Norman. "Dissent on Palestine Refugee
Schools." Integrated Education (N-D,
1971):50.

Simon, Rita James. Continuity and Change: A
Study of Two Ethnic Communities in Israel.
New York: Cambridge U. Press, 1978.

Slann, Martin Wayne. "Jewish Ethnicity and the
Integration of an Arab Minority in Israel."
Human Relations 26(1973):359-370.

_____. "The Political Integration of East and
West Jerusalem: Arab and Jewish Community
Cooperation." Doctoral dissertation, U. of
Georgia, 1970. Univ. Microfilms Order No.
71-13,128.

Smith, Colin. The Palestinians. London:
Minority Rights Group, My, 1975.

Smith, Pamela Ann. "Aspects of Class Structure
in Palestinian Society, 1948-1967."
In Israel and the Palestinians. Edited by
Uri Davis and others. London: Ithaca Press,
1975.

Smith, Terence. "Israel's Arabs Are Neither
Pariahs Nor Fully Accepted." New York Times,
N 16, 1975.

Smooha, S., and Hofman, J. "Some Problems of
Arab-Jewish Coexistence in Israel." Middle
East Review 9(1976/1977):5-14.

Smythe, Hugh H., and Urass, James A. "Arabs in
Israel--Literature, Themes and Current Surveys
About Youth, Social Change, and Education."
Journal of Human Relations, Fourth Quarter,
1967.

Soen, D. "Arabs, Social Change and Ethnicity in
Israel." Orient (Opladen) 4(D, 1976):109-122.

Sofer, Arnon, and Bar-Gal, Yoram. "Urban Elements in Non-Jewish Villages in the North of Israel." In Geography in Israel, pp. 275-296. Edited by D. H. K. Amiran and Y. Ben-Arieh. Jerusalem: International Georgraphical Union, 1976.

"Sons of the Village." Journal of Palestine Studies 8(Autumn, 1978):167-171. [Arab local groups in Israel]

Spector, D. "The Arabs of Israel." Jewish Affairs 8(Ja-F, 1978):3-5.

"The Squeeze on Nazareth." Journal of Palestine Studies 8(Autumn, 1978):134-135. Social and community services in Nazareth

Stendel, Ori. The Minorities in Israel. Trends in the Development of the Arab and Druze Communities, 1948-1973, My, 1973. The Israel Economist, P.O. Box 7052, Jerusalem, Israel.

Stock, Ernest. "Jewish State and Arab Citizens." Forum 26(1977):42-51.

"The Struggle for Equality; Israel's Arab Citizens." New Outlook 18(N, 1975) entire issue.

Tessier, Arlette. Gaza. Beirut: N.p., 1971.

Tessler, Mark A. "The Identity of Religious Minorities in Non-Secular States: Jews in Tunisia and Morocco and Arabs in Israel." Comparative Studies in Society and History 20(Jl, 1978):359-373.

_____. "Israel's Arabs and the Palestinian Problem." Middle East Journal 3(Summer, 1977):313-329.

_____. Three Nonassimilating Minorities. Jews in Tunisia and Morocco and Arabs in Israel. New York: Praeger, 1977.

Teveth, Shabtai. The Cursed Blessing: The Story of Israel's Occupation of the West Bank. New York: Random House, 1971.

Tilbawi, Abdullatif L. Arab Education in Mandatory Palestine. London: Luzac and Co., 1956.

Tillman, Seth. "The West Bank Hearings. Israel's Colonization of Occupied Territory." Journal of Palestine Studies 7 (Winter, 1978):71-87.

Toledano, Samuel. "Israel's Arabs: A Unique National Minority." International Problems 12(Je, 1973):39-43.

_____. The Status of Israel's Arabs Following the Yom Kippur War. New York: Institute of Human Relations, American Jewish Committee, Mr, 1974.

Trabulsi, Fawwaz. "The Palestine Problem: Zionism and Imperialism in the Middle East." New Left Review 57(S-O, 1969):53-90.

Tuma, Elias H. "The Arabs in Israel: An Impasse." New Outlook (Tel Aviv), Mr-Ap, 1966.

_____. "The Economic Viability of a Palestine State." Journal of Palestine Studies 7 (Spring, 1978):102-124.

Turki, Fawaz. The Disinherited: Journal of a Palestinian Exile. N.p.: N.p., 1972.

U.S. Congress, 95th, 1st session, House of Representatives, Committee on International Relations, Subcommittee on International Organization. Israeli Settlements in the Occupied Territories: Hearings... Washington, DC: GPO, 1978.

U.S. Congress, 95th, 1st session, Senate, Committee on the Judiciary, Subcommittee on Immigration and Naturalization. The Colonization of the West Bank Territories by Israel: Hearings... Washington, DC: GPO, 1978.

Ursan Kilani, Majed. Zionist Inspiration in Curricula for the Arabs in Israel. Amman: N.p., 1972.

Van Arkadie, Brian. Benefits and Burdens: A Report on the West Bank and Gaza Strip Economies Since 1967. New York: Carnegie Endowment for International Peace, 1977.

_____. "The Impact of the Israeli Occupation on the Economies of the West Bank and Gaza." Journal of Palestine Studies 6(Winter, 1977).

Wasserstein, David. The Druzes and Circassians of Israel. London: Anglo-Israel Association, 1976.

Watzman, Herbert M. "Stakes Are High, Political Activity Is Low on Israel's Campuses." Chronicle of Higher Education, D 4, 1978. [Arabs in Israeli universities]

Weigert, Gideon. Arabs and Israelis: Life Together. Jerusalem: Gideon Weigert, 1973.

Weinstock, Nathan. "The Impact of Zionist Colonization on Palestinian Arab Society before 1948." Journal of Palestine Studies 2(Winter, 1973).

Weitz, J. "A Solution to the Refugee Problem: The State of Israel with a Small Arab Minority." In Documents from Israel: Readings for a Critique of Zionism. Edited by Uri Davis and N. Mezvinsky. London: Ithaca Press, 1975.

Wistrich, Robert S. The Myth of Zionist Racism. London: World Union of Jewish Students, 1976.

Yousuf, Abdulgadir Mohammad. "The British Educational Policy in the Arab Public Schools of Palestine during the Mandate." Doctoral dissertation, Indiana U., 1956. Univ. Microfilms Order No. 17,991.

Zahlan, Antoine B. "Palestine's Arab Population." Journal of Palestine Studies 3(Summer, 1974).

Zahlan, Antoine B., and Zahlan, Rosemarie. "The Palestinian Future: Education and Manpower." Journal of Palestine Studies 6(Summer, 1977):103-112.

Zahri, Shaul, and Achiezra. The Economic Conditions of the Arab Minority in Israel. Givat Haviva: Center for Arab and Afro-Asian Studies, 1966.

Zaid, K. "Israel's Arabs after Twenty-five Years." New Outlook 16(Jl-Ag, 1973): 11-16.

Zayyad, Tawfiq. "The Fate of the Arabs in Israel." Journal of Palestine Studies 6 (Autumn, 1976).

Zelizer, B. "Employment Problems for Educated Arabs." Israel Economist 32(D, 1976): 19-20.

Zenner, W., and Kasdan, L. "The Israeli Druzes: Economics and Identity." Midstream 23 (My, 1977):34-37.

Zionism and Racism: Proceedings of An International Symposium. Tripoli: International Organization for the Elimination of All Forms of Racial Discrimination, 1977.

Zogby, James Joseph. "Arabs in the Promised Land: The Emergence of Nationalist Consciousness Among the Arabs in Israel." Doctoral dissertation, Temple U., 1975.

Zureik, Elia T. "Israeli Youth Perceptions of the Palestinians." Journal of Palestine Studies 4(Winter, 1975).

_____. "Toward a Sociology of the Palestinians." Journal of Palestine Studies 6 (Summer, 1977):3-40.

_____. "Transformation of Class Structure Among the Arabs in Israel: From Peasantry to Proletariat." Journal of Palestine Studies 6(Autumn, 1976).

Oriental Jews in Israel

Ackerman, Walter. "Reforming Israeli Education." In Israel: Social Structure and Change, pp. 397-408. Edited by Michael Curtis and Mordechai Chertoff. New Brunswick, NJ: Dutton, 1973.

Adler, Chaim. "The Israeli School as a Selective Institution." In Integration and Development in Israel, pp. 287-301. Edited by S. N. Eisenstadt and others. New York: Praeger, 1970.

Adler, Chaim, Kahane, Reuven, and Avgar, Amy. The Education of the Disadvantaged in Israel. Comparisons, Analysis and Proposed Research. Jerusalem: National Council of Jewish Women Research Institute for Innovation in Education, Hebrew U., Summer, 1975.

Alport, E. A. "The Integration of Oriental Jews into Israel." World Today, Ap, 1967.

Arieli, Mordecai, and Kshti, Yitzhak. "The Socially Disadvantaged Peer Group in the Israeli Residential Setting." Jewish Journal of Sociology 19(D, 1977).

Arzi, Yehudit, and Amir, Yehuda. "Intellectual and Academic Achievements and Adjustments of Underprivileged Children in Homogenenous and Heterogeneous Classrooms." Child Development 48(Je, 1977):726-729.

Ayash, Edward. "The Unknown Culture of Sephardic Jews." Jewish Currents 26(D, 1972):22-25.

Bar-Moshe, Itzhak. "The Integration of Iraqi Jews." Challenge (Supplement of Bama' aracha) 1(Mr-Ap, 1976):17-18.

Bellos, Susan. "Integrating the Disadvantaged." Jerusalem Post, D 25, 1970.

Ben-Gal, S. Affective Biology for the So-Called Culturally Disadvantaged, A Strategy of Change. Jerusalem: Project Mabat, Israel Scoence Teaching Centre, Hebrew U., 1977.

ben Levy, Shalom. "Israeli Education System Unfair to Oriental Jews." Davka 1(Mr-Ap, 1971):14-16.

Ben-Meir, G. "Oriental Jews in Israel: Problems and Prospects." Jewish Frontier 33(O, 1966):15-20.

Bensimon-Donath, Doris. "L'intégration des juifs nord-africains en Israël. Dispersion et Unité, 1970.

Bi-Annual Report, 1973-1974. Jerusalem: National Council of Jewish Women Center for Research in Education of the Disadvantaged, Hebrew U., 1974.

Bi-Annual Report, 1975-1976. Jerusalem:
National Council of Jewish Women Research
Institute for Innovation in Education of
the Disadvantaged. 1976

Bilski-Cohen, Rachel, with Melnik, Noah. The
Use of Creative Movement for Promoting the
Development of Concept Formation and In-
tellectual Ability in Young Culturally Dis-
advantaged Children. Jerusalem: National
Council of Jewish Women Research Institute
for Innovation in Education, Hebrew U.,
Jl, 1974.

"Black Panthers in Israel." Race Today 7(Je,
1975):129-130.

Blackstone, Tessa. "Education and the Underprivileged in Israel." Jewish Journal of
Sociology 13(1971):173-188.

Brude, Rita Zemach. "Educating Israel's
Majority." Harvard Graduate School of
Education Association Bulletin 20(Spring-
Summer, 1o76):13-15.

Burstein, P. "Social Cleavages and Party
Choice in Israel: A Log-Linear Analysis."
American Political Science Review 72(Mr,
1978):96-109.

Chouraqui, Andre. "Les Juifs d'Afrique de
Nord Entre l'Orient et l'Occident."
Etudes Maghrebines, No. 5. Paris:
Centre d'Etudes des Relations Inter-
nationales, 1965. [Education and other
aspects of immigrant life in Israel]

"Closing the Social and Economic Gap."
Challenge 1(F, 1976):4-8.

Cohen, Claudine. "Grandir au quartier kurde.
Rapports de générations et modèles
culturels d'un groupe d'adolescents
israéliens d'origine kurde." Doctoral
dissertation, U. of Paris I, 1972.

_____. Grandir au quartier Kurde: Rapports
de générations et modèles culturels
d'adolescents israéliens d'origine
kurde. Paris: Institute d'Ethnologie-
Museé de l'Homme, 1975.

Cohen, Erik. "The Black Panthers and Israeli
Society." Jewish Journal of Sociology 14
(Je, 1972):93-110.

Cohen, Hayyim. "Integrating Israel's Underprivileged Immigrants. The Jewish Migration from Africa and Asia." Wiener Library
Bulletin 25(1972):3-12.

_____. Absorption Problems of Jews from
Asia and Africa in Israel. Jerusalem:
World Sephardi Federation Executive of
Israel, 1974. [English translation from
Ha'universita, Journal of the Hebrew U.,
19A (Mr, 1974)]

Cohen, Hayyim J., and Yehuda, Zvi (comps.).
Asian and African Jews in the Middle East,
1860-1971. Jerusalem: Hebrew U. and Ben-
Zvi Institute, 1976.

Cohen, Percy. "Ethnic Group Differences in
Israel." Race, Ja, 1968.

_____. "Ethnic Hostility in Israel." New
Society, F 28, 1963.

_____. "Israel's Ethnic Problem." Jewish
Journal of Sociology, Je, 1967.

Coleman, James S. "Social and Cultural Inte-
gration and Educational Policy." In
Rethinking Urban Education, pp. 124-132.
Edited by Herbert J. Wallberg and Andrew T.
Kopan. San Francisco, CA: Jossey-Bass,
1972.

Davis, Dan, and Kugelmass, Judith. Home
Environment: The Impact of the Home
Instruction Program for Preschool Youngsters
(HIPPY) on the Mother's Role as Educator.
Jerusalem: National Council of Jewish Women
Center for Research on the Disadvantaged,
Hebrew U., My, 1974.

Davis, Uri. "The Oriental Jews." In
Israel: Utopia Incorporated. A Study of
Class, State, and Corporate Kin Control,
pp. 33-44. London: Zed Press, 1977.

Deshen, Shlomo. "Is the Business of Ethnicity
Finished?" In The Election in Israel, 1969,
pp. 278-304. Edited by A. Arian. Jerusalem:
Academic Press, 1972.

Deshen, Shlomo, and Shokeid, Moshe. The Pre-
dicament of Homecoming: Cultural and Social
Life of North African Immigrants in Israel.
Ithaca, NY: Cornell U. Press, 1974.

Donat, D. "Social Integration of North-
African Jews in Israel." Dispersion and
Unity, 1971.

Dutter, L. E. "Eastern and Western Jews:
Ethnic Divisions in Israeli Society."
Middle East Journal 31(Autumn, 1977):
451-468.

Eisenstadt, S. N. "The Changing Institutional
Setting and Social Problems of the Israeli
Educational System." Acta Sociologica 9
(1965).

_____. "The Oriental Jews in Israel." Jewish
Social Studies 12(1950):199-222.

_____ (ed.). The Integration of Immigrants
from Different Countries of Origin.
Jerusalem: Magnes Press, 1969.

Eliachar, Elie. "'Born to Fail': Israel's
Communal Problem." New Outlook (Tel Aviv,
Israel) 17(Mr-Ap, 1974): 68-74, 79.

Eliachar, Elie and others. The Sephardim in Israel, 1971. The Council of the Sephardi Community, 12A Hassolel Street, Jerusalem, Israel.

Eliyahu, E. "Keeping the Oriental Jews Down." Middle East International 87(S, 1978):23-24.

Elkaim, Mony. Panthères noires d'Israel. Paris: François Maspero, 1972.

Elon, Amos. "The Black Panthers of Israel." New York Times Magazine, S 12, 1971.

Eshel, Yohanan, and Klein, Zev. "The Effects of Integration and Open Education on Mathematics Achievement in the Early Grades in Israel." American Educational Research Journal 15(Spring, 1978):319-323.

Etzioni-Halevy, Eva. "Protest Politics in the Israeli Democracy." Political Science Quarterly 90(Fall, 1975):497-520. [Black Panthers]

Feitelson, D., and Krown, S. The Effects of Heterogeneous Grouping and Compensatory Measures on Culturally Disadvantaged Pre-School Children in School. Jerusalem: Paul Baerwald School of Social Work, Hebrew U., 1969.

Frankenstein, Carl. They Think Again... Summary of an Educational Experiment with Disadvantaged Adolescents. Jerusalem: School of Education, Hebrew U., 1972.

Friendly, Alfred. Israel's Oriental Immigrants and Druzes. London: Minority Rights Group, Ag, 1972.

Gardner, Marilyn. "How Jerusalem Faces School Integration." Milwaukee Journal, S 24, 1976.

Geffner, Edward. Sephardi Problems in Israel. Jerusalem: The World Sephardi Federation, 1972.

Ghareeb, E. "Israel's Black Panthers Expose Social Contradictions." Arab Palestinian Resistance 4(Je, 1972):82-90.

Gillboa, Yehoshua A. "Israel's Ethnic Gap." Jewish Spectator 42(Summer, 1977).

Gitelman, Z., and Naveh, D. "Elite Accommodation and Organizational Effectiveness: The Case of Immigrant Absorption in Israel." Journal of Politics 38(N, 1976):963-986.

Glubb, F. "The Israeli Black Panther Movement and the Palestinian People." Palestine Bulletin 3(N 1, 1977):10-13.

_____. "Zionism and the Oriental Jews." Palestine 3(Ja, 1977):74-77.

Goldberg, H. "The Mimouna and the Minority Status of Moroccan Jews." Ethnology 17 (1978):75-88.

Goldberg, Harvey E. Cave Dwellers and Citrus Growers: A Jewish Community in Libya and Israel. New York: Cambridge U. Press, 1972.

Gross, Morris B. "Israeli Disadvantaged." Record 72(S, 1970):105-110.

Heller, Celia S. "Ethnic Differentiation Among the Jews of Israel." In Migration and Development. Edited by Helen I. Safa and Brian M. Du Toit. Chicago: Aldine, 1975.

Hoffmitz, L. "North African Jewry in Israel." Jewish Frontier 43(F, 1976):17-21.

Home Instruction Program for Preschool Youngsters. Jerusalem: National Council of Jewish Women Center for Research in Education of the Disadvantaged, Hebrew U., S, 1973.

Inbar, M. "Immigration and Learning: The Vulnerable Age." Canadian Review of Sociology and Anthropology 14(My, 1977):218-234.

Inbar, Michael, and Adler, Chaim. Ethnic Integration in Israel. A Comparative Case Study of Moroccan Brothers Who Settled in France and Israel. New Brunswick, NJ: Transaction, 1977.

_____ and _____. "The Vulnerable Age: A Serendipitous Finding." Sociology of Education 49(J1, 1976):193-200. [Children of Moroccan immigrants in Israel and France]

Iris, Mark. "Systems in Crisis: American and Israeli Response to Urban Ethnic Protest." Doctoral dissertation, Northwestern U., 1978. Univ. Microfilms Order No. 7903283. [Black Panthers]

Mark, Iris, and Shama, Avraham. "Black Panthers: The Movement." Society 9(My, 1972):37-44.

_____ and _____. Immigration without Integration. Cambridge, MA: Schenkman, 1977. [Sephardi immigrants in Israel]

"Is High School a Luxury?" Challenge 3(Ja-F, 1978):6.

Israel. Ministry of Education and Culture. Projects for the Educationally Disadvantaged from Low-Income Groups and the Population of Disadvantaged Areas--A 10-Year Survey. Jerusalem: The Ministry, My, 1971.

"Israel's Oriental Jews: A Statistical Survey." Journal of Palestine Studies 1(1972):144-155.

"Israeli Black Panthers. Up Against the Wailing World." MERIP Reports 1(O, 1971). [Middle East Research and Information Project]

Josepthal, Giora. "The Integration of Israeli Immigrants: New Methods." Jewish Frontier, Je, 1956.

Kashti, Y. "Socially Disadvantaged Youth in Residential Education in Israel." Doctoral dissertation, U. of Sussex, n.d.

Katzir, Yael. "The Effects of Resettlement on the Status and Role of Yemeni Jewish Women: The Case of Ramat Oranim, Israel." Doctoral dissertation, U. of California, Berkeley, 1976. Univ. Microfilms Order No. 77-4494.

Keller, Cathy Grossman. "The Dark Side of Israel." Tropic (Miami Herald), Ja 1, 1978.

Khazzoom, J. Daniel. "Toward Political Action for Israeli Sephardim." Reconstructionist 39(Ja, 1974):11-14. [By a Jew from Iraq]

Klein, Franke S. "Abkulturationsprobleme der jemenitischen Juden in Israel." Anthropos 62(1967).

Klein, Zev. "Some Issues Involved in Integration in Israel." Council Woman (National Council of Jewish Women) 38(Jul-S, 1976): 8-10.

Klein, Zev, and Eshel, Yohanan. A Study of an Integration and Special Intervention Project in Elementary Schools. Jerusalem: National Council of Jewish Women, Research Institute for Innovation in Education of the Disadvantaged, Hebrew U., 1971.

Klein, Z., and Eshel, Y. A Further Investigation of the Effects of Integration and Special Educational Intervention in the Early Primary Grades. Jerusalem: NCJW Research Institute for Innovation in Education, School of Education, Hebrew U., 1976.

Kleinberger, Aharon. "Problems of Equality." In Society, Schools, and Progress in Irsrael. London: Pergamon, 1969.

Kraft, Joseph. "Letter from Israel." New Yorker 49(Ap 7, 1973):63-89.

Krown, Sylvia. Three's and Four's Go To School. Englewood Cliffs, NJ: Prentice-Hall, 1974. [Oriental Jewish children in Israel]

Kushner, Gilbert. Immigrants from India in Israel: Planned Change in an Administered Community. Tucson: U. of Arizona Press, 1973.

_____. "Planned Change in an Administered Community: Immigrants from India to Israel." Doctoral dissertation, U. of Arizona, 1967.

Levin, Meyer. "The Last of the Falashas?" Midstream 21(Je-Jl, 1975):44-49.

Levin, Nehemia. "The Attitudes of Jewish Administrators of Russian, Polish and Israeli Descent in Institutions of Higher Education in Israel Toward Students of Askkenozic and Sephardic or Oriental Background." Doctoral dissertation, U. of Connecticut, 1977.

Lewis, Arnold Jay. "Sharonia: Education and Social Inequality in an Israeli Town." Doctoral dissertation, Columbia U., 1977. Univ. Microfilms Order No. 7804374.

Lewy, Arieh. "Differences in Achievement: A Comparison over Time of Ethnic Group Achievement in the Israeli Elementary School." Evaluation in Education: International Progress 1(1977).

Lewy, Arieh, and Chen, Michael. "Differences in Achievement: A Comparison over Time of Ethnic Group Achievement in the Israeli Elementary School." Evaluation in Education: International Progress 1(1977): 3-72.

Louvish, Misha. "Poverty and Panthers." Jewish Frontier 38(Je, 1971):5-6.

Lumer, Hyman. "Corral Dark-Skinned Sephardic of Israel, Into Hopeless Hells." Muhammad Speaks, Ag 6, 1971.

Marx, Emanuel. The Social Context of Violent Behaviour: A Social Anthropological Study in an Israeli Immigrant Town. London: Routledge, 1976.

Mittelmann, Alexander. "Educational Problems of Newcomers in Israel, 1948-1958." Doctoral dissertation, U. of Pittsburgh, 1963.

Mooney, Ross L. Israel and the Education of the Culturally Deprived. ERIC ED 011 271.

Nachmias, Chava. "The Issue of Saliency and the Effect of Tracking on Self-Esteem." Urban Education 12(O, 1977):327-344.

Nachmias, D. "Status Inconsistency and Political Opposition: A Case Study of an Israeli Minority Group." Middle East Journal 27(Autumn, 1973):456-470. [Moroccan Jews]

Nadel, Baruch. "The Black Panthers of Israel: Reaping the Fruits of Neglect." Israel Horizons, My, 1971.

"North African Immigrants Call for an End to Discrimination." Israel's Oriental Problem, Je, 1968.

Ogbu, John U. "Oriental Jews in Israel." In Minority Education and Caste, pp. 321-342. New York: Academic Press, 1978.

The Oriental Ethnic Communities in Israeli Society. Jerusalem: Ministry of Education and Culture, 1957.

Ortar, Gina R., and Carmon, H. Components of Mother's Language Contributing to Children's IQ. Jerusalem: School of Education, Hebrew U., 1973.

Ortar, Gina R., and Frankenstein, C. "How to Develop Abstract Thinking in Immigrant Children from Oriental Countries." In Between Past and Future, pp. 291-316. Edited by C. Frankenstein. Jerusalem: Henrietta Szold Foundation, 1953.

Peleg, Rachel, and Adler, Chaim. "Compensatory Education in Israel. Conceptions, Attitudes, and Trends." American Psychologist 32(N, 1977):945-958.

_____ and _____. Evaluation of Experimental and Research Results in Compensatory Education. Jerusalem: National Council of Jewish Women, Research Institute for Innovation in Education of the Disadvantaged, Hebrew U., 1975.

Peres, Yochanan, and Schrift, Ruth. "Intermarriage and Interethnic Relations: A Comparative Study." Ethnic and Racial Studies 1(0, 1978):428-451.

Proceedings of the Second Marcus Converence, January 1975: New Ventures in the Care of Disadvantaged Youth. Jerusalem: National Council of Jewish Women, Research Institute for Innovation in Education of the Disadvantaged, Hebrew U., 1975.

Rapaport, Chanan and others. "Early Child Care in Israel." Early Child Development and Care 4(1976).

"Reform in Education." Israel's Oriental Problem, N, 1968. [Ability-grouping in Israeli schools]

Rejwan, N. "The Two Israels: A Study in Europe-ocentrism." Judaism 16(Winter, (1967):97-108.

Ribon, Nathan. "Israel's Educational Gap." Challenge (Supplement of Bama' aracha) 1 Mr-Ap, 1976):21-23.

Roumani, Maurice M. "The Integration of Oriental Jews." In On Ethnic and Religious Diversity in Israel. Edited by Solomon Poll and Ernest Krauz. Romat Gan: Institute for the Study of Ethnic and Religious Groups, Bar Ilan U., 1975.

Rubenstein, Aryeh. "Israel's Integration Problem." Midstream, Mr, 1963.

Sabar, N., and Kaplan, E. H. Developing a Seventh Grade Biology Curriculum for Heterogeneous Classes Containing Disadvantaged Students in Israel. Tel Aviv: Tel Aviv U., 1975.

Sachs, Shimon. Aus Nomandenkindern werden Schuler. Erzielungeprobleme orientalischer Ein wandererkinder in Israel. Bern, Switzerland: Verlag Hans Huber, 1967.

Sadan, E. and others. "Education and Economic Performance of Occidental and Oriental Family Farm Operators." World Development 4 (My, 1976).

Samuel, E. "Integration in Israel." Jewish Spectator 30(N, 1965):12-14.

Schanche, Don A. "Egyptian-Born Jews in Israel Ignoring Sadat's Call to Return." Los Angeles Times, Jl 31, 1977.

Selzer, Michael. The Outcasts of Israel: Communal Tensions in the Jewish State. Jerusalem: The Council of the Sephardi Community, 1965.

Sephardi, A. "Israel's Oriental Jews." Jewish Currents, My, 1968.

The Sephardim in Israel. Problems and Achievements, 1972. Council of the Sephardi Community, Jerusalem, P.O.B. 10, Israel.

Shama, Avraham. Immigration without Integration: Third World Jews in Israel. Cambridge, MA: Schenckman, 1976.

Shapiro, Raphael. "Zionism and Its Oriental Subjects. Part 1: The Oriental Jews in Zionism's Dialectical Contradictions." Khamsin 5(1978).

Shmueli, Eliezer. "Problems in Educating Oriental Jewish Children in Israel." Integrateducation 15(My-Je, 1977).

Shokheid, Moshe. The Dual Heritage. Immigrants from the Atlas Mountains in an Israeli Village. Manchester, England: Manchester U. Press, 1971.

Shuval, Judith T. "Self-Rejection Among North African Immigrants to Israel." Israel Annals of Psychiatry and Related Disciplines 4(1966):101-110.

Simon, Aryeh (ed.). Ba'ayot Hinukh Bevotai-Sefer Leyaldai Olim (Educational Problems of the Immigrant Children). Volume 2 of Mikraot Pedagogiyot. Edited by Haim Ormian. Tel-Aviv: Otsr Hamoreh, 1961.

Simon, Rita James, and Gurevitch, Michael. "Some Intergenerational Comparisons in Two Ethnic Communities in Israel." Human Organization 30(Spring, 1971):79-88.

Smilansky, Moshe. Education of the Disadvantaged in Israel, 1974. Mediax, Inc.,
N. Charles Street, Westport, CT 06880.

Smooha, Sammy. "Black Panthers: The Ethnic
Dilemma." Society 9(My, 1972):30-36.

_____. "Ethnic Stratification and Allegiance
in Israel: Where Do Oriental Jews Belong?"
Il Politico 41(1976):635-651.

Smooha, S., and Peres, Y. "The Dynamics of
Ethnic Inequalities: The Case of Israel."
Social Dynamics 1(1975):63-80.

Soen, Dan. "Les groupes ethniques orientaux
en Israël. Leur place dans la stratification sociale." Revue francaise de
Sociologie 12(1971):218-227.

Sohlberg, S. C. Psychologische en sociale
aspecten van intelligentie en schoolaan-
passing bij oriëntaalse immigranten-
kinderen in Israël. Assen, the Netherlands: Van Gorcum, 1970.

Strizower, S. "The 'Bene Israel' in Israel."
Middle Eastern Studies 2(1971):123-143.

Strouse, Evelyn. "Where Integration Works."
Jerusalem Post Magazine, N 24, 1978.
[Rehavia, Jerusalem, project]

Syrkin, M. "Oriental Jews in Israel." Jewish
Frontier, Ap, 1952.

Tajfel, H., Jahoda, G., Nemeth, C., Run, Y.,
and Johnson, N. "The Devaluation by
Children of their Own National and Ethnic
Group: Two Case Studies." British Journal
of Social and Clinical Psychology 11(1972):
235-243.

Teller, Judd L. (ed.). Acculturation and
Integration. New York: American
Histadrut Cultural Exchange Institute,
1965.

Wall, H. Daniel. "Dissenter in the Desert."
Jerusalem Post, Ag 11, 1978. [Michael
Kaplan, architect in Dimona]

Weingrod, Alex. "Recent Trends in Israeli
Ethnicity." Ethnic and Racial Studies 2
(Ja, 1978):55-65.

Weiss, Sol. "Educating the Disadvantaged,
Israeli Style." Urban Education 7(J1,
1972):181-197.

Wexler, Philip. "Children of the Immigrants:
A Study of Education, Ethnicity and Change
in Israel." Doctoral dissertation, Princeton U., 1972.

Yosef, R. Bar, and Padan, D. "Oriental Ethnic
Groups in the Crystallization of the Classes
in Israel." Molad, N, 1964. [In Hebrew]

Zeneer, Walter Paul. "Syrian Jewish Identifica-
tion in Israel." Doctoral dissertation,
Columbia U., 1965. Univ. Microfilms Order
No. 66-8536.

Zuriel, Y. "School Integration." Jewish
Frontier 39(J1-Ag, 1972):20-21.

General

Acculturation and Integration. New York:
American Histadrut Cultural Exchange
Institute, n.d.

Adler, Chaim. "Education and Integration of
Immigrants in Israel." International Migration Review 3 (Summer, 1969):3-19.

_____. "Social Stratification and Education
in Israel." Comparative Education Review 18
(F, 1974):10-23.

Al-Qazzaz, Ayad "Army and Society in Israel."
Pacific Sociological Review (Ap, 1973):
143-165.

Amir, Yehuda and others. "Attitude Change in
Desegregated Israeli High Schools."
Journal of Educational Psychology 70(Ap,
1978):129-136.

Arian, Asher. "Consensus and Community in
Israel." Jewish Journal of Sociology 12
(Je, 1970).

Avi-Yonah, Michael. The Jews of Palestine.
New York: Schocken, 1975.

Bachi, Roberto. The Population of Israel.
Jerusalem: Institute of Contemporary
Jewry, Hebrew U., 1977.

Bar-Gal, Y. "Changes in the Structure of
Minority Villages in Israel--Outline and
Reasons." Sociologica Ruralis 15(1975):
173-188.

Barham, Randolph L. Israel: A Modern Education. Washington, DC: GPO, 1967.

Bar-Yosef, Rivka Weiss. "Desocialization and
Resocialization: The Adjustment Process of
Immigrants." International Migration
Review, Summer, 1968.

Ben Yehuda, Shaleak. Black Hebrew Israelites
from America to the Promised Land. N.p.:
Vantage Press, 1975.

Bender, Jay. "World Jewish Student Conference."
Jewish Currents 25(D, 1971):22-26. [Sept.
2-7, 1971, Zieglerville, PA]

Ben-Israel, Asiel. "The Original Hebrew Israelite Nation" (interview). Black World 24 (My, 1975):62-85.

Benor, J. L. "Christian Education in Israel." Christian News from Israel, Je, 1958, pp. 39-43.

Ben-Or, T. Integration in the Hebrew School System in the State of Israel (in Hebrew). Jerusalem: Ministry of Education and Culture, 1973.

Bensimon, Doris, and Errera, Eglal. Israel et ses populations. Brussels: Complexe (PUF), 1977.

Bentwich, J. S. Education in Israel. London: Routledge, 1965.

Ben Yoseph, Jacob. "A Study of Secondary School Education in Israel, 1948-1966." Doctoral dissertation, New York U., 1967.

Berkson, Isaac B. "A Centralized System of Jewish Education in Palestine." Jewish Education 2(Ja, 1930):29-41.

_____. "The Hebrew School System in Palestine and Decentralization." Jewish Education 6 (O-D, 1934):151-161.

Bloom, Sophie. "Israeli Reading Methods for Their Culturally Disadvantaged." Elementary School Journal, Mr, 1966.

Borsten, Joan and others. "The Roots of a Cult." Jerusalem Post, Ja 19, 1979-Ja 25, 1979. [Series of five articles on the Black Hebrews]

Breus, Fyodor. "Nazism, Zionism, Maoism: National Policy." Daily World, S 18, 1978. [Reprinted from Navosti]

Broder, Jonathan. "Chicago Blacks Seek Election in Israel." Chicago Tribune, Ja 9, 1977. [Black Israelites]

Burg, Blanka. "Mental Abilities of Israeli Children from Different Socio-Cultural Groups." Doctoral dissertation, Yeshiva U., 1972.

Burstein, Moshe. Self-Government of the Jews in Palestine since 1900. Tel-Aviv: N.p., 1934.

Cameron, Sue. "Israel's Other Battlefront." Times Educational Supplement, O 26, 1973.

Carpenter, James W. "The Jewish Educational System in Palestine During the Time of Jesus." Doctoral dissertation, American U., 1958.

Chen, Michael. "Educational Concomitants of Adolescent Participation in Israeli Youth Organizations." Doctoral dissertation, U. of Pittsburgh, 1967.

Cohen, Carl. "Democracy in Israel." Nation, Jul 20, 1974.

Cohen, Percy S. "Ethnic Hostility in Israel." New Society, F 28, 1963.

Cohen, Yehudi A. A Transnational Study of Formal Education: Its Relationship to the Social System and Its Consequences, Social Structure and Education in Israel and the United States. New Brunswick, NJ: Rutgers U., 1969.

"The Communal Front." Israel's Oriental Problem, N, 1968.

Darwaza, Muhammad Izzat. The History of the Children of Israel from their Books. Cairo, Egypt: Al-Dar al-Qawmiyya lil-Tiba's wa-al-Nashr, 1960. [In Arabic]

Davis, Uri. Israel: Utopia Incorporated. London: Zed Press, 1977.

Dinstein, Yoram, and Shapiro-Libai, Nitza (eds.). Israel Yearbook on Human Rights. Vol. I. Tel-Aviv, Israel: Faculty of Law, Tel-Aviv U., 1972.

Dore, R. P. "Educational Normative Standards in Israel: A Comparative Analysis." International Review of Education 4(1958):389-408.

Drummond, William J. "Ethiopian Jews Given Recognition." Los Angeles Times, Ap 30, 1975.

_____. "Israel School Integration, Busing Evoke No U.S.-Type Protests." Los Angeles Times, Ap 11, 1976.

Dushkin, A. M., and Frankenstein, C. (eds.). Studies in Education. Jerusalem: Hebrew U., 1964 or 1965.

Eaton, Joseph W. "Reaching the Hard-to-Reach in Israel." Social Work, Ja, 1970.

Eaton, Joseph W., with Chen, Michael. Influencing the Youth Culture: A Study of Youth Organizations in Israel. Beverly Hills, CA: Sage, 1970.

Eisenstadt, S. N. The Absorption of Immigrants: A Comparative Study Based Mainly on the Jewish Community of Palestine and the State of Israel. Glencoe, IL: Free Press, 1955.

Eisenstadt, S. N., Bar-Yosef, Rivka, and Adler, Chaim. Integration and Development in Israel. New York: Praeger, 1970.

Eisenstadt, S. N., Bar-Yosef, R., and Adler, C. Integration and Development in Israel. Jerusalem: Jerusalem U. Press, 1970.

Eisenstadt, S. N. and others (eds.). Stratification in Israel. Jerusalem: Academon, 1968.

Emanuel, Muriel (ed.). Israel: A Survey and Bibliography. New York: St. Martin's Press, 1972.

Etzioni-Halevy, Eva, with Shapira, Rina. Political Culture in Israel: Cleavage and Integration Among Israeli Jews. New York: Praeger, 1977.

Falah, Salman A. "Druze Children Go to School." New Outlook, F, 1966, pp. 36-39.

Feitelson, Dina and others. "Social Interactions in Heterogeneous Preschools in Israel." Child Development 43(D, 1972): 1249-1259.

Feuerstein, Reuven, Krasilowsky, David, and Rand, Yaacov. "Innovative Educational Strategies for the Integration of High-Risk Adolescents in Israel." Phi Delta Kappan 55 (Ap, 1974):556-558.

Flapan, Simha. "National Inequality in Israel." New Outlook, N-D, 1964, pp. 24-36.

Frankenstein, Carl (ed.). Teaching as a Social Challenge. Jerusalem: School of Education, Hebrew U., 1977.

Friedmann, Georges. The End of the Jewish People? Tr. Eric Mosbacher. Garden City, NY. Doubleday, 1968.

Fuss, Alisa. "Arbeit mit nicht-angepassten, gemeinschaftschwierigen Kindern in Israel." Praxis der Kinderpsychologie und Kinderpsychiatrie 20(Ag, 1971):306-315.

Gerber, Israel J. The Heritage Seekers, 1978. Jonathan David Publishers, 68-22 Eliot Ave., Middle Village, NY 11379. [Black Jews in Israel, the "Original Hebrew Israelite Nation"]

Ghilan, Maxim and others. "Israel a Racist State?" Jewish Currents 29(F, 1975):14-23.

Glasman, Naftaly S. Governance and Politics of Education in Israel: Culture Bound or Free?, 1970. ERIC ED 043 125.

Globerson, Arye. Higher Education and Employment in Israel. Lexington, MA: Lexington Books, 1978.

Goldman, Judy. "Problems of Ethnic Integration in Israel." Millennium 1(Ag, 1971):54-66.

Gray, Francine du Plessix. "Jerusalem Journal." New Yorker, Je 14, 1976.

Great Britain. Colonial Office. The System of Education of the Jewish Community in Palestine. Colonial No. 201. London: HMSO, 1946.

Handelman, D., and Deshen, S. (comps.). The Social Anthropology of Israel: A Bibliographical Essay with Primary Reference to Loci of Social Stress. Tel Aviv: Institute for Social Research, Tel Aviv U., 1975.

Hanegbi, Haim, Machover, Moshe, and Orr, Akiva. "The Class Nature of Israeli Society." New Left Review 65(Ja-F, 1971):3-26.

Hattis, Susan Lee. "The Bi-national Idea in Palestine During Mandatory Times." Doctoral dissertation, U. of Geneva, 1970.

_____. The Bi-National Idea in Palestine during Mandatory Times. Haifa, Israel: Shikmona Publishing Co., 1970.

The Hebrew University. "Schools and Social Integration in Israel." Integrated Education 9(My-Je, 1971):27-31.

Herman, Simon N. American Students in Israel. Ithaca, NY: Cornell U. Press, 1971.

Herman, S. N. and others. The Identity and Cultural Values of High School Pupils in Israel. Jerusalem: Hebrew U., 1967, 246 pp. ERIC ED 017 003.

Herman, S. N. Israelis and Jews. New York: Random House, 1970.

Hofman, J. E. "The Ethnic Identity of Jewish Youth in Israel." Megamoth 16(1970):5-14.

Hofman, John E. "Identity and Intergroup Perception in Israel." International Journal of Intercultural Relations 1(F, 1977):79-102. [Review of research]

Hofman, John E., and Zak, Itai. "Interpersonal Contact and Attitude Change in a Cross-Cultural Situation." Journal of Social Psychology, Ag, 1969.

Hofman, John E., and Debbiny, Sami. "Religious Affiliation and Ethnic Identity." Psychological Reports 26(Je, 1970):1014.

Hofstein, Avi and others. "Some Correlates of the Choice of Educational Streams in Israeli High Schools." Journal of Research in Science Teaching 14(My, 1977):241-247.

Ichilov, Orit. "Alternatives to Nonschooling: Youth Outside School in Israel." Adolescence 13(Spring, 1978):45-54.

Inbar, Dan E. "Perceived Authority and Responsibility of Elementary School Principals in Israel." Journal of Educational Administration 15(My, 1977):80-91.

Isaac, J. "Israel--A New Melting Pot?" In W. D. Borrie and others, The Cultural Integration of Immigrants, pp. 234-266. Paris: UNESC, 1959.

Jarus, A., Marcus, J., Oren, J., and Rapaport, C. (eds.). Children and Families in Israel: Some Mental Health Perspectives. Jerusalem: Szold Foundation, 1970.

Jonas, Serge. "Les classes sociales en Israël." Cahiers internationaux de sociologie 38(1965):221-230.

Kaniel, Soshana. The Social Background of Students and Their Prospect of Success at School. Israel National Commission for UNESCO, My, 1971. ERIC ED 060 274.

Kaplan, Eugene H. "A Model Biology Curriculum for Heterogeneous Seventh Grade Biology Classes Containing Culturally Deprived Students" (2 parts). Science Education 59 (J1-S, 1975):313-320, 321-332.

Katznelson, K. The Ashkenazic Revolution. Tel Aviv, Israel: Anach, 1964. [In Hebrew]

Kaufman, T. "Be Fruitful and Multiply: Population Growth in Israel." Israel Economist 33(O-N, 1977):28-29.

Klaff, Vivian Z. "Ethnic Patterns of Residence as an Indicator of Social Integration in Israel: A Macrosocietal Approach." Population Index 41(J1, 1973).

_____. "Ethnic Segregation in Urban Israel." Demography 10(My, 1973).

_____. "The Impact of Ethnic Internal Migration Patterns on Population Distribution in Israel: Observed and Projected." International Migration Review 11(Fall, 1977):300-325.

_____. "Residence and Integration in Israel: A Mosaic of Segregated Peoples." Ethnicity 4(Je, 1977):103-121.

Kleinberger, Aharon F. Society, Schools and Progress in Israel. Oxford, England: Pergamon Press, 1969.

Kramer, Ralph M. Community Development in Israel and the Netherlands. A Comparative Analysis. Berkeley, CA: U. of California, Institute of International Studies, 1970, 164 pp. Available from Publications Office, Institute of International Studies, U. of California, Berkeley, CA 94720.

Kugelmass, Sol, Lieblich, Amia, and Ehrlich, Chedvah. "Perceptual Exploration in Israeli Jewish and Bedouin Children." Journal of Cross-Cultural Psychology 3(D, 1972):345-352.

Kushner, Gilbert. Immigrants from India in Israel. Planned Change in an Administered Community. Tucson, AZ: U. of Arizona Press, 1972.

Lador, M. "Integration and Education." Near East Report, Supplement B, My, 1966, pp. 10-11.

Landau, Jacob M. "Cultural Change and Its Reflection in Politics." In The Arabs in Israel. A Political Study, pp. 39-68. New York: Oxford U. Press, 1969.

Laqueur, Walter. "Zionism, the Marxist Critique, and the Left." Dissent 18(D, 1971):560-574.

Lerner, Natan. "Equality of Rights Under Israeli Law." Patterns of Prejudice 9 (N-D, 1975):1-4.

_____. Las Minorias en Israel. Buenos Aires: Congreso Judío Latin-americano, 1976.

Lewy, Arieh, and Chen, Michael. "Closing or Widening the Achievement Gap: A Comparison over Time of Ethnic Group Achievement in the Israeli Elementary School." In Studies in Educational Administration and Organization 4(1976), published by the Israeli Ministry of Education and Culture. [In Hebrew; summary in English]

Lieblich, Amia and others. "Effects of Ethnic Origins and Parental SES on WPPSI Performance of Pre-School Children in Israel." Journal of Cross-Cultural Psychology 3(Je, 1972):159-168.

Lipset, Seymour Martin. "Education and Equality: Israel and the United States Compared." Society 11(Mr-Ap, 1974):56-66.

Lissak, Moshe. Social Mobility in Israel Society. Tr. Batya Stein. Jerusalem: Israel Universities Press, 1969.

Lombard, Avima. "Early Schooling in Israel." In Norma D. Feshbach, John I. Goodlad, and Avima Lombard, Early Schooling in England and Israel, pp. 63-102. New York: McGraw-Hill, 1973.

McCullough, William Stewart. The History and Literature of the Palestinian Jews from Cyrus to Herod, 550 B.C. to 4 B.C. Toronto: U. of Toronto Press, 1975.

Marmorstein, Emile. "European Jews in Muslim Palestine." Mid. E. Studies 11(Ja, 1975): 74-87.

Matras, Judah, Rosenfeld, J. M., and Salzburger, Lotte. "On the Predicaments of Jewish Families in Jerusalem." International Journal of Comparative Sociology 10(1969): 234-250.

Michman, Joseph. Cultural Policy in Israel. Paris: UNESCO, 1973.

Minkovich, A., Davis, D., and Bashi, J. An Evaluation Study of Israeli Elementary Schools. Jerusalem: School of Education, Hebrew U., Je, 1977.

Mittelmann, Alexander. "Educational Problems of Newcomers in Israel, 1948-1958." Doctoral dissertation, U. of Pittsburgh, 1963.

Morris, Benny. "Poor Marks for Minorities Education." Jerusalem Post, My 16, 1978.

Moskin, J. Robert. "Israeli Youth: The Coming Explosion." Look 35(Je 15, 1971):21-26.

Nadel, Elizabeth and others. "English in Israel: A Sociolinguistic Study." Anthropological Linguistics 19(Ja, 1977): 26-53.

Nardi, Noach. Education in Palestine, 1920-1945. Washington, DC: Zionist Organization of America, 1945.

Ormian, Haim (ed.). Education in Israel. Jerusalem: Ministry of Education and Culture, 1973.

Ortar, Gina R. "Educational Achievement of Primary School Graduates in Israel as Related to their Socio-cultural Background." Comparative Education 4(1967): 23-34.

Patai, Raphael. Israel Between East and West: A Study in Human Relations. 2nd ed. Westport, CT: Greenwood, 1970.

Peres, Yochanan. Ethnic Identity and Ethnic Relations in Israel. Washington, DC: H.E.W., 1967.

_____. "Ethnic Identity and Inter-Ethnic Relations." Doctoral dissertation, Hebrew U., 1968.

_____. "Ethnic Relations in Israel." American Journal of Sociology 76(My, 1971): 1021-1047.

_____. "Ethnic Relations in Israel." In People and Politics in the Middle East. Edited by Michael Curtis. New Brunswick, NJ: Rutgers U. Press, 1971.

Peretz, Don. "Israel 1973: Reform or Rebellion?" New Politics 10(Spring, 1973): 28-36.

Perlberg, Arye, and Rom, Yael. "A Compensatory Program on the Higher Education Level--An Israeli Case Study." Educational Forum, Mr, 1969.

Poll, Solomon, and Krausz, Ernest (eds.). On Ethnic and Religious Diversity in Israel. Ramat Gan: Bar-Ilan U., 1975.

Preale, Ilane and others. "Perceptual Articulation and Task Effectiveness in Several Israel Subcultures." Journal of Personality and Social Psychology 15(Jl, 1970):190-195.

Rauch, Max. "Higher Education in Israel." Doctoral dissertation, U. of Southern California, 1971.

Remba, O. "The Ethnography of Rich and Poor in Israel." New Middle East 49(O, 1972): 36-39.

Rim, Y., and Aloni, R. "Stereotypes According to Ethnic Origin, Social Class and Sex." Acta Psychologica (Amsterdam) 31(1969): 312-325.

Rinott, Moshe. "The Educational Activities of the Hilfsverein der deutschen Juden in Palestine, 1901-1918." Doctoral dissertation, Hebrew U., 1969.

Rodinson, Maxine. Israel: A Colonial-Settler State? New York: Monad Press, 1973.

Rosenzweig, Rafael, and Tomarin, Georges. "Israel's Power Elite." Trans-action 7(Jl-Ag, 1970):26-33, 38-42.

Rubin, Morton. The Walls of Acre: Intergroup Relations and Urban Development in Israel. New York: Holt, Rinehart & Winston, 1974.

Schmelz, U. O., and Bachi, R. "Hebrew as Everyday Language of the Jews in Israel--Statistical Appraisal." In Salo Wittmayer Baron: Jubilee Volume, On the Occasion of His Eightieth Birthday, I. New York: Columbia U. Press, 1975.

Schnall, David J. Radical Dissent in Contemporary Israeli Politics. New York: Praeger, 1979.

Segre, V. D. Israel: A Society in Transition. New York: Oxford U. Press, 1971.

Selzer, Michael. "Nation Building and State Building: The Israeli Example." Phylon 32 (Spring, 1971):4-22.

_____. The Organization of the Jewish State. New York: Black Star, 1968.

Semyonov, Moshe. "Community, Ethnicity and Achievement: Toward Understanding Contextual Effects." Doctoral dissertation, State U. of New York at Stony Brook, 1978. Univ. Microfilms Order No. 7824690.

Shahak, Israel. Civil Rights in Israel Today. London: N.p., 1972.

Shapira, Rina, and Etzioni-Halevy, Eva. Who Is the Israeli Student? Tel Aviv: N.p., 1973.

Sharan, Shlomo, and Calfee, Robert. "The Relation of Auditory, Visual, and Auditory-Visual Matching to Reading Performance of Israeli Children." Journal of Genetic Psychology 130(Je, 1977):181-189.

Sharan, Shlomo, and Weller, Leonard. "Classification Patterns of Underprileged Children in Israel." Child Development 42(Je, 1971): 581-594.

Shumsky, Abraham. The Clash of Cultures in Israel; a Problem for Education. New York: Teachers College, Columbia U., 1955.

Shuval, J. T. "Emerging Patterns of Ethnic Strain in Israel." Social Forces 40(1962).

Skea, Susan, Draguns, Jruis G., and Phillips, Leslie. "Ethnic Characteristics of Psychiatric Sympotomatology Within and Across Regional Groupings: A Study of an Israeli Child Guidance Clinic Population." Israel Annals of Psychiatry and Related Disciplines 7(Ap, 1969):31-42.

Smilansky, Moshe. "Fighting Deprivation in the Promised Land." Saturday Review 49(O 15, 1966).

_____. First Definitions Toward Development-Planning Advancement of Disadvantaged Pupils in the Decade 1975-1985, 1974. ERIC ED 094 013.

Smilansky, Moshe, and Smilansky, Sarah. "Deprivation and Disadvantage: Israel. Intellectual Advancement of Culturally Disadvantaged Children: An Israeli Approach for Research and Action." In Deprivation and Disadvantage. Nature and Manifestations, pp. 187-209. Edited by A. Harry Passow. Hamburg, Germany: UNESCO Institute for Education, 1970.

_____ and _____. "Intellectual Advancement of Culturally Disadvantaged Children: An Israeli Approach for Research and Action." International Review of Education 13(1967).

Smilansky, Moshe. The Intellectual Development of Kibbutz-Born Children, 1974. Mediax, Inc., 21 Charles St., Westport, CT 06880.

Smilansky, M. and others. Secondary Boarding School for Gifted Students from Disadvantaged Strata, Technical Report No. 2, the Socio-Economic Background of the Students and Their Success in Secondary School, A Follow-Up Study. Jerusalem, Israel: National Institute for Research in the Behavioral Sciences; Tel-Aviv U. Research and Development Lab. for the Study of the Disadvantaged, Ap, 1971, 193 pp. ERIC ED 054 239.

Smooha, Sammy. Israel: Pluralism and Conflict. London: Routledge & Kegan Paul, 1978.

_____. "Pluralism: A Study of Intergroup Relations in Israel." Doctoral dissertation, U. of California, Los Angeles, 1973.

Smythe, Hugh H., and Weintraub, Sandra. "Intergroup Relations in Israel." In People and Politics in the Middle East. Edited by Michael Curtis. New Brunswick, NJ: Rutgers U. Press, 1971.

Soen, Dan, and Tishler, Izhak. Urban Renewal: Social Surveys, Mr, 1968. Institute for Planning and Development, Israel. [Touches on inter-ethnic relations in two urban neighborhoods in Israel]

Solomon, G. Educational and Psychological Effect of Television on Children: Sesame Street in Israel. Jerusalem: Department of Communications and School of Education, 1973.

Spilerman, Seymour, and Habib, Jack. Development Towns in Israel: The Role of Community in Creating Ethnic Disparities in Labor Force Characteristics, 0, 1974. ERIC ED 101 033.

Standel, Uri. Minorities. Jerusalem: Ministry of Education and Culture, 1970.

Stern, Deborah S. "Mental Health and Socio-Cultural Origins and Change in a Peri-Urban Settlement in Israel." Master's thesis, Brandeis U., 1972.

Talmon, J. L. "The New Anti-Semitism." New Republic, S 18, 1974.

Thompson, Era Bell. "How Israel Solves its Cultural Lag." Ebony, N, 1965.

Tinker, Hugh. "Indians in Israel: The Acceptance Model and Its Limitations." Race 13(J1, 1971):81-84.

Turner, Bryan S. "Avineri's View of Marx's Theory of Colonialism: Israel." Science and Society 40(Winter, 1976-1977):385-409.

U.S. Congress, 91st, 2nd session, House of Representatives, Committee on Education and Labor, Select Subcommittee on Education. Education in Israel. Report... Washington, DC: GPO, 1970.

Walker, David. "Survival the Aim as Campuses Learn to Live With Less." Times Higher Education Supplement, Ja 14, 1977.

Weinberg, Meyer. "Inequality in Israeli Education." Research Review of Equal Education 2 (Winter, 1978):3-36.

Weinrod, Alex. Israel Group Relations in a New Society. New York: Praeger, 1965.

Weinrod, Alex, and Gurevitch, Michael. "Who Are the Israeli Elites?" Jewish Journal of Sociology 19(Je, 1977):67-77.

Weller, Leonard. "Education." In Sociology in Israel, pp. 50-77. Westport, CT: Greenwood Press, 1974.

Yuchtman (Yoar), Ephriam, and Samuel, Yitzhak. "Determinants of Career Plans: Institutional Versus Interpersonal Effects." American Sociological Review 40(Ag, 1975):521-531.

Italy

Acquaviva, S. S., and Santuccio, M. _Social Structure in Italy: Crisis of a System_. London: Martin Robertson, 1976.

Alcock, Antony Evelyn. "The History of the South Tyrol Question." Doctoral dissertation, U. of Geneva, 1970.

Anello, Michael. " The Education of the Poor and Disadvantaged in Italy." in _Education and the Many Faces of the Disadvantaged: Cultural and Historical Perspectives_, pp. 368-376. Edited by William A. Brickman and Stanley Lehrer. New York: Wiley, 1972.

Bernardini, Gene. "The Origins and Development of Racial Anti-Semitism in Fascist Italy." _Journal of Modern History_ 49 (S, 1977):431-453.

Burtig, G. "Employment Problems and the Educational System in Italy." _International Labour Review_ 114(Jl-Ag, 1976.

Borrelli, Mario. _The School and Capitalist Development_, Ap, 1972. The Secretary, Nuffield Teacher Enquiry, U. of York, York YO1 5DD, England.

Caffaz, Ugo. _L'antisemitismo italiano sotto il fascismo_. Firenze: La Nuova Italia, 1975.

Clough, Patricia. "Open Access Has 'Not Helped' Equality of Opportunity." _Times Higher Education Supplement_, S 17, 1976.

Cole, John W., and Wolf, Eric R. _The Hidden Frontier. Ecology and Ethnicity in an Alpine Valley_. New York: Academic Press, 1974.

Di Nola, Alfonso M. _Antisemitismo in Italia, 1962-1972_. Florence, Italy: Vallecchi, 1973.

Felice, Renzo de. _Storia degli ebrei italiani sotto il fascismo_. 2nd ed. Torino, Italy: N.p., 1972.

Fenet, Alain. "La Question du Tyrol du sud. Une Probleme de droit international." Doctoral dissertation, U. of Lille, 1968.

de Francesco, Corrado. "The Growth and Crisis of Italian Higher Education During the 1960s and 1970s." _Higher Education_ 7(My, 1978): 193-212.

Galli, Giorgio. "The Student Movement in Italy." _The Human Context_ 2(D, 1970): 494-505.

Gatterer, Claus. _Im Kampf gegen Rom: Buerger, Minderheiten und Autonomien in Italien_. Vienna: N.p., 1968.

Gerhardi Bon, Silva. _La persecuzione anti-ebraica a Trieste (1938-1945)_. Udine: Del Bianco, 1972.

Grassi, Corrado. "Deculturization and Social Degradation of the Linguistic Minorities in Italy." _Linguistics_ 191(My 24, 1977):45-54.

Gross, Feliks. _Ethnics in a Borderland: An Inquiry Into the Nature of Ethnicity and Reduction of Ethnic Tensions in a One-Time Genocide Area_. Westport, CT: Greenwood Press, 1978. [Trentino-Alto Adige, Italy]

Hallenstein, Dalbert. "Minority Groups Call for More Language Rights." _Times Educational Supplement_, S 10, 1976.

Ingrao, Chiara. "The School Movement in Rome." _New Left Review_, Mr-Ap, 1969.

Johnson, Anthony. "The Special Classes Racket." _Times Educational Supplement_, Ag 13, 1971.

Mark, Peter. "Africans in Venetian Renaissance Painting: The Social Status of Black Men in Late Fifteenth Century Venice." _Renaissance Q_ 4(1975):7-11.

Michaelis, Meir. "The 'Duce' and the Jews: An Assessment of the Literature on Italian Jewry under Fascism 1922-1945." In _Yad Vashem Studies, XI_. Edited by Livia Rothkirchen. Jerusalem: Yad Vashem, 1976.

_____. _Mussolini and the Jews_. New York: Oxford U. Press, 1978.

Moorehead, Caroline. "Italian Notebook." _Times Educational Supplement_, Je 30, 1972.

Morfogo, Ahron. _Hebrew Education_ (in Hebrew). Jerusalem: N.p., 1951. [Jewish education under Mussolini and after]

Pan, Christoph. _Suedtirol als volkisches Problem: Grundriss einer Ethno-Soziologie_. Vienna: N.p., 1971.

Papi, Massimo D. "Studi e problemi sull' antigiudaismo medievale." _Arch. stor. ital._ 135(Nos. 1-2, 1977):141-164.

Peluffo, N. "Culture and Cognitive Problems." _International Journal of Psychology_ 2(1967): 187-198.

Pergola, Sergio Della. _Anatomia dell'ebraismo italiano..._ Roma: Carrucci, 1976.

Perreau, Pietro. _Educazione e cultura degli Israeliti in Italia nel Medioevo_. Corfu: G. Nacamulli, 1885.

Preti, Luigi. "Fascist Imperialism and Racism." In _The Ax Within. Italian Facism in Action_. Edited by Roland Sarti. New York: Watts, 1974.

Sacerdoti, G. "Jewish Rights Under a New Italian Concordat." _Patterns of Prejudice_ 12 (Ja-F, 1978):26-28.

The Schoolboys of Barbiana. Letter to a
Teacher. Tr. Nora Rossi and Tom Cole.
New York: Random House, 1970.

Schwarzenberg, Claudio. "Fascismo e legislo-
zione razziale." R. stor. diritto contemp.
1 (No. 1, 1978):35-49.

Shulvass, Moses A. The Jews in the World of
the Renaissance. Tr. Elvin I. Kose.
Leiden: Brill, 1973.

Stobart, Janet. "Children in the North."
New Society, S 25, 1975.

Toaff, Elio and others. 1870 la breccia del
Ghetto. Rhome: Barulli, 1971. History of
Jews in Italy

Toscano, Mario. Alto Adige-South Tyrol. Ed.
by George A. Carbone. Baltimore, MD:
Johns Hopkins U. Press, 1975.

Tuohy, William. "Their Tongue is Friulian, Not
Italina." Los Angeles Times, S 13, 1976.

Waagenaar, Sam. The Pope's Jews. LaSalle, IL:
Open Court, 1974.

Ivory Coast

Alalade, Felix O. "The Role of French in Sym-
bolizing and Exacerbating Social Differences
in the Ivory Coast." A Current Bibliography
on African Affairs 10(L977-78):163-176.

Charlick, Robert B. "Access to 'Elite' Education in the Ivory Coast--The Importance of
Socioeconomic Origins." Sociology of Education 51(J1, 1978):187-200.

Chazan, N. "The Manipulation of Youth Politics
in Ghana and the Ivory Coast." Geneve-Afr.
15(1976):38-63.

Clignet, Remi. The Fortunate Few. Evanston,
IL: Northwestern U. Press, 1966.

Fuller, Hoyt W. "Our Literary Colonialism--
in Africa and America." Black World 23(D,
1973):49-50, 90. [U. of Abidjan, Ivory
Coast]

Mao, N'Guessan. "La protection de l'enfant en
droit civil iroiren." R. jur. pol. 31
(Ap-Je, 1977):279-286.

Saint-Vil, Jean. "L'immigration scolaire et
ses consequences sur la démographie urbaine
en Afrique Noire: l'exemple de Gagnoa
(Côte d'Ivoire)." Cahiers d'Outre-Mer 28
(1975):376-387.

Scovitch, Joseph. "West African Anomaly:
Jewish Influences in the Evolution of the
Ivory Coast." Ecumene 9(1977):29-34.

Triaud, Jean-Louis. "La question musulmane
en Côté d'Ivoire." R. fr. hist. outre-mer
61, No. 4(1974):542-571.

Japan

Abrams, Arnold. "The Shantytowns of Japan."
Bridge 3(My, 1975):17-20. [Koreans in Japan]

Alber, Heinz Hugo. Die Aufstände der Ainu und
deren geschichtlicher Hintergrund. Vienna,
Austria: Institut für Japanologie, 1975.

Ben-Dasan, Isaiah. The Japanese and the Jews.
New York: Weatherhill, 1972.

Brameld, Theodore. Japan: Culture, Education
and Change in Two Communities. New York:
Holt, Rinehart & Winston, 1968.

Butterfield, Fox. "New Militance Bringing Gains
for Japan's 'Outcasts.'" New York Times,
D 11, 1974. [Burakumin]

Chiba, M. "Relations Between the School District
System and the Feudalistic Village Community
in Nineteenth-Century Japan." Law and Society
Review, F, 1968.

Cornell, John B. "Ainu Assimilation and
Cultural Extinction: Acculturation Policy in
Hokkaido." Ethnology 11(1964):287-304.

Cummings, William K. The Secret of Japanese
Education. The Role of Education in Socio-
economic Achievement: A Comparative Study,
Ag 31, 1977. ERIC ED 147 202.

De Vos, George A. Japan's Outcastes--The Problem
of the Burakumin, Mr, 1971. Minority
Rights Group, 36 Craven Street, London WC 2,
England.

De Vos, George, and Wagatsuma, Hiroshi. Japan's
Invisible Race. Caste in Culture and Personality. Berkeley: U. of California Press,
1966.

Donoghue, John D., with Acitelli-Donoghue, Anna.
Pariah Persistence in Changing Japan: A Case
Study. Washington, DC: U. Press of America,
1977. [Burakumin]

Duke, Benjamin C. "The Pacific War [1941-1945]
in Japanese and American High Schools: A
Comparison of the Textbook Teachings."
Comparative Education, F, 1969.

Forrer, Stephen E. and others. Measuring
Japanese Racial Attitudes, 1975. ERIC ED
120 593 [Toward blacks and Koreans]

_____. "Racial Attitudes of Japanese University
Students." Research in Higher Education 6
(1977):125-137.

Fox, John P. "Japanese Reactions to Nazi
Germany's Racial Legislation." Wiener Library
Bulletin 23(1969):46-50.

Geiser, Peter. "The Contemporary Ainu: A People
in Search of Society." Human Organization 30
(1971):31-38.

Goldberg, Faye J. "The Question of Skin Color and Its Relation to Japan." Psychologia 16 (1973):132-146.

Grisdale, John. "A Stepping Stone to Status." Times Educational Supplement, Ag 2, 1974. [Teaching at a private senior high school in Japan]

Hitchcock, Romyn. The Ainus of Yezo, Japan. Report of the U.S. National Museum for 1890, pp. 429-502.

Iwawaki, Saburo and others. "Color Bias Among Young Japanese Children." Journal of Cross-Cultural Psychology 9(Mr, 1978):61-73.

Japanese National Commission for UNESCO. The Role of Education in the Social and Economic Development of Japan. Tokyo, Japan, 1966.

Jo, Moon Hwan. "The Problems of the Korean Minority in Japan: Goal Conflict and Assimilation." Doctoral dissertation, New York U., 1974. Univ. Microfilms Order No. 74-29,998.

Lee, Changsoo. "Chosoren: An Analysis of the Korean Communist Movement in Japan." Journal of Korean Affairs 3(Jl, 1973):3-32. [The General Association of Korean Residents in Japan]

_____. "The Politics of the Korean Minority in Japan." Doctoral dissertation, U. of Maryland, 1971. Univ. Microfilms Order No. 72-4141.

Marginalization of Peoples. Racial Oppression in Japan, Political Repression in South Korea, Economic Slavery in Brazil. New York: Idoc/North America, 1974.

Masui, Shigeo. "The Problem of the Comprehensive Secondary School in Japan." International Review of Education 17(1971):27-37.

Michio, Nagai. Higher Education in Japan--Its Takeoff and Crash. Tr. J. Dusenburg. Tokyo, Japan: U. of Tokyo Press, 1972.

Minomiya, Shigeaki. "An Inquiry Concerning the Origin, Development, and Present Situation of the Eta in Relation to the History of Social Classes in Japan." Transactions of the Asiatic Society of Japan, New series 10 (1933):47-154.

Mitchell, Richard H. The Korean Minority in Japan, 1910-1963. Berkeley, CA: U. of California, 1968.

Nee, Brett. "Sanya: Japan's Internal Colony." Bulletin of Concerned Asian Scholars 6 (S-O, 1974):12-18. [Tokyo]

Newell, William H. "Some Problems of Integrating Minorities into Japanese Society." Journal of Asian and African Studies, Jl-O, 1967.

Oberdorfer, Don. "It's a Joyful Spring for Tiger of Kyoto." Washington Post, Mr 17, 1974.

Ogbu, John U. "The Buraku Outcastes of Japan." In Minority Education and Caste, pp. 307-320. New York: Academic Press, 1978.

Ohnuki-Tierney, Emiko. The Ainu of the Northwest Coast of Southern Sakhalin. New York: Holt, Rinehart & Winston, 1974.

Pae, S. "[Legal Status of the Korean Residents (Minority) in Japan]." Pophak (Seoul) 13 (S, 1972). [In Korean; summary in English]

Rohlen, Thomas P. "Is Japanese Education Becoming Less Egalitarian? Notes on High School Stratification and Reform." Journal of Japanese Studies 3(Winter, 1977):37-70.

_____. Is Japanese Education Becoming Less Egalitarian? Notes on High School Statification and Reform, 1975. ERIC ED 129 932.

Rubin, Arnold. Black Nanban: Africans in Japan during the Sixteenth Century. Bloomington, IN: African Studies Program, Indiana U., 1974.

Ruyle, Eugene E. "Ghetto and Schools in Kyoto, Japan." Integrated Education 11(Jl-O, 1973):29-34.

_____. "The Political Economy of the Japanese Ghetto." Doctoral dissertation, Columbia U., 1971.

Ryoke, Minoru. "The Nature of the Distribution of Outcaste Communities." Kwansei Gakuin University Annual Studies 14(1965).

Saar, John. "Japan's Outcasts Fight Back." Washington Post, Je 12, 1977. [The Burakumin]

Sala, Gary Clark. "Protest and the Ainu of Hokkaido." Japan Interpreter 10(Summer, 1975):44-65.

Saxonhouse, Gary R. "The Supply of Quality Workers and the Demand for Quality in Jobs in Japan's Early Industrialization." Explorations in Economic History 15(1978):40-68.

Shimahara, Nobuo. Burakumin: A Japanese Minority and Education. The Hague: Martinus Nijhoff, 1971.

Shimahara, Nobuo. "A Study of the Enculturative Roles of Japanese Education." Doctoral dissertation, Boston U., 1967.

Shimizu, Yoshihiro. "Entrance Examinations: A Challenge to Equal Opportunity in Education." Journal of Social and Political Ideas in Japan, D, 1963.

Shinichiro, Takakura. The Ainu of Northern Japan. A Study in Conquest and Acculturation. Philadelphia: American Philosophical Society, Ap, 1960.

Smythe, Hugh H., and Naitoh, Yashimasa. "The Eta Caste in Japan." Phylon 13(1953).

Smythe, H. H., and Tsuzuki, C. "The Eta: Japan's Indigenous Minority." Sociology and Social Research 37(1952-1953):112-114.

Sovik, Arne. "Japanese Prejudices." Patterns of Prejudice 10(N-D, 1976):36-37.

Sternberg, Leo. "The Ainu Problem." Anthropos 26(1929):755-799.

Taira, Koji. "Education and Literacy in Meiji Japan: In Interpretation." Explorations in Economic History 8(Summer, 1971):371-394.

Teichler, Ulrich Christian. "Bildungsexpansion und Statusdistribution: Das Beispiel Japans." Doctoral dissertation, Bremen U., 1975.

Thompson, Lawrence. Some Are Crowned with Thorns. Tokyo: Japan Christian Social League, 1976. [Burakumin]

Thurston, Donald R. Teachers and Politics in Japan. Princeton, NJ: Princeton U. Press, 1974.

Unger, Jonathan. "Foreign Minorities in Japan." Journal of Contemporary Asia 3, n.d.

Wagtsuma, Hiroshi. "The Social Perception of Skin Color in Japan." Daedalus, Spring, 1967.

Watanabe, Hitoshi. The Ainu Ecosystem. Environment and Group Structure. Rev. ed. Seattle: U. of Washington Press, 1972.

Whymont, Robert. "The Untouchables Point the Finger." Manchester Guardian, Je 28, 1975. [Burakumin]

Yamamoto, Akira. "Communication in Culture Spaces: A Study of the Buraku." Doctoral dissertation, Indiana U., 1974. Univ. Microfilms Order No. 74-14,188.

Jordan

Lancaster, Fidelity. "Bedouin by Adoption." New Society, Ja 31, 1974.

Kenya

Abbott, S. P. "The African Education Policy of the Kenya Government, 1909-39." Master's thesis, London School of Economics, 1969.

Abreu, Elsa. "The Challenge in Kenya's Colonial History: The Role of Voluntary Organisations in Education." Kenya His. R. J. 4, No. 2(1976):207-222.

Anderson, John E. The Struggle for the School: The Interaction of Missionary, Colonial Government and Nationalist Enterprises in the Development of Formal Education in Kenya. London: Longmans, 1970.

Atieno-Odhiambo, E. J. "The Political Economy of the Asian Problem in Kenya, 1888-1939." Transafric. J. Hist. 4(1974):135-149.

Bowden, Edgar. "Perceptual Abilities of African and European Children Educated Together." Journal of Social Psychology 79(D, 1969): 149-154.

Court, David. "The Education System as a Response to Inequality in Tanzania and Kenya." Journal of Modern African Studies 14(1976).

Court, David, and Ghai, Dharam (eds.). Education, Society and Development: New Perspectives from Kenya. London: Oxford U. Press, 1975.

Cowen, M. Some Problems of Income Distribution in Kenya. Nairobi: Nairobi U., 1977.

Fields, Gary S. "Higher Education and Income Distribution in a Less Developed Country." Oxford Economic Papers 27(Jl, 1975):244-259.

Foran, W. R. A Cuckoo in Kenya. London: Hutchinson, 1936.

Franklin, Donald B. "Education and Nationalism in Kenya, 1945-1963." Master's thesis, Teachers College, Columbia U., 1966.

Frost, R. A. "Trusteeship Discrimination and Attempts to Promote Inter-racial Cooperation in Kenya, 1945-63." Doctoral dissertation, Oxford U., 1972.

Furedi, Frank. "The Development of Anti-Asian Opinion in Nakuru District, Kenya." African Affairs 73(Jl, 1974):347-358.

Gavin, R. "Correcting Racial Imbalance in Employment in Kenya." International Labor Review, Ja-F, 1967.

Githara, Henry Kamanú. "The Development of African Secondary Education in the Republic of Kenya (1924-1968)." Doctoral dissertation, Catholic U. of America, 1970.

Goldthorpe, E. An African Elite: Makerere College Students, 1922-1960. Nairobi: Oxford U. Press, 1965.

Greaves, L. B. Carey Francis of Kenya. London: Rex Collings, 1969.

Gregory, Robert G. India and East Africa: A History of Race Relations within the British Empire, 1890-1939. New York: Oxford U. Press, 1971.

Hodd, M. "Income Distribution in Kenya (1963-72)." Journal of Developmental Studies 12 (Ap, 1976).

Huxley, Elspeth J. G. Race and Politics in Kenya: A Correspondence between Elspeth Huxley and Margery Perlam. New ed. Westport, CT: Greenwood, 1975.

Kay, Stafford. "African Roles, Responses, and Initiatives in Colonial Education: The Case of Western Kenya." Paedagogica Historica 16 (1976):272-293.

Keller, E. J. "Education Policy, Inequality and the Political Economy of Rural Community Self-Help in Kenya." Journal of African Studies 4(1977):86-106.

Kenya Education Commission Report, Part 1. Nairobi, Kenya: English Press Ltd., 1964.

Kenyatta, J. Facing Mount Kenya: The Tribal Life of the Gikuyu. London: Seeker & Warburg, 1938.

Kinanjui, A. "The Kikuyu Independent Schools, 1920-1955." Bachelor's thesis, Makerere U. College, 1967.

King, K. J. "Kenya's Educated Unemployed." MURA 7(1974):45-63.

Kipkorir, Benjamin Edgar. "The Alliance High School and the Origins of the Kenya African Elite, 1926-62." Doctoral dissertation, U. of Cambridge, 1970.

Kiteme, Kamuti. "The Impact of a European Education upon Africans in Kenya: 1846-1940." Doctoral dissertation, Yeshiva U., 1970. Univ. Microfilms Order No. 71-05687.

Kovar, Michael H. "The Kikuyu Independent Schools Movement: Interaction of Politics and Education in Kenya (1923-1953)." Doctoral dissertation, U. of California at Los Angeles, 1970.

Laughton, W. H. Teaching About Our People. Cambridge: Cambridge U. Press, 1965.

LeVine, Robert A. "Western Schools in Non-Western Societies: Psychosocial Impact and Cultural Response." Teachers College Record 79(My, 1978):749-755. [The Gusii in Kenya]

Leys, Norman. Kenya. London: Hogarth Press, 1924.

McCormack, Richard T. "Asians in Kenya. Conflicts and Politics." Doctoral dissertation, U. of Freiburg, Switzerland, 1971.

Maleche, Matthew Kaluna. "Unemployment of Youth in Kenya: Implications for Primary School Curriculum." Doctoral dissertation, Columbia U., 1976. Univ. Microfilms Order No. 76-27708.

Morris, Peter. "Nairobi Divides." New Society, Mr 7, 1968. [Indians in Kenya]

Mutiso, G. C. M. "Kenya: The Structure of Inter-Ethnic and Inter-Racial Interaction." Joliso. The East African Journal of Literature and Society 1(1973).

Njoroge, Hganga. "An Outline of the Historical Development of Primary Education in Kenya 1844-1970." Doctoral dissertation, Ohio U., 1972. Univ. Microfilms Order No. 72-22063.

Odinga, O. Not Yet Uhuru: An Autobiography. London: Oxford U. Press, 1933.

Olson, J. B. "Secondary Schools and Elites in Kenya: A Comparative Study of Student s in 1961 and 1968." Comparative Education Review 16(F, 1972):44-53.

Rothchild, Donald. Citizenship and National Integration: The Non-African Crisis in Kenya. Denver, CO: Graduate School of International Studies, U. of Denver, 1970.

_____. "Ethnic Inequalities in Kenya." Journal of Modern African Studies 7(1969): 609-711.

_____. Racial Bargaining in Independent Kenya. A Study of Minorities and Decolonization. New York: Oxford U. Press, 1973.

Schilling, Donald Gilmore. "British Policy for African Education in Kenya, 1895-1939." Doctoral dissertation, U. of Wisconsin, 1972. Univ. Microfilms Order No. 72-23334.

_____. "Local Native Councils and the Politics of Education in Kenya, 1925-1939." Int. J. Afric. Hist. Stud. 9(1976):218-247.

Schott, J. R. "The European Community of Kenya." 2 vols. Doctoral dissertation, Harvard U., 1964.

Sheffield, James R. "Policies and Progress in African Education in Kenya, 1949-63." Doctoral dissertation, Columbia U., 1964.

Sifuna, D. N. "European Settlers as a Factor Influencing Government Policy and Practice in African Education in Kenya, 1900-1962." Kenya Hist. R. J. 4(1976):63-83.

Stabler, Ernest. Education Since Uhuru: The Schools of Kenya. Middletown, CT: Wesleyan U. Press, 1969.

Tangri, R. K. "A Political History of the Asians in Kenya." Master's thesis, U. of Edinburgh, 1966.

Truman, Robert Hayward. "The Origins and Development of Racial Pluralism in the Educational System of Kenya from 1895 to 1925." Doctoral dissertation, U. of Illinois, 1973. Univ. Microfilms Order No. 73-17657.

Turton, E. R. "The Introduction and Development of Educational Facilities for the Somali in Kenya." History of Education Quarterly 14 (Fall, 1974).

Urch, George E. F. "The Africanization of the Curriculum in Kenya." Doctoral dissertation, U. of Michigan, 1967. Univ. Microfilms Order No. 68-07746.

_____. "Education and Colonialism in Kenya." History of Education Quarterly, Fall, 1971.

_____. "Language and the Schools in Kenya." School and Society 99(O, 1971):373-377.

van Zwanenberg, R. "The Background to White Racialism in Kenya." Kenya Hist. Rev., 1974, pp. 5-12.

_____. "History and Theory of Urban Poverty in Nairobi: The Problem of Slum Development." Canadian Journal of African Studies 6(1972):379-402.

Ward, Kevin. "Evangelism or Education? Mission Priorities and Educational Policy in the African Inland Mission, 1900-1950." Kenya Hist. R. J. 3, No. 2(1975):243-260.

Korea

Auh, Paul (Chunsuk). "Education as an Instrument of National Assimilation: A Study of the Educational Policy of Japan in Korea." Doctoral dissertation, Columbia U., 1931.

Bang, Hung Kya Harry. "Japan's Colonial Educational Policy in Korea, 1905-1930." Doctoral dissertation, U. of Arizona, 1972. Univ. Microfilms Order No. 72-31,848.

Chen, I-te. "Japanese Colonialism in Korea and Formosa: A Comparison of Its Effects Upon the Development of Nationalism." Doctoral dissertation, U. of Pennsylvania, 1968.

Dong, Wonmo. "Japanese Colonial Policy and Practice in Korea, 1905-1945: A Study in Assimilation." Doctoral dissertation, Georgetown U., 1965.

Kim, Che-won. Die Volksschule in Korea: Die japanische Assimilationerziehung. Antwerp, Belgium: De Sikkel, 1934.

Lee, Sung-hwa. "The Social and Political Factors Affecting Korean Education, 1885-1950." Doctoral dissertation, U. of Pittsburgh, 1958.

Nahm, Andrew C. (ed.). Korea Under Japanese Colonial Rule: Studies of the Policy and Techniques of Japanese Colonialism. Kalamazoo: Center for Korean Studies, Western Michigan U., 1973.

Rim, Han Young. "The Development of Higher Education in Korea during the Japanese Occupation (1919-1945)." Doctoral dissertation, Columbia U., 1952.

Sang-Chul Suh. Growth and Structural Changes in the Korean Economy, 1910-1940: The Korean Economy Under the Japanese Occupation. Cambridge, MA: Harvard U. Press, 1978.

Toby, Ronald. "Education in Korea under the Japanese: Attitudes and Manifestation." Occasional Paps. Korea 1(Ap, 1974):55-64.

Kuwait

Observer. "Oil for Underdevelopment and Discrimination: The Case of Kuwait." Monthly Review 30(N, 1978):12-21.

Laos

Emling, Marjorie Elaine. "The Education System in Laos During the French Protectorate, 1893 to 1945." Master's thesis, Cornell U., 1969.

Halpern, Joel Martin. Government, Politics and Social Structure in Laos: A Study of Tradition and Innovations. New Haven, CT: Yale U., 1964.

_____. "Laos and Her Tribal Problems." Michigan Alumnus Quarterly Review 67 (D 3, 1960):59-67.

Halpern, Joel Martin, and Tursman, Marilyn Clark. "Education and Nation Building in Laos." Comparative Education Review 10 (O, 1966):499-507.

Halpern, Joel M., and Kunstadter, Peter. "The Role of the Chinese in Lao Society." Journal of the Siam Society 49(1961):21-46.

Iwata, Keiji. "Minority Groups in Northern Laos, Especially the Yao." Edited by Joel M. Halpern. Wooster, OH: Bell and Howell, Micro Photo, 1961.

Langer, Paul F. Education in the Communist Zone of Laos. AD-742 387. Springfield, VA: National Technical Information Service, D, 1971.

Phoneke, Khamphao. "The Loation Challenge: A 'Non-Polluting' Education System." Prospects 5(Spring, 1975):87-95.

Lebanon

Dubar, Claude. "Structure confessionnelle et classes sociales au Liban." Revue française de Sociologie 15(1974):301-328.

Hanna, Suhail Ibn-Salim. "Al-Jamiah Al-Amrikiyya." Saturday Review 55(My 27, 1972): 38-47. [The American U., Beirut, Lebanon]

Liberia

Akpan, M. B. "Black Imperialism: Americo-Liberian Rule Over the African People of Liberia." Canadian Journal of African Studies 7(1973):217-236.

Berman, Edward H. "Tuskegee-In-Africa." Journal of Negro Education 41(Spring, 1972): 99-112.

Carlon, S. Jabaru. "Black Civilization and the Problem of Indigenous Education in Africa: The Liberian Experience." Présence african africaine (1975):253-268.

Lave, Jean. "Cognitive Consequences of Traditional Apprenticeship Training in West Africa." Anthropology and Education Quarterly 8(Ag, 1977):177-180.

Livingston, Thomas W. "The Exportation of American Higher Education to West Africa: Liberia College, 1850-1900." Journal of Negro Education 45(Summer, 1976):246-274.

Nelson, Randle W., and Hlophe, Stephen S. "Education and Politics in Liberia and the United States: A Socioeconomic Comparison of Colony and Colonizer." Umoja 1(Spring, 1977):55-71.

Libya

Folayan, Kola. "Italian Colonial Rule in Libya." Tarikh 4(1974):1-10.

Goldberg, Harvey E. Cave Dwellers and Citrus Growers. A Jewish Community in Libya and Israel. London: Cambridge U. Press, 1972.

Segre, Claudio G. Fourth Shore. The Italian Colonization of Libya. Chicago, IL: U. of Chicago Press, 1974.

Luxembourg

Thomas, David. "Immigrants in Belgium and Luxembourg." New Community 1(0, 1971):11-15.

Malagasy

Bardonnet, D. "Minorités asiatiques à Madagascar." Annuaire Francais de Droit International 10(1964).

Delvol, Raymond. "The Indians in Madagascar." Kroniek Afrika 6(1975):250-257.

Esoavelomandroso, Faranirina v. "Langue, culture et colonisation à Madagascar: malagache et français dans l'enseignement officiel (1916-1940)." Omaly Si Anio: R. ét hist. (Jl-D, 1976):105-166.

Filliot, J.-M. La traite des esclaves vers les Mascareignes au XVIIIe siècle. Paris: Orstom, 1974

Mutibwa, P. M. The Malagasy and the Europeans. London: Longman, 1975.

Paillard, Yon P. "Faut-il mettre les jeunes indigenes dans les collèges francais de Madagascar (1913)?" L'information historique, My-Je, 1971.

Poirier, Jean. "Les groupes ethniques de Madagascar." RFEPA 100(1974):31-40.

Malawi

Dotson, Floyd, and Dotson, Lillian O. The Indian Minority of Zambia, Rhodesia and Malawi. New Haven, CT: Yale U. Press, 1968.

Heyeneman, S. P. "The Formal School as a Traditional Institution in an Underdeveloped Society: The Case of Northern Malawi." Paedagogica Historica 12(1972):460-472.

Kayira, Legson. I Will Try. London: Longmans, 1966.

Mpakiti, Attati. "Malawi: The Birth of a Neo-Colonial State." Afric. R. 3(1973):33-68.

Malaysia

Alatas, Hussein Syed. Intellectuals in Developing Societies. London: Cass, 1977.

_____. The Myth of the Lazy Native: A Study of the Image of the Malays, Filipinos and Javanese from the 16th to the 20th Century and Its Function in the Ideology of Colonial Capitalism. London: Cass, 1977.

Ambalavanar, Rajeswary. "Tamil Education in Malaya, 1920-1941." Journal of Tamil Studies 1(1969):89-114.

Amin, Mohamed, and Caldwell, Malcolm (eds.). Malaya: The Making of a Neo-Colony. Nottingham, England: Spokesman Books, 1977.

Anand, S. "Aspects of Poverty in Malaysia." Review of Income and Wealth 23(Mr, 1977).

Andri, F. M. "Poverty and Tax Incidence in West Malaysia." Public Finance Quarterly 5(Jl, 1977).

Arasaratnam, Sinnappah. Indians in Malaysia and Singapore. London: Oxford U. Press, 1970.

Arlès, J. "Ethnic and Socio-economic Patterns in Malaysia." International Labour Review 104(D, 1971).

Bamadhaj, Halinah. "The Impact of the Japanese Occupation of Malaya on Malay Society and Politics (1941-1945)." Master's thesis, U. of Auckland, 1975.

Barr, Pat. "At Rice Roots Level." Times Educational Supplement, Ap 16, 1976.

Bock, John C. "Countervailing Outcomes of Malaysian Education: National Identity and Political Alienation." Education and Urban Society 10(F, 1978):113-144.

_____. Education and Social Integration: A Case Study of Institutional Effect on Malaysia, F 7, 1971. ERIC ED 049 976.

Carey, Iskander. Orang Asli: The Aboriginal Tribes of Peninsular Malaysia. New York: Oxford U. Press, 1976.

Cham, B. N. "Class and Communal Conflict in Malaysia." Journal of Contemporary Asia 5(1975):446-461.

_____. "Colonialism and Communalism in Malaysia." Journal of Contemporary Asia 7 (No. 2, 1977):178-199.

Colletta, N. J. "Malay Education in the Plantation Milieu--Cultural Chauvinism or Social Class Consciousness?" Asian Profile 4(Ag, 1976):333-362.

_____. "Malaysia's Forgotten People: Education, Cultural Identity, and Socio-Economic Mobility among South Indian Plantation Workers." Contributions to Asian Studies 7 (1975):87-182.

Cooke, D. F. "The Mission Schools of Malaya, 1815-1942." Paedogogica Historica 6 (1966):364-399.

Eberhard, W. "The Cultural Baggage of Chinese Emigrants--Studies and Novels Read by Chinese Students in Malaya." Asian Survey 2(My, 1971):445-462.

Elegant, Robert S. "Malays Travel Bumpy Road to Racial Equality." Los Angeles Times, Jl 14, 1974.

Enloe, Cynthia H. Multi-Ethnic Politics: The Case of Malaysia. Berkeley, CA: Center for South and Southeast Asia Studies, U. of California, 1970.

Fook-Seng, Philip Loh. "A Review of the Educational Developments in the Federated Malay States to 1939." J.S.E. Asian Studies 5 (S, 1974):225-238.

Freedman, M. "The Growth of a Plural Society in Malaya." Pacific Affairs 33(1969).

Gungwu, Wang. "Chinese Politics in Malaya." China Quarterly (Jl-S, 1970):1-30.

Hirschman, Charles. "Educational Patterns in Colonial Malaya." Comparative Education Review 16(O, 1972):486-502.

_____. Ethnic Stratification in Peninsular Malaysia. Washington, DC: American Sociological Association, 1975.

Hoerr, O. D. "Education, Income, and Equity in Malaysia." Economic Development and Cultural Change, Ja, 1973.

Hsu, William Chang Nang. "Chinese Education in Malaya: One Dimension of the Problems of Malayan Nationhood." Master's thesis, U. of British Columbia, 1969.

Issalys, Pierre Francois. "Ethnic Pluralism and Public Law in Selected Commonwealth Countries." Doctoral dissertation, U. of London, 1972.

Kessler, C. S. "Islam and Politics in Malay Society: Kelantan, 1886-1969." Doctoral dissertation, London School of Economics, n.d.

Kim, Khoo Kay. "Malay Society, 1974-1920." J. S. E. Asian Studies 5(S, 1974):171-198.

Koon, Yeon Chee. "Education and National Integration in Malaysia." Journal of Political and Social Science, S, 1972.

Lee, Ah C. "Policies and Politics in Chinese Schools in the Straits Settlements and the Federated Malaya States, 1786-1941." Master's thesis, Singapore U., 1958.

Lee, Edwin. The Towkays of Sabah: Chinese Leadership and Indigenous Challenge in the Last Phase of British Rule. Singapore: Singapore U. Press, 1976.

Ling, Lee Sow. "Education and National Unity in a Bi-Cultural Society: Malaya." Master's thesis, U. of London, Institute of Education, 1967.

Loh, Philip. "British Politics and the Education of Malays, 1909-1939." Paedagogica Historica 14(1974):355-384.

Loh, Philip Fook Seng. Seeds of Separation: Educational Policy in Malaya, 1874-1940. New York: Oxford U. Press, 1976.

Mac Dougall, John Arthur. "Shared Burdens: A Study of Communal Discrimination by the Political Parties of Malaysia and Singapore." Doctoral dissertation, Harvard U., 1968. Univ. Microfilms Order No. 68-13449.

Mahajani, Usha Ganesh. The Role of Indian Minorities in Burma and Malaya. Bombay: Vora, 1960.

"Malaya's Linguistic Maze." Race Today 4(Ja, 1972):21-22.

Means, G. P. Malaysian Politics. London: U. of London Press, 1970.

Milne, R. J. "Politics, Ethnicity and Class in Guyana and Malaysia." Social and Economic Studies 26(Mr, 1977):18-37.

Nagata, Judith A. "Perception of Social Inequality in Malaysia." Contrib. Asian
Studies 7(1975):113-136.

_____. "What Is a Malay? Situational Selec-
tion of Ethnic Identity in a Plural
Society." American Ethnologist 1(1974):
331-333.

Nam, Tae Y. Racism, Nationalism, and Nation-
building in Malaysia and Singapore.
Meerut: Sadhna Prakashan, 1973.

Nash, Manning. "Ethnicity, Centrality, and
Education in Pasir Mas, Kelantan." Comparative Education Review 16(F, 1972):
4-15. [Malay Peninsula]

Netto, G. Indians in Malaya: Historical Facts
and Figures. Singapore: N.p., 1962.

Purcell, Victor W. W. S. The Chinese in
Malaya. New York: N.p., 1948.

Rabushka, Alvin. "Affective, Cognitive, and
Behavioral Consistency of Chinese-Malay
Interracial Attitudes." Journal of Social
Psychology 82(O, 1970):35-41.

_____. "Integration in a Multi-Racial In-
stitution: Ethnic Attitudes Among Chinese
and Malay Students at the University of
Malaya." Race, Jl, 1969.

_____. Race and Politics in Urban Malaya.
Stanford, CA: Hoover Institution Press,
1973.

_____. "Racial Stereotypes in Malaya."
Asian Survey, Jl, 1971.

"Race Relations in the Campus." Malaysian
Digest, Jl 15, 1971.

Radcliffe, David J. "Education and Cultural
Change Among the Malays, 1900-1940."
Doctoral dissertation, U. of Wisconsin,
1970.

Ratnam, K. J. Communalism and the Political
Process in Malaya. Singapore: U. of
Singapore Press, 1965.

Roff, W. R. The Origins of Malay Nationalism.
Kuala Lumpur: U. of Malaya Press, 1967.

Rudner, Martin. "Education and the Political
Process in Malaysia and Singapore."
Doctoral dissertation, Hebrew U., 1974.

Salleh, Awang Had b. "Malay Teacher Training
in British Malaya, 1878-1941." Bachelor's
thesis, U. of Malaya, 1967.

Sandhu, Kermal Singh. Indians in Malaya.
Cambridge: Cambridge U. Press, 1969.

Schwarz, Ute. "Interethnische Beziehungen der
Semang, Sendi und Jakun (Malaya)."
Doctoral dissertation, U. of Freiburg in
Breisgan, 1971.

Sevrugian, Emanuel. "Zum Problem einer
asiatischen Minderheit: Die Chinesen in
Malaysia." Saeculum 24(1973):167-190.

Sharma, C. L. Ethnicity, Communal Relations,
and Education in Malaysia, F, 1977.
ERIC ED 139 089.

Snodgrass, D. R. "Trends and Patterns in
Malaysian Income Distribution, 1957-70."
In Readings on Malaysian Economic Develop-
ment. Edited by D. Lim. Kuala Lampur:
N.p., 1975.

Stenson, Michael. "Class and Race in West
Malaysia." Bulletin of Concerned Asian
Scholars 8(Ap-Je, 1976):45-54.

Stevenson, Rex. Cultivators and Administrators:
British Educational Policy Towards the
Malays, 1875-1906. New York: Oxford U.
Press, 1976.

Stroebe, Margaret Susan. "The Development of
Equivalence Judgements in Malaysian
Children." Doctoral dissertation, U. of
Bristol, 1972.

Takei, Yoshimitsu, Bock, John C., and Saunders,
Bruce. "Educational Sponsorship by
Ethnicity: Preliminary Analysis of the West
Malaysian Experience." Ohio University
Papers in International Studies 28(1973):
1-37.

Thillainathan, R. "Inter-Racial Balance in
Malaysian Employment and Wealth: An Evalu-
ation of Distributional Targets." Dev. Ec.
(S, 1976):239-260.

Villiers, C. S. "Education and National Building in a Plural Society: The Malaysian
Case." Master's thesis, Manchester U.,
1972.

von Vorys, Karl. Democracy Without Consensus:
Communalism and Political Stability in
Malaysia. Princeton, NJ: Princeton U.
Press, 1975.

Wiebe, Paul D., and Mariappen, S. "Ethnic
Insularity and National Identification in a
Plural Society: Indian Malaysians--A Case
Study." Economic and Political Weekly 10
(S 13, 1975):1477-1485.

Yew Yeok Kim. "Education and the Acculturation
of the Malaysian Chinese: A Survey of Form
IV Pupils in Chinese and English Schools in
West Malaysia." Philippines Sociological
Review 24(1976):93-126.

Mali

N'Diaye, Amadou. "La condition de l'enfant dans la société contemporaine au Mali." R. jur. pol. 31(Ap-Je, 1977):329-352.

Zolberg, Vera L. "National Goals, Social Mobility, and Personal Aspirations: Students in Mali." R. Can. Ét. Africa 10 (1976):125-142.

Mauritius

Benedict, Burton. "Education Without Opportunity: Education, Economics, and Communalism in Mauritius." Human Relations 11(1958): 315-329.

Bennoune, Mahfoud. "Mauritania: A Neo-colonial Desert." Dialectical Anthropology 3(1978):43-66.

Issalys, Pierre Francois. "Ethnic Pluralism and Public Law in Selected Commonwealth Countries." Doctoral dissertation, U. of London, 1972.

Mexico

Aguirre Beltran, Gonzalo. Cuijla, esbozo etnografico de un pueblo negro. Mexico, D.F.: Fundo de cultura Economica, 1958.

_____. Obra Polémica. Mexico, D.F.: Centro de Invesitgaciones Superiores, Instituto de Antropología e Historia, 1976. [History and critique of Mexico's Indian policy]

_____. La población negra de México, 1519-1810. 2nd ed. Mexico: Fondo de Cultura Económica, 1972.

_____. "Races in 17th Century Mexico." Phylon 6(1945):212-218.

Anderson, Arthur J. O., Berdan, Frances, and Lockhart, James (eds.). Beyond the Codices. The Nahua View of Colonial Mexico. Berkeley, CA: U. of California Press, 1976.

Barkin, David. "Acceso a la educación en México." Revista Mexicana de Sociología 33 (1971):33-50.

_____. "Acceso a y beneficios de la educación superior en México." Revista del Centro de Estudios Educativos 3(1971).

_____. "Education and Class Structure: The Dynamics of Social Control in Mexico." Pol. Soc. 5(1975):185-200.

Bartra, Roger. "El problema indígena y la ideologia indigenista." Revista Mexicana de Sociología 36(1974):459-482.

Basauri, Carlos. La Población Negroide Mexicana. México: Instituto Nacional de Antropología e Historia, 1943.

Beals, Ralph L. "Mexico's Persistent Indians." Current History 66(My, 1974).

Bejar Navarro, R. "Prejuicio y discriminación racial en México." R. Mexic. Sociol. 31 (1969):417-433.

Benitez, Fernando. Los Indios de Mexico. Mexico City: Ediciones Era, 1970.

Borah, Woodrow. "Race and Class in Mexico." Pacific Historial Review 23(1954):331-342.

Bowser, Frederick P. "The Free Person of Color in Mexico City and Lima: Manumission and Opportunity, 1580-1650." In Race and Slavery in the Western Hemisphere: Quantitative Studies, pp. 331-368. Edited by Stanley L. Engerman and Eugene D. Genovese. Princeton, NJ: Princeton U. Press, 1975.

Brack, Gene M. "La opinión mexicana, el racismo norteamericano y la guerra de 1846." Anglia, 1971.

Britton, John A. "Indian Education, Nationalism, and Federalism in Mexico, 1910-1921." The Americas 32(Ja, 1976):445-458.

_____. "Urban Education and Social Change in the Mexican Revolution, 1931-40." Journal of Latin American Studies 5(N, 1973):233-245.

Carroll, Patrick J. "Mandinga: The Evolution of a Mexican Runaway Slave Community, 1735-1827." Comparative Studies in Society and History 19(O, 1977):489-505.

_____. "Mexican Society in Transition: The Blacks in Veracruz, 1750-1830." Doctoral dissertation, U. of Texas, 1975.

Caso, Alfonso. "El Indigenismo Mexicano." Journal of World History 10(1967).

_____. Nietodos y resultados de la política indigenista en México. Mexico City: Instituto Nacional Indigenista, 1954.

Cervantes Hernandez, José. "Social Class and Educational-Occupational Aspirations: An Exploratory Study in Two Regions of Mexico." Doctoral dissertation, Catholic U. of America, 1970. Univ. Microfilms Order No. 71-1460.

Chance, John K. "Race and Class in a Colonial Mexico City: A Social History of Antequera, 1521-1800." Doctoral dissertation, U. of Illinois, 1974.

_____. Race and Class in Colonial Oaxaca. Stanford, CA: Stanford U. Press, 1978.

_____. "The Urban Indian in Colonial Oaxaca." American Ethnologist 3(1976):603-632.

Chance, John K., and Taylor, William B. "Estate and Class in a Colonial City: Oaxaca in 1792." Comparative Studies in Society and History 19(O, 1977):454-487.

Comel, Gabriele. "Das Problem der integration der indianer Sonoras, Mexiko, in den ersten Jahrzehnten des 19. Jahrhunderts." Doctoral dissertation, Cologne U., 1973.

Cook, Sherburne F., and Borah, Woodrow. Essays on Population History. Vol. I: Mexico and the Caribbean. Berkeley, CA: U. of California Press, 1971.

_____ and _____. Essays in Population History. Mexico and the Caribbean. Vol. II. Berkeley, CA: U. of California Press, 1974. [Deals with race mixture in Mexico]

Corwin, Arthur F. "Mexican Emigration History, 1900-1970: Literature and Research." Latin American Research Review 8(Summer, 1973):3-24.

Crumrine, N. Ross. The Maya Indians of Sonora, Mexico: A People Who Refuse to Die. Tucson: U. of Arizona Press, 1977.

Davidson, David M. "Negroes in Colonial Mexico, 1519-1650." Master's thesis, U. of Wisconsin, 1965.

de la Fuente, Julio. Relaciones Interétnicas. Mexico City, Mexico: Instituto Nacional Indígenista, 1965.

Delhumeau, Antonio. "Elites culturales y educación de masas en México." Revista Mexicana de Ciencia Política 19(1973).

Dillman, C. Daniel. "Urban Growth along Mexico's Northern Border and the Mexican National Border Program." Journal of Developing Areas 4(Jl, 1970):487-508.

Dobson-Ingram, John R. A. Formal Schooling and the Aspirations of Stratified Rural Youth, 1973. ERIC ED 121 546.

Drake, Diana Mack. "Bilingual Education Programs for Indian Children in Mexico." Modern Language Journal 62(S-O, 1978):239-248.

Dusenberry, William H. "Discriminatory Aspects of Legislation in Colonial Mexico." Journal of Negro History 33(Jl, 1948):284-302.

Echánove Trujíllo, Carlos. Sociología mexicana. 2nd ed. Mexico: Editorial Poncia, 1963.

Eckstein, Susan. The Poverty of Revolution: The State and the Urban Poor in Mexico. Princeton, NJ: Princeton U. Press, 1977.

Estudios sobre las relaciones interetnica en México. Mexico City: UNESCO, Jl, 1974.

Fish, Warren R. "The Food Plight of the Mexican Poor." In Latin America: Search for Geographic Explanations, pp. 65-74. Conference of Latin Americanist Geographers. Edited by R. J. Tata. Chapel Hill, NC: U. of North Carolina, 1976.

Forbes, Jack D. "Nationalism, Tribalism, and Self-Determination: Yuman-Mexican Relations, 1821-1848." Indian Historian 6(Spring, 1973): 18-22.

Friedlander, Judith. Being Indian in Hueyapan. A Study of Forced Identity in Contemporary Mexico. New York: St. Martin's Press, 1975.

Friedman, Harold, and Friedman, Helen. "Letter from Mexico." Integrateducation 14(Jl/Ag, 1976).

Gamio, Manuel. Consideraciones Sobre El Problema Indígena. Mexico City: Instituto Indigenista Interamericano, 1966.

Garrard, James L. "A Survey of the Education of the Indians of Mexico as a Factor in their Incorporation into Modern Mexican Society." Doctoral dissertation, U. of Washington, 1956.

Gerhard, Peter A. "A Black Conquistador in Mexico." Hispanic American Historical Review 58(Ag, 1978):451-459.

Gibson, C. "The Transformation of the Indian Community in New Spain, 1500-1810." Journal of World History 2(1954-1955):581-607.

Gill, Clark C. Education in a Changing Mexico. Washington, DC: GPO, 1969.

González Casanova, Pablo. Democracy in Mexico. New York: Oxford, 1970.

_____. "L'evolution du système des classes aux Mexique." Cahiers internationaux de sociologie 39(1965):113-136.

Haussman, Fay. "Teaching the Indians." Times Educational Supplement, O 13, 1978.

Heath, Shirley Brice. Telling Tongues: Language Policy in Mexico. Colony to Nation. New York: Teachers College Press, 1972.

Hellbom, Anna-Britta. "Cultural Continuity and Differentiated Acculturation as Revealed in Language: Some Examples of Nahuatl-speaking Mestizos." Folk 10(1968):29-36.

_____. La Participacion cultural de las Mujeres Indias y Mesitzas en el Mexico precortesiano y postrevolucionario. Stockholm: Ethnografiska Museet, 1967.

Høivik, Tord. "Social Inequality: The Case of Mexico." Journal of Peace Research 2, 1971.

Israel, Jonathan I. Race, Class, and Politics in Colonial Mexico, 1610-1670. London: Oxford U. Press, 1975.

Ivie, Stanley D. "Multicultural Education: The Mexican Experience." Educational Forum 42(My, 1978):441-449.

Jacobsen, J. V. Educational Foundations of the Jesuits in Sixteenth Century New Spain. Berkeley, CA: N.p., 1938.

Jäklein, K. J. "Sentences by Mexican Indian Peasants." Journal of Peasant Studies 2 (Ja, 1975):226-228.

"[Jewish] Education in Mexico." World Jewry 9(My-Je, 1966):30.

Kolack, Shirley, and Kolack, Sol. "The Ambiguous Status of Jews in Mexico." Conservative Judaism 31(Fall-Winter, 1976-77):78-85.

Krause, Corinne A. "The Jews in Mexico: A History with Special Emphasis on the Period from 1857 to 1930." Doctoral dissertation, U. of Pittsburgh, 1970. Univ. Microfilms Order No, 71-8418.

Ladd, Doris M. The Mexican Nobility at Independence, 1780-1826. Austin, TX: Institute of Latin American Studies, U. of Texas, 1976.

Lafaye, Jacques. Quetzalcóatl and Guadalupe: The Formation of Mexican National Consciousness 1531-1813. Tr. Benjamin Keen. Chicago: U. of Chicago Press, 1977.

Lesser, Harriet Sara. "A History of the Jewish Community of Mexico City, 1912-1970." Doctoral dissertation, New York U., 1972. Univ. Microfilms Order No. 73-11,731.

Levitz, Jacob. "The Jewish Community in Mexico: Its Life and Education." Doctoral dissertation, Dropsie College, 1954.

_____. "Jewish Education in Mexico." Jewish Education 26(Spring, 1956):35-41.

Liebman, Seymour. The Jews in New Spain: Faith, Flame, and the Inquisition. Coral Gables, FL: U. of Miami Press, 1970.

Lios, Peggy K. Mexico Under Spain, 1521-1556: Society and the Origins of Nationality. Chicago, IL: U. of Chicago Press, 1975.

Maloof, Louis J. "A Sociological Study of Arabic-speaking People in Mexico." Doctoral dissertation, U. of Florida, 1959. Univ. Microfilms Order No. 61-5498.

Martinez, Hector. "Los Promotores Sociales en los Programmas de Integracion." America Indigena, Ap, 1965.

Martínez Jimenez, Alejandro. "La educacíon elemental en el Porfiriato." Historia Mexicana 22(Ap-Je, 1973):514-552.

Martinez Saldaña, Tomás, and Gándara Mendoza, Leticia. Política y sociedad en México: El caso de Los Altos de Jalisco. Mexico: SEP/INAH, 1976.

Meisler, Stanley. "Mexico's Indians on Margin of Society." Los Angeles Times, Ag. 24, 1975.

Mir-Araujo, Adolf. "Ecological Inequalities in Educational Attainment in Mexico." Doctoral dissertation, U. of Texas, 1970. Univ. Microfilms Order No. 70-18,272.

Modiano, Nancy. The Indian Schools of the Chiapas Highlands: Bilinguals and Reading. New York: Holt, Rinehart, and Winston, 1973.

Moone, Janet Ruth. "Tarascan Development: National Integration in Western Mexico." Doctoral dissertation, U. of Arizona, 1969.

Moreno, Dorinda (ed.). La Mujer—en pie de lucha. Mexico City, Mexico: Espina del Norte Publications, 1973.

Muñoz Izquierdo, Carlos, and Lobo, José. "Expansión Escolar, Mercado de Trabajo y Distribución del Ingreso en México." Revista del Centro de Estudios Educativos 4(1974):9-30.

Nash, June, and Rocca, Manuel María. Dos mujeres indígenas. México: Instituto Indigenista Interamericano, 1976.

Orbe, Gonzola R. "Educacíon e Integracion de Grupos Indigenas." American Indigena, Ap, 1965.

Palmer, Colin A. "Negro Slavery in Mexico, 1570-1650." Doctoral dissertation, U. of Wisconsin, 1970.

_____. Slaves of the White God: Blacks in Mexico, 1570-1650. Cambridge, MA: Harvard U. Press, 1976.

Paulín de Siade, Georgina. "Mapos del monolingüismo y el bilingüismo de los indígenes de Oaxaca en 1960." Revista Mexicana de Sociología 36(1974):807-856.

Peña, G. de la. Aspiraciones escolares y nivel socioeconómico. Mexico City: Centro de estudios educativos, 1968.

Perissinotto, Giorgio. "Educational Reform and Government Intervention in Mexico." Current History 66(My, 1974).

Raby, David L. "Los principios de la educacíon rural en México: el caso de Michoacan, 1915-1929." Historia Mexicana 22(Ap-Je, 1973):553-581.

"Reflexiones sobre la desnutrición en México." Comercio Exterios, Banco Nacional de Comercio Exterior, S.A. 28(F, 1978).

Reynolds, Alfred W. "The Alabama Negro Colony in Mexico: 1894-96." Alabama Review 5(0, 1952):243-268; 6(Ja, 1953):31-58.

Roncal, Joaquin. "The Negro Race in Mexico." Hispanic American Historical Review 24(Ag, 1944):530-540.

Schwartz, Rosalie. Across the Rio to Freedom: U.S. Negroes in Mexico. El Paso, TX: Texas Western Press, U. of Texas, 1975.

_____. "Across the Rio to Freedom: U.S. Negroes in Mexico." S.W. Stud. 44(1975): 3-64.

Secretaria de Educacion Publica. La Casa del Estudiante Indígena. México, D.F.: The Secretaría, n.d.

Secretaria de Educacion Pública, Consejo Nacional Técnico de la Educación. La Coordinación y la Ampliación de la Obra Cultural y Educativa en Beneficio de la Poblacion Indígena. Mexico, D.F.: The Secretaría, 1962.

Secretaria de Educacion Pública. La Educacion Pública en México. Vol. I. México, D.F.: The Secretaria, 1966.

Serron, Luis A. Some Thoughts on Mexican Poverty Viewed from the Perspective of the World Population Plan of Action, Ag, 1977. ERIC ED 152 611.

Shugasser, Bernard. "Colegio Israelita De Mexico." Jewish Education 24(Spring, 1953): 55-60.

Silva Herzog, Jesus. "Los problemas de la Universidad Nacional de Mexico." Cuadernos Americanos 33(Ja-F, 1974):60-93.

Tella, Torcuato S. Di. "The Dangerous Classes in Early Nineteenth-Century Mexico." Journal of Latin American Studies 5(My, 1973):79-105.

Thompson, Richard A. The Winds of Tomorrow: Social Change in a Maya Town. Chicago: U. of Chicago Press, 1974. [Ticul, Yucatán]

Tyler, Ronnie C. "Fugitive Slaves in Mexico." Journal of Negro History 57(Ja, 1972):1-12.

UNESCO. Race and Class in Post-Colonial Society: A Study of Ethnic Group Relations in the English-speaking Caribbean, Bolivia, Chile and Mexico. Paris: UNESCO, 1977.

Uribe Villegas, Oscar. "Monolingües indígenas de Mexico: Su distribución territorial y su dispersión sociolingüistica." Revista Mexicana de Sociologia 35(1973):585-600.

Vaughn, Mary K. "Schools for Social Control: Mexican Educational Policy and Programs, 1880-1928." Doctoral dissertation, U. of Wisconsin, 1973.

Vasquez de Knauth, Josefina. "Mexico: Education and National Integration." In Education and Social Structure in the Twentieth Century. Edited by Walter Laqueur and George L. Mosse. New York: Harper & Row, 1967.

_____. Nacionalismo y educación en Mexico. Mexico, D.F.: Colegio de Mexico, 1970.

Warner, Truman Augustine. "The School and Community of Ixmiquilpan: A Case Study in Mexican Education." Doctoral dissertation, Columbia U., 1966. Univ. Microfilms Order No. 67-5552.

Wolf, Monika. "Probleme des Indigenismus und der Minoritätenpolitik in Mexiko." Ethnographisch-Archäologische Zeitschrift 11(1970):275-281.

X., Marvin. "Anthropologist Traces Black Man in Mexico." Muhammad Speaks, O 27, 1972.

Zubryn, Emil. "Ambitious Plans Fail to Reach Poor." Times Educational Supplement, My 27, 1977.

Morocco

Asher, S. Bar (ed.). The Jews of Morocco Under the Sheriffs' Rule. Jerusalem: Zalman Shazar Foundation, Hebrew U., n.d.

Ben-Ami, Issachar. Yahadut Maroke, Perakim beheker tarbutam. Jerusalem: Rubin Mass., 1975. [Moroccan Judaism. Ethnocultural Studies; in Hebrew with French summary]

Bidwell, Robin. Morocco Under Colonial Rule: French Administration of Tribal Areas, 1912-1956. London: Cass, 1973.

Bishtawi, K. "The Jews of Morocco: Testimony to Security." Mid. E. (My, 1978):50-53.

Brownfield, A. "The Jews of Morocco and the Zionist Philosophy of Nationality." Arab World, S-O, 1970.

Corcos, David. Studies in the History of the Jews of Morocco. Jerusalem: Rubin Mass, 1976.

Damis, John. "Early Moroccan Reactions to the French Protectorate: The Cultural Dimension." Humaniora Islamica 1(1973):15-31.

Eickelman, Dale F. "The Art of Memory: Islamic Education and Its Social Reproduction." Comparative Studies in Society and History 20(O, 1978):485-516.

Fenyvesi, Charles. "Clever Merchants and Honest Folk." Jerusalem Post, Ag 18, 1978. [Jews in Morocco]

_____. "Moroccan Interlude." Jerusalem Post, Jl 21, 1978.

Foster, Badi. "The Moroccan Power Structure as Seen from Below: Political Participation in a Casablancan Shantytown." Doctoral dissertation, Princeton U., 1974.

Goldberg, Harvey E. "The Mimuna and the Minority Status of Moroccan Jews." Ethnology 17(Ja, 1978):75-88.

Griffin, K. B. "Income Inequality and Land Redistribution in Morocco." Bangladesh Development Studies 3(Jl, 1975).

Halstead, John P. Rebirth of a Nation: The Origins and Rise of Moroccan Nationalism, 1912-1944. Cambridge, MA: N.p., 1969.

Jacobs, Milton. "The Moroccan Jewess: A Study in Culture Stability and Change." Doctoral dissertation, Catholic U., 1957.

Malka, V. "La politique juive du roi Hassan II." L'Arche 244(Jl, 1977):28-29.

Michaux-Bellaire, E. "L'enseignement indigène au Maroc." Revue du Monde Musulman 15 (1911):422-452.

Rabinovich, Abraham. "Appointment in Rabat." Jerusalem Post Magazine, D 22, 1978. [Jews in Morocco]

Rivet, D. "École et colonisation au Maroc: La politique de Lyautey au début des années 20." Cah. hist. 20(1976):173-198.

Rosen, Lawrence. "Muslim-Jewish Relations in a Moroccan City." International Journal of Middle East Studies 3(S, 1972).

Schanche, Don R. "Immigration From Israel Called Moroccan Mirage." Washington Post, Je 23, 1977.

_____. "'Very Few' Jews Return to Morocco." Los Angeles Times, My 1, 1977.

Sundiata, I. K. "Beyond Race and Color in Islam." Journal of Ethnic Studies 6(Spring, 1978):1-23.

Taib, Saab Eddin. "Linguistic and Cultural Conflicts in Modern Morocco." Federal Linguist 4(Fall-Winter, 1972):1-7.

Tessler, Mark A. "The Identity of Religious Minorities in Non-Secular States: Jews in Tunisia and Morocco and Arabs in Israel." Comparative Studies in Society and History 20(Jl, 1978):359-373.

_____. Three Nonassimilating Minorities. Jews in Tunisia and Morocco and Arabs in Israel. New York: Praeger, 1977.

Toledano, Yoseph. "The Lost History of Moroccan Jewry." Challenge (Supplement of Bama' aracha) 1(Mr-Ap, 1976):4-5.

Wagner, Dan. "Memories of Morocco: The Influence of Age, Schooling, and Environment on Memory." Cognitive Pyschology 10(1978): 1-28.

Zafrani, Haim. "La Vie intellectuelle juive au Maroc de la fin du 15eme au debut du 20eme siecle." Doctoral dissertation, U. of Paris, 1971.

_____. "La vie intellectuelle juive au Maroc de la fin du 15ème au debut du 20ème siècle." Revue de l'Occident musulman et de la Mediterranée Aix-en-Provence 9(1971).

Mozambique

Alpers, Edward H. "Ethnicity, Politics, and History in Mozambique." Africa Today 21 (Fall, 1974):39-52.

Azvedo, Mario J. "The Legacy of Colonial Education in Mozambique (1876-1976)." A Current Bibliography on African Affairs 11 (1978-1979):3-16.

Lefort, Rene. "The Party Stays on a War Footing." Guardian, S 5, 1976.

Mondlane, Eduardo C. "Race Relations and Portuguese Colonial Policy, with Special Reference to Mozambique." Objective: Justice I, 1(1969). [Written in 1967]

Fita-Ferreira, Antonio. "The Ethno-History and the Ethnic Grouping of the Peoples of Mozambique." S. Afric. J. Afric. Aff. 3 (1973):56-76.

Torres, J. L. Ribeiro. "Race Relations in Moçambique." Zambezia 3(D, 1973):39-52.

Namibia

Fraenkel, Peter. The Namibians of South West Africa. Rev. ed. London: Minority Rights Group, Jl, 1974.

International Commission of Jurists. "Apartheid in Namibia." Objective: Justice 6(Ja-F, 1974):16-24.

Nujoma, Sam. "Namibians Want Immediate End to South Africa's Rule." Objective: Justice 4(Ja-Mr, 1972):6-8, 33.

O'Callaghan, Marion. Namibia: The Effects of Apartheid on Culture and Education. Paris: UNESCO, 1977.

Nepal

Milward, C. A. "Red Brick Among the Rice Fields." Times Educational Supplement, Ag 9, 1977. [Budhanilkantha School in Nepal]

Netherlands

Amersfoort, Johannes M. M. v. "Immigratie en winderheidsvorming. Een analyse van de Nederlands situatie, 1945-1973." Doctoral dissertation, U. of Amsterdam, 1974. [Immigrants in the Process of Becoming a Minority... Summary in English]

_____. Surinamese Immigrants in the Netherlands. The Hague: State Printing House for the Ministry of Culture, Recreation and Social Work, 1969.

_____. "West Indian Migration to the Netherlands." In Foreigners in Our Community. Edited by Hans van Houte and Willy Melgert. Amsterdam, The Netherlands: Keesing, 1972.

Bagley, Christopher. Community Relations in the Netherlands: A Model for Britain?, 1972. The Society of Friends, Friends House, Euston Road, London NW1 2BJ, England.

_____. The Dutch Plural Society. A Comparative Study in Race Relations. London: Oxford U. Press, 1973.

_____. "Holland Unites." New Society, Mr 7, 1968. [Indonesians in Holland]

_____. "Holland's 'Red Niggers.'" Race Today 5(F, 1973):61-62. [Surinamers in Amsterdam]

_____. "Immigrant Minorities in the Netherlands: Integration and Assimilation." International Migration Review 5(Fall, 1970).

_____. "Immigration and Social Policy in the Netherlands." New Community 1(O, 1971): 25-28.

Beeson, Trevor. "Dutch Prescription for Racial Harmony." Christian Century, S 6, 1972.

Bovenkerk, Frank. [Letter on Surinamese migration to the Netherlands] Race 15 (O, 1973):248-253.

_____. Review of Bagley, The Dutch Plural Society. Race 15(O, 1973):261-264.

Brennan, Paul. "Surinamers in Holland." New Society, N 6, 1975.

Buve, R. T. J. "Surinaamse slaven en vrije negers in Amsterdam gedurende de 18^e eeuw." Bijdragen Tot de Taal, Land en Volkenkunde 119(S'-Gravenhage, 1963).

Darragh, A. "Residential Segregation of Ethnic Groups in Rotterdam, The Netherlands." Master's thesis, Queen's U., Kingston, 1978.

Deakin, Nicholas. "The Dutch Experiment Revisited." Institute of Race Relations Newsletter, Mr, 1968. [Integration of 300,000 Indonesians in Holland]

Den Boer, A. W. "De Molukkers in Nederland." Spiegel Hist. 12(O, 1977):526-534.

Drewe, P. and others. "Segregation in Rotterdam: An Explorative Study on Theory, Data and Policy." Tijdschrift voor Economische en Sociale Geografie 66(1975):204-216.

Ebbeling, G. "Minorities in Holland." Race Today 3(N, 1971):381.

Emmanuel, Isaac S., and Emmanuel, Suzanne. History of the Jews of the Netherlands Antilles. 2 vols. New York: Ktav Publishing House, 1970.

Fishman, Joel. "The Jewish Community in Post-War Netherlands, 1944-1975." Midstream 22 (Ja, 1976):42-54.

Florin, Frits. "Refugee Students in the Netherlands." Higher Education and Research in the Netherlands 19(1975):19-23.

Friedler, Ya'acov. "The Children of Burgerwijshuis." Jerusalem Post, D 8, 1978.

Friedman, Harold, and Friedman, Helen. "Letter From Bijlmereer, The Netherlands." Integrateducation 13(Jl-Ag, 1975):21-23.

Gans, Mozes Heiman. Memorbook. History of Dutch Jewry from Renaissance to 1940. London: Georg Prior, 1977.

Green, Vera M. "Aspects of Interethnic Integration in Aruba, Netherlands Antilles." Doctoral dissertation, U. of Arizona, 1969.

Hartlye, Bryan. "Dutch Citizens." New Society, F 8, 1973. [South Moluccans in Holland]

Kappen, Olav van. "Geschiedenis der zigeuners in Nederland. De ontwikkeling van de rechtspositie van de Heidens of Egyptenaren in de Noordelijke Nederlanden (1420 - ± 1750." Doctoral dissertation, U. of Utrecht, 1965. [History of the Gypsies in the Netherlands...; an English summary is provided]

Kuper, Jessica. "After the Holocaust." New Society, Mr 15, 1979. [Jews in the Netherlands]

Lennards, Joseph L. The Secondary School System in the Netherlands: Some Social Consequence of Streaming, Ja, 1969. ERIC ED 029 365.

_____. "Streaming and Status Socialization in the Dutch Secondary School System." Doctoral dissertation, Princeton U., 1978. Univ. Microfilms Order No. 7807481.

Lijphart, Arend. The Politics of Accommodation. Pluralism and Democracy in the Netherlands. 2nd. ed. Berkeley, CA: U. of California Press, 1975.

Marien, M. "South Moluccan Radicalism in the Netherlands: Nationalist or Emancipation Movement." Sociologia Neerlandica 9(1973): 77-87.

Michman, Joseph (ed.). Studies on the History of Dutch Jewry. Vol. I. Jerusalem: Magnes Press, Hebrew U., 1975.

Moorman, Paul. "Socialist Minister Gets Universities' Blood Up." Times Higher Education Supplement, N 12, 1976.

Peschar, Julien Lambert. "Equal Opportunity in the Netherlands: The Influence of Social Class on Education and Occupation: An Ex-Post-Facto Study 1958-73." Sociologia Neerlandia 11(1975):60-75.

_____. "Milieu, school, beroep. Een achteraf-experiment over de periode 1958-1973 naar de invloed van het sociaal milieu op school--en beroepsloopbaan." (The influence of social class on educational and occupational career. An ex-post-facto study, 1958-1973.) Doctoral dissertation, U. of Groningen, 1975. [English summary included]

Popa-Radix, P. J. A. Reception and Social Guidance of Migrant Workers. The Hague: Migrant Groups Division, Ministry of Cultural Affairs, Recreation and Social Welfare, 1968.

Presser, J. Downfall: The Persecution and Extermination of the Dutch Jewish Community, 1940-1945. Hague, Netherlands: National Institute of War Archives, 1965.

"Pride and Prejudice." Newsweek, N 17, 1969.

Rose, Leesha. The Tulips Are Red. New York: Barnes, 1979. [Netherlands under Nazi occupation]

Saenger-Ceha, Maria Magdalena. "Psychological and Social Factors in Student Drop-Out." Doctoral dissertation, U. of Groningen, 1970.

Sander, Gordon F. "Innocence Lost." New York Times Magazine, Ag 22, 1976. [Deals with, among other things, racial prejudice in the Netherlands]

Sijes, B. A. "The Position of the Jews during German Occupation of the Netherlands." Acta Hist. Neerlandicae 9(1976):170-192.

Tholenaar-Van Raalte, J. "De integratie van Westindische immigraten in Groot-Brittanië en in Nederland." Nieuwe West-Indische Gids 46 (1968):150-163.

Uidriks, G. Social Disadvantages and Educational Opportunity: Examination of 50 Children from Two Working Class Neighborhoods. Utrecht: Institute of Education, State U., 1969.

Vellinga, M. L., and Wolters, W. G. "De Chinezen." In Allochtonen in Nederland, pp. 214-228. Edited by H. Verwey Jonker. Staatsuitgeverij's-Gravenhenge, 1971. [Chinese]

Verduin-Muller, Henriette. On Cross-Cultural Education in the Netherlands, S, 1976. ERIC ED 132 103. [Children of migrant workers]

Verwey-Jonker, H. (ed.). Allochtonen in Nederland. The Hague: State Printing House for the Ministry of Culture, Recreation and Social Work, 1971.

Weeren, Donald. "Historical and Contemporary Aspects of Inter-religious Relations in Dutch Education and Society." Doctoral dissertation, Columbia U., 1967.

Whitney, Craig R. "Placid Dutch Town Is Swept by Fear--and Prejudice." New York Times, My 25, 1977. [Bovensmilde]

_____. "Police Isolate Moluccans of Dutch Town Struck by Terrorists." New York Times, My 26, 1977. [Bovensmilde]

Wilder, J. S. "Indonesian Women in the Hague: Colonial Immigrants in the Netherlands." Doctoral dissertation, New York U., 1967.

Willems, Fredericus. "Manisfcstations of Discrimination in the Netherlands." In Foreigners in Our Community, pp. 71-77. Edited by Hans van Houte and Willy Melgert. Amsterdam, The Netherlands: Keesing, 1972.

New Zealand

Adams, Peter. Fatal Necessity: British Intervention in New Zealand, 1830-1847. New York: Oxford U. Press, 1978.

Archer, Dave, and Archer, Mary. "Maoris in Cities." Race 13(0, 1971):179-185.

_____ and _____. "Race, Identity, and the Maori People." Journal of the Polynesian Society 79(1970):201-218.

Ausubel, David P. The Fern and the Tiki: An American View of New Zealand and National Character, Social Attitutdes, and Race Relations. 2nd ed. North Quincy, MA: Christopher, 1977.

_____. Maori Youth. Wellington, NJ: Price Millburn, 1961.

Barham, I. H. The English Vocabulary and Sentence Structure of Maori Children. Wellington, New Zealand: New Zealand Council for Educational Research, 1965.

Barnett, J. Ross. "Race and Physician Location: Trends in Two New Zealand Urban Areas." New Zealand Geographer 34(Ap, 1978):2-12.

Barney, David. Who Gets to Pre-School? The Availability of Pre-School Education in New Zealand. Wellington: New Zealand Council for Educational Research, 1975.

Barrington, John M. "Cultural Adaptation and Maori Educational Policy: The African Connection." Comparative Education Review 20(F, 1976):1-10.

_____. "Education, Labor Force, and Race in New Zealand." Sociology and Social Research 55(J1, 1971):449-453.

_____. "Educational Administration in the Multiracial Society: A Report on New Zealand." Race 14(J1, 1972):59-68.

_____. "Maori Education and Society, 1867-1940." Master's thesis, Victoria U. (Wellington), 1965.

_____. "[Marori Scholastic Achievement]: A Historical Review of Policies and Provisions." New Zealand Journal of Educational Studies 1(1966):1-14.

Barrington, John, and Beaglehole, T. H. Maori Schools in a Changing Society. Wellington: New Zealand Council for Educational Research, 1974.

Barrington, John M., and Ewing, John L. "Human Problems in Administrative Change: A New Zealand Case Study." Journal of Educational Administration 11(1973):88-95.

Beaglehole, T. H. "Maori Schools, 1816-1880." Master's thesis, Victoria U. of Wellington, 1955.

Bender, Byron W. Linguistic Factors in Maori Education. Wellington: New Zealand Council for Educational Research, 1971.

Bray, D. H. "Extent of Future Time Orientation: A Cross-Ethnic Study among New Zealand Adolescents." British Journal of Educational Psychology 40(Je, 1970):200-208.

Bray, Douglas H., and Hill, Clement. Polynesian and Pakeha in New Zealand Education. 2 vols. London: Heinemann Educational Books, 1973.

Bray, D. H., and Jordan, J. E. "Ethnic Intergroup Levels Among New Zealand Teachers College Students." Journal of the Polynesian Society 82(1973):266-280.

Brookes, R. H., and Kawharu, I. H. (eds.). Administration in New Zealand's Multiracial Society. Wellington, N.Z.: New Zealand Institute of Public Administration, 1967.

Brown, Douglas W. F. "Maori Scholastic Underachievement as a Challenge to Methodology." Master's theis, U. of Canterbury, 1962.

Buck, Peter. The Coming of the Maori. Wellington: Whitcome and Tombs for Maori Purposes Fund Board, 1949.

Butchers, A. G. Education in New Zealand. Wellington: Coulls, Somerville, Wilkie, Ltd., 1930

_____. Young New Zealand; A History of the Early Contact of the Maori Race with the European. Dunedin, N.Z.: Coulls, Somerville, Wilkie, Ltd., 1929.

Butterworth, Graham V. The Maori People in the New Zealand Economy. Palmerston North, N.Z.: Department of Social Anthropology and Maori Studies, Massey U., 1974.

Caselberg, John (ed.). Maori Is My Name... Historical Maori Writings in Translation. Dunedin, N.Z.: J. McIndoe, 1975.

Clark, Paul. "Hauhau": The Pai Mauire Search for Maori Identity. Auckland: Auckland U. Press, 1975.

Clay, Marie M. "Early Childhood and Cultural Diversity in New Zealand." Reading Teacher 29(Ja, 1976):333-342.

Collette, C., and O'Malley, P. "Urban Migration and Selective Acculturation: The Case of the Maori." Human Organization 33(S, 1974).

Coutts, P. J. F. "Merger on Takeover: A Survey of the Effects of Contact between European and Maori in the Foveaux Strait Region." Journal of the Polynesian Society 78(1969): 495-516.

Curson, P. H. "Migration of Cook Islanders to New Zealand." South Pacific Bulletin 23 (1973):15-25.

_____. "Polynesians and Residence in Auckland." New Zealand Geographer 26(1970): 162-173.

Elley, W. B. "Changes in Mental Ability in New Zealand School Children, 1936-1968." New Zealand Journal of Educational Studies 4(1969):140-155.

Ewing, J., and Shallcross, J. (eds.). Introduction to Maori Education. Wellington: New Zealand U. Press, 1970.

Fitzgerald, Thomas K. Education and Identity: A Reconsideration of Some Models of Acculturation and Identity. Washington, DC: American Educational Research Association, 1970. ERIC ED 048 050.

_____. Education and Identity: A Study of the New Zealand Maori Graduate. Wellington, N.Z.: New Zealand Council for Educational Research, 1977.

_____. "The First Generation of Maori University Graduates: A Historical Sketch." New Zealand Journal of Educational Studies 5(1970):46-62.

_____. Integration, Race, and the Maori of New Zealand, Ap, 1971. ERIC ED 049 332.

_____. "The Maori University Graduate and the Sentiment System." Anthropological Quarterly 47(Ap, 1974):169-181.

_____. "The Social Position of Maori University Graduates." Polynesian Studies 7 (1968).

_____. "What Is 'Integration'?" New Zealand Monthly 5(Jl, 1968).

Fong, Ng Bickleen. Chinese in New Zealand: A Study in Assimilation. Hong Kong: Hong Kong U., 1959.

Foster, John, and Ramsay, Peter D. "Migration, Education and Occupation: The Maori Population 1936-1956." In Social Process in New Zealand, pp. 198-232. Edited by John Forster. Milford, N.Z.: Longman Paul, 1969.

Franklin, S. Harvey. Trade, Growth and Anxiety. New Zealand Beyond the Welfare State. London: Methuen, 1978.

Goldman, Lazarus M. History of the Jews in New Zealand. New York: Heinman, 1958.

Green, Roger C. "Adaptation and Change in Maori Culture." In Ecology and Biogeography in New Zealand. Edited by G. Kuschel. The Hague: Dr. W. Junk, 1974.

Greif, Stuart W. The Overseas Chinese in New Zealand. Singapore: Asia Pacific Press, 1974.

_____. "The Historical, Social and Political Development of the Chinese of New Zealand." Doctoral dissertation, U. of California, Berkeley, 1972.

Greenaway, George H. "New Zealand: Education Among the Maoris." Education Panorama 8(1966).

Harker, Richard K. "Maori Education and Research." Australian and New Zealand Journal of Sociology 7(Ap, 1971):46-57.

_____. "Maori Enrolment at N.Z. Universities 1956-68." New Zealand Journal of Educational Studies 5(1970):142-152.

_____. "Social Class Factors in a New Zealand Comprehensive School." Educational Research 13(F, 1971):155-158.

_____. "Some Aspects of Maori University Education in New Zealand." Master's thesis, Victoria U. of Wellington, 1970.

Harre, John. "The Interracial Mixing of a Group of Young Zealand Adults." Race, Ja, 1966.

_____. Maori and Pakeha. A Study of Mixed Marriages in New Zealand. London: Pall Mall Press, 1966.

Hawthorn, H. B. "The Maori: A Study in Acculturation." American Anthropological Association, Memoirs 64(Ap, 1944).

Heuer, Berys. Maori Women. Wellington, N.Z.: A. H. and A. W. Reed, 1972.

Hohepa, P. W. "Cultural Minorities in Auckland." in Equality of Opportunity through Education, pp. 16-24. Wellington: Association for the Study of Childhood, 1972.

Hooper, Anthony B. "Social Relations among Cook Islanders in New Zealand." Master's thesis, U. of New Zealand (Auckland), 1959.

Huttenback, Robert A. Racism and Empire. White Settlers and Colored Immigrants in the British Self-Governing Colonies, 1830-1910. Ithaca: Cornell U. Press, 1976.

Jackson, Brian. "Maori and Paheka: New Zealand's Race Bomb." New Society, Ja 30, 1975.

Jackson, M. D. "Literacy, Communication and Social Change: the Maori Case, 1830-1870." Master's thesis, U. of Auckland, 1967.

Jackson, P. M. Maori and Education, or the Education of Natives in New Zealand and its Dependencies. Wellington: N.p., 1931.

Kawharu, I. H. Maori Land Tenure: Studies of a Changing Institution. Oxford: Clarendon Press, 1977.

_____. Orakei: A Ngati Whatua Community. Christchurch, N.Z.: Whitcoulls Ltd., 1975.

_____ (ed.). Conflict and Compromise: Essays on the Maori since Colonisation. Wellington: Reed, 1975.

Keith, K. J. "Race Relations and the Law in New Zealand." R. Dr. Homme (1973):329-368.

Kernot, Clifton B. J. "Leadership Among Migrant Maoris." Master's thesis, U. of Auckland, 1963.

Kohere, Reweti. The Autobiography of a Maori. Wellington: Reed, 1951.

Lovegrove, M. N. "A Cross-Cultural Study of Scholastic Achievement and Selected Determiners." Doctoral dissertation, U. of Auckland, 1965.

_____. "Maori Underachievement." Journal of the Polynesian Society 73(1964):70-72.

_____. "The Scholastic Achievement of European and Maori Children." New Zealand Journal of Educational Studies, My, 1966.

_____. "What History Tells Us About the Ability of the Maori." Journal of the Australian and New Zealand History of Education Society 1(1972):21-32.

Lyttle, John. "Anti-discrimination Law in New Zealand and Britain." New Community 1 (Autumn, 1972):451-452.

McCreary, J. R. "Reading Tests With Maori Children." New Zealand Journal of Educational Studies, My, 1966.

McDonald, Geraldine. Maori Mothers and Pre-School Education. Wellington: New Zealand Council for Educational Research, 1973.

McKean, W. A. Essays on Race Relations and the Law in New Zealand. Wellington: Sweet and Maxwell, 1971.

McKenzie, David. "The Changing Concept of Equality in New Zealand Education." New Zealand Journal of Educational Studies 10 (1975).93-110.

Mackenzie, Mary (comp.). Maori Education 1960-69: A Bibliography. Wellington: New Zealand Council for Educational Research, 1970.

McLaren, Ian A. Education in a Small Democracy: New Zealand. London: Routledge & Kegan Paul, 1974.

MacLeod, A. "Maoris--New Awareness, New Strains." Far Eastern Economic Review 72 (My 15, 1971):34-39.

Maracle, Carmen. "Maori and [Canadian] Indian People Share Common Problems and Aspirations." Indian News (Ottawa, Canada) 16 (O, 1973):5.

Metge, Joan. "Education." In The Maoris of New Zealand. Routahi, pp. 151-170. 2nd ed. London: Routledge & Kegan Paul, 1976.

Miller, Harold. "Maori and Pakeha, 1814-1865." In The Maori People Today: A General Survey. Edited by I. L. G. Sutherland. London: Oxford U. Press, 1940.

_____. Race Conflict in New Zealand 1814-1865. Auckland: Blackwood & Janet Paul, 1966.

Miller, John. Early Victorian New Zealand: A Study of Racial Tension and Social Attitudes, 1839-1852. London: Oxford U. Press, 1958.

Minoque, W. J. D. "The Social Heritage and Educational Systems of Hawaii and New Zealand: Comparisons and Contrasts." New Zealand Journal of Educational Studies, N, 1968.

Mitcalfe, Barry. Maori Poetry: The Singing Word. Wellington: Price Milburn, 1974.

Mol, J. J. "Integration versus Segregation in the New Zealand Churches." British Journal of Sociology, Je, 1965.

Morrison, S. R. "Socially Handicapped--The Maoris of New Zealand." Integrated Education, D, 1966-Ja, 1967.

Murray, Saana. Te Karanga a Te Kotuku. Maori Organization on Human Rights, Box 19036, Wellington, New Zealand, n.d. [Efforts of Te Kihu o te Ika people to retain their land]

Nathan, Judith. "An Analysis of an Industrial Boarding School: 1847-1860. A Phase in Maori Education." New Zealand Journal of History 7(Ap, 1973):47-59.

New Zealand. Government White Paper on Proposed Amendments to the Maori Affairs Act 1953, the Maori Affairs Amendment Act, 1967, and Other Related Acts. Wellington, N.Z.: Government Printer, 1973.

New Zealand Council for Educational Research. Research Needed in the Education of Maori Children. Wellington, N.Z.: The Council, 1961.

New Zealand Education Institute. Report and Recommendations on Maori Education. Wellington, N.Z.: The Institute, 1967.

New Zealand National Advisory Committee on Maori Education. Report on Maori Education. Wellington: Government Printer, 1971.

New Zealand Post-Primary Teachers' Organization. Interim Report on Maori Education. Wellington, N.Z.: The Organization, 1970.

Ngata, Apirana T. The Past and Future of the Maori. Christchurch: N.p., 1893.

O'Connor, P. S. "Keeping New Zealand White, 1908-1920." New Zealand Journal of History 2 (Ap, 1968):41-65.

Ogbu, John U. "Maoris in New Zealand." In Minority Education and Caste, pp. 265-285. New York: Academic Press, 1978.

O'Malley, Patrick. "The Amplification of Maori Crime: Cultural and Economic Barriers to Equal Justice in New Zealand." Race 15 (Jl, 1973):47-57.

Oppenheim, Roger. "Maori Children in Auckland School." The New Era, England, D, 1964.

Parr, C. J. "Maori Literacy 1843-67." Journal of the Polynesian Society 72(1963):211-234.

Parsonage, William. "The Education of Maoris in New Zealand." Journal of the Polynesian Society 65(1956):5-11.

Pitt, David C., and Macpherson, Cluny.
Emerging Pluralism: The Samoan Community
in New Zealand. Auckland: Longman Paul,
1974.

_____ (ed.). Social Class in New
Zealand. N.p.: N.p., n.d.

Pool, D. I. "Estimates of New Zealand Maori
Vital Rates from the Mid-Nineteenth
Century to World War I." Population
Studies 27(Mr, 1973):117-125.

_____. The Maori Population of New Zealand
1769-1971. New York: Oxford U. Press,
1978.

Powell, Guy. "The Maori School: A Cultural
Dynamic?" Journal of the Polynesian
Society 64(1955):259-266.

Ramsay, Peter D. K. "A Question of Control:
The Administration of Maori Schools."
New Zealand Journal of Educational Studies
7(1972):119-129.

Ritchie, James E. "The Evidence for Anti-
Maori Prejudice." Victoria University
of Wellington Publications in Psychology
16(1964):85-99.

_____. "Human Problems and Educational
Change in a Maori Community: A Case Study
in the Dynamics of a Social Decision."
Journal of Polynesian Society 65(1956):13-
34.

_____. The Making of a Maori. Wellington:
A. H. and A. W. Reed, 1963.

_____ (ed.). Race Relations: Six New
Zealand Studies. Wellington, N.Z.:
Department of Psychology, Victoria U.,
1964.

Ritchie, Jane. Childhood in Rakau: The First
Five Years of Life. Wellington: Victoria
U., 1957.

_____. Maori Families. Wellington: Victoria
U., 1964.

Rowland, D. T. "Maori Migration to Auckland."
New Zealand Geographer 27(Ap, 1971):21-37.

_____. "Processes of Maori Urbanisation."
New Zealand Geographer, Ap, 1972.

Sage, C. B. "A Study in Community. Elements
of Racial Discrimination in the Township
of Pukekohe, New Zealand, with Particular
Reference to the Construction of a
Segregated Maori School." Master's thesis,
U. of New Zealand (Auckland), 1952.

St. George, Ross. "Beating the System: Some
Issues in Maori Schooling." Delta 7(Ag,
1970):26-33.

_____. "Maori and European Psycholinguistics
Abilities: A Resolution of Results in
Conflict with Similar Studies." Australian
Journal of Psychology 24(Ap, 1972):9-11.

Schwimmer, Erik (ed.). The Maori People in the
Nineteen-Sixties--A Symposium. New York:
Humanities Press, 1969.

_____. The World of the Maori. Wellington,
N.Z.: A. H. and A. W. Reed, 1966.

Scott, Dick. Ask That Mountain. N.p.:
Heinemann Education, n.d. [Treatment of
Maoris by Pakeha governments]

Sinclair, Keith. "Why Are Race Relations in
New Zealand Better than in South Africa,
South Australia or South Dakota?" New
Zealand Journal of History, 0, 1971.

Sorrenson, M. P. K. "Colonial Rule and Local
Response: Maori Responses to European Domination in New Zealand since 1860."
J. Imperial Commonwealth History 4(Ja, 1976):
127-137.

_____. "How to Civilize Savages: Some
'Answers' from Nineteenth-Century New
Zealand." New Zealand Journal of History 9
(0, 1975):97-110.

_____. Maori and European since 1870--A Study
in Adaptation and Adjustment. London:
Heinemann, 1967.

Spoonley, Paul. "Inciting Racial Disharmony in
New Zealand." New Community 7(Winter,
1978/9):111-113.

Stewart, Robert A. C. (ed.). Adolescence in New
Zealand. II: Wider Perspectives.
Auckland: Heinemann Education, 1976.
[Touches on Maori-Pakeha differences]

St. George, Ross. "Racial Intolerance in New
Zealand: A Review of Studies." In Schools
in New Zealand Society. Edited by G. H.
Robinson and B. T. O'Rourke. Sydney:
Wiley, 1973.

Sutherland, I. L. G. "Maori and Pakeha."
In New Zealand, pp. 48-72. Edited by H.
Belshaw. Los Angeles, CA: U. of California
Press, 1947.

Sutherland, O. R. W. and others. Justice and
Race: A Monocultural System in a Multi-
Cultural Society. Hamilton: New Zealand
Race Relations Council, 1973.

Thompson, Richard. "After Three Years: New
Zealand's Race Relations Act in Operation."
New Community 4(Summer, 1975):232-235.

_____. "The All White All Blacks of 1970."
Race Today, Je, 1970.

_____. "The New Zealand Race Relations Act."
New Community 1(Summer, 1972):314-317.

_____. Race Discrimination in Sport--A New Zealand Controversy. National Council of Churches in New Zealand, 1969.

_____. "Race Relations in Transition." Race Today, N, 1969.

_____. "Report from New Zealand." New Community 3(Winter-Spring, 1974):144-146.

_____. "Young Maoris Face Problems." Race Today 2(1970):82-84.

Vaughn, Graham M. "Development of Ethnic Awareness in Maori and Pakeha School-children." Victoria University of Wellington Publications in Psychology 16(1964): 41-50.

_____. "Ethnic Attitudes and Awareness among New Zealand Children." New Era, My, 1967.

_____. Racial Issues in New England. Auckland: Akarana Press, 1972.

Vaughn, G. M., and Thompson, R. H. T. "New Zealand Children's Attitudes toward Maoris." Journal of Abnormal and Social Psychology 62(1961):701-704.

Walker, Ranginui J. "Education for a Multi-Cultural Society." Multi-Cultural School 1 (1975):5-13.

_____. "The Social Relationships of the Maori Students at Auckland Teachers' College." Master's thesis, U. of Auckland, 1965.

_____. "There Are Maori Solutions for Some Maori Problems in City Schools." National Education, F, 1969, pp. 16-19.

Ward, Alan. A Show of Justice: Racial 'Amalgamation' in Nineteenth Century New Zealand. Toronto: U. of Toronto Press, 1974.

_____. "Law and Law-Enforcement on the New Zealand Frontier, 1840-1893." New Zealand Journal of History 5(0, 1971):128-149.

Watson, John. Accommodating the Polynesian Heritage of the Maori Child. Wellington: New Zealand Council of Educational Research, 1972.

Watson, J. E. Horizons of Unknown Power: Some Issues in Maori Schooling. Wellington: New Zealand Council on Educational Research, 1967.

Webb, Stephen D., and Collette, John (eds.). New Zealand Society: Contemporary Perspectives. New York: Wiley, 1973.

Williams, John Smith. Maori Achievement Motivation. Wellington: Department of Psychology, Victoria U., 1960.

Whitney, Craig R. "Tashkent Absorbs Tatars and Germans Uprooted by Stalin." New York Times, D 27, 1977.

Williams, J. A. Politics of the New Zealand Maori: Protest and Cooperation 1891-1909. London: Oxford U. Press, 1969.

Williams, J. S. Maori Achievement Motivation. Wellington, N.Z.: Department of Psychology, Victoria U., 1960.

Williams, John A. Politics of the New Zealand Maori: Protest and Cooperation, 1891-1909. Seattle, WA: U. of Washington Press, 1969.

Winiata, Maharaia. The Changing Role of the Leader in Maori Society. Auckland: Blackwood and Janet Paul, 1967.

Nigeria

Abernathy, David B. The Political Dilemma of Popular Education--An African Case. Palo Alto, CA: Stanford U. Press, 1969.

Adeoina, Segun. "Power Structures and Education Decision Making in Nigeria." Journal of Negro Education 41(Summer, 1972):216-226.

Adesina, Sylvester Adesegun. "An Analysis of Nigeria's Educational Plans and Actual Educational Development between 1945 and 1970." Doctoral dissertation, Columbia U., 1974. Univ. Microfilms Order No. 74-15968.

Agbowuro, Joseph. "Nigerization and the Nigerian Universities." Comparative Education 12(0, 1976):243-254.

Awoniyi, Timothy A. "Problems Related to Curriculum Development and Teaching the Mother Tongues in Nigeria: A Historical Survey, 1800-1974." Audio-Visual Language Journal 13(Spring, 1975):31-41.

_____. "The Role and Status of the Yoruba Language in the Formal School System of Western Nigeria, 1846-1971." Doctoral dissertation, U. of Ibadan, n.d.

_____. "The Yoruba Language and the Formal School System: A Study of Colonial Language Policy in Nigeria, 1882-1952." International Journal of African Historical Studies 8 (1975):63-80.

Babalola, Adelboye. "The Role of Nigerian Languages and Literature in Fostering National Cultural Identity." Présence afric. 2 (1975):53-83.

Baikie-Abdallah, D. Adamu. "Wanted: A Programme of Education for Mutual Understanding in Nigeria." West African Journal of Education 14(F, 1970). [Inter-tribal relations]

Bamidele, Michael O., and Peil, Margaret. "Education in Lagos: Expectation and Achievement." W. Afric. J. Sociol. Pol. Sci. 2(Nos. 1-2, 1976-77):73-98.

Bamisaiye, A. "Ethnic Politics as an Instrument of Unequal Socio-economic Development in Nigeria's First Republic." African Notes 2(1971).

Bandiare, Ali. "L'enfant dans la société nigérienne." R. jur. pol. 31(Ap-Je, 1977): 371-380.

Bloom, Leonard. "Values and Attitudes of Young Nigerians: Responses to Social Change." West African Journal of Sociology and Political Science 2(1976/77).

Bolade, A. "An Investigation of the Concept of Internal Colonialism in Nigeria's Recent Economic Development." Master's thesis, Queen's University, Kingston, 1977.

Boyan, Douglas Robert. "Educational Policy Formulation in the North of Nigeria, 1900-1969." Doctoral dissertation, U. of Wisconsin, 1972. Univ. Microfilms Order No. 72-31665.

Daudu, Patrick Cyrus Adamola. "The Management of Ethnic Conflicts in Northern States of Nigeria, 1968-1973." Doctoral dissertation, U. of Pittsburgh, 1974. Univ. Microfilms Order No. 75-06342.

Daum, David A. "The National Language Question." West African Journal of Education 18(O, 1974):355-362.

Diaku, P. A. "The Role of the British Colonial Government in the Provision of Education for Nigerians, 1887-1910: An Analysis of Performance and Impact." Master's thesis, U. of Wales, Bangor, 1976.

Diamond, Stanley. "The Ibo's Plight." New York Review of Books 18(F 24, 1972):46 (letter).

_____. Nigeria: Model of a Colonial Failure. New York: American Committee on Africa, 1967.

Doi, R. "Islamic Education in Nigeria (11th Century to 20th Century)." Islamic Culture 1(1972).

Ekong, Ekong E. "The Fictiveness of Class Analysis in Contemporary Nigerian Society." West African Journal of Sociology and Political Science 2(1976/77).

Eze, Onyeabo. "Nigeria-Biafra Conflict. Social and Economic Background." Doctoral dissertation, U. of Basle, 1971.

Fafunwa, A. "Education in the Mother-Tongue: A Nigerian Experiment--The Six-Year (Yoruba Medium) Primary Education Project at the University of Ife, Nigeria." West African Journal of Education 19(Je, 1975): 218-228.

Fajana, Ade. "Colonial Control and Education: The Development of Higher Education in Nigeria, 1900-1950." Journal of the Historical Society of Nigeria 6(1972):323-340.

_____. "Educational Policy in Nigerian Traditional Society." Phylon 33(Spring, 1972):33-48.

_____. "Lugard's Educational Policy in Nigeria, 1912-18." West African Journal of Education 19(Je, 1975):179-198.

Fuchs, Estelle. "The Compatability of Western Education with Ibo Culture: An Examination of the Complex Dynamics Involved in the Successfull Diffusion of Literacy and Schooling to the Ibo of Eastern Nigeria." Doctoral dissertation, Columbia U., 1964.

Graham, Sonia. Missions and Government in Northern Nigeria, 1900-1919... Ibadan, Nigeria: Ibadan United Press, 1966.

Gutkind, Peter C. W. "The View from Below: Political Consciousness of the Urban Poor in Ibadan." Cah. ét. afric. 15(1975):5-36.

Hansford, Keir and others. "A Provisional Language Map of Nigeria." Savanna 5 D, 1976):115-126.

Hubbard, James P. "Education Under Colonial Rule: A History of Katsina College, 1921-1942." Doctoral dissertation, U. of Wisconsin, 1973.

Imoagene, O. Social Mobility in Emergent Society: The New Elite in Western Nigeria. Canberra: Australian National U., 1976.

Isichei, Elizabeth. A History of the Igbo People. London: Macmillan, 1976.

_____. The Ibo People and the Europeans. New York: St. Martin's Press, 1974.

Koehl, Robert. "The Uses of the University: Past and Present in Nigerian Educational Culture. Part I." Comparative Education Review 15(Je, 1971):116-131.

Kurtz, Donn M. "Education and Elite Integration in Nigeria." Comparative Education Review, F, 1973.

Marjasan, J. A. "Traditional Systems of Education in the Cultures of Nigeria." Présence Afric. 3(1975):322-368.

Njoku, Scholastica Ibari. "The Development of the British System of Education in Nigeria, 1882-1929." Doctoral dissertation, U. of Oregon, 1969. Univ. Microfilms Order No. 70-09462.

Nnoli, Okwudiba. "Education and Ethnic Politics." Africa Development 1(1976): 37-53.

Nwa-Chil, C. C. "The Spread of 'Western Education' in Nigeria." J. E. Afric. Res. Dev. 3(1973):145-166.

Nwabachili, Chudi C. Education in Nigeria. (A Study of Attitudes Toward "Modern" Education). Lund, Sweden: Department of Sociology, U. of Lund, 1970.

Nwabara, S. N. Iboland: A Century of Contact with Britain, 1860-1960. Atlantic Highlands, NJ: Humanities, 1978.

Nwagwu, N. A. (ed.). Universal Primary Education in Nigeria: Issues, Prospects and Problems. Benin City, Nigeria: Ethiope Publishing Corp., 1976.

O'Connell, James, and Beckett, Paul. Education and Power in Nigeria. New York: Holmes and Meier, 1977.

Ogunlade, J. O. "Ethnic Identification and Preference of Some School Children in Western Nigeria." Sociology and Social Research 56 (Ja, 1972):195-201.

Okedijii, Francis O. "The Cultural Conditions of the Preschool Child in Nigeria." Les Carnets de l'enfance 21(Ja-Mr, 1973):19-33.

Olatunbosun, D. Nigeria's Neglected Rural Majority. Ibadan: Oxford U. Press, 1975.

Omolewa, Michael. "The English Language in Colonial Nigeria, 1862-1960. A Study of the Major Factors Which Promoted the Language." J. Nigerian Eng. Stud. Assoc. 7(D, 1975): 103-117.

Onah, J. Onuora, and Iwiyi, E. C. "Urban Poverty in Nigeria." Genève-Afrique 14 (1975):74-82.

_____ and _____. "Urban Poverty in Nigeria." South African Journal of Economics 44(Je, 1976):185-193.

Osaji, Debe. "Language Imposition: Sociolinguistic Case Study of the Hansa Language in Nigeria." Afric. Lang. 3(1977):117-129.

Otite, Onigu. "Resource Competition and Inter-Ethnic Relations in Nigeria." In Ethnicity and Resource Competition in Plural Societies. Edited by Leo A. Despres. Chicago, IL: Aldine, 1975.

Paden, John N. Religion and Political Culture in Kano. Berkeley, CA: U. of California Press, 1973.

Pell, Margaret. "Three Years After Biafra." New Society, Mr 15, 1973.

Price-Williams, D. R. "Abstract and Concrete Modes of Classification in a Primitive Society." British Journal of Educational Psychology 32(1962):50-61.

Rogers, Cyril A. "A Study of Race Attitudes in Nigeria." Rhodes-Livingstone Journal 26 (1959):51-64.

Salamone, Frank A. "Structure, Stereotypes, and Students: Implications for a Theory of Ethnic Interaction." Council on Anthropology and Education Quarterly 8(My, 1976):6-13. [Northwestern Nigeria]

Seibel, H. D. "Some Aspects of Inter-Ethnic Relations in Nigeria." Nigerian Journal of Social and Economic Studies 9(1967).

Smock, Audrey S. Ibo Politics: The Role of Ethnic Unions in Eastern Nigeria. Cambridge, MA: Harvard U. Press, 1971.

Taiwo, C. O. "Nigeria: Language Problems and Solutions." Propsects 6(1976):406-415.

Taiwo, O. "The Nigerian Novel and Indigenous Culture Problems of Communication." Doctoral dissertation, U. of Stirling, 1972.

Tinuoye, Olufemi Omolaoye. "Ends and Means of Reducing Inequality of Educational Opportunity in Nigeria: A Heuristic Approach to an Analysis of Public Policy." Doctoral dissertation, U. of Michigan, 1975. Univ. Microfilsm Order No. 75-20463.

Tseayo, Justin I. "Aspects of National Integration in Nigeria: The Tiv Case." Doctoral dissertation, U. of Sussex, 1973.

University of Lagos, Human Resources Research Unit. Socio-Economic Background of Nigerian University Students. Lagos: U. of Lagos, 1973.

Van Den Berghe, Pierre L. "Pluralism at a Nigerian University: A Case Study." Race 12 (Ap, 1971):429-441. [U. of Ilosho]

Williams, G. "The Social Stratification of a Neo-Colonial Economy: Western Nigeria." In African Perspectives. Edited by C. Allen and R. W. Johnson. London: Cambridge U. Press, 1970.

Wolpe, Howard. Urban Politics in Nigeria: A Study of Port Harcourt. Berkeley, CA: U. of California Press, 1974.

Norway

Belding, Robert E. "The Lapps: An Educational Study of a Minority Group." Clearing House 48(Ap, 1974):501-507.

Brown, Ross. "Norway Keeps the Gypsies Moving." Race Today 4(Jl, 1972):248.

_____. "Norway--Reserved or Xenophobic?" Race Today 4(Mr, 1972):92.

Coombs, L. Madison, and Boon, Inez. The Pedagogical Situation in the North with Special Reference to Alaska and the Lapps in Norway. Montreal, Canada: Alaska U., College; Arctic Institute of North America, Ag, 1969. Available from the Arctic Institute of North America, 3458 Redpath Street, Montreal 25, P.Q. Canada. ERIC ED 039 985.

Eidheim, Harald. Aspects of the Lappish Minority Situation. Oslo: Universitets-forlaget, 1974.

Forsius, Harriett, and Seitamo, Leila. "Mental State of Skolt Lapp Children: A Preliminary Report." Arctic Anthropology 7(1970):6-8.

Gordon, Gerd S. "The Norwegian Resistance During the German Occupation 1940-1945: Repression, Terror, and Resistance: The West Country of Norway." Doctoral disser-tation, U. of Pittsburgh, 1978. Univ. Microfilms Order No. 790 2755.

Guggenheim, F., and Hoem, A. "Cross-Cultural and Intracultural Attitudes of Lapp and Norwegian Children." Journal of Social Psychology, 0, 1967.

Hansen, Robert Eugene. "The Democratization of Norwegian Education." Doctoral disserta-tion, Harvard U., 1952.

Hill, R. G. P. (ed.). The Lapps Today in Finland, Norway and Sweden, I. Paris: Mouton, 1960.

Hill, R. G. P., and Nickul, K. (eds.). The Lapps Today, in Finland, Norway and Sweden, II. Oslo-Bergen-Tromsø: Universitets-forlaget, 1969.

Jonassen, Christen T. Community Conflict in School District Reorganization: A Cross-Cultural Study. Oslo, Norway: Universitets-forlaget, 1968.

Karadia, Chliotu. "Cold Comfort for Norway's Pakistanis." Race Today 3(0, 1971):344-345.

Langlo, Jon. "Teacher's Attitudes and the School Context: The Case of Upper-Secondary Teachers in Norway." Comparative Education Review 20(F, 1976):61-78.

Manbeck, John B. "American Indians and Lapps: A Comparative Study." American Scandanavian Review 59(1971):365-373.

Nesheim, A. Introducing the Lapps. Oslo: N.p., 1963.

Nickul, Karl. "Administrative Situations and the Lapp Population." In Education in the North. pp. 107-111. Edited by Frank Darnell. Arctic Institute of North America, U. of Alaska, 1972.

Nordic Lapp Council. The Lapps Today in Finland, Sweden, and Norway, II. Oslo: Universititetsforlaget, 1969.

Slaatto, Erling, and Kielland, Sigrid. "The Education of Lapp Children in Norway." Educational Horizons 51(Spring, 1973):127-129.

Spencer, Arthur. The Lapps. New York: Crane, Russak, 1978.

Ulfsby, Inez Boon. "Norwegian Cross-Cultural Programs for Lapp Societies." In Education in the North, pp. 269-272. Edited by Frank Darnell. Arctic Institute of North America, U. of Alaska, 1972.

Pakistan

Farenga, Cynthia. "On Being an American Khanabadoosh." Northwestern Report 5(F, 1976):14-18. [Qualander gypsies in West Pakistan]

Shah, Farhat. "Socio-Psychological Determinants of Academic Achievement of Children in Pakistan." Dissertation Abstracts Inter-national 31 (12-A)(Je, 1971):6288.

Ziring, Lawrence. "Dilemmas in Higher Educa-tion in Pakistan: A Political Perspective." Asian Affairs: An American Review 5(My-Je, 1978):307-324.

Panama

Biesanz, John, and Smith, Luke. "Race Relations in Panama and the Canal Zone: A Comparative Analysis." American Journal of Sociology 57(1951):7-14.

Biesanz, John, and Biesanz, Mavis. "Schools in the Panama Canal Zone." Michigan Education Journal 33(1953):432-434.

Blauch, Lloyd E., and Iversen, William L. "Educational Facilities in the Canal Zone." In Education of Children on Federal Reserva-tions. Washington, DC: GPO, 1939.

Comptroller General of the United States. "Canal Zone Housing and Schools." In Study of Various Personnel Policies of the Canal Organization and Other Federal Agencies in the Canal Zone, pp. 159-188. Washington, DC: General Accounting Office, My 28, 1975.

DeWitt, Donald L. "Social and Educational Thought on the Development of the Republic of Panama, 1903-1946: An Intellectual History." Doctoral dissertation, U. of Arizona, 1972.

Johnson, Lawrence. "The Upward Extension of the Canal Zone Schools for Native Colored Children." Doctoral dissertation, Stanford U., 1949.

Joly, Luz Gracie. "Notes on the Historical, Ethnographical, and Social Status of the Negro in Panama." Notes in Anthropology 13 (1968):5-18.

Malcioln, José V. "Panama." Freedomways 4 (1964):383-391.

_____. "Panama and the Canal." Freedomways 18(1978):87-89.

Massaquol, Hans J. "Panama. It's Much More Than Just a Canal." Ebony 33(Jl, 1978):44-56.

Medina H., Andrés. "El indo en el contexto de la sociedad panameña." América Indígena 32 (1972)

Neisler, Stanley. "Blacks in Canal Zone Embarrassing to U.S." Los Angeles Times, Mr 14, 1974.

_____. "The Blacks of Panama." Nation, Je 22, 1974, [Apparent reprint of preceding item]

Morton, Allen Glenn. "The Private Schools of the British West Indians in Panama." Doctoral dissertation, George Peabody College, 1966. Univ. Microfilms Order No. 66-11,244.

_____. "The Private Schools of the British West Indians in Panama." Doctoral dissertation, George Peabody College, 1972.

Sahota, G. S. "The Distribution of the Benefits of Public Expenditure in Panama." Public Finance Quarterly 5(Ap, 1977).

U.S. Congress, 93rd, 2nd session, House of Representatives, Committee on Merchant Marine and Fisheries, Subcommittee on Panama Canal. Canal Zone Policies and Problems. Hearings... Serial No. 93-48. Washington, DC: GPO, 1975.

Westerman, George W. "Gold vs. Silver Workers in the Canal Zone." Common Ground 8(Winter, 1948):92-95. [Racial discrimination in employment and schools]

_____. "Historical Notes on West Indians on the Isthmus of Panama." Phylon 22(1961): 340-350.

Papua-New Guinea

Australian College of Education. Educational Perspectives in Papua New Guinea, 1974. ERIC ED 133 808.

Berndt, Catherine H. "Social and Cultural Change in New Guinea: Communication, and Views About 'Other People.'" Sociologus 7 (1957):38-57.

Boyle, Barbara. "A Nation of 700 Tribes-- and Troubles." Washington Post, N 25, 1973.

Burton-Bradley, B. G. "Mixed Race Society in Port Moresby." New Guinea Research Bulletin 23(1968):1-49.

Clarke, A. "Education, Economy and Society in Papua New Guinea." Master's thesis, U. of Nottingham, n.d.

Colebatch, H. K. "Educational Policy and Political Development in Australian New Guinea." Melbourne Studies in Education, 1967, pp. 102-147.

Conroy, J. D. "Occupational Prestige and Labour Market Behaviour in Papua New Guinea." Economic Record 50(S, 1974).

Curtain, Richard. "Labor Migration in Papua New Guinea: Primary School Leavers in the Towns--Present and Future Significance." In Migration and Development. Edited by Helen I. Safa and Brian M. Du Toit. Chicago, IL: Aldine, 1975.

Foster, Philip. "Dilemmas of Educational Development: What We Might Learn from the Past." Comparative Education 19(O, 1975): 375-392.

Friedlaender, Jonathan S. Patterns of Human Variation: The Demography, Genetics, and Phenetics of Bougainville Islanders. Cambridge, MA: Harvard U. Press, 1975.

Groves, William C. Native Education and Culture-Contact in New Guinea: A Scientific Approach. New York: AMS Press, 1977, orig. 1936.

Gwyther-Jones, Roy E. "Some Literacy Problems in the Territory of Papua and New Guinea." Literacy Discussion 2(Winter, 1971):7-16.

Hoglin, Ian (ed.). Anthropology in Papua New Guinea. Melbourne, Australia: Melbourne U. Press, 1973.

Inglis, Amirah. The White Women's Protection Ordinance. Sexual Anxiety and Politics in Papua, 1920-1934. New York: St. Martin's Press, 1975.

Inglis, K. "Island Without History?" New Guinea 2(1968):8-26.

Ison, Barry (ed.). Pukari: Voices of Papua New Guinea. San Diego, CA: Tofua Press, 1976. [By the Expressive Arts Department of Sogeri Senior High School]

Joyce, J. T. C. "A Preliminary Study of Cultural Differences in Values Influencing Western Education in the Enga District" (2 parts). New Guinea Psychologist 6(1974): 9-16, 63-77.

Khan, Iltija. "The Politics of Integration: Papua New Guinea." Australian Journal of Political History 20(D, 1974):360-369.

Kiki, Albert Maori. Kiki, Ten Thousand Years in a Lifetime, a New Guinea Autobiography. Melbourne, Australia: N.p., 1968.

Lampl, Michelle and others. "The Effects of Protein Supplementation on the Growth and Skeletal Maturation of New Guinean Schoolchildren." Annals of Human Biology 5(1978): 219-227.

Maddock, M. N. "The Culture Gap--What Is Formal Schooling with Its Science Education Component Doing to Papua New Guinea." Australian Science Teachers Journal 21(My, 1975):93-97.

Mair, Lucy. Australia in New Guinea, 1970. 2nd ed. International Scholarly Book Services, Inc., P.O. Box 4347, Portland, OR 97208.

Malcolm, L. A. "Some Biosocial Determinants of the Growth, Health and Nutritional Status of Papua New Guinean Preschool Children." In Biosocial Interrelations in Population Adaptation. Chicago, IL: Aldine, 1975.

Mamak, Alexander, and Bedford, Richard. Bougainvillean Nationalism: Aspects of Unity and Discord. Christchurch, New Zealand: Department of Geography, U. of Canterbury, 1974.

Mead, Margaret. "The Rights of Primitive Peoples: Papua-New Guinea, A Crucial Instance." Foreign Affairs, Ja, 1967.

Nelson, H. Papua New Guinea: Black Unity or Black Chaos. Ringwood, Victoria: Penguin, 1972.

Olewala, N. Ebia. "The Attainment of Self-Government in Papua New Guinea." Objective: Justice 6(Ja-F, 1974):6-8.

Pearse, Richard. Intergroup Attitude Change in a Tribal Society: An Experimental Study in a New Guinea School, 1970. ERIC ED 043 542.

Powell, J. P. "The Rise and Fall of U.P.N.G." Vestes: Australian Universities' Review 18 (N, 1975):111-117. [U. of Papua New Guinea]

Powell, J. P., and Wilson, Michael (eds.). Education and Rural Development in the Highlands of Papua New Guinea, 1974. ERIC ED 149 876.

Prince, J. R. Science Concepts in a Pacific Culture. Sydney: Angus and Robertson, 1969.

Prudom, K. "Out of the Stone Age." Times Educational Supplement, Ag 16, 1974.

Ralph, R. C. "Education in Papua-New Guineau: Integration Whither?" In Education in Comparative and International Perspectives, pp. 415-432. Edited by Kalil I. Gezi. New York: Holt, Rinehart & Winston, 1971.

Rowley, Charles D. The New Guinea Villager: The Impact of Colonial Rule on Primitive Society and Economy. New York: Praeger, 1966.

Seifert, William H. "Adjustment to Urbanization in Papua-New Guinea." Doctoral dissertation, Catholic U. of America, 1975. Univ. Microfilms Order No. 75-21,538.

Sharp, Nonie. "On the Politics of Ignorance: Notes on the Colonial Mentality." Arena (Australia) 41(1976). [White Australians and Papua New Guineans]

Smith, Geoffrey. Education in Papua New Guinea. Carlton South, Victoria: Melbourne U. Press, 1975.

Smith, R. "Social Relations in a Papua New Guinea Primary School." Journal of Education (Konedobu, Papua New Guinea), O, 1975.

Thomas, E. Barrington (ed.). Papua New Guinea Education. New York: Oxford U. Press, 1976.

Torrey, Barbara Boyle. "Australian Imperialism in Papua New Guinea." Bulletin of Concerned Asian Scholars 6(S-O, 1974):2-6.

Valentine, Charles A. "Changing Indigenous Societies in New Guinea." In Readings in Anthropology. Edited by Ian H. Hogbin. Melbourne, Australia: N.p., 1973.

Van der Veur, Karol, and Richardson, Penelope. Education Through the Eyes of an Indigenous Urban Elite. Canberra, Australia: New Guinea Research Unit, Australian National Unit, Australian National U., 1966.

Ward, R. G., and Lea, D. A. M. (eds.). An Atlas of Papua and New Guinea. Glasgow: Collins, 1970.

Weeks, Sheldon G. "Distribution of Educational Opportunities at Tertiary Level in Papua New Guinea." Australian Geographer 14(My, 1978): 46-49.

White, O. Parliament of 1000 Tribes. London: Heinemann, 1965.

Wilby, Peter. "Where Lecturers Earn Twice the v-c's Salary." Times Higher Education Supplement, O 22, 1976. [Universities in Papua New Guinea]

Wolfers, Edward P. Race Relations and Colonial Rule in Papua New Guinea. Sydney: Australia and New Zealand Book Co., 1975.

Wu, David Yen-Ho. "An Ethnic Minority: The Adaptation of Chinese in Papua New Guinea." Doctoral dissertation, Australian National U., 1974.

Young, R. E. "Papua New Guinea: A New Paternalism." Australian Journal of Education 20(Je, 1976):149-159.

Zable, Arnold. "Neo-Colonialism and Race Relations: New Guinea and the Pacific Rim." Race 14(Ap, 1973):393-441.

Paraguay

"The Aché Indians: Genocide in Paraguay." Akwesasne Notes 5(Early Winter, 1973):26-27.

Arens, Richard. The Forest Indians in Stroessner's Paraguay: Survival or Extinction? London: Survival International, Ja, 1978.

Arens, Richard. "Paraguayan Indian Hunt." Nation (S 24, 1973):266-268.

_____ (ed.). Genocide in Paraguay. Philadelphia: Temple U. Press, 1976.

Barreiro, Jose. "The Destruction of the Aché." Akwesasne Notes 9(Late Spring, 1977):18-19.

Carvalho-Neto, Paulo de. Antología Negro del Paraguayo. Quito, Ecuador: Anales, Editorial Universitaria, 1962.

_____. El Negro Uruguayo (Hasta la Abolición). Quito, Ecuador: Editorial Universitaria, 1965.

Corvalán, G. "El Bilinguismo en el Paraguay." Revista Paraguaya de Sociologia 13(D, 1976): 7-35.

Chase-Sardi, Miguel, and Rehnfeldt, Marilyn. "Project Marandu." American Indian Journal 3(Jl, 1977):9-14. [Indians in Paraguay]

Hack, Hendrik. "Die Kolonisation der Mennoniten in paraguayischen Chaco." Doctoral dissertation, U. of Amsterdam, 1961.

Kroeker, Peter. "Lenguas and Mennonites: A Study of Cultural Change in the Paraguayan Chaco, 1928-1970." Master's thesis, Wichita State U., 1970.

Lernoux, Penny. "Paraguay: Aborigines Face Destruction." Washington Post, Je 14, 1977.

Melia, Bartomeu (comp.). "Bibliografia sobre el 'bilinguismo' del Paraguay." Estudios Paraguayos 2(D, 1974):73-82.

Muenzel, Mark. The Aché Indians: Genocide in Paraguay. Copenhagen, Denmark: International Work Group for Indigenous Affairs, 1973.

Rubin, J. National Bilingualism in Paraguay. The Hague: Mouton, 1968.

Smith, Robert Jerome, and Melia, Bartomeu. "Genocide of the Aché-Guyaki. A Continuing Report on the Conditions of Natural World People in Paraguay." Akwesasne Notes 11 (Late Winter, 1979):25-26.

Williams, John Hoyt. "Black Labor and State Ranches: The Tabapí Experience in Paraguay." Journal of Negro History 62 (O, 1977):378-389.

_____. "Esclavos y pobladores: observaciones sobre la historia parda del Paraguay en el sighlo XIX." Revista paraguaya de la Sociología 31(S-D, 1974):7-29.

Peru

Alfaro Lagoria, Consuelo, and Zegarra Ballón, Lourdes. "Peru: Institutionalizing Zuechua." Prospects 6(1976):424-429.

Arguedas, José Maria. Deep Rivers. Tr. Frances Horning Barraclough. Austin: U. of Texas Press, 1977. [Novel]

Blanco, Hugo. Land or Death. New York: Pathfinder Press, 1973.

Bourricaud, Francois. Power and Society in Contemporary Peru. New York: Praeger, 1970.

Bowser, Frederick P. The African Slave in Colonial Peru, 1524-1650. Stanford, CA: Stanford U. Press, 1973.

_____. "The Free Person of Color in Mexico City and Lima: Manumission and Opportunity 1580-1650." In Race and Slavery in the Western Hemisphere: Quantitative Studies, pp. 331-368. Edited by Stanley L. Engerman and Eugene G. Genovese. Princeton, NJ: Princeton U. Press, 1975.

Caceres, Baldomero. "La reforma de la educación en el Perú." Educación Hoy 6(1976):52-66.

Campbell, Leon G. "Black Power in Colonial Peru: The 1779 Tax Rebellion of Lambayeque." Phylon 33(Summer, 1972):140-152.

Carruthers, Ben F. "Peru: End of a Black Trail." Black Enterprise 4(O, 1973):64.

Davies, Thomas M., Jr. Indian Integration in Peru: A Half Century of Experience, 1900-1948. Lincoln, NB: U. of Nebraska Press, 1974.

_____. "Indian Integration in Peru, 1820-1948." The Americas 30(O, 1973):184-208.

De Sagasti, Heli E. E. "Social Implications of Adult Literacy: A Study Among Migrant Women in Peru." Doctoral dissertation, U. of Pennsylvania, 1972. Univ. Microfilms Order No. 73-1374.

Drysdale, Robert S. "Education for Rural Society in Transition: The Case for Peru." Canadian and International Education 3(D, 1974):74-98.

Epstein, Erwin H. "Education and Peruanidad: 'Internal' Colonialism in the Peruvian Highlands." Comparative Education Review 15 (Je, 1971):188-201.

Espinoza-Llanos, Nicéforo Enrique. "Exploratory Analysis of Some Key Influences on Children in Southern Indian Communities of Peru with Implications for Education in Rural Schools." Doctoral dissertation, U. of Maryland, 1953.

Faron, Louis C. "Ethnicity and Social Mobility in Chancay Valley, Peru." In Actas y Memorias del XXXVII Congreso Internacional de Americanistas. Buenos Aires, 1966, I. N.p.: N.p., n.d.

Flores Ochoa, Jorge A. "Mistis and Indians: Their Relations in a Micro-region of Cuzco." International Journal of Comparative Sociology 15(1974):182-192

Fuenzalida, F. and others. El Indio y el poder el Perú. Lima: Moncloa-Campodónico, 1970.

Gerhards, Ernst. "Das Bild des Indio in der peruanischen Literatur." Doctoral dissertation, U. of Berlin, 1972.

Gilbert, Dennis L. "The Oligarchy and the Old Regime in Peru." Doctoral dissertation, Cornlell U., 1977. Univ. Microfilms Order No. 77-28,351. Ca. 1850-1968

Harth-Terre, Emilio. Negros e indios. Lima: Ed. Juan Mejia Baca, 1973.

Hoggarth, Pauline F. "Bilingualism in Calca, Department of Cuzco, Peru." Doctoral dissertation, U. of St. Andrews, 1974.

Instituto Nacional de Cultura. Cultural Policy in Peru. Paris: UNESCO, 1978.

Lewis, R. A. "Employment and Income in Low-Income Settlements of Lima, Peru." Review of Social Economy 33(O, 1975).

Lowenthal, Abraham F. (ed.). The Peruvian Experiment: Continuity and Change under Military Rule. Princeton, NJ: Princeton U. Press, 1976.

Mariategui, José Carlos. Seven Interpretive Essays on Peruvian Reality. Tr. Marjory Urquidi. Austin, TX: U. of Texas Press, 1971.

Martin, Luis. "Indian Education in Colonial Peru." Indian Education 6(Summer, 1973): 44-47.

Martin, Luis, and Pettus, Jo Ann Gewin. Scholars and Schools in Colonial Peru. Dallas, TX: School of Continuing Education, Southern Methodist U., 1973.

Martínez, Hector. "Perú: educación en las communidades indígenas." América Indígene 33(Ap-Je, 1973):539-560.

Mason, Philip. "Gradualism in Peru: Some Impressions on the Future of Ethnic Group Relations." Race, Jl, 1966.

Matos Mar, J. "Les 'Barriadas' de Lima: Un Exemple d'Integration a la Vie Urbaine." l'Urbanisation en Amerique Latine. Paris: UNESCO, 1962.

Normano, J. F., and Gerbi, Antonello. Japanese in South America. New York: Day, 1943. [Especially Peru]

Núñez del Prado, Oscar, with Whyte, William F. Kuyo Chico: Applied Anthropology in an Indian Community. Chicago, IL: U. of Chicago Press, 1973.

Paulston, Rolland G. Society, Schools and Progress in Peru. London: Pergamon, 1971.

_____. "United States Educational Intervention in Peru, 1909-1968." Paedagogica Historica 11(1971):426-454.

"Peru's Rural Reform Plans Seem to Bypass Indian Village." New York Times, D 24, 1976. [La Merced de Chaute]

Piel, Jean. "L'importation de main-d'oeuvre chinoise et le développment agricole au Pérou au XIXème siècle." Cahiers des Ameriques Latines 9-10(1974):87-104.

Primov, George P. "Ethnicity in Highland Peru." Doctoral dissertation, U. of Washington, 1975.

_____. "The School as an Obstacle to Structural Integration among Peruvian Indians." Education and Urban Society 10(F, 1978):209-22 222.

Smith, Richard Chase. The Amuesha People of Central Peru: Their Struggle to Survive. Copenhagen: International Work Group for Indigenous Affairs, 1974.

Spalding, Karen W. "Indian Rural Society in Colonial Peru: The Example of Huarochirí." Doctoral dissertation, U. of California, Berkeley, 1967.

Stein, William W. Modernization and Inequality in Vicos, Peru: An Examination of the "Ignorance of Women." Buffalo: Council on International Studies, State U. of New York at Buffalo, 1975.

Stewart, Watt. Chinese Bondage in Peru: A History of the Chinese Coolie in Peru, 1849-1974. Durham, NC: Duke U. Press, 1951.

Tigner, James L. "The Ryukyuans in Peru, 1906-1952." The Americas 35(Jl, 1978): 20-44.

Van den Berghe, Pierre L. "Education, Class, and Ethnicity in Southern Peru: Revolutionary Colonialism." In Education and Colonialism, pp. 270-298. Edited by Philip G. Altbach and Gail P. Kelly. New York: Longman, 1978.

_____ (ed.). Class and Ethnicity in Peru. Leiden, The Netherlands: E. J. Brill, 1974.

Varallános, José. El cholo y el Peru. Buenos Aires: Imprenta Lopez, 1962.

Varese, Stefano. The Forest Indians in the Present Political Situation of Peru. Copenhagen, Denmark: International Work Group for Indigenous Affairs, 1972.

Wachtel, Natan. La vision des vaincus: Les indiens du Pérou devant la Conquête espagnole. Paris: Gallimard, 1971.

_____. The Vision of the Vanquished: The Spanish Conquest of Peru through Indian Eyes, 1530-1570. London: Harvester Press, 1977.

Walter, John P. Deprived Urban Youth: An Economic and Cross-Cultural Analysis of the United States, Colombia, and Peru. New York: Praeger, 1975.

Webb, Richard Charles. Government Policy and the Distribution of Income in Peru, 1963-1973. Cambridge, MA: Harvard U. Press, 1977.

Phillipines

Agoncillo, Teodoro. "The Cultural Aspect of the Japanese Occupation." Philippine Social Science and Humanities Review 28(1963): 351-394.

_____. A Short History of the Philippines. New York: Mentor, 1969.

Agoncillo, T. M., and Alfonso, O. M. A Short History of the Filipino People. Quezon City, P.I.: U. of the Philippines, 1960.

Alatas, Hussein S. The Myth of the Lazy Native: A Study of the Image of the Malays, Filipinos and Javanese from the 16th to the 20th Century and Its Function in the Ideology of Colonial Capitalism. London: Cass, 1977.

Alexander, Carter. "A Transplanted Educational Administration--the Philippine School System." School and Society 23(Je 5, 1926): 697-707.

Alzona, Encarnación. A History of Education in the Philippines, 1565-1930. Manila: U. of Philippines Press, 1932.

_____. The Filipino Woman, 1565-1937. Manila, P.I.: N.p., 1937.

Amyot, Jacques. "The Chinese Community of Manila..." Doctoral dissertation, U. of Chicago, 1960.

Ang, Teresita. "Research Studies on the Chinese Minority in the Philippines. A Selected Survey." Philippines Sociological Review 24 (1976):25-50.

Arcilla, José S. "Philippine Education: Some Observations from History." Philippine Studies 20(1972):273-286.

Arong, Jose R. T. "Schooled in Conflict: The Impact of Education and Culture in Ethno-Religious Conflict in Southern Philippines." Doctoral dissertation, Stanford U., 1976. Univ. Microfilms Order No. 76-18,744. [Suli]

Baban, Nicolas Paez. "A History of Education in the Philippines, 1898-1904." Master's thesis, Silliman U., Philippines.

Baumgartner, Joseph. "The National Language, Bilingualism and Literacy: Some Questions on the Current Policy." Philippine Quarterly of Culture and Society 5(1977): 266-270.

Bazaco, Evergisto. History of Education in the Philippines. Vol. I: Spanish Period--1565-1898. Manila: U. of Santo Tomas Press, 1939.

Benabarre, B. "Public Funds for Private Schools in a Democracy." Doctoral dissertation, Centro Escolar U., Manila, 1958.

Benitez, C. History of the Philippines. Boston: Ginn, 1954.

Bernad, Miguel A. "The Structure and Culture of Philippine Society Before the Spanish Conquest." Asian Pacific Quarterly, Summer, 1972.

Blaker, James Ronald. "The Chinese in the Philippines: A Study of Power and Change." Doctoral dissertation, Ohio State U., 1970. Univ. Microfilms Order No. 70-26252.

Blondin, Jacqueline Eugenie. "Development and Testing of a Model for the Adaptation of a Learning System from an American Culture to a Philippine Culture." Doctoral dissertation, Michigan State U., 1974.

Blount, James H. American Occupation of the Philippines, 1898-1912. New York: Putnam's, 1912.

_____. American Occupation of the Philippines. Manila, P.I.: Malaya Books, 1968.

Cabrera, Agustin A. "Status of the Education of the Badjaos of Sulu." Master's thesis, U. of Santa Tomas, 1967.

Calog, Doris S. "Historical Survey of Philippine Education under American Occupation, 1898-1934." Master's thesis, Dominican College, San Rafael, CA, 1967.

Cariño, Benjamin V. "Hope or Despair: A Comparative Study of Slum and Squatter Communities in Five Philippine Cities." Philippine Planning Journal 8(1971):8-14.

Castaneda, Esperanza Aurora G. "Survey of Philippine Educators' Views Concerning the Language Problem of the Philippines." Doctoral dissertation, United States International U., CA, 1968. Univ. Microfilms Order No. 69-19827.

Catapang, Vincent R. The Development of the Present Status of Education in the Philippine Islands. Boston, MA: The Stratford Company, 1926.

Constantino, Renato. Dissent and Counter-Consciousness. Quezon City, Philippines: Malaya Books, 1970.

Corpuz, Onofre D. "Western Colonization and the Filipino Response." Journal of Southeast Asia History 3(Mr, 1962):1-23.

Counts, George S. "Education in the Philippines." Elementary School Journal 26 (O, 1925):94-106.

Darrach, Marie L. "Manila and English." Commonweal 12(Ag 20, 1930):401-403.

Doeppers, Daniel F. "Ethnicity and Class in the Structure of Philippine Cities." Doctoral dissertation, Syracuse U., 1971.

_____. "'Ethnic Urbanism' and Philippine Cities." Annals of the Association of American Georgraphers 64(D, 1974):549-559.

Dulatre-Padilla, Luz. "The Status of Chinese Secondary Schools in the City of Manila." Master's thesis, U. of the Philippines, 1954.

Engel, Charles. "Health Problems in the Philippines in the American Era." Bull. Am. Hist. Collect. (Manila) 4(Jl, 1976):18-32.

Escultura, Edgar E. "The Roots of Backwardness: An Analysis of the Philippine Condition." Science and Society 38(Spring, 1974):49-76.

Fe Jamias, Maria and others. "Ethnic Awareness in Filipino Children." Journal of School Psychology 83(Ap, 1971):157-164.

Feliciano, Gloria D. "Toward an Effective Medium of Communication for the Filipino Masses." Asian Studies 8(1970):196-202.

Felix, Alfonso L., Jr. "Colonial Society in the Philippines." Bull. Am. Hist. Collect. (Manila) 6(Ja-Mr, 1978):30-51.

Flores, Dominador A., Jr. "Colonial Education and the Political Acculturation of the Filipinos." Doctoral dissertation, Indiana U., 1969.

Foley, Douglas E. "Colonialism and Schooling in the Philippines from 1898 to 1970." In Education and Colonialism, pp. 69-95. Edited by Philip G. Altbach and Gail P. Kelly. New York: Longman, 1978.

_____. Philippine Rural Education: An Anthropological Perspective. Dekalb, IL: Center for Southeast Asian Studies, Northern Illinois U., 1976.

Forbes, W. C. The Philippine Islands. 2 vols. Boston, MA: Houghton Mifflin, 1928.

Fox, Robert B., and Flory, Elizabeth H. (comps.). The Filipino People: Differentiation and Distribution Based on Linguistic, Cultural and Racial Criteria. Manila: National Museum of the Philippines, 1974. [Five-color map]

Francisco, Luzvininda. "The First Vietnam: The U.S.-Philippine War of 1899." Bulletin of Concerned Asian Scholars 5(D, 1973):2-16.

Frei, Ernest J. "The Historical Development of the Philippine National Language." Philippine Social Sciences and Humanities Review 14-15 (1949-1950).

Fuchs, Elinor, and Antler, Joyce. Year One of the Empire. Boston, MA: Houghton Mifflin, 1973. [Filipino rebellion, 1899]

Gates, John M. Schoolbooks and Krags. The United States Army in the Philippines, 1898-1902. Westport, CT: Greenwood Press, 1973.

Gonzalez Garcia, Alfonso. "An Historical Study of the Legal and Constitutional Bases of Public Elementary Education in the Philippines." Doctoral dissertation, U. of Michigan, 1959. Univ. Microfilms Order No. 59-2116.

Giesecke, Len. "History of American Economic Policy in the Philippines During the American Colonial Period, 1900-1935." Doctoral dissertation, U. of Texas, 1974.

Gonzalez, Andrew B. "The 1973 Constitution and the Bilingual Education Policy of the Department of Education and Culture." Philippine Studies 22(1974):325-337.

Gowing, Peter Gordon. "Mandate in Moroland: The American Government of Muslim Filipinos, 1899-1920." Doctoral dissertation, Syracuse U., 1968.

_____. "Muslim Filipinos Between Integration and Secession." South East Asia Journal of Theology 14(1973):64-77.

_____. "Of Different Minds: Muslim and Christian Perceptions of the Mindanao Problem." Philippine Quarterly of Culture and Society 5(1977):243-252.

Graff, H. F. American Imperialism and the Philippine Insurrection. Boston, MA: N.p., 1969.

Green, Justin J. "Children and Politics in the Philippines: Socialization for Stability in a Highly Stratified Society." Asian Survey 17(J1, 1977):667-678.

Guerrero, Amado. Philippine Society and Revolution. Hong Kong: Ta Kung Pao, 1971.

Guerrero, Amor C. "The Socio-Economic Composition of the Student Body in the University of the Philippines Quezon City." Master's thesis, U. of the Philippines, 1955.

Guthrie, G. M. The Filipino Child and Philippine Society. Manila: Philippine U. Press, 1961.

Hidalgo, Cesar A. (comp.). "Linguistic Problems in Minority/Majority Group Relations in Southeast Asian Countries: Selected Works." J. Siam Soc. 63(J1, 1975):145-155.

Hidalgo, Mariano O. "Social Classes in the Philippines and their Implications for Education." Educational Quarterly 5(D, 1957-Mr, 1958):258-272.

Hunt, Chester L. "'Americanization' Process in the Philippines." India Quarterly 12(1956):117-130.

_____. "Cotabato: Melting Pot of the Philippines." Philippine Social Sciences and Humanities Review 19(1954):40-72.

Jamais, M. F., Pablo, R. Y., and Taylor, D. M. "Ethnic Awareness in Filipino Children." Journal of Social Psychology 83(1971).

Jensen, Khin Khin Myint. "The Chinese in the Philippines during the American Regime, 1898-1946." Doctoral dissertation, U. of Wisconsin, 1956.

Lear, Elmer Norton. "Education in Guerrilla Territory under a Regime of Enemy Occupation." History of Education Quarterly 7(Fall, 1967): 312-328 [Leyte]

_____. The Japanese Occupation of the Philippines, Leyte, 1941-1945. Ithaca, NY: Cornell U. Press, 1961.

Mahajani, Usha. Philippine Nationalism: External Challenge and Filipino Response, 1565-1946. Brisbane, Australia: Queensland U. Press, 1971.

Jenks, A. E. "Assimilation in the Philippines, as Interpreted in Terms of Assimilation in America." American Journal of Sociology 19(1913-1914):773-791.

Jensen, Irene K. K. M. The Chinese in the Philippines During the American Regime: 1898-1946. San Francisco, CA: R and E Research Associates, 1975.

Jornacion, George William. "The Time of the Eagles: United States Army Officers and the Pacification of the Philippine Moros, 1899-1913." Doctoral dissertation, U. of Maine, 1973. Univ. Microfilms Order No. 74-10,112.

Eng Kist Koh. "American Educational Policy in the Philippines and the British Policy in Malaya, 1898-1935." Comparative Education Review, Je, 1965.

Lacuesta, Y., and Gascon, Manuel. "The History of the Preparation of High School Teachers in the Philippines, 1901-1941." Doctoral dissertation, Columbia U., 1958. Univ. Microfilms Order No. 58-02693.

Landa-Jocano, Felipe. "Philippines at Spanish Contact: An Essay in Ethnohistory." In Brown Heritage: Essays on Philippine Cultural Tradition and Literature, pp. 49-89. Edited by Antonio G. Manuud. Quezon City, P.I.: Ateneo de Manila U. Press, 1967.

Landa-Jocano, F. Slum As a Way of Life. Quezon City, Philippines: U. of the Philippines Press, 1975. [Manila]

Lear, Elmer Norton. "Collaboration, Resistance, and Liberation: A Study of Society and Education in Leyte, The Philippines, Under Japanese Occupation." Doctoral dissertation, Columbia U., 1951. Univ. Microfilms Order No. 00-03358.

Lebar, Frank M. (ed.). Ethnic Groups of Insular Southeast Asia. Vol. II: Philippines and Formosa. New Haven, CT: Human Relations Area Files Press, 1975.

Liban, Pura T. "The Culture of the Ybang: Its Educational Implications." J. N. Luzon 4(J1, 1973):1-54.

Lim, Benito. "The Silent Majority." Philippine Sociological Review 24(1976):17-24.

Lopez, Violetta B. "Culture Contact and Ethnogenesis in Mindoro up to the End of the Spanish Rule." Asian Stud. 12(Ap, 1974):1-39.

Luna, Severino N. Born Primitive in the Philippines. Ed. Irene Murphy. Carbondale, IL: Southern Illinois U. Press, 1975.

McBeath, Gerald A. Political Integration of the Philippine Chinese. Berkeley, CA: Center for South and Southeast Asia Studies, U. of California, 1973.

Magdalena, Federico v. "Intergroup Conflict in the Southern Philippines: An Empirical Analysis." Journal of Peace Res. 14(1977): 299-314.

Mahajani, Usha. Philippine Nationalism: External Challenge and Filipino Response, 1565-1946. St. Lucia, Queensland: U. of Queensland Press, 1971.

Mahmoud, M. F. "The Muslim Problem and the Government's Response." Philippine Journal of Public Administration 18(J1, 1974):215-225.

Manuud, Antonio G. (ed.). Brown Heritage: Essays on Philippine Cultural Tradition and Literature. Quezon City, P.I.: Ateneo de Manila U. Press, 1967.

May, Glenn A. "Social Engineering in the Philippines: Aims and Execution of American Educational Policy, 1900-1913." Philippine Stud. 24(1976):135-183.

Medina, Ricardo C. "The Extent and Causes of Dropouts of Mohammedan Pupils in Zamboanga City." Master's thesis, U. of the Philippines, 1961.

Molony, Carol Hodson. "Multilingualism and Social Behavior in the Southern Philippines." Doctoral dissertation, Stanford U., 1969. Univ. Microfilms Order No. 70-01577.

Morales, Alfredo T. "Anthropology and Education Change in the Philippines." In Anthropology: Range and Relevance (A Reader for Non-Anthropologists). Edited by Mario Zamora and Zeus A. Salazar. Quezon City: Kayumanggi, 1975.

Niu, Paul. "A Study of the Curricular Problems in Philippine-Chinese Schools." Master's thesis, Ateneo de Manila U., 1964.

Noble, Lela Garner. "The Moro National Liberation Front in the Philippines." Pacific Affairs 49(Fall, 1976):405-424.

Oades, Rizalino A. "The Social and Economic Background of Philippine Nationalism, 1830-1892." Doctoral dissertation, U. of Hawaii, 1974. Univ. Microfilms Order No. 74-27,686.

O'Shaughnessey, Thomas J. "How Many Muslims Has the Philippines?" Philippine Stud. 23 (1975):375-392.

Osias, Camilo. Barrio Life and Barrio Education. Yonkers-on-Hudson, NY: World Book Company, 1921.

_____. Our Education and Dynamic Filipinism. Manila, P.I.: Oriental Commercial Company, Inc., 1927.

Owen, Norman G. Comprador Colonialism: Studies on the Philippines under American Rule. Ann Arbor: U. of Michigan Papers on South and Southeast Asia, 1971.

Palanca, Ellen H. "The Economic Position of the Chinese in the Philippines." Philippine Stud. 25(1977):80-94.

Pascasio, Emy M. "Bilingual Competence for the Filipinos: A Realistic Educational Goal." Regional English Language Centre Journal 4(Je, 1973):9-24.

_____. "The Language Situation in the Philippines from the Spanish Era to the Present." In Brown Heritage: Essays on Philippine Cultural Tradition and Literature, pp. 225-252. Edited by Antonio G. Manuud. Quezon City, P.I.: Ateneo de Manila U. Press, 1967.

Pecson, Geronima T., and Racelis, Maria (eds.). Tales of the American Teachers in the Philippines. Manila: Carmelo and Bauerman, 1959.

Perlman, Daniel H. "Higher Education in the Philippines: An Overview and Current Problems." Peabody Journal of Education 55 (Ja, 1978):119-126.

Phelan, John Leddy. The Hispanization of the Philippines: Spanish Aims and Filipino Responses, 1565-1700. Madison, WI: U. of Wisconsin Press, 1959.

Philippine Islands Board of Educational Survey. A Survey of the Educational System of the Philippine Islands. Manila: Bureau of Printing, 1925.

Ragsdale, Jane S. "Coping With the Yankees: The Filipino Elite, 1898-1903." Doctoral dissertation, U. of Wisconsin, 1975. Univ. Microfilms Order No. 75-9994.

Ramos Peña, Laura. "The Public School Systems of Puerto Rico and the Philippine Islands: An Introductory Comparative Study (Historical Approach)." Master's thesis, U. of Puerto Rico, n.d.

Romero, René C. "The Flowering of Philippine Education under the American Regime (1898-1923)." Bull. Am. Hist. Collect. (Manila) 4(Ap, 1976):14-24.

Rutland, Lolita Garcia. "The History of Teacher Education in the Philippines to 1955." Doctoral dissertation, U. of Florida, 1955. Univ. Microfilms Order No. 00-14328.

Saber, Mamitua. "Majority-Minority Situation in the Philippines." Solidarity 10(J1-Ag, 1975):36-47.

Salamanca, Bonifacio S. "The Filipinos and American Educational Policies." In The Filipino Reaction to American Rule 1901-1913, pp. 76-95. N.p.: Shoe String Press, 1968.

Sals, Florent Joseph. "A Study of Primitive Education Among the Ifugaos." Master's thesis, Ateneo de Manila U., 1952.

San Agustin, Araceli. "The Moro Way of Life and the Philippine Public School System." Master's thesis, U. of the Philippines, 1959.

Santiago, Domingo C. "History of Philippine Education During the Japanese Occupation." Master's thesis, U. of the Philippines, 1951.

Schirmer, Daniel B. Republic or Empire. American Resistance to the Philippine War. Cambridge, MA: Schenkman, 1972.

Schumacher, John N. "Philippine Higher Education and the Origins of Nationalism." Philippine Studies 23(1975):53-66.

Schwartz, Karl. "Filipino Education and Spanish Colonialism: Toward an Autonomous Perspective." Comparative Education Review 15(Je, 1971):202-218.

Scott, William Henry. The Discovery of the Igorots: Spanish Contacts With the Pagans of Northern Luzon. Quezon City, Philippines: New Day Publishers, 1974.

Silliman, Rachel Gadiane. "The Visayans and Pilipino: A Study of Regional Elite Attitudes, Nationalism, and Language Planning in the Philippines." Doctoral dissertation, Claremont Graduate School, 1976. Univ. Microfilms Order No. 76-16639.

Simbulan, Dante C. "A Study of the Socio-Economic Elite in Philippine Politics and Government 1946-1963." Doctoral dissertation, Australia National U., 1965.

Smith, Mary Ann and others. "An Adult Education Programme for the Igorot Women of Northern Philippines." Convergence 8(1975): 16-22.

The Social Background of Students and Their Prospects for Success at School. Philippines National Commission for UNESCO, My, 1971. ERIC ED 060 275.

Social Integration of the Philippines. Manila, P.I.: Philippine Independence Commission, 1924.

Stanley, Peter W. A Nation in the Making. The Philippines and the United States, 1899-1921. Cambridge, MA: Harvard U. Press, 1974.

Steen, John P. Van de. "Critical Issues in Bontoc Education." Master's thesis, Ateneo de Manila U., 1956.

Stone, Richard L. "Some Aspects of Muslim Social Organization." In Brown Heritage: Essays on Philippine Cultural Tradition and Literature, pp. 90-133. Edited by Antonio G. Manuud. Quezon City, P.I.: Ateneo de Manila U. Press, 1967.

Survey of the Educational System of the Philippine Islands. Board of Educational Survey created under acts 3162 and 3196 of the Philippine Legislature. Manila: Bureau of Printing, 1925.

Tadaoan, Pio M. "A Critical Study of the Educational Problems of the Non-Christian Tribes of the Mountain Province." Master's thesis, U. of the Philippines, 1953.

_____. "Education in the Mountain Province." Sagada Social Studies 4(Je, 1955):1-61. [Sagada, Mt. Province]

Tan, Antonio S. "The Emergence of Philippine Chinese National and Political Consciousness, 1880-1935." Doctoral dissertation, U. of California, 1969.

Tan, Samuel Kong. "The Muslim Armed Struggle in the Philippines, 1900-1941." Doctoral dissertation, Syracuse U., 1973. Univ. Microfilms Order No. 74-17,633.

Taylor, D. M., and Gardner, R. C. "Role of Stereotypes in Communication Between Ethnic Groups in the Philippines." Social Force, D, 1970.

Terrenal, Regina C. "A Socio-Economic and Educational Study of the Tinguians of Central Abra." Master's thesis, U. of San Carlos, 1964.

Thomas, Ralph Benjamin. "Muslim But Filipino: The Integration of Philippine Muslims, 1917-1946." Doctoral dissertation, U. of Pennsylvania, 1971. Univ. Microfilms Order No. 72-6242.

Tilman, Robert O. "The Impact of American Education on the Philippines." Asia (N.Y.C.), Spring, 1971.

Tovera, David Garcia. "A History of English Teaching in the Philippines: From Unilingualism to Bilingualism." Doctoral dissertation, Northwestern U., 1975. Univ. Microfilms Order No. 75-29771.

Ulack, Richard. "Migration to the Slum and Squatter Communities of Cagayan de Oro City, the Philippines." International Migration Review 10(Fall, 1976):355-376.

Utrecht, Ernst. "The Separatist Movement in the Southern Philippines." Race and Class 16(Ap, 1975):387-403.

Villamin, Arceli M. "Bilingual Research in the Philippines." Reading Teacher 31(N, 1977): 189-192.

Weightman, George H. "Anti-sinicism in the Philippines." Asian Studies 5(Ap, 1967): 220-231.

Wery, R. and others. "Population, Employment, and Poverty in the Philippines." World Development 6(Ap, 1978).

Whitwell, Charles Garland. "Spanish Educational Policy in the Philippine Islands." Doctoral dissertation, U. of Texas, 1940.

Wickberg, Edgar B. The Chinese in Philippine Life, 1850-1898. New Haven, CT: Yale U. Press, 1965.

_____. "The Chinese Mestizo in Philippine History." Journal of Southeast Asian History 5(Mr, 1964):62-100.

Worchester, D. C. Philippines, Past and Present. New York: The Macmillan Company, 1930.
Yabes, Leopoldo. "The Filipino Scholar." Philippine Social Science and Humanities Review 28(1963):319-350.

Zamora, Mario D. "The Hispanization Process: Traditions and Methods in Colonial Change in Village Philippines." Eastern Anthropologist 28(Jl-S, 1975).

Poland

Apenszlak, Jacob and others. The Black Book of Polish Jewry: The Martyrdom of Polish Jewry under the Nazi Occupation. American Federation for Polish Jews, 1943.

Bak, Józef. "Count Stanislaw Sharbek's Foundation at Drohowyz. An Historical Outline of the Education of Orphans to 1914." Stud. Hist. 1(1975):71-100. [In Polish, with English summary]

Bartoszewski, Wladyslaw, and Lewin, Zofia. The Samaritans: Heroes of the Holocaust. Ed. Alexander T. Jordan. New York: Twayne, 1972. [Polish aid to Jews during Nazi occupation of Poland during World War II]

Bohdanowicz, L. "The Muslims in Poland--Their Origin, History, and Cultural Life." Journal of the Royal Asiatic Society, O, 1942.

Bojarska, B., and Pospieszalski, K. "The German Schools for Polish Children in Occupied Poznán." Przeglad Zachodni 1(1972). [In Polish; English summary]

Bojarska, Barbara. Extermination of the Polish Intelligentsia in the Gdańsk-Pomerania Region (in Polish). Poznan: Instytut Zachodni, 1972.

Chalasinski, Jozef. The Young Rural Generation in the Polish People's Republic: Autobiographies, Personalities. Things and Events, Biography and History, Ag, 1976. ERIC ED 135 511.

Ciolkosz, Adam. "'Anti-Zionism' in Polish Party Politics." Wiener Library Bulletin 22 (Summer, 1968):2-9.

Czepulis-Rastenis, Ryszarda. "La structure et la situation sociale de l'intelligentsia du Royaume de Pologne dans la période entre l'insurrection de 1830 et celle de 1863." Acta Poloniae Hist. 33(1976):69-92.

Davis, Horace B. (ed.). The National Question. Selected Writings by Rosa Luxemburg. New York: Monthly Review Press, 1977.

Dobroszycki, Lucjan. "Restoring Jewish Life in Post-War Poland." Soviet Jewish Affairs 3(1973):58-72.

Dobroszycki, Lucjan, and Kirschenblatt-Gimblett, Barbara. Image Before My Eyes: A Photographic History of Jewish Life in Poland, 1864-1939. New York: Schocken, 1977.

Drozdowski, Marian. "The National Minorities in Poland in 1918-1939." Acta Poloniae Historica 22(1970).

Druker, Abraham. "Fight Against Ghetto Benches in Polish Universities" and "Ghettos for Jewish Students in Warsaw Colleges." School and Society 46(1937):502, 591.

Eisenstein, Miriam. Jewish Schools in Poland, 1919-1939: Their Philosophy and Development. New York: King's Crown Press, 1950.

Eitzen, D. Stanley. "Two Minorities: The Jews of Poland and the Chinese of the Philippines." Jewish Journal of Sociology, D, 1968.

Firkowska, Anna and others. "Cognitive Development and Social Policy." Science 200(Je, 1978):1357-1362.

Fishman, Joshua A. (ed.). Studies on Polish Jewry, 1919-1931: The Interplay of Social, Economic and Political Factors in the Struggle of a Minority for Its Existence. New York: Yivo Institute for Jewish Research, 1974.

Fiszman, Joseph R. "Education and Equality of Opportunity in Eastern Europe, with Special Focus on Poland." Politics and Society 7 (1977).

_____. "Education and Social Mobility in People's Poland." Polish Review 16(Summer, 1971):5-31.

_____. Revolution and Tradition in People's Poland: Education and Socialization. Princeton, NJ: Princeton U. Press, 1972.

Furie, William B. "A History of Jewish Education in Poland Before 1765." Doctoral dissertation, Boston U., 1939.

Galeski, Boguslaw (ed.). Rural Sociology in Poland, 1976. ERIC ED 135 578.

Gitman, Joseph. "The Jews and Jewish Problems in the Polish Parliament, 1919-1939." Doctoral dissertation, Yale U., 1963. Univ. Microfilms Order No. 67-10,345.

Goldberg, Itche, and Suhl, Yuri (eds.). The End of a Thousand Years. The Recent Exodus of the Jews from Poland, 1971. Committee for Jews of Poland, 1 Union Square, W., Room 409, New York, NY 10003.

Goldberg, Jacob. "Poles and Jews in the 17th and 18th Centuries. Rejection and Acceptance." Jb. Gesch. Osteuropas 22 (1974):248-282.

Golebiowski, Bronislaw. The Young Generation's Aspirations and Orientations, Ag, 1976. ERIC ED 135 512.

Goodhart, Arthur L. Poland and the Minority Race. New York: Brentano's, 1920.

Gross, Jan Tomasz. Polish Society under German Occupation: the Generalgouvernement, 1939-1944. Princeton, NJ: Princeton U. Press, 1979.

Groth, Alexander J. "Dimoski, Pilsudski, and Ethnic Conflict in Pre-1939 Poland." Canadian Slavic Studies, Spring, 1969.

Gurdus, Luba Krugman. The Death Train: A Personal Account of a Holocaust Survivor. New York: National Council on Art in Jewish Life, 1978. [Nazi-occupied Poland]

Hauptkommission zur Untersuchung der Naziverbrechen in Polen. Verbrechen an Polnischen Kindern, 1939-1945. Warschau: Polnischer Verlag der Wissenschaften, 1973. [Nazi persecution of Polish children, mainly Jews]

Heller, Celia S. On the Edge of Destruction: The Jews of Poland Between the Two World Wars. New York: Columbia U. Press, 1976.

Horak, Stephan. Poland and Her National Minorities, 1919-39. New York: Vantage, 1961.

Jalowiecki, Bohdan. "Applied Sociology as an Instrument for Area Planning." Polish Sociological Bulletin (Warsaw) 15(1967). [Deals with the concept of neighborhood]

Jedruszczak, Tadeusz. "Anti-Nazi Organizations of the Resistance Movement in Poland (1939-1945)." Polish W. Aff. 2(1975):168-204.

Kar, Anthony L. "The Response of the People to the Use of Formal Education in the Attempted Denationalization of Poland, 1795-1914." Doctoral dissertation, U. of Michigan, n.d.

Katz, Alfred. Poland's Ghettos at War. New York: Twayne, 1971.

Klessman, Christoph. Die Selbstbehauptung einer Nation: Nationalsozialistische Kulturpolitik und polnische Widerstandsbewegung im Generalgouvernement, 1939-1945. Düsseldorf: Bertelsmann Universitats-verlag, 1971.

Kloskowska, Antonina. "The Negroes as Seen by Polish Children." International Journal of Comparative Sociology 3(1962):189-199.

Kolankiewicz, George. "The Technical Intelligentsia." In Social Groups in Polish Society. Edited by David Lane and George Kolankiewicz. New York: Columbia U. Press, 1973.

Korczak, Janusz Goldszmit, Henryk . Ghetto Diary. New York: Schocken, 1978. [Jewish children in the Warsaw ghetto]

Korzec, Pawel. "Polen unter der Minderheitenschutz Vertag (1919-1934)." Jb. Gesch. Osteuropas 22(No. 4, 1974):515-555.

Kowalewski, Z. "Ecological Aspects of Intellectual and Cultural Divisions in People's Poland." Kultura i Spoleczenstwo 10(1966). [In Polish]

Kozakiewicz, Mikolaj. Theoretical and Practical Implications of the Different Meanings of Unequal Access to Education, Ag, 1976. ERIC ED 135 513.

Krakowski, S. "The Slaughter of Polish Jewry--A Polish 'Reassessment.'" Wiener Library Bulletin 26(1972-1973):13-20.

Krekeler, Norbert. Revisionsanspruch und geheime Ostpolitik der Weimarer Republik. Die Subventionierung der deutschen Minderheit in Polen. Stuggart: Deutsche Verlags-Anstalt, 1973.

Kwilecki, Andrzej. "Polish Western Territories in Sociological Research and Theory." Polish Sociological Bulletin 2(1968):61-68.

Lane, David, and Kolankiewicz, George (eds.). Social Groups in Polish Society. New York: Colubmia U. Press, 1973.

Lichtenstein, Erwin. "Der Kulturbund der Juden in Danzig, 1933-1938." Z. Gesch. Juden 10 (1973):181-190.

Ligman, Mary T. "The League of Nations and German Minorities in Poland." Master's thesis, De Paul U., 1936.

McKinley, Jane. "A Survey of the Status of the Jews and the Germans in Poland Up to 1939." Master's thesis, Loyola U., Chicago, 1948.

Majewski, Sanislaw. "Nazi School Politics in the District of Kielce, 1939-45." Studia Hist. 1(1978):91-106. [In Polish with English summary]

Matejko, Alexander. Social Change and Stratification in Eastern Europe: An Interpretive Analysis of Poland and Her Neighbors. New York: Praeger, 1974.

Maurer, Jadwiga. "The Jew in Contemporary Polish Writing." Wiener Library Bulletin 21 (Autumn, 1967):26-30.

Mendelsohn, Ezra. "The Politics of Agudas Yisroel in Inter-War Poland." Soviet Jewish Affairs 2(1972):47-60.

Miaso, Jozef. "Clandestine Education in Poland in the Years of the Nazi Occupation, World War II." Polish W. Aff. 1(1978):104-112.

Mikula, Mary F. "The Fate of the Jews in Poland During World War II." Master's thesis, Marquette U., 1962.

Moorman, Paul. "Coming Top of the Form Sets Poles Apart." Times Educational Supplement, Ap 1, 1977.

_____. "Shake-Up Puts Learning Society in Vanguard of New Revolution." Times Educational Supplement, Ja 11, 1974.

_____. "Warsaw Notebook." Times Educational Supplement, D 14, 1973.

Motzkin, Leo. La campagne antisémite en Pologne. Paris: Rousseau, 1932.

Nakielska, Zofia. Social Obstacles Towards Success of Pupils in Polish Primary Schools, Ag, 1976. ED 128 123.

Nowacki, Tadeusz. "Die Lehrer und die Volksbildung in Polen während der Hitler-okkupation von 1939 bis 1944." Vergleichende Pädagogik 2(1966):67-79.

Nowak, Irena. "Some Differences of Social Contact Patterns among Various Social Strata." Polish Sociological Bulletin 2 (1966):135-143.

Nowakowski, Stefan. "Egalitarian Tendencies and the New Social Hierarchy in an Industrial-Urban Community in the Western Territories." Polish Sociological Bulletin 2(1964).

_____. "Social Integration in the Opole District in Western Territories." Polish Sociological Bulletin 2(1963):58-66.

Pleśniarski, Boleslaw. "Die polnische Bildung und polnische Schule in den Jahren der Hitlerbesatzung (1939-1945)." Vierteljahrsschrift für Wissenschaftliche Pädagogik 52(1976):213-225.

Pougatch-Zalcman, Léna. Les enfants de Vilna. Une expérience pédagogique. Tournai, France: Casterman, 1970. [Tarbut schools]

Rabinowicz, Harry M. The Legacy of Polish Jewry: A History of Polish Jews in the Inter-War Years 1919-1939. New York: Thomas Yoseloff, 1965.

Radziejowski, Janusz. "Roman Rosdolsky: Man, Activist and Scholar." Science and Society 42(Summer, 1978):198-210. [Ukranians in Poland]

Ringelblum, Emanuel. Polish-Jewish Relations During the Second World War. New York: Fertig, 1976.

Ronge, Wolfgang. "Der Wandel der Klassen-struktur und die Umgestaltung der Intelligenz in Polen." Doctoral dissertation, U. of Muenster, 1972.

Rosenfeld, Max. "Secularism and Our Heritage. The Jewish Secular School Movement in Poland." Jewish Currents 30(Je, 1976):26-29.

Rosenthal, Harry K. German and Pole: National Conflict and Modern Myth. Gainesville, FL: U. Presses of Florida, 1976.

_____. "Poles, Prussians, and Elementary Education in Nineteenth-Century Posen." Can.-Am. Slavic Stud. 7(S, 1973):209-218.

Sarapate, Adam. "Stratification and Social Mobility in Poland." In Empirical Sociology in Poland. Warsaw: Polish Scientific Publishers, 1966.

Segal, Simon. The New Poland and the Jews. New York: N.p., 1938.

Serwánski, Edward, and Walczak, Marian. "The Extermination of Teachers in Great Poland during the Nazi Occupation, 1939-1945" (in Polish). Przeglad Zachodni 5-6(1972):41-75.

Shapiro, David G. "The Beginning of Polish Jewry." Master's thesis, Yeshiva U., 1969.

Simon, Maurice David. "Students, Politics and Higher Education in Socialist Poland." Doctoral dissertation, Stanford U., 1972.

Singer, Isaac Bashevis. A Day of Pleasure: Stories of a Boy Growing Up in Warsaw. New York: Farrar, Straus and Giroux, 1977. [1908-1918]

Slomczynski, Kazimierz, and Krauze, Tadeusz (eds.). Class Structure and Social Mobility in Poland. Tr. Anna M. Furdyna. White Plains, NY: M. E. Sharpe, 1978.

Szafar, Tadeusz. "'Endecized' Marxism: Polish Communist Historians en Recent Polish Jewish History." Soviet Jewish Affairs 8 (Spring, 1978).

Szczepanski, Jan. "Les classes sociales de la societe polonaise contemporaine." Cahiers internationaux de sociologie 39(1965):197-216.

_____. "Sociological Aspects of Higher Education in Poland." In Social and Political Transformation in Poland. Edited by S. Ehrlich. Warsaw: N.p., 1964.

Tellenback, Sten. "Patterns of Stratification in Socialist Poland." Acta Sociologica 17 (1974-1975):25-47.

Tims, R. W. Germanizing Prussian Poland. New York: Columbia U., 1941.

Tomala, Jerzy and others. The Access to Higher Schools in Poland (In the Aspect of Social Equality and Economic Development), Ja, 1976. ERIC ED 128 125.

Trendowski, Thomas. "Ukranian Minority in Poland, 1920-1932." Master's thesis, Wayne State U., 1938.

Turowski, Jan, and Szwengrub, Lili Maria (eds.). Rural Social Change in Poland, Ag, 1976. ERIC ED 135 510.

Tuwim, Julian. "Prewar Polish Anti-Semitism." Jewish Currents 29(F, 1975):28-30.

Vincour, Earl. Polish Jews: The Final Chapter. New York: McGraw-Hill, 1977.

Wandycz, Piotr S. The Lands of Partitioned Poland, 1795-1918. Seattle, WA: U. of Washington Press, 1975.

Weinryb, Bernard D. The Jews of Poland: A Social and Economic History of the Jewish Community in Poland from 1100 to 1800. Philadelphia: Jewish Publication Society of America, 1973.

Wesclowski, W., and Slomczyuski, K. Social Stratification in Polish Cities. Belgrade: Institut Drustvenih Nauka, 1967.

Wesolowska, Eugenia Anna. "The Role of Adult Functional Literacy in Poland." Literacy Discussion 8(Summer, 1977):25-46.

Wieliczko, Mieczyslaw. "History as a Teaching Subject in the Underground School System during the Hitlerite Occupation." An. U. Mariae Curie-Sklodowska (Sect. F) 24(1974): 279-292. [In Polish; summaries in French and Russian]

Wisniewski, Wieslaw. "The Academic Progress of Students of Different Social Origin." Polish Sociological Bulletin 1(1970):135-144.

Wyczanski, Andrzej. "Alphabétisation et structure sociale en Pologne au XVIe siècle." Annales 29(My-Je, 1974).

Wynot, Edward D., Jr. "The Case of German Schools in Polish Upper Silesia." Polish Review 2(1974):47-69.

_____. "'A Necessary Cruelty': The Emergence of Official Anti-Semitism in Poland. 1936-39." American Historical Review 76(O, 1971): 1035-1058.

_____. "The Polish Germans, 1919-1939: National Minority in a Multinational State." Polish Review, Winter, 1972.

Wysocki, B. A., and Cankardas, A. A. "A New Estimate of Polish Intelligence." Journal of Educational Psychology 48(1957):525-533.

Zagorski, Kryzystof. "Social Mobility and Education in Poland." Polish Sociological Bulletin 2(1971):5-16.

_____. "Organization and Resulting Changes in Class Structure and Education." International al Journal of Sociology 7(1977-78):48-58.

Zamoyski, Adam. "The Jews in Poland. Part I: 1264-1795." History Today 26(F, 1976):73-82.

Zurawicka, J. "The Structure of the Warsaw Intelligentsia at the End of the XIXth Century." Journal of European Economic History 5(Winter, 1976).

Portugal

Almeida, Raymond A., and Nyhan, Patricia. Cape Verde and Its People: A Short History. Part I [and] Folk Tales of the Cape Verdean People, 1976. ERIC ED 137 152.

Herzlich, Guy. "Education in Portugal." Guardian, N 30, 1975.

Russell- Wood, A. J. R. "Iberian Expansion and the Issue of Black Slavery: Changing Portuguese Attitudes, 1440-1770." American Historical Review 83(F, 1978):16-42.

Yerushalmi, Yosef H. The Lisbon Massacre of 1506 and the Royal Image in the Shebet Yehudah. Cincinnati, OH: Hebrew Union College, Jewish Institute of Religion, 1976.

Rhodesia (See: Zimbabwe)

Rumania

Boia, Lucian. Relationships between Romanians, Czechs and Slovaks, 1848-1914. Tr. Sanda Michailescu. Bucharest: Editura Academiei Republicii Socialiste, Romania, 1977.

Castellan, G. "The Germans of Rumania."
Journal of Contemporary History 6(1971):
52-75.

Gilberg, Trond. "Ethnic Minorities in
Romania under Socialism." East European
Quarterly 7(1973):435-458.

Király, Károly. "An Ethnic-Hungarian Communist
in Rumania Complains to His Party About
Bias." New York Times, F 1, 1978.

Nanay, Julia. Transylvania: The Hungarian
Minority in Rumania. Astor, FL: Danubian
Press, 1976.

Petyt, K. M. "Romania--A Multilingual Nation."
Linguistics 158(Ag 15, 1975):75-102.

Sneersohn, Hyam Z. Palestine and Roumainia:
A Description of the Holy Land and the Past
and Present State of Roumania and the
Roumanian Jews. New York: Arno, 1977,
orig. 1872.

Sozan, Michael. "Ethnocide in Rumania."
Current Anthropology 18(D, 1977):781-782.
[Hungarian minority, the Szeklers of
Transylvania]

Ussoskin, Moshe. Struggle for Survival.
Jerusalem: Academic Press, 1975. [Jews in
Romania, 1910-1950]

Volgyes, Ivan. "The Treatment of Minority
Nationalities in Romania: The Case of
Ceasescu's Hungarians." Nationalities
Papers 5(Spring, 1977):79-90.

Rwanda

Brain, J. L. "The Tutsi and the Ha: A Study
in Integration." J. Asian Afric. Stud.
8(Ja-Ap, 1973):39-49.

Codere, Helen (ed.). The Biography of an
African Society. Rwanda 1900-1960 Based
on Forty-Eight Rwandan Autobiographies.
Tervuren, Belgium: Musée Royal De
L'Afrique Centrale, 1973.

Erny, Pierre. "L'Enseignement au Rwanda de
1916 à 1948." Dialogue (Kipali, Rwanda)
(Mr-Ap, 1976):24-49.

Habrimana, Bonaventure. "L'enfant dans la
société rewandaise." R. jur. pol. 31
(Ap-Jl, 1977):381-406.

Kuper, Leo. The Pity of It All: Polarisation
of Racial and Ethnic Relations. London:
Ducksworth, 1977.

Shyirambere, Spiridion. "Contribution a l'etude
sociolinguistique du bilangüisme. Le
Kinyarwanda et le francais au Rwanda."
Doctoral dissertation, U. of Louvain
(U.C.L.), 1973.

Saudi Arabia

Munro, John. "'God Loves Those Who Do Their
Work Properly.'" Times Higher Education
Supplement, My 10, 1974.

Senegal

Bouche, Denise. "L'enseignement dans les
territoires français de l'Afrique
occidéntale de 1817 à 1920: mission
civilisatrice ou formation d'une élite?"
2 vols. Doctoral dissertation, U. of
Paris, I, F, 1974. [Mainly Senegal]

_____. "Le participation des missionaires au
développement de l'enseignement dans les
colonies françaises d'Afrique occidentale
de 1817 à 1940." Ét. hist. afric. 8(1976):
173-198.

Crowder, Michael. Senegal--A Study of French
Assimilation. Rev. ed. London: N.p.,
1967.

Diarra, Fatoumata-Agnès and others. Two Studies
on Ethnic Group Relations in Africa.
Senegal. The United Republic of Tanzania.
Paris: UNESCO, 1974.

Idowu, H. Oludare. "Assimilation in 19th-
Century Senegal." Cahiers d'Etude
Africaines 9(1969):194-218.

_____. "Café au Lait: Senegal's Mulatto
Community in the Nineteenth Century."
Journal of the Historical Society of
Nigeria 6(D, 1972):271-288.

Obichere, Boniface I. "Colonial Education
Policy in Senegal. A Structural Analysis."
Black Academy Review 1(Winter, 1970):17-24.

O'Brien, Rita Cruise. White Society in Black
Africa: The French of Senegal. London:
Faber, 1972.

Samb, A. "L'éducation islamique au Sénégal."
Notes afr. 136(1972):97-101.

Unser, Gunther. "Intelligenzia und Politik im
Senegal von den Anfangen bis zur Unabhängig-
keit im Jahre 1960." Doctoral dissertation,
U. of Aachen, 1971.

Sierra Leone

Anderson, Eugene Christian. "The Development
of Government Policy for Education in
Sierra Leone, 1881 to 1961." Doctoral
dissertation, U. of Michigan, 1964. Univ.
Microfilms Order No. 65-05875.

Anderson, E. Christian. "Early Muslim Schools
and British Policy in Sierra Leone."
West African Journal of Education, O, 1970.

Ayandele, E. A. "James Africanus Beale Horton: Pioneer Philosopher of Western Education in West Africa." West African Journal of Education 16(Je, 1972):115-121.

Caulker, Patrick S. "The Autochthonous Peoples, British Colonial Policies, and the Creoles in Sierra Leone: The Genesis of the Modern Sierra Leone Dilemma of National Integration." Doctoral dissertation, Temple U., 1976. Univ. Microfilms Order No. 76-11988.

Dawson, John. "Race and Inter-group Relations in Sierra Leone." Race 6(1964-1965):83-99, 217-231.

Fyle, Clifford A. "A National Languages Policy and the Teacher of English in Sierra Leone." Sierra Leone Journal of Education 10(0, 1975):6-11.

Harding, Gladys Modwyn Cicely. "Education and Democracy in West Africa with Particular Reference to Sierra Leone." Doctoral dissertation, Northwestern U., 1971. Univ. Microfilms Order No. 72-06974.

Harrell-Bond, Barbara E. Modern Marriage in Sierra Leone: A Study of the Professional Group. The Hague: Mouton, 1976.

Imig, David Gregg. "An Analysis of Social Factors Affecting Education in Sierra Leone, 1951-1966." Doctoral dissertation, U. of Illinois, 1969. Univ. Microfilms Order No. 70-13360.

Ketkar, Suhas L. "The Economics of Education in Sierra Leone." J. Mod. Afric. Stud. 15 (Je, 1977):301-309.

Porter, Arthur T. Creoledom. New York: Oxford U. Press, 1963.

Sawyerr, Ebunolorun Samuel. "The Development of Education in Sierra Leone in Relation to Western Contact." Master's thesis, McGill U., 1969.

Sinclair, J. S. "Education and Changing Social Structure in Sierra Leone." Doctoral dissertation, U. of Edinburgh, 1976.

_____. "Educational Assistance, Kinship and the Social Structure in Sierra Leone." Africana Research Bulletin 2(1972):30-62.

Skinner, David E. "Islam and Education in the Colony and Hinterland of Sierra Leone (1750-1914)." Canadian Journal of African Studies (1976):499-520.

Spitzer, Leo. The Creoles of Sierra Leone: Responses to Colonialism, 1870-1945. Madison, WI: U. of Wisconsin Press, 1974.

Walker, James W. St. G. The Black Loyalists: The Search for a Promised Land in Nova Scotia and Sierra Leone, 1783-1870. New York: Holmes and Meier, 1976.

Singapore

Ahlek, Chou See (pseud.). "In Lee Kuan Yew's Singapore, Prosperity Rides on Rails of Repression." Harvard Crimson, My 13, 1975.

Ahmed, Zahoor. "Analysis of the Effects of Changes in Administrative Policies of the Singapore Ministry of Education on the Operation of the Singapore School System, 1960-1972." Doctoral dissertation, U. of Kansas, 1973. Univ. Microfilms Order No. 74--2515.

Arasaratnam, Sinnappah. Indians in Malaysia and Singapore. London: Oxford U. Press, 1970.

Beaulieu, Peter Dennis. "Singapore: A Case Study of Communalism and Economic Development." Doctoral dissertation, U. of Washington, 1975. Univ. Microfilms Order No. 76-17396.

Bedlington, Stanley Sanders. "The Singapore Malay Community: The Politics of State Integration." Doctoral dissertation, Cornell U., 1974. Univ. Microfilms Order No. 74-29893.

Busch, Peter Alan. Legitimacy and Ethnicity: A Case Study of Singapore. Lexington, MA: Lexington Books, 1974.

Busch, Peter Alan. "Political Unity and Ethnic Diversity: A Case Study of Singapore." Doctoral dissertation, Yale U., 1972. Univ. Microfilms Order No. 72-29523.

Chen, George Wan-Hsin. "The Social Bases of Political Development and Integration: The Case of Singapore." Doctoral dissertation, U. of Oregon, 1974. Univ. Microfilms Order No. 75-12527.

Chew, Sock Foon, and MacDougall, John A. Forever Plural: The Perception and Practice of Inter-communal Marriage in Singapore. Athens, OH: Center for International Studies, Ohio U., 1977.

Fatt, Yong Ching. "Leadership and Power in the Chinese Community in Singapore during the 1930's." J. S. E. Asian Stud. 8(S, 1977): 195-209.

Fong, Pang Eng. "Growth, Inequality and Race in Singapore." International Labour Review 111(Ja, 1975):15-28.

George, T. J. S. Lee Kuan Yew's Singapore. London: Andre Deutsch, 1974.

Hassan, Riaz. "Inter-Ethnic Marriage in Singapore: A Study in Inter-Ethnic Relations." Inst. S. E. Asian Studies, Occasional Papers 21(My, 1974).

Hu, Shi Ming. Education in a Multi-Cultural Society: The Republic of Singapore, 1974. ERIC ED 095 058.

Hwa, Cheng Siok. "The Non-Citizen Population of Singapore." Nanyang Quarterly 3(D, 1973):38-57.

Juve, Richard G. "Education as an Integrating Force in Singapore, A Multi-Cultural Society." Doctoral dissertation, Rutgers U., 1975. Univ. Microfilms Order No. 76-01116.

Khatena, Joe. "Relative Integration of Selected Ethnic Groups in Singapore." Sociology and Social Research 54(J1, 1970): 460-465.

Kuo, Eddie C. Y. "Language Status and Literacy Trend in a Multilingual Society—Singapore." RELC Journal 5(Je, 1974):1-15.

_____. "Population Ration, Intermarriage and Mother Tongue Retention." Anthropological Linguistics 20(F, 1978):85-93.

Kuo, Peter A. "Religion, Educational Aspirations, and Career Choice Among Chinese Teenagers in Singapore." Doctoral dissertation, U. of Notre Dame, 1966. Univ. Microfilms Order No. 65-09894.

Lee Poh Ping. "Chinese Society in Nineteenth- and Early Twentieth-Century Singapore: A Socioeconomic Analysis." Doctoral dissertation, Cornell U., 1974. Univ. Microfilms Order No. 74-17,117.

_____. Chinese Society in Nineteenth-Century Singapore. New York: Oxford U. Press, 1978.

Lind, Andrew W. Nanyang Perspective: Chinese Students in Multiracial Singapore. Honolulu, HI: Asian Studies Program, U. of Hawaii, 1974.

MacDougall, John Arthur. "Shared Burdens: A Study of Communal Discrimination by the Political Parties of Malaysia and Singapore." Doctoral dissertation, Harvard U., 1968. Univ. Microfilms Order No. 68-13449.

Murray, Douglas Patterson. "Multilanguage Education and Bilingualism: The Formation of Social Brokers in Singapore." Doctoral dissertation, Stanford U., 1971. Univ. Microfilms Order No. 72-11627.

Nam, Tae Y. Racism, Nationalism, and Nation-Building in Malaysia and Singapore. Meerut: Sadhna Prakashan, 1973.

Pang, E. F. "Growth, Inequality and Race in Singapore." International Labour Review 111 (Ja, 1975).

Rao, V. V. B., and Ramakrishnan, M. K. "Economic Growth, Structural Change and Income Inequality, Singapore, 1966-1975." Malayan Economic Review 21(O, 1976).

Rudner, Martin. "Education and the Political Process in Malaysia and Singapore." Doctoral dissertation, Hebrew U., 1974.

Saw, Swee-Hock. Singapore Population in Transition. Philadelphia: U. of Pennsylvania Press, 1970.

Turnbull, Constance M. A History of Singapore, 1819-1975. New York: Oxford U. Press, 1978.

Wee, Ann. "The Chinese Daughters of Indian Parents." New Society, N 10, 1977.

Wilson, Harold Edmund. "Educational Policies in a Changing Society: Singapore, 1918-1959." Doctoral dissertation, U. of British Columbia, 1975.

_____. "Education as an Instrument of Policy in Southeast Asia: The Singapore Example." J. S. E. Asian Stud. 8(Mr, 1977):75-84.

Yeh, S. H. K. "Housing Conditions and Housing Needs in Singapore." Malayan Economic Review 19(O, 1974).

Somalia

Davidson, Basil. "Somalia: Towards Socialism." Race and Class 17(Summer, 1975): 19-37.

Ghalib, Omer Arteh [Interview]. Africa Report 22(Mr-Ap, 1977):43-49. [Somalia Minister of Higher Education and Culture]

Pestalozz, Luigi. The Somalian Revolution. Tr. Peter Glendening. Paris: Editions Afrique Asie Amerique Latine, 1974.

South Africa

Abdul-Hadi, Hafex. "La question des Hindous en Afrique du Sud." Doctoral dissertation, U. of Paris, 1950.

"Academic Apartheid; Segregation of South African Universities." Round Table 198 (Mr, 1960):134-139.

"Academic Freedom in South Africa: The Open Universities in South Africa and Academic Freedom 1957-1974." Minerva 13 (Autumn, 1975).

Adam, Heribert. "The Rise of Black Consciousness in South Africa." Race 15(O, 1973): 149-165.

Adam, Kogila. "Dialectic of Higher Education for the Colonized: The Case of Non-White Universities in South Africa." In South Africa: Sociological Perspectives, pp. 197-213. Edited by Heribert Adam. London: Oxford U. Press, 1971.

Administration of South West Africa. Report of the Commission of Enquiry into Non-European Education in South West Africa, Part I: Native Education. Part II: Coloured Education. Windhoek, N, 1958.

"Afrikaner Academics Show Signs of Dissent from Nationalist Policy." Times Higher Education Supplement, F 4, 1972.

Ainslie, Rosalynde. Children of Soweto. London: South Africa Racial Amity Trust, 1978.

Alvesson, Hoyt S. "Minority Group Autonomy and the Rejection of Dominant Group Racial Mythologies: the Zulu of South Africa." Afric. Stud. 33(1974):3-24.

Anti-Apartheid Movement. Racism and Apartheid in Southern Africa: South Africa and Namibia... Paris: UNESCO, 1974.

"Apartheid in South African Learned Societies." Native 196(D 29, 1962):1241-1242.

Arnold, Millard (ed.). Steve Biko: Black Consciousness in South Africa. New York: Random House, 1978.

Aschheim, Steven E. "The Communal Organization of South African Jewry." Jewish Journal of Sociology 12(D, 1970).

Ashley, M. J. "Academic Contrasts in South Africa." Sociology of Education 42(Summer, 1969):284-291.

Atmore, Anthony, and Westlake, Nancy. "A Liberal Dilemma: A Critique of the Oxford History of South Africa." Race 14(O, 1972): 107-136.

Auerbach, F. E. The Power of Prejudice in South African Education. Cape Town: A. A. Balkema, 1966. [History textbooks in the Transvaal]

Bach, Theresa. Recent Progress of Education in the Union of South Africa. Bulletin 1919, No. 49. Department of the Interior Bureau of Education. Washington, DC: GPO, 1919.

Bagley, Christopher. "Alienation and Human Fulfillment: A Case Study of South Africa." Journal of Human Relations 17(1969):12-25.

Ballinger, Margaret. From Union to Apartheid--A Trek to Isolation. Folkestone: Bailey Brothers and Swinfen, Ltd., 1969.

Barnett, P. A. "Problems and Perils of Education in South Africa." Royal Colonial Institute Proceedings 36(1904-1905):130-155.

"Basic Statistics, 1972-1975." Bantu Education Journal 22(F, 1976):20-21.

"Basic Statistics: Schools, Number of Teachers." Bantu Ed. J. 23(Mr, Ap, 1977):20-21, 20-21.

Behr, Abraham L. "Three Centuries of Coloured Education. Historical and Comparative Studies of the Education of the Coloured People in the Cape and the Transvaal, 1652-1951." Thesis, Potchefstroom U. of Christian Higher Education, 1952.

Behr, A. L., and MacMillan, R. G. Education in South Africa. Pretoria: J. L. van Schaik, 1966.

Biesheuvel, S. "Black Industrial Labour in South Africa." South African Journal of Economics 42(S, 1974).

Biko, B. S. (ed.). Black Viewpoint, 1972. Spro-Cas Black Community Programmes, 86 Beatrice Street, Durban, South Africa.

"Blacks Outside the Homelands." Bantu 24 (Ag, 1977):3-33.

Bloom, Leonard. "The Coloured People of South Africa." Phylon, Summer, 1967.

_____. "Education for Africans in South Africa." Integrated Education, Ag-N, 1965.

_____. "Self-Concepts and Social Status in South Africa: A Preliminary Cross-Cultural Analysis." Journal of Social Psychology 51(1960):103-112. [South African university students, black and white]

Botha, M. C. "Compulsory Education for Black Children." Bantu 24(Mr, 1977):2-7.

Bradlow, Frank R. "A Jewish View of the Just Society in South Africa." Patterns of Prejudice 12(Jl-Ag, 1978):20-24, 29.

Braithwaite, Edward R. Honorary White. New York: McGraw-Hill, 1975.

Brandel-Syrier, Mia. Reeftown Elite. London: Routledge & Kegan Paul, 1972.

Breytenbach, Breyten. "The Fettered Spirit." UNESCO Courier, Mr, 1967. [Apartheid as the death of cultural life]

Brickhill, Joan. "Students Who Face a Trial of Ideas Rather Than Actions." Times Higher Education Supplement, S 5, 1975. [Black student leaders in South Africa]

Brickman, William W. "Racial Segregation in Education in South Africa." School and Society 88(1960):258-269.

Brindley, Marianne. Western Coloured Township: Problems of an Urban Slum. Johannesburg: Ravan Press, 1976. [Near Johannesburg]

Brookes, Edgar H. Apartheid--A Documentary Study of Modern South Africa. New York: Barnes and Noble, 1968.

_____. The History of Native Policy in South Africa from 1830 to the Present Day. Pretoria, S.A.: J. L. Van Schaik, Ltd., 1927.

_____. White Rule in South Africa 1830-1910: Varieties in Governmental Policies Affecting Africans. Pietermaritzburg, South Africa: U. of Natal Press, 1974.

Browett, J. G., and Hart, T. "The Distribution of White Minority Groups in Johannesburg." So. Afric. Geog. 5(Ap, 1977):404-412.

Bryant, A. T. "Mental Development of the South African Native." Eugenics Review 9 (1917):42-49.

Bryer, Keith. "White Students and Black African Power." Times Higher Education Supplement, Ap 21, 1972.

Burns, John F. "'Separate But Equal' Is Still a Dream in South Africa." New York Times, Ja 8, 1978.

_____. "South Africa Schools: Separate, Unequal." New York Times, Jl 15, 1976.

Burchell, D. E. "African Higher Education and the Establishment of the South African Native College, Fort Hare." S. Afric. Hist. J. (N, 1976):60-83.

Cape Colony. Department of Public Education. The Native Primary School: Suggestions for the Consideration of Teachers, Capetown, Cape Times, 1924.

Carlson, Joel. No Neutral Ground. New York: Crowell, 1973.

Carstens, Peter. The Social Structure of a Cape Colored Reserve: A Study of Racial Integration and Segregation in South Africa. New York: Oxford U. Press, 1966.

Chimutengwende, Chenhamo C. South Africa: The Press and the Politics of Liberation. London: Barbican Books, 1978.

Chisholm, J. (ed.). Robert Kennedy in South Africa. Johannesburg, South Africa: Rand Daily Mail, Ag, 1968.

Clwyd, Ann. "Homeland Fires." Guardian, Je 7, 1975.

Colman, Andrew M., and Lambley, Peter. "Authoritarianism and Race Attitudes in South Africa." Journal of Social Psychology 82(D, 1970):161-164.

Counter Information Services, London. Black South Africa Explodes. Washington, DC: Transnational Institute, 1977.

Couzens, T. J. "The Black Press and Black Literature in South Africa, 1900-1950." Eng. Stud. Africa 19(S, 1976):93-99.

Crijns, Arthur G. J. "Race Relations and Race Attitudes in South Africa. A Socio-psychological Study of Human Relationships in a Multiracial Society." Doctoral dissertation, U. of Nimwegen, 1959.

Daniel, J. "NUSAS." South African Outlook 104 (Ja, 1974):3-13.

Danziger, K. "The Psychological Future of an Oppressed Group." Social Forces, O, 1963. [African high school students]

Davenport, T. R. H. The Beginnings of Urban Segregation in South Africa... Grahamstown, South Africa: Rhodes U., 1971.

Davie, T. B. Education and Race Relations in South Africa. The Interaction of Educational Policies and Race Relations in South Africa. Johannesburg, S.A.: South African Institute of Race Relations, 1955.

Davies, Robert. "The White Working-Class in South Africa." New Left Review 82(N-D, 1973):40-59.

Desai, B., and Marney, C. The Killing of the Iman. London: Quartet Books, 1978. [Muslim leader in South Africa]

Douglas-Home, Mark. "Students v. Vorster." New Society 20(Je 15, 1972):556.

Dubb, Allie A. Jewish South Africans: A Sociological View of the Johannesburg Community. Grahamstown, South Africa: Institute of Social and Economic Research, Rhodes U., 1977.

Du Toit, A. S. "Kontak en Assosiasie van Kleurling met Bantoe in die Kappse Skiereland." Doctoral dissertation, Stellenbosch U., 1958.

Du Toit, Brian M. "Color, Class, and Caste in South Africa." Journal of Asian and African Studies 1(1966):197-212.

Duffy, Patrick S. "Government Control of Education in South Africa." Catholic Educational Review, F, 1969.

Duming, P. A., and Van Schaik, J. L. (eds.). Trends and Challenges in the Education of the South African Bantu. Fort Hare U. Press, 1967.

Duncan, H. F. and others. A Study of Pictorial Perception Among Bantu and White Primary School Children in South Africa. Johannesburg: Witwatersrand U. Press, 1973.

Edelstein, Melville. What Do Young Africans Think? Johannesburg: Institute of Race Relations, 1973.

Education and the South African Economy.
Johannesburg: Witwatersrand U. Press, 1966.

Education Commission of the Study Project on
Christianity in Apartheid Society. *Educa-*
tion Beyond Apartheid, 1971. Christian
Institute of Southern Africa, Posbus/P.O.
Box 31134, Braamfontein, Transvaal.

Eisenberg, P. S. "Bantu Education in the
Union of South Africa." B. Litt. thesis,
Oxford U., 1957.

Elphick, Richard. *Kraal and Castle: Khoikoi*
and Founding of White South Africa. New
Haven, CT: Yale U. Press, 1977.

Eriksson, Lars-Gunnar. "Education and
Training Programs for Southern Africans."
Objective: Justice 5(O-D, 1973):39-46.

Evalds, Victoria K. "The 'Bantu Education'
System: A Bibliographic Essay." *A Current*
Bibliography on African Affairs 10(1977-
78):219-242.

February, V. "The Afrikaans Language--
Afrikanerizing Instrument." *Afric.*
Perspectives 1(1976):11-24.

Feinstein, Martin. "Expulsion Fears Over Non-
Whites Recede..." *Times Educational*
Supplement, O 27, 1978 [White private
schools]

Feit, Ewald. "Community in a Quandary:
The South African Jewish Community and
Apartheid." *Race* 8(Ap, 1967).

_____. "Conflict and Communication: An
Analysis of the 'Western Areas' and 'Bantu-
Education' Campaigns of the African Nation-
al Congress of South Africa based on
Communication and Conflict Theories."
Doctoral dissertation, U. of Michigan,
1965. Univ. Microfilms Order No. 66-06602.

Foisie, Jack. "S. Africa Plan for Plural
Societies Omits Chinese." *Los Angeles*
Times, N 27, 1977.

Franz, G. H. and others. *Bantu Education:*
Oppression or Opportunity? Stellenbosch:
South African Bureau of Racial Affairs,
1955.

Freund, W. M. "Race in the Social Structure
of South Africa, 1652-1836." *Race and*
Class 18(Summer, 1976):53-67.

Geary, Kevin. "Indicators of Educational
Progress--A Markov Chain Approach Applied
to Swaziland." *Jr. Mod. Afric. Stud.* 16
(Mr, 1978):141-152.

Geber, Beryl A. "Education Under Apartheid."
Patterns of Prejudice 10(N-D, 1976):25-29.
[Soweto]

Gerhart, Gail M. *Black Power in South*
Africa. The Evolution of an Ideology.
Berkeley: U. of California Press, 1978.

Ginwala, F. N. "Class, Consciousness and
Control--Indian South Africans, 1860-1946."
Doctoral dissertation, Oxford U., 1974.

Glass, Y. "Industrialization and Urbanization
in Southern Africa." In *Problems of Trans-*
ition: Proceedings. Edited by J. F.
Holleman. Pietermaritzburg: Natal U. Press,
1964.

Goguel, A. M. "L'enseignment en Afrique du
Sud." *RFEPA* 103(1974):34-54.

Great Britain. Colonial Office. *Report on*
Native Education in South Africa, Part III.
Education in the Protectorates, by
E. B. Sargant. London, 1908.

Greenberg, D. S. "South Africa: II."
Science 169(J1, 1970):260-267. [Race and
the universities]

Greenstein, Lewis J. "Slave and Citizen: The
South African Case." *Race* 15(J1, 1973):25-
46.

Gregor, A. James. "Apartheid." In
Contemporary Radical Ideologies. New York:
Random House, 1968.

Gregor, A. James, and McPherson, D. A. "Racial
Preference and Ego-Identity among White
and Bantu Children in the Republic of South
Africa." *Genetic Psychology Monographs* 73
(1966):217-254.

Gregor, Carol. "Jo'burg's Shadow City."
New Society, Je 5, 1975. [Soweto]

Hahlo, K. G. "A European-African Worker
Relationship in Africa." *Race*, J1, 1969.

Hall, Edward T. "An American Headmaster in an
African School." *Independent School*
Bulletin 35(F, 1976):49-52. [Multiracial
Maru a Pulu school in Gabarone, Botswana]

Hammond-Tooke, W. D. (ed.). *The Bantu-Speaking*
Peoples of South Africa. Boston, MA:
Routledge & Kegan Paul, 1974.

Hampel, Rainer, and Krupp, Burkhard. "The
Cultural and the Political Framework of
Prejudice in South Africa and Great Britain."
Journal of Social Psychology 103(1977):193-
202.

Hart, T. "Patterns of Black Residence in the
White Residential Areas of Johannesburg."
South African Georgraphical Journal 58(1976):
141-150.

Hartshorne, K. B. *Native Education in the Union*
of South Africa... Johannesburg: South
African--Institute of Race Relations, 1953.

Hawarden, Eleanor. Prejudice in the [South African] Classroom. Johannesburg: N.p., 1966.

Haynes, George E. "South Africans Face Their Race Problems." Crisis, N, 1930.

Heaven, Patrick C. L. "A Historical Survey and Assessment of Research into Race Attitudes in South Africa: 1930-1975." South African Journal of Sociology (S, 1977):68-75.

Heese, J. A. Die Herkoms von die Afrikaner. 1657-1867. Cape Town: N.p., 1971.

Hellmann, Ellen. "The Progress of Apartheid." Patterns of Prejudice 5(Ja-F, 1971):1-7.

Hepple, Alex. South Africa: Workers Under Apartheid. London: Christian Action Publications Ltd., 1969.

Herbstein, Denis. "Death and School in Soweto." Guardian, Je 27, 1976.

_____. White Man, We Want to Talk to You. N.p.: Penguin, 1978. [The Je 1976 uprising in Soweto]

Herrman, Louis. A History of the Jews in South Africa, from the Earliest Times to 1895. Westport, CT: Greenwood, 1975, reprint of 1935 ed.

Hey, P. D. The Rise of the Natal Indian Elite. Pietermaritzburg: Privately printed, 1962.

Hoaglund, Jim. "Black Consciousness in S. Africa: No Longer Passive." Washington Post, Ja 12, 1977.

Hoge, J. "Rassenmischung in Südafrika in 17. und 18. Jahrhundert." Zeitschrift für Rassenkunde 8(1938).

Horrell, M. A Decade of Bantu Education. Johannesburg: N.p., 1964.

_____. The Education of the Coloured Community in South Africa 1652-1970. Johannesburg: South African Institute of Race Relations, 1970.

Horrell, Muriel, and Horner, Dudley (comps.). A Survey of Race Relations in South Africa. Johannesburg, S.A.: South African Institute of Race Relations, Ja, 1974.

Howard, Brian. "Education, Vorster-Style." Race Today 4(Jl, 1972):231.

Hugo, Pierre J. "Academic Dissent and Apartheid in South Africa." Journal of Black Studies 7(Mr, 1977):243-262.

Hunter, Archibald Peter. "The Reorientation of Educational Policy in South Africa since 1948." Doctoral dissertation, U. of California, Los Angeles, 1963. Univ. Microfilms Order No. 63-03871.

Hurwitz, N. The Economics of Bantu Education in South Africa. Johannesburg: N.p., 1964.

Huttenback, Robert A. Racism and Empire. White Settlers and Colored Immigrants in the British Self-Governing Colonies, 1830-1910. Ithaca, NY: Cornell U. Press, 1976.

Innes, Duncan. "South Africa: Our Country, Our Responsibility." Objective: Justice 2(Jl, 1970):29-31.

Innes, Duncan and others. Apartheid and Education. No. 13/70. New York: United National Special Committee on the Policies of Apartheid, My, 1970.

"Inside South Africa Today. A Talk With Khotso Seatlholo." Militant, Mr 18, 1977. [President, Soweto Students Representative Council, Ag 1976-Ja 1977]

Ireland, Ralph. "Apartheid and the Education of the Coloureds in the Republic of South Africa." Plural Societies 5(Summer, 1974): 9-24.

_____. "Apartheid and the Education of the Indian Community in the Republic of South Africa." Plural Societies 6(Summer, 1975): 3-18.

_____. "Current Status of Non-White Education in South Africa." School and Society, O, 1969.

_____. "Education for What? A Comparison of the Education of Black South Africans and Black Americans." Journal of Negro Education 41(Summer, 1972):227-240.

_____. "Specialized Educational Facilities for the Bantu in South Africa." Intellect 102(Ja, 1974):265-269.

_____. "TRANSKEI: The Signficance of Education for the Republic of South Africa's First 'Bantustan.'" Plural Societies 3(Spring, 1972):39-58.

Jacgz, Jane W. Refugee Students from Southern Africa. New York: African-American Institute, 1967.

Jacobson, Dan, and Segal, Ronald. "Apartheid and South African Jewry: An Exchange." Commentary 24(N, 1957).

"Jews' Future in South Africa." Patterns of Prejudice 11(Mr-Ap, 1977):19-22.

Johnson, Robert Edward. "Indians and Apartheid in South Africa: The Failure of Resistance." Doctoral dissertation, U. of Massachusetts, 1973. Univ. Microfilms Order No. 74-7587.

Johnstone, Frederick A. Class, Race and Gold: A Study of Class Relations and Racial Discrimination in South Africa. Boston: Routledge & Kegan Paul, 1975.

_____. "White Prosperity and White Supremacy in South Africa Today." *African Affairs* 69(1970):124-140.

Jones, Robert Carless. "The Development of Attitudes Leading to the Nationalist 'Apartheid' Philosophy of Bantu Education in the Republic of South Africa." Doctoral dissertation, U. of Oklahoma, 1966. Univ. Microfilms Order No. 66-08092.

Jordaan, Ken. "The Origins of the Afrikaners and their Language, 1652-1720: A Study in Miscegenation and Creole." *Race* 15(Ap, 1974):461-495.

Kaplinsky, R. "Industrialization, Race Relations and the Future of South Africa." *Radical* (U. of Cape Town) 2(1969).

Keirn, Susan Middleton. "Scuttling: The Social Mosaic of Urban Black South Africans." Doctoral dissertation, U. of Florida, 1975. Univ. Microfilms Order No. 76-12,228.

Kgware, W. M. *Education for Africans.* Johannesburg: South African Institute of Race Relations, 1969.

_____. "Education of the Africans in South Africa." *So. Africa Int.* 5(O, 1974):75-86.

_____. "In Search of an Educational System: Critical Appraisal of the Past and Present Administration of Bantu Education." *Publ. U. College N.* (Ser. C, No. 8, 1973):3-23.

Kinloch, Graham C. "Racial Prejudice in Highly and Less Racist Societies: Social Distance Preferences Among White College Students in South Africa and Hawaii." *Sociology and Social Research* 59(O, 1974):1-13.

Kitzinger, Sheila. "Having a Baby in South Africa." *New Society*, Jl 24, 1975.

Knight, J. B., and McGrath, M. D. "An Analysis of Racial Wage Discrimination in South Africa." *Oxford Bulletin of Economics and Statistics* 39(N, 1977).

Koka, Drake. "'Our Policy Is To Break the Spine of Apartheid'" (interview). *Militant*, N 10, 1978. [General secretary, Black Allied Workers Union of South Africa]

Kumbula, Tendayi. "S. Africa's Education Geared to Apartheid." *Los Angeles Times*, Je 27, 1976.

Kuper, Leo. *The College Brew.* Durban, South Africa: N.p., 1960. Segregated universities for blacks

_____. "Race, Class and Power: Some Comments on Revolutionary Change." *Comparative Studies in Society and History* 14(S, 1972): 400-421. South Africa and Algeria

La Guma, Alex (ed.). *Apartheid: A Collection of Writings on South African Racism.* London: Lawrence and Wishart, 1972.

Lambley, Peter. "Racial Attitudes and the Maintenance of Segregation: A Study of Voting Patterns of White, English-speaking South Africans." *British Journal of Sociology* 25(1974):494-499.

Lavin, Deborah. "The Dilemma of Christian-National Education in South Africa." *World Today*, O, 1965.

Leary, P. M., and Lewis, J. E. S. "Some Observations on the State of Nutrition of Infants and Toddlers in Sekukuniland." *South African Medical Journal* 39(1965).

Lee, Franz J. T. "Bantu Education in South Africa." *International Socialist Review*, Autumn, 1966.

Legassick, Martin. *The National Union of South African Students: Ethnic Cleavage and Ethnic Integration in the Universities.* Los Angeles, CA: African Studies Center, U. of California, 1967.

Legassick, M., and Shingler, J. "South Africa." In *Students and Politics in Developing Nations*, pp. 103-145. Edited by D. Emmerson. London: Pall Mall, 1968.

Legum, Colin. "Color and Power in the South African Situation." *Daedalus*, Spring, 1967.

Leonard, Leo D. "Apartheid and Bantu Education Since 1948." Master's thesis, Utah State U., 1966.

Leonard, Leo Donald. "Apartheid and Education in the Republic of South Africa." Doctoral dissertation, Utah State U., 1970. Univ. Microfilms Order No. 70-10936.

Leonie, Andrew. "The Development of Bantu Education in South Africa, 1652-1954." Doctoral dissertation, U. of Montana, 1965.

Le Roux, C. du P. "Vooroordele en Sterotipes in die Rasselhoudings van Kleurlinge." Master's thesis, Stellenbosch, 1969.

Lever, Henry. *Ethnic Attitudes of Johannesburg Youth.* Johannesburg: Witwatersrand U. Press, 1968.

_____. "Some Problems in Race Relations Research in South Africa." *Soc. Dynamics* 1 (Je, 1975):31-44.

Lever, Henry, and Wagner, O. J. M. "Ethnic Preferences of Jewish Youth in Johannesburg." *Jewish Journal of Sociology*, Je, 1967.

Lewin, P. "The Black-White Wage Gap, 1951-1969." South African Journal of Economics 44(Je, 1976):171-184.

Lewsen, Phyllis. "The Cape Liberal Tradition--Myth or Reality?" Race 13(Jl, 1971):65-80.

Loram, Charles Templeman. "Dissertation on the Education of the South Africa Native." Teacher College Record 17(My, 1916):268-273.

_____. The Education of the South African Native. New York: Columbia U., 1915.

_____. "Native Education in South Africa: The Community Outlook." School and Society 33(Ja 17, 1931):69-73.

Lunn, B. "Libraries for Non-Whites in the Republic of South Africa." Libri 13(1963).

Lystad, Mary H. "Adolescent Social Attitudes in South Africa and Swaziland." American Anthropologist 72(D, 1970):1389-1397.

Maasdorp, G. T., and Pillay, P. N. The East Rand Indian Community: A Socio-Economic Survey Conducted for the Benoni Town Council. Durban, S.A.: Department of Economics, U. of Natal, 1970.

MacCrone, I. D. "Psychological Factors Affecting the Attitude of White to Black in South Africa." South African Journal of Science 27(1930):591-598.

_____. Race Attitudes in South Africa. London: Oxford U. Press, 1957.

MacMillan, William. Bantu, Boer and Britain: The Making of the South African Native Problem. N.p.: Oxford, 1963.

_____. The Cape Color Question--A Historical Survey. New York: Humanities Press, 1968.

Magona, Sindliwe. "Capetown Sister Visits Here." Wree-View 3(S-O, 1978) interview. [Black teacher and social worker]

Magubane, Bernard. The Political Economy of Race and Class in South Africa. New York: Monthly Review Press, 1979.

Malherbe, E. G. Bantu Manpower and Education. Johannesburg, South Africa: South African Institute of Race Relations, 1969.

_____. "The Non-White Universities of South Africa." Reality 1(1970).

Manganyi, N. C. Alienation and the Body in Racist Society: A Study of the Society that Invented Soweto. New York: NOK Publishers, 1977.

Marais, J. S. The Cape Coloured People, 1652-1937. Johannesburg: N.p., 1962.

Maree, Lynn. "Black Future?" Times Educational Supplement, Jl 16, 1976. [Soweto]

Marks, Shula. "Natal: The Zulu Royal Family and the Ideology of Segregation. Jr. S. Afric. Stud. 4(Ap, 1978):172-194.

Mashile, G. G., and Pirie, G. H. "Aspects of Housing Allocation in Soweto." S. Afric. Geog. J. 59(S, 1977):139-149.

Mashinini, Tsietsi. "Behind the Growing Upsurge in South Africa." Militant, N 26, 1976. [Interview of O 9, 1976, with the president of the Soweto Students Representative Council]

Maud, Ruan. "Racialism in Rag Time: The Psychology of Capitulation in South Africa." Universities Quarterly 27(Summer, 1973):407-419. [Rhodes U.]

Mbata, J. Congress. "Race and Resistance in South Africa." In The African Experience. Vol. I: Essays, pp. 210-232. Edited by John N. Paden and Edward W. Soja. Evanston, IL: Northwestern U. Press, 1970.

Mbokazi, Simon. "The Role of Bhekunzulu College in the Training of Chiefs and Headmen in Kwazulu." Africanus 7(S, 1977):21-32.

Medlicott, Paul. "Black Education in South Africa." New Society, My 1, 1975.

Meyer, Lysle E. "A Report on South Africa's Black Univiersities." Issue 4(Fall, 1974):12-18.

_____. "Oppression or Opportunity? Inside the Black Universities of South Africa." Journal of Negro Education 45(Fall, 1976):365-382.

Mgzashe, Mxolisi. "South African Students Organize Independent of Liberal Whites." African World 1(S 18, 1971):5.

Mhlongo, S. "Une analyse des classes en Afrique du Sud." Temps. Mod. 31(N, 1975):687-728.

Morlan, Gail. "The Student Revolt against Racism in South Africa." Africa Today, My-Je, 1970.

Morrison, Douglas. "Widening Gulf Divides South African Students." Times Higher Education Supplement, Ag 2, 1974.

Morse, Stanley J., and Peele, Stanton. "'Coloured Power' or 'Coloured Bourgeoisie'? Political Attitudes Among South African Coloureds." Public Opinion Quarterly 38 (Fall, 1974):317-334.

Morse, Stanley J., and Orpen, C. (eds.). Contemporary South Africa. Social Psychological Perspectives. Cape Town, South Africa: Juta & Co., 1974.

Mphahlele, Ezekiel. "Back to Ancestral Ground." First World 1(My-Je, 1977):13-17.

Msomi, James E. B. "The Development of African Education in South Africa: 1954-1977." Doctoral dissertation, Syracuse U., 1978. Univ. Microfilms Order No. 7823581.

Muir, R. K. "Leadership in a Dual Cultural Setting: A Sociometric Study of Cleavage Between English and Afrikaans--Speaking School Children and the Role of the Leaders in Bridging It." British Journal of Educational Psychology, N, 1963.

Muir, R. K., and Tunmer, R. "The Africans' Drive for Education in South Africa." Comparative Education Review, O, 1965.

Mukheji, S. B. Indian Minority in South Africa. New Delhi, India: People's Publishing House, 1959.

Murphy, Emmett Jefferson. "Bantu Education in South Africa: Its Compatibility with the Contrasting Objectives of African Self-Development or White Domination." Doctoral dissertation, U. of Connecticut, 1973. Univ. Microfilms Order No. 73-24421.

_____. Schooling for Servitude. Some Aspects of South Africa's Bantu Education System, 1972. ERIC ED 091 309.

Murray, A. V. The School in the Bush. London: Macmillan, 1929.

Nannan, Billy. "Discrimination and Segregation in South African Education." Objective: Justice 3(Jl-S, 1971):30-33.

Nash, Roy. "History As She Is Writ." New Society, Ag 3, 1972. [The treatment of South Africa in English junior school textbooks]

Neame, L. E. The History of Apartheid. London: Pall Mall Press, 1962.

Nengwekhulu, R. "Education for Blacks in South Africa: A Radical Alternative." Free Southern Africa 1(1973):42-50.

Neville, Mary H. "Reading in Capetown Schools: A Comparative View." Comparative Education 10(Je, 1974):115-120.

Nieuwoudt, J. M. and others. "White Ethnic Attitudes After Soweto: A Field Experiment." South African Journal of Sociology (S, 1977):1-12.

Nkoana, Matthew. "Nationalism's Revolutionary Potential." Race Today 6(Ap, 1974):119-120.

Nkondo, G. M. (ed.). Turfloop Testimony: The Dilemma of A Black University in South Africa. Johannesburg: Raven Press, 1976.

Nkosi, Lewis. "The Forbidden Dialogue." UNESCO Courier, Mr, 1967.

Natantala, Phyllis. An African Tragedy. The Black Woman Under Apartheid. Detroit: Agascha Productions, 1976.

Olivier, N. J. J. "Apartheid or Integration?" In Africa in Transition. Edited by P. Smith. London: Reinhardt, 1958.

Orpen, Christopher. "Internal-External Control and Perceived Discrimination in a South African Minority Group." Sociology and Social Research 56(O, 1971):44-48.

_____. "Prejudice and Adjustment to Cultural Norms Among English-Speaking South Africans." Journal of Psychology 77 (Mr, 1971):217-218.

_____. "Prejudice and Personality in White South Africa: A 'Differential Learning' Alternative to the Authoritarian Personality." Journal of Social Psychology 87 (Ag, 1972):313-314.

Ottaway, David B. "S. Africa's Embattled Universities." Washington Post, S 5, 1976.

Pachai, Bridglal. The South African Indian Question, 1860-1971. Capetown, South Africa: N.p., 1971.

Parker, Franklin. "Revisiting Segregated South Africa." Kappa Delta Pi Record 9 (D, 1972):50-53.

_____. "Separate Schools and Separate People of South Africa." Journal of Negro Education 41(Summer, 1972):266-275.

Paton, Alan. "The Price of Segregation." UNESCO Courier, Mr, 1967. [Effects of apartheid on cultures in South Africa]

_____. "White South Africa's Only Hope for Survival." New York Times Magazine, My 13, 1973.

Patterson, Sheila. "Some Speculations on the Status and Role of the Free People of Colour in the Western Cape." In Studies in African Social Anthropology. Edited by Meyer Fortes and Sheila Patterson. New York: Academic Press, 1975.

Payne, Les. "Black South African Student Leader in Hiding; Others Flee." Los Angeles Times, N 25, 1976. [Tlhopheto Modise, chairman, Soweto Student Representative Council]

_____. "Protests Spread Out from Johannesburg." Los Angeles Times, N 25, 1976. [Lerothodi High School, Bethanie, South Africa]

Peteni, R. L. The African Teachers' Associations of South Africa: An Official
History. Algonac, MI: Reference Publications, 1978.

Peterson, Robert W. (ed.). South Africa and
Apartheid. New York: Facts on File, 1971.

Phillips, Ray E. The Bantu in the City: A
Study of Cultural Adjustment on the
Witswatersrand. New York: AMS Press,
1977; orig. 1938.

Pieterse, J. E. (ed.). Jeug en Kultuur.
Johannesburg, South Africa: Voortrek-
kerpers, 1967.

Pillay, Bala. British Indians in the Transvaal: Trade, Politics and Imperial
Relations, 1885-1906. London: Longman,
1977.

Pogrund, Benjamin. "South Africa's Coloureds."
New Republic, Ag 7, 1976.

Pollak, Hansi. Education for Progress.
Johannesburg, S.A.: South African
Institute of Race Relations, 1971.

Poortinga, Y. H. Cross-Cultural Comparison of
Maximum Performance Tests; Some Method-
ological Aspects and Some Experiments with
Simple Auditory and Visual Stimulus.
Johannesburgh, S.A.: National Institute for
Personnel Research, 1971.

Preston-Whythe, Eleanor. "Race Attitudes and
Behaviour: The Case of Domestic Employment
in White South African Homes." Afric. Stud.
35 (1976):71-90.

"The Problem of Bantu Education in South
Africa." South African Association of
Science Report (1903):334-340.

Rabalao, L. J. "The Use of Space to Control
Racial/Cultural Groups in Metropolitan
Praetoria, South Africa." Master's thesis,
U. of Western Ontario, 1971.

Randall, Peter (ed.). Anatomy of Apartheid,
1970. Christian Institute of Southern
Africa, Posbus/P.O. Box 31134, Braamfontein,
Transvaal.

_____ (ed.). Apartheid and the Church.
Johannesburg, S.A.: Church Commission
of the Study Project on Christianity in
Apartheid Society, 1972.

_____ (ed.). Directions of Change in South
African Politics, 1971. Christian Institute
of Southern Africa, Posbus/P.O. Box 31134,
Braamfontein, Transvaal.

_____ (ed.). Power, Privilege and Poverty.
Johannesburg, South Africa: Economics
Commission of the Study Project on
Christianity in Apartheid Society, 1972.

_____ (ed.). Some Implications of Inequality,
1971. Christian Institute of Southern
Africa, Posbus/P.O. Box 31134, Braamfontein,
Transvaal.

_____ (ed.). South Africa's Minorities, 1971.
Christian Institute of Southern Africa,
Posbus/P.O. Box 31134, Braamfontein,
Transvaal.

_____ (ed.). South Africa's Political
Alternatives. Johannesburg, South Africa:
Report of the Political Commission of the
Study Project on Christianity in Apartheid
Society, 1973.

_____ . A Taste of Power. The Final, Coor-
dinated Spro-Cas Report. Johannesburg,
South Africa: The Study Project on
Christianity in Apartheid Society, 1973.

_____ (ed.). Towards Social Change, 1971.
Christina Institute of Southern Africa,
Posbus/P.O. Box 31134, Braamfontein,
Transvaal.

Rauche, G. A. "Black Universities--A Challenge."
South African Journal of African Affairs
6 (1976):3-9.

Raum, J. W. "Das Bantuschulwesen in der
Südafrikanischen Union." Doctoral
dissertation, U. of Munich, 1963.

Raum, O. F. "South Africa: A Bantu Urban
Residential Area." In The World Year
Book of Education 1970. Education in
Cities, pp. 42-71. Edited by Joseph A.
Lauwerys and David G. Scanlon.
New York: Harcourt, Brace and World,
1970. [Mamelodi, near Pretoria] .

Rex, John. "The Plural Society: The South
African Case." Race 12(Ap, 1971):401-413.

Rhoodie, N. J. Apartheid and Racial Partner-
ship in Southern Africa. Pretoria/Cape
Town, South Africa: Academica, 1969.
[Defense of government policy]

Rhoodie, N. J., and Ventu, H. J. Apartheid: A
Socio-Historical Exposition of the Origin
and Development of the Apartheid Idea.
Cape Town: N.p., 1959.

Robertson, Neville L., and Robertson, Barbara
L. Education in South Africa. Bloomington,
IN: Phi Delta Kappa Educational Foundation,
1977.

Rose, Brian W. "Bantu Education as a Facet of
South African Policy." Comparative Education Review, Je, 1965.

_____ (ed.). Education in Southern Africa.
London: Collier-Macmillan, 1970.

Ross, Robert. Adam Kok's Griquas: A Study in the
the Development of Stratification in South
Africa. New York: Cambridge U. Press,
1977.

Rubin, Neville. "Law, Race and Colour in South Africa." Objective: Justice 6(Ja-F, 1974): 29-35.

Sabbagh, M. Ernest. "Some Geographical Characteristics of a Plural Society: Apartheid in South Africa." Geographical Review 58 (1968):1-28.

Sachs, Albie. Justice in South Africa. London: Heinemann, 1973.

_____. South Africa: The Violence of Apartheid. London: Christian Action Publications, Ltd., 1969.

Schlemmer, Lawrence. Social Change and Political Policy in South Africa. Johannesburg, South Africa: South African Institute of Race Relations, 1970.

_____. "Urban Violence in South Africa." New Society, S 2, 1976.

Scully, Malcolm G. "South Africa's Isolated Universities." Chronicle of Higher Education, Mr 20, 1978.

_____. "South Africa's Jarring Contrasts." Chronicle of Higher Education, Ap 10, 1978.

_____. "South Africa's 3 Black Campuses." Chronicle of Higher Education, Mr 27, 1978.

Segal, Ronald. "The Dying Minds." UNESCO Courier, Mr, 1967.

Seidman, Gay W. "Khotso Seatholo: Fighting for Freedom in South Africa." Harvard Crimson, Mr 7, 1977.

Serote, Mongane. "Feeling the Waters." First World 1(Mr-Ap, 1977):22-25.

Setai, Bethuel. The Political Economy of South Africa: The Making of Poverty. Washington, DC: U. Press of America, 1977.

Sevry, Jean. "Éducation et Apartheid en Afrique du Sud." Présence africaine (1976): 60-80.

Shedd, Steven. "Socioeconomic Status of Urban Coloured and Asian Communities in the Republic of South Africa." Master's thesis, Michigan State U., 1972.

Shingler, John David. "Education and Political Order in South Africa, 1902-1961." Doctoral dissertation, Yale, U., 1973. Univ. Microfilms Order No. 74-11883.

Sigxashe, W. W. "Two Decades of Bantu Education in South Africa." Sechaba (Jl, 1973):13-17.

_____. "Two Decades of Bantu Education in South Africa." In Join Struggle Against Apartheid, pp. 3-16. Edited by World Federation of Teachers' Unions. Prague: World Federation of Teachers' Unions, 1973. [1953-1973]

Sikakane, Joyce. A Window on Soweto. London: International Defence and Aid Fund, 1977.

Simons, H. J., and Simons, R. E. Class and Colour in South Africa, 1850-1950. Baltimore, MD: Penguin, 1970.

Singh, R. N. "Indian and Coloured Education in the Cape." Master's thesis, U. of London, Insitute of Education, 1961.

Sofer, C. "Some Recent Trends in the Status History of the Coloured People of South Africa." Master's thesis, London School of Economics, 1949.

Sorrenson, Keith. Separate and Unequal. Cultural Interaction in South Africa 1919-1961. London: Heinemann Educational, 1977.

"Special Issue on Apartheid." Objective: Justice, Ja, 1970.

Spuy, H. J. van der. "The Psychology of South Africa." New Society, D 12, 1974.

Stacey, R. D. "Some Observations on the Economic Implications of Territorial Segregation in South Africa." South African Journal of Economics, Mr, 1965.

"Statistics--Black Schools, Teachers, Pupils, and Population: 1925-1976." Bantu Educa. Journal 23(D, 1977):28.

Steinberg, Bernard. "Jewish Education in South Africa." Jewish Education 39(D, 1969):14-22.

Steinhart, Edward K. "White Student Protests in South Africa: The Privileged Fight for Their Rights." Africa Today 19(Summer, 1972).

Stepping Into the Future. Education for South Africa's Black, Coloured and Indian Peoples, 1975. Erudita Publications (Pty) Ltd., P.O. Box 25111, Marshalltown, Johannesburg, Republic of South Africa 2107.

Stevens, Richard P. "Zionism, South Africa and Apartheid: The Paradoxical Triangle." Phylon 32(Summer, 1971):123-142.

Strauss, Johann. "Identity and Social Change." Patterns of Prejudice 9(S-O, 1975): 1-10.

Stubbs, Ached (ed.). I Write What I like/ Steve Biko: A Selection of His Writings. New York: Harper & Row, 1979.

"Students." Southern Africa 5(Je-Jl, 1972): 22-23.

Tabata, I. B. Education for Barbarism in South Africa. Bantu (Apartheid) Education. London: Pall Mall Press, 1960.

Timol, Razia, and Mazibuko, Tutuzile. <u>Soweto:
A People's Response. Sample Survey of the
Attitudes of People in Durban to the Soweto
Violence of June 1976</u>. Durban: Institute
for Black Research, 1977.

Tiryakian, Edward A. "Sociological Realism:
Partition for South Africa?" <u>Social Forces</u>,
D, 1967.

Troup, Freda. <u>Forbidden Pastures: Education
Under Apartheid</u>. London: International
Defence and Aid Fund, 1976.

Tunmer, Raymond. "The African Urban High
School Pupil--His Background and
Aspirations." Doctoral dissertation, U. of
Witwatersrand, 1970.

_____. <u>Race and Education</u>. Johannesburg,
South Africa: Institute for the Study of
Man in Africa, n.d.

United Nations. <u>Apartheid and Racial Discrimination in Southern Africa</u>. No. OPI/316.
Sales Section, United Nations, NY, n.d.

_____. <u>Segregation in South Africa</u>. Ques-
tions and Answers on the Policy of
Apartheid. Sales No. E 69. I 15, New
York, n.d.

United Nations, Department of Political and
Security Council Affairs, Unit on Apartheid.
<u>Repressive Legislation of the Republic of
South Africa</u>. ST/PSCA/SER. A/7.
United Nations, NY, 1969.

United Nations, General Assembly, Official
Records, Twenty-Third Session, Agenda Item
31. <u>Report of the Special Committee on the
Policies of Apartheid of the Government of
the Republic of South Africa</u>. A/7254.
New York: United Nations, 1968.

United Nations Unit on Apartheid. <u>Student Movements in South Africa</u>. New York: Unit on
Apartheid, United Nations, My, 1970.

UNESCO. <u>Apartheid. Its Effects on Education,
Science, Culture, and Information</u>, 1967.
UNESCO Publications Center, 317 E. 34th
Street, New York, NY 10016.

_____. <u>Apartheid. Its Effects on Education,
Science, Culture, and Information</u>. 2nd
ed., revised and enlarged, 1972. Unipub,
Inc., P.O. Box 433, New York, NY 10016.

"University Unrest in South Africa." <u>Race
Today</u> 4(Ag, 1972):270-271.

Unterhalter, B. "A Content Analysis of the
Essays of Black and White South African High
School Pupils." <u>Race</u> 14 (Ja, 1973):311-329.

Van Den Berghe, Pierre L. "Race Segregation in
South Africa: Degrees and Kinds." <u>Cahiers
d'Etudes Africaines</u>, Cahier 3, 1966.

Van der Horst, Sheila. <u>Progress and Retro-
gression in South Africa: A Personal View</u>.
Johannesburg, South Africa: South African
Institute of Race Relations, 1971.

Van der Merwe, H. W., and Welsh, David (eds.).
<u>Student Perspectives on South Africa</u>.
Cape Town, South Africa: Philip, 1972.

Van der Spuy, H. I. J. "National Psychology
and Racial Discrimination." <u>Patterns of
Prejudice</u> 8(N-D, 1974):10-17.

Watson, Graham. <u>Passing for White: A Study
of Racial Assimilation in a South African
School</u>. New York: Barnes & Noble, 1970.

Watson, Stanley G. S. "School for Pass-Whites."
Doctoral dissertation, Simon Fraser U., 1968.

Watson, Stanley G., and Hampkin, H. "Race and
Socio-Economic Status as Factors in the
Friendship Choices of Pupils in a Racially
Heterogeneous South African School." <u>Race</u>,
O, 1968.

Watters, Edmond Arthur III. "Botswana: The
Roots of Educational Development and the
Evolution of Formal and Informal Education."
Doctoral dissertation, Lehigh U., 1973.
Univ. Microfilms Order No. 74-06706.

Weaver, Leon. "Apartheid and the Coloured
Dilemma." <u>Africa Report</u> 21(S-O, 1976):7-11.

Weeks, Sheldon G. "Race and Retrogression in
Education: African Education in South
Africa." <u>Africa Today</u> 14, No. 2, n.d.

Welsh, David. <u>The Roots of Segregation: Native
Policy in Natal</u>. Cape Town, South Africa:
Oxford U. Press, 1971.

Wicker, Tom. "Still 'Bantu Education.'" <u>New
York Times</u>, D 17, 1978.

Wilson, Francis, and Perrot, Dominique (eds.).
<u>Outlook on a Century: South Africa, 1870-
1970</u>, 1973. SPRO-CAS, P.O. Box 31134, Braamfontein, South Africa.

Wolfson, J. G. E. "The Ideology and Provision of
Racially Segregated Education in South
Africa, 1948 to 1972--a Survey of Some
Aspects of Bantu Education." Master's thesis,
U. of Birmingham, 1976.

_____. "Medium of Instruction as an Ideological
Issue in South African Black Schools."
<u>J. Educ.</u> 8 (Jl, 1976):3-16.

Wolpe, Harold. "Capitalism and Cheap Labour
Power in South Africa: From Segregation to
Apartheid." <u>Economy and Society</u> 1(1972).

_____. "The Theory of Internal Colonialism:
The South African Case." In <u>Beyond the
Sociology of Development</u>. Edited by Ivar
Oxall. London: Routledge and Kegan Paul,
1975.

Woods, Donald. Biko. New York: Paddington Press, 1978.

World Conference for Action Against Apartheid. Report of the World Conference Against Apartheid. 2 vols. New York: United Nations, 1977.

Zille, Helen. "An Exiled Professor Returns to South Africa." Chronicle of Higher Education, My 8, 1978. [Ezekiel Mphahlele]

_____. "Student Politics in South Africa: Black-White Contrast." Chronicle of Higher Education, S 11, 1978.

Zungu, Yeyedwa. "The Education for Africans in South Africa." Journal of Negro Education 46 (Summer, 1977):202-218.

Spain

Almarcha, Amparo. "La Sociologia de la educación en España." Revista Española de Investigaciones Sociologicas 2 (Ap-Je, 1978

Baer, Itzhak. A History of the Jews in Christian Spain. Philadelphia: N.p., 1961.

Batista I. Roca, J.-M. "The Catalan National Movement." Institute of Race Relations Newsletter, S, 1967.

Beltza. El Nacionalismo Vasco. Hendaya: Ediciones Mugalde, 1974.

Beneria, Lourdes. "The Allocation of Resources to Education: Spain, 1940-1972." Doctoral dissertation, Columbia U., 1975.

Boswell, John. The Royal Treasure. Muslim Communities Under the Crown of Aragon in the Fourteenth Century. New Haven, CT: Yale U. Press, 1977.

Carlson, Charles Lawrence. "The Vulgar Sort: Common People in Siglo de Oro Madrid." Doctoral dissertation, U. of California, Berkeley, 1977.

Cazorla Perez, José. "Minorias marginadas en España: el caso de los gitanos." Revista Espanola de la Opinion Publica 45 (Jl-S, 1976).

Douglas, William A. Echalar and Murelaga. Opportunity and Rural Exodus in Two Spanish Basque Villages. New York: St. Martin's Press, 1975.

Ferrar, Robert. "'Les autres catalan': le proletariat urbain à Barcelone." Revue Géographique des Pyrénées et du Sud-Ouest 48(1977):191-198.

Garcia Venero, M. Historia del Nacionalismo Vasco. Madrid: N.p., 1969.

Heiberg, Marianne. "Insiders/Oursiders: Basque Nationalism." Archives Européenes de Sociologie 16(1975):169-193.

Hopkins, Adam. "Basques Hope for End to Tongue Trouble." Times Educational Supplement, Ap 30, 1976.

Lévi-Provencal, E. Histoire de l'espagne musulmane. 3 vols. Paris: G.-P. Maisonneuve, 1950-1963.

McGrath Grubb, E. E. "Attitudes towards Black Africans in Imperial Spain." Legon J. Humanities 1(1974):68-90.

Martz, L. M. "Poverty and Welfare in Hapsburg Spain: The Example of Toledo." Doctoral dissertation, U. of London, Kings College, n.d.

Mayo, Patricia Elton. The Roots of Identity: Three National Movements in Contemporary European Politics. London: Allen Lane, 1974. [Basques]

Meisler, Stanley. "Spain Gypsies Get Help but Biases Linger." Los Angeles Times, S 28, 1978.

Moore, Kenneth. Those of the Street: The Catholic-Jews of Mallorca. Notre Dame, IN: U. of Notre Dame Press, 1977.

Ortizi. Historia de Eukadi: el nacionalismo vasco Yeta. Paris: Ruedo Ibérico, 1975.

Payne, Stanley G. Basque Nationalism. Reno: U. of Nevada Press, 1975.

Pike, Ruth. "Sevillian Society in the Sixteenth Century: Slaves and Freedmen." Hispanic American Historical Review 47 (1967):344-359.

Quintana, Bertha B., and Floyd, Lois G. ¡Que Gitano! Gypsies of Southern Spain. New York: Holt, Rinehart & Winston, 1972.

Sicroff, Albert A. "Les Statuts de pureté de sang en Espagne aux XVe et XVIIe siecles." Doctoral dissertation, U. of Paris, 1955.

da Silva, Milton M. "The Basque Nationalist Movement: A Case Study in Ethnic Nationalism." Doctoral dissertation, U. of Massachusetts, 1972.

_____. "Modernization and Ethnic Conflict. The Case of the Basques." Comparative Politics 7(Ja, 1975):227-251.

Thomas, Ned. "Self-Help Nurseries Can Save Basques." Times Educational Supplement, Ja 4, 1974.

Thompson, Billy Russell. "Bilingualism in Moorish Spain." Doctoral dissertation, U. of Virginia, 1970. Univ. Microfilms Order No. 70-26,581.

Sri Lanka

Abeysekera, G. "The Distribution of Income in Sri Lanka, 1953-73: Its Structure, Trends, and Interpretation." Doctoral dissertation, U. of Wisconsin, 1975.

Beteille, Andre. "The Future of the Backward Classes: The Competing Demands of Status and Power." In India and Ceylon: Unity and Diversity, pp. 83-120. Edited by Philip Mason. New York: Oxford U. Press, 1967.

Corca, A. "One Hundred Years of Education in Ceylon." Modern Asian Studies, Ap, 1969.

De Silva, K. M. "Some Aspects in the Development of Social Policy in Ceylon, 1840 to 1855." Doctoral dissertation, U. of London, 1961.

Farmer, B. H. "The Social Basis of Nationalism in Ceylon." Journal of Asian Studies 25(My, 1965):431-430.

Fernando, Chitra. "English and Sinhala Bilingualism in Sri Lanka." Language in Society 6(D, 1977):341-360.

Fernando, Quintus Godfrey. "The Minorities in Ceylon, 1926-1931, with Special Reference to the Donoughmore Commission." Doctoral dissertation, U. of London, 1973.

Gnanamuttu, G. A. Education and the Indian Plantation Worker in Sri Lanka. Colombo: The author, 1977 4 Chelsea Gardens, Colombo 3, Sri Lanka

Goonetileke, H. A. I. (comp.). A Bibliography of Ceylon. A Systematic Guide to the Literature on the Land, People, and Culture Published in Western Languages from the Sixteenth Century to the Present Day. Vols. I and II. Zug, Switzerland: Inter Documentation Company AG, 1970.

_____. A Bibliography of Ceylon. Vol. III. Zug, Switzerland: Inter Documentation Comapny, 1976.

Harrison, Paul. "Land and Labour in Ceylon." New Society, My 29, 1975.

Jayasuriya, J. E. Education in Ceylon. Columbo: Associated Educational Pub., 1969.

Jayaweera, Swarna. "British Educational Policy in Ceylon in the Nineteenth Century." Paedagogica Historica 9(1969):68-90.

_____. "Language and Colonial Educational Policy in Ceylon in the Nineteenth Century." Mod. Ceylon Stud. 2(J1, 1971):123-150.

Kapferer, Judith. "Four Schools in Sri Lanka: Equality of Opportunity for Rural Children?" Comparative Education 11(Mr, 1975):31-41.

Kearney, Robert N. "Language and the Rise of Tamil Separation in Sri Lanka." Asian Survey 18(My, 1978):521-534.

Mahroof, M. M. M. "Muslim Education in Ceylon, 1780-1880." Islamic Culture, Ap, 1972.

_____. "Muslim Education in Ceylon 1881-1901." Islamic Culture 47(O, 1973):301-325.

Mukherjee, Sadhan. Ceylon. Island that Changed. New Delhi, India: People's Publishing House, 1971.

Pieris, P. R. "The Sociological Consequences of Imperialism, with Special Reference to Ceylon." Doctoral dissertation, London School of Economic, 1950.

"Problems of Muslim Minorities." Dawn (Karachi, Pakistan), Ag 29, 1976. [Sri Lanka, Nepal, Ghana]

Ruberu, T. R. A. "Educational Developments Under the British in Ceylon During the Period 1796-1834." Doctoral dissertation, U. of London, Institute of Education, 1960.

_____. "Educational Tradition Indigenous to Ceylon." Paedagogica Historica 14(1974):106-117.

Schwarz, Walter. The Tamils of Sri Lanka. Lodnon: Minority Rights Group, S, 1975.

Sharma, C. L. Ethnicity, Communal Relations, and Education in Sri Lanka, 1976. ERIC ED 125 143.

Sivanandan, A. "The Politics of Language: 3. Ceylon: An Essay in Interpretation." Race Today, Je, 1970.

Thurairatnam, Dante. "Education and National Development: Sri Lanka, A Case Study." Doctoral dissertation, Bowling Green State U., 1978. Univ. Microfilms Order No. 7901456.

Uswatte-Aratchi, G. "University Admissions in Ceylon: Their Economic and Social Background and Employment Expectations." Modern Asian Studies 8(J1, 1974):289-318.

Wesumperuma, D. "The Migration and Conditions of Immigrant Labour in Ceylon, 1880-1910." Doctoral dissertation, U. of London, School of Oriental and African Studies.

Wickremesinghe, C. K. "The Sociological Implications of Educational Policies in Ceylon Since 1947." Bachelor's thesis, Oxford U., 1967.

Sudan

Albino, Oliver. The Sudan: A Southern Viewpoint. London: Oxford U. Press, 1970.

Balamoan, G. A. Policies in the Anglo-Egyptian Sudan. 1884-1956. Cambridge, MA: Center for Population Studies, Harvard U., 1976.

Beshir, Mohamed. The Southern Sudan: From Conflict to Peace. New York: Barnes & Noble, 1975.

Collins, Robert O. The Southern Sudan in Historical Perspective. Tel Aviv: U. of Tel Aviv Students Association, 1975.

Deng, Francis Mading. Africans of Two Worlds. The Dinka in Afro-Arab Sudan. New Haven, CT: Yale U. Press, 1977,

El-Badrawi, Abdul Monem. "Die Entwicklung der Demokratie im Sudan von 1936 bis 1968." Doctoral dissertation, U. of Bonn, 1971.

Meisler, Stanley. "Ten Years of Fratricide." Nation, D 6, 1971.

O'Neill, Norman. "Imperialism and Class Struggle in Sudan." Race and Class 20 (Summer, 1978):1-19.

Roden, D. "Regional Inequality and Rebellion in the Sudan." Geographical Review 64(1974): 498-516.

Sanderson, Lilian M. "Education and Administrative Control in Colonial Sudan and Northern Nigeria." Afric. Aff. (London) 74(O, 1975): 427-441.

_____. "Education in the Southern Sudan, 1898-1948." Doctoral dissertation, U. of London, External, 1966.

Sarkesian, Sam C. "The Southern Sudan: A Reassessment." African Studies Review, Ap, 1973.

Sconyers, David Joseph. "British Policy and Mission Education in the Southern Sudan: 1928-1946." Doctoral dissertation, U. of Pennsylvania, 1978. Univ. Microfilms Order No. 7816355.

Sommer, John W. "The Sudan: A Geographical Investigation of the Historical and Social Roots of Political Dissension." Doctoral dissertation, Boston U., 1968.

Tajelanbia, A. E. D. "An Analysis of Cultural and Social Heterogeneity of a Sudanese Town El Obeid." Doctoral dissertation, U. of Manchester, 1971.

Surinam

De Groot, Silvia W. Djuka Society and Social Change: History of an Attempt to Develop a Bush Negro Community in Surinam, 1919-1926. New York: Humanities Press, 1969.

_____. "Djuka Society and Social Change. History of an Attempt to Develop a Bush Negro Community in Surinam, 1917-1926." Doctoral dissertation, U. of Amsterdam, 1969.

_____. From Isolation towards Integration: The Surinam Maroons and their Colonial Rulers: Official Documents Relating to the Djukas (1845-1863). The Hague: Martinus Nijhoff, 1977.

Dew, Edward. "Surinam: The Struggle for Ethnic Balance and Identity." Plural Societies 5 (Autumn, 1974).

Grodd, Gabriele. "Kulturwandel der indonesischen Einwanderer in Surinam." Doctoral dissertation, U. of Freiburg in Breisgau, 1971.

Hellinga, W. G. Language Problems in Surinam: Dutch as the Language of the Schools. Amsterdam: North-Holland Pub. Co., 1955.

Herskovits, Melville Jean, and Herskovits, Frances S. Rebel Destiny: Among the Bush Negroes of Dutch Guiana. New York: McGraw-Hill, 1934.

Hoetink, H. "Surinam and Curacao." In Neither Slave Nor Free. The Freedmen of African Descent in the Slave Societies of the New World, pp. 59-83. Edited by David W. Cohen and Jack P. Greene. Baltimore, MD: Johns Hopkins U. Press, 1972.

Kloos, Peter. The Akuriyo of Surinam. A Case of Emergence from Isolation. Copenhagen: International Work Group for Indigeneous Affairs, My, 1977.

Lamur, Humphrey Ewald. "The Demographic Evolution of Surinam, 1920-1970. A Socio-demographic Analysis." Doctoral dissertation, U. of Amsterdam, 1973.

Lamur, H. E. The Demographic Evolution of Surinam 1920-1970: A Socio-Demographic Analysis. Tr. Dirk H. van der Elst. The Hague: Martinus Nijhoff, 1973.

Lichtveld, Lou. "The Social and Economic Background of Education in Surinam and the Netherlands Antilles." Vox Guyanae 1 (1954-1955):35-58.

Lier, Rudolf A. J. van. _Sarnenleving in een Grensgebied_. The Hague: N.p., 1949. [History of Surinam until 1940.]

Malefijt, Annemarie de Waal. _The Javanese of Surinam: Segment of a Plural Society_. Assen, Netherlands: Van Gorcum, 1963.

Price, Richard. _The Guiana Maroons. A Historical and Bibliographical Introduction_. Baltimore: Johns Hopkins U. Press, 1976.

_____. _Saramaka Social Structure: Analysis of a Maroon Society in Surinam_. Rio Piedras, Puerto Rico: Institute of Caribbean Studies, U. of Puerto Rico, 1975.

Speckmann, Johan Dirk. "The Indian Group in the Segmented Society of Surinam." _Caribbean Studies_ 3(Ap, 1963):3-17.

Van Lier, R. A. J. _Frontier Society: A Social Analysis of the History of Surinam_. The Hague, Netherlands: Martinus Nijhoff, 1971.

Swaziland

Kuper, H. _The Uniform of Color: A Study of White-Black Relationships in Swaziland_. Witwatersrand U. Press, 1947.

Lewis-Jones, H. "Education for Inferiority: Two Decades of Bantu Education." _Free Southern Africa_ 1(1973):36-41.

Sweden

Allardt, Erik. "Finns and Swedes as Minorities in Sweden and Finland." _Scandanavian Review_ 66(Mr, 1978):17-23.

Anderson, C. Arnold. "Expanding Educational Opportunities: Conceptualization and Measurement." _Higher Education_ 4(N, 1975): 393-408.

_____. "Lifetime Inter-Occupational Mobility Patterns in Sweden." _Acta Sociologica_ 1 (1956):168-202.

Andersson, Berit, Arnman, Göran, Jönsson, Ingrid, and Swedner, Harald. _Social Segregation in Grundskolan_. Sociologiska Institutionen, Lunds Universitet, F, 1975.

Austrup, Gerhard. "Aktuelle Wanderungsprobleme zwischen Finnland und Schweden. Ein Beitrag zum europäischen Migrations--und Gastarbeiterproblem." _Geographische Rundschau_ 29(1977):235-240.

Boye-Moller, M. "Language Training for Immigrant Workers in Sweden." _International Labour Review_ 109(D, 1973).

Duckenfield, Mike. "Immigration Policy Faces Language Hurdle." _Times Education Supplement_, Mr 24, 1978.

Duner, Anders. "A Longitudinal Study of the Career Process." In _Vad skall det bliva?_, pp. 323-336. Stockholm: Allmänna Förlaget, 1972.

Ekstrand, Lars Henric. _Adjustment among Immigrant Pupils in Sweden: Social, Emotional and Linguistic Variables and their Relationship_. Educational and Psychological Interactions, 1974. ERIC Ed 125 282.

_____. _Migrant Adaptation--A Cross Cultural Problem. A Review of Research on Migration, Minority Groups and Cultural Differences_, with Special Regards to Children, 1977. ERIC ED 144 368.

Fischer, Ludwig. _Die Produktion von Kopfarbeitern: Spätkapitalistische Bildungspolitik am Beispiel den schweidischen Hochschulwesens_. Berlin: Verlag für der Studium der Arbeiterbewegung, 1974.

Friedman, Helen, and Friedman, Harold. "Letter from Malmö, Sweden." _Integrateducation_ 13 (Ja-F, 1975):14-16.

Fulcher, James. "Class Conflict in Sweden." _Sociology_ 7(1973):49-70.

Grundin, Hans U. _Läs-och skrivförmagans utveckling genom skolaren_. Stockholm: Liber Läromedel, 1975. [English-language summary, pp. 137-142]

Grundin, Hans U. _The Reading and Writing Abilities of Swedish Pupils: A Survey of the Development from Grade 1 to Grade 12_, 1975. ERIC ED 134 977.

Haavio-Mannilo, Elina, and Stenius, Kerstin. _Mental Health Problems of New Ethnic Minorities in Sweden_. Helsinki, Finland: Institute of Sociology, U. of Helsinki, 1974.

_____ and _____. "Mental Health Problems of the New Ethnic Minorities in Sweden." _Acta Sociologica_ 17(1974-1975):367-392.

Hammar, T. _The First Immigrant Election_. Stockholm: Commission on Immigration Research, 1977.

_____. "Sverige at svenskarna." Doctoral dissertation, U. of Stockholm, 1964. [See English summary: "Sweden for the Swedes: Immigration policy, aliens control and right of asylum 1900-1932."]

Härnqvist, Kjell. "Social Factors and Educational Choice: A Preliminary Study of Some Effects of the Swedish School Reform." _International Journal of Educational Reform_, Vol. I, pp. 87-102.

Herz, L. "A Note on Identification Assimilation among Forty Jews in Malmö." Jewish Journal of Sociology 11(D, 1969):165-173.

Heymowski, A. Swedish "Travellers" and Their Ancestry. A Social Isolate or an Ethnic Minority? Uppsala, Sweden: Almquis-Wiksell, 1969. [Gypsies and others]

Hill, Michael J. "Sweden's White Migrants Face Trouble." Race Today 3(N, 1971): 379-380.

Hill, R. G. P. (ed.). The Lapps Today in Finland, Norway and Sweden, I. Paris: Mouton, 1960.

Hill, R. G. P., and Nickul, K. (eds.). The Lapps Today in Finland, Norway and Sweden, II. Oslo-Bergen-Tromso, Norway: Universitetsforlage, 1969.

Hufford, Larry. Sweden's Power Elite. Washington, DC: U. Press of America, 1977.

Hughes, William E. Relations Between Swedes and Black Ethnic Groups. A Historical Survey: 1624-1970. Stockholm: Institute of Education, U. of Stockholm, n.d.

Hughes, William E. Relations Between Swedes and Black Ethnic Groups: A Pilot Study. Stockholm: Institute of Education, U. of Stockholm, Ag, 1969.

_____. Relations Between Swedes and Black Ethnic Groups: Some Theoretical and Methodological Perspectives and Considerations. Stockholm: Institute of Education, U. of Stockholm, 1969.

_____. Skin Color Identification and Preference Among Children in Sweden and America: A Comparative Analysis. Uppsala: Pedagogiska institutionen, U. of Uppsala, 1975.

Husen, T. Problems of Differentiation in Swedish Compulsory Schooling. Stockholm: Scandanavian U. Books, 1962.

_____. "The Relation Between Selectivity and Social Class in Secondary Education." Educational Sciences, F, 1966.

_____. "Responsiveness and Resistance in the Educational System to Changing Needs of Society: Some Swedish Experiences." International Review of Education 15(1969): 476-487.

_____. Social Background and Educational Career. Research Perspectives on Equality of Educational Opportunity. Paris: Organization for Economic Cooperation and Development, 1972.

Immigrant Pupils and Immigrant Teaching in Sweden: Some Findings of Surveys in 1975, 1976 and 1977. Vallingby, Sweden: National Central Bureau of Statistics, 1977.

Jaakkola, Magdalena. "Diglossia and Bilingualism among Two Minorities in Sweden." Linguistics 183(D, 1976):67-84. [Finns]

Johannesson, I. "Bilingual-Bicultural Education of Immigrant Children in Sweden." International Review of Education 21(1975): 347-355. [Finnish children in Malmoe]

Johansson, H. B. "Samerna och Sameunde visningen i Sverige." Doctoral dissertation, Umea U., 1977. The Saamees and Sami Education in Sweden, Lapps

Juttner, Egon. "Der Kampf um die schwedische Schulreform." Doctoral dissertation, U. of Berlin, 1970.

Koblik, Steven (ed.). Sweden's Development from Poverty to Affluence, 1750-1970. Tr. Joanne Johnson. Minneapolis: U. of Minnesota Press, 1975.

Kokot, Eugene. "Swedish Reindeer Lapps: A Minority within a Minority." Scandanavian Review 66(Mr, 1978):28-35.

Korhonen, Olavi. "Linguistic and Cultural Diversity among the Saamis and the Development of Standard Saamish." Linguistics 183(D, 1976):51-65.

Korpi, Walter. "Poverty, Social Assistance and Social Policy in Post-War Sweden." Acta Sociologica 18(1975):120-141.

Kramer, Jane. "The Invadrare." New Yorker, Mr 22, 1976. [Foreign workers in Sweden]

Lipp, Ellen. "Bilingualism and Bilingual Education Among the Second Generation Estonians in Stockholm." Master's thesis, American U., 1977. Univ. Microfilms Order No. 13-10,390.

Majava, Altti. Migration Between Finland and Sweden from 1946 to 1974. Helsinki: Planning Division, Ministry of Labor, 1975.

Marklund, Sixten. "Comparative School Research and the Swedish School Reform." International Review of Education 17(1971):39-48.

Markovits, Andrei S. Educational Reform and Class Cleavages in Social Democratic Regimes: The Case of Sweden, S, 1976. ERIC ED 137 202.

Mellbin, Tore. "The Children of Swedish Nomad Lapps." Acta Paediat. 51, suppl. 131(1962).

_____. The Children of Nomad Swedish Lapps. A Study of their Health, Growth, and Development. Uppsala: N.p., 1962.

Meurle, Kristina, and Andríc, Mile. Background to the Yugoslav Migration to Sweden. Case Study of a Group of Yugoslav Workers at a Factory in Sweden. Lund, Sweden: Sociologiska institionen, U. of Lund, 1971.

"Minorities." Scandanavian Review, 1978, pp. 1-112.

Moberg, Verne. "The Great Swedish School Reform." Saturday Review of Education, Mr, 1973.

Nyland, Bella. "The Debate on Freedom and Equality in Swedish Education, 1909-1928." Doctoral dissertation, U. of Uppsala, 1975.

Öberg, K. "Treatment of Immigrant Workers in Sweden." International Labour Review 110 (Jl, 1974).

Paulston, Christina Bratt. Linguistic Aspects of Emigrant Children, 1977. ERIC ED 144 340 Finnish children

Paulston, Christina Bratt, and Paulston, Rolland G. Language and Ethnic Boundaries, S, 1976. ERIC ED 136 556. Swedish Lapps and others

Paulston, Rolland G. "Ethnic Revival and Educational Conflict in Swedish Lapland." Comparative Education Review 20(Je, 1976): 179-192.

_____. Separate Education as an Ethnic Survival Strategy: The Finlandssvenka Case, N, 1976. ERIC ED 134 489. [Swedes in Finland]

_____. Swedish Comprehensive School Reform, 1918-1950: The Period of Formulation and Adoption. New York: Teachers College Press, 1968.

Polack, A. The Jews of Sweden. Jerusalem: N.p., 1961. [In Hebrew]

Ruong, Israel. "Lapp Schools, Teacher Education and Trans-Cultural Studies." In Education in the North, pp. 325-332. Arctic Institute of North America, U. of Alaska, 1972.

_____. The Lapps in Sweden. Stockholm: The Swedish Institute for Cultural Relations with Foreign Countries, Victor Pettersons Bokindustri AB, 1967.

Sandberg, Lars G. "The Case of the Impoverished Sophisticate: Human Capital and Swedish Economic Growth before World War I." Journal of Economic History 39(Mr, 1979): 225-241.

Scase, Richard. Social Democracy in Capitalist Society. Totowa, NJ: Rowman and Littlefield, 1977.

_____.(ed.). Swedish Class Structure. New York: Pergamon, 1976.

Schwartz, David. Identitet och Minoritet. Stockholm: Almqvist & Wiksell, 1971.

_____. Svenska Minoriteter. Stockholm: Aldus, n.d.

[Special issue on Gypsies in Malmö]. Synpunkten 13(1976):1-52.

Standing Conference of European Ministers of Education, Strasbourg. Ad Hoc Committee on the Education of Migrants. Country Report (Sweden), D 7, 1974. ERIC ED 094 900.

Stjarne, Kerstin. "A Report from Sweden." Interracial Books for Children 5(1974):15. [On racism in Swedish children's literature]

Stockfelt-Hoatson, Britt-Ingrid. "The Teaching of Bilingual Infant Immigrants in a Swedish Town." Linguistics 198(O, 1977):119-125.

Svensson, Tom G. Ethnicity and Mobilization in Sami Politics. Stockholm: Department of Anthroplogy, U. of Stockholm, 1976.

Sweden. Ministry of Labour. Immigrants in Sweden: A Summary of Swedish Immigration Policy. Stockholm: Ministry of Labour, 1975.

Swedner, Harald. "The Swedish Immigrant Problem: There Exist No Simple Radical Solutions." In Les travailleurs étrangers en Europe occidentale, pp. 121-133. Edited by Philippe J. Bernard. Paris: Mouton, 1976.

Takman, John, with Lindgren, Lars. The Gypsies in Sweden. A Socio-Medical Study. Stockholm: Liber Förlag, 1976.

Therborn, Göran. "Power in the Kingdom of Sweden." International Socialist Journal 2 (1965):51-63.

Thomas, David. "Newcomers in Sweden." New Community 1(O, 1971):29-31.

Thulstrup, Ake. "'Freedom Movements' in Sweden. Nazi Influence." Wiener Library Bulletin 19(Autumn, 1965):27-30.

Tillhagen, C. H. Zigenare I Severige. Stockholm: N.p., 1965.

Tomasson, Richard F. "From Elitism to Egalitarianism in Swedish Education." Sociology of Education, Ap, 1965.

_____. "Radical Restructuring of Higher Education in Sweden." Educational Record 56 (Spring, 1975):78-88.

Trankell, Arne, and Trankell, Ingrid. "Problems of the Swedish Gypsies." Scandinavian Journal of Educational Research (1968):141-214.

Wadensjö, E. "Remuneration of Migrant Workers in Sweden. International Labour Review 112 (Jl, 1975).

Wigoder, Geoffrey. "The Polish Jews of Sweden." Jerusalem Post, F 2, 1979.

Willke, I. "Schooling of Immigrant Children in West Germany, Sweden, England." International Review of Education 21(1975): 357-382.

Willmann, Bodo. "Economic Change, Educational Needs, and Secondary School Reform in Sweden." Western European Education 9 (Summer, 1977):3-112.

Switzerland

Belding, Robert E. "The Swiss Unsystem of Education." Bulletin of the NASSP 55(N, 1971):23-31.

Braun, Rudolf. Sozio-kulturelle Probleme der Eingliederung italienischer Arbeitskräfte in der Schweiz. Erlenbach-Zürich, Switzerland: Eugen Rentsch, 1970.

Carter, Vincent O. The Bern Book: A Record of a Voyage of the Mind. New York: John Day, 1973. [A black American writer in Switzerland]

Dürrenmatt, Peter. "Kontrolle und Assimilierung." Basler Nachrichten, F 18-19, 1967.

Egger et Boillat. "L'éducation des enfants de travailleurs migrants en Suisse. Problemes et solutions." International Review of Education 21 (1975).

Hagmann, Hermann-Michel. Les travailleurs étrangers chance et tourment de la Suisse. Lausanne: Payot, 1966.

Hoffmann-Novotny, Hans Joachim. "Immigrant Minorities in Switzerland: Sociological, Legal, and Political Aspects." Paper presented to Annual Meeting of the Society for the Study of Social Problems, Montreal, Ag, 1974.

_____. Soziologie des Fremdarbeiterprobleme. Eine Theoretische und empirische Analyse am Beispiel der Schweiz. Stuttgart, Germany: Ferd. Enke, 1973.

Im Hof, Ubrich. "Die Viersprachigkeit der Schweiz als Minoritätenproblem des 19. und 20. Jahrhunderts." In Geschichte und politische Wissenschaft... Edited by Beat Junker et al. Bern: Francke Verlag, 1975.

Johnston, R. J., and White, P. E. "Reactions to Foreign Workers in Switzerland: An Essay in Electoral Geography." Tijdschrift voor Economische en Sociale Geografie (1977):341-354.

Kulling, Friedrich. Bei Uns wie überall? Antisemitismus in der Schweiz 1866-1900. Zurich: SIG, 1977.

Michel-Adler, E. "Schule ohne Chance-gleichheit." Profil 51(1972):72-83.

Munz, E. "Die Schule, der Schularzt und des freundsprachige Kind." Präventiv-medizin (Ja-F, 1963).

Perrenoud, P. Stratification Culturelle et Réussite Scolaire. Geneva, Switzerland: N.p., 1970.

Rovere, Giovanni. Testi di italiano popolare: autobiografie di lavoratori e figli di lavatori emigranti. Rome: Centro Studi Emigrazione, 1977. [Italian workers in Switzerland]

Steiner, H. "Unsere Ausländerkinder und die Schulen." Neue Zürchen Zeitung, Ja 20, 1966.

Wallimann, Isidor. "Toward a Theoretical Understanding of Ethnic Antagonism: The Case of the Foreign Workers in Switzerland." Zeitschrift für Soziologie 3(1974):84-94.

Weidler-Steinberg, Augusta. Geschichte der Juden in der Schweiz vom 16. Jahrhundert bis nach der Emanizipation. 2 vols. Edited and enlarged by Florence Guggenheim-Grunberg. Zurich: Schweyerischen Israelitischer Gemeindebund, 1966, 1970.

Syria

Armel, Kayla (ed.). Syria: A Prison to 4500 Jews. Toronto, Canada: Beth Tzedec Congregation, N 27, 1974.

Fein, Leonard, and Daoudi, Adib. "Syria's Jews. An Exchange of Correspondence." Moment 3(Ap, 1978):29-33.

Friedman, Saul S. "The Anguish of Syrian Jewry." Midstream 21(Je-Jl, 1975):14-22.

Haddad, Robert M. Syrian Christians in Muslim Society: An Interpretation. Princeton, NJ: Princeton U. Press, 1970.

Murphy, Kevin. "The Forgotten Jews Who Live in Prison City." Evening News (London), O 25, 1978. [Damascus]

Persoff, Menachem (ed.). The Jews in Syria. 2 vols. Jerusalem: WZO, Youth and Hechalutz Dept. and the Dept. of Sephardic Communities in conjunction with the Israel Council for Jews in Arab Lands, 1976.

Sanjian, Avedis K. The Armenian Communities in Syria Under Ottoman Dominion. Cambridge, MA: Harvard U. Press, 1965.

Sawdayee, Maurice M. "The Impact of Western European Education on the Jewish Millet of Baghdad: 1860-1950." Doctoral dissertation, New York U., 1977. Univ. Microfilms Order No. 7803136.

Shestack, Jerome. "Persecution of Syrian Jews." Bulletin of International League for the Rights of Man, S, 1974.

Siegel, Judy. "The Nightmare of Syrian Jews." Jerusalem Post, Ap 19, 1974.

Vanly, Ismet Scheriff. The Kurdish Problem in Syria. London: N.p., 1968.

_____. Le Kurdistan irakien, entité nationale. Neuchâtel: N.p., 1970.

Tanzania

Barkan, Joel D. An African Dilemma: University Students, Development and Politics in Ghana, Tanzania and Uganda. New York: Oxford U. Press, 1976.

Cameron, John. "The Integration of Education in Tanganyika." Comparative Education Review, F, 1967.

Court, David. "The Education System as a Response to Inequality in Tanzania and Kenya." Journal of Modern African Studies 14(1976).

Dodd, William. "Centralization in Education in Mainland Tanzania." Comparative Education Review 12(1968):268-280.

Dolan, Louis Francis. "Transition from Colonialism to Self-reliance in Tanzanian Education." Doctoral dissertation, U. of Michigan, 1970.

Furley, O. C., and Watson, Tom. "Education in Tanganyika Between the Wars: Attempts to Blend Two Cultures." South Atlantic Quarterly 65(Autumn, 1966):471-490.

Gottneid, A. Church and Education in Tanzania. Nairobi: EAPN, 1976.

Gould, W. T. S. "Patterns of School Provision in Colonial East Africa." Ét. hist. afric. 8(1976):131-148.

Guilotte, Joseph Valsin III. "Becoming One People: Social and Cultural Integration in a Multi-Ethnic Community in Rural Tanzania." Doctoral dissertation, Tulane U., 1973. Univ. Microfilms Order No. 74-10688.

Hector, Henry J. "The Government's Role in African Post Primary Education in Tanganyika, 1919-1939." Master's thesis, Teachers College, Columbia U., 1967.

Hirji, Karim. "School Education and Underdevelopment in Tanzania." Maji Maji 12 (S, 1973).

Konter, J. H. "An Analysis of an African Rural Economy of Poverty at Grass Roots Level." Cult. et Devt. 8(1976):607-622.

Kuper, Leo. The Pity of It All: Polarisation of Racial and Ethnic Relations. London: Ducksworth, 1977.

Mbilinyi, Marjorie J. "Basic Education: Tool of Liberation or Exploitation?" Prospects 7(1977):489-503.

_____. "Education, Stratification, and Sexism in Tanzania: Policy Implications." African Review 3(Je, 1973):327-340.

Report of Education Conference, 1925. Together with the Report of the Committee for the Standardization of the Swahili Language. Dar-es-Salaam: Government Printers, 1925.

Rodney, Walter. "Class Contradictions in Tanzania." Panafricanist 6(1975):15-29.

Samoff, Joel. Education in Tanzania: Class Formation and Reproduction, S, 1976. ERIC ED 137 201.

Shivji, Issa G. Class Struggles in Tanzania. New York: Monthly Review Press, 1976.

_____. Tanzania: The Silent Class Struggle. Dar es Salaam and Lund, Sweden: N.p., 1971.

Smith, A. S. "The Contribution of the Missions to the Educational Structure and Administrative Policy in Tanganyika, 1918-1961." Master's thesis, Sheffield U., 1962.

_____. "British Colonial Education Policy--Tanganyika: A Variation on the Theme." Paedagogica Historica 2(1965):435-454.

Swatman, J. E. D. "Access to Education: The Changing Pattern in the Location of Schools." Tanzania Notes Rec. (D, 1976):107-114. [1863-1969]

Thompson, A. E. "Partnership in Education in Tanganyika, 1919-1961." Master's thesis, U. of London, Institute of Education, 1965.

Walji, Shirin Remtulla. " A History of the Ismaili Community in Tanzania." Doctoral dissertation, U. of Wisconsin, 1974.

Thailand

Andelman, David A. "Thai Moslems, Oppressed Minority, Strive to Find Way in Secular World." New York Times, Jl 1, 1975.

Brand, Arie. "Education and Social Mobility in Thailand." Sociologische Gids 15 (1968):355-367.

Chantarapunya, Panomporn. "The Extent of Equalization of Educational Opportunity in Public Secondary Schools in Thailand." Doctoral dissertation, U. of Illinois, 1976. Univ. Microfilms Order No. 76-24054.

Coughlin, Richard J. Double-Identity: The Chinese in Modern Thailand. Hong Kong: Hong Kong U. Press, 1960.

Dassé, Martial. "Les rébellions ethnique du nord de la Birmanie et de la Thaïlande (Part 1)." Monde Asiatiques (Summer, 1976): 233-250.

Dautremer, J. "Les races de l'Indochine, III: Thai du royaume de Siam." L'Ethnographie 4 (Jl, 1914):31-42.

Dibble, Charles Ryder. "The Chinese in Thailand Against the Background of Chinese-Thai Relations." Doctoral dissertation, Syracuse U., 1961. Univ. Microfilms Order No. 62-01097.

Evers, Hans-Dieter (ed.). Loosely Structured Social Systems: Thailand in Comparative Perspective. New Haven, CT: Yale U. Southeast Asian Studies, 1969.

Flanagan, P. Imperial Anthropology--Thailand. Sydney: N.p., 1972.

Flood, E. Thadeus. "The Vietnamese Refugees in Thailand. Minority Manipulation in Counterinsurgency." Bulletin of Concerned Asian Scholars 9(Jl-S, 1977):31-47.

Foster, Brian Lee. "Ethnicity and Economy: The Case of the Mons in Thailand." Doctoral dissertation, U. of Michigan, 1972. Univ. Microfilms Order No. 73-11113.

Frederickson, Charles K. "Alternatives for Bilingual Education in Thailand: Theory and Practice." Doctoral disseration, Loyola U. of Chicago, 1975. Univ. Microfilms Order No. 75-14508.

Geddes, William R. Migrants of the Mountains: The Cultural Ecology of the Blue Miao (Hmong Njua) of Thailand. Oxford: Clarendon Press, 1976. [Miao people]

Gua, Bo. "Opium, Bombs and Trees: The Future of the H'Mong Tribesmen in Northern Thailand." Journal of Contemporary Asia 5 (1975):70-81.

Gurevich, Robert. "Language, Minority Education, and Social Mobility: The Case of Rural Northeast Thailand." Journal of Research and Development in Education 9(Summer, 1976):137-144.

Guskin, Alan Edward. "Changing Identity: The Assimilation of Chinese in Thailand." Doctoral dissertation, U. of Michigan, 1968. Univ. Microfilms Order No. 69-12115.

Haemindra, Natawan. "The Problem of the Thai-Muslims in the Four Southern Provinces of Thailand (Part 1)." J.S.E. Asian Studies 7 (S, 1976):197-225.

_____. "The Problem of the Thai-Muslims in the Four Southern Provinces of Thailand (Part 2)." J.S.E. Asian Stud. 8(Mr, 1977): 85-105.

Kerdpibule, Udom. "Education and Social Stratification: A Thai Study." Social Science Review 8(Mr, 1971):78-85.

Keyes, Charles F. "Buddhism and National Integration in Thailand." Journal of Asian Studies 30(My, 1971):551-567.

Keyes, Charles. Isan: Regionalism in Northern Thailand. Ithaca, NY: Cornell U. Press, 1967.

Keyes, Charles F. (ed.). Ethnic Adaptation and Identity: The Karen on the Thai Frontier With Burma. Phiadelphia: Institute for the Study of Human Issues, 1978.

Kraft, Richard John. Education in Thailand: Student Background and University Admission. Bangkok: Educational Planning Office, Ministry of Education, 1968.

_____. "Student Background, University Admission, and Academic Achievement in the Universities of Thailand." Doctoral dissertation, Michigan State U., 1968. Univ. Microfilms Order No. 69-05899.

Labmala, Surasugdi. "A Model for Evaluation of Educational Opportunity in the Public Schools of Thailand." Doctoral dissertation, U. of Illinois, 1973. Univ. Microfilms Order No. 74-12,277.

Landon, K. P. The Chinese in Thailand. London: Oxford U. Press, 1941.

Marks, Thomas A. "The Meo Hill Tribe Problem in Thailand." Asian Survey 13(O, 1973).

Maxwell, William E. "The Ethnic Identity of Male Chinese Students in Thai Universities." Comparative Education Review 18(F, 1974): 55-69.

Minority Groups in Thailand. Washington, DC: Center for Research in Social Systems, American U., n.d.

Nguyen-Van-Khoi, Joseph. "A Study of the Impact of Christian Missionaries on Education in Thailand, 1662-1910." Doctoral dissertation, St. Louis U., 1972. Univ. Microfilms Order No. 72-23983.

Noranitiphadungkarn, Chakrit. "Community Elites and the Power Structure: A Comparative Study of Two Communities in Thailand." Doctoral dissertation, U. of Pittsburgh, 1968. Univ. Microfilms Order No. 69-04100.

Punyodyana, Boonsanong. "The Changing Status and Future Role of the Chinese in Thailand." In Trends in Thailand, pp. 59-69. Edited by M. Rajaretnam and Lim So Jean. Singapore: Institute of Southeast Asian Studies, 1973.

_____. "The Chinese in Thailand: A Synopsis of Research Approaches." Philippines Sociological Review 24(1976):57-61.

_____. Chinese-Thai Differential Assimilation in Bangkok: An Exploratory Study. Ithaca, NY: Southeast Asia Program, Cornell U., 1971.

_____. "Later-Life Socialization and Differential Social Assimilation of the Chinese in Urban Thailand." Social Forces 50(D, 1971):232-238.

Schrock, J. L. and others. Minority Groups in Thailand. Pamphlet No. 550-107, Ethnographic Study Series. Washington, DC: U.S. Army Headquarters, 1970.

Shurke, Astri. "Loyalists and Separatists: The Muslims in Southern Thailand." Asian Survey 17(Mr, 1977):237-250.

Skinner, G. William. "Change and Persistence in Chinese Culture Overseas: a Comparison of Thailand and Java." Journal of the South Seas Society (1960):86-100.

_____. "The Thailand Chinese: Assimilation in a Changing Society." Asia, Autumn, 1964.

The Social Background of Students and Their Prospect of Success at School. Thailand National Commission for UNESCO, My, 1971. ERIC ED 060 276.

Suepsaman, Banchong. "The Study of Stress in Thai Children: An Epidemiological Study of School Children in Bangkok, Thailand." Doctoral dissertation, U. of North Carolina, 1973. Univ. Microfilms Order No. 74=15397.

Suhrke, Astri. "The Thai Muslims: Some Aspects of Minority Integration." Pacific Affairs 43(Winter, 1970-71).

Suthasasna, Arong. "Ruling Elite, Higher Education, and Thai Society." Doctoral dissertation, U. of Illinois, 1973. Univ. Microfilms Order No. 74-12,205.

Tirrell, Raymond Francis. "An Analysis of Factors That are Assumed to Influence Acculturation and Assimilation of Tribal Minorities in Northern Thailand." Doctoral dissertation, Syracuse U., 1972. Univ. Microfilms Order No. 73-09569.

Tobias, Stephen F. "Buddhism, Belonging, and Detachment--Some Paradoxes of Chinese Ethnicity in Thailand." J. Asian Stud. 36 (F, 1977):303-326.

Valenti, Jasper J., and Gutek, Gerald L. Education and Society in India and Thailand. Washington, DC: U. Press of America, 1977.

Watson, J. K. P. "A Conflict of Nationalism: The Chinese and Education in Thailand, 1900-1960." Paedagogica Historica 16(1976): 429-451.

Wongswadiwat, Jirawat. "The Psychological Assimilation of Chinese University Students in Thailand." Doctoral dissertation, U. of Illinois, 1973. Univ. Microfilms Order No. 74-12,257.

Wongyai, Prasan. "Elites and Power Structure in Thailand." Doctoral dissertation, Florida State U., 1974. Univ. Microfilms Order No. 75-00983.

Wyatt, David Kent. "The Beginnings of Modern Education in Thailand, 1868-1910." Doctoral dissertation, Cornell U., 1966. Univ. Microfilms Order No. 67-01442.

_____. "Education and the Modernization of Thai Society." In Change and Persistence in Thai Society: Essays in Honor of Lauriston Sharp. Edited by G. William Skinner and A. Thomas Kirsch. Ithaca, NY: Cornell U. Press, 1975.

_____. The Politics of Reform in Thailand: Education in the Reign of King Chulalongkorn. New Haven, CT: Yale U. Press, 1969.

Togo

Delval, R. "Les musulmans aux Togo." L'Afr. et l'Asie 10(1974):4-21.

Tunisia

Allman, J. "La mobilité sociale et l'éducation de masse dans la Tunisie indépendante." R. Occident musulman Méditerr 19(1975):17-28.

_____. Social Mobility and Educational Access in Tunisia. Leiden: Brill, 1977.

Bacha, Najet. "L'éducation en Tunisie depuis la reformé de 1958." Revue Tunisienne de Sciences Sociales 9(1972):167-188.

Freund, W. Die Djerbi in Tunesien: soziologische Analyse einer nordafrikanischen Minderheit. Meisenheim-am-Glan: A. Hain, 1970.

Lelong, Michel. "Le Patrimoine musulman dans l'enseignement tunisien apres l'independance." Doctoral dissertation, U. of Titograd, 1971.

Pirson, Ronald. "Déstructuration et reconstruction de la société tunisienne: du groupe à la classe sociale." Cahiers Internationaux de Sociologie 64(1978):147-178.

Roy, Bruno. "Contribution à l'étude des communautés juives du Sud-Et de la Tunisie." Doctoral dissertation, U. of Montpellier, 1969.

Soumille, P. "L'idée de race chez les Européens de Tunisie pendant les années 1890-1910." R. hist. Maghrébine (Ja, 1976): 59-66.

Tessler, Mark A. "The Identity of Religious Minorities in Non-Secular States: Jews in Tunisia and Morocco and Arabs in Israel." Comparative Studies in Society and History 20(Jl, 1978):359-373.

_____. Three Nonassimilating Minorities: Jews in Tunisia and Morocco and Arabs in Israel. New York: Praeger, 1977.

Toumi, Mohsen. "La scolarisation et le tissu social en Tunisie." R. fr. et pol. afric. (Ja, 1975):32-61.

Zoughlami, Younes. "L'enseignement en Tunisie vingt ans après la Réforme de 1958: L'évolution de la scolarisation." Maghreb (O-D, 1977):44-51.

Turkey

Bedoukiah, Kerop. The Urchin: An Armenian's Escape. London: John Murray, 1979.

Boyajian, Dickran H. Armenia: The Case for a Forgotten Genocide. Westwood, NJ: Educational Book Crafters, 1972.

Haim, Sylvia G. "Aspects of Jewish Life in Baghdad under the Monarchy." Middle E. Studies 12(My, 1976):188-208.

Kansu, Sevket Aziz. "Rassengeschichte der Türkei." Belleten 159(Jl, 1976):353-386.

Kazarian, Haigazn. "Opening of the Turkish Genocide of 1915-18: Arrest and Murder of the Armenian Intellectuals." Armenian Review 3(1971).

_____. "The Turkish Genocide of the Armenians: A Premeditated and Official Assault." Armenian Review 30(Spring, 1977): 3-25.

Krikorian, Mesrob K. Armenians in the Service of the Ottoman Empire 1860-1908. London: Routledge & Kegan Paul, 1977.

Nalbandian, Louise. The Armenian Revolutionary Movement. Berkeley, CA: U. of California Press, 1963.

Paine, Suzanne. Exporting Workers: The Turkish Case. London: Cambridge U. Press, 1975.

Sarkissian, A. O. "Genocide in Turkey." History of the First World War 48 (1970). [Massacre of Armenians]

Toynbee, Arnold J. Treatment of the Armenians in the Ottoman Empire. London: Canston & Sons, 1916.

Abadan-Unak, N. "La migration turque et la mobilite sociale." Studi Emigrazione (Rome) 10(Je, 1973):236-252.

Uganda

Adams, Bert N. "Urban Skills and Religion: Mechanisms for Coping and Defense Among the Ugandan Asians." Social Problems 22 (O, 1974):28-42.

Barkan, Joel D. An African Dilemma: University Students, Development and Politics in Ghana, Tanzania and Uganda. New York: Oxford U. Press, 1976.

Bass, James David. "British Colonial Policy in Uganda." Doctoral dissertation, U. of Virginia, 1975. Univ. Microfilms Order No. 75-26090.

Battle, Vincent Martin. "Education in Eastern Uganda, 1900-1939: A Study of Initiative and Response During the Early Colonial Period." Doctoral dissertation, Columbia U., 1974. Univ. Microfilms Order No. 74-28482.

Carter, Felice Vernon. "Education in Uganda, 1894-1945." Doctoral dissertation, U. of London, 1967.

_____. "The Education of African Muslims in Uganda." Uganda Journal 29(1965):193-199.

Currie, Janice. "The Occupational Attainment Process in Uganda: Effects of Family Background and Academic Achievement on Occupational Status Among Ugandan Secondary School Graduates." Comparative Education Review 21(F, 1977):14-28.

Dahlberg, F. M. "The Asian Community [in Lira]." Sociologus 26(1976):29-42.

Doornbos, Martin R. "Ethnicity, Christianity, and the Development of Social Stratification in Colonial Ankole, Uganda." Int. J. Afric. Hist. Stud. 9, No. 4(1976):555-575.

Farrant, M. R. and others. Kampala's Children..., 1972. UNICEF, Eastern Africa Regional Office, Amber House, P.O. Box 7047, Kampala, Uganda.

Fuller, Thomas. "African Labor and Training in the Uganda Colonial Economy." Int. Journal of African Historical Studies 10(1977):77-95.

Heyneman, Stephen P. "A Brief Note on the Relationship Between Socioeconomic Status and Test Performance Among Ugandan Primary School Children." Comparative Education Review 20 (F, 1976):42-47.

_____. "Differences in Construction, Facilities, Equipment and Academic Achievement Among Ugandan Primary Schools." International Review of Education 23(1977):35-46.

Hoorweg, Jan. Protein-Energy Malnutrition and Intellectual Abilities: A Study of Teen-Age Ugandan Children. The Hague: Mouton, 1976.

International Commission of Jurists. Violation of Human Rights and the Rule of Law in Uganda, 1974.

Jamal, Vali. "Asians in Uganda, 1880-1972: Inequality and Expulsion." Economic History Review 29(N, 1976):602-616.

_____. "Taxation and Inequality in Uganda, 1900-1964." Journal of Economic History 38 (Je, 1978):418-438.

Jensen, Jürgen. "Interethnische Beziehungen und Akkulturation in der frühen Kolonialzeit von Uganda." Sociologus 16(1966):39-53. [English summary, p. 53]

Kabwegyere, T. B. "The Asian Question in Uganda: 1894-1972." Kenya Hist. R. 2(1974): 189-204.

Kasozi, A. B. K. "The Impact of Koran Schools on the Education of African Muslims in Uganda, 1900-1968." Dini Na Mila 4(My, 1970):1-21.

Kirunda, C. R. A. "The Implications of the Colonial System of Education for an Independent Uganda." Res. Abstracts Newslett. 1(Jl, 1973):89-102.

Mamdani, Mahmood. Politics and Class Formation in Uganda. New York: Monthly Review Press, 1976.

Marshall, James. A School in Uganda. London: Gollancz, 1976.

Mason, David. The Crisis for British Asians in Uganda. London: British Council of Churches, O, 1970.

Morris, H. S. The Indians in Uganda. London: Weidenfeld and Nicolson, 1968.

Mukherjee, Radhakrishna. Uganda: The Problem of Acculturation. Berlin: Akademie-Verlag, 1956.

Oded, Arye. Islam in Uganda: Islamization through a Centralized State in Pre-Colonial Africa. New York: Wiley, 1974.

Plender, Richard. "The Expulsion of Asians from Uganda: Legal Aspects." New Community 1(Autumn, 1972):420-427.

Twaddle, Michael (ed.). Expulsion of a Minority: Essays on Ugandan Asians. London: Athlone Press, 1975.

Uziogwe, G. N. "Inter-Ethnic Cooperation in Northern Uganda." Tarikh 2, 1970.

Watson, Tom. "A History of Church Missionary Society High Schools in Uganda, 1900-1924. The Education of a Protestant Elite." Doctoral dissertation, U. of East Africa, 1969.

Wood, Alfred Wallace. "Educational and Social Development in Uganda, 1935-1946." Master's thesis, U. of London Institute of Education, 1967.

                      USSR

Ailtounian, Jeanine. "Comment peut-on être Arménien?" Les Temps Modernes 353(D, 1975).

Ainsztein, Reuben. "Anti-Semitism--the New Soviet Religion." Jerusalem Post Magazine, D 29, 1978. [Reprinted from New Statesman]

Akademiia Pedagogicheshikh Nauk RSFSR. Natsional'nye shkoly RSFSR (Schools of Russian Minorities in the Russian RSFSR). Moscow: Izdatel'stvo APN, 1962.

"Abkhazians' Protest." Peking Review, Ag 4, 1978.

Allworth, Edward. "La rivalté entre le russe et les langues orientales dans les territoires asiatiques de l'U.R.S.S." Cahiers du Monde Russe et Sovietique, O-D, 1966.

_____ (ed.). Central Asia: A Century of Russian Rule. New York: Columbia U. Press, 1967.

_____ (ed.). Nationality Group Survival in Multi-Ethnic States. Shifting Support Patterns in the Soviet Baltic Region. New York: Praeger, 1977.

Alston, Patrick L. Education and the State in Tsarist Russia. Palo Alto, CA: Stanford U. Press, 1969.

Altshuler, Mordecai. "Georgian Jewish Culture Under the Soviet Regime." Soviet Jewish Affairs 5(1975).

_____. "Jewish Studies in the Ukraine in the Early Soviet Period." Soviet Jewish Affairs 7(Spring, 1977).

_____. "The Jews in the Scientific Elite of the Soviet." Jewish Journal of Sociology 15 (Je, 1973).

Armstrong, John A. Ukranian Nationalism. 2nd ed. New York: Columbia U. Press, 1963.

Armstrong, Terence. "The Administration of Northern Peoples: The U.S.S.R." In The Arctic Frontier, pp. 57-88. Edited by St. J. Macdonald. Toronto: U. of Toronto Press, 1966.

Aronson, I. Michael. "The Attitudes of Russian Officials in the 1880's Toward Jewish Assimilation and Emigration." Slavic Review 34(Mr, 1975):1-18.

_____. "Nationalism and Jewish Emancipation in Russia: The 1880's." Nationalities Papers 5(Fall, 1977):167-182.

Arutyunyan, Y. V. A Comparative Study of Rural Youth in the National Regions of the U.S.S.R.: General and Specific Features, Ag, 1976. ERIC ED 128 121.

_____. "Development of National Culture in the U.S.S.R.: Some Tendencies and Observations." In Race and Peoples. Contemporary Ethnic and Racial Problems, pp. 139-156. Moscow: Progress Publishers, 1974.

_____. "A Preliminary Socioethnic Study," Soviet Sociology 9(Winter, 1970-1971). [Tatar ASSR]

Aspaturian, Vernon. "The Non-Russian Nationalities." In Prospects for Soviet Society, pp. 143-198. Edited by Allen Kassoff. New York: Praeger, 1968.

Azimov, Pigan, and Desheriev, Yunus. "Soviet Experience in the Development of National Cultures." In Central Asia in Modern Times. Edited by B. G. Gafurov and others. Moscow: Novosti Press, 1975.

Azrael, Jeremy R. "Bringing Up the Soviet Man: Dilemmas and Progress." Problems of Communism, My-Je, 1968.

_____. Emergent Nationality Problems in the USSR. Santa Monica, CA: Rand, S, 1977.

_____ (ed.). Soviet Nationality Policies and Practices. New York: Praeger, 1978.

Bacon, Elizabeth E. Central Asia under Russian Rule. A Study in Cultural Change. Ithaca, NY: Cornell U. Press, 1966.

Baraheni, Reza and others. In Defense of Mustafa Dzhemilev, D, 1976. Mutafa Dzhemilev Defense Committee, 853 Broadway, Room 414, New York, NY 10003. [Tatars in the USSR]

Baron, Salo W. The Russian Jew Under Tsars and Soviets. 2nd ed. New York: Macmillan, 1975.

Bartley, Diana E. Soviet Approaches to Bilingual Education. Philadelphia: Center for Curriculum Development, 1971.

Belikov, L. V. "Training of Teachers for the Far North of the U.S.S.R." In Education in the North, pp. 283-290. Edited by Frank Darnell. Arctic Institute of North America, U. of Alaska, 1972.

Benningsen, Alexandre. Islam in the Soviet Union. New York: Praeger, 1967.

_____. "Muslims in Tsarist Russia, 1865-1917." Integrated Education 12(Ja-F, 1974): 46-48.

Benningsen, Alexandre, and Winbush, S. Enders. Muslim National Communism in the Soviet Union. Chicago: U. of Chicago Press, 1979.

Berls, Robert E., Jr. "The Russian Conquest of Turkmenistan: 1869-1885." Doctoral dissertation, Georgetown U., 1972.

Bettleheim, Charles. "The Problem of the Nationalities." In Class Struggles in the USSR. First Period: 1917-1923. Tr. Brian Pearce. New York: Monthly Review Press, 1976.

Bilinsky, Yaroslav. "The Education Laws of 1958-9 and Nationality Policy." Soviet Studies 14(O, 1962):138-157.

_____. "Education of the Non-Russian Peoples in the U.S.S.R., 1917-1967: An Essay." Slavic Review 27(S, 1968):411-437.

_____. "Russian Dissenters and the Nationality Question." In Nationalism and Human Rights: Processes of Modernization in the USSR. Edited by Ihor Kamenetsky. Littleton, CO: Libraries Unlimited, 1977.

Birch, Julian. The Ukranian Nationalist Movement in the USSR since 1956. London: Ukranian Publishers, 1971.

Birch, Julian. "The Ukranian Nationalist Movement in the USSR Since 1956." Ukranian Review 17(1970).

Birnbaum, Henrik. "On Some Evidence of Jewish Life and Anti-Jewish Sentiments in Medieval Russia." Viator 4(1973):225-255.

Blakely, Allison. "The Negro in Imperial Russia: A Preliminary Sketch." Journal of Negro History 61(O, 1976):353-361.

Bociurkiw, B. R. "Soviet Nationalities Policy and Dissent in the Ukraine." World Today 30(My, 1974):214-226.

Bociurkiw, B., and Strong, John W. (eds.). Religion and Atheism in the USSR and Eastern Europe. London: Macmillan, 1975.

Boiko, V. I. "Direction and Motivation of Potential Migration of the Peoples of the Lower Amur." Soviet Sociology 9(Spring, 1971):567-578.

Bourdeaux, Michael, Matchett, Kathleen, and Gerstenmaier, Cornelia. Religious Minorities in the Soviet Union (1960-70), D, 1970. Minority Rights Group, 36 Craven Street, London WC2, England.

Braginsky, Joseph. "Talking with Americans About Soviet Jews." New World Review 40 (Fall, 1972):86-96.

Bratcher, John. "Problems of Rural Education in the Soviet Union: The Little Red Schoolhouse." Peabody Journal of Education 50 (Jl, 1973):283-290.

Bromley, Y. V., and Kozlov, V. I. "National Processes in the U.S.S.R." In Races and Peoples. Contemporary Ethnic and Racial Problems, pp. 116-138. Moscow: Progress Publ

Bruk, S. I. "Ethnodemocratic Processes in the USSR." Soviet Sociology 10(Spring, 1972).

Brym, Robert I. "Strangers and Rebels: The Russian-Jewish Intelligentsia in Marxist Social Movements at the Turn of the Twentieth Century." Doctoral dissertation, U. of Toronto, 1976.

Butkevich, M. N. "Why a Student Does Not Arrive at the Finish." Soviet Review, Spring, 1966. [A study of dropouts from institutions of higher learning in Sverdlovsk]

Cang, Joel. The Silent Millions: A History of the Jews in the Soviet Union. New York: Taplinger, 1970.

Carlisle, Donald S. "Modernization, Generations, and the Uzbek Soviet Intelligentsia." In The Dynamics of Soviet Politics. Edited by Paul Cocks and others. Cambridge, MA: Harvard U. Press, 1976.

Carrère d'Encausse, Helène. Réforme et révolution chez les musulmans de l'Empire russe, Bukhara, 1867-1924. Paris: A. Colin, 1966.

Chauhan, Sivdan S. Nationalities Question in USA and USSR: A Comparative Study. New Delhi: Sterling Publishers, 1976.

Chauncey, Henry (ed.). Soviet Preschool Education. 2 vols. New York: Holt, Rinehart, and Winston, 1969.

Chechinski, Michael. "Soviet Jews and Higher Education." Soviet Jewish Affairs 3(N, 1973).

Chekoeva, S. "The Russian Language in the National Schools of the Russian Federation." Soviet Education 18(My, 1976):64-77.

Chepelev, V. I. (ed.). Public Education in the Ukranian S.S.R. Tr. by J. Weir and Olena Marko-Suvorova. Kiev: "Radyanska Shkola" Publishing House, 1970.

Chermouxamedov, S. Ch. The Historical Development of Education in Uzbekistan, 1975. ERIC ED 133 857.

Choseed, Bernard J. "Reflections of the Soviet Nationalities Policy in Literature. The Jews. 1938-1948." Doctoral dissertation, Columbia U., 1948.

Clem, Ralph S. "Assimilation of Ukranians in the Soviet Union, 1959." Master's thesis, Columbia U., 1972.

_____. "The Changing Geography of Soviet Nationalities and Its Socioeconomic Correlates: 1926-1970." Doctoral dissertation, Columbia U., 1975.

_____ (ed.). The Soviet West: Interplay between Nationality and Social Organization. New York: Praeger, 1975.

Connor, Walter D. Socialism, Politics, and Equality. Hierarchy and Change in Eastern Europe and the USSR. New York: Columbia U. Press, 1979.

Conquest, Robert. The Nation Killers: The Soviet Deportation of Nationalities. London: Macmillan, 1970.

_____. The Soviet Deportation of Nationalities. N.p.: N.p., 1960.

_____ (ed.). Soviet Nationalities Policy in Practice. London: Bodley Head, 1967.

Cox, Terence M. Rural Sociology in the Soviet Union. New York: Holmes & Meier, 1978.

Curtiss, Mina. "Some American Negroes in Russia in the Nineteenth Century." Massachusetts Review (Spring, 1968):268-278.

Danilov, Alexandre I. "Cultural Situations and Education in the Soviet North." In Education in the North, pp. 59-72. Edited by Frank Darnell. Arctic Institute of North America, U. of Alaska, 1972.

Davis, Horace B. "The National Question in the Soviet Union." In Toward a Marxist Theory of Nationalism, pp. 88-134. New York: Monthly Review Press, 1978.

Demko, George J. The Russian Colonization of Kazakhstan, 1896-1916. Bloomington, IN: Research Center for the Language Sciences, Indiana U., 1969.

Dennis, Peggy. "Anti-Semitism, Still Strong and Officially Sanctioned, Blights Soviet Policy." In These Times, D 20, 1978.

Desheriev, I., and Melikiian, M. "Development and Mutual Enrichment of the Languages of the Nations of the USSR." Digest of the Soviet Ukranian Press 2(1966):23-25.

Desheriyev, Yunus, and Mikhalchenko, Vita Y. "A Case in Point: the Soviet Experience with Languages." Prospects 6(1976):388-392.

DeWitt, Nicholas. The Status of Jews in Soviet Education. New York: The American Jewish Congress, 1964.

Diakiv-Hornovy, Osyp. The USSR Unmasked: A Collection of Articles and Essays on Soviet Russian Repression in Ukraine. Tr. by Walter Dushuyek and Vasyl Diakiv. New York: Vantage Press, 1976.

Dijur, I. M. "Jews in the Russian Economy." In Russian Jewry 1860-1917 pp. 120-143. New York: Yoseloff, 1966.

"Discussion of the Concept of Nation and Nationality." Current Digest of the Soviet Press 18(Je 15, 1966):14-21.

Dragadze, Tamara. "Family Life in Georgia." New Society, Ag 19, 1976.

Dumont, P. and others. "Problèmes de nationalités en Russie et en URSS." Cah. monde russe soviétique 3-4(1974): 315-374.

Dunn, Dennis J. (ed.). Religion and Moderni- zation in the Soviet Union. Boulder, CO: Westview Press, 1977.

Dunn, Ethel. "Educating the Small Peoples of the Soviet North: The Limits of Cultural Change." Arctic Anthropology, 1968.

_____. "Education and the Native Intelli- gentsia in the Soviet North: Further Thoughts on the Limits of Culture Change." Arctic Anthropology 6(1970):112-122.

Dunn, Stephen P. "New Departures in Soviet Theory and Practice of Ethnicity." Dialectical Anthropology 1(N, 1975):61-70.

Dunn, Stephen P., and Dunn, Ethel. "Education and Social Mobility." In The Peasants of Central Russia, chapter 3. New York: Holt, Rinehart and Winston, 1967.

_____ and _____ (eds.). Introduction to Soviet Ethnography. 2 vols. Berkeley, CA: Highgate Road Social Science Research Station, 1974.

Dziuba, Ivan. Internationalism or Russifica- tion? A Study in the Soviet Nationalities Problem. 3rd ed. New York: Monad Press, 1975.

Education in the U.S.S.R. An Annotated Bibliography of English-Language Materials. Washington, DC: GPO, 1975.

Eminov, Mumunali Mumun. "The Development of Soviet Nationality Policy and Current Soviet Perspectives--on Ethnicity." Doctoral dissertation, Indiana U., 1976. Univ. Microfilms Order No. 76-21,576.

Epstein, Erwin H. "Ideological Factors in Soviet Educational Policy Toward Jews." Education and Urban Society 10(F, 1978): 223-254.

"Exploitation and Oppression of Non- Russian People in Central Asia." Peking Review 20(Mr 4, 1977):21-23.

Farmer, Kenneth C. "Language and Linguistic Nationalism in the Ukraine." Nationalities Papers 6(Fall, 1978):125-149.

_____. "Ukranian Dissent: Symbolic Politics and Sociodemographic Aspects." Ukranian Quarterly, Spring, 1978.

Firstenberg, Barbara. "An Aspect of Soviet Jewry: Anti-Semitism and Birobidzhan." Master's thesis, Adelphi U., 1972.

Fish, Daniel. "The Jews in Syllabuses of World and Russian History: What Soviet School Children Read About Jewish History." Soviet Jewish Affairs 8(Spring, 1978).

Fisher, Alan W. The Crimean Tatars. Stanford, CA: Hoover Institution Press, 1978.

Fisher, Dan. "Ethnic Problem Heats Up in Soviet Union." Los Angeles Times, Je 28, 1978. [Abkhazian Autonomous Republic]

_____. "Return to Crimean Homes Unlikely for Most Tartars." Los Angeles Times, D 23, 1977.

Forgus, Silvia P. "Estonian Nationalism and Primary Education 1860-1905." Doctoral dissertation, U. of Illinois, 1974.

_____. "Nationality Question in the Resolutions of the Communist Party of the Soviet Union 1898-1964." Nationalities Papers 5(Fall, 1977):183-201.

Friedberg, Maurice. "Anti-Semitism As a Policy Tool in the Soviet Union." New Politics 9 (Fall, 1971):61-79.

Gales, Tatiana P. The Role of Language Instruc- tion in Bilingual Education in the Soviet Union, Ap 14, 1977. ERIC ED 142 094.

Garunov, E. "Schools With a Multinational Composition." Soviet Education 13(D, 1970): 4-16.

Gellner, Ernest. "Soviet Anthropology and Ethnicity." European Journal of Sociology 18(1977).

Gilboa, Yehoshua. The Black Years of Soviet Jewry. Boston, MA: Little, Brown, 1972. [1939-1953]

Gill, R. R. "Minderheitenprobleme in der Sowjetunion." Europa Archiv 27(1972): 314-322.

Gitelman, Zvi Y. Jewish Nationality and Soviet Politics. The Jewish Sections of the CPSU, 1971-1930. Princeton, NJ: Princeton U. Press, 1972.

"Gili Ebrei Nell'MRSS." Sovietica, Ap, 1977, pp. 3-71. [Jews in the U.S.S.R.]

Glukhov, A. "Basic Problems of the Economics of Public Education." Problems of Economics 18(Ja, 1976).

Golden-Hanga, Lily. Africans in Russia. Moscow: Novosti Press, 1966.

Goldhagen, Erich (ed.). Ethnic Minorities in the Soviet Union. New York: Praeger, 1968.

Graham, Loren R. "Science and Values: The Eugenics Movement in Germany and Russia in the 1920's." American Historical Review 82 (D, 1977):1133-1164.

Green, Warren Paul. "The Nazi Racial Policy Towards the Karaites." Soviet Jewish Affairs 8(Autumn, 1978). [Crimea]

Greenberg, Louis. The Jews in Russia. 2 vols. New Haven, CT: Yale U. Press, 1944-1951.

Grochev, Ivan. La Question Nationale en U.R.S.S.: Expérience et Solutions. Moscow: Editions der Progrès, 1968.

Gurova, R. G. "A Study of the Influence of Sociohistorical Conditions on Child Development (Comparative Investigation, 1929 and 1966)." Soviet Review 12(Fall, 1971):229-252. [Altai and Northern Baikal]

Gurvich, I. S. Contemporary Ethnic Processes in Siberia. IXth International Congress of Anthropological and Ethnological Sciences, A-S, 1973.

Guthier, Steven L. "The Belorussians: National Identification and Assimilation, 1897-1970." Soviet Studies 29(19770:270-283.

H. H. "Education and Social Mobility in the USSR." Soviet Studies 18(Jl, 1966):57-65.

Halevy, Zvi. Jewish Schools Under Czarism and Communism: A Struggle for Cultural Identity. New York: Springer, 1976.

_____. "Jewish Students in Soviet Universities in the 1920's." Soviet Jewish Affairs 6(1976).

Halevy, Zvi, and Halevy, Eva Etzioni. "The 'Religious Factor' and Achievement in Education." Comparative Education 10(0, 1974): 193-199.

Halperin, Charles J. "Judaizers and the Image of the Jew in Medieval Russia: A Polemic Revisited and a Question Posed." Canadian-American Slavic Studies 9(Summer, 1975):141-155.

Hasiotis, Arthur C., Jr. "A Comparative Study of the Political and Economic Policies Pursued by the USSR and Communist China in their Attempt to Consolidate their Respective Positions Within Russian Central Asia (1917-1934) and Sinkiang (1949-late 1957)." Master's thesis, Columbia U., 1965.

Hayit, Baymirza. Turkestan zwischen Russland und China. Amsterdam: Philo Press, 1971.

Haywood, Harry. "A Student in Moscow." In Black Bolshevik. Autobiography of an Afro-American Communist, pp. 148-175. Chicago: Liberator Press, 1978.

Henriksson, Anders H. "The Riga German Community: Social Change and the Nationality Question, 1860-1905." Doctoral dissertation, U. of Toronto, 1978.

Hetmanek, Allen. "Islam Under the Soviets." Doctoral dissertation, Georgetown U., 1965.

Hirszowicz, Lukasz. "Jewish Cultural Life in the USSR--A Survey." Soviet Jewish Affairs 7 (Autumn, 1977).

_____. "The Soviet Union and the Jews during World War II." Soviet Jewish Affairs 4(1974): 73-89.

Hoffmann, Joachim. Deutsche und Kalmyken, 1942 bis 1945. Freiburg: Verlag Rombach, 1974.

_____. Die Ostlegionen, 1941-1943: Turko-tataren, Kaukaiser und Wolgafinnen in deutschen Heer. Freiburg: Verlag Rombach, 1976.

Holdsworth, M. "Soviet Central Asia, 1917-1940." Soviet Studies 3(Ja, 1952):258-277.

Howell, Wilson N., Jr. "The Soviet Union and the Kurds: A Study of National Minority Problems in Soviet Policy." Doctoral dissertation, U. of Virginia, 1965. Univ. Microfilms Order No. 66-3151.

Isayev, I. National Languages in the USSR: Problems and Solutions. Moscow: N.p., 1977.

Israel, Gerard. The Jews in Russia. Tr. Sanford L. Chernoff. New York: St. Martin's Press, 1975.

Jacoby, Susan. "Toward an Educated Elite: the Soviet Universities." Change 3(N, 1971):33-39.

Jennison, Earl W., Jr. "The Neglected 'Ethnics' in Russian History Surveys." History Teacher 8(My, 1975):437-451.

Jesman, Czeslaw. "Early Russian Contacts with Etheopia." Proceedings of the Third International Conference of Etheopian Studies, 1966. Addis Ababa: Institute of Etheopian Studies, Haile Selassie I U., 1969.

"Jews in the Soviet Union." Soviet Life, Mr, 1977.

Jones, Lesya, and Pendzey, Luba (comps.). "Dissent in Ukraine: Bibliography." Nationalities Papers 6(Spring, 1978):64-70.

Jones, Lesya, and Yasen, Bohdan (eds.). Dissent in Ukraine: An Underground Journal from Soviet Ukraine. Baltimore, MD: Smoloskyp Publishers, 1977.

Jones, T. Anthony, and Matthews, Mervyn (comps.). Soviet Sociology, 1964-75. New York: Praeger, 1977.

Junusov, M. S. and others (eds.). The Theory and Practice of Proletarian International- ism. Moscow: Progress Publishers, 1976. [See chapters 6 and 7, on Soviet nationalities.]

Kamentsky, Ihor. Hitler's Occupation of Ukraine, 1941-1944: A Study of Totalitarian Imperialism. Milwaukee: Marquette U. Press, 1956.

_____ (ed.). Nationalism and Human Rights: Process of Modernization in the USSR, 1977. Order from Prof. Andris Skreija, U. of Nebraska, Omaha, NB 68101.

Kamosko, L. V. "Changes in the Class Struggle of Students of Intermediate and Higher Schools in Russia (1830's to 1880's)." Voprosy Istorii 10(1970). [In Russian]

Karklins, Rasma. "La Révolution mondiale et les allemands d'Union Soviétique." Cah. monde russe soviétique (Jl-D, 1975): 425-553.

Kass, Ilana. "Between Hammer and Crescent." Jerusalem Post Magazine, F 23, 1979. [Muslims in the USSR]

Katz, Josef. One Who Came Back. The Diary of a Jewish Survivor. Tr. by Hilda Reach. New York: Herzl Press, 1973. [Jewish ghettos in Latvia]

Katz, Zev. Patterns of Social Mobility in the USSR. Cambridge, MA: Center for Inter- national Studies, M.I.T., 1972.

_____. "Sociology in the Soviet Union." Problems of Communism 20(My-Je, 1971):22-40.

Katz, Zev and others (eds.). Handbook of Major Soviet Nationalities. New York: Free Press, 1975.

Keenan, Edward L. "Soviet Time Bomb." New Republic, Ag 21, 1976. [Ethnic minorities in the U.S.S.R.]

Kirimal, Edige. Der nationale Kampf der Krim Türken. Emsdetten: Leske Verlag, 1952.

Klier, John D. "The Ambiguous Legal Status of Russian Jewry in the Reign of Catherine II." Slavic Review 35(S, 1976):504-517.

_____. "The Illustratsiia Affair of 1858: Polemics on the Jewish Question in the Russian Press." Nationalities Papers 5(Fall, 1977):117-135.

_____. "The Origins of the Jewish Minority Problem in Russia, 1772-1812." Doctoral dissertation, U. of Illinois, 1975.

Koch, Fred C. The Volga Germans: In Russia and America from 1763 to the Present. University Park: Pennsylvania State U. Press, 1977.

Kolasky, John. Education in Soviet Ukraine. A Study in Discrimination and Russification. Toronto, Canada: Peter Martin Associates, 1968.

Korey, William. "Jews As Non-Persons in Soviet Textbooks." American Zionist 60(Mr-Ap, 1970).

_____. "The Origins and Development of Soviet Anti-Semitism." Slavic Review, Mr, 1972.

_____. "Quotas and Soviet Jewry." Commentary 57(My, 1974):55-57. [In relation to higher education]

_____. "The Soviet Jewish Future. Some Ob- servations on the Recent Census." Midstream 20(N, 1974):37-50.

_____. "Soviet Jewry: Plight and Prospect." Midstream 23(Ap, 1977):18-27.

_____. The Soviet Cage. Anti-Semitism in Russia. New York: Viking, 1973.

Korey, William, and Schlesinger, Ina. Jews As Non-Persons: A Study of Soviet History Textbooks in Elementary and Secondary Schools, 1970. B'Nai B'Rith International Council, 1640 Rhode Island Avenue, N.W., Washington, DC 20036.

Koropeckyi, I. S. (ed.). The Ukraine Within the USSR. New York: Praeger, 1977.

Koszeliwec, Iwan. Mykola Skrypnk. New York: Suchasmist, 1972. [Ukraine]

Kotylar, Alexander. "Problems of Younger Workers in the USSR." International Labour Review 109(Ap, 1974):359-371.

Kotze, Dirk A. "The Rise and Decline of Native Administration." Teaching Political Science 4(Ja, 1977):235-246.

Krader, Lawrence. Peoples of Central Asia. 2nd ed. Bloomington, IN: Indiana U. Publica- tions, 1966.

Krawchenko, Bohdan. "Ukrainian Studies in Canada." Nationalities Papers 6(Spring, 1978):26-43.

Kreusler, A. "Bilingualism in Soviet Non-Russian Schools." Elementary School Journal 62(1961):94-99.

Kriendler, Isabelle T. "Education Policies Toward the Eastern Nationalities in Tsarist Russia: A Study of Il' minskii's System." Doctoral dissertation, Columbia U., 1970.

Krivickas, Vladas. "The Polish Minority in Lithuania, 1918-1926." Slavonic E. Europ. Review 53(Ja, 1975):78-91.

Kulichenko, Mikhail. "Economic and Social Development of Soviet Peoples: A Factual Survey." New World Review 40(Fall, 1972): 97-114.

Kumanev, V. A. "Experience of the USSR in Implementing a Nationalities Policy." In Races and Peoples. Contemporary Ethnic and Racial Problems, pp. 95-115. Moscow: Progress Publishers, 1974.

_____. Socialism and Universal Literacy: Liquidation of Mass Illiteracy in the U.S.S.R. Moscow: Navka, 1967.

Kupchinsky, Roman (ed.). The Nationalities Question in the U.S.S.R.: A Collection of Documents (in Russian). Munich: Suchasnist, 1975.

Kuzin, N. P. and others. Education in the USSR. Moscow: Progress Publishers, 1972.

Lane, Christel O. "Socio-political Accommoda-tion and Religious Decline: The Case of the Molokan Sect in Soviet Society." Com-parative Studies in Society and History 17 (Ap, 1975):221-237.

Lane, David S. "Ethnic and Class Stratifica-tion in Soviet Kazakhstan, 1917-39." Comparative Studies in Society and History 17(Ap, 1975):165-189.

_____. "The Impact of Revolution: The Case of Selection of Students for Higher Education in Soviet Russia, 1917-1928." Sociology 7(1973):241-252.

_____. Politics and Society in the USSR. 2nd ed. New York: New York U. Press, 1978.

Lane, David S., and O'Dell, Felicity. The Soviet Industrial Worker: Social Class, Education, and Control. New York: St. Martin's Press, 1978.

Lantzeff, George, and Pierce, Richard. Eastward to Empire. Montreal: McGill-Queen's U. Press, 1973.

Lazzerini, Edward J. "Ismail Bey Gasprinskii and Muslim Modernism in Russia, 1878-1914." Doctoral dissertation, U. of Washington, 1975.

Le Compte, Garé. "Soviet Muslims and the Afro-Asian World." Doctoral dissertation, American U., 1971. Univ. Microfilms Order No. 72-9156.

Lederhendler, Eli M. "Resources of the Ethnically Disenfranchised." In Nationality Group Survival in Multi-Ethnic States. Edited by Edward Allworth. New York: Praeger, 1977. [Jews in USSR]

Lenin, V. I. Critical Remarks on the National Question. The Right of Nations to Self-Determination. Moscow: Progress Publishers, 1971.

_____. Ueber Wissenschaften and Hochschul wesen. Berlin: Dietz Verlag, 1969.

"'Let Us Go'--The Cry of Soviet Jews." Jews in Eastern Europe, Ja, 1970.

Levin, Dov. "Estonian Jews in the USSR (1941-1945)." In Yad Vashem Studies XI. Edited by Livia Rothkirchen. Jerusalem: Yad Vashem, 1976.

Lewis, E. Glyn. Multilingualism in the Soviet Union: Aspects of Language Policy and Its Implementation. Edited by Joshua Fishman. Hague: Mouton, 1972.

Lewis, Robert A., and Rowland, Richard H. "East is West and West is East... Population Redistribution in the USSR and its Impact on Society." International Migration Review 11(Spring, 1977):3-29.

Lewis, Robert A. and others. Nationality and Population Change in Russia and the USSR: An Evaluation of Census Data, 1897-1970. New York: Praeger, 1976.

Lilge, Frederic. "Lenin and the Politics of Education." Slavic Review 27(Je, 1968):230-257.

Lipset, Harry. "Education of Moslems in Tsarist and Soviet Russia." Comparative Education Review 12(1968):310-322.

_____. "Jewish Schools in the Soviet Union, 1917-1947: An Aspect of Soviet Minorities Policy." Doctoral dissertation, Columbia U., 1966.

_____. "The Status of National Minority Languages in Soviet Education." Soviet Studies 19(O, 1967):181-189.

Low, Alfred D. Lenin on the Question of Nationality. New York: Bookman, 1958.

McAuley, Alastair. Economic Welfare in the Soviet Union: Poverty, Living Standards, and Inequality. Madison: U. of Wisconsin Press, 1979.

_____. Soviet Anti-Poverty Policy, 1955-1975, Mr, 1977. ERIC ED 146 245.

McKenna, Francis R. "Education for Elite Development in Soviet Uzbekistan." Doctoral dissertation, U. of Michigan, 1969.

McLeish, John. "The Soviet Conquest of Illiteracy." Alberta Journal of Educational Research 18(D, 1972):307-326. [1917-1934]

Margulies, Sylvia. The Pilgrimage to Russia: The Soviet Union and the Treatment of Foreigners, 1924-1937. Madison: U. of Wisconsin Press, 1968.

Massell, Gregory J. "Modernization and National Policy in Soviet Central Asia: Problems and Prospects." In The Dynamics of Soviet Politics. Edited by Paul Cocks and others. Cambridge, MA: Harvard U. Press, 1976.

_____. The Surrogate Proletariat. Moslem Women and Revolutionary Strategies in Soviet Central Asia, 1919-1929. Princeton, NJ: Princeton U. Press, 1974.

Matthews, Mervyn. Class and Society in Soviet Russia. New York: Walker, 1972.

_____. "Class Bias in Russian Education." New Society, D 19, 1968.

_____. "Poverty in Russia." New Society, Ja 27, 1972.

_____. Privilege in the Soviet Union: A Study of Elite Life-Styles Under Communism. Boston: G. Allen & Unwin, 1978.

_____. "Russian School-Leavers." New Society, Ja 6, 1972.

_____. "The Soviet Elite." New Society, Je 12, 1975.

Mazlakh, S., and Shakhrai, V. (eds.). On the Current Situation in the Ukraine. Ann Arbor: U. of Michigan Press, 1970.

Medlin, William K. and others. Education and Development in Central Asia: A Case Study on Social Change in Uzbekistan. The Hague: Leiden/E. J. Brill, 1971.

Medvedyev, Roy A. "Jews in the U.S.S.R.: Problems and Prospects." Survey 17(1971): 185-200.

Mehta, V. Soviet Economic Policy. Income Differentials in the USSR. New Delhi: Radiant Publishers, 1977.

Mendelsohn, Ezra. Class Struggle in the Pale: The Formative Years of the Jewish Workers' Movement in Tsarist Russia. London: Cambridge U. Press, 1970.

Murray, G. J. A., Jr. "Minorities in the Soviet Union: A Black Perspective." Interracial Books for Children 5(1974).

Mustafina, F. "The Rural School in Bashkira." Soviet Education 13(D, 1970):68-77.

Mykula, W. "Soviet Nationalities Policy in Ukraine, 1920-1930." Ukranian Review, 1972-1973.

Mylleyniemi, Seppo. Die Neuordnung der baltischen Länder 1941-1944. Zum national-sozialistischen Inhalt der deutschen Besatzungspolitik. Helsinki: U. Press, 1973.

Naby, Eden. "Les assyriens d'Union Soviétique." Cah. monde russe soviétique (Jl-D, 1975):445-457.

Namsons, Andrivs. "Die Universität Lettlands und ihre Reorganisation in der Zeit von 1940-1972." Acta Balt. 13(1974):102-133.

"Nationalities and Nationalism in the U.S.S.R." Problems of Communism, S-O, 1967.

Nekrich, Aleksandr M. The Punished Peoples: The Deportation and Fate of Soviet Minorities at the End of the Second World War. Tr. George Saunders. New York: Norton, 1978.

Newth, J. A. "Jews in the Soviet Intelligentsia." Bulletin on Soviet Jewish Affairs, Jl, 1968.

Noah, Harold (ed.). The Economics of Education in the U.S.S.R. New York: Praeger, 1969.

Orbach, Alexander. "Jewish Intellectuals in Odessa in the Late Nineteenth Century: The Nationalist Theories of Ahad Ha'am and Simon Dubnow." Nationalities Papers 6(Fall, 1978):109-123.

Orbach, Wila. "The Destruction of the Jews in the Nazi-Occupied Territories of the USSR." Soviet Jewish Affairs 6(1976).

Parming, Tonu, and Jarvesoo, Elmar (eds.). A Case Study of a Soviet Republic: The Estonian SSR. Boulder, CO: Westview Press, 1978.

Pennar, Jaan, Bakalo, Ivan I., and Bereday, George Z. F. Modernization and Diversity in Soviet Education with Special Reference to Nationality Groups. New York: Praeger, 1971.

Pierce, Richard A. Russian Central Asia, 1867-1917. Berkeley, CA: U. of California Press, 1957.

Pinkus, Benjamin. "The Campaign Against Jewish Nationalism and Cosmopolitanism in the Soviet Union, 1946-53." Soviet Jewish Affairs 4(Autumn, 1974).

Pipes, Richard. "Catherine II and the Jews: The Origins of the Pale of Settlement." Soviet Jewish Affairs 5, No. 2(1975):3-20.

_____. The Formation of the Soviet Union: Communism and Nationalism, 19717-1923. 2nd ed. Cambridge, MA: Harvard U. Press, 1964.

Plakans, Andrejs. "Peasants, Intellectuals, and Nationalism in the Russian Baltic Province, 1820-90." Journal of Modern History 46(S, 1974):445-475.

Pool, Jonathan. "Developing the Soviet Turkic Tongues: The Language of the Politics of Language." Slavic Review 35(S, 1976).

_____. Some Observations on Language Planning Azerbaijan and Turkmenistan, My, 1976. ERIC ED 126 715.

Pospielovsky, Dmitry V. "The Jewish Question in Russian Samizdat." Soviet Jewish Affairs 8(Autumn, 1978).

_____. "Nationalism as a Factor of Dissent in the Contemporary Soviet Union." Canadian Review of Studies in Nationalism 2 (Fall, 1974):91-116.

Potichnyj, Peter J. "The Struggle of the Crimean Tatars." In Nationalism and Human Rights: Processes of Modernization in the USSR. Edited by Ihor Kamenetsky. Littleton, CO: Libraries Unlimited, 1977.

Powell, David E. Antireligious Propaganda in the Soviet Union: A Study of Mass Persuasion. Cambridge, MA: MIT Press, 1975.

Rakowska-Harmstone, Teresa. "The Dialectics of Nationalism in the USSR." Problems of Communism 23(My-Je, 1974):1-22.

_____. "The Dilemma of Nationalism in the Soviet Union." In The Soviet Union under Brezhnev and Kosygin: The Transition Years, pp. 115-134. Edited by John W. Strong. New York: Van Nostrand, 1971.

_____. "Ethnic Autonomy in the Soviet Union." Society 12(Ja-F, 1975):44-49.

_____. Russia and Nationalism in Central Asia. The Case of Tadzhikistan. Baltimore, MD: Johns Hopkins Press, 1970.

von Rauch, George. The Baltic States: Estonia, Latvia, Lithuania. The Years of Independence, 1917-1940. Berkeley, CA: U. of California Press, 1974.

Reddaway, Peter. "The KGB in Georgia." New York Review of Books 24(Mr 31, 1977):35.

Redlich, Shimon. "The Jews Under Soviet Rule During World War II." Doctoral dissertation, New York U., 1968.

_____. "Soviet Uses of Jewish Nationalism During World War II: The Membership and Dynamics of the Jewish Antifascist Committee in the USSR." Nationalities Papers 5(Fall, 1977):136-166.

Remer, Claus. "Die Faschistischen Pläne und ihr Scheitern am Ende des zweiten Weltkrieges." Jb. Gesch. sozial. Lander Eur. 19(No. 2, 1975):185-200.

Rhinelander, Laurens H., Jr. "The Incorporation of the Caucasus into the Russian Empire: The Case of Georgia, 1801-1854." Doctoral dissertation, Columbia U., 1972.

Riordan, James. "Survey Shows Russians Share Western Problem." Times Higher Education Supplement, S 6, 1974. [Study by E. K. Vasilieva]

Rogers, James Allen. "Racism and Russian Revolutionists." Race 14(Ja, 1973):279-289.

Rogger, Hans. "Tsarist Policy on Jewish Emigration." Soviet Jewish Affairs 3(1973): 26-36.

Robich, Azade-Ayse Murat. "Transition into the 20th Century: Reform and Secularization among the Volga Tatars." Doctoral dissertation, U. of Wisconsin, 1976.

Rosen, Seymour M. The Development of People's Friendship University in Moscow. Washington, DC: GPO, 1973.

Rozek, Edward J. "The Problems of National Minorities in the USSR." In Case Studies in Human Rights and Fundamental Freedoms. A World Survey, vol. 4. Edited by Willem A. Veenhoven, Winifred Crum Ewing, and others. The Hague: Nijhoff, 1976.

Rubel, Paula G. The Kalmyk Mongols: A Study in Continuity and Change. Bloomington, IN: Indiana U. Press, 1967.

Rubenstein, Alvin Z. "Lumumba University: An Assessment." Problems of Communism 20(N-D, 1971):64-69. [Patrice Lumumba People's Friendship U., Moscow]

Rubin, B., and Kolesnikov, I. U. Student through the Eyes of the Sociologist. Rostov on the Don: Izdatelstvo Rostovskogo Universiteta, 1968.

Russischer Kolonialismus in der Ukraine: Berichte und Dokumente. Munich: Ukrainischer Verlag, 1962.

Rutkevich, M. N. (ed.). The Career Plans of Youth [in the Soviet Union]. White Plains, NY: International Arts and Sciences Press, 1968.

_____ (ed.). The Career Plans of Youth. White Plains, NY: International Arts and Sciences Press, 1969.

Scuik, Olena, and Yasen, Bohdan (eds.). Ethnocide of Ukrainians in the USSR. Baltimore: Smoloskyp Publishers, 1976.

Sahaydak, Maksym (comp.). The Ukranian Herald, Issue 7-8: Ethnocide of Ukranians in the U.S.S.R. Tr. by O. Sciuk and B. Yasen. Baltimore: Smoloskyp Publishers, 1976.

Sawyer, Thomas E. "The Jewish Minority in the Soviet Union: A Critical Study." 2 vols. Doctoral dissertation, Georgetown U., 1978. Univ. Microfilms Order No. 7901786.

Schmelz, U. O. "New Evidence on Basic Issues in the Demography of Soviet Jews." Jewish Journal of Sociology 16(D, 1974).

Schneider, Gertrude. "The Riga Ghetto, 1941-1943." Doctoral dissertation, CUNY, 1973.

Schoenman, Ralph. "In Defense of Mustafa Dzhemilov: Socialism and Liberty Are Inseparable." Militant, S 10, 1976. [Imprisoned Crimean Tatar activist]

Schulman, Elias. History of Jewish Education in the Soviet Union. New York: Ktav Publishing House, 1971.

_____. "The Jewish School System in the Soviet Union, 1918-48." Doctoral dissertation, Dropsie College, 1965.

Schwarz, Solomon. "Birobidzhan: An Experiment in Jewish Colonization." In Russian Jewry, pp. 342-395. Edited by Gregory Aronson and others. New York: Thomas Yoseloff, 1969.

_____. "Education and the Working Class: Expansion and Advance." Survey 65(O, 1967):15-34.

Semiskin, T. "A School in the Arctic." Soviet Union Review, N, 1931.

Shabad, Theodore. "Ethnic Results of the 1970 Soviet Census." Soviet Geography 12(S, 1971):435-457.

_____. "Unrest Is Spurring Soviet to Meld Its 100 Nationalities." New York Times, Jl 31, 1972.

Sheehy, Ann. The Crimean Tatars and Volga Germans: Soviet Treatment of Two National Minorities. London: Minority Rights Group, Ag, 1971.

Shevchenko Scientific Society. Ukraine: A Concise Encyclopedia, II. Toronto: U. of Toronto Press, n.d.

Shimoniak, Waslyl. "Education of Minorities in the U.S.S.R." School & Society 100 (Ja, 1972):58-66.

_____. "A Study of Soviet Policies in Uzbekistan and Their Implications for Educational and Social Change." Doctoral dissertation, U. of Michigan, 1963.

Shorish, M. Mobin. "Education in the Tajik Soviet Socialist Republic: 1917-1967." Doctoral dissertation, U. of Chicago, 1972.

Shtromas, A. "The Legal Position of Soviet Nationalities and Their Territorial Units According to the 1977 Constitution of the USSR." Russian Review (Jl, 1978):265-272.

Shubkin, V. N. and others. "Quantitative Methods in Sociological Studies of Problems of Job Placement and Choice of Occupation," Part I. Soviet Sociology, Summer, 1968. [Novosibirsk oblast]

Shumiatcher, Abraham Isaac. "My Years in Russia: Some Memories." Ed. by A. A. Levin and H. C. Klassen. Canadian Ethnic Studies 2(D, 1970):1-5.

Siegelbaum, Lewis H. "Another 'Yellow Peril': Chinese Migrants in the Russian Far East and the Russian Reaction before 1917." Mod. Asian Stud. 12(No. 2, 1978):307-330.

Silver, Brian David. "Bilingualism and Maintenance of the Mother Tongue in Soviet Central Asia." Slavic Review 35(S, 1976).

_____. "Ethnic Identity Change Among Soviet Nationalities: A Statistical Analysis." Doctoral dissertation, U. of Wisconsin, 1972.

_____. "Ethnic Intermarriage and Ethnic Consciousness Among Soviet Nationalities." Soviet Studies (Ja, 1978):107-116.

_____. "The Impact of Urbanization and Geographical Dispersion on the Linguistic Russification of Soviet Nationalities." Demography 11(F, 1974).

_____. "Levels of Sociocultural Development Among Soviet Nationalities: A Partial Test of the Equalization Hypothesis." American Political Science Review 68(D, 1974):1618-1637.

_____. "Social Mobilization and the Russification of Soviet Nationalities." American Political Science Review 68(Mr, 1974):45-66.

_____. "The Status of National Minority Languages in Soviet Education: An Assessment of Recent Changes." Soviet Studies 26(Ja, 1974):28-40.

Simirenko, Alex. "From Vertical to Horizontal Inequality: The Case of the Soviet Union." Social Problems 20(Fall, 1972):150-161.

Simmonds, George W. (ed.). Nationalism in the U.S.S.R. and Eastern Europe in the Era of Brezhnev and Kosygin. Detroit, MI: U. of Detroit Press, 1977.

Smal-Stocki, Roman. The Captive Nations: Nationalism of the Non-Russian Nations in the Soviet Union. New York: Bookman Associates, 1960.

Smolar, Boris. Soviet Jewry Today and Tomorrow. New York: Macmillan, 1972.

Sociar'naja sreda ucascihsja i ih sansy na uspevaemos st' (The Social Background of Students and Their Prospect of Success at School). Ushinsky (K.D.) State Scientific Library of the Academy of Pedagogical Sciences, Moscow (USSR), S, 1971. ERIC ED 060 279.

Solchanyk, Roman. "The 'Sophistication' of Soviet Nationality Policy in the Ukraine." Ukranian Quarterly 24 (Winter, 1968).

Soule, Mason. "Linguistic Assimilation of Non-Russian Nationalities in the USSR." Master's thesis, Kent State U., 1978.

Sovetkin, F. F. (ed.). Natsionalie shkoli RSFSR 2A 40 Let. Moscow: Izdatelstvo Akademii Pedagogicheskikh Nauk RSFSR, 1958.

Soviet Anti-Semitic Propaganda. London: Institute of Jewish Affairs, 1978.

Stetsko, Slava. "National Persecution in the USSR." Ukranian Review (1976):31-55.

Stumpp, Karl. "Die Volksdeutschen in der Sowjetunion." Zahlen der Volkszählung von 1970." Osteuropa (N, 1975):935-940.

Svensson, Frances. "The Final Crisis of Tribalism: Comparative Ethnic Policy on the American and Russian Frontiers." Ethnic and Racial Studies 1(Ja, 1978):100-123.

Symmons-Symonolewicz, Konstantin. The Non-Slavic Peoples of the Soviet Union: A Brief Ethnographical Survey. Meadville, PA: Maplewood Press, 1972.

Tartakower, A., and Kolitz, Z. (eds.). Jewish Culture in the Soviet Union. Jerusalem, Israel: Cultural Department of the World Jewish Congress, 1973.

Taylor, Telford. Courts of Terror: Soviet Criminal Justice and Jewish Emigration. New York: Simon and Schuster, 1976.

Tillett, Lowell. The Great Friendship: Soviet Historians on the Non-Russian Nationalities. Chapel Hill, NC: U. of North Carolina Press, 1969.

Toth, Robert C. "Jews Have Own 'State' in Soviet Union." Los Angeles Times, Je 14, 1977. [Jewish Autonomous Region, Birobijan]

_____. "African Students Assail Soviet Society." Los Angeles Times, N 23, 1975.

_____. "Germans in Russia: Many Want to Stay." Los Angeles Times, Ap 24, 1976.

_____. "Sociology in Russia: Party Line Takes Precedence Over Science." Los Angeles Times, O 10, 1976.

_____. "Soviet Jews Survive in 'Lost Place.'" Los Angeles Times, Je 27, 1976. [Ilinka]

"Tough Fight for Coveted Places." Times Higher Education Supplement, Ja 3, 1975. [Higher education in the U.S.S.R.]

Tepper, Leopold. The Great Game. New York: McGraw-Hill, 1977. [Jews in the USSR]

Tsamerian, I. P., and Ronin, S. L. Equality of Rights Between Races and Nationalities in the U.S.S.R. Nijmegen: N.p., 1962.

U.S. Congress, 92nd, 1st session, House of Representatives, Committee on Foreign Affairs, Subcommittee on Europe. Soviet Jewry. Hearings... Washington, DC: GPO, 1972.

U.S. National Institute of Mental Health. Special Report: The First U.S. Mission on Mental Health to the U.S.S.R. Washington, DC: GPO, F, 1969.

U.S.S.R. Academy of Sciences. "National Relations in the U.S.S.R.: Theory and Practice." Problems of the Contemporary World 4(1974).

Uvachan, V. N. The Peoples of the North and Their Road to Socialism. Moscow: Progress Publishers, 1975.

Vardys, V. S. "Geography and Nationalities in the USSR: A Commentary." Slavic Review 30 (1972).

Vasil'eva, E. K. "An Ethnodemographic Characterization of Family Structure in Karanin 1967." Soviet Review 12(Winter, 1971/72):301-322.

Vishniak, Mark. "Anti-Semitism in Tsarist Russia." In Essays on Anti-Semitism. Edited by Koppel Pinson. New York: N.p., 1946.

Vorob'yev, V. V. "The Settling of Eastern Siberia Before the Revolution." Soviet Geography 16(F, 1975):75-85.

Voronel, Alexander. "The Search for Jewish Identity in Russia." Soviet Jewish Affairs 5(1975).

Vucinich, Wayne S. (ed.). Russia and Asia: Essays on the Influence of Russia on the Asian Peoples. Stanford, CA: Hoover Institution Press, 1972.

We Are From Friendship University. Moscow:
Progress Publishers, 1965.

Weinrich, Uriel. "The Russification of Soviet
Minority Languages." Problems of Communication 2(1953).

Weinryb, B. D. "Antisemitism in Soviet
Russia." In The Jews in Soviet Russia Since
1917. Edited by Lionel Kochan. New York:
Oxford U. Press, 1970.

Wheeler, Geoffrey E. "The Muslims of Central
Asia." Problems of Communism 16(S-O,
1967):72-81.

_____. Racial Problems in Soviet Muslim
Asia. London: Oxford U. Press, 1960.

_____. "The Turkic Languages of Soviet
Muslim Asia: Russian Linguistic Policy."
Mid. E. Stud. 13(My, 1977):208-217.

Wixman, Ronald. "Assimilation of Ethnic Groups
of the Caucasus which Lack Native Ethnic
Institutions (1926-1959)." Master's thesis,
Columbia U., 1972.

Woltner, M. Das wolgadeutsche Bildungswesen
und die russische Schulpolitik.
Vol. I: Von der Begründung der Wolgakolonien
bis zur Einführung des gesetzlichen
Schulzwanges. Leipzig: N.p., 1937.

Yanowitch, Murray. Social and Economic Inequality in the Soviet Union: Six Studies.
White Plains, NY: M. E. Sharpe, 1977.

_____ (ed.). The Career Plans of Youth.
White Plains, NY: International Arts and
Sciences Press, 1971.

Yanowitch, Murray, and Dodge, Norton T. "The
Social Evaluation of Occupations in the
Soviet Union." Slavic Review 28(D, 1969):
619-643.

_____ and ____. "Social Class and Education:
Soviet Findings and Reactions." Comparative
Education Review, O, 1968.

Yanowitch, Murray, and Fisher, Wesley A. (eds.).
Social Stratification and Mobility in the
USSR. White Plains, NY: International Arts
and Sciences Press, 1973.

Yarmolinky, Avrahm. The Jews and Other Minor
Nationalities under the Soviets. New York:
Vanguard, 1928.

Zamborsky, Laura L. "The Plight of the Jews
in the Soviet Union 1960-1970." Doctoral
dissertation, John Carroll U., 1971.

Zinchensko, I. "The National Composition and
the Languages of the Population of the USSR
According to the Data of the 1970 Census."
Soviet Education 16(S-O, 1974):33-45.

Zwicker, Peter. Comparative Politics 8(1976).
[Soviet minorities]

Uraguay

Carvalho-Neto, Paulo de. El Negro Uruaguayo
(hasta la abolicion). Quito, Ecuador:
Editorial Universitaria, 1965.

Pereda Valdés, Ildefonso. El Negro en el
Uruguay: Pasado y Presente. Montevideo:
Revista del Instituto Histórico y Geográfico
del Uruguay, 1965.

Rama, Carlos M. Los Afro-Uruguayos.
Montevideo: El Sigo Instrado, 1967.

Venezuela

Acosta Saignes, Miguel. Vida de los escalvos
negros en Venezuela. Caracus, Venezuela:
Hesperides, 1967.

Bertrán Prieto Figueroa, Luis. De una
educación de castas a una educación de
masas. Havana: N.p., 1951.

Coppens, Walter. The Anatomy of a Land Inva-
sion Scheme in Yekuana Territory,
Venezuela. Copenhagen, Denmark:
International Work Group for Indigenous
Affairs, 1972.

Lizot, Jacques. The Yanomami in the Face of
Ethnocide. Copenhagen: IWGIA, 1976.

Lombardi, John V. "The Abolition of Slavery in
Venezuela" A Nonevent." In Slavery and
Race Relations in Latin America, pp. 228-
252. Edited by Robert T. Toplin. Westport,
CT: Greenwood Press, 1974.

_____. "Race, Sex, Marriage, and Children."
In People and Places in Colonial Venezuela,
pp. 67-87. Bloomington, IN: Indiana U.
Press, 1976.

Pollack-Eltz, Angelina. The Black Family in
Venezuela. Wien: Ferdinand Berger &
Sohne, 1974.

_____. "La incorporación de los indígenas a
la vida moderna en Venezuela." Suplemento
Antropológico de la Revista del Ateno
Paraguayo 6(1970).

Silvert, Kalman H., and Reissman, Leonard.
Education, Class and Nation: The Experi-
ences of Chile and Venezuela. N.p.:
Elsevier, 1978.

Watson-Franke, Maria-Barbara. "Traditional
Educational Concepts in the Modern World:
The Case of the Guajiro Indians of Vene-
zuela." Sociologus 24(1974):97-116.

Wright, Winthrop R. "Elitist Attitudes Toward Race in Twentieth-Century Venezuela." In Slavery and Race Relations in Latin America, pp. 325-347. Edited by Robert B. Toplin. Westport, CT: Greenwood Press, 1974.

Vietnam

An Outline of the Institutions of the Democratic Republic of Viet Nam. Hanoi: Foreign Languages Publishing House, 1974.

Benedict, Paul K. "Languages and Literatures of Indochina." Far Eastern Quarterly 6 (1946-1947):379-389.

Brocheux, P. "Vietnamiens et Minorities en Cochinchine Pendant la Période Coloniale." Modern Asian Studies, 0, 1972.

Buttinger, Joseph. "The Ethnic Minorities in the Republic of Vietnam." In Problem of Freedom: South Vietnam Since Independence, pp. 99-121. Edited by Wesley R. Fishel. New York: Free Press of Glencoe, 1961.

Coyle, Joanne Marie. "Indochinese Administration and Education: French Policy and Practice, 1917 to 1945." Doctoral dissertation, Fletcher School of Law and Diplomacy, 1963.

De Francis, John. Colonialism and Language Policy in Viet Nam. New York: Mouton, 1977.

Dremuk, Richard, and Hurley, Marvin. "Vietnam, Laos and Cambodia." In Report of the Training Workshop on the Evaluation of Asian Educational Credentials. Honolulu, HI: National Association for Foreign Student Affairs, East-West Center, Ag, 1968.

Ethnic Minorities of North Vietnam. JPRS/DC-198. Washington, DC: U.S. Joint Publication Research Service, Jl, 1958.

Finman, Byron G., Borus, Jonathan F., and Stanton, M. Duncan. "Black-White and American-Vietnamese Relations Among Soldiers in Vietnam." Journal of Social Issues 31 (1975):39-48.

Gregerson, Marilyn. "The Ethnic Minorities of Vietnam." South East Asia, Winter, 1972.

Hickey, Gerald Cannon. The Major Ethnic Groups of the South Vietnamese Highlands. A.R.P.A., 1972.

_____. "Social Systems of Northern Vietnam." Doctoral dissertation, U. of Chicago, 1958.

Johnston, Howard J. "The Tribal Soldier: A Study of the Manipulation of Ethnic Minorities." Naval War College Review 19(Ja, 1967):98-143.

Kahin, George McT. "Minorities in the Democratic Republic of Vietnam." Asian Survey (Jl, 1972):580-586.

Kelly, Gail P. "Colonial Schools in Vietnam: Policy and Practice." In Education and Colonialism, pp. 96-121. Edited by Philip G. Altbach and Gail P. Kelly. New York: Longman, 1978.

Kelly, Gail P. "Colonial Schools in Vietnam, 1918-1938." Proc. Fr. Colonial Hist. Soc. 2(1977):96-106.

_____. "Franco-Vietnamese Schools, 1918-1938." Doctoral dissertation, U. of Wisconsin, 1975. Univ. Microfilms Order No. 76-08211.

Ky, Luong Nhi. "The Chinese in Vietnam: A Study of Vietnamese-Chinese Relations with Special Attention to the Period 1862-1961." Doctoral dissertation, U. of Michigan, 1963. Univ. Microfilms Order No. 63-04983.

Laffey, John F. "Racism in Tonkin before 1914: The Colons' View of the Vietnamese." French Colonial Studies 1(Spring, 1977):65-81.

Levin, Libian et al. Skola och Samhialle i Kina, Kuba, Tanzania och Vietnam. Stockholm, Sweden: Raben & Sjogren, 1970.

Long, Ngo Vinh. Before the Revolution: The Vietnamese Peasants Under the French. Cambridge, MA: MIT Press, 1973.

Luong Nhi Ky. "The Chinese in Vietnam: A Study of Vietnamese-Chinese Relations With Special Attention to the Period 1862-1961." Doctoral dissertation, U. of Michigan, 1962.

Malleret, Louis. Ethnic Groups of French Indochina. JPRS: 12359. Washington, DC: Joint Publications Research Office, 1962.

Marr, David G. Vietnamese Anticolonialism, 1885-1925. Berkeley, CA: U. of California Press, 1971.

Maw-Kuey, Tsai. Les Chinois au Sud-Vietnam. Paris: Bibliothèque Nationale, 1968.

Miller, John Francis, Jr. "Diglossia: A Centrifugal Force in Socio-Cultural Relationships. The Case of the Khmer Minority in South Vietnam." Doctoral dissertation, Southern Illinois U., 1975. Univ. Microfilms Order No. 76-13273.

Minority Groups in the Republic of Vietnam. Washington, DC: GPO, 1967.

Minority Rights Group. The Montagnards of South Vietnam. London: Minority Rights Group, 1972.

Osborne, Milton E. The French Presence in
Cochin China and Cambodia: Rule and
Response (1859-1905). Ithaca, NY: Cornell
U. Press, 1969.

Schrock, Joann L., Gosier, Dennis E., Marton,
Diane S., McKenzie, Virginia S., and Murfin,
Gary D. Minority Groups in North Vietnam.
Washington, DC: GPO, Ap, 1972.

Turton, Andrew. "National Minority Peoples in
Indochina." Journal of Contemporary Asia 4
(1974):336-342.

Van, Pham-Thi. "L'histoire du Viêt-nam sous
l'oeil des historiens français, 1870-1968."
Master's thesis, Montréal U., 1970.

Vannsak, Keng. "Recherches d'un fonds
culturel khmer." Doctoral dissertation,
U. of Paris IV, 1971.

Vella, Walter F. (ed.). Aspects of Vietnamese
History. Honolulu, HI: U. Press of
Hawaii, 1973.

Vien, Nguyen Khac. Ethnographical Data, vol.
1. Vietnamese Studies, No. 32. Hanoi:
Xunhasaba, 1972.

_____ (ed.). General Education in the
D.R.V.N. Vietnamese Studies, No. 30.
Hanoi: Xunhasaba, 1971.

Vu-Duc-Bang. "The Dong Kinh Free School
Movement, 1907-1908." In Aspects of
Vietnamese History, pp. 30-95. Edited by
Water Vella. Honolulu: U. of Hawaii
Press, 1973.

Vu-Tam-Ich. A Historical Survey of Educational Developments in Vietnam. Lexington, KY:
U. of Kentucky, 1959.

Wickert, Frederic. "The Tribesmen." In
Viet-Nam: The First Five Years, pp. 126-
140. Edited by Richard W. Lindholm.
East Lansing, MI: Michigan State U. Press,
1959.

Woodruff, Lance. "Unfortunately Black."
Chicago Defender, D 30, 1967. Children
of Negro American soldiers and Vietnamese
women

Yemen

Kapeliuk, Menajem. Los Judios del Yemen.
Tr. by Beraja Barsky de Maizlis. Buenos
Aires, Argentina: Congreso Judio Latin-
americano, 1971.

Tobi, Josef. The Jews of Yemen. Jerusalem:
Zalman Shazar Centre, Historical Society of
Israel, 1975.

Yesha' Yahu, Yisrael, and Tobi, Josef (ed.).
The Jews of Yemen. Studies and Researches.
Jerusalem: Yad Izhak Ben-Zvi, 1975.

Yugoslavia

Banac, Ivo. "The National Question in
Yugoslavia's Formative Period: 1918-1921."
Doctoral dissertation, Stanford U., 1975.

Baucic, I. Social Aspects of External Migration of Workers and the Yugoslav Experience
in the Social Protection of Migrants.
Geneva: United Nations Office, 1975.

Bennett, William S., Jr. "Elitism and
Socialist Goals in Yugoslav Education."
Notre Dame Journal of Education 3(F, 1972):
267-277.

Bertsch, Gary K. "The Revival of Nationalism."
Problems of Communism 22(N-D, 1973):1-15.

Burks, R. V. The National Problem and the
Future of Yugoslavia. Santa Monica, CA:
Rand Corporation, 1971.

_____. The National Problem and the Future
of Yugoslavia. AD-741 594. Springfield,
VA: National Technical Information Service,
O, 1971.

Chinese Journalist Group. "Unity Among
Nationalities." Peking Review 21(F 24,
1978):24-26.

Chirot, Daniel. Social Change in a Peripheral
Society: The Creation of a Balkan Colony.
New York: Academic Press, 1976. [Wallachia]

Davis, Horace B. "'Solving the National Ques-
tion' in Yugoslavia." In Toward a Marxist
Theory of Nationalism, pp. 135-164.
New York: Monthly Review Press, 1978.

Dedijer, Vladimir and others. History of
Yugoslavia. Tr. Kordija Kveder. New York:
McGraw-Hill, 1974.

Denitch, Bogdan Denis. "The Institutionalization of Multinationalism." In The Legitimation of a Revolution. The Yugoslav Case,
pp. 105-148. New Haven, CT: Yale U. Press,
1976.

Djodan, Sime. "The Evolution of the Economic
System of Yugoslavia and the Economic
Position of Croatia." Journal of Croatian
Studies (N.Y.C.) 13(1972):3-102.

Doder, Dusko. "Albanian Influence Grows in
Backward Yugoslav Province [of Kosovo]."
Washington Post, Je 5, 1975.

Dyker, David A. "The Ethnic Muslims of
Bosnia--Some Basic Socio-Economic Data."
Slavonic and East European Review 50
(Ap, 1972):238-256.

Freidenreich, Harriet Pass. "Belgrade, Zagreb,
Sarajevo: A Study of Jewish Communities
in Yugoslavia before World War II."
Doctoral dissertation, Columbia U., 1973.

Gavrilovic, Z., and Vlahovic, P. (eds.). Racism, Races and Race Prejudice (in Serbo-Croatian). Belgrade: Yugoslav Anthropological Association, 1974.

Harriman, Helga H. Slovenia Under Nazi Occupation, 1941-1945. New York: Studia Slovenica, 1977.

Hoffman, George W. "Migration and Social Change." Problems of Communism 22(N-D, 1973):16-31.

Hondius, Fritz. The Yugoslav Community of Nations. The Hague: Mouton, 1968.

Jelinek, Yeshayahu. "The 'Final Solution'-- the Slovak Version." East European Quarterly 4(Ja, 1971).

_____. "Slovakia and Its Minorities 1939-1945: People With and Without National Protection." Nationalities Papers 4(Spring, 1976):1-15.

Jončić, Koca. Relations Among the Peoples and National Minorities in Yugoslavia. Belgrade: n.p., 1969.

Karaman, Igo (ed.). Zur Geschichte der Burgen- ländischen Kroaten. Zagreb: Institute of Croatian History, U. of Zagreb, 1977.

Kintzer, Frederick C. "Educational Reforms in Yugoslavia." Educational Record 59(Winter, 1978):87-104.

Lang, Nicholas R. "The Dialectics of De- centralization: Economic Reform and Regional Inequality in Yugoslavia." World Politics 27(Ap, 1975):309-335.

Levntal, Z. (ed.). The Crimes of the Fascist Occupiers and their Assistants Against the Jews in Yugoslavia. Belgrade: Savez jevrejskih opstina Jugoslavije, 1952. [In Serbo-Croatian with English summary]

Lockwood, William G. European Moslems: Economy and Ethnicity in Western Bosnia. New York: Academic Press, 1975.

Mandic, Oleg. "La stratification sociale en Yugoslavie et la notion de classe." Cahiers internationaux de sociologie 39 (1965):171-184.

Milic, Vojin. "General Trends in Social Mobil- ity in Yugoslavia." Acta Sociologica 9 (1965).

"The Nationalities Question in Yugoslavia." International Journal of Politics 2(Spring, 1972). [Four articles by Yugoslav writers]

Pantic, D. Ethnic Distance in S.F.R. Yugo- slavia (in Serbo-Croatian). Belgrade: Institut drustvenih nauka, 1967.

Petrovich, Michael B. "Continuing Nationalism in Yugoslav Historiography." Nationalities Papers 6(Fall, 1978):161-177.

_____. "Yugoslavia: Religion and the Tensions of a Multi-National State." East European Quarterly 6(Mr, 1972).

Prifti, Peter R. "Minority Politics: The Albanians in Yugoslavia." Balkanistica 2 (1975):7-18.

Prinmorac, Igor. "Race Research in Yugoslavia." Patterns of Prejudice 10(Ja-F, 1976):35-37.

"Problems of Muslim Minorities." Dawn (Karachi, Pakistan), Ag 29, 1976.

Robinson, Gertrude Joch. "Mass Media and Ethnic Strife in Multi-National Yugoslavia." Journalism Quarterly 51(Autumn, 1974):490- 497.

Rogel, Carole. The Slovenes and Yugoslavism, 1890-1914. New York: Columbia U. Press, 1977.

Roucek, Joseph S. "Yugoslavia's History of Education Before 1918." Paedagogica Historica 13(1973):66-84.

Russinow, Dennison. The Crisis in Croatia. New York: American Univerities Field Staff, 1972.

Seferagic, Dusica. "Scientific Work in Yugo- slavia on Migrant Returnees and Their Impact on the Mother Country." International Migration Review 11(Fall, 1977):363-374.

Shoup, Pal. Communism and the Yugoslav National Question. New York: Columbia U. Press, 1968.

Simic, Andrei. The Peasant Urbanites. A Study of Rural-Urban Mobility in Serbia. New York: Academic Press, 1972.

Stavrou, Nikolaos A. "Unity, Brotherhood and Manipulation. Language and Minorities in Yugoslavia." Society 12(Ja-F, 1975):75-78.

Tolicic, Ivan, and Zorman, Leon. Achievement and Personality Characteristics of School Children in Relation to Environment, Je, 1977. ERIC ED 146 211.

Tomasic, Dinko. "Nationality Problems in Partisan Yugoslavia." Journal of Central European Affairs 6(Jl, 1946).

Ulrih-Atena, Ela. "National Linguistic Minorities: Bilingual Basic Education in Slovenia." Prospects 6(1976):430-438.

Vuskovic, Boris. "Social Inequality in Yugoslavia." New Left Review 95(Ja-F, 1976): 26-44.

Zaire

Bokamba, Eyamba G. "Authenticity and the Choice of a National Language: The Case of Zaire." Présence Afric. 3-4(1976):104-142.

De Schsevel, M. "Les Forces politiques de la decolonisation congolaise jus qu à la veille de l'independance." Doctoral dissertation, U. of Louvain, 1970.

Emoungu, P. A. N. "The Concept of Educational Adaptation and Development in the Congo, 1920-60." Doctoral dissertation, U. of Illinois, 1973.

L'enseignement aux indigenes: documents officiels precedes de notices historiques-Congo belge, colonies portugaises, colonies francaises. Brussels: Institut Colonial International, 1910, 2 vols.

Gingrich, Newton Leroy. "Belgian Education Policy in the Congo, 1945-1960." Doctoral dissertation, Tulane U., 1971. Univ. Microfilms Order No. 72-03881.

Rideout, William Milford, Jr. "Education and Elites: The Making of the New Elites and the Formal Education System in the Congo." Doctoral dissertation, Stanford U., 1971. Univ. Microfilms Order No. 72-11648.

Rossie, Jean-Pierre (comp.). "Bibliographie commentee de la communaute Musulmane au Zaire des origines a 1975." Cah. CEDAF 6 (1976):1-38.

Samba, Kaputo Wa Maluta. "Phenomene d'ethnicité et conflits tribaux dans les centres urbains du Zaire." Doctoral dissertation, U. of Brussels (U.L.B.), 1974.

UKendo-Mpasi, P. "Réflexions sur la problematique de la langue d'enseignement au Congo." Revue Congolaise der Sciences Humaines 2(1971).

Zambia

Burawoy, M. "Consciousness and Contradiction: A Study of Student Protest in Zambia." British Journal of Sociology 27(1976):78-98.

Christensen, J. E. "Occupational Education in Zambia, 1885-1970." Doctoral dissertation, U. of California, Los Angeles, 1972.

Coombe, Trevor. "The Origins of Secondary Education in Zambia," 2 parts. African Social Research 3(1967):173-205; 4(1967(283-315.

Dotson, Floyd, and Dotson, Lillian O. The Indian Minority of Zambia, Rhodesia and Malawi. New Haven, CT: Yale U. Press, 1968.

Gann, L. H. "The Growth of a Plural Society--Social, Economic, and Political Aspects of Northern Rhodesian Development, 1890-1953, with Special Reference to the Problem of Racial Relations." Doctoral dissertation, Oxford U., 1963.

Hall, Richard. The High Price of Principles: Kaunda and the White South. London: Hodder & Stoughton, 1969.

_____. "Zambia's Racial Make-Up." Race Today, 0, 1969.

Henderson, Ian. "The Limits of Colonial Power: Race and Labour Problems in Colonial Zambia, 1900-1953." Imperial Commonwealth History 2(My, 1974):294-307.

Irvine, S. A. "African Education in Northern Rhodesia--The First Forty Years." Teacher Education (London) 2(1961-1962):36-50. [1885-1925]

Matejko, Alexander. "The Upgraded Zambian." Phylon 36(Fall, 1975):291-308.

Meehlo, H. S. Reaction to Colonialism. Manchester, England: Manchester U. Press, 1973. [Northern Zambia until World War II]

Molteno, R. Zambia: The Educational and Student Scene. Lukasa, Zambia: School of Humanities, U. of Zambia, 1970.

Okonji, M. O. "The Development of Logical Thinking in Preschool Zambian Children: Classification." Journal of Genetic Psychology 125(D, 1974):247-256.

Parker, Franklin. "The Inception of the Department of African Education in Northern Rhodesia." Paedagogica Historica 4(1964):149-162.

Peters, Harold Eugene. "The Contributions of Education to the Development of Elites Among the Plateau Tonga of Zambia: A Comparative Study of School-Leavers from Two Mission Schools 1930 to 1965." Doctoral dissertation, U. of Illinois, 1975. Univ. Microfilms Order No. 76-16181.

Ragsdale, John Paul. "The Educational Development of Zambia as Influenced by Protestant Missions from 1880 to 1954." Doctoral dissertation, Lehigh U., 1973. Univ. Microfilms Order No. 73-23815.

Rotberg, Robert I. Black Heart: Gore-Brown and the Politics of Multiracial Zambia. Berkeley: U. of California Press, 1977.

Scarritt, James, and Hatter, John. Racial and Ethnic Conflict in Zambia. Vol. 2, No. 2, Studies in Race and Nations, 1970-1971 series. Center on International Race Relations, U. of Denver, Denver, CO.

Serpell, Robert. "Language in Zambia." Race Today 3(Je, 1971):207.

Zimbabwe

Arrighi, Giovanni. "The Political Economy of Rhodesia." New Left Review 39(S-O, 1966): 35-65.

Atkinson, Norman. Teaching Rhodesians: A History of Educational Policy in Rhodesia. London: Longman, 1972.

Austin, Reginald. Racism and Apartheid in Southern Africa: Rhodesia, A Book of Data. Paris: UNESCO Press, 1975.

Barnes, Helene. "Multi-racial University 'a Facade.'" Times Higher Education Supplement, Jl 13, 1973. [U. of Rhodesia]

Berger, Elena L. Labour, Race and Colonial Rule: The Copperbelt from 1924 to Independence. Oxford, England: Clarendon Press, 1974.

"Black Rhodesian Academics Map Out Africanization." Times Higher Education Supplement, Mr 17, 1978.

Bone, R. C. African Education in Rhodesia: The Period to 1927. Salisbury, Rhodesia: U. College of Rhodesia, 1970.

Bowman, Larry W. Politics in Rhodesia. White Power in an African State. Cambridge, MA: Harvard U. Press, 1973.

Chalbiss, R. J. "The Origins of the Educational System of Southern Rhodesia." Rhodesian History 4(1973):57-77.

Chelwaluza, Clifford. "No Entry." Race Today, Je, 1970.

Chimutengwende, Chenhamo. "The Rhodesian Crisis and the Liberation Movement." Race Today, Jl, 1969.

Christie, Michael. Black Paper on Rhodesia. London: Institute of Race Relations, 1972.

Clarke, D. G. "Settler Ideology and African Underdevelopment in Postwar Rhodesia." Rhodesian Journal of Economics 8(Mr, 1974): 17-38.

Colquin, Ethel Maud (Cookson). The Real Rhodesia. London: Hutchinson & Co., 1924.

Cubitt, Verity S., and Riddell, Roger C. The Urban Poverty Datum Line in Rhodesia: A Study of Minimum of Consumption Needs of Families. Salisbury: Faculty of Social Studies, U. of Rhodesia, 1974.

Davies, C. S. "African Education in Rhodesia." NADA (The Southern Rhodesia Native Affairs Department Annual) 10(1969).

Davies, Dorothy Keyworth. "Education." In Race Relations in Rhodesia. A Survey for 1972-73. London: Rex Collings, 1975.

Dotson, Floyd, and Dotson, Lillian O. The Indian Minority of Zambia, Rhodesia and Malawi. New Haven, CT: Yale U. Press, 1968.

Duignan, Peter James. "Native Policy in Southern Rhodesia, 1890-1923." Doctoral dissertation, Stanford U., 1961. Univ. Microfilms Order No. 62-05515.

Frank, David. "Eretz Rhodesia." Jerusalem Post, Ag 22, 1978. [Jewish community in Zimbabwe]

_____. "Road from Rhodesia." Jerusalem Post Magazine, Ja 19, 1979. [Jews in Zimbabwe]

Good, Kenneth. "Education for the Colonized." New Society, N 1, 1973. [U. of Rhodesia]

_____. "The Last White Christmas for Rhodesia?" New Society, F 8, 1973.

Grant, G. C. The Africans' Predicament in Rhodesia. London: Minority Rights Group, Ja, 1972.

Gray, Richard. The Two Nations--Aspects of the Development of Race Relations in the Rhodesias and Nyasaland. London: Oxford U. Press, 1960.

Harris, P. B. "Pragmatism Versus Protest at the University College of Rhodesia." Universities Quarterly 25(Winter, 1970): 71-82.

Henderson, Ian. "College Crackdown in Rhodesia." New Republic, N 19, 1966.

Honey, J. R. de S. "University of Rhodesia." Times Higher Education Supplement, D 26, 1975. [Letter]

Hopkins, Adam. "Too Little, Too Late." Times Educational Supplement, F 25, 1977. [Black education in Rhodesia]

International Labour Office. Labour Conditions and Discrimination in Southern Rhodesia (Zimbabwe). London: ILO, 1977.

James, Leslie A. L. "Education in the Rhodesias and Nyasaland, 1890-1963." Doctoral dissertation, New York U., 1965.

Jenni, H. P. Rassismus in Rhodesien. Enlarged ed., Jl, 1972. Arbeitsgruppe Dritte Welt, Postfach 1007, 3001 Bern, Switzerland.

Jessen, K. V. "Some Aspects of Library Provision in African Townships: The Bulawayo Township Libraries." Rhodesian Librarian 5 (Ap, 1973).

Kaufamann, Laura. "Sailing between Scylla and Charybdis." Times Higher Education Supplement, N 3, 1972. [Higher education in Rhodesia]

Kay, George. Distribution and Density of the African Population in Rhodesia. Hull: Hull U. Geography Department, 1972.

Kileff, Clive. "Black Suburbanites: Adaptation to Western Culture in Salisbury, Rhodesia." Doctoral dissertation, Rice U., 1970. Univ. Microfilms Order No. 70-23540.

Kinloch, Graham C. "Changing Black Reaction to White Domination." Rhodesian History 5 (1974):67-78.

_____. "Changing Rhodesian Race Relations: A Study of Demographic and Economic Factors." Proc. Am. Phil. Soc. 122(F, 1978):18-24.

_____. "Social Types and Race Relations in the Colonial Setting: A Case Study of Rhodesia." Phylon 33(Fall, 1972):276-289.

Krikler, D. M. "The Jews of Rhodesia." Institute of Race Relations Newsletter, Ja, 1969.

Krikler, Dennis M. "The Pioneering Jews of Rhodesia." Wiener Library Bulletin 22 (Autumn, 1968):19-24.

Lacy, Creighton. "'Christian' Racism in Rhodesia." Christian Century, Mr 15, 1972.

Loney, Martin. Rhodesia, White Racism and Imperial Response. Harmondsworth: Penguin, 1975

McAdam, Anthony. "The Limits of Dissent in Rhodesia." Race Today 3(My, 1971):151-152.

McHarg, James. "Influences Contributing to the Education and Culture of the Native People in Southern Rhodesia from 1900 to 1961." Doctoral dissertation, Duke U., 1962. Univ. Microfilms Order No. 63-03598.

Mackenzie, John M. "Colonial Labour Policy in Rhodesia." Rhodesian Journal of Economics 8 (Mr, 1974).

Makura, Nicholas G. G. "The Historical Development of African Education in Rhodesia: Administration of African Education from 1928 to 1973." Doctoral dissertation, U. of Illinois, 1978. Univ. Microfilms Order No. 7820997.

Martin, Christopher. "Educational Need in Rhodesia." Race Today 3(Ja, 1971):19-20.

Mashingaidze, E. K. "Government-Mission Cooperation in African Education in Southern Rhodesia Up to the Late 1920's." Kenya Hist. R. J. 4, No. 2(1976):265-281.

Mazobere, Crispin Christopher Godzo. "Racial Conflict in Rhodesia." Doctoral dissertation, Boston U., 1973. Univ. Microfilms Order No. 73-14163.

Mlambo, Eshmael. Rhodesia: The Struggle for a Birthright. London: Hurst, 1972.

Morrison, Douglas. "'It's Not Going to Be Another Mozambique.'" Times Educational Supplement, My 28, 1976.

Mungazi, Dickson Adlai. "The Change of Black Attitudes Toward Education in Rhodesia, 1900-1975." Doctoral dissertation, U. of Nebraska, 1977. Univ. Microfilms Order No. 7809160.

Murphree, B. J. "Socio-Economic Factors Influencing the Aspirations and Achievement of African Secondary Pupils in Rhodesia." Doctoral dissertation, U. of Rhodesia, n.d.

Murphree, Marshall W. "Diffisionism or Extinction: The Stark Alternatives." Times Higher Education Supplement, S 21, 1973. [Dean of faculty of social science, U. of Rhodesia]

_____. "Race and Power in Rhodesia." In Politics of Race. Edited by D. G. Baker. Farnborough: Saxon House, D. C. Heath Ltd., 1975.

_____. "Whites in Black Africa: Their Status and Role." Ethnic and Racial Studies 1(Ap, 1978):154-174.

_____. Employment Opportunity and Race in Rhodesia. Denver, CO: Graduate School of International Studies, U. of Denver, 1973.

_____ (ed.). Education, Race and Employment in Rhodesia. Salisbury: Artca Publications, 1975.

Mutasa, Didymus. Rhodesian Black Behind Bars. London: Mowbray, 1976.

Muzorewa, Abel T. Rise Up and Walk: The Autobiography... Edited by Norman E. Thomas. Nashville, TN: Abingdon, 1978.

Ndolvu, S. "Student Protest in Salisbury." Africa Today 21(1974):39-42.

O'Callaghan, Marion. Southern Rhodesia: The Effects of a Conquest Society on Education, Culture and Information. New York: Unipub, 1977.

O'Leary, John. "What Kind of [Educational] System After Rhodesian War is Over?" Times Higher Education Supplement, Jl 7, 1978.

O'Meara, Patrick. Rhodesia. Racial Conflict or Coexistence? Ithaca, NY: Cornell U. Press, 1975.

Orpen, Christopher. "The Effect of Race and Similar Attitudes on Interpersonal Attraction Among White Rhodesians." Journal of Social Psychology 86(F, 1972):143-145.

Palley, Claire. "A Note on the Development of Legal Inequality in Rhodesia: 1890-1962." Race 12(Jl, 1970):87-93.

_____. Constitutional History and Law of Southern Rhodesia. Oxford: Clarendon Press, 1966.

_____. "Law and the Unequal Society: Discriminatory Legislation in Rhodesia under the Rhodesian Front from 1963 to 1969. Part 1." Race 12(Jl, 1970):15-47.

_____. "Law and the Unequal Society: Discriminatory Legislation in Rhodesia under the Rhodesian Front from 1963 to 1969. Part 2." Race 12(O, 1970):139-167.

Palmer, Robin. Land and Racial Domination in Rhodesia. London: Heinemann Educational, 1977.

Parker, Franklin. "African Community Development and Education in Southern Rhodesia, 1920-1935." International Review of Missions 51(1962):336-347.

_____. African Development and Education in Southern Rhodesia. Columbus, OH: Ohio State U. Press, 1960.

_____. "Education of Africans in Southern Rhodesia." Comparative Education Review 3 (1959-1960):27-32.

Partridge, Nan. Not Alone. A Study for the Future of Rhodesia, 1972. SCM Press, 56-58 Bloomsbury Street, London WC1B 3QX, England.

Passmore, Gloria C. The National Policy of Community Development in Rhodesia. Salisbury: U. of Rhodesia, 1972.

Phelps, William. "African Secondary School Education in Zimbabwe. From the Student's Perspective." Renaissance 2, Issue 3 [1973] 29-34. [Kuregai Secondary School, Mangwana Tribal Trust Land]

Phillips, Alan. "Where Black Is Not So Beautiful." Times Higher Education Supplement, D 5, 1975. [U. of Rhodesia]

Pichon, Roland. Le Drame Rhodésien, Résurgence du Zimbabwe. Paris: IDOC, 1975.

Pollak, O., and Pollak, K. (comps.). Rhodesia and Zimbabwe: An International Bibliography. Boston: G. K. Hall, 1977.

Randolph, R. H. Church and State in Rhodesia, 1969-1971. Gwelo: N.p., 1971.

Ranger, T. O. The African Voice in Southern Rhodesia, 1898-1930. New York: International Publications Service, 1970.

"Rhodesia--Teachers on Trial." Race Today 3 (My, 1971):163-164.

Rhodesia: Why Minority Rule Survives. London: Christian Action Publications, Ltd., 1969.

Rogers, Cyril A., and Frantz, Charles. Racial Themes in Southern Rhodesia: The Attitudes and Behavior of the White Population. New Haven, CT: Yale U. Press, 1962.

Steele, M. C. "The Foundations of a 'Native' Policy: Southern Rhodesia, 1923-1933." Doctoral dissertation, Simon Fraser U., 1972.

Sutcliffe, R. B. "Stagnation and Inequality in Rhodesia, 1946-1968." Bulletin of the Oxford University Institute of Economics and Statistics 33(1971).

Taylor, J. R. African Education: The Historical Development and Organization of the System. Salisbury: Ministry of Information, 1970.

Taylor, R. African Education: The Historical Development and Organization of the System. Salisbury: Government Printer, 1970.

Vambe, Lawrence. An Ill-Fated People: Zimbabwe Before and After Rhodes. Pittsburgh, PA: U. of Pittsburgh Press, 1973.

_____. From Rhodesia to Zimbabwe. London: Heinemann, 1976. Autobiography

Van Onselen, Charles. Chibaro: African Mine Labour in Southern Rhodesia. London: Pluto Press, 1976.

Warhurst, P. R. "The History of Race Relations in Rhodesia." Zambezia 3(D, 1973):15-19.

Weinrich, A. K. H. Black and White Elites in Rural Rhodesia. Manchester, England: Manchester U. Press, 1973.

_____. Mucheke: Race, Status, and Politics in a Rhodesian Community. New York: Holmes & Meier, 1977.

Whaley, W. R. "Race Policies in Rhodesia." Zambezia 3(D, 1973):31-37.

Whitehead, R. M. "The Aborigines' Protection Society and the Safeguarding of African Interests in Rhodesia, 1889-1930." Doctoral dissertation, Oxford U., 1975.

ZAPU. "The Deprivation of the African in Zimbabwe." Zimbabwe Review 23(1974):1-5.

Other Education Studies

Adelman, Irma, and Morris, Cynthia Taft. Economic Growth and Social Equity in Developing Countries. Stanford, CA: Stanford U. Press, 1973.

Alcock, Anthony E. and others (eds.). The Future of Cultural Minorities. New York: St. Martin's Press, 1979.

Allen, Sheila. "Plural Society and Conflict." New Community 1(Autumn, 1972):389-392.

Altbach, Philip G. "Education and Neocolonialism." Teachers College Record 72(My, 1971): 543-558.

Ammoun, Charles D. Study of Discrimination in Education. New York: United Nations, Ag, 1957.

Anderson, C. Arnold. "Sociology of Education in a Comparative Framework." International Review of Education 16(1970):147-160.

Archer, Margaret S. (ed.). Students, University and Society. London: Heinemann, 1972.

Asad, Talal (ed.). Anthropology and the Colonial Encounter. London: Ithaca Press, 1974.

Ashworth, Georgina (ed.). World Minorities 1. London: Minority Rights Group, 1977.

The Assault on World Poverty: Problems of Rural Development, Education, and Health. Baltimore: Johns Hopkins U. Press, 1975.

Bagley, Christopher and others. "The Orthogonality of Religious and Racialist/Punitive Attitudes in Three Societies." Journal of Social Psychology 92(Ap, 1974):173-179. [Netherlands, Britain, and New Zealand]

Banton, Michael. Racial Minorities. London: Fontana, 1972.

Bereday, George Z. F. "Social Stratification in Industrial Countries." Comparative Education Review 21(Je-O, 1977):195-210.

Bloom, Len. The Social Psychology of Race Relations. London: Allen & Unwin, 1971.

Bodley, John H. Victims of Progress. Menlo Park, CA: Cummings, 1975.

Boudon, Raymond. Education, Opportunity, and Social Inequality: Changing Prospects in Western Society. New York: Wiley, 1974.

Braunert, Horst. "Jüdische Diaspora und Judenfeindschaft in Altertum." Gesch. Wiss. Unter. 26(S, 1975):531-547.

Brickman, William W. "Education of the Poor from Ancient Times to 1800 in International Perspective." In Education and the Many Faces of the Disadvantaged: Cultural and Historical Perspectives, pp. 325-348. Edited by William W. Brickman and Stanley Lehrer. New York: Wiley, 1972.

Brimer, M. A., and Pauli, L. Wastage in Education. A World Problem, 1971. Unipub, Inc., P.O. Box 433, New York, NY 10016

Callaway, Archibald. Educational Planning and Unemployed Youth. Paris: UNESCO, 1971.

Campbell, Persia Crawford. Chinese Coolie Emigration to Countries Within the British Empire. London: Cass, 1923.

Canham, G. William (ed.). Mother-Tongue Teaching. Hamburg, Germany: UNESCO Institute for Education, 1972.

Carceles, Gabriel. "World Public Expenditure: Education and Armaments, 1965-74." Prospects 7(1977):581-587.

Carlon, S. J. and others. "Civilisation noire et pédagogie." Présence Africaine 95 (1975).

Caudill, William, and Tsung-Yi Lin (eds.). Mental Health Research in Asia and the Pacific. Honolulu: N.p., 1969.

Chabaud, Jacqueline. The Education and Advancement of Women. Paris: UNESCO, 1970.

Chang, Stephen. The Chinese Around the World. Mountain View, CA: World Chinese Publishing Association, 1970.

Char, Tin-Y Uke. "Legal Restrictions on Chinese in English-speaking Countries of the Pacific." Master's degree, U. of Hawaii, 1932.

Chernyak, Y. Advocates of Colonialism. Tr. Taras Kapustin. Ed. Roger Silverman. Moscow: Progress Publishers, 1968.

Choppin, Bruce. "Social Class and Educational Achievement." Educational Research, Je, 1968. [An international study]

Clignet, Remi. "Damned If You Do, Damned If You Don't: The Dilemmas of Colonizer-Colonized Relations." Comparative Education Review 15(O, 1971):296-312.

_____. Liberty and Equality in the Educational Process: A Comparative Sociology of Education. New York: Wiley, 1974.

Coleman, B. I. "The Incidence of Education in Mid-Century." In Nineteenth Century Society. Essays in the Use of Quantitative Methods for the Study of Social Data. Edited by E. A. Wrigley. London: Cambridge U. Press, 1972.

Connor, Walker. "A Nation Is a Nation, Is a State, Is an Ethnic Group Is a..." Ethnic and Racial Studies 1(O, 1978):377-400.

Cumming, P. A. and others. "Rights of Indigenous Peoples: A Comparative Analysis." American Society of International Law, Proceedings 68(1974):265-301.

Curtin, Philip D. "The Black Experience of Colonialism and Imperialism. Daedalus 103 (Spring, 1974):17-29.

Dale, R. R., and Miller, P. McC. "Can Sex Affect Academic Achievement?" Times Higher Educational Supplement, D 10, 1971.

Das, K. "Measures of Implementation of the International Convention on the Elimination of All Forms of Racial Discrimination with Special Reference to the Provisions Concerning Reports from States Partner to the Convention." In En l'honneur de. in honour of, Egon Schwelb. Edited by René Cassin, Polys Modinos and Karel Vasak. Paris: A. Pedove, 1971.

Davenport, Manuel M. "The Moral Paternalism of Albert Schweitzer." Ethics 84(Ja, 1974): 116-127.

De Reuck, Anthony, and Knight, Julie (eds.). Caste and Race: Comparative Approaches. Boston: Little, Brown, 1967.

De Vaux de Foletier, F. Mille ans d'histoire des Tsiganes. Paris: Fayard, 1971.

De Vos, George A., and Romanucci-Ross, Lola (eds.). Ethnic Identity: Cultural Continuities and Change. Palo Alto, CA: Mayfield Publishing Co., 1975.

Del Boca, Angelo, and Giovana, Mario. Fascism Today. New York: Pantheon, 1968.

Despres, Leo A. (ed.). Ethnicity and Resource Competition in Plural Societies. The Hague: Mouton, 1975.

De Villefosse, L. Geographie de la Liberte. Les Droits de l'Homme dans le Monde, 1953-1964. Paris: R. Laffont, 1965.

"La Dinamizacion Cultural." Convergence 6 (1973):28-44. [Aymara Indian peoples of Bolivia, Peru, and Chile]

"Domination coloniale et mouvement nationalitaires." Revue Algerienne des sciences Juridques Politiques et Economiques 9(1972): entire issue.

Domnitz, Myer. "Efforts of Eliminating Prejudice in Textbooks." Patterns of Prejudice 5(My-Je, 1971):7-10.

Dunbar, Ernest. The Black Expatriates. New York: Dutton, 1968. [Interviews with sixteen black Americans living abroad]

Durojaiye, M. O. A. Education for Racial Integration. Kampala, Uganda: Makerere Institute of Social Research, D, 1971.

Eide, Ingrid (ed.). Students As Links Between Cultures. Paris: UNESCO, 1970.

El-Ghannam, Mohammed A. Education in the Arab Region Viewed from the 1970 Marrakesh Conference, 1971. Unipub, Inc., P.O. Box 433, New York, NY 10016.

Eldridge, Albert F. (ed.). Legislatures in Plural Societies: The Search for Cohesion in National Development. Durham, NC: Duke U. Press, 1977.

Emmanuel, Arghiri. "White Settler Colonialism and the Myth of Investment Imperialism." New Left Review 73(My-Je, 1972):35-57.

Equal Educational Opportunity: 1. A Statement of the Problem, with Special Reference to Recurrent Education, 1971. ERIC ED 055 267.

"Equal Opportunity Through Education. National Reports." Educational Panorama, VII, No. 3, 1965. [Australia, Malaya, Cameroon, Panama, Japan, France and Kenya]

Esman, Milton J. Ethnic Conflict in the Western World. Ithaca, NY: Cornell U. Press, 1977.

Evetts, Julia. The Sociology of Educational Ideas. London: Routledge & Kegan Paul, 1973.

Fallers, Lloyd A. (ed.). Immigrants and Associations. The Hague: Mouton, 1967.

Fattal, Antoine. Le Statut légal des non-musulmans en Pays d'Islam. Beirut: n.p., 1958.

Fitzgerald, Thomas K. "Education and Identity: A Reconsideration of Some Models of Acculturation and Identity." New Zealand Journal of Educational Studies 7(1972).

Flora, Peter. "Historische Prozesse sozialer Mobilisierung. Urbanisierung und Alphabetisierung, 1850-1965." Zeitschrift für Soziologie 1(1972):85-117. [World]

Foster, Philip J. "Education and Social Differentiation in Less-Developed Countries." Comparative Education Review 21(Je-O, 1977):211-229.

Francois, Louis. The Right to Education. UNESCO, 1968.

Galtung, Johan. "Educational Growth and Educational Disparity." Prospects 5(1975): 323-328.

Gellner, Ernest. "Nationalism." In Thought and Change. London: N.p., 1964.

Gerstl, Joel, and Perrucci, Robert. "Educational Channels and Elite Mobility: A Comparative Analysis." Sociology of Education, Ap, 1965.

Gist, Noel P., and Dworkin, Gary (eds.). The Blending of Races, Marginality, and Identity in World Perspectives. New York: Wiley, 1972.

Goitein, S. D. A Mediterranean Society. The Jewish Communities of the Arab World as Portrayed in the Documents of the Cairo Geniza. Vol. II: The Community. Berkeley, CA: U. of California Press, 1971.

Golladay, Fredrick L. and others. Education and Distribution of Income: Some Exploratory Forays. Technical Reports. Conference on Policies for Educational Growth (Paris, France, June 3-5, 1970), My 20, 1970. ERIC ED 063 686.

Gotlieb, A. (ed.). Human Rights, Federalism and Minorities. Toronto: Canadian Institute of International Affairs, 1970.

Gordon, David C. Self-Determination and History in the Third World. Princeton, NJ: Princeton U. Press, 1971. [Contemporary Arab historiographers]

Gough, Ian. "State Expenditure in Advanced Capitalism." New Left Review 92(Jl-Ag, 1975):53-92.

Greenough, Richard. "Worldwide Failure to Provide Equal Educational Opportunity." School and Society, Mr, 1972.

Griffin, K., and Khan, A. R. "Poverty in the Third World: Ugly Facts and Fancy Models." World Development 6(Mr, 1978).

Grove, D. John. "A Test of the Ethnic Equalization Hypothesis: A Cross-National Study." Ethnic and Racial Studies 1(Ap, 1978):175-195. [Nine countries]

Haq, Khadija (ed.). Equality of Opportunity Within and Among Nations. New York: Praeger, 1977.

Halasz, Jozsef (ed.). Socialist Concept of Human Rights. Budapest: Akademiai Kiado, 1966.

Halloran, James D. and others. Race As News. Paris: UNESCO Press, 1974. [Covers English-speaking and French-speaking countries]

Hanssen, B. Integration Processes in Complex Societies. IXth International Congress of Anthropological & Ethnologists, Ag-S, 1973.

Hargreaves, David H. Interpersonal Relations and Education. London: Routledge, 1972.

Haupt, G., Löwy, M., and Weill, C. Les marxistes et la question nationale 1848-1914. Paris: Maspéro, 1974.

Heindel, Richard H. "Equality of Opportunities Among Natives." Intellect 105(Mr, 1977).

Heligman, Larry and others. Measurement of Infant Mortality in Less Developed Countries. Washington, DC: GPO, 1978.

Henriques, Fernando. Children of Caliban: Miscegenation. London: Secker and Warburg, 1974.

Hepburn, A. C. (ed.). Minorities in History. New York: St. Martin's Press, 1979.

Hollister, Robinson. Education and Distribution of Income, VII. Conference on Policies for Educational Growth (Paris, France, June 3-5, 1970), 1970. ERIC ED 063 651.

Holly, Douglas. Society, Schools and Humanity: The Changing World of Secondary Education. London, England: McGibbon & Kee, 1971.

Hon Chan, Chai. Planning Education for a Plural Society, 1971. Unipub, Inc., P.O. Box 433, New York, NY 10016.

_____. "Planning Education for National Integration in Plural Societies." Journal of Research and Development in Education 4 (Summer, 1971):91-106.

Hourani, A. H. Minorities in the Arab World. London: Oxford U. Press, 1947.

Hunt, Chester L., and Walker, Lewis. Ethnic Dynamics: Patterns of Intergroup Relations in Various Societies. Homewood, IL: Dorsey, 1974.

Husen, Torsten. "The Comprehensive versus Selective School Issue." International Review of Education 17(1971):3-10.

Hymes, Dell (ed.). Pidginization and Creolization of Languages. London: Cambridge U. Press, 1971.

Institute of Jewish Affairs. The Jewish Communities of the World. 3rd rev. ed. London: Andre Deutsch, 1971.

International Labour Office. Indigenous Peoples. Living and Working Conditions of Aboriginal Populations in Independent Countries. Geneva: I.L.O., 1953.

Isaacs, Harold R. "Color in World Affairs." Foreign Affairs, Ja, 1969.

Jacobs, William R. "The Fatal Confrontation: Early Native-White Relations on the Frontiers of Australia, New Guinea, and America--A Comparative Study." Pacific Historical Review 40(Ag, 1971):283-309.

Jayawardena, C. "Migration and Social Change: A Survey of Indian Communities Overseas." Geographical Review 58(1968): 426-449.

Journal of Negro Education. "The Education Subject and Under Privileged Peoples." 3(Ja, 1934).

Kedar, Y. "Comparison of Patterns of Aggression in the Reactions to Frustration in Different Ethnic Groups." Master's thesis, Bar-Ilan U., Ramat-Gan, 1970.

Kiernan, V. S. The Lords of Human Kind. London: Weidenfeld & Nicholson, 1969.

Kolpakov, A., and Soroko-Tsyupa, O. "The National Question in the Developed Capitalist Countries." In Races and Peoples. Contemporary Ethnic and Racial Problems, pp. 159-181. Moscow: Progress Publishers, 1974.

Korotun, L., and Belov, P. "Along the Road of Internationalism." Soviet Education 13 (D, 1970):17-28.

Kuper, Leo. "Continuities and Discontinuities in Race Relations: Evolutionary or Revolutionary Change." Cahiers d'études Africaines 3, 1970.

_____. Race, Class, and Power. Ideology and Revolutionary Change in Plural Societies. Chicago: Aldine, 1975.

Labbens, J. "International Symposium on Unadapted Families. Paris, February, 1965." International Social Science Journal XVI, No. 4, 1964. [Poverty and deprivation in comparative perspectives]

Lane, David. The End of Equality? Stratification Under State Socialism. London: Penguin, 1971.

Langeveld, M. J., and Bolleman, G. "Some Aspects of the Role and Atitude of the Teacher in Relation to the Socially Disadvantaged Child." Paedagogica Europea 146 (1969). [Gypsy children]

League of Nations. Permanent Mandates Commission. A Comparative Study of Education in Mandated Territories. Mme. Bugge-Wicksell. In Annexes to the Minutes of the Third Session, 1923:239-56

Le Gall, A., Lauwerys, J. A., Holmes, B., Dryland, A. B., and Mattsson, S. Present Problems in the Democratization of Secondary and Higher Education. Paris: UNESCO, 1973.

Leon-Portilla, Miguel. "Anthropology and the Endangered Cultures." In American Anthropolical Association, Annual Report, 1974. Washington, DC: American Anthropological Association, Ap, 1975.

Lerner, Nathan. The U.N. Convention on the Elimination of all Forms of Racial Discrimination. Leyden, Netherlands: A. W. Sythoff, 1970.

Lewis, Diane. "Anthropology and Colonialism." Current Anthropology 14(D, 1973):581-591, 599-602.

Lewis, Harold O. "American Education and Civil Rights in an International Perspective." Journal of Negro Education, Summer, 1965.

Liegeois, Jean-Pierre. "Naissance du pouvoir tsignae." Revue francaise de Sociologie 16 (1975):295-316.

[London] Times News Team. The Black Man in Search of Power: A Survey of the Black Revolution Across the World. New York: Nelson, 1969.

Lowe, John, Grant, N., and Williams, T. D. (eds.). Education and Nation Building in the Third World. London: Chatto & Windus, 1971.

Lyon, Michael H. "Ethnic Minority Problems: An Overview of Some Recent Research." New Community 2(Autumn, 1973):329-352.

Mackey, William F., and Verdoodt, Albert (eds.). The Multinational Society: Papers of the Ljubijana Seminar. Rowley, MA: Newbury, 1975.

Mason, Philip. Patterns of Dominance. New York: Oxford U. Press, 1970.

Mason, Philip. "Regionalism, Black Power, and the Revolt of Youth." Race Today, Je, 1969.

Mazrui, Ali A. "Educational Techniques and Problems of Identity in Plural Societies." International Social Science Journal 24 (1972).

_____. World Culture and the Black Experience. Seattle, WA: U. of Washington Press, 1974.

Meyer, John W. Comparative Research on the Relationships between Politics and Educational Institutions. Department of Sociology. Stanford U., Ag, 1970.

Minority Education in Global Perspective: Proceedings of the World Education Workshop at the University of Connecticut. Storrs, CT: School of Eduction, U. of Connecticut, 1972.

Mittelman, James H. "Student Activism and Social Change in America and Africa." Afro-American Studies 2(Je, 1971):53-60.

Modeen, Tore. The International Protection of National Minorities. Abo: Abo Akademi, 1969.

Monks, T. G., and Kawwa, T. "Social Psychological Aspects of Comprehensive Education." International Review of Education 17(1971):66-74.

Morris, H. S. "Some Aspects of the Concept of Plural Society." MAN, N.S. 2(1967): 169-184.

Morrock, Richard. "Heritage of Strife: The Effects of Colonialist 'Divide and Rule' Strategy Upon the Colonized Peoples." Science & Society 37(Summer, 1973):129-151.

Munford, Luther. "Rhodes Scholars: No Longer All White." Chronicle of Higher Education, Ja 17, 1972.

Nam, Charles. Group Disparities in Educational Participation and Achievement, IV. Conference on Policies for Educational Growth (Paris, France, June 3-5, 1970), 1971. ERIC ED 063 650.

Noonan, Richard D. School Resources, Social Class, and Student Achievement. A Comparative Study of School Resource Allocation and the Social Distribution of Mathematics Achievement in Ten Countries. New York: Halsted, 1976.

Orans, Martin. "Caste and Race Conflict in Cross-Cultural Perspective." In Race, Change, and Urban Society, pp. 83-150. Edited by Peter Orleans and William Russell Ellis, Jr. Beverly Hills, CA: Sage, 1971. [India, Japan, and U.S.]

Orum, Bente. Social baggrund, intellektuelt niveau og placering i skolesystemey (The Relationship between Social Background, the Intellectual Level of Pupils, and Their Situation in the School System at the Age of 14), S, 1971. ERIC ED 060 284.

Passow, A. Harry. "Comprehensive versus Selective Education: The New Equality." International Review of Education 17(1971): 11-24.

Passow, A. Harry and others. The National Case Study: An Empirical Comparative Study of Twenty-One Educational Systems. New York: Wiley, 1976.

Passow, A. Harry (ed.). Deprivation and Disadvantage. Nature and Manifestations. Hamburg, Germany: UNESCO Institute for Education, 1970.

Patai, Raphael. The Diaspora--Yesterday and Today. Englewood Cliffs, NJ: Prentice-Hall, 1972.

Patterson, Orlando. The Sociology of Slavery. N.p.: N.p., 1969.

_____. "Toward a Future that Has No Past--Reflections on the Fate of Blacks in the Americas." Public Interest 27(Spring, 1972): 25-62.

Platt, William J. "Policy Making and International Studies in Educational Evaluation." Phi Delta Kappan 55(Mr, 1974):451-456.

Plotnicov, Leonard, and Tudden, Arthur (eds.). Essays in Comparative Social Stratification. Pittsburgh, PA: U. of Pittsburgh Press, 1970.

Podmore, Chris. "Private Schools--An International Comparison." Canadian and International Education 6(D, 1977):8-33.

Poliakov, Leon. The History of Anti-Semitism. Vol. II: From Mohammed to the Marranos. Tr. Natalie Gerardi. New York: Vanguard Press, 1974.

Prinz, Jachim. The Secret Jews. New York: Random House, 1973.

Psacharopoulos, G. "Unequal Access to Education and Income Distribution: An International Comparison." De Economist 125 (1977).

Puxon, Grattan. "The First World Romani Congress." Race Today 3(Je, 1971):192-194. ["Gypsies"]

Resnikoff, Moses B. "Social Aspects of Jewish Elementary Education in the First Centuries of the Christian Era." Doctoral dissertation, Columbia U., n.d.

Rivkin, Ellis. The Shaping of Jewish History. New York: Scribner's, 1972.

Roberts, K. "The Organization of Education and the Ambitions of School Leavers: A Comparative Review." Comparative Education, Mr, 1968.

Robertson, A. H. Human Rights in the World. Manchester, England: Manchester U. Press, 1971.

Ruhlen, Merritt. A Guide to the Languages of the World. Stanford, CA: Department of Linguistics, Stanford U., 1975.

Ryba, Raymond. "Aspects of Territorial Inequality in Education." Comparative Education 12(O, 1976):183-197.

Sanders, Douglas E. The Formation of the World Council of Indigenous Peoples. Copenhagen: International Work Group for Indigenous Affairs, Ag, 1977.

Santa Cruz, Hernan. Racial Discrimination. E/CN.4/Sub. 2/307/Rev. 1. New York: United Nations, 1971.

Scharfstein, Zevi. Toledot Ha-hinuch B'Yisrael B'Dorot Ha-Aharonim. 3 vols. New York: Ogen, 1945-1949. [History of Jewish education over the world]

"Schooling for the Children of Migrant Workers." Western European Education 4 (Spring-Summer, 1972):132-135.

Searle, Chris. The Forsaken Lover: White Words and Black People. London: Routledge & Kegan Paul, 1972.

Seaton, W. H. Schools in Travail. New York: The Carnegie Corporation, Visitors' Grants Committee, 1932.

Sen-Dou, Chang. "The Distribution and Occupation of Overseas Chinese." Geographical Review (Ja, 1968):89-107.

Sengstock, Mary C. "Differential Rates of Assimiliation in an Ethnic Group: In Ritual, Social Interaction, and Normative Culture." International Migration Review, Spring, 1969.

Sevilla-Casas, Elias (ed.). Western Expansion and Indigenous Peoples. Chicago: Aldine, 1977.

Sharf, Andrew. Byzantine Jewry: From Justinian to the Fourth Crusade. New York: Schocken, 1971. [527-1204]

Schimoniak, Wasyl. Communist Education: Its History, Philosophy and Politics. Chicago: Rand McNally, 1970.

Singh, Baldave. "Socio-Economic Inequalities Between Ethnic and Racial Groups: An Exploratory Comparative Study." Doctoral dissertation, U. of Denver, 1978. Univ. Microfilms Order No. 7823798.

S-Mehta. Minority Rights and Obligation, 1972. Canada Research Bureau, P.O. Box 605, Ottawa, Canada.

Sohlman, Asa. Difference in School Achievement and Occupational Opportunities: Explanatory Factors. A Survey Based on European Experience. Conference on Policies for Educational Growth (Paris, France, June 3-5, 1970), 1971. ERIC ED 063 685.

Spurgeon, John H. and others. "Body Size and Form of Children of Predominantly Black Ancestry Living in West and Central Africa, North and South America, and the West Indies." Annals of Human Biology 5(1978): 229-246.

Steenberger, Evert. "Equal Opportunity Through Education. Synthesis of National Reports." Education Panorama, VII, No. 3, 1965.

Stone, Lawrence (ed.). The University in Society. Vol. I. Oxford and Cambridge from the 14th to the Early 19th Century. Vol. II. Europe, Scotland, and the United States from the 16th to the 20th Century. Princeton, NJ: Princeton U. Press, 1974.

Suyin, Han. "Race Relations and the Third World." Race 13(Jl, 1971):1-20.

Swartz, M. "The Position of Jews in Arab Lands Following the Rise of Islam." Muslim World, Ja, 1970.

Tatz, Colin M. "Four Kinds of Dominion." Patterns of Prejudice 7(Mr-Ap, 1973):1-8. [Australia, Canada, New Zealand, and South Africa]

Tax, Sol. "The Education of Underprivileged Peoples in Dependent and Independent Territories." Journal of Negro Education 15 (1946):336-345.

Tilly, Charles. An Urban World. Boston: Little, Brown, 1974.

Tinker, Hugh. The Export of Indian Labour Overseas, 1830-1920. London: Oxford U. Press, 1974. [Mauritius, S. Africa, Caribbean, Guyana, and Fiji]

_____. Race, Conflict and the International Order: From Empire to United Nations. London: Macmillan, 1977.

UNESCO. Comparative Study of Co-education. UNESCO/ED/MD/15 Paris: UNESCO, O 30, 1970.

UNESCO. Cultural Rights As Human Rights. New York: Unipub, 1970.

_____. "The Qualitative Aspects of Educational Planning." Integrated Education 9(Ja-F, 1971):35-45.

United Nations Educational, Social and Cultural Organization (UNESCO). World Survey of Education, 1955-1971. Paris: UNESCO, 1971.

UNESCO. Statistics of Educational Attainment and Illiteracy. 1945-1974. Paris: UNESCO, 1977.

UNESCO Office of Statistics. A Statistical Study of Wastage at School. New York: Unipub, 1972.

U.S. Congress, 92nd, 1st session, Senate, Report No. 92-275. "Year of World Minority Language Groups", Jl 21, 1971.

U.S. Congress, 93rd, 2nd session, House of Representatives, Committee on Foreign Affairs, Subcommittee on International Organizations and Movements. Human Rights in the World Community: A Call for U.S. Leadership. Washington, DC: GPO, Mr 27, 1974.

Valentine, Paul W. "The Fascist Specter Behind the World Anti-Red League." Washington Post, My 28, 1978. [World Anti-Communist League]

Van den Berghe, Pierre L. Race and Racism: A Comparative Perspective. 2nd ed. New York: Wiley, 1978.

Veenhoven, Willem A. (ed.). Case Studies on Human Rights and Fundamental Freedoms. 2 vols. The Hague: Martinus Nijhoff, 1975.

Voegelin, C. F., and Voegelin, F. M. Classification and Index of the World's Languages. New York: Elsevier North-Holland, 1976.

Weekes, Richard V. (ed.). Muslim Peoples: A World Ethnographic Survey. Westport, CT: Greenwood Press, 1978.

Wesley, Charles H. "Rise of Negro Education in the British Empire." Journal of Negro Education 1(O, 1932):354-366 and 2(Ja, 1933):68-82. [1732-1840]

West, Katharine. "Stratification and Ethnicity in 'Plural' New States." Race 13(Ap, 1972):487-495.

Williamson, Bill. Education, Social Structure and Development. A Comparative Analysis. London: Macmillan, 1979.

Yates, Alfred. The Organization of Schooling. A Study of Educational Grouping Practices. London: Routledge & Kegan Paul, 1971.

Ye'or, Bar. Dhimmi Peoples: Oppressed Nations. Geneva: Editions de l'Avenir, 1978. [Non-Arab and Non-Muslims in Muslim countries]

Education Studies by Area

Africa

Abdel-Rahman, Mohamed E. "Interactions Be-. tween Africans North and South of the Sahara." Journal of Black Studies 3(D, 1972):131-147.

Africa Information Service (ed.). Return to the Source. Selected Speeches by Amilcar Cabral, Ag, 1973. Africa Information Service, 112 West 120th Street, New York, NY 10027.

Africa Research Group. Race to Power. The Struggle for Southern Africa. Garden City NY: Anchor Books, 1974.

Amiji, Hatim. "The Asian Minorities." In Islam in Africa, pp. 139-181. Edited by James Kritzeck and William H. Lewis. New York: Van Nostrand-Reinhold, 1969.

Amin, Samir. "Lutte des classes en Afrique." Révolution 1(N, 1963).

_____. Neo-Colonialism in West Africa. Tr. by Francis McDonagh. New York: Monthly Review Press, 1973.

Ankomah, Kofi. "The Colonial Legacy and African Unrest." Science and Society 34 (1970):129-145.

Anumonye, Amechi. African Students in Alien Cultures, 1970. Black Academy Press, Inc., Box 366, Ellicott Station, Buffalo, NY 14205.

Arens, William, Changing Patterns of Ethnic Identity and Prestige in Contemporary East Africa. IXth International Congress of Anthropological and Ethnological Sciences, Ag-S, 1973.

"Asian Minorities in East Africa and Britain." New Community 1(Autumn, 1972):406-416.

Asiwaju, A. I. Western Yorubaland Under European Rule, 1889-1945. London: Longman, 1976. [French and British rule in West Africa]

_____. "Formal Education in Western Yorubaland, 1889-1960: A Comparison of the French and British Colonial Systems." Comparative Education Review 19(O, 1975): 434-450.

Bagley, Christopher. "Pluralism, Development and Social Conflict in Africa." Plural Societies 3(1972):13-32.

Balandier, Georges. Sociology of Black Africa. Social Dynamics in Central Africa. New York: N.p., 1970.

Balmer, W. T. "Text-books: a study with an African background." International Review of Missions 14(Ja, 1925):37-44.

Bamgbose, A. (ed.). Mother Tongue Education: The West African Experience. London: Hodder & Stoughton, 1976.

Bates, Robert. Ethnicity in Contemporary Africa. Syracuse, NY: Program of Eastern African Studies, Syracuse U., 1973.

Beck, Ann. "Colonial Policy and Education in British East Africa." Journal of British Studies 5(My, 1966):115-138.

van den Berghe, Pierre L. (ed.). Race and Ethnicity in Africa. Nairobi: East African Publishing House, 1975.

Berman, Edward H. "American Influence on African Education: The Role of the Phelps-Stokes Fund's Education Commissions." Comparative Education Review 15(Je, 1971): 132-145.

_____. "Education in Africa and America: History of the Phelps-Stokes Fund, 1911-1945." Doctoral dissertation, Columbia U., 1970.

_____ (ed.). African Reactions to Missionary Education. New York: Teachers College Press, 1975.

Bharati, Agehanda. The Asians in East Africa: Jayhind and Uhuru. Chicago: U. of Chicago Press, 1972.

Bharati, Agehananda. "Patterns of Identification among the East African Asians." Sociologus 15(1965):128-142.

Bolibaugh, Jerry Bevoly. French Educational Strategies for Sub-Saharan Africa: Their Intent, Derivation, and Development. Stanford, CA: School of Education, Stanford U., 1964.

Bond, Horace Mann. "Critical Summary." Journal of Negro Education, Summer, 1961. [On African education]

_____. "The European Heritage: Approaches to African Development, Comment on Paul Henry's Paper." In Africa Today. Edited by C. Grove Haines. Baltimore: The Johns Hopkins Press, 1954:141-146.

_____. "Forming African Youth: A Philosophy of Education." Africa Seen by American Negroes. Paris: Presence Africaine, 1956: 247-262.

_____. "Observations on Education in West Africa." Educational Record 31(Ap, 1950): 129-140.

_____. "Reflections, Comparative, on West African Nationalist Movements." Presence Africaine, Vol. VIII-IX-X, No. Special, Ie Ier Congress International des Ecrivains et Artistes Noire, Paris-Sorbonne, Vol. 19 (S, 1956):22-28.

Bouche, Denise. L'enseignement dans les territoires francais de l'Afrique occidentale de 1817 à 1920: Mission civilisatrice ou formation d'une élite? 2 vols. Paris: Librairee Honore Champion, 1975.

Boxer, Charles R. Race Relations in the Portuguese Colonial Empire, 1415-1825. Oxford, England: Clarendon Press, 1963.

Brewer, Marilyn, and Campbell, Donald T. Ethnocentrism and Intergroup Attitudes East African Evidence. New York: Halstead, 1977.

Brooks, Hugh, C., and Ayouty, Yassin El (eds.). Refugees South of the Sahara. Westport, CT: 1970.

Brown, Godfrey N. "British Educational Policy in West and Central Africa." Journal of Modern AFrican Studies 2(1964):365-377.

Brown, Godfrey N., and Hiskett, Mervyn (eds.). Conflict and Harmony in Education in Tropical Africa. London: Allen and Unwin, 1975.

Brown, Leon Carl. "Color in Northern Africa." Daedalus, Spring, 1967.

Brunschwig, Henri. "De La Resistance Africaine a l'Imperialisme Européen." Journal of African History 15(1973).

Buckley, J. K. "The Growth of African Education in Botswana, Lesotho, Swaziland, Malawi, Zambia, Rhodesia and South Africa, 1950-1970." Educ. Botswana, Lesotho, and Swaziland (Mr, 1974):21-33.

Bugnicourt, J. "Disparités scolaires en Afrique." Revue Tiers-Monde 12(1971).

Buijtenhuijs, R. "Psychologie et pédagogie africaines." Kroniek Afrika 1(1971).

Calvet, Louis-Jean. "Le Francais d'Afrique et l'enseignement du francais en Afrique." Francais dans le Monde 138(Jl, 1978):29-32, 41-42.

Campbell, Donald T. and others (eds.). Ethnocentrism and Intergroup Attitudes: East African Evidence. New York: Wiley, 1976.

Chaka, Malik. "Frelimo Secondary School: Toward the New Mozambican." IFCO News, Jl-Ag, 1973.

Chouraqui, André. Between East and West: A History of the Jews of North Africa. Tr. by Michael M. Bernet. Philadelphia, PA: Jewish Publication Society of American, 1968.

Clignet, Remi. "Education and Elite Formation." In The African Experience. Edited by John N. Paden and Edward W. Soja. Vol. I: Essays. Evanston, IL: Northwestern U. Press, 1970.

_____. "Ethnicity, Social Differentiation, and Secondary Schooling in West Africa." Cahiers d'Etudes Africaines. Cahier 2, 1967.

_____. "Inadequacies of the Notion of Assimilation in African Education." Journal of Modern African Studies 8(1970):425-444.

_____. "The Legacy of Assimilation in West African Educational Systems: Its Meaning and Ambiguities." Comparative Education Review, F, 1968.

Clignet, Remi, and Foster, Philip. "French and British Colonial Education in Africa." Comparative Educational Review 8(1964):191-198.

Cohen, Abner (ed.). Urban Ethnicity. London: Tavistock, 1974. [Mostly Africa]

Calcough, C. "Formal Education Systems and Poverty-Focused Planning." JMAS 15(1977): 569-589.

Colonna, Fanny. "Enseignement des indigenes et enseignement du peuple aux XIX siecle: un projet commun." R. fr. et pol. afric. (Ja, 1975):62-74.

Corbett, Edward M. The French Presence in Black Africa. Washington, DC: Black Orpheus Press, 1972.

Court, D. "East African Higher Education from the Community Standpoint." Higher Education 6(1977):45-66.

_____. "The Education System as a Response to Inequality." JMAS 14(1976):661-690. [East Africa]

Davis, Horace B. "Social Classes and the Formation of Nations: Fanon, Cabral, and the African Liberation Struggle." In Toward a Marxist Theory of Nationalism. New York: Monthly Review Press, 1978, pp. 202-239.

De Granda, G. "A Socio-Historical Approach to the Problem of the Portuguese Creole in West Africa." International Journal of the Sociology of Language 7(1976):11-22.

Delf, George. Asians in East Africa. London: Oxford, 1963.

De Marco, Roland R. Italianization of African Natives: Government Native Education in the Italian Colonies, 1890-1937. New York: Teachers College, 1943.

Deltar, G. "Problems of Library Service to Africans." Rhodesian Librarian 1(Ap, 1969).

Diop, Cheikh Anta. L'Afrique noire précoloniale. Paris: N.p., 1960.

Don Nanjiri, Daniel D. C. The Status of Aliens in East Africa: Asians and Europeans in Tanzania, Uganda, and Kenya. New York: Praeger, 1976.

Doob, Leonard W. "Psychology." In The African World. Edited by Robert A. Lystad. New York: Praeger, 1966.

Dotson, Floyd, and Dotson, Lillian O. "The Economic Role of Non-Indigenous Ethnic Minorities in Colonial Africa." In Colonialism in Africa, 1870-1960. Vol. IV. The Economics of Colonialism. Edited by Peter Duignan and L. H. Gann. New York: Cambridge U. Press, 1975.

DuToit, Brian M. (ed.). Ethnicity in Modern Africa. Boulder, CO: Westview Press, 1977.

D'Souza, D. Henry. "External Influences on the Development of Educational Policy in British Tropical Africa from 1923 to 1939." Afric. Stud. R. 17(S, 1975):35-44.

Dubois, H. M. "La pedagogie apliquee a nos noirs d'Afrique." Africa (1929):381-403.

DuBois, W. E. B. "Education in Africa." Crisis, Je, 1926.

_____. "The Sort of Education Africans Need." Negro World, Ag 14, 1926.

East African Institute of Social and Cultural Affairs. Racial and Communal Tensions in East Africa. Kenya: East African Publishing House, 1966.

Eliou, Marie. "Educational Inequality in Africa: An Analysis." Prospects 6(1976): 558-570. [French-speaking areas]

Erny, Pierre. Childhood and Cosmos: The Social Psychology of the Black African Child. Tr. Laexandre Mboukou. New York: Black Orpheus Press and New Perspectives, 1973.

Evans, Judith L. Children in Africa: A Review of Psychological Research. New York: Teachers College Press, 1970.

"The Expulsion of West African Aliens." Journal of Modern African Studies 9(1971):205-230.

Fafunwa, Babs. "Race Prejudice in Textbooks." Africa 43(Mr, 1975):56-57.

Fellows, Lawrence. "The Duka-Wallas Are Outcasts in Africa." New York Times Magazine, Je 25, 1967. [Asian shopkeepers in Africa]

Ferreira, Eduardo de Sousa. Portuguese Colonialism in Africa: The End of an Era: The Effects of Portuguese Colonialism on Education, Science, Culture and Information. Paris: UNESCO, 1974.

Feuerstein, R., and Richelle, M. Children of the Mellah. Jerusalem: Jewish Agency and Szold Foundation, 1953. [Jewish children in North Africa]

Forrest, Leon. "Black Historians Condemn U.S. Africa Policy." Muhammad Speaks, N 6, 1970.

Fosh, Patricia. "Equality and Inequality in East Africa--A Research Note." Sociological Review 26(F, 1978):139-145.

Foster, P. Education and Social Differentiation in Africa. New York: Conference on Inequality in Africa, 1976.

Frank, Lawrence. The Politics of Race in Lesotho. Vol. 2, No. 3, Studies in Race and Nations, 1970-1971 series. [Center on International Race Relations, U. of Race Relations, U. of Denver, Denver, CO]

Frazier, E. Franklin. "Education and the African Elite." Transactions of the Third World Congress of Sociology Vol. 5. Changes in Education. Amsterdam, 1956:90-96.

_____. "Impact of Colonialism on African Social Forms and Personality." Publications of Norman Wait Harris Memorial Foundation Lectures on Africa in the Modern World, 1955: 70-96.

_____. "The Impact of Western Education on the African's Way of Life." Africa Today, 1955:166-171.

Furley, Oliver C. "Education and the Chiefs in East Africa in the Interwar Period." In U. of East Africa Social Sciences Conference, 1968/1969. History Papers. Kampala, Uganda: Institute of Social Research, 1969.

_____. "The Struggle for Transformation in Education in Kenya since Independence." East Africa Journal 9(Ag, 1972):14-24.

"Further Notes on the Asian Minorities of East Africa." New Community 1(Autumn, 1972):417-419.

Gardinier, David E. "Education in French Equatorial Africa, 1842-1945." Proc. Fr. Colonial Hist. Soc. (1977):121-138.

Gerber, Jane Satlow. "Jewish Society in Fez: Studies in Communal and Economic Life." Doctoral dissertation, Columbia U., 1972.

Ghai, Dharam P. (ed.). Portrait of a Minority. Asians in East Africa. New York: Oxford U. Press, 1966.

Goody, Esther N., and Groothues, Christine Muir. "The West Africans: The Quest for Education." In Between Two Cultures. Migrants and Minorities in Britain. Edited by James L. Watson. Oxford: Basil Blackwell, 1977:151-180.

Gordon, D. C. North Africa's French Legacy, 1954-1962. Cambridge, MA: Harvard U. Press, 1962.

Görög-Karady, Veronika. "Préference parentale et inégalite raciale: étude d'un thème idéologique dans la littérature orale africaine." Res. Afric. Lit. 8(S, 1977):54-82.

Gregory, Robert G. India and East Africa: A History of Race Relations within the British Empire, 1890-1939. Oxford, England: Clarendon Press, 1972.

Grimaud, Nicole. "Les juifs d'Afrique du Nord, leur situation et leurs problèmes en 1968." Revue Occident musulman. Special number, 1970.

Hanna, William John. "Student Protest in Independent Black Africa." Annals 395(My, 1971):171-183.

_____ (ed.). University Students and African Politics. New York: Africana Pub. Co., 1975.

Hardy, G. Une conquete morale: l'enseignement en Afrique occidentale francaise. Paris: N.p., 1917.

Hawes, Hugh W. R. and others. Curriculum and Reality in African Primary Schools. London: Longman, 1978.

Heggoy, Alf Andrew. "North Africa: European Penetration and the Colonial Period: A Syllabus." Improving College and University Teaching 23(Spring, 1975):108-112.

Heine, Bernd. Status and Use of African Lingua Franca. New York: N.p., 1970.

Hetherington, Penelope. British Paternalism and Africa, 1920-1940. London: Frank Cass, 1978.

Hilliard, F. H. A Short History of British West Africa. London, Nelson, 1957.

Hirschberg, H. Z. A History of the Jews in North Africa. Vol. I: From Antiquity to the 16th Century. Leiden: Brill, 1974.

Hoernle, A. A. "An Outline of the Native Conception of Education." Africa 4(1931):145-163.

Hollingsworth, L. W. The Asians of East Africa. London: Macmillan, 1960.

Hopkins, Elizabeth. "Racial Minorities in British East Africa." In The Transformation of East Africa. Edited by Stanley Diamond and Fred Burke. London: Basic Books, 1966:85-153.

Hornsby, George. "German Educational Achievement in East Africa." Tanganyika Notes and Records 62(Mr, 1964):83-90.

Houis, Maurice. "The Problem of the Choice of Languages in Africa." Prospects 6(1976):393-405.

Huxley, Julian S. Africa View. New York: Harper & Row, 1931.

Indire, F. F. "Education and Black Civilization." Présence Africaine 1(1974):28-39.

Institute for Advances Study and the Academic Committee of the World Jewish Congress. Proceedings of the Seminar on Muslim-Jewish Relations in North Africa. New York: Waldon Press, 1975.

Irvine, S. H. "Ability Testing in English-speaking Africa: An Overview of Predictive and Comparative Studies." Rhodes Livingstone Journal, D, 1963.

_____. "Contributions of Ability and Attainment Testing in Africa to a General Theory of Intellect." In Biosocial Aspects of Race. Edited by G. A. Harrison and John Peel. Oxford: Blackwell Scientific Publications Ltd., 1969.

Ishumi, A. G. "Student Activism on the Educational Scene: An Historical and Social Profile." Utafiti 1(1976):189-208.

Ismagilova, R. N. "The Ethnic Factor in Modern Africa." In Races and Peoples. Contemporary Ethnic and Racial Problems. Moscow: Progress Publishers, 1974:121-256.

Jackson, Miles M. "Culture Shock and the Black Librarian Abroad." Wilson Library Bulletin 49(N, 1974):235-237.

Jahoda, Gustav. "Culture Conflict and Education: Some Comments in the Light of Psychological Research." Afrika Spectrum 11, No. 2(1976):173-186.

Jenkins, David. Black Zion. The Return of Afro-Americnas to Africa. London: Wildwood House, 1975.

Jolly, Richard (ed.). Education in Africa--Research and Action. Kenya: East Africa Publishing House, 1969.

Jones, G. Howard. "Educational Needs in West Africa." Journal of the African Society 26 (J1, 1927):341-367.

Jones, Hayden. "Ethnocentrism in Four Contemporary General Works on Africa." Mazungumzo, Spring, 1971.

Kabongo, Ilunga. "Pluralisme et integration-Reflections sur la dynamique politique en Afrique noire post-coloniale." Cahiers Economiques et Sociaux (France), Mr, 1967.

Kelly, Michael. "The Africanization of Syllabuses in Education in Anglophone and Francophone Countries of West Africa." Teacher Education in New Countries 11(F, 1971):229-238.

Kenny, James A. "Statistical Classification of African Ethnic Units." J. Asian Afric. Studies 11(J1-Oc, 1976):180-193.

Kibirige, Harry M. "Public Libraries in East Africa in the Mid-1970's: A Comparative Critique." UNESCO Bulletin for Libraries 31(N-D, 1977):331-339.

Kilbride, Janet E., Robbins, Michael C., and Kilbride, Philip L. "The Comparative Motor Development of Baganda, American White, and American Black Infants." American Anthropologist 72(D, 1970):1422-1428.

King, Kenneth J. "Africa and the Southern States of the U.S.A.: Notes on J. H. Oldham and American Negro Education for Africans." Journal of African History 10 (1969).

_____. "The American Background of the Phelps-Stokes Commissions, and their Influences in Education in East Africa." Doctoral dissertation, U. of Edinburgh, Je, 1968.

_____. "Education and Ethnicity in the Rift Valley: Masai, Kipsigis and Kikuyu in the School System." Educ. E. Africa 5, No. 2 (1975):197-218.

_____. PanAfricanism and Education. A Study of Race Philanthropy and Education in the Southern States of American and East Africa. London: Oxford U. Press, 1971.

Kitching, G. Economic and Social Inequality in Rural East Africa: The Present as a Clue to the Past. Swansea: Centre for Development Studies, U. College, 1977.

_____. "The Concept of Class and the Study of Africa." Africa Review 2(1972):327-350.

Klineberg, Otto, and Zavalloni, Marisa. Nationalism and Tribalism Among African Students. A Study of Social Identity. Paris: International Social Science Council, 1969.

Knight, Eleanor G. "Education in French North Africa." Islamic Quarterly 2(D, 1955):294-308.

Kofele-Kale, Ndiva. "Our Colonial Mentality: Europe's Legacy to Africa." Pan-Africanist, D, 1971.

Kubat, Daniel (ed.). The Politics of Migration Policies. The First World in the 1970's. Staten Island, NY: Center for Migration Studies, 1978.

Kumene, Daniel P. "African Vernacular Writing: An Essay on Self-Devaluation." African Social Research 9(Je, 1970):639-659.

Kuper, Leo, and Smith, M. G. (eds.). Pluralism in Africa. Berkeley: U. of California Press, 1969.

Lacoste, Yves. "General Characteristics and Fundamental Structures of Medieval North African Society." Economy and Society 3(F, 1974):1-17.

Lang, Brian. "The East African Europeans." New Society, Ja 20, 1972.

Lema, Anza. "Black Civilization and Education." Présence Africaine 3(1973):143-155.

Leys, Norman. The Colour Bar in East Africa. London: Hogarth, 1941.

Liu, W. "African Education in British Africa." Master's thesis, U. of Reading, 1966.

Livingston, Thomas W. Education and Race: A Biography of Edward Wilmot Blyden. N.p.: Boyd and Fraser, 1975.

Logan, Rayford W. "Education in Former French West and Equatorial Africa and Madagascar." Journal of Negro Education 30(1961):277-285.

Lugard, F. O. "Education in Tropical Africa." Edinburgh Review 242(1925):1-19.

Lunga, Sylvester H. W. "The Nguni and the Colonizer: A Study of the Dehumanization of a Race, 1870-1880." Master's thesis, McGill U., 1971.

Lyons, Charles H. "The Educable African: British Thought and Action, 1835-1865." In Essays in the History of African Education. Edited by Vincent M. Battle and Charles H. Lyons. New York: Teachers College Press, 1970, pp. 1-31.

Lyons, Charles H. and others. Education for What? British Policy versus Local Initiative. Syracuse, NY: Program of Eastern African Studies, Syracuse U., 1973.

MacDonald, R. J. "A History of African Education in Nyasaland: 1875-1945." Doctoral dissertation, U. of Edinburgh, 1968.

McFie, J. "The Effect of Education on African Performance on a Group of Intellectual Tests." British Journal of Educational Psychology 31(1961):232-240.

McLaughlin, Stephen D. "Cognitive Processes and Learning: A Review of Research on Cognition in Africa." African Studies Review (Ap, 1976):75-93.

Macrae, P. "Race and Class in Southern Africa." Afric. R. 4(1974):237-258.

Magubane, Bernard. "Crisis in African Sociology." East Africa Journal 5(D, 1968):21-40.

_____. "A Critical Look at Indices Used in the Study of Social Change in Colonial Africa." Current Anthropology 12(O-D, 1971): 419-445.

_____. "Pluralism and Conflict Situations in Africa: A New Look." African Social Research 7(Je, 1969):529-554.

Malinowski, Bronislaw. "Native Education and Culture Contact." International Review of Missions 25(1936):480-515.

Mangat, J. S. A History of the Asians in East Africa, 1886 to 1945. London: Oxford U. Press, 1969.

Maquet, Jacques. Africanity. The Cultural Unity of Black Africa. New York: Oxford U. Press, 1972.

Marchand, Claude. "Idéologie coloniale et enseignement en Afrique Nord francophone." Canadian Journal of African Studies, 1971.

Margarido, Claude. "L'enseignement en Afrique dite Portugaise." Revue Francaise d'Etudes Politiques Africaines, Ag, 1970.

Martin, B. G. "Notes on Some Members of the Learned Classes of Zanzibar and East Africa in the Nineteenth Century." African Historical Studies, 1971.

Martin, Jean-Yves. "Sociologie de l'enseignement en Afrique Noire." Cahiers internationaux de sociologie 53(1972):337-362.

Mazrui, Ali A. Cultural Engineering and Nation-Building in East Africa. Evanston, IL: Northwestern U. Press, 1972.

_____. Political Values and the Educated Class in Africa. Berkeley: U. of California Press, 1978.

_____. World Culture and the Black Experience. Seattle, WA: U. of Washington Press, 1974.

Mbilinyi, M. Who Goes to School in East Africa? Dar es Salaam: Institute of Education, 1976.

Mehnert, Wolfgang. "Schulpolitik im Dienste der Kolonialherrschaft des deutschen Imperialismus in Afrika (1884-1914)." Doctoral dissertation, Karl-Marx-U., Leipzig.

Melvyn, P. "Youth Unemployment in Industrialised Market Economy Countries." International Labour Review 116(Jl-Ag, 1977):23-38.

Meyer, John W. and others. "The World Educational Revolution, 1950-1970." Sociology of Education 50(O, 1977):242-258.

Mkhize, M. "Thought on Race Consciousness." African Communist 57(1974):71-83.

Molnos, Angela. "Die Sozialwissenschaftliche Erforschung Ostafrikas 1954-1963." Ostafrika (Berlin)

Morris, H. S. "Indians in East Africa: A Study of a Plural Society." British Journal of Sociology 7(1956):194-211.

Morrison, Donald G., and Stevenson, Hugh Michael. "Cultural Pluralism, Modernization and Conflict: Sources of Political Instability in Black Africa." Canadian Journal of Political Science, Mr, 1972.

Moumini, Abdou. Education in Africa. Tr. Phyllis N. Ott. New York: Praeger, 1968.

Murray, Albert B. School in the Bush: A Critical Study of the Theory and Practice of Native Education in Africa. New York: Longmans, Green and Co., 1929.

Nanjira, Daniel D. C. Don. The Status of Aliens in East Africa. Asians and Europeans in Tanzania, Uganda, and Kenya. New York: Praeger, 1976.

Ndumbu, Abel. Prospects of Tailoring Racial Harmony. A Study of Racial Preference and Identification in An Unpolarised African Setting. Kampala, Uganda: Social Psychology Section, Department of Sociology, Makerere U., 1972.

Nnoli, O. The Dynamics of Interethnic Socio-economic Gap in Africa. New York: Conference on Inequality in Africa, 1976.

Nwagwu, Nicholas A. "Equalization of Educational Opportunities in African Countries." Journal of Educational Administration 14(0, 1976):270-278.

Nyaggah, Mougo. "Asians in East Africa: The Case of Kenya." J. Afric. Stud. 1(Summer, 1974):205-233.

Obichere, Boniface I. "African Critics of Victorian Imperialism: An Analysis." Journal of African Studies 4(Spring, 1977): 1-20.

Obiechina, Emmanuel. "Perceptions of Colonialism in West African Literature." Ufahamu 5 (1974):45-70.

Ogot, B. A. "Racial Consciousness among Africans." East Africa Journal, Ap, 1965.

Ogungbesan. Kolawole. "Antobiographies in Africa." Savanna 2(Je, 1973):1-10.

Oloruntimehin, B. Olatunji. "Education for Colonial Dominance in French West Africa from 1900 to the Second World War." J. Hist. Soc. Nigeria 7(1974):347-356.

Orbell, S. F. W. "The Role of Environmental Factors in the Education of African Pupils." Zambezia 1(1970).

Otieno, N. Antipa. "Outline of History of Education in East Africa, 1844-1925." Doctoral dissertation, Teachers College, Columbia U., 1963.

Palmer, R., and Parsons, N. (eds.). The Roots of Rural Poverty in Central and Southern Africa. London: Heinemann, 1977.

Pieterse, Cosmo, and Munro, Donald (eds). Protest and Conflict in African Literature. New York: Africana Pub. Corporation, 1969.

Plender, Richard. "The Exodus of Asians from East and Central Africa: Some Comparative and International Law Aspects." American Journal of Comparative Law 19(1971).

Povey, John F. "American Education and French Assimilation: A Comparison." Midwest Quarterly 11(1970):265-279.

_____. "Education Through the Eyes of African Writers." Educational Forum, N, 1966.

"Pre-Colloquium on 'Black Civilization and Education.'" Présence Africaine 3(1973):5-142.

"Problèmes posés par des étudiants négro-africains à l'étranger." Annales Médico-Psychologiques 1(1969):487.

Ranger, T. O. "African Attempts to Control Education in East and Central Africa, 1900-1939." Past and Present 32(D, 1965).

Read, Margaret. Education and Social Change in Tropical Areas. London: Nelson, 1955.

Richards, Audrey I. The Multicultural States of East Africa. Montreal: McGill-Queen's U. Press, 1969.

Rivière, Claud. "Classes et stratification sociales en Afrique noire." Cah. int. Sociol. 55(D, 1975):285-314.

_____. "De l'Objectivité des classes sociales en Afrique noire." Cahiers internationaux de sociologie 39(1965):197-216.

Rodney, Walter. "Class and Nationalism in Africa." Race Today 6(Ag, 1974):231-233.

_____. "Education for Underdevelopment." and "Development by Contradiction." How Europe Underdeveloped Africa. London: Bogle-L'Ouverture Publications, 1972.

_____. "Education in Africa and Contemporary Tanzania." In Institute of the Black World (ed.). Education and the Black Struggle: Notes from the Colonized World. Cambridge, MA: Harvard Educational Review, 1974.

Rose, Brian (ed.). Education in Southern Africa. London: Collier-Macmillan, 1970.

Rothchild, Donald. "African Nationalism and Racial Minorities." East Africa Journal, D, 1965.

Sabatier, Peggy Roark. "Educating a Colonial Elite: The William Ponty School and Its Graduates." Doctoral dissertation, U. of Chicago, 1977. [French West Africa]

Salifou, André. "L'education africaine traditionnelle." Présence Africaine 1(1974): 3-14.

Samuels, Michael A. "The FRELIMO School System." Africa Today 18(Jl, 1971):69-73.

Samuels, Michael A., and Bailey, Norman A. "Education, Health, and Social Welfare." In Portuguese Africa: A Handbook, Part I. Edited by David M. Abshire and Michael A. Samuels. New York: Praeger, 1969.

Sanda, A. O. "Ethnic Pluralism and Intra-Class Conflicts in Four West African Societies." Civilisations Nos. 1-2(1977):65-80.

Scanlon, David G. (ed.). Traditions of African Education. New York: Columbia U. Press, 1964.

Schlemmer, Lawrence. "Political Adaptation and Reaction Among Urban Africans." Social Dynamics 2(1976).

Schrank, Gilbert Isaac. "German South West Africa: Social and Economic Aspects of Its History, 1884-1915." Doctoral dissertation, New York U., 1974. Univ. Microfilms Order No. 74-30044.

Scott, Benjamin F. "The Technology of Liberation." Black World 21(Jl, 1972):29-39. [Proposed Pan-African Academy of Science and Technology]

Sharp, Evelyn. African Child: An Account of the International Conference on African Children. New York: Longmans Green Co., 1931.

Shepherd, George W., Jr. "The Growth of Counterracism among New African Politics." In Racial Influences on American Foreign Policy. Edited by George W. Shepherd, Jr. New York: Basic Books, 1976.

Simuyu, Vincent G. "Traditional Methods of Education in East Africa." Présence Africaine 3(1973):178-196.

Singh, Rajkumar Y. "A Study of the Problems of Indians in East Africa." 2 parts. Quarterly Review of Historical Studies 1-2 (1971-1972).

Smith, Woodruff D. "The Ideology of German Colonialism, 1840-1906." Journal of Modern History 46(D, 1974):641-662.

Spencer, John (ed.). The English Language in West Africa. London: Longman, 1971.

Spivey, Donald. "The African Crusade for Black Industrial Schooling." Journal of Negro History 63(Ja, 1978):1-17.

Tandon, Yash. The Future of the Asians in East Africa. London: Rex Collings, 1973.

Tessler, Mark A. "Problems of Measurement in Comparative Research: Perspectives from an African Survey." Social Science Information 12(Je-Ag, 1973).

"Textbooks for African Schools." Africa 1(Ja, 1923):13-22.

Thomas, L. V. "Acculturation et nouveaux milieux sccio-culturels en Afrique noire." Bull. IFAN 36(1974):164-215.

Traore, Sekou. Responsabilités historiques des étudiants africains. Paris: Editions Anthropos, 1973.

Trimingham, J. Spencer. A History of Islam in West Africa. Oxford: N.p., 1970.

Turner, Harold W. "African Independent Churches and Education." Journal of Modern African Studies 13(Je, 1975).

Turner, Victor (ed.). Colonialism in Africa, 1870-1960. Vol. 3: Profiles of Change: African Society and Colonial Rule. Cambridge U. Press, 1971.

Umbina, W. E. (comp.). Research in Education on East Africa (Kenya, Tanzania, and Uganda)-- Periodical Articles, Theses and Research Papers, 1900-1976. Nairobi: U. of Nairobi, 1977.

United Nations Economic and Social Council, Commission on Human Rights. Report of the Ad Hoc Working Group of Experts Prepared in Accordance with Resolution 21 (XXV) of the Commission on Human Rights E/CN.4/1050. 2 F 1971. New York: UNESCO, 1971. [Southern Africa and Portuguese territories]

U.S. Congress, 92nd, 2nd session, House of Representatives, Committee on Foreign Affairs. The Faces of Africa: Diversity and Progress; Repression and Struggle. Washington, DC: GPO, 1972.

van den Berghe, Pierre L. (ed.). Race and Ethnicity in Africa. Nairobi: East African Publishing House, 1975.

Van Der Laan, Laurens (ed.). "Asian Minorities in Africa: Indians and Lebanese." Kroniek Van Afrika 6(1975). [Afrika-Studiecentrum, Leiden-Nederland]

vander Ploeg, Arie J. "Education in Colonial Africa: The German Experience." Comparative Education Review 21(F, 1977):91-109.

Vengroff, Richard. "Neo-Colonialism and Policy Outputs in Africa." Comparative Political Studies 8(Jl, 1975):234-250.

Wallerstein, I. M. "Ethnicity and National Integration in West Africa." Cahiers d' Etudes Africaines 3(O, 1960):129-139.

Wansborough, John. "The Decolonization of North African History." Journal of African History 10(1968):643-650.

Wazaki, Yoiche. "Tribal Mixing in East African Societies." Africa-Kenkyu 8(1969): 1-20.

Westermann, Diedrich. "The Place and Function of the Vernacular in African Education." International Review Missions 14(Ja, 1925): 25-36.

Willey, Helen O. "The Distribution of Non-Moslem Groups in the Middle East and North Africa Since 1830." Master's thesis, Kent State U., 1969.

Williams, John E., Morland, J. Kenneth, and Dinderwood, W. L. "Connotations of Color Names in the United States, Europe, and Asia." Journal of Social Psychology 82 (1970):3-14.

Wiseman, John. "Peaceful Outsiders." New Society, Mr 7, 1974. [Bushmen of Botswana]

Wober, Mallory. Psychology in Africa. London: International African Institute, 1975.

Arctic

Armstrong, Terence E. and others. The Circumpolar North: A Political and Economic Geography of the Arctic and Sub-Arctic. New York: Wiley, 1978.

Darnell, Frank (ed.). Education in the North. Selected Papers of the First International Conference on Cross-Cultural Education in the Circumpolar Nations and Related Articles. Fairbanks, AK: Center for Northern Educational Research, U. of Alaska, 1972.

Lantis, M., and Anderson, R. J. "Some Demographic, Social and Economic Factors of the Polar Regions." Medicine and Public Health in the Arctic and Antarctic. Geneva: World Health Organization, 1963.

Richards, Bill. "Near the Pole, Eskimos Ponder Political Unity." Washington Post, Je 14, 1977.

Schaeffer, Otto. "Eskimo Personality Yesterday and Today." Arctic 28(1975).

Wonders, William C. The Arctic Circle. Toronto: Longman, 1976.

Asia

Abdushelishvily, M. B. Certain Problems of Ethnic Anthropology in South-West Asia in the Light of the Latest Research. IXth International Congress of Anthropological and Ethnological Sciences, Ag-S, 1973.

Alexander, Garth. Silent Invasion: the Chinese in South-East Asia. London: Macdonald and Jane's, 1973.

Bennett, Don C. "Southeast Asian Indigenous Minorities." Journal of Geography 69(0, 1970):428-433.

Bruk, S. I., Cheboksarov, N. N., and Chesnov, Y. V. "National Processes in Asian Countries Outside the USSR." Races and Peoples. Contemporary Ethnic and Racial Problems. Moscow" Progress Publishers, 1974.

Casal, Gabriel, and Grant, Alex I. "A Survey of Ethnic Groups in Southeast Asia." Impact (Manila) 10(Je, 1975):197-209.

Chang, David W. "Current Status of Chinese Minorities in Southeast Asia." Asian Survey 13(Je, 1973):587-603.

Connor, Walker. "An Overview of the Ethnic Composition and Problems of Non Arab Asia." Journal of Asian Affairs 1(Spring, 1976): 9-25.

Davidi, A. "Some Cultural Changes in the Chinese Minority Communities in Southeast Asia: A Study in Political Geography, with Special Reference to Singapore." Doctoral dissertation, U. of London, School of Oriental and African Studies.

Embree, John F. and others. Ethnic Groups of Northern Southeast Asia. New Haven, CT: Yale U. Press, 1950.

Esman, M. J. "Communal Conflicts in Southeast Asia." In Ethnicity, Theory and Experience. Edited by Nathan Glazer and Daniel P. Moynihan. Cambridge, MA: Harvard U. Press, 1975.

Fawcett, James T. and others. The Value of Children in Asia and the United States: Comparative Perspectives. Honolulu: East-West Population Institute, U. of Hawaii, 1974.

Freedman, Maurice, and Willmott, William E. "Recent Research on Race Relations: South-East Asia, With Special Reference to the Chinese." International Social Science Journal 13(1961):245-270.

Furnivall, John S. Educational Progress in Southeast Asia. New York: AMS Press, 1978; orig. 1943.

_____. Netherlands India. Cambridge, England: Cambridge U. Press, 1939.

Giap, The Siauw. "Religion and Overseas Chinese Assimilation in Southeast Asian Countries." Révue de Sud-Est Asiatique 2(1965): 67-83.

Hassan, Riaz. "National and Ethnic Identities in South-East Asia." Int. Asienforum 1-2 (My, 1978):155-164.

Haynes, Rodney. "Political Participation by Ethnic Minorities in East Asia, 1950-1970." Master's thesis, U. of British Columbia, 1976.

Heidhues, Mary F. Somers. Southeast Asia's Chinese Minorities. New York: Longman, 1974.

Hunter, Guy. South East Asia--Race, Culture, and Nation. London: N.p., 1966.

Irwin, Graham W. (ed.). Africans Abroad. New York: Columbia U. Press, 1977.

Jackson, James C. "The Chinatowns of Southeast Asia: Traditional Components of the City's Central Area." Pacific Viewpoint 16(1975): 45-77.

Johns, Anthony H. "Islam in Southeast Asia: Reflections and New Directions." Indonesia 19(Ap, 1975):33-57.

Kang, Tai S. (ed.). Nationalism and the Crises of Ethnic Minorities in Asia. Westport, CT: Greenwood, 1979.

Kee, Francis Wong Hoy. Comparative Studies in Southeast Asian Education. London: Heinemann, 1974.

Khan, Azizur R. and others. Poverty and Landlessness in Rural Asia. Geneva: International Labour Office, 1978.

Krejci, J. "Ethnic Problems in Europe." In Contemporary Europe: Social Structures and Cultural Patterns. Edited by S. Giner and M. S. Archer. London: Routledge and Kegan Paul, 1978.

Kunstadter, Peter (ed.). Southeast Asia Tribes. Minorities and Nations. 2 vols. Princeton, NJ: Princeton U. Press, 1967.

Lebar, Frank M. and others. Ethnic Groups of Mainland Southeast Asia. New Haven, CT: Human Relations Area Files, 1964.

Llamzon, Teodoro A. "The Problems of Group versus National Identity in the Development of National Languages in Southeast Asia." J. Siam Soc. 63(J1, 1975):4-21.

Madan, T. N. (ed.). Muslim Communities of South Asia: Culture and Society. New Delhi: Vikas Pub. House, 1976.

Medlin, William K., Carpenter, F., and Cave, W. Education and Social Change: A Study of the Role of the School in a Technically Developing Society in Central Asia. Ann Arbor, MI: U. of Michigan Press, 1965.

Murray, Douglas P. "Chinese Education in Southeast Asia." China Quarterly (O-D, 1964):67-95.

Orr, Kenneth (ed.). Appetite for Education in Contemporary Asia. Australian National U., 1978.

Palmer, Leslie. "Educational Systems of Southern Asia and Social Stratification." In Papers in the Sociology of Education in India. Edited by S. M. Gore and I. P. Desai. New Delhi: National Council of Educational Research and Training, 1967.

Peacock, James L. "Plural Society in Southeast Asia." High School Journal 56(O, 1972):1-10.

Rodrigues, L. A. "The Indo-European Miscegenation." B. Inst. Menezes Braganca 108(1975): 21-38. [South Asia]

Rothermund, Dietmar (ed.). Islam in Southern Asia: A Survey of Current Research. Wiesbaden: Franz Steiner, 1975.

Rotter, G. "Die Stellung des Negers in der islamisch-arbischen Gesellschaft bis zum XVI Jahrhundert." Doctoral dissertation, U. of Bonn, 1967.

Shapiro, Michael C., and Schiffman, Harold F. Language and Society in South Asia, S, 1975. ERIC ED 127 806.

Thompson, Virginia M. Minority Problems in Southeast Asia. Stanford, CA: Stanford U. Press, 1955.

UNESCO. Literacy in Asia: A Continuing Challenge. Paris: UNESCO, 1978.

Europe

Abadan-Unat, Nermin. "Educational Problems of Turkish Migrants' Children." International Review of Education 21(1975).

Abadan-Unat, Nermin and others. Turkish Workers in Europe, 1960-1975; A Socio-Economic Reappraisal. Leiden: E. J. Brill, 1976.

Abbott, George D. Israel in Europe. 2nd ed. New York: Humanities Press, 1972.

Abramovich, Stanley. Survey of Jewish Education in Western Europe. Geneva, Switzerland: Joint Distribution Committee, 1966.

Access to Higher Education in Europe. Comparative Background Documents and Report of the Conference. Paris, France. United Nations Education, Scientific, and Cultural Organization, 1968. ED 029 569.

Ahmad, Khurshid. "Islam and Muslims in Europe Today." European Judaism 17(Ja, 1975).

_____. Muslims in Europe. An Interim Report presented to the Secretary General of the Islamic Council of Europe. London: Islamic Council of Europe, 1976.

Ainsztein, Reuben. Jewish Resistance in Nazi-Occupied Eastern Europe. New York: Barnes and Noble, 1974.

Archer, Margaret S., and Giner, Salvador (eds.). Contemporary Europe: Class, Status and Power. London: Weidenfeld and Nicolson, 1971.

Arnold, Hermann. Die Zigeuner. Freiburg im Breisgau: Walter-Verlag Olten, 1965.

Ascher, Abraham and others (eds.). The Mutual Effects of the Islamic and Judeo-Christian Worlds. The East European Pattern. New York: Columbia U. Press, 1978.

Bachrach, Bernard S. Early Medieval Jewish Policy in Western Europe. Minneapolis: U. of Minnesota Press, 1977.

Bahro, Rudolf. The Alternative. New York: Times Books, 1978. [Eastern Europe]

Ball, Robert. "How Europe Created Its 'Minority Problem.'" Fortune 88(D, 1973):130-133, 136,138-139, and 142.

Barnich, M. "Les conditions de logement des travailleurs migrants dans les pays de la communaté européenne." Consommation 24 (Ap-Je, 1977).

Barou, Jacques. "Rôle des cultures d'origine et adaptation des travailleurs africain en Europe." In Les travailleurs étrangers en Europe occidentale. Edited by Bernard J. Philippe. Paris: Mouton, 1976.

Barta, Johannes. "Die jüdische Familienerziehung in der zweiten Hälfte des 19. Jahrhunderts in Mittel-und Osteuropa." Doctoral dissertation, U. of Tübingen, 1972.

Bernard, Cheryl. "Migrant Workers and European Democracy." Political Science Quarterly 93 (Summer, 1978):277-299.

Berger, John. A Seventh Man: Migrant Workers in Europe. New York: Viking, 1975.

Bernard, Phillippe J. (ed.). Les travailleurs étrangers en Europe occidentale. Paris: Mouton, 1976.

Biddiss, Michael D. "Myths of the Blood." Patterns of Prejudice 9(S-O, 1975):11-19. [European racist ideology 1850-1945]

Blaug, Mark, and Woodhall, Maureen. "Patterns of Subsidies to Higher Education in Europe." Higher Education 7(Ag, 1978):331-361.

Bloch, Marc. Slavery and Serfdom in the Middle Ages. Tr. William R. Beer. Berkeley, CA: U. of California Press, 1975.

Bodermann, Michael. "Comments on Oppenheimer's 'The Subproletariat.'" Insurgent Sociologist 4(Spring, 1974):53. [Guest workers in Europe]

Böhning, W. R. Mediterranean Workers in Western Europe: Effect on Home Countries and Countries of Employment. Geneva: World Employment Programme, International Labour Organization, S, 1975.

Bok, W., and Schmelz, U. O. (eds.). Démographie et identité juives dans l'Europe contemporaine. Brussels: Editions de l'Universite de Bruxelles, 1972.

Bortuiker, Elijah. "Report on Jewish Education in Europe." Jewish Education 29(Spring, 1959):35-44 and 29(Fall, 1959):49-59.

Brownlow, William Robert Bernard. Lectures on Slavery and Serfdom in Europe. New York: Negro Universities Press, 1969.

Burks, R. V. East European History: An Ethnic Approach. Washington, DC: American Historical Association, n.d.

Castells, M. "Immigrant Workers and Class Struggles in Advanced Capitalism: The Western European Experience." Politics and Society 5(1975):33-66.

Castles, Stephen. "Some General Features of Migration to Western Europe." New Community 1(Spring, 1972):183-188.

Castles, Stephen, and Kosack, Godula. "The Education of Immigrant Children." Immigrant Workers and Class Structure in Western Europe. London: Oxford U. Press, 1973.

_____. "The Function of Labour Immigration in Western European Capitalism." New Left Review 73(My-Je, 1972):3-21.

_____. "Immigrants: West Europe's Industrial Reserve Army.'" New Society, N 30, 1972.

Centre for Multiracial Studies and le Centre d'Etudes des Relations Interethniques de Nice. Anglo-French Conference on Race Relations in France and Great Britain. Paris: Mouton, 1972.

Centre Internationale de l'Enfance. Les Enfants de Travailleurs Migrants en Europe. Paris: Les Editions ESF, 1974.

Chairoff, Patrice. Dossier Néo-nazisme. Paris: J-P Ramsey, 1977.

Cinanni, Paolo. Emigration and Imperialisms: Zur Problematik und Arbeitsemigranten. Munich, Germany: Verlagskooperative Trikont, 1970.

Cohen, Gloria. "What's Happening in Eastern European Schools." Bulletin of the NASSP 55(N, 1971):40-52. [Denmark, U.S.S.R. and Hungary]

Collinder, Bjorn. The Lapps. New York: Oxford U. Press, 1949.

Collins, Doreen. Social Policy of the European Economic Community. New York: Wiley, 1975. [Migrant labor]

Commission of the European Communities. The Children of Migrant Workers. Brussels: CEEC, 1977.

Congress of European Nationalities. Sitzungs-beiricht des Kongressess der organisierten nationalen Gruppen in den Staaten Europas. 13 vols. Wien, Leipzig: In Kommission bei Wilhelm Branmüller Universitäts-Verlagsbuch-handlung, 1926-1938.

Connor, Walker. "The Political Significance of Ethnonationalism within Western Europe." In Ethnicity in an International Context. Edited by Abdul Said and Luiz Simmons. Edison, NY: Transaction Books, 1976.

Connor, Walter D. Socialism, Politics, and Equality. Hierarchy and Change in Eastern Europe and the USSR. New York: Columbia U. Press, 1979.

Council for Cultural Cooperation. The Integra-tion of Migrant Children Into Pre-school Education, 1977. ERIC ED 140 963.

Council of Europe. Ad Hoc Conference on the Education of Migrants, J1, 1974. ERIC ED 096 051.

_____. Record of the Proceeding of the Ad Hoc Conference on the Education of Migrants. Strasbourg: Documentation Centre for Educa-tion in Europe, 1974.

_____. Unemployment among Young People and Its Social Aspects. London: HMSO, 1975.

Council for Europe, Council for Cultural Cooperation. Reform and Development of High-er Education: A European Symposium. Windsor, Berks: NFER Publishing Co., 1978.

Cozannet, Françoise. "Gypsies and the Problem of Acculturation." Diogenes 95(Fall, 1976): 68-92.

Damon, W. A. "Educational Adaptation of Per-manent Migrants." International Migration 12(1974):270-292.

Deakin, Nicholas (ed.). Immigrants in Europe. London: Fabian Society, 1972.

DeCoster, S. "L'enfant étranger dans un nouveau monde: L'école." Documents Hommes et migration 23(1972):3-28.

Decouple, L. "Les enfants des travailleurs migrant en Europe occidentale." Courrier de la Recherche Pédagogique 10(1959):87-96.

DeGeorge, Richard T., and Scanlan, James P. (eds.). Marxism and Religion in Eastern Europe. Boston: D. Reidel Pub. Co., 1975.

de Montvalon, R. The Aspirations of Young Mi-grant Workers in Western Europe, 1976. ERIC ED 134 673.

Downey, Glanville. "'Un-Roman Activities': The Ruling Race and the Minorities." Anglican Theol. Review 58(1976):432-443.

Dvorjetski, M. "Psychosociological Problems of Jewish Children Hidden by Non-Jews During the Holocaust." Medica Judaiea 1(J1, 1970): 36-37.

Education, Inequality and Life Chances. 2 vols. London: HMSO, 1975. [An OECD Seminar]

Eidheim, Harald. "The Lappish Movement: An Innovative Political Process." In Local-Level Politics. Edited by Marc J. Swartz. Chicago, IL: Aldine, 1968.

Ermacora, F. "Über den Minderheitenschutz in europäischen Südosten." Jahrbuch fur internationales Recht 13(1967).

"Europe: Students and the University in the Capitalist Countries and the Democratiza-tion of Education." Democratic Education (Prague) 2(1973):3-27.

"Europe Report. Education." New Society, My 29, 1975.

European Economic Community. The Perception of Poverty in Europe. London: EEC, 1977.

_____. Social Indicators for the European Economic Community. London: EEC, 1978.

Fejto, François. Les Juifs et l'Antisémitisme dans les pays communistes. Paris: 1960.

Finley, Moses I. (ed.). Slavery in Classical Antiquity: Views and Controversies. Cam-bridge, England, 1960.

Fishman, I. "The History of Jewish Education in Central Europe from the Beginning of the Seventeenth Century to 1782 (the Edict of Toleration Issued by Joseph II of Austria)." Doctoral dissertation, U. of London, 1941.

Forbes, C. A. "The Education and Training of Slaves in Antiquity." Transactions of the American Philological Association 86(1955): 321-360.

Garnsey, Peter. Social Status and Legal Pri-vilege in the Roman Empire. New York: Oxford U. Press, 1970.

Geiger, Theodor. "Der Intellektuelle in der europäischen Gesellschaft von Heute." Acta Sociologica 1(1956):62-74.

Geipel, John. The Europeans: An Ethno-Histori-cal Survey. London: Longmans Green, 1969.

Giner, Salvador, and Archer, Margaret S. Contemporary Europe: Social Structures and Cultural Patterns. London: Routledge and Kegan Paul, 1978.

Girard, Alain, and Charbit, Yves. Les Enfants de Travailleurs Migrants en Europe. Paris: Les Editions ESF for the Centre International de'l Enfance, 1974.

Gokalp, Atan. "Des ghettos culturels à la fiction intégrationniste: repenser l'immigration familiale des migrants méditerranéens." In Les travalleurs étrangers en Europe occidentale. Edited by Philippe J. Bernard. Paris: Mouton, 1976.

Goshko, John M. "Children Without a Country." Washington Post, Jl 29, 1974. (Reprinted in Integrateducation, Ja-F, 1975). [Children of migrant workers in Europe]

_____. "Efforts to Ease Their Plight." Washington Post, Jl 29, 1974. [Education of migrant children in Europe]

Güdemann, Moritz. Geschichte des Erziehungs-wesens und der kultur der abendländischen Juden während des Mittelalters und der neuren Zeit. Vienna: N.p., 1880-1888.

Hake, Barry (ed.). "Compensatory Education." Paedagogica Europaea: Review of Education in Europe 9(1974): entire issue.

Halsall, Elizabeth. "Intelligence, School and Social Context: Some European Comparisons." Comparative Education, Je, 1966. [Belgium, Holland and England]

Hartl, H. Nationalitätenprobleme in heutigen Südosteuropa. Munich: Oldenbourg, 1973.

Heidenheimer, Arnold J. "The Politics of Public Education, Health, and Welfare in the U.S.A. and Western Europe: How Growth and Reform Potentials Have Differed." British Journal of Political Science 3(Jl, 1973): 315-340.

Hill, Robert F., and Stein, Howard F. "Ethnic Stratification and Social Unrest in Contemporary Eastern Europe and America." Nationalities Papers 1(1972).

Hindus, Milton. A World at Twilight: A Portrait of the Jewish Communities of Eastern Europe Before the Holocaust. New York: Macmillan, 1971.

Hoëm, Anton. "Escuelas nacionales y minorías etnicas en Escandinavia, una comparacíon." Revista Mexicana de Sociología 36(1974):889-909.

Hroch, Miroslav. Die Vorkaempfer der nationalen Bewegung bei den kleinen Voelkern Europas. Eine vergleichende Analyse zur gesellschaftlichen Schichtung der patriotischen Gruppen. Prag: Universita Karlova, 1968.

Hüfner, Klaus. "Education, Vocational Training and Migration: A European Problem." In Foreigners in Our Community. Edited by Hans van Houte and Willy Melgert. Amsterdam, The Netherlands: Keesing, 1972.

_____. "Problems of Education and Vocational Training of Migrant Workers and Their Children." In Foreigners in Our Community. Edited by Hans van Houte and Willy Melgert. Amsterdam, The Netherlands: Keesing, 1972.

Husén, Torsten. Social Background and Educational Career. Research Perspectives on Equality of Educational Opportunity. Paris: Organization for Economic Cooperation and Development, 1972. [Europe]

"Les immigrés." Revue francaise d'études politiques méditarraneennes (Paris) (Je, 1975):38-116. [Several articles]

"Les immigrés en Europe." Croissances des jeunes Nations (Je, 1973):5-27.

Janowsky, Oscar J. The Jews and Minority Rights, 1898-1918. New York: Columbia U. Press, 1933.

Jelavich, Charles. The Establishment of the Balkan National States, 1804-1920. Seattle: U. of Washington Press, 1977.

"Jews in Eastern Europe." Reports on the Foreign Scene 12(Ag, 1972):1-14. Published by the American Jewish Committee.

John, Gus. "Education and Community Organization." In Foreigners in Our Community. Edited by Hans van Houte and Willy Melgert. Amsterdam, The Netherlands: Keesing, 1972.

Kahn, Alfred J., and Kamerman, Sheila B. Not for the Poor Alone. European Social Services. Philadelphia: Temple U. Press, 1975.

Katona, George, Btrumpel, Burkhard, and Zahn, Ernest. Aspirations and Affluence: Comparative Studies in the United States and Western Europe. New York: McGraw-Hill, 1971.

Katz, Jacob. Out of the Ghetto. The Social Background of Jewish Emancipation, 1770-1870. Cambridge, MA: Harvard U. Press, 1973.

Kautsky, Karl. Are the Jews a Race? New York: International, 1927.

Kay, Joseph. The Social Conditions and Education of the People in England and Europe. Vol. 2: The Education of the People. Clifton, NJ: Augustus M. Kelley, 1973 (orig., 1850).

Kayser, Bernard. "European Migrations: The New Pattern." International Migration Review 11(Summer, 1977):232-240.

Kedward, H. R. Fascism in Western Europe, 1900–1945. Glasgow: Blackie, 1973.

Kehr, Helen (ed.). Persecution and Resistance Under the Nazis. London: Institute of Contemporary History, 1978.

Kenrick, Donald, and Puxon, Grattan. The Destiny of Europe's Gypsies. London: Heinemann, 1972.

Kestenberg–Gladstein, Ruth. Neuere Geschichte der Juden in den böhmischen Ländern. Pt. 1: Das Zeitalter der Aufklärung 1780–1830. Tübingen, Germany: J.C.B. Mohr, 1969.

King, Edmund J. "Comparative Research for the 16–19 Age Group in Western Europe." International Review of Education 21(1975):149–163. [England, Germany, France, Italy, and Sweden]

King, Robert R. Minorities Under Communism. Nationalities as a Source of Tension Among Balkan Communist States. Cambridge, MA: Harvard U. Press, 1973.

Kiraly, Bela K. (ed.). Tolerance and Movements of Religious Dissent in Eastern Europe. New York: Columbia U. Press, 1975.

Kisch, G. "Nationalism and Race in Medieval Law." Seminar (1943):48–73.

Klee, Ernst. Die Nigger Europas. Düsseldorf, F.R.D.: Pädagogischer Verlag Schwann, 1973.

Kocev, Nikokj. "The Question of Jews and the So-Called Judáizers in the Balkans from the 9th to the 14th Century." Bulgarian Hist. R. 6(No. 1, 1978):60–79.

Kohler, Max J., and Wolf, Sunon. Jewish Disabilities in the Balkan States. Philadelphia, PA: American Jewish Historical Society, 1916.

Kosiuski, Lesnak A. (ed.). Demographic Development in Eastern Europe. New York: Praeger, 1977.

Kröll, K. "Das Phänomen Armut. Wandlungen des Begriffs in Zeitablauf unter besonderer Berücksichtigung mittel alterlicher Armenplegemassnahmen im Vergleich zu Heute." Doctoral dissertation, U. of Cologne, 1973.

Kruijsen, Joep. "Atlas Linguarum Europaea." Higher Education and Research in the Netherlands 21(Spring, 1977):3–12.

Langmuir, Gavin I. "Majority History and Post-Biblical Jews." Journal of the History of Ideas 27(Ja, 1966).

[The last decade of labor migration in Europe] ICMC Migration News 27(1978):1–43.

Lawton, John. "Moslems in Europe Test Social Systems, Local Customs." Washington Post, Ap 2, 1979.

Leibholz, G. "Some Remarks on the Protection of Racial and Linguistic Minorities in Europe During the Nineteenth Century." Internationales Recht und Diplomatie (1972): 119–129.

Lendvai, Paul. Anti-Semitism Without Jews. Communist Eastern Europe. Garden City, NY: Doubleday, 1971.

_____. Eagles in Cobwebs: Nationalism and Communism in the Balkans. Garden City, NY: Doubleday, 1969.

Lessing, O. E. Minorities and Boundaries. The Hague: Nijhoff, 1931.

Levin, Henry M. "Educational Opportunity and Social Inequality in Western Europe." Social Problems 24(D, 1976):148–172.

Lewis, Flora. "Western Europe's Militant Minorities Find Common Cause in Secret Meeting." New York Times, Jl 8, 1975.

Lis, C., and Soly, H. Poverty and Capitalism in Pre-Industrial Europe. Hassocks, Sussex: Harvester Press, 1979.

Levi Bacci, Massimo (ed.). The Demographic and Social Pattern of Emigration from the Southern European Countries. Firenze: Comitato Italiano per lo Studio dei Prolemi della Popolazione, 1972.

Lossowski, P. "National Minorities in the Baltic States, 1919-1940." Acta Poloniae Historica 25(1972).

Macdonald, Ian. "Immigration and Class." Race Today 5(Ap, 1973):107–8.

Mahler, Rapael. A History of Modern Jewry, 1780-1815. New York: Schocken Books, 1971.

Majava, Altti (ed.). Migration Research in Scandanavia. Helsinki: Ministry of Labour, Planning Division, 1973.

Marcus, Jacob R. (ed.). The Jew in the Medieval World: A Source Book, 315-1791. Westport, CT: Greenwood, 1975. Reprint of 1938 ed.

Marquit, Erwin. The Socialist Countries. General Features of Political, Economic, and Cultural Life. Minneapolis, MN: Marxist Educational Press, 1978. [Dept. of Anthropology, U. of Minnesota]

Marrus, Michael R. "European Jewry and the Politics of Assimilation: Assessment and Reassessment." Journal of Modern History 49 (Mr, 1977):89–109.

Matejko, Alexander. Social Change and Stratification in Eastern Europe: An Interpretive Analysis of Poland and Her Neighbors. New York: Praeger, 1974.

Matthijssen, M. A., and Verwoort, C. E. (eds.). Education in Europe, Sociological Research. The Hague: Mouton, 1969.

Matzozky, Eliyho (comp.). From Shtetl to Destruction: The Jewish Experience in Eastern Europe. Monticello, IL: Council of Planning Librarians, 1977.

M'Bow Amadou-Mahtar. "Problems and Prospects. The Education of Migrant Workers--Where Do We Stand?" Prospects 4(Autumn, 1974):344-347. [Followed by additional articles on allied subjects]

Mesinger, Jonathan. "The Changing Cultural Geography of the Jews in Eastern Europe, 1897-1926." Master's thesis, Syracuse U., 1972.

Mistrorigo, L. "L'integrazione scolastica dei figli degli emigrati nella comunità europea." Orientamenti Sociali (Rome) 31(D, 1976):3-17.

Mitchell, B. R. European Historical Statistics 1750-1970. New York: Columbia U. Press, 1978.

Modeen, Tore. "The International Protection of National Minorities in Europe." Acta Academiae Aboensis 37(1969).

Moller, Herbert. "Youth As A Force in the Modern World." Comparative Studies in Society and History, Ap, 1968.

Montvalon, Robert de. The Aspirations of Young Migrant Workers in Western Europe. Paris: UNESCO, 1976.

Moore, Robert. "Immigrant Workers in Europe." Patterns of Prejudice 7(Jl-Ag, 1973):1-5.

Moorman, Paul. "The Great Obstacle to Equal Opportunity is Inherited Wealth." Times Higher Education Supplement, Ja 24, 1975.

Morris, Rosemary. "The Powerful and the Poor in Tenth-Century Byzantium: Law and Reality." Past and Present 73(N, 1976):3-27.

Mosse, George L. Toward the Final Solution: A History of European Racism. New York: Fertig, 1979.

"Muslims in Europe." Patterns of Prejudice 7 (S-O, 1973):5-8. [Conference of Islamic Centres and Bodies in Europe, My 17-19, 1973]

Neave, Guy. Patterns of Equality: The Influence of New Structures in European Higher Education Upon the Equality of Educational Opportunity. Windsor, Berks: NFER Publishing Co., 1977.

Neuburg, Paul. The Hero's Children: The Postwar Generation in Eastern Europe. London: Constable, 1972.

Nikolinakos, M. "New Dimensions in the Employment of Foreign Workers." Journal of Hellenic Diaspora 3(Ja, 1976):5-15.

O.E.C.D. Education, Inequality and Life Chances. 2 vols. Paris: O.E.C.D., 1975.

O'Boyle, Lenore. "A Possible Model for the Study of Nineteenth-Century Secondary Education in Europe." Journal of Social History 12(Winter, 1978):236-247.

_____. "The Problem of an Excess of Educated Men in Western Europe, 1800-1850." Journal of Modern History 42(D, 1970):471-495.

Oppenheimer, Martin. "The Sub-Proletariat: Dark Skins and Dirty Work." Insurgent Sociologist 4(Winter, 1974):6-20.

Organization for Economic Cooperation and Development. Education Policies and Trends in the Context of Social and Economic Development Perspectives, 1977. ERIC ED 143 591.

_____. Entry of Young People into Working Life. General Report, 1977. ERIC ED 145 075.

Ouazzini, Mustapha. "Défense et développement des cultures d'origine." Les travailleurs étrangers en Europe occidentale. Paris: Mouton, 1976.

Padrun, Ruth, and Guyot, Jean (eds.). Migrant Women Speak. London: Search Press, 1978.

Paikert, Geza Charles. The Danube Swabians. German Populations in Hungary, Rumania and Yugoslavia and Hitler's Impact on Their Patterns. The Hague, Netherlands: Nijhoff, 1967.

Pan, C. Südtirol als volkisches Problem: Grundriss einer Südtiroler Ethno-Soziologie. Wien-Stutgart: Wilhelm Braumuller, 1971.

"Pan-European Conference of Migrant Workers, Beekbergen, 21-24 November 1974: Statement of the Preparatory Committee." Race and Class 16(O, 1974):207-213.

Parkin, Frank. "Class Stratification in Socialist Societies." British Journal of Sociology 20(1969):355-374.

"La participation des travailleurs migrants a la vie communale." Hommes et Migrations Special number, 1976.

Patlagean, Evelyne. Pauvreté économique et pauvreté sociale a Byzance, 4e-7e siècles. Paris: Mouton, 1977.

Pepermans, G. M. A. "Antisemitisme in de Latijnse literatuur." Hermeneus 4(1976): 192-197.

Petersen, W. "On the Subnations of Western Europe." In Ethnicity, Theory and Experience. Edited by Nathan Glazer and Daniel P. Moynihan. Cambridge, MA; Harvard U. Press, 1975.

Pi-Sunyer, Oriol (ed.). The Limits of Integration: Ethnicity and Nationalism in Modern Europe. Amherst, MA: Department of Anthropology, U. of Massachusetts, 1971.

Poliakov, Léon. The Aryan Myth: A History of Racist and Nationalist Ideas in Europe. Tr. Edmund Howard. New York: New American Library, 1977.

_____. Histoire de l'antisémitisme. L'Europe Suicidaire, 1870-1933. Paris: Calmann Levy, 1977. [4th vol. of his study]

Poupinot, Yann. Les Bretons a l'heure de l'Europe. Paris: Nouvelles Editions Latines, 1961.

Psacharopoulos, George. Earnings and Education in OECD Countries. Paris: OECD, 1976.

Puxon, Grattan. "Gypsies: Blacks of East Europe." Nation, Ap 17, 1976.

_____. "Forgotten Victims. Plight of the Gypsies." Patterns of Prejudice 11 (Mr-Ap, 1977):23-28.

Ringer, Fritz K. Education and Society in Modern Europe. Bloomington: Indiana U. Press, 1978.

Robinson, Donald W. "European Textbooks and America's Racial Problem." Social Education, Mr, 1969.

Safrai, Ahmud. "Elementary Education, Its Religious and Social Significance in the Talmudic Period." Journal of World History 11(1968).

Salvi, Sergio. Le nazioni proibite: Guida a dieci colonie interne dell' Europa occidencale. Florence, Italy: Vallecchi, 1973.

Samardzie, Radovan. "Stages of Development of Balkan Culture and Education under the Ottomans in the Balkans in the Eighteenth Century." E. Eur. Q. 9(Winter, 1975):405-414.

Schieder, Theodor (ed.). Sozialstruktur und Organisation europäischer Nationalbewegungen. Munich: R. Oldenbourg, 1971.

Schloh, B. "Bericht des Europarates über die Nationalen Minderheiten." Jahrbuch für internationales Recht 9(Jl, 1960).

Seeger, Murray. "Gypsies in East Europe Poor, Hated." Los Angeles Times, S 29, 1977.

"Seminar on Adaptation and Integration of Permanent Immigrants." International Migration 12(1974):109-308.

Sevenster, J. N. The Roots of Pagan Anti-Semitism in the Ancient World. Leiden: E. J. Brill, 1975.

Shanks, Michael. European Social Policy. Today and Tomorrow. New York: Pergamon Press, 1977.

Shapiro, Joseph. "Education among early Hebrews with emphasis on Talmudic period." Doctors dissertation, 1938. U. of Pittsburgh.

Sherwin-White, A. N. Racial Prejudice in Imperial Rome. London: Cambridge U. Press, 1967.

Shulvass, Moses A. Jewish Culture in Eastern Europ. New York: Ktav Publ. House, 1975.

Sijes, B. A. Studies over Jodenvervolging. Assen: Van Gorcum, 1974.

Simmonds, George W. (ed.). Nationalism in the U.S.S.R. and Eastern Europe in the Era of Brezhnev and Kosygin. Detroit, MI: U. of Detroit Press, 1977.

Snowden, Frank M., Jr. Blacks in Antiquity: Ethiopians in the Greco-Roman Experience. Cambridge: Harvard U. Press, 1970.

Sorensen, Aage B. "Equality of Educational Opportunity in an Expanding Educational System." Acta Sociologica 14(1971):151-161.

"Specialists on the Problems of Training Migrant Workers Meet in Geneva." Labour Education 26(O, 1974):8-20.

Stephens, Meic. Linguistic Minorities in Western Europe. Llandysul: Gomer Press, 1977.

Stukat, Karl G. Current Trends in European Pre-School Research. Windsor: NFER, 1976.

Sugar, Peter F. (ed.). Native Fascism in the Successor States, 1918-1945. Santa Barbara, CA: American Bibliographical Center, 1971.

Sugar, Peter F., and Lederer, Ivo J. (eds.). Nationalism in Eastern Europe. Seattle, WA: U. of Washington Press, 1969.

Sundberg-Weitman, Brita. Discrimination on Grounds of Nationality: Free Movement of Workers and Freedom of Establishment under the EEC Treaty. New York: North-Holland Pub. Co., 1976.

Swedner, Harald. "Some Thoughts on Receptors and Regulators." Acta Sociologica 15(1972): 109-123. [European worker-immigrants]

Szajkowski, Zosa. An Illustrated Sourcebook on the Holocaust, Vol. I. New York: Ktav. Publishing House, 1978. [Collection of anti-semitic illustrations]

Szczepanski, Jan. Higher Education in Eastern Europe. New York: International Council for Educational Development, 1974.

Thompson, Ann. "The Jews and the Minorities Treaties, 1918, 1929." Doctoral dissertation, Catholic U. of America, 1966.

Thompson, Margaret Regina. "The Jews and the Minorities Treaties, 1918-1929." Doctoral dissertation, Catholic U. of America, 1966. Univ. Microfilms Order No. 67-6862.

Titze, Hartmut. Die Politisierung der Erziehung: Untersuchungen über die soziale und politische Funktion der Erziehung von der Aufklärung bis zum Hochkapitalismus. Frankfurt am Main: N.p., 1973.

Tomasek, Hans, and Bjorkquist, David. "Industrial Education for Youth in the Socialistic Nations of Eastern Europe." Journal of Industrial Teacher Education 12(Spring, 1975):5-11.

Trunck, Isaiah E. "Internal Living Conditions in the Ghettos of Eastern Europe Under Nazi Rule." Doctoral dissertation, Jewish Teachers Seminary-Herzlia, 1969. [Written in Yiddish]

Trunk, Isaiah. Judenrat. New York: Stein and Day, 1978.

Trunk, Isaiah, and Levine, Herbert S. "The Jewish Councils in Eastern Europe under Nazi Rule (An Attempt at a Synthesis)." Societas, Summer, 1972.

Tsawriyon, T. M. "Die hebräische Presse in Europa (ein Spiegel der Geistesgeschichte des Judentums..." 2 vols. Doctoral dissertation, U. of Munich, 1951.

Turner, Henry A., Jr. (ed.). Reappraisals of Fascism. New York: New Viewpoints, 1975.

UNESCO. Access to Higher Education in Europe, 1968. New York: Unipub., P.O. Box 433, New York, NY 10016.

Urbach, E. E. "The Talmudic Sage--Character and Authority." Journal of World History 11(1968).

Vago, Bela. The Shadow of the Swastika: The Rise of Fascism and Anti-Semitism in the Danube Basin, 1936-1939. Farnborough, Hants: Saxon House for the Institute of Jewish Affairs, 1975.

Vago, Bela, and Mosse, George L. (eds.). Jews and Non-Jews in Eastern Europe, 1918-1945. New York: Wiley, 1975.

Vander Planck, Pieter Hendrikus. "The Linguistic Assimilation of Language Minorities in Europe." Monda linguo-problemo 4(1972): 96-105.

_____. "Taalassimilatie van Europese taalminderheden. Een inventarisierende en hypothesevormende studie naar assimilatieverschinjuselen onder Europese taalgroepen." Doctoral dissertation, U. of Rotterdam, 1971. ["Assimilation of European language minorities..." See English summary.]

Van Houte, Hans, and Melgert, Willy (eds.). Foreigners in Our Community. A New European Problem to be Solved. Amsterdam, The Netherlands: Keesing, 1972.

Vogt, Joseph. Ancient Slavery and the Ideal of Man. Tr. Thomas Wiedemann. Cambridge, MA: Harvard U. Press, 1975.

Ward, Antony. "European Migratory Labor: A Myth of Development." Monthly Review 27 (D, 1975):24-38.

Warzee, Louis. "Education of Migrant Workers' Children." Education and Culture 27 (Spring, 1975):31-37.

Watts, W. J. "Race Prejudice in the Satires of Juvenal." Acta. Class. 19(1976):83-104.

Weinryb, Bernard Dov. Jewish Vocational Education. History and Appraisal of Training in Europe. New York: J.T.S.P. U. Press, 1948.

Weisbord, Robert G. "Scandanavia: A Racial Utopia?" Journal of Black Studies 2(Je, 1972):471-488.

Widgren, J. "The Social Situation of Migrant Workers and Their Families in Western Europe." Studi Emigrazione--Etudes Migrations (Rome) 8(Je, 1976):159-201.

Wiesen, David S. "Juvenal and the Blacks." Class. Med. 36:132-150.

Weissmann, Ann B. "Widening the Base for Higher Education: A Study of Scandanavian Institutions." Western European Education 2(Summer, 1974):3-85.

Wihtol de Wenden, C. Les immigrés dans la Cité: La répresentation des immigrés dans la vie publique en Europe. Paris: La Documentation Française, 1978.

Zielinski, Henryk. "National Minorities in Central Europe and the Problem of European Security, 1918-1939." Dzieje Najnowsze 4 (1974):3-18. [In Polish, with English summary]

Latin America

Aguilar, Luis E. (ed.). Marxism in Latin America. Rev. ed. Philadelphia: Temple U. Press, 1978.

Aguirre Beltran, Gonzalo. Regiones De Refugio: El Desarrollo De La Communidad y El Proceso Dominical en Mestizo America. Mexico City: Instituto Indigenista Interamericano, 1967.

Albo, Xavier. The Future of the Oppressed Languages in the Andes. IXth International Congress of Anthropological and Ethnological Sciences, Ag-S, 1973.

Barnes, Earl, and Barnes, Mary. "Education Among the Aztecs." In Studies in Education. Edited by Earl Barnes. Palo Alto: Stanford U. Press, 1897.

Bastide, Roger. African Civilisations in the New World. London: Hurst, 1972.

_____. Les Ameriques Noires, les civilisations africaines dans le nouveau monde. Paris: Payot, 1967.

_____. "La femme de couleur en Amérique Latine." L'Homme et la Societe. 31-32 (Ja-Je, 1974).

_____. "The Present Status of Afro-American Research in Latin America." Daedalus 103 (Spring, 1974):111-123.

_____ (ed.). La femme de couleur en amérique latine. Paris: Editions Anthropos, 1974.

Bastien, Remy. "Estructura de la adaptacion del negro en America Latina y del afroamericano en Africa." America Indigena 29(1969):587.

Bauer, Arnold J. "Rural Workers in Spanish America: Problems of Peonage and Oppression." Hispanic American Historical Review 59(F, 1979):34-63.

Beller, Jacob. Jews in Latin America. New York: N.p., 1969.

Benet, William and Others. "Illiteracy in Latin America--Trends and Issues." Literacy Work 4(Ap-Je, 1975):43-68.

Benitez Centeno, Raúl (ed.). Las clases sociales en América Latina. Mexico City: Siglo XXI, 1978.

Bernard, L. L., and Bernard, J. S. "The Negro in Relation to Other Races in Latin America." Annals 140(1928):306-318.

Bone, Louis W. Secondary Education in the Guianas. Chicago, IL: Comparative Education Center, U. of Chicago, 1962.

Bonfil Batalla, Guillermo. "El concepto de indio en América: una categoria de la situacion colonial." Anales de Antropología 9(1972).

Bowser, F. B. "The African in Colonial Spanish America: Reflections on Research Achievements and Priorities." Latin American Res arch Review 7(Spring, 1972):77-94.

_____. "Colonial Spanish America." In Neither Slave Nor Free. The Freedmen of African Descent in the Slave Societies of the New World. Edited by David W. Cohen and Jack P. Greene. Baltimore, MD: Johns Hopkins U. Press, 1972.

Breton, F. "Working and Living Conditions of Migrant Workers in South America." International Labour Review 114(N-D, 1976).

Bryan, Patrick. "The African in Latin America." Bulletin African Studies Association West Indies 4(D, 1971):40-56.

Calderón Quigano, José Antonio. "Poblacion raza en Hispanoamérica." An. estud. Am. 27(1970).

Carrasco, Pedro and others. Estratificación social en la Mesoamérica prehispánica. México: SEP/INAH, 1976.

de Carvalho-Neto, Paulo. "Folklore of the Black Struggle in Latin America." Latin American Perspectives 5(Spring, 1978):53-88.

_____. "Historia del folklore de las luchas sociales en America latina." Caudernos Americanos 189(Jl-Ag, 1973):133-156.

Chandler, David L. "Health Conditions in the Slave Trade of Colonial New Granada." In Slavery and Race Relations in Latin America. Edited by Robert B. Toplin. Westport, CT: Greenwood Press, 1974:51-88.

Chang, Ching Chieh. "The Chinese in Latin America, A Preliminary Geographic Survey With Special Reference to Cuba and Jamaica." Doctoral dissertation, U. of Maryland, 1956. Univ. Microfilms Order No. 17,794.

Cohen, David W., and Greene, Jack P. (eds.). Neither Slave Nor Free. The Freedmen of African Descent in the Slave Societies of the New World. Baltimore, MD: Johns Hopkins U. Press, 1972.

Cohen, Jacob Xenab. Jewish Life in South America. New York: Bloch, 1941.

Cohen, Martin A. (ed.). The Jewish Experience in Latin America... 2 vols. New York: Ktav Publishing House, 1971.

Comas, Juan. Relaciones inter-raciales en America Latina: 1940-1960. Mexico City: U. Nacional Autonoma de Mexico, 1961.

Cardoso, Roberto De Oliveira. Urbanizacao e Tribalismo: A Integracao dos Indois Terena Numa Sociedade de Classes. Rio De Janeiro: Zahar Editores, 1968.

Davis, Horace B. "Latin America: Nationalism or Revolution?" In Toward a Marxist Theory of Nationalism. New York: Monthly Review Press, 1978, pp. 182-201.

Davis, Shelton H., and Mathews, Robert O. The Geological Imperative. Anthropology and Development in the Amazon Basin of South America. Irvine, CA: Program in Comparative Culture, U. of California, F, 1977.

De Costa, Miriam (ed.). Blacks in Hispanic Literature. Port Washington, NY: Kennikat Press, 1977.

Denevan, William M. (ed.). The Native Population of the Americas in 1492. Madison: U. of Wisconsin, 1976.

Diggs, Irene. "Color in Colonial Spanish America." Journal of Negro History 38(O, 1953):403-427.

Dossick, Jesse J. "Education Among the Ancient Aztecs." Doctoral dissertation, Harvard U., 1941.

Dostal, W. (ed.). The Situation of the Indians of South America. Geneva, Switzerland: World Council of Churches, 1972.

Drimmer, Melvin. "Thoughts on the Study of Slavery in the Americas and the Writing of Black History." Phylon 36(Summer, 1975): 125-139.

Escobar, Alberto. Lenguaje y Discriminacion Social en America Latina. Lima, Peru: Milla Batres, 1972.

Feder, Ernest. "Poverty and Unemployment in Latin America: A Challenge for Socio-Economic Research." The Rural Society of Latin America Today 2(1973):29-67. [Published by the Institute of Latin American Studies, Stockholm]

"The First International Congress of Central American Indians." Indígena, Summer, 1977.

Fox, Hugh (ed.). First Fire: Central and South American Indian Poetry. Garden City, NY: Anchor, 1978.

Franco, Jose Luciano. "La Presencia Negra en el Nuevo Mundo." Casa de las Americas 7 (1968):7-135.

Frank, Andrew G. Urban Poverty in Latin America. St. Louis, MO: Social Science Institute, Washington U., 1966.

González Casanova, Pablo. "Sociedad plural, colonialismo interno y desarrollo." América Latina 6(1963).

Gorinsky, Conrad. "The Amerindian Situation." Race Today, Ag, 1969.

Gräbener, Jürgen (ed.). Zur Marginalisierung des Afro-Amerikaners in Lateinamerika. Düsseldorf: Bertelsmann Universitaets-uerlog, 1971.

Greaves, Thomas C. "Pursuing Cultural Pluralism in the Andes." Plural Societies (Summer, 1972):33-49.

Gross, Daniel R. (ed.). Peoples and Cultures of Native South America: An Anthropological Reader. Garden City, NY: Doubleday, 1973.

Harris, Marvin. Patterns of Race in the Americas. New York: Walker, 1964.

Hawkins, John N. Teacher's Resource Handbook for Latin American Studies: An Annotated Bibliography of Curriculum Materials Preschool Through Grade Twelve. Los Angeles: Latin American Center, U. of California, 1975.

Heath, Dwight B. (ed.). Contemporary Cultures and Societies of Latin America: A Reader in the Social Anthropology of Middle and South America. 2nd ed. New York: Rnadom House, 1974.

Henry, Frances (ed.). Ethnicity in the Americas. Chicago: Aldine, 1976.

Herbert, Jean-Loup, Bookler, Carlos G., and Quan, Julio. Indianité et Lutte des Classes. Paris: Union General D'Editions, 1972.

Herskovits, Melville J. The New World Negro: Selected Papers in Afro-American Studies. Bloomington: U. of Indiana Press, 1966.

Hilton, Ronald. "The Languages of Latin America and the Caribbean: A Holistic Analysis." Hispania 60(Mr, 1977):88-100.

Hoetink, H. Slavery and Race Relations in the Americas: Comparative Notes on their Nature and Nexus. New York: Harper & Row, 1973.

Hudson, Randall O. "The Status of the Negro in Northern South America, 1820-1860." Journal of Negro History 49(1964):225-239.

"Indians From Two Continents Find Common Problems." Navajo Times, S 29, 1977:A-9 to A-19. [Conference on Discrimination Against Indigenous Populations in the Americas--1977]

Instituto de Estudios Africanos. "Facetas del Esclavo Africano en America Latina." America Indigena 29(1969):665-697.

Irwin, Graham W. (ed.). Africans Abroad. New York: Columbia U. Press, 1977.

Itsigsohn, Jose A. "The Jewish Communities of Latin America." Olam (Spring, 1976).

Jackson, Richard. The Black Image in Latin American Literature. Albuquerque: U. of New Mexico Press, 1977.

de Janvry, Alain, and Garrauión, Carlos. "The Dynamics of Rural Poverty in Latin America." Journal of Peasant Studies 4(1977):206-216.

Jones, Rhett S. "Race Relations in the Colonial Americas: An Overview." Humboldt Journal of Social Relations, Spring, 1974.

_____. "Slavery in the Colonial Americas." Black World 26(F, 1975):28-39.

Kamen, Henry. "El negro en Hispanoamerica (1500-1700)." Anuario de Estudios Americanos 28(1971):121-137.

Knight, Franklin W. The African Dimension in Latin American Societies. New York: Macmillan, 1974.

Knudson, Jerry W. "Antisemitism in Latin America (1). Barometer of Social Change." Patterns of Prejudice 6(S-O, 1972):1-11. [Mexico, Bolivia, and Cuba]

Konetzke, R. (ed.). Colección de documentos para la historia de la formacíon social de Hispanoamérica, 1493-1810. Madrid, 1959.

_____. Süd-und Mittelamerika. I. Die Indianer-kulturen und die spanish-portugiesische Kolonialherrschaft. Frankfurt a. M., 1965.

Kossok, Manfred. "Common Aspects and Distinctive Features in Colonial Latin America." Science and Society 37(Spring, 1973):1-30.

LaBelle, Thomas J. (ed.). Educational Alternatives in Latin America: Social Change and Social Stratification. Los Angeles: UCLA Latin American Center, U. of California, 1975.

Lerner, Natan. "Nationalism and Minorities in Latin America." Patterns of Prejudice 11 (Ja-F, 1977):17-22.

Lipschutz, Alejandro. El Indio-Americanismo y el Problema Racial en las Americas. Santiago, Chile: Editorial Nascumento, 1944.

_____. "Indoamericanism y raza india." Perfil de Indoamerica de nuestro tiempo. Santiago de Chile: Andres Bello, 1968.

_____. El Problema racial en la Conquista de America y el mestizaje. 2nd ed. Santiago de Chile: Andres Bello, 1967.

MacLachlan, Colin M. "African Slave Trade and Economic Development in Amazonia, 1700-1800." In Slavery and Race Relations in Latin America. Edited by Robert B. Toplin. Westport, CT: Greenwood Press, 1974:112-145.

_____. "The Indian Directorate: Forced Acculturation in Portuguese America (1757-1799)." The Americas (Ap, 1972):357-387.

Mark, Y. "Impressions of the Jewish Schools in Argentina and Brazil." Jewish Education 34 (Summer, 1964):248-250.

Maybury-Lewis, David. "Don't Put the Blame on Anthropologists." New York Times, Mr 15, 1974. [Indians in Latin America]

Meagher, Arnold J. The Introduction of Chinese Laborers to Latin America: The Coolie Trade, 1847-1874. San Francisco: Chinese Materials Center, 1977.

Meiklejohn, Norman A. "The Implementation of Slave Legislation in Eighteenth-Century New Granada." In Slavery and Race Relations in Latin America. Edited by Robert B. Toplin. Westport, CT: Greenwood Press, 1974:176-203.

Meiners, Evelyn P. "The Negro in the Rio de la Plata." Doctoral dissertation, Northwestern U., 1948.

Mellafe, Rolando. Negro Slavery in Latin America. Berkeley, CA: U. of California Press, 1975.

Mendez, Jose Luis. "El poder negro y las ciencias sociales americanas." Revista de Ciencias Sociales 17(S, 1973).

Mesa Lago, Carmelo. Social Security in Latin America: Pressure Groups, Stratification, and Inequality. Pittsburgh: U. of Pittsburgh Press, 1978.

Mörner, Magnus. "Legal Equality--Social Inequality: A Post-Abolition Theme." Revista/ Review Interamericana 3(1973).

_____ (ed.). Race and Class in Latin America. New York: Columbia U. Press, 1969.

_____. Race Mixture in the History of Latin America. Boston: Little, Brown, 1967.

Olaechea Labayen, Juan B. "Acceso del mestizo hispanoindiano a Universidades y Colegios." Revista Española de Pedagogía 34(1976):277-306.

Omang, Joanne. "Where White Makes Right." Washington Post, Ag 29, 1976. [Racial prejudice in Latin America]

Pescatello, Ann M. (ed.). The African in Latin America. New York: Knopf, 1975.

_____. Old Roots in New Lands: Historical and Anthropological Perspectives on Black Experiences in the Americas. Westport, CT: Greenwood, 1977.

Pitt-Rivers, Julian. "Mestizo or Ladino?" Race Ap, 1969. [Latin America]

_____. "Race, Color, and Class in Central America and the Andes," Daedalus, Spring, 1967.

_____. "Race in Latin America: The Concept of 'Raza.'" Archives Européennes de Sociologie 14(1973):3-31.

Portes, Alejandro, and Walton, John. Urban Latin America: The Political Condition from Above and Below. Austin: U. of Texas Press, 1976.

Rama, German W. "Educación media y estructura social en América Latina." Revista Latino Americana de Ciencias Sociales 3(Je, 1972).

Reinaga, Ramiro. Ideología y Raza en América Latina. Mexico City: Privately printed, 1972.

Renaud, Andre. "South America, 1968." North-ian, Ja, 1969. [Problems of Indians in South and Central America]

Renner, Richard R. "Poverty and Education in Latin America." In Education and the Many Faces of the Disadvantaged: Cultural and Historical Perspectives. Edited by William W. Birckman and Stanley Lehrer. New York: Wiley, 1972, pp. 349-362.

Ricard, R. "Le Probléme de l'enseignement du castillan aux Indiens d'Amérique durant la période coloniale." Bulletin de la Faculté des Lettres de Strasbourg 39(1961):281-296.

Rogler, Lloyd H. "Slum Neighborhoods in Latin America." Journal of Inter-American Studies 9(1967).

Rosenblat, Angel. La Poblacion indigena y el mestizaje en America. 2 vols. Buenos Aires: 1954. [1492-1950]

Rout, Leslie B., Jr. The African Experience in Spanish America. 1502 to the Present Day. New York: Cambridge U. Press, 1976.

Russell-Wood, A. J. R. "Technology and Society: The Impact of Gold Mining on the Institution of Slavery in Portuguese America." Journal of Economic History 37(Mr, 1977):59-83.

Sable, Martin H. (comp.). Latin America Jewry: A Research Guide. Cincinnati, OH: Hebrew Union College Press, 1978.

Sánchez-Albornoz, Nicolás. The Population of Latin America. Berkeley, CA: U. of California Press, 1974.

"Selected Papers on Education Presented at the VIIth Latin-American Congress of Sociology, 1964." Social and Economic Studies. Jamaica, 1965.

Serafini, Oscar. "La educación en los barrios populares urbanos de América Latina." Revista Paraguaya de Sociologia 9(1972).

Service, Elman R. "Indian-European Relations in Colonial Latin America." American Anthropologist 57(Je, 1955):411-425.

Sherman, William L. Forced Native Labor in Sixteenth Century Central America. Lincoln: U. of Nebraska Press, 1979.

Silvert, Kalman H. "Race and National Cohesion in Latin America." In Racial Influences on American Foreign Policy. Edited by George W. Shepherd, Jr. New York: Basic Books, 1970.

Solaun, Mauricio, and Kronus, Sidney. Discrimination Without Violence: Miscegenation and Racial Conflict in Latin America. New York: Wiley, 1973.

Spalding, Karen. "The Colonial Indian: Past and Future Research Perspectives." Latin American Research Review, 1972,

Stavenhagen, Rodolfo. Classes, Colonialism, and Acculturation in Mezoamerica. "Studies in Comparative International Development: vol. I." 1965. Social Science Institute, Washington U., St. Louis, MO 63130.

Steward, T. Dale. "The Indians of the Americas: Myths and Realities." Revista/Review Interamericana 3(1973).

Symposium on Equality of Opportunity in Employment in the American Region. Equality of Opportunity in Employment in the American Region.... Geneva: International Labour Office, 1974.

Symposium on Inter-Ethnic Conflict in South America. "The Declaration of Barbados: For the Liberation of the Indians." Current Anthropology 14(Je, 1973):267-269. [Ja 30, 1971]

Tigner, James L. "The Okinawans in Latin America." Doctoral dissertation, Stanford U., 1956. Univ. Microfilms Order No. 17,742.

Toplin, Robert B. (ed.). Slavery and Race Relations in Latin America. Westport, CT: Greenwood Press, 1974.

Touraine, Alain, and Becaut, Darriel. Working Class Consciousness and Economic Development in Latin America. "Studies in Comparative International Development." vol. III. 1967-1968. Social Science Institute, Washington U., St. Louis, MO 63130.

Turner, Frederick C. "Minority Groups in Latin America." Patterns of Prejudice 7(Mr-Ap, 1973):19-22.

Uzcategui, Emilio. Historia de la educación en Hispanoamérica. Quito, Ecuador, 1973.

Valle, M. M. "La Errada Interpretacion Europeo Frente a la Autentica Concepcion Indigena." Nueve Perspective del Imperio de los Reyes Incas, 36th Congresso Internacional de Americanistas, Madrid, 1964.

Villamarin, Juan A., and Villamarin, Judith E. Indian Labor in Mainland Colonial Spanish America. Newark: Latin American Studies Program, U. of Delaware, 1975.

Wagley, Charles, and Harris, Marvin. Minorities in the New World: Six Case Studies.

Weisskopf, Thomas E., and Figueroa, Adolfo. "Traversing the Social Pyramid: A Comparative Review of Income Distribution in Latin America." Latin American Research Review 11(1976):71-112.

Wendt, Herbert. The Red, White and Black Continent. Tr. by Richard and Clara Winston. Garden City, NY: Doubleday, 1966.

Wesley, Charles H. (ed.). The Negro in the Americas. Washington, DC: N.p., 1940.

Wilbert, Johannes (ed.). Enculturation in Latin America: An Anthology. Los Angeles: Latin American Center, U. of California, 1976.

Wilkie, James W. (ed.). Statistical Abstract of Latin America. Los Angeles: Latin American Center, U. of California, 1977.

Wolf, Eric R., and Hansen, Edward C. The Human Condition in Latin America. New York: Oxford U. Press, 1972.

Wyckoff, Theodore. "Race, Color, and Prejudice: Solutions from Three Countries." Journal of Negro Education 41(Summer, 1972):195-201. [Brazil, Jamaica, and Mexico]

Zavala, Silvio. "Relaciones históricas entre indios y Negros en Ibero-america." Revista de las Indias 88(Ap, 1946).

Zelinsky, Wilbur. "The Historical Geography of the Negro Population of Latin America." Journal of Negro History 34(Ap, 1949):153-221.

Middle East

Abdo, Ali Ibrahim, and Kasmieh, Khairieh. Jews of Arab Countries. Beirut: N.p., 1971.

Betts, Robert Brenton. "The Indigenous Arabic-speaking Christian Communities of Greater Syria and Mesopatamia....Lebranon, Syria, Jordan, Israel, and Iraq...." Doctoral dissertation, Johns Hopkins U., 1968. Univ. Microfilms Order No. 68-10,562.

Caploe, David. "Discrimination by Law." Middle East International, Jl, 1974.

Cohen, Hayyim J., and Yehuda, Zui (comp.). Asian and African Jews in the Middle East, 1860-1971. Jerusalem: Hebrew U. and Ben-Zvi Institute, 1976.

Frankl, Ludwig A. The Jews in the East. Tr. P. Beaton from 1859 edition. Westport, CT: Greenwood, 1975.

Gordon, David C. History and Identity in Arab Text-Books: Four Cases. Princeton, NJ: Program in Near Eastern Studies, Princeton U., 1971. [Saudi Arabia, Syria, Tunisia, and Lebanon]

Green, Robert L. Report of Sabbatical Trip to the Middle East and East Africa. December 10, 1971-January 17, 1972. East Lansing, MI: Center for Urban Affairs, Michigan State U., 1972. [Israel, Kenya, and Tanzania]

Hirschberg, H. Z. "The Jewish Quarter in Muslim Cities and Berber Areas." Judaism 17(Fall, 1968):405-421.

Landshut, Siegfried. Jewish Communities in the Muslim Countries of the Middle East: A Survey. Westport, CT: Hypecion Press, 1975 reprint of 1950 edition.

Lewis, Bernard. "Race and Colour in Islam." Encounter, Ag, 1970.

_____. Race and Color in Islam. New York: Harper & Row, 1971.

Luca, Costa [pseud.] "Legal Discrimination Among Arabs." Patterns of Prejudice 10 (Jl-Ag, 1976):1-14.

Lutfiyya, Abdulla M., and Churchill, Charles W. (eds.). Readings in Arab Middle Eastern Societies and Cultures. The Hague, The Netherlands: Mouton Publishers, 1970.

Memmi, Albert. Jews and Arabs. Chicago, IL: J. Philip O'Hara, 1975. [Middle East]

Suad, Joseph, and Pillsbury, Barbara L. K. (eds.). Muslim-Christian Conflicts: Economic, Political, and Social Origins. Boulder, CO: Westview Press, 1978.

Szliowicz, Joseph S. Education and Modernization in the Middle East. Ithaca, NY: Cornell U. Press, 1973.

UNRWA/Unesco Institute of Education. Better Teachers. 1970. UNIPUB, Inc., P.O. Box 433, New York, NY 10016. [Professional training for untrained Palestine refugee teachers in schools of the United Nations Relief and Works Agency for Palestine Refugees in the Near East (UNRWA)]

Willey, Helen O. "The Distribution of Non-Moslem Groups in the Middle East and North Africa Since 1830." Master's thesis, Kent State U., 1969.

Oceania

Aames, Jacqueline S. "The Role of Education in Affecting Changes in Attitudes and Values Toward Strategies of Elite Selection: Micronesia Under an American Administration." Doctoral dissertation, U. of California, Santa Barbara, 1976. Univ. Microfilms Order No. 77-5232.

Alkire, William H. An Introduction to the Peoples and Cultures of Micronesia. 2nd ed. Menlo Park, CA: Cummings, 1977.

Amichandra, Pundit. "Primary Education of Indians in Fiji." Master's thesis, U. of New Zealand (Auckland), 1946.

Anttila, Elizabeth K. "A History of the People of the Trust Territory of the Pacific Islands and their Education." Doctoral dissertation, U. of Texas, 1965.

Ballendorf, Dirk A. "Coming Full Circle: A New School for Micronesia." British Journal of Educational Technology 5(My, 1974):81-88.

Barrington, J. R. "Higher Education in New Zealand's Pacific Territories." Master's thesis, Victoria U. (Wellington), 1967.

Beauchamp, Edward. "Educational Policy in Eastern Samoa: An American Colonial Outpost." Comparative Education 11(Mr, 1975): 23-30.

_____. "A Regional University in the South Pacific." Intellect (formerly School and Society) 101(O, 1972):60-62. [University of the South Pacific, Suva, Fiji]

Bellwood, Peter. "The Prehistory of Oceania." Current Anthropology 16(Mr, 1975):9-28.

Brammall, J., and May, R. (eds.). Education in Melanesia. Canberra: Australian National U., 1975.

Brookfield, H. C. Colonialism, Development and Independence: The Case of the Melanesian Islands in the South Pacific. New York: Cambridge U. Press, 1972.

Brown, Carolyn H. "Coolie and Freemen: From Hierarchy to Equality in Fiji." Doctoral dissertation, U. of Washington, 1978. Univ. Microfilms Order No. 7824439.

_____. "Ethnic Politics in Fiji: Fijian-Indian Relations." Journal of Ethnic Studies 5(Winter, 1978):1-17.

Browne, Roosevelt. "Black Nationalism in the South Pacific." Black World 25(Mr, 1976): 32-40. [Interview by Gayleatha B. Cobb]

Burgess, H. J., and Burgess, Ann P. "Malnutrition in the Western Pacific Region." WHO Chronicle 30(1976):64-69.

Butterfield, Fox. "The Improbable Welfare State." New York Times Magazine, N 27, 1977. [Micronesia]

Calman, Donald. "History of the Indians in Fiji, 1916-1949." Master's thesis, U. of Sydney, 1952.

Capizzi, Elaine, Hill, Helen, and Macey, Dave. "FRETILIN and the Struggle for Independence in East Timor." Race and Class 17(Spring, 1976):381-395.

Carroll, Vern (ed.). Pacific Atoll Populations. Honolulu, Hawaii: U. Press of Hawaii, 1975.

Cato, A. Cyril. "A Survey of Native Education in Fiji, Tonga and Western Samoa, with Special Attention to Fiji." Doctoral dissertation, U. of Melbourne, 1951.

Clammer, J. R. Literacy and Social Change: A Case Study of Fiji. Leiden: E. J. Brill, 1976.

_____. "Literacy and Social Change in Fiji Since 1835." Doctoral dissertation, U. of Oxford, 1971.

Cochrane, D. G. "Racialism in the Pacific: A Descriptive Analysis." Oceania 40(S, 1969): 1-12. [The Solomon Islands]

Cockrum, Emmett Erston. "The Emergence of Modern Micronesia." Doctoral dissertation, U. of Colorado, 1970. Univ. Microfilms Order No. 71-5878.

Coletta, Nat. "Ponape: Cross-Cultural Contact, Formal Schooling, and Foreign Dominance in Micronesia." In Topics in Culture Learning. Edited by Richard W. Brislin and Michael P. Hamnett. Vol. 5., Ag, 1977. ERIC ED 145 706.

Congress in Micronesia. Report on the First Trust Territory Low-Cost Housing Conference (Held at) Ponape, September 10-17, 1971. Saipan: Congress of Micronesia, 1971.

Decker, John A. Labor Problems in the Pacific Mandates. New York: AMS Press, 1978, orig. 1948.

Dutton, Tom, and Lynch, John. "Languages of the Pacific: Distribution, Classification and Cultural Historical Implications." In The Melanesian Environment. Edited by John H. Winslow. Canberra: Australian National U. Press, 1977.

Eliss, James D. "Some Problems Concerning the Chinese in Oceania." Doctoral dissertation, U. of London, 1955.

Evans, Grant. "Timor: The Dynamics of Underdevelopment and Independence." Intervention (Australia) 5(Jl, 1975).

Fischer, Joseph L. "The Japanese Schools for the Natives of Truk, Caroline Islands." In Education and Culture. Edited by George D. Spindler. New York: Holt, Rinehart & Winston, 1961.

Forman, Charles W. "Theological Education in the South Pacific Islands: A Quiet Revolution." Journal de la Société des Océanistes 25(1969):151-167.

Francis, Russell. "Paradise Lost and Regained: Educational Policy in Melanesia and Polynesia." Comparative Education 14(Mr, 1978): 49-64.

Galo, N. "The Social Determinants of Education in Western Samoa." Master's thesis, Victoria U. (Wellington), 1967.

Gibson, Graham H. "Native Education by the Methodist Mission in the New Britain District, 1875-1950, with Particular Reference to New Ireland and the Coastal Areas of the Gazelle Peninsula of New Britain." Master's thesis, U. of Melbourne, 1961. [Bismarck Archipelago]

Gillion, Kenneth L. O. The Fiji Indians. Challenge to European Dominance. 1920-1946. Canberra: Australian National U. Press, 1977.

_____. Fiji's Indian Immigrants. Melbourne: Oxford U. Press, 1962.

Gilson, R. P. Samoa 1830 to 1900: The Politics of a Multi-Cultural Community. New York: Oxford U. Press, 1970.

Heine, Carl. Micronesia at the Crossroads: A Reappraisal of the Micronesian Political Dilemma. Honolulu: U. Press of Hawaii, 1974.

Hempenstall, P. J. "Indigenous Resistance to German Rule in the Pacific Colonies of Samoa, Ponape, and New Guinea, 1884-1914." Doctoral dissertation, U. of Oxford, 1974.

Hogbin, H. I. "Education on Ontong Java, Soloman Islands." American Anthropologist 33 (1931):601-615.

Howe, K. R. The Loyalty Islands: A History of Culture Contacts, 1840-1900. Honolulu: U. Press of Hawaii, 1977.

Howells, William. The Pacific Islanders. New York: Scribner, 1973.

Hughes, C. A. A. "Racial Issues in Fiji." Doctoral dissertation, Oxford U., 1965.

Highes, Daniel T., and Lingenfelter, Sherwood G. (eds.). Political Development in Micronesia. Columbus, OH: Ohio State U. Press, 1974.

Johnson, James Curtis. "Native Education in the Territories under British Mandata." Master's thesis, U. of Texas, 1930.

Kennedy, Paul M. The Samoan Tangle. A Study in Anglo-German-American Relations, 1878-1900. New York: Barnes and Noble, 1973.

King, Frank P. (ed.). Oceania and Beyond: Essays on the Pacific Since 1945. Westport, CT: Greenwood, 1976.

Labby, David. The Demystification of Yap. Dialectics of Culture on a Micronesian Island. Chicago: U. of Chicago Press, 1976.

Lamb, David. "Many Young Samoans Would Flee Paradise." Los Angeles Times, O 2, 1974.

Laracy, Hugh. Marists and Melanesians: A History of Catholic Missions in the Solomon Islands. Honolulu: U. Press of Hawaii, 1976.

Latu, N. M. "The Social Determinants of Education in Western Samoa." Master's thesis, Victoria U. (Wellington), 1966.

Levy, Robert I. Tahitians. Mind and Experience in the Society Islands. Chicago: U. of Chicago Press, 1975.

Lieber, Michael D. (ed.). Exiles and Migrants in Oceania. Honolulu: U. Press of Hawaii, 1977.

Lunel, R. "Les écoles françaises en Polynésie." L'Education National 22(Mr 24, 1966):12-14.

Lyon, Robin Ray. "The Social and Ethnic Geography of Tahiti." Master's thesis, Brigham Young U., 1967.

Ma' Ia' I, Fana' afi. "A Study of the Developing Pattern of Education and the Factors Influencing that Development in New Zealand's Pacific Dependencies." Master's thesis, U. of New Zealand (Wellington), 1958.

Macbeth, Alastair M. "A Study of the Changes in Social Attitudes of Secondary School Pupils in the British Solomon Islands Protectorate." Doctoral dissertation, U. of Oxford, 1973.

_____. "Influence of Schools on Economically Disadvantageous Attitudes: A Solomon Islands Study." Human Relations 29(1976):367-383.

McGath, Vicky L. (comp.). General Introduction to Polynesian Cultures. Honolulu: Hawaii Bicentennial Commission, 1976.

Mamak, Alexander. "Pluralism and Social Change in Suva City, Fiji: A Summary of Findings." Plural Societies 8(1977):53-66.

Managreve, Mamao. "A Critical Examination of Education in Rotuma." Master's thesis, U. of Auckland, 1958.

Mann, C. W. Education in Fiji. Melbourne, 1935.

Masland, L., and Masland, G. "The Samoan ETV Project: Some Cross-Cultural Implications of Educational Television, Part II." Educational Broadcasting 8(My-Je, 1975):23-28.

May, Walther. "Die Erziehung in Mikronesien." Doctoral dissertation, U. of Bonn, 1957.

Mayer, Adrian C. Indians in Fiji. London: Oxford U. Press, 1963.

Milburn, D. and others (eds.). "Perspectives on the South Pacific: An Island View of Curriculum Development." Canadian and International Education 5(Je, 1976):109-119.

Norton, Robert Edward. Race and Politics in Fiji. New York: St. Martin's Press, 1978.

Oliver, Douglas L. Ancient Tahitian Society. 3 vols. Honolulu: U. Press of Hawaii, 1974.

Niederholzer, Robert C. "Youth Education in the Cook Islands." Doctoral dissertation, U. of California, Berkeley, 1962.

Ostheimer, John M. (ed.). The Politics of the Western Indian Ocean Islands. New York: Praeger, 1975.

Ostor, A. A. "Europeans and Islanders in the Western Pacific, 1520-1840." Master's thesis, U. of Melbourne, 1967.

Puchkov, P. I. "Ethnic Processes in Oceania." Races and Peoples. Contemporary Ethnic and Racial Problems. Moscow: Progress Publishers, 1974:257-271.

Ramarui, David. "Education in Micronesia: Practicalities and Impracticalities." In The Impact of Urban Centers in the Pacific. Edited by Roland W. Force and Brenda Bishop. Honolulu: Pacific Science Association, 1975.

Richstad, Jim, and McMillan, Michael. "The Pacific Islands Press." Journalism Quarterly 51(Autumn, 1974):470-477.

Rokotuivuna, Amelia and Others. Fiji: A Developing Australian Colony. Victoria, Australia: I. D. A., 1973.

Ross, Angus (ed.). New Zealand's Record in the Pacific Islands in the Twentieth Century. New York: Humanities Press, 1969.

Saemala, Francis J. "Educational Challenge to the Island-States." Integrated Education (N-D, 1973):14-16.

Salū, Lazarus E. "Liberation and Conquest in Micronesia." In Oceania and Beyond: Essays on the Pacific Since 1945. Edited by F. P. King. Westport, CT: Greenwood, 1977.

Sanchez, Pedro. "Education in American Samoa." Doctoral dissertation, Stanford U., 1955.

Schipper, George. "A Study of the Past, Present, and Future Needs of Elementary Education in American Samoa." Master's thesis, Chapman College, 1972.

Smith, Donald Francis. Education for More than One Culture: Fostering Cultural Pluralism in Micronesia, J1, 1976. ERIC ED 132 107.

_____. "Education of the Micronesian with Emphasis On the Historical Development." Doctoral dissertation, American U., 1968. Univ. Microfilms Order No. 68-14968.

_____. "Micronesian Culture vs. American Education." School and Society 99(Summer, 1971):279-282.

_____. "Micronesian Education: A Decade of Change." Educational Leadership 28(F, 1971): 494-496.

Tate, Merze, and Foy, Fidele. "Slavery and Racism in South Pacific Annexations." Journal of Negro History 50(Ja, 1965):1-21.

Thomas, R. Murray. "A Scheme for Assessing Unmet Educational Needs: The American Samoa Example." International Review of Education 23(1977):59-78.

Topping, Donald M. "A Bilingual Education Program for Micronesia." Linguistic Reporter 17(My-Je, 1975).

U.S. Congress, 94th, 2nd session, House of Representatives, Committee on Interior and Insular Affairs, Subcommittee on Territorial and Insular Affairs. Current Problems in the Marshall Islands. Hearing.... Washington, DC: GPO, 1976.

"U.S. Expands West in the Pacific." Akwesasne Notes 7(Late Summer, 1975):32-34.

Valentine, Charles A. "Social Status, Political Power, and Native Responses to European Influence in Oceania." Anthropological Forum 1(1963):3-55.

Wood, John L. S. "Education Policy in British South Pacific Islands: A Comparative Survey of Education Policy in Fiji, Western Samoa, and Papua-New Guinea." Doctoral dissertation, U. of California, Los Angeles, 1964.

Yanihara, Tadao. Pacific Islands Under Japanese Mandate. New York: AMS Press, 1977 (orig. 1940).

West Indies

Alleyne, Mervin C. "Language and Society in St. Lucia." Caribbean Studies 1(Ap, 1961): 1-10. [Reprinted in Lowenthal and Comitas (eds), Consequences of Class and Color, below]

Anttila, Earl. "United States Educational Policies in the Caribbean." Doctoral dissertation, U. of Texas, 1953. [Cuba, Haiti, Santa Domingo, Virgin Islands, and Puerto Rico]

Armet, A. "Equisse d'une sociologie politique de la Martinique--de l'Assimilation au Sentiment National." Doctoral dissertation, Ecole des Hautes Etudies, 1969.

Baksh, Ishmael J. "The Development of Public Secondary Education in Trinidad and Tobago." International Education 4(1975):10-19.

_____. "Some Factors Related to Educational Expectation Among East Indian and Negro Students Attending Public Secondary School in Trinidad." Doctoral dissertation, U. of Alberta, 1974.

Best, Lloyd. "Black Power and National Reconstruction in Trinidad and Tobago." Afro-American Studies 2(Je, 1971):71-81.

Bird, Edris. "Adult Education and the Advancement of Women in the West Indies." Convergence 8(1975):57-64.

Blouet, Olwyn Mary. "Education and Emancipation in Barbados, 1823-1846. A Study in Cultural Transference." Doctoral dissertation, U. of Nebraska, 1977. Univ. Microfilms Order No. 77-29, 476.

Bough, James A., and Macridis, Roy C. (eds.). Virgin Islands: America's Caribbean Outpost. Wakefield, MA: Walter F. Williams Publishing Co., 1970.

Bowen, W. "Development, Immigration and Politics in a Pre-Industrial Society: A Study of Social Change in the British Virgin Islands in the 1960s." Caribbean Studies 16(Ap, 1976):67-85.

Braithwaite, Lloyd. "Social Stratification in Trinidad." Social and Economic Studies 2(1952):5-175.

_____. "The Development of Higher Education in the British West Indies." Social and Economic Studies 7(Mr, 1958):1-64.

_____. "The Problem of Cultural Integration in Trinidad." Social and Economic Studies 3(Je, 1954):82-96. [Reprinted in Lowenthal and Comitas (eds.). Consequences of Class and Color, below]

Bramson, Leon. Society and Education on St. Croix: The Danish Period, Ag, 1975. ERIC ED 155 103.

Brathwaite, Edward. The Development of Creole Society in Jamaica, 1770-1820. New York: Oxford U. Press, 1972.

Brown, Susan Ellen. "Coping With Poverty in the Dominican Republic: Women and their Mates." Doctoral dissertation, U. of Michigan, 1972. Univ. Microfilms Order No. 73-6800.

Bynoe, Jacob Galton. "Social Change and High School Opportunity in Guyana and Jamaica: 1957-1967." Doctoral dissertation, U. of British Columbia, 1972.

Camejo, Acton. "Racial Discrimination in Employment in the Private Sector in Trinidad and Tobago." Social and Economic Studies, S, 1971.

Campbell, Alfred A. St. Thomas Negroes: A Study in Personality and Culture. Psychological Monographs Vol. 55, No. 5. Evanston, IL: American Psychological Association, 1943.

Campbell, Carl. "Social and Economic Obstacles to the Development of Popular Education in Post-Emancipation Jamaica, 1834-1865." Journal of Caribbean History 1(1970):57-88.

_____. "Towards an Imperial Policy for the Education of Negroes in the West Indies after Emancipation." Jamaican Historical Review 7(1967):68-102.

Campbell, Horace. "Jamaica: The Myth of Economic Development and Racial Tranquility." Black Scholar 4(F, 1973):16-23.

Campbell, Mavis Christine. The Dynamics of Change in a Slave Society: A Sociopolitical History of the Free Coloreds of Jamaica, 1800-1865. Rutherford, NJ: Fairleigh Dickinson U. Press, 1976.

Clarke, Colin G. Kingston, Jamaica. Urban Growth and Social Change, 1692-1962. Berkeley, CA: U. of California Press, 1975.

Clarke, Edith. My Mother Who Fathered Me. London: Allen and Unwin, 1957, 1962 new issue. [Jamaica]

Collin, Claude, and Lanfrey, Jean-Francois. "La Martinique, department ou colonie?" Les Temps Modernes 345(Ap, 1975).

Collings, Walter. Jamaican Migrant. London: Routledge and Kegan Paul, 1965.

Comitas, Lambros, and Loewnthal, David (eds.). Slaves, Free Men, Citizens, West Indian Perspectives. Garden City, NY: Anchor, 1973.

Coombs, Orde (ed.). Is Massa Day Dead? Black Moods in the Caribbean. Garden City, NY: Doubleday, 1974.

Corbin, Carlyle G., Jr. Institutional Consequences of Imported Education to the U.S. Virgin Islands. Kingshill, St. Croix: International Institute, Caribbean Regional Office, 1975.

Craig, Dennis R. "Bidialectal Education: Creole and Standard in the West Indies." Linguistics 175(J1, 1976):93-134.

Creque, Darwin D. The U.S. Virgins and the Eastern Caribbean. Philadelphia, PA: Whitmore Publishing Co., 1968.

Cross, Malcolm. "Race, Pluralism and Power in the West Indies." New Community 1(Summer, 1972):290-297.

_____ (ed.). West Indian Social Problems: A Sociological Perspective. Port-of-Spain, Trinidad: Columbus, 1970.

Crowley, Daniel J. "Cultural Assimilation in a Multiracial Society." Annals of the New York Academy of Sciences 83(Ja, 1960).

DePestre, Rene. "Problems of Identity for the Black Man in the Caribbean." Caribbean Quarterly 19(S, 1973):51-61.

Dejnozka, Edward L. "American Educational Achievement in the Virgin Islands, 1917-1963." Journal of Negro History 57(O, 1972): 385-394.

_____ . "Navajos and Virgin Islanders: Educational Parallels." Integrated Education (N-D, 1973):17-19.

Deonanan, Carlton R. A Historical Perspective: Curriculum Development and Instrumentalism in the Educational System in the British West Indies, O, 1975. ERIC ED 124 617.

_____ . "Education and Imperialism." Journal of Negro Education 45(Fall, 1976):472-478. [Trinidad]

Desai, Patricia and others. "The Social Background of Malnutrition in Jamaica." Cajanus 2(1969):303-318.

Dey, Mukul K. "The Indian Population in Trinidad and Tobago." International Journal of Comparative Sociology 3(1962):245-253.

Duncker, Sheila J. "The Free Coloured and Their Fight for Civil Rights in Jamaica, 1800-1830." Master's thesis, U. of London, 1961.

Dyer, P. B. "The Effect of the Home on the School in Trinidad." Social and Economic Studies (Jamaica), D, 1968.

The Educational Setting in the Virgin Islands With Particular Reference to the Education of Spanish-Speaking Children. Rio Piedras, Puerto Rico: Social Sciences Research Center, U. of Puerto Rico, n.d.

Ehrlich, Allen S. "Race and Ethnic Identity in Rural Jamaica: The East Indian Case." Caribbean Quarterly 22(Mr, 1976):19-27.

Elisabeth, Leo. "The French Antilles." In Neither Slave Nor Free. The Freedmen of African Descent in the Slave Societies of the New World. Edited by David W. Cohen and Jack P. Greene. Baltimore, MD: Johns Hopkins U. Press, 1972.

Evans, Luther H. The Virgin Islands from Naval Base to New Deal. Ann Arbor, MI: J. W. Edwards, 1945.

Farrell, Joseph P. "Education and Pluralism in Selected Caribbean Societies." Comparative Education Review, Je, 1967.

Figueroa, John J. "Education for Jamaica's Needs." Caribbean Quarterly 15(Mr, 1969): 5-33.

_____ . Society, Schools and Progress in the West Indies. London: Pergamon, 1971.

Figueroa, Peter M. E., and Persaud, Ganga Sociology of Education: A Caribbean Reader. London: Oxford U. Press, 1976.

Foner, Nancy. "Competition, Conflict, and Education in Rural Jamaica." Human Organization 31(Winter, 1972).

_____ . Status and Power in Rural Jamaica. A Study of Educational and Political Change. New York: Teachers College Press, 1973.

Forsythe, Dennis. "Race, Color, and Class in the British West Indies." Journal of Social and Behavioral Sciences 20(Fall, 1974):58-68.

_____ . "Repression, Radicalism and Change in the West Indies." Race 15(Ap, 1974):401-429.

_____ . "The Ruling Class in Jamaica." Black Liberator 2(Ja, 1975-Ag, 1976):351-357.

Franco, Franklin J. Los negros, los mulatos y la nacion dominicana. Santo Domingo, Dominican Republic: Editora Nacional, 1969.

Frazier, E. Franklin. "Race Relations in the Caribbean." The Economic Future of the Caribbean, Seventh Annual Conference of the Division of the Social Sciences, 1944:27-31.

Gerber, Stanford N. (eds.). Proceedings of the Second Conference on the Family in the Caribbean. Rio Piedras: Institute of Caribbean Studies, U. of Puerto Rico, 1973.

Gervan, Norman. Aspects of the Political Economy of Race in the Caribbean and the Americas. Kingston, Jamaica: Institute of Social and Economic Research, 1975.

Gooding, Earl M. "Education in Trinidad: Past and Present." Doctoral dissertation, U. of Connecticut, 1961.

Goossen, J. G. "Kin to Eath Other: Integration in Guadeloupe." Doctoral dissertation, Columbia U., 1970.

Gordon, Shirley C. A Century of West Indian Education: A Source Book. London: Longmans, 1963.

_____. "The Negro Education Grant, 1835-1845: Its Application in Jamaica." British Journal of Educational Studies 6(1957-1958):140-150.

_____. Reports and Repercussions in West Indian Education, 1835-1933. London: Ginn, 1968.

Gorsuch, Richard L., and Barnes, M. Louis. "Stages of Ethical Reasoning and Moral Norms of Carib Youth." Journal of Cross-Cultural Studies 4(S, 1973):283-301.

Green, Helen B. "Values of Negro and East Indian School Children in Trinidad." Social and Economic Studies 14(1965):204-216.

Green, Vera M. Migrants in Aruba: Interethnic Integration. Assen: Van Gorcum, 1973.

Gresle, François. "Les enseignants et l'école: une analyse socio-démographique des instituteurs et des professeurs de la Martinique." Cahiers de Centre d'Études Régionales Antilles-Guyana 19(1969).

Gullick, C. J. M. R. "Carib Ethnicity in a Semi-Plural Society." New Community 5(Autumn) (Autumn, 1976):250-258. [St. Vincent]

_____. Exiled from St. Vincent: The Development of Black Carib Culture in Central America up to 1945. Malta: Progress Press, 1976.

_____. "Tradition and Change Amongst the Caribs of St. Vincent." Doctoral dissertation, Oxford U., 1974.

Hall, Douglas. "Jamaica." In Neither Slave Nor Free. The Freedmen of African Descent in the Slave Societies of the New World. Edited by David W. Cohen and Jack P. Greene. Baltimore, MD: Johns Hopkins U. Press, 1972.

Hall, Gwendolyn Midlo. "Saint Dominique." In Neither Slave Nor Free. The Freedmen of African Descent in the Slave Societies of the New World. Edited by David W. Cohen and Jack P. Greene. Baltimore, MD: Johns Hopkins U. Press, 1972:172-192.

Hamid, Idris. "'Church' Schools Accused of Breeding Racism." Trinidad Guardian, F 16, 1971. [Trinidad]

Hammond, S. A. "Education in the British West Indies." Journal of Negro Education 15 (Summer, 1946).

Hamshere, Cyril. The British in the Caribbean. London: Weidenfeld and Nieholson, 1973.

Handler, Jerome S. The Unappropriated People. Freedmen in the Slave Society of Barbados. Baltimore, MD: Johns Hopkins U. Press, 1974.

Handler, Jerome, and Lange, Frederick W. Plantation Slavery in Barbados. Cambridge, MA: Harvard U. Press, 1978.

Handler, Jerome S., and Sio, Arnold A. "Barbados." In Neither Slave Nor Free. The Freedmen of African Descent in the Slave Societies of the New World. Edited by David W. Cohen and Jack P. Greene. Baltimore, MD: Johns Hopkins U. Press, 1972.

Hayot, Emile. "Les gens de couleur libres du Fort-Royal (1679-1823)." Revue française d'histoire d'outre-mer 56(1969):1-163.

Hertzig, M. E. and others. "Intellectual Levels of School Children Severely Malnourished During the First Two Years of Life." Pediatrics 49(1972):814-824. [Jamaica]

Higman, Barry W. "The Chinese in Trinidad, 1806-1838." Caribbean Studies, O, 1972.

_____. "The Slave Populations of the British Caribbean: Some Nineteenth-Century Variations." In Eighteenth-Century Florida and the Caribbean. Edited by Samuel Proctor. Gainesville: U. Presses of Florida, 1976.

Hodgson, Eva N. Second Class Citizens: First Class Men. Amalgamated Bermuda Union of Teachers, Hamilton, Bermuda.

Hoetink, H. The Two Variants in Caribbean Race Relations. A Contribution to the Sociology of Segmented Societies. New York: Oxford U. Press, 1967.

Hopkin, A. G. "The Development of Government Policy in Education in Fiji, 1916-1966." Doctoral dissertation, U. of London, 1977.

Hosein, Everold N. "The Problem of Imported Television Content in the Commonwealth Caribbean." Caribbean Quarterly 22(D, 1976): 7-25.

Irwin, Graham W. (ed.). Africans Abroad. New York: Columbia U. Press, 1977.

James, C. L. R. "Race Relations in the Caribbean." Newsletter of the Institute of Racial Relations, Mr, 1964:19-23.

Jarvis, J. Antonio. The Virgin Islands and Their People. Philadelphia, PA: Dorrance, 1944.

Jha, J. C. "Indian Heritage in Trinidad." Eastern Anthropologist 27(Ap-Je, 1974).

_____. "Indian Pressure Groups in Trinidad (West Indies), 1897-1921." Q. R. Hist. Stud. 14(1974-75):138-156.

_____. "Indians in the West Indies." Q. R. Hist. Stud. 14(1974-1975):12-18.

Johnston, Franklin A. J. "Education in Jamaica and Trinidad in the Generation After Emancipation." Doctoral dissertation, U. of Oxford, 1971.

Keagy, Thomas J. "The Poor Whites of Barbados." R. hist. am. 73-74(Ja-De, 1972):9-52.

Keith, Sherry. "An Historical Review of the State and Educational Policy in Jamaica." Latin American Perspectives 5(Spring, 1978): 37-52.

Kirkaldy, John. "'Equal Up Yourself'--Jamaica's Literacy Drive." New Society, S 25, 1975.

_____. "Patois, Education and Jamaica." New Society, O 4, 1973.

Klass, Morton. East Indians in Trinidad: A Study in Cultural Persistence. New York: Columbia U. Press, 1961.

Knight, Franklin W. The Caribbean, the Genesis of a Fragmented Nationalism. New York: Columbia University Press, 1978.

Kopytoff, Barbara. "The Development of Jamaican Maroon Ethnicity." Caribbean Quarterly 22 (Je-S, 1976):33-50.

_____. "The Incomplete Polities: An Ethnohistorical Account of the Jamaica Maroons." Doctoral dissertation, U. of Pennsylvania, 1973.

Kovats-Beaudoux, Edith. "Une minorité dominante: les blancs créoles de la Martinique." Doctoral dissertation, U. of Paris, 1969.

Kuper, Adam. Changing Jamaica. London: Routledge and Kegan Paul, 1976.

LaGuerre, John Gaffar. "Afro-Indian Relations in Trinidad and Tobago: An Assessment." Social and Economic Studies 25(1976):291-306.

_____. Calcutta to Caroni. The East Indians of Trinidad. London: Longman, 1974.

Laguerre, Michael S. "The Black Ghetto as an Internal Colony: Socio-Economic Adaptation of a Haitian Urban Community." Doctoral dissertation, U. of Illinois, 1976.

Layne, Derrick S. "Politics and Educational Expansion in Barbados, 1961-1975." Master's thesis, U. of Calgary, 1976.

Lewis, Gordon K. The Virgin Islands. A Caribbean Lilliput. Evanston, IL: Northwestern U. Press, 1972.

Lewis, S., and Mathews, T. H. Caribbean Integration--Papers on Social, Political, and Economic Integration. Rio Piedras: Institute of Caribbean Studies, U. of Puerto Rico, 1967.

Lind, Andrew W. "Adjustment Patterns Among the Jamaican Chinese." Social and Economic Studies 7(1958):144-164.

López Yustos, A. (comp.). "Education in the West Indies." Revista/Review Interamericana 2(1972).

Lowenthal, David. "Black Power in the Caribbean Context." Economic Geography 48(Ja, 1972): 116-134.

_____. "Conflict and Race in the Caribbean." Integrated Education (S-O, 1971):42-48.

_____. "Free Colored West Indians: A Racial Dilemma." In Racism in the Eighteenth Century. Edited by Harold E. Pagliaro. Cleveland, OH: Press of Case Western Reserve U., 1973.

_____. "Race and Color in the West Indies." Daedalus, Spring, 1967.

_____. West Indies Societies. New York: Oxford U. Press, 1972.

Lowenthal, David, and Comitas, Lambros (eds.). The Aftermath of Sovereignty: West Indian Perspectives. Garden City, NY: Doubleday, 1973.

_____. Consequences of Class and Color. West Indian Perspectives. Garden City, NY: Anchor Books, 1973.

McFarlane, Milton C. Cudjoe of Jamaica: Pioneer for Black Freedom in the New World. Short Hills, NJ: R. Enslow, 1977.

Mahabir, Harold Gilks. "A Study of Elementary Students Coming From Varying Socio-Economic Backgrounds in Trinidad-Tobago and the Effect These Backgrounds Have on National Examinations." Doctoral dissertation, 1973.

Malik, Tygendra K. East Indians in Trinidad. A Study in Minority Politics. London: Oxford U. Press, 1971.

Manyoni, J. R. "Stratification in Barbados. (A Study in Social Change)." Doctoral dissertation, U. of Oxford, 1973.

Miller, Errol L. "Body Image, Physical Beauty and Colour among Jamaican Adolescents." Social and Economic Studies 18(Mr, 1969): 72-89.

Mintz, Sidney W. "The Caribbean Region." Daedalus 103(Spring, 1974):45-71.

_____. Caribbean Transformations. Chicago, IL: Aldine, 1974.

Mintz, Sidney W., and Price, Richard. An Anthropological Approach to the Afro-American Past: A Caribbean Perspective. Philadelphia: Institute for the Study of Human Issues, 1976.

Morrissey, Marietta. "Imperial Designs: A Sociology of Knowledge, Study of British and American Dominance in the Development of Caribbean Social Science." Latin American Perspectives 3(Fall, 1976):97-116.

Morrow, P. "Chinese Adaptation in Two Jamaican Cities." Honors thesis in Anthropology, Harvard U., 1972.

Nelson, Cecil. "Class Structure in Jamaica." Black Liberator 2(Je, 1974-Ja, 1975):217-226.

Nettleford, Rex. Mirror Mirror: Identity, Race and Protest in Jamaica. London: Collins, 1971.

_____. "National Identity and Attitudes to Race in Jamaica." Race 7(Jl, 1965):59-72.

Newson, Linda A. Aboriginal and Spanish Colonial Trinidad. New York: Academic Press, 1976.

Nicholls, David G. "A Work of Combat: Mulatto Historians and the Haitian Past, 1847-1867." J. Interam. Stud. World Aff. 16(F, 1974):15-38.

_____. "Biology and Politics in Haiti." Race 13(O, 1971):203-214.

_____. "East Indians and Black Power in Trinidad." Race 12(Ap, 1971):443-459.

Norton, Graham. "The West Indies As Centres for Migration. Black British Adventures." The Round Table 242(Ap, 1971):273-281.

Nosel, José. "Les étudiants à la Martinique." In "Problèmes universitaires des Antilles-Guyane françaises." Cahiers de Centre d' Etudes Regionales Antilles-Guyana 18(1969): 36-71.

O'Neill, Edward A. Rape of the American Virgins. New York: Praeger, 1972. [American Virgin Islands]

Oxaal, Ivar. Race and Revolutionary Consciousness: A Documentary Interpretation of the 1970 Black Power Revolt in Trinidad. Cambridge, MA: Schenkman, 1971.

Palmer, Godfrey. "Handsworth: Caribbean Black Country." Times Education Supplement, Je 16, 1972.

Palmer, Ransford W. "A Decade of West Indian Migration to the United States, 1962-1972: An Economic Analysis." Social and Economic Studies 23(1974):571-587.

Parris, Ronald G. "Race, Inequality and Underdevelopment in Barbados, 1627-1973." Doctoral dissertation, Yale U., 1974.

Patterson, H. Orlando. "Outside History: Jamaica Today." New Left Review 31(My-Je, 1965):35-43.

_____. "Slavery, Acculturation, and Social Change: The Jamaican Case." British Journal of Sociology 17(1966):151-164.

Pearse, Andrew C. "Education in the British Caribbean: Social and Economic Background." Vox Guyanae 2(F, 1956):9-24.

Pope, Polly. "Danish Colonialism in the West Indies." In War. Its Causes and Correlates. Edited by Martin A. Nettleship and Others. Chicago, IL: Aldine, 1975.

Prince, G. Stewart. "Mental Health Problems in Pre-School West Indian Children." Maternal and Child Care, Je, 1967.

Pujadas, Leo. "A Note on Education Development in Trinidad and Tobago, 1956-1966." Trinidad and Tobago Central Statistical Office Research Papers 6(1969):1-46.

Racine, Marie M. B. "French Creole in the Caribbean." CLA Journal 18(Je, 1975):491-500.

Ramcharan-Crowley, Pearl. "Creole Culture: Outcast in West Indian Schools." School Review 69(1961):429-436. [St. Lucia and Dominica]

Ramesar, Marianne D. "The Impact of the Indian Immigrants on Colonial Trinidad Society." Caribbean Quarterly 22(Mr, 1976):5-18.

Rennie, Bukkha. "The Caribbean Revolution De-Mystified." Race Today 6(My, 1974):142-146.

Rich, Cynthia Jo. "Election Year in the Virgin Islands." Race Relations Reporter 6(Ja-F, 1974):33-41.

Richardson, Stephen A. "Physical Growth of Jamaican Children Who Were Severely Malnourished Before 2 Years of Age." Journal of Biosocial Science 7(1975):445-462.

Riviere, Bill. Oppression and Resistance: The Black Condition in the Caribbean. Ithaca, NY: Africana Studies and Research Center, Cornell U., 1976.

Robert, Michel. "Les musulmans à Madagascar et dans les Mascareignes." R. fr. ét. pol. afric. (Je-Jl, 1977):46-71.

Roberts, G. W. "A Note on Recent Migration from the West Indies to Canada." Canada West Indies Trade. Kingston: U. of the West Indies, 1967.

_____. Some Aspects of Emigration From the West Indies to the United Kingdom. Third Annual Race Relations Conference. London, S 19, 1968.

Rodney, Walter. The Groundings With My Brothers. London: Bogle-L'Ouverture, 1975.

Romaine, R. I. "Negro Education in the British West Indies: Attitudes and Policy After Emancipation, 1834-50." Doctoral dissertation, Cambridge U., St. Catherine's, 1961.

Rubenstein, Hymie. "Black Adaptive Strategies: Coping with Poverty in an Eastern Caribbean Village." Doctoral dissertation, U. of Toronto, 1976. [St. Vincent]

Rubin, Vera, and Zavolloni. We Wish to Be Looked Upon: A Study of the Aspirations of Youth in a Developing Society. New York: Teachers College Press, 1969. [Trinidad]

Ryan, Selwyn Douglas. "Decolonization in a Multi-racial System: A Case Study of Trinidad and Tobago." Doctoral dissertation, York U., 1967.

_____. Race and Nationalism in Trinidad and Tobago. A Study of Decolonization in a Multi-racial Society. Toronto, Canada: U. of Toronto Press, 1972.

_____. "The Struggle for Afro-Indian Solidarity in Trinidad and Tobago." Trinidad and Tobago Index 4(S, 1966):3-28.

Salkey, Andrew (ed.). Caribbean Essays. London: Evans, 1973.

Saunders, Emmanuel. "Black American Settlers in Trinidad, 1800-1865." Doctoral dissertation, Howard U., 1975.

Seaga, Edward P. G. "Parent-Teacher Relationships in a Jamaican Village." Social and Economic Studies 4(S, 1955):289-302. [Reprinted in Lowenthal and Comitas (eds.). Consequences of Class and Color, above]

Sealy, Clinton. "Shepherd's Bush Social and Welfare Association." Race Today 4(N, 1972): 355. [Night school for West Indian children]

Sheppard, Jill. "A Historical Sketch of the Poor Whites of Barbados: From Indentured Servants to 'Redlegs.'" Caribbean Studies 14(O, 1974).

_____. The "Redlegs" of Barbados. Millwood, New York: NTO Press, 1977.

Silin, R. A. "A Survey of Selected Aspects of the Chinese in Jamaica." Honors thesis in Anthropology, Harvard U., 1962.

Simmons, Peter. "Red Legs": Class and Color Contradictions in Barbados." Studies in Comparative International Development 11 (Spring, 1976).

Singham, A. W., and Singham, N. L. "Cultural Domination and Political Subordination: Notes towards a Theory of the Caribbean Political System." Comparative Studies in Society and History 15(Je, 1973):258-288.

Smith, M. G. "Education and Occupational Choice in Rural Jamaica." Social and Economic Studies 9(1960). [Reprinted in Lowenthal and Comitas (eds.). Consequences of Class and Color, above]

_____. The Plural Society in the British West Indies. Berkeley: U. of California Press, 1965.

Smith, Robert Jack. "Muslim East Indians in Trinidad: Retention of Ethnic Identity Under Acculturative Conditions." Doctoral dissertation, U. of Pennsylvania, 1963. Univ. Microfilms Order No. 64-3506.

Special Correspondent. "Black Power in the Caribbean." Race Today, D, 1959.

Stone, Carl. Class, Race and Urban Politics in Jamaica. Institute of Social and Economic Research, U. of the West Indies, 1973.

Taylor, C. E. Leaflets from the Danish West Indies. Westport, CT: Negro Universities Press, 1970, orig., 1888.

Thomas, Clive. "Black Exploitation in the Caribbean." In Is Massa Day Done? Edited by Orde Coombs. Garden City, NY: Anchor Books, 1974.

Thomes-Hope, E. "An Approach to the Delimitation of School Districts: The Example of Primary Schools in the Parish of St. Ann, Jamaica." Social and Economic Studies 24 (S, 1975).

Tolentino, Hugo. Raza e historia en Santo Domingo. 1. Los orígenes del prejuicio racial en América. Santo Domingo: Universidad Antónoma, 1974.

Totten, Ashley L. "The Truth Neglected in the Virgin Islands." Messenger 8(Jl, 1926): 204-206, 8(Ag, 1926):244-245.

Trillin, Calvin. "U.S. Journal: St. Croix, American Virgin Islands." New Yorker 50 (F 25, 1974):111-116.

UNESCO. Race and Class in Post-Colonial Society: A Study of Ethnic Group Relations in the English-speaking Caribbean, Bolivia, Chile, and Mexico. Paris: UNESCO, 1977.

Walters, Elsa H., and Castle, E. B. Principles of Education: With Special Reference to Teaching in the Caribbean. London: George Allen and Unwin, 1967.

Westergaard, Waldemar C. The Danish West Indies Under Company Rule. New York: Macmillan, 1917.

"White School Closes Rather than Allow Student to Wear Afro." African World, Ap 15, 1972. [St. Mary's Academy, Roseau, Dominica]

Whitelock, Otto V. St. "Social and Cultural Pluralism in the Caribbean." Annals of the New York Academy of Sciences 83(Ja 20, 1960: 761-916.

Williams, Eric. "The Blackest Thing in Slavery Was Not the Black Man." Revista/Review Interamericana 3(1973).

_____. Education in the British West Indies. New York: New York U. Place Book Shop, 1968.

_____. From Columbus to Castro: The History of the Caribbean 1492-1969. New York: Harper & Row, 1970.

_____. "The Historical Background of Race Relations in the Caribbean." Miscelanea de estudios dedicados a Fernando Ortiz. Havana, Cuba, 1957.

Wilson, Peter J. Crab Antics: The Social Anthropology of English-Speaking Negro Societies in the Caribbean. New Haven, CT: Yale U. Press, 1973.

Wolf, Donna Marie. "The Caribbean People of Color and the Cuban Independence Movement." Doctoral dissertation, U. of Pittsburgh, 1973.

Bibliographies

Abler, Thomas S., Sanders, Douglas E., and Weaver, Sally M. and others (comps.). A Canadian-Indian Bibliography, 1960-1970. Toronto: U. of Toronto Press, 1974.

Ajaegbu, Hyacinth I. (comp.). African Urbanization: A Bibliography. London: International Africal Institute, 1972.

Alcala, V. O. (comp.). A Bibliography of Education in the Caribbean. Port-of-Spain, Caribbean Commission, 1959.

Allworth, Edward. Soviet Asia, Bibliographies: A Compilation of Social Science and Humanities Sources on the Iranian, Mongolian, and Turkic Nationalities, With an Essay on the Soviet-Asian Controversy. New York: Praeger, 1975.

Altbach, Philip G., and Kelly, David H. (comps.). Higher Education in Developing Nations: A Selected Bibliography, 1969-1974. New York: International Council for Educational Development, 1976.

Anchish, M., Connell, R., Fisher, J., and Koloff, M. (comps.). "A Descriptive Bibliography of Published Research and Writing on Social Stratification in Australia, 1946-1967." Australian and New Zealand Journal of Sociology 5(1969):128-152.

Apanasewic, Nellie, and Rosens, Seymour (comps.). Eastern European Education: A Bibliography of English-Language Materials. Washington, DC: U.S. Office of Education, 1966.

_____ (comps.). Soviet Education. A Bibliography of English-Language Materials. Washington, DC: U.S. Office of Education, 1964.

Avakian, Anne M. (comp.). America and the Armenians in Academic Dissertations: A Bibliography, 1974. Professional Press, 2727 Parker, Berkeley, CA.

Baa, Enid M. (comp.). Theses on Caribbean Topics, 1958-1968. San Juan, Puerto Rico: Institute of Caribbean Studies, U. of Puerto Rico, 1970.

Baldus, Herbert (comp.). Bibliografica critica da Ethnologia Brasileira, 2 vols. Hamburg, 1954-1968.

Baron, George (comp.). A Bibliographical Guide to the English Educational System, 3rd ed. N.p.: Athlone Press, 1965.

Beham, Alisa (comp.). Selected Bibliography of Israel Educational Materials. Vol. I. Jerusalem: School of Education, Hebrew U., 1966.

Behn, Wolfgang (comp.). The Kurds in Iran: A Selected and Annotated Bibliography, 2nd ed. London: Mansell, 1977.

Behrendt, Richard F. W. (comp.). Bibliography of National Minorities in Chile. Washington, DC: N.p., 1943.

Bell, Robert R. (comp.). A Bibliography on the Lower Class Negro Family in the West Indies, the United States, and Great Britain. Philadelphia, PA: Department of Sociology, Temple U., 1968.

Bendix, Dorothy and others (comps.). "The Open University: An Annotated Bibliography." Drexel Library Quarterly 11(Ap, 1975):68-90.

Besterman, Theodore (comp.). A World Bibliography of African Bibliographies. Rev. by J. D. Pearson. Totowa, NJ: Powman and Littlefield, 1975.

Beyer, Barry (comp.). Africa South of the Sahara. A Resource and Curriculum Guide. New York: Crowell, 1969.

"Bibliography: Class Structure and Stratification Processes in Poland, 1956-1976." International Journal of Sociology 7(1977-1978):189-210.

Binkley, Joanne (comp.). Off the African Shelf. An Annotated Bibliography on Society and Education, 1970. Clearinghouse for Education and Social Science, 970 Aurora, Boulder, CO 80302.

Boily, Robert (comp.). Quebec 1940-1969 Bibliographie: le systeme politique quebecoise et son environement. Montreal: Les Presses de l'université de Montreal, 1971.

Bons, J. J. (comp.). Selected Bibliography on Eskimo Ethnology with Special Emphasis on Acculturation. Compiled at the Stefansson Collection, Baker Library, Dartmouth College, Hanover, NH, Je, 1956.

Bradley, Ian L. (comp.). "A Bibliography of Indian Musical Culture in Canada." Northian 12(Summer, 1976):4-10.

Brembeck, Cole S., and Keith, John P. (comps.). Education in Emerging Africa. East Lansing, MI: Michigan State U., 1963.

Breyfogle, D., and Dworaczek, M. (comps.). Blacks in Ontario: A Selected Bibliography 1965-1976. Toronto: Research Library, Ontario U. of Labour, 1977.

British Columbia Centennial Committee. Ethnic Groups in British Columbia: A Selected Bibliography. Victoria, B.C.: 1953.

Brooks, I. R. (comp.). Native Education in Canada and the United States: A Bibliography. Calgary: Office of Educational Development, Indian Students U. Program Services, U. of Calgary, 1976.

Brown, E. Leonard, and Snarr, D. Neil (comps.). "Dissertations Concerning Social Change and Development in Central America and Panama (1960-1974): An Annotated Bibliography." Rural Sociology 40(F, 1975):284-318.

Buang, Zahrah (comp.). "Linguistic Problems in Minority/Majority Relations in Southeast Asian Countries: An Annotated Bibliography-- Malaysia." J. Siam Soc. 63(Jl, 1975):110-132.

Buchanan, John (comp.). Black Britons: A Selective Bibliography on Race... London: Borough of Lambeth, 1972.

Camps, Juan Comas (comp.). Bibliografía selection de las culturas indígenas de America. Mexico: Instituto Panamericano de Geografía e Historia, Comision de Historia, 1953.

Carney, R. J., and Ferguson, W. O. A Selected and Annotated Bibliography on the Sociology of Eskimo Education. With a foreword by B. Y. Card. Edmonton, Boreal Institute with the Dept. of Educational Foundations, U. of Alberta, 1965.

Carty, James and others. "Writings on Irish History." Irish Historical Studies. Dublin: N.p., 1936.

Carvalho-Neto, Paulo de. "Bibliografía Afro-Ecuatoriana." Boletín Ecuatoriano de Antropología, 1963, pp. 5-19.

Choudhury, N. C., and Ray, Shaymal Kumar (comps.). Bibliography of Anthropology of India. Calcutta: Juanodaya, 1976.

Cobb, Martha K. "Bibliographical Essay: An Appraisal of Latin American Slavery Through Literature." Journal of Negro History 58 (O, 1973):460-469.

Coleman, Marion M. Polish Literature in English Translation, 960-1960. Cheshire, CT: Cherry Hill, 1963.

Comitas, Lambros (comp.). The Complete Caribbeana, 1900-1975: A Bibliographic Guide to the Scholarly Literature, 4 vols. Milwood, NY: KTO Press, 1977.

Community Relations Commission (comp.). Race Relations in Britain. London: The Commission, 1973.

Conover, Helen (comp.). Africa, South of the Sahara: A Selected Annotated List of Writings. Washington, DC: GPO, 1963.

Coppell, W. G. (comp.). World Catalogue of Theses and Dissertations About the Australian Aborigines and Torres Strait Islanders. Sydney U. Press, 1977.

Cordeiro, Daniel Raposo (comp.). A Bibliography of Latin American Bibliographies--Social Sciences and Humanities. Metuchen, NJ: Scarecrow, 1979.

Craig, Beryl F. (comp.). Central Australian and Western Desert Regions: An Annotated Bibliography. Canberra, Australia: Australian Institute of Aboriginal Studies, 1969.

Craigie, James (comp.). A Bibliography of Scottish Education, 1872-1972. London: U. of London Press, 1974.

Davis, Lenwood G. (comp.). "Pan-Africanism: An Extensive Bibliography." Genève-Afrique 11 (1972):82-110.

Department of Social Anthropology, University of Edinburgh. African Urbanization. London: International African Institute, 1965.

Deutsch, Richard R. (comp.). Northern Ireland 1921-1974. A Select Bibliography. New York: Garland, 1975.

Dinstel, Marion (comp.). List of French dissertations on Africa, 1884-1961. Boston, MA: G. K. Hall, 1966.

Disadvantaged Children in Canada. Bibliographies in Education, Number 9. Ottawa, Canada: Canadian Teacher's Federation, Ap, 1970. ERIC ED 041 965.

Drake, Howard (comp.). Bibliography of African Education, South of the Sahara. Aberdeen, Scotland: Aberdeen U. Press, 1942.

Duignan, Peter and others. Africa South of the Sahara: A Bibliography for Undergraduate Libraries. Pittsburgh, PA: National Council of Associations for International Studies; Albany, NY: New York State Education Dept., 1971. ERIC ED 050 000.

Duignan, Peter, and Gann, L. H. (comps.). Colonialism in Africa. Vol. 5: A Bibliographical Guide to Colonialism in Sub-Saharan Africa. New York: Cambridge U. Press, 1974.

Duby, Leslie C., Robb, Andrew, and Spira, Thomas (eds.). "Annotated Bibliography of Works on Nationalism: A Regional Selection." Canadian Review of Studies in Nationalism 1(1974). [Bibliographic Supplement]

Easterbrook, David L. (comp.). Bibliography of Africana Bibliographies, 1965-1975." Afric. J. 7(1976):101-148.

Eicher, Joanne B. (comp.). African Dress. A Selected and Annotated Bibliography of Subsaharan Countries. East Lansing, MI: African Studies Center, Michigan State U., 1969.

Engleman, Uriah Zevi. Jewish Education in Europe, 1914-1962. Annotated Bibliography. Jerusalem: Hebrew U., 1965.

An Ethnographic Bibliography of New Guinea. 3 vols. Canberra, Australia: Australian National U. Press, 1968.

"Evaluation of Achievement in the Socialist Countries of Eastern Europe." Educational Documentation and Information 191(2nd quarter, 1974):14-78. [A bibliography]

Feeney, Joan V. (comp.). Peasant Literature: A Bibliography of Afro-American Nationalism and Social Protest from the Caribbean. Monticello, IL: Council of Planning Librarians, 1975.

Fermoselle Lopez, Rafael (comp.). "The Blacks in Cuba: A Bibliography." Caribbean Studies 12(O, 1972).

Florescano, Enríque (comp.). Bibliografía de la historia demografica de Mexico (época prehispanica--1910)." Hist. Mex., Ja-Mr, 1972.

Fluk, Louis R. (comp.). Jews in the Soviet Union. Rev. ed. New York: American Jewish Committee, 1975.

Fraser, Stewart, and Fraser, Barbara J. (comps.). "Scandanavian Education: A Bibliography of English Language Materials." Western European Education 5(1973-1974).

Fraser, Stewart E., and Hsu, Kuang-liang (comps.). "Chinese Education and Society: A Bibliographic Guide. The Cultural Revolution and Its Aftermath." Chinese Education 5(Fall-Winter, 1972-1973):1-204.

_____ (comps.). Chinese Education. The Cultural Revolution and Its Aftermath--A Bibliographical Guide. New York: International Arts and Sciences Press, 1972.

Fuerst, Rene (comp.). Bibliography of the Indigenous Problem and Policy of the Brazilian Amazon Region (1957-1972). Copenhagen, Denmark: International Work Group for Indigenous Affairs, 1972.

Galván Lafarga, Luz Elena (comp.). "Bibliografía Comentada sobre la Educacion en México, en las Epocas Prehispánica y Colonial." Revista del Centro de Estudios Educativos 4 (1974):101-127.

Garigue, Philip. A Bibliographical Introduction to the Study of French Canada. Montreal: Dept. of Sociology and Anthropology, McGill U., 1956.

Garigue, Philippe, and Savard, Raymonde. Bibliographie du Quebec, 1955-1965. Montreal: Presses de l'Universite de Montreal, 1967.

Gibson, Gordon D. (comp.). "A Bibliography of Anthropological Bibliographies: Africa." Current Anthropology 10(1969):527-566.

Glazier, Kenneth M. (comp.). Africa South of the Sahara; a Selected and Annotated Bibliography--1958-1963. Stanford, CA: Stanford U. Press, 1964.

_____ (comp.). Africa South of the Sahara; a Selected and Annotated Bibliography, 1964-1968. Stanford, CA: Stanford U. Press, 1969.

Gordon, Leonard H. D., and Shulman, Frank J. (comps.). Doctoral Dissertations on China. A Bibliography of Studies in Western Languages, 1945-1970. Seattle, WA: U. of Washington Press, 1972.

Gräbener, Jürgen, and Preker, Bernhard (comps.). Karibische Studien in Europa, Ja, 1970. Fakultät für Soziologie der Universität Bielefeld, 48 Bielefeld, Voltmannstrasze 28a, Germany. [In German, English, French, and Spanish]

Greaves, Monica Alice (comp.). Education in British India, 1698-1947. London: Institute of Education, U. of London, 1967.

Gregorovich, Andrew (comp.). Canadian Ethnic Groups Bibliography. A Selected Bibliography of Ethno-cultural Groups in Canada and the Province of Ontario. Toronto: Department of the Provincial Secretary and Citizenship of Ontario, 1972.

Gregory, Peter B., and Krenkel, Noele (comps.). China: Education Since the Cultural Revolution. A Selected, Partially Annotated Bibliography of English Translations, 1972, Evaluation and Research Analysts, 245-30th Street, San Francis, CA 94131.

Griffiths, A. (comp.). Some Recent British Research on the Social Determinants of Education: An Annotated Bibliography. Leeds: Institute of Education, U. of Leeds, 1971.

Hachten, William A. (comp.). Mass Communication in Africa: An Annotated Bibliography, 1971. ERIC ED 136 285.

Hanson, John W., and Gibson, Geoffrey W. (comps.). African Education and Development Since 1960. East Lansing, MI: Michigan State U., 1966.

Harris, Robin, and Grandpre, Marcel de (comps.). "Select Bibliography of Higher Education in Canada." Canadian Journal of Higher Education 3(1974):175-182.

Hart, Donn V. (comp.). An Annotated Bibliography of Philippine Bibliographies: 1965-1974. DeKalb, IL: Center for Southeast Asian Studies, Northern Illinois U., 1975.

Henthorn, William E. (comp.). A Guide to Reference and Research Materials on Korean History. An Annotated Bibliography. Honolulu, HI: Center for Cultural and Technical Interchange between East and West, U. of Hawaii, 1968.

Hill, Janet (ed.). Books for Children: The Homelands of Immigrants in Britain. London: Institute of Race Relations, 1971. [Annotated; deals with Africa, Cyprus, India, Pakistan, Ireland, Italy, Poland, Turkey, and the West Indies]

Hoorweg, Jan, and Marais, H. C. (comps.). Psychology in Africa: A Bibliography. Leyden, The Netherlands: Afrika-Studie-Centrum, 1969.

Jain, S. K. (comp.). East Indians in Canada. The Hague: Research Group for European Migration Problems, 1971.

Hundsdorfer, V. (comp.). Bibliographie zur sozialwissenschaftlichen Erforschungs Tansanias. Munich: Welttorum Vertig, 1974.

Jackson, Robin (comp.). "A Bibliography: Development of the Multicultural Policy in Canada." Canadian Library Journal 33(Je, 1976):237-243.

Jaquith, James R. (comp.). "Bibliography of Anthropological Bibliographies of the Americas." América Indígena 30(1970):419-469.

Johnson, F. Henry. "A Select Bibliography." A Brief History of Canadian Education. Toronto: McGraw-Hill, 1968.

Jones, David Lewis (comp.). "Theses on Welsh History Presented before 1970." Welsh Historical Review, Je, 1971.

Kay, Stafford, and Nystrom, Bradley (comps.). "Education and Colonialism in Africa: An Annotated Bibliography." Comparative Education Review 15(Je, 1971):240-259.

Kehr, Helen (ed.). Prejudice. Racial-Religious-Nationalist. London: Vallentine, Mitchell, 1971.

Khalidi, Walid (comp.). Palestine and the Arab-Israeli Conflict. An Annotated Bibliography, 1974. Institute for Palestine Studies, Box 329, R.D. 1, Oxford, PA 19363.

Klingelhofer, E. L. (comp.). A Bibliography of Psychological Research and Writing in Africa. Uppsala: Scandanavian Institute of African Studies, 1967.

Knez, Eugene I., and Swanson, Chang-Su (comps.). A Selected and Annotated Bibliography of Korean Anthropology. Korea: National Assembly Library, 1968.

Koentjaraningrat (comp.). Anthropology in Indonesia: A Bibliographical Review. s'Gravenhage: Martinus Nijhoff, 1975.

Lambeth Central Library (comp.). Black Britons, 1972. Lambeth Central Library, Brixton Oval, London SWL, England.

Lehmann, Ruth P. (comp.). Nova Bibliotheca Anglo-Judaica: A Bibliographic Guide to Anglo-Jewish History, 1937-1960. London: Jewish Historical Society of England, 1961.

Leitner, Erich (comp.). "Selected Bibliographies on Research into Higher Education: An International Inventory." Higher Education 7(Ag,

Levy, Goldie (comp.). European Education in South Africa, 1922-1946. A Select Bibliography. Cape Town, S.A.: U. of Cape Town, 1946.

Liber, George, and Mostovych, Anna (comps.). Nonconformity and Dissent in the Ukranian SSR, 1955-1075: An Annotated Bibliography. Cambridge, MA: Harvard Ukranian Research Institute, 1978.

Linquist, Harry M. (comp.). "A World of Bibliography of Anthropology and Education, with Annotations." In Anthropological Perspectives on Education. Edited by Murray L. Wax, Stanley Diamond, and Fred O. Gearing. New York: Basic Books, 1971.

A List of American Doctoral Dissertations on Africa. Washington, DC: GPO, 1962.

Lomné, Josette (comp.). El problema indio. Paris: Masson, 1973.

McCarthy, Joseph M. (comp.). Guinea-Bissau and Cape Verde. A Comprehensive Bibliography. New York: Garland, 1977.

Macdonald, Alexandra M. (comp.). Contribution to a Bibliography on University Apartheid. Cape Town, S.A.: School of Librarianship, U. of Cape Town, 1959.

Mackey, W. F. (comp.). International Bibliography on Bilingualism. Montreal, Canada: Université Laval, 1972.

McNeill, Malvina R. (comp.). Guidelines to Problems of Education in Brazil. A Review and Selected Bibliography. New York: Teachers College Press, 1970.

Mallea, J. R., and Philip, L. (comps.). "Canadian Cultural Pluralism and Education: A Select Bibliography." Canadian Ethnic Studies 8(1976):81-88.

Malycky, Alexander (ed.). [Bibliographical data on ten Canadian ethnic groups] Canadian Ethnic Studies 1(Ap, 1969): entire issue.

Marais, J. M. (comp.). European Education in South Africa (1946-1955). Cape Town, S.A.: U. of Cape Town, 1957.

Marshall, Mac, and Nason, James D. (comps.). Micronesia 1944-1974: A Bibliography of Anthropological and Related Source Materials. New Haven, CT: Human Relations Area Files, 1975.

Martinez, Héctor, Cameo, Miguel C., and Ramirez, Jesús S. (comps.). Bibliografia indigena andina peruana (1900-1968). Lima, Peru: Centro de Estudios de Poblacion y Desarrolo, 1969.

Matthews, Daniel G. (comp.). Current Bibliography on African Affairs. Greenwood Periodicals, Inc., 51 Riverside Avenue, Westport, CT 06880.

Matthews, William (comp.). Canadian Diaries and Autobiographies. Berkeley, CA: U. of California Press, 1950.

Maxwell, Constantia. Short Bibliography of Irish History. London: N.p., 1921.

Milano, Attilio (comp.). Bibliotheca Historica Italo-Judaica. Firenze: Sansoni, 1954. Supplemento 1954-1963. Firenze: Sansoni, 1964.

Mutibwa, Olivia M. N. (comp.). Education in East Africa 1970. A Select Bibliography. Kampala, Uganda: Makerere U. Library, 1971.

Mutiso, Gideon-Cyrus M. (comp.). Messages: An Annotated Bibliography of African Literature for Schools. Upper Montclair, NJ: Montclair State College Press, 1970.

Narang, H. L. (comp.). "Canadian Research on Indian Education." Northian 11(Spring, 1975):11-12. [Theses and dissertations until 1971]

Nevadomsky, Joseph-John, and Li, Alice (comps.). The Chinese in Southeast Asia. A Selected and Annotated Bibliography of Publications in Western Languages, 1960-1970. Berkeley, CA: Center for South and Southeast Asia Studies, U. of California, Berkeley, 1970.

Nenberg, Assia (comp.). The State of Israel, 1946-1968. An Annotated Bibliography. Jerusalem, Israel: Graduate Library School, Hebrew U., 1970.

Nock, David (comp.). "A Partial Inventory of Books by French Canadian Sociologists 1960-1971." Insurgent Sociologist 4(Je, 1974): 28-29.

Oberem, Odo (comp.). "Auswahlbibliographie zu dem thema 'Indianer unter europäisher Herrschaft in der Kolonialzeit.'" Wiener Ethnohistorische Blätter 8(1974).

Ojo-Ade, Femi. Analytic Index of Presence Africaine, 1947-1972. Washington, DC: Three Continents Press, 1977.

O'Leary, Timothy J., and Steffens, Joan (comps.). Lapps Ethnographic Bibliography. 2 vols. New Haven, CT: Human Relations Area Files, 1975.

Ouvrard, M. C. "Recherche Bibliographique et Documentaire d'une part sur l'immigration Antillaise en Frances, d'outre-part sur les Organismes s'occupant de l'acceuil des Antillais." Doctoral dissertation, Conservatoire des Artes et Métiers, Institut National des Techniques de la Documentation, 1968.

Paden, John N., and Soja, Edward W. (comps.). The African Experience. Vol. IIIA: Bibliography. Evanston, IL: Northwestern U. Press, 1970.

Panofsky, Hans E. (comp.). A Bibliography of Africana. Westport, CT: Greenwood, 1975.

Paple, H. (comp.). Les Travailleur Étrangers en France." Hommes et Migrations--Études (Paris) 120(1973):3-196.

Paraprofessional School Personnel. Bibliographies in Education, No. 16. Ottawa, Canada: Canadian Teachers' Federation, D, 1970. ERIC ED 048 102.

Parker, Franklin, and Parker, Betty (comps.). American Dissertations on Foreign Education: A Bibliography with Abstracts: Africa. New York: Whitestone Publishing Co., 1974.

Passin, Herbert (comp.). Japanese Education: A Bibliography of Materials in the English Language. New York: Teachers College Press, 1970.

_____ (comp.). "Japanese Education: Guide to a Bibliography in the English Language." Comparative Education Review 9(1965):81-101.

Paulston, Rolland G. (ed.). Folk Schools in Social Change: A Partisan Guide to the International Literature. Pittsburgh, PA: U. Center for International Studies, U. of Pittsburgh, 1974.

Pearson, J. D., and Jones, Ruth (eds.). The Bibliography of Africa. New York: African Publishing Corporation, 1970. [101 Fifth Avenue, New York, NY 10003]

Pelzer, Karl J. (comp.). West Malaysia and Singapore: A Selected Bibliography. New Haven, CT: Human Relations Area Files, 1971.

Phommasouvanh, Bounlieng (comp.). "Annotated Bibliography of Researches and Studies on the Minority/Majority Languages in Laos." J. Siam. Soc. 63(J1, 1975):133-144.

Pidduck, William (ed.). Radical Right and Patriotic Movements in Britain: A Bibliographical Guide. Brighton: Harvester Press, 1978.

Plomley, N. J. B. (comp.). An Annotated Bibliography of the Tasmanian Aborigines. Royal Anthropological Institute of Great Britain and Ireland. Occasional Paper No. 28, 1969.

Porter, Dorothy B. (comp.). Afro-Braziliana: A Working Bibliography. Boston: G. K. Hall, 1978.

Poston, Susan L. (comp.). Nonformal Education in Latin America: An Annotated Bibliography. Los Angeles: Latin American Center, U. of California, Los Angeles, 1976.

Price, Charles A. (comp.). Australian Immigration: A Bibliography and Digest. Canberra: Australian National U., 1966.

_____ (comp.). Australian Immigration. A Bibliography and Digest No. 2. Canberra: Australian National U., 1971.

Ragatz, Lowell J., and Ragatz, Janet E. A Bibliography of Articles, Descriptive, Historical, and Scientific, on Colonies and Other Dependent Territories, Appearing in American Geographical and Kindred Journals. 2nd ed., 2 vols. Washington, DC: Educational Research Bureau, 1951.

Ramos, Roberto (comp.). Bibliografía de la historia de México. 2nd ed. Mexico: Instituto Mexicano de Investigaciones Economicas, 1965.

Reeves, Susan C., and Dudley, May. New Guinea Social Science Field Research and Publications 1962-67. Canberra: New Guinea Research Unit, Australian National U., 1969.

Reinecke, John E. and others (comps.). A Bibliography of Pidgin and Creole Languages. Honolulu: U. Press of Hawaii, 1975.

Research: Annotated Bibliography of New Canadian Studies. Toronto, Canada: Toronto Board of Education, 1969. ERIC ED 061 136.

Richmond, W. Kenneth (comp.). The Literature of Education: A Critical Bibliography, 1945-1970. 2 vols. London: Methuen, 1972.

Richstad, Jim, and McMillan, Michael (comps.). Mass Communication and Journalism in the Pacific Islands. Honolulu: U. Press of Hawaii, 1978.

Robinson, Jacob, and Friedman, Philip (comps.). Guide to Jewish History under Nazi Impact. New York: Ktav Publishing House, 1973.

Roper, T. (comp.). "A Select Bibliography on Aboriginal Education." In Aboriginal Education. The Teacher's Role. Edited by T. Roper. North Melbourne, Victoria: National Union of Australian U. Students, 1969, pp. 223-231.

Rosenberg, Louise Renee (comp.). Jews in the Soviet Union. An Annotated Bibliography 1967-1971. New York: American Jewish Committee, 1971.

Roth, Cecil (comp.). Magna Bibliotheca Anglo-Judica: A Bibliographical Guide to Anglo-Jewish History. New ed. London: Jewish Historical Society of England, 1937.

Rothenberg, Joshua (comp.). Judaica Reference Materials. A Selective Annotated Bibliography. Preliminary edition. Waltham, MA: Library, Brandeis U., 1971.

Rousseau, M. H. A Bibliography of African Education in the Federation of Rhodesia and Nyasaland (1890-1958). Capetown, S.A.: Capetown School of Librarianship, U. of Capetown, 1958.

Saito, Shiro (comp.). Philippine Ethnography. A Critically Annotated and Selected Bibliography. Honolulu: Hawaii: U. Press of Hawaii, 1972.

Sardesai, D. R., and Sardesai, B. D. (comps.). Theses and Dissertations on Southeast Asia. An International Bibliography in Social Sciences, Education, and Fine Arts. Zug, Switzerland: Inter Documentation Co., 1970.

Schapera, Isaac (comp.). Select Bibliography of South African Native Life and Problems. London: Oxford U. Press, 1941.

Sharma, Jagdish S. (comp.). India's Minorities: A Bibliographical Study. Delhi: Vikes Pub. House, 1975.

Schwarz, David (comp.). Invandrar-och minoritets frogor. Nordsk bibliographie. (Bibliography of Nordic Migration and Ethnic Minority Issues.) Stockholm: Sociologiska Institutionen, Stockholm Universitet, 1976.

Shields, James J. (comp.). A Selected Bibliography on Education in East Africa, 1941-1961. Kampala, Uganda: Makerere U. College, 1962.

Shulman, Frank J. (comp.). Japan and Korea: An Annotated Bibliography of Doctoral Dissertations in Western Languages, 1977-1969. Chicago, IL: American Library Association, 1971.

Singerman, Robert (comp.). The Jews in Spain and Portugal: A Bibliography. New York: Garland, 1975.

Sivanandan, A. Coloured Immigrants in Britain: A Select Bibliography. 3rd ed. London: Institute of Race Relations, 1970.

Sivanandan, A., and Waters, Hazel (comps.). Register of Research on "Commonwealth Immigrants" in Britain 1970. London: Institute of Race Relations, 1970.

Skinner, G. William (comp.). Modern Chinese Society, Vol. I. Stanford, CA: Stanford U. Press, 1974.

Slesinger, Zalmen (comp.). Jewish Education Index. Jewish Education 25(Winter, 1954-1955: supplement. [1929-1954]

Snow, Philip A. (comp.). A Bibliography of Fiji, Tonga, and Rotuma: A Preliminary Working Edition. Honolulu, Hawaii: U. of Hawaii Press, 1969.

Soon, Lau Teik (comp.). "A Bibliography on the Malaysian-Singapore Chinese." Philippines Sociological Review 24(1976):81-91.

Strowbridge, Nancy A. (comp.). Education in East Africa 1962-1968. A Selected Bibliography. Kampala, Uganda: Makerere U. College Library, 1969.

_____ (comp.). Education in East Africa 1969. Kampala, Uganda: Makerere U. College Library, 1970.

Strupp, Karl. Bibliographie du droit des gens et des relations Internationales. Leyden: Sitjthoff, 1938.

Sukhum, Parichart (comp.). "The Chinese in Thailand: An Annotated Bibliography." Philippines Sociological Review 24(1976): 63-71.

Swift, Donald F., and Acland, Henry. "The Sociology of Education in Britain, 1960-1968: A Bibliographical Review." Social Science Information, Ag, 1969.

Szwed, John F., and Abrahams, Roger D. (comps.). Afro-American Folk Culture: An Annotated Bibliography of Materials from North, Central and South America and the West Indies. Volume I: North America. Volume II: The West Indies, Central and South America. Philadelphia: Institute for the Study of Human Issues, Je, 1977.

Tairas, J. N. B. (comp.). Indonesia: A Bibliography of Bibliographies. New York: Oleander Press, 1975.

Taylor, Clyde R. H. (comp.). Bibliography of Publications on the New Zealand Maori and Moriori of the Chatham Islands. London: Oxford U. Press, 1973.

_____ (comp.). A Pacific Bibliography: Printed Matter Relating to the Native Peoples of Polynesia, Melanesia, and Micronesia. Wellington, New Zealand: The Polynesian Society, 1951.

Teacher Education Programs for Native Peoples, 1975. Canadian Teachers' Federation, 110 Argyle Street, Ottawa K2P 1B4, Canada.

Thomas, R. Murray, Arbi, Sutan Zanti, and Soedijarto (comps.). Indonesian Education: An Annotated Bibliography. Vol. I. Santa Barbara, CA: ABC-CLIO, 1973.

Trelles y Govín, Carlos Manuel (comp.). Bibliografía social cubana. Havana: Biblioteca Nacional José Marti, 1969.

Uchida, Naosaku (comp.). Overseas Chinese. Bibliography... Stanford, CA: Stanford U. Press, 1959.

United Nations Secretariat. Apartheid. A Selective Bibliography on the Racial Policies of the Government of the Republic of South Africa. ST/LIB/22/Rev. 1. New York: UN Secretariat, F 16, 1970.

University of London Institute of Education. Catalogue of the Collection of Education in Tropical Areas. 3 vols. London: G. K. Hall, 1964.

Valdes, Nelson P., and Edwin (comps.).
The Cuban Revolution: A Research-Study
Guide (1959-1969). Albuquerque, NM: U. of
New Mexico Press, 1971.

Van Warmelo, N. J. (ed.). Anthropology of
Southern Africa in Periodicals to 1950.
Johannesburg: Witwatersrand U. Press, 1977.

Wainwright, Hester H., and Fraser, M. (comps.).
English as a Second Language in Multiracial
Schools: A Bibliography. London: National
Book League, 1977. [Great Britain]

Webbert, Charles A. (comp.). The Basque
Collection. A Preliminary Checklist.
Moscow, ID: Library, U. of Idaho, 1971.

Weinman, Paul L. A Bibliography of the
Iroquoian Literature, Partially Annotated,
D, 1969. ERIC ED 055 724.

Welch, Ruth L. (comp.). Migration Research and
Migration in Britain. Birmingham, England:
The Centre for Urban and Regional Studies,
U. of Birmingham, 1971.

Wieschhoff, Heinrich A. (comp.). Anthropological Bibliography of Negro Africa. New
Haven, CT: American Oriental Society,
1948.

Wiles, M. (comp.). Books About the Education
of Immigrants. Leeds: ATEPO, 1971.

Williams, Helen M. (comp.). Micronesia, Poly-
nesia, and Australasia. Supplement I,
Ap 15, 1971. Hickam Air Force Base, APO
San Francisco, CA 96552.

Yates, C. J. C., and Sword, J. L. Philosophi-
cal Analysis and Educational Priority Areas,
Ap, 1972. The Secretary, Nuffield Teacher
Enquiry, U. of York, York YO1 5DD, England.
[Great Britain]

AUTHOR INDEX

A

Aames, Jacqueline, 1347
Aaron, Cindy, 294
Aaron, Leroy, 49
Aarons, Alfred C., 717
Aarons, Alfred C., 632.
Abad, Vincente, 475
Abadan-Unat, Nermin, 1299, 1334
Abajian, James, 221
Abarca, Tony, 492
Abassi, Mahmoud, 1220
Abbey, Brian, 1004, 1083
Abbey, Harlan, 330
Abbey, Sue Wilson, 205
Abbie, Andrew A., 1075
Abbot, Simon, 1004, 1178
Abbott, Carl, 228
Abbott, Edith, 260
Abbott, George D., 1334
Abbott, Grace, 607
Abbott, Joan, 1177
Abbott, Kenneth A., 579, 581
Abbott, L. J., 381
Abbott, Martin, 3, 393
Abbott, Mary Lee, 402
Abbott, Ralph, and others, 301
Abbott, S. P., 1242
Abbott, William L., 37, 252, 588
Abboushi, W. F., 1220
'Abd-al-'Ariz' Abd-al-Qadir Kamil, 827
Abdee, Nino, 1165
Abdel-Rahman, Mohamed E., 1325
Abderholden, Jack W., 219
Abdo, Ali Ibrahim, 1346
Abdul, Raoul, 632
Abdul-Hadi, Hafex, 1278
Abdullah Muhammad S., 1150
Abdullah, Taufik, 1217
Abdushelishvily, M. B., 1333
Abe, Clifford, 449
Abe, Shirley, 252
Abeel, Erica, 897
Abel, David, 788
Abel, Emily K., 873
Abell, W. A., 561
Abelson, Paul, 607
Abelson, Willa D., 692
Aber, Elaine M., 895
Aberbach, Joel D., 301, 764, 843
Aberdeen, David, 72
Aberdeen, F. D., 70
Aberle, David F., 509
Aberle, Sophie D. (ed.), 556
Abernathy, David B., 1259
Abeysekera, G., 1290
Abir, Mordechai, 1140
Abler, Thomas S., 1356
Ablon, Joan, 523, 550, 600, 707
Abner, Edward V., 135
Abney, Everett E., 241, 684
Abney, Glenn, 311
Abou, Selim, 1074
Aboud, Frances E., 93, 1096
Abraham, Ansley A., 241
Abraham, Cleo, 230
Abraham, Roger D., 385
Abraham, Sidney, 29
Abraham, Theodore, 36

Abrahams, Ina, 553
Abrahams, Paul P., 917
Abrahams, Roger D., 42, 632, 1004, 1362
Abrahamson, Harold J., 827
Abram, Morris B., 888
Abramovich, Stanley, 1334
Abramowitz, Jack, 632
Abramowitz, Karen, 338
Abrams, Arnold, 1240
Abrams, Carol, and others, 208
Abrams, Charles, 835, 1004
Abrams, Elliott, 810
Abrams, Mark, 1200
Abrams, Roger I., 289
Abramson, Edward E., 93
Abramson, Harold J., 230, 607
Abramson, Joan, 746
Abramson, Marcia, 158
Abramson, Paul R., 93
Abramson, Stephen A., 937
Abreu, Elsa, 1242
Abt, Lawrence E., 189
Abubadika, Muvlina Imiri (Sonny Carson), 338
Abu Ghazaleh, Adnan Mohammad, 1220
Abu-Ghosh, Subhi, 1220
Abu Hanna, Anis, 1220
Abu-Laban, Baha, 416, 1100
Abu-Lughod, Ibrahim, 636, 1220
Abu Shilbaya, Mohammad, 1220
Ace, M. E., 36
Acevedo, Homero, 449
Aceves, Edward A. (comp.), 449
Achabel, Dale, 742
Achiezra, 1228
Acholonu, Constance Williams, 632
Achor, Shirley Coolidge, 438
Acitelli-Donoghue, Anna, 1240
Ackerman, Bruce L., 835
Ackerman, Donald, 1004
Ackerman, Marc J., 659
Ackerman, Walter, 1228
Ackley, Randall, 905
Ackley, Sheldon, 937
Acland, H. D., 93
Acland, Henry, 70, 1178, 1362
Acock, A. C., 1065
Acosta, Adela M., 475
Acosta-Belen, Edna, 475
Acosta Marin, Eugene, 427
Acosta Saignes, Miguel, 1311
Acquaviva, S. S., 1239
Acton, Thomas A., 1178
Acuña, Rodolfo, 93, 448, 449
Adachi, Christina, 590
Adachi, Ken, 1113
Adair, Alvis Van-Ressealeas, 93
Adair, Augustus A., 246
Adair, John, 520, 530
Adair, Mildred L., 509
Adam, Barry, 986, 1004
Adam, H., 1150
Adam, Heribert, 1278
Adam, Kogila, 1278
Adam, R. S., 1083
Adam, Ruth, 385
Adam, Uwe Dietrich, 1150
Adams, Adrian, 1141
Adams, Arvil V., 398, 729, 746, 750
Adams, Barbara, 1178
Adams, Bert N., 1160, 1299

Furst, Randy, 347, 395, 900
Furstenberg, Frank F., Jr., 179
Furth, H. G., 55
Furuya, Kazuko K., 592
Fuschillo, Jean, 237
Fusco, Gene C., 116, 723
Fusco, Liz, 347, 770
Fuss, Alisa, 1235
Fussell, Richard, 196
Futransky, David L., 495
Fyle, Clifford A., 1277

G

Gaarder, Alfred Bruce, 89
Gabb, Sally, 314
Gabbard, Ann V., 279
Gabert, Glen, Jr., 829
Gable, Robert K., 116, 171
Gabler, R., 117
Gabourie, F. W., 551
Gabriel, Richard A., 392
Gabriner, Vickie, 358, 585
Gaby, Daniel, 327
Gad, Finn, 1206
Gaertner, Samuel, 41
Gaffney, Michael, 696
Gagala, Kenneth L., 992
Gage, N. L., 55
Gagnon, L., 1094
Gaida, P., 1117
Gaier, Eugene L., 950
Gaikwad, V. S. R. R., 1212
Gaile, Sandra L., 253
Gaillard, Faye, 609
Gaillard, Frye, 320, 347, 456, 508, 517, 524,
    525, 538, 542, 560, 617, 852, 912, 950
Gaines, Harold L., 377
Gaines, John S., 456
Gaines, Loretta, 710
Gaines, Miriam, 279
Gaines, Richard L., 294
Gaines, William A., 1026
Gaither, Gerald, 913
Gaitskell, Julia, 1167, 1200
Gaitz, Charles M., 753
Gal, Susan, 1086
Galabus, Kenneth E., 950
Galambos, Eva, 805
Galamison, Milton, 347, 770, 1025
Galanty, Ervin, 347
Galarza, Ernesto, 215, 456, 469
Galatioto, Rocco G., 343
Galbraith, Francis Templeton, 215
Galbraith, John Kenneth, 747, 1025
Galchus, Donna S., 950
Gale, G. Fay, 1077, 1078, 1183, 1187
Gale, Jim, 1078
Gale, Mary Ellen, 196-197, 248, 862
Galedo, Lillian, 589
Gales, Tatiana P., 1303
Galeski, Boguslaw, 1273
Galimore, Judith, 132
Galindez, Jesús de, 480
Galitzi, Christine A., 609
Galitzine, Elizabeth S., 700

Gall, Peter, 815, 821
Gallagher, Buell G., 42, 248, 922, 950
Gallagher, James J., 259
Gallagher, John, 215
Gallagher, Sr. Marie Patrice, 333
Gallaway, Lowell E., 754
Gallegos, Katherine Powers (ed.), 560
Gallegos, Mario, 480
Gallegos, Samuel, Jr., 873
Gallessich, June, 470
Galli, Giorgio, 1239
Galli, Marcia J., 542
Galli, Nicholas, 480
Gallimore, Ronald, 132, 253, 256
Gallissot, René, 1073
Galloway, Charles G., 560, 566, 1104
Galloway, Gladys G., 9
Galloway, Joel D., 114
Galloway, Oscar F., 885
Galloway, Russell, 830
Galloway, Wilda, 1104
Gallup, George, 1025
Galo, N., 1348
Galphin, Bruce, 283
Galston, Arthur W., 1131
Galtung, Johan, 1320
Galuzzi, W. E., 560
Galván, Robert A., 440
Galván Lafarga, Luz Elena, 1358
Galvin, Raymond T., 293
Gambill, Jerry T., 1104
Gambino, Richard, 609, 625
Gamble, George R., 51
Gamble, H. F., 738
Gamble, Leo M., 430
Gamboa, Erasmo, 456
Gambone, James V., 494
Gamel, Nona N., 696
Gamio, Manuel, 456, 1249
Gammon, Tim, 382
Gándara Mendoza, Leticia, 1250
Gandy, John M., 412, 916
Gangware, Wenana B., 667
Gani, Leon, 1145
Ganley, William, 829
Gann, L. H., 1315, 1358
Gannett, William C., 395
Gannon, Arthur Seymour, 829
Gannon, James F., 754
Gannon, James P., 347
Gannon, Roger, 1098
Gannon, Thomas M., 347, 770, 829
Gans, Herbert J., 696, 723, 770, 851, 852,
    1025
Gans, Mozes Heiman, 1253
Ganschow, Thomas W., 582
Gansneder, Bruce M., 667
Gant, Lisbeth, 185
Gantt, Walter N., 116
Ganz, Richard L., 37
Gao, Ren-Ying, 582
Gappa, Judith M., 950
Gara, Larry (ed.), 242
Garafalo, Charles, 242
Garbarino, James, 294
Garbarino, Merwyn S. (ed.), 517
Garber, Alex, 1026
Garber, Howard, 57
Garber, Lee O., 794, 815
Garcia, Alejandro, 456

H

Hayashi, Wayne, 993
Hayball, H., 1123
Hayden, Gaylord V., 979
Hayden, J. Carleton, 1030
Hayden, Jessie, 431
Hayden, R. G., 458
Hayden, Robert C., 739
Hayden, Tom, 327, 771
Haydon, Caroline, 1168
Hayduk, Leslie Alec, 113
Hayes, Annamarie G., 642, 953
Hayes, Arthur Batiest, 395
Hayes, Arthur S., 327, 642
Hayes, Charles L., 1030
Hayes, Christopher A., 294
Hayes, Edward C., 216
Hayes, Edward J., 123, 953, 981
Hayes, Edward M., 123
Hayes, Eloise, 254
Hayes, James V., 441
Hayes, John Gregory, 274
Hayes, John M., 266
Hayes, Laurie, 889
Hayes, Lucy Agnes, 350
Hayes, Marie Therese, 123
Hayes, Marilyn E., 412
Hayes, Susanna Adella, 539
Hayes-Bautista, David E., 458
Haygood, Atticus G., 1030
Hayit, Baymirza, 1128, 1304
Hayles, V. Robert, 974
Hayner, N., 562
Hayner, U., 562
Haynes, Arthur Vertrease, 11
Haynes, Carrie Ayers, 181, 686
Haynes, Elizabeth Ross, 181, 248
Haynes, George Edmund, 350, 1282
Haynes, Judith M., 1162, 1189
Haynes, Kingsley E., 441
Haynes, Leonard L., Jr., 829
Haynes, Leonard L., III, 923
Haynes, M. Alfred, 287, 739
Haynes, Robert V., 405
Haynes, Rodney, 1333
Haynes, Rose Mary F., 405
Hayot, Emile, 1352
Häyrynen, Yrjö-Paavo, 57
Hayward, Gerald C., 708
Haywood, Harry, 11, 325, 1304
Haywood, Jacquelin S., 283
Haywood, Jeff, 66, 998
Haywood, John W., 913
Hazard, Leland, 853
Hazen, Henry H., 739, 875
Heacock, Don, 123
Head, Simon, 1219
Head, Wilson A., 1098
Headlee, Judy A., 642
Headley, Dave, 1189
Heald, James E., 1030
Healy, Gary W., 123, 493
Healy, Timothy S., 816, 901, 953
Heaney, Thomas W., 828
Heap, James L., 1121
Heard, Marvin Eugene, 516
Hearn, Robert Wesley, 1030
Hearnden, Arthur, 1153
Heaston, Patricia Y. W., 181
Heath, Dwight B. (ed.), 1343
Heath, G. Louis, 11, 123, 216, 258, 524, 562, 869, 882, 953

Heath, Robert W., 668, 729
Heath, Shirley Brice, 1249
Heath, Tony, 1175
Heathman, James E., 28, 500, 577, 1069
Heaton, William R., Jr., 1128
Heaven, Patrick C. L., 1282
Heavner, Robert O., 387
Hebdon, Truman R. A., 538
Heber, Rick, 57, 114, 697
Hechinger, Fred, 771
Hechinger, Fred N., 719, 953, 1030
Hechinger, Fred W., 642
Hechinger, Grace, 1030
Hecht, Edward, 387
Hecht, James L., 837
Hecht, Kathryn A., 203, 521, 697
Hechter, Michael, 1175
Heckel, Benno, 1128
Heckel, Robert V., 143, 954
Hecker, Lena B., 203
Heckman, L. B., 1030
Heckman, Richard Allen, 885
Hector, Henry J., 1296
Hedayatullah, M., 1162
Hedegard, J. M., 892
Hedensheimer, Walker Jon, 378
Hedgeman, Anna Arnold, 11
Hedgepeth, William, 816, 1030
Hedges, Janice N., 731, 733
Hedin, Naboth, 607
Hedlay, Carolyn, 474
Hedman, A. R., 668
Hedrick, James, 923
Heemstra, Gerritt, 562
Heer, David M., 181, 1030
Heerman, Charles E., 540
Heese, J. A., 1282
Hefferman, Arthur J., 231
Heffernan, Helen, 458
Heffernon, Andrew, 682
Hefner, James A., 248, 739
Hegudüs, András, 1209
Heggen, James R., 755
Heggie, Sarah, 863
Heggoy, Alf Andrew, 1073, 1074, 1328
Heginbotham, H., 1189
Hegmann, Franz, 1153
Heiberg, Marianne, 1289
Heidenheimer, Arnold J., 1337
Heider, Eleanor R., 123
Heidhues, Mary F. Somers, 1333
Heifetz, Robert, 333
Height, Dorothy I., 993
Heilbrun, James, 350
Heiligman, Avron C., 993
Heimer, Franz-Wilhelm, 1074
Hein, R. N., 1095
Hein, Virginia H., 248
Heindel, Richard H., 1321
Heine, Bernd, 1328
Heine, Carl, 1348
Heineman, Benjamin W., 1189
Heineman, Robert B., 1030
Heins, Marjorie, 274, 431
Heintz, W. F., 629
Heinz, Ann, 123
Heisler, Martin, 1087
Heiss, Jerold, 123, 181
Heitzmann, William Ray, 24
Heiwich, June Sark, 562

Hinton, William H., 914
Hinze, Richard H., 254
Hipin, John, 1193
Hipkins, John, 1190
Hippler, Arthur E., 110, 203, 217, 521, 576
Hirabayashi, James, 593
Hirabayaski, Gordon K., 1114
Hirai, Bernice K. Y.,
Hirata, Lucie C., 582
Hirata, Lucie Cheng, 254, 603
Hirbour, Rene, 1105
Hirischi, Melvin, 521
Hirji, Karim, 1296
Hiro, Dilip, 236, 603, 642, 1162, 1168, 1190,
    1212
Hirsch, Arnold R., 266
Hirsch, Ernest A., 81
Hirsch, Herbert, 441, 795, 853
Hirsch, Jay G., 100, 125
Hirsch, Jerry, 57
Hirsch, N. D. M., 617
Hirsch, Werner Z., 806, 816, 954
Hirschberg, H. Z., 1328, 1346
Hirschfelder, Arlene B., 532, 576
Hirschman, Charles, 1246
Hirschoff, M.-W. U., 795
Hirshberg, Richard Irwin, 1207
Hirszowicz, Lukasz, 1304
Hist, Albert B., 531
Hitchcock, Dale C., 43
Hitchcock, Romyn, 1241
Hitchings, Phil, 772
Hitti, Philip K., 626
Hixson, Eugene E., 1042
Hixson, Judson, 954, 993
Hixson, William B., 772
Hjelmseth, Donald E., 529
Hlophe, Stephen S., 1245
Ho, James K., 739
Ho, Man Keung, 565
Hoaglund, Jim, 911, 1282
Hoaglund, Ralph P., III, 752
Hoar, George Frisbie, 870
Hoard, C. M., 322
Hoare, Quintin, 1190
Hoay, Kwee Tek, 1217
Hobart, C. W., 1138
Hobart, Charles W., 563, 1105, 1206
Hobart, Thomas Y., 1031
Hobbs, A., 1161
Hobbs, Gardner J., 686
Hobbs, Louise, 739
Hobbs, Maurice, 1190
Hobby, Frederick Douglass, Jr., 642
Hobby, Selma Ann Plowman, 207
Hoben, Thomas, 162
Hobsbawm, E. J., 772
Hobson, Carol Joy, 1031
Hobson, Elizabeth C., 181
Hobson, Julius, 711
Hobson, Julius, Jr., 236
Hobson, Julius W., 236, 718, 816
Hočevar, T., 89
Hoch, Dean E., 220
Hochberg, J., 42
Hochschild, Arlie, 1135
Hodd, M., 1242
Hodgart, Robert L., 378
Hodge, Clair C., 731
Hodge, Jacqueline G., 217

Hodge, John L., 993
Hodge, Marie G., 494
Hodge, Patricia Leavey, 1031
Hodge, Robert W., 1031
Hodge, William H., 531, 576
Hodges, C. V., 248
Hodges, Jimmy, 691
Hodges, Walter F., 698
Hodgins, B. W., 1101
Hodgkins, Benjamin J., 125, 723, 1031
Hodgkins, Mary C., 1084
Hodgkinson, C. J., 1105
Hodgson, Eva N., 1352
Hodgson, Godfrey, 1031
Hodkinson, Raymond, 1168
Hody, Maud, 1121
Hoe, Ban Seng, 1114
Hoeber, Elizabeth, 837
Hoedemaker, Sally B., 322
Hoem, A., 1262
Hoëm, Anton, 1337
Hoepfner, 124
Hoepfner, Ralph, 43, 217
Hoerder, Dirk, 26
Hoernle, A. A., 1328
Hoerr, O. D., 1246
Hoetink, H., 1291, 1343, 1352
Hoetker, James, 125
Hoeveler, Diane L., 181
Hoexter, Corinne K., 582
Hoff, George A., 533
Hoffecker, Carol E., 233
Hoffius, Steve, 395
Hoffman, Abbie, 767
Hoffman, Abraham, 448
Hoffman, Clive, 217
Hoffman, Daniel Ronald, 266
Hoffman, Dean K., 563
Hoffman, Edwin O., 395
Hoffman, Ellen, 237
Hoffman, George W., 1314
Hoffman, Gerard, 481
Hoffman, Géza, 610
Hoffman, James, 1010
Hoffman, Jeffry, 333
Hoffman, Joachim, 1304
Hoffman, Joan, 395
Hoffman, Julius J., Judge, 258, 267
Hoffman, Lois W., 181, 1031
Hoffman, Louis J., 412
Hoffman, Martin, 232
Hoffman, Martin L., 1031
Hoffman, Marvin, 315, 351
Hoffman, Philip E., 820
Hoffman, Randall W., 901
Hoffman, Virginia, 511
Hoffman, W. L., 302
Hoffman, Wayne L., 375
Hoffmann, Earl, 669
Hoffman-Novotny, Hans Joachim, 1295
Hoffmitz, L., 1230
Hoffnitz, L., 1223
Hofley, John R., 1121
Hofman, J., 1226
Hofman, John E., 610, 1223, 1235
Hofmann, Gale E., 169
Hofmann, Gerhard, 77, 81, 125
Hofstead, John A., 610
Hofstein, Avi, 1235
Hofstetter, C. Richard, 907